THE NETWORK PRESS
ENCYCLOPEDIA OF NETWORKING
THIRD EDITION

THE NETWORK PRESS®
ENCYCLOPEDIA OF NETWORKING
THIRD EDITION

Werner Feibel

NETWORK PRESS
SYBEX

SAN FRANCISCO • PARIS • DÜSSELDORF • SOEST • LONDON

Associate Publisher: Guy Hart-Davis
Contracts and Licensing Manager: Kristine O'Callaghan
Developmental Editor: Linda Lee
Acquisitions Editor: Bonnie Bills
Editors: Lisa Auer, Elizabeth Hurley-Clevenger
Project Editor: Gemma O'Sullivan
Technical Editors: Mark J. Kovach, Steven Thomas
Book Designer: Maureen Forys, Happenstance Type-O-Rama
Graphic Illustrators: Tony Jonick, Jerry Williams
Electronic Publishing Specialists: Maureen Forys, Happenstance Type-O-Rama, and Kate Kaminski
Project Team Leader: Leslie Higbee
Proofreaders: Jennifer Campbell, Rich Ganis, Patrick J. Peterson, Amey Garber, Carson Brown, Nancy Riddiough
Indexer: Matthew Spence
Companion CD: Ginger Warner, Keith McNeil
CD Coordinator: Kara Schwartz
Cover Designer: Archer Design
Cover Illustrator/Photographer: FrontPage International

To my wife Luanne, daughter Molly,
and son Stefan, with all my love.

—Werner

"Well, in our country," said Alice, still panting a little, "you'd generally get to somewhere else—if you ran very fast for a long time, as we've been doing."

"A slow sort of country!" said the Queen. "Now, here, you see, it takes all the running you can do, to keep in the same place. If you want to get somewhere else, you must run at least twice as fast as that!"

> Lewis Carroll, Through the Looking Glass
> The red queen was a wide-eyed optimist.

[In] a certain Chinese encyclopedia... it is written that animals are divided into:
  (a) those belonging to the Emperor
  (b) those that are embalmed
  (c) tame ones
  (d) suckling pigs
  (e) sirens
  (f) fabulous ones
  (g) stray dogs
  (h) those included in the present classification
  (i) those that tremble as if mad
  (j) innumerable ones
  (k) those drawn with a very fine camelhair brush
  (l) others
  (m) those that have just broken the water pitcher
  (n) those that look like flies from a long way off

> Jorge Luis Borges

Acknowledgments

As was the case with the first two editions of this book, this could never have been completed without the help of the many other people involved in the project. This special group of people deserves many, many, many thanks and heartfelt appreciation for all their hard work, dedication, and the long hours they spent on the pages you see before you.

Once again, thanks to Guy Hart-Davis for convincing me to do a third edition, and to Acquisitions and Development Editors Bonnie Bills, Neil Edde, and Linda Lee for the excellent job they did of prodding me along and reminding me to keep busy. They were always polite, encouraging, and supportive—particularly Linda who inherited the project in mid-frenzy, but who always managed to be helpful and to keep her good humor. If patience is a virtue, these are some of the most virtuous people on the planet. I am grateful to all of them, and wish them easier tasks for their future projects.

Tech Editors Mark J. Kovach and Steven Thomas went through each entry diligently and made sure that it was technically in tune. They pointed out idiocies and inconsistencies—but did so in a polite manner. They also suggested topics and entries that should be covered, and made sure that my treatment of other topics covered multiple perspectives, rather than being biased in favor of certain approaches. Any improvements in this edition are due to their expertise and to their willingness to offer suggestions; any errors, shortcomings, or omissions are due to my obtuseness and shortsightedness in not taking their advice.

I'm also grateful to Dan Schiff and Kate Kaminski for all their efforts in retrieving (and in many cases recreating) old material for the editors and myself. Thanks also to Gemma O'Sullivan, Project Editor, who started the formidable task of getting the book into production. Lisa Auer, Editor, did a superb job of editing this huge project and of keeping track of pages and pages of new material. She managed to find cross-references that led nowhere, catch my grammatical and stylistic lapses, decipher my verbal handwaving, and clear up passages that just didn't make any sense. Thanks, Lisa, for helping the book flow more smoothly and make more sense.

Editor Elizabeth Hurley-Clevenger inherited the chaos that was this project as it lurched along the production track, with various parts in different states of completion and entropy. She did a fantastic job of making sense of queries, pulling responses out of me, tracking down lost art, and generally dealing with the various crises and obstacles encountered along the way. That she was able to do this calmly and with good humor is proof that she can handle any professional challenge that comes along.

Project Team Leader, Leslie Higbee complemented this effort by doing a wonderful job of keeping close watch over the pages and art as they came into production and floated from proofreader to proofreader. Heartfelt thanks also to the many people who worked as proofreaders on this project: Jennifer Campbell, Rich Ganis, Patrick J. Peterson, Amey Garber, Carson Brown, and Nancy Riddiough. The work these folks do rarely gets the recognition it deserves. The painstaking efforts the proofreaders make to check even the tiniest details are what keep a good book from becoming a goof book, a page-turner from turning into a pale-burner, and a hit tune from ending up as a hat tuna.

Also, many thanks to Maureen Forys, Electronic Publishing Specialist and the book's designer. She did a magnificent job of displaying patience and courage while simultaneously marrying the art with the words.

Finally, many thanks to my wife, Luanne, and to our daughter, Molly, for their patience; and a hearty welcome to Stefan, who arrived while this revision was going on, and who doesn't know anything yet about patience. They always make things much easier and much more fun.

Table of Contents

Introduction

What You'll Find in This Book

Each edition of this book has been larger than the previous one. For example, this one is about 30-40 percent larger than its predecessor; it has more pages and smaller type than the second edition. As in earlier editions of this book, I've tried to provide a comprehensive, straightforward introduction to the basic concepts, facts, and approaches related to networks and networking.

Networking has been defined broadly to cover configurations ranging from those with just a couple of computers in a single room to networks with thousands (or even millions) of machines attached at locations all around the world. This broad definition is simple, but affords lots of possibilities.

To make things even more intriguing, the range of devices that can be elements in a network also keeps growing. Originally, network elements were either computers (large or small) or special purpose resource devices (such as printers, scanners, or storage elements). Now, you can connect to a network using a cellular phone, a handheld device such as a personal digital assistant (PDA), or even some fancy wristwatches. Soon, household appliances such as your refrigerator, toaster, or microwave will be able to connect to a network or to form local area networks by communicating with each other. Even your clothes will be able to connect to a network—although it's not clear what such elements will have to say when connected to a network. Clearly, things are getting more complicated,...er, I mean interesting.

The details of how such devices connect to and use a network can be quite different; however, the basic principles used to establish a connection and to transmit actual commands and data remains the same for many types of network elements. So, even though some things relating to networks have changed considerably, other aspects change very little. These "constants" include the fundamental concepts and principles that underlie networking.

In this book, I've tried to focus on these concepts, rather than on "how-to" instructions. For example, you'll learn what defines and distinguishes different types of networks, rather than how to set up such networks. Similarly, you'll learn what different types of network-related programs (such as browsers) do, rather than learning specific commands when using such programs.

Many aspects of networks have changed in major ways since the previous edition. Some topics and technologies have literally come into being since the last edition. Areas that have changed dramatically, and that have consequently been beefed up, include: the World Wide Web, the Internet, intranets and extranets, satellite and other wireless technologies, and networking protocols.

In all cases, I've tried to provide the information necessary to understand at least the basics about the topic. However, the key word here is "tried," since some of these topics or areas are developing so rapidly that they change almost daily. For example, between the time the entry for

Iridium—a satellite communications project—was written and the time the chapter containing the entry went into galleys, the Iridium project consortium filed for bankruptcy. In that case I was able to add information about this turn of events; in other cases, it was not possible to keep things quite so up to date.

The facts and information you'll find here are certainly available in other places. However, I've tried to present this information in a clear manner, and to show how different concepts and facts relate to each other. Also, I don't know of any other book or source that provides so much network-related information in one place and in such a conveniently accessible form. To find all the information included in this book, you would have to check hundreds of books, disks, or other sources. So, if nothing else, this book can save you the very considerable time and effort you'd have to spend rounding up the information yourself.

Opening Doors...And Keeping Them Open

By making the longer entries as self-contained as possible, I've tried to make it possible for any level of reader—even a networking novice—to get a quick introduction to networking topics. This book can serve as a gateway or portal—both networking terms, by the way—for those interested in learning about network-related topics.

By making such entries as complete as possible—and by including shorter entries about more specialized and esoteric concepts—I've tried to make the book equally useful for intermediate and advanced network users. Entries about state of the art technologies and topics are included mainly for the more advanced reader, but I've tried to relate these to existing concepts for the benefit of readers who are still trying to get an overview of the field.

By putting all this information on paper and binding the pages, Sybex has created a hefty book, which can also be useful in other ways. You might say that the encyclopedia's content can open doors and the medium can hold them open. And, with the electronic version that's included on the CD-ROM, your browser can provide a window on a door, while the hard copy can serve as a doorstop. How's that for multifunction devices?

"Oh, what a tangled web we perceive,

When once we practice to receive."

Despite its size, this encyclopedia just scratches the surface of what there is to know about networking. In fact, it probably makes a smaller scratch in the body of knowledge about the current state of networking than the previous edition did for networking back then. To give you some idea of the magnitude of the task that awaits anyone starting out to research a topic on their own, consider the following. The World Wide Web had about 10 million pages when the second edition of this book came out a few years ago. Since then, the Web has grown to about 800 million pages—an 80-fold increase, with an average growth rate of about 300,000 pages per day!

Even if the proportion of networking-related material on this larger Web we know today is only one-tenth as high as the proportion in the old 10 million page Web—almost certainly a conservative estimate—this would still be an 8-fold increase. This book would have to be about 10,500 pages long to provide a commensurate increase in coverage.

So, Why a Book?

Given the hopelessness of staying up to date, why even bother with a book of this sort? Well, as I said, there are over 800 million Web pages you could search through—clearly neither an attractive nor a feasible alternative. Granted, about 750 million of these pages are advertisements—mostly self-serving fluff, with very few containing actual information.

Still, that leaves millions and millions of pages that might contain relevant information. Rather than having to navigate this Web from the start, I think you'll find it easier to learn about networking by beginning with a source that has the basic information all in one place—for example, this book. Once you have an understanding of the main points, you can go to the Web to get more specific information or to find out what's happened in the few weeks, days, or hours since you last checked.

Throughout the book, I've tried to include references to Web pages where you can go to look for more information about specific topics covered in this book. I've also included several lists of such references pointing you to Web pages for periodicals, standards organizations, and interest groups about specific topics.

My hope is that you'll be able to find what you need either in this book or by following some of the leads I've included. If you can't find something you think should be there, please let us know. Also contact us via the Sybex Web site at `http://www.sybex.com` if you find something but it's not clearly presented.

Happy reading!

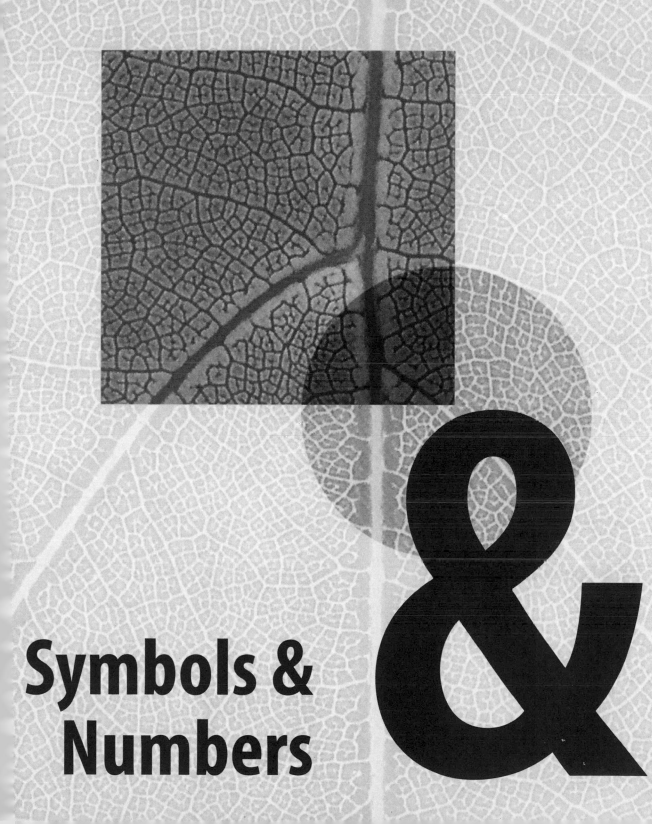

Symbols &
Numbers

& (Ampersand)

The ampersand is used to indicate special characters in HTML (Hypertext Markup Language) and XML (eXtensible Markup Language) documents—that is, documents for the World Wide Web. A semicolon (;) ends the character specification. For example, & specifies the ampersand character(&); ö specifies a lowercase o with an umlaut, or dieresis, mark (ö).

In the UNIX operating system, an ampersand is used to run a program in the background.

In programming languages such as C, C++, Java, and Perl, the ampersand is used as a bitwise AND operator. (A bitwise operator is one that operates separately on the individual bits or bit pairs in a value—as opposed to evaluating the entire value as a whole.) This binary operator takes two bit patterns as operands, and it returns the result of carrying out AND operations on the corresponding bits in each value. The bitwise AND operator returns a 1 if both corresponding bits in each pair are 1, and returns a 0 otherwise. For example, 10101010 & 01011010 yields 00001010.

In C and C++, the ampersand does double duty and also serves as the address operator. When used before a variable name in these languages, the expression returns the address at which storage for the variable has been allocated.

< > (Angle Brackets)

Angle brackets are used in pairs to surround *markup tags* in HTML (Hypertext Markup Language) and XML (eXtensible Markup Language) documents—that is, documents for the World Wide Web. For example, <P> indicates a paragraph break; <B> and </B> indicate the start and end of a section that is to be displayed in boldface.

<! -- --> (Angle Brackets, Bang Sign)

In HTML (Hypertext Markup Language) and XML (eXtensible Markup Language) files, <!-- begins a comment and --> ends one. The browser ignores any material between these delimiters, with one exception that's discussed below. Comments may continue over more than one line.

While browsers are designed to ignore material within comments, newer browsers will check the comment body to see whether the comment includes style definitions, such as those created in style sheets. Some older browsers don't support style sheets, and these browsers would process the style definitions as ordinary text. To avoid this, in-file style definitions—that is, those included in the document file rather than placed in a separate file—should be put within comments. Browsers that support style sheets will recognize the material as style definitions and will process it accordingly. Browsers that don't support them will simply ignore the comment.

<? ?> (Angle Brackets, Question Mark)

In XML (eXtensible Markup Language) documents, <? and ?> mark the beginning and end, respectively, of a processing instruction to the XML processor (which interprets an XML file). A processing instruction provides information or a directive to the XML processor.

For example, the following XML processing instruction indicates the version of XML being used in a file:

```
<?XML version = "1.0" ?>
```

→ *Broader Category* XML (eXtensible Markup Language)

&

* (Asterisk)

In several operating systems, the asterisk serves as a wildcard character to represent one or more characters, such as in a file name or extension. For example, a* matches act, actor, and and, but not band.

In pattern matching involving regular expressions, the asterisk matches the occurrences of the single character immediately preceding it. For example, ba*th matches bth, bath, and baaaaath, but not bbath.

In e-mail and in other contexts that use plain text, asterisks are sometimes used around words or phrases to indicate emphasis. For example, "I *really* want to emphasize the second word in this sentence."

In most programming languages (as in high school algebra), an asterisk is used to indicate multiplication. For example, 35 * 15 yields a product of 525.

In C and C++, the asterisk is also used to define a pointer variable and as a dereferencing operator. For example, the following lines in a C or C++ program define *intptr* as a pointer to an integer, define *myint* as an integer, assign the value 37 to *myint*, and assign the address of *myint* (indicated by *&myint*) to the *intptr* variable. (In programming parlance, after the assignment statement, *intptr* points to, or *references*, the variable *myint*.)

```
/* define a pointer to int;
   note asterisk */
int *intptr;
/* define an integer variable */
int myint;
/* miscellaneous code */
...
/* set myint to the value 37 */
myint = 37;
/* assign address of myint to intptr;
   no asterisk */
intptr = &myint;
/* display contents of myint;
   note asterisk   */
printf("%d\n", *intptr);
```

In these languages, the content of a pointer variable is an address, which represents the location of a variable of the appropriate type—namely, the variable *myint* in the example. After the statements in the example, both **intptr* (a dereferenced value) and *myint* have the value 37, whereas *intptr* still has as its value the address of *myint*. In the example, the dereferencing operator returns the contents of the variable located at the address contained in *intptr*.

@ (At Sign)

The at sign is used to separate the username from domain specifiers in e-mail addresses. For example, mels@golemxiv.mit.edu would indicate someone with username mels on a computer named golemxiv at MIT.

In Perl, the at sign is used to indicate an array variable. For example, @AWSHUCKS refers to an array named AWSHUCKS.

\ (Backslash)

In some operating systems, such as DOS, OS/2, and NetWare, the backslash character separates directory names or directory and file names in a path statement. By itself, the backslash represents the root directory in these operating systems.

In various programming and editing contexts, the backslash is used to escape the character that follows. For example, \n is an escape code to indicate a newline character in many operating environments.

&& (Double Ampersand)

Double ampersands are used at the beginning and end of a variable name in arguments for server-side include commands. Server-side includes are elements inserted into HTML files, and they are used to specify commands that the Web server is expected to carry out before sending the document to a browser. Such commands are used to update the document based on environment variables or values entered into a form by a user. HTML files with server-side inserts (SSIs) are identified by special extensions, with the specific extensions depending on the Web server on which the file is stored:

- .SSI for NetWare servers
- .SHTML for Apache servers
- .STM for Microsoft Internet Information servers

The following represents a variable that might be included in such commands: *&&myvariable&&*.

In programming languages such as C, C++, Perl, and Java, a double ampersand (&&) is used as a logical AND operator. This operator combines two values and returns a nonzero value only if both of the operands are nonzero. If either value is zero, the logical AND operator returns 0. For example, 35 && 67 yields a nonzero value (usually 1), whereas 35 && 0 yields 0.

// (Double Slash)

In *URLs* (Uniform Resource Locators), double slash characters separate the protocol from the site and document names. For example, if it existed,

`http://examplehost.ucsc.edu/filename.html`

would refer to a file named `filename.html` residing on the examplehost machine at the University of California at Santa Cruz. To get to this file, you would use a server that supports HTTP (Hypertext Transfer Protocol).

In various programming languages, including C++ and Java, the double slash characters are used to begin a one-line comment. The compiler ignores any text following the double slashes on the same line.

μ (Mu)

Used as an abbreviation for the prefix *micro*, as in μsec for microsecond and μm for micrometer. The order of magnitude represented by mu corresponds to one-millionth, which is $10^{\mu 6}$ in base 10. When using a binary number system, a millionth portion is represented by $2^{\mu 20}$.

→ *See Also*   Order of Magnitude

% (Percent Sign)

Extended HTML (Hypertext Markup Language) files may contain tags that are not recognized by HTML. These additional tags are intended for programs or libraries that can recognize and process these tags—for example, for the `httpodbc.dll` library, which provides tools for dealing with databases. In such tags, the percent sign is used to indicate the beginning and end of the tag's content. Extended HTML files have .HTX as their extension.

In programming languages such as Perl, C, C++, and Java, the percent sign is used as the modulus binary operator. This operator takes two whole numbers (A and B) as its operands, and returns the remainder when A is divided by B, using whole number division. For example, 49 % 6 = 1, 6 % 20 = 6, and 20 % 6 = 2 because these are the remainders when whole number division is performed on the values.

. and .. (Period and Double Period)

In hierarchically organized directory systems, such as those used by UNIX, DOS, and OS/2, . and .. refer to the current and the parent directories, respectively. The period and double period are used when specifying relative path names.

In pattern matching involving regular expressions, the . matches any single character, except a newline character.

(Pound Sign)

The pound sign, also known as a hash mark, is used to indicate the beginning of a comment in various scripting and programming languages (such as Perl or AWK). In such languages, any text from the pound sign to the end of a line is treated as a comment and is ignored.

In other languages, such as C and C++, the pound sign is used to indicate the start of a preprocessor directive. A statement such as

```
#include filename.ext
```

is an instruction that tells the preprocessor to replace the directive with the actual contents of the file named `filename.ext`. Similarly, a statement such as

```
#define IDENTIFIER 35
```

is an instruction that tells the preprocessor to replace every occurrence of *IDENTIFIER* with the value 35.

In HTML, the pound sign is used when referring to an *anchor* (a named cross-reference location) in the current document or to a specific anchor within a different HTML document. For example, the first of the following statements specifies a link to a location (named `anchorsHERE`) in the same document as the reference, and the second specifies a link to a particular location (`anchorsAWAY`) in an HTML file named `wildblueyonder.html`.

```
<A HREF="#anchorsHERE">

<A HREF="wildblueyonder.html
#anchorsAWAY">
```

? (Question Mark)

In many operating systems, a question mark serves as a wildcard character that represents a single character, such as in a file or directory name.

/ (Slash)

The slash (also known as a *forward slash* or a *virgule*) separates directory levels in some operating systems (most notably UNIX), in addresses for gopher, and in *URLs* (Uniform Resource Locators). For example, the following URL specifies the name and location of a hypertext version of the jargon file, which contains definitions for terms and events that have helped define the computer culture:

```
http://www.phil.uni-sb.de/fun/jargon/
index.html
```

In this URL, the file is named `index.html`, and it is located in the `/fun/jargon` directory on a machine in Germany (de).

In other operating systems, such as DOS, OS/2, and NetWare, a slash is sometimes used to indicate or separate command line switches or options for a command.

In an HTML (Hypertext Markup Language) markup tag, a slash is used to indicate the end of the tag. For example, a section of text that is displayed in boldface would begin with the `<B>` tag, and end with the `</B>` tag.

/* */ (Slash, Asterisk)

In cascading style sheets (CSS) for HTML (Hypertext Markup Language) files, the /* and */ start and end comments, respectively. The browser will ignore any material between these delimiters when it processes the style sheet information.

~ (Tilde)

A tilde is used to indicate a user's subdirectory when specifying a URL (Uniform Resource Locator). For example, the following URL indicates that a browser should look for file `theinfo.html` in the user subdirectory of the user with login name myelin at the www.thesite.com Web site:

http://www.thesite.com/~myelin/theinfo.htm

In some programming languages—most notably, Perl and AWK—a tilde is used to signal a bitwise negation. This means that all 1s in a bit pattern become 0s; similarly, all erstwhile 0s become 1s.

1+1 Switching

In SONET (Synchronous Optical Network) architectures, 1+1 switching helps ensure that transmissions reach their destinations without error. In 1+1 switching, the same packet is sent along each of the two rings in a SONET architecture. If both versions of the packet reach their destination, the better packet (that is, the one with fewer errors) is accepted and the other is discarded.

1Base5

The IEEE 802.3 committee's designation for an Ethernet network that operates at 1Mbps and that uses unshielded twisted-pair (UTP) cable. This configuration uses a physical bus, with nodes attached to a common cable. AT&T's StarLAN is an example of a 1Base5 network.

→ *See Also* 10BaseX, 10Broad36; 100BaseT

2B+D

2B+D refers to the two B (bearer) and one D (data) channels provided in ISDN's Basic Rate Interface (BRI). The B channels have 64Kbps bandwidths, and can be used for voice, data, or video. The D channel operates at 16Kbps, and is generally used for signaling and control transmissions. The D channel can also be used for low-speed data transmissions.

→ *Broader Categories* BRI (Basic Rate Interface); ISDN (Integrated Services Digital Network)

→ *Compare* 23B+D

2B1Q Encoding

In ISDN (Integrated Services Digital Network) and other digital communications technologies (such as ADSL, for Asymmetric Digital Subscriber Line), 2B1Q is the line code (signal encoding method) used to represent 0s and 1s in a digital signal at the physical level. 2B1Q is an ANSI standard and has replaced the alternate mark inversion (AMI) method used in older versions of ISDN.

2B1Q (which stands for 2 binary, 1 quaternary) is also a data-translation scheme. It encodes two binary bit values into a single quaternary digit (known as a *quat*) in a four-value range. Because any of four possible values can be encoded in a single signal, 2B1Q is known as a four-level line code. While 2B1Q is generally regarded as an improvement over AMI, its usefulness is already limited, because of the high speeds and large distances involved in many digital connections. As a result, even more complex line code schemes are coming into use—for example, carrierless amplitude/phase modulation (CAP) and discrete multitone (DMT).

See the table "Common Data-Translation Methods" in the *4B/5B Encoding* entry, for a comparative summary of some of the more widely used data-translation schemes.

→ *See Also* ADSL (Asymmetric Digital Subscriber Line); Encoding, Signal; ISDN (Integrated Services Digital Network)

→ *Compare* CAP (Carrierless Amplitude/Phase Modulation); DMT (Discrete Multitone)

4B/5B Encoding

4B/5B encoding is a data-translation scheme that serves as a preliminary to signal encoding in FDDI (Fiber Distributed Data Interface) networks and also in 100Base-TX Ethernet networks. In 4B/5B, every group of four bits is represented as a five-bit symbol. This symbol is associated with a bit pattern that is then encoded using a standard signal-encoding method, usually NRZI (non-return to zero inverted). This preprocessing makes the subsequent electrical encoding 80 percent efficient. For example, using 4B/5B encoding, you can achieve a 100Mbps transmission rate with a clock speed of only 125MHz.

In contrast, the Manchester signal-encoding method, which is used in Ethernet and other types of networks, is only 50 percent efficient. For example, to achieve a 100Mbps rate with Manchester encoding, you need a 200MHz clock speed.

The table "Common Data-Translation Methods" provides a comparative summary of several common schemes for prepping data for transmission.

COMMON DATA-TRANSLATION METHODS

Method	Translation	Used in
2B1Q	2 binary values to 1 quaternary value	ADSL, ISDN
4B/5B	4-bit blocks to 5-bit blocks	100BaseTX, FDDI
5B/6B	5-bit blocks to 6-bit blocks	100VG-AnyLAN
8B/6T	8-bit binary blocks to 6-trit ternary blocks	100BaseT4
8B/10B	8-bit blocks to 10-bit blocks	1000Base-T, Fibre Channel, SNA

4CIF (4× Common Intermediate Format)

4CIF refers to an image format for videoconferencing. 4CIF is a higher bandwidth (and higher resolution) variant of the CIF format, which has become a de facto standard for videoconferencing images. 4CIF's 704 × 576 resolution has double the resolution on each side compared to the CIF (352 × 288). Doubling vertical and horizontal resolution produces four times the number of pixels, hence the 4 in 4CIF.

→ **Broader Category** Videoconferencing

→ **See Also** CIF (Common Intermediate Format)

5B/6B Encoding

A data-translation scheme that serves as a preliminary to signal encoding in 100VG-AnyLAN networks. In 5B/6B, every group of five bits is represented as a six-bit symbol. This symbol is associated with a bit pattern that is then encoded using a standard signal-encoding method, such as NRZ (non-return to zero).

See the table "Common Data-Translation Methods" in the *4B/5B Encoding* entry, for a comparative summary of several of the more commonly used data-translation methods.

5ESS

In telecommunications, 5ESS refers to a commonly used electronic switching system (ESS) for central offices. 5ESS is used to route calls for ISDN (Integrated Services Digital Network) systems.

Originally developed and manufactured by AT&T, 5ESS is now handled by Lucent, and is also known as Lucent 5ESS. ISDN users may be connected to the 5ESS switch by any of three types of interfaces:

T interface   Provides a direct, four-wire connection between user and 5ESS—that is, a connection without an NT1 unit mediating. T interfaces can be at most 3,300 feet, which represents a signal loss of 6dB at 96kHz.

U interface   Provides a mediated, two-wire connection between user and 5ESS—that is, a connection with an NT1 unit at the user's end. U interfaces can be at most 27,000 feet, which represents a signal loss of 42dB at 40kHz. U interfaces can use either a proprietary AMI line card or a 2B1Q line card. The former is a proprietary standard, which is on its way out; the latter is an ANSI standard line-coding technique.

Z interface   Makes it possible to connect an analog device to the 5ESS switch. Z interfaces may be necessary for pay phones or for phones in a remote area. The Z interface is inefficient because the 5ESS switch must perform extra tasks to make the connection and communication possible.

→ *Broader Category*   ISDN (Integrated Services Digital Network)

→ *See Also*   2B1Q Encoding

7-Bit ASCII

7-bit ASCII is also known as standard ASCII (American Standard Code for Information Interchange), and is in contrast to extended ASCII, which uses 8 bits. 7-bit ASCII represents the coding for a character set consisting of 128 different symbols—generally consisting of 32 control characters, digits, upper- and lowercase letters, punctuation, and other special symbols. The eighth bit in a byte encoding a standard ASCII character is generally used for parity.

8B/6T Encoding

A data-translation scheme in which each block of eight binary values (bits) is recoded into a single block of six ternary (three-valued) digits, or *trits*—that is, symbols in a three-valued system. The resulting trit sequence—a ternary value—is then transmitted as a block.

8B/6T encoding is used in the 100BaseT4 variant of fast Ethernet. See the table "Common Data-Translation Methods," in the *4B/5B Encoding* entry, for a comparative summary of several commonly used data-translation methods.

8B/10B Encoding

A physical-layer data-translation scheme that is related to 4B/5B encoding. The 8B/10B scheme recodes eight-bit patterns into 10-bit symbols. 8B/10B encoding is used, for example, in IBM's SNA (Systems Network Architecture) networks. It is also used in Fibre Channel and in 1000Base-T Ethernet architectures. In fact, the Fibre Channel scheme was adopted for use in Gigabit Ethernet. In order to achieve a 1Gbps transmission rate, the 10-bit blocks must be transmitted at 1.25Gbps.

See the table "Common Data-Translation Methods" in the *4B/5B Encoding* entry, for a comparative summary of several of the more commonly used data-translation methods.

9-Track Tape

A tape storage format that records along nine parallel tracks on $\frac{1}{2}$-inch, reel-to-reel magnetic tape. Eight tracks are used for data, and one track is used for parity information. These tapes are often used as backup systems on minicomputer and mainframe systems; digital audio tapes (DATs) are more common on networks.

10/100

10/100 indicates that a device (for example, a router or switch) can support variants of either the traditional 10Mbps Ethernet standard (for example, 10BaseT) or the faster 100Mbps Ethernet standard (for example, 100BaseT). Most newer devices support both these speeds.

10BaseF

→ *See* 10BaseX

10BaseFB

→ *See* 10BaseX

10BaseFL

→ *See* 10BaseX

10BaseFP

→ *See* 10BaseX

10BaseX

The designations 10Base2, 10Base5, 10BaseF, and 10BaseT refer to various types of baseband Ethernet networks.

10Base2

10Base2 uses thin coaxial cable. This version can operate at up to 10Mbps and can support cable segments of up to 185 meters (607 feet). It is also known as *thin Ethernet, ThinNet*, or *CheaperNet*, because thin coaxial cable is considerably less expensive than the thick coaxial cable used in 10Base5 networks.

10Base5

10Base5 uses thick coaxial cable. This version is the original Ethernet. It can operate at up to 10Mbps and support cable segments of up to 500 meters (1640 feet). It is also known as *thick Ethernet* or *ThickNet*.

10BaseF

10BaseF is a baseband 802.3-based Ethernet network that uses fiber-optic cable. This version can operate at up to 10Mbps.

Standards for the following special-purpose versions of 10BaseF are being formulated by the IEEE 802.3:

10BaseFP (fiber passive)   For desktops.

10BaseFL (fiber link)   For intermediate *hubs* and workgroups.

10BaseFB (fiber backbone)   For central facility lines between buildings.

10BaseT

10BaseT is a baseband 802.3-based Ethernet network that uses unshielded twisted-pair (UTP) cable and a star topology. This version can operate at up to 10Mbps. It is also known as *twisted-pair Ethernet* or *UTP Ethernet*.

→ **Broader Category**   Ethernet

→ **See Also**   1Base5; 10Broad36; 100BaseT

10Broad36

10Broad36 is a broadband, 802.3-based Ethernet network that uses 75-ohm coaxial (CATV) cable and a bus or tree topology. This version can operate at up to 10Mbps and support cable segments of up to 1800 meters (about 6000 feet).

A 10Broad36 network uses differential phase shift keying (DPSK) to convert the data to analog form for transmission. Because of the encoding details, a 10Broad36 network actually needs 18 megahertz (MHz) for each channel: 14MHz to encode the 10Mbps signal and 4MHz more for collision detection and reporting capabilities.

In a 10Broad36 network, throughput is 10Mbps in each direction; that is, a total bandwidth of 36MHz is needed. This bandwidth can be provided in a single cable or in two separate cables.

&

A split-cable approach uses half the cable for each direction, which means the cable must have a 36MHz bandwidth. A dual-cable approach uses separate cables for each direction, so that each cable needs only an 18MHz bandwidth.

→ *Broader Categories* Ethernet; Network, Broadband

→ *See Also* 1Base5, 10BaseX; 100BaseT

16CIF (16× Common Intermediate Format)

16CIF refers to an image format for videoconferencing. 16CIF is a higher bandwidth (and higher resolution) variant of the CIF format, which has become a de facto standard for videoconferencing images. 16CIF's 1408 × 1152 resolution has four times the resolution on each side—compared to the CIF (352 × 288). Quadrupling vertical and horizontal resolution produces 16 times the number of pixels, hence the 16 in 16CIF.

→ *Broader Category* Videoconferencing

→ *See Also* CIF (Common Intermediate Format)

23B+D

23B+D refers to the 23 B (bearer) and one D (data) channels provided in ISDN's Primary Rate Interface (PRI). The B channels have 64Kbps bandwidths, and can be used for voice, data, or video. The D channel operates at 16Kbps, and is generally used for signaling and control transmissions. The D channel can also be used for low-speed data transmissions.

→ *Broader Category* PRI (Primary Rate Interface); ISDN (Integrated Services Digital Network)

→ *Compare* 2B+D

24×7

When referring to sales, service, or support, 24×7 indicates that something is available or accessible anytime—that is, 24 hours a day, 7 days a week. When referring to operation or functioning, the term indicates that the system, network, or other device is expected to be available (up and running) continuously— that is, with no downtime.

25-Pair Cable

This refers to bundles of unshielded twisted pair (UTP) wire in which 25 wire pairs are grouped together within a single trunk to a common location—generally a punch-down block. At this block, individual wire pairs are "broken out" to make it possible to group and connect them to specific devices. For example, two or four pairs might be connected to a telephone.

25-pair cables are used in situations in which multiple connections must be possible. For example, such cables might be used to connect multiport switches or repeaters in Ethernet networks. As another example, early keysystems needed 25-pair cables to connect to the multiple phone lines. (A keysystem is a telephone configuration that makes it possible to handle multiple lines automatically. Keysystems are used in small- to medium-sized businesses; larger businesses generally use a private branch exchange, or PBX.)

32-Bit Word

A 32-bit word uses four bytes to represent a value. With 32 bits, a range of over 4 billion integer values can be represented:

- From 0 to 4,294,967,245 if using unsigned values—that is, non-negative values only

- From −2,147,483,648 to 2,147,483,647 if using signed values—that is, both positive and negative values

32-bit words are the standard for 32-bit processors (such as the Pentium family) and data buses.

50/125μ (Micron) Multimode Fiber

50/125μ multimode refers to a type of optical fiber that is widely used in Europe and Asia. Such fiber consists of a glass or plastic *core*, surrounded by a plastic cover, known as the *cladding*. Because the cladding and core have different refractive indexes, the cladding keeps a light signal contained within the core. In multimode fiber, the core is wide enough that the light can take several paths (known as *modes*). The numbers in the name refer to the diameter (in microns) of the fiber's core and cladding, respectively.

Of the three main types of optical fiber—50/125μ multimode, 62.5/125μ multimode, and single mode—the properties of 50/125μ fiber lie between those of the more expensive single-mode fiber and the less expensive (but noisier) 62.5/125μ fiber.

→ **Broader Category** Cable, Fiber-Optic

→ **Compare** 62.5/125μ Multimode Fiber; Single-Mode Fiber

56K Line

A digital telephone circuit with a 64Kbps bandwidth, but with a bandwidth of only 56Kbps data, with the other 8Kbps being used for signaling. Also known as switched 56K, as an *ADN* (Advanced Digital Network) or a *DDS* (Dataphone Digital Service) line.

56K Modem

56K modems support downloads (for example, from an Internet service provider, or ISP) at speeds approaching 56Kbps. Uploads from the end user's PC can't be faster than 33.6Kbps.

The general consensus among industry experts and pundits is that 56K-modem technology represents the last gasp for analog modems. Strictly speaking, 56K modems are already hybrids: to

achieve their high download speeds, they transmit digitally to the central office of the end user's telephone service provider.

Properties and Performance

56K modems use ordinary telephone lines; however, these lines must be clean and they cannot be multiplexed. (Multiplexed lines are found in densely populated areas, where signals for multiple customers may share a common line. A multiplexed arrangement produces too much noise for a 56K connection.) Because the signal must be clean, the customer's equipment can't be too far from the phone company's central office—no more than a mile or two.

A 56K connection requires 56K modems at both ends. Furthermore, the download cannot involve any analog-to-digital conversions, since the signal would become too noisy to support 56Kbps transmission. This means that the download modem—that is, the ISP's—must send its signal digitally to the phone company's central office (CO). The last part of the transmission—from central office to customer premises—involves a digital-to-analog conversion at the CO. One such conversion is allowed.

When things are going right, 56K modems operate at different speeds (and in different ways) for uploading and downloading. Upstream connections—that is, those for uploading to an ISP—operate at a maximum speed of 33.6Kbps. The upstream connection is just like any other modem connection.

The downstream connection is where 56K modems earn their name. Transmissions from an ISP to an end user can operate at a maximum speed of 56Kbps—at least on paper. In practice, the fastest download speed allowed is 53.3Kbps. The 53.3K ceiling exists because the Federal Communications Commission (FCC) limits the amount of power that can be sent down a telephone line.

Even the 53.3Kbps speed is just an ideal, though. You're likely to reach it only under idealized conditions—for example, in a test lab. In practice, speeds between 40 and 50Kbps are the rule in the real world. The actual session speed will depend on the quality of the connection, and the maximum speed can be achieved only over short distances. If the connection is too noisy, the modem switches down to 33.6Kbps.

Modem Operation

Ordinarily, signals from a customer to the phone company travel in analog form along the local loop to the CO. The analog signals are digitized at the CO before being sent over trunks to an interexchange carrier (IXC) or to another CO. The illustration "56K modems in operation" shows how such modems work. Notice the asymmetry in the performance of the user's and the service provider's modems. A 56K modem connection works as follows:

1. A subscriber's 56K modem sends analog signals upstream to the phone company's central office (CO). The upstream connection is just a 33.6Kbps connection.

2. The analog signal is converted to digital form at the CO, is multiplexed with signals from other subscribers, and is sent on to the Internet Service Provider (ISP) on a line whose speed depends on the ISP's connection. This will generally be a T-1 (1.544Mbps) or even a T-3 (44.736Mbps) line.

3. Subscribers' signals—now in digital form—are demultiplexed and processed individually so that the appropriate responses can be made.

4. The ISP's responses are multiplexed and sent, in digital form, to the CO over the ISP's connection.

5. At the CO, the ISP's digital signals are again demultiplexed and converted to analog form before being sent on to the appropriate subscribers.

6. The downstream analog signal is sent at a nominal rate of 56Kbps, but realistically it is more likely to be in the 40 to 50Kbps range and is never higher than 53Kbps.

Some customers—in particular, those with a high traffic volume—have digital lines to the CO. An ISP will almost certainly have a digital connection. In that case, instead of having to translate digital data into an analog signal, a 56K modem can (and does) send digital signal samples downstream to the phone company CO or to a digital internetwork switch.

The digital samples are encoded using pulse code modulation (PCM) and are sent at the rate of 8000 8-bit samples per second. Although 8000 samples of this size actually yield a 64Kbps rate, the effective transmission rate is only 56Kbps. Noise in the system makes it necessary to use one bit from each byte for nondata purposes.

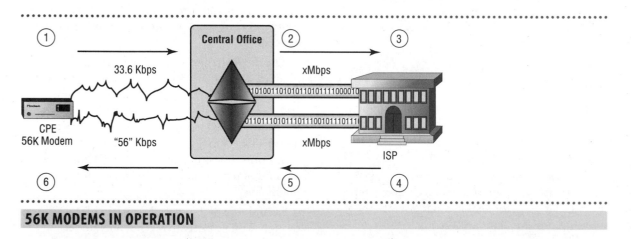

56K MODEMS IN OPERATION

56K Modem Standards

56Kbps modems were originally developed using either of two competing—and incompatible—technologies: *x2* (from U.S. Robotics) and *K56flex* (from Rockwell International and Lucent Technology). The incompatibility imposed rather severe restrictions on modem users. For example, because like could communicate only with like, a user with an x2 chip set modem could not use a service provider that used modems based on K56flex technology.

In 1997, the various interest groups involved eventually formulated a common modem design and signaling standard. This was known as V.pcm during its unofficial status, and was adopted eventually as the V.90 standard by the ITU (International Telecommunications Union) in September of 1998. All new modems will support the V.90 standard.

V.90 modems are still based on chip sets from the major modem manufacturers, and they are still built on either x2 or K56flex technology. Because of this, V.90 modems also support either x2 or K56flex, depending on the chip set. This is useful because not all 56Kbps connections will be upgraded immediately to V.90. For example, an ISP may still be working with either x2 or K56flex (or even with both), and may upgrade to V.90 only over time.

Many pre-V.90 modems have been or can be modified to make them V.90 compliant. Such modifications are done either through flash upgrades or through chip replacement. In most cases, these upgrades are free or cost a nominal sum. They were offered by modem manufacturers in order to stimulate modem sales before the V.90 standard was adopted.

Miscellaneous

56K modem technology is much like lower speed modem technology in some ways, and it is fraught with problems and dangers in other ways. Most of the problems have to do with lines and connections.

Several conditions must be met for a 56K connection to operate at anything close to that rate:

- As mentioned, a line must be sufficiently noise free to support 56K transmissions. You can test whether your line meets this criterion. Using a V.34-compliant modem, you can call a special number. See `www.3com.com/ need4_56k/linetest.html` for details on how to do this. It's a good idea to do this *before* investing in a 56K modem—although most new computers include 56K modems. If your line doesn't support 56Kbps connections, your 56K modem will work nicely as a 33.6K modem.

- The modem at the other end of the connection—for example, the ISP's—must also be a 56K modem. In addition to supporting a 56Kbps connection, the ISP must have a digital connection to the phone company's central office.

- Both 56K modems must be V.90-compliant. If not, the noncompliant modem must be based on the same chip set as the V.90 modem. That is, the V.90 modem's fallback mode (x2 or K56flex) must be the same as the other modem's (only) mode.

One way to get around the (less than) 56Kbps speed limit on V.90 modems is to connect with two modems at the same time. This is known as *modem bonding*, or *aggregation*. It can double the effective connection speed. Prefabricated bonded modems are available. These come with double chip sets and double connectors.

To be useful, the customer must have an available telephone line for each modem. Also, the ISP must support bonded-modem connections.

Alternative high-speed technologies include cable and ISDN modems, ADSL (Asymmetric Digital Subscriber Line) or another type of DSL connection, and satellite connections.

→ *Broader Category* Modem

62.5/125μ (Micron) Multimode Fiber

62.5/125μ multimode refers to a type of optical fiber that is widely used in North America. Such fiber consists of a glass or plastic *core*, surrounded by a plastic cover, known as the *cladding*. Because the cladding and core have different refractive indexes, the cladding keeps a light signal contained within the core. In multimode fiber, the core is wide enough that the light can take several paths (known as *modes*). The numbers in the name refer to the diameter (in microns) of the fiber's core and cladding, respectively.

Of the three main types of optical fiber—62.5/125μ multimode, 50/125μ multimode, and single mode—62.5/125μ is the least expensive to manufacture. However, its optical properties are not as good as for the other two types of fiber.

➜ *Broader Category* Cable, Fiber-Optic

➜ *Compare* 50/125μ (Micron) Multimode Fiber; Single-Mode Fiber

64K Line

A digital telephone circuit with a 64Kbps bandwidth. Also known as a DS0 (digital signal, level 0) line. When the entire 64Kbps are allocated for the data, the circuit is known as a *clear channel*. This is in contrast to a circuit in which 8Kbps are used for signaling, leaving only 56Kbps for data.

66-Type Punch-Down Block

A device for terminating wires, with the possibility of connecting input and output wires. This type of punch-down block can handle wires with up to 25 twisted pairs. The 66-type have generally been superseded by 110-type punch-down blocks.

➜ *See Also* Punch-Down Block

80/20 Rule

In connection with LAN traffic analysis, the 80/20 rule states that 80 percent of (inter)network traffic travels within a network segment, and that the remaining 20 percent travels along the backbone. It is arguable whether this rule still applies today—specifically, whether backbone traffic increases as the size of internetworks increases.

100BaseFX

A 100BaseT basal type variant that runs over multimode or single-mode fiber-optic cable and uses SC or ST connectors. 100BaseFX technology is generally used for high-speed Ethernet backbones, rather than for connecting individual nodes to the backbone. Nodes on a 100BaseFX network using multimode cable and repeaters can be up to 2 kilometers apart; for networks using single-mode cable, nodes can be up to 10 kilometers apart. This variant is also written *100Base-FX*.

➜ *See* 100BaseT

➜ *Compare* 100BaseT2; 100BaseT4, 100BaseTX

100BaseT

This is the general name for any of four 100Mbps Ethernet variants. 100BaseT Ethernet is one of the candidates trying to become *the* standard 100Mbps Ethernet. This version was developed and proposed originally by Grand Junction, in collaboration with several other corporations.

The term *Fast Ethernet* is often used for this version. This is unfortunate, since that term is also used to refer to any Ethernet implementation that supports speeds faster than the official 10Mbps standard. To add to the confusing terminology, a software product (no longer available) was also named fastEthernet.100BaseT Ethernet retains Ethernet's CSMA/CD (Carrier Sense Multiple Access, Collision Detect) media access method—in contrast to the 100VG-AnyLAN variant (now officially, IEEE 802.12)—which is the other major 100Mbps Ethernet available.

The main differences between fast (100Mbps) Ethernet and standard (10Mbps) Ethernet are:

- A 100BaseT Ethernet allows a much shorter gap between signals. For example, the interframe gap (IFG) has been decreased from 9.6 to 0.96 microseconds.

- A 100BaseT Ethernet requires either higher-grade cable or more wire pairs. It can run at 100Mbps speeds on Category 3 or 4 cable—provided four pairs are available; Category 5 cable requires only two pairs.

- Currently, a 100BaseT Ethernet can support a network that is only about a tenth of the length allowed for an ordinary Ethernet network. For networks that use copper (as opposed to fiber-optic) cabling: Two nodes of a 100BaseT4 network can be no further apart than 205 meters—regardless of whether the nodes are next to each other.

- 100BaseT networks can support up to 1,024 nodes per network segment.

- 100BaseT networks must use a star topology, according to the IEEE 802.3u specifications.

The following variants of 100BaseT Ethernet have been defined:

100BaseFX Runs over multimode fiber-optic cable. Nodes on a 100BaseFX network can be up to two kilometers apart.

100BaseTX Uses two wire pairs, but requires Category 5 unshielded or shielded twisted pair (UTP or STP) wire.

100BaseT4 Can use category 3, 4, or 5 UTP cable. The T4 in the name comes from the fact that four wire pairs are needed: two for sending and two for receiving. Uses an 8B/6T data-translation scheme for greater efficiency.

100BaseT2 Can use category 3, 4, or 5 UTP cable. The T2 indicates that 100BaseT2 uses two wire pairs, each of which sends and receives.

In some configurations, fast and ordinary Ethernet nodes can share the same network. Fast Ethernet devices identify themselves as such by sending a series of FLPs (fast link pulses) at startup.

→ *Primary Sources* IEEE 802.3u committee publications

→ *Broader Categories* Ethernet

→ *Compare* 100VG-AnyLAN

100BaseT2

A 100BaseT Ethernet variant that uses two pairs of category 3 (or higher) unshielded twisted-pair (UTP) cable and RJ-45 connectors. Each wire pair is used for both sending and receiving. Nodes can be up to 500 meters apart. 100BaseT2 is only now becoming an 820.3u standard.

→ *See* 100BaseT

→ *Compare* 100BaseFX; 100BaseT4; 100BaseTX

100BaseT4

A *100BaseT Ethernet* variant that can use category 3, 4, or 5 unshielded twisted-pair (UTP) cable and RJ-45 connectors. The T4 means that four wire pairs are needed: two for sending and two for receiving. Two nodes of a 100BaseT4 network can be no further apart than 205 meters, regardless of whether the nodes are next to each other. 100BaseT transmits over multiple wires at the same time and uses 8B/6T encoding, which makes it possible to use a lower signal frequency. This variant is sometimes written *100Base-T4*.

→ *See* 100BaseT

→ *Compare* 100BaseFX; 100BaseT2; 100BaseTX

100BaseTX

A *100BaseT Ethernet* variant that uses two wire pairs (one to send and one to receive), but requires Category 5 UTP or STP wire. 100BaseTX can also use IBM type 1A cable. Like its copper-wire cousins, this variant uses RJ-45 connectors. Two nodes of a 100BaseTX network can be no further apart than 205 meters—regardless of whether the nodes are next to each other. This variant is sometimes written *100Base-TX*.

→ *See* 100BaseT

→ *Compare* 100BaseFX; 100BaseT2; 100BaseT4

100BaseVG

→ *See* 100VG-AnyLAN

100BaseX

100BaseX (sometimes written as 100Base-X) is a function that translates between the FDDI (Fiber Distributed Data Interface)-based physical layer and the CSMA/CD-based data-link layer in a 100Mbps Ethernet proposed by Grand Junction Networks. The term was used more generally to refer to a 100Mbps Ethernet developed by Grand Junction, among others. This proposed specification has since become known as Fast Ethernet, and has been refined into the following variants:

100BaseFX Runs over fiber-optic cable.

100BaseT4 Runs over unshielded twisted-pair (UTP) cable rated at category 3 or higher—provided there are four available wire pairs.

100BaseT2 Runs over category 3 or higher UTP cable but requires only two wire pairs.

100BaseTX Runs over category 5 UTP cable.

These variants all use the standard CSMA/CD (Carrier Sense Multiple Access/Collision Detection) medium access scheme used by classic Ethernet. (In contrast, the 100VG-AnyLAN variant proposed by Hewlett-Packard and other companies uses a demand priority access scheme.) Specifications and standards for the Fast Ethernet versions have been debated by the IEEE 802.3u subcommittee, and were just approved in June 1995.

→ *Broader Category* Ethernet

→ *See Also* Fast Ethernet

→ *Compare* 100VG-AnyLAN

100Mbps Ethernet

Any of several proposed 100Mbps implementations of the Ethernet network architecture. Three different approaches have been proposed: 100VG-AnyLAN, 100BaseX, and fastEthernet. These implementations differ most fundamentally in the media-access methods and types of cable they use.

100VG-AnyLAN

100VG-AnyLAN is an Ethernet-like, shared-media LAN architecture developed by Hewlett-Packard (HP) and AT&T Microelectronics, and later modified by HP and IBM. 100VG-AnyLAN has been adopted as a standard by an IEEE 802.12 committee. Like 100BaseT, one of its high-speed LAN competitors, 100VG-AnyLAN is an extension of 10BaseT Ethernet that supports transmissions of up to 100Mbps over voice-grade (category 3) twisted-pair wire. 100VG-AnyLAN is expected to eventually support speeds as high as 4Gbps. The VG in the name stands for voice grade.

Differences from 10Mbps and 100Mbps Ethernet

100VG-AnyLAN differs from ordinary (10Mbps) and fast (100Mbps) Ethernet in the following major ways:

- It uses demand priority (rather than CSMA/CD) as the media access method. Demand priority is collisionless, and it allows for minimal prioritization of packets.

- Like 100BaseT, 100VG-AnyLAN uses ordinary (category 3) unshielded twisted-pair (UTP) cable, provided that the cable has at least four wire pairs. Ordinary Ethernet uses only two pairs: one to send and one to receive. (A working group is investigating ways in which 100VG-AnyLAN can be made to operate over two-pair UTP cable.)

- It uses quartet signaling to provide four transmission channels (wire pairs) instead of just one. All wire pairs are used in the same direction at a given time. Currently, 100VG-AnyLAN is a half-duplex technology, but a study group is investigating ways to allow full-duplex connections.

- It uses the more efficient 5B/6B NRZ signal encoding, as opposed to the Manchester encoding scheme used by ordinary Ethernet. (100BaseT4, a 100BaseT variant, also uses a more efficient 8B/6T encoding scheme.)

- For category 3 cable, a VG-AnyLAN network can be at most 600 meters from end to end—and only 200 meters if all hubs in the network are connected in the same wiring closet. These values increase by 50 percent—that is, to 900 and 300 meters, respectively—when category 5 shielded twisted-pair (STP) cable is used. For VG-AnyLANs using fiber-optic cable, the most widely separated network nodes can be up to 2,000 meters, or 2 kilometers, apart.

- It supports both Ethernet and token ring networks.

Demand Priority

Demand priority is arguably the most controversial aspect of 100VG-AnyLAN. Demand priority makes it necessary to redefine the MAC (media access control) layer, which uses CSMA/CD (Carrier Sense Multiple Access/Collision Detection) to control access in Ethernet networks. In contrast to CSMA/CD, demand priority is a collisionless access method.

Demand priority ensures that each node has fair access to the network, makes it unnecessary to check for collisions, and makes it unnecessary to use a token in token ring networks. The demand priority scheme is operated from a hub or switch, which will control access to the network.

The hub or switch polls each network node in succession. If the node has something to send, it is allowed to send a single packet—except in cases discussed later in this section. If a node has nothing to send it simply skips a turn.

Nodes may be either end users or hubs. For purposes of access, a hub is treated just like a workstation by the access controller. That is, the hub will get access to the network whenever the hub gets polled. Once the hub has access to the network, however, it is treated differently. The hub gets to send one packet for each port on which it has a connection. Thus, if a hub has five workstations attached, the hub will be able to send five packets—one for each workstation—when the hub gets its turn. To the hubs below it, the hub that gets them access to the network through the access controller is known as the *root hub* for the nodes.

Nodes may indicate that their packets are high priority. Such nodes get serviced sooner and are allowed to send more than a single packet. This preferential treatment makes it possible to set up a very simple prioritization scheme in VG-AnyLAN networks—which makes such an architecture more attractive than Ethernet for sending real-time or other time-sensitive data.

&

Upgrading to 100VG-AnyLAN

100VG-AnyLAN is designed to provide an easy upgrade path from 10Mbps Ethernet. An upgrade requires two new components:

- A 100VG-AnyLAN network interface card (NIC) for each node being upgraded. This NIC replaces the 10Mbps version in the node.

- A 100VG-AnyLAN hub to replace the 10Mbps hub. This type of hub is plug-compatible with a 10Mbps hub, so that the upgrade requires simply unplugging a node from one hub and plugging it into the 100VG-AnyLAN hub. This can all take place in the wiring closet.

If you are already using twisted-pair Ethernet cabling, you may not need any new wiring, provided that the cable has four wire pairs.

In addition to Ethernet, 100VG-AnyLAN also supports token ring architectures, and it can be used with either Ethernet or Token Ring cards (but not both at the same time or in the same network). An appropriate bridge or router is needed to allow communication between an Ethernet and a token ring LAN.

Because the demand priority access method can be deterministic, the 100VG-AnyLAN architecture could handle isochronous data—that is, data (such as voice or video) that requires a constant transmission rate. In general, 100VG-AnyLAN can handle multimedia data more efficiently than 100BaseT Ethernet.

The 100VG-AnyLAN Forum is the advocacy group for this LAN architecture. This consortium includes over 20 members, including Apple, Compaq, and IBM. 100VG-AnyLAN is also known simply as VG or AnyLAN.

→ *Broader Category* Ethernet; Network Architecture

→ *See Also* Demand Priority; HSLAN (High-Speed Local-Area Network)

→ *Compare* 100BaseT

110-Type Punch-Down Block

A device for terminating wires, with the possibility of connecting input and output wires. This type of punch-down block has generally replaced the older 66-type blocks originally used by the telephone company.

→ *See Also* Punch-Down Block

193rd Bit

In a T1 communications channel, a framing bit that is attached to every group of 192 bits. These 192 bits represent a single byte from each of the 24 channels multiplexed in a T1 line.

→ *See Also* T1

500 Telephone Set

In phone company parlance, a 500 telephone set refers to a single-line telephone with a rotary dial. In short, a 500 telephone set is the telephone company's name for an older telephone.

→ *Compare* 2500 Telephone Set

802.x

→ *See* IEEE 802.x

1000Base-CX

In Gigabit Ethernet technology, 1000Base-CX represents a physical layer used to connect clusters of nodes. The specification for 1000Base-CX is based on the definition of the Fibre Channel physical layer. This variant uses two pairs of balanced, shielded 150-ohm copper cable—commonly known as twinax cable. The maximum distance between links is only 25 meters with copper cable.

Because of this, 1000Base-CX is generally used for short distance connections—for example, between nearby rooms or between a wiring closet and a room.

→ **Broader Categories** Ethernet; Gigabit Ethernet

→ **See Also** 1000Base-LX; 1000Base-SX; 1000Base-T

1000Base-LX

In Gigabit Ethernet technology, 1000Base-LX represents a physical layer used for horizontal cabling within a building. The 1000Base-LX specification is based on the physical layer definition for Fibre Channel. 1000Base-LX uses a pair of fiber-optic cables for its medium, and long-wavelength light for its signal. If single-mode fiber is used, the maximum distance between links is 3 kilometers; if multimode fiber is used, the maximum distance is either 440 or 550 meters—depending on whether 62.5 or 50 micron fiber used.

→ **Broader Categories** Ethernet; Gigabit Ethernet

→ **See Also** 1000Base-CX; 1000Base-SX; 1000Base-T

1000Base-SX

In Gigabit Ethernet technology, 1000Base-SX represents a physical layer used for backbone cabling. The 1000Base-SX specification is based on the physical layer definition for Fibre Channel. This variant uses two multimode fiber optic cables for a medium, and short-wavelength light for signaling. The maximum distance between links is either 260 or 525 meters—for 62.5 and 50 micron multimode fiber, respectively.

→ **Broader Categories** Ethernet; Gigabit Ethernet

→ **See Also** 1000Base-CX; 1000Base-LX; 1000Base-T

1000Base-T

1000Base-T, also known as Gigabit Ethernet, is the name for an Ethernet variant that operates at 1000Mbps

→ **Broader Category** Ethernet

→ **See Also** 1000Base-CX; 1000Base-LX; 1000Base-SX; Gigabit Ethernet

1000Base-X

This is used as a general term to refer to the physical layer in a Gigabit Ethernet network. At the physical control sublayer (PCS)—which is the interface between the media access control (MAC) sublayer of the data-link layer above and the physical medium attachment (PMA) sublayer below—1000Base-X supports three different media:

1000Base-CX Uses two pairs of copper cable.

1000Base-LX Uses one pair of optical fibers using long-wavelength light.

1000Base-SX Uses one pair of optical fibers using short-wavelength light.

→ **Broader Category** Gigabit Ethernet

→ **See Also** 1000Base-CX; 1000Base-LX; 1000Base-SX

1003.x

→ **See** POSIX (Portable Operating System for UNIX)

2500 Telephone Set

In phone company parlance, a 2500 telephone set refers to a dual-tone multifrequency (DTMF) telephone with a touch-tone keypad. This type of phone is what most customers currently use.

→ *Compare* 500 Telephone Set

3172

The 3172 is an IBM network controller. It connects to a LAN on one side and to a mainframe on the other. The LAN may use any of several architectures, including Ethernet, Token Ring, or FDDI (Fiber Distributed Data Interface).

3174

A cluster control unit for the IBM 3270 family of display terminals.

3270

The 3270 designation is used for a line of terminals, communications controllers, and printers that are used with IBM mainframes. The 3270 devices use synchronous communications protocols, either SDLC (Synchronous Data Link Control) or BSC (Binary Synchronous Communication), to communicate with the host.

In order for a stand-alone PC to communicate with an IBM mainframe, it must have an add-in board that enables the PC to emulate a 3270 terminal.

3270 Data Stream

In IBM's SNA (Systems Network Architecture) environment, a stream in which characters are converted and/or formatted, as specified through control characters and attribute settings.

3274

The designation for a cluster controller that can serve as a front end for an IBM mainframe host. Devices, such as 3270 terminals or printers, communicate with the host through this controller. The 3274 cluster controllers have been replaced by 3174 establishment controllers in newer configurations.

3278

The designation for a popular IBM terminal used to communicate with IBM mainframes.

3279

The designation for a color version of the 3278 terminal used to communicate with IBM mainframes.

3705

The designation for a computer that serves as a data communications controller for IBM's 370-series mainframes. The 3705 also has ports for asynchronous access over dial-up lines.

3745

The IBM 3745 is a communications controller that is used, for example, as a front-end processor for an IBM SNA (System Network Architecture) network.

3780

The IBM 3780 is a remote job-entry terminal that can be used as a remote card reader or a printer for an IBM mainframe. 3780 devices communicate using the binary synchronous (BSC) protocol or the Synchronous Data Link Control (SDLC) protocol.

3780 also refers to the batch language protocol used for communication with remote terminals.

6611

The 6611 is a multiprotocol router from IBM. The 6611 supports APPN (Advanced Peer-to-Peer Networking, IBM's peer networking software), AppleTalk, DECnet, IPX (Internetwork Packet Exchange), NetBIOS, and TCP/IP (Transmission Control Protocol/Internet Protocol).

41449

This is AT&T's name for its version of the ISDN (Integrated Services Digital Network) primary rate interface (PRI). 41449 is not identical to the ANSI T1.607 specification, which defines ISDN PRI.

&

A

A1 Security Level

A1 represents the highest level of security in the U.S. government's Orange Book specifications on computer security.

→ **See Also** Security

A5

A5 is a cipher (that is, an encryption method) used in GSM (Global System for Mobile Communications) cellular communications to encrypt transmissions between a digital mobile phone and a base station. Other parts of a mobile phone connection (such as the connection between two base stations or between a base station and the telephone company's central office) are not encrypted.

A5 is an example of a stream cipher—that is, one in which a transmission is encrypted a byte (or even a bit) at a time. The algorithm is considered basically sound (based on statistical tests); however, "simple" versions (that is, those using short registers in the encryption process) can be deciphered by exhaustive search.

→ **See Also** Encryption

AA (Auto Answer)

Auto answer is a feature by which a modem, fax machine, or other device can automatically respond to an incoming call and establish a connection.

AAL (ATM Adaptation Layer)

The AAL is the topmost of the three layers defined for the ATM network architecture. The AAL mediates between the ATM layer and the various communication services involved in a transmission. Separate AAL protocols are defined for the different quality of service (QoS) classes supported in ATM. These protocols are known as AAL 1 through AAL 5.

→ **See Also** ATM (Asynchronous Transfer Mode)

AAR (Automatic Alternate Routing)

In X.25 and other networks, AAR is the process by which the network automatically routes traffic—to maximize throughput, minimize distance, or balance channel usage.

AARP (AppleTalk Address Resolution Protocol)

→ **See** Protocol, AARP (AppleTalk Address Resolution Protocol)

ABM (Asynchronous Balanced Mode)

In the ISO's HDLC (High-Level Data-Link Control) protocol, ABM is an operating mode that gives each node in a point-to-point connection equal status as senders and receivers.

ABP (Alternate Bipolar)

A signal-encoding method.

→ **See Also** Encoding, Signal

ABR (Available Bit Rate)

In ATM (Asynchronous Transfer Mode), ABR is one of the two best-effort service classes. ABR is used for bursty data, and it makes use of any available bandwidth—within limits. Unlike unspecified bit rate (UBR), the other best-effort service class, ABR uses traffic management and checks for congestion. ABR will slow down transmission if traffic is heavy and the network is congested to avoid dropped cells. ABR does not guarantee delivery of

ATM cells, but it does guarantee a minimum transmission rate for a user.

When an application requests ABR service, the network first determines the peak cell rate (PCR) and the minimum cell rate (MCR). The PCR is the fastest speed possible without the risk of cell loss. The PCR is the highest available rate the service class will use. The MCR is the lowest rate the application will accept. This value may be negotiated based on the needs of the application, or it may be the network's default value. Once the PCR and MCR have been negotiated, the ABR service class will operate within these limits.

To ensure that it can operate within its specified bounds, an ABR session uses closed-loop congestion management (to monitor traffic and adjust the rate when necessary) and a rate-based flow control mechanism (to ensure that the ABR session gets its share of the bandwidth). ATM switches play an important role in congestion management and, therefore, also in rate control. For example, in the simplest congestion management plan, an ATM switch may set a congestion indication bit in an ATM cell, to tell the receiving station of congestion on the line. The end station will then send a resource management cell to the sending station to have it lower the transmission rate. In a more sophisticated management scheme, some or all of the ATM switches in a connection may serve as virtual end stations, which enables them to play a more direct role in controlling the transmission rate. (See the entry on Closed-Loop Congestion Management for more details.)

Also, to minimize data loss under possibly variable transmission conditions, ATM switches capable of handling ABR traffic generally include large buffers. Cells are stored in these buffers, while a switch waits for bandwidth to open up or for confirmation that the cells successfully reached their destination. For the most effective operation, each virtual connection through the switch should have its own buffer. (Each of these can be proportionately smaller than—and taken from—the switch's global buffer.)

→ **Broader Category** ATM (Asynchronous Transfer Mode)

→ **Compare** CBR (Constant Bit Rate); UBR (Unspecified Bit Rate); VBR (Variable Bit Rate)

→ **See Also** Best-Effort Service; Closed-Loop Congestion Management

Abstract Syntax

An abstract syntax is a machine-independent set of language elements and rules used to describe objects, communications protocols, and other items. For example, Abstract Syntax Notation One (ASN.1) was developed as part of the OSI reference model; Extended Data Representation (XDR) was developed as part of Sun Microsystems' Network File System (NFS).

Abstract Syntax Notation One (ASN.1)

→ **See** ASN.1 (Abstract Syntax Notation One)

AC (Access Control)

A field in a token-ring token or data frame.

AC (Alternating Current)

AC (alternating current) is a power supply whose polarity (direction of flow) switches periodically. AC is the type of electrical power supplied for homes and offices.

With AC, the actual amount of power being supplied at any given moment depends on where in the switching process you are. When plotted over time, a "pure" AC power supply produces a sine wave.

Not all countries use the same switching rate. For example, in North America, the current switches polarity 60 times per second; in most European countries, the rate is 50 times per second. These values are indicated as cycles per second, or hertz (Hz).

Thus, electrical power in the United States alternates at 60 Hz.

Not all devices can use AC. In some cases the AC power must be converted to direct current (DC), which provides a constant voltage level and polarity. All digital systems (such as computers) must use DC.

→ *Compare* DC (Direct Current)

AC (Application Context)

In the OSI reference model, AC (application context) is a term for all the application service elements (ASEs) required to use an application in a particular context.

More specifically, in network management, the AC provides the ground rules that serve to define the relationship between two applications during a temporary connection. These ground rules will determine the types of services that can be invoked during the connection and also the manner in which information will be exchanged. Such a context is important for defining the systems management services provided by a CMISE (Common Management Information Service Element).

→ *See Also* ASE (Application Service Element); CMISE (Common Management Information Service Element)

Acceptable Use Policy (AUP)

→ *See* AUP (Acceptable Use Policy)

Acceptance Angle

In fiber optics, the acceptance angle is a value that measures the range over which incoming light will be reflected and propagated through the fiber. The size of this angle depends on the relative refractive indexes of the fiber core, the cladding, and the surrounding medium (which is generally air). "Acceptance angle and cone" illustrates this concept and its three-dimensional counterpart, the acceptance cone.

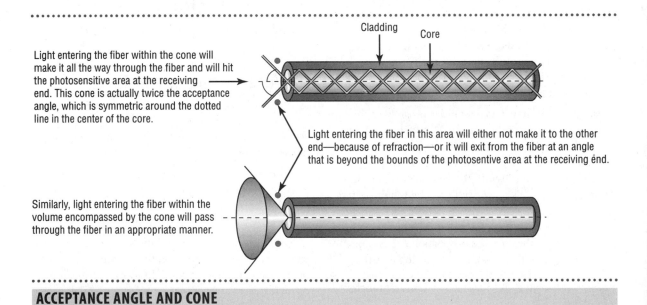

Cladding Core

Light entering the fiber within the cone will make it all the way through the fiber and will hit the photosensitive area at the receiving end. This cone is actually twice the acceptance angle, which is symmetric around the dotted line in the center of the core.

Light entering the fiber in this area will either not make it to the other end—because of refraction—or it will exit from the fiber at an angle that is beyond the bounds of the photosentive area at the receiving end.

Similarly, light entering the fiber within the volume encompassed by the cone will pass through the fiber in an appropriate manner.

ACCEPTANCE ANGLE AND CONE

Light entering the fiber within the acceptance angle will make it all the way through the fiber and will hit the photosensitive area at the receiving end. Note that the total acceptable area is actually twice the acceptance angle, which is symmetric around the dotted line in the center of the core, as seen in the illustration. In the three-dimensional case, light entering the fiber at an angle that lies outside the acceptance cone volume will either not make it to the other end—because of refraction—or it will exit from the fiber at an angle that is beyond the bounds of the photosensitive area at the receiving end. In contrast, light entering the fiber within the volume encompassed by the cone will pass through the fiber in an appropriate manner.

Acceptance Cone

In fiber optics, an acceptance cone is the three-dimensional analog of an acceptance angle. The cone is generated by revolving the acceptance angle 360 degrees with the center of the fiber's core as the cone's point. The illustration "Acceptance angle and cone" depicts this cone, as well as the two-dimensional angle.

Access Component

An access component is one of the three major parts of a data warehouse environment—the other two are the acquisitions and storage components. The access component represents the front end of the data warehouse, and this is the part that a user will work with when querying, mining, or adding to the database.

The access component may include various applications for performing the required tasks. Front-end applications for accessing a data warehouse may include the following:

- Those that provide interfaces for "simple" queries—for example, stand-alone query

managers, query management capabilities built into other products (such as standard spreadsheet or database programs), and also report generators. Since data warehouses generally have huge amounts of data, such programs may have trouble dealing with and paring down the quantities of information returned by even simple queries.

- Data-mining applications, including advanced statistical analysis programs, neural network or other (quasi-) artificial intelligence packages, simulation and visualization programs (which try to help the miner get a handle on the information mined by providing and presenting it in a dynamic or visual way). Despite their greater sophistication, such programs might still place a considerable analytical burden on the user.

- Special-purpose applications (such as finance, inventory, or human resource packages) that are designed for use in other contexts and to work with certain kinds of information. Even though they are designed for other purposes, users may still expect them to be usable for providing access to warehouse data. Information of use to such packages may be included in the data warehouse, but not necessarily in the form (or format) required by the application.

- Custom applications designed and built to order—generally in-house or possibly through outsourcing—which are intended to work as effectively and efficiently as possible with the contents and format of the warehouse of interest.

→ *Broader Category* Data Warehousing

→ *Compare* Acquisition Component; Storage Component

Access Control

An operating system uses access control to determine the following:

- How users or resources can interact with the operating system
- What a specific user or group of users may do when interacting with the operating system
- Who can access a file or directory and what that user can do after accessing it
- How system or network resources can be used

At the lowest levels, hardware elements and software processes can obtain limited access to the system through mechanisms such as interrupts or polling. For example, low-level access to DOS is through IRQs (interrupt request lines) and through software interrupts, such as INT 21H, which provide programs with access to DOS capabilities and to certain hardware resources.

Access-control measures can be associated with users, files and directories, or resources. When assigned to users or groups of users, these control measures are known as *access rights*, *access privileges*, *trustee rights,* or *permissions*. When associated with files and directories, the access-control elements are known as *attributes* or *flags*. Resources and other system objects generally have an associated access control list (ACL), which contains all the users who may use the resource.

Access control is generally specified by a system administrator or by the owner of a particular file or resource. Some access privileges are determined for users during network configuration; others may be assigned when the user logs on to a network or begins a session with an operating system.

Access-control issues can be complex, particularly if multiple operating environments are involved, as on an internetwork. One reason is that operating environments differ in the access-control measures they support. Because there are overlaps, omissions, and definition differences, mapping access controls between environments may be complicated.

→ *See Also* Access Rights

Access Control Decision Function (ACDF)

→ *See* ACDF (Access Control Decision Function)

Access Control Enforcement Function (ACEF)

→ *See* ACEF (Access Control Enforcement Function)

Access Control Entry (ACE)

→ *See* ACE (Access Control Entry)

Access Control Information (ACI)

→ *See* ACI (Access Control Information)

Access Control List (ACL)

→ *See* ACL (Access Control List)

Access Interface Unit (AIU)

→ *See* AIU (Access Interface Unit)

Access Line

In PSTNs (Public Switched Telephone Networks)—that is, in ordinary telephone connections—the access line connects the end user to the central office (CO). Also known as the *local loop*, this connection is generally analog.

At the CO, the connection from the access line is generally converted to digital form, and is then switched to the appropriate circuits. This is either a circuit within the same exchange (for a local call) or the appropriate trunk for connection to another exchange or to a toll office (for extended area service or long-distance calls, respectively).

Access Log

An access log is a record of efforts to access a network or a resource on that network. Access logs are often kept on a firewall, and the log represents one element in the security services provided by the firewall. The specific contents of an access log depend on the firewall or on other elements of the server's security system. The process of adding to such a log file is known as *access logging*.

Access Mask

In Windows NT, an access mask is used to specify the operations, or services, that are allowed to a particular user or group. An access mask is associated with an object, and the details of a mask depend on the particular object of interest. For example, an access mask for a file object may include such operations as Read, Write, Run (execute), Delete, or Change.

→ *Broader Category* Windows NT

Access Network

A network attached to the trunk of a backbone network. This type of connection usually requires a gateway or a router, depending on the types of networks that comprise the backbone network.

Access Permission

→ *See* Permissions

Access Rights

Access rights are properties associated with files or directories in a networking environment; also known as *access privileges, access permissions,* or *trustee rights*. Access rights determine how users and network services can access and use files and directories. All networking environments and operating systems use some type of access rights settings to control access to the network and its resources.

Access rights are similar to security attributes, which specify additional properties relating to a file or directory. Security attributes can override access rights. In general, rights are assigned to a user for a specific file or directory. Attributes are assigned to a file or directory and control access by any user, regardless of that user's rights. The set of rights a user has been assigned to a file or directory is called his or her *trustee assignment*.

The number of access rights is relatively small. The terminology and particular combination of rights vary from system to system. For example, in Novell's NetWare 3.*x* and 4.*x*, access rights may be associated with directories or files or both, and a right may apply to all the files in a directory or only to individual ones. In NetWare 2.*x*, rights apply only to directories. See the table "Novell NetWare Access Rights" for descriptions of the access rights associated with NetWare.

NOVELL NETWARE ACCESS RIGHTS

Access Right	Usage Allowed
Access Control (A)	Allows you to modify the trustee assignments and inherited rights mask (IRM) for a file. With Access Control rights, you can grant other users any rights except Supervisory rights.
Create (C)	Allows you to create subdirectories or files within a directory. Also allows you to salvage a file if it is deleted.
Erase (E)	Allows you to delete a file or directory.
File Scan (F)	Allows you to see a file or directory name when listing the parent directory.

Continued on next page

NOVELL NETWARE ACCESS RIGHTS (continued)

Access Right	Usage Allowed
Modify (M)	Allows you to change the name and attributes of a file or directory.
Read (R)	Allows you to open and read a file.
Supervisory (S)	Allows you to exercise all rights to a file or directory, including the right to grant Supervisory privileges to the file or directory to other users. (This right does not exist in NetWare 2.x.)
Write (W)	Allows you to open, edit, and save a file.

The meaning or effect of a specific privilege may also be system-dependent. For example, in an AppleShare environment, the following access privileges are defined:

- See Files, which allows a user to see, open, and copy files.

- See Folder, which allows a user to see a folder (but not necessarily the folder's contents). If this privilege is not set, the folder does not even appear on the user's screen.

- Make Changes, which allows the user to change the contents of a file or folder. Even drastic changes such as deletions are allowed.

These AppleShare environment privileges may be granted to any of the following:

- Owner: The user who created (and, hence, owns) the file or folder.

- Group: The collection of users to whom the privilege is granted. This may be a single user.

- Everyone: All users with access to the file server.

In UNIX, owners, groups, and others may be granted read, write, or execute permissions for a file or a directory, as follows:

- Read access for a file allows a user to read or display the contents of a file. Read permission for a directory means the user can generate a directory listing.

- Write access for a file means the user can edit the file or redirect output to it. Write access for a directory allows the user to create a file or a subdirectory.

- Execute access for a file allows the user to use the file name as a command. Execute permission for a directory means the user can pass through the directory to subdirectories.

In Windows NT, access rights can be associated with folders (that is, directories) and files. Administrators generally find it easier to work at the folder level because files within the folder have the same rights associated with them as the folder does. The following access rights can be defined for folders in NT networks that use the NTFS file system:

No Access   User has no access rights to the folder or any of its files. This overrides any other access or other rights the user might have. This can also be a file access right.

List   User can view a directory or subdirectory list and can switch to a subdirectory.

Read   User has List rights and, in addition, can view the contents of data files and run applications. This can also be a file access right.

Add   User can add files and subdirectories to a directory.

Add & Read   User has both Read and Add rights.

Change   User has Add & Read rights and, in addition, can change the contents of data files and can delete files and subdirectories. This can also be a file access right.

Full Control   User has all of the above rights and, in addition, can change permission settings on files and subdirectories and can become owner of files or subdirectories. This can also be a file access right.

A

Special Directory Access   User can customize rights to be assigned for a directory. Special Directory Access rights include Read, Write, Delete, Execute, Change Permissions, and Take Ownership.

Special File Access   User has rights analogous to Special Directory Access, except that they apply to files instead of directories.

When a single machine or network includes more than one environment, there must be a well-defined rule for assigning and determining access rights. For example, in NetWare for Macintosh, the NetWare access rights supersede the AppleShare access privileges.

Similarly, there are mechanisms for ensuring that access rights are applied only as broadly as intended. For example, NetWare uses an Inherited Rights Mask (version 3.x) or Inherited Rights Filter (version 4.x) to specify which access rights for a directory are also applicable in a subdirectory.

→ **Broader Category**   Access Control

→ **See Also**   Attribute; IRM (Inherited Rights Mask)/IRF (Inherited Rights Filter)

Access Time

In hard-disk performance, access time refers to the average amount of time it takes to move the read/write heads to a specified location and retrieve data at that location. The lower this value, the better the performance. Currently, hard disks with access times around 10 milliseconds are common.

Access Token (AT)

→ **See**   (AT) Access Token

Access Unit (AU)

→ **See**   AU (Access Unit)

Account

An account describes and represents a user for a network. The account includes information associated with the user such as the following: user name, password, groups of which the user is a member, and the user's access rights. Any restrictions on the form such information can or must take (for example, password format) are specified in the account policies for the network.

Accounting

A process by which network usage can be determined and charges assessed for use of network resources, such as storage, access, and services. Accounting measures include blocks read, blocks written, connect time, disk storage, and service requests.

Most network operating systems include an accounting utility or support an add-on accounting package. For example, NetWare 3.11 has an accounting option in its SYSCON utility.

Accounting Management (AM)

→ **See**   AM (Accounting Management)

Account Lockout

In Windows NT, account lockout is a value that specifies the number of incorrect or invalid login attempts allowed before a (would-be) user's account is frozen and the user is locked out from any future login attempts. This value, and its consequent lockout, is used as a very basic security measure. The main effectiveness of account lockout is to prevent someone from using a dictionary or other brute force attack to guess a password. (For the sake of hopeless typists, access to a locked account generally can be restored by the system administrator.) In Novell NetWare environments, the analogous security measure is known as *intruder detection*.

Account Metering Function (AMF)

→ *See* AMF (Account Metering Function)

Account Policy

In networking and other multiuser environments, a set of rules that determines whether a particular user is allowed to access the system and what resources the user may use. In Windows NT Advanced Server, the account policy determines the way in which passwords may be used in a domain (a group of servers with a common security policy and database).

Accumaster Integrator

A network management program from AT&T.

ACD (Automatic Call Distributor)

In a PBX (private branch exchange) or other telephone service, an ACD is a device that automatically switches an incoming call to the next available line.

ACDF (Access Control Decision Function)

In open systems, a function that uses various types of information, such as ACI (access control information), and guidelines to decide whether to grant access to resources in a particular situation.

ACE (Access Control Entry)

In Windows NT, an ACE is an element of an Access Control List (ACL). The ACE specifies permission to carry out an operation or use a service defined for a particular resource or object. Within such a list, the ACE is associated with a particular user or group, and it helps to define the permissions granted to that user (or group).

→ *Broader Category* Windows NT

ACE (Adverse Channel Enhancement)

In telecommunications, an ACE is a modem-adjustment method that allows the modem to compensate for noisy lines. For example, the modem might lower the operating speed if the transmission error rate gets too high.

ACEF (Access Control Enforcement Function)

In open systems, a function that enforces the decision made by the ACDF (access control decision function).

ACF (Advanced Communications Function)

ACF (Advanced Communications Function) is the base name for several IBM software packages that operate under IBM's SNA (Systems Network Architecture). In some cases, the programs are revisions or extensions of older programs.

The following programs are included:

ACF/NCP (Advanced Communications Function/Network Control Program) Resides in a communications controller. It provides and controls communications between the host machine and the network devices.

ACF/TCAM (Advanced Communications Function/Telecommunications Access Method) Serves as an ACF/VTAM application and provides message handling and other capabilities.

ACF/VTAM (Advanced Communications Function/Virtual Telecommunications Access Method) Provides and controls communications between a terminal and host programs. ACF/VTAM supersedes and adds capabilities to the older VTAM software.

ACF/VTAME (Advanced Communications Function/Virtual Telecommunications Access Method Entry) An obsolete program that has been superseded by ACF/VTAM.

→ *Broader Category* SNA (Systems Network Architecture)

ACI (Access Control Information)

In the CCITT's X.500 directory services model, ACI refers to any information used in controlling access to a file or directory.

ACID (Atomicity, Consistency, Isolation, and Durability)

In transaction processing (TP), the ACID acronym summarizes the attributes that are desirable for a transaction.

Atomicity Means that either the entire transaction must be completed or it must seem as if nothing at all was done. That is, either all the steps required for the transaction must be completed or the transaction processing program must roll back the state of the system to the point just before any of the transaction was begun. For example, if a customer decides to cancel an ATM (automatic teller machine) transaction, after inserting an ATM card and entering a PIN (personal identification number), the program

must forget that the person even entered any information.

Consistency Means that a completed transaction must take the system from one consistent state to another. For example, the consistency criterion means that making a cash withdrawal from an ATM machine should leave the user's account with a balance that is less than the original balance by the amount of the withdrawal (plus any fees for the transaction). The user should not be left without an account or with a balance larger than before the transaction.

Isolation Means that the final outcome of a transaction carried out concurrently with lots of other transactions should be the same as if the transactions were carried out individually and in sequence instead of concurrently. That is, the final outcomes should be the same as if each transaction were carried out in its entirety before any other transaction is begun.

Durability Means that, when a transaction is completed, it should leave the transaction elements (for example, the user) in a new state and that this state should persist over time—at least until there is another transaction. For example, once a cash withdrawal is made, the person's bank balance should reflect the withdrawal, but then should not immediately change to new values without any reason.

The ACID criteria should be transparent to a user engaged in a transaction. That is, a transaction passes the ACID test exactly when everything goes smoothly—regardless of whether the transaction is completed or not.

ACK

In telecommunications, a control character that indicates that a packet has been received without an error. In certain network architectures, ACK is the name for a frame that sends such an acknowledgment. The ASCII ACK character has value 6.

ACL (Access Control List)

In some networking environments, the ACL is a list of services available on a network, along with the users and devices that are allowed to use each service. This list provides one way to control access to network resources.

In NetWare Directory Services (NDS), each object in the directory has a property called the ACL, which lists all the other objects that have trustee assignments (rights) to that object.

Acquisition Component

An acquisition component is one of the three major parts of a data warehouse environment—with the other two being the access and storage components. The acquisition component is the back end of the data warehouse environment, and refers to the tools and processes required to create the data warehouse.

This component needs to work with the data (which may come from any of several types of sources), with the records containing the data (which may contain duplicate, discrepant, or obsolete records), and with the keys used to characterize and organize the data and records. It also needs to be able to interact with the sources of the data—for extracting the information and also for passing back corrections to the source of the extracted data. To accomplish all these things, an acquisition component needs the following kinds of capabilities, which correspond to various phases in the creation of the warehouse:

Data extraction This involves actually removing the data from the source, which may be a legacy system (such as the corporate database or databases), purchased or rented materials (such as mailing lists), or materials that are acquired on an ongoing basis (such as field reports or sales information from field workers). Once extraction methods have been developed for a set of data from a given source, and once these have been tested and fine-tuned, they should be

turned into functions that can be automated—to make it possible to extract similar data as the source materials grow or change and as new data become available. Data extraction may involve various types of hardware environments (mainframes, stand-alone or networked PCs, tapes, and so forth); similarly, the extraction process may need to deal with various types of software and files (organized databases, scanned data, and so forth)—all of which add to the challenge of successfully extracting the information that is to become part of the data warehouse.

Data cleaning This entails eliminating inaccuracies (such as incorrect values in addresses, IDs, and so forth), inconsistencies (such as multiple, but not identical, records for the same person or item), and impossibilities (such as record values out of range). For successful cleaning, it's necessary to have a basis for making decisions (for example, determining the correct value, establishing criteria for selecting among inconsistent data, agreeing how to deal with impossible data) and then a means of implementing these decisions. As with data extraction, the first phase needs to be relatively hands-on, and may require decisions on a record-by-record basis. Once the initial materials have been cleaned and stored, a set of general methods must be developed to make it feasible to update materials that have already been included, and also to acquire new information. Data cleaning concerns primarily the content of the data, in contrast to the next component, which is concerned with the structure of the data. If you've ever gotten multiple pieces of bulk mail with just minor differences in the name or address, you've experienced directly the fact that this aspect of creating a data warehouse is often sadly neglected.

Data formatting Data cleaning tries to ensure that the material going into (and, as a result, also coming out of) the warehouse is true and accurate. In contrast, data formatting is concerned with ensuring that the structure of the information (format, field sizes, and so forth) is consistent and compatible. For example, an acquisitions component needs to be able to ensure that field sizes, field sequencing, and data types all conform to the desired standards.

Integrating keys   Keyed data from various sources may need to be integrated with each other and into the data warehouse so that a user can search all the information easily and with a reasonable expectation of getting reliable results. Since the keys used to organize the data from various sources are likely to reflect the priorities of the respective database administrators (for example, sales or marketing as opposed to technical support), integrating the keys may be a formidable task, and must be done carefully and intelligently.

Merging records and files   Even if the keys to the records can be integrated and merged, there is still the task of combining the information that is to be found at the end of those keys. Depending on the format and accuracy of this information, this may be a very major task indeed.

Purging records   When multiple databases are merged, duplicate records may be found, and these will need to be purged—both to keep the volume of information in the warehouse down and also to prevent future errors from creeping in. If this is not done, one copy of a record may be updated but not the other, which could lead to problems at a later point.

Loading the warehouse   Once everything has been organized, cleaned, and tidied, the information can be put into the data warehouse.

Updating the data source (back-flush capabilities)   *Back-flushing* refers to feedback or corrections that flow from the data warehouse to the source databases from which the warehouse was filled. Such feedback should be provided for several reasons: to show common courtesy to the keepers of the original database, to keep users of the databases (as opposed to the warehouse)

from getting incorrect information from their database, and also to prevent the erroneous records from being reintroduced to the warehouse at a later date—for example, if the warehouse is updated from the original sources.

→ *Broader Category* Data warehouse

→ *See Also* Access Component; Storage Component

ACR (Available Cell Rate)

The ACR is a measure of bandwidth in ATM (Asynchronous Transfer Mode) networks. More specifically, the ACR value represents the number of cells that are available or allowed per second for a specified quality of service (QoS) class.

ACR is also known as the *allowed cell rate*.

→ *Broader Categories* ATM (Asynchronous Transfer Mode); QoS (Quality of Service)

ACS (Asynchronous Communications Server)

An ACS is usually a dedicated PC or expansion board that provides other network nodes with access to any of several serial ports or modems. The ports may be connected to mainframes or minicomputers.

To access a modem or a port, the workstation user can run an ordinary communications program in a transparent manner. However, in order for this to work, one of the following must be the case:

- The communications program must include a redirector to route the communication process to the appropriate ACS.

- The workstation must have a special hardware port emulation board installed, which takes up one of the workstation's expansion slots. In this case, the communications package does not need any special rerouting capabilities.

- The user must run a redirection program before starting the communications package. To work with a software-based redirector, the communications package must be able to use DOS interrupt INT 14H. Unfortunately, many communications programs bypass this interrupt to access the UART (universal asynchronous receiver/transmitter) directly for faster operation.

→ *Broader Category* Server

ACSE (Association Control Service Element)

In the OSI reference model, an application-level service that establishes the appropriate relationship between two applications, so that they can cooperate and communicate on a task, such as exchanging information.

Active

When used to describe hardware or a configuration, *active* generally means that the hardware does some signal processing—cleaning, boosting, or both. For example, an active hub boosts and cleans a signal before passing it on.

Active Content

Active content refers to material on a Web page that can behave differently depending on what the user does or on specific conditions existing at runtime. For example, the date at runtime may determine which version of active content is displayed—or whether any content is displayed at all. Similarly, values in a cookie file may determine what a user sees. For interactive pages, the user's responses will determine how the content develops.

Several possibilities exist for creating active content. These include Dynamic Hypertext Markup Language (DHTML), ActiveX controls, and Java applets for working at the level of the actual document. Various tools and resources—including Web page editors, class or control libraries, and so forth—exist for creating active content using any of these approaches (that is, Java, ActiveX, and so forth).

Because active content needs to execute on the user's machine, the active components may pose a security threat. For example, an ActiveX control may cause malicious or inadvertent damage to the user's files or system. Because they execute within their own "sandbox," Java applets cannot cause such damage. (In fact, it is possible to get applets to spill out of the sandbox, but such efforts have not yet gone beyond research labs.)

Active Directory

Microsoft's Active Directory is the global distributed directory service included with Windows 2000 (formerly known as NT 5). Active Directory is based on, and compatible with, X.500 directory standards, but it also includes proprietary extensions. When Windows 2000 is released, Active Directory will be able to provide hierarchical, distributed directory services for NT networks and internetworks, and will be able to work with other directory services based on open standards (for example, Novell Directory Services, or NDS).

Active Directory supports the LDAP (Lightweight Directory Access Protocol) in native mode, and provides such directory services as the following:

- Adding or modifying user accounts

- Locating printers and other network resources

- Managing network resources, user entries, and also distributed components

Support for distributed components is provided through Microsoft's DCOM (Distributed Component Object Model), which has been developed along with COM (Component Object Model).

The ADSI (Active Directory Services Interface) provides a unified interface to directory services for developers. This enables developers to create applications that can work with whatever directory service is in use on a network—for example, LDAP or NDS.

→ *Broader Category* DS (Directory Service)

Active Directory Services Interface (ADSI)

→ *See* ADSI (Active Directory Services Interface)

Active Hub

In an ARCnet and other networks, an active hub is a component that makes it possible to connect additional nodes to the network and also to boost signals that go through the hub.

→ *See Also* Hub

Active Link

In an ARCnet network, a box used to connect two cable segments when both cable segments have high-impedance network interface cards (NICs) connected.

Active Monitor (AM)

→ *See* AM (Active Monitor)

Active Monitor Present (AMP)

→ *See* AMP (Active Monitor Present)

Active Platform

Active Platform is the name given to a family of products created by Microsoft for network clients and servers to facilitate connectivity over intranetworks and the Internet. Active Platform includes Microsoft Internet Explorer (IE) on the client side and Microsoft Windows NT Server and Internet Information Server (IIS) on the server side. Also included on the server side are Microsoft Active Directory (which provides X.500 compliant directory services using LDAP, or Lightweight Directory Access Protocol) and Microsoft Transaction Server (which provides transaction monitoring and object request broker, or ORB, services). Not all of these components have been completed, but they are all expected to be available by the time Windows 2000 (formerly known as NT 5) is released.

In addition, Microsoft's implementation of the HTML (Hypertext Markup Language) and Dynamic HTML standards, its COM (Component Object Model), and also DCOM (Distributed Component Object Model), are part of Active Platform, along with Active Server Pages (ASPs).

For various reasons, Microsoft is dropping the name Active Platform, and is now using the name Distributed interNetworking Applications Architecture (DNA) to describe essentially the same technology.

Active Server Pages (ASP)

→ *See* ASP (Active Server Pages)

Active Star

A network configuration in which the central node of a star topology cleans and boosts a signal.

→ *See Also* Topology, Star

Active Text

In HTML (Hypertext Markup Language) and XML (eXtensible Markup Language) files, active text is content that represents a hypertext link. When the file is displayed on a Web page, active text generally will be highlighted or marked in some special way. When the user moves the mouse pointer over active text, the pointer and/or the text should change to indicate that the content is a link. If the user clicks on active text, the browser should retrieve and display the document (or document section) associated with the link.

ActiveVRML

ActiveVRML (Virtual Reality Markup Language) is used to display interactive animation. It is an add-on for Microsoft Internet Information Server (IIS). Once installed in IIS, ActiveVRML can automatically handle both stand-alone VRML files and also VRML code embedded in Web pages. ActiveVRML is available over the Web from http://www.microsoft .com/ie.

→ *See Also*   VRML (Virtual Reality Markup Language)

ActiveX

Microsoft ActiveX is a software technology whose components make it possible to do neat things in Web pages—such as making them interactive. The technology can also be used to enable documents to launch viewer, help, or other types of programs from within the document. ActiveX accomplishes these things by using a version of Microsoft OLE (object linking and embedding) technology that has been streamlined and extended to make the technology more suitable for use over the Internet or an intranet. OLE and ActiveX are both based on Microsoft's Component Object Model (COM), which specifies how objects are to be defined and how they can be manipulated. (One of Microsoft's

own Web pages describes ActiveX as essentially a packaging technology for COM objects.)

ActiveX is still evolving, as is the larger context within which ActiveX fits—namely Microsoft's architecture for working with objects on the Internet and over intranets. This larger framework includes Microsoft's COM, DCOM (Distributed Component Object Model), and its newer DNA (Distributed interNetworking Applications Architecture). While details and capabilities are still changing, the main components of the ActiveX technology are in place. These include ActiveX controls, ActiveX documents, ActiveX scripting capabilities (with Microsoft's own Java Virtual Machine, or JVM), and ActiveX server-side resources.

ActiveX Controls

The main element in ActiveX is the ActiveX control. This is essentially a small, self-contained, compiled program or module that can be embedded in a Web page and then executed when the page is displayed by an appropriate browser (such as Microsoft Internet Explorer 3 and later).

ActiveX controls are native code, and are generally delivered as DLLs (dynamic-link libraries). As native code, controls have the same capabilities and rights as other Windows programs—for example, accessing files or peripherals on the user's machine. (Such capabilities make controls more powerful, but also more susceptible to security abuses, as discussed below.)

For input and output tasks, ActiveX controls use the application in charge of the file in which the control is embedded. In the case of Web pages, this will generally be a browser. ActiveX controls play the same kind of role in Microsoft's browser environment as Java applets do in Netscape's Web technology. However, because controls are compiled into a native format, they are not platform independent, as applets are.

ActiveX controls can carry out actions on objects. Controls are defined in generic form so that the same control can be used in various situations. The details of the control's functioning can be specified and controlled using parameters. For example, the Filter control can take an image file and do such things to it as blurring, inverting, flipping (horizontally or vertically), or adding shadows—depending on the parameter selections and values. Similarly, the Structured Graphics control makes it possible to display text at specified angles or even to create simple drawings on the screen.

Many ActiveX controls—more than 6000, according to Microsoft—are available from various (commercial and noncommercial) sources. Many generic ActiveX controls are included with Microsoft Internet Explorer. Any others must be downloaded, installed on your machine, and registered with the operating system before you can use them in your Web pages or other programs. (If a required control is unavailable on your machine, it is downloaded and installed automatically.)

You can write your own controls by using an appropriate programming environment (such as Microsoft Visual C++). Various tools—for example, APIs (application programming interfaces), DLLs (dynamic-link libraries), and special resources such as Microsoft's ATL (ActiveX Template Library)—are available to help users create ActiveX controls.

In their functionality, ActiveX controls are comparable to Java applets or, more precisely, to JavaBeans—which are code modules that can be used in applets or applications. Unlike platform-independent applets, however, ActiveX controls are tied to a particular platform. Although Microsoft has promised to make ActiveX technology available on other platforms, the current reality is that ActiveX controls run almost exclusively on Windows platforms.

Even after ActiveX technology becomes available on multiple platforms, any new controls or refinements to the ActiveX technology will have to be adapted and compiled for the non-Windows platforms, which will probably involve a time lag.

Arguably, most ActiveX controls are defined and used for enhancing Web pages, and such enhancement controls constitute the main type. However, controls can also be defined to serve as substitutes for browser or other application plug-ins written in Java or other programming languages. For example, controls could be written to do image processing or to play sound files.

Using ActiveX Controls

ActiveX controls can be included in HTML files, programs, or script files. In an HTML file, you can embed an ActiveX control directly, by defining the control inside the <OBJECT> and </OBJECT> tags. Generally such a definition will include several parameters, which provide the details for the control.

You can also include ActiveX controls in an HTML file through the use of a script—using a scripting language such as VBScript. The details of the ActiveX control call are specified within the script, which is included between the <SCRIPT> and </SCRIPT> tags.

When a browser displays the HTML file, the embedded controls will be activated at the appropriate time or under the appropriate conditions. For example, a control may produce some type of effect if the user clicks on the screen or on a particular spot on the screen, or if the user gives a response to a form entry. ActiveX controls can, therefore, be used to make an HTML page interactive.

However, only certain browsers can display the effects of ActiveX controls. Such a browser must be what is known as an *ActiveX container*—which essentially means that the browser has the resources to interpret the controls. The browser must know how to interpret the control's effects in order to display them. Beginning with version 3, Microsoft Internet Explorer (IE) was designed as an ActiveX container. As a result, IE can handle ActiveX controls directly. Other browsers—for example, Netscape Navigator—must be supplemented with a plug-in module before they can be considered ActiveX containers.

If a required control is not installed on a browser's or an application's machine, the control is automatically downloaded, installed, and registered. It will then execute as required for the page display or other service. Once downloaded and installed, the control becomes resident on the machine—that is, it remains installed. "ActiveX at Work" shows the steps and decisions involved in getting an ActiveX control to execute.

These steps are as follows:

1. A Web page, most likely, an HTML file, delivered by the Web server contains an ActiveX control.

2. The client's browser checks whether the control is available on the client machine. If not, the browser requests the ActiveX control, and the Web server delivers it.

3. The ActiveX control then executes in the Web page.

4. The control is now resident on the client's machine.

The advantage of the control being resident on the machine is that the control will then be available if

needed at some future point. The disadvantage is, of course, that all this may be done completely without the user's control. In light of the security issues relating to ActiveX controls, automatic downloads can create problems. (It is possible to set your browser to check before downloading a control. However, unless the user is familiar with the controls of interest, this discretionary power is unlikely to be of any more value than deciding at random whether to download a control.)

ActiveX Security Issues

Perhaps the most significant drawback to ActiveX technology has to do with security. Because they are treated—and can function—like Windows programs, ActiveX controls can access files and other system resources. This also means that the controls can damage files or other system resources. Such damage can be inadvertent (due to incompetent or buggy programming) or deliberate (due to malicious programming).

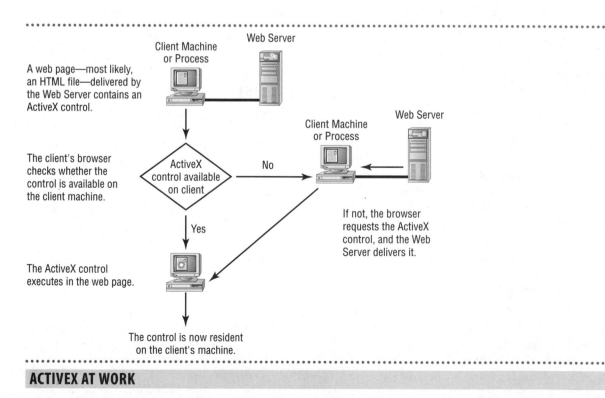

A web page—most likely, an HTML file—delivered by the Web Server contains an ActiveX control.

The client's browser checks whether the control is available on the client machine.

ActiveX control available on client

The ActiveX control executes in the web page.

If not, the browser requests the ActiveX control, and the Web Server delivers it.

The control is now resident on the client's machine.

Controls can even be created to perform very subtle actions that may never be detected—or that remain unnoticed for a long time. To demonstrate the capabilities and the potential dangers of ActiveX controls, a group of hackers in Germany created a control that would download invisibly to any client machine running IE 3.1. Once installed on the client machine, the control would check the machine for a particular version of a popular electronic banking package. If found, the control would use the package to transfer funds (in small amounts) from the user's account to the hackers' accounts. (This example also illustrates the importance of taking software versions into consideration and also suggests the advantages of using the latest version possible of a piece of software. Since the hackers' feat was dependent on a particular version of IE, it's likely that the security hole the hackers exploited was patched in later versions of the browser.)

Similarly, the Exploder control—developed by Fred McLain, also to prove a point about ActiveX security—will shut down Windows 95 on any machine to which it downloads, and will turn off the power on energy-conserving PCs.

This ActiveX ability to access (and possibly damage) files is in contrast to the sandbox model that provides security for Java applets. In the sandbox model, each applet gets its own sandbox—that is, working area—within which it can execute. The applet is denied access to anything outside the sandbox. This means that an applet cannot get access to any files or other resources on the user's machine, at least in theory. (Researchers, hackers, and inept programmers have discovered ways of getting around the Java security model.)

To provide a measure of security—or, perhaps more accurately, a security blanket—ActiveX supports Authenticode. This is an authentication system that uses digital signatures to verify a file's authenticity and integrity. The authenticity test shows that the file is, indeed, from the purported source; the integrity test shows that the file has not been tampered with at any point in its transit.

Thus, as a security measure, Microsoft encourages ActiveX developers and clients to use digital signatures. Such signatures verify that the code's author is who they claim to be and that the code has not been tampered with since it was created. Authors should include a digital signature with their work. Clients should use only ActiveX controls with valid and trusted digital signatures.

Note, however, that these security measures certify only that the control is authentic. The signatures cannot tell you whether an applet is either well designed or correct. Thus, a valid digital signature guarantees only that you'll know whom to blame if a control does damage to your system or other files. Probably, Authenticode is best regarded as a necessary but not sufficient security element.

ActiveX Documents

One of the things that makes ActiveX attractive, particularly among business users, is the fact that it can work with data in various formats without needing to convert these data to any sort of standard format (such as HTML, for example). Thus, an ActiveX control can display Excel spreadsheets or PowerPoint or Access files, to name just three possibilities. This means you can view an Excel spreadsheet with your browser, for example.

ActiveX documents are embeddable objects. ActiveX controls can be used in such documents to work with various types of files—in their native formats.

Such flexibility is possible because of the streamlined OLE technology at the core of ActiveX. Essentially, when ActiveX controls are included in an ActiveX document (such as an HTML file), the file becomes a little Windows program with OLE edit-in-place capabilities. Using OLE, applications can be launched simply by clicking on a file generated by the application. Because OLE has been refined for use on the Internet or intranets, these applications need not be on the same machine as the file or the control. Rather, the application can be elsewhere on the network.

Using ActiveX in Script Files

Another way to get ActiveX controls into Web pages is by including the controls in script files—that is, in files created using a Web scripting language such as JavaScript, JScript (Microsoft's flavor of JavaScript), or VBScript. Scripts can help make Web pages interactive, and the same scripts can be used with multiple files.

One of the main advantages of script files is that they can be handled on the client side of a network session. That is, the client machine can carry out the processing work specified in the script. This frees the server's resources for other uses.

To make it possible to integrate ActiveX controls with Java applets, Microsoft has created a Java Virtual Machine (JVM) which implements Microsoft's flavor of Java and its scripting model.

ActiveX on Web Servers

In light of the flexibility provided by ActiveX technology—especially its ability to handle different file formats—it shouldn't be surprising that ActiveX is also used on the server side of a network connection. Microsoft ActiveX Server Framework is designed to give Internet clients access to applications running on the server. It also makes it possible to deliver special services—for example, for handling streaming media—and make them available to Internet clients.

Internet Information Servers, which provide access to Web pages on an intranet or on certain Internet sites, are becoming very popular. Many of these use ActiveX components. To get access to such servers, applications can use Microsoft Internet Server Application Programming Interface (ISAPI). This is a dynamic-link library (DLL) containing objects and resources for use in ActiveX controls.

The resources in ActiveX and in the ISAPI enable Web programmers to create ISAPI filters, which are similar to CGI (Common Gateway Interface) scripts, and which are used to enable applications (including browsers) to talk with Web servers. However, whereas CGI scripts are limited to handling predefined file formats, ISAPI filters can handle any file formats for which an appropriate application is accessible.

This capability alone should help make ISAPI filters popular with businesses and others who need to work with lots of different file formats. However, such filters can also provide digital signature- or password-based security measures—over and above any security measures taken on the server.

→ **See Also** COM (Component Object Model); DCOM (Distributed Component Object Model); DNA (Distributed interNetworking Applications Architecture)

→ **Compare** Applet

ActiveX Data Object (ADO)

→ **See** ADO (ActiveX Data Object)

ACU (Autocall Unit)

An ACU is a device that can dial telephone numbers automatically. Just about anyone who owns a phone probably has been, on one or more occasions, the target of an ACU.

AD (Administrative Domain)

In the Internet community, an AD consists of a collection of nodes, routers, and connectors that is managed by a common administrator, such as an organization or a company.

Adapter

An adapter is a board that plugs into an expansion bus, and that provides special capabilities, such as video, fax, modem, network access, and so on.

Besides functionality, adapters are distinguished by the width of the data bus between the adapter and the PC. Adapters may have 8-, 16-, or 32-bit—or even wider—connections.

Adapter Support Interface (ASI)

→ **See** ASI (Adapter Support Interface)

Adaptive Directory

In message routing, an adaptive directory, also known as a *dynamic directory,* is one that may be updated during a user's session. A bridge or router uses such a directory (also known as a routing table) to determine the path a message should take to reach its destination. Adaptive directories are generally (but not necessarily) used for adaptive routing.

→ **Compare** Fixed Directory

→ **See Also** Adaptive Routing

Adaptive Routing

To determine a path for a message, a bridge or router makes use of network information in a directory, or routing table. Such a table may be fixed (updated at the start of a user session, and static thereafter) or adaptive (possibly updated during a user session as well as at the session start). Adaptive routing, also known as *dynamic routing,* uses an adaptive directory to determine a path. That is, adaptive routing makes use of information about changes in network topology or traffic when defining a route for a message. Thus, paths for two different messages to the same destination during a session may take different routes because the routing table changed in the time between messages.

→ **Compare** Fixed Routing

Adaptive Speed Leveling

Adaptive speed leveling is a modem technology that enables modems to deal with noisy lines and other transient problems that can increase the error rate in a transmission. By using adaptive speed leveling, a modem can "downshift" to a slower transmission speed if the error rate exceeds a preset threshold. Once the line problem disappears, the modem will try to continue transmitting at a higher speed.

ADC (Analog-to-Digital Converter)

An ADC is a device that converts an analog signal into digital form. The ADC does this by sampling the analog signal and assigning a binary value to each sample, based on the signal's level in the analog transmission. The number of distinct values that can be assigned depends on the number of bits allocated for each sample. If one byte is allocated, any of 256 possible values can be assigned.

To capture the information in the analog signal with sufficient fidelity, the signal must be sampled at a rate that is twice the maximum frequency range for the analog signal. For example, the human voice covers about 4000 Hertz (4KHz). By sampling the voice signal 8000 times per second, the voice message can be faithfully reproduced in digital form.

ADCCP (Advanced Data Communications Control Procedure)

→ **See** Protocol, ADCCP (Advanced Data Communications Control Procedure)

ADDMD (Administrative Directory Management Domain)

In the CCITT's X.500 directory services model, a collection of directory system agents (DSAs) under the control of a single authority.

→ **See Also** DSA (Directory System Agent)

Address

An address is a value used to specify a location. The location may be an area of local or shared memory, or it may be a node or other device on a network.

Network-Related Addresses

Several types of addresses are distinguished for network locations. The type of address used in a particular context depends partly on which protocol or device is creating the address. Address information may be maintained in any of several ways, such as in look-up tables or directories.

Some common types of network-related addresses are hardware, network, node, Internet, and e-mail (electronic mail). There are other types of addresses, and not all types of addresses are used in the same conceptual model. Devices that connect networks or network segments generally get network and/or node addresses on each network they connect.

Hardware Address

A hardware address, also known as a *physical address* or a *MAC address*, is a unique numerical value assigned to a network interface card (NIC) during the manufacturing process or by setting jumpers or switches during network installation. One part of this address is assigned to the manufacturer by the IEEE (Institute of Electronics Engineers) and is common to all components from that manufacturer; the second part of the hardware address is a unique value assigned by the hardware manufacturer.

Network Address

A network address is an arbitrary value that is assigned identically to each station in a particular network. As long as there is only a single network, this value is automatically unique. If two or more networks are connected, each must have a different network address. If a station (for example, a server) connects to two networks, that station will have two different network addresses.

A network address is also known as a *network number* or an *IPX external network number*.

Node Address

In addition to a common network address, each station in a network has a unique node address. This value identifies a particular node, or more specifically, the NIC assigned to each node, in a particular network. This address is also known as a *node number* or *station address*.

When specified as a source or destination, a network server or workstation may be identified by a network and a node address or by a hardware address.

The node addresses for Ethernet cards are factory-set, and no two cards have the same number. The node addresses for ARCnet and Token Ring cards are set by changing jumpers or switches on the cards. If a node contains two NICs, the node will have two different network addresses.

Internal Address

An internal address is a unique value that specifies a node with respect to a particular server in a network, which is useful in networks that have multiple servers. This is a logical address. Only certain network operating systems, such as NetWare, support internal addresses.

See the illustration entitled "Examples of network addresses" for an illustration of the kinds of addresses discussed so far.

Internet Address

An Internet address is a network-layer address that uniquely identifies a node on an internet or on the Internet. This type of address uses four bytes of storage, and it is generally represented as four decimal values separated by decimal points, as in 12.34.56.78. Certain bits from an Internet address can be masked to identify a subnetwork that contains some of the nodes in the internetwork.

Special protocols, such as the Address Resolution Protocol (ARP), are used to convert from an Internet to a hardware address; other programs, such as the Reverse ARP (RARP), convert from a hardware to an Internet address.

A

E-Mail Address

An e-mail (electronic-mail) address is an application-layer address that identifies a user's mailbox location in a message-handling system. These addresses have little in common with the other types of addresses mentioned; however, the e-mail address must be associated with the station's network and node address or with its hardware address in order for messages to be transferred from a sender to a receiver.

Memory-Related Addresses

Several different formats are used for memory addresses in personal computers: flat address space, segmented address, and paged address.

Flat Address Space

An address in a flat address space is a simple numerical value in the range between 0 and the highest address value. For example, in a machine with 1 megabyte of memory, the addresses range from 0x00000 to 0xfffff.

Segmented Address

An address in a segmented address space consists of a segment and an offset value. The segment value represents a (usually 16-byte) location that is aligned on a paragraph boundary. The offset value represents the number of bytes to shift from this segment address. DOS uses segmented addresses.

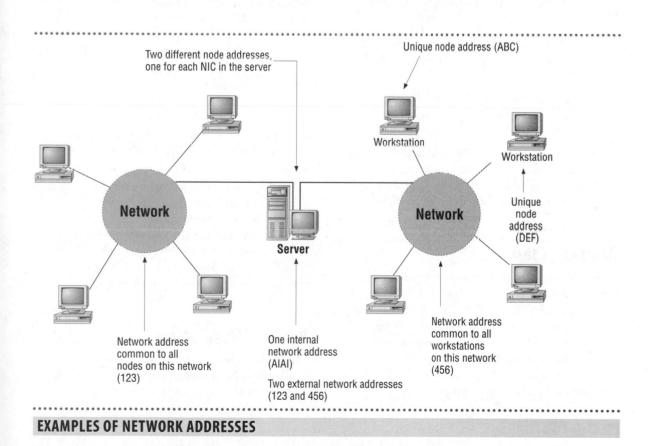

Two different node addresses, one for each NIC in the server

Unique node address (ABC)

Workstation

Workstation

Network

Network

Server

Unique node address (DEF)

Network address common to all nodes on this network (123)

One internal network address (AIAI)

Two external network addresses (123 and 456)

Network address common to all workstations on this network (456)

EXAMPLES OF NETWORK ADDRESSES

Paged Address

Certain types of address space actually consist of two types of values. For example, in expanded memory, locations in a special set of chips, and hence, in a special set of addresses, are mapped into special memory buffers. These buffers are broken into pages of a specific size.

Virtual memory also uses paged addresses.

Address Bus

An address bus is the electrical signal lines over which memory locations are specified. Each line carries a single bit, so the number of lines on the bus determine the number of possible addresses:

- 20 lines allow access to 1 megabyte (MB) of memory. Examples include Intel's 8086 and 8088 processors.

- 24 lines provide access to 16MB. Examples include Intel's 80286 and Motorola's 68000 processors.

- 32 lines provide access to 4GB. Examples include Intel's 80386, 80486, and Pentium, and Motorola's 68020 and later processors.

- 64 lines provide access to 16 exabytes (EB). (An exabyte is a billion billion, or a quintillion, bytes.) Digital Equipment Corporation's Alpha APX chip is an example of a 64-bit address bus.

Address, Classless

A classless address is an IP (Internet Protocol) address that does not simply use one of the address classes (A, B, C, and D) defined for IP addresses. A classless address generally uses a subnet mask to distinguish bits used to identify a network address from those used to identify a machine within this network (that is, a local address). In a classless address such masks do not fall on byte boundaries.

Address Mask

In the IP (Internet Protocol) addressing scheme, a group of selected bits whose values identify a subnetwork; also known as a *subnet mask*. All the members of that subnetwork share the same mask value. Using an address mask makes it easier for the system to reference a member of a particular subnet.

Address Translation

Address translation refers to a process by which the information (that is, the address) used to identify a network or a machine on a network is converted from one format to another. This occurs, for example, when a communication goes from one type of network to another—for example, from an address used in TCP/IP-based networks to a non-TCP/IP network which uses a different addressing scheme.

Address translation is also necessary in networks that have a gateway or a proxy server through which the network is accessed. In such a case, the gateway or proxy server will have something like a mailing address to which communications are addressed. This device will then have further addresses for the individual machines behind the gateway or proxy server.

Finally, address translation is used in networks that use subnetting to allow extra machines on a TCP/IP-based network without using up precious addresses in a particular address class. See the entries on IP (Internet Protocol) Address; Address, Classless; and Subnetting for more information about how addresses work in subnetting.

Address Resolution

The process of mapping one type of address to another; specifically, mapping a network (local) address to a hardware-dependent address. The most widely used method of address resolution is the Address Resolution Protocol (ARP) or a variation of that protocol.

Adjacent Channel

An adjacent channel is a frequency band immediately below or above the current channel. For example, a channel between 100MHz and 500MHz and a channel between 700MHz and 900MHz are both adjacent to the channel between 500MHz and 700MHz.

ADMD (Administration Management Domain)

In the CCITT's X.400 Message Handling System (MHS) model, an ADMD (Administration Management Domain) is a network or network section operated by the CCITT (Consultative Committee for International Telegraphy and Telephony) or a national PTT (Post, Telegraph, and Telephone). Specific examples of ADMDs include MCImail and AT&Tmail in the United States, British Telecom Gold400mail in Britain.

ADMDs are public carriers, unlike PRMDs (private management domains), which are run by private organizations or companies. In accordance with CCITT guidelines, ADMDs handle any international connections; PRMDs communicate through a local ADMD. ADMDs can connect PRMDs, but a PRMD cannot connect ADMDs. Because all ADMDs run under the auspices of CCITT, the conglomeration of ADMDs in the world forms the backbone for a global X.400 network.

→ *Broader Categories* MD (Management Domain); X.400

→ *Compare* PRMD (Private Management Domain)

Administration

Administration involves the management and maintenance of a computer system, network, or environment.

Administrative Tasks

An administrator's responsibilities may be grouped into several general categories:

Configuration management Handling tasks such as user accounts, hardware settings, access rights, and security.

Data-flow management Monitoring performance, managing memory and resources, making sure applications and data files are accessible, and generally ensuring that data is flowing properly.

Hardware maintenance Installing, maintaining, and diagnosing hardware components.

Software maintenance Installing applications and other software, software version control, bug reporting and resolution, and so on.

Help Training users, providing documentation for using the system resources and applications, and offering other support.

Levels of Administration

Various levels of administration are distinguished, including the following:

System Refers to a particular division in a company or a particular type of hardware, such as mainframes or database servers. System administration responsibilities do not necessarily involve networking issues; that is, a system administrator may or may not need to attend to issues relating to the connections between machines, as well as to the machines themselves.

Network   Usually refers to a LAN (local area network), but may encompass machines in a larger range, provided these machines are all connected by a common architecture. In addition to the individual machines, a network administrator must keep track of the connections between the machines.

Internetwork   Refers to multiple networks. Some or all of these networks may use different architectures. An internetwork administrator should be able to assume that any subnetworks are under the control of network administrators, so that the internetwork administrator can concentrate on the connections between networks rather than those between machines.

Administration Management Domain (ADMD)

→ *See*   ADMD (Administration Management Domain)

Administrative Directory Management Domain (ADMD)

→ *See*   ADMD (Administrative Directory Management Domain)

Administrative Domain (AD)

→ *See*   AD (Administrative Domain)

Administrator Account

In Windows NT, the Administrator (note initial cap) account is a special account with full privileges and complete security permissions. The owner of

this account can assign or remove permissions for any user or group, and can also create accounts for other administrators.

While the Administrator account is the most powerful in an NT network, it is often also the most vulnerable to attack by outsiders—or even by insiders if the Administrator is careless when logged in with this account. The account's vulnerability to attack derives from the fact that this account has the same user name on almost all Windows NT networks. Consequently, a would-be intruder can usually take the user name for granted, and only needs to guess the password. The Administrator account can be vulnerable to insider attacks if the Administrator leaves the account logged in while not actually using it.

One strategy for defending against attacks is to leave the Administrator account as a shell account with limited privileges, while creating a new account—with a different name, but with the full Administrator permissions and privileges. By doing this, the Administrator can hide (at least for a time) the real account from attacks aimed at the Administrator account. This strategy might be called the puppet government approach, because the true power lies behind the puppet facade. If using this strategy, however, it is essential to plan out the transfer of administration as completely as possible, and to carry out the transfer as carefully as possible—to avoid locking oneself out inadvertently. A shell Administrator account is still needed because Windows NT demands it.

Functionally equivalent accounts exist in other networking environments. For example, on UNIX systems the account is Root, in NetWare 3.*x* it is Supervisor, and in NetWare 4.0 and later it is NWAdmin.

ADO (ActiveX Data Object)

An ADO is an ActiveX component. Collections of ADOs are used to work with material from databases or other data providers that have

OLE DB-compliant interfaces. OLE-DB (for object linking and embedding for databases) is Microsoft's new technology for programming and interacting with databases or other types of (possibly anonymous) data stores.

In short, a collection of ADOs works much like an API (application programming interface) for interacting with OLE-DB. That is, the ADOs sit between an application program and the OLE-DB interface. This interface, in turn, sits between the ADO actions or requests and some type of data store. In OLE-DB terminology, the ADOs are *data consumers* and the OLE-DB drivers serve as *data providers*.

Drivers are, or will be, available to serve as OLE-DB data providers for data stored using ODBC (Open Database Connectivity), Oracle, SQL, Microsoft Access and Exchange Server, and IBM AS/400 systems. As the OLE-DB interface becomes more widely established, third-parties are expected to provide OLE-DB drivers to serve as data providers for their products.

→ **Broader Categories** ActiveX; COM (Component Object Model)

→ **See Also** OLE-DB (Object Linking and Embedding for Databases)

ADSI (Active Directory Services Interface)

In Windows 2000 (formerly known as NT 5), ADSI provides a unified interface for Microsoft's new Active Directory, which will provide X.500 compliant, distributed directory services. Such a unified interface will enable network administrators to manage resources on the network—even if different network operating systems and different directory services are involved.

ADSI also makes it easier for developers to create applications that need to work with a network directory regardless of what directory service—for example, NDS (Novell Directory Services), LDAP (Lightweight Directory Access Protocol), or Active Directory—is being used. Because the developer uses the ADSI, an application need never know what directory service is actually providing the services.

→ **Broader Categories** Active Directory; DS (Directory Service)

ADSL (Asymmetric Digital Subscriber Line)

ADSL is one of a family of DSL (digital subscriber line) variants, and it is described in the ANSI T1.413 specification. DSL technology provides digital access over ordinary telephone lines. Of the DSL variants, ADSL has the brightest expected future because it can deliver a range of high-speed download and upload speeds in a versatile manner over such lines. You do need a special modem, however, and your local phone company office must support ADSL service. (That's because the part about using ordinary telephone lines is only partly true.)

ADSL Performance

The performance figures for ADSL services range all over the place. This is because several factors can have considerable influence on the performance in an ADSL connection. In particular, the following will affect the bandwidth available for upstream and downstream transmissions:

- Distance between the end user and the telephone company's central office (CO)—that is, the length of the local loop. The greater the distance, the lower the maximum bandwidth. For example, the maximum downstream speed is about 1.544Mbps from 18,000 feet, whereas a maximum speed of 8.448Mbps is possible if the distance is only 9000 feet. 18,000 feet is the maximum distance over which ADSL services can be provided without boosting the signal in some way. Less than 80 percent of the telephone connections in the United States are within this distance of a CO.

- Thickness, or gauge, of the wire in the local loop. The thicker the wire—that is, the lower the gauge—the shorter the distance over which a particular bandwidth is supported. For example, the 18,000-foot maximum distance mentioned above holds only for AWG 24 wire; for the thinner 26 AWG wire (which also has higher resistance), the maximum distance is only 15,000 feet.

- The strength of the signal from the telephone company to the end user. Part of the reason ADSL connections support such high speeds has to do with the fact that the signal is much stronger than for an ordinary telephone call.

- The way in which the total bandwidth is split into upstream and downstream channels. Generally, making downstream the larger (and faster) channel makes the most sense, since most users will be more likely to download long files than to upload them. Upstream speeds can range from 64Kbps to about 1.2Mbps; downstream speeds can consume the remaining bandwidth for the connection.

The actual effect of each of these factors will depend on the particular circumstances of each individual user. For example, even if you and I have exactly the same PC configurations, one of us might have a maximum download speed almost six times that of the other under the right circumstances.

ADSL supports traffic in both directions. The ADSL specification defines support for up to seven bearer channels. Of these, four are simplex channels, which transmit only downstream; the remaining three can be duplex channels, which can transmit in both directions.

Simplex Channels (Downstream)

Within the ADSL specification, any bearer channel can be configured to carry any multiple of 32Kbps—within the range limits allowed for ADSL. However, to impose at least some structure on the rate picture, the ADSL specification defines four transport classes—1, 2, 3, and 4—for downstream traffic. These classes correspond to data rates that are multiples of 1.536Mbps, which is the bandwidth of the user data portion of a T1 line in the United States. (A T1 line actually has a bandwidth of 1.544Mbps, but 8Kbps is used for administrative and control functions.) The transport classes are as follows:

Transport class 1   Supports up to a maximum of 6.144Mbps. This data rate can be provided in any of several ways: one 6.144Mbps bearer channel, one 4.608Mbps and one 1.536Mbps channel; two 3.072Mbps channels, one 3.072Mbps channel and two 1.536Mbps channels, four 1.536Mbps channels. Support for transport class 1 is mandatory in an ADSL device.

Transport class 2   Supports up to a maximum of 4.608Mbps. Again, this rate can be attained in any of several ways: one 4.608Mbps channel, one 3.072 and one 1.536Mbps channel; three 1.536Mbps channels. Support for transport class 2 is optional.

Transport class 3   Supports up to a maximum of 3.072Mbps, which can be in the form of one 3.072Mbps channel or two 1.536Mbps channels. Support for transport class 3 is optional.

Transport class 4   Supports one 1.536Mbps channel. Support for transport class 4 is mandatory.

The ADSL forum has also defined transport classes for use in Europe and other places in which the higher-bandwidth E1 lines serve as the basic bandwidth unit for high-speed transport. An E1 line has a bandwidth of 2.048Mbps. Specifically, the following three optional transport classes have also been defined:

Transport class 2M-1   Supports a maximum of 6.144Mbps, which can be delivered as one 6.144Mbps channel; one 4.096Mbps and one 2.048Mbps channel; or three 2.048Mbps channels. This class corresponds roughly to transport class 1 in the U.S. model.

Transport class 2M-2   Supports a maximum of 4.096Mbps, which can be in the form of a single 4.096Mbps channel or two 2.048Mbps channels. This class lies between transport classes 2 and 3 in the U.S. model.

Transport class 2M-3   Supports a maximum of 2.048Mbps, which can be in the form of a single 2.048Mbps channel. This class corresponds to transport class 4 in the U.S. model.

It's important to note that the quoted speeds assume optimal conditions and sufficient proximity to the CO. Not all transport classes will be available to all ADSL subscribers. For example, if you live over three miles (that is, close to 18,000 feet) from the CO, you shouldn't expect to use transport class 1—or even classes 2 or 3, for that matter.

Duplex Channels (Upstream and Downstream)

The duplex channels can carry traffic in both directions simultaneously. In practice, however, they will be used almost exclusively for upstream traffic—since the simplex channels provide sufficient bandwidth for the downstream traffic. The possible rates for the duplex channels depend on the transport class being used.

Of the three duplex channels, one must be a control channel—known as the C channel. This channel is used to transmit signaling and setup messages. For (the slowest) transport classes (4 and 2M-3), the C channel operates at a mere 16Kbps; for the other transport classes the C channel operates at 64Kbps.

One of the other duplex bearer channels operates at 160Kbps, and the third can operate at either

384Kbps or 576Kbps, depending on the transport class in use. Table "Duplex Bearer Channels" summarizes the possible configurations for the bidirectional bearer channels.

DUPLEX BEARER CHANNELS

Transport Classes	C Channel Bandwidth	Channel Configurations
1, 2M-1	64Kbps	One 576Kbps, or one 384Kbps and one 160Kbps
2, 3, 2M-2	64Kbps	One 160Kbps, or one 378Kbps
4, 2M-3	16Kbps	One 160Kbps

Note that only transport classes 1 and 2M-1 can have all three duplex bearer channels in use at the same time. The other transport classes have only the C channel and one of the other bearer channels in operation at a time.

As stated earlier, these rates are defined to make the picture a bit more manageable. In fact, most ADSL projects allow rates in between those specified, and some ADSL providers have managed to squeeze even higher bandwidth out of the local loop.

Structure of an ADSL connection

An ADSL connection between an end user and a telephone company or an ISP (Internet Service Provider) requires the following extra components:

ADSL modems (required at each end)   These components sit at opposite ends of the local loop and communicate with each other. The modems also do two other important things. In a modem component known as the *channel separator*, they split the bandwidth into upstream and downstream channels. (Note that the two modems don't split the bandwidth the same way. After all, one modem's up is another modem's down.) The modems also handle both voice and data communications—in a component known as the *POTS* (for Plain Old Telephone Service) *splitter*. The sender's splitter slips (try saying that quickly a few times) the voice signal into the bandwidth below 4000Hz and sends the data at higher frequencies. (Because they occupy nonoverlapping frequency ranges, both voice and data can be sent over the wires at the same time, without interfering with each other.) The receiving modem disentangles the two frequency bands and sends each signal toward the appropriate destination. (Note that two end users with ADSL modems cannot call each other directly. Each end user must connect to a CO modem.)

Ordinary analog telephone line with copper wire connection (user end, possibly CO end)
The ADSL transmissions are just pumped over ordinary copper wire, with lots of power—so that even high bandwidth signals won't get lost or go bad during their journey. The attenuation (signal weakening) and interference during the transmission over the wire make ADSL signals so sensitive to distance.

DSLAM (at CO)   At the CO, the user's upstream data component is split from the voice transmission. The voice portion is sent off to a PSTN (Public Switched Telephone Network) The data portion is sent to a DSLAM (Digital Subscriber Line Access Multiplexer). The DSLAM is—as the multiplexer in its name suggests—a device at which multiple (ADSL data) signals are combined into a single transmission stream.

ATM (or other high-speed) connection (at CO)
Very often, the multiplexed ADSL data streams are sent on over an ATM (Asynchronous Transfer Mode) line—or over some other high-speed connection (for example, frame relay). This line usually connects to an ISP, which is what the ADSL end users were trying to access in the first place. The ATM connection usually marks the end of the copper line, as the transmission will generally continue over higher-bandwidth optical fiber.

Operation of an ADSL Connection

"An ADSL connection at work" summarizes the steps involved when communicating over an ADSL connection. First, the sender's POTS splitter combines any voice and data signals for transmission as a single signal. This signal is sent along one of the upstream bearer channels maintained by the channel separator.

Even though it travels out on a single channel and over a single set of wires, a signal leaving an ADSL modem at the subscriber's end is split for transmission in separate frequency bands for voice and data (1). The bottom 4KHz frequency band is used for the voice transmission; frequencies above this band are used for the data transmission. This separation also is carried out by the POTS splitter.

At the telephone company's CO (2), the signals on the two channels are sent to the appropriate devices at the CO. The voice signal is sent on the telephone network; the data signal is sent to a DSLAM—a device that multiplexes signals from multiple ADSL modems into a single stream.

The DSLAM sends its stream over an electrical connection using copper wire to an ATM switch or hub (3). The ATM component is connected, usually by a very high speed fiber optic connection, to the Internet or some other high-speed network by means of an appropriate provider (4).

The ADSL signals are sent using either of two modulation strategies: DMT (discrete multitone) or CAP (carrierless amplitude/phase) modulation. These modulation methods are not compatible, which means that DMT modems can only speak with other DMT modems, and CAP modems can only speak with other CAP modems. DMT is both an ANSI and an ITU standard, but CAP claims a larger user base.

At the CO end, the receiving modem's channel separator feeds the transmission of the POTS splitter. The splitter separates the voice and data signals, sending the voice to a PSTN connection and the data to a DSLAM.

At the DSLAM, ADSL signals from several ADSL modems are multiplexed into a giant stream. The individual ADSL data transmissions are then sent on to their ultimate destination over a very high speed line.

Going in the other direction, a high-bandwidth data stream comes in from the Internet through an ATM or other high-speed connection. This stream is sent into the DSLAM, where the individual ADSL sessions are demultiplexed and sent on the appropriate ADSL modem.

At the modem, the ADSL data stream is merged with any voice transmission, and the combined signal is sent—with as much power as possible—along the local loop to the end user's modem. Being the receiver this time, the user's modem sends the transmission over a downstream channel through the channel separator. From there it is fed into the POTS splitter, which separates the signal into its voice and data elements.

The voice transmission will go to the telephone, and the data transmission will go to the user's PC.

ADSL's Variants and Future

As stated, ADSL is arguably the DSL variant with the brightest future. Already, however, variants on ADSL itself have been developed. These each have features that are particularly useful for certain purposes or groups. The two that have received the most attention are RADSL (for Rate-Adaptive ADSL) and CDSL (for Consumer DSL).

RADSL is essentially the same as ADSL except that an RADSL connection is smart enough to adjust its transmission rate in response to line noise or other conditions that threaten to increase transmission errors.

CDSL refers to a not-yet-standardized set of ideas about how to make ADSL technology simpler and less expensive—thereby making it more appealing as a mass market service. In general terms, CDSL connections will operate at slower speeds than ADSL. On balance, however, CDSL modems will not need splitters and will be much less expensive to manufacture than their ADSL counterparts. This makes it feasible to build consumer PCs with CDSL modems as an optional or standard component.

A "lite" version of ADSL, which would operate at lower speeds, would require less complex and less expensive equipment, and could develop into a consumer product, has been proposed by the Universal ADSL Working Group (UAWG), whose members include Microsoft, Intel, Compaq, GTE, Sprint, and all five RBOCs (Regional Bell Operating Companies).

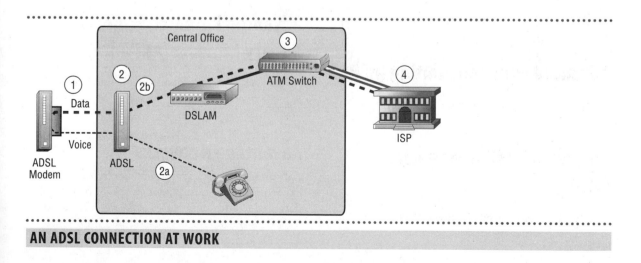

AN ADSL CONNECTION AT WORK

In January 1998, when ADSL service first began to appear in the United States, the technology was rather expensive. The modems cost several hundred dollars, and the monthly charges for the service were also several hundred to over a thousand dollars.

In contrast, at the start of 1999, ADSL modems are under $300, and monthly charges are in the $50–$200 range.

→ *See Also* CAP (Carrierless Amplitude/Phase) Modulation; DMT (Discrete Multitone)

ADSL Termination Unit (ATU)

→ *See* ATU (ADSL Termination Unit)

ADSP (AppleTalk Data Stream Protocol)

→ *See* Protocol, ADSP (AppleTalk Data Stream Protocol)

Advanced Communications Function (ACF)

→ *See* ACF (Advanced Communications Function)

Advanced Function Printing (AFP)

→ *See* AFP (Advanced Function Printing)

Advanced Intelligent Network (AIN)

→ *See* AIN (Advanced Intelligent Network)

Advanced Mobile Phone Service (AMPS)

→ *See* AMPS (Advanced Mobile Phone Service)

Advanced Peer-to-Peer Networking (APPN)

→ *See* APPN (Advanced Peer-to-Peer Networking)

Advanced Program-to-Program Communications (APPC)

→ *See* APPC (Advanced Program-to-Program Communications)

Advanced Research Projects Agency (ARPA)

→ *See* ARPA (Advanced Research Projects Agency)

Advanced Research Projects Agency Network (ARPAnet)

→ *See* ARPAnet (Advanced Research Projects Agency Network)

Advantage Networks

Advantage networks represent a networking strategy from Digital Equipment Corporation (DEC), designed to add support for protocols such as the TCP/IP suite to DEC's OSI-compliant DECnet Phase V architecture.

Adverse Channel Enhancement (ACE)

→ *See* ACE (Adverse Channel Enhancement)

Advertising

The process by which a network service makes its presence and availability known on the network. For example, Novell NetWare services use the SAP (Service Advertising Protocol).

AE (Application Entity)

In the OSI reference model, an entity (process or function) that runs all or part of an application. An AE may consist of one or more application service elements (ASEs).

AEP (AppleTalk Echo Protocol)

→ *See* Protocol, AEP (AppleTalk Echo Protocol)

AFI (Authority and Format Identifier)

In the OSI reference model, part of the address for the network-layer service access point (NSAP). The AFI portion specifies the authority, or administrator, that is allocating the IDI (initial domain identifier) values. The AFI also specifies the format of the IDI and the DSP (domain specific part), which are other parts of the NSAP address.

AFP (Advanced Function Printing)

In IBM's SAA (Systems Applications Architecture) environments, the ability to print text and images; that is, to use all points addressable (APA) printers.

AFP (AppleTalk Filing Protocol)

→ *See* Protocol, AFP (AppleTalk Filing Protocol)

AFS (Andrew File System)

→ *See* Protocol, AFS (Andrew File System)

AFT (Application File Transfer)

In the International Standardized Profile (ISP) grouping, a prefix that identifies FTAM (file transfer, access, and management) profiles. For example, AFT11 represents basic file transfer.

Agent

In general, an agent is a program that can perform a particular task automatically, when appropriate or upon request by another program. An agent is commonly used to provide information to an application, such as a network management program. An agent may be machine- or function-specific.

The following are some of the agents that are found in networking-related contexts:

- In a client-server networking model, an element that does work on behalf of a client or a server application. For example, in Novell's SMS (storage management system) backup architecture, a special backup agent, called a *TSA* (*target service agent*), is loaded on every node that you want to back up from a centralized location. The agent allows the central backup program to access and back up the data on that node.

- In an IBM Token Ring architecture, an element on the network interface card that monitors certain aspects of the node and ring performance, and that reports this information to a network management program or to a Ring Error Monitor (REM).

- In network management and monitoring, a terminate-and-stay-resident (TSR) program that runs on a workstation to monitor activity and report this to a network management program.

- On the World Wide Web (WWW), several kinds of agent programs are used for various retrieval tasks. Spiders, Web robots, and wanders search Web pages for specified information; Web commerce agents—known as *shopbots*—can do price comparison or real shopping over the internet.

- Chatterbots and MUD agents can answer user queries. Originally developed for use in Multiuser Dungeons (or Dimensions) games, such agents can be adapted to provide information about other domains or topics.

- Microsoft's FrontPage uses bots, or Webbots, to carry out various tasks.

- Viruses and worm programs are less benign agents. They traverse a network with minimal help, just like other agents. However, rather than carrying out a particular task or retrieving information, such programs try to create and leave copies of themselves everywhere they can. These malicious agents may also have other tasks, such as destroying data.

Agent technology can be adapted for just about any purpose, and agents can be developed to help out with any sort of task. Work on using agents as personal assistants is a hot topic at universities and research labs all around the world.

The data collected by an agent is organized and processed by an agent handler. In network management, an agent handler may organize and analyze data concerning some network function or component.

Aging

A process by which old items or table entries are removed in a systematic manner, such as first in,

first out. This process serves both to update such tables and to speed up access.

Agoric System

An agoric system is a networking environment in which decision making, allocation of certain resources, and information gathering are decentralized, and may be distributed over an entire network or internetwork. Based on the metaphor of the Greek *agora*, or marketplace, network hosts and programs can act like buyers and sellers of resources (such as processor time, bandwidth, or storage). Buyers seek applications and servers to carry out required tasks, and sellers offer to carry out these tasks for a price. If properly implemented, such a system can provide more efficient use of available resources.

Suppose an application needs something done—for example, multicasting a large file to hundreds of sites or computing interest payments for a million clients. In an agoric system, such an application could send a request indicating this need to a buyer process. The request might include conditions or stipulations. For example, the application might be willing to pay $100 if the files can be sent within 10 minutes, $5 if they are sent within an hour, and $0 if the file transfer takes more than one hour.

The buyer process will, in turn, send the request to seller processes. Sellers can submit bids on the task. For example, seller A may be willing to send the files within 5 minutes for the promised $100, seller B may charge $20 to send them within 30 minutes, and seller C may offer to send them for free within 2 hours. The application can decide which, if any, offer to accept, and matters can proceed accordingly.

In an agoric system, hosts with high bandwidths can carry out such a task—to the mutual benefit of the host doing the work and the application requesting it. In an ordinary distributed environment, such a host's bandwidth might be underutilized most of the time.

Several agoric systems have been implemented. These vary in their details and capabilities. Some

A

systems, for example, allow buyers and sellers to play dual or interchangeable roles. For example, a seller for a particular task might also function as a buyer for that same task—by subcontracting out some or all of the task to another seller.

In some systems, hosts can take a proactive role. For example, if a host notices that a particular database is searched or used frequently, the host may buy a copy of the database—essentially, as an investment. With the database, the host's seller process can get in on the action surrounding the database—by serving as a seller to some of the many buyers of this database.

Agoric systems are still a nascent technology, so it remains to be seen whether this "free-market" approach to distributed computing will catch on.

AI (Authentication Information)

In network security, information used to determine whether a user is legitimate and authorized to access the system.

AIM (Analog Intensity Modulation)

In communications using light (rather than electrical) signals, a modulation method in which the intensity of the light source varies as a function of the signal being transmitted.

AIN (Advanced Intelligent Network)

In telecommunications, the name for a sophisticated digital network of the future.

AIS (Alarm Indication Signal)

A signal used in the OSI network management model and also in broadband ISDN networks to indicate the presence of an alarm or error somewhere on the network.

AIU (Access Interface Unit)

An AIU is a software product from Lucent Technologies. It is used in telephone switching situations—in particular, to separate online and voice calls—that is, calls to an access provider and telephone conversations. It is also used to route the online calls (which will generally tie up a circuit for a much longer time than a voice call) to a special set of circuits. This makes it possible to use the available circuits more efficiently and intelligently. For example, in practice, an AIU rarely blocks (is unable to complete) a call

Currently, AIUs work only with proprietary (AT&T) digital switches.

AL (Application Layer)

The topmost of the seven layers in the OSI reference model.

→ **See** OSI Layer

Alarm

In various network environments, particularly network management, an alarm is a signal used to indicate that an abnormality, a fault, or a security violation has been detected. Alarms may be distinguished by type, such as performance, fault, or security, and also by the severity of the event that caused the alarm.

At one extreme are critical events that represent immediate threats to continued network operation; for example, when a crucial LAN (local area network) node or a server goes down. In some network management environments, such critical alarms may trigger automatic response by the network management package.

At the other extreme are events that are not currently serious, but that may eventually become serious enough to threaten network operation; for example, when network traffic is getting close to the network's bandwidth limit. Such events generally do not require immediate correction but should be monitored.

Alarm Indication Signal (AIS)

→ *See* AIS (Alarm Indication Signal)

Alarm Reporting Function (ARF)

→ *See* ARF (Alarm Reporting Function)

Alert

In network management, an alarm sent by an agent to the administrator. An alert reports that a problem has arisen or that a threshold has been reached.

Algorithm

An algorithm is a predefined set of instructions for accomplishing a task. An algorithm is guaranteed to produce a result in a finite amount of time. Algorithms are used in many ways in networking. For example, there are hashing algorithms for finding file names in a directory and timing algorithms for deciding how long to wait before trying to access a network.

In most cases, the algorithms are of little interest to either the casual or intense network user. However, several algorithms have escaped from behind the scenes and have actually become items in marketing literature and other product discussions. The following are a few of the better-known algorithms:

Auto-partition An algorithm by which a repeater can automatically disconnect a segment from a network if that segment is not functioning properly. This can happen, for example, when a broken or unterminated cable causes too many collisions. When the collisions have subsided, the network segment can be reconnected.

Bellman-Ford An algorithm for finding routes through an internetwork. The algorithm uses distance vectors, as opposed to link states. The Bellman-Ford algorithm is also known as the *old ARPAnet* algorithm.

Distance-vector A class of computation-intensive routing algorithms in which each router computes the distance between itself and each possible destination. This is accomplished by computing the distance between a router and all of its immediate router neighbors, and adding each neighboring router's computations for the distances between that neighbor and all of its immediate neighbors. Several commonly used implementations are available, such as the Bellman-Ford algorithm and the ISO's Interdomain Routing Protocol (IDRP).

DUAL (Diffusing Update Algorithm) This is a distance-vector algorithm developed by Cisco Systems and actually embedded in their proprietary Enhanced Interior Gateway Routing Protocol (E-IGRP). The algorithm aims to find the shortest path to a specified destination by working its way toward the destination by always taking the shortest next step.

Hot potato In networks, a routing algorithm in which a node routes a packet or message to the output line with the shortest queue.

Link-states A class of routing algorithms in which each router knows the location of and distance to each of its immediately neighboring routers, and can broadcast this information to all other routers in a link state packet (LSP). If a router updates its LSP, the new version is broadcast and replaces the older versions at each other router. The scheme used to distribute the LSP greatly influences the performance of the routers. These types of algorithm are an alternative to distance-vector algorithms; rather than storing actual paths, link-state algorithms store the information needed to generate such paths. The ISO's open shortest path first (OSPF) algorithm is an example of a link-state algorithm.

Spanning-tree An algorithm that is used to compute open paths (paths without loops) among networks. The algorithm can generate all such paths and select one. If that path becomes inoperative because a node has gone down, the algorithm can find an alternate path. This type of algorithm is used by bridges to find the best path between two nodes in different networks, and to ensure that no path loops occur in the internetwork. This algorithm is defined in the IEEE 802.1 standard.

Alias

In a computer environment, a name that represents another, usually longer, name. In NetWare Directory Services (NDS), an alias is an object in one part of the Directory tree that points to the real object, which is located in a different part of the tree. Users can access the real object through the alias.

In various operating systems—for example, MacOS, Windows 95, Windows 98, and Windows NT—an alias is an icon that provides a direct path to a file or directory elsewhere on a disk (for example, one that may be buried many levels deep in a hierarchical directory structure) or on a different disk. Just as the map is not the territory, an alias is not necessarily the same as the location to which it provides access. For example, the properties of an alias in Windows 95, Windows 98, and Windows NT (at least up to NT 4) are just that—the properties of the alias and not of the file or directory to which the alias provides access. In Windows environments, an alias is generally referred to as a *shortcut*.

Alignment Error

In an Ethernet or other network, an error in which a packet has extra bits; that is, the packet does not end on byte-boundaries and will have invalid CRC (cyclic redundancy check) values. An alignment error may be caused by a faulty component, such as a damaged network interface card (NIC), transceiver, or cable.

Allocation Unit

In Novell's NetWare, areas that are used to store information from files and tables. Two types of storage are distinguished: blocks, which are used to store data on disk, and buffers, which hold data in RAM temporarily.

→ *See Also* Block; Buffer, Fiber-Optic Cable; Buffer, Memory.

Allowed Cell Rate (ACR)

→ *See* ACR (Available Cell Rate)

Alternate Bipolar (ABP)

A signal-encoding method.

→ *See Also* Encoding, Signal

Alternate Mark Inversion (AMI)

→ *See* AMI (Alternate Mark Inversion)

Alternate Route Selection (ARS)

→ *See* ARS (Alternate Route Selection)

Alternate Routing

This term describes the use of an alternative communications path, such as a telephone connection, when the primary one is not available.

Alternating Current (AC)

→ *See* AC (Alternating Current)

AM (Accounting Management)

One of five OSI (Open Systems Interconnection) network management domains defined by the ISO (International Standardization Organization)and CCITT (Consultative Committee for International Telegraphy and Telephony), now the ITU-T (International Telecommunications Union—Telecommunication Standardization Sector). This domain is concerned with the administration of network usage, costs, charges, and access to various resources.

→ *See Also*   Network Management

AM (Active Monitor)

In a token-ring network, the node that is responsible for creating, passing, and maintaining the token. The performance of the AM is monitored constantly by standby monitors (SMs) to ensure that the token-passing process is not interrupted.

Amdahl's Rule

A rule of thumb concerning computer performance, Amdahl's rule states that

- Each instruction cycle requires one bit of I/O (input/output), and

- One byte of memory should be available for each instruction a processor can execute in a second.

For example, this rule suggests that a processor with a 500MHz clock speed should be fed at the rate of 500Mbps of input; similarly, a processor capable of performing 1 billion instructions per second (BIPS) should have 1GB of memory.

AME (Asynchronous Modem Eliminator)

An AME, also known as a *null modem*, is a serial cable and connector with a modified pin configuration (compared to an ordinary RS-232 cable). This cable enables two computers to communicate directly; that is, without modems as intermediaries.

American National Standards Institute (ANSI)

→ *See*   ANSI (American National Standards Institute)

American Standard Code for Information Interchange (ASCII)

→ *See*   ASCII (American Standard Code for Information Interchange)

American Wire Gauge (AWG)

→ *See*   AWG (American Wire Gauge)

America Online (AOL)

→ *See*   AOL (America Online)

AMF (Account Metering Function)

In the OSI network management model, the function that keeps track of every user's resource usage.

AMH (Application Message Handling)

In the International Standardized Profile (ISP) model, the prefix used to identify MHS (Message Handling System) actions.

AMI (Alternate Mark Inversion)

A signal-encoding scheme in which a 1 is represented alternately as positive and negative voltage, and 0 is represented as zero voltage. It does not use transition coding, but can detect noise-induced errors at the hardware level.

→ *See Also* Encoding, Signal

AMP (Active Monitor Present)

In token-ring networks, a packet issued every three seconds by the active monitor (AM) on the ring to indicate that the AM is working and is still in charge.

Amplifier

A device for boosting an analog signal. The same service is provided by a repeater for digital signals.

Amplitude

The magnitude, or level, of a signal. For an electrical signal, it is expressed in volts (voltage) or amperes (current). In computer contexts, current is more likely to be expressed in milliamperes.

AMPS (Advanced Mobile Phone Service)

A cellular telephone service. AMPS is a wireless analog communications service that operates in the 825 to 890MHz range. For many years, AMPS was the dominant cellular technology in North and South America. However, as cellular communications move to digital technology, AMPS is being replaced by the digital GSM (Global System for Mobile Communications) technology.

→ *Compare* GSM (Global System for Mobile Communications)

Analog Communication

A telecommunications system that uses analog (that is, continuous, sinusoidal) signals to represent information. An example of an analog communication system is the classic voice-based telephone system (which is being replaced by the newer, digital systems).

Analog Intensity Modulation (AIM)

→ *See* AIM (Analog Intensity Modulation)

Analog Signal

→ *See* Signal, Analog

Analog-to-Digital Conversion

The process of converting an analog signal (one that can take on any value within a specified range) to digital form. An analog-to-digital converter (ADC) is a device that converts an analog signal to digital form.

Analog-to-Digital Converter (ADC)

→ *See* ADC (Analog-to-Digital Converter)

Analog Simultaneous Voice/Data (ASVD)

→ *See* ASVD (Analog Simultaneous Voice/Data)

Anchor

In HTML (Hypertext Markup Language) documents, an anchor is an element that is used to name a specific location within an HTML page (that is, a specific section in a document). To create an anchor, the text that represents the start of the anchored section must be placed between `<A>` (for anchor) and `</A>` (for end of anchor) tags. In addition, a name for the anchor must be specified as an attribute within the `<A>` tag. For example, the following HTML excerpts each create an anchor named YouAreHere, and indicate that the text "My location" begins the section associated with this anchor.

```
<A NAME="YouAreHere">My location</A>
<H3><A NAME="YouAreHere">My location
</A></H3>
```

The second excerpt shows a common strategy for creating anchors—namely, defining them inside some structural element of the document (a number 3 head in the example). Note that HTML manuals emphasize that you can place an anchor within a document element (such as a head or a title)—as in the second excerpt—but that you should not place a document element inside the text for an anchor. Thus, the following variant on the second excerpt should *not* be used.

```
<A NAME="YouAreHere"><H3>My location
</H3></A>
```

HTML links may point to a different HTML page (that is, document) or to a location within the same HTML page as the link. In the first case—that is, pointing to a different HTML page—the link can send the browser to the start of the referenced page or to a specific location on that page. Only the document name is needed to reference the top of an HTML page. In contrast, to reference a particular section in the same or different document, the link also needs to include an anchor name.

Links use the same `<A>` and `</A>` tags as anchors, but use an `HREF` attribute instead of `NAME` in the `<A>` tag. The following HTML excerpts show the three different forms a link can take:

```
<A HREF="ThatDoc.HTML">Start of other
document</A>
```

```
<A HREF="ThatDoc.HTML#YouAreHere">
Section in OTHER document</A>
<A HREF="#YouAreHere">Section in THIS
document</A>
```

The first excerpt points to the start of the file `ThatDoc.HTML`, with "Start of other document" being the text you click to get the browser to display `ThatDoc.HTML`. (This text is known as the link's *hot spot,* and will be highlighted in the HTML file in which the link is found.) Note that the first excerpt points to an HTML page, rather than to an anchor.

The second excerpt points to the YouAreHere anchor in the `ThatDoc.HTML` file. The pound sign (#) serves to separate the document and anchor names.

The third excerpt points to the YouAreHere anchor in the same file as the link. The pound sign indicates that YouAreHere represents an anchor rather than a document. "Anchors away" illustrates the three different uses of the anchor tag.

Anchors are also used in other markup languages such as SGML (Standardized General Markup Language) and XML (eXtensible Markup Language).

→ *Broader Category* HTML (Hypertext Markup Language)

Ancillary Control Process

An ancillary control process is one that serves as an interface or intermediary between a program (for example, an application) and an I/O (input/output) driver.

ANF (AppleTalk Networking Forum)

A consortium of developers and vendors working to encapsulate AppleTalk in other protocols; for example, within the TCP/IP suite.

ANI (Automatic Number Identification)

In ISDN and some other telecommunications environments, a feature that includes the sender's identification number, such as telephone number, in the transmission, so that the recipient knows who is calling; also known as *caller ID*.

Annex D

In frame-relay technology, a document that specifies a method for indicating permanent virtual circuit (PVC) status. The document is part of the ANSI T1.617 standard.

Annotation Bot

In Microsoft FrontPage, an annotation bot enables a user to include notes or placeholders in a Web page. These annotations will not be visible to a browser examining the document but can be seen using FrontPage.

→ *Broader Categories* Bot; Microsoft FrontPage

Anonymous FTP

On the Internet, a protocol that allows a user to retrieve publicly available files from other networks. By using the special user ID, "anonymous" users can transfer files without a password or other login credentials. (FTP is an application-layer protocol in the Internet's TCP/IP protocol suite.)

Anonymous Remailer

An Internet service that can be used to hide the origins of an e-mail message being sent to someone. The anonymous remailer removes any source address information from a message, substitutes any specified pen name, and then sends the message on to the specified destination.

A

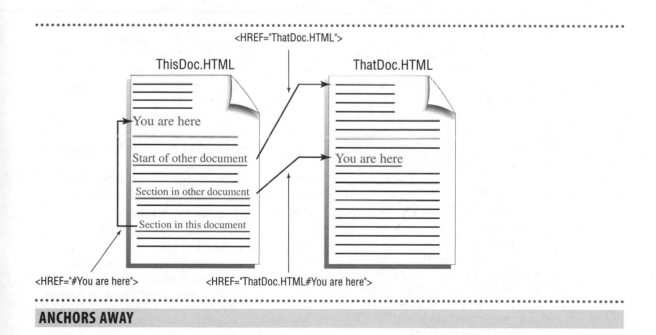

ANCHORS AWAY

ANSI (American National Standards Institute)

The United States representative in the ISO (International Standardization Organization). ANSI creates and publishes standards for programming languages, communications, and networking. For example, the standard for the FDDI network architecture is ANSI X3T9.5.

Table "Selected ANSI Standards" lists some of the standards that have been developed under the auspices of this organization.

SELECTED ANSI STANDARDS

Standard	Description
T1.101	Synchronous interface standards for digital networks
T1.102	Electrical interfaces for the digital hierarchy
T1.103	Format specifications for synchronous DS3 lines in the digital hierarchy
T1.103a	Updated version of T1.103
T1.105	Optical interface rates and format specifications for the digital hierarchy
T1.110	General information for Signaling System Number 7 (SSN7) (Same as ITU Q.700)
T1.113	SSN7, Integrated Services Digital Network (ISDN) User Part
T1.116	SSN7, Operations, Maintenance, and Administration Part (OMAP)
T1.219	ISDN management—overview and principles
T1.413	Physical layer operation for Asymmetric Digital Subscriber Line (ADSL)
T1.602	ISDN Data-Link layer (DLL) signaling specifications for application at the user-network interface (UNI)
T1.603	ISDN minimal set of bearer services for the Primary Rate Interface (PRI)
T1.604	ISDN minimal set of bearer services for the Basic Rate Interface (BRI)
T1.610	Digital Subscriber Signaling System Number 1 (DSS1), generic methods for controlling ISDN supplementary services
T1.613	ISDN, call waiting supplementary services
X3.1	Synchronous data transmission signaling rates (Similar to ITU V.6 and V.7)
X3.4	7-bit ASCII character set
X3.15	Bit sequencing of ASCII characters in serial transmissions
X3.16	Character structure and parity sense for serial transmission of ASCII characters
X3.24	Signal quality for synchronous data terminal equipment/data circuit-terminating equipment (DTE/DCE) interfaces (Similar to EIA-RS-334)
X.3.25	Character structure and parity for parallel communication of ASCII characters
X3.28	Procedures for the use of ASCII control characters
X3.32	Graphic representation of ASCII control characters
X3.36	Signaling rates for high-speed communications between DTE and DCE
X3.44	Determining the performance of data communications systems
X3.66	Advanced data communication and control procedures (ADCCP)
X3.92	Data Encryption Algorithm (DEA)
X3.105	Data Link Encryption
X3.106	Modes of operation for DEA
X3.139	Token ring MAC (media access control) for the Fiber Distributed Data Interface (FDDI)
X3.140	Connection-oriented Transport layer protocol specification for Open Systems Interconnection (OSI)
X3.148	Token ring Physical layer protocol for FDDI
X3.153	Basic connection-oriented session protocol specification for OSI
X3.166	Physical layer medium dependent (PMD) specification for FDDI
X9.8	Personal information number (PIN) management and security
X9.9	Message authentication for wholesale financial institutions
X9.17	Key management for wholesale financial institutions
X9.19	Retail message authentication
X9.23	Message encryption for financial institutions
X9.24	Retail key management
X9.26	Financial institution sign-on authentication for wholesale financial transactions
X9.30	Public key cryptography using irreversible algorithms for the financial services industry
X9.31	Public key cryptography using reversible algorithms for the financial services industry

Answer Mode

In telecommunications, a modem in answer mode can handle the process of connecting to a calling modem automatically. Specifically, the modem can detect and answer an incoming call, determine the protocol the calling modem is using, and then synchronize the session with the calling modem.

Antenna

In wireless communications, an antenna is a device that radiates electromagnetic signals during transmission and that captures such signals during reception.

Anti-Virus Program

An anti-virus program is used for detecting or removing a computer virus. Such a program looks for suspicious activity, such as unnecessary disk access, attempts to intercept a BIOS or other low-level call, and attempts to format or delete files. In some cases, the anti-virus program detects a bit pattern characteristic of a particular virus.

Some anti-virus programs are TSR (terminate-and-stay-resident) programs, which monitor computer activity constantly, looking for indications of a virus. In some cases, these types of programs can be extremely annoying and very processor intensive. Users have been known to remove an anti-virus TSR program from memory out of frustration.

Other anti-virus programs are designed to run periodically. When they are run, the programs look for the tell-tale signs (known as *signatures*) of particular viruses. These programs are minimally disruptive; on the other hand, their effectiveness is directly proportional to the frequency with which they are used.

Because the coding for computer viruses is constantly changing, anti-virus programs must also be updated regularly. It is important to test anti-virus programs thoroughly, which means that every new release must be tested. Make sure an anti-virus program performs to your expectations before installing it on a network. Some programs can eat up a significant amount of working memory.

Another, newer, type of anti-virus program takes a more probabilistic approach. Such programs use quasi-intelligent strategies (for example, expert system rules, fuzzy logic, or neural nets) in an effort to identify viruses. In some cases, the program may actually lay out special code to "trap" a virus.

The appearance, over the past few years, of macro viruses and, more recently, of viruses that look for network machines to invade has made it much easier to spread viruses, and has also made the task of keeping anti-virus technology ahead of—or at least not too far behind—the virus writers more challenging.

→ *Broader Category* Data Protection

→ *Related Article* Virus

AOL (America Online)

America Online is a commercial online service like CompuServe (now owned by AOL) and the Microsoft Network (MSN). In fact, AOL is the largest online service, with a subscriber base of over 13 million members. AOL provides a range of services (mail, news, reference, financial, entertainment, Internet access, and so forth) for subscribers operating in DOS, Windows (3.1 and later), and Macintosh environments. In the most recent version of its access software, AOL has integrated version 4 of Microsoft Internet Explorer.

Subscribers can pay about $22 per month for an unlimited access service plan, or they can use a limited plan, in which they can get five hours per week for $10 and then pay for additional hours on a per-use basis.

AOM (Application OSI Management)

In the International Standardized Profile (ISP) model, the prefix for functions and services related to network management.

AOW (Asia and Oceania Workshop)

One of three regional workshops for implementers of the OSI reference model. The other two are EWOC (European Workshop for Open Systems) and OIW (OSI Implementers Workshop).

Apache Web Server

Apache is a very popular World Wide Web server for UNIX platforms. Apache is a fully functional Web server whose popularity stems from its easy installation, full feature set, performance, and price (free). The Apache Web server source code is available at www.apache.org.

Recently, IBM announced that it will support the use of Apache Web servers on its systems.

AP (Application Process)

In the OSI reference model, a program that can make use of application layer services. Application service elements (ASEs) provide the requested services for the AP.

APD (Avalanche Photodiode)

A detector component in some fiber-optic receivers. The APD converts light into electrical energy. The "avalanche" refers to the fact that the detector emits multiple electrons for each incoming photon (light particle).

APDU (Application Protocol Data Unit)

A data packet at the application layer; also called *application-layer PDU*.

→ *See Also* OSI Reference Model

API (Application Program Interface)

An API is an abstract interface to the services and protocols offered by an operating system, usually involving a published set of function calls. Programmers and applications can use the functions available in this interface to gain access to the operating system's services. The table "Example APIs" lists some of the APIs currently available for specific purposes.

EXAMPLE APIS

API Name	Comments
HLLAPI (High-Level Language API)	Provides an interface between PC applications and IBM mainframes
IDAPI (Integrated Database API)	Proposed to provide an interface between front-end applications and back-end programs that access databases
ISAPI (Internet Server API)	Provides resources for adding to the functionality of Microsoft Internet Information Server (IIS)
JavaBeans	A collection of more specialized APIs; provides resources for creating interactive applets and Java programs
JMAPI (Java Management API)	Provides resources for programming network management tools in Java
JTAPI (Java Telephony API)	Provides resources for programming telephony services using Java
MAPI (Messaging API)	Provides resources for creating messaging services
MFC (Microsoft Foundation Class)	Provides access to resources in Microsoft Visual Programming Languages environments
NSAPI (Netscape API)	Provides resources for programming extension to Netscape Web tools
SAPI (Speech API)	Provides resources for creating applications for speech processing
TAPI (Telephone API)	Microsoft's collection of resources for creating telephony applications
TSAPI	Novell and other companies' collection of resources for creating telephony applications
WinCAPI (Windows Crypto API)	Provides resources for creating encryption tools

APIA (Application Program Interface Association)

A group that writes APIs for the CCITT's X.400 Message Handling System (MHS).

APPC (Advanced Program-to-Program Communications)

In IBM's SAA (Systems Application Architecture), APPC is a collection of protocols to enable executing applications to communicate directly with each other as peers (without intervention by a mainframe host).

APPC is defined at a level comparable to the session layer in the OSI reference model. It can be supported in various networking environments, including IBM's SNA (System Network Architecture), Ethernet, Token Ring, and X.25.

APPC/PC (Advanced Program-to-Program Communications/Personal Computers) is a PC-based version of APPC.

AppleDouble

In the Macintosh world, a file format that uses separate files for the data and resource forks that make up a Macintosh file. This enables the files—or at least the data portion—to be used on different platforms.

→ *Compare* AppleSingle

AppleShare

A network operating system from Apple. AppleShare runs on a Macintosh network server, providing file and printer services. AppleShare uses the AppleTalk protocol suite to carry out its tasks.

→ *See Also* AppleTalk

AppleSingle

In the Macintosh world, a file format that stores both a file's contents (data fork) and its resources (resource fork) within a single file. Because data and resources are mixed in a proprietary format, such a file cannot be used on other platforms.

→ *Compare* AppleDouble

Applet

An applet is a client-oriented Java program that can execute on an HTML (Hypertext Markup Language) page when the page is displayed. However, the page must be read by a "Java-enabled" browser program—that is, one that includes or has access to a Java interpreter, and that can, therefore, execute Java programs. An applet performs some function (such as displaying an animation sequence, providing an interactive form for the user to complete, performing static or dynamic calculations or graphical displays) appropriate for the Web page on which it executes.

When a Java-enabled browser encounters an HTML reference to an applet, the browser retrieves the applet from its location (generally, a Web server)—just as the browser would retrieve an image to be displayed on the page. Once retrieved, the applet can execute on the client's machine when the HTML page is displayed.

Since applets are programs that may be downloaded from unreliable sites, an applet generally has several restrictions that apply to it. These restrictions prevent the applet from reading or writing to the client machine's file system, loading or executing programs, or communicating with any machines other than the server from which the applet was retrieved.

Java applets are created using Java's applet class. Applets are comparable in their operation to ActiveX controls.

→ *Broader Concept* Java

→ *Compare* ActiveX; Servlet

AppleTalk

AppleTalk is Apple's proprietary protocol suite for Macintosh network communications. It provides a multilayer, peer-to-peer architecture that uses services built into the operating system. This gives every Macintosh networking capabilities. AppleTalk can run under any of several network operating systems, including Apple's AppleShare, Novell's NetWare for Macintosh, and Sun Microsystems' TOPS.

AppleTalk was developed in the mid-1980s with the goal of providing a simple, portable, easy-to-use, and open networking environment. To access such a network, a user just needs to "plug in, log in, and join in."

A newer version, Phase 2, was released in 1989. This version provided some new capabilities and extended others.

AppleTalk Layers

AppleTalk is a comprehensive, layered environment. It covers networking services over almost the entire range of layers specified in the OSI reference model. "The AppleTalk protocol hierarchy" shows the organization of the AppleTalk layers, as well as the protocols in the AppleTalk Protocol Suite.

Physical and Data-Link Layers

There are AppleTalk implementations for the following network architectures at the physical and Data-Link layers:

- Apple's 230Kbps

- LocalTalk architecture. LocalTalk provides a media-access method and a cabling scheme for AppleTalk. The architecture uses twisted-pair cables and RS-422 connections, allows nodes to be separated by as much as 305 meters (1000 feet), and can transmit at up to 230.4Kbps. The term LocalTalk is sometimes used to refer to an AppleTalk network.

- EtherTalk, Apple's implementation of the 10 megabit per second (Mbps) Ethernet architecture. Two versions of EtherTalk exist. The earlier one, EtherTalk Phase 1, is modeled on the Blue Book Ethernet 2 (as opposed to the version specified in the IEEE 802.3 documentation). Its successor, Phase 2, is modeled on the IEEE 802.3 standard. Because these two variants of Ethernet define packets somewhat differently, Phase 1 and Phase 2 nodes cannot communicate directly with each other. EtherTalk has replaced LocalTalk as the default networking capability in newer Macintosh models.

- TokenTalk, Apple's implementation of the token-ring architecture. AppleTalk supports both the 4-Mbps version specified by IEEE 802.5 and the 16-Mbps version from IBM. The token-ring architecture is supported only in AppleTalk Phase 2.

- FDDITalk, Apple's implementation of the 100Mbps FDDI architecture.

For each of these architectures, a Link Access Protocol (LAP) is defined: LLAP for LocalTalk, ELAP for EtherTalk, TLAP for TokenTalk, and FLAP for FDDITalk.

Network Layer

All AppleTalk networks use the DDP (Datagram Delivery Protocol) at the Network layer, regardless of the architecture operating at the Data-Link layer. This protocol makes a best effort at packet delivery, but delivery is not guaranteed.

Note also the AARP (AppleTalk Address Resolution Protocol) at this layer. The AARP maps AppleTalk (network) addresses to Ethernet or Token Ring (physical) addresses.

Higher Layers

For reliable packet delivery, the ADSP (AppleTalk Data Stream Protocol) and ATP (AppleTalk

Transaction Protocol) are available. Each of these protocols is appropriate under different conditions.

The NBP (Name Binding Protocol) and ZIP (Zone Information Protocol) help make addressing easier. NBP associates easy-to-remember names (used by users) with the appropriate address.

ZIP is used mainly on larger networks or internetworks, which are more likely to be divided into zones. A zone is a logical grouping of nodes which together make up a subnetwork. The concept of a

zone was introduced to allow for larger networks with more than 255 nodes, and also to make addressing and routing tasks easier.

Applications access an AppleTalk network through the AFP (AppleTalk Filing Protocol); they access printer services by shipping PostScript files through the PAP (Printer Access Protocol).

A few protocols make use of services from more than one lower-level protocol. For example, ZIP relies on ATP and DDP services.

A

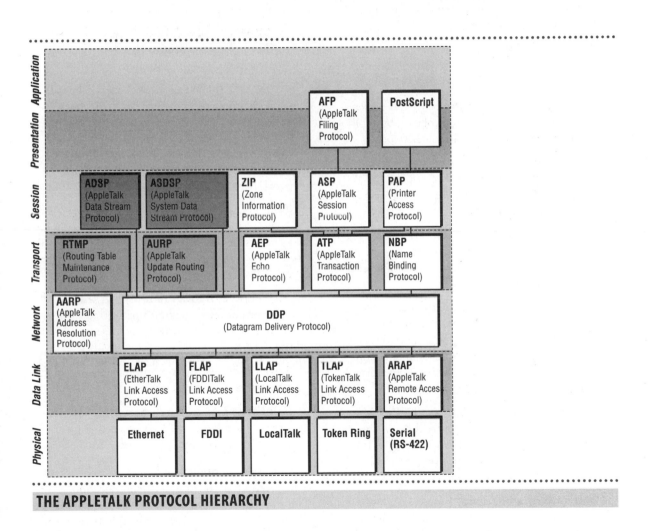

THE APPLETALK PROTOCOL HIERARCHY

AppleTalk Protocol Suite

The following protocols make up the AppleTalk Protocol Suite (see the illustration "The AppleTalk protocol hierarchy," earlier in this article):

AARP (AppleTalk Address Resolution Protocol)   A network-layer protocol that maps AppleTalk (network) addresses to physical addresses.

ADSP (AppleTalk Data Stream Protocol)   A session-layer protocol that allows two nodes to establish a reliable connection through which data can be transmitted.

AEP (AppleTalk Echo Protocol)   A transport-layer protocol used to determine whether two nodes are connected and both available.

AFP (AppleTalk Filing Protocol)   A presentation/application-layer protocol used by applications to communicate with the network.

ASDSP (AppleTalk Safe Data Stream Protocol)   A session-layer protocol that is similar to ADSP but that provides additional security against unauthorized use.

ASP (AppleTalk Session Protocol)   A session-layer protocol used to begin and end sessions, send commands from client to server, and send replies from server to client.

ATP (AppleTalk Transaction Protocol)   A transport-layer protocol that can provide reliable packet transport. Packets are transported within the framework of a transaction (an interaction between a requesting and a responding entity [program or node]).

AURP (AppleTalk Update Routing Protocol)   A transport-layer routing protocol that is similar to RTMP (Routing Table Maintenance Protocol) but that updates the routing table only when a change has been made to the network.

DDP (Datagram Delivery Protocol)   A network-layer protocol that prepares and routes packets for transmission on the network.

LAP (Link Access Protocol)   Works at the Data-Link layer, converting packets from higher layers into the appropriate form for the physical transmission. Each network architecture needs its own LAP:

ELAP (EtherTalk Link Access Protocol) The link-access protocol used for Ethernet networks.

FLAP (FDDITalk Link Access Protocol) The link-access protocol used for FDDI networks.

LLAP (LocalTalk Link Access Protocol) The link-access protocol used for LocalTalk networks.

TLAP (TokenTalk Link Access Protocol) The link-access protocol used for Token Ring networks.

ARAP (AppleTalk Remote Access Protocol) A link-access protocol for accessing the network from a remote location over a serial line.

NBP (Name Binding Protocol)   A transport-layer protocol that associates device names with network addresses. If the NBP is successful, this binding process will be completely transparent to the user.

PAP (Printer Access Protocol)   A session-layer protocol for creating a path from the user or application to a printer.

RTMP (Routing Table Maintenance Protocol) A transport-layer routing protocol for moving packets between networks.

ZIP (Zone Information Protocol)   A session-layer protocol used to help find a node; for example, in a large internetwork.

If installed, an AppleShare server runs on top of these protocols at the uppermost (application) layer. The AppleShare server uses the AFP to provide centralized file sharing for its clients, and can use the PAP to provide printer sharing.

Numbers and Zones

In AppleTalk networks, every node has an official numerical address. In addition, a node may be part of a named group of nodes, which somehow belong together.

Network and Node Numbers

Each AppleTalk network is assigned a unique network number, and each node in that network is assigned this number. Packets addressed to a node on the network must include the network number.

In addition to a network number, each node has a node number that is unique within that network. This is an 8-bit number and can be any value between 1 and 254, inclusive (0 and 255 are reserved as node numbers). However, servers must have node numbers within the range of 128 to 254, and workstations must have numbers in the 1 to 127 range.

Zones

A *zone* is a logical grouping of nodes. The basis for the grouping can be any criterion that is useful for a particular configuration, as in the following examples:

- Geographical, such as all machines on the second floor

- Departmental, such as all machines in the marketing department

- Functional, such as all machines that can provide access to printers

By restricting routing or searches to machines in a particular zone, network traffic and work can be reduced considerably. Accessing resources by zones also makes it easier to determine what is available for specific needs.

A node may belong to more than one zone at the same time, or not be part of any zone. A zone can cross network boundaries; that is, a zone can consist of parts of two or more different networks or include multiple networks.

Phase 2 AppleTalk

Phase 2, an updated version of AppleTalk, was released in 1989. This version provides several improvements over Phase 1, including the following:

- Allows more than 254 nodes per network

- Allows a network to be assigned more than one network number

- Introduced the AppleTalk Internet Router, which allows up to eight AppleTalk networks to be connected

Network Numbering in Phase 2

In AppleTalk Phase 2, a network can be assigned a range of network numbers. A particular node on this network can be associated with any one number in this range. By providing multiple network numbers for a single network, it is possible to have more than the 254 nodes allowed in a Phase 1 network, because each network number can support 253 (yes, 253) individual nodes.

When you are assigning number ranges, a rough rule of thumb is to assign one network number for every 25 to 50 nodes. If you expect a lot of growth, use a smaller number. For example, assigning two network numbers for a 100-node network leaves room for 406 additional nodes.

When a network is part of an internetwork, there are several restrictions on what can be connected and how. These restrictions concern routers and bridges, and the networks they can connect, as follows:

- All routers connected to a particular network must use the same network number range for the interface with that network. For example, if a router thinks the network uses numbers 1000 to 1009, another router connected to the same network cannot use 1002 to 1008.

- Routers must connect networks with different number ranges that do not overlap. This means that routers cannot connect a network to itself and that networks with overlapping network numbers cannot interact with each other.

- A bridge must connect network segments with the same number range.

"Rules for connecting AppleTalk Phase 2 internetworks" illustrates these rules.

AppleTalk Networking Forum (ANF)

→ *See* ANF (AppleTalk Networking Forum)

AppleTalk Print Services (ATPS)

→ *See* ATPS (AppleTalk Print Services)

Application

An application is a program that calls operating system services and performs work, such as data creation or manipulation, for the user. Applications may be stand-alone, network-based, distributed, or part of an integrated package.

Stand-Alone Applications

A stand-alone application can execute only one version of itself at a time and can support only a single user at a time. This type of application executes on a single machine, which may or may not be connected to a network. Single-user versions of spreadsheet, graphics, and database programs are examples of stand-alone applications.

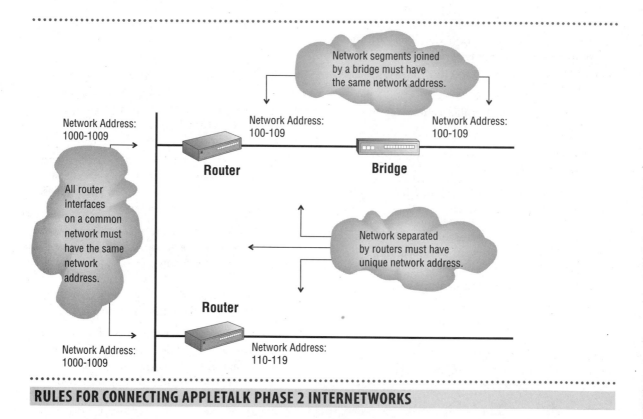

RULES FOR CONNECTING APPLETALK PHASE 2 INTERNETWORKS

Network-Based Applications

A network-based application executes on a network and is aware of the network, which means that it can use networking conventions, elements, resources (such as print spoolers and cache buffers), and devices (such as printers, modems, and backup devices).

This type of application can be used by multiple users at the same time. Applications differ in the number of allowable users and in the measures taken to enforce restrictions and to make sure users do not ruin other users' data. Network and data protection measures include the use of flags, access rights, and lock-outs. These serve to help ensure that data is used correctly, only as needed, and with fair access to all users.

Network-based applications may execute on a single machine or be distributed over multiple machines. Client/server computing is an example of a distributed arrangement in which part of an application (the front end) executes on the workstation to provide an interface for the user, and another part (the back end) executes on a server to do the actual work, such as searching a database.

A network-based application may be multiuser or multilaunch. Only one copy of a multiuser application executes, but multiple users can access files in this executing program. A multilaunch application allows multiple users to execute the program separately but at the same time. In effect, each user gets a private version of a multilaunch application.

Distributed Applications

Distributed applications may have executable components on different machines in a network or internetwork. Network-based and distributed applications have much in common; in many cases, the difference between the two is one of degree, rather than substance.

To the client that launches a distributed application, the application's execution should look the same as if the application were running entirely on the client machine.

Integrated Applications

An integrated application is part of a collection, or suite, of programs. Ideally, these programs complement each other in their functionality and allow easy exchange of data. Microsoft Office, Lotus SmartSuite, and Corel's PerfectOffice are examples of such integrated applications.

Accessing Networks from Applications

Users may access networks through or for applications. For example, an application may use a network resource or may need to communicate with an application on another machine. Or a user may log in to a network with the specific intention of using an application available on that network.

Regardless of the details, such network accesses are through the topmost layer in the OSI reference model: the application layer. This layer provides users and programs with an interface to the network. At this layer, both the user and the application are isolated from the details of network access and communication.

SHARING DATA AMONG APPLICATIONS

Separate applications can also communicate and exchange data. Using pipes, in which the output from one program is simply "piped" in as input to another program is one of the simplest ways to share data.

OLE (object linking and embedding) is a more sophisticated method, which provides much greater flexibility. OLE makes it possible for updates to be carried over automatically to whatever applications use the updated items.

Application Context (AC)

→ *See* AC (Application Context)

Application Entity (AE)

→ *See* AE (Application Entity)

Application File Transfer (AFT)

→ *See* AFT (Application File Transfer)

Application Layer

The topmost layer in the seven-layer OSI reference model. Content for use by and in applications is transported and delivered at this layer.

→ *See Also* OSI Reference Model

Application-Level Proxy

An application-level proxy is a program that sits between applications and requested network services. In particular, the proxy serves as a transparent intermediary between client applications requesting services and the (remote) servers that are providing them. For the servers, the proxy pretends that requests from all the clients going through the proxy actually come from the proxy.

Thus, servers know only about the existence of a single client for the application-level services. For example, all requests for Web pages would be routed to the proxy. All the actual clients are hidden behind this proxy. The client thinks it is talking to the server when in fact it is talking to the proxy. "An application-level proxy at work" shows how such a proxy works.

The elements in the illustration are as follows:

1. Genuine request: By client A for a document or service from server Y

1a. Proxied request: By qA for a document or service from Y

2. Genuine response: By Y to request from qA

2a. Proxied response: By qY to request from A

3. Genuine request: By B for a document or service from Z

3a. Proxied request: By qB for a document or service from Z

4. Genuine response: By Z to request from qB

4a. Proxied response: By qZ to request from B

The proxy generally runs on a firewall, but this is not necessary. Such a proxy is designed to help prevent a would-be intruder from sneaking in by hijacking a TCP or other lower-level connection. An application-level proxy does this by limiting network traffic passing through it to the higher-level protocols (for example, HTTP, FTP, or SMTP) for which the proxy is set up. This means that any TCP/IP datagrams trying to sneak in will simply be dropped. Each application requires a separate application proxy.

As is the case for a proxy server, an application-level proxy may change mailing headers or other source addresses so that outgoing messages or requests appear to come from the device on which the proxy is running.

→ *Compare* Circuit-level proxy

→ *See Also* Proxy; Server, Proxy

Application Message Handling (AMH)

→ *See* AMH (Application Message Handling)

Application OSI Management (AOM)

→ *See* AOM (Application OSI Management)

Application Process (AP)

→ *See* AP (Application Process)

Application Program Interface (API)

→ *See* API (Application Program Interface)

Application Program Interface Association (APIA)

→ *See* APIA (Application Program Interface Association)

Application Protocol Data Unit (APDU)

→ *See* APDU (Application Protocol Data Unit)

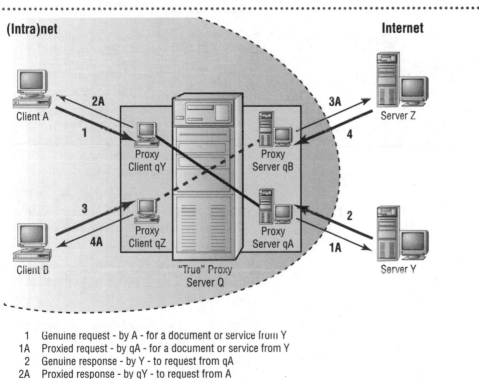

1   Genuine request - by A - for a document or service from Y
1A Proxied request - by qA - for a document or service from Y
2   Genuine response - by Y - to request from qA
2A Proxied response - by qY - to request from A
3   Genuine request - by B - for a document or service from Z
3A Proxied request - by qB - for a document or service from Z
4   Genuine response - by Z - to request from qB
4A Proxied response - by qZ - to request from B

AN APPLICATION-LEVEL PROXY AT WORK

Application Sharing

Application sharing is a feature of videoconferencing and dataconferencing environments. It allows two people to work together on the same application, even though the application is running on only one of their machines. Although launched from only one machine, the application appears to run simultaneously on both machines, and each user can interact with the program.

Application-Specific Integrated Circuit (ASIC)

→ *See* ASIC (Application-Specific Integrated Circuit)

APPN (Advanced Peer-to-Peer Networking)

APPN is a network architecture defined within IBM's SAA (Systems Application Architecture) environment. APPN allows peer-to-peer communications between computers without requiring a mainframe in the network.

APPN is also supported within IBM's SNA (Systems Network Architecture) environment. Unlike standard SNA, however, APPN supports dynamic routing of packets.

APPN was designed to provide the peer-to-peer services and the flexibility that SNA lacked. Toward that end, APPN allows LU-LU (logical unit to logical unit) and CP-CP (control point to control point) connections. LU-LU connections represent basic connections between very generic devices. The CP-CP connections allow for the exchange of management information about resources available for the nodes involved in the connection. APPN also provides intermediate session routing (ISR), which enables two nodes to communicate even if they are not directly connected. Most important, APPN can do all of these things without the need for a main-

frame or other master controller; rather, an APPN network can be built of just PCs, loaded with the appropriate software.

APPN Components

An APPN network includes the following main types of nodes, as well as more specialized ones:

APPN Network Nodes (APPN NNs) These elements

- Provide (the very generic) LU-LU service for logical units attached to the NNs.

- Effectively function as servers for the APPN ENs and the LEN (client) ENs attached to the NN. (These components are discussed later in this list.)

- Can attach APPN or LEN ENs to the network by connecting the element to the NN.

- Select routes and perform directory searches. Unlike components in an SNA network, APPN NNs can do dynamic routing, which means that a route can be determined as needed, rather than having to be defined at the start of a session and remaining unchanged throughout.

- Provide intermediate session routing (ISR)— that is, paths between NNs or between the NN and another EN—to pass material from a connection to a different area of the network.

- Use T2.1 protocols, such as those for SNA, but with enhancements for the APPN environment.

- Can use CP-CP connections to communicate with other nodes of the appropriate type.

APPN End Nodes (APPN ENs) These elements

- May be attached to multiple NNs, each via a different link.

- Can and must register as LUs with the NNs to which particular ENs are attached.

- Can perform limited directory services within their own nodes, and can report the results of such actions when requested by an NN.

- Use T2.1 protocols, including enhancements.

- Can use CP-CP connections to communicate with NNs, but only with one NN at a time. (The APPN EN can, however, be attached to more than one NN at a time.)

- Cannot use CP-CP connections to communicate with another APPN EN.

Low-End Network End Nodes (LEN ENs)
These elements

- Cannot register as LUs with NNs to which the LEN ENs are attached. Instead, LEN ENs must be able to be assigned and make use of predefined LUs—that is, LUs that have already been created and registered. This means that LEN ENs can work only with predefined connections.

- Use the same (T2.1) protocols as the other components, but without being able to use any particular enhancements supported by APPN.

- Cannot use CP-CP connections; instead, LEN ENs must use LU-LU connections when communicating.

The following types of nodes are also important for certain kinds of APPN network configurations:

Peripheral border nodes (PBNs)   Can establish an LU connection between two adjacent subnetworks, but do not support intermediate network routing. Thus, a peripheral border node can establish a connection between a logical unit in one network and a logical unit in an adjacent network, but the node cannot route the connection to another network node.

Extended border nodes (EBNs)   Support intermediate networking, but only for predefined subnetworks. That is, an extended border router can help establish a connection between logical units in different subnetworks, even if these subnetworks are not adjacent.

APPN subarea interchange nodes (INs)   Make it possible to connect an APPN network to an SNA network. INs are actually type 5 devices—PU 5, in IBM's parts terminology, as described in the SNA entry—and these INs effectively serve as gateways between the related but not identical networking architectures.

APPN Node Structure

APPN nodes all have the same general structure, but not the same functionality. Nodes have the following general components:

Data link control (DLC)   Provides an interface between the components. This component consists of two parts:

- The DLC element, which is responsible mainly for moving data to and from the physical medium, retransmitting data if necessary, and communicating with the path control component described elsewhere in this list.

- The DLC manager, which activates the link between the node and another node (so that the transmission will be possible), and then activates the DLC element to do its work. Once the work is done, the DLC manager deactivates the DLC element and the link in turn. The DLC manager also passes information to the control point component.

Path control (PC)   Checks and massages messages going to or coming from the DLC component, and also starts and ends a communications session. Like the DLC, the PC has two main components:

- The PC element, which deals with packets to and from the DLC—including error checking and packet prioritization—and which also routes messages between the PC manager and other components in the node.

- The PC manager, which connects and disconnects the session, controls the flow of traffic, and communicates with the control point component.

Control point (CP) Manages resources for the node. Depending on the type of node, the CP may also provide services for other nodes and may exchange management information with other nodes. The CP has numerous components, including configuration, directory, management, session, and topology and routing services, as well as address space management. See the *CP (Control Point)* entry for more information on these components.

Intermediate session router (ISR) Moves network traffic between intermediate nodes—that is, nodes other than the source and destination. The ISR has two components:

- The session connector (SC), which routes packets through intermediate nodes, reassembles packets and basic information units (BIUs), if necessary, does error checking for the session, and controls the pacing of the transmissions.

- The session connector manager (SCM), which is responsible for establishing and breaking connections with the intermediate nodes involved in the session, reserving buffers for the session traffic, and connecting the SC to the path control component. The SCM also communicates with the control point and with the node operator facility component (described later in the list).

Logical unit (LU) Communicates with the path control and other node components, and also with logical units in other nodes. The actual transmission of user packets (as opposed to management or routing packets) takes place mainly through the LU, and through LU-LU connections in particular. The LU has the following components which, together, provide the necessary session and presentation services:

- LU-LU half session (HS), which is responsible for the data flow and transmission controls for one end of a session connection. The data flow control (DFC) component creates the request/response headers (RHs) that are added to packets (known as request/response

units, or RUs). This component also makes sure the proper parameter values are included in the header. The DFC element also chains together RUs that belong together and that will be sent in sequence during a session. Such RU chains are known as brackets, and the DFC manages the bracket protocol that is used to transmit RU chains. The transmission control (TC) component is responsible for assembling the request/response units (RUs) that are exchanged during a session. If encryption is being used in the session, the TC element does the encrypting and decrypting, and also manages sender and encryption verification. The TC element is also responsible for the pacing of the session.

- Session manager (SM), which does what is needed to enable a session—or at least the node's half session end of it. This component sends and receives the requests to activate a session between LUs. (Such a request is known as a BIND in APPN-speak.) The SM also helps establish parameters when negotiating the details of a BIND. Once a link has been activated for a session, the SM creates a half session instance, and connects this half session to the node's path control component. Should a session connection be broken, the SM informs the resource manager component.

- Presentation services, which work with the transaction programs that use the LU6.2 protocol—IBM's peer-to-peer upper-level protocol—to communicate with each other. (Communications between transaction programs are known as *conversations*.) In particular, this component calls and loads an appropriate transaction program—in the LU, this will be a service transaction program. The presentation services component also packages data into logical records, and performs other kinds of mappings. This component works closely with the LU's resource manager component, which is described in the next item.

- Resource manager (RM), which manages the resources for conversations between transaction programs. The RM is also responsible for session-level security and for creating the security header. The RM creates and destroys conversation resources, and also connects these resources to presentation services and to the half session. Finally, the RM creates presentation service instances for a session, and destroys these when they are no longer needed.

- Service transaction programs (STPs), which converse with application transaction programs (ATPs) within the node (but outside the LU component) and with other STPs in other nodes.

Application transaction programs (ATPs) Communicate with applications on one side and with STPs in the LU on the other side. These programs provide the necessary translations between applications and the LU6.2 protocol used to communicate between nodes.

Node operator facility (NOF) Responsible for the tasks related to the node as a network element. These include activating the link to attach the node to another node (and to the network), creating and deleting LUs to identify a logical entity for the network, and defining such things as the contents of the directory, parameters for various elements and for the node. The NOF also interacts with transaction programs

→ *Broader Category* SAA (Systems Application Architecture)

ARA (Attribute Registration Authority)

In the X.400 Message Handling System (MHS), the organization that allocates unique attribute values.

ARAP (AppleTalk Remote Access Protocol)

→ *See* Protocol, ARAP (AppleTalk Remote Access Protocol)

Archie

An Internet service that can find the location of specified files based on the file's name or description. An Archie server gets its information by using the FTP program to do a listing of files on accessible servers and also by getting file description information. Currently, Archie servers have data about over 2.5 million files on over 1000 servers.

Archie servers are scattered throughout the Internet, and are accessible using services such as telnet or gopher, through e-mail, or by using Archie client programs. Archie servers should be equivalent (except for minor differences arising because not all servers are updated at the same time), so selecting a server is just a matter of convenience. See the table "Example Archie Servers" for a list of some of the available servers.

EXAMPLE ARCHIE SERVERS

Servers	Location
archie.ac.il	Israel
archie.au	Australia
archie.doc.ic.ad.uk	United Kingdom
archie.edvz.uni-linz.ac.at	Austria
archie.funet.fi	Finland
archie.kr	Korea
archie.mcgill.ca	Canada (McGill University)
archie.ncu.edu.tw	Taiwan
archie.rediris.es	Spain
archie.rutgers.edu	USA (Rutgers University)
archie.sura.net	USA (SURAnet is a service provider)
archie.switch.ch	Switzerland
archie.th-darmstadt.de	Germany
archie.unipi.it	Italy
archie.univ-rennes1.fr	France
archie.unl.edu	USA (University of Nebraska, Lincoln)
archie.wide.ad.jp	Japan

Useful Archie Commands

Once a connection has been established with the Archie server, various commands are available. The following list summarizes some useful ones.

Help	Displays a list of available commands.
Manpage	Displays the reference manual for Archie.
List	Displays a list of the anonymous STP servers whose contents are listed in Archie's database. If this command is followed by a regular expression, the command displays only the servers that match the expression.
Servers	Displays a list of all the available Archie servers.
Version	Displays the version number of the Archie server you're querying. Such information will come in handy if you need to get help with the program.

Various other commands and configuration possibilities are available to make Archie more useful and more convenient to use.

Architecture

Architecture is an amorphous term in the area of networking. The term can refer to both the physical layout (topology) of the network and also the protocols (communication rules and data elements) used to communicate.

Architecture can also refer to the basic structure of a networking service, such as a print service architecture. Used this way, it generally indicates the overall scheme of APIs (Application Program Interfaces), agents, and so on, used to fit different pieces of the service together.

You will hear references to network architectures, such as ARCnet, Ethernet, and Token Ring, which are all defined primarily at the two lowest layers of the OSI model: the physical and Data-Link layers. Each architecture includes an implicit topology.

In the context of hardware, the term refers to the manner in which a computer is constructed. The architecture includes the type of processor (for example, Intel 80x86 or Pentium, Motorola 680xx, or RISC chip) and the type of bus that is used to transmit data and other signals to the computer's components and peripherals.

In the IBM PC world, which is currently dominated by Intel processors, the three major buses are ISA (Industry Standard Architecture), EISA (Extended Industry Standard Architecture), and MCA (Microchannel Architecture). However, two newer bus designs—VL (VESA Local) and PCI (Peripheral Component Interconnect)—are growing in popularity and are likely to become the dominant bus architectures.

→ **See Also** Network Architecture

Archive

As a noun, a repository for data, applications, and so forth. These materials may be master copies or regular backups of the current hard disk contents. As a verb, the act of backing up data files to provide a safe copy in case of a disaster.

Archive Site

On the Internet, a node that provides access to a collection of files.

ARCnet (Attached Resource Computer Network)

ARCnet is a baseband network architecture originally developed as a proprietary network by Datapoint Corporation in the late 1970s. ARCnet became very popular when Standard Microsystems Corporation (SMC) developed a chip set for PCs. The

A

architecture has been used for years and has become a de facto standard. However, it has not become as popular as other network architectures, such as Ethernet. ARCnet is popular for smaller networks because it is relatively simple to set up and operate, its components are inexpensive (street prices for ARCnet boards are among the lowest), and the architecture is widely supported.

ARCnet has a transmission rate of 2.5Mbps. ARCnet Plus is a newer, 20Mbps version. A third-party, 100Mbps architecture based on ARCnet is also available from Thomas-Conrad. Although ARCnet Plus was developed by Datapoint Corporation alone, current and future development of ARCnet standards is under the aegis of the ATA (ARCnet Trade Association), a consortium of vendors that market ARCnet products.

ARCnet uses token passing to control access to the network. Each node in an ARCnet network has a unique address (between 1 and 255), and the token is passed sequentially from one address to the next. Nodes with successive addresses are not necessarily next to each other in the physical layout.

Officially, ARCnet uses a bus topology, but in practice ARCnet networks can use a star or a bus wiring scheme. These two types of networks use slightly different components, and they are sometimes referred to as low-impedance and high-impedance ARCnet, respectively.

"Context and properties of ARCnet" summarizes the characteristics of this architecture.

ARCnet Network Components

The hardware components needed in an ARCnet network include an ARCnet network interface card, cable, connectors, hubs, active links, and baluns.

ARCnet Network Interface Card (NIC)

ARCnet NICs include chips to handle the ARCnet protocols and packet formats, as well as a transceiver (usually with a BNC connector) on the card. Most ARCnet NICs have a low-impedance transceiver, which is best suited for a star or tree topology. (A tree topology has features of both star and bus topologies.)

Cards with high-impedance transceivers are suitable for a bus topology.

ARCnet cards do not come with hardware addresses in a ROM chip. Instead, they have jumpers that can be set to specify an address for the node in which the card is installed. The network administrator needs to set this address (which must be between 1 and 255) for each card in the network. Each node must have a unique address. The network administrator also needs to set the IRQ (interrupt) and I/O (input/output) addresses on the card. The hardware address is network-dependent; the IRQ and I/O addresses are machine-dependent.

Context

```
Network Architecture
   Shared-Media
      ARCnet ─────────┐
      Ethernet        │
      Token Ring      │
   Switched Media     │
                      ▼
```

ARCnet	
Description	Shared-media, baseband network
Topology	Bus (high-impedance ARCnet) Star (low-impedance ARCnet)
Access method	Token passing
Speed	Up to 2.5 Mbps
Cable	RG-62 coaxial (93-ohm) Unshielded twisted-pair Fiber-optic
Frame size	Up to 508 data bytes
Variants	High-impedance ARCnet Low-impedance ARCnet Mixed-impedance ARCnet ARCnet Plus

CONTEXT AND PROPERTIES OF ARCNET

Cable

ARCnet cable can be coaxial, twisted-pair, or even fiber-optic. Coaxial ARCnet networks generally have RG-62 cable, which has a 93-ohm impedance. Other types of coaxial cable, such as RG-59U or RG-11U, are also used.

An ARCnet network might include unshielded twisted-pair (UTP) or IBM's special-design cables (Types 1 and 3), but only if the NIC has the appropriate connectors or if an appropriate adapter is available. If UTP cabling is used, nodes are arranged in a daisy chain, and one end of the chain is connected to a hub or to an adapter that connects to coaxial cable. Similar converters can convert from coaxial to fiber-optic cable.

The last node in an ARCnet network must be terminated with a resistor of appropriate strength: 93 ohm for coaxial networks, and 105 ohm for networks using twisted-pair wiring.

Connectors, Active Links, and Baluns

For coaxial cable, BNC connectors are used. For twisted-pair cable, the connectors are either the modular RJ-11/RJ-45 telephone type, or the D-shell type used for standard serial and parallel ports.

Active links are boxes used to connect two cable segments when both cable segments have high-impedance NICs connected.

Baluns are used to connect coaxial and twisted-pair cabling.

Hubs

Hubs serve as wiring concentrators. Three types of hubs can be used:

Active hubs These types of hubs have their own power supply. They can clean and boost a signal and then relay it along the network. An active hub serves as both a repeater and a wiring center. Active hubs usually have 8 ports, but they can have as many as 64. The type of hub used must be appropriate for the type of cable being used. Active hubs can extend the maximum distance between nodes.

Passive hubs Passive hubs simply relay signals, without cleaning or boosting them. These types of hubs collect wiring from nodes, and they must be connected to an active hub. Passive hubs have four ports, and are used only in low-impedance networks. Passive hubs cannot be used to extend the distance between nodes.

Intelligent hubs Intelligent hubs are active hubs that use a low-frequency signal band to monitor the status of a link. These hubs can have up to 16 ports.

ARCnet Operation

ARCnet data transmissions are broadcast to all nodes on the network (a feature characteristic of both bus and star topologies), but the transmitted packets are (presumably) read only by the node(s) to which the destination address applies. Note that even though all nodes can listen at the same time, only one node can transmit.

Structure of an ARCnet Packet

ARCnet has several different types of frames, or packets, which are listed on the table "ARCnet Packets." The illustration "ARCnet frame structure" shows the makeup of ARCnet frames.

ARCNET PACKETS

Packet Type	Function
ITT (Invitation to Transmit)	The token, which determines the node that is allowed to transmit
FBE (Free Buffer Enquiry)	The frame that is used to ask whether the destination node is able to receive packets
ACK (Acknowledge)	The packet used to indicate that a packet was received as transmitted
NAK (Negative Acknowledge)	The packet used to indicate that a packet was not received correctly and should be retransmitted
PAC	The actual ARCnet data frame

The data, control, or check bytes that make up the frame are known as ISUs (information symbol units). ISUs are defined differently in ARCnet and in ARCnet Plus.

All ARCnet frames begin with a six-bit alert signal, and all bytes begin with the bit sequence 110, so that each byte actually requires 11 bits in an ARCnet transmission.

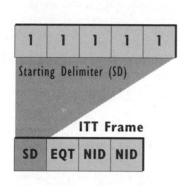

ITT Frame

FBE Frame

ACK Frame

NAK Frame

PAC Frame

SD	SOH	SID	DID	DID	CP	SC	DATA	FSC

(1 or 2, 1 or 2, 0-508, 2)

Frame components are symbols containing the following:

SD Starting delimiter, a special bit pattern of six consecutive 1bits, to indicate the start of the frame

EQT ASCII 0x04, which indicates the frame type

NID The address of the next node to get the token

ENQ ASCII 0x85, which identifies the frame type

DID The address of the destination node for the enquiry

ACK ASCII 0x86, indicating that the packet was recieved correctly

NAK ASCII 0x15, indicating that the packet was not recieved correctly

SOH ASCII 0x01, indicating the start of the header

SID The address of the source node sending the frame

CP A continuation pointer value, indicating the number of data bytes

SC System code

DATA Up to 508 symbols containing system code and data

FCS Frame check sequence, verifying the integrity of the frame

ARCNET FRAME STRUCTURE

ARCnet data frames consist of data, header, and trailer. Originally, an ARCnet frame could have up to 252 bytes of data. Almost all ARCnet implementations now support an expanded frame of up to 508 bytes of data (plus a dozen or so header bytes).

An ARCnet header for a PAC frame includes the following:

- A start of header byte

- Source and destination addresses, with values between 1 and 255 (a destination address of 0 indicates that the frame is being broadcast to all nodes)

- One or two bytes indicating the number of data bytes

The trailer is a 16-bit CRC (cyclic redundancy check) value.

Data Frame Transmission

The transmission of data frames in an ARCnet network is controlled by a token, which is a special data frame. This token, in turn, is dispensed by the network's controller, which is the node with the lowest address. The controller is determined when the network is first activated. Each node broadcasts its address, and the node with the lowest address becomes the controller. This reconfiguration process, which takes less than a tenth of a second, is repeated each time a new node joins the network.

The controller passes the token sequentially from one address to the next. The node with the token is the only node allowed to transmit, with some exceptions.

Frame transmission is a complicated process in ARCnet. A node (the source) waiting to send a message to another node (the destination) needs to do several things, in the following order:

1. The source waits for the token (ITT).

2. Once it has the token, the source sends an FBE packet to the destination to make sure the destination has room for the frame.

3. The source waits for a positive reply.

4. Once the source gets a positive response (ACK) to the FBE packet, the source broadcasts the frame.

5. The source waits for an acknowledgment from the intended destination. The destination node must acknowledge receipt of the frame. Since acknowledgement is required, ARCnet can guarantee frame delivery.

6. Once the frame has been received at the destination, the controller passes the token to the next address.

Disrupting Data Transmission

Unless something is wrong on the network, every node gets the token at least once every 840 milliseconds. If a node has not seen the token within that time, that node can disrupt the network and force the creation of a new token by sending a reconfiguration burst—a predefined bit pattern sent hundreds of times in succession—to destroy the existing token. After a period, the token is regenerated, the network nodes reannounce themselves, and the network begins transmitting again.

New nodes on an ARCnet network also send a reconfiguration burst. This pattern announces their presence on the network, and possibly establishes a new node as controller.

Communicating with Higher Layers

ARCnet's small frame size causes compatibility problems with some network-layer protocols, such as Novell's IPX protocol. IPX passes 576-byte packets (known as *datagrams*) to the architecture operating at the Data-Link layer. This packet size is too large, even for an extended ARCnet frame.

To enable IPX to talk to ARCnet, the fragmentation layer was developed. At this layer, the source node breaks an IPX packet into two smaller frames for ARCnet. At the destination's fragmentation layer, the datagram is reassembled before being passed to IPX.

High-Impedance ARCnet

High-impedance ARCnet networks use a bus topology, as illustrated in the illustration "Layout for a high-impedance ARCnet network." The high-impedance NICs make it possible to daisy chain nodes and active hubs. The active hubs serve as collectors for other hubs and nodes.

The following restrictions apply to high-impedance ARCnet networks:

- No single cable segment connecting nodes can be more than 305 meters (1000 feet) long.

- Only *active* (or intelligent) hubs may be used.

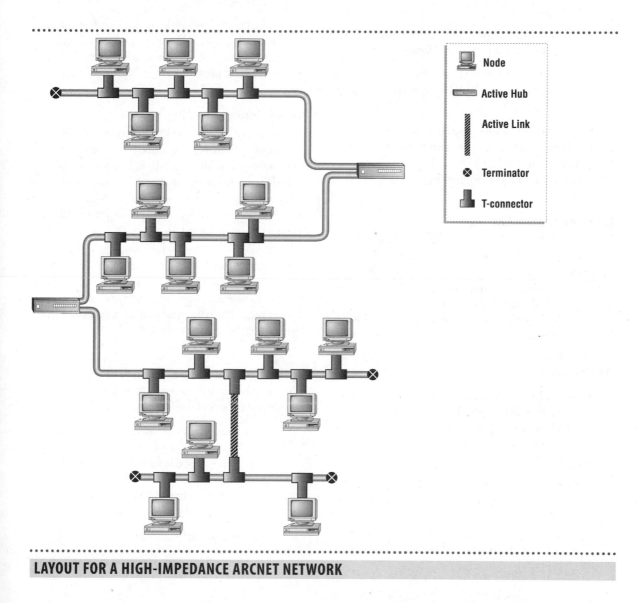

LAYOUT FOR A HIGH-IMPEDANCE ARCNET NETWORK

- Adjacent active hubs (hubs with no intervening nodes) must be within 610 meters (2000 feet).

- Nodes are connected to the trunk cable using BNC T-connectors. The node's NIC must be connected directly to the T-connector; that is, drop cable is not allowed.

- T-connectors must be at least 1 meter (3.25 feet) apart on the cable.

- At most, eight nodes can be connected in a series (with no intervening hubs).

- Both ends of a cable segment must be terminated with either a BNC terminator or an active hub (or link).

- The cabling cannot loop back on itself. For example, the cable cannot go from an active hub through other hubs and eventually connect back into the original hub.

Low-Impedance ARCnet

Low-impedance ARCnet networks use a star topology, in which passive hubs serve to collect nodes, as illustrated in "Layout for a low-impedance ARCnet network." Each passive hub is connected to an active hub. Active hubs can be linked with each other, and they can also be linked directly with nodes. In the latter case, the active hub also acts as a wiring center.

The following restrictions apply to low-impedance ARCnet networks:

- Active hubs can be connected to nodes, active hubs, or passive hubs. The active hub must be within 610 meters (2000 feet) of an active hub or a node, or within 30 meters (100 feet) of a passive hub.

- Passive hubs can be used only between a node and an active hub; two passive hubs cannot be next to each other. A passive hub must be within 30 meters (100 feet) of an active hub and within 30 meters (100 feet) of a node.

- Nodes can be attached anywhere on the network, provided the node is within the required distance of an active or passive hub: within 610 meters (2000 feet) of an active hub or within 30 meters (100 feet) of a passive hub.

- Unused hub ports must be terminated on a passive hub and should be terminated on an active hub.

- The cabling cannot loop back on itself. For example, the cable cannot go from an active hub through other hubs and eventually connect back into the original hub.

Mixed-Impedance ARCnet

A mixed ARCnet network is one that includes both high- and low-impedance components in the same network, as illustrated in "Layout of a mixed-impedance ARCnet network, with low-impedance and high-impedance components." In this type of network, all the restrictions for both impedance levels must be observed.

Perhaps the most important constraint for a mixed-impedance ARCnet is that high-impedance NICs can be used in place of low-impedance cards, but the reverse is not possible. Because of this restriction, it is crucial that you keep track of what kind of NIC is in each node.

Restrictions on ARCnet Networks

The following restrictions apply to both high- and low-impedance ARCnet networks:

- The maximum length of a cable segment depends on the type of cable. The general restriction is that the signal attenuation must be less than 11 dB over the entire cable segment at a frequency of 5MHz. In practice, this leads to the following maximum distances:

- Coaxial cable: 450–600 meters (1500–2000 feet)

- UTP and IBM Type 3 (unshielded) cable: 100 meters (330 feet)

A

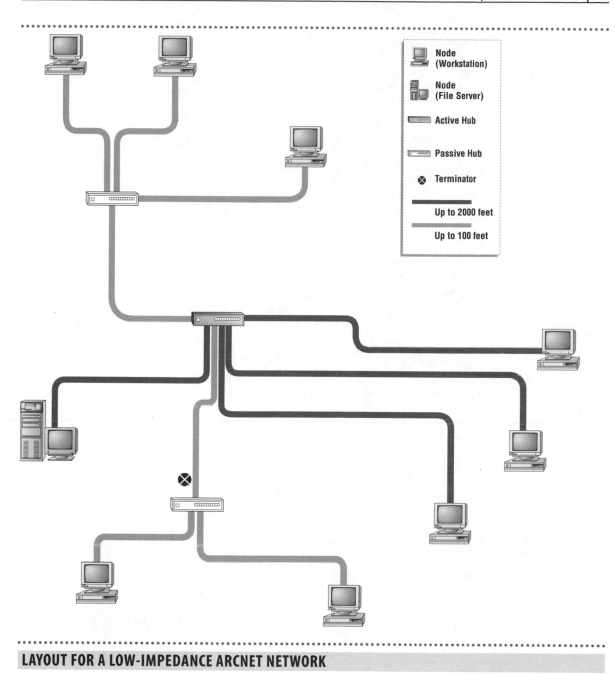

Node
(Workstation)

Node
(File Server)

Active Hub

Passive Hub

Terminator

Up to 2000 feet

Up to 100 feet

LAYOUT FOR A LOW-IMPEDANCE ARCNET NETWORK

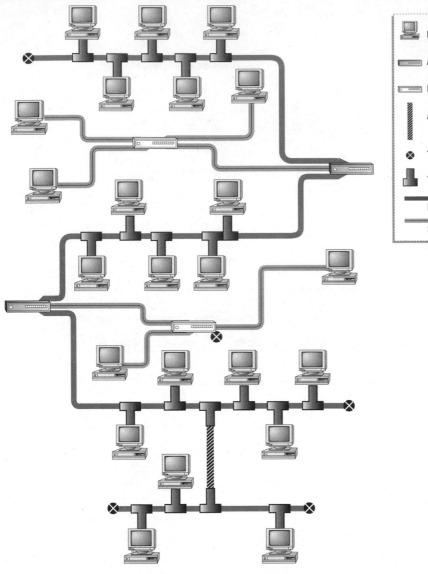

Legend:
- Node
- Active Hub
- Passive Hub
- Active Link
- Terminator
- T-connector
- Bus Cable
- Star Cable

LAYOUT OF A MIXED-IMPEDANCE ARCNET NETWORK, WITH LOW-IMPEDANCE AND HIGH-IMPEDANCE COMPONENTS

- IBM Type 1 (shielded) cable: 200 meters (660 feet)

- The maximum cable length for the entire network is 6000 meters (20,000 feet).

- The maximum number of cable segments in a series is three. If UTP cable is used, the series of segments can be at most about 130 meters (430 feet); for coaxial cable, the maximum length is about 300 meters (990 feet).

- Each cable segment must be terminated at both ends by being connected to an active hub or terminator.

- An ARCnet network can have a maximum of 255 nodes. Each active hub counts as a node.

- At most, 10 nodes are allowed in a series when UTP cable is used; 8 nodes if coaxial cable is used.

- The maximum distance between any two nodes on the network is determined by the constraint that no ARCnet signal can have a propagation delay of more than 31 microseconds. The total propagation delay is determined by adding the propagation delays in all the devices (nodes, hubs, and cable) connecting the nodes. Network components generally have propagation delays of less than 0.5 microseconds, and much less in some cases.

ARCnet Advantages

ARCnet has the following advantages:

- Components are relatively inexpensive. Street prices for basic ARCnet NICs usually are less than those for Ethernet or Token Ring NICs.

- Because the ARCnet architecture and the chip set have been around a long time, the hardware has become stable, so that there are few compatibility or reliability problems with ARCnet components.

- Wiring is very flexible, allowing lots of leeway in placing nodes.

- It is relatively easy to use different types of cabling in an ARCnet network (but adapters must be used to avoid connection incompatibilities).

- A star layout makes diagnostics easy in low-impedance networks.

- Except for the extra cabling a star topology requires, installation is relatively inexpensive.

ARCnet Disadvantages

ARCnet has the following disadvantages:

- Its data transmission is inefficient. ARCnet sends three overhead bits for every byte. Also, administrative exchanges (such as ACK or NAK packets) between source and destination are done on the data bandwidth, which degrades performance further.

- Actual throughput is much less than the maximum 2.5Mbps. Even for small networks, the throughput is less than 65 percent of maximum, and this value decreases as more nodes are added to the network.

- The network administrator must manually set a unique address by adjusting switches on every NIC in the network. If two nodes have the same address, the administrator will need to track down the conflicting boards by tedious examination of each NIC.

- Because of throughput and addressing restrictions, ARCnet is not particularly well-suited for internetworking.

ARCnet Plus

Datapoint's ARCnet Plus is a 20Mbps version of the ARCnet standard. ARCnet Plus has the following features:

- Backward-compatibility with ARCnet

- Ability to communicate with both ARCnet and ARCnet Plus nodes

- Support for transmission rates of up to 20Mbps
- Support for data frames up to 4224 bytes long
- Use of the same RG-62 cable as ordinary ARCnet
- New frames, with enhanced frame formats and command sets
- Support for up to 1MB of buffer space

ARCnet Plus achieves its greater speed by cutting the time interval for a symbol in half and by using phase and amplitude shifting to encode four bits in every signal; that is, the basic symbol in ARCnet Plus is actually a nibble.

Like its predecessor, ARCnet Plus regulates much network activity by timing. The allowable intervals are much smaller with ARCnet Plus, however. For example, a bit interval is half as long in ARCnet Plus as in regular ARCnet.

Another extension of this type of architecture is TCNS, offered by Thomas-Conrad, which is a 100Mbps, copper-based network.

→ **Broader Category** Network Architecture

→ **See Also** TCNS (Thomas-Conrad Network System)

TIPS ON ARCNET ADDRESSES

Keep accurate addresses. Make sure you have up-to-date records of the address set for each ARCnet node's NIC. When you need to find duplicate addresses or add nodes, you'll be glad you did.

If you're the administrator, never let anyone else change the node addresses, because you may have to deal with the problems caused by their sloppiness.

Assigning the low address is particularly important. The network controller will be the node with the lowest address, so make sure this machine is fast enough to handle the controlling role. In general, it's best to assign the lowest addresses to servers, bridges, and routers.

ARCnet Trade Association (ATA)

→ **See** ATA (ARCnet Trade Association)

ARDIS

ARDIS is a wireless wide area network that uses packet radio technology. It is billed as a wide area packet data network that provides service in over 425 metropolitan areas and over 10,000 cities and towns.

Designed primarily for transmitting small files (less than 10KB or so), ARDIS breaks transmissions up into 240-byte packets. These are sent using either of two protocols:

- MDC4800, which operates at 4800bps
- RDLAP (Radio Data Link Access Protocol), which operates at 19.2Kbps

ARDIS networks are designed to provide good in-building service—that is, to allow connections even from within buildings. (Some radio-based networks perform poorly indoors, so this feature makes ARDIS particularly attractive.)

ARF (Alarm Reporting Function)

In the OSI network management model, a service that reports failures, faults, or problems that might become faults.

ARM (Asynchronous Response Mode)

In the ISO's HLDC (High-Level Data Link Control) protocol, ARM is a communications mode in which a secondary (slave) node can initiate communications with a primary (master) node without first getting permission from the primary node.

ARM's operation is in contrast to NRM (normal response mode), in which the primary node must initiate any communication, and to ABM (asynchronous balanced mode), in which the two nodes are equal.

→ **Broader Category** HDLC (High-Level Data Link Control)

ARP (Address Resolution Protocol)

→ **See** Protocol, ARP (Address Resolution Protocol)

ARPA (Advanced Research Projects Agency)

The agency that was largely responsible for what eventually became the Internet. Now called DARPA (for Defense ARPA).

ARPAnet (Advanced Research Projects Agency Network)

ARPAnet was the first large-scale, packet-switched, wide area network (WAN). It was originally developed in the early 1970s under the auspices of the U.S. Department of Defense's Defense Advanced Research Projects Agency (DARPA).

Many of the most commonly used networking protocols, including TCP/IP, were developed as part of the ARPAnet project. The ARPAnet was decommissioned in 1991, but parts of the network have become part of the Internet.

ARQ (Automatic Repeat Request)

In communications, a control code that indicates an error in transmission and that requests a retransmission.

ARS (Automatic Route Selection)

In telephony, a process by which a path is selected for a transmission; also called alternate route selection.

AS (Autonomous System)

Essentially, an autonomous system refers to a network that is locally maintained, but that is also connected to a larger internetwork. More specifically, in the Internet world, AS (autonomous system) is a term for a collection of routers that are part of a larger network but that are under the control of a single organization. The routers, or *gateways* as they are called in the older Internet terminology, communicate with each other using a common protocol, known as an interior gateway protocol (IGP). Currently, the two most widely supported IGPs in the Internet community are the OSPF (Open Shortest Path First) and the Integrated IS-IS protocols.

ASs communicate using an exterior gateway protocol (EGP), such as EGP (Exterior Gateway Protocol) and BGP (Border Gateway Protocol).

In the OSI reference model, an autonomous system is known as a *routing domain*, IGPs are known as *intradomain routing protocols*, and EGPs are known as *interdomain routing protocols*.

AS/400

A minicomputer line from IBM. The AS/400 was introduced in 1988 to replace the System/36 and System/38 series.

ASCII (American Standard Code for Information Interchange)

ASCII is the character-encoding system used most commonly in local area networks (LANs). The standard ASCII characters are encoded in seven bits and have values between 0 and 127. The remaining

128 characters form the extended ASCII character set, whose elements may be defined differently depending on the language being used. See the tables "Standard ASCII Character Set" and "Extended ASCII Character Set (IBM PC)."

In common usage, ASCII is used to refer to a text-only file that does not include special formatting codes.

→ *Broader Category* Encoding

→ *Compare* EBCDIC

STANDARD ASCII CHARACTER SET

Decimal	Character	Decimal	Character
0	NUL (null)	30	RS (record separator)
1	SOH (start of heading)	31	US (unit separator)
2	STX (start of text)	32	space
3	ETX (end of text)	33	!
4	EOT (end of transmission)	34	"
5	ENQ (enquire)	35	#
6	ACK (acknowledge)	36	$
7	BEL (bell)	37	%
8	BS (backspace)	38	&
9	HT (horizontal tab)	39	'
10	LF (line feed)	40	(
11	VT (vertical tab)	41	)
12	FF (form feed)	42	*
13	CR (carriage return)	43	+
14	SO (shift out)	44	,
15	SI (shift in)	45	-
16	DLE (data link escape)	46	.
17	DC1 (device control 1)	47	/
18	DC2 (device control 2)	48	0
19	DC3 (device control 3)	49	1
20	DC4 (device control 4)	50	2
21	NAK (negative acknowledge)	51	3
22	SYN (synchronous idle)	52	4
23	ETB (end transmission block)	53	5
24	CAN (cancel)	54	6
25	EM (end of medium)	55	7
26	SUB (substitute)	56	8
27	ESC (escape)	57	9
28	FS (file separator)	58	:
29	GS (group separator)	59	;

STANDARD ASCII CHARACTER SET (continued)

Decimal	Character	Decimal	Character
60	<	94	^
61	=	95	_
62	>	96	`
63	?	97	a
64	@	98	b
65	A	99	c
66	B	100	d
67	C	101	e
68	D	102	f
69	E	103	g
70	F	104	h
71	G	105	i
72	H	106	j
73	I	107	k
74	J	108	l
75	K	109	m
76	L	110	n
77	M	111	o
78	N	112	p
79	O	113	q
80	P	114	r
81	Q	115	s
82	R	116	t
83	S	117	u
84	T	118	v
85	U	119	w
86	V	120	x
87	W	121	y
88	X	122	z
89	Y	123	{
90	Z	124	|
91	[	125	}
92	\	126	~
93	]	127	DEL

A

EXTENDED ASCII CHARACTER SET

Decimal	Character	Decimal	Character
001	☺	136	ê
002	☻	137	ë
003	♥	138	è
004	♦	139	ï
005	♠	140	î
006	♣	141	ì
007	•	142	Ä
008	◘	143	Å
009	○	144	É
010	◙	145	æ
011	♂	146	Æ
012	♀	147	ô
013	♪	148	ö
014	♫	149	ò
015	☼	150	û
016	►	151	ù
017	◄	152	ÿ
018	↕	153	Ö
019	‼	154	Ü
020	¶	155	¢
021	§	156	£
022	▬	157	¥
023	↨	158	₧
024	↑	159	ƒ
025	↓	160	á
026	→	161	í
027	←	162	ó
028	∟	163	ú
029	↔	164	ñ
030	▲	165	Ñ
031	▼	166	ª
032–127	Same as standard ASCII character set	167	º
128	Ç	168	¿
129	ü	169	⌐
130	é	170	¬
131	â	171	½
132	ä	172	¼
133	à	173	¡
134	å	174	«
135	ç	175	»

EXTENDED ASCII CHARACTER SET (continued)

Decimal	Character	Decimal	Character
176	░	216	╪
177	▒	217	┘
178	▓	218	┌
179	│	219	█
180	┤	220	▄
181	╡	221	▌
182	╢	222	▐
183	╖	223	▀
184	╕	224	α
185	╣	225	β
186	║	226	Γ
187	╗	227	π
188	╝	228	Σ
189	╜	229	σ
190	╛	230	μ
191	┐	231	τ
192	└	232	Φ
193	┴	233	Θ
194	┬	234	Ω
195	├	235	δ
196	─	236	∞
197	┼	237	φ
198	╞	238	ε
199	╟	239	∩
200	╚	240	≡
201	╔	241	±
202	╩	242	≥
203	╦	243	≤
204	╠	244	⌠
205	═	245	⌡
206	╬	246	÷
207	╧	247	≈
208	╨	248	°
209	╤	249	∙
210	╥	250	·
211	╙	251	√
212	╘	252	ⁿ
213	╒	253	²
214	╓	254	■
215	╫	255	

A

ASCIIbetical Sorting

A sorting strategy that uses the ASCII character set as the basis for the ordering. In ASCII, numbers and special symbols precede letters, and uppercase letters precede lowercase ones.

ASE (Application Service Element)

In the OSI reference model, an ASE (application service element) is any of several elements that provide the communications and other services at the application layer. An application process (AP) or application entity (AE) requests these services through predefined interfaces, such as those provided by APIs (Application Program Interfaces).

ASEs are grouped into common application service elements (CASEs) and specific application service elements (SASEs). The CASEs provide services for many types of applications; the SASEs represent or provide services for specific applications or genres.

CASE

The following CASEs are commonly used:

ACSE (Association Control Service Element) This element establishes the appropriate relationship between two applications (AEs) to enable the applications to cooperate and communicate on a task. Since all associations or relationships must be established through the ACSE, and since applications must establish a relationship to communicate, the ACSE is needed by all applications.

CCRSE (Commitment, Concurrency, and Recovery Service Element) This element is used to implement distributed transactions, which may require multiple applications. The CCRSE helps ensure that distributed data remains consistent by making sure that applications do not interfere with each other when doing their work and that actions are performed completely or not at all.

ROSE (Remote Operations Service Element) This element supports interactive cooperation between two applications, such as between a client and a server. ROSE provides the services needed for the reliable execution of requested operations and transfer of data.

RTSE (Reliable Transfer Service Element) This element helps ensure that PDUs (protocol data units), or packets, are transferred reliably between applications. RTSE services can sometimes survive an equipment failure, because they use transport-layer services.

SASE

The following SASEs are commonly used:

DS (Directory Service) This element makes it possible to use a global directory, which is a distributed database with information about all accessible network entities in a communications system.

FTAM: (File Transfer Access and Management) This element enables an application to read, write, or otherwise manage files on a remote machine.

JTM (Job Transfer and Manipulation) This element enables an application to do batch data processing on a remote machine. With JTM, a node could, for example, start a computation on a supercomputer at a remote location and retrieve the results when the computation was done.

MHS (Message Handling System) This element enables applications to exchange messages; for example, when using electronic mail.

MMS (Manufacturing Message Service) This element enables an application on a control computer to communicate with an application on a slave machine in a production line or other automated operation.

VT (Virtual Terminal) This element makes it possible to emulate the behavior of a particular terminal, which enables an application to communicate with a remote system without considering the type of hardware sending or receiving the communications.

The entire set of ASEs required for a particular application is known as the application context (AC) for that application.

→ **Broader Category** AC (Application Context)

ASI (Adapter Support Interface)

ASI (Adapter Support Interface) is a standard interface developed by IBM for enabling Token Ring adapters to talk to any of several higher-level protocols. The most recent version of ASI is marketed as LAN Support Program.

Like other adapter interfaces, such as NDIS (Network Driver Interface Specification) by Microsoft and ODI (Open Data-Link Interface) by Novell, ASI includes at least the following two components:

- A data-link-layer driver to talk to the network interface card (NIC)

- A network-layer driver to talk to the network-level protocols

Asia and Oceania Workshop (AOW)

→ **See** AOW (Asia and Oceania Workshop)

ASIC (Application-Specific Integrated Circuit)

Special-purpose chips, with logic designed specifically for a particular application or device. ASICs are also known as *gate arrays*, and they are constructed from standard circuit cells from a library.

ASN.1 (Abstract Syntax Notation One)

In the OSI reference model, ASN.1 (Abstract Syntax Notation One) is a notation used to describe data structures, such as managed objects in a network management system.

ASN.1 is machine-independent and is used in many networking contexts. For example, it is used to describe application-layer packets in both the OSI network management framework and in the Simple Network Management Protocol (SNMP) from the Internet TCP/IP protocol suite.

ASN.1 serves as a common syntax for transferring information between two end systems (ESs) that may use different encoding systems at each end.

→ **Primary Sources** CCITT recommendations X.208 and X.209; ISO documents 8824 and 8825

→ **Broader Category** Abstract Syntax

→ **See Also** BER (Basic Encoding Rules)

ASPs (Active Server Pages)

ASPs are an extension to Microsoft Internet Information Server (IIS) 3 and later. This extension makes it possible to create HTML (Hypertext Markup Language) documents dynamically—based on user input or other information and relying on ActiveX controls. The documents are generated by running back-end (that is, server-side) scripts created using VBScript or JScript. By using such scripts it is possible, for example, to ensure that delivered Web pages are always up-to-date. ASPs also make it possible to interface with legacy system data (such as product catalogs) over the Web or over an extranet.

For example, a potential customer might want information on pricing for certain products available from a vendor. Using static HTML pages, the customer might get back information from the most recent version of the company's standard catalog. This information probably would not, for example, indicate whether a product is in stock. In contrast, when making the same query to a server that uses ASPs, the customer might get back a list of only the items that are currently in stock. Controls or scripts could be used to search inventory information as well as the product catalog in order to return such a customized response.

ASPs are compatible with other Web programming languages, such as Perl, Python, and REXX.

→ *See Also*   Microsoft IIS (Internet Information Server)

ASP (AppleTalk Session Protocol)

→ *See*   Protocol, ASP (AppleTalk Session Protocol)

Asserted Circuit

A circuit that is closed; that is, a circuit with a voltage value. Depending on the logic being used, an asserted circuit can represent a 1 (usually) or 0 (rarely).

Assigned Number

In the Internet community, a numerical value that serves to distinguish a particular protocol, application, or organization in some context. For example, assigned numbers distinguish the different flavors of Ethernet protocols used by different implementers. Assigned numbers, which are not addresses, are assigned by the Internet Assigned Numbers Authority (IANA).

Association Control Service Element (ACSE)

→ *See*   ACSE (Association Control Service Element)

ASVD (Analog Simultaneous Voice/Data)

A proposed modem standard that can be used to transmit multimedia materials—voice, video, etc.—over ordinary (analog) telephone lines. The ASVD specifications are being finalized by the ITU (International Telecommunication Union, formerly known as the CCITT).

ASVD is offered as an inexpensive (and slower) alternative to ISDN (Integrated Services Digital Network). The bandwidth for ASVD is considerably more limited than for ISDN. The version under consideration supports modem speeds of up to 14.4Kbps, but somewhat slower speeds for multimedia data.

Asymmetrical Multiprocessing

Asymmetrical multiprocessing characterizes (multiple processor) architectures in which processors are not treated equally. For example, certain processors may be used to different extents or for specific execution threads. Such an asymmetrical architecture is easier and less expensive to implement than a symmetrical multiprocessing architecture, but makes it harder to scale the architecture up simply by adding processors.

→ *Broader Category*   Multiprocessing

→ *Compare*   Symmetrical multiprocessing

Asymmetric Digital Subscriber Line (ADSL)

→ *See*   ADSL (Asymmetric Digital Subscriber Line)

Asymmetric Digital Subscriber Line Terminal Unit (ATU)

→ *See*   ATU (ADSL Terminal Unit)

Asynchronous

Asynchronous describes a communications strategy that uses start and stop bits to indicate the beginning and end of a character, rather than using constant timing to transmit a series of characters. In a sense, asynchronous transmissions actually synchronize for each character. "A data word sent by asynchronous transmission" shows the bits used in this communications method.

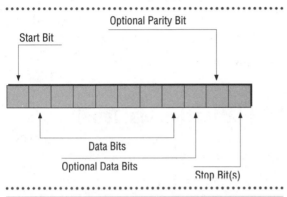

Start Bit

Optional Parity Bit

Data Bits

Optional Data Bits

Stop Bit(s)

A DATA WORD SENT BY ASYNCHRONOUS TRANSMISSION

Asynchronous communications methods are generally less efficient but more resistant to disruption than synchronous communications. Asynchronous methods are more efficient for situations in which traffic comes in bursts (rather than moving at a regular pace). Common examples of asynchronous communications devices are modems and terminals.

Asynchronous Balanced Mode (ABM)

→ *See* ABM (Asynchronous Balanced Mode)

Asynchronous Communications Server (ACS)

→ *See* ACS (Asynchronous Communications Server)

Asynchronous Modem Eliminator (AME)

→ *See* AME (Asynchronous Modem Eliminator)

Asynchronous Response Mode (ARM)

→ *See* ARM (Asynchronous Response Mode)

Asynchronous Time Division Multiplexing (ATDM)

→ *See* ATDM (Asynchronous Time Division Multiplexing)

Asynchronous Transfer Mode (ATM)

→ *See* ATM (Asynchronous Transfer Mode)

AT (Access Token)

In Windows NT, an access token is associated with a process (for example, a program or a service request), and is used to determine whether the process is to be allowed to perform the desired operations on the resource or object for which access is requested. This is determined by checking the access token when the process makes its request. For such access to be granted, the process must have the appropriate permissions, the user for whom the process is running must also have permission to access the resource, and there must be nothing associated with the resource of interest that forbids such access.

When a process makes its request, NT's Security Reference Monitor (SRM) checks the access token for the process. The SRM does this by comparing the token with the resource's Discretionary Access Control List (DACL), which lists the services available to processes when they try to use the object or resource of interest.

→ *Broader Category* Windows NT

→ *See* Access Token (AT)

ATA (ARCnet Trade Association)

A consortium of vendors and other organizations that manages ARCnet specifications.

AT Command Set

The AT command set was developed by Hayes Microcomputer Products to operate its modems. The AT in the name is short for attention. This signal precedes most of the commands used to get a modem to do its work. For example, ATDP and ATDT (for attention dial pulse and attention dial tone, respectively) are used to dial a number on either a pulse or Touch Tone phone.

The AT command set quickly became a de facto standard. It is now used by most modem manufacturers, and is supported on virtually every modem on the market.

→ *See Also* Modem

ATCON

A Novell NetWare program that monitors the AppleTalk protocol stack in a multiprotocol network. It reports statistics about the performance of AppleTalk devices and services.

ATDM (Asynchronous Time Division Multiplexing)

ATDM is a multiplexing technique used in (usually) digital telecommunications. Multiple transmissions can be handled by slicing a carrier signal into small time slices and allocating these time slices to parts of different transmissions. In ordinary time division multiplexing (TDM), the slots are allocated to the transmissions in a predefined sequence. In contrast, in ATDM, the slots are allocated to specific transmissions as needed.

→ *See Also* TDM (Time Division Multiplexing)

ATDP (Attention Dial Pulse)

In the Hayes modem command set, a command to dial a number using a pulse (rotary) telephone.

→ *See Also* AT Command Set

ATDT (Attention Dial Tone)

In the Hayes modem command set, a command to dial a number using a Touch Tone phone.

→ *See Also* AT Command Set

ATM (Asynchronous Transfer Mode)

ATM (Asynchronous Transfer Mode) is a packet-switched (more specifically, cell-switched), broadband network architecture that is expected to become an established standard by the late 1990s. It forms the core of a broadband ISDN (BISDN) architecture, which extends the digital transmission capabilities defined by ISDN to allow data, voice, and multimedia transmissions on the same lines. It is also known as *cell relay*, to distinguish it from frame relay. (Arguably, ATM is also the technology with the largest number of acronyms and abbreviations associated with it. A disproportionate number of the entries in Appendix A come from the ATM world.)

ATM is a real-time architecture that can provide very high bandwidths as needed. Implementations currently operate at speeds ranging from special, slow-speed versions of 12.96Mbps or 25Mbps up to 622.08Mbps. Speeds as high as 2.488Gbps will eventually be supported.

The very high bandwidth and the ability to transmit multiple media make ATM an attractive, high-speed architecture for both local area networks (LANs) and wide area networks (WANs). It is useful for enterprise networks, which often connect LANs over wide areas and which may need to transport large amounts of data over very long distances.

Long-haul, high-bandwidth capabilities are particularly attractive for WANs, which have until now been shackled by the relatively low bandwidths over long-distance lines. FDDI (Fiber Distributed Data Interface) is a good architecture for LANs, and frame relay has possibilities for WANs, but neither of these architectures is suitable for both LANs and WANs. Note that ATM can still be rather expensive, although inexpensive versions have been designed.

"Context and properties of ATM" summarizes the characteristics of this architecture.

A

Context

Network Architecture
   Shared-Media
   Switched-Media
      Circuit
      Message
      Packet
         Fixed-Size
         ATM (Cell Relay) ────────┐
     Variable-Size
     Frame Relay

ATM

Properties	Structure		
	Layers	**Planes**	**Cells**
Broadband	Physical	Users	Constant Size (53 Octets)
Core of BISDN	(Two Sublayers)	Management	(48-Octet Payload)
Useful for LANs and WANs	ATM Layer	Control	(5-Octet Header)
Uses short- or long-haul fiber-optic	(Service Independent)		Not Byte-Bound/Oriented
cable	AAL		
Initial speeds up to 166.62 Mbps	(Two Sublayers)		
(eventural speeds up to 2.49	(Four Service Classes)		
Gbps)	A: for Voice, Data		
Can always operate at top speed	B: for Video, etc.		
(provided there is enough traffic)	C: for Connection-		
Can transmit voice, video, data	Oriented Mode		
(simultaneously, if necessary)	D: for Connectionless		
	Mode		

CONTEXT AND PROPERTIES OF ATM

ATM Features

ATM has the following features:

- Transmission over fiber-optic lines. These can be local or long-distance, public or private lines. Long-distance lines can be leased or dial-up. Slower-speed variants using copper wire (including unshielded twisted pair, or UTP, wiring) have been developed as entry-level products.

- Versions for different transmission rates can be implemented on a range of Physical layer interfaces, including CEPT4 (part of a European transmission standard with a speed hierarchy comparable to the North American Digital Signal, or DS, hierarchy), DS3 (Digital Signal 3), FDDI (Fiber Distributed Data Interface), and SONET/SDH (Synchronous Optical Network/Synchronous Digital Hierarchy).

- Capability for parallel transmissions, because ATM is a switching architecture. In fact, each node can have a dedicated connection to any other node.

- Operation at maximum speed at all times, provided there is enough network traffic to give the required throughput.

- Use of fixed-length (53-byte) packets, which are known as *cells*.

- Error correction and routing in hardware, partly because of the fixed cell sizes.

- Transmission of voice, video, and data at the same time. The fixed-length cells also make voice transmission more accurate, because there is less timing variation.

- Easier load balancing, because the switching capabilities make it possible to have multiple virtual circuits between sender and receiver.

- Support for quite a range of LAN emulation modes, which means that many local area network architectures can communicate over ATM without having to deal with the details of the ATM architecture and signaling. The

emulation makes the ATM segment disappear for the two ends of the communication.

- LAN emulation allows even legacy systems to communicate over ATM.

ATM Structure

The ATM architecture is organized into layers, as are other network architectures, and also into planes, which specify domains of activity. See "Structure of the ATM architecture" for a graphic representation of the organization of the planes and layers.

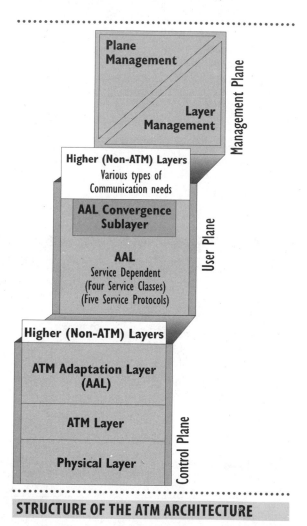

STRUCTURE OF THE ATM ARCHITECTURE

Physical Layer

The ATM Physical layer corresponds to the OSI reference model Physical layer. It is concerned with the physical medium and interfaces, and with the framing protocols (if any) for the network.

The Physical layer has two sublayers. The lower sublayer is the physical medium (PM), or physical-medium dependent (PMD) layer. It includes the definition for the medium (optical fiber, in most versions) and the bit-timing capabilities.

The upper sublayer, transmission convergence (TC), is responsible for making sure valid packets or frames are created and transmitted—for whatever physical interface (such as SONET, FDDI, and so forth) is being used. This involves breaking off individual cells from the data stream of the higher layer (the ATM layer), checking the cell's header, and encoding the bit values for the appropriate physical interface.

The user-network interface (UNI) is specified by the ATM forum, an organization dedicated to defining and implementing ATM. UNI allows for various types of physical interfaces for ATM networks, including the following:

- SONET connections at 155.52Mbps (OC-3, STS-3, or in CCITT terminology, STM-1)

- DS3 connections at 44.736Mbps

- 100Mbps connections using 4B/5B encoding

- 155Mbps connections using 8B/10B encoding

These interfaces all use optical fiber which, initially, was the only medium specified for ATM. A special, slower-speed (12.96Mbps and 25Mbps) version—known as ATM25—has been designed for use over category 3, unshielded twisted pair (UTP) copper wire.

ATM Layer

The ATM layer is a service-independent layer at which outgoing cell headers and trailers are created, virtual channels and paths are defined and given unique identifiers, and cells are multiplexed or demultiplexed. The ATM layer creates the cells and then uses the Physical layer to transmit them. Headers in received cells are verified at this layer. Headers and trailers are also removed from incoming cells. The ATM layer is also responsible for traffic and network management.

AAL (ATM Adaptation Layer)

The topmost layer, AAL is service-dependent. It provides the necessary protocol translation between ATM and the other communication services (such as voice, video, or data) involved in a transmission. For example, the AAL translates between elements from a pulse-code modulation (PCM) transmission (which encodes voice data in digital form) and ATM cells. ATM transmissions may be connection-oriented or connectionless. In a connection-oriented transmission, a path between the source and destination must be established before transmission begins. In a connectionless transmission, no predefined path is necessary. Rather, cells can be transmitted along different paths if necessary. By default, ATM sessions are connection oriented.

ATM transmission modes can be selected to guarantee a specified quality of service (QoS). The following service classes, which each use different AAL protocols, are defined at the AAL:

- Class A is suited for constant bit rate (CBR), connection-oriented transmission and provides circuit-switching emulation. This is appropriate for voice and other isochronous data. Because of the constant bit rate, end-to-end timing is important. The protocol is AAL 1.

- Class B is for real-time variable bit rate (VBR-RT, or VBRrt, also RT-VBR), connection-oriented data. For example, compressed data, such as packetized voice or video transmissions during teleconferences, may be sent using this service class. Although a variable bit rate is allowed, end-to-end timing is still important because of the kinds of data being sent. The protocol is AAL 2. Use of this service class is relatively rare, and is becoming rarer, because of the lower overhead needed for the AAL 5 protocol (see below).

- Class C is suited for non-real-time variable bit rate (VBR-NRT, or VBRnrt, also NRT-VBR) data transmissions—that is, for bursty data. Although ATM is a connection-oriented architecture, it can also operate in connectionless modes. X.25 WAN connections may use this class of service. Since data may come in bursts, end-to-end timing serves little purpose for this class of service. The protocol is either AAL 3/4 or AAL 5; the former provides error detection, but the latter does not. (AAL3 and AAL4 were originally distinct protocols, with the former being for connection-oriented and the latter for connectionless transmissions. The two protocols have been combined into the single AAL3/4.)

- Class D is suited for VBRnrt, connectionless data transmissions, and for available bit rate (ABR) transmissions. Neither end-to-end timing nor error detection is needed for this class of service. The protocol is either AAL 3/4 or AAL 5, with AAL 5 being the more likely candidate—among other reasons, because it has no error detection overhead (in contrast to AAL 3/4), and so allows for more efficient transmissions. In fact, because of its lack of overhead, the AAL5 protocol is also known as SEAL (for simple and efficient adaptation layer).

- Class X provides for user-defined quality of service specifications. Both the bit rate qualities (that is, CBR, VBR, and so forth) and the issue of end-to-end timing can be specified by the user. An unspecified bit rate (UBR) is often used for this user-defined service class. Class X transmissions are connection oriented.

The AAL 5 protocol supports service classes C and D more efficiently than does AAL 3/4.

AAL Sublayers

The AAL has two sublayers:

- CS (convergence sublayer) is the upper sublayer, which provides the interface for the various services. Users connect to the CS through service access points (SAPs). No protocol data units (PDUs) are defined for this level, because the data passing through is application- and service-dependent. The CS may deal with two types of functions, depending on the higher-level service being used. The common part convergence sublayer (CPCS) is used for all transmissions—to do such things as padding cells and adding headers and trailers before passing a cell to the SAR sublayer. For certain kinds of higher-layer services (such as switched multimegabit digital service, or SMDS, frame relay, or for signaling), a service-specific convergence sublayer (SSCS) is also used.

- SAR (segmentation and reassembly) is the sublayer that packages variable-size packets into fixed-size cells at the transmitting end, and repackages the cells at the receiving end. The SAR sublayer is also responsible for finding and dealing with cells that are out of order or lost.

A separate PDU is defined for each class of service. Each PDU contains 48 octets, which are allocated for the header, trailer, and data (with the latter known as *payload* in ATM terminology). Of these, the AAL 5 PDU can carry the most data at a time: a 48-octet payload. AAL 1 is next, with a 46- or 47-octet payload, then AAL2 with 45 octets, and finally AAL 3/4 with 44-octet payloads. These PDUs become the data (payload) for the ATM cells that are created and transmitted. (Actually, AAL 5 is not completely free of overhead. The last cell in an AAL5 transmission will have fewer octets.)

ATM Planes

Three domains of activity, known as planes, are distinguished for ATM:

- The control plane, on which calls and connections are established and maintained. This plane uses signaling AAL (SAAL) to move signaling or control packets between higher layers and the ATM layer. For such cells, the service-specific coordination function (SSCF) mediates between the higher-layer packets and the service-specific connection-oriented protocol (SSCOP). The SSCOP provides end-to-end error detection (and, possibly, also correction), cell resequencing and, sometimes, even cell recovery. The use of SAAL makes it possible to provide very reliable transmissions. At the top of the control plane, ATM uses the ITU (International Telecommunications Union) Q.2931 signaling protocol and the UNI 3.1 and 4 specifications to establish connections between applications and the ATM network.

- The user plane, on which users, or nodes, exchange data. This is the plane at which ordinary user services are provided. In other words, the user plane is where actual ATM transmissions take place. The other planes are concerned with monitoring or managing the ATM session.

- The management plane, on which network-management and layer-management services are provided. This plane coordinates the three planes, and manages resources for the layers. The management plane (or M-plane, as it is often called) manages both the other planes and the ATM layers. The plane management is layer independent and involves coordinating the actions and needs of the three ATM planes. For layer management, the management plane provides operation, administration, and maintenance (OAM) services. In addition to OAM services, several other protocols are used by or available to the management plane. These include: an ATM Local Management Interface (LMI) protocol, the Internet's Simple Network Management Protocol (SNMP), and the OSI-defined Common Management Information Protocol (CMIP).

ATM Operation

The illustration "ATM transmission elements" shows the elements used as a transmission gets onto an ATM network. The top part of the illustration represents the higher (non-ATM) service layers; the bottom part represents the ATM and Physical layers in the ATM model. The ATM node does the work of the AAL and much of the ATM layer.

Data from the various types of services (voice, video, data, and so forth) is handled at the AAL layer in an ATM node. The data is converted into ATM cells, regardless of the types of packets that came in. The data is handled by the appropriate class of service. For example, the Class A or B services will handle voice or video data; Class C or D services will handle data from a network, and so forth.

Data comes down into the AAL as packets of varying sizes, but leaves as fixed-size (48-octet) SAR PDUs. The details of these PDUs depend on the type of service (Class A, B, C, or D) and the AAL protocol being used. The SAR sublayer does the necessary chopping and packing.

The SAR PDUs from the various services are wrapped into ATM cells at the ATM layer and multiplexed for transmission onto the ATM cell stream. These ATM cells contain the virtual channel and path identification (VCI and VPI, respectively) required for the cell to reach its destination. The ATM switch uses channel and path information to send the cell out through the appropriate port. Once built, the ATM cells are passed down to the Physical layer for transmission.

The cell stream contains bits and pieces of various types of packets, all in separate cells. The cells may be routed, or switched, at various points on their path, as appropriate for maintaining connections at the required quality of service.

The cell stream is encoded and transmitted over the physical medium connecting the ATM network. At the receiving end, the ATM layer routes the cells to the appropriate services at the AAL. The cells are repackaged into the appropriate packet form by the AAL service. This service also checks that the entire packet has been received and that everything is correct.

At the receiving end, the transmission sequence is undone, with the services at the topmost (for ATM) sublayer unpacking the ATM cells to reveal the various types of data, which are passed out to the services that handle the data.

A

ATM Interfaces

The ATM architecture distinguishes among several functional interfaces, depending on the elements involved:

- The user-network interface (UNI), which connects an end user to the network via an ATM switch or other device. This interface supplies network access. A further distinction is made between UNIs for private and public networks. The rationale for this distinction is that private networks may want to use different addressing schemes—for example, to provide special addresses to local machines. The UNI 3.1 (and later) specifications provide protocols and guidelines for both public and private UNIs. (The interface for private networks is known as a private UNI, and is specified as PUNI or P-UNI.) A variant of the UNI specifications has been created for LAN emulation for ATM. These are the L-UNI specifications.

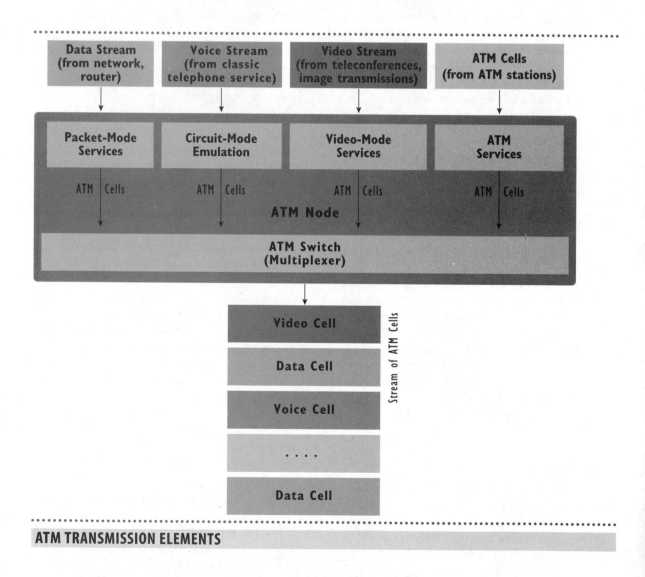

ATM TRANSMISSION ELEMENTS

A

- The network-node interface (NNI), which connects network nodes—in this case, ATM switches—to each other. This interface makes network routing possible. As with UNIs, separate interfaces are defined for public and private networks. The latter are known as private NNIs, and specified as PNNI or P-NNI. As with UNIs, a variant of the NNI specifications has been created for LAN emulation over ATM. These are the L-NNI (or LNNI or LENNI) specifications.

- The data exchange interface (DXI), which connects a data terminal equipment (DTE) device (for example, a router) with a data service unit (DSU) device at the user's end. To increase transmission efficiency, the DTE sends formatted frames to the DSU. These frames can be of different lengths, which enables the DTE to make more efficient use of the available bandwidth. Before sending the content of these frames over the ATM network, the DSU reassembles them into the official ATM cell format.

- Broadband Intercarrier Interface (B-ICI), which allows ATM networks in disparate locations to communicate and cooperate even though they must do so over a WAN (wide area network). A range of end-to-end services can be made available over this connection, including frame relay, circuit simulation, and SMDS.

- Frame UNI (FUNI), which also uses variable-sized frame cells for greater transmission efficiency. Such an interface is particularly useful when the network is using a slow-speed connection. As with DXI, the frames are repackaged into cells at the ATM SAR sublayer.

Cell Structure

ATM cells are not byte oriented. Even though cells are defined as a specific number of octets, the fields within such a cell often cross byte boundaries.

ATM cells consist of a five-octet header and a 48-octet data, or payload, section. The payload section is an SAR PDU, to which a five-octet ATM header is added. See the illustration "Structure of an ATM cell at the UNI."

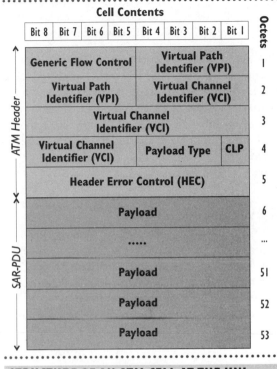

STRUCTURE OF AN ATM CELL AT THE UNI

Most of the bits in the header are used for virtual path and channel identification. The CLP (cell loss priority) bit indicates whether the cell can be discarded if network traffic volume makes this advisable. If the flag is set, the cell is expendable.

Because header fields can extend over multiple octets—for example, the VPI or VCI fields—the ATM specifications include guidelines for how bits are to be arranged within a field.

- Within an octet, bit order goes from left to right. For example, in octet 1, the VPI bits are—from highest to lowest—bits 4, 3, 2, and 1, with 1 being the least significant bit within that octet.

- Across octets, bit order goes downward as octets go upward. Thus, the lowest order bit in the VPI field is bit 5 in octet 2. Similarly, the lowest order bit for the VCI field is bit 5 in octet 4; the highest order bit in this field is bit 4 in octet 2, and the bits in octet 3 are between the high- and low-order quartets.

The cell-structure shown in the illustration applies to cells that travel onto the network across the UNI. When cells are moving across the NNI—that is, for routing purposes—the VPI field is extended to encompass the entire first octet. That is, cells at the NNI use 12 bits for VPI and 16 for VCI. There is no generic flow control (GFC) field for cells traveling across the NNI.

ATM Variants

Because ATM's progress toward becoming the dominant high-speed architecture has been much slower than anticipated, several variants on the basic technology have been proposed—as a means of getting at least some form of ATM into more markets and networks. Two of the more interesting variants are ATM25 and ATM LAN emulation.

ATM25

ATM25 is a 25Mbps version intended as a low-end and (relatively) low-priced entry into ATM technology. This version was proposed by the Desktop ATM25 Alliance, which includes IBM and Apple among its members. This variant can run on ordinary UTP (unshielded twisted-pair) cables, and allows 25Mbps transmissions in both directions. The ATM Forum approved the ATM25 specifications, and various products are currently available to enable ATM25 networks to communicate in a transparent manner with other, faster-speed ATM networks.

ATM LAN Emulation (LANE)

This variant uses software to fool a network operating system into thinking that an ATM interface card is actually an Ethernet or Token Ring adapter. This software may be included as a driver on the workstation, or client machine. Additional software runs

a LAN emulation server—either on an ATM switch or on a separate PC.

With ATM LAN emulation (LANE or LE), an ATM device can be made to look like an Ethernet or a Token Ring node to a network server. Below the surface, however, the virtual Ethernet device, for example, is able to operate at blazing ATM speeds by breaking the Ethernet packets into ATM cells before sending them on. The packets might be sent across an ATM network to a receiving device that also supports LAN emulation. The packets could then be reassembled at the receiving end, and passed transparently to a receiving Ethernet device. Information in the header area identifies packets as coming from a LAN emulation device. Such an emulation makes ATM devices independent of higher-level protocols (such as TCP/IP or IPX).

LANE makes it possible to provide an ATM bridge between two nodes that share a common network architecture. This bridge is provided at the MAC (media access control) sublayer of layer two (data-link control) in the OSI connectivity model—which is a relatively low-level connection.

The ATM Forum has defined LAN emulation user-network and network-network interfaces (LUNI or L-UNI and LNNI or L-NNI or LENNI) to ensure that LAN emulations from various vendors will be compatible and able to work together.

IP over ATM

Like LAN emulation, IP over ATM (also known as Classical IP over ATM) is designed to enable end-users working with other network architectures to communicate over ATM. Unlike LANE, however, IP over ATM does this only for networks using the Internet TCP/IP protocol stack. Also in contrast to LANE, IP over ATM is not transparent to the end users using ATM.

IP over ATM is much more limited and restrictive than LAN emulation. For example, IP over ATM does not currently take advantage of the QoS capabilities afforded by ATM; rather, only a best-effort approach is supported. Similarly, there is limited support for routing, which means there are restrictions on which end users can use the TCP/IP protocols to communicate with which other users over ATM.

Such limitations are being addressed, and new capabilities are being added, in a newer set of specifications for IP over ATM. One direction in which work is proceeding is in the creation of better routing capabilities. Toward this end, a Next Hop Routing Protocol (NHRP) has been developed. Such improvements have not been officially approved, however.

Multiprotocol over ATM (MPOA)

The MPOA project is more ambitious than any of the ATM variants discussed in the preceding paragraphs. The goal set for MPOA is to provide transparent connectivity (over ATM) for networks running any of various protocol stacks—as LANE does. However, unlike LANE, MPOA is being designed to provide such connectivity at the Network layer—thus making it possible to route communications between endpoints. (In contrast, LANE provides limited routing capabilities because the connectivity is provided at the MAC sublayer of the data-link control layer in the OSI protocol stack.) In a sense, MPOA can be regarded as the next step in the evolution of LAN emulation capabilities.

MPOA is still a work in progress because the technical and design challenges are formidable and disagreements on the details are based on the commercial interests of competing vendors. For example, MPOA will entail (ATM) switching as well as (network-level) routing. Moreover, the routing and switching will need to be coordinated. For example, if the destination for a communication can only be reached by routing, the ATM switching path will need to get the communication from its starting location to an address from which the communication can be routed. Another unresolved technical issue concerns the handling of nonroutable protocols (for example, NetBIOS and SNA, or System Network Architecture).

Commercial interests are involved in the design and planning of protocols for implementing MPOA. These interests are creating coalitions whose decisions are made on the basis of competitors' decisions, rather than on the technical merits of a particular position.

ATM Resources

The ATM Forum is a consortium of several hundred vendors, researchers, and other involved parties. The Forum's charter is to help develop and promote the use of ATM-related products and services. Toward this end, the forum provides information about ATM, helps develop specifications for ATM products and use, and generally keeps ATM on the minds of the appropriate people and groups.

Forum members are companies that are interested in developing or using ATM technology. These companies are readying products for various facets of an ATM network, such as nodes, switches, PBXs, and routers.

Various combinations of forum members/vendors have formed partnerships to create and market ATM components. Companies such as Sprint and AT&T will offer ATM services to their customers.

While many aspects of the ATM technology and specifications are still in flux, significant portions have been tested and proven viable. Vendors have forged ahead and are selling ATM products. They are still quite expensive, however, partly because the absence of finalized specifications has led to vendor-specific implementations. This, of course, makes interoperability more elusive, and customers more reluctant.

ATM variants and emulation schemes have been proposed in an effort to make ATM better known. Major ATM vendors have been cutting their prices, which is also expected to help the established base grow.

→ **Broader Categories** Network Architecture; Network, Cell-Switched; Network, Packet-Switched

→ **See Also** ABR (Available bit rate); QoS (Quality of Service)

ATM25 (Asynchronous Transfer Mode 25Mbps)

ATM25 is a version of ATM (Asynchronous Transfer Mode) networking technology defined to run over copper wire at a rate of 25Mbps. The wire must be at least category 3 unshielded twisted pair (UTP) wire. Only one pair of wires is needed.

ATM25 differs from standard ATM in two significant ways:

Speed   ATM was originally designed to operate at speeds ranging from 155Mbps to 2.488Gbps. However, since this original formulation, several slower-speed variants have been defined, including ATM25 and a 100Mbps version that uses Fiber Distributed Data Interface (FDDI) technology at the Physical layer.

Medium   Since it is a high-speed network technology, standard ATM is designed to use fiber-optic cable. In contrast, ATM25 is designed to operate over lower-priced (and lower bandwidth) copper wire.

ATM25 was designed to provide a low-cost entry into ATM technology.

→ *Broader Category*   ATM (Asynchronous Transfer Mode)

ATM Adaptation Layer (AAL)

→ *See*   AAL (ATM Adaptation Layer)

Atomicity, Consistency, Isolation, and Durability (ACID)

→ *See*   ACID (Atomicity, Consistency, Isolation, and Durability)

ATP (AppleTalk Transaction Protocol)

→ *See*   Protocol, ATP (AppleTalk Transaction Protocol)

ATPS (AppleTalk Print Services)

An NLM (NetWare Loadable Module) that provides NetWare nodes with access to printers and Macintosh nodes with access to NetWare print queues. Settings for this module are in the ATPS.CFG file.

ATTACH

In Novell's NetWare 2.x and 3.x, the ATTACH command tells a file server that a workstation exists and wants to join the network. The server will assign the workstation a connection number.

Once attached, the user at the workstation can access any of the server's services (assuming that the user has the necessary access rights to those services). The ATTACH command cannot be used to connect to the network initially. The LOGIN command must be used for the first server. Then the ATTACH command can be used to attach to additional servers. ATTACH does not execute a login script or redefine the workstation's environment. The ATTACH command is not included in NetWare 4.x.

→ *Broader Category*   NetWare

Attached Resource Computer Network (ARCnet)

→ *See*   ARCnet (Attached Resource Computer Network)

Attachment

In electronic mail, an attachment is a file that is sent along with a regular e-mail message. Attachments usually consist of data files (images, spreadsheet files, and so forth) but may also be executable programs.

Attachment Unit Interface

→ *See* AUI (Attachment Unit Interface)

Attack Scanner

An attack scanner is a software package used to probe UNIX networks for security problems or flaws. The package will essentially play the role of an intruder trying to steal or force access to a network. The use of such programs is somewhat controversial.

In April 1995, a controversial attack scanner product—SATAN (Security Analysis Tool for Auditing Networks) by Wietse Venema and Dan Farmer—was posted to the Internet. Such a product can be used by *crackers* (users trying to break into systems for malicious purposes) as well as by system administrators and security people. As a result, the Internet community is divided as to whether such a product should be made freely available.

Attention Dial Pulse (ATDP)

→ *See* ATDP (Attention Dial Pulse)

Attention Dial Tone (ATDT)

→ *See* ATDT (Attention Dial Tone)

Attenuation

Attenuation is the loss of signal strength over distance. It is measured in decibels (dB) per kilometer (expressed as dB/km) or per 100 feet. In the logarithmic decibel scale, a 3 dB loss means a 50 percent loss in power, as computed in the following equation. Specifically, the formula for power loss is

$$db = 10 \log_{10} \frac{Power_{out}}{Power_{in}}$$

In this equation, a 50 percent loss would actually yield a result of −3 dB. Under certain conditions, the coefficient in the equation will be 20, in which case a result of −6 dB would indicate a 50 percent loss. When describing losses, however, the negative sign is dropped, so that a result of −6 dB is expressed as a 6 dB loss.

Attenuation depends on several factors, including the wire composition and size, shielding, and frequency range of the signal. For copper cable, attenuation increases with signal frequency; for optical fiber, attenuation is relatively constant over a large frequency range.

Fiber-optic cable has the least attenuation, usually fractions of a decibel per kilometer. Unshielded untwisted-pair cable (such as the silver, flat-satin cables used in short-distance telephone and modem lines) has the most attenuation of any cable types used in telecommunications, and this type of cable is not used directly in networks.

Attenuation Factor

A value that expresses the amount of a signal lost over a given distance, such as decibel loss per kilometer (expressed as dB/km).

Attribute

An attribute is a feature or property associated with an entity. For example, objects in network management and entries in an X.500 Directory Services database have attributes.

An attribute has a type and a value associated with it. The type constrains the form the value can take. For example, an INTEGER type may have only a whole number value, or a BOOLEAN may have only a value that evaluates to TRUE or FALSE.

Much network management or monitoring activity consists of determining or changing attribute values. Attribute values are read or set by functions that provide the relevant network services.

File and Directory Attributes

Among the most important attributes are those associated with files and directories, because these ultimately limit what can be done on a network. The attributes are generally represented as single-bit flag values, with the flag either set or not set.

The specific attributes defined vary from system to system, but attributes are used in every operating system and networking environment. Certain attributes assume or replace others, and certain attributes override access rights. See the table "Novell NetWare File and Directory Attributes" for descriptions of NetWare attributes associated with files and directories.

NOVELL NETWARE FILE AND DIRECTORY ATTRIBUTES

Attribute	Description
A (Archive needed)	Set automatically when a file is changed after its most recent backup. (NetWare 2.x, 3.x, 4.x)
C (Copy inhibit)	Set to keep Macintosh files from being copied. Does not apply to DOS files. (NetWare 3.x, 4.x)
Cc (Can't compress)	Set automatically when a file cannot be compressed because it would not save a significant amount of space. (NetWare 4.x)
Co (Compressed)	Set automatically to show that a file has been compressed. (NetWare 4.x)
Di (Delete inhibit)	Set to keep users from deleting a file or directory. (NetWare 3.x, 4.x)
Dc (Don't compress)	Set to prevent a file from being compressed. (NetWare 4.x)
Dm (Don't migrate)	Set to prevent a file from being migrated to a secondary storage medium, such as an optical disk drive. (NetWare 4.x)
X (Execute only)	Set to keep a file from being copied, deleted, changed, or backed up. Since this setting cannot be changed, it's necessary to keep a backup (nonrestricted) copy of the program before freezing it. Assigning this attribute is not recommended; the same effect can be accomplished with the Ro attribute. (NetWare 2.x, 3.x, 4.x)
H (Hidden)	Set to keep a file or directory from being displayed in a directory listing. (NetWare 2.x, 3.x, 4.x)
I (Indexed)	Set to make it faster to access a file with many clusters on a hard disk. (NetWare 2.x, 3.x, 4.x)
Ic (Immediate compress)	Set to make sure that a file is compressed immediately. (NetWare 2.x, 3.x, 4.x)
M (Migrate)	Automatically set to show that a file has been migrated to a secondary storage medium. (NetWare 4.x)
P (Purge)	Set to make sure a file or directory is purged (zeroed) immediately after deletion, so that no data from the file is available. (NetWare 3.x, 4.x)
R (Rename inhibit)	Set to make sure a file or directory name is not changed. (NetWare 3.x, 4.x)
Ra (Read audit)	Supported but not used.
Ro/Rw (Read only/Read write)	Set to specify whether a file can be modified. (NetWare 2.x, 3.x, 4.x)
S (Shareable)	Set to indicate that multiple users or processes can access a file simultaneously. (NetWare 2.x, 3.x, 4.x)
Sy (System)	Set to indicate that a file or directory is a NetWare or DOS system file or directory. (NetWare 2.x, 3.x, 4.x)
T (Transactional)	Set to allow NetWare's Transactional Tracking System (TTS) to protect a file. (NetWare 2.x, 3.x, 4.x)
Wa (Write audit)	Supported but not used.

Document Element Attributes

In markup languages such as HTML (Hypertext Markup Language), attributes are used to distinguish elements of the same type by their details. Elements may be distinguished on the basis of different values for the same attribute or by using different attributes.

For example, different instances of the anchor element will have different names. These differences are specified as different values for the NAME attribute associated with instances of this element. In contrast, anchor elements used as links (references to other locations in the same or different document) differ from elements used as anchors (signposts for locations to which links can refer).

Links use the HREF attribute, and are distinguished from each other by the values associated with HREF (that is, by the location to which the links refer); in contrast, anchors use the NAME attribute, as shown above, in the entry for Anchor.

Table "HTML Attributes" lists some of the attributes defined in HTML and provides brief descriptions of what they do. Those marked with an asterisk are deprecated in HTML 4.0. This means they are still supported, but their use is not encouraged because their function has been replaced by another attribute or language element. Deprecated attributes will eventually be declared obsolete.

→ **See Also** Access Rights

HTML ATTRIBUTES

Attribute	Description
ACTION	For <FORM> element, specifies the URL (Uniform Resource Locator) that will receive the data from a submitted form; specifies that the form data should be emailed, and to whom it should be mailed.
ALIGN*	Specifies how an element (image, table, etc.) should be aligned in relation to surrounding text.
ALINK*	Specifies the color for a hypertext link while the mouse is clicking on the link.
ALT	Specifies alternative material as text—for browsers that cannot load or support a specified image.
BACKGROUND*	Specifies a picture to use as a background for the displayed Web page.
BGCOLOR*	Specifies the background color for the Web page.
CLASS	Specifies a class name for an element, and associates this element with a style sheet.
HREF	In <LINK> and <A> (anchor) elements, specifies the URL of a referenced file.
HREFLANG	Specifies the language used in the file referenced by HREF. (HREF must be defined.)
ID	Specifies a unique name for an element in either a style sheet or on a Web page.
LANG	Specifies the language for an element.
LINK*	Specifies the color of unvisited hypertext links.
MEDIA	For <DIV> element, specifies the output device to be used (for example, SCREEN, PRINT, BRAILLE, SPEECH, etc.).
NAME	Specifies a name for a property on a Web page.
SIZE	Specifies the height of an element. For example, for <HR> (horizontal rule), SIZE specifies the height of the rule.
STYLE	Specifies style information for an element. Information is specified as a property or a set of properties for the element.
TARGET	Specifies a window or frame into which a new Web page can be loaded.
TEXT*	Specifies the color for text on a page.
TITLE	Specifies a title for an element.
TYPE*	Specifies a look for bullet lists
VLINK*	Specifies the color for hypertext links that have been defined.
WIDTH	Specifies the width of an element. For example, with <HR> (horizontal rule), specifies the width of the rule.

Attribute Registration Authority (ARA)

→ *See* ARA (Attribute Registration Authority)

ATU (ADSL Termination Unit)

In ADSL (Asymmetric Digital Subscriber Line) technology, an ATU is the device that is responsible for creating the signaling and frame packaging for an ADSL session. Each end of the connection (the end user's home and the telephone company's central office) needs an ATU. The ATU-C (for central office) and the ATU-R (for remote) actually represent the ADSL connection since these devices are responsible for creating and interpreting the line coding method used to represent bit values, and also for packaging the bit streams into ADSL frames or superframes.

In most installations, the POTS (for Plain Old Telephone Service) splitter (which combines voice and data into a single signal at one end and separates then at the other end) is built into the ATU. The ATU is commonly built into an ADSL modem. This can cause turf problems in some cases because the user's modem must be in the home, which contains the customer's (and not the phone company's) equipment and wiring.

→ *Broader Category* ADSL (Asymmetric Digital Subscriber Line)

AU (Access Unit)

In the 1988 version of the CCITT's X.400 Message Handling System (MHS), an AU is an application process that provides a CCITT-supported service, such as faxing, with access to a Message Transfer System (MTS). The MTS can deliver a message to users or services at any location accessible through the MHS.

AUs supplement user agents (UAs), which give human users access to an MTS.

→ *Broader Category* X.400

→ *Compare* PDAU; UA (User Agent)

Audio Frequency Range

The range of frequencies that the human ear can hear, which goes from a frequency of 20 hertz to about 20 kilohertz (although few people can hear the extremes well). People can produce sounds within only a small portion of this range, from about 100 to 3000 hertz, which is the bandwidth of the ordinary, acoustically based telephone system.

Audit

An examination of network activity to make sure that the network monitoring and data gathering are working correctly. Although this is a management activity, it is done independently of the network management package in some environments (for example, in NetWare). An independent audit can check the reliability of the management software.

Audit Policy

In Windows NT, an audit policy is used to specify and determine which user events are to be tracked for security purposes. The System Access Control List (SACL) associated with a network object or resource specifies which services or operations will be audited if a user tries to access them.

Audit Trail

An audit trail is a record of all transactions that occur on a network. This record can be studied (by the system administrator) to identify such activities as efforts to sneak into the network to track the progress of an item of data, and so forth.

AUI (Attachment Unit Interface)

One component of the Physical layer, as defined in the IEEE 802.x specifications and in the OSI reference model. The other two components are the Physical layer signaling (PLS) above the AUI and the physical medium attachment (PMA) below it.

→ *See Also* Connector, AUI

AUP (Acceptable Use Policy)

An AUP represents guidelines established for the use of a network, of the Internet or of the services from a particular provider. For example, in the early days, commercial traffic was not allowed on the Internet, according to the NSF's (National Science Foundation) AUP. Internet service providers may also stipulate AUPs. For example, providers may restrict or prohibit distribution of newsletters or other postings to large subscriber lists.

AURP (AppleTalk Update Routing Protocol)

→ *See* Protocol, AURP (AppleTalk Update Routing Protocol)

Authentication

In network security and other operations, authentication is the process of determining the identity and legitimacy of a user, node, or process. Various authentication strategies have been developed. Among the simplest are the use of user IDs and passwords.

A relatively new authentication scheme, called *digital signatures*, is very effective and almost impossible to fool (unless one has access to the private encryption key of one party). In digital signatures, a user (user A) uses another user's (user B's) public key to encrypt the transmission, and uses user A's private key to "sign" it. At the receiving end, user B uses user A's public key to validate the signature, and user B's private key to decrypt the transmission.

The CCITT distinguishes two levels of authentication for directory access in its X.509 recommendations:

- Simple authentication, which uses just a password and works only for limited directory domains.

- Strong authentication, which uses a public key encryption method to ensure the security of a communication.

Recently, the idea of biometric authentication has become quite popular and of considerable interest in banking and other areas in which authentication is widely used. In biometric authentication, some physical characteristic of the user is examined. Such characteristics include fingerprints, handprints, or the corneal area of the eye—all of which are unique for each individual. ATM machines are currently being tested that examine a customer's eye for authentication.

In Windows NT, Microsoft Internet Information Server (IIS) supports three types of authentication:

- **Anonymous:** This is, effectively, no authentication at all. It allows users to browse (selected) contents on a Web server. Anonymous authentication should get a user access only to public materials—that is, materials that anyone should be able to see. The network administrator should make sure that anonymous accounts don't have access permission to any restricted files.

- **Clear text:** This allows users to log in with a username and a password. Such authentication is generally used for Web servers that provide information for downloading. One problem with clear text authentication is that snoops can capture usernames and passwords. If these same authentication elements give the user access to other (possibly restricted or sensitive) files and directories on the server, any snoop who captures them will also have access to these locations.

- **Windows NT challenge/response**: This provides the most stringent authentication and should be used when setting up a Web server for internal use—that is, a server on which users may need to have access to restricted materials.

→ *Broader Category* Security

→ *See Also* Microsoft IIS (Internet Information Server); Windows NT Challenge/Response

Authentication, Biometric

In biometric authentication, a unique physical characteristic of the user is examined. Features that are being used for such authentication include fingerprints, handprints, and the patterns in the central part of the eye. Because such features are unique for each individual, they offer the possibility of (almost) completely foolproof authentication criteria—barring, of course, coercive measures such as kidnapping.

→ *See Also* Authentication

Authentication Information (AI)

→ *See* AI (Authentication Information)

Authentication System

An authentication system is a server whose job is to check the validity of all identities on the network and of their requests. Most of the work is done automatically, without requiring any explicit human intervention.

One example of an authentication system is Kerberos, which was created for Project Athena at MIT. Kerberos is a distributed authentication system, which verifies that a user is legitimate when the user logs in and every time the user requests a service. Kerberos uses special keys, called *tickets*, to encrypt transmissions between Kerberos and a user.

→ *Broader Category* Network Security

Authenticode

Authenticode is a security feature of Microsoft Internet Explorer. Designed for authentication of ActiveX controls and other types of distributed code, Authenticode helps users ensure that a downloaded application is intact and has not been tampered with and that it actually came from the developer whose digital signature it bears.

To accomplish this, Authenticode uses X.509 digital certificates, with which developers "sign" their code. Such certificates for Authenticode can be purchased from Verisign or GTE or they can be generated by a private certificate authority (CA).

Distributed code should not be used until the signature can be verified. Even if verified, however, the code may still be malicious. It's important to note that Authenticode can only ensure that the code comes from the claimed developer and that it has not been tampered with during distribution. The verification cannot ensure that the contents of the code will not cause damage—either by the programmer's intent or through incompetence.

→ *Broader Category* Authentication

→ *See Also* Code Signature

Authority and Format Identifier (AFI)

→ *See* AFI (Authority and Format Identifier)

Auto Answer (AA)

→ *See* AA (Auto Answer)

Autocall Unit (ACU)

→ *See* ACU (Autocall Unit)

AUTOEXEC.BAT

Under DOS, `AUTOEXEC.BAT` is a special batch file that is executed automatically when the computer boots or reboots. The commands in the file can be used to configure a working environment. For example, commands in an `AUTOEXEC.BAT` file may load drivers or other files, set a command line prompt, set environment variables, load a network operating system, and so on.

Various solutions have been developed to allow some flexibility in booting to an environment. For example, OS/2 version 2.*x* allows each DOS process to have its own automatically executed file. For DOS, various programs have been developed to allow conditional processing in the `AUTOEXEC.BAT` file.

→ **Broader Category** Boot

→ **See Also** AUTOEXEC.NCF; CONFIG.SYS

AUTOEXEC.NCF

On a NetWare server, `AUTOEXEC.NCF` is an executable batch file that is used to configure the NetWare operating system and to load the required modules. The following are some of the tasks of `AUTOEXEC.NCF`:

- Store the server name and IPX internal network number.

- Load local area network (LAN) drivers and the settings for the network interface cards (NICs).

- Bind protocols to the installed drivers.

- Load NetWare Loadable Modules (NLMs).

- Set time-zone information on the network.

- Execute certain server commands.

→ **Compare** AUTOEXEC.BAT

Automated Attendant

In computer telephony, an automated attendant can provide services such as presenting a menu of choices to callers, determining the buttons pressed by a caller, responding with a personalized greeting to a call, and so forth. The functions of an automated attendant are made available through a PC telephony card working with the appropriate software.

→ **Broader Category** CTI (Computer-Telephony Integration)

Automatic Alternate Routing (AAR)

→ **See** AAR (Automatic Alternate Routing)

Automatic Call Distributor (ACD)

A device that automatically switches an incoming call to the next available line.

Automatic Number Identification (ANI)

→ **See** ANI (Automatic Number Identification)

Automatic Repeat Request (ARQ)

→ **See** ARQ (Automatic Repeat Request)

Automatic Rollback

In NetWare's Transaction Tracking System (TTS), a feature that restores the starting state of a database if a transaction fails before completion.

Automatic Route Selection (ARS)

→ **See** ARS (Automatic Route Selection)

Autonegotiation

With the development of 100Mbps Ethernet, it became necessary to find a way for 10Mbps and 100Mbps network adapters to identify their capabilities—so that these two different types of adapters could operate together on the same network. For example, if a 100Mbps card needs to coexist with 10Mbps cards on a network, the faster card will slow down its operation as necessary.

Autonegotiation was included in the 100Base-T specifications to enable network cards to determine each other's capabilities. Devices that are autonego-tiation compliant must be able to send and receive Fast Link Pulse (FLP) bursts, which are used to indicate the capabilities of the card. The timing on the FLPs is such that a 100Mbps device can identify the pulse elements as FLPs, but a 10Mbps device will see them as ordinary pulses, known as Normal Link Pulses (NLPs).

The FLPs are very rapid sequences made up of a series of alternating data and timing pulses. The timing pulses are mandatory, the data pulses are optional. If present, the data pulses make up a 16-bit Link Code Word (LCW). The contents of this word identify the device and its capabilities. "Link Code Word" shows the details of this information.

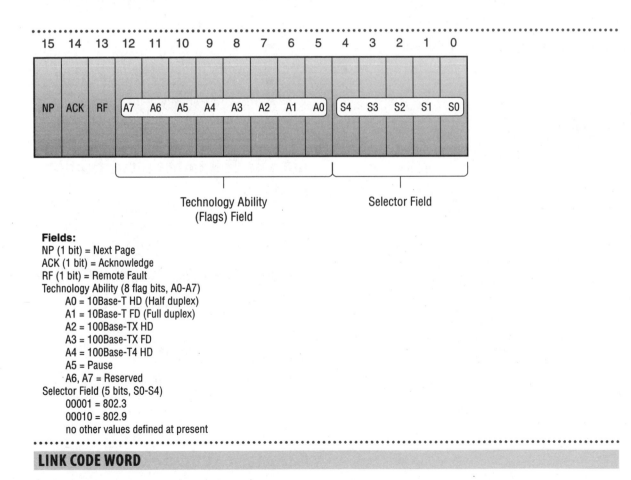

Fields:
NP (1 bit) = Next Page
ACK (1 bit) = Acknowledge
RF (1 bit) = Remote Fault
Technology Ability (8 flag bits, A0-A7)
    A0 = 10Base-T HD (Half duplex)
    A1 = 10Base-T FD (Full duplex)
    A2 = 100Base-TX HD
    A3 = 100Base-TX FD
    A4 = 100Base-T4 HD
    A5 = Pause
    A6, A7 = Reserved
Selector Field (5 bits, S0-S4)
    00001 = 802.3
    00010 = 802.9
    no other values defined at present

LINK CODE WORD

The LCW contains values for five fields:

Selector field (5 bits) This identifies the type of device. Currently, only two values are specified, to identify 802.3- and 802.9-compliant devices.

Technology Ability field (8 bits) Individual bits in this field are used to identify the type of technology supported (for example, 10Base-T operating at half- or full-duplex, 100Base-T4, and so forth). The technologies defined so far for this field fall into a priority list, which the computer can use to identify the best mode of operation for the devices involved in a negotiation. For example, of the existing 10Mbps and 100Mbps Ethernet technologies, 100Base-T2 operating in full-duplex mode has the highest priority—because it has the simplest requirements for 100Mbps operation.

Remote Fault (RF, 1 bit) field This field is set if the device's counterpart at the other end of the link has detected an error somewhere.

Acknowledge (ACK, 1 bit) field This bit is set when the device has received three successful transmissions of the LCW from the device at the other end of the connection.

NextPage (NP, 1 bit) field This bit is set if a device wants to send more LCWs—for example, to communicate additional information.

The original autonegotiation specifications were developed for 100Mbps Ethernet—to deal with 10Mbps and 100Mbps devices operating over twisted-pair wire. More specifically, autonegotiation was designed for connections using twisted-pair wire *and* RJ-45 connectors.

When the Gigabit Ethernet standard was developed, autonegotiation was retained, but it had to be adapted to work with optical fiber and with the 1000Mbps speeds in Gigabit Ethernet. Since the FLP was unsuitable for use with optical fiber, the standard 8B/10B data translation scheme is used for autonegotiation between a Gigabit Ethernet device and either a 10Mbps or 100Mbps device.

Autonomous System (AS)

→ *See* AS (Autonomous System)

Auto-Partition Algorithm

An algorithm by which a repeater can automatically disconnect a segment from a network if that segment is not functioning properly. This can happen, for example, when a broken or unterminated cable causes too many collisions. When the collisions have subsided, the network segment can be reconnected.

A/UX

An implementation of the UNIX operating system on a Macintosh, enhanced with some Macintosh-specific features, such as support for the Macintosh Toolbox. A/UX is based on System V Release 2 (SVR2) of AT&T's UNIX.

AUX

In DOS, AUX is the logical name for an auxiliary device. This is usually the serial communications board, which is more commonly known as *COM1*.

Availability

In network performance management, the proportion of time during which a particular device, program, or circuit is ready for use. Specifically, the availability of a device is the ratio of MTBF to (MTBF + MTTR), where MTBF and MTTR are mean time before failure and mean time to repair, respectively. A device is considered available even if it is in use.

Available Bit Rate (ABR)

→ *See* ABR (Available Bit Rate)

Available Cell Rate (ACR)

→ *See* ACR (Available Cell Rate)

Avalanche Photodiode (APD)

→ *See* APD (Avalanche Photodiode)

Avatar Chat

An avatar chat is a high bandwidth descendant of the (text-based) chat rooms available on the Internet. Participants in a chat room can chat with each other in real time—by typing their comments for distribution to other "chatters." Each participant in an avatar chat can choose an image (the avatar) to represent the chatter. These images can interact with each other in a 3-D virtual world. Thus, chat participants can see each other's images in this world. Communication within the avatar chat is still done by typing, however.

Needless to say, moving around in 3-D worlds is a very high bandwidth activity. Consequently, an avatar chat requires a high-speed connection—such as ISDN (Integrated Services Digital Network).

→ *Compare* IRC (Internet Relay Chat)

AWG (American Wire Gauge)

AWG (American Wire Gauge) is a classification system for copper wire. The system is based on the gauge, or diameter, of the conducting wire. The lower the gauge, the thicker the wire and the lower the resistance per unit length. The table "Diameter and Resistance Values for Selected Wire Gauges" shows some gauge values and corresponding diameters.

Note that resistance values depend on the details of the wire's composition.

DIAMETER AND RESISTANCE VALUES FOR SELECTED WIRE GAUGES

AWG Value (gauge)	Diameter (mm)	Resistance (ohms/meter)
30	0.26	0.346
24	0.51	0.080
22	0.64	0.050
20	0.81	0.032
18	1.02	0.020
16	1.29	0.012
14	1.63	0.008
12	2.05	0.005

B.x Service Level

B.x is used to specify a level of service for traffic on Public Switched Telephone Networks (PSTNs). The x in the name represents a percentage expressed in decimal form. For example, B.05 signifies a 5 percent level of service and B.5 signifies a 50 percent level.

This percentage represents the probability that a call attempt will be blocked—that is, unsuccessful. Thus, a B.05 service level means that, on average, 5 percent of the call attempts through a trunk of (potentially) available lines will be blocked because no line is available when the call attempt is made.

In telephony, a *trunk* is a collection of telephone wire groups that run between two central offices (COs) or between a CO and an intermediate routing station known as a *tandem*. When a call comes into a CO from a home or business phone, the CO uses an available line in the trunk to continue the connection toward the call's destination. If no line is available, the call attempt is said to be blocked.

The lines in a trunk that are available and that connect COs with each other are used to make connections between the calls coming in from home or business phones to a central office.

The B.x value is used by a telephone company or other service provider when designing its trunk lines. In order to obtain licenses, a company's lines must meet the quality of service guidelines established by communications regulators who have jurisdiction over the region in which the company operates.

Based on estimates of traffic volume and patterns over time and on information in the Erlang B traffic tables, the telephone company can determine how many lines it needs to group in a trunk to satisfy the specified service network. The issues involved are quite complex, and the conclusions depend strongly on several assumptions about the properties of a typical telephone call.

For example, a typical conversation call is very different from a typical call to an Internet Service Provider (ISP) or other online service. Voice calls tend to be short and to occupy the line almost full time during their duration. In contrast, data calls last much longer and often have bursty traffic patterns—that is, periods of idleness (for example, while a buffer is filling) interspersed with periods of rapid transmissions (for example, while a file is being sent).

Similarly, large trunks—those consisting of many lines—can be used to higher capacity than those with fewer lines while still meeting a given service level. For example, a 200-line trunk can be operating at almost 95 percent capacity and still meet a B.05 service level; in contrast, a 25-line trunk can operate at only about 75 percent capacity while still satisfying this service level. However, the service level for large trunks degrades more quickly than for smaller trunks when traffic increases. Increasing traffic by less than 8 percent on a 200-line trunk can degrade the service level from B.05 to B.1; in contrast, traffic on a 25-line trunk can increase by almost 15 percent before the service level degrades to B.1.

B8ZS (Bipolar with 8 Zero Substitution)

A signal-encoding scheme in which a 1 is represented alternately as positive and negative voltage, and 0 is represented as zero voltage. For timing purposes, B8ZS requires at least one bit of every eight to be a 1. If the eight-bit restriction is violated, B8ZS sends an invalid 1—that is, a 1 with the same polarity (voltage direction) as the previous 1. Since successive 1s must have opposite polarity, the second 1 will be interpreted as a violation signal, rather than as a data bit.

B8ZS is also expanded as Binary 8—Zero Substitution.

→ *See Also* Encoding, Signal

Babble

In telephony and telecommunications, babble is interference in the form of crosstalk from multiple communications channels.

BAC (Basic Access Control)

In the CCITT X.500 directory services model, the more comprehensive of two sets of access-control guidelines. The less comprehensive set is called SAC (Simplified Access Control).

→ *See Also* X.500

Backbone

In a hierarchically arranged distributed system, the backbone is the top-level, or central, connection path shared by the nodes or networks connected to it.

The backbone manages the bulk of the traffic, and it may connect several different locations, buildings, and even smaller networks. The backbone often uses a higher-speed protocol than the individual local area network (LAN) segments.

Backbone Cable

→ *See* Cable, Backbone

Backbone Closet

In the premises wiring for a building, the backbone closet is the location at which the backbone cable is terminated. At this location, the cable may be cross-connected to either backbone cable from another location or to horizontal cable, which runs to locations throughout the building.

Backbone Device

A backbone device is a network node (for example, a hub, router, or switch) that is connected only to other network nodes. Backbone devices are in contrast to edge devices, which are nodes with an interface to at least one user.

→ *Compare* Edge Device

Backbone Network

A backbone network is one with a central cabling scheme (the backbone) to which other networks are attached. Nodes in one network can talk to nodes in other networks by sending packets across the backbone network.

The networks attaching to the backbone are known as *access networks*. Access networks may require a gateway or router to attach to the backbone network.

A backbone network can be useful in decentralized corporations. For example, a backbone network might be used in a company in which each department has set up its own network, and several different architectures are used. Since the backbone network leaves the access networks intact, those networks can continue operating as if they were not on the larger network. However, the backbone gives each of the networks access to the resources and data of the other access networks.

One obstacle to a successful backbone network is the high bandwidth that may be required to handle potentially heavy traffic. Because of this consideration, fiber-optic cable is the most sensible cabling for backbone networks. The illustration "An example backbone network" shows such a structure.

B

Backbone-to-Horizontal Cross-Connect (BHC)

→ *See* BHC (Backbone-to-Horizontal Cross-Connect)

Back End

In a client/server architecture, the portion of an application that runs on the server and does the actual work for the application. The *front end* runs on the client machine and provides an interface through which the user can send commands to the back end.

Back-Flush

In data warehousing, back-flush refers to the process of feeding corrected data to the legacy system or other systems that were the source of the (now-cleaned) data warehouse contents. As information is acquired for warehousing from the legacy system and other sources, the information must be checked and possibly corrected before being added to the warehouse. During the back-flush process, corrected data are generally written to a separate file. This file can be accessed and used for corrections by the administrator of the legacy system.

→ *Broader Category* Data Warehousing

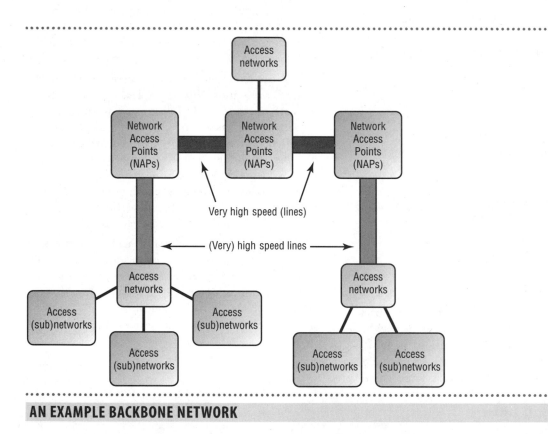

AN EXAMPLE BACKBONE NETWORK

Background Process

A process or program that executes incidentally, while another process or program is operating in the foreground. The foreground process gets the main attention of the CPU (central processing unit), and the background process takes CPU cycles when the foreground process is temporarily idle.

Backing Out

In NetWare's TTS (Transaction Tracking System), the process of abandoning an uncompleted database transaction, leaving the database unchanged. TTS takes this action to ensure that the database is not corrupted by information from an incomplete transaction.

→ *See Also* TTS (Transaction Tracking System)

Back-Off

In a shared-media LAN using collision detection, back-off refers to the action that a node takes if it detects a collision when the node tries to send a packet. For example, an Ethernet node (which uses Carrier Sense Multiple Access/Collision Detection, or CSMA/CD) may detect a collision because there is already a packet in transit. When this happens, the colliding node immediately stops trying to transmit for some specified period of time. The duration of this back-off period is determined by a predefined set of rules, known as the back-off algorithm. Generally, this algorithm will generate a random time period—one that may be weighted if packets can have priorities. The transmission protocol being used determines the details of the back-off period.

The back-off algorithm is defined as part of the IEEE 802.3 specification. Recently, an alternative algorithm—the Binary Logarithmic Access Method, or BLAM—has been proposed for handling collision situations.

→ *Broader Category* Collision Detection and Avoidance

Backplane

A backplane is a circuit board with slots into which other boards can be plugged, as illustrated in "A backplane," which shows a simplified board. The motherboard in a PC is a backplane.

A *segmented backplane* is a backplane with two or more buses, each with its own slots for additional boards.

Backplate

The metal bracket at one end of a circuit board, usually at the back where the board is plugged into an expansion slot. The backplate, also known as an *end bracket* or *mounting bracket*, typically has cutouts for connectors and switches. PCs usually come with blank backplates over each expansion slot, which are removed when you plug a board into the slot.

Backscattering

In a fiber-optic transmission, light that is reflected back in the direction from which the light came. In radio transmissions, backscattering occurs when the incident and scattered waves travel in opposite directions relative to a reference plane.

Back-to-Back Connection

In a back-to-back connection, the output from a transmitting device is connected directly to the input for a receiving device. Such connections are useful for troubleshooting or running benchmarks on the connections or the devices.

Backup

A backup is an archival copy that is stored on an external medium. For example, a backup might contain the contents of a hard disk or a directory.

The creation of regular backups is essential in a networking environment. An effective backup system ensures that data stored on the network can be recreated in the event of a crash or another system failure.

Networking packages differ in the type of backup supported, in the media to which material can be backed up, and in the ease with which parts of the archived material can be restored. Backups are generally made to tape or to erasable optical (EO) media. No serious network should be backed up to floppy disks.

Recently, various companies have begun offering offsite backup. In this arrangement, a company's data would be encrypted, compressed, and transmitted (via the Internet) to one or more

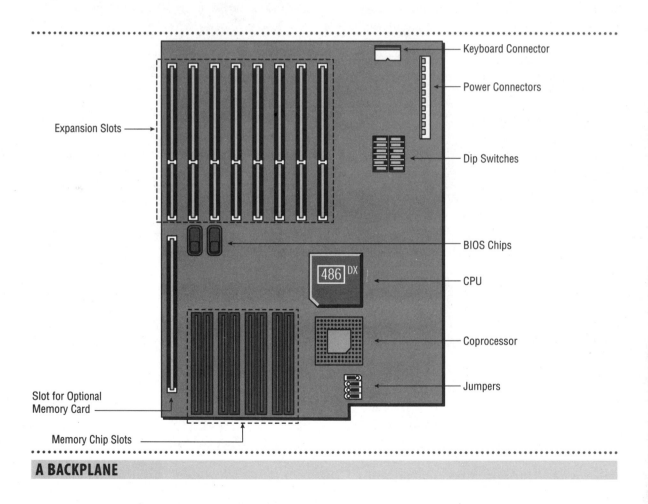

Expansion Slots

Slot for Optional
Memory Card

Memory Chip Slots

Keyboard Connector

Power Connectors

Dip Switches

BIOS Chips

486 DX

CPU

Coprocessor

Jumpers

A BACKPLANE

secure storage locations administered by the company selling the service.

Various types of backups are distinguished, including full, differential, and incremental. In full backups, a copy is made of all the data.

In differential and incremental backups, only the data that has been added or changed since the previous backup is included. Differential and incremental backups assume a full backup has been done and they merely add to this material. Such backups use the Archive flag (attribute), which is supported by DOS and most networking environments. This flag is associated with a file and is set whenever the file is changed after the file is backed up.

The backed up material should generally be stored in a different physical location from the original material, and should be protected from disasters such as fire, flood, magnets, theft, and so on.

Backup operations should be done at a time when the network is not being used for its ordinary activity, which generally means outside regular working hours. One reason for this is that most backup programs will not back up a file that is open. Truly, the work of a system administrator is never done.

When you restore the data, you restore the last full backup first, then restore each incremental backup made since the last full backup.

BACKUP TIPS

- Keep multiple copies of backups; redundancy should be a part of your backup plan.

- Test your backups to make sure that they are what you think they are.

- Store your backups in a secure, off-site location.

- Replace your backup media on a regular basis.

- Consider making incremental backups of critical data at more frequent intervals.

→ *See Also* Archive

→ *Related Articles* Data Protection; Disk Duplexing; Disk Mirroring

Backup Domain Controller (BDC)

→ *See* BDC (Backup Domain Controller)

Backward Channel

In telecommunications and other types of transmissions, a backward channel is a secondary channel that is used to transmit in a direction opposite to the main transmission. Such a channel is generally—but not always—used to send control, acknowledgement, and other types of administrative signals, whereas the *primary*, or *forward*, *channel* is used to transmit data or information.

Since it is used primarily for administrative purposes, the backward channel generally has a smaller bandwidth than the forward channel, although this is not necessarily the case. Access to the backward channel is often controlled by circuits for the forward channel.

The backward channel is also known as the *reverse channel*, but this term is used more commonly when referring to the channel arrangement in cellular communications. More specifically, the reverse (that is, backward) channel is the one going from the mobile unit (for example, a cellular phone) to the base station. Clearly, this is an instance in which the backward channel can also convey information.

→ *Broader Category* Telecommunications

→ *Compare* Forward Channel

Backward Error Correction (BEC)

→ *See* BEC (Backward Error Correction)

B

Backward Explicit Congestion Notification (BECN)

→ **See** BECN (Backward Explicit Congestion Notification)

Bad-Block Revectoring

In data protection, the process by which material written to a defective area of the hard disk is retrieved and rewritten to a different, nondefective area of storage. The defective area is identified as such in a bad block table, so that future writes will not be made to the area. Bad-block revectoring is also known as bad-block redirection and is known as a *Hot Fix* in Novell's NetWare, and as Sector Sparing in the Windows NT file system (NTFS).

Bad Block Table

In storage management, a table in which all known defective areas of a hard disk are listed to ensure that nothing will be written to these areas. The process of protecting data in this manner is known as *bad-block revectoring*, or *Hot Fix* in Novell's NetWare.

Balun

A balun is a hardware device used to adjust impedances in order to connect different types of cable. The name comes from *bal*anced/*un*balanced, because the device is often used to connect twisted pair (balanced) to coaxial (unbalanced) cable. Such wiring configurations are found primarily in IBM Cabling Systems. Baluns may have different connectors at each end to make them compatible with the cable types being connected. For example, a balun might have a BNC connector at one end and an RJ-45 connector at the other.

A balun makes it possible to use twisted-pair wiring that may already be installed in parts of a building or office in conjunction with coaxial cable that is coming from elsewhere or that has been installed more recently. The balun controls the electrical signal's passage from one cable type to the

WHAT TO LOOK FOR IN A BALUN

Baluns may include a stretch of cable (at extra cost, of course). Here are some things to consider when you're shopping for a balun:

- Baluns work most reliably when the cable has low capacitance (20 picofarads/foot or less) and when the cable impedance is not too high.

- Baluns are available in different qualities, based on the type and gauge (thickness) of cable at either end. Make sure the balun you select supports the cable properties and distances you need and then some. To be on the safe side, don't use a balun (or any other kind of connector, for that matter) at the maximum rated length.

- Some network interface card manufacturers recommend specific baluns for their boards. Similarly, some manufacturers suggest that you *do not* use baluns with their hubs or cards. Check with the manufacturer to determine whether either is the case with the network interface card or hub you plan to use.

- When using a balun on a network, you'll almost certainly want a balun designed for data transmission, because this type is made for direct (rather than reversed) pin-to-pin connections.

- Baluns pass signals on, so the balun's reliability depends on the signal's quality. For this reason, it's not a good idea to use a balun with passive hubs, which don't clean and strengthen the signal before passing it on.

other, but does not change the signal in any other way. Similarly, a balun enables you to connect a network interface card designed for use with coaxial cables to a hub that uses twisted-pair cabling.

Baluns vary with respect to the cable gauge (thickness) supported and to the maximum cable distance over which the signal is supported. This distance may be as high as 360 to 460 meters (1200 to 1500 feet). Coaxial boosters may be used to increase signal strength in the coaxial cable, and thus increase the distance over which the signal will be supported by the balun. However, such boosters can cost up to ten times as much as a balun, and will only double the supported distance.

→ *Broader Categories* Connector; Intranetwork Link

Band

In telecommunications and other fields involving electrical signaling, a band refers to a range of frequencies. The term is generally used with qualifiers, as in frequency band or bandwidth. Bands are distinguished by the size of the frequency range involved (the width) or by the magnitudes of the frequencies (for example, kilohertz as compared to megahertz or gigahertz).

Less commonly, band can refer to other types of ranges as well—for example, a range of time, or a duration.

Bandpass Filter

A bandpass filter is one that allows transmissions *within* a specified frequency band to pass but that blocks out transmissions at any other frequencies. This is in contrast to a *bandstop filter*, which *stops* transmissions within a bandwidth, while allowing higher or lower frequencies to pass.

→ *Compare* Bandstop Filter

Band Splitter

A band splitter is any device that divides a frequency (or other type of) range—the band—into smaller and distinct subchannels. A *frequency division multiplexer* (FDM), for example, divides the frequency bandwidth into smaller bands and allocates each of these bands to a different transmission. A less obvious example of a band splitter is a *time division multiplexer* (TDM). Such a device divides the continuously flowing timestream into discrete intervals and assigns each interval to a different transmission.

With an FDM, each transmission gets full-time control of part of the bandwidth; with a TDM, each transmission gets part-time control of the full frequency bandwidth.

Bandstop Filter

A bandstop filter is one that blocks frequencies within a specified bandwidth but allows other frequencies—those at a higher or a lower frequency range—to pass. This is in contrast to a *bandpass filter*, which allows transmissions within a frequency range to pass but that blocks all higher and lower frequencies. Together, a bandstop and a bandpass filter make a complete filter that blocks all frequencies.

→ *Compare* Bandpass Filter

→ *See Also* FDM (Frequency Division Multiplexing); TDM (Time Division Multiplexing)

Bandwidth

Bandwidth refers to the amount of data a cable can carry; measured in bits per second (bps), for digital signals, or in hertz (Hz), for analog signals, such as sound waves. An analog bandwidth is computed by subtracting the lower frequency from the higher one. For example, the bandwidth of the human voice is roughly 2700Hz (3000–300).

A larger bandwidth means greater potential data-transmission capability. For digital signals, a higher bit rate represents a larger bandwidth. However, the higher the frequency, the shorter the wavelength. A higher bandwidth (that is, a higher signal frequency) means faster transmission, which means a shorter signal. With a short signal, there is a smaller margin for error in interpreting the signal. This means that the effects of attenuation and other signal distortion must be kept to a minimum.

A signal traveling along a cable degrades with distance. It is possible to connect the cable to special components that can clean up and rejuvenate a signal. High-frequency electrical signals must be cleaned up frequently, which means single cable segments must be short.

Some commonly used frequency bands for analog transmissions are shown in the table "Bandwidths on the Electromagnetic Spectrum."

BANDWIDTHS ON THE ELECTROMAGNETIC SPECTRUM

Name	Bandwidth (Frequency Range)	Wavelength	Comments
Ultra-low frequency (ULF)	.001Hz (hertz)–1Hz	300Gm (gigameters, or billions of meters)–300Mm (megameters, or millions of meters)	Subsonic
Extra low frequency (ELF)	30Hz–300Hz	10Mm–1Mm	
Voice frequency (VF)	300Hz–3kHz (kilohertz)	1Mm–100km (kilometers)	Audible spectrum
Very low frequency (VLF)	3kHz–30kHz	100km–10km	
	20kHz–100kHz	150km–30km	Ultrasonic
Low frequency (LF)	30kHz–300kHz	10km–1km	Long wave
Medium frequency (MF)	300kHz–3MHz (megahertz)	1km–100m	Medium wave
High frequency (HF)	3MHz–30MHz	100m–10m	
Very high frequency (VHF)	30MHz–300MHz	10m–1m	
Ultra-high frequency (UHF)	300MHz–3GHz (gigahertz)	1m–10cm (centimeters)	Ultra-shortwave
Super high frequency (SHF)	3GHz–30GHz	10cm–1cm	
Extremely high frequency (EHF)	30GHz–300GHz	1cm–1mm (millimeters)	
	300GHz–300THz (terahertz, or trillions of hertz)	1mm–1 micron	Ultramicrowave
Infrared (IR)	300GHz–430THz	1mm–0.7 micron	
Visible	430THz–750THz	0.7 micron–0.4 micron	Visible spectrum
Ultraviolet (UV)	750THz–30PHz (petahertz, or quadrillions of hertz; a quadrillion is 10^{15}, or roughly 2^{50})	400nm–10nm (nanometers, or billionths of a meter)	Ultraviolet
X-ray	30PHz–30EHz (exahertz, or quintillions of hertz; a quintillion is 10^{18}, or roughly 2^{60})	10nm–0.01nm	X-ray

Radio Spectrum Bandwidths

Very low frequency (VLF) through super high frequency (SHF) are considered the radio spectrum. The bandwidths are used as follows:

- AM radio broadcasts in the medium frequency (MF) range (535 to 1605kHz).

- FM radio and VHF television broadcast in the very high frequency (VHF) range (88 to 108MHz for FM; the split ranges from 54 to 88MHz and from 174 to 216MHz for VHF television).

- Cable stations broadcast over several bands (frequency ranges) in the VHF and ultra high frequency (UHF) ranges (108 to 174MHz in the VHF range; 216 to 470MHz in the VHF and UHF ranges).

- UHF television broadcasts in the UHF range (470 to 890MHz).

- Radar operates at 10 different bands over a huge frequency range (230MHz to 3THz).

Digital Transmission Bandwidths

For digital transmissions, bandwidths range considerably. Here are some examples of bandwidth values for digital transmissions:

- Some digital telephone lines: less than 100kbps

- ARCnet networks: 2.5Mbps

- ARCnet Plus networks: 20Mbps

- Ethernet networks: 10Mbps

- Fast Ethernet networks: 100Mbps

- Token Ring networks: 1, 4, or 16Mbps

- Fast Token Ring networks: 100Mbps

- Fiber-optic (FDDI) networks: About 100Mbps, but can theoretically be several orders of magnitude higher

- ATM networks: about 655Mbps, with speeds as high as 2.488 gigabits per second (Gbps) in the future

- Gigabit Ethernet networks, with speeds of up to 1Gbps

Bandwidth-Bound

In telecommunications, a transmission or an application is said to be bandwidth-bound if its performance can be improved by adding extra bandwidth for the communication. For example, the transfer of a large file can be made faster by providing extra bandwidth. In contrast, adding bandwidth will not improve the performance of a delay-bound transmission such as a voice conversation—assuming, of course, that the initial bandwidth is sufficient to carry the voice call adequately.

→ *Compare* Delay-Bound

Bandwidth Exchange

In telecommunications, bandwidth exchange allows unused bandwidth to be made available as needed to communications providers. Bandwidth exchange helps to improve overall performance by allowing those who need it to get access to bandwidth from those who have it but aren't using it.

This process is handled by bandwidth exchange brokers, such as Arbinet, Band-X, Min-X, and RateXchange. These brokers find available bandwidth—for example, in the massive trunks of the large telephone companies—and offer it as available to smaller communication providers.

Bang Path

In UNIX circles, the exclamation point character is referred to as a bang character. On the Internet, a bang path is a series of names that specifies a path between two nodes. A bang path is used in uucp (UNIX-to-UNIX copy program) and sometimes for e-mail (electronic mail) or communications on BITNET. The path consists of domain or machine names separated by exclamation points (!). For example, in a bang path such as hither!thither!yon, *hither* might be a gateway, *thither* a computer, and *yon* a user.

Bang paths go back to the days before automatic routing, because explicit paths were needed when sending to or communicating with another location.

Banner Page

A banner page is output by a printer in a network environment to separate print jobs. A banner page is also known as a *job separator page*. Printing of this page is controlled by the network operating system.

A banner page might indicate the name of the user who printed the file and other information. You can eliminate banner pages in NetWare and in most other network operating systems.

Barrel Connector

→ *See* Connector, Barrel

Base64

In MIME (Multipurpose Internet Mail Extension) technology, Base64 is a system for encoding binary data into a format that can be sent using the Simple Mail Transfer Protocol (SMTP).

→ *Broader Category* MIME (Multipurpose Internet Mail Extension)

Base Address

In memory allocation, a base address defines the starting or reference location for a block of contiguous memory. The memory may be general-purpose, or it may serve as cache or port memory. Here are some of examples of different types of base addresses:

- A base I/O (input/output) address is the starting location for the memory area allocated for an I/O port. The processor uses this address to find the correct port when the processor needs to communicate with a device.

- A base memory address is the starting location for a block of memory, such as a buffer area.

- A base video address is the starting location for video memory.

Baseband

In networking, a baseband connection is one that uses digital signals, which are sent over wires without modulation; that is, binary values are sent directly as pulses of different voltage levels rather than being superimposed on a carrier signal (as happens with modulated transmissions). Baseband networks can be created using twisted-pair, coaxial, or fiber-optic cable.

Even though only a single digital stream is transmitted over a baseband connection, it is possible to transmit multiple signals. This is done by multiplexing (combining several signals in a transmission by interleaving the signals using, for example, time slices).

This digital signaling is in contrast to broadband, in which analog signals are sent over multiple channels at the same time. Each channel is allocated a different frequency range.

Baseline

In performance analysis, a reference level, or the process of determining this level. For example, in a networking context, a baseline measures performance under what is considered a normal load.

Commonly used baseline measures include transmission rate, utilization level, and number of lost or erroneous packets.

Basic Access Control (BAC)

→ *See* BAC (Basic Access Control)

Basic Encoding Rules (BER)

→ *See* BER (Basic Encoding Rules)

Basic Information Unit (BIU)

→ *See* BIU (Basic Information Unit)

Basic Input/Output System (BIOS)

→ *See* BIOS (Basic Input/Output System)

Basic Link Unit (BLU)

→ *See* BLU (Basic Link Unit)

Basic Mode

In an FDDI II network, a mode of operation in which data can be transmitted using packet-switching. This is in contrast to hybrid mode, in which both data and voice can be transmitted.

→ *See Also* FDDI (Fiber Distributed Data Interface)

Basic Rate Access (BRA)

→ *See* BRA (Basic Rate Access)

Basic Rate Interface (BRI)

→ *See* BRI (Basic Rate Interface)

Basic Telecommunications Access Method (BTAM)

→ *See* BTAM (Basic Telecommunications Access Method)

Basic Transmission Unit (BTU)

→ *See* BTU (Basic Transmission Unit)

Baud Rate

The baud rate is the measure of the number of times an electrical signal can be switched from one state to another within a second. Each baud represents one such signal transition. The faster a switch can occur, the higher the baud rate.

The relationship between baud and bit transfer rates depends on the number of bit values that are encoded in a single signal. When each signal represents one bit, the bit and baud rates are equal; when a signal encodes multiple bits, the bit rate is a multiple of the baud rate.

The term *baud* comes from Baudot, the name of a French telegraph operator who developed a five-bit encoding system in the late 19th century. This Baudot code is still used, and it is officially known as International Telegraph Alphabet #1.

Since it is a violation of the bylaws for workers in computers and communications to pass up an opportunity to create an acronym, the term also doubles as the acronym for *bits at unit density*.

→ *Compare* Bit Rate

BBS (Bulletin Board System)

A BBS is one or more computers set up with modems so that users can access those computers from remote locations. Users dialing into the BBS can send messages, get technical support from a vendor, upload or download files, and so on.

Many BBSs are set up by vendors to provide users with a forum for communication and with delayed access to technical support. Some BBSs are set up to provide services to a specialized market, generally for a fee. (Fee-based BBSs are often given more aggrandized names, such as Information Services.)

BCC (Block Check Character)

In longitudinal redundancy checks (LRCs), a character inserted at the end of a block to provide error-detection capabilities. Each of the character's bits is a parity bit for a column of bits in the block.

→ **See Also** CRC (Cyclic Redundancy Check)

BCD (Binary Coded Decimal)

An encoding scheme in which each digit is encoded as a four-bit sequence.

B Channel

In an ISDN system, the bearer channel, which can carry voice or data at 64 kilobits per second in either direction. This is in contrast to the D channel, which is used for control signals and data about the call. Several B channels can be multiplexed into higher-rate H channels.

→ **See Also** BRI (Basic Rate Interface); PRI (Primary Rate Interface)

BCN (Beacon)

A frame used in a Token Ring network to indicate that a hard error (one that is serious enough to threaten the network's continued operation) has occurred in the node sending the beacon frame or in this node's nearest addressable upstream neighbor (NAUN).

BCP (Byte-Control Protocols)

BCPs are protocols that are character (rather than bit) oriented.

BDC (Backup Domain Controller)

A backup domain controller is a server that can take over network services (including user authentication) if the primary domain controller (PDC) fails. In order to be ready to take over, the BDC gets replicas of the PDC's security and user database files. These files are always synchronized with those of the PDC.

Actually, the BDC is even more versatile. It can be used to offload logon authentication from the PDC, which is particularly important for avoiding traffic congestion in networks with many users. The BDC can also be used to log users onto the network—for example, in domains in remote locations.

→ **Compare** PDC (Primary Domain Controller)

Beacon (BCN)

→ **See** BCN (Beacon)

BEC (Backward Error Correction)

Error correction in which the recipient detects an error, and requests a retransmission. The amount of material that needs to be retransmitted depends on the type of connection, how quickly the error was detected, and the protocols being used. Compare BEC with FEC (forward error correction).

BECN (Backward Explicit Congestion Notification)

In frame relay networks, a BECN cell is sent backward—that is, against the data traffic—to the source node. Essentially, the BECN cell is sent upstream, against the data traffic coming downstream. This control cell is generated, either by the destination node or by the network itself, when the network traffic upstream from the source node is congested. The source node—that is, the node receiving the BECN cell—is expected to make adjustments to deal with the congestion.

→ *Broader Category* Frame Relay

→ *Compare* FECN (Forward Explicit Congestion Notification)

Bel

A bel is a unit for measuring the relative intensity of two levels for an acoustic, electrical, or optical signal. The bel value is actually proportional to the logarithm (to base 10) of this ratio.

For example, if one voltage is 10 times as strong as another, the higher voltage is one bel higher than the lower one; similarly, if one sound is 100 times as loud as another, the louder sound is two bels louder. The decibel, a tenth of a bel, is used more commonly when computing such values.

Bellman-Ford Algorithm

An algorithm for finding routes through an internetwork. The algorithm uses distance vectors, as opposed to link states. The Bellman-Ford algorithm is also known as the *old ARPAnet* algorithm.

→ *See Also* Algorithm

Bend Loss

In fiber optics, bend loss refers to signal attenuation that results when light waves bounce off the side of the fiber. This occurs when a fiber is curved and also when it develops microbends because the cable is twisted, stretched, or crinkled.

BER (Basic Encoding Rules)

In the ISO's Abstract Syntax Notation One (ASN.1), the BER are the rules for encoding data elements. Using the BER, it is possible to specify any ASN.1 element as a byte string. This string includes three components, and the encoding may take any of three forms, depending on the information being encoded.

Components of BER

The components of BER are the Type, Length, and Value fields.

The Type, or identifier, field, indicates the class of object, as well as the string's form. Examples of ASN.1 types include BOOLEAN, INTEGER, BIT STRING, OCTET STRING, CHOICE, and SEQUENCE OF. Of these, the first two are primitive, the next three may be primitive or constructed types, and the SEQUENCE OF type is always constructed. (A primitive object consists of a single element of a particular type of information, such as a number or logical value; a constructed type is made up of other simpler elements, such as primitive objects or other constructed types.)

The Length field indicates the number of bytes used to encode the value. Values actually may have a definite or an indefinite length. For the latter case, a special value is included in the last byte.

The Value, or contents, field represents the information associated with the ASN.1 object as a byte string. For primitive types, this is a single value; for constructed types, there may be several values, possibly of different types, involved.

BER Encoding

The encoding may be any of the following:

- Primitive/fixed length, which consists only of a primitive object and which is always a fixed length. For example, an integer variable is of this type.

- Constructed/fixed length, which consists of a group of objects and values, with a fixed total length. For example, this might be a record with only predefined components, all of which have a fixed and known length.

- Constructed/variable length, which consists of a group of objects whose total size may vary from case to case, so that a special value is needed to indicate the end of the value.

The BER can provide an encoding for any valid ASN.1 object. One difficulty is that the rules can sometimes provide more than one. In this case, the rules may be too general, because all the "synonymous" rules eat up overhead.

BER Variants

Several variants of the BER have been proposed and are being developed. In general, these are designed to provide faster, simpler, and/or more generic encodings. The following are some of the alternatives that have been proposed:

- CER (canonical encoding rules), which represent a subset of the BER. With the canonical rules, it should be possible to eliminate any redundant paths, which can slow down performance considerably.

- DER (distinguished encoding rules), which are also a subset of BER.

- LWER (lightweight encoding rules), which make faster encoding possible, but may result in larger transmissions.

- PER (packed encoding rules), which are used to compress the information about an object.

→ *Primary Sources* CCITT recommendation X.209; ISO document 8825

→ *Broader Category* ASN.1

BER (Bit Error Rate)

Number of erroneous bits per million (or billion or trillion) bits in a transmission or a transfer (as from a CD to memory). The BER depends on the type and length of transmission or on the media involved in a transfer. Compare this with the block error rate.

Berkeley Internet Name Domain (BIND)

→ *See* BIND (Berkeley Internet Name Domain)

Berkeley Software Distribution UNIX (BSD UNIX)

→ *See* BSD UNIX (Berkeley Software Distribution UNIX)

BERT (Bit Error Rate Tester)

A hardware device for checking a transmission's bit error rate (BER), or the proportion of erroneous bits. The BERT sends a predefined signal and compares it with the received signal. BERTs are moderately expensive devices that are used most commonly for troubleshooting wiring. Compare BERT with BLERT.

Best-Effort Service

In TCP/IP and other packet-based communications technologies, best-effort refers to a quality of service (QoS) class that, surprisingly, makes no guarantees regarding either delivery or speed. Best-effort service applies to connectionless transmissions—that is, those for which no explicit path between the source and destination needs to be established before transmission can begin.

Essentially, a best-effort service will take steps to get a packet from a source to a destination—for example, rerouting or buffering as necessary. However, if there is no path between the source and destination or if it takes too long to deliver the packet, the service may simply discard it. Even if the packet is delivered, it may get there late or out of sequence.

In ATM (Asynchronous Transfer Mode) networks, unspecified bit rate (UBR) and available bit rate (ABR) are examples of best-effort services.

BGP (Border Gateway Protocol)

→ *See* Protocol, BGP (Border Gateway Protocol)

BHC (Backbone-to-Horizontal Cross-Connect)

In premises wiring, the BHC is the location at which the backbone cable is connected to the horizontal wiring that will run to locations throughout the building or campus.

BIA (Burned-In Address)

A hardware address for a network interface card. Such an address is assigned by the manufacturer and is unique for each card.

BIB (Bus Interface Board)

An expansion board. In particular, a network interface card (NIC), which serves as an interface between the node (computer) and the network medium.

Big-Endian

In data transmission and storage, big-endian is a term that describes the order in which bytes in a word are processed (stored or transmitted). The term comes from Jonathan Swift's *Gulliver's Travels*, in which a war is fought over which end of an egg should be cracked for eating. This ordering property is also known as the processor's *byte-sex*.

In big-endian implementations, the high-order byte is stored at the lower address. Processors in mainframes (such as the IBM 370 family), some minicomputers (such as the PDP-10), many RISC machines, and also the 68000 family of processors use big-endian representations. The IEEE 802.5 (token ring) and the ANSI X3T9.5 FDDI standards use big-endian representations. In contrast, the 802.3 (Ethernet) and 802.4 (token bus) standards use little-endian ordering.

The term is used less commonly to refer to the order in which bits are stored in a byte.

→ *Compare* Little-Endian; Middle-Endian

Binary Coded Decimal (BCD)

Binary Coded Decimal is an encoding scheme in which each digit is encoded as a unique four-bit sequence.

BIND (Berkeley Internet Name Domain)

In the Internet community, a domain name system (DNS) server developed at the University of California, Berkeley, and used on many Internet machines.

Bindery

In Novell's NetWare products, the bindery is a database maintained by the network operating system (NOS) on each server. The bindery is located in the SYS:SYSTEM directory and contains information about all the users, workstations, servers, and other objects recognized by the server.

The bindery information determines the activities possible for the user or node. In the bindery, this information is represented as a flat database.

The bindery has three types of components:

Objects   Users, devices, workgroups, print queues, print servers, and so on. Most physical and logical entities are regarded as objects.

Properties   Attributes, specifically, as assigned to bindery objects, such as full name, login restrictions, or group membership information.

Property data sets   The values that will be stored in an object's property list.

The bindery has been replaced in NetWare 4.x by the NetWare Directory Services (NDS), in which information is represented hierarchically, in tree format.

However, version 4.x includes bindery-emulation capabilities, which makes it possible to integrate bindery-based objects into a network based on NDS. In NetWare 4.1, the *Bindery services* utility creates a bindery context within which the bindery objects appear as a flat database—as required by earlier versions of NetWare. This perspective is valid in only a limited context, which makes it possible to integrate the bindery information into the NDS while still providing a pre-4.x server with access to the bindery's contents.

Another 4.1 utility, NetSync, makes it possible to manage up to 12 NetWare 3.x servers within a NetWare 4.1 network. This makes all 12 servers look like a single server to users—a user would need only one login to access as many of the NetWare 3.x servers as desired. (As always, such access assumes that the user has the necessary privileges.) With NetSync, it also becomes easier to update resources on different machines.

→ *Broader Category*   NetWare

Bindery Emulation

In Novell NetWare 4.x, bindery emulation is a NetWare Directory Service that makes the Directory database emulate a flat database.

In NetWare 2.x and 3.x, information about all network objects is stored in a flat database, called the *bindery*. A flat database is one in which all objects in the database exist as entities of equal standing; an object cannot contain another object. In NetWare 4.x, network objects and their related information are contained in a hierarchical database, called the Directory. A hierarchical database can contain several levels of objects, which means that objects can contain other objects.

Bindery emulation allows programs that were written to run under the NetWare bindery to find the network object information they need in NetWare 4.x's Directory by making the information in the Directory appear as a flat structure.

Such bindery emulation is provided by the Bindery services utility, which makes the bindery's contents look appropriate for whatever server is querying it (i.e., 3.x or 4.x).

→ *Broader Category*   NetWare

Binding and Unbinding

In a local area network (LAN), binding is the process of associating a communication protocol, such as TCP/IP, IPX/SPX, or AppleTalk, and a network interface card (NIC). Unbinding is the process of dissociating the protocol from the NIC.

The LAN driver for a card must have *at least* one communication protocol associated with it. The LAN driver will be able to process only those packets that use the associated protocol.

The term is also used to describe the behavior of remote programs using remote procedure calls (RPCs) to communicate. Such programs bind with each other by establishing a connection and then exchanging command requests.

BIOS (Basic Input/Output System)

The BIOS is a collection of services on a ROM (read-only memory) chip. The BIOS services enable hardware and software, operating systems and applications, and also applications and users to communicate with each other. The BIOS services are loaded automatically into specific addresses, and they should always be accessible.

BIOS services are updated and expanded to handle newer devices and greater demands. To get a newer BIOS, you simply need to replace the ROM chip in your computer with an appropriate upgrade chip.

BIOS Extensions

A collection of services that supplement those provided by the standard BIOS (Basic Input/ Output System). Like the standard BIOS, BIOS extensions are implemented on a ROM (read-only memory) chip, located on the motherboard or on an expansion board.

Bipolar with 8 Zero Substitution (B8ZS)

→ See B8ZS (Bipolar with 8 Zero Substitution)

BISDN (Broadband ISDN)

BISDN is an extension of the ISDN (Integrated Services Digital Network) to allow multiple types of information to be transmitted. BISDN can handle voice, video, and graphics, as well as data.

Whereas ISDN networks generally use some form of time division multiplexing (TDM) for actual transmissions, BISDN networks generally use ATM (asynchronous transfer mode) as their transmission technology. ATM is often erroneously regarded as being equivalent to BISDN.

BISDN Services

The illustration "BISDN services" summarizes the kinds of capabilities that have been defined for BISDN networks. The services are grouped into two main groups, each with multiple service classes.

- *Interactive services* are those in which the user can initiate the service and influence its direction. Three classes are distinguished, and each class includes several examples. For example, conversational services include videoconferencing and videotelephony (for shopping, learning, etc). Online research is included among interactive services.

- *Distribution services* are those in which information (in the form of video, documents, or data) can be broadcast to whoever has the resources and rights to receive the broadcast. Distribution services are divided into those for which the user has no control over the presentation (other than to turn it on or off) and those where the user can control which elements are received. Examples of the former include TV programming and electronic newspapers; examples of the latter include retrieval of selected news items and certain online courses.

→ *Primary Sources* BISDN is discussed in more than a few of the documents in the ITU-T I.xxx document series. For example, I.113 provides a vocabulary for BISDN, and I.121 provides a list of the documents that discuss BISDN or ATM or both. These include I.150 (ATM for BISDN), I.211 (BISDN services), I.311 (general BISDN networking aspects), I.327 (BISDN functional architecture), I.361, I.362, and I.363 (ATM layers), I.413 and I.432 (BISDN user-network interface), and I.610 (operation and maintenance for BISDN). In some cases, these recommendations must be read in relation to their ISDN counterparts, whose numbers are generally lower than the corresponding BISDN document. For example, I.210 discusses ISDN services.

→ *Compare* ISDN (Integrated Services Digital Network)

Bit

A binary digit; the smallest unit of information. A bit can have a value of 0 or 1 in a digital system. All but the low-level protocols move information in larger chunks, such as bytes, which consists of multiple bits.

→ *Compare* Dibit; Quadbit; Quat; Tribit; Trit

Bit Duration

In digital communications, the bit duration is the amount of time it takes a single bit to pass a specified point on the transmission path. Bit duration is used to measure delays in a connection. The term is used primarily in high-speed communications.

Bit Error Rate (BER)

→ *See* BER (Bit Error Rate)

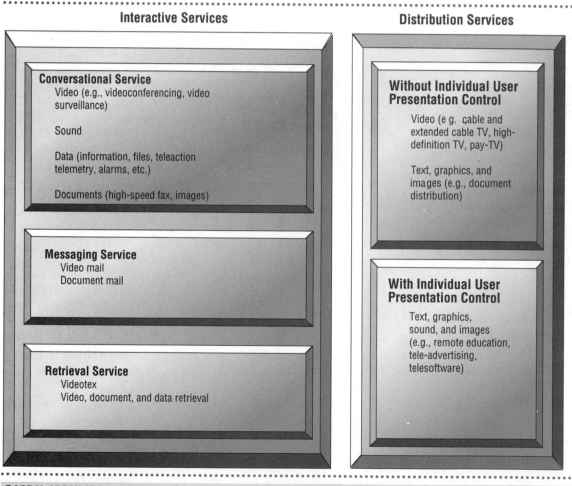

Interactive Services

Conversational Service
Video (e.g., videoconferencing, video surveillance)

Sound

Data (information, files, teleaction telemetry, alarms, etc.)

Documents (high-speed fax, images)

Messaging Service
Video mail
Document mail

Retrieval Service
Videotex
Video, document, and data retrieval

Distribution Services

Without Individual User Presentation Control
Video (e.g. cable and extended cable TV, high-definition TV, pay-TV)

Text, graphics, and images (e.g., document distribution)

With Individual User Presentation Control
Text, graphics, sound, and images (e.g., remote education, tele-advertising, telesoftware)

BISDN SERVICES

Bit Error Rate Tester (BERT)

→ *See* BERT (Bit Error Rate Tester)

Bit Interval

Bit interval, also known as *bit time*, refers to the amount of time a digital signal is left at a particular voltage level to indicate a value. Usually, the level will indicate the value of a single bit, but it is possible to encode more than a single bit in a voltage level, thereby transmitting more than one bit in a single bit interval.

In general, the longer the bit interval, the slower the transmission rate. For example, when encoding a single bit at a time, a bit interval of .01 second means a transmission rate of only 100 bits per second (bps).

→ *Related Articles* Bit Rate; Encoding, Signal

BITNET (Because It's Time Network)

BITNET is a computer network that connects many educational institutions in North America and Europe. BITNET was set up through EDUCOM, a nonprofit educational consortium. It is designed to provide communication facilities and easy access to files—even from remote locations—provided that the user has the appropriate access privileges. Today, BITNET connects more than 1000 locations.

Partly because the early nodes were predominantly IBM mainframes, BITNET still uses the RSCS (Remote Spooling Communications Subsystem) and NJE (Network Job Entry) protocol suites. Because of this, a gateway is needed to communicate with other networks, such as the Internet.

Once a gateway between the Internet and BITNET is known, it is relatively easy to send a message to a user on BITNET from most Internet installations. An address such as `user@computer.bitnet` will suffice, because most Internet mail programs recognize *bitnet* as a pseudo domain name.

In Canada, BITNET is known as NetNorth, and in Europe it is known as EARN (for European Academic Research Network).

Bit-Oriented Protocol (BOP)

→ *See* Protocol, BOP (Bit-Oriented Protocol)

Bit Rate

Bit rate is a measure of throughput, or rate of data transfer. It represents the number of bits that are transmitted in a second in a digital communication, measured in bits per second (bps). The faster the bit rate, the shorter the bit interval (the interval to signal a bit value). For example, at a bit rate of 5000bps, each bit interval can be at most .0002 second when a single bit is transmitted in each bit interval.

Bit rate is often used interchangeably with baud rate, but these two measurements are not exactly the same. *Baud rate* refers to the number of electrical signal transitions made in a second. If a single bit is encoded in each signal, the bit rate and baud rate will be equal. However, if multiple bits are encoded in a single signal, the bit rate will be higher than the baud rate.

Bit Stuffing

In data transmission, a technique for ensuring that specific bit patterns do not appear as part of the data in a transmission. For example, if six consecutive 1 values are encountered in the transmitted data, a 0 bit would be inserted after the fifth consecutive 1 bit. The receiver removes any inserted bits when processing the transmission.

B

BIU (Basic Information Unit)

In SNA network communications, a packet of information created when the transmission control layer adds a request/response header (RH) to a request/response unit (RU). This unit is passed to the path control layer.

→ *See Also* SNA (Systems Network Architecture)

BIU (Bus Interface Unit)

An adapter card. In particular, a network interface card (NIC), which acts as an interface between a node (computer) and the network.

Blackout

A blackout is a total loss of electrical power. Blackouts can be caused by cut or broken power lines, lightning strikes, and other natural and man-made disasters.

→ *See Also* Power Disturbances

BLER (Block Error Rate)

In communications, an error rate based on the proportion of blocks with errors. Compare it with BER (bit error rate), which is based on the number of erroneous bits per million (or billion or trillion) bits in a transmission.

BLERT (Block Error Rate Tester)

A hardware device for determining a transmission's block error rate (BLER), which is the proportion of blocks with erroneous bits. This device is also known as a BKERT.

Block

A block is an area of memory or storage with a fixed size. A network operating system block can be anywhere from 4 to 64 kilobytes (KB). DOS blocks are typically a multiple of 2KB. NetWare blocks are typically 4KB. However, the actual block size depends on the size of the volume on which storage is being allocated.

In some environments, such as in NetWare, a block represents the smallest chunk of storage that can be allocated at a time. (In NetWare, you can accept the suggested block size, which is based on the size of the volume, or you can specify the block size you want to use.)

Two types of blocks are distinguished:

Disk-allocation block   Used to store network data, at least temporarily.

Directory-entry block   Used to store directory information.

NetWare 4*x* and later support block suballocation, in which a block can be broken into 512-byte chunks. These chunks can be used to store the ends of several files. For example, with a 4 kilobyte (KB) block size, three 5KB files would fit into four blocks. Each of the files would use one block and two 512-byte chunks in the fourth block. In contrast, these files would require six blocks (two per file) in NetWare 3*x*.

Block Check Character (BCC)

→ *See* BCC (Block Check Character)

Block Error Rate (BLER)

→ *See* BLER (Block Error Rate)

Block Error Rate Tester (BLERT)

→ *See* BLERT (Block Error Rate Tester)

Blown Fiber

→ *See* Fiber, Blown

BLU (Basic Link Unit)

In IBM's SNA (Systems Network Architecture) networks, a block, or packet, of information at the data-link layer.

→ *See Also* SNA (Systems Network Architecture)

Blue Book Ethernet

Ethernet version 2.0. This term is sometimes used to distinguish Ethernet 2.0 from the similar, but not identical, Ethernet variant defined in the IEEE 802.3 standard.

→ *See Also* Ethernet

Bluetooth

Bluetooth is the name for a new short-range wireless technology from Ericsson, Nokia, IBM, Intel, and Toshiba. Using radio technology, Bluetooth is designed to enable PDAs, cellular phones, notebook PCs, and other mobile devices to communicate with each other over short distances—within 10 meters in a base configuration or within 100 meters with an amplifier. Devices can communicate at speeds of up to 1Mbps, and can exchange voice or data signals. Bluetooth technology uses low-power microwave signals that hop among frequencies in the 2.45GHz frequency band. This band is part of the unlicensed ISM range, which is dedicated to use for industrial, scientific, and medical purposes. Devices using Bluetooth to communicate do not have to be in each other's line of sight.

Products with support for Bluetooth should be available by the time you are reading this, as major manufacturers for the various affected devices have indicated they plan to bring Bluetooth-compliant products to market by early 1999. Bluetooth-compliant products will need to have an embedded chip with a radio transceiver.

The product gets its name from Harald Bluetooth, a Danish king who united the country in the 10th century.

→ *Broader Category* Wireless Communication

Bookmark

In browser environments on the World Wide Web or on an intranet web, a bookmark is used to store the URL (Uniform Resource Locator, or address) of a frequently visited Web page. By saving URLs as bookmarks, the user gets one-click access to the Web pages at the stored URLs. Microsoft Internet Explorer refers to these frequently visited URLs as *favorites*.

In gopher environments on the Internet, a bookmark is used to mark a specific menu or directory on a gopher server. Once the bookmark has been created and placed at the desired location, it's possible to get almost immediate access to that location, rather than having to work your way through layers of menus.

→ *See Also* Browser; Gopher

Boot

The process by which a computer is started up and its operating system kernel is loaded into RAM (random-access memory) is called the *boot,* or *bootstrap,* process. Although the details may differ when booting to different disk operating systems or network operating systems, the basic steps are the same:

1. Execute a hardware self-test.

2. Look in a predefined place for the boot sector and load this code.

3. Execute the boot sector program to load other programs.

4. Execute these programs to load still other programs or to configure the operating environment.

5. Repeat the previous step as often as dictated by the programs being loaded and by their initialization code.

DOS BOOT: THE DOS BOOTSTRAP PROCESS

1. A program (the ROM-BIOS) in ROM (read-only memory) executes. This program checks the hardware components by doing a POST (power-on self-test).

2. The ROM-BIOS program loads and executes a program from the boot sector on a floppy or hard disk.

3. This boot sector program loads hidden files, which, in turn, load the basic device drivers for DOS (keyboard, disk, and display) and execute the DOS initialization code. Part of this initialization loads the DOS kernel.

4. The DOS kernel builds various tables it will need, initializes device drivers, and executes instructions found in CONFIG.SYS, if this file exists.

5. The DOS kernel loads COMMAND.COM, the DOS command processor.

BOOTP (Bootstrap Protocol)

→ **See** Protocol, BOOTP (Bootstrap Protocol)

Boot Partition

On a hard disk, the boot partition is the logical disk section that contains the files needed to start up, or boot, the computer.

In the Microsoft Windows NT Server environment, the boot partition contains the NT system files. By default, these system files are placed in the WINNT directory.

In addition to the boot partition, an NT Server also needs a system partition. The system partition, interestingly enough, contains the hardware-specific files needed to boot (that's right, boot) the server.

→ **Compare** System Partition

Boot ROM

A ROM (read-only memory) chip used in diskless workstations to enable these machines to boot and connect to a network.

Bootstrap Protocol (BOOTP)

→ **See** Protocol, BOOTP (Bootstrap Protocol)

BOP (Bit-Oriented Protocol)

→ **See** Protocol, BOP (Bit-Oriented Protocol)

Border Gateway Protocol (BGP)

→ **See** Protocol, BGP (Border Gateway Protocol)

Bot

A bot is a program that can be activated for, or dropped into, a session in order to provide a specific kind of capability or to carry out a particular task. For example, bots can be used for such things as counting the number of hits at a Web site, rounding up price comparisons for a particular product, navigating across the Web, and so forth. Many Web-based applications include bots for particular purposes related to the application.

For example, Microsoft FrontPage includes the following bots:

Annotation bot Allows users to add private notes to a Web page. These notes can be seen in FrontPage but not by a browser.

Confirmation bot Echoes information entered by a user to allow the user to confirm the accuracy of the information.

HTML markup bot Makes it possible to add HTML codes, even nonstandard codes, to a Web page.

Include bot Makes it possible to import the contents of a file into an HTML document.

Scheduled image bot Makes it possible to specify a time period and to display an image only during the specified time period. Outside the specified time period, the bot is idle.

Scheduled include bot Makes it possible to specify a time period and to display the contents of an included file only during the specified time period. Outside the specified time period, the bot is idle.

Search bot Makes it possible to search a local web for pages containing a specified string.

Substitution bot Makes it possible to display the value of an environment variable in a document.

Table of contents bot Makes it possible to generate a table of contents (that is, an outline) of a local web.

Timestamp bot Makes it possible to mark the time and date when a Web page was last edited.

Bots are also known as *webbots*.

Bounce

A term for the action of returning an undeliverable e-mail message. In such a case, the postmaster on the system returns the message, along with a *bounce message*, to the sender.

BRA (Basic Rate Access)

Access to an ISDN Basic Rate Interface (BRI), an interface with two 64 kilobits per second (kbps) B channels (for voice and data) and one 16kbps D channel (for call and customer information). Compare it with PRA, which is access to a PRI (Primary Rate ISDN).

Bracket

In IBM's SNA (Systems Network Architecture) and APPN (Advanced Peer-to-Peer Networking) environments, a bracket consists of one or more sequences of response units (RUs, which are essentially packets) that are exchanged by participants in a session. The bracket includes both the RUs and the responses to them.

The elements of a bracket make up a transaction, so the entire bracket must be completed before the next bracket can begin. A database query, together with the response, is an example of a bracket.

Bracket Protocol

→ *See* Protocol, Bracket

Braid Shield

In coaxial cable, a braid or mesh conductor, made of copper or aluminum, that surrounds the insulation and foil shield. The braid helps protect the carrier wire from electromagnetic and radio frequency interference.

→ *See Also* Cable, Coaxial

Breakout Box

A breakout box is a diagnostic tool that can be used to reconnect wires or pins between a device (for example, a computer or modem) and a cable. With the breakout box, a particular connection can be turned off or reconnected to pair different wires. With an RS-232 breakout box you can create a null-modem connection, which some printers and other devices use.

BRI (Basic Rate Interface)

A BRI is an interface between a user and an ISDN (Integrated Services Digital Network) switch. The BRI specifies two 64 kilobit per second (kbps) B channels (for voice and data) and one 16kbps D channel (for customer and call information).

This channel combination is sometimes denoted as *2B+D*. It can be compared with PRI (Primary Rate Interface).

Access to a BRI is provided by a BRA (basic rate access).

Bridge

The term *bridge* generally refers to a hardware device that can pass packets from one network to another. Bridges operate at the OSI Reference Model's second lowest layer, the data-link layer. A bridge makes the networks look like a single network to higher level protocols or programs.

A bridge serves both as a medium (the bridge part) and as a filter. It allows packets from a node on one network to be sent to a node on another network. At the same time, the bridge discards any packets intended for the originating network (rather than passing these to the other network).

Bridges versus Routers, Brouters, and Repeaters

The terms *bridge* and *router* are often used interchangeably. In fact, in older documentation, Novell referred to its routers as bridges. A router is a device that can send packets to network segments on the way to their destination. Unlike bridges, routers operate at the network layer of the OSI Reference Model. However, bridges and routers have come to take on some of each others' properties. In fact, a brouter (for *bridging router*) is a device that has the capabilities of both a bridge and a router.

A bridge's capability to segment, or divide, networks is one difference between a bridge and a repeater. A repeater is a device that moves all packets from one network segment to another by regenerating, retiming, and amplifying the electrical signals. The main purpose of a repeater is to extend the length of the network transmission medium beyond the normal maximum cable lengths.

Protocol Independence of Bridges

A bridge is independent of, and therefore can handle packets from, higher level protocols. This means that different higher level protocols can use the same bridge to send messages to other networks.

To protocols at higher OSI layers (most immediately, the network layer), the presence of a bridge is transparent. This means that two networks connected by a bridge are treated as part of the same logical network by protocols such as Novell's IPX/SPX, IBM's NetBIOS, or the widely used TCP/IP. This transparency makes it possible to access a logical network that is much larger than the largest physical network allowed.

Packet Transmission

Because it operates at the data-link layer, a bridge just checks the address information in a packet to determine whether to pass the packet on. Beyond that checking, a bridge makes no changes to a packet.

A bridge sees each packet that is transmitted on each of the networks the bridge connects. If a packet from network A is addressed to a local node (that is, to one in network A), the bridge discards the packet, since the packet will be delivered internally through the network. On the other hand, if a packet from network A is addressed to a remote node (on network B), the bridge passes the packet over to network B. The figure "A simple local bridge" shows how a bridge can connect two networks.

The bridge greatly reduces traffic on both networks by protecting each network from the other network's local messages. This makes each of the smaller networks faster, more reliable, and more secure, while retaining transparent communication with the other network (or networks).

When routing packets, a bridge uses only node addresses; it does not take network addresses into account. A node address is a physical address, associated with a network interface card (NIC), rather than with a particular network.

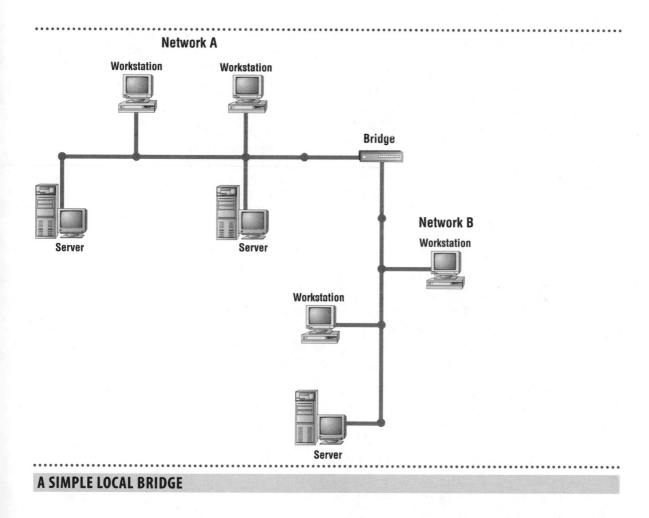

A SIMPLE LOCAL BRIDGE

Types of Bridges

Bridges can be categorized by several different features. The table "Bridge Groupings" summarizes the various categories.

BRIDGE GROUPINGS

Feature	Grouping
Level	LLC (logical link control) layer versus MAC (media access control) layer
Operation	Transparent versus source routing
Location	Internal (card) versus external (stand-alone)
Bridged distance	Local versus remote

LLC-Layer versus MAC-Layer Bridges

MAC-layer bridges operate at the media-access control (MAC) sublayer, the lower sublayer into which the IEEE divides the data-link layer of the OSI Reference Model. These bridges can connect only networks using the same architecture (Ethernet to Ethernet, Token Ring to Token Ring, and so on), because the bridge expects to handle a particular packet format, such as Ethernet or ARCnet.

LLC-layer bridges operate at the upper sublayer of the data-link layer, the logical link-level control (LLC) sublayer. These types of bridges can connect different architectures (such as Ethernet to Token Ring), because these architectures use the same LLC sublayer format, even if they use different formats at the MAC sublayer.

Most older bridges are of the MAC-layer type and can connect only same-architecture networks; most newer products are of the LLC-layer type and can connect dissimilar architectures.

Transparent Routing versus Source Routing

The manner in which a bridge routes packets depends largely on the architectures involved. Bridges connecting Ethernet networks use transparent routing, a packet-routing method in which

the bridge determines a route. Transparent bridges determine "on the fly" where a packet belongs. Such bridges learn and store the location of each node, and route packets accordingly. A transparent bridge can carry out its routing without explicit instruction or attention from the user. The bridge builds a routing table (known as a *filtering database*), and looks in this table to determine the location of a destination node. Based on this information, the bridge can determine whether to ignore the packet or to pass it on.

To avoid infinite loops, only one route can be allowed between any source and destination combination. The spanning tree algorithm can be used to identify a route with no loops between any pair of nodes.

In contrast, most bridges connecting Token Ring networks use source routing. This is a deterministic routing method in which the source node must provide the route as well as the destination for the packet. The source node learns the available routes through route discovery. The routing information is inserted by the sender, and can be determined by sending a discovery packet. This packet uses the spanning tree algorithm to find the most efficient route to the destination, and reports this route to the sender.

Source routing bridges determine an explicit path to the destination node and include this routing information in the packet. Surprisingly, the requirements for source routing capabilities are considerably more complex than for transparent bridges. Accordingly, source routing capabilities are generally available as options for a bridge. Although source routing requires more work to find the path initially, it is more efficient once the path has been established, because there is no longer any reason for the bridge to find a path.

According to the IEEE 802.3 specifications, all bridges should be capable of using transparent routing. Some can also do source routing. A bridge can distinguish between the two approaches by checking the packet being sent. Depending on the value of a particular bit in the source address field, a packet may include source-routing information.

To enable source routing bridges to communicate with transparent bridges that might be on the same network—and at the same time to satisfy the IEEE requirement about transparent routing—IBM developed *source routing transparent (SRT)* bridges. These bridges use source routing if the packet allows it; otherwise the bridges use transparent routing.

Internal versus External Bridges

A bridge may be internal or external. An *internal bridge* is on a card plugged into an expansion slot in a server. The server is part of both networks. An internal bridge gets its power from the PC's bus. Internal bridges generally include multiple types of connectors. A special type of internal bridge is used to connect to wide area networks (WANs). This type of bridge will have connectors for modem or telephone connections, such as D-shell or RJ-type connectors.

An *external bridge* is a stand-alone component to which each network is connected by cable. The external bridge is part of both networks. An external bridge generally has multiple connectors; for example, BNC for coaxial cable (as in Ethernet or ARCnet networks), modular (RJ-*xx*) for twisted-pair cable, and possibly DB-9 or DB-25 (for serial connection to a modem). External bridges need their own power supply, and they usually include a connector for accessing WANs.

Local versus Remote Bridges

A bridge may be local or remote. A *local bridge* connects two networks in the same geographical location, such as networks on either side of the hall or on either side of an office floor. Usually, these types of bridges are added to break a large, busy network into two smaller networks. This reduces network traffic on each of the newly formed networks.

By using the spanning tree algorithm specified in the IEEE 802.1 standard, local bridges can ensure that only a single path is used to send a packet between a source and a destination. If this path is not usable, the algorithm can find an alternate path.

A *remote bridge* connects two networks separated by considerable geographical distance, large enough to require a telecommunications link. Remote bridges must be used in pairs, with one at each end of the link, as shown in the illustration "A simple configuration involving remote bridges."

A remote bridge connects to a local area network at one end and to a switching network, such as one with an X.25 interface, at the other end. Each remote bridge is connected to a network at one port and to a network cloud at another port. (A *cloud* is a working concept that is used to indicate a connection that is taken for granted, for purposes of the discussion and whose details are not specified.)

The interfaces are likely to be different at these two ports. For example, a remote bridge may connect to an Ethernet network at one port and to a serial interface (such as RS-232) at the other. The cloud represents the point-to-point link between the two remote bridges.

Remote bridges also need a protocol to communicate with each other. For example, if the remote bridges communicate over an ISDN or an X.25 line, the bridge at each end needs to be able to communicate using the switched network (ISDN or X.25) protocol.

The throughput in a remote bridge is likely to be limited by the long-distance connection. At the local end, the bridge will generally have the same nominal speed as the network (10Mbps for Ethernet, 4 or 16Mbps for Token Ring, and so on). At the remote end, the throughput will depend on the type of connection. At this end, possible speeds may run from a few kilobits per second to several megabits per second.

Translational Bridges

Translational bridges enable communications between different kinds of networks. For example, a translational bridge can make it possible for a token ring node to communicate with a node on an Ethernet network. The bridge does any necessary conversions between packet or byte formats.

Learning Bridges versus Static Bridges

A *learning bridge* is one that automatically builds a table of node addresses, based on the NICs the bridge finds on the network. The bridge builds the table by using the information broadcast when a new node logs on and by checking on the source and destination addresses as packets pass through the bridge.

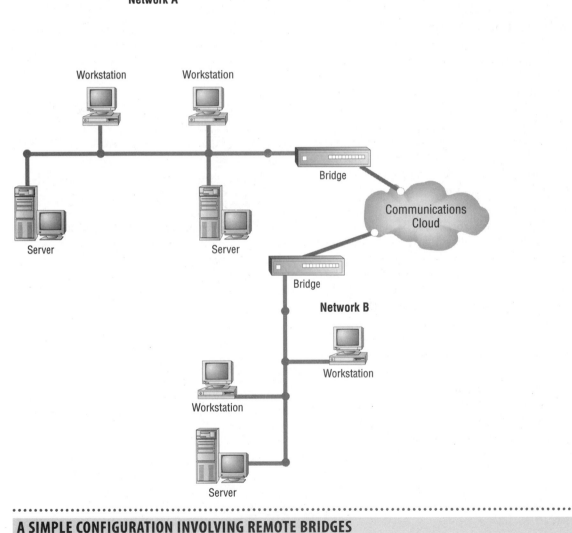

Network A

Workstation

Workstation

Bridge

Communications Cloud

Server

Server

Bridge

Network B

Workstation

Workstation

Server

A SIMPLE CONFIGURATION INVOLVING REMOTE BRIDGES

The performance of a learning bridge improves over time as the bridge completes its table of node locations. Until it knows the location of a node, the bridge assumes the node is on the remote network and so passes on the packets. The bridge is constantly updating its table—adding new addresses and dropping addresses that have not been mentioned within a period of time.

In contrast, a *static bridge* is one that cannot build its own address table. Instead, the addresses must be entered by hand. Fortunately, static bridges have all but disappeared. Just about all modern bridges are learning bridges, since static bridges do not meet IEEE 802.1 specifications.

Multiple Bridges and the Spanning-Tree Algorithm

Multiple bridges may be used to connect several networks. Any one bridge connects only two networks directly, but may connect more than two networks indirectly. The bridge is attached to each network by a port.

B

WHAT TO LOOK FOR IN A BRIDGE

When you're investigating bridges, you'll want to get details about bridge features and capabilities. Vendors should be able to provide both marketing and technical information about their products. Make sure to get the technical information. The vendors' materials should provide information about at least the following:

- Whether the bridge is local or remote.

- Whether the bridge is internal or external.

- Media and architecture supported for the local network; for example, twisted-pair Ethernet, fast Ethernet, 16Mbps Token Ring, or FDDI. It's a good idea to ask explicitly about your particular configuration and to get the answer in writing.

- If applicable, what interface the bridge supports for a remote connection. For example, it may support RS-232, RS-422, V.35, T1, or DSx.

- Number of ports.

- Transmission speeds, both local and long distance, if applicable. The smaller of these values is the critical one. Number of packets passed is generally a more useful figure than the actual bit-transfer rate.

- Whether the bridge supports load balancing.

- Whether the bridge can collect network performance data, such as number of packets received, forwarded, and rejected, number of collisions, and errors during a transmission. Such network management services may require additional software (which may cost several thousand dollars).

- Price, which can range from a few hundred dollars to over $10,000.

When you're selecting a remote bridge, you need to worry about compatibility with the network and also with the long-distance services that will be used. Keep in mind that you may need to budget for two remote bridges if you're responsible for the networks at both ends of the connection.

For more specific and more advanced questions, such as about a bridge's compatibility with a particular network configuration, you may need to talk to the bridge vendor's technical support staff. In many cases, the network vendor (Novell, Banyan, and so on) will have a database of hardware that has been explicitly tested with the vendor's networking products. Be forewarned that these vendors may want to charge you for revealing this information.

If there are multiple bridges, the bridges communicate with each other and establish a layout in order to find a spanning tree for all the networks. A *spanning tree* is one that includes paths to all nodes that can be reached on the network but includes no more paths than are necessary to completely interconnect the nodes and networks involved. Most important, a spanning tree does not include any loops (closed paths), which could trap a packet, thereby effectively shutting down the network.

Because larger network clusters make multiple paths possible, there is the danger that the same message will get broadcast all over the networks through multiple paths. This will produce a great deal of extraneous network traffic and can, in fact, bring down the network. A closed path, or loop, among the networks could be damaging because it could start an unending packet-passing process. The spanning-tree algorithm, specified in IEEE 802.1, is applied to provide a path between every pair of accessible nodes on the network and ensure that there are no loops in the paths to be used by the bridge.

Although the spanning tree algorithm ensures that the same packet won't take multiple paths to the same destination, the algorithm doesn't rule out the possibility of multiple paths being used to transmit *different* packets between the same source and destination. Higher-end bridges include the ability to do load balancing, by distributing traffic over more than one path between a source and destination.

Recently, wireless bridges have become available for limited-distance remote connections. Remote bridges that use radio waves can be up to 25 or 30 miles apart—provided the terrain and weather allow it, and provided the two bridges have directional antennas available. Remote bridges using lasers can be up to about 3500 feet apart. Since focused signals must be sent in both cases, such bridges must be within each other's line of sight.

Wireless remote bridges are susceptible to two kinds of interference:

- Inward interference, which can occur when another device is operating in the same bandwidth and the two signals interact with each other.

- Outward interference, in which the device under consideration is causing interference in a different device.

→ **Broader Category** Internetwork Link

→ **See Also** Brouter; Gateway; Repeater; Router; Switch

Broadband ISDN (Integrated Digital Services Network)

→ **See** BISDN (Broadband ISDN)

Broadband Transmission

A broadband transmission is an analog communication strategy in which multiple communication channels are used simultaneously. The data in a broadband transmission is modulated into frequency bands, or channels, and is transmitted in these channels.

Guard bands, which are small bands of unused frequencies, are allocated between data channels. These provide a buffer against interference due to signals from one data channel drifting or leaking over into a neighboring one. The illustration "A broadband transmission" shows how data channels and guard bands are used.

For example, cable TV (CATV) uses broadband transmission, with each channel getting a 6 megahertz (MHz) bandwidth. Broadband transmissions use coaxial or fiber-optic cable, and they can transmit voice, data, or video.

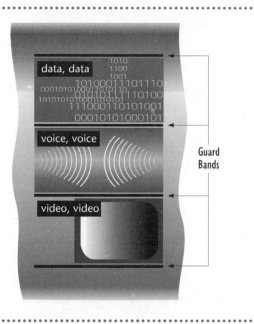

Guard
Bands

A BROADBAND TRANSMISSION

When digital data is being transmitted, a modem or other device demodulates the signals back into digital form at the receiving end. A modem used for broadband transmissions needs two bands of at least 18MHz bandwidth each: one band for sending and the other for receiving.

Broadcast

In a network transmission, sending a message to all connected nodes. This is in contrast to a transmission that is targeted at a single node. Most packet formats have a special address value to indicate a packet that is being broadcast. Compare broadcast with *multicast*.

Broadcast Storm

In network traffic, a condition in which packets are broadcast, received, and then broadcast again by one or more of the recipients. The effect of a broadcast storm is to congest a network with redundant traffic. Broadcast storms can arise, for example, in bridged networks that contain loops (closed paths).

Broadcast Transmission

In an AppleTalk network that uses the LocalTalk architecture and its LocalTalk Link Access Protocol (LLAP), a transmission sent to each node in the network. Compare broadcast transmission with directed transmission.

Brouter

A brouter (also known as a *bridging router* or, less commonly, as a *routing bridge*) is a device that combines the features of a bridge and a router. A brouter can work at either the data-link layer or the network layer.

Working as a bridge, a brouter is protocol independent and can be used to filter local area network traffic. Working as a router, a brouter is capable of routing packets across networks.

→ *Broader Categories* Bridge; Internetwork Link; Router

Brownout

A short-term decrease in voltage level, specifically when the voltage is more than 20 percent below the nominal RMS voltage. Brownouts can occur when a piece of heavy machinery is turned on and temporarily drains the available power, or when everyone feels the need to run their air conditioners at the same time.

→ *See Also* Power Disturbance

B

Browser

A browser is a hypertext file reader. That is, a browser is a program that can display material containing links to other material (perhaps located in other files or even on other machines), and that can provide quick and easy access to the contents associated with such links.

Browsers may be text, graphics, or multimedia based. Multimedia browsers can be divided into first and second generations, with the second-generation browsers being enhanced (or, rather, *enabled*, as the marketers have called them) through the inclusion of any of several types of interpreters, as described below.

- A text-based, or line-oriented, browser is able to display only rudimentary graphics, and is generally line-oriented. However, text browsers can still switch to any material that is formatted in a suitable manner for the browser. WWW and Lynx are examples of such browsers. Both are accessible on the Internet.

- Graphics browsers can handle both text and graphics, require a mouse, and generally have a much nicer display than line-oriented browsers. Cello and Mosaic are examples of graphics-based browsers.

- First-generation multimedia browsers can display sound and video, in addition to having all the capabilities of graphics browsers. Early versions of Netscape Navigator are first-generation multimedia browsers. In fact, Navigator is arguably the browser that helped turn Web surfing into a global pastime. Mosaic is also a multimedia browser. Variants of the Mosaic browser are available for several computing environments. For example, xMosaic is a browser for the X Window System.

- HotJava, a browser from Sun Microsystems, marks the advent of the second generation of multimedia browsers. HotJava is a multimedia browser with a built-in Java interpreter. HotJava is said to be *Java-enabled*.

The interpreter allows HotJava to run *applets* (programs that can be embedded in Web pages, and executed when the Web pages are displayed). Java applets make Web pages dynamic because they can be changed on the fly by running an appropriate applet. HotJava also includes security capabilities and object concepts of the Java programming environment. Other enabled browsers include the newer versions of Netscape Navigator and Microsoft Internet Explorer.

Forms-capable browsers allow users to fill in information on forms or questionnaires. Most graphics-based browsers are forms-capable.

Browsers have long been used in programming environments—for example, in the SmallTalk environment created at Xerox PARC in the 1970s and 1980s. These readers have really come into widespread use with the growth of the World Wide Web (WWW) on the Internet.

First and foremost, browsers are display tools. However, the rapid pace of developments on the Web, together with the intense competition between browser manufacturers, has also turned them into cutting edge technologies that have produced advances in several areas. For example, through their race to add features to their browsers, Microsoft and Netscape have brought about major enhancements and revisions in the definition of HTML (Hypertext Markup Language), the language of choice for creating Web pages. In fact, the newest version of the language, HTML 4.0, has incorporated many of the features that just a year or two ago could only be tacked on externally using enabled browsers. Developments in browser technology have also led to advances in scripting languages such as JavaScript and VBScript.

Competition in the development of browser features has also spurred the development of document object models, which makes it easier to identify and distinguish between structural and content elements. This has led to the development of Dynamic HTML, or DHTML, which helps make documents (inter)active, and of cascading style sheets and other markup models that strive to separate document markup from document content. By separating markup and content, it becomes possible to create the appropriate style sheets for each browser without having to create and maintain two separate versions of documents. Style sheets can be reused for multiple documents, which also saves development time.

The next arena for competition among browser developers will probably have to do with implementing XML (eXtensible Markup Language) support in the browser. (XML is the more powerful and flexible successor to HTML.)

The terms *browser* and *browsing* are also used in a somewhat different sense in Microsoft Windows NT networks. In NT networks, a browser provides information about the domains, servers, and resources that are available to a particular network domain. Such information is made available through browse lists, and browsing simply refers to the act of requesting such lists from an appropriate browser.

NT networks can have several types of browsers, including the following:

- One Domain Master Browser, which maintains the master browse list containing information about all servers and resources in all domains of the network. The Domain Master Browser role will be played by the network's primary domain controller (PDC).

- Zero or more Master Browsers, which are needed in domains that use the TCP/IP protocol suite and that span more than a single subnet. Master Browsers make it possible to exchange browser lists across domains— despite the fact that the browser lists that are broadcast by the Domain Master Browser are filtered out by routers in TCP/IP networks. (In networks that use other protocol stacks, such as IPX/SPX, the broadcasts are passed across the routers, so that there is no need for Master Browsers to exchange lists.)

- Zero or more Backup Browsers, which are used to offload traffic from the Domain Master Browser, and which can also become a Domain Master Browser if necessary.

- Zero or more Potential Browsers, which are machines that do not function as browsers, but that could be configured to do so if necessary or desirable. Potential Browsers participate in selecting browsers for a network.

→ *See Also* Applet; HotJava; Microsoft Internet Explorer; Netscape Navigator; WWW (World Wide Web)

BSD Socket Layer

In BSD UNIX, the layer that represents the API (Application Program Interface) between user applications and the networking subsystem in the operating system kernel.

BSD UNIX (Berkeley Software Distribution UNIX)

A UNIX version implemented at the University of California, Berkeley. BSD UNIX introduced several enhancements to AT&T's original implementation, including virtual memory, networking, and interprocess communication support.

BTAM (Basic Telecommunications Access Method)

An early access method for communications between IBM mainframes and terminals. BTAM is still used, but is largely obsolete because it does not support IBM's SNA (Systems Network Architecture). ACF/VTAM has replaced BTAM as the method of choice for remote communications with IBM mainframes.

Btrieve

In Novell's NetWare 3.0 and later, Btrieve is a key-indexed record management program that allows you to access, update, create, delete, or save records from a database. Btrieve is a program (actually several programs) that can run in either of two versions: client- or server-based.

In addition to record-management capabilities, Btrieve includes the following:

- Communications facilities, for both local and remote communications between a program and a record base. The Btrieve Message Routers (BROUTER.NLM and BDROUTER.NLM) handle outgoing requests; BSPXCOM handles incoming requests from a remote source (a workstation or another server).

- Requesters (DOS, OS/2, and so on), which provide Btrieve access for applications running on workstations. The requesters are: BREQUEST.EXE (for DOS), BTRCALLS .DLL (for OS/2), and WBTRCALL.DLL (for Windows).

- Utilities for setting up, monitoring, and maintaining the record base, among other things. These utilities are mentioned briefly in the next section.

- Special data-protection measures for dealing with the record base in case of system failure. In addition to the standard ones such as record locking, data-protection measures include *logging*, which records any changes made to designated files so that the changes can be undone later, if necessary. The *roll forward* modules mentioned in the next section provide the mechanism for such corrections. Data-protection measures also include *shadow paging*, in which page images are saved before making any changes on the page. Btrieve can back up files even while they're in use by using *continuous operation*.

- Support for NetWare Directory Services (NDS), which are new with NetWare 4.*x*. This support is available only beginning with version 6.1 of Btrieve.

- Security measures such as the ability to encrypt and decrypt data and also the ability to assign ownership to files.

- Memory management and caching capabilities to help speed up access and other operations.

Btrieve creates and maintains a key-indexed record base (or database). A key-indexed database is one in which keys, or record fields, are used as the basis for creating an index, which is information that guides access to a database.

A Btrieve record base uses a specially defined data format, which is also supported by database programs and other applications from third-party vendors.

Btrieve-Related Modules

The Btrieve programs are provided in NetWare Loadable Modules (NLMs). The most fundamental of these are BTRIEVE.NLM and BSPXCOM.NLM.

BTRIEVE contains the Record Manager program that does the work on the server. This program performs disk I/O (input/output) for Btrieve files on the server. This program must be loaded on any server that has Btrieve files.

BSPXCOM handles requests to the server from any workstation or another remote source. BSPXCOM must be loaded on any server that needs to communicate with a Btrieve requester program on a workstation.

Such a Btrieve requester must be loaded on any workstation that needs to communicate with a Btrieve record base. This program relays requests from the user or from an application to the Record Manager on the appropriate server.

Other NLMs handle more specialized duties. For example, BROUTER.NLM and BDROUTER .NLM handle Btrieve-related requests from a server to a remote server. The illustration "Relationships of Btrieve elements" shows how the various Btrieve elements fit together.

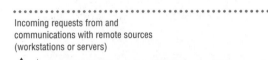

Incoming requests from and communications with remote sources (workstations or servers)

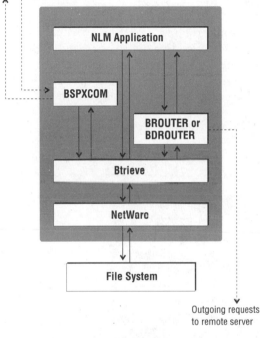

Outgoing requests to remote server

RELATIONSHIPS OF BTRIEVE ELEMENTS

Several Btrieve utilities provide the more nitty-gritty services needed to handle the record bases:

- BTRMON.NLM monitors Btrieve activity on the server.

- BSETUP.NLM and BREBUILD.NLM are used to change configurations and to update Btrieve data files from version 5.x to 6.x, respectively.

- BUTIL.NLM imports and exports Btrieve data, and transfers data between Btrieve files.

- BDIRECT.NLM provides support for the NDS in NetWare 4.x. This NLM is available only in Btrieve versions 6.1 and later.

- BROLLFWD.EXE (for DOS), PBROLL .EXE (for OS/2), and WBROLL.EXE (for Windows) are the roll forward utilities. These are used to restore a Btrieve file in case of some type of system failure.

Server- and Client-Based Btrieve

The server-based version runs the Btrieve Record Manager on the server and a special (operating system dependent) requester program on the workstation. The Record Manager handles the I/O for the database; the requester handles the I/O between workstation and server.

The client-based version does all its processing on the workstation, and makes I/O calls (calls involving the record base) through the workstation's operating system. The client-based version is available only to developers who want to create applications that can use Btrieve data files.

If the calls are for the server's record base, the Btrieve requester redirects the calls to the server. The illustration "A client and server using Btrieve" shows this situation. Note that the Btrieve requester is provided as part of a server-based Btrieve implementation.

→ *Broader Category* NetWare

BTU (Basic Transmission Unit)

In IBM's SNA communications, an aggregate block of one or more path information units (PIUs) that all have the same destination. Several PIUs can be combined into a single packet, even if they are not all part of the same message. BTUs are created at the path-control layer.

→ *See Also* SNA (Systems Network Architecture)

B

Buffered Distributor

In Gigabit Ethernet, a buffered distributor is used to help avoid collisions while giving each network user full bandwidth. Also known as a full-duplex repeater, a buffered distributor can provide 1Gbps connections in full-duplex mode for each user connected to the network.

If a collision is detected on the network, the buffered distributor can hold the contents of a transmission (that is, buffer it) until the medium is available. Or the distributor can send the material in the other direction on the network—that is, in the direction opposite to the traffic already in transit.

A buffered distributor can check for traffic congestion and monitor flow control; however, it cannot guarantee a given quality of service. Such a device is less expensive than a true gigabit switch, but the distributor also lacks some of the switch's

capabilities. Specifically, the switch can operate at layer 3 (the network layer), whereas the buffered distributor operates at layer 2. The switch can also guarantee quality of service.

The full-duplex distributor is more expensive, but also more powerful, than a half-duplex repeater. The latter can provide less than 1Gbps bandwidth, cannot do flow control, and cannot avoid collisions.

Buffer, Fiber-Optic Cable

In fiber-optic cabling, a layer immediately surrounding the cladding (which surrounds the fiber core). The tighter this buffer is wrapped around the cladding, the less opportunity the cladding and core have to move around in the cable.

→ *See Also* Cable, Fiber-Optic

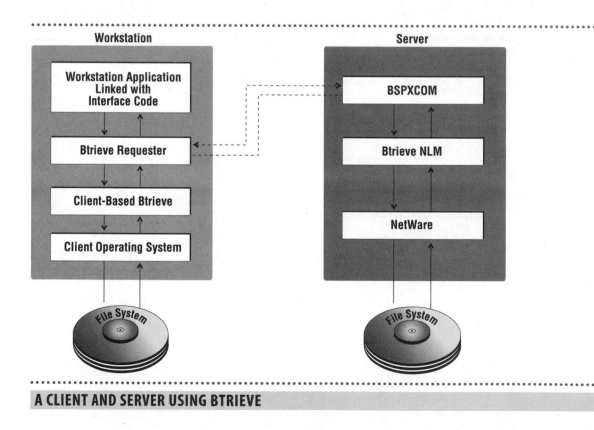

A CLIENT AND SERVER USING BTRIEVE

Buffer, Memory

In memory or storage applications, a buffer is a temporary storage location that is generally used to hold intermediate values, or other types of data, until they can be processed. The storage may be allocated in ordinary RAM (random access memory), on a hard disk, or in special memory registers (such as on a UART chip, which is used for serial communications).

A print buffer is one common example. A spooler program saves a file to be printed in the print buffer, and deals with the file as CPU (central processing unit) availability allows. Buffers provide faster access to stored data.

Three types of buffer allocations are distinguished:

File-cache buffer   Used to store disk-allocation blocks temporarily.

Directory-cache buffer   Used to store the DET (directory-entry table) blocks.

Packet-receive buffer   Used to hold incoming packets until they can be processed.

Buffered Repeater

In a network cabling scheme, a buffered repeater is a device that can clean and boost signals before sending them on. A buffered repeater can hold a message temporarily, for example, when there is already a transmission on the network. In Ethernet networks, a buffered repeater can help prevent collisions by holding traffic when the repeater detects a packet already on the network.

→ *See Also*   Repeater

Bulletin Board System (BBS)

→ *See*   BBS (Bulletin Board System)

Bundle

In cabling, a bundle is a group of wires or optical fibers within a cable. The wires (or fibers) in a bundle have the same electrical (or optical) specifications.

Burned-In Address (BIA)

→ *See*   BIA (Burned-In Address)

Burst

In communications, a burst is a sequence of signals that are transmitted together, without interruption. For example, a transmitting device with a buffer may wait until the buffer reaches a predefined level; once this happens, the device may then transmit continuously until the buffer is empty. A device transmitting in this way is said to be in *burst mode*.

A burst is in contrast to a continuous stream of data transmitted at a constant rate.

Burstiness

In the CCITT recommendations for BISDN, a measure of the distribution of data over time. The definition for the term has not yet been finalized. One definition being considered is the ratio between maximum, or peak, and mean (average) bit rate.

Burst Mode

A high-speed transmission mode in which the transmitter takes control of the communications channel temporarily, until its transmission is complete. This mode is used in internal communications, such as between hard disk and bus, and also in communications between devices. The term is also used to refer to the packet burst protocol in NetWare.

Burst Speed

The maximum speed at which a device can operate without interruption, generally only for short periods. This is in contrast to *throughput*, which indicates the average speed at which a device can operate under ordinary conditions, such as when transmitting or printing an entire file.

Bursty Data

Transmissions that come in variable-sized blocks arriving at irregular intervals are said to consist of bursty data. The expected burstiness of network traffic can have important consequences for network planning and design and for traffic management on an existing network.

Bus

In computer hardware, a *bus* is a path for electrical signals, generally between the CPU (central processing unit) and attached hardware. Buses differ in the number of bit values they can carry at a time, in their speed, and in their control mechanisms.

Bit values   In the PC world, 8-, 16-, and 32-bit data buses are common. On workstations and larger machines, 64- and 80-bit buses are common.

Speed   The speed of a bus depends on the system clock. Bus speed is generally measured in megahertz (MHz). The IBM-PC bus has gone from a 4.77MHz clock speed in the original PC to 100MHz in today's high-end machines. Other types of chips can support clock speeds of well over 100MHz.

Control   Buses may be controlled through interrupts or through polling.

In networking, bus refers to a logical and physical network topology in which messages are broadcast along the main cable, so that all nodes receive each transmission at the same time. Standard Ethernet and certain ARCnet networks use a bus topology.

→ *See Also*   Topology, Bus

Bus Interface Board (BIB)

→ *See*   BIB (Bus Interface Board)

Bus Interface Unit (BIU)

→ *See*   BIU (Bus Interface Unit)

Bus Mastering

In general, bus mastering is a bus-access method in which a card or device takes control of the bus in order to send data onto the bus directly, without help from the CPU (central processing unit). In a network, the network interface card takes control of the bus.

Generally, MCA (Microchannel Architecture) and EISA (Extended Industry Standard Architecture) machines support bus mastering, but ISA (Industry Standard Architecture) machines do not. VL (VESA local) and PCI (Peripheral Component Interconnect) buses also support bus mastering.

Bus mastering can improve throughput considerably, but only if the board and the computer support the same bus-mastering method, *and* if the bus mastering doesn't conflict with the hard-disk controller.

Several types of transfer modes are possible with bus mastering, including burst mode, streaming data mode, and data duplexing. A particular bus-mastering scheme may support some or all of these modes.

Bus Topology

→ *See* Topology, Bus

Bypass

In telephony, a bypass is a connection with an interexchange carrier (IXC) that does not go through a local exchange carrier.

Byte

A collection of—usually eight—bits (but rarely worth a dollar anymore). A byte generally represents a character or digit.

Bytecode

In Java programming, bytecode is an intermediate code format that provides a platform-independent version of a compiled Java program. The bytecode file is created from Java source code by the Java compiler. The bytecode file can be executed on any platform for which a platform-specific bytecode interpreter is available. This bytecode interpreter is known as the Java Virtual Machine (JVM).

The JVM is built into browsers that support Java. The JVM enables the browser to run applets encountered in HTML (Hypertext Markup Language) files.

Bytecode files are interpreted during execution. This is generally a slower process than executing a program that has been compiled to a platform-specific native format. One way to help get extra speed—but at the cost of portability—is to use a just-in-time (JIT) compiler to convert the bytecode to a native format. Once this is done, however, the compiled file will no longer be portable.

→ *Broader Category* Java

Byte-Control Protocols (BCP)

BCPs are protocols that are character-oriented, as opposed to bit-oriented.

Byte-Oriented Protocol

→ *See* Protocol, Byte-Oriented

Byte-Sex

For a processor, byte-sex is a feature that describes the order in which bytes are represented in a word. Processors may be little-endian, big-endian, or bytesexual.

In little-endian representations, the low-order byte in a word is stored at the lower address. In big-endian processors or contexts, the high-order byte is stored first. *Bytesexual* is a term used to describe a process that is capable of using either little-endian or big-endian representations for information, depending on the value of a flag bit.

→ *See Also* Big-Endian; Little-Endian; Middle-Endian

Byzantine Failure/Byzantine Robustness

In networking, a situation in which a node fails by behaving incorrectly or improperly, rather than by breaking down completely and disappearing from the network. A network that can keep working even if one or more nodes is experiencing Byzantine failure has *Byzantine robustness*.

B

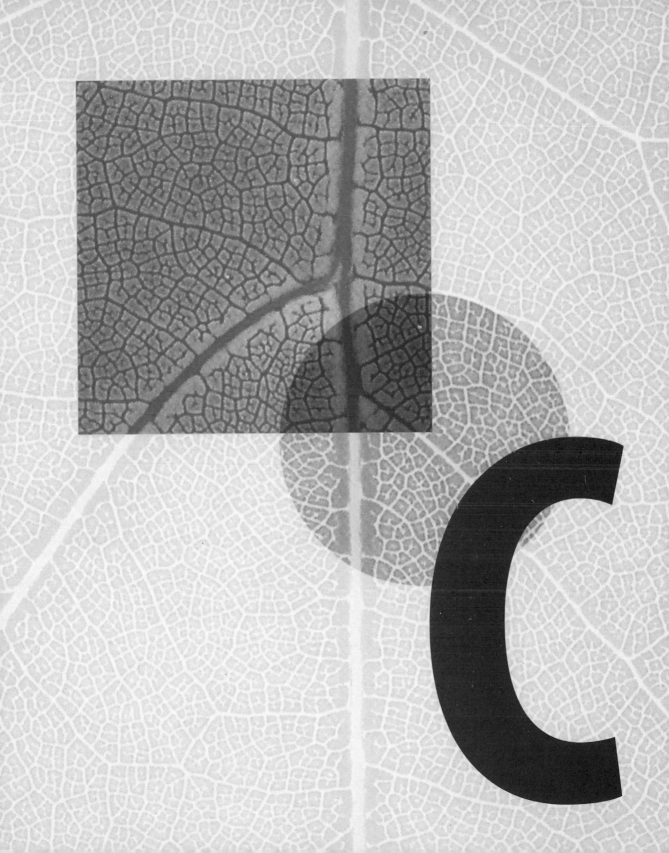

C

C is a high-level programming language that has had great popularity and influence because it gives programmers considerable access to low-level machine structures and very powerful capabilities for creating and using data structures. These capabilities, together with its speed, make C a suitable language for systems programming.

Originally developed at AT&T's Bell Labs by Brian Kernighan and Dennis Ritchie, C was used to program an early version of the UNIX operating system—both to implement the operating system and to demonstrate the viability of C for such systems programming tasks.

C remains an active programming language, but it has largely been superseded by C++, its object-oriented successor. *The C Programming Language* by Kernighan and Ritchie (1978, Prentice-Hall) provides a summary of the language by its creators, and it also happens to be one of clearest programming language books you're ever likely to see.

→ *See Also* C++

C++

C++ is an object-oriented programming language developed by Bjarne Stroustrup at AT&T Bell Labs. Most generally, C++ is the C language augmented with a concept of classes. This class component, which gives C++ its object-oriented capabilities, was borrowed from the earlier Simula programming language. (The language's name is a play on notation: ++ is the C-language increment operator, which adds 1 to the variable being incremented. C++ can be viewed as C with something added.)

C++ is widely used for both general and systems programming tasks. In fact, until Java was developed, C++ was arguably the most commonly used programming language for Web-related programming. For a somewhat rambling and very personal account of the language and its creation, see Stroustrup's

The Design and Evolution of C++ (1994, Addison-Wesley). The book provides excellent insights into the concepts and issues important for designing, understanding, and using an object-oriented programming language.

→ *See Also* C

CA (Certificate Authority)

A certificate (or certification) authority is an entity that can create signed encrypted certificates, which are used to authenticate services, transactions, or users on a network. Essentially, a CA creates a certificate for a client and then signs it to vouch for the client. The entire package is encrypted to make it (virtually) impossible to forge.

Because it is creating products used for security purposes, a certificate authority must itself be trusted and secure. It must be able to generate keys for encryption, and must be able to ensure the integrity of these keys. Commercial CAs include Verisign (which still does many of the certificates currently in circulation), GTE, and the U.S. Postal Service.

"Official" CAs have, in turn, certified other CAs—at a lower level in the trust hierarchy. This certificate authority hierarchy serves to provide quality control over the CAs so that clients of these later generation CAs can have confidence in the certificates they issue. Despite the existence of such hierarchies, it is easy to set up a CA that has not been certified.

→ *See Also* Certificate Server

Cable

It took about 100 years for wire to replace the kite string as a medium for electrical power, but the change was heartily welcomed, particularly by researchers. The first electrical wires were heavy, thick, naked, and noisy iron lines. The wire was about as thick as coat hanger wire, and was unshielded. Eventually, copper became the medium of choice for electrical wiring, and shielding was developed to insulate the wires. It then became feasible to group multiple wires together and cover them with an outer casing. And, voilà, the cable is born. Cables are currently the most popular medium for transmitting information between nodes in a network, although wireless transmission schemes (radio, infrared, and microwave communications) are becoming more widely used.

Network Cabling Schemes

In a network, the cabling scheme connects nodes (or stations) and also gives the network its characteristic shape (topology) and features. Network cabling schemes distinguish between main and auxiliary cables. The main cable provides the path and defines the shape for the network; the auxiliary cables connect nodes to the main path or to wiring centers that are connected to the main path. Depending on the architecture, the terminology for such cables differs.

Ethernet Trunk and Drop Cables

For Ethernet networks, the main cable is referred to as the *trunk cable*, and the auxiliary cables are called *drop cables*. Trunk cable forms the backbone, or main cabling scheme of an Ethernet network. Because of its role and location, trunk cable is sometimes called *backbone cable*. Drop cable may be used to attach an individual node to a network trunk cable. Nodes can also be connected to the cable indirectly through a connector or transceiver rather than with drop cable. The different types of connectors are discussed in a separate article.

IBM Token Ring

IBM Token Ring networks distinguish between the main ring path and patch cables. In this context, patch cables attach nodes (called *lobes* in Token Ring networks) to wiring centers. The wiring centers are called multistation attachment units (MAUs) in such networks. The patch cables can also attach to patch panels, which are, in turn, connected to MAUs.

Cable Types

Four main types of cable are used in networks:

- Coaxial cable, also called coax, which can be thin or thick.

- Twisted-pair cable, which can be shielded (STP) or unshielded (UTP).

- IBM cable, which is essentially twisted-pair cable, but designed to somewhat more stringent specifications by IBM. Several types are defined, and they are used primarily in IBM Token Ring networks.

- Fiber-optic cable, which can be single-mode, multimode, or graded-index multimode.

Coaxial, IBM, and twisted-pair cables transmit electricity. Fiber-optic cables transmit light signals. Each of the cable types is subdivided into more specialized categories and has its own design and specifications, standards, advantages, and disadvantages.

Cable types differ in price, transmission speed, and recommended transmission distance. For example, twisted-pair wiring is currently the cheapest (and also the most limited in performance). Fiber-optic cable is more expensive but much faster and more robust. Coaxial cable lies between these two types on most performance and price features.

This article discusses network cabling in general. The specific cable types (coaxial, twisted-pair, IBM, and fiber-optic) are covered in more detail in separate articles. In addition to this cabling, there is a cable infrastructure behind the walls, in shafts, and under the ground. These cables are discussed under the headings "Cable, Horizontal" and "Cable, Backbone."

Cable Components

The different cable types have the following components in common:

- A conductor to provide a medium for the signal. The conductor might be a copper wire or a glass tube.

- Insulation of some sort around the conductor to help keep the signal in and interference out.

- An outer sheath, or jacket, to encase the cable elements. The jacket keeps the cable components together, and may also help protect the cable components from water, pressure, or other types of damage.

In addition to these common features, particular types of cable have other components. Coaxial cable has one or more shields between the insulation and the jacket. Twisted-pair cable has two conductor wires twisted around each other. Fiber-optic cable may include material to help protect the fiber from pressure.

Conductor

For electrical cable, the conductor is known as the *signal*, or *carrier*, *wire*, and it may consist of either solid or stranded wire. Solid wire is a single thick strand of conductive material, usually copper. Stranded wire consists of many thin strands of conductive material wound tightly together.

Signal wire is described in the following terms:

- The wire's conductive material (for example, copper)

- Whether the wire is stranded or solid

- The carrier wire's diameter, expressed directly (for example, in inches, centimeters, or millimeters), or in terms of the wire's gauge, as specified in the AWG (American Wire Gauge) tables (see the AWG article for a summary of gauges)

The total diameter of the strand determines some of the wire's electrical properties, such as resistance and impedance. These properties, in turn, help determine the wire's performance.

For fiber-optic cable, the conductor is known as the *core*. The core is a glass or plastic tube that runs through the cable. The diameter of this core is expressed in microns (millionths of a meter).

Insulation Layer

The insulating layer keeps the transmission medium's signal from escaping and also helps to protect the signal from outside interference. For electrical wires, the insulation is usually made of a dielectric (nonconductor), such as polyethylene. Some types of coaxial cable have multiple protective layers around the signal wire.

For fiber-optic cable, the insulation is known as *cladding* and is made of material with a lower refraction index than the core's material. The refraction index is a measure that indicates the manner in which a material will reflect light rays. The lower refraction index ensures that light bounces back off the cladding and remains in the core.

Plenum Cable Jacket

The outer casing, or jacket, of the cable provides a shell that keeps the cable's elements together. Two main classes of jacket are plenum and nonplenum. For certain environments, plenum cable is required by law. It must be used when the cable is being run "naked" (without being put in a conduit) inside walls, and should probably be used whenever possible.

Plenum jackets are made of nonflammable fluoropolymers (such as Teflon or Kynar). They are fire-resistant and do not give off toxic fumes when burning. They are also considerably more expensive (by a factor of 1.5 to 3) than cables with nonplenum jackets. Studies have shown that cables with plenum jackets have less signal loss than nonplenum cables.

Plenum cable used for networks should meet the NEC's CMP (National Electric Code's communications plenum cable) or CL2P (class 2 plenum cable) specifications. The cable should also be UL-listed for UL-910, which subjects plenum cable to a flammability test. The NEC and UL specifications are discussed in the Cable Standards article.

Nonplenum Cable Jacket

Nonplenum cable uses less expensive material for jackets, so it is considerably less expensive than cable with plenum jackets, but it can be used only under restricted conditions. Nonplenum cable jackets are made of polyethylene (PE) or polyvinylchloride (PVC), which will burn and give off toxic fumes.

PVC cable used for networks should meet the NEC's CMR (communications riser cable) or CL2R (class 2 riser cable) specifications. The cable should also be UL-listed for UL-1666, which subjects riser cable to a flammability test. See the Cable Standards article for a discussion of cable safety standards and performance levels.

Cable Packaging

Cables can be packaged in different ways, depending on what it is being used for and where it is located. For example, the IBM cable topology specifies a flat cable for use under carpets. Some fiber-optic trunks contain thousands of fibers, each of which can carry multiple messages.

The following types of cable packaging are available:

Simplex cable   One cable within one jacket, which is the default configuration. The term is used mainly for fiber-optic cable to indicate that the jacket contains only a single fiber.

Duplex cable   Two cables, or fibers, within a single jacket. In fiber-optic cable, this is a common arrangement. One fiber is used to transmit in each direction.

Multifiber cable   Multiple cables, or fibers, within a single jacket. For fiber-optic cable, a single jacket may contain thousands of fibers; for electrical cable, the jacket will contain at most a few dozen cables.

Cable Properties

Cable is described in terms of the size and makeup of its components, as well as in terms of the cable's performance. For example, electrical cable specifications include the gauge, or diameter, of the signal wire.

The cable's electrical and physical properties determine the performance you can expect and the range of conditions under which you can use the cable. Cables differ in the electrical properties (signal loss, impedance, and so on) they offer. The table "Cable Properties" lists some of the features that distinguish cables.

CABLE PROPERTIES

Property	Measurement or Description	Comment
Size		
Conductor wire diameter	Millimeters (mm), inches (in), or gauge (AWG)	For stranded wire, this represents the total diameter of the entire cluster of strands.
Core fiber diameter	Microns	In optical fiber, some core diameters have desirable properties in terms of the paths certain wavelengths of light take in the core. For example, diameters of 62.5 and 100 microns for multimode fiber and of under 10 microns for single-mode fiber are common.
Wire insulation diameter	Millimeters or inches	The diameter of the cable's insulation layer is needed to calculate certain electrical properties of a cable.
Cladding diameter	Microns	For optical fiber, the cladding diameter varies much less than the core diameter, partly because the cladding helps to make the fiber easier to package if the cladding is of an approximately constant size.
Wire shield diameter	Millimeters, inches, or gauge	
Jacket diameter	Millimeters or inches	The diameter of the jacket can be important when installing the cable because it may determine space requirements.

Continued on next page

C

CABLE PROPERTIES (continued)

Property	Measurement or Description	Comment
Composition		
Conductor wire composition	Materials; Solid vs. stranded (# of strands)	Conductor wires may be solid or stranded, or of different types of conductive material (usually copper alone or in some variant). If the wire is stranded, the specifications should note the number of strands.
Wire insulation composition	Materials	
Shield composition	Materials; % area covered by shield mesh	For coaxial cable only, shield composition refers to the makeup of the protective shield around the conductor wire.
Jacket composition	Materials; plenum vs. non-plenum	
Electrical Properties		
DCR (DC Resistance)	Ohms (&o) per distance (100 or 1000 feet)	Refers to the DC resistance for the conductor wire.
Shield DCR	Ohms (&o) per distance (100 or 1000 feet)	Refers to the DC resistance for the shield.
Impedance	Ohms	The measure of a wire's inertial resistance to changes in electrical current, which helps determine the wire's attenuation properties. Most networks use cable with a characteristic impedance level. There are devices for connecting cable segments that have different impedances.
Capacitance	Picofarads per foot (pF/ft)	The measure of the cable's ability to store up electrical charge or voltage. This charge storage distorts a signal as it travels along its course; the lower the capacitance the better.
Attenuation	Maximum decibels per distance at given frequency; common distances include 100 feet, 1000 feet, and 1 kilometer, e.g., dB/1000 ft at 5MHz	The measure of the signal loss over distance. Data sheets may include several attenuation values for different frequencies. This distinction can be important because attenuation of an electrical signal increases with signal frequency.
Crosstalk (NEXT)	Minimum decibels per distance (1000 or 100 feet) (dB/distance)	NEXT (near-end crosstalk) is a common measure of interference by a signal from a neighboring cable or circuit. The higher the decibel value, the less crosstalk.
Velocity of Propagation	% (values should be about 60%; preferably above 80%)	Specifies the maximum signal speed along the wire, as a proportion of the theoretical maximum (the speed of light).
Other Properties		
Weight	Unit weight per distance (oz/ft; gm/m) Maximum recommended cable segment range	Distance (feet, meters, or kilometers).
Bandwidth	Megahertz (MHz) or megabits per second (Mbps)	
Price	Dollars per distance (100 or 1000 feet)	The price of the actual cable is often insignificant compared to the price of installation.
Performance/Safety Ratings	NEC CL2, CMP, and CMR; EIA/TIA-568 Categories 1-5; UL Levels 1-5; ETL ratings	See the Cable Standards article for information about these cable safety standards.

You can obtain the specifications for a specific type of cable from the cable manufacturer or vendor. The table "Cable Component Abbreviations" lists some common abbreviations used in cable specifications or data sheets.

CABLE COMPONENT ABBREVIATIONS

Abbreviation	Feature	Component(s)
AD	Air dielectric	Insulation
AL	Aluminum braid	Shield
ALS	Aluminum sheath	Shield
AWG	American Wire Gauge (AWG) value for wire	Carrier wire
BC	Bare copper braid	Carrier wire; shield
CCAL	Copper-clad aluminum	Carrier wire
CCS	Copper-covered steel	Carrier wire
FEP	Fluorinated ethylene propylene (Teflon)	Insulation; jacket
FFEP	Foamed fluorinated ethylene propylene (Teflon)	Insulation
FP	Foamed polyethylene	Insulation
K	Kynar/polyvinylidene fluoride (plenum)	Jacket
PE	Polyethylene (solid)	Insulation; jacket
PVC	Polyvinylchloride	Jacket
PVDF	Generic polyvinylidene fluoride (plenum)	Jacket
SC	Silvered copper braid	Carrier wire; shield
TC	Tinned copper braid	Carrier wire; shield
x%	Percentage of surface area covered by braid	Shield
#cond	Number of conductors	Carrier wire

Factors Affecting Cable Performance

Cables are good media for signals, but they are not perfect. Ideally, the signal at the end of a stretch of cable should be as loud and clear as at the beginning. Unfortunately, this will not be true.

Any transmission consists of signal and noise components. Even a digital signal degrades when transmitted over a wire or through an open medium. This is because the binary information must be converted to electrical form for transmission, and because the shape of the electrical signal changes over distance.

Signal quality degrades for several reasons, including attenuation, crosstalk, and impedance.

Attenuation

Attenuation is a decrease in signal strength, and it is usually measured in decibels (dB) per 100 feet or per kilometer. Such loss happens as the signal travels over the wire. Attenuation occurs more quickly at higher frequencies and when the cable's resistance is higher.

In networking environments, repeaters are responsible for cleaning and boosting a signal before passing it on. Many devices are repeaters without explicitly saying so. For example, each node in a token-ring network acts as a repeater. Since attenuation is sensitive to frequency, some situations require the use of equalizers to boost different frequency signals the appropriate amount.

Crosstalk

Crosstalk is interference in the form of a signal from a neighboring cable or circuit; for example, signals on different pairs of twisted wire in a twisted-pair cable may interfere with each other. A commonly used measure of this interference in twisted-pair cable is near-end crosstalk (NEXT), which is represented in decibels. The higher the decibel value, the less crosstalk and the better the cable.

Additional shielding between the carrier wire and the outside world is the most common way to decrease the effects of crosstalk.

Impedance

Impedance, which is a measure of electrical resistance to change in current, is not directly a factor in a cable's performance. However, impedance can become a factor if it has different levels at different locations in a network. In order to minimize the disruptive effects of different impedances in a network, special devices, called *baluns*, are used to equalize impedance at the connection (at the balun location).

Impedance does reflect performance indirectly, however. In general, the higher the impedance, the higher the resistance. And, the higher the resistance, the greater the attenuation at higher frequencies.

Cable Imperfections

Cables bend, twist, crack, get cut, and corrode. All of these changes from the cable's pristine state affect the cable's performance. A bend or twist in a cable can bring wires closer to each other, which can increase the effects of interference between them. In optical fiber, a bend—even a microbend of less than a millimeter or so—can bounce the light signal in a manner that is detrimental to the quality of the main signal.

CABLE TIPS

Here are some tips on purchasing and installing cabling:

- Cables have quite a few properties that should be considered in making decisions. You can find information about these cable properties in cable specifications or data sheets, which are available from cable vendors.

- In general, cable that meets military specifications (MIL-SPECS) is designed to more stringent requirements, and so is a good choice for networks. This is even more true for connectors, because the military specifications insist on durable and reliable connectors. (Connectors are particularly prone to shoddy construction.)

- Fiber-optic connectors are especially tricky to attach because fiber optics has such exact alignment requirements. It's probably worth your while to let a professional attach these connectors.

- When you're ordering cable, make sure it's clear whether you want cable with connectors or "raw" (bulk) cable.

- Make sure the cable is good quality. Otherwise, you'll have trouble after a while, as the insulation within and outside the cable breaks down.

- Test cable both *before* and *after* installing it.

- While present needs are obviously the major determinant of cabling decisions, future plans should also be taken into consideration. In general, at least consider installing cable one level more powerful than you think you'll need.

- When adding cable to an existing cabling system, find out exactly what kind of cable is already in place. The safest thing is to get the actual part and specification information from the cable jacket, then order exactly that from the same distributor (or a certified equivalent from a different manufacturer).

- Before adding to existing cable, test it as thoroughly as possible. If the cable seems likely to have a major breakdown within a few months, it's almost certainly better to replace it now.

- Protect the cable as much as possible. Such measures should include protecting the cable from temperature or moisture changes, which can cause the cable to crack or melt.

- Support the cable as much as possible, so that a hanging cable doesn't stretch because the cable's own weight is pulling it downward.

- Velcro cable ties can help make things neater, by enabling you to collect multiple loose wires into a single cluster. The Rip-Tie Company in San Francisco is one vendor that offers these neatness aids.

Cracks or complete breaks in wire can lead to short circuits or to the circuit being broken. Corrosion in the shielding or wire can lead to signal interference.

Selecting Cable

Cables are used to meet all sorts of power and signaling requirements. The demands made on a cable depend on the location in which the cable is used and the function for which the cable is intended. These demands, in turn, determine the features a cable should have.

Function and Location

Here are a few examples of considerations involving the cable's function and location:

- Cable designed to run over long distances, such as between floors or buildings, should be robust against environmental factors (moisture, temperature changes, and so on). This may require extra jackets or jackets made with a special material. Fiber-optic cable performs well, even over distances much longer than a floor or even a building.

- Cable that must run around corners should bend easily, and the cable's properties and performance should not be affected by the bending. For several reasons, twisted-pair cable is probably the best cable for such a situation (assuming it makes sense within the rest of the wiring scheme). Of course, another way to get around a corner is by using a connector; however, connectors may introduce signal-loss problems.

- Cable that must run through areas in which powerful engines or motors are operating (or worse, being turned on and off at random intervals) must be able to withstand magnetic interference. Large equipment gives off strong magnetic fields, which can interfere with and disrupt nearby signals. In commercial and residential settings, this can be a problem with cable that is run, for example, through the elevator shaft. Because it is not affected by such

electrical or magnetic fluctuations, fiber-optic cable is the best choice in machinery-intensive environments.

- If you need to run lots of cables through a limited area, cable weight can become a factor, particularly if all that cable will be running in the ceiling above *you*. In general, fiber-optic and twisted-pair cables tend to be lightest.

- Cables being installed in barely accessible locations must be particularly reliable, and they should probably be laid with backup cable during the initial installation. Some consultants and mavens advise laying a second cable whenever you are installing cable, on the assumptions that the installation is much more expensive than the cable and that installation costs for the second cable add only marginally to the total cost. Generally, the suggestion is to make at least the second cable optical fiber.

- Cables that need to interface with other worlds (for example, with a mainframe network or a different electrical or optical system) may need special properties or adapters. For example, UTP cable in a Token Ring network needs a media filter between the cable and the MAU (media access unit) to which the cable is attached. The kinds of cable required will depend on the details of the environments and the transition between them.

Main Cable Selection Factors

Along with the function and location considerations, cable selections are determined by a combination of factors, including the following:

- The type of network you plan to create (Ethernet, Gigabit Ethernet, Token Ring, or another type). While it is possible to use just about any type of cable in any type of network, certain cable types have been more closely associated with particular network

C

types. For example, Token Ring networks use twisted-pair cable.

- The amount of money you have available for the network. Keep in mind that cable installation can be an expensive part of the network costs.

- Whatever cabling resources are already available (and usable). You will almost certainly have available wiring that could conceivably be used for a network. It is almost equally certain, however, that at least some of that wire is defective or is not up to the requirements for your network.

- Building or other safety codes and regulations.

Connected versus Bulk Cable

You can get cable with or without connectors at either end. Both connected and bulk cable have advantages and drawbacks. Whether connected or bulk cable is better depends on how you are going to use the cable.

You have much more flexibility to cut or reroute with bulk cable, because you are not restricted to a precut cable segment. On the other hand, you (or someone you trust) will need to attach the connectors. This requires special tools and involves stripping the end of the cable and crimping the connector to this bare wire.

Cable Prices

Cable prices depend on factors such as the following:

- Type of cable (coaxial, twisted-pair, fiber-optic). In general, fiber-optic cable is the most expensive but the price is dropping rapidly. Fiber-optic cable is followed closely by thick coaxial cable. STP and thin coaxial follow in roughly that order, but with considerable overlap in prices. UTP is the least expensive type of cable.

- Whether cable comes in bulk or with connectors at either end. While price is an issue, this

question will be answered mainly by your needs for the cable.

- Whether the cable is plenum or nonplenum. Plenum versions can cost from 1.5 to 3 times as much as the nonplenum version.

Cable prices change, so do not be surprised to find considerable variation in prices when you start getting quotes.

UTP cable is grouped into voice- and data-grade. Most telephone wire is just voice-grade. Prices for data-grade UTP cable are a few cents higher per foot.

Cabling Tools

Installation tools for handling cables include wire strippers, dies, and crimping tools for attaching connectors to the end of a stretch of bulk cable. Such tools are often included in adapter kits, which are configured for building particular types of cable (for example, coaxial cable or cable for RS-232 connections). Depending on how comprehensive the toolkit is, expect to pay anywhere from about $30 to $500.

Testing tools for cables include a whole range of line scanners and monitors. The simplest of these can tell you whether there is any electrical activity between one location in a network (or a cable installation) and another. The most sophisticated can do just about everything except tell you where you bought the cable. Oddly enough, not even the best testing tools can tell you much about the wire within 20 feet or so of the tool. This is because the times involved for electrical or light signals to traverse this distance are too short to be reliably measured.

The top-of-the-line scanners can test any kind of copper-based cable not only for faults, but also for performance specifications (NEXT, attenuation, and so on). These types of scanners know about the electrical requirements of the most popular network architectures (such as Ethernet/802.3 and Token Ring) and are capable of finding faults or deviations from specifications at just about any location on the network. Of course, you will pay several thousand dollars for this capability.

Cable Vendors and Resources

Many companies sell both electrical and fiber-optic cable, as well as connectors, installation, and testing tools. Some vendors specialize in fiber-optic products, others in copper-based products, and still others offer both.

When you are ready to start looking for cabling and other components, it will be worthwhile getting the cabling guides and catalogs from several vendors. The guides offer useful general-purpose hints and guidelines for selecting and installing cable.

Here are some cable vendors and their telephone numbers:

AMP Incorporated   (800) 522-6752; (717) 564-0100

Andrew Corporation   (800) 328-2696; Fax (708) 349-5673

Berk-Tek   (800) 237-5835

Black Box Corporation   (800) 552-6816; (412) 746-5500

Comm/Scope   (800) 982-1708; (704) 324-2200; Fax (704) 459-5099

CSP (Computer System Products)   (800) 422-2537; (612) 476-6866; Fax (612) 476-6966

FIS (Fiber Instrument Sales)   (800) 445-2901; (315) 736-2206; Fax (315) 736-2285

Jensen Tools   (800) 426-1194; (602) 968-6231; Fax (800) 366-9662

Trompeter Electronics   (800) 982-2639; (818) 707-2020; Fax (818) 706-1040

→ *See Also*   Cable, Backbone; Cable, Coaxial; Cable, Fiber-Optic; Cable, Horizontal; Cable, IBM; Connector; Connector, Fiber-Optic

Cable, Adapter

Cable used to connect a Token Ring network interface card (NIC) to a hub or multistation access unit (MAU). IBM Type 1 and Type 6 cable can be used for this purpose. The IBM cables have a DB-9 or DB-25 connector at the NIC end and an IBM data connector at the MAU end.

Cable, Backbone

Backbone cable refers to the cable that forms the main trunk, or backbone, of a network, particularly an Ethernet network. Individual nodes and other devices may be connected to this cable using special adapters (such as transceivers) and a separate stretch of cable (called the *drop cable* in an Ethernet network) to the node.

More generally, backbone cable is defined by the EIA/TIA-568 committee as any "behind the scenes" cable—cable running behind walls, in shafts, or under the ground—that is not classified as horizontal cable. (Horizontal cable is defined by the EIA/TIA-568 committee as any cable that goes from a wiring closet, or distribution frame, to the wall outlet in the

EIA/TIA-568 MAIN AND OPTIONAL TYPES OF BACKBONE CABLE

Cable Type	Main	Optional
UTP	100-ohm, multipair UTP cable, to be used for voice-grade communications only	
STP	150-ohm STP cable, such as that defined in the IBM Cable System (ICS)	100-ohm STP cable
Coaxial	50-ohm thick coaxial cable, such as the cable used in thick Ethernet networks	75-ohm (broadband) coaxial cable, such as CATV cable
Optical fiber	62.5/125-micron (step- or graded-index) multimode optical fiber	Single-mode optical fiber

work area). This includes cable used to connect wiring closets and equipment rooms.

The EIA/TIA-568 recognizes four main types of backbone cable, and several optional variants. These types are listed in the table "EIA/TIA-568 Main and Optional Types of Backbone Cable."

→ *Compare* Cable, Horizontal

→ *See Also* Cable

Cable, Broadcast-Oriented

Cable that is designed to carry video signals sent from one location in the network, known as the *head-end*. This type of cable is generally designed for one-way communication, which makes it of limited value for use as network cable.

Cable, Category *x*

A five-level rating system for telecommunications wiring, specified in the EIA/TIA-568 documents. These categories describe minimum performance capabilities for unshielded twisted-pair cable. The five current categories are likely to be augmented with two additional categories—6 and 7—sometime over the next year or so.

→ *See Also* Cable Standards

Cable, CATV (Community Antenna Television, or Cable Television)

Wiring used for the transmission of cable television signals. CATV is broadband coaxial cable and is generally wired for one-directional transmission; that is, from the cable station, or a head-end, to the consumer. If the CATV cable is not one-directional, it may be possible to use it for network cabling.

Cable, Coaxial

Coaxial cable, often called coax, is used for data transmissions. This cable's remarkably stable electrical properties at frequencies below 1GHz (gigahertz) makes the cable popular for cable television (CATV) transmissions and for creating local area networks (LANs). Not surprisingly, coax is also used with the higher-speed cable modems, which the cable companies hope to make the method of choice for accessing the Internet from the home. Telephone company switching offices also use coaxial cable to route long-distance calls. "Context and properties of coaxial cable" summarizes the features of this type of cable.

Coaxial Cable Components

A coaxial cable consists of the following layers (moving outward from the center):

Carrier wire A conductor wire (the carrier, or signal, wire) is in the center. This wire is made of (or contains) copper and may be solid or stranded. There are restrictions regarding the wire composition for certain network configurations. The diameter of the signal wire is one factor in determining the attenuation (loss) of the signal over distance. The number of strands in a multistrand conductor also affects the attenuation.

Insulation An insulation layer consists of a dielectric (nonconductor) around the carrier wire. This dielectric is usually made of some form of polyethylene or Teflon.

Foil shield A thin foil shield around the dielectric. This shield usually consists of aluminum bonded to both sides of a tape. Not all coaxial cables have foil shielding; some have two foil shield layers, interspersed with braid shield layers.

Braid shield   A braid, or mesh, conductor, made of copper or aluminum, that surrounds the insulation and foil shield. This conductor can serve as the ground for the carrier wire. Together with the insulation and any foil shield, the braid shield protects the carrier wire from electromagnetic interference (EMI) and radio frequency interference (RFI). The braid and foil shields provide good protection against electrical interference, but only moderate protection against magnetic interference.

Jacket   An outer cover that can be either plenum (made of Teflon or Kynar) or nonplenum (made of polyethylene or polyvinylchloride).

The illustration "A coaxial cable has five layers" shows the makeup of a coaxial cable. The layers surrounding the carrier wire also help prevent signal loss due to radiation from the carrier wire. The signal and shield wires are concentric, or coaxial, hence the name.

C

Context

```
Cable
    Electrical
        Twisted-Pair
        Coaxial  ─────────────────────────┐
    Optical                                │
        Fiber-Optic                        │
                                           ▼
```

Coaxial Properties
Stable and predictable electrical properties
At least one shield around conductor wire
Subject to electromagnetic interference
Variable impedance levels
Thin and thick varieties
Broadband and baseband varieties
Thin coaxial uses BNC/TNC connectors; thick coaxial uses N-series connectors
Twinaxial runs two cables within a single jacket
Triaxial and quadrax have extra shielding for special uses

Coaxial Uses
Ethernet networks
ARCnet networks
Cable TV lines
Video cable
IBM mainframe and midrange-based networks (twinaxial)
Telephone switching offices

CONTEXT AND PROPERTIES OF COAXIAL CABLE

Conductor Wire
Made of copper, copper treated with tin or silver, or aluminum or steel covered with copper.

Dielectric
Made of a nonconductive material (such as polyethylene or Teflon), which may be solid or filled with air.

Foil Shield
Made of a polypropylene or polyester tape coated with aluminum on both sides.

Braid Shield
Made of flexible conductive wire braided around the dielectric (and foil shield). Braid may be made of aluminum or bare or treated copper. Braid is described in terms of the percentage coverage it gives. For example, 95% SC means 95% coverage with silvered copper.

Jacket
Made of polyvinylchloride or polyethylene for non-plenum cable; made of Teflon or Kynar for plenum cable.

A COAXIAL CABLE HAS FIVE LAYERS

Coaxial Cable Performance

The main features that affect the performance of coaxial cable are its composition, width, and impedance.

The carrier wire's composition determines how good a conductor the cable will be. Copper is among the best materials for this purpose. The IEEE specifies stranded copper carrier wire with tin coating for thin coaxial, and solid copper carrier wire for thick coaxial.

Cable width helps determine the electrical demands that can be made on the cable. In general, thick coaxial can support a much higher level of electrical activity than thin coaxial.

Impedance is a measure of opposition to the flow of alternating current. The properties of the dielectric between the carrier wire and the braid help determine the cable's impedance. Each type of network architecture uses cable with a characteristic impedance.

Impedance helps determine the cable's electrical properties and also limits the contexts in which the cable can be used. For example, Ethernet and ARCnet architectures can both use thin coaxial cable, but they have different impedances; therefore, Ethernet and ARCnet cables are not compatible. In networks, the impedances range from 50 ohms (for an Ethernet architecture) to 93 ohms (for an ARCnet architecture).

Coaxial Cable Connectors

A segment of coaxial cable has an end connector at each end. The cable is attached through these end connectors to a T-connector, a barrel connector, another end connector, or to a terminator. Through these connectors, another cable or a hardware device is attached to the coaxial cable.

In addition to their function, connectors differ in their attachment mechanism and components. For example, BNC connectors join two components by plugging them together and then turning the components to click the connection into place. Different-sized coaxial cable requires a different-sized connector.

For coaxial cable, the following types of connectors are available:

- A BNC (bayonet nut connector) is used for thin coaxial cable.

- The N-series connectors are used for thick coaxial cable.

- A TNC (threaded nut connector) may be used in the same situations as a BNC, provided that the other connector is also using TNC.

Connectors for coaxial cable should be plated with silver, not tin. This improves the contact and the durability of the connector.

Thin versus Thick Coaxial

Descriptively, coaxial cable is grouped mainly into thin and thick varieties. Thin coaxial cable is $^3/_{16}$-inch in diameter and is used for various network architectures, including thin Ethernet (also known as 10Base2 or CheaperNet) and ARCnet. When using this configuration, drop cables are not allowed. Instead, the T-connector must be connected directly to the network interface card (NIC). This means the NIC must have an on-board transceiver, known as a medium attachment unit (MAU) in the IEEE 802.3 standard.

Thick coaxial cable is $^3/_8$-inch in diameter. It is used for thick Ethernet (also known as 10Base5 or Thick-Net) networks, cable TV (CATV), and other connections. Thick coaxial is expensive and is notoriously difficult to install and work with. It is more likely to be inherited than selected for use in a network.

Cable Content Descriptions

Other descriptions of coaxial cable are based on the contents of the cable, rather than its size, as follows:

Twinaxial Also known simply as twinax, this coaxial cable has two carrier wires, each with its own dielectric, or insulation, layer. The wires are generally twisted around each other, which helps reduce magnetic interference, and are surrounded by a shield and a jacket whose properties run the same gamut as for ordinary coaxial cable. This type of cable is used in IBM and AppleTalk networks. For example, twinaxial cable is used to connect IBM 5250 terminals to System/36 or AS/400 computers.

Triaxial Also known simply as triax, this coaxial cable has extra shielding: an inner braid surrounded by an inner (nonplenum) jacket, surrounded by an outer copper braid. This outer braid is, in turn, surrounded by the outer jacket. The extra shielding makes a big difference because of the grounding and improved protection.

Quadrax This cable is a hybrid of triaxial and twinaxial cable. Quadrax has the extra carrier wire with dielectric, and also has the extra shielding of triaxial.

Quad shield This cable has four layers of shielding: alternating layers of foil and braid shields. Quad shield cable is used in situations where heavy electrical interference can occur; for example, in industrial settings.

Baseband versus Broadband Cable

Functionally, coaxial cable is grouped into baseband and broadband varieties.

Baseband coaxial cable has one channel over which a single digital message can be sent, at speeds of up to 80Mbps. Thin coaxial is used for baseband cable.

Broadband coaxial cable can carry several analog signals (at different frequencies) simultaneously. Each of these signals can be a different message or a different type of information. Thick coaxial cable can be used for broadband transmissions in a network.

Broadband coaxial can use a single cable or multiple cables. In single-cable broadband coaxial, frequencies are split; for example, into 6MHz channels for each station. Some channels are allocated for bidirectional communication. Dual-cable broadband coaxial uses one cable for sending and one for receiving data; each cable has multiple channels.

Note that broadband coaxial requires much more planning than baseband coaxial. For example, a broadband setup will probably need amplifiers for dealing with the different broadband signals.

Coaxial Cable Designations

The following designations are used for coaxial cable used in networks. These are just a few of the available coaxial cable types.

RG-6 Used as a drop cable for CATV transmissions. It has 75 ohms impedance, is a broadband cable, and is often quad-shielded.

RG-8 Used for thick Ethernet. It has 50 ohms impedance. The thick Ethernet configuration requires other cable and a MAU (transceiver).

C

The other cable required is a twisted-pair drop cable to the NIC. The drop cable off RG-8 cable uses a 15-pin DIX (or AUI) connector. RG-8 is also known as N-Series Ethernet cable.

RG-11   Used for the main CATV trunk. It has 75 ohms impedance and is a broadband cable. This cable is often quad shielded (with foil/braid/foil/braid around the signal wire and dielectric) to protect the signal wire under even the worst operating conditions.

RG-58   Used for thin Ethernet. It has 50 ohms impedance and uses a BNC connector.

RG-59   Used for ARCnet. It has 75 ohms impedance and uses BNC connectors. This type of cable is used for broadband connections and also by cable companies to connect the cable network to an individual household.

RG-62   Used for ARCnet. It has 93 ohms impedance and uses BNC connectors. This cable is also used to connect terminals to terminal controllers in IBM's 3270 system configurations.

Advantages of Coaxial Cable

Coaxial cable has the following advantages over other types of cable that might be used for a network. The advantages are general and may not apply in a particular situation. Note also that advantages change or disappear over time, as technology advances and products improve.

- Broadband coaxial can be used to transmit voice, data, and even video.
- The cable is relatively easy to install.
- Coaxial cable is reasonably priced compared with other cable types.

Disadvantages of Coaxial Cable

Coaxial cable has the following disadvantages when used for a network:

- It is easily damaged and sometimes difficult to work with, especially in the case of thick coaxial.

- Coaxial is more difficult to work with than twisted-pair cable.
- This type of cable cannot be used with token-ring network architectures.
- Thick coaxial can be expensive to install, especially if it needs to be pulled through existing cable conduits.
- Connectors can be expensive.
- Baseband coaxial cannot carry integrated voice, data, and video signals.

USING EXISTING COAXIAL CABLE

It may be tempting to try to use existing coaxial cable—which is likely to be CATV cable—for a network. If you're considering this, here's an important point to keep in mind: Not all CATV cables are the same.

Broadcast-oriented cables are designed to carry video signals sent from one location in the network, known as the head-end. Such cables are designed for one-way communication, which makes them useless for data networks. Even if a bidirectional CATV cable is available, several other considerations must be taken into account before you can use this cable for a local area network.

If the cable will still be used to transmit TV channels, you need to find two frequency bands that won't be used for TV channels. Each of these bands must have at least 18MHz bandwidth. The bands are used by a modem, which modulates network data into the appropriate frequency band at one end. A second modem demodulates this signal at the other end. The TV and data networks will be independent of each other.

Because your network may be grafted onto an existing CATV topology, you need to make sure your system can deal with this. Typically, a CATV network uses a tree topology. The head-end is the root, and the signal is transmitted along successive branches. For this setup, you need to make sure that limitations on cable length are not exceeded.

Tools for Working with Coaxial Cable

Almost all cable testers can deal with coaxial cable (see the Cable article for a discussion of the tools used for cable testing). For more specialized tasks requiring tools, such as crimpers and dies for attaching connectors to cable, you will need versions specifically designed for coaxial cable.

When in doubt, of course, ask the vendor explicitly whether a particular tool will work with coaxial cable.

A COAXIAL CABLE

→ *See Also* Cable; Cable, Fiber-Optic; Cable, Twisted-Pair; Connector

Cable, Data-Grade

Twisted-pair cable of sufficiently high quality to use for data transmission. In contrast, voice-grade cable is more susceptible to interference and signal distortion. In the EIA/TIA-568 cable specifications, Categories 2 through 5 are data-grade cable.

→ *See Also* Cable, Twisted-Pair

Cable, Distribution

In broadband networks, a term for cable used over intermediate distances (up to a few hundred yards) and for branches off a network trunk, or backbone. RG-11 cable is commonly used for this purpose.

Cable, Drop

Cable used to connect a network interface card (NIC) to a transceiver on a thick Ethernet network. Drop cable, also known as AUI cable or transceiver cable, has a 15-pin AUI, or DIX, connector at the NIC cnd and an N-series connector at the transceiver end. This term may also be applied loosely to other cables that connect a network node to a wiring center of some sort.

→ *See Also* Cable

Cable, Enhanced Unshielded Twisted-Pair (EUTP)

→ *See* Cable, EUTP (Enhanced Unshielded Twisted-Pair)

Cable, EUTP (Enhanced Unshielded Twisted-Pair)

Cable that fits into Categories 4 and 5 in the EIA/TIA-568 specifications has considerable performance advantages over cable in the lower categories. For this reason, Category 4 and 5 cable is sometimes known as enhanced unshielded twisted-pair (EUTP) cable. See the entry on Cable Standards for a summary of the EIA/TIA cable categories.

→ *Broader Category* Cable, Twisted-Pair

Cable, Feeder

A 25-pair cable that can be used for carrying both voice and data signals. This cable can run from equipment to distribution frame.

Cable, Fiber-Optic

Fiber-optic cable, also known as optical fiber, provides a medium for signals using light rather than electricity. Cables of this type differ in their physical dimensions and composition and in the wavelength(s) of light with which the cable transmits. The illustration "Context and properties of fiber-optic cable" summarizes the features of this type of cable.

Because fiber-optic communication uses light signals, transmissions are not subject to electromagnetic interference. This, and the fact that a light signal encounters little resistance on its path (relative to an electrical signal traveling along a copper wire), means that fiber-optic cable can be used for much longer distances before the signal must be cleaned and boosted.

Some fiber-optic segments can be several kilometers long before a repeater is needed. In fact, scientists have sent signals over fiber-optic lines for thousands of kilometers without any signal boosters. In 1990, researchers sent a 1Gbps signal almost 8000 kilometers (about 5000 miles) without a boost! A project—FLAG (for Fiber-Optic Link Around

Context

```
Cable
    Electrical
        Twisted-Pair
        Coaxial
    Optical
        Fiber-Optic ─────────────┐
                                 ▼
```

Fiber-Optic Properties
Medium for light signals
Light at certain wavelengths is best for signaling purposes
Comes in single-mode (thin fiber core; single light path) and multimode (thick fiber core; multiple light paths) versions
Multimode can be step-index or graded-index
Cable is very lightweight
Very high bandwidth
Immune to electromagnetic inteference, eavesdropping
Very long cable segments possible

Fiber-Optic Uses
FDDI networks
Gigabit Ethernet
ATM
Long-haul lines
To connect network segments or networks
To connect mainframes to peripherals
To connect high-speed, high-performance workstations

CONTEXT AND PROPERTIES OF FIBER-OPTIC CABLE

the Globe)—is currently underway to lay optical fiber completely around the world.

In principle, data transmission using fiber optics is many times faster than with electrical methods. Speeds of over 10Gbps are possible with fiber-optic cable. In practice, however, this advantage is still more promise than reality, because the cable is waiting for the transmission and reception technology to catch up. With the increasing popularity of Gigabit Ethernet, this is beginning to happen.

Nevertheless, fiber-optic connections deliver more reliable transmissions over greater distances, although at a somewhat greater cost. Fiber-optic cables cover a considerable price and performance range.

Uses of Fiber-Optic Cable

Currently, fiber-optic cable is used less often to create a network than to connect two networks or network segments. For example, cable that must run between floors is often fiber-optic cable, most commonly of the 62.5/125 variety with an LED (light-emitting diode) as the light source.

Being impervious to electromagnetic interference, fiber is ideal for such uses because the cable is often run through the elevator shaft, and the elevator motor puts out strong interference when the elevator is running.

One reason fiber-optic networks are slow to catch on is price. Network interface cards (NICs) for fiber-optic nodes can cost several thousand dollars, compared to street prices of about $100 for some Ethernet and ARCnet cards. However, when selecting optical fiber, it is not always necessary to use the most expensive fiber-optic connections. For short distances and slower bandwidths, inexpensive cable is just fine. In general, a fiber-optic cable will always allow a longer transmission than a copper cable segment.

Fiber-Optic Cable Components

The major components of a fiber-optic cable are the core, cladding, buffer, strength members, and jacket. Some types of fiber-optic cable even include a conductive copper wire. This can be used to provide power—for example, to a repeater. The illustration "Components of a fiber-optic cable" displays the makeup of this type of cable.

Fiber-Optic Core and Cladding

The core of fiber-optic cable consists of one or more glass or plastic fibers through which the light signal moves. Plastic is easier to manufacture and use but works over shorter distances than glass. The core can be anywhere from about two to several hundred microns. (A micron, also known as a micrometer, is a millionth of a meter, or about $1/25{,}000$ of an inch.)

In networking contexts, the most popular core sizes are 50, 62.5, and 100 microns. Most of the fiber-optic cable used in networking has two core fibers: one for communicating in each direction.

The core and cladding are actually manufactured as a single unit. The cladding is a protective layer (usually of plastic) with a lower index of refraction than the core. The lower index means that light that hits the core walls will be redirected back to continue on its path. The cladding will be anywhere between a hundred microns and a millimeter (1000 microns) or so.

GIPOF (Graded-Index Plastic Optical Fiber)

In recent years, an optical fiber with a plastic core, but with high-performance specs, has been introduced. The plastic core is more flexible than glass, and so makes such fiber easier to install than fiber with a glass core. GIPOF is also less expensive to make than fiber with a glass core; in fact, the price of GIPOF cable is comparable to the cost of Category 5 unshielded twisted-pair (UTP) cable.

With the decrease in cost comes a decrease in range, however. The specifications for GIPOF cable claim that it can transmit at 100Mbps for a distance of 150 meters. This is in comparison to 2000 meters for optical fiber with a glass core, to 100 meters for Category 5 cable, and to a mere 50 meters for the previous generation of plastic optical fiber.

It remains to be seen whether this type of cable will catch on.

C

Fiber-Optic Buffer

The buffer of a fiber-optic cable is one or more layers of plastic surrounding the cladding. The buffer helps strengthen the cable, thereby decreasing the likelihood of microcracks, which can eventually grow into larger breaks in the cable. The buffer also protects the core and cladding from potential corrosion by water or other materials in the operating environment. The buffer can double the diameter of some cable.

A buffer can be loose or tight. A loose buffer is a rigid tube of plastic with one or more fibers (consisting of core and cladding) running through it. The tube takes on all the stresses applied to the cable, buffering the fiber from these stresses. A tight buffer fits snugly around the fiber(s). A tight buffer can protect the fibers from stress due to pressure and impact, but not from changes in temperature.

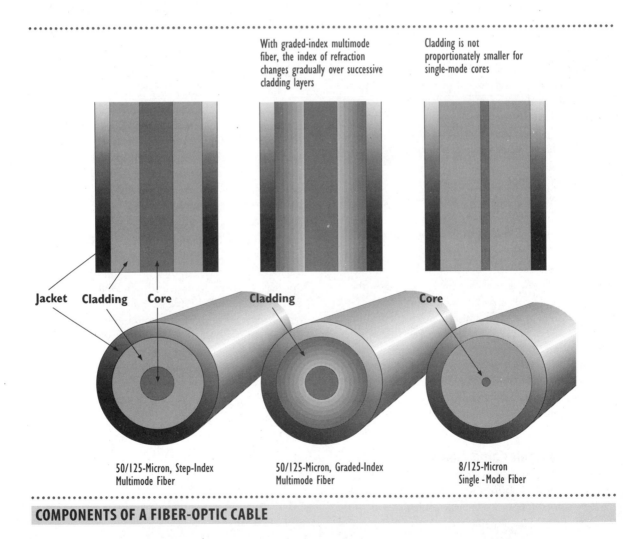

With graded-index multimode fiber, the index of refraction changes gradually over successive cladding layers

Cladding is not proportionately smaller for single-mode cores

Jacket   Cladding   Core

Cladding

Core

50/125-Micron, Step-Index Multimode Fiber

50/125-Micron, Graded-Index Multimode Fiber

8/125-Micron Single-Mode Fiber

COMPONENTS OF A FIBER-OPTIC CABLE

Strength Members

Fiber-optic cable also has strength members, which are strands of very tough material (such as steel, fiberglass, or Kevlar) that provide extra strength for the cable. Each of the substances has advantages and drawbacks. For example, steel attracts lightning, which will not disrupt an optical signal but may seriously disrupt the people or machines sending or receiving such a signal.

Fiber-Optic Jacket

The jacket of a fiber-optic cable is an outer casing that can be plenum or nonplenum, as with electrical cable. In cable used for networking, the jacket usually houses at least two fiber/cladding pairs: one for each direction.

Single-Mode versus Multimode Cable

Fiber-optic cable can be either single-mode or multimode. (Modes are the possible paths for the light through a cable.)

Single-Mode Cable

In single-mode fiber-optic cable, the core is so narrow (generally less than 10 microns) that the light can take only a single path through it. Single-mode fiber has the least signal attenuation, usually less than 2 decibels (dB) per kilometer. This type of cable is the most difficult to install, because it requires the greatest precision, and it is the most expensive of the major fiber-optic types. However, transmission speeds of 50Gbps and higher are possible. To get a sense of this magnitude, note that a 10Gbps line can carry 130,000 voice channels.

Even though the core of single-mode cable is shrunk to very small sizes, the cladding is not reduced accordingly, nor should it be. For single-mode fiber, the cladding diameter should be about ten times the core diameter. This ratio makes it possible to make the cladding the same size as for popular multimode fiber-optic cable. This helps create a de facto size standard. Keeping the cladding large also makes the fiber and cable easier to handle and more resistant to damage.

Multimode Cable

Multimode fiber-optic cable has a wider core, so that a beam of light has room to follow multiple paths through the core. Multiple modes (light paths) in a transmission produce signal distortion at the receiving end.

One measure of signal distortion is modal dispersion, which is represented in nanoseconds (billionths of a second) of tail per kilometer (ns/km). This value represents the difference in arrival time between the fastest and slowest of the alternate light paths. The value also imposes an upper limit on the bandwidth, since the duration of a signal must be larger than the nanoseconds of a tail value. With step-index fiber, expect between 15 and 30 ns/km. Note that a modal dispersion of 20 ns/km yields a bandwidth of less than 50Mbps.

Gradation of Refraction: Step-Index Cable versus Graded-Index Cable

One reason optical fiber makes such a good transmission medium is because the different indexes of refraction for the cladding and core help to contain the light signal within the core. Cable can be constructed by changing abruptly from the core refractive index to that of the cladding, or this change can be made gradually. The two major types of multimode fiber differ in this feature.

Step-Index Cable

Cable with an abrupt change in refraction index is called step-index cable. In step-index cable, the change is made in a single step. Single-step multimode cable uses this method, and it is the simplest, least expensive type of fiber-optic cable. It is also the easiest to install. The core is usually between 50 and 125 microns in diameter; the cladding is at least 140 microns.

The core width gives light quite a bit of room to bounce around in, and the attenuation is high (at least for fiber-optic cable): between 10 and 50 dB/km. Transmission speeds between 200Mbps and 3Gbps are possible, but actual speeds are much lower.

Graded-Index Cable

Cable with a gradual change in refraction index is called graded-index cable, or graded-index multimode. This fiber-optic cable type has a relatively wide core, like single-step multimode cable. The change occurs gradually and involves several layers, each with a slightly lower index of refraction. A gradation of refraction indexes controls the light signal better than the step-index method. As a result, the attenuation is lower, usually less than 15 dB/km. Similarly, the modal dispersion can be 1 ns/km and lower, which allows more than ten times the bandwidth of step-index cable. Graded-index multimode cable is the most commonly used type for network wiring.

Fiber Composition

Fiber core and cladding may be made of plastic or glass. The following list summarizes the composition combinations, going from highest quality to lowest:

Single-mode glass Has a narrow core, so only one signal can travel through.

Graded-index glass Not tight enough to be single-mode, but the gradual change in refractive index helps give more control over the light signal.

Step-index glass The abrupt change from the refractive index of the core to that of the cladding means the signal is less controllable.

Plastic-coated silica (PCS) Has a relatively wide core (200 microns) and a relatively low bandwidth (20MHz).

Plastic This should be used only for very short distances.

To summarize, fiber-optic cables may consist of glass core and glass cladding (the best available). Glass yields much higher performance, in the form of higher bandwidth over greater distances. Single-mode glass with a small core is the highest quality. Cables may also consist of glass core and plastic cladding. Finally, the lowest grade fiber composition is plastic core and plastic cladding. Step-index plastic is at the bottom of the heap in performance.

FIBER-OPTIC CABLE QUALITY

Here are a few points about fiber-optic cable (other things being equal):

- The smaller the core, the better the signal.

- Fiber made of glass is better than fiber made of plastic.

- The purer and cleaner the light, the better the signal. (Pure, clean light is a single color, with minimal spread around the color's primary wavelength.)

- Certain wavelengths of light behave better than others.

Fiber-Optic Cable Designations

Fiber-optic cables are specified in terms of their core and cladding diameters. For example, a 62.5/125 cable has a core with a 62.5 micron diameter and cladding with twice that diameter.

The following are some commonly used fiber-optic cable configurations:

8/125 A single-mode cable with an 8 micron core and a 125 micron cladding. This type of cable is expensive and currently used only in contexts where extremely large bandwidths are needed (such as in some real-time applications) or where large distances are involved. An 8/125 cable configuration is likely to broadcast at a light wavelength of 1300 or 1550nm.

62.5/125 The most popular fiber-optic cable configuration, used in most network applications. Both 850 and 1300nm wavelengths can be used with this type of cable.

100/140 The configuration that IBM first specified for fiber-optic wiring in a Token Ring network. Because of the tremendous popularity of the 62.5/125 configuration, IBM now supports both configurations.

Make sure you buy fiber-optic cable with the correct core size. If you know what kind of network you plan to build, you may be constrained to a particular core size. IBM usually specifies a core of 100 microns for Token Ring networks; other networks more commonly use cable with a 62.5 micron core.

Components of a Fiber-Optic Connection

In addition to the cable itself, a fiber-optic connection needs a light source to generate the signal, as well as connectors, repeaters, and couplers to route and deliver the signal. The illustration "Components of a fiber-optic connection" shows how this works.

Transmitter

Fiber-optic transmitters convert an electronic signal into light and send this light signal into the fiber core. The transmitter's light source and output optical power are crucial elements in determining the transmitter's performance.

The transmitter's output power depends on several things, including the fiber and cladding sizes and the fiber's numerical aperture (NA). The NA is a measure of the fiber's ability to gather light and is determined by the angle over which light hitting the fiber will move through it.

Output power values range from less than 50 to over 200 microwatts. Smaller cores generally have lower output power, but also less signal attenuation and higher bandwidth. Output power values should not be too high, since this increases energy requirements and also risks frying the components at the receiving end.

Transmitters use either digital or analog modulation. Analog modulation is used for voice, video, and even radar signals, which require bandwidths ranging from tens of kilohertz to hundreds of megahertz, and even as high as a gigahertz. Digital modulation is used in computer networks and in long-haul telephone systems, which require

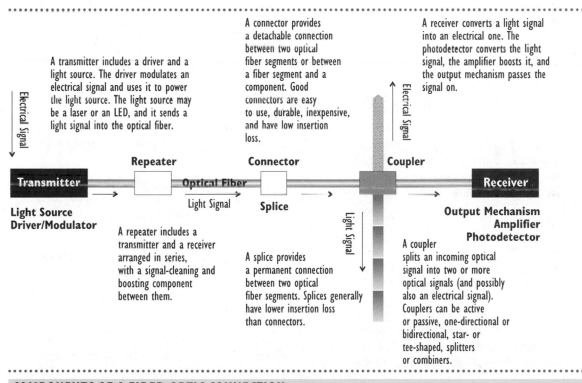

COMPONENTS OF A FIBER-OPTIC CONNECTION

transmission speeds ranging from tens of kilobits to more than a gigabit per second. Transmitters differ in speed. Not surprisingly, the faster ones are also more expensive.

Light Source

The light source will be a laser or a light-emitting diode (LED). A good light source in a fiber-optic connection should have the following characteristics:

- Fast rise and fall times. The rise time is the time required for a light source to go from 10 to 90 percent of the desired level. This time limits the maximum transmission rate, so it should be as short as possible. Lasers have a rise time of less than a nanosecond; the rise time for LEDs ranges from a few nanoseconds to a few hundred nanoseconds.

- A narrow spectral width. The spectral width refers to the range of wavelengths emitted by the light source, and it should be as narrow as possible. Spectral widths for lasers are 1 to 3nm; for LEDs, they are from 30 to 50nm.

- Light emission at a central wavelength with minimal spectral width. The central wavelength is the primary wavelength of the light being emitted. For various reasons, wavelengths of 820, 850, 1300, and 1550nm have all been used. LEDs are used for the first three of the wavelengths, but rarely for 1550nm. Lasers can be used at all of these wavelengths, and single-frequency lasers (possible at the two highest wavelengths) make it possible to emit at a particular wavelength with minimal spectral width.

- A good relationship between the emitting area and acceptance angle. The emitting area is the opening through which the transmitter emits its light. This should be small in relation to the fiber core's acceptance angle, so that all the light emitted by the transmitter will enter the core. Not surprisingly, lasers have a much smaller emitting area than LEDs.

- Steady, strong output power. The higher the output power, the stronger the signal and the further it can travel without becoming too weak. Laser output can be as much as 1000 times that of LEDs.

- A long lifetime. The lifetime of a light source is the amount of time before the source's peak output power is half its original level. This is generally in the millions of hours (longer than ours) and is typically longer for LEDs than for lasers!

Although lasers are clearly the light source of choice, LEDs are generally the light source of record. The most likely reason for this is price; transmitters that use LEDs are usually much less expensive. This is not a problem for networking purposes, however, because LEDs operating at 820 or 850nm are fine for the short-distance, fiber-optic connections currently most popular. Despite their performance shortcomings compared with lasers, LEDs are more reliable and less prone to breakdowns.

Receiver

Fiber-optic receivers undo the work of transmitters: They accept a light signal and convert this to an electrical signal representing information in analog or digital form. A receiver's performance depends on how well its three main components work. The following are the main components of a fiber-optic receiver:

- The photodetector, which "sees" the optical signal and converts it into electrical form. This produces a current that is proportional to the level of light detected.

- The amplifier, which boosts the signal and gets it into a form ready for processing.

- The processor, which tries to reproduce the original signal.

The receiver also includes interfaces for the cable carrying the light signal and the device to which the electrical signal is being passed.

The photodetector and amplifier processes are essentially identical for analog and digital signals. The main differences are in the processor.

There are several classes of photodetectors, each suitable for different speed and distance configurations. The receiver sensitivity specifies the weakest signal that the photodetector can detect. This information may be expressed as an absolute value, such as 10 microwatts, or as a microwatt level needed for a given bit error rate (BER).

Duty Cycle

A duty cycle specifies the ratio of high to low signal values in a digital transmission. This is not necessarily equal to the proportion of 0 and 1 bit values in the message, because some signal-encoding methods will encode a 1 as high at one point in a transmission and as low in another point. (See the Encoding, Signal article for examples of such methods.) The ideal duty cycle is 50 percent.

The duty-cycle value is important because receivers use a reference level as the threshold between high and low values. Some receivers adjust this reference during a transmission. If a duty-cycle value deviates from the 50 percent ideal, the altered threshold level could lead to more erroneous values. For example, if a threshold is adjusted downward because of a 20 percent duty cycle, low signals that are marginally but not significantly higher than normal may be misinterpreted as high values. There are two strategies for getting around the potential error problem: signal encoding and reference levels.

Certain signal-encoding methods, such as the Manchester and differential Manchester methods used in Ethernet and Token Ring networks, always have a 50 percent duty cycle. The tradeoff for this nice behavior is that these encoding methods require a clock that runs at twice the data rate (since every interval is associated with two electrical levels).

It is possible to build a receiver that has an absolute reference level; that is, one that will always correspond to the level of a 50 percent duty cycle. This is accomplished by coupling the receiver to a DC power supply. The tradeoff for this is that the receiver has higher power requirements; it requires a signal that is 6 to 8 dB (roughly, four to eight times) stronger than for an ordinary receiver.

Transceiver

A fiber-optic transceiver includes both a transmitter and a receiver in the same component. These are arranged in parallel so that they can operate independently of each other. Both the receiver and the transmitter have their own circuitry, so that the component can handle transmissions in both directions.

Repeater

Like a transceiver, a fiber-optic repeater includes both a transmitter and a receiver in the same component. However, in the repeater, these components are arranged in series, separated by circuitry for cleaning and boosting the signal. The receiver gets the signal and passes it through the booster to the transmitter.

Connectors and Splices

Connectors serve to link two segments of cable or a cable and a device. A connector is used for temporary links. To link two sections of cable permanently, use a splice; to link more than two sections of cable, use a coupler. In general, use a splice when possible; use a connector when necessary.

A good connector or splice should have the following properties:

- Low power loss. There should be minimal loss of signal power going across the connection or splice. For networks and short-distance connections, the loss should be less than 1 dB; for long-haul connections, there should be less than 0.2 dB loss.

- Durability. The connector should be capable of multiple matings (connections) without loosening or becoming unreliable. Durability values typically range between about 250 and 1000 matings.

- Ease of use. The connector or splice should be easy to install.

- Low price. The less expensive, the better, provided all the preceding features are satisfactory.

There are many types of connector designs used for fiber-optic cable. Some of the most commonly used ones in networking are BFOC (bayonet fiber-optic connector), SC (subscriber connector), ST (straight tip), SMA (sub-miniature assembly), and the MIC (medium interface connector) specified for the FDDI (Fiber Distributed Data Interface) network architecture. See the Connectors, Fiber-Optic article for more information about fiber-optic connectors.

If a fiber-optic connection is more or less permanent, it may make more sense to splice the cable segments together. Splicing techniques are more reliable and precise than connectors. Because of this, signal loss at splices is much lower (almost always less than 1 dB, and often less than 0.25 dB) than at connectors. Splicing is almost always used for long-haul, fiber-optic cable.

The two most common splicing methods are fusion and mechanical splices. Of the two, fusion gives the better splices.

A fusion splice welds the two fibers together using a high-precision instrument. This type of splice produces losses smaller than 0.1 dB. The equipment for such splicing is quite expensive, however.

A mechanical splice is accomplished by fitting a special device over the two fibers to connect them and lock them into place. The device remains attached to the splice area to protect the splice from environmental effects, such as moisture or pressure. Mechanical splices have higher signal losses than fusion splices, but these losses may still be less than 0.25 dB.

Couplers

Fiber-optic couplers route an incoming signal to two or more outgoing paths. Couplers are needed in fiber-optic networks. When an electrical signal is split and sent along parallel paths, each derived signal is the same strength. This is not the case with light signals.

After the signal is split, the derived optical signals are each weaker than the original signal. For example, if a fiber-optic coupler splits a signal into two equal signals, each of those derived signals loses 3 dB relative to the original signal, just from the signal halving. Couplers can be designed to split a signal equally or unequally. See the Coupler, Fiber-Optic article for more information.

Optical Switches

Couplers used in networks need some type of bypass mechanism, so that the coupler can be disconnected if the coupler's target nodes are not on the network. This disconnection capability is accomplished with an optical switch, which allows the light to bypass a node and to continue on around the network.

Fiber-Optic Cable Signal Loss

As mentioned earlier, light signals can be diminished by coupling. In addition, factors that contribute to signal loss across a stretch of cable include the following:

Pulse dispersion If the cable's core width is large compared with the light's wavelength, light enters the core at different angles and will travel different distances to the destination. As explained earlier, the difference in arrival times between the fastest and slowest signals in a group is measured in nanoseconds of tail over the distance the light must travel. This value limits the maximum transmission rate, because signal pulses must be separated by at least the nanoseconds of tail time. For example, if a signal acquires 10 nanoseconds of tail over the required distance, the maximum transmission rate is 100Mbps.

Attenuation Loss of signal strength that occurs because some of the light is absorbed by the cladding, and some light is scattered as a result of imperfections in the fiber.

Fiber bending Signal loss can occur because the fiber is bent in particular ways. Multiple bands of light (known as modes) enter a core, each at slightly different angles. Bending the fiber can enable certain modes to escape from the core. Since the modes that escape will not be random, fiber bending can introduce systematic loss of certain signal components. Simply rolling fiber cable onto a spool for distribution can introduce fiber bending. Cable manufacturers design their cable spools carefully, and some even publish specifications for the spool.

Microbending   Microbends are tiny kinks that can arise in the cable as a result of various stresses (for example, attaching a connector at the end of a cable). Microbends in the fiber can cumulate, and the presence of many kinks can significantly increase the signal loss from bending.

Fiber ovality   If the fiber's core and cladding are not round, the nonuniform shape will distort the signal. This can happen, for example, if the cable was squashed with a heavy weight, so that the core and cladding are partially flattened.

Advantages of Fiber-Optic Cable

Fiber-optic connections offer the following advantages over other types of cabling systems:

- Light signals are impervious to interference from EMI or electrical crosstalk. Light signals do not interfere with other signals. As a result, fiber-optic connections can be used in extremely adverse environments, such as in elevator shafts or assembly plants, where powerful motors and engines produce lots of electrical noise.

- Fiber-optic lines are much harder to tap, so they are more secure for private lines.

- Light has a much higher bandwidth, or maximum data-transfer rate, than electrical connections. (This speed advantage has yet to be realized in practice, however.)

- The signal has a much lower loss rate, so it can be transmitted much further than it could be with coaxial or twisted-pair cable before boosting is necessary.

- Optical fiber is much safer, because there is no electricity and so no danger of electrical shock or other electrical accidents.

- Fiber-optic cable is generally much thinner and lighter than electrical cable, and so it can be installed more unobtrusively. (Fiber-optic cable weighs about an ounce per meter; coaxial cable weighs nearly ten times that much.)

- Cable making and installation are much easier than they were in the early days.

Disadvantages of Fiber-Optic Cable

The disadvantages of fiber-optic connections include the following:

- Fiber-optic cable is currently more expensive than other types of cable.

- Other components, particularly NICs, are very expensive.

- Certain components, particularly couplers, are subject to optical crosstalk.

- Fiber connectors are not designed to be used as often as you would like. Generally, they are designed for fewer than a thousand matings. After that, the connection may become loose, unstable, or misaligned. The resulting signal loss may be unacceptably high.

- Many more parts can break in a fiber-optic connection than in an electrical one.

Fiber-Optic Cable Tools

It is only fitting that the most complex wiring technology should also have the most sophisticated tools. Optical fiber undergoes an extensive set of tests and quality-control inspections before it even leaves the manufacturer.

The manufacturers' tests are designed to get complete details about the cable's physical and optical properties. Optical properties include attenuation, dispersion, and refractive indexes of the core and cladding layers. Physical properties include core and cladding dimensions, numerical aperture and emitting areas, tensile strength, and changes in performance under extreme temperature and/or humidity conditions (or as a result of repeated change in temperature). The values for these properties are used to evaluate cable performance.

The equipment you might need to test fiber-optic cables in a network setting includes the following:

- An installation kit—a general-purpose tool set for dealing with optical fiber. Such a toolkit will include cable strippers, scissors, crimping tools, epoxy, pliers, canned air (for cleaning fibers after polishing), inspection microscope, polishing materials, and so on.

- Optical power meter, which is a device that can read levels of optical signals on a fiber-optic line. Using sensors attached to the cable, this device can report absolute or relative signal levels over a range of 110 dB (which means that the weakest and strongest detectable signals differ by a factor of over 10 billion). An optical power meter can also be used to measure light at specific wavelengths.

- An OTDR (optical time domain reflectometer), which is a device that can measure the behavior of the light signals over time and create graphical representations of these measurements. An OTDR can be used to measure signal loss along a stretch of cable and to help locate a fault in a fiber-optic connection.

- Splicer, which is used to create splices, or permanent connections in an optical fiber. Fusion splicers are the most expensive devices of this sort.

- Polishers, which are used to prepare fiber ends for splicing or connection.

- A microscope, so you can inspect the results of a splicing or polishing operation. A microscope may be included in an installation toolkit.

Fiber-Optic Cable Vendors

Many vendors sell both electrical and fiber-optic cable, as well as connectors, installation, and testing tools. The following vendors offer an extensive selection of fiber-optics products. (See the Cable article for other cable vendors.)

AMP Incorporated (800) 522-6752; (717) 564-0100

CSP (Computer System Products) (800) 422-2537; (612) 476-6866; Fax (612) 476-6966

FIS (Fiber Instrument Sales) (800) 445-2901; (315) 736-2206; Fax (315) 736-2285

→ *See Also* Cable; Cable, Coaxial; Cable, Twisted-Pair; Connector, Fiber-Optic; Coupler, Fiber-Optic; FDDI (Fiber Distributed Data Interface)

Cable, Foil Twisted-Pair (FTP)

→ *See* Cable, Twisted-Pair

Cable, FTP (Foil Twisted-Pair)

→ *See* Cable, Twisted-Pair

Cable, GIPOF (Graded-Index Plastic Optical Fiber)

→ *See* Cable, Fiber-Optic

Cable, Graded-Index Plastic Optical Fiber (GIPOF)

→ *See* Cable, Fiber-Optic

Cable, Horizontal

Horizontal cable is defined by the EIA/TIA-568 committee as any cable that goes from a wiring closet, or distribution frame, to the wall outlet in the work area. Distribution frames from a floor or building are connected to other frames using backbone cable.

In a sense, horizontal cable is the most crucial in the entire network cabling structure. Since it is installed in the walls, floors, ceiling, or ground, the installation process can be difficult and expensive. Moreover, the cable should be able to handle future standards and technology.

The EIA/TIA-568 recognizes four main types of horizontal cable, and several optional variants. These types are listed in the table "EIA/TIA-568 Main and Optional Types of Horizontal Cable." The EIA/TIA specifications call for at least two cables from this list to be run to every wall outlet. At least one of these should be unshielded twisted-pair (UTP).

→ *Compare* Cable, Backbone

→ *See Also* Cable

EIA/TIA-568 MAIN AND OPTIONAL TYPES OF HORIZONTAL CABLE

Cable Type	Main	Optional
UTP	100-ohm, four-pair UTP cable	100-ohm, 25-wire-pair UTP cable
STP	150-ohm STP cable, such as that defined in the IBM Cable System (ICS)	100-ohm STP cable
Coaxial	50-ohm, thin coaxial cable, such as the cable used in thin Ethernet networks	75-ohm (broadband) coaxial cable, such as CATV cable
Optical fiber	62.5/125-micron (step- or graded-index) multi-mode optical fiber	Multimode fiber with other core/cladding ratios of 50/125-micron, 100/140-micron, etc.
Undercarpet		Flat cable (such as Type 8 in the ICS) that can be run under carpet without posing a hazard

Cable, IBM

The IBM Cable System (ICS) was designed by IBM for use in its Token Ring networks and also for general-purpose premises wiring. The illustration "Context and properties of the IBM Cable System" summarizes the features of this type of cable.

IBM has specified nine types of cable, mainly twisted-pair, but with more stringent specifications than for the generic twisted-pair cabling. The type taxonomy also includes fiber-optic cable, but excludes coaxial cable. The twisted-pair versions differ in the following ways:

- Whether the type is shielded or unshielded

- Whether the carrier wire is solid or stranded

- The gauge (diameter) of the carrier wire

- The number of twisted pairs

Specifications have been created for seven of the nine types, as well as for two variants on types. Types 4 and 7 are undefined; presumably, they are reserved for future use.

Type 1 Cable

Type 1 cable is shielded twisted-pair (STP), with two pairs of 22-gauge solid wire. It has an impedance of 150 ohms and a bandwidth of 20MHz. It is used for data-quality transmission in IBM's (4Mbps) Token Ring network and also in 10BaseT Ethernet networks. It can be used for the main ring or to connect lobes (nodes) to multistation attachment units (MAUs), which are wiring centers.

Although not required by the specifications, a plenum version is also available, at about twice the cost of the nonplenum cable. The plenum cable can be used in air ducts. The riser cable can be used in elevator shafts, mail chutes, and other paths running vertically through a building. Type 1 cable can also be used outdoors.

Compare Type 1 with Type 6.

C

Type 1A Cable

Type 1A represents a new cable standard in IBM's taxonomy. It is made the same way as Type 1 cable, but has been enhanced to allow a frequency bandwidth of 300MHz at the designated impedance of 150 ohms for Type 1 cable. With this bandwidth, Type 1A cable can be used for any of 4, 16, or 32Mbps Token Ring, 10BaseT, or 100BaseT networks.

Type 1A cable can be used indoors or outdoors. If you're going to be installing new cable, this type should be high on your list of candidates.

Type 2 Cable

Type 2 is a hybrid consisting of four pairs of unshielded 22-gauge solid wire (for voice transmission) and two pairs of shielded 22-gauge solid wire (for data). Type 2 cable can support a voice connection as well as two Token Ring connections simultaneously. This type of cable can be used in 4Mbps Token Ring networks or in 10BaseT Ethernet networks.

Type 2 cable is for indoor use only. Although not required by the specifications, a plenum version is also available, at about twice the cost.

Context

```
Cable
    Electrical
        Twisted-Pair
        Coaxial
    Optical
        Fiber-Optic
```

IBM Cable System Properties

Comprises Types 1 through 9 (of which all types but 4 and 7 are defined)

Type 5 is fiber-optic

Type 3 is unshielded twisted-pair (UTP)

Remaining types are shielded twisted-pair (STP)

Type 1 is most common in Token Ring Networks

Type 1a can be used indoors or outdoors, and is suitable even for 100 Mbps networks

Type 2 is for indoor use and supports networks up to 10Mbps

Type 3 is not recommended for 16 Mbps networks

Type 3 cable generally requires a media filter

Type 6 is used mainly as short-distance patch cable

Type 8 is flat cable for use under a carpet

IBM Cable System Uses

IBM Token Ring networks

10BaseT Ethernet networks

100BaseT Ethernet networks

ARCnet networks

ISDN lines

Some IBM 3270 networks

CONTEXT AND PROPERTIES OF THE IBM CABLE SYSTEM

Type 2A Cable

Type 2A cable is an enhanced version of Type 2 cable, designed to provide a 300MHz bandwidth at a resistance of 150 ohms. Because of its greater bandwidth, Type 2A cable can be used for the same range of networks as Type 1A cable: 4, 16, or 32Mbps Token Ring, and 10BaseT or 100BaseT Ethernet networks.

Type 2A cable is for indoor use.

Type 3 Cable

Type 3 is unshielded twisted-pair (UTP), with two, three, or four pairs of 22- or 24-gauge solid wire. The pairs have at least two twists per foot. This category requires only voice-grade capabilities, and so may be used as telephone wire for voice transmissions. Type 3 is not recommended for 16Mbps Token Ring networks, but it can be used in 10BaseT, 100BaseT, or 100VG-AnyLAN networks.

Type 3 cable is for indoor use only. Although not required by the specifications, a plenum version is also available, at about twice the cost.

Type 3 cable is becoming more popular as adapter cable, which is used to connect a node to a MAU. You must use a media filter if you are using Type 3 cable to connect a node to a MAU or if you need to switch between UTP and STP in a Token Ring network. However, you should not mix Type 1 and 3 cable in the same ring. Mixing cable types makes trouble-shooting difficult.

Some manufacturers offer higher-quality Type 3 cable for greater reliability. Such cable has more twists per foot, for greater protection against interference. Many vendors recommend that you use (EIA/TIA-568) Category 4 cable (with 12 twists per foot). This category of cable costs about 20 percent more than ordinary Type 3 cable, but is rated for higher speeds. The category value represents a classification system for the performance of UTP cable. See the Cable Standards article for more information.

Type 5 Cable

Type 5 is fiber-optic cable, with two glass fiber cores, each with a 100-micron diameter and a 140-micron cladding diameter. (IBM also allows the more widely used 50/125- and 62.5/125-micron fibers.)

This type is used for the main ring path (the main network cabling) in a Token Ring network to connect MAUs over greater distances or to connect network segments between buildings. Type 5 cable can also be used for 10BaseF and 100BaseF Ethernet networks.

Type 5 cable may be used indoors or outdoors, but must be installed in a conduit if used outdoors. Plenum versions of Type 5 cable are available at only a slightly higher cost.

Type 6 Cable

Type 6 is STP cable, with two pairs of 26-gauge stranded wire. This type is commonly used as an adapter cable to connect a node to a MAU. In that type of connection, the PC end of the cable has a male DB-9 or DB-25 connector, and the MAU end has a specially designed IBM data connector.

Type 6 cable is also used as a patch cable; for example, to connect MAUs. For this use, the cable has IBM data connectors at each end.

Type 6 cable is for indoor use only. Because Type 6 is used mostly for shorter distances, the price per foot tends to be higher than for other cable types.

Type 8

Type 8 is STP cable, with two pairs of flat, 26-gauge solid wire. This type is specially designed to be run under a carpet, so the wires are flattened. This makes the cable much more prone to signal loss than Type 1 or Type 2 cable; however, the performance of Type 8 cable is adequate for the short distances usually involved in under-the-carpet cabling.

Type 8 cable is for indoor use only, and may be used in 4 or 16Mbps Token Ring or 10BaseT Ethernet networks.

Type 9

Type 9 is STP cable, with two pairs of 26-gauge solid or stranded wire. This type is covered with a plenum jacket and is designed to be run between floors. Type 9 cable can be used for 4 or 16Mbps Token Ring networks or for 10BaseT and 100BaseT Ethernet networks.

Type 9 cable is for indoor use only.

→ *See Also* Cable, Twisted-Pair

Cable Modem

→ *See* Modem, Cable

Cable, Patch

Cable used to connect two hubs or multistation attachment units (MAUs). IBM Type 1 or Type 6 patch cables can be used for Token Ring networks.

→ *See Also* Cable, IBM

Cable, Plenum

Cable that has a fire-resistant jacket, which will not burn, smoke, or give off toxic fumes when exposed to heat. The cable goes through a plenum—that is, a conduit, or shaft, running inside a wall, floor, or ceiling. Fire regulations generally stipulate that cable running through such conduits must be fireproof.

→ *See Also* Cable

Cable, Quadrax

A type of coaxial cable. Quadrax cable, sometimes known simply as quadrax, is a hybrid of triaxial and twinaxial cable. Like twinaxial cable, quadrax has the extra carrier wire with dielectric; like triaxial cable, quadrax has extra shielding.

→ *See Also* Cable, Coaxial

Cable, Quad Shield

A type of coaxial cable with four layers of shielding: alternating layers of foil and braid shields. Quad shield cable, sometimes known simply as quad shield, is used in situations where heavy electrical interference can occur, such as in industrial settings.

→ *See Also* Cable, Coaxial

Cable Retransmission Facility (CRF)

→ *See* CRF (Cable Retransmission Facility)

Cable, Riser

Cable that runs vertically; for example, between floors in a building. Riser cable often runs through available shafts (such as for the elevator). In some cases, such areas can be a source of electrical interference. Consequently, optical fiber (which is impervious to electromagnetic interference) is generally used as rise cable.

Cable, Screened Twisted-Pair (ScTP)

→ *See* Cable, Twisted-Pair

Cable, ScTP (Screened Twisted-Pair)

→ *See* Cable, Twisted-Pair

Cable, Shielded Twisted-Pair (STP)

→ *See* Cable, Twisted-Pair

Cable Signal Fault Signature (CSFS)

→ *See* CSFS (Cable Signal Fault Signature)

Cable Standards

Several cable standards are concerned with the performance and reliability of cables under actual working conditions. In particular, these standards specify the cable's minimal acceptable behavior under standard and adverse working conditions; for example, in manufacturing or industrial environments, where heavy machinery is turned on and off during the course of operations. Such actions can generate strong interference and power-supply variations. Cable environments are often distinguished in terms of the demands made on the cable. The standards also specify the minimum behavior required under extreme conditions, such as fire.

The most commonly used safety standards in the United States are those specified in the National Electric Code and in documents from Underwriters Laboratories. Other standards are specified by the Electronic Industries Association (EIA)/Telecommunications Industries Association (TIA), Electrical Testing Laboratory, and Manufacturing Automation Protocol. For international standards, the International Standardization Organization (ISO) has developed specifications in conjunction with the International Electrotechnical Commission (IEC). The ISO/IEC 11801E specification is similar to the EIA/TIA 568 standards described in a later section.

The National Electric Code (NEC)

The NEC is published by the National Fire Protection Agency (NFPA, 617-770-3000), and specifies safety standards for general-purpose cables in commercial and residential environments, and also specifically for cables used for communications. The Class 2 (CL2x) standards apply to general-purpose cables, and the Communications (CMx) standards apply to special-purpose cables capable of carrying data.

Of the CL2 standards, the most stringent ones apply to Class 2 plenum cable (CL2P). Cable that meets or exceeds these standards is said to be CL2P compliant. CMP-compliant cable meets the corresponding standard for plenum communications cable.

The less stringent CL2R standards apply to riser cable (cable that can be used, for example, in a vertical utility shaft between floors in a building). The corresponding standard for communications riser cable is CMR.

Be wary if you intend to use cable that is neither CMx- nor CL2x-compliant. Older cable that is already in the walls may be noncompliant.

Underwriters Laboratories (UL)

UL tests cable and other electrical devices to determine the conditions under which the cable or device will function safely and as specified. UL-listed products have passed safety tests performed by inspectors at the Underwriters Laboratories.

Two tests are most directly relevant to network cable:

UL-910 Tests smoke emissions and the spread of flames for plenum cable. This test corresponds to the CL2P level of safety standards. A cable that passes the UL-910 test is rated as OFNP (optical fiber, nonconductive plenum) by UL.

UL-1666 Tests the performance of riser cable in a fire. This test corresponds roughly to the CL2R level of safety standards. A cable that passes the UL-1666 test is rated as OFNR (optical fiber, nonconductive riser) by UL.

UL also uses a system of markings to categorize cable as falling into one of five levels (I through V). Cables that meet level I and II standards meet minimum UL safety requirements, but the performance of these cables may be inadequate for networking purposes. Cables that meet level III, IV, or V standards meet both safety and various performance requirements. Higher levels allow for less attenuation and interference due to crosstalk than lower levels.

Cable should be UL-listed, and just about every cable is. However, you need to find out which listing applies. For example, OFNR cable is UL-listed

C

but is not suitable for environments that demand fire protection.

For most networking applications, cable that meets requirements for UL level III or above should be adequate.

UNDERWRITERS LABORATORIES (UL) PHONE NUMBERS

East Coast: (516) 271-6200

Central: (708) 272-8800

West Coast: (408) 985-2400

Electronic Industries Association/ Telecommunications Industries Association (EIA/TIA)

A committee for EIA/TIA has created yet another classification system for specifying the performance of unshielded twisted-pair (UTP) cable. The EIA/TIA taxonomy—specified in the EIA/TIA-568 and 568B standards, and also in TIA/EIA-568A—includes the following categories (1 through 5, with 6 and 7 currently in development) whose criteria correspond roughly to the performance criteria specified for the UL levels:

Category 1 Voice-grade, UTP telephone cable. This describes the cable that has been used for years in telephone communications. Category 1 cable uses 22 or 24 gauge wire— AWG 22 or 24, in the American Wire Gauge, or AWG, classification—and can have a wide range of impedances. Officially, such cable is not considered suitable for data-grade transmissions (in which every bit must get across correctly). In practice, however, it works fine over short distances and under ordinary working conditions.

Category 2 Data-grade UTP, capable of supporting transmission rates of up to 4Mbps. Category 2 also uses AWG 22 or 24 wire. Common

uses for this category include AppleTalk networks and IBM 3270 data transmissions. IBM Type 3 cable falls into this category.

Category 3 Data-grade UTP, capable of supporting transmission rates of up to 10Mbps— which make it suitable for either 4Mbps Token Ring or 10Mbps Ethernet networks. Even though its nominal limit is 10Mbps, many vendors are using this type of cable to transmit at much higher speeds. (Operating at these higher speeds can lead to higher error rates and also to increased electromagnetic emissions from the wires.) Category 3 cable uses AWG 24 wire, has a frequency range of 16 to 25MHz, and a 100-ohm impedance. A 10BaseT network requires such cable.

Category 4 Data-grade UTP, capable of supporting transmission rates of up to 16Mbps with its 20MHz frequency range. As with Category 3 cable, vendors are pushing cable in this category to higher speeds—in some cases up to ATM speeds (155Mbps). A 16Mbps IBM Token Ring network requires such cable.

Category 5 Data-grade UTP, capable of supporting transmission rates of up to 155Mbps (but officially only up to 100Mbps). Category 5 cable uses AWG 22 or 24 wire, and has a 100MHz frequency range and a 100-ohm impedance. The wires in a Category 5 cable are wrapped together extra tightly, which helps give this cable type its high bandwidth. CDDI (Copper Distributed Data Interface) networks and 100BaseX network architectures require such cable. Specifications for a more stringent category 5E (for enhanced) have been developed by the TIA and released as an addendum to TIA/EIA 568A. These specifications tighten up the performance requirements, and it is strongly recommended that all new cable being installed should conform to the category 5E specifications.

Cable in Categories 4 and 5 is sometimes known as enhanced unshielded twisted-pair (EUTP) cable.

Working groups have been developing specifications for two additional categories that are designed to handle the next generation of networks. These new categories are characterized by their high bandwidths (200–250MHz and 600MHz)

Category 6   The specifications for this category represent the limits of what can be expected of UTP and screened twisted-pair wire. Category 6 cable is expected to support a frequency range that covers at least 200MHz, and possibly as high as 250MHz. Such cable is expected to support transmission rates for Gigabit Ethernet while remaining back compatible with lower categories. Category 6 cable is expected to use the same types of connectors as current cabling. Specifications for Category 6 cable are being developed by both TIA/EIA and by ISO/IEC.

Category 7   This specification is for STP cable, which will support a 600MHz frequency range. However, Category 7 cable will probably require an entirely new type of connector, and the working group is currently considering proposals for such connectors. Only an ISO/IEC working group is developing the Category 7 specification; however, it is expected that the TIA/EIA standards group will go along with the ISO/IEC specifications.

As stated, international standards for wiring are developed by the ISO/IEC. The ISO/IEC 11801 specification is similar to the TIA/EIA work except that the ISO/IEC specification distinguishes four performance classes—A through D—rather than the five categories found in the TIA/EIA documents. For the new categories, the ISO/IEC specifications refer to classes E and F, which correspond to Categories 6 and 7, respectively.

Performance Levels

Many cable vendors also use a five-level system to categorize their UTP cable. Just as there is overlap in the paths to enlightenment in various religious traditions, there is some overlap between these levels and the other systems discussed here. For example, the references to Level 4, Category 4 cable identify the cable according to the features described here and also according to the features in the EIA/TIA specifications.

Level 1   Voice-grade cable, which is suitable for use in the "plain old telephone system" (or POTS). Such cable can handle data at up to 1Mbps.

Level 2   Data-grade cable that is capable of transmission speeds as high as 4Mbps. This level corresponds roughly to the Type 3 cable described in IBM's Cabling System (see the Cable, IBM article). Level 2 cable also meets the requirements for the 1Base5 (StarLAN) Ethernet network developed by AT&T.

Level 3   Data-grade cable that is capable of transmission speeds as high as 16Mbps. This level corresponds to Category 3 cable in the EIA/TIA-568 specifications. Level 3 cable is used in 4Mbps or 16Mbps Token Ring networks, and also in 10BaseT Ethernet/802.3 networks.

Level 4   Data-grade cable that is capable of transmission speeds as high as 20Mbps. This level corresponds to Category 4 cable in the EIA/TIA-568 specifications. Level 4 cable is used for ARCnet Plus, a 20Mbps version of the ARCnet network architecture.

Level 5   Data-grade cable that is capable of transmission speeds as high as 100Mbps. This level corresponds to Category 5 cable in the EIA/TIA-568 specifications. Level 5 cable is used for CDDI (or TPDDI), which are copper-based implementations of the 100Mbps FDDI network architecture. 100BaseX, a 100Mbps version of Ethernet, is also intended to run on this type of cable.

Electrical Testing Laboratory (ETL)

The ETL is an independent laboratory that tests and rates products for manufacturers. Vendors specify if their cable has been tested and verified by ETL.

C

Manufacturing Automation Protocol (MAP)

The most commonly observed performance standards, arguably, are those associated with the MAP. Among other things, this standard specifies the expected performance for cables in the highly automated and machinery-heavy industrial working environments of the future.

Cable that meets MAP standards generally has quad shields; that is, four layers of shielding around the central core in a coaxial cable. The four layers of shielding help protect the cable against signal loss from the conductor wire and against electromagnetic interference from the outside world; for example, from heavy machinery being turned on and off. See the MAP article for more information.

Cable, STP (Shielded Twisted-Pair)

→ **See** Cable, Twisted-Pair

Cable, Telephone Twisted-Pair (TTP)

→ **See** Cable, Twisted-Pair

Cable Tester

An instrument for testing the integrity and performance of a stretch of cable. Cable testers run various tests to determine the cable's attenuation, resistance, characteristic impedance, and so on. High-end testers can test cable for conformity to various network architecture specifications, and can sometimes even identify a particular type of cable.

Because of measurement limitations, the 20 or so feet of cable nearest to the tester cannot be reliably examined.

Cable, Transceiver

Cable used to connect a network interface card to a transceiver, mainly in Ethernet architectures. A transceiver cable usually has an AUI connector at one end and an N-series or other type of connector at the other end. Coaxial transceiver cable comes in thick and thin versions. You can also get special cable with a built-in right angle.

Cable, Triaxial

A type of coaxial cable. Also called triax, this cable has an inner braid surrounded by an inner (non-plenum) jacket, surrounded by an outer copper braid. The extra shielding makes a big difference because of the grounding and improved protection.

→ **See Also** Cable, Coaxial

Cable, TTP (Telephone Twisted-Pair)

→ **See** Cable, Twisted-Pair

Cable, Twinaxial

A type of coaxial cable. Also called twinax, this cable has two insulated carrier wires, generally twisted around each other, which helps cut down considerably on magnetic interference. Twinaxial cables are used in IBM and AppleTalk networks.

→ **See Also** Cable, Coaxial

Cable, Twisted-Pair

Twisted-pair cable is very widely used, inexpensive, and easy to install. It can transmit data at an acceptable rate (up to 100Mbps in some network architectures). The best-known example of twisted-pair wiring is probably telephone cable, which is unshielded and is usually voice-grade, rather than the higher-quality data-grade cable used for networks. The illustration "Context and properties of twisted-pair cable" summarizes the features of this type of cable.

Context

```
Cable
    Electrical
        Twisted-Pair ──────────────┐
        Coaxial                    │
    Optical                        │
        Fiber-Optic                │
                                   ▼
```

Shielded Twisted-Pair (STP) Properties
Includes shield around twisted pairs
150 ohm impedance
Information in differential signal between wires in a pair
Subject to near-end crosstalk (NEXT)
Subject to electromagnetic interference
Generally uses RJ-xx connectors

Shielded Twisted-Pair (STP) Uses
IBM Token Ring networks
ARCnet networks
Rarely in Ethernet networks

Unshielded Twisted-Pair (UTP) Properties
No shield around twisted pairs
100 ohm impedance
Information in differential signal between wires in a pair
Subject to near-end crosstalk (NEXT)
Subject to electromagnetic interference
Generally uses RJ-xx connectors
Performance grades specified in EIA/TIA-568 Categories 1-5

Unshielded Twisted-Pair (UTP) Uses
10BaseT Ethernet networks
ARCnet networks
Certain sections of IBM Token Ring networks
Telephone lines (voice-grade)

CONTEXT AND PROPERTIES OF TWISTED-PAIR CABLE

In a twisted-pair cable, two conductor wires are wrapped around each other. A signal is transmitted as a differential between the two conductor wires. This type of signal is less prone to interference and attenuation, because using a differential essentially gives a double signal, but cancels out the random interference on each wire.

Twisting within a pair minimizes crosstalk between pairs. The twists also help deal with electromagnetic interference (EMI) and radio frequency interference (RFI), as well as signal loss due to capacitance (the tendency of a nonconductor to store up electrical charge). The performance of a twisted-pair cable can be influenced by changing the number of twists per foot in a wire pair.

IBM has developed its own categorization system for twisted-pair cable, mainly to describe the cable supported for IBM's Token Ring network architecture. The system is discussed in the Cable, IBM article.

Twisted-Pair Cable Components

A twisted-pair cable has the following components:

Conductor wires   The signal wires for this cable come in pairs that are wrapped around each other. The conductor wires are usually made of copper. They may be solid (consisting of a single wire) or stranded (consisting of many thin wires wrapped tightly together). A twisted-pair cable usually contains multiple twisted-pairs; 2, 4, 6, 8, 25, 50, or 100 twisted-pair bundles are common. For network applications, 2- and 4-pair cables are most commonly used.

Shield   Shielded twisted-pair (STP) cable includes a foil shield around each pair of conductors.

Jacket   The wire bundles are encased in a jacket made of polyvinylchloride (PVC) or, in plenum cables, of a fire-resistant material, such as Teflon or Kynar.

The illustration "Components of twisted-pair cable" shows the makeup of this type of cable. Note that the shield is not included for unshielded twisted-pair cable.

Conductor Wire
Made of copper, copper treated with tin or silver, or aluminum or steel covered with copper.

Dielectric
Made of a nonconductive material (such as polyethylene or Teflon), which may be solid or filled with air.

Foil Shield
Made of a polypropylene or polyester tape coated with aluminum on both sides (STP only).

Braid Shield
Made of flexible conductive wire braided around the dielectric (and foil shield). Braid may be made of aluminum or bare or treated copper. Braid is described in terms of the percentage coverage it gives. For example, 95% SC means 95% coverage with silvered copper (STP only).

Jacket
Made of polyvinylchloride or polyethylene for non-plenum cable; made of Teflon or Kynar for plenum cable.

COMPONENTS OF TWISTED-PAIR CABLE

Twisted-pair cable comes in two main varieties: shielded (STP) and unshielded (UTP). STP contains an extra shield or protective screen around each of the wire pairs to cut down on extraneous signals. This added protection also makes STP more expensive than UTP. (The price of coaxial cable actually lies between UTP and STP prices.)

Shielded Twisted-Pair (STP) Cable

STP cable has pairs of conductors twisted around each other. Each pair is covered with a foil shield to reduce interference and minimize crosstalk between wire pairs.

STP can handle high-speed transmissions, but the cable itself is relatively expensive, can be quite bulky and heavy, and is rather difficult to work with.

STP is used in ARCnet and Token Ring networks, although the special cable versions developed by IBM are more likely to be used in the Token Ring networks. Several of the types specified in the IBM Cable System are STP: Types 1, 2, 6, 8, and 9 (see the Cable, IBM article).

STP cable is sometimes known as data-grade cable or data-grade media (DGM).

Unshielded Twisted-Pair (UTP) Cable

UTP cable—also known as telephone twisted-pair (TTP) cable—does not include any extra shielding around the wire pairs. This type of cable is used in some Token Ring networks, usually those working at slower speeds. UTP can also be used in Ethernet and ARCnet architectures.

UTP is not the primary choice for any network architecture, but the IEEE has approved a standard for a 10BaseT Ethernet network that uses UTP cabling at 10Mbps. Networking mavens are divided as to whether 10BaseT and the use of UTP cable in general are welcome additions or dead-ends.

Because it lacks shielding, UTP is not as good at blocking noise and interference as STP or coaxial cable. Consequently, UTP cable segments must be shorter than when using other types of cable. For standard UTP, the length of a segment should never exceed 100 meters (about 330 feet).

On the other hand, UTP is quite inexpensive, and is very easy to install and work with. The price and ease of installation make UTP tempting, but keep in mind that installation is generally the major part of the cabling expense (so saving on the cable won't necessarily help cut expenses very

much) and that other types of cable may be just as easy to install.

To distinguish varieties of UTP, the EIA/TIA has formulated five categories. These are summarized in the Cable Standards article. Cable in Categories 4 and 5—which are the higher end, with respect to performance—is sometimes known as enhanced unshielded twisted-pair (EUTP) cable.

USING EXISTING TELEPHONE CABLE WIRES

Most telephone cable is UTP, and many telephone cables have extra wires because the cable comes with four pairs and the telephone company needs only two of the pairs for your telephone connection. (Any additional lines or intercoms require their own wire pairs.)

If there are unused wire pairs, you may be able to use these for your network cabling. While this is a tempting possibility, consider the following points carefully:

- The cable might not run conveniently for your needs, so you may need to add cable segments.

- Make sure you test all the cable you'll be using, and don't be surprised if some of it is defective.

- The telephone cable may be the lower-quality, voice-grade type, and you really should be using data-grade cable, unless you're transmitting over very short distances.

If you're going to use already installed cable for your network, make sure all of it works properly. Use a cable tester, which can provide detailed information about the cable's physical and electrical properties. When you're dealing with a long cable system, the chances are good that at least parts of it will be faulty. Find and replace the bad cable before you set everything up.

Hybrid Cable

In recent years, a hybrid class of cable has begun to appear in this country. Screened twisted-pair (ScTP)—also known as foil twisted-pair (FTP)—is a combination of shielded and unshielded twisted-pair cable.

C

ScTP cable consists of unshielded twisted-pair wires wrapped in aluminum ribbon. Proponents of this cable type claim that this wrapper provides at least some shielding from electromagnetic interference (EMI), which allows the cable to transmit at a faster rate—comparable to the 100Mbps possible with Category 5 UTP. This cable type remains largely untested in the United States.

ScTP cable is just beginning to appear in North America, but it has been used in Europe for a while. It is quite widely used in France and Germany, and has been endorsed by France Telecom and also Groupe Bull.

Performance Features

Twisted-pair cable is described in terms of its electrical and performance properties. The features that characterize UTP and STP cable include the following:

Attenuation   This value indicates how much power the signal has lost and is dependent on the frequency of the transmission. Attenuation is measured in relation to a specified distance; for example, 100 meters, 1000 feet, or 1 kilometer. Attenuation per 1000 feet values range from under 10 dB (for Category 4 cable running at 1MHz) to more than 60 dB (for Category 5 cable running at 100MHz). With attenuation, a lower value is better.

Capacitance   This value indicates the extent to which the cable stores up charge (which can distort the signal). Capacitance is measured in picofarads (pF) per foot, and lower values indicate better performance. Typical values are between 15 and 25 pF/ft.

Impedance   All UTP cable should have an impedance of 100 +/- 15 ohms.

NEXT   The near-end crosstalk (NEXT) indicates the degree of interference from neighboring wire pairs. This is also measured in decibels per unit distance, but because of notation and expression conventions, a high value is better for this feature. NEXT depends on the signal frequency and cable category. Performance is better at lower frequencies and for cables in the higher categories.

Twisted-Pair Cable Advantages

Twisted-pair cable has the following advantages over other types of cables for networks:

- It is easy to connect devices to twisted-pair cable.

- If an already installed cable system, such as telephone cable, has extra, unused wires, you may be able to use a pair of wires from that system. For example, in order to use the telephone cable system, you need telephone cable that has four pairs of wires, and there can be no intercoms or second lines to use the two pairs not needed for the telephone connection.

- STP does a good job of blocking interference.

- UTP is quite inexpensive.

- UTP is very easy to install.

- UTP may already be installed (but make sure it all works properly and that it meets the performance specifications your network requires).

Twisted-Pair Cable Disadvantages

Twisted-pair cable has the following disadvantages compared with other types of cable:

- STP is bulky and difficult to work with.

- UTP is more susceptible to noise and interference than coaxial or fiber-optic cable.

- UTP signals cannot go as far as they can with other cable types before they need cleaning and boosting.

- A skin effect can increase attenuation. This occurs when transmitting data at a fast rate over twisted-pair wire. Under these conditions, the current tends to flow mostly on the outside surface of the wire. This greatly decreases the cross-section of the wire being used for moving electrons, and thereby increases resistance. This, in turn, increases signal attenuation, or loss.

Selecting and Installing Twisted-Pair Cable

When you are deciding on a category of cable for your needs, take future developments—in your network and also in technology—into account. It is a good idea to buy the cable at least one category above the one you have selected. (If you selected Category 5 cable to begin with, you should seriously consider fiber-optic cable.)

Check the wiring sequence before you purchase cable. Different wiring sequences can lurk behind the same modular plug in a twisted-pair cable. (A wiring sequence, or wiring scheme, describes how wires are paired up and which locations each wire occupies in the plug.) If you connect a plug that terminates one wiring scheme into a jack that continues with a different sequence, the connection may not provide reliable transmission. See the Wiring Sequence article for more information.

You should find out which wiring scheme is used before buying cable, and buy only cable that uses the same wiring scheme. If you are stuck with existing cable that uses an incompatible wiring scheme, you can use a cross wye as an adapter between the two schemes.

If any of your cable purchases include patch cables (for example, to connect a computer to a wallplate), be aware that these cables come in two versions: straight through or reversed. For networking applications, use straight-through cable, which means that wire 1 coming in connects to wire 1 going out (rather than to wire 8 as in a reversed cable), wire 2 connects to wire 2 (rather than to wire 7), and so on. The tools for installing

and testing twisted-pair cable are the same as those used generally for network cables (see the Cable article for a discussion of cable tools).

→ **See Also** Cable; Cable, Coaxial; Cable, Fiber-Optic

Cable, Unshielded Twisted-Pair (UTP)

→ **See** Cable, Twisted-Pair

Cable, UTP (Unshielded Twisted-Pair)

→ **See** Cable, Twisted-Pair

Cable Vault

In the central office (CO) of a local telephone company, the cable vault is the location in which all the lines and trunks connected to the CO enter the premises. The cable vault is almost always underground for various logistical and aesthetic reasons. In COs in large city areas, the central vault may be the entry point for 30,000 to 40,000 lines and trunks.

Cable, Voice-Grade

Old-time, unshielded twisted-pair, telephone cable; Category 1 in the EIA/TIA-568 specifications. This cable is suited to the transmission of voice signals. Officially, such cable is not considered suitable for data-grade transmissions. In practice, it generally works fine at low speeds, over short distances, and under ordinary working conditions.

→ **See Also** Cable, Twisted-Pair

Cache

As a noun, a cache, also known as a disk cache, is an area of RAM (random-access memory) set aside for holding data that is likely to be used again. By keeping frequently used data in fast RAM, instead of on a hard or floppy disk with much slower access, a system's performance can be improved greatly.

As a verb, cache refers to the process of putting information into a cache for faster retrieval. Directory information and hard disk contents are examples of data likely to be cached. The illustration "Disk cache" shows an example of this process.

Cache Buffer Pool

In Novell's NetWare, the cache buffer pool is the amount of memory available for the network operating system (NOS) after the server module has been loaded into memory. The memory in this pool can be allocated for various purposes:

- To cache the file allocation tables (FATs) for each NetWare volume

- To create a hash table containing directory information

- To provide memory for NetWare Loadable Modules (NLMs) that are needed

CAL (Client Access License)

In the Microsoft Windows NT networking environment, client access licensing is used for arrangements in which the licensee is charged for the largest number of clients who could access the network at one time—an arrangement known as *per-seat licensing*. In this arrangement, the network must pay for each client, and each client can then access any server.

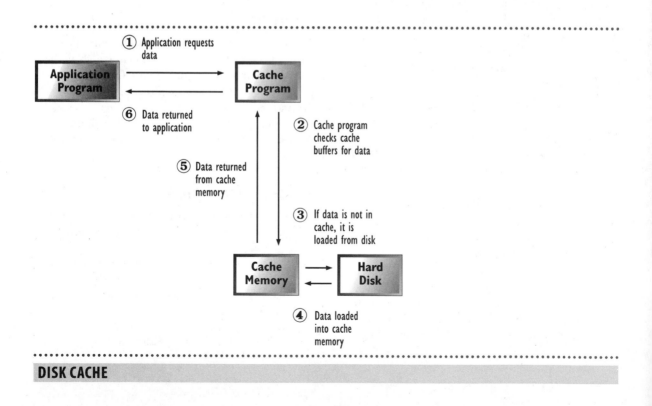

DISK CACHE

CAL is generally a practical arrangement for enterprise networks. This licensing scheme is in contrast to the more traditional *per-server licensing*, in which a license is required for each server, with the server licensing price being dependent on the number of clients who will access that server.

→ *Broader Category* Windows NT

Call

A request from one program or node to begin a communication with another node. The term is also used to refer to the resulting communications session.

Call Duration

In telephone communication, call duration represents the amount of time a telephone call lasts. In the PSTN (Public Switched Telephone Network—that is, the telephone system), the circuit over which the call is connected remains tied up until the call ends.

The average, or expected, call duration is used in analyses and models of telephone network traffic. This information is used to plan for upgrades and increases in line and trunk capacity.

The current telephone network infrastructure is based, in part, on traffic models in which the average call lasts about 3 minutes. With this kind of traffic, there can be lots of calls because lines and trunk space are always becoming available as calls are constantly terminated.

In contrast, calls to an Internet Service Provider (ISP) last much longer than a typical voice call. A telephone network filled with such calls would have a very different traffic pattern. One reason for this is that lines are turned over much less slowly because the typical session call lasts over 30 minutes.

The combination of the current telephone system and the long call durations of Internet access calls are putting considerable strain on the phone system.

This is one of the reasons you may have trouble logging on to the Internet at times.

Call duration is also known as *holding time*.

Caller ID

In ISDN and some other telecommunications environments, a feature that includes the sender's identification number (such as telephone number) in the transmission so that the receiver knows who is calling. Caller ID is also known as *ANI (automatic number identification)* and *CLID (calling line identification)*.

Calling Line Identification (CLID)

→ *See* CLID (Calling Line Identification)

Call Setup Time

The amount of time needed to establish a connection between two nodes so they can communicate with each other.

Campus Area Network (CAN)

→ *See* CAN (Campus Area Network)

Campus-Wide Information System (CWIS)

→ *See* CWIS (Campus-Wide Information System)

CAN (Campus Area Network)

A network that connects nodes (or possibly departmental local area networks) from multiple locations, which may be separated by a considerable distance. Unlike a wide area network, however, a campus network does not require remote communications facilities, such as modems and telephones.

Capacitance

Capacitance is the ability of a dielectric (nonconductive) material to store electricity and to resist changes in voltage. In the presence of a signal (a voltage change), the dielectric will store some of the charge. Capacitance is usually measured in microfarads or picofarads (millionths or trillionths of a farad, respectively).

Other things being equal, the lower the capacitance, the better the cable. A higher capacitance means that more of the charge can be stored in the dielectric between two conductors, which means greater resistance. At higher frequencies, high capacitance results in greater signal attenuation.

→ *See Also* Cable

Capacitor

An electrical component in line conditioners, surge protectors, and other equipment. Capacitors help clean incoming power by absorbing surges and noise from electromagnetic and radio frequency interference. Compare it with inductor and MOV (metal oxide varistor).

CAP (Carrierless Amplitude/Phase Modulation)

In digital subscriber line (DSL) technology—for example, in ADSL (asynchronous digital subscriber line)—CAP is used as a line coding method. Line coding is what determines how 0 and 1 values are represented electronically when they are transmitted. With CAP, four binary bit values can be encoded in a single signal.

With CAP, both the amplitude (strength) and phase (timing) of a signal are varied to produce the 16 possible combinations of four bits (that is, from 0000 through 1111). In this way, CAP is very similar—in fact, identical to—quadrature amplitude modulation (QAM), which has been used in medium to high-speed modems for years. CAP and QAM differ, however, because CAP does not use a carrier signal, whereas QAM does. Instead, only the offset values—that is, just the values that would be added to the carrier signal in QAM—are transmitted. Circuitry at the receiving end must be able to add a carrier signal in order to permit further processing of the signal.

CAP is one of the two commonly used line encoding strategies that are popular for ADSL and HDSL (high-speed digital subscriber line). The other is discrete multitone (DMT). Compared with DMT, CAP is considered simpler, faster, and more established (because of its similarity to the venerable QAM).

DMT, in contrast, is considered better at handling noise and at adapting the transmission rate in case of noisy (and error-prone) connections. DMT is also the official line coding method for ADSL, but there are movements to get CAP approved as an official alternative line coding method.

→ *Broader Categories* Encoding, Signal

→ *See Also* DMT (Discrete Multitone)

Carrier Band

A communications system in which the entire bandwidth is used for a single transmission and in which a signal is modulated before being transmitted. This is in contrast to baseband systems, which do not modulate the signal, and to broadband systems, which divide the total bandwidth into multiple channels.

Carrier Detect (CD)

→ *See* CD (Carrier Detect)

Carrier Frequency

The rate at which the carrier signal repeats, measured in cycles per second, or hertz. In communications, the carrier signal is modulated, or altered, by superimposing a second signal, which represents the information being transmitted. In an acoustic signal, the frequency represents the signal's pitch.

Carrierless Amplitude/Phase Modulation (CAP)

→ *See* CAP (Carrierless Amplitude/Phase Modulation)

Carrier On

In carrier sense, multiple access (CSMA) media-access methods, a signal that indicates the network is being used for a transmission. When a node detects this signal, the node waits a random amount of time before trying again to access the network.

Carrier Pulse

A signal, consisting of a series of rapid, constant pulses, used as the basis for pulse modulation; for example, when converting an analog signal into digital form.

Carrier Sense Multiple Access/ Collision Avoidance (CSMA/CA)

→ *See* CSMA/CA (Carrier Sense Multiple Access/Collision Avoidance)

Carrier Sense Multiple Access/ Collision Detect (CSMA/CD)

→ *See* CSMA/CD (Carrier Sense Multiple Access/Collision Detect)

Carrier Serving Area (CSA)

→ *See* CSA (Carrier Serving Area)

Carrier Signal

An electrical signal that is used as the basis for a transmission. This signal has well-defined properties, but conveys no information (content). Information is sent by modifying (modulating) some feature of the carrier signal, such as the amplitude, frequency, or timing, to represent the values being transmitted.

Carrier-Switched Multiplexer (CS-MUX)

→ *See* CS-MUX (Carrier-Switched Multiplexer)

Carrier Wire

A conductive wire (capable of carrying an electrical signal); for example, the central wire in a coaxial cable, which serves as the medium for the electrical signal.

→ *See Also* Cable

Cascading Style Sheets (CSS)

→ *See* CSS (Cascading Style Sheets)

C

Cascading Style Sheets Level 1 (CSS1)

→ *See* CSS (Cascading Style Sheets)

Cascading Style Sheets Level 2 (CSS2)

→ *See* CSS (Cascading Style Sheets)

CAS (Communicating Application Specification)

An interface standard for fax modems developed by Intel and DCA. This proposed standard competes with the Class x hierarchy developed by EIA.

CAT (Common Authentication Technology)

In the Internet community, CAT is a specification for distributed authentication under development. CAT supports authentication measures based on either public- or private-key encryption strategies.

With CAT, both client and server programs must use the services of a common interface, which will provide the authentication services. This interface will connect to either DASS (Distributed Authentication Security Service), which uses public-key encryption, or Kerberos, which uses private-key encryption.

→ *Broader Category* Authentication

→ *See Also* DASS (Distributed Authentication Security Service); Kerberos

Cathedral versus Bazaar

In this phrase, cathedral and bazaar represent two models of programming development. In a paper entitled "The Cathedral and the Bazaar," Eric Raymond distinguishes between the cathedral style of programming (which characterizes program development in most software companies) and the bazaar style (which characterizes the development of the Linux operating system as a serious competitor to Windows).

Cathedral Programs

Cathedral programs are created by (more or less) official programming teams who do all the work, and who don't release the program until it is (reasonably) bug-free. The program's source code is an asset because it contains corporate secrets—information that the company wants to keep from others. Project managers for cathedral programs release the program only when it's ready or when the press releases and public opinion make it impossible to delay any longer. The cathedral style

- Is secretive vis-à-vis its user base. The source code and other program details are made available only to the members of the development team and to select individuals who may need access to the program or some of its components. A cathedral program is a mysterious entity. It is created by a priesthood of initiates and its details are known only to its creators.

- Releases code only when it is considered bug-free—that is, infrequently. Since only the code priests can fix the code, it is important to make sure all known problems are fixed before the product is released to end users. Since no program is ever bug-free, revisions will be necessary; since the revision is held until it is (once again) bug-free, users may need to wait months for fixes. (Note that many software cathedrals are beginning to release patches at more frequent intervals. Customers can download such patches from the companies' Web sites.)

- Deals with programming or deadline problems by adding developers to the project. Because bugs are what keep a product from being released, they are considered deep problems that can be solved only by experienced, specialist programmers. However, most studies of programming methodology find that adding developers does not solve the problem. As a result, most cathedral programs come out behind schedule.

Bazaar Programs

In contrast to cathedral programs, bazaar programs are created by individuals with a need or an idea. These original program creators are assisted by an ill-defined and ever changing cadre of end users with programming skills and with opinions about what they want. Keepers of bazaar programs tend to release early and release often. The bazaar approach

- Releases source code to end users. Since some of these end users will turn out to be contributors to the final program, making the source code available to them is a sensible step. As it turns out, it is also essential for enabling the development process that characterizes bazaar programs. Linus Torvalds—the creator of Linux—released the source code to the kernel he created, and this code has been worked on by hundreds, probably thousands, of contributors.

- Releases intermediate versions frequently. Such releases are known and acknowledged to contain bugs. As end users work with the releases, they will find the bugs and some will find solutions. The solutions may be programmed by the end users and submitted to the program's director (the person who released the original program and who maintains the official version). As soon as a bug is found and fixed, a new release of the program is likely to be distributed. Versions of bazaar programs can sometimes be released daily or even more frequently. In his Linux releases, Torvalds distinguishes between stable and not-yet-stable versions. End users may take the safe route and update only to the stable versions, or they may live dangerously, and grapple with even the flakier releases.

- Generally has no deadline problems, and deals with programming problems by making use of the insights, skills, and suggestions of debuggers. Bazaar programs such as Linux have benefited from the contributions of end users who work with the intermediate releases. In fact, many of the features in Linux are the result of cooperative efforts by people who possibly have never met face-to-face. Since bazaar programs are distributed in a more or less continuous series of releases, they aren't plagued by the kinds of deadline issues that cathedral programs must face. With a bazaar program there are never end users who have been waiting months for a new release with needed bug fixes.

→ *Primary Sources* Raymond's fascinating and insightful paper is available at `http://www .tuxedo.org/~esr/writings/cathedral-bazaar-1.html`.

CAU (Controlled Access Unit)

In IBM Token Ring networks, the term for an intelligent hub. CAUs can determine whether nodes are operating, connect and disconnect nodes, monitor node activity, and pass data to the LAN Network Manager program.

CAU/LAM (Controlled Access Unit/Lobe Attachment Module)

In IBM Token-Ring networks, a hub (the CAU) containing one or more boxes (the LAM) with multiple ports to which new nodes can be attached.

C Band

The C band is a portion of the electromagnetic spectrum using frequencies in the 4 to 7GHz range. This bandwidth is used for satellite communications.

Transmissions to a satellite (uplinks) use the 6GHz bands; transmissions from the satellite (downlinks) use the 4GHz bands.

CBC (Cipher Block Chaining)

An operating mode for the DES.

→ *See* DES (Data Encryption Standard)

CBEMA (Computer Business Manufacturers Association)

An organization that provides technical committees for work being done by other organizations; for example, the committee for the FDDI standard published by ANSI.

CBMS (Computer-Based Messaging System)

CBMS is an older term for a message handling system (MHS), or for electronic mail.

→ *See* E-Mail

CBR (Constant Bit Rate)

A CBR transmission is provided by an ATM (Asynchronous Transfer Mode) connection that uses Class A service, which is designed for voice or other data that are transmitted at a constant rate.

→ *Compare* ABR (Available Bit Rate); UBR (Unspecified Bit Rate); VBR (Variable Bit Rate).

CC (Clearing Center)

In EDI, a message-switching element through which documents are passed on the way to their destinations.

→ *See Also* EDI (Electronic Document Interchange)

CCC (Cisco Career Certification)

Cisco Systems is one of the world's major suppliers of networking and internetworking hardware, particularly routers and switches. The CCC program represents a way to provide necessary skills and to ensure a minimal level of skill for people who must administer and maintain networks and internetworks. To gain a certificate in a specified topic area, students must complete coursework in the specialty area and in related topics, and they must pass an exam.

Cisco offers a number of tracks, specialty subareas within some of the tracks, and three levels of expertise to which students can aspire. The tracks deal with routing and other internetworking topics, and students can work for Associate, Professional, or Expert status—with Expert being the most advanced level.

Cisco offers certification in the following tracks:

Internetworking For professionals working with internetworks consisting of LANs, WANs, or both. The CCIE (Cisco Certified Internetwork Expert) is the most comprehensive program in this track. It also includes specializations in routing and switching, in ISP dial (for remote connections), and in WAN switching.

Networking For professionals working primarily with networks that include Cisco components (routers or switches, for example). This track includes CCNA (Cisco Certified Network Associate) and CCNP (Cisco Certified Network Professional).

Design For professionals hoping to design networks or internetworks. The CCDA (Cisco Certification Design Associate) is one of the certificates available in this track.

WAN Switching For professionals working with internetworks that include WAN switches. This topic is a specialty area for all the other tracks. Thus, there are CCIE-WAN Switching, CCNA-WAN Switching, and CCDP-WAN Switching certificates, for example.

CCIR (International Consultative Committee for Radiocommunication)

An ITU (International Telecommunication Union) agency that is responsible for defining standards for radio communications. In 1993, the CCIR—together with the IFRB (International Frequency Registration Board)—was replaced by the ITU-R (International Telecommunication Union—Radiocommunication Standardization Sector).

→ *See Also* ITU

CCIS (Common Channel Interoffice Signaling)

In telephone communications, a transmission method that uses different channels for voice and control signals. The control signals are sent by a fast, packet-switched method, which makes it possible to include extra information (such as caller ID and billing information) in the control channel.

→ *See Also* CCS 7

CCITT (Consultative Committee for International Telegraphy and Telephony)

The CCITT is a permanent subcommittee of the ITU (International Telecommunications Union), which operates under the auspices of the United Nations. The committee consists of representatives from 160 member nations, mostly from national PTT (Postal, Telephone, and Telegraph) services.

The CCITT is responsible for dozens of standards used in communications, telecommunications, and networking, including the X.25 and X.400 standards, the V.42 and V.42bis standards for modems, and the I.xxx series of documents on ISDN (Integrated Services Digital Network).

The CCITT works closely with the ISO (International Standardization Organization), so that many standards and recommendations will appear in documents from both groups. CCITT recommendations appear every four years, with 1992 (the white books) being the most recent.

In March 1993, the CCITT was officially renamed the International Telecommunication Union-Telecommunication Standardization Sector (ITU-T, sometimes written as ITU-TS or ITU-TSS). However, since the CCITT name is so familiar and is likely to remain in widespread use for some time, the older name is used throughout this book.

CCRSE (Commitment, Concurrency, and Recovery Service Element)

In the OSI reference model, an application-layer service that is used to implement distributed transactions among multiple applications.

→ *See* ASE (Application Service Element)

CCS (Common Channel Signaling)

A signaling method in which control signals are sent across different channels than voice and data signals. This makes it possible to include various types of extra information in the control signal.

→ *See Also* CCS 7

CCS (Common Communications Support)

One of the pillars of IBM's SAA specifications. CCS includes support for data links, application services, session services, and data streams.

→ *See Also* SAA (Systems Application Architecture)

CCS (Continuous Composite Servo)

A compact disc recording technique in which the contents are stored on separate tracks laid out in concentric circles.

→ *Compare* SS (Sampled Servo)

CCS (Hundreds of Call Seconds)

In telephone communications, a measure of line activity. One CCS is equivalent to 100 seconds of conversation on a line, so that an hour of line usage is 36 CCS; 36 CCS is equal to one Erlang, and indicates continuous use of the line.

CCS 7 (Common Channel Signaling 7)

A version of the CCITT's Signaling System 7 (SS7); a transmission method in ISDN that makes special services (such as call forwarding or call waiting) available anywhere in a network. CCS 7 is an extension of the CCIS method for transmitting control information.

CD (Carrier Detect)

A signal sent from a modem to a PC, to indicate that the modem is online and ready for work.

CD (Compact Disc)

Compact discs are the product of a recording and storage technology that makes it possible to fit over half a gigabyte of digital data on a disc about the size of a floppy disk. Unlike floppy or hard disks, which use magnetic technology, compact discs are recorded using optical methods.

To produce a master disc for commercially-produced CDs, a laser literally burns the information into the disc by creating tiny pits in the surface. This changes the reflective properties of the disc at these locations relative to the surrounding surface. The information is read by using a laser so that there is never any physical contact during the reading process. The information on a CD is actually contained in the transitions between the pits and the non-pit areas (known as the lands).

CD technology has undergone several revisions and advancements since the first digital audio (DA) discs were developed over 10 years ago.

CD Variants

The following standards and variants have been created and used over the years. Most of these standards are still in use, and many current CD drives can read several of the standards. In addition, newer standards (such as CD-XA) are often back-compatible with earlier standards (such as CD-ROM).

CD standards are distinguished by the color of the laser used in that particular technology—for example, red, yellow, and green. Collectively, these standards documents are known as the Rainbow Books. The following standards are among the most popular:

CD-DA (Digital Audio) (Red Book) This was the first compact disc standard, and was developed for recording musical discs. CD-DA discs can hold about 74 minutes of music recorded at 44,100 samples per second (known as the scanning frequency), using **PCM (pulse code modulation)** as the digitization method, and allocating 16 bits for each sample. (With 16 bits, each sample can take on any of 65, 536 (or $2 \char`^ 16$ values). These bits can be allocated in whatever manner one chooses, provided the resulting split is meaningful. For example, by allocating 8 bits to each channel, you can get stereo. CD-DA was not developed for recording data. CD-DA is what everyone correctly thinks of as audio CD.

CD-ROM (Read only memory) (Yellow Book) This standard was designed to enable CD technology to be used with computers—and for storing huge amounts of data. Because error rate requirements for data are much more stringent than for music, the bits in a CD-ROM sector are allocated differently than for a musical performance. Whereas a CD-DA sector has 2352 bytes available for storing music in each sector, CD-ROM has only 2048, because 280 extra bits had to be allocated for error-detection and correction. CD-ROM actually does have a less stringent mode, known as mode 2 (in contrast to the mode 1 used for data). This makes 2336 bytes per sector available for use (at the cost of a considerable amount of error correcting).

CD-ROM/XA (Extended Architecture) (Yellow Book and some of the Green Book)

This standard was designed to provide a more efficient and flexible storage method, but one that could be made back-compatible with earlier standards. In addition to providing a new, more flexible sector format, CD-ROM/XA uses a different digitization method and compresses the audio data—decompressing the audio on the fly if the audio should ever be needed. At its lowest scanning frequency and highest compression, a CD-ROM/XA disc can hold over nine hours of stereo music—compared to just under 1.25 hours for CD-DA. In addition, CD-ROM/XA uses a new sector format, which allows a file to be nested inside another. Even though it uses special hardware, CD-ROM/XA technology is back-compatible with CD-DA and ordinary CD-ROM. (Fortunately, most CD drives available today include this extra hardware, so that these drives can read most kinds of CDs.) CD-ROM discs can hold up to 660MB of data.

Photo-CD This disc format was created by Kodak to provide a way for customers to digitize their photos and to use them at work or home. The Photo-CD technology combines the XA standards with multisession technology. A session is a recording period. Originally, CDs could record only once, which meant that all data or pictures had to be recorded in a single session. With a multisession disc, on the other hand, a customer can have pictures recorded several times up to the disc's capacity.

CD-WO (Write Once) and CD-MO (Magneto-optical) (Orange Book) These are specifications for recordable CDs. CD-WO—also known as CD-WORM (Write once, read many)—is the older standard. It can create discs with capacities of 128MB, 650MB, or 6.5GB, depending on the disc's size. CD-WO discs require a magneto-optical drive and are not compatible with CD-ROM technology. CD-MO discs can hold 128-, 230-, 600-, 650-, or 1300MB, and they must also be read by a special magneto-optical drive. Unlike CD-WO, however, CD-MO discs can be recorded multiple times. Because of this, MO discs are also known as EO (erasable optical) discs.

CD-R (Recordable) (Orange Book) This is a variant of the WO standard. Unlike CD-WO, however, discs recorded using CD-R technology can be read on ordinary CD-ROM drives. Until recently, CD-R machines were much too expensive for personal use; this has changed, and such devices are becoming very popular for business use. Discs for use in a CD-R drive are distinguished by their gold surface, as opposed to the silvery surface of a commercially produced disc. One reason for this is that CD-R discs are created using a somewhat different process than commercial CDs. Instead of burning pits into the surface, the recording laser in a CD-R drive simply changes the optical properties of an organic paint in the disc's recording surface. This makes it possible to work with a much weaker laser. CD-R discs can hold up to 660MB of information. These discs are, in essence, just ordinary CD-ROM discs produced by special means. CD-R's future may be limited, however, by the newer CD-RW technology (described in the next item), which can do everything CD-R can and more.

CD-RW (Rewritable) (Orange Book II) This variant uses a somewhat different recording technology than CD-R. Using what is known as phase change technology, CD-RW has a 780nm infrared laser that burns small pits into the disc.

The result is a disc with a somewhat lower reflectivity than a CD-R disc (making it harder to read), but one that can be written and erased up to 1000 times. Discs created with CD-RW drives use the Universal Disc Format (UDF), which differs from the layout of a standard CD-ROM, but which is also being used by the new DVD-ROM technology. CD-RW technology supports packet writing, which allows you to edit files on disc, drag and drop files to a CD-RW disc, and generally treat the discs as ordinary reusable media. (True random erasing, however, is still not available with all CD-RW drivers.) While CD-RW drives can read CD-R discs, the converse generally is not true. Only newer CD-ROM drives, with genuine Multi-Read capabilities (as specified by the OSTA, or Optical Storage Technology Association), can reliably read CD-RW discs. Partly these reading difficulties exist because of the lower reflectivity of CD-RW discs. CD-RW drives can also write CD-R discs, but not with packet writing capabilities. Discs for CD-RW cost in the $15–25 range, which is several times the cost of a CD-R disc. However, the reusability makes the CD-RW disc potentially much more economical. CD-RW was originally known as CD-E (for CD erasable).

CD-I (Interactive) (Green Book) This standard allows branching based on interaction between the user and the material. CD-I drives connect to a television set. Any computing capabilities required to run the software are built into the drive. You cannot use or even read CD-I discs in ordinary CD-ROM drives. 3DO is a proprietary variant of the CD-I standard.

High density CD (Blue Book) This technology is still being developed. When perfected, this standard is expected to increase the capacity of a disc tenfold—to about 6.5GB. In general, the shorter the wavelength of the laser light, the higher the storage capacity. Each time the wavelength is halved, possible storage capacity is increased fourfold. The problem is creating cost-effective blue lasers that have a sufficiently long life and sufficiently low energy requirements. As of early 1999,

violet lasers were just on the verge of making their way down the production cost chain toward commercial viability.

Hybrid standards Several variants have been developed for special purposes or to make use of particular technology. In general, such discs require special hardware. Hybrids include CD+G, CD-MIDI, CD-EB, and CD-V. CD+G (for graphics) is basically an audio CD with additional information such as text or graphics. CD-MIDI (for Musical Instrument Digital Interface) is an audio disc with MIDI information. CD-EB (for Electronic Book) is special size and format that is used mainly to store reference materials. CD-V (for video) is an audio disc with video information recorded in analog form. The laserdisc is actually a CD-V variant.

The logical structure of the material on a CD is defined in the ISO 9660 documents. These, in turn, are based on the earlier High Sierra specifications.

The market penetration for CD-ROM technology is stupendous—in part because just about every PC that has shipped in the past few years has included a CD-ROM drive. Also, just about every software product is distributed on CD-ROM by default.

Because of this penetration, there is every reason to expect the demand to remain high for at least the rewritable variants of CD-ROM technology (CD-R and CD-RW). The read-only part of the technology is rapidly being replaced by the much higher capacity DVD (digital versatile disc) technology.

➤*Compare* DVD (Digital Versatile Disc)

CDDI (Copper Distributed Data Interface)

CDDI is a networking configuration that implements the FDDI architecture and protocols on unshielded twisted-pair (UTP) cable—that is, on electrical (rather than optical) cable. A related implementation is SDDI (shielded distributed data interface), which uses shielded twisted-pair (STP) cable. Also known as copper-stranded distributed data interface and as TPDDI (twisted-pair DDI).

→ *See Also* FDDI (Fiber Distributed Data Interface)

CDF (Channel Definition Format)

CDF is an XML (eXtensible Markup Language) application from Microsoft. CDF provides a set of elements and definitions that enable you to create channels using instructions in a simple text file. In this context, a *channel* refers to a stream of materials (generally, Web pages) that are delivered according to some set of instructions or inclusion criteria. Generally, these instructions are specified as meta-content—either in a separate file or as markup instructions within the content file.

Separating content and metacontent has many advantages. For example, it is much easier to update and maintain a channel if all the instructions are in a separate file, where they can be read, evaluated, and edited easily—as opposed to being hidden among the (possibly considerable) content.

With CDF you can create such a *channel definition file,* also known as a *CDF control file*. This file specifies which Web pages should be delivered in a channel, using push technology. In addition to specifying what is to be delivered, the channel definition file can also specify how—in what order, in what format (for example, screen saver, full-screen, etc.), and to whom (for example, only to subscribers). In this file, you can also specify how often users should check the channel for new material.

A channel definition file is an XML file containing elements and attributes defined in the CDF document type definition (DTD). For example, such a file would have specifications for one or more channels.

Each channel's specification would be within the <CHANNEL> and </CHANNEL> tags. Various attributes—for example, the channel's name, a description, a URL (Uniform Resource Locator) to which users can go for more information, the location of the channel definition file, and so forth—must or could be defined for the channel.

The core of the channel definition, however, will be a list of elements between <ITEM> and </ITEM> tags. Each item will specify the location and attributes for a Web page to be included in the channel. Attributes for an ITEM element include or add the following: Title (a name for the item), HREF (the URL, or location, of the Web page), Show (how to display the Web page), Precache (whether to store the page in a cache before displaying), and Authenticate (whether to require a password). The presentation can be made as fancy or as simple as intelligent design principles permit for your particular storage and delivery requirements.

Other features of a channel can also be specified—for example, scheduling details.

To change the content or delivery of the channel, all you need to do is to make the appropriate changes in the CDF control file. For example, to show a different Web page, you just need to insert the new ITEM and remove the old ITEM entry from the file.

A CDF control file specifies the contents and presentation of Web pages. The actual content is delivered using push technology, or webcasting. JavaScript can be used to specify material for delivery via push technology, but the separation between instructions and content are not as clean as with CDF control files.

→ *See Also* Push Technology

CDFS (CD-ROM File System)

A file structure used for storing information on a compact disc. The file allocation table (FAT) system may not be efficient or even feasible for such a disc because of the large number of files the disc may contain.

CDMA (Code Division Multiple Access)

In cellular communications, CDMA is a proposed transmission method that uses special codes to fit up to ten times as much information into a channel. Each signal that comes in on a given frequency is "spread" using a different code. When the receiver decodes the received signals, only the signal with the appropriate spread will be meaningful; the other signals will be received as noise.

CDMA uses a soft-handoff when switching a transmission from one cell to another to ensure that no bits are lost in the transmission. In this type of handoff, both cells transmit the transitional bits at the same time and on the same frequency. This way, one of the transmissions will be within range of the receiver.

Also known as spread-spectrum technology, this method is not compatible with the TDMA (time division multiple access) method that was adopted as a standard in 1989. Interestingly, the actress Hedy Lamarr and the musician and composer George Antheil hold a patent (for jam-proof radio control of torpedoes) that specifies the fundamental principles of spread-spectrum technology.

→ *Broader Category* Cellular Communications

→ *Compare* TDMA (Time Division Multiple Access)

CDP (Cisco Discovery Protocol)

→ *See* Protocol, CDP (Cisco Discovery Protocol)

CDPD (Cellular Digital Packet Data)

CDPD is a cellular communications technology that sends digital data over unused analog cellular (voice) channels. CDPD data can be transmitted at 19.2Kbps, but only in service areas that support CDPD. The number of CDPD subscribers has grown at a regular rate since 1995, to a current level of over a million subscribers, and just about all areas are now accessible for CDPD connections.

A CDPD connection involves three main components and two optional elements of a more general nature:

- Mobile End System (M-ES), which can be a PC or other device equipped with a CDPD modem.

- Mobile Data Base Station (MDBS), which acts as a relay between the M-ES and the MDIS (see next item). The MDBS also keeps M-ESs within its range informed of whether the communications channel is currently available or whether someone is transmitting.

- Mobile Data Intermediate System (MDIS), which serves as the control point for the CDPD connection.

- Cellular relay towers (optional, depending on range and location), which amplify and pass on cellular signals within their region (cell) and to adjacent regions.

- Communications network (optional), which can serve as part of a connection—particularly if the MDBS and MDIS are widely separated.

The M-ES and MDBS communicate with each other over two channels using the Digital Sense Multiple Access (DSMA) Protocol. The *forward channel* goes from the MDBS to the M-ES, and is used by the MDBS to transmit status information and also data to M-ESs. For example, the MDBS uses the forward channel to indicate whether the communications channel is busy or idle. The *reverse channel* goes from M-ES to MDBS, and is used to transmit data.

When an M-ES wants to transmit—for example, to send an e-mail or a fax—the M-ES checks the forward channel (from the MDBS) to see whether it is busy or idle. If it's idle, the M-ES begins transmitting; if it's busy, the M-ES waits a random amount of time before trying again.

The MDIS has two main functions. In the *mobile home function*, the MDIS keeps track of the home location of each M-ES, and also provides forwarding information to the M-ESs as these move within the range of different MDBSs. The MDIS also manages the handoff between MDBSs as the M-ES moves between MBDS coverage regions. In its *mobile serving function*, the MDIS does various management and administrative tasks, such as authenticating subscribers, monitoring account usage and billing, monitoring line usage and performance, and so forth.

CDPD can be used as a mobile computing strategy to stay connected with the company network back at the office. It is also useful for credit card authorizations and other point-of-sale transactions. Essentially, a mobile user needs a special CDPD modem and the appropriate software. The user gets an IP (Internet protocol) address, which makes it possible to communicate as well as to make use of Internet services.

Mobile users can remain connected even when they are not using their computers and even when they are outside the range of a cell that supports CDPD. The CDPD specifications support a "sleep" mode for the computer. The network signals periodically to sleeping devices, and a device will "wake" if the signal includes the device's name or address. The monitoring for each device is done by the MDIS.

Similarly, the MDIS allows a user to remain connected even beyond areas that support CDPD through a technology known as switched CDPD. If the user is outside a service area with CDPD capabilities when called, the MDIS opens a circuit-switched connection over the channel. The connection is circuit-switched as far as the cellular network is concerned, but is essentially packet-switched as far as the device is concerned. This is because the MDIS closes the connection whenever there is silence, and reopens it whenever there is activity.

CDPD supports data compression and encryption. This cuts down on transmission times (and costs) and also helps keep snoopers from getting access to the data. In the CDPD specification, the data are first compressed and then encrypted.

The CDPD specifications are formulated under the auspices of the CDPD Forum, which you can contact at http://www.cdpd.org or at 800-335-CDPD (2373).

→ *See Also* Cellular Communications

CD-ROM Drive

CD-ROM stands for compact-disc, read-only memory. A CD-ROM drive is a peripheral device for reading CDs, which have a huge capacity (660MB).

Several features distinguish CD-ROM drives from each other:

- Transfer rate, which represents the amount of data that the drive can read from the disc in a second. Speeds are based on a base rate of 150KB per second, which is known as a single-speed drive. Double speed (2×) and quad-speed (4×) drives can transfer 300 and 600KB per second, respectively. Currently, drives in the 20× to 32× range are common. These have transfer rates of between 3 and 4.8MB per second. When reading such numbers, however, it's important to realize that different parts of a compact disc can be accessed at different maximum rates. In most cases, the vendor will include the drive's best specifications. Caveat emptor. Also, being able to read programs at such speeds doesn't necessarily lead to performance gains. Most programs are written to perform optimally with 2× or 4× drives—since those were the dominant drive speeds in the consumer market when the programs were developed. These programs will not necessarily perform any faster in faster drives.

- Access time, which represents the average time it takes to find a specified item of information on the disc. Currently, access times of less than 200 msec are considered standard.

- Compatibility with various CD standards, which indicates the types of CDs the drive can read. The CD (compact disc) article summarizes these. Briefly, drives should be able to read CD-XA (extended architecture) discs and should support multisession formats. The OSTA (Optical Storage Technology Association) has created a new MultiRead specification for CDs that is designed to ensure that newer drives can read the various rewritable CD formats that are currently available. These include CD-R and CD-RW, and are discussed in the CD (Compact Disc) entry.

- Number of discs the drive can handle. Multidisc systems can hold 3, 6, 18, or even 100 discs, and can switch between them within a few seconds. The drive can only read one disc at a time, however.

A CD-ROM drive may be connected to a network, making any available CDs shareable resources. With the appropriate server and drivers, users can share access to the disc currently loaded in the drive. A CD-ROM drive can be accessed just like any other volume, except that you can only read from it. If there are licensing restrictions on use of a disc, it is essential that the server software be able to restrict simultaneous access to the licensed number of users.

Like any other type of hardware device, CD-ROM drives require hardware drivers to communicate. In addition, a special driver containing extensions is required. These extensions are specific to the operating system, such as DOS, OS/2, or NT, with which the CD-ROM is working. Microsoft has provided such a driver for MS-DOS, called MSCDEX, which can be used with most CD-ROM drives. Some hardware manufacturers have also created their own proprietary drivers. If you are connecting a CD-ROM drive to a workstation, you will need to load both the driver's regular hardware driver and either MSCDEX or the manufacturer's own extensions driver.

If you want to make a CD-ROM drive available as a shared volume on a NetWare 3.12 or NetWare 4.x network, you do not load the MSCDEX driver.

Instead, load the CD-ROM driver's regular hardware drivers and Novell's CDROM.NLM. This NLM manages the interface between the drive and NetWare and enables the CD-ROM device to be viewed and accessed by multiple users, just like any other NetWare volume.

Note that the drivers available for a given CD-ROM drive may or may not work with your system. Verify that the drive is compatible before you install it.

CD-ROM File System (CDFS)

→ *See* CDFS (CD-ROM File System)

CDSL (Consumer Digital Subscriber Line)

CDSL is a digital subscriber line (DSL) variant that is designed to provide (relatively) high-speed connections to (actually, from) the Internet for home users. Like ADSL (asymmetric DSL), its more powerful (and more expensive) cousin, CDSL provides a higher downstream speed (that is, from the Internet Service Provider or, strictly speaking, from the phone company central office) than upstream speed (that is, from home user to central office).

CDSL will provide downstream speeds of 1Mbps and upstream speeds ranging between 16 and 128Kbps. Unlike ADSL and the other DSLs, CDSL will not need a component called a splitter, which makes it possible to combine voice and data transmissions at one end and to separate them at the other end. Being able to leave out the splitter technology will make CDSL modems much easier and less expensive to build, and will make it feasible to include them in consumer-level PCs. The omission of the splitter, however, also makes CDSL unable to handle voice calls.

→ *See Also* ADSL (Asymmetric Digital Subscriber Line)

Cell

In communications or networking, a packet, or frame, of fixed size. In general, fast packet-switching technologies—such as ATM (asynchronous transfer mode) and SDMS (switched multimegabit digital service)—use cells. Slower packet-switching technologies—such as X.25—are more likely to use variable-sized packets.

In cellular communications, a cell refers to a geographic area. Each cell has its own transmitter and receiver, through which signals can be distributed throughout the cell. Transmissions must be "handed off" from one cell to another when a mobile telephone or networking caller actually moves from one cell to another.

Cell, ATM

In the broadband ATM (Asynchronous Transfer Mode) network architecture, *cell* refers to a packet. ATM cells are each 53 octets, of which five octets are header and 48 are data.

→ *See Also* ATM (Asynchronous Transfer Mode)

Cell Loss Priority (CLP)

In an ATM network, the CLP is a bit value that specifies whether a cell can be discarded if advisable; for example, if the network gets too busy. A value of 1 indicates an expendable cell.

→ *See Also* ATM (Asynchronous Transfer Mode)

Cellular Communications

Cellular communications is a wireless communications technology. The communications area is divided into smaller areas, called cells, and transmissions are passed from cell to cell until they reach their destinations. Each cell contains an antenna and transmission facilities to pick up signals from another cell or from a caller and to pass them on to an adjacent cell or to a callee within the cell. Cells can be anywhere from a few kilometers to 32 kilometers (20 miles) in diameter.

One cellular communications method, called CDPD (Cellular Digital Packet Data) transmits data over any cellular channels that are not being used. CDPD uses telephone (voice) channels, but can switch to a new frequency, if necessary, when a voice transmission begins in the cell being used. CDPD was developed to provide data communications in the cellular frequency range without interfering with voice calls.

Cellular Digital Packet Data (CDPD)

→ *See* CDPD (Cellular Digital Packet Data)

CELP (Code Excited Linear Predictive Coding)

A variant of the LPC voice encoding algorithm. CELP can produce digitized voice output at 4800 bits per second.

→ *See Also* LPC (Linear Predictive Coding)

Central Office (CO)

The telephone switching station nearest to a customer (residential or business). Customers are connected directly to a CO, which connects them to other points in the telecommunications hierarchy. The CO provides services such as switching, dial tone, private lines, and Centrex.

Central Office Terminal (COT)

→ *See* COT (Central Office Terminal)

Central Processing

Central processing, also known as centralized processing, is a network configuration in which a single server processes tasks for multiple stations, all of which can communicate with the server. In such a setup, the nodes must share the computing power of the central processor. One consequence is that the more tasks, the slower things get done.

Central processing can be compared with distributed processing, in which tasks are performed by specialized nodes somewhere on a network. A station that needs something done sends a request onto the network. The server responsible for the service takes on the task, does it, and returns the results to the station. The client station need never know who actually did the work.

Central Processing Unit (CPU)

→ *See* CPU (Central Processing Unit)

CERT (Computer Emergency Response Team)

In the Internet community, CERT is a group formed in 1988 (by DARPA) to help respond to and deal with security problems that may arise on the Internet. The group also provides Internet administrators with information and assistance to help avoid security problems.

Tools and documents related to network security are available through Anonymous FTP from CERT's database in `www.cert.org`. See the Protocol, FTP article for more information.

→ *Broader Category* Network Security

Certificate

A certificate is a unique electronic file that is used to authenticate a user, program, provider, service,

or transaction. Usually, the certificate consists of a file containing (among other things) a copy of the user's or the service's public encryption key along with the signature of a trusted person verifying that the key does, indeed, belong to the user or service claimed. A certificate is created by a certificate (or certification) authority, which is a trusted entity with the resources and permission to create certificates. A certificate is encrypted in a way that makes it impossible to forge.

Certificates are used in various types of transactions and for various network protocols. For example, certificates are used for privacy enhanced mail (PEM), with X.509 protocols (which are concerned with authentication across networks), and for allowing the Secure Sockets Layer (SSL) protocols to encrypt online transactions (for example, when doing business on the Internet). A key with a certificate is required to even install SSL capabilities on a network. "Certificate elements" shows the kinds of information included in an X.509 authentication certificate.

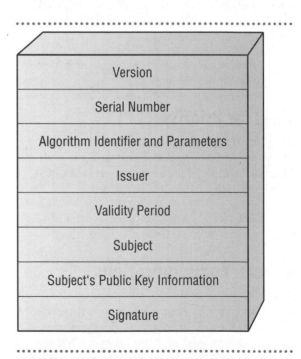

| Version |
| Serial Number |
| Algorithm Identifier and Parameters |
| Issuer |
| Validity Period |
| Subject |
| Subject's Public Key Information |
| Signature |

CERTIFICATE ELEMENTS

While certificates do offer a certain amount of security, they are by no means foolproof, for the following reasons:

- Both certificates and keys should expire and should be replaced periodically. This does not happen frequently enough, so keys are left in circulation longer than they should be. Similarly, invalid or expired certificates may not be recognized as such by someone examining them. (A list of invalid certificates is published in a certificate revocation list, or CRL, but not everyone checks this in a timely fashion.)

- The faith you can place in a certificate depends on your degree of trust for the person or authority issuing the certificate. Ideally, a certificate authority should be a trusted entity because it is authorized by a trusted party that has been appointed by a trusted party. In short, you should trust the certificate authority because it is at the bottom of a certificate authority hierarchy (CAH) whose elements are all trusted entities. This is a reasonable action—*provided* the certificate authority has, in fact, been "certified" by a trusted entity. It's possible—and actually quite easy—to become a certificate authority without getting certified. All it really takes is the right software. For example, the Windows NT Option Pack includes a Certificate Server program, which enables the server running it to become a certificate authority and to issue certificates. While these certificates are just as valid (from an algorithmic and encryption standpoint) as those issued by a certified certificate authority, they are being generated by a program that you may have no reason to trust.

- The value of a certificate also depends on the accuracy of the information used by the certificate authority to validate the user or service. Unless the certificate authority has independent ways of checking on the certification "candidate," the information available may not be completely reliable. In many cases, the certificate authority must rely on information provided by the candidate to make an assessment. If this information is incorrect or misleading, the subsequent validation may be called into question.

A less formal alternative to certificates is used for managing distributed keys when using the PGP (Pretty Good Privacy) encryption method. Rather than getting an official certificate to become validated, users collect signatures on their public keys from trusted friends. The idea behind this approach is that the more signatures you have attesting to your authenticity, the more likely it will be that an examiner will recognize and *trust* one of your signers. These signers are known as *introducers* because their signatures serve to "introduce" you to someone who needs to check on you.

→ **Broader Category** Authentication

Certificate Authority (CA)

→ **See** CA (Certificate Authority)

Certificate Revocation List (CRL)

→ **See** CRL (Certificate Revocation List)

Certificate Server

In the Microsoft Windows NT Option Pack, Certificate Server is a program that installs the software needed to set up a (noncertified) certificate authority—an entity that creates and issues certificates—on a server. Once installed, the certificate authority can begin to generate and distribute keys and certificates. Note, however, that a certificate authority created in this way has no claim for being trusted. In contrast, "certified" certificate authorities are created under the auspices of a hierarchy of trusted entities whose job is to validate new certificate authorities.

Certification Server

→ *See* Certificate Server

Certified NetWare Administrator (CNA)

→ *See* CNA (Certified NetWare Administrator)

Certified NetWare Engineer (CNE)

→ *See* CNE (Certified NetWare Engineer)

Certified NetWare Instructor (CNI)

→ *See* CNI (Certified NetWare Instructor)

CFB (Cipher Feedback)

An operating mode for the DES.

→ *See* DES (Data Encryption Standard)

CGI (Common Gateway Interface)

An interface specification that defines the rules of communication between information servers, such as HTTP (Hypertext Transport Protocol) servers on the World Wide Web and gateway programs. More specifically, the CGI is used when such a server needs to pass a user request to a gateway program. Being able to pass work off to the gateway program helps take some of the workload off the server.

The gateway program is generally designed to provide a mechanism for getting input from a user—for example, so an authorized user can complete an authentication form in order to get access to restricted areas. Among other things, the CGI specifications define the mechanisms by which

information can pass from the server to the gateway program and back.

The CGI specifications, along with many of the other specifications related to HTTP environments, are constantly undergoing revisions.

→ *Primary Sources* You can find the current form of the CGI specifications at `http://hoohoo .ncsa.uiuc.edu.cgi/overview.html`

→ *See Also* ISAPI (Internet Server Applications Programming Interface)

Challenge Handshake Authentication Protocol (CHAP)

→ *See* Protocol, CHAP (Challenge Authentication Protocol)

Channel

A channel is a physical or logical path for a signal transmission. Two particularly important channels in networking are the communications channel and the disk channel.

A communications channel is a path through which data or voice can be transmitted, for example, in a network or a telephone call. In telecommunications, a single cable may be able to provide multiple channels.

A disk channel, in a hard-disk configuration, consists of the components that connect a hard disk drive to an operating environment, such as DOS, OS/2, NetWare, or VINES. These components include cables and a hard disk adapter or controller. A single channel can accommodate multiple hard disks. A computer may have multiple disk channels.

On the World Wide Web, a channel is a thematically organized stream of information that can be accessed easily by an appropriate search engine, or delivered automatically—using push technology—to an end user. For example, Microsoft Internet

Explorer provides several such channels using Microsoft Channel Definition Format (CDF), including a Disney channel and a sports channel. In fact, Microsoft hosts a Channel Guide that provides access to hundreds of such channels through their CDF definitions.

In cabling and wiring, a channel is a trough for holding cables. The channel makes it easier to guide cables, keep them from getting tangled, and keep them organized.

→**Compare** Circuit

Channel Bank

A device that multiplexes low-speed signals into a single high-speed signal.

Channel Definition Format (CDF)

→**See** CDF (Channel Definition Format)

Channel Service Unit (CSU)

→**See** CSU (Channel Service Unit)

CHAP (Challenge Handshake Authentication Protocol)

→**See** Protocol, CHAP (Challenge Authentication Protocol)

Character

A byte with an identity. A group of bits—usually, seven or eight—that represents a single letter, digit, special symbol, or control code in an encoding scheme, such as ASCII or EBCDIC.

Character-Oriented Windows (COW) Interface

→**See** COW (Character-Oriented Windows) Interface

Character Set

A character set refers to the collection of characters (letters, digits, special symbols, escape codes, and so forth) associated with a particular encoding scheme. The standard (seven-bit) and extended (eight-bit) ASCII (American Standard Code for Information Interchange) character sets represent two examples. In these schemes, particular characters are associated with specific numerical values (for example, 65 for *A* and 97 for *a*).

Alternatives to ASCII encoding exist—for example, EBCDIC (Extended Binary Coded Decimal Interchange Code). In addition, there are also variants on both standard and extended ASCII character sets.

These variants will differ from the standard sets by replacing one or more characters in the standard set with characters or symbols that are needed for a particular language or content area. For example, a character set for German keyboards may include characters with an umlaut (such as ö); a character set for French may include characters with a cedilla (as in français); a Spanish character set may include an *n* with a tilde (as in mañana).

Many software packages let you select the language you want to use in the package. This selection will determine what character set is used for screen display and also when printing the file.

Checksum

Checksum is a simple error-detection strategy that computes a running total based on the byte values transmitted in a packet, and then applies a simple operation to compute the checksum value.

Checksums are very fast and easy to implement, and they can detect about 99.6 percent of errors in a packet. This reliability level is acceptable for most simple communications situations, but is less reliable than the more sophisticated CRC (cyclical redundancy check) calculations, which have an accuracy of more than 99.9 percent.

The receiver compares the checksums computed by the sender and by the receiver. If they match, the receiver assumes the transmission was error-free. If they do not match, there was an error.

→ *Broader Category* Error Detection and Correction

→ *Compare* CRC (Cyclical Redundancy Check); Parity

Chemical Markup Language (CML)

→ *See* CML (Chemical Markup Language)

Chromatic Dispersion

In a fiber-optic transmission, the dispersion of a light signal because of the different propagation speeds of the light at different wavelengths; also known as material dispersion. The wavelengths around which dispersion is minimal, such as those around 1300 or 830 nanometers, are commonly used for signaling.

CHRP (Common Hardware Reference Platform)

A set of specifications for PowerPC systems. CHRP is being developed by Apple, IBM, and Motorola, and is designed to enable such a machine to run multiple operating systems and cross-platform applications.

While specifications have not been finalized, a minimum machine will have at least 8MB of RAM and a 1MB cache; CHRP machines will use the PowerPC 604 or later chip, and will support the PCI (Peripheral Component Interconnect) bus

standard. CHRP machines will support at least the following environments:

- AIX (IBM's UNIX port)
- IBM OS/2 for PowerPC
- Mac OS (Apple's new Macintosh operating system)
- Novell NetWare
- Solaris (from SunSoft)
- Microsoft Windows NT

CICS (Customer Information Control System)

A terminal that provides transaction processing capabilities for IBM mainframes. CICS supports the SNA (Systems Network Architecture).

CIDR (Classless Interdomain Routing)

CIDR is a routing strategy that was developed as a partial solution to two difficulties that have developed as the number of networks connected to the Internet has grown very large. One problem was that routers had to deal with too many network addresses and were choking on their routing tables. The second problem was that the supply of Class B network addresses was being used up too quickly. Class B networks can have up to 65,536 hosts, but there can be only 16,384 Class B network addresses. This address class (see IP Address for a more detailed discussion) is useful for companies or organizations that have large networks with thousands of hosts for each network. While there are many companies with a few thousand hosts on their networks, there are few that have anywhere near 65,000.

Because of the way address classes are defined, this situation leads to a lot of potential addresses being wasted. The next address class—C—supports networks with 256 or fewer hosts. There can be more than 2 million Class C addresses. So, whereas Class B address spaces are too big, those for Class C are somewhat small for many businesses and organizations. When a mid-size company asks for an Internet address, it must be given either a Class B address from a dwindling supply or several (perhaps several dozen) Class C addresses. For example, a company with just over 8000 hosts would need 32 Class C addresses. In contrast, by taking a Class B address, it would waste more than 55,000 potential addresses.

CIDR is designed to make a happy medium possible by assigning consecutive Class C addresses to organizations or corporations that have more than 256 machines but that may not be large enough to merit a Class B address. CIDR takes advantage of the assignment scheme and treats the cluster of Class C networks as belonging to the same "supernetwork"—as indicated by their common value in the higher-order address bits (known as the *prefix* bits in this context). By routing just on the (fewer) higher order bits, routers can fulfill their functions without having to store all the networks to which they are routing.

For CIDR to be successful, several things are required:

- The internal and external gateway protocols need to be able to represent the "supernetwork cluster" groupings. Earlier gateway protocols (such as BGP-3, IGRP, and RIP-1) cannot do this; newer versions (such as BGP-4, EIGRP, IS-IS, OSPF, and RIP-2) can. The protocol situation is in transition because newer protocols are, in some cases, just becoming available.

- Class C addresses must be assigned consecutively, as assumed in the CIDR strategy. While this can be done easily in some areas, it's much more difficult in others. One important and sticky issue is how to deal with address owners who move, as such a move could entail a switch in providers, which would undoubtedly lead to routing changes. If the address that's moving happens to be in the middle of a "supernetwork," the abbreviated addressing scheme falls apart.

- An effective strategy must be worked out for assigning addresses. Two possible basic approaches are *provider-based* and *geographically based*. In the former, networks that share a provider get addresses close to each other, regardless of whether these networks are physically near each other. The geographically based approach would assign addresses within a block to networks in the same geographical area. The current Internet is closer to the provider-based variant.

CIF (Common Intermediate Format)

The Common Intermediate Format (CIF) is the de facto standard for videoconferencing images. This standard specifies a resolution of 352×288 pixels.

Two higher-resolution variants of the CIF have also been developed. 4CIF specifies a 704×576 resolution, which gives 4× the number of pixels—hence the name. The second high-resolution variant is 16CIF, which specifies a 1408×1152 resolution. This yields 16× the pixels of CIF.

Two lower-resolution variants are also used sometimes. QCIF (for quarter-CIF) has half the resolution in each dimension (176×144), which yields one-fourth the number of pixels compared to CIF. The lowest-resolution variant is SQCIF (for sub-quarter CIF), which has an 88×72 resolution.

→ *Broader Category* Videoconferencing

→ *See Also* 4CIF (4x Common Intermediate Format); 16CIF (16x Common Intermediate Format); QCIF (Quarter Common Intermediate Format); SQCIF (Sub-Quarter Common Intermediate Format)

Cipher Block Chaining (CBC)

An operating mode for the DES.

→ *See* DES (Data Encryption Standard)

Cipher Feedback (CFB)

An operating mode for the DES.

→ *See* DES (Data Encryption Standard)

Ciphertext

Text that has been encrypted to make it unintelligible to anyone who lacks essential information about the encryption scheme. The required information is generally a specific value, known as the encryption (or decryption) key. Conventional-, public-, or private-key encryption strategies may be used to create ciphertext.

→ *See Also* Plaintext

CIR (Committed Information Rate)

In frame-relay networks, a bandwidth, or information rate, that represents the average level for a user. If the user's network activity exceeds this rate, the frame-relay controller will mark the user's extra packets to indicate that they can be discarded if necessary.

Circuit

A closed path through which electricity can flow. The term is also used to refer to components (such as chips) capable of creating such a path.

In communications, a circuit refers to a logical stream of data between two nodes on a network.

Circuit-Level Proxy

A circuit-level proxy is a program that intercepts network traffic using a specified transport protocol on a particular port (for example, from a client on a network) and decides whether each packet should be sent on to its destination outside the network. If so, the proxy repackages the packet to make it appear as if it comes from the proxy (rather than from the client, who remains hidden from the other end of the connection by the proxy). In essence, a circuit-level proxy serves as a stand-in for a client, to make it look as if the server is, in fact, dealing with the proxy.

Circuit-level proxies operate at the middle networking levels (3, 4, and 5), and are in contrast to the higher-level *application-level proxies*, which serve as stand-ins for traffic relating to a particular application.

→ *Compare* Application-Level Proxy

→ *See Also* Proxy; Server, Proxy

Circuit-Switched Network

→ *See* Network, Circuit-Switched

CIS (CompuServe Information Service)

CIS, better known simply as CompuServe, is the oldest of the major online services. It was, for several years, the largest online service, but that position has been taken over by America Online (AOL). In fact, AOL has also taken over CompuServe, but has kept it running as a separate online service. CompuServe supports DOS, Windows, and Macintosh users. It offers the usual forums, electronic mail, financial and news services, and software to download or use online. For a flat monthly fee, users have unlimited access to basic services; special services incur additional fees. Users can also get access to the Internet.

→ *See Also* AOL (America Online)

CISC (Complex Instruction Set Computing)

CISC is a processor design strategy that provides the processor with a relatively large number of basic instructions, many of which are complex but very powerful. These complex instructions may require several clock cycles to complete, which can slow down overall processing.

CISC is in contrast to the RISC (reduced instruction set computing) design strategy. A RISC chip uses a small number of simple operations to do its work. These simple operations are optimized for speed, and most require only a single clock cycle for completion.

Cisco Discovery Protocol (CDP)

→ *See* Protocol, CDP (Cisco Discovery Protocol)

CIX (Commercial Internet Exchange)

CIX is an association of domestic Internet access providers that provides connection points between commercial traffic and the Internet. The CIX was formed to route commercial traffic back when such traffic was not allowed according to the AUP (acceptable use policy) for the Internet. CIX members agree to carry each others' traffic when requested. Contact Gopher or Web servers at www.cix.org for more information about CIX.

Cladding

In fiber-optic cable, the material (usually plastic or glass) surrounding the fiber core. The cladding has a lower index of refraction than the core, which means that light hitting the cladding will be reflected back into the core to continue its path along the cable.

→ *See Also* Cable, Fiber-Optic

Clamping Time

In power protection, the amount of time needed for a surge protector to deal with a voltage spike or surge; that is, to bring the voltage within acceptable levels.

Class

In Java and other object-oriented programming environments, a class is an abstract element that serves as a generic template for defining objects (which are specific instances of that class). A class will have properties and actions, or methods, associated with it. The objects defined in reference to a class will share the properties specified for the class.

Classes can be defined in terms of other classes, and these derived classes can inherit properties of the parent class, and can have additional or special properties of their own. In fact, classes are often organized into class hierarchies, and they can be collected into class libraries.

By importing a class library into a program, the program gets access to any classes contained in the library. The program can include definitions of objects or derived classes based on the library classes. For example, Java applets—programs that are embedded into Web pages—are based on the predefined Applet class.

In markup languages such as HTML (Hypertext Markup Language) or XML (eXtensible Markup Language), CLASS is a universal attribute that can be used with most tags to specify how a document element is to be handled. This is done by associating the element with a definition of a class in a style sheet. The style sheet can contain definitions that will be applied when the specified element is displayed by a browser program.

→ *Broader Categories* HTML (Hypertext Markup Language); Java

Class A Certification

An FCC certification for computer or other equipment intended for industrial, commercial, or office use, rather than for personal use at home. The Class A commercial certification is less restrictive than the Class B certification.

Class A Domain

→ *See* IP (Internet Protocol) Address

Class B Certification

An FCC certification for computer equipment, including PCs, laptops, and portables intended for use in the home rather than in a commercial setting. Class B certification is more restrictive than the commercial Class A certification.

Class B Domain

→ *See* IP (Internet Protocol) Address

Class C Domain

→ *See* IP (Internet Protocol) Address

Class D Domain

→ *See* IP (Internet Protocol) Address

Classless Interdomain Routing (CIDR)

→ *See* CIDR (Classless Interdomain Routing)

Class *x* Service

In ATM (Asynchronous Transfer Mode) networks, several classes of service are defined. These service classes are designed for delivering different types of data using a variety of connections. The service classes are provided at the ATM Adaptation Layer (AAL), and protocols have been developed to handle the different classes.

Table "ATM Service Classes" summarizes the different classes.

→ *Broader Category* ATM (Asynchronous Transfer Mode)

ATM SERVICE CLASSES

Class	Properties	Example Data
A	Real-time; Constant bit rate (CBR); Connection-oriented (guaranteed delivery); AAL 1 protocol two-way audio	Voice, Video;
B	Real-time; Variable bit rate (VBR); Connection-oriented (guaranteed delivery); AAL 2 protocol; Rarely used because class D is superior	Videoconferencing; One-way audio
C	Non-real-time; VBR; Connection-oriented (guaranteed delivery) AAL 3/4 or AAL 5 protocol	Reservation systems or other bursty data
D	Non-real-time; Available bit rate (ABR); Connectionless (no guaranteed delivery) AAL 3/4 or AAL 5 protocol	Reservation systems or other bursty data
X	User-defined; Unspecified bit rate (UBR); Connection-oriented or connectionless; Special protocol	Bursty data

Clearing Center (CC)

→ See CC (Clearing Center)

Clear to Send (CTS)

→ See CTS (Clear to Send)

CLEC (Competitive Local Exchange Carrier)

The Telecommunications Act of 1996 decreed that competition to provide telephone services should be allowed at all levels of service. With respect to local telephone service, the existing service provider—known as the local exchange carrier (LEC)—would be known as the incumbent LEC (ILEC). In most cases, this is a Regional Bell Operating Company (RBOC). Competing providers of local service would be known as competitive LECs (CLECs) or other LECs (OLECs). These are independent carriers, in most cases.

→ Broader Category PSTN (Public Switched Telephone Network)

CLID (Calling Line Identification)

In ISDN and some other telecommunications environments, a feature that includes the sender's identification number (such as telephone number) in the transmission so that the receiver knows who is calling. It is also known as ANI (automatic number identification) and caller ID.

Client

A client is a machine that makes requests of other machines (servers) in a network or that uses resources available through the servers.

For example, workstations are network clients because they use services from the server. As another example, a client application is an application that makes requests of other applications, on the same or on different machines, for services, information, or access to resources.

→ Compare Server

→ See Also Workstation

Client Access License (CAL)

→ See CAL (Client Access License)

Client-Based Application

An application that executes on the client machine (the workstation) in a network.

Client/Server Computing

Client/server computing is a networking arrangement with the following characteristics:

- Intelligence, defined either as processing capabilities or available information, is distributed across multiple machines.

- Certain machines—the clients—can request services and information from other machines—the servers. For example, a server may have quick access to huge databases that can be searched on behalf of the client.

- The server does at least some of the processing for the client.

Applications capable of running in a client/server environment can be split into a front end that runs on the client and a back end that runs on the server. The front end provides the user with an interface for giving commands and making requests. The application's real work is done by the back end, which processes and carries out the user's commands.

Client/server computing allows for several types of relationships between the server and client, including the following:

- Stand-alone (non-networked) client applications which do not request access to server resources. For example, a local word processor might be a stand-alone client application.

- Applications that run on the client but request data from the server. For example, a spreadsheet program might run on a workstation and use files stored on the server.

- Programs where the physical search of records takes place on the server, while a much smaller program running on the client handles all user-interface functions. For example, a database application might run this way on the server and client.

- Programs that use server capabilities to share information between network users. For example, an electronic-mail system may use the server this way.

The illustration "Client/server computing arrangements" is an example of these different arrangements.

→ *See Also* Back End; Front End

Client/Server Database

→ *See* Database

Client Services for NetWare (CSNW)

→ *See* CSNW (Client Services for NetWare)

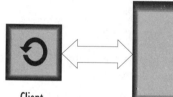

Client

Server

Although the client and server may be connected, the application runs entirely on the client machine.

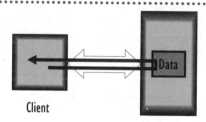

Client

Server

The program executes on the client machine, but uses files or data from the server.

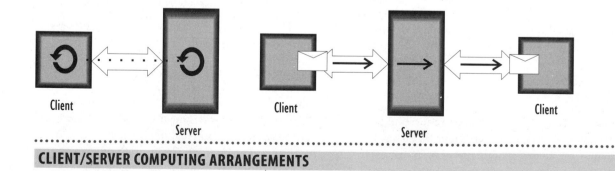

CLIENT/SERVER COMPUTING ARRANGEMENTS

CLNS (Connectionless Mode Network Service)

In the OSI reference model, CLNS is a network-layer service in which data transmission can take place without a fixed connection between source and destination. Individual packets are independent, and they may reach the destination through different paths and in a mixed order. In this type of transmission service, each packet must carry its own destination address and information about the packet's relative position in the message.

CLNS is the most common operating mode for local area networks (LANs). In contrast, for wide area networks (WANs), CONS (connection-oriented network service) is more popular.

→ *Primary Source* ISO document 8348

→ *Broader Category* Connectionless Service

→ *Compare* Connection-Oriented Service

Cloaking

Cloaking refers to the practice of hiding the actual source of an e-mail message by using an anonymous remailer or by otherwise disguising the source address. Cloaking has legitimate uses, but is arguably used most often by spam and scam artists.

Clock Speed

Activities carried out by and for the processor must all be carefully timed and coordinated. To make this possible, each processor has a clock associated with it. This clock serves as a timing reference by slicing time into very short intervals. The clock speed is defined as the number of such slices in a second.

Clock speed is expressed in millions of cycles per second (megahertz, or MHz). For example, the CPU in the original IBM had a clock speed of 4.77MHz. This is painfully slow when compared to today's processors, with clock speeds that can be in the 600-700MHz range.

While processor clock speeds keep going up, this does not result in a linear increase in computing speed. One reason for this is that the processor is not the only component with a clock. For example, the system bus with which the processor must interact—either directly or indirectly—also has a clock associated with it. This clock is considerably slower than the processor's. Bus speeds have been 33 or 66MHz; only recently have chip sets appeared that can support 100MHz bus speeds. Because of these great speed differences, processors must sometimes remain idle until the bus responds. Such idle clock cycle times are known as *wait states*.

Closed-Loop Congestion Management

Closed-loop congestion management is used in a certain class of service available in ATM (Asynchronous Transfer Mode) connections. Specifically, this traffic control method is a required part of ABR (available bit rate) service. ABR service is used for bursty data that need not be transmitted in real time, but that cannot have too much delay. ABR service uses any available bandwidth, and it provides a guaranteed minimum bandwidth.

The congestion management is part of the intelligence used by ABR to monitor network traffic and to slow down the connection if there is congestion on the network or a danger of cells being dropped as a result.

The following elements are involved in closed loop congestion management:

- Two physical *end stations*: the source, or sender, and the destination, or receiver.

- *ATM switches*, which relay cells across the connection between the end stations.

- *Resource management cells*, which are transmitted to convey control information between end stations.

- A *congestion indication bit* in a resource management cell header.

Using these parts, congestion management can be handled in any of several ways—depending on the kinds of information switches can pass (feedback) and on which switches do the passing (loop handling). For example, in the simplest case, switches pass on only an indication that there is congestion (by setting the congestion indication bit) and the loop is handled only by the end stations (who negotiate changes in transmission rate). The following feedback arrangements are used:

EFCI (explicit forward congestion indication) When warranted, switches set the congestion indication bit in a resource management cell header. Otherwise, switches just pass on (data and resource management) cells. If the bit is set, the destination end station sends rate adjustment requests in a resource management cell to the source end station. Loop handling for EFCI must be end-to-end, since only the end stations have anything to say about the rate.

ERM (explicit rate marking) When warranted and possible, switches may add weight to rate adjustment requests made by end stations. Although switches do put in their two cent's worth to the end stations, the actual loop handling is still end-to-end.

VS/VD (virtual source/virtual destination) A switch can function as if it were an end station—that is, the switch can include rate adjustment information in resource management cells and can negotiate with its neighboring (real or virtual) end stations. Feedback models in which only certain switches function in this way are known as *segmented VS/VD*; those in which each switch functions this way are known as *hop-to-hop VS/VD*. With this feedback model, the physical end stations are not as crucial for congestion management. As a result, it is possible to create a firewall between the physical end stations and the network between them.

Three basic loop handling strategies are available for ABR connections:

End-to-end In this strategy, a cell transmission is not considered complete until the destination end station has replied and indicated that all was received. That is, in end-to-end loop handling, the congestion indicator must reach the destination end station before any resource management message can be sent to the source. Over long or noisy paths, such a strategy can become very inefficient because the intermediate switches may need to buffer lots of cells while confirmation information works its way between the physical end stations.

Segmented loop handling In this strategy, certain intermediate switches play an end-station role for purposes of transmission control and pacing. For example, the virtual end station ATM switches can request rate adjustments, so that traffic management can occur more quickly and on a smaller scale.

Hop-by-hop loop handling This is similar to segmented loop handling, except that every switch plays the same virtual end-station role. That is, each switch can send resource management messages to its neighbor to control traffic flow.

The illustration "Loop handling strategies" illustrates the three ways of handling the communications loop in an ABR connection.

→ **Broader Category** ATM (Asynchronous Transfer Mode)

→ **See Also** ABR (Available Bit Rate)

Cloud

→ **See** Network Cloud

End-to-End

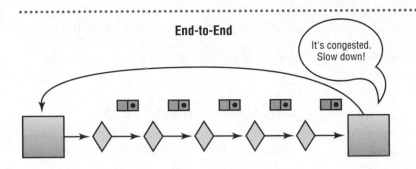

Segmented

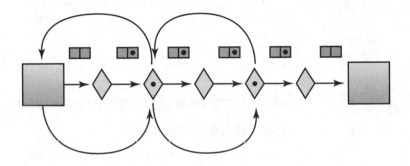

Hop-by-Hop

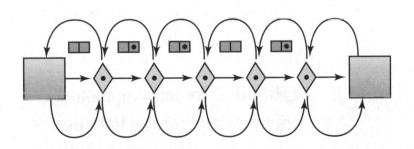

General Legend

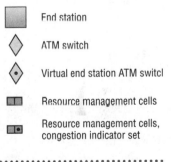

End station

ATM switch

Virtual end station ATM switch

Resource management cells

Resource management cells, congestion indicator set

LOOP HANDLING STRATEGIES

CLP (Cell Loss Priority)

In an ATM network, a bit value that specifies whether a cell can be discarded if advisable; for example, if the network gets too busy. A value of 1 indicates an expendable cell.

→ *See Also*　ATM (Asynchronous Transfer Mode)

CLTS (Connectionless Transport Service)

In the OSI reference model, a transport-layer service that does not guarantee delivery, but makes a best effort, does error checking, and uses end-to-end addressing.

CLU (Command Line Utility)

In Novell's NetWare and in other operating and networking environments, a program that can be executed at the appropriate command-line prompt. Examples of command line utilities in NetWare include NCOPY and FLAG for manipulating files and file attributes, respectively.

Cluster

In a network, particularly in a mainframe-based network, a group of I/O (input/output) devices, such as terminals, computers, or printers, that share a common communication path to a host machine. Communications between the devices in a cluster and the host are generally managed by a cluster controller, such as IBM's 3274 controller.

Cluster Controller

A device that serves as an intermediary between a host machine, such as a mainframe, and a group (cluster) of I/O (input/output) devices, such as terminals, computers, or printers. The IBM 3274 is an example of such a device. This controller has been superseded by the 3174 establishment controller.

CMC (Common Mail Calls)

An API (Application Program Interface) developed by the X.400 API Association (XAPIA) to enable message-handling agents—for example, in an e-mail system—to communicate with message stores, or post offices. The calls in the API are designed to be independent of hardware platforms, operating systems, e-mail systems, and messaging protocols. The API is also referred to as common messaging calls.

CMIP (Common Management Information Protocol)

A network management protocol for the OSI reference model. CMIP, pronounced "see-mip," defines how management information can be communicated between stations. CMIP is functionally comparable to the older, and arguably more widely used, SNMP (Simple Network Management Protocol).

→ *See Also*　Network Management

CMIPDU (Common Management Information Protocol Data Unit)

In the OSI network management model, a packet that conforms to the CMIP. The packet's contents depend on the requests from a CMISE, which relies on the CMIP to deliver the user's requests and to return with answers from the appropriate application or agent.

→ *See Also*　CMISE (Common Management Information Service Element); NetworkManagement

CMIPM (Common Management Information Protocol Machine)

In the OSI network management model, software that accepts operations from a CMISE user and initiates the actions needed to respond and sends valid CMIPDUs (CMIP packets) to a CMISE user.

→ *See Also* CMISE; Network Management

CMIS (Common Management Information Service)

In the OSI network management model, a standard for network monitoring and control services. CMIS, pronounced "see-miss," is documented in CCITT recommendation X.710 and ISO document 9595.

→ *See Also* CMISE, Network Management

CMISE (Common Management Information Service Element)

In the OSI network management model, a CMISE is an entity that provides network management and control services. Seven types of CMISEs, pronounced "see-mize," are specified:

- Event report
- Get
- Cancel get
- Set
- Action
- Delete
- Create

The services provided by CMISEs are used by the system management functions (SMFs). The SMFs are in turn used to carry out the tasks specified for the five system management functional areas (SMFAs)

defined in the OSI network management model. "Major components in the ISO-OSI network management model" shows this relationship.

→ *See Also* Network Management

CML (Chemical Markup Language)

CML is an XML (eXtensible Markup Language) application created by Peter Murray-Rust. CML provides a document model (in the form of an XML Document Type Definition, or DTD) and markup tags for presenting content having to do with chemistry. With CML, it's possible, for example, to create diagrams of molecules and use them as if they were ordinary document elements—and, in a sense, that's exactly what they are within CML. CML allows the user to manipulate document elements like objects, based on the rules defined in the DTD.

CML includes elements for representing, among other things, atoms, molecules, atomic bonds, and chemical formulas. Each element can have zero or more attributes associated with it. For example, the ATOM element has attributes for specifying an atom's atomic number (ATOMNO), its type (ATTYPE), its element symbol (ELSYM), an isotope number (ISOTOPE), and coordinates for representing the atom in either 2-D (X2 and Y2) or 3-D space (X3, Y3, and Z3).

Elements can be used inside other elements. For example, when defining a molecule, you can specify atoms and bonds as part of the molecule definition.

To read a document created with CML, you need a special viewer, which can be either a browser plug-in or a stand-alone viewer. One such viewer—CMLViewer—is available as either a Java applet or an application.

→ *Broader Categories* SGML (Standard Generalized Markup Language); XML (eXtensible Markup Language)

→ *Compare* CDF (Channel Definition Format); MathML (Mathematical Markup Language); OSD (Open Software Description); SMIL (Synchronized Multimedia Integration Language)

CMOS (Complementary Metal-Oxide Semiconductor)

CMOS, pronounced "see-moss," is a logic family for digital circuits. CMOS logic is not exceptionally fast, but it has relatively low power consumption, which makes it ideal for such items as battery-powered PCs.

CMOS is used for RAM chips that need to retain information, such as configuration data or date and time information. The values stored in these RAM chips are maintained by battery power, and they are generally not accessible to the operating system.

→ **Compare** TTL (Transistor-Transistor Logic)

CMOT (Common Management Information Services and Protocol over TCP/IP)

An effort to implement the OSI framework's CMIS and CMIP services on the Internet community's TCP/IP protocol suite, rather than on OSI layer protocols. For various reasons, including the popularity of SNMP and the difficulty of porting the OSI model to a TCP/IP environment, CMOT was never completed.

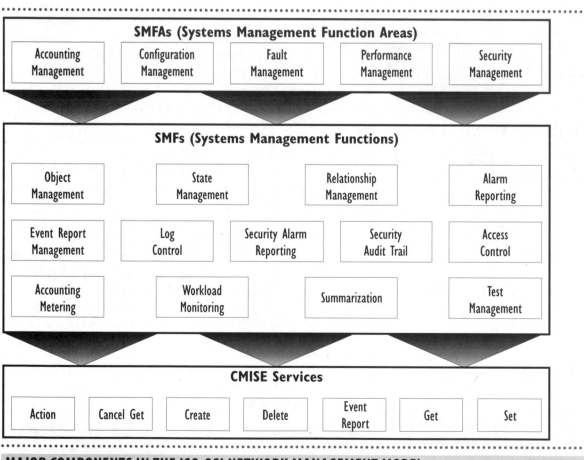

SMFAs (Systems Management Function Areas)

| Accounting Management | Configuration Management | Fault Management | Performance Management | Security Management |

SMFs (Systems Management Functions)

Object Management	State Management	Relationship Management	Alarm Reporting
Event Report Management	Log Control	Security Alarm Reporting	Security Audit Trail	Access Control
Accounting Metering	Workload Monitoring	Summarization	Test Management

CMISE Services

| Action | Cancel Get | Create | Delete | Event Report | Get | Set |

MAJOR COMPONENTS IN THE ISO-OSI NETWORK MANAGEMENT MODEL

CMS (Conversational Monitor System)

CMS is an interactive subsystem in IBM's SNA (Systems Network Architecture).

→ **See** SNA (Systems Network Architecture)

CN (Common Name)

In the NetWare Directory Services (NDS) for Novell's NetWare 4.x, a name associated with a leaf object in the NDS Directory tree. For a user object, this would be the user's login name.

CNA (Certified NetWare Administrator)

A title given to people who successfully complete Novell-authorized courses on administering a NetWare network and/or pass a comprehensive exam about this topic. The CNA program is designed for people who are responsible for the day-to-day operations and high-level maintenance of their networks. CNAs must know how to add and remove users, grant user rights, load applications, do backups and other maintenance tasks, and maintain network security. Separate tests are required and degrees are offered for NetWare 2.2, 3.11, and 4.x environments.

CNAs are discussed in *CNA Study Guide for IntranetWare* (Second Edition, by Michael Moncur and James Chellis, Network Press, 1997) and *CNA Study Guide for NetWare 4* (Michael Moncur, James Chellis, and James Chavez, Network Press, 1997).

→ **See Also** CNE; CNI; ECNE

CNE (Certified NetWare Engineer)

A title given to people who successfully complete a whole series of Novell-authorized courses on becoming technicians or consultants for NetWare networks and/or pass a comprehensive exam about this topic. The CNE program is designed for people who are responsible for designing and installing NetWare networks, and also for the low-level maintenance tasks such as diagnostics, troubleshooting hardware or networking software, and so forth. Separate tracks are available for NetWare 2.2, 3.11, and 4.x. In addition to demonstrating mastery of basic and advanced topics related to NetWare, successful CNE candidates must demonstrate mastery of networking technology and operating system concepts.

→ **See Also** CNA; CNI; ECNE

CNI (Certified NetWare Instructor)

A title given to people who successfully complete a comprehensive and rigorous training program in order to teach Novell courses. Candidates who are accepted for the CNI program must demonstrate a proficiency in their area of specialization by attending each course they want to teach and passing the course test at a more stringent level than is required of ordinary (CNA or CNE) students.

As a final requirement, candidates must pass an IPE (instructor performance evaluation). Among other things, candidates must set up a classroom or lab, and then teach a 45- to 60-minute section of the course for which the candidate wants to become an instructor. Candidates do not know which section they will be asked to teach until the day before their evaluation.

→ **See Also** CNA; CNE; ECNE

CO (Central Office)

The telephone switching station nearest to a customer (residential or business). Customers are connected directly to a CO, which connects them to other points in the telecommunications hierarchy. The CO provides services such as switching, dial tone, private lines, and Centrex.

...thens the signal in a coaxial
...g it possible to run a cable over

Coaxial Cable

→ **See** Cable, Coaxial

COCF (Connection-Oriented Convergence Function)

In the DQDB (Distributed Queue Dual-Bus) network architecture, a function that prepares data coming from or going to a connection-oriented service. The service first establishes a fixed, but temporary, connection, then transmits the data, and finally breaks the connection.

Cochannel Cell

In cellular communications, cochannel cells are those that use the same frequencies for communications. Such cells must be separated by a distance large enough that transmissions involving cochannel cells do not interfere with each other.

→ **Broader Category** Cellular Communications

Codec

A codec is a device for converting analog signals to digital form. For example, codecs are used in digital telephone systems, such as ISDN (Integrated Services Digital Network), so that voice signals can be transmitted over digital lines. The name is a contraction of coder/decoder.

To make the conversion, a codec must use some type of signal-sampling technique. These samples are converted into discrete signals for transmission across the digital lines.

The most common conversion method is PAM (pulse amplitude modulation), in which samples of the analog signal's amplitude are converted into discrete signals whose amplitude corresponds to the analog signal's amplitude at sampling time. To reproduce the original signal accurately, PAM devices must sample the analog signal at a rate at least twice the frequency's signal. For example, for voice signals, which have a 4KHz bandwidth, the PAM device must sample at least 8000 times.

The discrete amplitude value is modulated one more time to make it compatible with the digital circuits. PCM (pulse code modulation) converts the PAM signals into a stream of binary values. To make this conversion, the range of amplitudes in a PAM signal is divided into 128 discrete quantizing levels.

To represent 128 possible amplitude values, seven bits are needed for each PAM signal. This means that PCM must work at 56Kbps or faster. Digital channels in North America provide a 64Kbps capacity, which means 8Kbps can be used for administrative and system control purposes.

→ **Broader Category** Digital Communication

→ **See Also** Modulation

Code Division Multiple Access (CDMA)

→ **See** CDMA (Code Division Multiple Access)

Code Excited Linear Predictive Coding (CELP)

→ **See** CELP (Code Excited Linear Predictive Coding)

Code Signature

A code signature is a digital signature (a unique numerical value that supposedly cannot be forged) associated with a program. The signature is included for security reasons—to authenticate the program's sender (or creator) and the program's origin. Because the code signature cannot be forged, it guarantees that the program was created or sent by the person who signed it. The code signature cannot, however, guarantee that the program is benign or competently written.

→ **See Also** Digital Signature

Coding

Coding is a general term for a representation, usually by means of a predefined syntax or language. For example, in the OSI reference model, an application layer packet, or protocol data unit (APDU), will have a coding that depends on the application involved.

ASCII and EBCDIC are two widely used coding schemes. Abstract Syntax Notation One (ASN.1) coding is used in many contexts that adhere to the OSI reference model, such as in network management tasks.

In a communications setting, several types of coding are distinguished, and each type may occur dozens of times:

Source The coding used by the application that initiates a transmission. That application must be running on an end system—that is, on a network node capable of using all seven layers in the OSI reference model.

Target The coding used by the application that receives a transmission. The receiving application must be running on an end system.

Transfer A coding used by the applications at both ends of the connection or by the translation program. Transfer coding may be needed if the source and target codings are different.

→ **See Also** ASCII; ASN.1; EBCDIC

Cold Boot Loader

In Novell's NetWare, a program on the file server's hard disk that will automatically load NetWare after a cold boot.

Collision Detection and Avoidance

In an Ethernet network, a collision is the simultaneous presence of signals from two nodes on the network. A collision can occur when two nodes each think the network is idle and both start transmitting at the same time. Both packets involved in a collision are broken into fragments and must be retransmitted.

Collision Detection

To detect a collision, nodes check the DC voltage level on the line. A voltage level two or more times as high as the expected level indicates a collision, since this means there are multiple signals traveling along the wires at the same time. Collision detection in broadband networks involves a separate bandwidth for collision detection and is somewhat more complex, since there may not be any DC voltage to test.

In the CSMA/CD (carrier sense multiple access/collision detection) media-access method, for example, collision detection involves monitoring the transmission line for special signals that indicate that two packets were sent onto the network at the same time and have collided. When this happens, special actions are taken (as described in the CSMA/CD article).

Collision Avoidance

To avoid collisions, nodes can send special signals that indicate a line is being used for a transmission. For example, the CSMA/CD media-access method uses RTS (Ready to Send) and CTS (Clear to Send) signals before sending a frame onto the network. A node transmits only after the node has requested access to the line and been granted access. Other

of the RTS/CTS transmission
ransmit at the same time.

CSMA/CD (Carrier Sense
lision Detect); Ethernet

Collision Domain

In Ethernet networks, the collision domain marks the maximum extent of a network segment. This extent is essentially determined by how long it takes to send the shortest valid Ethernet frame, which is 64 bytes in classic (10Mbps) Ethernet. Specifically, the collision domain is the size of the largest round-trip a signal can make in the time it takes to send the minimum packet. For classic Ethernet networks, this is about 200 meters, but is much shorter for the higher speed (100Mbps and 1Gbps) networks. One way high-speed networks extend the collision domain is by increasing the minimum frame size. For example, carrier extension pads the minimum frame to 512 bytes, which extends the collision domain. This is often supplemented with packet bursting, which allows a single node to transmit up to 3KB of frames in succession. In such a packet burst, only the first frame needs to be padded.

COM (Component Object Model)

COM is an object-oriented, open architecture that is intended to allow client/server applications to communicate with each other in a transparent manner, even if these applications are running on different platforms. Objects can also be distributed over different platforms.

The COM model was originally developed as a joint project of Microsoft and Digital Equipment Corporation (DEC). Their original goal was to allow networks or machines that use Microsoft's Object Linking and Embedding (OLE) technology to communicate transparently with networks or machines that use DEC's ObjectBroker technology. Thus, COM was intended as a platform-independent technology along the lines of, but more versatile and more powerful than, OLE.

Since its inception, COM has become primarily an object model for Windows-based environments. The COM model specifies how objects are to be defined and how they can be used. The model also specifies the interfaces through which objects can communicate and through which services can be requested and provided. This interface and the services behind it are available to such resources as ActiveX controls.

ActiveX is the main vehicle for manipulating COM objects on the Windows desktop. DCOM (Distributed Component Object Model) provides the required extensions for distributed computing environments—for example, over a network or an intranet.

Microsoft would like to establish COM/DCOM as the standard object model for both local and distributed computing. As such, COM/DCOM is competing against the Object Management Group (OMG) CORBA (Common Object Request Broker Architecture). CORBA has been around longer, and so has the advantage of priority. Furthermore, COM/DCOM is platform-dependent, since it is supported—with a few exceptions—on only one platform. Of course, Windows is the dominant PC computing platform, with over 80 percent of PCs being Windows-based.

→ *Compare* CORBA (Common Object Request Broker Architecture); ObjectBroker; OLE (Object Linking and Embedding)

COM1, COM2, COMx

On a PC, the names associated with successive serial ports. Devices that might be connected to such a port include modems, pointer devices, and some printers. Compare these ports with LPT1.

Combiner

A combiner is a fiber-optic coupler (optical signal splitter and redirector) that combines multiple incoming signals into a single outgoing signal.

A particular type of combiner is an essential element for WDM (wavelength division multiplexing), in which signals from multiple channels are sent over the same output channel. The input channels are all transmitting at different wavelengths, and the coupler's job is to combine the signals in the proper manner. A combiner is sometimes known as a combiner coupler.

→ *See Also* Coupler

Command Line Utility (CLU)

→ *See* CLU (Command Line Utility)

Commerce Solution Provider (CSP)

→ *See* CSP (Commerce Solution Provider)

Commercial Internet Exchange (CIX)

→ *See* CIX (Commercial Internet Exchange)

Committed Bytes

In the world of memory, the committed bytes value represents the number of memory bytes allocated and in use by application programs.

Committed Information Rate (CIR)

→ *See* CIR (Committed Information Rate)

Commitment, Concurrency, and Recovery Service Element (CCRSE)

→ *See* CCRSE (Commitment, Concurrency, and Recovery Service Element)

Common Authentication Technology (CAT)

→ *See* CAT (Common Authentication Technology)

Common Carrier

A private company, such as a telephone company, that supplies any of various communications services (telephone, telegraph, Teletex, and so on) to the public.

Common Channel Interoffice Signaling (CCIS)

→ *See* CCIS (Common Channel Interoffice Signaling)

Common Channel Signaling (CCS)

→ *See* CCS 7 (Common Channel Signaling 7)

Common Channel Signaling 7 (CCS 7)

→ *See* CCS 7 (Common Channel Signaling 7)

Common Communications Support (CCS)

→ *See* CCS (Common Communications Support)

Common Gateway Interface (CGI)

→ *See* CGI (Common Gateway Interface)

Common Hardware Reference Platform (CHRP)

→*See* CHRP (Common Hardware Reference Platform)

Common Intermediate Format (CIF)

→*See* CIF (Common Intermediate Format)

Common Mail Calls (CMC)

→*See* CMC (Common Mail Calls)

Common Management Information Protocol (CMIP)

→*See* CMIP (Common Management Information Protocol)

Common Management Information Protocol Data Unit (CMIPDU)

→*See* CMIPDU (Common Management Information Protocol Data Unit)

Common Management Information Protocol Machine (CMIPM)

→*See* CMIPM (Common Management Information Protocol Machine)

Common Management Information Service (CMIS)

→*See* CMIS (Common Management Information Service)

Common Management Information Service Element (CMISE)

→*See* CMISE (Common Management Information Service Element)

Common Management Information Services and Protocol over TCP/IP (CMOT)

→*See* CMOT (Common Management Information Services and Protocol over TCP/IP)

Common Name (CN)

→*See* CN (Common Name)

Common Object Model (COM)

→*See* COM (Component Object Model)

Common Object Request Broker Architecture (CORBA)

→*See* CORBA (Common Object Request Broker Architecture)

Common Programming Interface for Communications (CPIC)

→ *See* CPIC (Common Programming Interface for Communications)

Common User Access (CUA)

→ *See* CUA (Common User Access)

Communicating Application Specification (CAS)

→ *See* CAS (Communicating Application Specification)

Communication, Asynchronous

Asynchronous communications are those in which a transmission may take place at a variable rate, and in which byte boundaries are indicated by a combination of start and stop bits. Transmission elements are distinguished by these special bits. This is in contrast to synchronous communication, in which transmission elements are identified by reference to a clock or other timing mechanism.

Examples of asynchronous processes include voice or data transmissions (commonly using modems), terminal-host communications, and file transfer. Modems, terminals, pointer devices, and printers are all devices that use asynchronous communications.

In asynchronous communication, the occurrence of the special start bit indicates that a byte is about to be transmitted. The duration of the start bit indicates the length of a bit interval (duration of a single signal value), which represents the speed at which that byte is going to be transmitted. In a sense, asynchronous transmissions synchronize for each byte.

With respect to the communication, both sender and receiver need to agree on the number of start and stop bits, and also on whether a parity bit will be used. This information is necessary to identify the transmission elements. If a parity bit is used, knowing what kind of parity is operating will help interpret the transmission contents.

Asynchronous transmissions are less efficient than synchronous (time-based) ones. For example, the start and stop bit around each byte represent 25 percent overhead for an asynchronous byte. Because of this lesser efficiency, asynchronous communications cannot attain the bandwidths possible with synchronous transmissions.

On the other hand, asynchronous transmissions are much more flexible, forgiving, and easier to correct than the faster moving synchronous transmissions.

→ *See Also* Communication, Synchronous

Communication, Bisynchronous

In bisynchronous, or bisync, communication a special (SYN) character is used to establish synchronization for an entire data block. Both sender and receiver must be synchronized. The receiver must acknowledge the receipt of each block with alternating ACK characters: ACK0 for one block, ACK1 for the next, ACK0 for the next, and so on. Two successive acknowledgments with the same ACK character indicates a transmission error.

Also known as BSC, bisynchronous communication is used in IBM mainframe environments. It is used primarily when transmitting data in EBCDIC format.

Communication Buffer

RAM set aside on a file server for temporarily holding packets until they can be processed by the server or sent onto the network. The RAM will be allocated as a number of buffers, each with a predetermined size. A communication buffer is also known as a routing buffer or packet receive buffer.

Communication Medium

The physical medium over which a communications signal travels. Currently, the most popular medium is cable. Wireless media, such as infrared wave, microwave, or radio wave, are also becoming more widely used.

Communication Server

→ *See* Server, Communication

Communication, Synchronous

Synchronous communications are those that depend on timing. In particular, synchronous transmissions are those that proceed at a constant rate, although this rate may change during different parts of a communication (or when the line quality changes).

In synchronous communications, transmission elements are identified by reference to either an external clock or a self-clocking, signal-encoding scheme. This is in contrast to asynchronous communication, in which transmission elements are identified by special signal values (start and stop bits).

Synchronous communications can achieve very large bandwidths, eventually allowing speeds of over 100Mbps. Unfortunately, as transmission rate increases, signal quality decreases, because each bit interval becomes extremely short.

External Clocks

When an external clock is used for synchronous communications, the duration of test bits are timed, and the resulting values are used as the bit-interval value. It is necessary to resynchronize the transmission occasionally to make sure that the parties involved do not drift apart in their timing. This is a real danger, because even tiny differences in timing can have a significant effect when millions of bits are transferred every second in a communication.

To avoid such a problem, many synchronous transmission methods insist that a signal must change at least once within a predetermined amount of time or within a given block size. For example, the B8ZS (bipolar with eight zero substitution) signal-encoding scheme is based on a requirement that a transmission can never contain more than seven 0 bits in succession. Before that eighth consecutive 0, a 1 bit will be inserted.

Self-Clocking Transmissions

Self-clocking, signal-encoding schemes have a transition, such as a change in voltage or current, in the middle of each bit interval. A self-clocking encoding method changes the signal value within every bit interval to keep the two parties in synch during a transmission. This works because each party can recalibrate its timing if it notices a drift.

Self-clocking methods avoid the need to insert extra bits (as in the B8ZS encoding scheme). On the other hand, a self-clocking machine needs a clock at least twice as fast as the transmission speed in order to accomplish the signal changes within each bit interval. Expressed differently, this means you will not be able to transmit any faster than at half the clock speed on a machine. (You can effectively increase the speed by compressing files before transmission, thereby sending more information than the bit rate would indicate.)

→ *Compare* Communication, Asynchronous

Communicator

→ *See* Netscape Communicator

Compact Disc (CD)

→ *See* CD (Compact Disc)

Compatibility

Compatibility is the ability of one device or program to work with another. Compatibility is sometimes built in to the product; in other cases, the compatibility is achieved through the use of drivers or filters.

For example, to ensure that a network interface card will work with a network software package, drivers are used. Rather than creating drivers for every adapter, a more common strategy is to create a more or less generic driver interface, and then try to get developers to adapt the interface for their products to this generic interface. Vendors may also adapt the generic drivers to handle the special features of particular products.

Competitive Local Exchange Carrier (CLEC)

→*See* CLEC (Competitive Local Exchange Carrier)

Complementary Metal-Oxide Semiconductor (CMOS)

→*See* CMOS (Complementary Metal-Oxide Semiconductor)

Complete Trust Domain Model

Windows NT uses a domain model as the basis for network administration and resource management. The accounts and resources in a Windows NT network can be administered as a single domain, or the network can be divided into separate domains. In a single domain, both accounts and resources will be administered from a central authority. In multiple-domain networks, account administration can be centralized or distributed. Resources will almost certainly be decentralized in a multiple-domain network—unless, by some accident or design decision, all resources are placed in a single domain.

The issue of interest concerns accessibility of resources—namely, who gets to use which resources. Access to resources is determined by a trust relationship. Simply put, if the resource trusts the user, the user can call on the resource.

Four administrative strategies are defined for the various possible configurations, with one of these strategies being the complete trust domain model. In this model, a network is divided into separate domains, each of which administers its own accounts and resources. Thus, in the complete trust domain model, both accounts and resources are decentralized. A user (account) from domain A can use a resource in domain B only if the user is trusted by the resource.

In a complete trust domain model, such decisions must be made separately for each possible pair of domains. This is because trust relationships are not transitive. Even if A trusts B and B trusts C, it's not correct to conclude that A should trust C. Instead, the trust relationship between A and C must be determined separately.

One advantage of such an arrangement is flexibility because each domain can establish its own policies and guidelines. In large networks, this potential flexibility also can become a logistical problem, however, because of the potentially large number of possible trust relationships. For example, with 10 domains, there are 90 possible relationships that need to be considered.

→*See Also* Domain Model

Complex Instruction Set Computing (CISC)

→*See* CISC (Complex Instruction Set Computing)

Component Object Model (COM)

→*See* COM (Component Object Model)

Compression

→ *See* Data Compression

CompuServe

→ *See* CIS (CompuServe Information Service)

CompuServe Information Service (CIS)

→ *See* CIS (CompuServe Information Service)

Computer

Networks consist of computers, along with some means for connecting the computers and enabling them to communicate with each other. The illustration "Context of computers in networks" shows the role of computers.

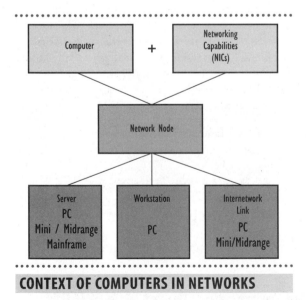

CONTEXT OF COMPUTERS IN NETWORKS

The individual computers that make up a network are known as nodes, or stations. Nodes can be PCs, minicomputers, or even mainframes.

The term PC can refer to any type of personal computer, but there are differences between, for example, a network using IBM PC and compatible machines and one using Macintoshes. Both of these networks will, in turn, differ somewhat from a network that uses Sun workstations.

Almost all PC-class machines are based on one of four processor architecture families:

- The Intel 80x86 family, including the analogous processors from third-party manufacturers (such as Cyrix and AMD), and Pentiums, the newest incarnation from Intel

- The Motorola 680x0 family, used in many machines from the Macintosh family of computers and in some higher-end workstations

- RISC (reduced instruction set computing) chips, used in special-purpose machines, number crunchers, and high-end workstations but starting to migrate down to lower-level machines

- PowerPC chips, which are being used in newer Macintoshes and also in some PCs from IBM

Unless otherwise stated, PC will refer to the IBM PC and compatible computers (as well as to IBM's own Micro Channel Architecture line of computers) based on the Intel architecture. Where the discussion concerns Macintoshes or Sun machines, this will be mentioned.

PCs

PCs can be servers, workstations, or inter-network links in a network. The whole gamut of PCs can be used in a network. You can even attach a palmtop computer to a network. Not all PCs can serve all functions in a network, however.

To work in a network, PCs need a special network interface card (NIC), or adapter. This component provides the appropriate chips and circuitry for translating commands or data into packets and then into electrical signals to be sent over the network. At the receiving end, the NIC captures the received transmission, and again translates, but this time from the electrical format used on the network to a format the networking software understands.

A node may function as a workstation, a server, or an internetwork link (which serves to connect two or more networks). In certain combinations, a computer can serve more than one of these functions at a time.

Server

A server provides access to resources or services, such as files, printers, fax machines, electronic mail, and so on. Servers may be distinguished by the elements to which they control access. For example, you will see references to file servers, print servers, fax servers, and communications servers. A file server generally runs the network, providing access to programs and data, and sometimes also to peripherals.

A network need not have a server. If each node is a workstation, then each node is accessible to other nodes. Networks in which all nodes are workstations are known as distributed, peer-to-peer, or simply peer networks. Artisoft's LANtastic, Novell's NetWare Lite, and Microsoft's Windows for Workgroups are examples of peer-to-peer network packages.

If there is a server, it may be dedicated or nondedicated. A dedicated server cannot be used as a workstation. Networks with a dedicated server are known as centralized networks or server-based networks.

Workstation

A workstation requests access to files, printers, and so on, from a server. Actually, the user simply requests such services as if they were available on the workstation itself. Special shell and redirection software will route the request to the server. Users can also use a workstation for non-network activity.

There is no inherent hardware difference between a server and a workstation. Practical performance considerations, however, dictate that servers should be faster, more powerful machines. In practice, workstations may be any level PC, with 80486 and Pentiums probably being the most common. You may even still see the occasional 80286 or 80386 being used as a workstation. These days, servers are almost always Pentium or Pentium II machines. In fact, some network operating systems require at least a Pentium-class processor for the server.

A special class of machines, called diskless workstations, can be used only as workstations on a network. These workstations have their boot instructions in ROM, boot to the network, and can be used only to do work on the network. Since they do not have disk drives, you cannot download any data to the workstations or upload data to the network.

Recently, a great deal has been written and said about low-cost (under $500) network computers, which are diskless machines designed to be hooked up to the Internet or to corporate intranets. Industry experts are divided in their prognostications about the prospects for such a device. These discussions have generated mostly heat and relatively little light—largely because much of the discussion has stemmed from vested interests rather than the technical merits of such a device.

Internetwork Link

An internetwork link serves to connect two networks with each other. A PC may serve as an internetwork link and as a server or workstation at the same time. Examples of internetwork links include bridges, routers, brouters, and gateways.

Non-PC

Networks can include minicomputers, such as the DEC VAX or the IBM AS/400 series, or mainframes, such as the IBM System/370 and System/390 families (although this is more common in older networks and in networks run by or from MIS departments).

C

Many networks, particularly those in large organizations, include minicomputers and mainframes. For example, it is not uncommon to see a minicomputer serving as a front-end processor (FEP) for a mainframe, to handle incoming transmissions from PCs or terminals.

Mainframe- and PC-based networks are very different worlds from each other, with different character codes, protocols, frame formats, and operating environments. Despite (or perhaps because of) the obstacles that have always existed to make PC-mainframe communication such a challenge, there are a frightening number of possible configurations in which a PC can talk to a mainframe or minicomputer. IBM alone has dozens of hardware and software products (such as the SNA architecture and the IBM Data Connector) for helping computers of various sizes communicate with each other.

→ *Broader Category* Hardware Network

Computer-Based Messaging System (CBMS)

A computer-based messaging system is an older term for a message handling system or for electronic mail.

Computer Business Manufacturers Association (CBEMA)

→ *See* CBEMA (Computer Business Manufacturers Association)

Computer Emergency Response Team (CERT)

→ *See* CERT (Computer Emergency Response Team)

Computer-Telephony Integration (CTI)

→ *See* CTI (Computer-Telephony Integration)

Computer-to-PBX Interface (CPI)

→ *See* CPI (Computer-to-PBX Interface)

Concentrator

Most generally, in the area of communications, a concentrator is a device that can take multiple input channels and send their contents to fewer output channels. In addition to these multiplexing capabilities, a concentrator can store data until an output channel becomes available.

In networking hardware, a concentrator is essentially an upscale hub. The terms *hub* and *concentrator* are often used interchangeably, and the term *wiring center* is often used to refer to either a hub or a concentrator.

As is the case for a hub, the main function of a concentrator is to serve as a termination point for cable running from individual nodes (stations) in a network. The cable connects to the network or to another wiring center.

A concentrator may have multiple boards or boxes mounted on a rack. Each board is essentially a hub—a wiring center for a single network's nodes. Such boards generally include LEDs (light-emitting diodes) to indicate the status of each port on the board.

The size and complexity of the concentrator depends on the number of boards that have been installed. Partly because of their versatility and power, high-end concentrators can cost as much as $50,000.

Hubs and concentrators can be viewed as the ends of a continuum. Hub manufacturers are likely to include concentrators in their product lines.

Concentrator Operation

Concentrators can be much more versatile than hubs in what they can connect. For example, a concentrator might connect network elements (or networks) with different cabling and perhaps even with different architectures.

Note that the concentrator might not necessarily be connecting these different architectures to each other. Rather, the concentrator may be serving as a wiring conduit for multiple (independent) networks simultaneously; for example, for networks running in different departments in a company. It is possible to include bridging or routing capabilities in the concentrator. With bridging or routing, a concentrator can connect different architectures to each other.

Concentrators are generally located in a wiring closet, which serves as a wire-collection location for a predefined area. In the closet, the concentrator may be connected to another concentrator, to an intermediate distribution frame (IDF), to a main distribution frame (MDF), or perhaps to a telephone line. IDFs collect the wiring from a limited area (such as a floor) and feed this to the MDF for the building. The MDF connects the building to the outside electrical world.

Concentrator Features

All concentrators provide connectivity, serving as wiring centers. Many concentrators also have their own processor and can serve as network activity monitors. Concentrators with processors save performance and other data in a management information base (MIB). This information can be used by network management software to fine-tune the network.

A board in the concentrator may have its own processor for doing its work. In such a case, the board is using the concentrator as a convenient location for as a base of operations.

→ **Broader Category** Intranetwork Link

→ **See Also** Hub; Wiring Center

Conductor

Any material (for example, copper wire) that can carry electrical current. Compare conductor with semiconductor or insulator.

→ **See Also** Cable

CONFIG.SYS

In DOS and OS/2 environments, CONFIG.SYS is a file that contains information about various types of configuration and driver settings. For example, CONFIG.SYS may include information about drivers and memory managers that are loaded into memory. The OS/2 configuration file can be quite long and complex.

Configuration Management

Configuration management is one of five OSI network management domains specified by the ISO and CCITT. Configuration management is concerned with the following:

- Determining and identifying the objects on the network and their attributes

- Determining states, settings, and other information about these objects

- Storing this information for later retrieval or modification

- Reporting this information if requested by an appropriate and authorized process or user

- Modifying the settings for objects, if necessary

- Topology management, which involves managing the connections and relationships among the objects

- Starting up and shutting down network operations

C

Identifying Objects and Determining Settings

The first task for configuration management is to identify objects such as stations, bridges, routers, and even circuits. Depending on the sophistication of the management package, this process may be automatic or it may be done manually.

Each object will have configuration states and other information associated with it. For example, a node might have the following settings:

- Interface settings, such as speed, parity, jumper settings, and so on

- Model and vendor information, including serial number, operating system, memory and storage, hardware address, and so on

- Miscellaneous other details, such as installed drivers and peripherals, maintenance and testing schedules, and so on

Similarly, leased lines or circuits will have information such as identification number, vendor (or leaser), speeds, and so on.

Operational States for an Object

Within the OSI model, four operational states are defined for an object:

Active   The object is available and in use, but has the capacity to accept services or requests.

Busy   The object is available and in use, but currently is not able to deal with any more requests.

Disabled   The object is not available.

Enabled   The object is operational and available, but not currently in use.

Such values must be determined—manually or automatically—and stored for easy access and updating (for example, in a relational database). If stored in a database, the information will generally be accessed using some type of query language. SQL (Structured Query Language) has become a standard means for accessing object operational state information. The configuration management capabilities include being able to report this information upon request.

Modifying Settings and States

The values and states associated with network objects may be changed. For example, they will be changed when trying to communicate with a network object, correct a fault, or improve performance. Certain values (for example, state information) may be changed automatically when an action is begun on the network. Other values may need to be changed by the system administrator.

→ *Broader Category*   Network Management

→ *See Also*   Accounting Management; Fault Management; Performance Management; Security Management

Configuration, Network

Network configuration consists of the equipment, connections, and settings in effect for a network at a particular time. Equipment generally refers to hardware (computers, peripherals, boards, cables, and connectors), but may also include software under certain circumstances.

Because compatibility and interoperability can sometimes be elusive in the networking world, a system administrator needs to have detailed knowledge about the equipment on the network. This information may include specific model numbers, memory specifications, enhancements, and so on. This information must be updated scrupulously or conflicts may occur. Fortunately, most networking systems include a utility for recording configuration information and for updating it as the network changes.

The current settings for each piece of equipment should also be recorded as part of the configuration information. When deciding on specific settings, it is important to avoid conflicts. A conflict can arise, for example, because two boards each want to use the same memory location or interrupt line. Again, most network operating systems include a utility to help keep this information organized and to spot potential conflicts before they are made official.

Conformance Requirements

The set of requirements a device or implementation must satisfy in order to be regarded as conforming to a particular specification or recommendation.

Conformance Testing Service (CTS)

→ *See* CTS (Conformance Testing Service)

Congestion

In data communications, a state in which the data traffic approaches or exceeds the channel's capacity, resulting in a severe performance degradation and, possibly, loss of packets.

Connection

A connection is an open link between two endpoints. The nature of the connection depends on the endpoints, on the devices at the endpoints, and on the details of the link between them. For example, you can make a connection between your telephone and the phone company's central office (CO); you can also make a connection through the CO between your phone at home and the phone at work. Similarly, a link between your computer at home and one at work or school is also a connection.

The mentioned connections are all examples of physical connections. That is, there is a direct relationship between the endpoints and the physical infrastructure that connects them.

In contrast, a connection between your PC and a Web site somewhere in the world is a logical, or

virtual, connection. There is a connection because material gets from one endpoint to the other. However, different parts of the material may traverse different paths to get from one endpoint to the other. Thus, there is no single physical connection that necessarily endures for any longer than a second or so. Similarly, links across a high-speed network (for example, ATM or Frame Relay) usually are also virtual connections.

Connectionless Mode Network Service (CLNS)

→ *See* CLNS (Connectionless Mode Network Service)

Connectionless Service

In network operations, a connectionless service is one in which transmissions take place without a pre-established path between the source and destination. This means that packets may take different routes between the source and destination. Connectionless services are defined at the Network and Transport layers, with the specifications in CLNS (Connectionless Mode Network Service) and CLTS (Connectionless Transport Service), respectively.

Because packets may arrive by different paths and in random sequences, there is no way to guarantee delivery in connectionless service. Instead, the higher layers, particularly the Transport layer, are left with the job of making sure packets reach their destination without error. Because it cannot guarantee delivery, a connectionless service is known as a *best-effort service*.

CLNP (Connectionless Network Protocol), CLTP (Connectionless Transport Protocol), IP (Internet Protocol), and UDP (User Datagram Protocol) are examples of protocols that support connectionless service.

→ *Compare* Connection-Oriented Service

Connectionless Transport Service (CLTS)

→ *See* CLTS (Connectionless Transport Service)

Connection-Mode Network Service (CONS)

→ *See* CONS (Connection-Mode Network Service)

Connection, Network

A network connection is a linkage between network elements. Network connections exist on two different levels:

Physical connections Concern the cables and connectors (used to create the physical topology of the network) and the machines connected. When building a network, you must first establish the physical connections.

Logical connections Concern the way in which nodes on the network communicate with each other. For example, the sequence in which a token is passed in an ARCnet or Token Ring network depends on the network's logical topology, not on the network's physical layout. Thus, node x may communicate with node y in the network, even though the two nodes are not adjacent machines in the physical network.

Connection Number

A number assigned to any node that attaches to a file server. The network operating system on the file server uses the connection number to control how nodes communicate with each other. A node will not necessarily be assigned the same connection number each time it attaches to the network.

Connection-Oriented Convergence Function (COCF)

→ *See* COCF (Connection-Oriented Convergence Function)

Connection-Oriented Service

In network operations, a connection-oriented service is one in which a connection (a path) must be established between the source and destination before any data transmission takes place. With this service, packets will reach their destination in the order sent, because all packets travel along the same, "no-passing" path. If they can establish a connection, connection-oriented services can guarantee delivery.

With this type of connection, the OSI Data-Link layer, for example, checks for errors, does flow control, and requires acknowledgment of packet delivery.

X.25 and TCP (Transmission Control Protocol) are two protocols that support connection-oriented services. Connection-oriented services are defined at the network (CONS) and transport (COTS) layers.

→ *Compare* Connectionless Service

Connectivity

The ability to make hardware and/or software work together as needed. The principles and details of how this happens comprise about half of this book and thousands of pages in other books.

Connector

A connector provides the physical link between two components. For example, a connector can link a cable and a network interface card (NIC), a cable and a transceiver, or two cable segments. For electrical cable, a connection is established whenever the conducting wires (or extensions) from the two connectors make and maintain contact. The signal can simply move across the contact.

For fiber-optic cable, good connections take much more work, because the degree of fit between the two fiber cores determines the quality of the connection. This fit cannot be taken for granted, because the diameters involved are smaller than a human hair.

Connectors differ in their shape, size, gender, connection mechanism, and function. These features influence, and sometimes determine, where a connector can be used. Where necessary, special adapters may be used for connections involving different connector combinations. For example, N-series to BNC adapters make it possible to connect thick to thin coaxial cable.

Connectors also differ in how sturdy they are, how easily and how often they can be attached and detached (how many matings they can survive), and in how much signal loss there is at the connection point.

The type of connector needed in a particular situation depends on the components involved and, for networks, on the type of cable and architecture being used. For example, an Ethernet network using coaxial cable will need different connectors between cable and NIC than an IBM Token Ring network using shielded twisted-pair (STP) cable.

The world of connectors includes its own miniworld of acronyms: N, BNC, DB, DIN, RJ, SC, SMA, ST, TNC, V.32, and so on. To make matters even more confusing, some connectors have more than one name.

About half a dozen types of connectors are used with electrical cable in some network-related context; about a dozen more types are used with fiber-optic cable. These connector types are discussed in separate articles. This article discusses connectors in general.

Connector Functions

A connector may be passing the signal along or absorbing it (as a terminator does). A connector that passes a signal along may pass it unmodified or may clean and boost it.

Connectors can serve a variety of purposes, including the following:

- Connect equal components, such as two segments of thin coaxial cable
- Connect almost equal components, such as thin to thick coaxial cable
- Connect unequal components, such as coaxial to twisted-pair cable
- Connect complementary components, such as an NIC to a network
- Terminate a segment; that is, connect a segment to nothing
- Ground a segment; that is, connect a segment to a ground

Connector Shapes

In this context, the term shape refers to the component, not to the connection. Specially shaped connectors are used for particular types of connections or for connections in particular locations. For example, a T-connector attaches a device to a cable segment; an elbow connector allows wiring to meet in a corner or at a wall.

The connector shapes used in networking setups are listed in the table "Cable Connector Shapes," and the illustration "Some connector shapes" shows examples.

CABLE CONNECTOR SHAPES

Shape	Description
Barrel	Used to link two segments of cable in a straight run; i.e., in a location where there are no corners or turns. In networking, BNC and N-series barrel connectors are used to connect sections of thin and thick coaxial cable, respectively.

Continued on next page

CABLE CONNECTOR SHAPES (continued)

DB- or D-type — Describes the connector's frame and refers to a whole family of connectors most commonly used for serial, parallel, and video interfaces. DB-9 and DB-25 connectors are used for serial ports on ATs and XTs. 9-pin versions are used for connecting a monitor to the video board. External network cards, which attach to the parallel port, use DB connectors.

Elbow — Connector with a right-angle bend, used to connect two sections of cable in a corner or to accomplish a change of direction.

RJ — Used to connect telephones to the wall or to modems. RJ-11 and RJ-45 are two commonly used types.

T — Used to attach a device to a section of cable. The horizontal bar of the T links two sections of cable, like a barrel connector; the vertical bar attaches the device. In networks, a T-connector is used to link a section of drop cable to the main cable segment in a thick Ethernet network.

Y — Sometimes used in multiplexers; for example, in a component that provides two ports from one. The shape is mainly a matter of convenience.

Miscellaneous — There are no inherent limitations in the shape a connector can have. Special-shaped connectors can be used when necessary.

Barrel Shape

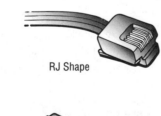

RJ Shape

T Shape

Y Shape

SOME CONNECTOR SHAPES

Connector Genders

Connector *gender* basically refers to whether a connector has plugs or sockets. The gender is important because the elements being connected must have complementary genders.

A male connector is known as a *plug*; the female connector is known as a *jack*. With a few notable exceptions, such as the IBM data connectors and certain fiber-optic connectors, all connector types have distinct genders. The illustration "Connector genders" shows examples of male and female connectors.

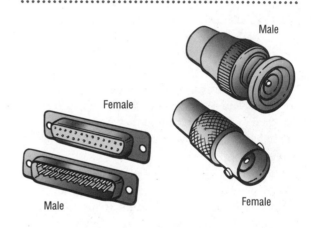

Male

Female

Male

Female

CONNECTOR GENDERS

Connection Mechanisms

The connection mechanism defines how the physical contact is made to allow the signal to pass from one side of the connection to the other.

Connection mechanisms differ considerably in how sturdy they are. For example, the pin-and-socket connection at a serial port can be wobbly without extra support from screws. On the other hand, fiber-optic connectors must be cut to precise proportions, and must not allow any play in the connection, since a cable thinner than a human hair does not need much room to move around.

Connectors are not necessarily named according to the connection mechanism. Rather, the names may have some other basis. The table "Selected Connector Types" illustrates the range of connection mechanisms.

COMPONENTS FOR OTHER TYPES OF LINKS

Connectors connect equal or complementary components. The following components make other types of links possible:

Cable Adapters: Connect almost equal components. Adapters mainly serve to allow size adjustments.

Terminators: Absorb a signal at the end of a network or cable segment to prevent the signal from being reflected back into the cable (thereby causing interference with newer signals traveling out on the cable). Networks have stringent rules about what must be terminated; it's very wise to observe these rules.

Grounded Terminators: Work just like regular terminators, except that grounded terminators have a pigtail or a small metal chain at the end. This needs to be attached to a suitable object to dissipate the charge and to prevent it from being stored up anywhere. (One end of any network or segment must be grounded as well as terminated.)

Baluns: Connect unequal components; that is components that have different electrical properties (impedances). Baluns are commonly used to connect coaxial to twisted-pair cable.

Transceivers: Connect components and also process signals. Transceivers are receivers and transmitters. Because their main function is passing information (rather than connecting), transceivers may be installed directly on the network interface card. Transceivers establish an electrical, rather than merely a physical, connection.

Repeaters: Clean and boost a signal before passing the signal on to the next cable segment or node. There are often limitations on how repeaters may be distributed on a network. For example, the IEEE 802.3 standards allow at most four repeaters on the signal path between any two stations on an Ethernet/802.3 network. Repeaters are primarily signal boosters, and are connectors only secondarily. Like transceivers, repeaters establish an electrical connection.

SELECTED CONNECTOR TYPES

Type	Description
BNC (bayonet nut connector)	Slide together and then lock into place. Ethernet networks with thin coaxial cable use BNC connectors. A variant on the standard BNC connectors is used for twinaxial cable. BNC connectors can survive many matings.
TNC (threaded nut connector)	Similar to BNC in construction, except that TNC has threads instead of notches, which create tighter connections.
N-series	Similar to TNC, except that the barrel is somewhat fatter and the plug is somewhat thinner. N-series connectors are used with thick coaxial cable in thick Ethernet networks. N-series connections are quite tight.
Centronics	Use teeth that snap into place. The printer end of a parallel PC-printer connection usually has this type of connector. IEEE-488 interfaces also use Centronics connectors. The term *Telco-type* is also used to describe certain Centronics connectors.
D-type	One of the three classes of connectors that use pins and sockets to establish contact between the elements involved. These are so named because the frame around the pins and sockets that make up the connection resembles a *D*. The connectors for the serial and parallel ports on most PCs use D connectors.
V.35 and M.50	Also use pins and sockets, but they are arranged somewhat differently than for the D-type connectors. V.35 connectors have more rectangular frames.
DIN	Round, but also use pins and sockets. The keyboard connector on most PCs is a DIN connector, as are two of the connectors used for LocalTalk networks.
RJ-*xx*	Connect by catching and locking a plug in place with an overhanging element in the jack connector. RJ-*xx*, or modular, connectors are used in telephone connections and also with twisted-pair cable in networks. Connector versions differ in the number of line pairs they support, e.g., RJ-11 connectors support two pairs; RJ-45 connectors support up to four pairs. A variant on this type is the MMJ (for modified modular jack) connector, which is used in some DEC networks.
IBM Data	A specially designed connector used in IBM Token Ring networks. The connector has a somewhat intricate connection mechanism that can short-circuit when disconnected, so that the network can preserve its structure even when nodes drop out.

C

These connection classes are all used for electrical cable. Several of the same connection principles also apply to fiber-optic cable. Numerous types of fiber-optic connectors exist, as discussed in the Connector, Fiber-Optic article.

Connector Mating and Insertion Loss

Attaching two connectors to each other is known as *mating*. Because they involve physical parts and are subject to wear and tear, connectors become less effective as they go through more matings. Because this can lead to increased signal degradation, your choice of connectors may depend on how often you expect to connect and disconnect network segments.

Another factor to consider is *insertion loss*. The signal will undergo a certain amount of loss and distortion at a connection point. This insertion loss will be expressed in decibels (dB). For electrical connections, this value can be 15 dB and more; for fiber-optic cable, this value will generally be less than 1 dB.

→ **See Also** Connector, AUI; Connector, BNC; Connector, Fiber-Optic

Connector, AUI (Attachment Unit Interface)

An AUI connector is a 15-pin, D-type connector that is used in some Ethernet connections. Typically, it is used to connect a drop cable to a network interface card (NIC). This type of connector is also known as a *DIX* (for Digital, Intel, Xerox) connector. The illustration "An AUI connector" shows an example.

The connection mechanism is the D-type pin and socket, just as for the RS-232 connectors found on most computers. In addition, an AUI connector includes a (sometimes fragile) slide mechanism that can lock the connection into place.

AN AUI CONNECTOR

Connector, Barrel

A connector used to link two pieces of identical cable, such as thin or thick coaxial cable. The name comes from the connector's shape. BNC barrel connectors link thin coaxial cable; N-series connectors link thick coaxial.

Connector, BFOC (Bayonet Fiber-Optic Connector)

→ **See** Connector, ST (Straight Tip)

Connector, Bayonet Fiber-Optic Connector (BFOC)

→ **See** Connector, ST (Straight Tip)

Connector, BNC

A BNC connector is used with coaxial cable in thin Ethernet networks, in some ARCnet networks, and for some video monitors. Its name may come from Bayonet-Neill-Concelnan, for its developers; from bayonet nut connector, for its attachment mechanism; or from bayonet navy connector, for one of its early uses. The illustration "A BNC connector" shows an example of this type of connector.

A BNC CONNECTOR

To connect a BNC connector, you insert the plug in the jack, and then lock in the connection by turning the connector. The simple plugging mechanism can survive many matings, and the lock makes the connection more stable.

BNC connectors come in the following shapes and versions:

Barrel connector Connects two pieces of thin coaxial cable. Each end of the barrel connector is typically female, which means the cable pieces must have a male BNC connector at the end being attached.

Elbow connector A BNC connector with a right angle in it, for use in corners or in other locations where the cabling needs to change direction.

T-connector Connects a network node to the cable segment. The T-connector usually has female connections at each end and a male BNC connection forming the descender in the *T*. A network machine is attached to the male connector; the other two ends are connected to the trunk cable segment for the network.

Terminator Prevents a signal from bouncing back from the end of the network cable and interfering with other signals. The terminator connects to a BNC connector at the end of the trunk cable segment.

Grounded terminator Grounds and terminates a thin Ethernet trunk segment. A grounded terminator connects to a BNC connector at the end of a trunk cable segment, but includes a ground cable at the end of the terminator. One end of each trunk cable segment must be grounded.

Connector, D-4

A fiber-optic connector that uses a threaded coupling nut for the connection.

→*See* Connector, Fiber-Optic

Connector, D-type

The D-type category of connectors is one of the three classes of connectors that use pins and sockets to establish contact between the elements involved. These are so named because the frame around the pins and sockets that make up the connection resembles a *D*. The connectors for the serial and parallel ports on most PCs use D-type connectors.

D-type connectors are distinguished by the number and arrangement of pins (and/or sockets, depending on the connector's gender) and by the size of the frame. Names such as DB-9, DB-25, or DB-37 refer to connectors with 9, 25, and 37 pins/sockets, respectively.

Common types of D-type connectors include the following:

- DB-9, which is used for some serial (RS-232) interfaces and also for video interfaces. The pin assignments are different for these two uses, so the connectors are not interchangeable.

- DB-15, which is used for video interfaces.

- DB-25, which is used for some serial (RS-232) interfaces and also for a parallel printer interface.

- DB-37, which is used for an RS-422 interface.

The illustration of "Examples of D-type connectors" shows some of these types of connectors. The actual pin assignments depend on the cable's use.

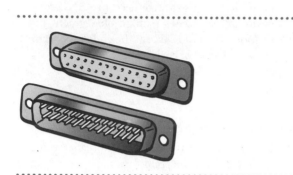

EXAMPLES OF D-TYPE CONNECTORS

In general, connections involving such connectors can be flimsy unless the connectors are locked into place with screws.

Special-purpose variants on the pin-and-socket mechanism (and the D frame) have special names. DIX (for Digital, Intel, and Xerox), or AUI (for attachment unit interface) connectors, are used in Ethernet networks. DIX connectors may also have a slide mechanism to help lock the connection into place.

Connector, Elbow

A connector with a right angle in it, designed for connecting wires in a corner or wherever a change of direction is needed.

Connector, ESCON (Enterprise System Connection Architecture)

A fiber-optic connector for use with multimode fiber in IBM's ESCON channel.

→ **See** Connector, Fiber-Optic

Connector, F

A connector used in 10Broad36 (broadband Ethernet) networks and also in the broadband versions of the (IEEE 802.4) token-bus architecture.

Connector, FC

A connector used for fiber-optic cable, which uses a threaded coupling nut for the attachment and 2.5 millimeter ceramic ferrules to hold the fiber.

→ **See** Connector, Fiber-Optic

Connector, Fiber-Optic

A fiber-optic connector must establish a physical link between two segments of optical core, which are just a few nanometers (billionths of a meter, or fractions of a human hair) in diameter. The degree of overlap between the core segments determines the quality of the connection, because this overlap controls how much light is lost or distorted in the crossover from one fiber to the other. "A fiber-optic connector" shows an example of this type of connector.

A FIBER-OPTIC CONNECTOR

A fiber-optic connection must not only be precise and smooth, it must also be as immobile as possible. Even the slightest movement can cause unacceptable signal loss. Fiber-optic connections should be put through as few matings as possible, because even a snug connection becomes less snug each time it is made and unmade. (A *mating* is the joining of two connectors.)

In fact, to encourage lifelong attachments (instead of random matings), splices are frequently used to make fiber-optic connections. (A *splice* is a permanent connection between two fiber segments.)

To establish a temporary but sound fiber-optic connection, the following tasks are necessary:

- Immobilize each fiber as completely as possible.

- Polish the section that will make contact to as smooth a finish as possible.

- Bring the fiber segments into maximum contact.

- Immobilize the connection.

Features of an Effective Fiber-Optic Connector

An effective connector is one that has very low insertion loss (signal loss that occurs as the signal passes through the connector) and very low return loss (signal that is reflected back through the fiber from which the signal came). Insertion losses of less than 1 decibel (dB), and usually less than 0.5 dB, are the rule with fiber-optic connectors. This means that almost 80 percent of the signal (almost 90 percent with a 0.5 dB loss) gets past the connector. In contrast, more than 90 percent of an electrical signal may be lost going through a connector.

The reflection loss indicates the amount of the signal that is reflected back; that is, the amount lost to reflection. A large negative decibel value means there was little loss to reflection. For example, a reflection loss of -40 dB means that 0.01 percent of the signal was reflected back. By convention, the negative sign is dropped when speaking of loss; the -40 dB value is simply 40 dB. In this case, and in several others involving signals, a large positive decibel value is better, even though the discussion involves loss.

Several components and steps are important for making a satisfactory fiber-optic connection. Ferrules help guide and immobilize the fiber. To make a good connection, the fiber ends must be properly and evenly polished.

Ferrules

A ferrule grabs the fiber and channels it to a point where it can be put in contact with another fiber. The ferrule (which is derived from a word for bracelet) is a thin tube into which a segment of fiber is inserted. The fiber will be trimmed and polished at the end of the ferrule.

The best (and most expensive) ferrules are made of ceramic. Ceramic is remarkably stable and well-behaved over the temperature range the connector is likely to encounter under ordinary conditions. Plastic is a poorer (and cheaper) material for ferrules. Stainless steel fits between these two extremes in performance and price.

Even if the ferrule is designed to fit as snugly as possible around the fiber, there may still be movement because of changes in temperature and humidity in the area around the cable. To minimize the movement produced by such climatic conditions, the fiber may be glued to the ferrule using epoxy, or wedged in more snugly by slightly crimping the ends of the ferrule.

Polishing

The fiber will be cut at the end of the ferrule. On the fiber's scale, such a cut will look very jagged and rough—unacceptable for making a connection. To smooth the cut, the end must be carefully and thoroughly polished.

Trying to polish the fiber ends to a completely flat surface is not always the best way to make a clean connection. It is virtually impossible to get both fiber ends smooth enough and angled in the same direction. In practice, there will always be gaps between two smooth and flat surfaces.

A gap between the fiber ends will not only result in a loss of the signal traveling on, it will also cause more of the original signal to be reflected back

C

along the fiber. The return reflection signal will interfere with the newer signals moving along the fiber. Return reflection loss is one of the values that should be as high as possible. The more of the reflected signal that is lost, the less will actually be reflected back. Losses of 30 to 40 dB are considered good for this variable.

A relatively effective polishing strategy aims for PC (physical contact) connections. In this strategy, the ends of the fibers are polished to rounded ends. Such fibers *will* be in physical contact, so there will be no air gap to weaken the outgoing signal and to reflect back much of this signal.

Polishing can be a delicate and tedious process, and is best left to the experts and the machines.

BUILDING YOUR OWN FIBER-OPTIC CABLE CONNECTORS

If you'll be building fiber-optic cable connectors yourself, keep in mind that both the epoxy glue and crimping methods require considerable skill and patience. Newer tools make the job somewhat easier, but you still need to make sure that the fiber is at exactly the right orientation before gluing or crimping.

The fiber protruding through the tube needs to be trimmed and polished so that the surface that connects to the fiber in the other connector will be as smooth as possible. The smoother the surface, the better the connection you can make.

Types of Fiber-Optic Connectors

Like electrical cable connectors, different types of fiber-optic connectors have different kinds of attachment mechanisms. The actual attachments between ferrule shells may be made by threading, snapping, or clicking.

In addition to attachment mechanisms, fiber-optic connectors differ in the following ways:

- The size of the ferrule.

- Whether the connector can be keyed. *Keying* is a technique for making a connector asymmetrical, usually by adding a notch or plug.

The asymmetry makes it impossible to plug the connector in incorrectly. It also ensures that the fibers in the connector ends always meet at the same orientation.

- The number of matings the connectors can endure without producing unacceptable signal loss.

- Whether the fiber must be twisted to make the connection. If it needs to be turned, multiple fibers cannot run through the same connector. Non-twisting connectors are becoming much more popular.

Connectors also differ in the way the fiber is attached to the connector itself. You can either use epoxy to glue the fiber into the connector (usually into a tube, or ferrule), or you can crimp the connector and the ferrule together using a special tool. In general, fiber that is attached to the connector using epoxy glue is more robust and less likely to be damaged than fiber attached by crimping.

Fiber-optic connectors can be a source of significant signal loss, so it is important to select connectors carefully. Find out how many matings a fiber connector is specified for. You should also make sure that the cables you are connecting are as similar as possible.

The table "Factors Contributing to Signal Loss at Fiber-Optic Connectors" summarizes problems that can arise with fiber-optic connections. The sum of all these losses is known as insertion loss and can be measured simply by taking readings of signal strength at either end of the connection.

Make sure all connectors in your network are compatible. Avoid core or cladding size mismatches if at all possible. Some mismatches won't work together at all; others will introduce unnecessary signal loss.

There are quite a few different types of fiber-optic connectors. One reason for this is that many groups and corporations developed their own during the early days of the technology, and most of these connector types are still around. The most common of types are described in the following sections.

FACTORS CONTRIBUTING TO SIGNAL LOSS AT FIBER-OPTIC CONNECTORS

Factor	Description
Core diameter	Connecting a core with a given diameter to a core with a *smaller* diameter. Depending on the degree of mismatch, you can lose anywhere from 1 dB to more than 10 dB. (Note that there is no loss of this type if the sender's smaller core is connected to a larger core at the receiving end.) This loss source is particularly bothersome for single-mode fiber, since the cores are so small to being with.
Core concentricity	Connecting two fiber-optic cables whose cores are not both centered in the cladding, so that there is spillage from the transmitter's core into the receiver's cladding.
Core ovality	Connecting cores one or both of which are elliptical rather than perfectly round. Again, this results in spillage from the sending core.
NA mismatch	Connecting a core with a given NA (numerical aperture) to a core with a smaller NA.
Lateral placement	Connecting two fiber-optic cables that are not properly aligned, which has the same effect as a diameter or concentricity mismatch.
Fiber cuts	Connecting fibers that are not cut cleanly and straight at the ends. The more of a gap, the more of the signal is lost. This potential signal loss is an excellent argument for having the fiber cut professionally, even if you will attach the connectors.
Connection angle	Connecting fibers at an angle. This not only can cause signal loss, it can also cause light to enter the second fiber at an angle different from its original path, which causes signal distortion.
Rough surface	If the surface of either connector end is rough, there will not be a complete union, which will leave space for light to escape.
Gaps	If the two fibers are not actually touching, light can escape into the open area between the fiber. This light is not only lost for the signal, but some of it can also be reflected back into the sender's fiber. Such reflected light can interfere with the signals traveling in the proper direction.
Contaminants	Allowing contaminants in the connector can interfere with the connection between the fibers.
Bends	Kinks or bends in the cable, near the connector.
Promiscuity	Using the connector too often; that is, for too many matings, which can loosen the connector and allow play between the two fibers.

ST Connector

An ST (straight tip) connector, developed by AT&T, is the most widely used type of fiber-optic connector. This type of connector is used in premises wiring and in networks, among other places. It is used in 10BaseFL (fiber link) networks, and is also allowed for 100BaseFX networks. The connector uses a BNC attachment mechanism, 2.5 mm ferrules (ceramic, steel, or plastic), and either single-mode or multimode fiber. An ST connector will last for about 1000 matings, *except* when plastic ferrules are used. In that case, the connector is good for only about 250 matings.

Insertion loss is 0.3 dB for ceramic ferrules, but can be more than twice that with plastic ferrules. A return reflection loss of 40 dB is typical with single-mode fiber.

Because this is such a widely used connector type, many other connectors are compatible or can be made compatible with a simple adapter. For example, adapters are available to connect SMA to ST connectors.

Also known as a bayonet fiber-optic connector (BFOC).

FC Connector

Originally developed in Japan for use in telecommunications, an FC connector uses a threaded coupling nut for the attachment, and 2.5 millimeter ceramic ferrules to hold the fiber. An FC connector works with either single-mode or multimode fiber, and will last for about 1000 matings.

Older style FC connectors used fibers polished to a flat surface. These connectors suffered from signal distortion and loss. Newer FC connectors use a PC polishing approach, which applies polish to a rounded surface to ensure physical contact between the fibers. With PC polished fibers, FC connectors have an insertion loss of about 0.3 dB and a return reflection loss of around 40 dB for single-mode fiber.

FC connectors are becoming obsolete. They are being replaced by SC and MIC connectors.

SC Connector

An SC (subscriber connector) connects two components by plugging one connector into the other. Once the two connectors are latched together, they cannot be pulled apart by sheer pressure. Instead, the connection must be broken (for example, by pressing a button to release a latch).

An SC connector works with either single-mode or multimode fiber, and will last for about 1000 matings. It has an insertion loss of 0.3 dB, and a return reflection loss of about 40 dB.

SC connectors have replaced the older FC and D-4 connectors used in telecommunications involving fiber-optic cable. SC connectors are also becoming more popular in networking contexts, although they are still not nearly as popular as ST connectors for this application. SC connectors are the recommended ones to use for the medium-dependent interface (MDI) in 100BaseFX networks. ST and MIC connectors are also allowed.

MIC Connector

An MIC (medium interface connector), also known as an *FDDI connector*, is a dual-fiber connector designed by an ANSI committee for use with fiber-optic cable in the FDDI (Fiber Distributed Data Interface) network architecture. The connector attaches two fibers that help make up the two rings specified in the FDDI architecture.

MIC connectors use a latching mechanism, similar to the one used for SC connectors. In order to ensure that connections are made properly, MIC connectors

are keyed as A, B, M, or S. MIC connectors can be used for the medium-dependent interface of 100BaseFX networks, but only if they are keyed as M.

An MIC connector works with either single-mode or multimode fiber, and will last for about 500 matings. It has an insertion loss of about 0.3 dB for single-mode fiber, and about 0.5 dB for multimode fiber. Reflection loss is 35 dB or higher, not quite as good as for SC connectors.

The connector is quite flexible and can be attached either to another MIC connector, to two ST connectors, or to a transceiver. Because of this flexibility, MIC connectors are becoming increasingly popular.

SMA Connector

An SMA connector uses a threaded coupling mechanism to make the connection. This type of connector was originally developed in the 1970s by the Amphenol Corporation for use with only multimode fiber; however, SMA connectors can now be used with either multimode or single-mode fiber.

SMA connectors last for only for about 200 matings, and they have a relatively high insertion loss of 1.5 dB (which means about 30 percent of the signal is lost).

SMA connectors come in two forms: the SMA-905 uses a straight ferrule, and the SMA-906 uses a ferrule with a step pattern, which is narrowest at the ferrule tip, and widest at the back end of the ferrule.

One reason for their popularity is that SMA connectors have been designed to meet very stringent military specifications.

Adapters are available to connect SMA to ST connectors.

D-4 Connector

A D-4 connector is just like an FC connector, except that the D-4 ferrule (which holds the fiber core in place) is only 2 millimeters. D-4 connectors can be used for single-mode or multimode cable, and will last for about 1000 matings.

ESCON Connector

An ESCON connector is similar to the MIC connector designed for FDDI, except that the ESCON connector uses a retractable cover to make it easier to attach a transceiver. The drawback is that the connection is less robust. An ESCON connector will last for about 500 matings, has a 0.5 dB insertion loss, and a reflection loss of at least 35 dB.

Connector, IBM Data

An IBM data connector is a type designed by IBM for use in its Token Ring networks. These connectors are used to attach a node (or *lobe*) to a multistation access unit (MAU), a wallplate, or a patch panel. MAUs group several lobes into a ring, and may connect to other MAUs. Patch panels serve as wiring way stations.

The attachment mechanism is genderless, and involves a relatively complex mechanism in which two connectors click together to establish the connection.

An IBM data connector is self-shorting, which means that there is a circuit across it even if there is nothing plugged in. This is important for maintaining the ring structure inside a MAU.

Connector, ISO 8877

A variant of the RJ-45 connector that is compatible with international standards.

→ *See Also* Connector, RJ-*xx*

Connector, MIC (Medium Interface Connector)

A dual-fiber connector designed by an ANSI committee for use with fiber-optic cable in the FDDI network architecture. MIC connectors are keyed with A, B, M, or S to ensure that the connections are made properly. M-keyed MIC connectors can be used for the medium-dependent interface (MDI) of 100BaseFX networks.

→ *See* Connector, Fiber-Optic

Connector, MMJ (Modified Modular Jack)

A special type of modular (RJ-*xx*) connector, developed by Digital Equipment Corporation (DEC) for use with its wiring scheme. An MMJ connector uses the same snap-in attachment mechanism as the RJ-*xx* connector, but the plug and the jack are keyed (made asymmetric).

Connector, N-Series

An N-series, or N-type, connector is used with thick coaxial cable, such as in thick Ethernet networks. N-series connectors come in male and female versions. The connection mechanism uses threads to couple the connectors. "An N-series connector" shows an example of this type of connector.

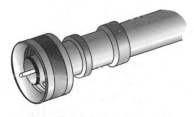

AN N-SERIES CONNECTOR

N-series connectors come in the following shapes and versions:

Barrel connector   Connects two pieces of thick coaxial cable. Each end of the barrel connector is usually female, which means the cable pieces must have a male N-series connector at the end being attached.

Elbow connector   A connector with a right angle in it, for use in corners or in other locations where the cabling needs to change direction.

Terminator   Prevents a signal from bouncing back from the end of the network cable and interfering with other signals. The terminator connects to a male N-series connector at the end of the trunk cable segment.

Grounded terminator   Grounds and terminates a thick Ethernet trunk segment. A grounded terminator connects to an N-series connector at the end of a trunk cable segment, but includes a ground cable at the end of the terminator. One end of each trunk cable segment must be grounded.

Connector, RJ-xx

An RJ-*xx* connector, also known as a *modular connector*, comes in a plastic plug that snaps into the appropriate socket, or jack. RJ-*xx* connectors are used with twisted-pair cable, such as for telephone cables.

The attachment mechanism involves pushing the plug into the jack until a tooth clicks into place to prevent the plug from coming out.

Several RJ-*xx* versions are available. The most common types are RJ-11, RJ-12, and RJ-45. RJ-11 and RJ-12 connectors are used with two- and three-pair (four- and six-wire) cables. RJ-45 connectors are used with four-pair (eight-wire) cable. Since they have eight wires, RJ-45 connectors are larger than RJ-11 or RJ-12 connectors.

An MMJ (modified modular jack) is a special type of RJ-*xx* connector developed by Digital Equipment Corporation (DEC) for use with its wiring scheme. An MMJ connector uses the same snap-in attachment mechanism as the RJ-*xx* connector, but the plug and the jack are keyed (made asymmetric).

An ISO 8877 connector is a variant of the RJ-45 connector. This type is compatible with international standards.

Connector, SC (Subscriber Connector)

A type of fiber-optic connector that connects two components by plugging one connector into the other. SC connectors are the recommended ones to use for the medium-dependent interface (MDI) of 100BaseFX networks.

→**See**   Connector, Fiber-Optic

Connector, SMA

A fiber-optic connector type that uses a threaded coupling mechanism to make the connection.

→**See**   Connector, Fiber-Optic

Connector, ST (Straight Tip)

A widely used fiber-optic connector developed by AT&T. This type of connector is used in premises wiring and in networks, among other places. ST connectors are also used for 10BaseFL wiring in 10BaseF networks, and also in 100BaseFX networks.

ST connectors are also known as bayonet fiber-optic connectors (BFOC).

→**See**   Connector, Fiber-Optic

Connector, T

A connector that generally links three pieces of cable. Specifically, a T-connector links a device or cable to another cable. In order to add the linked cable, the other cable must be spliced. The connector's name comes from its shape.

Connector, TNC (Threaded Nut Connector)

A connector similar to a BNC connector, except that the TNC connector is threaded and screws into the jack to make the connection. This type of connector is also called a threaded Neill-Concelnan or threaded navy connector.

CONS (Connection-Mode Network Service)

In the OSI reference model, a network-layer service that requires an established connection between source and destination before data transmission begins. The logical-link control and media-access control sublayers can do error detection, flow control, and packet acknowledgment. CONS is common in wide area networks, and is in contrast to the CLNS (connectionless-mode network service) more popular with local area networks.

Console

In a Novell NetWare environment, the monitor and keyboard from which the network administrator can control server activity is called the *console*. The administrator (or any other user, if there is a security breach) can give commands to control printer and disk services, send messages, and so on.

To prevent unauthorized use of the console, several steps are possible:

- Lock the console to prevent physical access to it.
- Use the lockup feature in the Monitor NLM (NetWare Loadable Module) to disable keyboard entry until the user enters the correct supervisor password.
- Use the Secure Console command to secure the console and also to prevent access to the debugger (which can be used to bypass security measures).

- Be on the lookout for unauthorized activity in the SYS:SYSTEM directory.
- Before loading an NLM, check to make sure it is approved, which means the module has been tested by Novell and was found to work.

→ *Broader Category* NetWare

Constant Bit Rate (CBR)

→ *See* CBR (Constant Bit Rate)

Consultative Committee for International Telegraphy and Telephony (CCITT)

→ *See* CCITT (Consultative Committee for International Telegraphy and Telephony)

Consumer Digital Subscriber Line (CDSL)

→ *See* CDSL (Consumer Digital Subscriber Line)

Container

A *container* is an element in the Directory tree for Novell's NetWare 4.*x*'s NetWare Directory Services (NDS). The Directory tree contains information about all the objects connected to all the servers in a NetWare network or internetwork. Containers help to group these objects into a hierarchical structure.

A container is an object that may contain other containers or leaf objects or both. Within the Directory tree, a container is allowed only below the root or below another container, as illustrated in "An example of an NDS Directory tree."

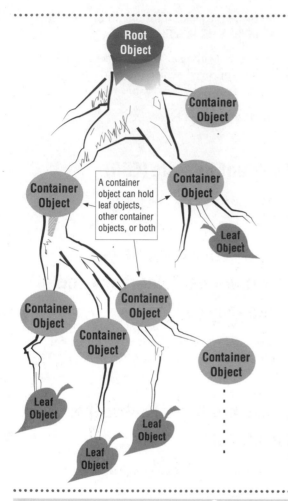

A container object can hold leaf objects, other container objects, or both

AN EXAMPLE OF AN NDS DIRECTORY TREE

In an actual network, a container generally corresponds to some meaningful level of organization or administration within the world connected by the network, such as a division or department of a company. A leaf object corresponds to information about a specific network element (node, peripheral, user, and so on).

Two types of container objects are commonly used:

O (Organizations)   Help to organize and group objects in the tree. There must be at least one organization in a directory tree. All organizations in a tree must be at the same level immediately below the root.

OU (Organizational Units)   Help to organize subsets of leaf objects in the tree. OU levels are not required in a Directory tree.

In Microsoft ActiveX Web resources technology, a container is a program that can process and execute ActiveX controls. That is, a device that supports ActiveX is said to be an ActiveX container.

→ *Broader Category*   ActiveX; NetWare

→ *See Also*   NDS (NetWare Directory Services)

Container Tag

In markup languages such as HTML (Hypertext Markup Language) and XML (eXtensible Markup Language), a container tag is one that requires a closing counterpart. For example, <UL>, which indicates the start of an unnumbered (bulleted) list, must be paired with its ending counterpart—</UL>—which indicates the end of the list. This is in contrast to a tag such as <LI>, which represents the start of an item in a list (for example, in a bulleted list). This is not a container tag, since no </LI> is required at the end of the item. Instead, the item end is determined by the presence of another <LI> tag (indicating the start of a new item) or by the </UL> ending the list.

→ *Broader Category*   HTML (Hypertext Markup Language); XML (eXtensible Markup Language)

Contention

The basis for a first-come-first-serve media access method. In a contention-based access method, the first node to seek access when the network is idle will get to transmit. Contention is at the heart of the CSMA/CD access method used in Ethernet networks. Compare it with the polling and token-passing methods.

Context

In the CCITT's X.500 Directory Services (DS) model, a portion of the Directory Information Tree (DIT), which contains information about all directory objects. In Novell's NetWare 4.*x* NDS, the current location in the Directory tree.

→ *See Also* NDS (NetWare Directory Services)

Continuous Composite Servo (CCS)

→ *See* CCS (Continuous Composite Servo)

Control Character

A control character is any of several character values that have been reserved for transmission and other control functions, such as cursor movement. For example, in the ASCII character set, the characters with codes below 32 are control characters. Character 9 (Ctrl-I) is a Tab code, character 7 (Ctrl-G) is the code for a beep, and so on.

Control characters are also known as *control codes*, *communication control codes*, or *communication control characters*.

Controlled Access Unit (CAU)

→ *See* CAU (Controlled Access Unit)

Controlled Access Unit/Lobe Attachment Module (CAU/LAM)

→ *See* CAU/LAM (Controlled Access Unit/Lobe Attachment Module)

Controller

In a mainframe environment, a controller is a device that communicates with a host computer and mediates between this host and the terminals accessing the host.

In a PC environment, a controller is a device, usually a board, that is responsible for accessing another device, and for writing and possibly retrieving material on this device. For example, a hard disk controller accesses the hard disk. Controllers, also called *controller boards*, mediate between the computer and a CD-ROM or tape drive. The controller board generally manages the connected device, including input and output.

The operating system uses a *controller address* to locate a disk controller. This value is usually set directly on the controller board, by setting jumpers or DIP switches.

Control Point (CP)

→ *See* CP (Control Point)

Control Point to Control Point (CP-CP) Connection

→ *See* CP-CP (Control Point to Control Point) Connection

Control Unit Terminal (CUT)

→ *See* CUT (Control Unit Terminal)

Convergence

Convergence has become a term widely used in several areas relating to computing and networks. In all cases, the term is used to refer to some sort of fusion or integration process.

In internetworking situations, convergence is a process by which network activity is resynchronized after a change in routing; for example, because a node was added or dropped. Thus, even a very simple change in the routing table can make it necessary to reestablish convergence. Routing algorithms differ in the speed with which they can produce convergence.

In business, the term is sometimes used to refer to the consolidation—taking place in various industries—that occurs when companies buy each other up, until there are only one or two huge conglomerates in the domain. It is also used in business contexts to refer to the process by which the various communications fields are merging—again through buyouts or partnerships. This happens, for example, when telecommunications companies buy or go into partnership with Internet Access Providers, news services, cable companies, and so forth.

Related to the second business sense, convergence is also used in the area of technology to refer to the evolution toward the all-in-one device, which can be used as a computer, telephone, pager, and so forth, and which will be usable anywhere the person finds him or herself.

Conversational Monitor System (CMS)

CMS is an interactive subsystem in IBM's SNA (Systems Network Architecture) technology.

→ *See* SNA (Systems Network Architecture)

CONVERT.EXE

In the Windows NT environment, CONVERT is a program for converting from the FAT (file allocation table) file system to the NTFS (new technology file system). Note that it is not possible to convert from NTFS back to FAT.

Cookie

A cookie is a sequence of bits that a browser may write to a user's hard disk at the request of a server. When a user visits a Web site with a browser, the owners of that Web site may want to keep track of the user, so as to be able to "recognize" the user when he or she visits the Web site again. By storing a cookie on the user's hard disk, the Web site will be able to check for the cookie when the user visits again.

The contents of a cookie can provide information that allows a Web server to customize materials displayed for the user when he or she visits. For example, if a user visits an online store Web site, the server may keep track of the types of products the user examines and buys. From this information the server may build a user profile, which can be stored in the cookie on the user's machine. When the user visits at some later date, the server may inform the user about new products or special deals in the user's areas of interest.

While the use of cookies can be very handy, the practice also raises some thorny and controversial issues, as well as creating a security risk. Most fundamentally, a cookie represents an access to the user's computer. In many cases—especially with older browsers—this access is unauthorized (and often unknown to the user). At the least, such an action represents a breach of good manners. At the worst, it can represent an attack on the user's machine. To give users back some control over their machines, newer (versions of) browsers will inform the user anytime a server wants to deliver a cookie, and will give the user the option of refusing the cookie.

Cooperative Processing

A program execution technology that allows different tasks in a program to be carried out on different machines. Cooperative processing is important for client/server computing, in which an application front end executes on a client (workstation), and a back end executes on the server.

Copper Distributed Data Interface (CDDI)

→ *See* CDDI (Copper Distributed Data Interface)

Coprocessor

A microprocessor chip that carries out a certain class of tasks on behalf of another processor (the central processing unit, or CPU), in order to leave the CPU available for other work. The most commonly used coprocessors do floating-point arithmetic. Other types are for graphics, disk management, and input/output.

CORBA (Common Object Request Broker Architecture)

A specification created by the Object Management Group (OMG) to provide a way for applications operating in object-oriented environments to communicate and exchange information, even if these applications are running on different platforms. By going through an ORB (object request broker), applications can make requests of objects or other applications without knowing anything about the structure of the called entity.

The ORB enables applications to communicate through an object-oriented front end, which makes it unnecessary to use application- or platform-specific RPCs (remote procedure calls) to make requests or to route and deliver responses.

In addition to ORB clients and servers, the CORBA specification includes an IDL (interface definition language) and APIs (application program interfaces). The IDL provides the ORB client with a way to specify each desired operation and any required parameters. CORBA makes provisions for two classes of APIs:

- A static invocation API, which can be used to specify requests and parameters in advance, so that these can be compiled directly into the application.

- A dynamic invocation API, which must be used to specify requests and parameters that will not be known until runtime.

While CORBA version 2.0 is new, CORBA-compliant products have been appearing almost since the original specification in 1992. For example, Digital's ObjectBroker software implements CORBA on a variety of platforms including various flavors of UNIX, Windows and Windows NT, DEC OSF/1, and Macintoshes. (ObjectBroker is implemented only partially on some of these platforms.) Microsoft is expected to develop a competing technology based on its OLE (Object Linking and Embedding) standard.

→ *Primary Source* OMG's Common Object Request Broker Architecture specification

Core

In fiber optics, the transparent central fiber (usually glass, but sometimes plastic) through which a light signal travels. The core is surrounded by cladding, which has a lower index of refraction than the core, so that light is reflected back into the core when it hits the cladding.

→ *See Also* Cable, Fiber-Optic

Core Gateway

On the Internet, any one of several key routers (*gateways*, in older Internet terminology). All networks on the Internet must provide a path from a core gateway to the network.

Corporation for Open Systems (COS)

→ *See* COS (Corporation for Open Systems)

Corporation for Research and Educational Networking (CREN)

→ *See* CREN (Corporation for Research and Educational Networking)

COS (Corporation for Open Systems)

The COS is a group concerned with the testing and promotion of products that support the OSI reference model.

COT (Central Office Terminal)

In local telephone service, the COT is one end of a digital connection—with the other being the remote terminal (RT)—over which the telephone company can connect 96 voice channels over a single trunk. This enables the phone company to get as far into the field as possible before switching to analog technology in the local loop to a subscriber. The COT-RT connection essentially extends the phone company's central office (CO) into the field so that the local loop between a subscriber and the CO can be shorter. A shorter loop means a cleaner connection.

→ *See Also* CSA (Carrier Serving Area)

Count to Infinity

In a distance-vector routing strategy, *count to infinity* is an artifact in which certain networks may come to be classified as unreachable because routers are relying on each others' incorrect information.

The *infinity* in this case refers to the distance to the network. In practice, this value will be one more than the maximum hop count allowed for a route. In a Novell NetWare network, 16 hops (steps to the destination) would be infinite, since at most 15 hops are allowed.

→ *Broader Category* Routing, Distance-Vector

Coupler, Fiber-Optic

Most generally, a coupler is a device for transferring energy between two or more channels. In fiber-optic networks, a coupler is a device that routes an incoming signal to two or more outgoing paths, or a device that routes multiple incoming signals into a single outgoing path.

Couplers are important in fiber-optic networks. When an electrical signal is split and sent along parallel paths, each derived signal is the same strength. This is not the case with light signals. After the signal is split, the derived optical signals are each weaker than the original signal.

For example, if a fiber-optic coupler splits a signal into two equal signals, each of those derived signals is half as strong; it loses 3 decibels (dB) relative to the original signal. Couplers can be designed to split a signal equally or unequally.

Couplers are often described in terms of the number of input and output signals. For example, a 3×5 coupler has three input and five output channels. If the coupler is bidirectional, you can also describe it as 5×3.

Under certain conditions, particularly when using wavelength as a basis for splitting or multiplexing a signal, couplers are subject to optical crosstalk. This can happen, for example, if the wavelengths being used are too similar, so that they are transformed in similar ways by the coupler. Generally, the wavelengths used will be made very different deliberately to minimize the possibility of crosstalk.

Fiber-optic couplers can be grouped in any of several ways, based on their form and function:

- Whether the coupler is created by using mirrors (CSR) or by fusing fibers (fused).

- Whether the coupler splits a signal (splitter) or combines multiple signals into a single one (combiner).

- Whether the coupler has its own power supply to boost signals (active) or simply splits signals (passive).

- Whether the coupler sends signals in one direction (directional) or both directions (bidirectional).

- Whether the coupler splits the signal into two (tee) or more (star) parts.

CSR versus Fused Couplers

CSR (centro-symmetrical reflective) couplers use a concave mirror that reflects the light from incoming fiber(s) to outgoing ones. By adjusting the mirror, the light distribution can be controlled.

In a fused coupler, incoming and outgoing fibers are gathered at a central point and wrapped around each other. By applying heat to the wrapping point, the fibers can be fused at this location, so that light from any of the incoming fibers will be reflected to all the outgoing ones.

Splitter versus Combiner Couplers

A splitter coupler breaks a signal into multiple derived signals. An important type of splitter is a wavelength-selective coupler, which splits an incoming signal into outgoing signals based on wavelength.

In contrast a combiner coupler, also known simply as a *combiner*, combines multiple incoming signals into a single outgoing one. A particular type of combiner is an essential element for WDM (wavelength division multiplexing), in which signals from multiple channels are sent over the same output channel. The input channels are all transmitting at different wavelengths, and the coupler's job is to combine the signals in the proper manner.

Active versus Passive Couplers

An active coupler has its own electrical power supply, which enables the coupler to boost each of the derived signals before transmitting it. Active couplers include electrical components: a receiver that converts the input signal into electrical form, boosting capabilities, and transmitters to convert the electrical signal into an optical one before sending it. An active coupler may also send the signal, usually in electrical form, to a node on a network.

A passive coupler simply splits the signal as requested and passes the weakened signals on to all fibers. There is always signal loss with a passive coupler.

Directional versus Bidirectional Couplers

A directional coupler can send a split signal in only one direction. A bidirectional coupler can send a split signal in both directions.

Tee versus Star Couplers

A tee coupler splits an incoming signal into two outgoing signals. This type of coupler has three ports and is used in bus topologies.

A star coupler splits the signal into more than two derived signals. Star couplers are used in star topologies.

Passive Star Couplers

A passive star coupler is an optical signal redirector created by fusing multiple fibers together at their meeting point. This type of coupler serves as the center of a star configuration. Because the fibers are fused, a signal transmitted from one node will be transmitted to all the other nodes attached when the signal reaches the coupler.

Passive star couplers are used for optical (IEEE 802.4) token-bus networks that have a passive star topology.

COW (Character-Oriented Windows) Interface

In OS/2, an SAA (Systems Application Architecture) compatible interface.

CP (Control Point)

In IBM's SNA (System Network Architecture) and APPN (Advanced Peer-to-Peer Networking) environments, a CP is the management component of a type 2.1 node (also known as a PU 2.1 or T 2.1). More specifically, the control point manages the available resources for such a node. (Control points are also defined for other node types—for example, type 4 or 5 nodes.)

In an APPN network, such nodes can be either APPN end nodes (ENs) or APPN network (that is, intermediate) nodes (NNs). APPN nodes can exchange management information by using a CP-CP connection. In contrast, the control points for low-end network end nodes (LEN ENs) cannot establish CP-CP connections. This means that CPs for LEN ENs can manage resources for their components, but they cannot exchange management information.

Control points manage the following types of resources for their components:

- **Address Space Management** (ASM), which is responsible for handling the addresses associated with each link between the node and another network element.

- **Configuration Services** (CS), which are responsible for establishing and maintaining the physical link between the node and whatever it's connected to.

- **Directory Services** (DS), which are responsible for searching, retrieving, and updating information related to resources and connections associated with the node. For example, the control point's directory service will locate a needed resource. The actual DS functions available depend on the type of node (that is, NN or EN, APPN or LEN node).

- **Management Services** (MS), which are responsible for the level of alertness and the type of logging associated with the node.

- **Session Services** (SS), which are responsible for initializing and ending sessions (CP-CP or LU-LU) between nodes. (CP-CP and LU-LU stand for control point to control point and logical unit to logical unit, respectively.)

- **Topology and Routing Services** (TRS), which are responsible for selecting routes and also for managing the network topology database. The TRS also manages the class-of-service database, which contains information about the transmission priority, bandwidth, and security levels requested by or given to a session.

Various types of control points are defined—depending on the type of node. For example, APPN ENs and NNs have ENCPs and NNCPs (for end node and network node control points), respectively.

Certain control points can also provide services to other nodes. For example, the system services control point (SSCP) in a type 5 node and a network node control point (NNCP) in an APPN NN can provide services. NNCPs can provide directory database information to neighboring nodes, and such information can be used to determine routes.

→ *Broader Categories* APPN (Advanced Peer-to-Peer Networking); SNA (System Network Architecture)

→ *See Also* CP-CP (Control Point to Control Point) Connection

CP-CP (Control Point to Control Point) Connection

In IBM's SNA (System Network Architecture) and particularly its APPN (Advanced Peer-to-Peer Networking) environments, CP-CP connections are used—by the appropriate types of nodes—to exchange resource management information.

Session details and the exchange of management information are handled by *service transaction programs* (STPs). The ten available transaction programs do such things as:

- Initiate and terminate CP-CP sessions

- Receive, and respond to search requests from adjacent nodes

- Send search requests to adjacent nodes

- Send information about changes in resource registrations to other NNs or to ENs which have requested such information or which need to be informed of changes

- Send and receive information from the routing topology database

While all nodes in an APPN network have control points, not all such nodes can use CP-CP connections. Low-end network end nodes (LEN ENs) must use LU-LU (logical unit to logical unit) connections to communicate with other nodes.

→ *Broader Categories* APPN (Advanced Peer-to-Peer Networking); SNA (System Network Architecture)

→ *See Also* CP (Control Point); LU-LU (Logical Unit to Logical Unit) Connection

CPE (Customer Premises Equipment)

Equipment used at the customer's location, regardless of whether this equipment is leased or owned.

CPI (Computer-to-PBX Interface)

In digital telecommunications, an interface through which a computer can communicate with a PBX (private branch exchange).

CPIC (Common Programming Interface for Communications)

APIs (Application Program Interfaces) for program-to-program communications in IBM's SAA (Systems Application Architecture) environment. The CPIC APIs are designed for LU 6.2 protocols; that is, for interactions in which the programs are equals.

CPU (Central Processing Unit)

The CPU is the main processor in a computer. The CPU chip (set) may be aided in its work by special-purpose chips, such as graphics accelerators and the UART (universal asynchronous receiver/transmitter).

In the networking world almost all the machines use CPUs from one of four main architectural lines:

- The 68000 family of processors from Motorola. This family includes the 68020, 68040, etc. 68K processors, as they are sometimes called, have been used in many members of the Macintosh collection.

- The PowerPC family of processors from IBM and Motorola. Power chips have been used in several new versions of the Macintosh line.

- The Intel family from Intel, which includes the 80*x*86 generation of processors, followed by the Pentium, Pentium II, and Pentium III chips. Also included here are Intel work-alikes—clone chips such as those made by AMD and Cyrix—which use the same general architecture as Intel's chip families. This architecture has become so successful largely because of the success of DOS and Windows. According to estimates, as many as 90 percent of network machines have such "Wintel" chips controlling them.

- Miscellaneous proprietary chips, such as the Alpha processor from Digital Equipment Corporation (DEC) and RISC (reduced instruction set computing) chips used in high-end workstations such as those built by Sun Microsystems and by IBM.

Chips are distinguished by, among other things, the processor's clock speed and the widths of the CPU's data and address buses. In the roughly 20-year history of the PC, CPUs have increased in speed from the 4.77MHz of the 8086 (actually 8088) chips used in the original IBM PC to speeds in the 600–700MHz range. Currently, the majority of CPUs are 32-bit components; although 64-bit processors have been available in higher-end workstations and are expected in PCs by sometime in 1999.

Cracker

A cracker is someone who tries to access computers or networks without authorization—generally with malicious intentions. In contrast, the term *hacker* is used to refer to someone who tries to access systems out of curiosity. The latter term, however, is also used as a general term for anyone trying to access a computer without authorization.

CRC (Cyclic Redundancy Check)

An error-detection method based on a transformation of the bit values in a data packet or frame.

→ **See** Error Detection and Correction

CREN (Corporation for Research and Educational Networking

Part of the Internet, along with the ARPAnet, MILnet, and several other research and government networks.

CRF (Cable Retransmission Facility)

In a broadband network, the CRF is the starting point for transmissions to end users. For example, the CRF might be the cable network's broadcast station. End user stations can generally transmit control and error information, but not data to the CRF.

Crimper

A tool for crimping the end of a piece of cable in order to attach a connector to the cable. This tool is essential if you plan to cut and fine-tune cable.

CRL (Certificate Revocation List)

A CRL is a list of invalid certificate numbers. Certificates are electronic documents that are created by a trusted source and that are used to authenticate a user or service. The CRL contains information about certificates that have expired or that have been revoked for other reasons. Guidelines for the creation and use of CRLs are provided in the X.500 directory services specifications.

→ **Broader Category** Authentication

→ **See Also** Certificate; CA (Certificate Authority)

Cross-Connect Device

A cross-connect device is a punch-down block. A *cross-connect* is a connection between two punch-down blocks. This device is used to establish a physical connection between the horizontal cable running from a machine and the cable running to the wiring center, or hub.

The device is used to terminate incoming wire pairs in an orderly manner, and to distribute these wires to end users or to wiring centers. By connecting a device, such as a node in a network, to the more accessible punch-down block instead of directly to a wiring center or to a hub, you can switch connections more easily; for example, to test different wiring configurations.

Crosstalk

Crosstalk is interference generated when magnetic fields or current from nearby wires interrupts electrical currents in a wire. As electrical current travels through a wire, the current generates a magnetic field. Magnetic fields from wires that are close together can interfere with the current in the wires. Crosstalk leads to *jitter*, or signal distortion.

Shielding the wire and twisting wire pairs around each other help decrease crosstalk. If twists are spaced properly, the magnetic fields in the wires cancel each other out. However, crosstalk can also be induced if the twists in a wire are badly spaced.

Crosstalk comes in near–and far-end varieties, known as NEXT and FEXT, respectively. FEXT (far-end crosstalk) is the interference in a wire at the receiving end of a signal sent on a different wire. NEXT (near-end crosstalk) is the interference in a wire at the transmitting end of a signal sent on a different wire. NEXT is the value generally measured when evaluating or testing cable.

Cross Wye

A cable used to switch the wiring arrangement from one sequence to another; for example, from USOC wiring to EIA-568B. This type of switch effectively changes the pin assignments of the incoming cable.

→ *See Also* Wiring Sequence

CSA (Carrier Serving Area)

A CSA is used to work around line length limitations and to make more efficient use of the wiring between the local telephone company offices and end users. The CSA combines digital and analog technology to enable the phone company to minimize the length of the local loop between a subscriber's home and the phone company's central office (CO). A shorter local loop can generally support a higher bandwidth. This is important because it allows the phone company to provide two subscriber lines over a single local loop connection. The demand for second lines has increased because people want to be able to log onto the Internet without cutting off the entire house (and the rest of the family) from the telephone.

Ninety-six digital voice channels are combined on a single trunk that connects a central office terminal (COT) to a remote terminal (RT) located in the middle of a cluster of subscribers. This trunk can be several miles long. The local loops to the individual subscribers connect to the RT. The maximum length of the local loop is limited—usually to about 12,000 feet—so installing an RT in a cluster of subscribers makes it possible to provide cleaner lines even to remote subscribers.

CSFS (Cable Signal Fault Signature)

In electrical line testing, a unique signal reflected back when using time domain reflectometry (TDR) to test the electrical activity of a line. Based on the CSFS, a trained technician may be able to identify the source and location of a problem.

CSMA/CA (Carrier Sense Multiple Access/Collision Avoidance)

CSMA/CA is a media-access method used in Apple's LocalTalk networks. CSMA/CA operates at the media-access-control (MAC) sublayer, as defined by the IEEE, of the Data-Link layer in the OSI reference model.

The CSMA/CA Process

When a node wants to transmit on the network, the node listens for activity (CS, or carrier sense). Activity is indicated by a carrier on signal. If there is activity, the node waits a period of time and then tries again to access the network. "Summary of the CSMA/CA process" illustrates how the method works.

The wait, known as the *deferral time*, depends on the following:

- The activity level of the network. The deferral time is longer if there is lots of network activity; it is shorter when there is little activity.

- A random value added to the base deferral time. This ensures that two nodes who defer at the same time do not try to retransmit at the same time.

If the network is currently idle, the node sends a Request To Send (RTS) signal. This signal is sent regardless of whether the node wants to send a directed transmission (one with a particular destination) or a broadcast transmission (one sent to each node on the network).

Directed versus Broadcast Transmissions

In a directed transmission, the RTS is addressed to a particular node, and the sending node waits for a Clear To Send (CTS) signal in reply from this node. The RTS and the CTS must be sent within a predefined amount of time; otherwise, the sending node assumes there is a collision and defers.

In Apple's LocalTalk network architecture, the minimum interframe gap (IFG)—the time between successive frames (such as RTS and CTS or between CTS and data transmission)—is 200 microseconds.

In a broadcast transmission, the RTS is addressed to a predefined address (255) that indicates broadcasts. The sending node does not wait for a CTS; instead, the node begins the transmission. In a broadcast transmission, the RTS serves more as a statement of intent than as a request.

Type of Access Method

CSMA/CA is a probabilistic and contentious access method. This is in contrast to the deterministic

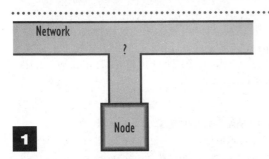

A node listens to the network activity for a carrier signal (CS) that indicates the network is in use. At any given time, multiple nodes may be listening. If a node hears a signal, the node defers (backs off) for an amount of time determined by network activity level and a random number generator.

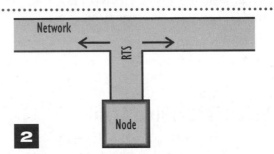

Hearing no CS, a node with something to say sends a Request to Send (RTS) signal onto the network. The signal is broadcast in both directions.

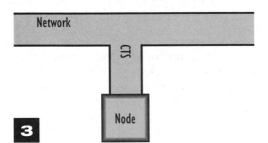

If it is sending to a particular node (directed transmission), the would-be sender waits for a Clear to Send (CTS) reply. If no reply is received within a predefined time, the node assumes there is a collision, and backs off for a random amount of time.

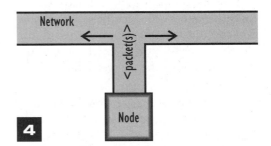

If a CTS is received, or if the message is intended as a broadcast transmission, the node begins sending its packet(s). In the case of a broadcast transmission, the node doesn't wait for a CTS.

SUMMARY OF THE CSMA/CA PROCESS

token-passing and polling methods. It is contentious in that the first node to claim access to an idle network gets it. CSMA/CA is probabilistic in that a node may or may not get access when the node tries. A disadvantage stemming from this probabilistic access is that even critical requests may not get onto the network in a timely manner.

Collision avoidance requires less sophisticated circuitry than collision detection, so the chip set is less expensive to manufacture. Collisions cannot always be avoided, however. When they occur, LocalTalk lets a higher level protocol handle the problem.

→ **Broader Category** Media-Access Method

→ **See Also** CSMA/CD; Polling; Token Passing

CSMA/CD (Carrier Sense Multiple Access/Collision Detect)

CSMA/CD is a media-access method used in Ethernet networks and in networks that conform to the IEEE 802.3 standards. CSMA/CD operates at the media-access-control (MAC) sublayer, as defined by the IEEE, of the Data-Link layer in the OSI reference model.

The following network architectures use this access method:

- Ethernet (and 802.3 compliant variants)
- EtherTalk, Apple's implementation of the Ethernet standard
- G-Net, from Gateway Communications
- IBM's PC Network, which is a broadband network
- AT&T's StarLAN

The CSMA/CD Process
In CSMA/CD, a node that wants to transmit on a network first listens for traffic (electrical activity) on the network. Activity is indicated by the presence of a carrier on signal on the line. "Summary of the CSMA/CD process" illustrates how the method works.

If the line is busy, the node waits a bit, then checks the line again. If there is no activity, the node starts transmitting its packet, which travels in both directions on the network cable.

The node continues monitoring the network. However, it is possible for two nodes to both detect no activity on the line and start transmitting at the same time. In that case, a collision occurs, and the network has packet fragments floating around.

When a collision is detected, a node follows this procedure:

1. Cancels its transmission by sending a jam signal (to indicate there is a collision and thereby prevent other nodes from joining the fun).

2. Waits a random amount of time (the *deferral time*), determined by a backoff algorithm.

3. Tries to access the network again.

Internally, nodes keep track of the number of unsuccessful transmission attempts for each packet. If this number exceeds some predefined value, the node decides the network is too busy and stops trying.

Each node in a network that uses CSMA/CD listens to every packet transmitted. The listener first checks whether the packet is a fragment from a collision. If so, the node ignores it and listens for the next packet.

If a packet is not a fragment, the node checks the destination address. The node will further process the packet if any of the following is the case:

- The destination address is the node's address.
- The packet is part of a broadcast (which is sent to every node).
- The packet is part of a multicast and the node is one of the recipients.

As part of this further processing, the destination node checks whether the packet is valid. (For a summary of invalid Ethernet packets, see the section on the Ethernet frame in the Ethernet article.)

Type of Access Method

CSMA/CD is a probabilistic, contentious access method, in contrast to the deterministic token-passing and polling methods. It is contentious in that the first node to claim access to an idle network gets it. CSMA/CD is probabilistic in that a node may or may not get access when the node tries. A disadvantage stemming from this probabilistic access is that even critical requests may not get onto the network in a timely manner.

CSMA/CD works best when most network activity is light. The access method works most poorly when the network traffic consists of many small messages, because nodes spend much of their time colliding, then waiting to retransmit.

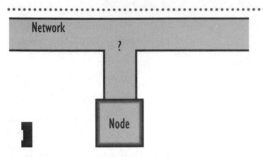

A node listens to the network activity for a carrier signal (CS) that indicates the network is in use. At any given time, multiple nodes may be listening. If a node hears a signal, the node defers (backs off) for an amount of time determined by network activity level and a random number generator.

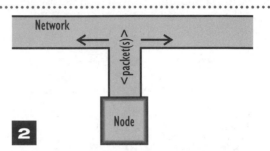

Hearing no carrier signal, a node with something to say sends its packet(s) onto the network. Note that the transmission moves in both directions along the bus. This is necessary to ensure that all nodes get the message at the same time, so that each node hears the same network.

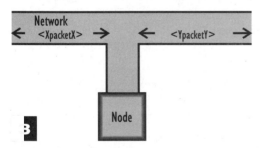

Because of the multiple access (MA) property, another node may have done the same thing, so that two messages are moving along the bus at the same time.

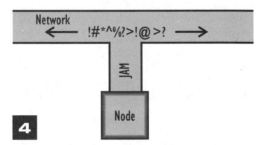

In such a case, a collision occurs. The packets are garbled, and electrical activity on the line is higher than usual. When a node hears a collision, the node starts sending a jam signal to indicate the collision. A node involved in a collision backs off for a randomly determined amount of time before trying again to access the network.

SUMMARY OF THE CSMA/CD PROCESS

To use this access method, a node must be able to detect network activity (carrier sense, or CS) and to detect collisions (collision detect, or CD). Both of these capabilities are implemented in hardware, on board the network interface card.

Because CSMA/CD is a contentious access method, any node can access the network, provided that node puts in the first request when the network line is idle. This makes the method multiple access (MA). Unlike CSMA/CA, a CSMA/CD node must be able to detect a collision on the line.

→ *Broader Category* Media-Access Method

→ *See Also* CSMA/CA; Polling; Token Passing

CS-MUX (Carrier-Switched Multiplexer)

In the FDDI (Fiber Distributed Data Interface) II architecture, CS-MUX is a component that passes time-dependent data, such as voice or video, to the architecture's media-access-control (MAC) layer. At that layer, the data is handled by a special isochronous media-access-control (IMAC) component.

The CS-MUX is not part of the FDDI II definition. Rather, the CS-MUX provides certain types of data for FDDI. Functionally, a CS-MUX operates at a level comparable to the logical-link-control (LLC) sublayer of the ISO model's Data-Link layer.

→ *Broader Category* FDDI (Fiber Distributed Data Interface)

CSNW (Client Services for NetWare)

CSNW is a Windows NT service that enables NT workstations (clients) to connect to NetWare file servers. CSNW works as a redirector, intercepting user or program commands and redirecting them to the NetWare server.

For such a service to be available, the user must have a valid account on the NetWare server.

Furthermore, the workstation must be running both the CSNW software and NWLink IPX/SPX, Microsoft's implementation of the NetWare protocol stack. The NT client can connect to NetWare servers that use either the bindery or the newer Novell Directory Services (NDS).

CSP (Commerce Solution Provider)

A CSP is an Internet Service Provider (ISP) that provides software and services to allow businesses to run an online store on the provider's host machine. Essentially, a CSP allows a business—small or large—to do business online, but without having to invest in the hardware and software required to run such an operation in-house.

CSS (Cascading Style Sheets)

Style sheets are used in HTML (Hypertext Markup Language) and XML (eXtensible Markup Language) documents. Style sheets give Web authors a means of getting more control over the appearance of their pages. In a style sheet, an author (or an editor) can specify the static appearance of a page (margins; font style, size, and color; foreground and background color; and so forth) and can also specify how various document elements (heads, lists, etc.) should look.

The convenient thing about style sheets is that you can put them in a separate file, and then just refer to this file in the HTML (or XML) file. In this way, the same style sheet can be used with lots of different documents, but the document files don't need to be bloated and muddied with the style specifications. Also, changing a style is very simple: just change the style sheet file. All documents that use the style sheet will automatically look different the next time they are displayed.

Once you make the style sheet available to an HTML file, you can apply any of the styles defined to any part of the HTML file. Wherever no style sheet elements are specified, the document will be displayed using the browser's default styles.

C

Style sheets are an improvement over older ways of controlling layout because they provide control while keeping this control out of the HTML file. There are serious advantages—for example, readability and modifiability—to keeping presentation separate from content in this way.

With *cascading style sheets*, you can use multiple style sheets in the same HTML document, and you can apply elements from different style sheets to different parts of the document. In short, you can cascade multiple style sheets onto each other—applying each as specified.

CSS1

The specifications for *cascading style sheets level 1* were developed by Hakon Lie and Bert Bos in 1996. The CSS1 specifications make it easier to keep things neat and tidy when fiddling with the layout. This first version provided resources mainly for manipulating the document layout, with more limited capabilities for specifying and controlling the devices on which a document is to be displayed. This latter area is addressed in CSS2.

The CSS1 specifications are supported—with some exceptions—by Netscape Navigator 4 and Microsoft Internet Explorer 4. Readers can also apply style sheets to HTML files before viewing them.

CSS2

In 1998, the CSS1 authors, along with Ian Jacobs and Chris Lillie, published the recommendations for CSS2. This version extends CSS1 by adding media-specific style sheets—that is, style sheets in which the display is defined for a particular output device—for example, a printer or a Braille typewriter. CSS2 also adds more refined control for positioning text and graphics, and better table handling. CSS2 is too new for any of the current batch of browsers to support it; however, both Netscape and Microsoft intend to support CSS2.

→ **Primary Sources** CSS1 specs are available at `http://www.w3.org/TR/REC-CSS1`; CSS2 specs are available at `http://www.w3.org/TR/REC-CSS2`.

CSS1 (Cascading Style Sheets Level 1)

→ **See** CSS (Cascading Style Sheets)

CSS2 (Cascading Style Sheets Level 2)

→ **See** CSS (Cascading Style Sheets)

CSU (Channel Service Unit)

A CSU is part of the integrated services unit (ISU) component that replaces a modem on a digital line. The CSU is mainly responsible for making the signals well-behaved and protecting the public carrier's lines from a malfunctioning data service unit (DSU).

In particular, a CSU prevents faulty customer-premises equipment (CPE), such as DSUs, from affecting a public carrier's transmission systems and ensures that all signals placed on the line are appropriately timed and formed. All CSU designs must be approved and certified by the FCC (Federal Communications Commission).

→ **Broader Category** Digital Communications

→ **See Also** DSU/CSU (Data Service Unit/Channel Service Unit)

CTI (Computer-Telephony Integration)

Computer-telephony (or computer-telephone) integration is a strategy for connecting standalone or networked computers to telephone switches in such a manner that the computer can receive, initiate, and route calls over the switch.

There are various strategies for accomplishing this. For example, a special connection—a *CTI link*—can be used to provide a single link between a network and a switch. All traffic passes through the CTI link, which may have a table or other means of determining which client is the recipient or initiator of a call.

Standards for CTI must be developed at two levels: the physical and the API, or programming, level.

- At the physical level, the rules for basic connections between computers and switches must be specified. For example, a standard must specify the electrical characteristics of such a connection. The CSTA (Computer-supported telecommunication applications) standard was developed by the ECMA (European Computer Manufacturers' Association). It has been around for a few years, and it is being implemented by several vendors. A competing standard—SCAI (Switch computer applications interface)—is still under development by ANSI.

- The API level provides functions that enable programmers to gain access to and use the capabilities of the lower level protocols. Little has been standardized at this level. Two widely used APIs are Microsoft's *TAPI* (Telephony Application Programming Interface) and Novell's *TSAPI* (Telephony Services API).

In addition to a CTI link, various other elements can be introduced into a configuration that integrates computers and telephony devices and services. For example, a CTI server can connect to the CTI link at one end and to APIs running on network nodes at the other end. This makes it easier to coordinate and control traffic between network and telephony services.

Data distributors, voice response units (VRUs), and automatic call distributors can also help make the services relying on CTI more efficient. For example, an ACD can help route incoming calls to the next available person in a technical support pool. As standards for Computer Telephony become more completely defined and accepted, we can expect considerable activity in this area.

→ *See Also* TAPI; TSAPI

CTS (Clear to Send)

CTS is a hardware signal sent from a receiver to a transmitter to indicate that the transmitter can begin sending. CTS is generally sent in response to a Request To Send (RTS) signal from the transmitter. The CTS signal is sent by changing the voltage on a particular pin.

CTS is used most commonly in serial communications, and is sent over pin 5 in an RS-232 connection. The RTS/CTS combination is used in the CSMA/CA (carrier sense multiple access/collision avoidance) media-access method used in Apple's LocalTalk network architecture.

→ *Broader Category* Flow Control

→ *See Also* RTS (Request To Send)

CTS (Conformance Testing Service)

A series of programs developed to create test methods for determining how well (or whether) a product implements a particular protocol correctly. CTS projects have developed or are developing test suites for LAN protocols (*CTS-LAN*), for wide area networks (*CTS-WAN*), and for such ISO or ITU standards as *FTAM* (File transfer, access, and management), X.400 (message handling), and X.500 (directory services). In general, the tests conform to guidelines for abstract test suites established by the ITU.

CUA (Common User Access)

In IBM's SAA environment, specifications for user interfaces that are intended to provide a consistent look across applications and platforms.

→ *See Also* SAA (Systems Applications Architecture)

Customer Information Control System (CICS)

→ *See* CICS (Customer Information Control System)

Customer Premises Equipment (CPE)

→ *See* CPE (Customer Premises Equipment)

CUT (Control Unit Terminal)

A terminal operating mode that allows only one session, such as running an application, per terminal. (If a CUT terminal is attached to an IBM 3174 establishment controller with multiple logical terminal support, it can support multiple sessions.) Compare this with DFT (distributed function terminal).

Cut-off Wavelength

In single-mode fiber optics, the shortest wavelength at which a signal will take a single path through the core.

Cut-through Switching

A switching method for Ethernet networks. The switch reads a destination address and immediately starts forwarding packets, without first checking the integrity of each packet. This reduces latency.

There are two switching strategies for implementing cut-through switches:

- Cross-bar switching, in which each input port (segment) establishes a direct connection with its target output port. If the target port is currently in use, the switch waits, which could back packets up at the input port.

- Cell-backplane switching, in which all ports share a common backplane (bus) along which all packets are sent. Incoming packets are broken up and repackaged with target addresses. These fragments are then sent onto the common backplane, from which the fragments will get themselves to the specified output port. The backplane should have a bandwidth at least as high as the cumulative bandwidths of all the ports.

→ *Compare* Store-and-forward switching

CWIS (Campus-Wide Information System)

An online repository of information about a particular school or campus. The CWIS contains information such as campus-event calendars, course listings, and job openings. Although they are created for use by students on the individual campuses, CWISs are accessible over the Internet.

Cycle, Periodic Analog Signal

One complete repetition of a periodic analog signal. A cycle goes from a high point (peak) in the signal's level to a low point (trough) and back to the peak. The cycles per second value defines the frequency of a periodic signal. Frequency is measured in hertz (Hz). For example, a 50 Hz signal travels at 50 cycles per second.

Cycle, FDDI II

In an FDDI (Fiber Distributed Data Interface) II network operating in hybrid mode, a cycle is a 12,500-bit protocol data unit (PDU), or packet, that provides the basic framing for the FDDI transmission. The cycle is repeated 8000 times per second, which yields 100Mbps of bandwidth for the network.

The cycle contains the following components:

Cycle header   Specifies how the cycle is to be used. One part of the information specified in the 12 bytes in the header is whether each of the wideband channels is being used for packet-switched or isochronous data.

DPG (dedicated packet group)   Used for packet-transfer control. The DPG consists of 12 bytes.

WBC (wideband channel)   Used for actual data transmission. There are 16 WBCs in each cycle. Each WBC consists of 96 bytes, or octets, and may be subdivided into subchannels. Depending on the number of bits allocated each cycle, subchannels may have bandwidths ranging from 8Kbps to 6.144Mbps. For example, an 8-bit-per-cycle subchannel yields a 64Kbps data rate, corresponding to a B channel in the ISDN telecommunications model; using 193 bits per cycle yields a 1.544Mbps T1 line. The default FDDI II WBC uses all 768 bits for a single channel.

→ *Broader Category*   FDDI (Fiber Distributed Data Interface)

Cyclic Redundancy Check (CRC)

→ *See*   CRC (Cyclic Redundancy Check)

Cylinder

On a hard disk, the term for the collection of concentric tracks at the same position on each of the hard disk platters.

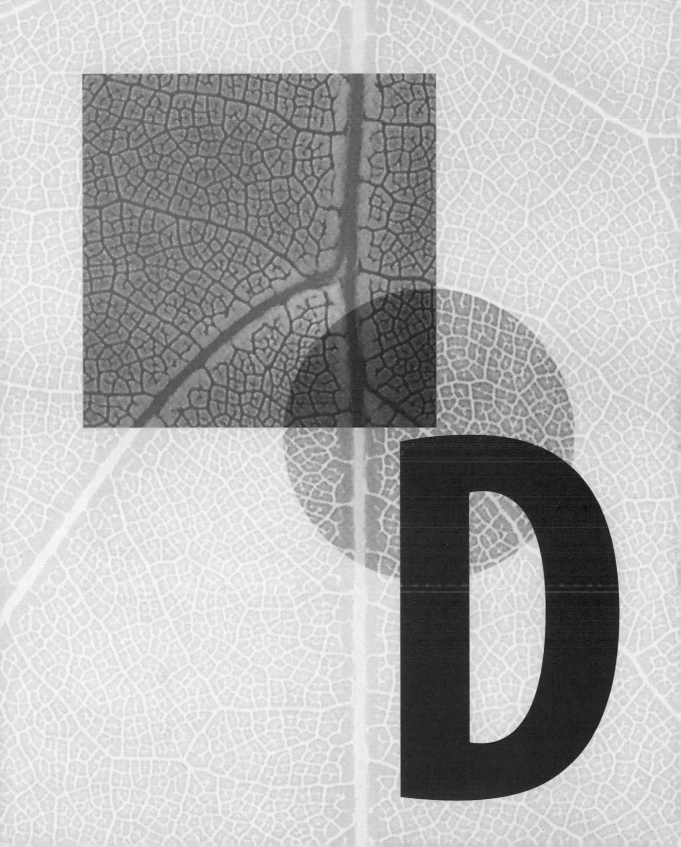

D

D4 Framing

In digital signaling, D4 framing is a method for identifying the individual channels in a DS1 channel or the individual T1 frames in a group or superframe.

D4 framing groups twelve 193-bit frames into one D4 superframe so that each DS1 channel consists of two D4 superframes.

Within each D4 superframe, the values in every one hundred ninety-third bit—in bits 193, 386, and so on—are used to identify the individual (DS0) channels. Also in each D4 superframe, the eighth bit in every channel of frames 6 and 12 is used for signaling between central offices. These are known as the A bit and the B bit, respectively. "Elements in D4 framing" illustrates this method.

→ **Compare** ESF Framing

DA (Destination Address)

In many types of packets, the destination address is found in a header field that specifies the address of the node to which the packet is being sent. Depending on the type of address involved, this field may be four, six, or more bytes. The address of the station that is sending the message is the *source address*.

→ **See Also** SA (Source Address)

DAA (Data Access Arrangement)

In telephony, a device required as protection for the public telephone network if the user's equipment does not meet FCC standards.

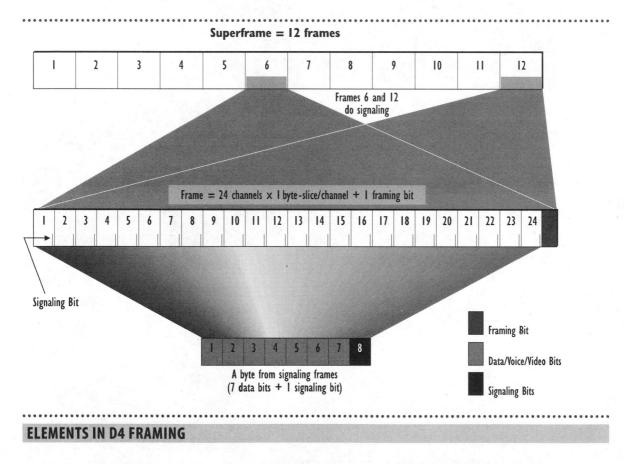

Superframe = 12 frames

| 1 | 2 | 3 | 4 | 5 | 6 | 7 | 8 | 9 | 10 | 11 | 12 |

Frames 6 and 12 do signaling

Frame = 24 channels × 1 byte-slice/channel + 1 framing bit

| 1 | 2 | 3 | 4 | 5 | 6 | 7 | 8 | 9 | 10 | 11 | 12 | 13 | 14 | 15 | 16 | 17 | 18 | 19 | 20 | 21 | 22 | 23 | 24 |

Signaling Bit

| 1 | 2 | 3 | 4 | 5 | 6 | 7 | 8 |

A byte from signaling frames
(7 data bits + 1 signaling bit)

Framing Bit

Data/Voice/Video Bits

Signaling Bits

ELEMENTS IN D4 FRAMING

DAC (Digital-to-Analog Converter)

A device for converting a digital signal to an analog one. An ADC (analog-to-digital converter) changes an analog signal to a digital signal.

DAC (Dual-Attachment Concentrator)

In an FDDI (Fiber Distributed Data Interface) network architecture, a concentrator used to attach single-attachment stations or station clusters to both FDDI rings.

DACS (Digital Access and Cross-Connect System)

In digital telecommunications, a DACS is a mechanism for switching a 64Kbps DS0 channel from one T1 line to another. The DACS makes it possible to connect input and output lines in software—that is, without having to physically connect the lines. Since it is a digital cross-connect system, the signal must first be digitized if it has come from the (analog) local loop.

Although the DACS method was originally developed for use in telephone company switching, it also has proven useful in networking contexts.

Daemon

In many operating environments, a background program that begins executing automatically when a predefined event occurs. Daemons (pronounced "demons") are common in the OS/2 and UNIX environments and are used in artificial intelligence work. Certain terminate-and-stay resident (TSR) programs in a DOS environment behave like daemon programs.

Similar elements are available on other platforms. For example, in Windows NT, such tasks are performed by services. Similarly, the analogous concept in NetWare is known as an NLM (NetWare Loadable Module), and in VMS (virtual memory system) it is known as a detached process.

Daisy Chain

A daisy chain is a method for connecting devices serially. In a daisy chain, one device (A) is connected to the computer, a second device (B) is connected to A, a third device (C) may be connected to B, and so forth, as in "An example daisy chain." SCSI devices are often connected in a daisy chain.

Depending on the electrical properties of the devices connected, the last device in the chain may need a special attachment that acts as an electrical terminator in order to prevent signals from bouncing back along the chain.

The connectivity provided through a daisy chain is also known as *cascading*.

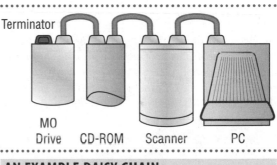

AN EXAMPLE DAISY CHAIN

DAL (Data Access Language)

In Macintosh-based client/server environments, an extension to the SQL database language. DAL is intended to provide a uniform access to any database that supports SQL.

DAL (Dedicated Access Line)

A DAL is a direct, private line between a subscriber and a local or long-distance access provider. Only the subscriber has access to the line, which may be digital or analog.

DAM (Data Access Manager)

In the System 7 operating system software for Macintoshes, DAM is a built-in capability for accessing databases on a network. The DAM mediates between an application and the database being accessed.

The DAM uses *database extensions* to communicate with the database. These are database-specific system files that contain the commands necessary to interact with a particular database.

→ *Broader Categories* Macintosh

DAMA (Demand-Assigned Multiple Access)

In telecommunications, a method for allocating access to communications channels. Idle channels are kept in a pool. When a channel capacity is requested, an idle channel is selected, allocated the requested bandwidth, and assigned to the requesting party.

DAN (Departmental-Area Network)

In government offices, a network that services a single government department.

Dark Fiber

→ *See* Fiber, Dark

DARPA (Defense Advanced Research Projects Agency)

The government agency largely responsible for the development of the ARPAnet government/university network, which eventually became part of the Internet. DARPA, originally known just as ARPA, is part of the U.S. Department of Defense (DoD).

DAS (Disk Array Subsystem)

The carriage, cabling, and circuitry for using multiple hard disks.

DAS (Dual-Attachment Station)

In an FDDI (Fiber Distributed Data Interface) network architecture, a station, or node, that is connected physically to both the primary and secondary rings. A station can be connected directly to the ring through a port on the DAS. In contrast, a SAS (single-attachment station) must be attached to a concentrator.

DAS (Dynamically Assigned Socket)

In an AppleTalk internetwork, a DAS is a unique socket value, assigned, upon petition, to a particular client.

A *socket* is an entity through which a program or process, known as a *socket client*, communicates with a network or with another process. Each AppleTalk socket is associated with an 8-bit value.

Values between 128 and 254, inclusive, are allocated for DASs. A process running on a node can request a DAS value. An available value in this range is assigned to the process. While this process is executing, the assigned value cannot be used for another socket.

DASs are in contrast to statically assigned sockets (SASs). SASs are allocated for use by various low-level protocols, such as NBP and RTMP in the AppleTalk protocol suite. Values between 1 and 127, inclusive, are used for SASs. Values between 1 and 63 are used exclusively by Apple, and values between 64 and 127 can be used by whatever processes request the values.

→ *Broader Category* Socket

DASS (Distributed Authentication Security Service)

DASS is a system for authenticating users logging into a network from unattended workstations. These workstations must be considered suspect, or untrusted, because their physical security cannot be guaranteed.

DASS uses public-key encryption methods, which support the more stringent strong authentication methods defined in the CCITT's X.509 specifications. In contrast to DASS, Kerberos is a distributed authentication system that uses a private-key encryption method.

→ *Broader Categories* Authentication; Encryption

→ *Compare* Kerberos

DAT (Digital Audio Tape)

A DAT is a popular medium for network and other backups. Information is recorded in digital form on a small audiotape cassette, originally developed by Sony and Hewlett-Packard (HP). The most common format is a 4-millimeter tape in a helical-scan drive, which can hold more than a gigabyte of information.

DATs use a logical recording format called *Data/DAT*. This format supports random data reads and writes. It also allows data to be updated in place, rather than requiring the modified data, and perhaps some of the unchanged data as well, to be rewritten to a new location.

Data Access Arrangement (DAA)

→ *See* DAA (Data Access Arrangement)

Data Access Language (DAL)

→ *See* DAL (Data Access Language)

Data Access Manager (DAM)

→ *See* DAM (Data Access Manager)

Database

A database is an indexed collection of information. The index imposes an order on the information and also provides access to the information in the database.

The information in a database can be accessed, modified, or retrieved using a query language. The most widely used query language is SQL (Structured Query Language), which forms the basis for most other query languages currently in use. See the SQL article for more information about this language.

The overwhelming majority of databases are still text based, rather than graphics or multimedia based, but this is changing. This development has implications, particularly for distributed databases. Until high-speed, long-distance telecommunications facilities are affordable for ordinary consumers, transmitting video over long-distance lines will seldom be worth the price.

Database types include flat file, relational, object-oriented, inverted-list, hierarchical, network, Internet, client/server, and distributed. These are not mutually exclusive categories. There is overlap between database types.

D

Flat File Database

In a flat file database, all the information is contained in a single file. A flat-file database consists of individual records that are, in turn, made up of fields. Each field may contain a particular item of information. There is not necessarily any relationship between records. The records are not organized in any particular way. Instead, lookup tables are created, and these are used to find and manipulate records.

A flat file database makes considerable demands of a user, who may need to "program" the required information into appropriate lookup tables.

NetWare versions prior to 4.x use a flat database, called the *bindery*, to store information about nodes and devices on the network.

Relational Database

In a relational database, the contents are organized as a set of tables in which rows represent records and columns represent fields. Certain fields may be found in multiple tables, and the values of these fields are used to guide searches. Database access and manipulation are a matter of combining information from various tables into new combinations. For example, a request might look for all records for people who work in a particular department and whose last raise was more than one year ago.

The overwhelming majority of databases currently available on PCs are relational databases. Fortunately, the theory of relational databases is well developed, so that robust DBMS (database management system) packages and powerful query and manipulation tools are available.

Object-Oriented Database

In an object-oriented database, the information is organized into objects, which consist of properties and allowable operations involving the objects.

Objects can be defined in terms of other objects (for example, as special cases or variants of a specific object), and can inherit properties from such "ancestor" objects. The Directory tree based on the information in the NetWare Directory Services (NDS) is an example of an object-oriented database.

Inverted-List Database

In an inverted-list database, the contents are also organized in tables, but these tables are more content-bound (less abstract) and therefore less easy to manipulate and modify.

In addition to tables, an inverted-list database also has records whose contents help simplify certain searches. For example, a database might have a record for each department in a corporation, and the contents of that record might be a listing of all the employees in that department. Indexes are used to keep track of records and to speed access.

Hierarchical Database

In a hierarchical database, the contents are organized hierarchically, as one or more trees. Each record in a tree has exactly one parent and may have children. Any two records in a hierarchical database are related in exactly one way.

The DOS directory and file system is an example of a hierarchical database. The relationships involved include "is a subdirectory of" and "in the same directory as."

Network Database

A network database is similar to a hierarchical database in that there are links between records. The main difference is that records in a network database may have no parents or one or more parents. This is because a network database consists essentially of records and links. These links do not necessarily form a hierarchically organized tree.

Note that the *network* in this label is not a computer network. It is a network in the mathematical sense: elements (records) connected by links (relationships).

Internet (HTML) Database

An Internet database is stored on the Internet. It may be a distributed database, or the entire database may be on a single host. Internet databases are often made up of HTML (Hypertext Markup Language) pages. In this case, the information may be called an *HTML database*. Such a database can take any of three forms:

- Static, in which the contents are prepared in advance and remain unchanged. Such databases may consist of static HTML pages. Such databases are output only and make little demand on the server's processing capabilities. They may require significant amounts of storage, however. Catalogs are often static databases.

- Dynamic, in which the contents are generated whenever a browser or other program wants to see material from the database. Generally, such output-only databases will consist of Dynamic HTML (DHTML) pages. A dynamic database requires processing power to generate the pages when requested and also for the database access functions. Parts or inventory lists, for which quantities may be updated constantly, are often dynamic databases.

- Interactive, in which the user may specify how materials are to be updated or used. Interactive databases are input and output. Interactive databases are generally controlled by CGI scripts, Active Server Pages (ASPs), or ISAPI (Internet Services Applications Programming Interface) applications. Such databases are the most computationally intensive of the three types: they must do everything a dynamic database does and must also run the server-side scripts, applications, or ASPs. Registration and other client lists may be stored as interactive databases.

Client/Server Database

A client/server database is distinguished by the manner in which the database is accessed, rather than by how the contents are organized. In this type of database, a client program makes a query or a request, and sends this request over a network to the server. A program on the server carries out the request, and sends the result back to the client. The client uses a front-end program to make the request, and the server uses a back-end program to fulfill it.

In such configurations, front- and back-end programs communicate using a standard database query language (for example, SQL, for Structured Query Language). Oracle and Informix are examples of client/server database programs. While there is nothing in the client/server definition that requires it, such databases generally work with the database contents arranged as a relational database.

Distributed Database

Any of the database types can be developed as a distributed database, because this is a matter of database storage rather than structuring. A distributed database is simply one whose contents are stored on multiple machines.

The fact that two employee records are on different machines does not change the relationship between the employees (for example, if both work in the same department). DBMS software will hide the distributed nature of the database from the user, so that users need not make any adjustments to their queries or methods for retrieving and changing data.

Database, Client/Server

→ *See* Database

Database, Distributed

→ *See* Database

Database, Flat File

→ *See* Database

Database, Hierarchical

→ *See* Database

Database, HTML (Hypertext Markup Language)

→ *See* Database

Database, Internet

→ *See* Database

Database, Inverted

→ *See* Database

Database Management System (DBMS)

→ *See* DBMS (Database Management System)

Database, Network

→ *See* Database

Database, Object-Oriented

→ *See* Database

Database, Relational

→ *See* Database

Data Bits

In asynchronous transmissions, the bits that actually comprise the data. Usually, 7 or 8 data bits are grouped together. Each group of data bits in a transmission is preceded by a start bit, then followed by an optional parity bit, as well as one or more stop bits.

Data Bus

The internal bus over which devices and system components communicate with the central processing unit (CPU) is called a *data bus*. Buses differ in their width, which is the number of data bits that can be transported at a time, and in their clock speed.

In general, maximum supported clock speeds keep getting higher, with 100 megahertz (MHz) speeds already available on some processors. While processor manufacturers continuously leapfrog each other's highest speeds, official bus standards change more slowly.

In the following summaries, the quoted clock speeds are those specified in the bus specifications or in de facto standards. You will be able to find faster processors than the ones discussed.

PC Data Bus Architecture

The following bus architectures are (or have been) popular for PCs:

ISA (Industry Standard Architecture)   The bus for the earliest PCs. Early PC versions were 8-bit and ran at 4.77MHz; later AT versions were 16-bit and ran at 8MHz.

EISA (Extended Industry Standard Architecture)   A 32-bit extension of the ISA bus. This architecture also runs at 8MHz.

MicroChannel   A 32-bit proprietary architecture from IBM, for use in most of its PS/*x* and Model *xx* series of computers. The MicroChannel bus operates at 10MHz.

VESA (Video Electronics Standards Association) An enhanced version of the EISA architecture, also known as *local bus*. The original version was 32-bit at 40MHz; the newer version is 64-bit at 50MHz.

PCI (Peripheral Component Interconnect) A newer architecture from Intel, PCI is 64-bit and operates at 33MHz.

These bus architectures are discussed in more detail in separate articles.

Macintosh Data Bus Architecture

In contrast, Apple's Macintosh line of computers has, for the most part used the NuBus architecture developed by Texas Instruments. This architecture is processor specific, which means that it is not applicable to an entire processor family.

→**See Also** EISA (Extended Industry Standard Architecture); ISA (Industry Standard Architecture); MicroChannel; PCI (Peripheral Component Interconnect); VESA (Video Electronics Standards Association)

Data Carrier Detect (DCD)

→**See** DCD (Data Carrier Detect)

Data Communications

Data communications is the transmission of data, commonly by electronic means over a physical medium. The data to be transmitted can be in analog or digital form. Similarly, the transmission method may be analog or digital. These two attributes are independent of each other—so that four possible data/transmission combinations are possible (analog-analog, analog-digital, digital-analog, digital-digital). Any potentially relevant Zen koans aside, it is generally agreed that, to be useful, data communications require both a sender and a receiver.

Components of Data Communications

The sender and receiver are also known as the *data source* and *data sink*, respectively. These are connected by a *data link*. The data link includes a transmission medium (for example, wire) and the appropriate transmission and receiving devices at the data source and sink. "Elements in data communications" shows these components.

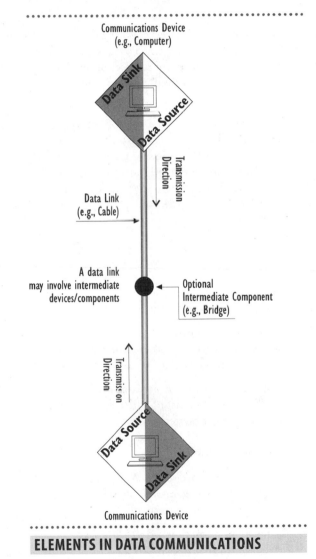

ELEMENTS IN DATA COMMUNICATIONS

The sender must encode and transmit the data, and the receiver must receive and decode the data. Data encoding may include special treatment, such as compression to eliminate redundancy or encryption to prevent, or at least discourage, eavesdropping.

Types of Data Transmission

The data transmission may be any of the following types:

Point-to-point, or direct   Over a direct (unmediated) link between sender and receiver. Point-to-point connections are commonly used in small networks and dedicated communications lines.

Mediated   Handled, and possibly modified, by intermediate stations or parties en route to the receiver. A transmission may be mediated simply because there are stations between the sender and the receiver. In such a case, all transmissions take the same path.

Switched   Mediated and possibly routed along different paths. A switched transmission may be diverted to any of multiple possible paths. Different transmission elements—fixed-size blocks, variable-sized packets, or entire messages—can be used as the basis for the switching.

Broadcast   Transmitted to any station or party capable of receiving, rather than to a specific receiver. A radio transmission is broadcast.

Multicast   Transmitted to any station on a stored or specified list of addresses. For example, electronic newsletters or mail from special interest groups are multicast when they are sent only to subscribers.

Stored and forwarded   Sent to a holding location until requested or sent on automatically after a predefined amount of time.

Time division multiplexed (TDM)   Combined with other transmissions. In this multiplexing method, transmissions share the entire capacity of a single channel. For example, the transmission might be divided into brief transmission slices that are interspersed in the channel.

Frequency division multiplexed (FDM)   Combined with other transmissions, as in TDM, but the multiplexed transmissions split a single channel, with each transmission taking some portion. For example, a transmission may use a small frequency range within the channel's entire range.

"Common data transmission schemes" shows the most common types of transmission.

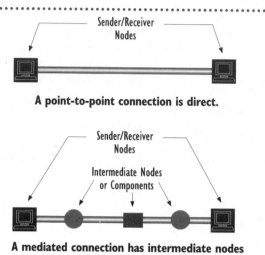

A point-to-point connection is direct.

A mediated connection has intermediate nodes or other components.

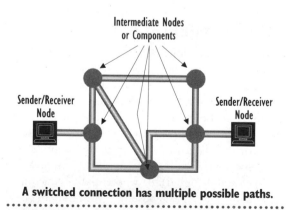

A switched connection has multiple possible paths.

COMMON DATA TRANSMISSION SCHEMES

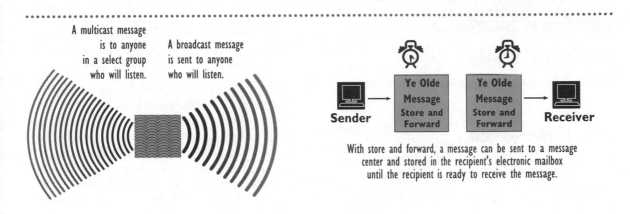

A multicast message is to anyone in a select group who will listen.

A broadcast message is sent to anyone who will listen.

Sender

Ye Olde Message Store and Forward

Ye Olde Message Store and Forward

Receiver

With store and forward, a message can be sent to a message center and stored in the recipient's electronic mailbox until the recipient is ready to receive the message.

D

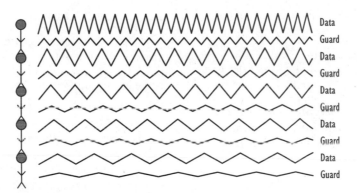

In frequency division multiplexing (FDM), each channel has its own frequency band, and each of these is part of the total bandwidth.
The data bands are separated from each other by guard bands.

Data
Guard
Data
Guard
Data
Guard
Data
Guard
Data
Guard

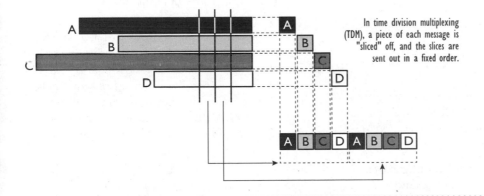

In time division multiplexing (TDM), a piece of each message is "sliced" off, and the slices are sent out in a fixed order.

A B C D

A B C D A B C D

COMMON DATA TRANSMISSION SCHEMES (continued)

Data Communications Equipment (DCE)

→ See DCE (Data Communications Equipment)

Data Compression

Data compression is a method of reducing the amount of data used to represent the original information. This can be accomplished by eliminating redundancy.

Compression Strategies

The basis for the compression can be any of the following:

- Repeated patterns or single-value runs in bit sequences, as in run-length limited (RLL) encoding.

- Probabilities of occurrences of particular byte values, as in Huffman, adaptive Huffman, or arithmetic coding. Commonly occurring values are encoded with a smaller number of bits than less common values.

- Commonly occurring words or phrases, as in the use of abbreviations or acronyms.

- Location of a sequence in a dictionary or other type of look-up table, as in dictionary-based algorithms such as LZ77, LZ78, and LZW.

- Similar pixel patterns or image elements that are repeated—possibly in different contexts or at different sizes. This is used in fractal compression.

- Smoothing of data by discarding extreme pixel values within a frame, as in JPEG compression. Strategies that compress only within a frame are known as intraframe, or spatial, compression strategies. The Discrete Cosine Transform (DCT), which forms the basis of a JPEG file does intraframe compression.

- Compression of data by looking for and storing only differences between successive frames. Such interframe, or temporal, compression strategies compress, in part, because difference values tend to lie within a smaller range and, hence, need fewer bits to be represented. DPCM (Differential Pulse Code Modulation) and ADPCM (Adaptive DPCM) are examples of temporal compression schemes.

Compression Classes

The two main classes of compression methods are lossless and lossy. In lossless compression, all the original information can be recovered. That is, when the compressed file is decompressed, the original image or sound will be reproduced. Lossless methods generally compress data to about 50 or 33 percent of the original size. These values represent compression ratios of 2:1 and 3:1, respectively. Lossless compression methods rarely reach ratios higher than 5:1 or so. Huffman coding, adaptive Huffman coding, LZW, and LZSS are examples of lossless compression algorithms.

In lossy compression, some of the original information will be lost. This means that the original image or other information is no longer reproducible from the compressed file. Lossy methods can attain compression ratios of 100:1 and even higher. JPEG, MPEG, and fractal compression are examples of lossy compression algorithms.

The table "Compression Methods" lists some of the compression methods that have been or are being used.

COMPRESSION METHODS

Method	Strategy	Comments
Adaptive Huffman coding	Variable-length bit coding, predictive model	Used in UNIX COMPACT program; modifies compression tree as new data comes in
ADPCM (Adaptive Differential Pulse Code Modulation)	Predictive model	Based on differences between consecutive samples. Used for compression of video, speech, or other sound information
Arithmetic coding	Variable-length bit coding	More efficient than Huffman because it can use fractional bit values when encoding
CDV (Compressed Digital Video)	DCT (Discrete Cosine Transform)	Used to compress video for satellite broadcast systems
DCLZ	Adaptive dictionary	Proposed as an alternative to QIC-122
DPCM (Differential Pulse Code Modulation)	Predictive model	Encodes differences between successive frames; used for compression of video or audio information
DVI (Digital Video Interactive)	DCT (Discrete Cosine Transform)	Developed by Intel and implemented in hardware; used for compressing and transmitting video
FIF (Fractal Image Format)	Self-similarity	Similar to fractal compression; implemented in hardware
Fractal compression	Self-similarity	Looks for repetition of similar patterns in image; compressed image stored as a mathematical equation
HDTV (high-definition television)	DCT (Discrete Cosine Transform)	For cable and satellite television
Huffman coding	Variable-length bit coding	Based on occurrence probabilities; first major compression algorithm (1952)
Indeo	DCT (Discrete Cosine Transform)	Developed by Intel for use in CD applications and for video playback; used in Microsoft Video for Windows and Apple QuickTime technologies
JPEG (Joint Photographic Experts Group); also JPG	DCT (Discrete Cosine Transform)	Used for image compression
LPC (Linear Predictive Coding)	Predictive model	Used for compression of speech information
LZ77 (Lempel-Ziv 77)	Sliding dictionary	Used in programs such as PKZIP and LHARC
LZ78/LZW (Lempel-Ziv 78/ Lempel-Ziv-Welch)	Adaptive dictionary	Used in UNIX COMPRESS program and in programs such as ARC and ARJ; LZW is a patented algorithm that improves on LZ78
LZSS (Lempel-Ziv)	Dictionary	Performance improvements over LZ77
MNP5	Adaptive Huffman coding	Used to compress modem signals
Motion compensation	Pixel averaging	Averages displacement of pixels from one frame to the next
MPEG-1 (Motion Picture Experts Group–1)	DCT (Discrete Cosine Transform)	Original standard for handling video and other multimedia
MPEG-2 (Motion Picture Experts Group–2)	DCT (Discrete Cosine Transform)	For high-speed and studio quality video
MPEG-4 (Motion Picture Experts Group–4)	DCT (Discrete Cosine Transform)	For low-speed video—e.g., over POTS (Plain Old Telephone Service)
Px64	DCT (Discrete Cosine Transform)	Forms the basis of ITU-T H.261 standard
QIC-122	Dictionary	Used in tape backups
Quality reduction	Compromise	Compresses by reducing one or more of image resolution, image size, or frame rate
Run length coding	Variable-length bit coding	Looks for repeated patterns
Shannon-Fano coding	Variable-length bit coding	Based on occurrence probabilities
V42bis	Dictionary	Alternative to, and improvement on, MNP5; uses LZW algorithm, which is patented
WIC (Wavelet Image Compression)	DWT (Discrete Wavelet Transform)	An alternative to JPEG

D

Data Country Code (DCC)

→ *See* DCC (Data Country Code)

Data Definition Language (DDL)

→ *See* DDL (Data Definition Language)

Data Description Packet (DDP)

→ *See* DDP (Data Description Packet)

Data Encryption Algorithm (DEA)

→ *See* DEA (Data Encryption Algorithm)

Data Encryption Key (DEK)

→ *See* DEK (Data Encryption Key)

Data Encryption Standard (DES)

→ *See* DES (Data Encryption Standard)

Data-Flow Control

The fifth layer in IBM's SNA.

→ *See* SNA (Systems Network Architecture)

Data Fork

The data fork is the data portion of a Macintosh file. It is the part of a Macintosh file that is transferred to non-Macintosh environments, such as DOS or UNIX.

→ *See Also* Macintosh

Data-Grade Media (DGM)

→ *See* Cable, Data-Grade

Datagram

A datagram is a packet that includes both source and destination addresses provided by the user, rather than by the network. A datagram can also contain data. A message might be sent as multiple datagrams, which may be delivered to the destination in nonconsecutive order. Receipt of a datagram is not acknowledged.

Datagram routing takes place at the Network layer of the OSI reference model. Datagram transmission takes place at the Data-Link layer.

Datagram services are provided in connectionless (as opposed to connection-oriented) transmissions. Because connectionless transmissions do not necessarily deliver datagrams in order, datagram services cannot guarantee successful message delivery. Receipt verification is the responsibility of a higher-level protocol, which must be able to assemble the message from the datagrams. Protocols that provide this type of service include UDP (User Datagram Protocol) in the Internet's TCP/IP protocol suite, CLNP (Connectionless Network Protocol) in the OSI reference model, and DDP (Datagram Delivery Protocol) in the AppleTalk protocol suite.

→ *See Also* Connectionless Service; Connection-Oriented Service

Data Interchange Standards Association (DISA)

→ *See* DISA (Data Interchange Standards Association)

Datakit VCS

A data-switch product from AT&T. Datakit VCS offers communications channels ranging from 9.6Kbps to 8Mbps and can be linked to X.25 networks.

Data Link

In communications, the components and medium necessary for communication between two stations or parties. The medium is generally (but not necessarily) a wire or fiber-optic cable, and the components are the transmitting and receiving facilities at either end of the link.

Data-Link Connection Identifier (DLCI)

→ *See* DLCI (Data-Link Connection Identifier)

Data-Link Control (DLC)

→ *See* DLC (Data-Link Control)

Data-Link Services (DLS)

The services provided at the Data-Link layer in the OSI reference model.

Data Mining

Data mining refers to the process of retrieving information for exploratory or analytic purposes from a data warehouse or a large database. The term *data mining* is used in a narrow and a broad sense. The main difference between the narrow and broad forms concerns the uses to which the mined data can be put.

According to the narrow definition of the term, only tools that make it possible to do statistical or other types of advanced analyses—for example, using neural nets or artificial intelligence (AI)—should be considered data mining tools. In fact, some practitioners define data mining (in the narrow sense) as a process that uses statistical and AI techniques to examine large bodies of information.

In the broader sense of the term, resources that provide descriptive or exploratory capabilities (for example, query managers or spreadsheets) are also considered data mining tools. The goal of data mining in this sense is often to identify patterns that can be used to generate models or hypotheses. The following kinds of tools can provide data mining capabilities:

- Query managers, through which a user can specify what information is to be retrieved. Currently, most query managers are either SQL-based or graphical programs. (SQL, or Structured Query Language, is the standard language for specifying database queries.) In a graphically based query manager, the user specifies a search by selecting the variables or attributes that define it.

- Report generators, which can be used to create a summary of the material retrieved from the data warehouse. Report generators are often included as components in other types of programs—for example, in query managers and many data analysis programs.

- Statistical analysis tools, which can be used to identify trends and to formulate hypotheses about possible causal relationships in the data. Various statistical packages are available, including SPSS (Statistical Package for the Social Sciences) and SAS (Statistical Analysis System). Such packages are considered data mining tools even in the narrow sense of the term.

- Graphical display and data visualization tools, which can provide visual summaries

D

or displays of information from a data warehouse. In some cases, such a picture can be worth several thousand words (and even more bytes). While any statistical package worth its salt will have some graphical display capabilities, special-purpose packages are much more powerful and can be used to present information in all sorts of ways. In fact data visualization is a very active research area from several perspectives, including information processing and (super)computing.

- Artificial intelligence tools, which use various strategies to organize or anticipate data. AI tools include neural nets (programs that "learn" by trial and error), expert systems (programs that "reason" by combining general-purpose, commonsense, and content-specific rules), and fuzzy logic systems (programs that can use ambiguous information and rules to formulate decisions or to develop concepts). Such tools also meet the more stringent criteria of the narrow definition of data mining.

- Spreadsheets, which have long been used to cross-tabulate and summarize information, and to identify trends in numerical and simple categorical data.

- Multidimensional databases, which essentially extend the descriptive capabilities of spreadsheets to higher levels of interaction between variables. A multidimensional database package makes it possible to create "virtual spreadsheets" by allowing a user to specify the variable combinations the user wants to examine.

Together, data mining and data warehousing have revolutionized database technology. Data warehousing provides a way for companies to organize, save, and make use of their legacy data—data that may have been scattered all over the corporation or that may have been hidden in the depths of a mainframe computer and is accessible only by MIS gurus.

Data mining makes such data warehouses accessible to Jane and John Doe—that is, to any end user with the necessary access rights. Data-mining tools provide powerful, (relatively) fast, and very flexible ways for such users to customize whatever queries they have.

→ Related Topics Data Warehousing

Data Network Identification Code (DNIC)

→ See DNIC (Data Network Identification Code)

Data over Voice (DOV)

→ See DOV (Data over Voice)

Data Packet

In general, a data packet is a well-defined block that contains user or application data. When transmitted, a data packet will also include a considerable amount of administrative information (not data) in the packet header and footer.

A data packet is defined for a particular protocol. The term is also used to refer to such packets within a particular protocol or architecture. For example, an X.25 data packet can contain up to 1024 bytes of user data.

Data-PCS (Data Personal Communications Services)

Data-PCS is a type of wireless communications service defined by Apple in a proposal to the FCC (Federal Communications Commission). The proposal was a petition to have the FCC set aside a 40MHz bandwidth in the 140MHz range between 1.85 and 1.99GHz.

The bandwidth is to be used for wireless communications using radio waves. Transmissions within the allocated bandwidth could have a maximum power of 1 watt. This maximum is strong enough for a 50-meter (165 feet) transmission range, but weak enough to allow multiple wireless networks to operate in different parts of the spectrum without interference.

→ *Broader Category* Transmission, Wireless

Dataphone Digital Service (DDS)

→ *See* DDS (Dataphone Digital Service)

Data Protection

Data protection involves the safeguarding of data being transmitted across the network or stored somewhere on the network.

Various steps can be taken to protect network data. Most of the measures cost money, but the more steps you take, the better protected your data is likely to be. This article summarizes techniques for protecting your data from equipment failures. See the Security article for information about how to protect data from unauthorized or malicious users.

Protecting Data Against Power Disturbance

The first line of defense—at the power lines—includes measures such as the following:

- Make sure the outlets you are using for the network machines are properly grounded. Without grounding, power protection measures may be pointless.

- Use a UPS (uninterruptible power supply) to ensure that a sudden power sag or failure does not cause the server or other crucial computers to crash. When a brownout or blackout occurs, the UPS provides emergency power from batteries. In case of a total power loss, the UPS should be able to power the server long enough to permit an orderly shutdown. A UPS can also clean a power signal (to make it closer to a pure waveform) before it reaches the networking hardware.

- Use surge protectors to protect against spikes (or surges) and sags. The former are very short bursts of very high voltage; the latter are temporary drops in voltage..When selecting surge protectors, be aware that the less expensive surge protectors are designed to protect against a single spike (or at most against a few spikes). These protectors are not designed to withstand repeated spikes. More expensive protectors will provide such long-term protection. Make sure surge protectors and all other electrical devices are UL listed.

- Use isolation transformers to protect against noise and static (smaller variations in voltage). These transformers clamp (suppress) any voltages that lie outside a predefined range.

UPS TIPS

If a UPS on every machine is too expensive, put one on just the most crucial network components. Make sure to protect at least the file servers. Put surge protectors on as many other nodes as possible.

When calculating costs, keep in mind that research has found that networks with UPSs have lower maintenance costs than networks with just surge protectors and isolation transformers.

Don't put a UPS on a printer. Not only is this unnecessary, it's also futile, since the printer's power demands will drain the UPS battery.

Backups, Diagnostic, and Anti-Virus Measures

Other data protection measures include the following:

- Doing regular backups, so that a minimum amount of data (such as no more than a day's worth) will ever be lost because of system failure. See the Backup article for more information.

- Running regular and rigorous diagnostics on your hard disks. Diagnostic programs will detect bad sectors or sectors that are about to go bad, will move any data from these sectors to safe areas of the disk, and will lock out the defective sectors. Some network packages can do this type of redirection on the fly. See the Diagnostic Program article for more information.

- Monitoring for viruses, and having well-defined recovery procedures in case of a virus attack. To reduce the possibility of virus infections, limit users' ability to upload software from personal floppy disks. See the Anti-Virus Program article for more information.

Data Protection through Software and Hardware

NetWare provides a variety of data-protection features that can be grouped into a category called *fault tolerance*. Other networking software may have similar features. NetWare's fault-tolerance features include the following:

Disk duplexing   Uses two hard disks attached to the server, and automatically copies all data to both hard disks. The disks are each accessed through separate channels (which means that each disk has its own controller board). If one disk or channel fails, the network operating system will notify the system administrator and will continue writing to the working disk. Not all network software packages support disk duplexing.

Disk mirroring   Also uses two hard disks and copies all data to both hard disks, but both disks share the same channel (which means that they are connected to the same controller board). Failure of the controller board makes both disks inaccessible.

Hot Fix   Uses a special area of the hard disk (called the *redirection area*) to hold data from defective areas. When a write operation indicates there is a problem at the location being written, the Hot Fix capability rewrites the data in question to the redirection area and stores the address of the defective location in a table set aside for that purpose.

Read-after-write verification   Checks newly written data before discarding the source data from memory. After writing data to the hard disk, the networking software reads the newly written data and compares it with the original data (which is still stored in RAM). If the new data and the original data match, the original data is discarded from RAM, and the next disk operation can take place. If there is a discrepancy, some corrective action (for example, a Hot Fix) is taken.

FAT duplication   Maintains duplicate file allocation tables (FATs) and directory entry tables (DETs). This method helps prevent files from becoming corrupted because of addressing errors (rather than because of media defects). FAT-duplication is done automatically by most networking software.

→ *See Also* Anti-Virus Program; Backup; Diagnostic Program; Security

Data rate

This refers to the speed at which data are transferred over a connection. The data rate will generally be lower than the throughput (total transfer rate) because the latter will also include signaling and other overhead bits.

Data Service Unit/Channel Service Unit (DSU/CSU)

→ *See* DSU/CSU (Data Service Unit/Channel Service Unit)

Dataset

In some network management programs, a term for a collection of data gathered by an agent (a program that performs a particular task automatically or on command). The data will generally pertain to a particular network function or device.

Data Set

In telecommunications, the telephone company's name for a modem.

Data Set Ready (DSR)

→ *See* DSR (Data Set Ready)

Data Sink

In data communications, the receiver of a data transmission. This is in contrast to the *data source*, which is the sender.

Data Source

In data communications, the sender of a data transmission. This is in contrast to the *data sink*, which is the receiver.

Data Stream Compatibility (DSC)

→ *See* DSC (Data Stream Compatibility)

Data Switch

A location or device in which data can be routed, or switched, to its destination. Data-switch devices are used in switching networks, in which data is grouped and routed on the basis of predetermined criteria or current network traffic.

Data Switching Equipment (DSE)

Equipment used in a switching network, such as X.25.

Data Terminal Equipment (DTE)

→ *See* DTE (Data Terminal Equipment)

Data Terminal Ready (DTR)

→ *See* DTR (Data Terminal Ready)

Data Transparency

Data transparency is a data-transmission strategy designed to ensure that data will not be interpreted as control signals. Bit or byte sequences that might be interpreted as flags or commands are modified before transmission and restored upon receipt.

For example, LLAP (LocalTalk Link Access Protocol), which is used in some AppleTalk networks, uses a data transparency method called *bit stuffing* to ensure that the data bit sequence 01111110 is never transmitted, since this specific value represents a flag. In bit stuffing, a 0 bit is inserted after the fifth 1 value in the 01111110 sequence.

Data under Voice (DUV)

In telecommunications, a strategy for transmitting voice and data over the same line.

→ *Compare* DOV (Data Over Voice)

Data Warehousing

An information management strategy in which all of a company's information is accessible through a single database. The corporate information may come from many sources and departments, may come in a variety of forms, and may be stored at different levels of detail. Corporate information includes such things as product, customer, and other "departmental" databases; sales, inventory, and other transaction data; archival, or legacy, data, and so forth.

The data warehouse will also contain *metadata*, which is information about the general organization of the warehouse, the format and location of the various materials in the warehouse, the operations or uses allowed for various items, and possibly connections between data items. The metadata needs to be updated whenever the actual data is changed.

The warehouse contents may be distributed over various machines and locations, but should be accessible in a transparent manner through a server. It is this transparent access of the entire corporate database with simple commands that makes data warehousing so attractive. By making the entire database accessible, it becomes easier to spot trends, coordinate updates, and generally keep the data organized and consistent.

Access to the data warehouse always assumes user authorization. That is, the integration of various databases should not make it possible for users to get access to data that was off limits before warehousing. Warehouse data should be accessible to authorized users in raw form or for analyses—and the necessary retrieval and analysis tools should be part of the data warehouse system.

Warehouse data will vary in level of detail, or *granularity*. Current data, which is more likely to be active and in flux, will be more detailed (finer-grained) than older materials, which may be just summary data. Other types of data may lie between these two extremes.

The material in a data warehouse need not all be online all the time. Dormant (or, at least napping) materials may be stored on secondary media (such as tapes or compact discs), which may need to be mounted before users can access them. For these materials to belong to the data warehouse, it's only necessary for the metadata to include information about these materials and their locations.

A Data Warehousing System

The components of a data warehousing system fall roughly into three categories: acquisition, storage, and access. These categories correspond roughly to input, administration, and output. Seen in these terms, the temporal relationship among the components also becomes clearer. At a very general level, the process of data warehousing occurs in three stages:

1. Getting the data into the warehouse during the acquisition, or input, phase. Various kinds of tools can be used during this phase, including data-entry programs, OCR (optical character recognition), database query programs (for getting information out of an existing database directly), and so forth.

2. Storing and administering the data once it's been input. Once the data is in, it needs to be indexed and stored. For the storage to be successful, the data warehouse hardware needs to have enough available space; for the storage to be useful, the information being stored needs to be organized and indexed in a suitable manner. Metadata—information about the data in the warehouse—needs to be created. This facilitates both the administration and the retrieval of information in the warehouse. Depending on the sources of the materials, the data in a warehouse may be left in their original, or legacy, form; or it may be homogenized into a standard, warehouse format. Each strategy has advantages and drawbacks.

3. Allowing users access to the contents of the warehouse. Data warehouses are created in order to simplify access to relevant information, regardless of the location or provenance of this information. Ideally, the access should be transparent. That is, the user should never need to worry about where the data is located or what format it has. For this data warehousing phase, users have access to various kinds of data mining tools. Such tools let users specify and retrieve the information they want. Some data mining tools allow the user to examine data from various perspectives—to get as complete a picture as possible. See the Data Mining entry for more information about such tools.

A complete data warehousing system should have resources for:

- Defining and organizing the warehouse contents, and storing information about the contents as metadata.

- Acquiring, displaying, and distributing data

- Managing and overseeing both the data and the warehouse operations

- Displaying information about the warehouse contents and organization

- Analyzing and manipulating the data

The advantages of data warehousing are many, as are the obstacles. One of the major issues that must be considered is how to organize and connect very heterogeneous information. The degree to which updates and reorganizations can be automated will depend strongly on the quality of the basic organization.

→ *See Also* Data Mining

dB (Decibel)

A decibel (abbreviated dB—from a unit named in honor of Alexander Graham Bell) is a tenth of a bel. It is a logarithmic unit used to measure relative signal intensity. (A logarithm, in case you've forgotten your algebra, is a mathematical construct that enables you to do multiplication and division by adding and subtracting the logarithms of the values involved.) Decibels are used to measure the relative intensity of acoustic, electrical, or optical signals.

Decibels are used to express the gain in signal power when a signal is passed through an amplifier. The relationship between the two values is expressed by a ratio: P_2/P_1, where P_1 is the original power level, and P_2 is the power level after the amplification.

A decibel value is computed by taking the logarithm (to base 10) of this ratio, and then multiplying this value by 10 (or 20, for some measures): $dB = 10 \log_{10}(P_2/P_1)$. For example, if the signal strength goes from 25 watts to 50 watts by going through an amplifier, the result would be $dB = 10 \log_{10}(50/25) = 10 \log_{10}(2) = 10 * 0.3010 = 3$ (roughly). If the signal strength increases from 10 to 1000 milliwatts (mW), the formula is: $dB = 10 \log_{10}(1000/10) = 10 \log_{10}(100) = 10 * 2 = 20$.

Thus, doubling the level of a magnitude (such as a wattage) represents a 3dB increase; increasing a magnitude a hundredfold is a 20dB increase. Because you can add logarithms, increasing a magnitude by a factor of 200 represents a 23dB increase.

Conversely, halving a level represents a gain of −3dB (also expressed as a *loss* of 3dB). This is true because the logarithm of 0.5 (that is, of one half) is −0.3010. Similarly, decreasing a level to one hundredth of its original value represents a −20dB gain (or a 20dB loss) because the logarithm of 0.01 (1/100) is −2.

The decibel value may be computed in terms of a reference level, such as a watt (W) or a milliwatt (mW). For such measures, the reference level is one of the values in the ratio. These referenced measures are denoted by dBW for decibel with reference to one watt, and dBm for decibel with reference to one milliwatt. See the dBm entry for more information on such referenced scales.

→ *See Also* dBm (Decibels Referenced to 1mW)

D-bit

In wide area networks and other communications using the X.25 protocol, the d-bit is set to 1 in a data or call request packet to indicate that the packet recipient should provide delivery confirmation.

→ *Broader Category* X.25

→ *See Also* M-bit

dBm (Decibels Referenced to 1mW)

In telecommunications, gain or loss in signal power is measured using a decibel (dB) scale. This is a logarithmic scale that expresses the ratio of two power values. Thus, the decibel scale measures relative signal strength. Specifically, signal gain (or loss) is expressed in the following formula: $dB = 10 \log_{10} (P_2/P_1)$, where P_1 and P_2 represent power levels 1 and 2, respectively, and $\log_{10}$ indicates that the logarithm to base 10 is being used. (In case you've forgotten your high school algebra, logarithms are handy tools that let you do multiplication by adding the logarithms for the numbers being multiplied.)

If a 10-watt signal goes into an amplifier and a 20-watt signal comes out, the gain in signal strength is expressed by: $dB = 10 \log_{10} (20/10) = 10 \log_{10} (2) = 10 * 0.3010 = 3$. (0.3010 is the base 10 logarithm of 2.) Thus, doubling a signal from 10 to 20 watts represents a 3dB gain. (Note that doubling a signal from 1000 to 2000 watts would also represent a 3dB gain since the ratio 2000/1000 also reduces to 2.)

Similarly, if a 50-watt signal is sent and a 25-watt signal is received, the signal gain is $dB = 10 \log_{10} (25/50) = 10 \log_{10} (0.5) = 10 * -0.3010 = -3$. (−0.3010 is the base 10 logarithm of one half.) Thus, halving a signal represents a gain of −3dB. This can also be expressed as a *loss* of 3dB. (Note, again, that halving the signal from 8000 to 4000 watts would also represent a −3dB gain—since the ratio 4000/8000 also reduces to 0.5.)

Because decibels are logarithmic values, you can add them. This makes it easy to compute the total gain (or loss) of a signal between any two points in the signal's journey.

By specifying a reference power level—in the case of dBm, 1 milliwatt (mW)—the (decibel) scale becomes an absolute one. In effect, P_1 in the equation is always 1mW. The equation for a referenced system becomes $dBm = 10 \log_{10} (P_2/1mW)$.

It turns out that the reference point has another useful property. A signal level of 1mW corresponds to 0dB. To see this, you just need to solve the equation. (In case you've forgotten, the base 10 logarithm of 1 is 0.)

The 1mW value was selected by convention, and because this magnitude lies within the range in which most telecommunications signals are transmitted. Most signals used in telecommunications are between 0.1mW and 10mW.

Other reference values are possible. For example, in a dBW system, the reference value would be 1 watt. This signal magnitude might be more appropriate for certain kinds of measurements.

Reference Level for Noise (dBrn)

The dBm system sets a reference level for *signal* strength. But any electrical transmission also includes a certain amount of noise from various sources. For signaling to be feasible, the noise level must be several orders of magnitude lower than the signal level.

By convention, the reference level for noise signals is the picowatt (pW). 1pW is a trillionth of a watt, which is equal to 10^{-12} watts. Rather than using dBp to refer to this system, it is known as *dBrn* (dB referenced for noise). Expressed in terms of the dBm scale, the (1pW) noise reference (0dBrn) is −90dBm. Conversely, the (1mW) signal reference (0dBm) is 90dBrn.

A rather specialized form of the noise system arises when testing signal gain or loss for analog voice transmissions. Since analog voice transmission uses only a limited frequency range—from 300 to 3400Hz—noise in any other frequency range can be ignored. Something called a *C message filter* can be used to allow only signals within the analog voice frequency range to pass through.

Filtering in this way also causes some signal loss. As a result, the calibration of the dBrn values in relation to dBm is thrown off. With such a filter, 0dBrn actually equals –91.5dBm. To adjust for the 1.5dB loss, the *dBrnC0* reference system is used. This system is known as a *C message weighted scale*. On this scale, 0dBrnC0 = –90dBm.

→ *See Also*   dB (Decibel)

DBMS (Database Management System)

A DBMS is application software that controls the data in a database, including overall organization, storage, retrieval, security, and data integrity. In addition, a DBMS usually has the following features:

- Support for formatting reports for printed output

- Support for importing and exporting data from other applications using standard file formats

- A data-manipulation language to support database queries

→ *See Also*   Database

dBrn (Decibels Referenced to Noise)

→ *See*   dBm (Decibels Referenced to 1mW)

dBrnC0 (Decibels Referenced to Noise through a C Message Filter at 0 Level)

→ *See*   dBm (Decibels Referenced to 1mW)

DBS (Direct Broadcast Satellite)

A DBS is a satellite that broadcasts signals directly to subscribers—that is, without going through a central station. Such broadcasts are already used for delivering digital TV signals, and various communications companies are betting billions of dollars that they will be used for delivering other kinds of services in the future.

There are two main categories of satellites: stationary and rotating, or orbiting. Satellites also differ in their distance from earth and—if rotating—in the shape of their orbits. Height is the major determinant for another feature that distinguishes satellite types: the satellite's footprint. The *footprint* represents the area that a satellite's beams can reach, so the bigger the footprint, the better.

Satellites are vulnerable to space debris, intense heat and cold, radiation, and several "natural" space phenomena. Two important nuisances are the Van Allen radiation belts (which ring the earth at distances of 300–500 miles and again at 2500–4000 miles above the earth) and asteroids (which orbit at over 10,000 miles from the earth). Signals passing through the Van Allen belts are subject to interference; satellites passing through the belts are subject to radiation.

Stationary satellites actually do orbit the earth; they just do it at the same speed as the earth's rotation. This makes such satellites appear stationary in relation to a particular point on earth. Only one type of satellite—*geosynchronous earth orbit (GEO)*—falls into this category. These stationary satellites orbit at about 22,300 miles above the earth. The idea of a geosynchronous satellite comes from a 1945 article by Arthur C. Clarke.

D

GEOs have been in use for over 30 years, and there are about 100 GEOs currently in orbit. GEOs are used for such things as broadcasting television signals, global positioning services (GPS), voice, video, and data communications, and telemetry services. The GEO orbital height is relatively debris- and radiation-free, and gravitational, centripetal, and centrifugal forces are balanced. These conditions give GEOs an expected life span of about 15 years—the longest of any satellite type. GEOs can handle data, voice, and video. Each GEO can cover half the earth; however, for various reasons, three satellites are actually needed to provide complete coverage of the entire earth. Transmissions involving a GEO have a delay of about 700 milliseconds, which can be made tolerable using echo cancellation techniques. Launching a GEO is very expensive, since a Titan-class rocket is needed.

Rotating satellites may orbit at different heights above the earth, and their orbits may be either spherical or elliptical. There are several types of rotating satellites, as described in the following paragraphs:

- HEO (high earth orbit): This type of HEO has a spherical orbit about 10,000 miles above the earth. This orbit is above the Van Allen radiation belts and below the asteroids that orbit the earth. High earth orbit satellites are similar to MEOs (medium earth orbit, see below), except that delays are longer; the HEO's footprint is larger, however. HEOs have a relatively long, 15-year expected life span.

- HEO (highly elliptical orbit): The orbit of this type of HEO is an ellipse, and a satellite's distance from earth may vary greatly—from an apogee (furthest point from earth) of over 24,000 miles, and a perigee (closest point to earth) of just over 600 miles. Three HEO satellites are needed for complete coverage. Such satellites were commonly used in the former Soviet Union, and several HEOs have been launched from Britain. The elliptical orbit has several disadvantages: the long orbit means that the satellite's signal will be subject

to Doppler shifts as well as changes in delay times. An elliptical orbit also passes twice through the Van Allen radiation belts, which surround the earth at two distances and which interfere with signal transmissions while the satellite is passing through the belt. The orbit also passes through asteroids and debris orbiting around the earth. HEOs have an expected life span of five years. New satellites must be launched from a Titan-class rocket.

- Big LEO (low earth orbit): Big LEOs are actually still in the design stages, but people have high expectations for the technology. These satellites have orbits that are only hundreds of miles above the earth. These orbits are close enough to the earth's atmosphere that friction will be a major force on the satellites, and the resulting heat will put considerable wear and tear on both the satellite and its components. Because of their relatively stressful orbits, LEOs have an expected life span of only about five years. On balance, however, launching LEOs is easy compared with launching a GEO, HEO, or MEO. LEOs can be launched from the back of a jumbo jet. Since they are low, LEOs must orbit the earth rapidly—about once every 90 minutes. LEOs will have very short delays—about 10 milliseconds. An LEO footprint will also be small, however, so 70 LEOs are needed for total earth coverage. Big LEOs differ from their little counterparts because of the frequency range in which each operates. Big LEO uses signals above 1GHz for voice and data communications; little LEO uses signals below 1GHz for data communications alone.

- Little LEO (low earth orbit): Like big LEOs, these satellites orbit just a few hundred miles above the earth. Whereas big LEOs use frequencies above 1GHz for signaling, little LEOs use the frequency range *below* 1GHz. Little LEOs are used for data communications, whereas big LEOs are intended for both voice and data.

- MEO (medium earth orbit): MEOs are a relatively new satellite technology. MEOs orbit at about 6000 miles above the earth, which is above the Van Allen belts but below the asteroids. This is a relatively safe orbit, with minimal required maintenance. As a result, MEOs have an expected life span of 15 years. The signal delay at this height is less than 100 milliseconds. Complete coverage of the earth would require 10 MEOs, but only 6 are needed to cover all but 5 percent of the earth.

"Satellite systems" shows some examples of satellites.

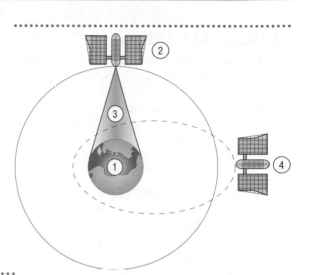

D

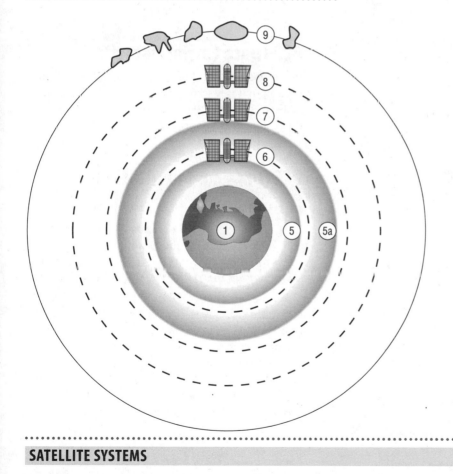

1. Earth
2. GEO satellite
3. GEO is stationary
4. HEO (Highly elliptical orbit)
5. Van Allen radiation belts
6. LEO
7. MEO
8. HEO
9. Asteroids/debris

SATELLITE SYSTEMS

DC (Direct Current)

Electrical power that travels in only one direction, as opposed to alternating current (AC), which changes directions many times a second. Batteries and most electronic components (such as computers) use DC power; power supplied for homes and offices is AC.

DCA (Document Content Architecture)

DCA is a data stream defined by IBM for using text documents in various computer environments. Three standard formats are specified for text transfer:

RFT (Revisable Form Text)   The primary format, in which text can still be edited.

FFT (Final Form Text)   The format in which text has been formatted for a particular output device and cannot be edited.

MFT (Mixed Form Text)   The format that contains more than just text, such as a document that also includes graphics.

→ *Compare*   DIA (Document Interchange Architecture)

DCB (Disk Coprocessor Board)

A DCB is an expansion board that serves as an interface between the central processing unit (CPU) and the hard disk controller. Because the DCB is intelligent, the CPU need not worry about reading and writing data. A DCB is also called an *HBA* (*host bus adapter*).

A disk channel consists of a DCB and other components needed to connect to one or more hard disks. Novell's NetWare supports up to four channels. For SCSI (Small Computer System Interface) drives, up to eight controllers can be associated with each DCB, and each controller can support two hard disks.

DCC (Data Country Code)

In WAN (wide area network) and other long-distance telecommunications that use X.25 technology, the DCC is a three-digit numerical code that identifies the country in which the communications element is located. This information is important, because it makes it possible to make the call format adjustments appropriate for the country.

→ *Broader Category*   X.25

DCD (Data Carrier Detect)

In telecommunications, a signal in an RS-232 connection that is asserted (True) when the modem detects a signal with a frequency appropriate for the communications standard the modem is using.

DCE (Data Communications Equipment)

DCE, which stands for data communications equipment or data circuit-terminating equipment, refers to a modem that is used in conjunction with a computer as the DTE (data terminal equipment).

More generally, a DCE is any device capable of communicating with the appropriate DTE, and of providing access to the appropriate type of line. For example, a modem can speak to a computer and can provide access to analog telephone lines. In digital telecommunications, a DSU (data service unit) and a CSU (communications service unit) together make up a DCE and provide access to the digital lines.

DCE (Distributed Computing Environment)

DCE is an open-networking architecture promoted by the Open Software Foundation (OSF), which is a consortium of vendors that includes Digital Equipment Corporation (DEC), Hewlett Packard (HP), and IBM. The DCE architecture provides the elements needed to distribute applications and their operation across networks in a transparent fashion.

If DCE is implemented, the entire network should appear to a user as one giant, very fast and powerful computer. Regardless of whether the network consists of two identical PCs or a few dozen different machines, DCE protects the user from any implementation details.

DCE sits on top of whatever network operating system is running, so that a user interacts with the DCE environment. This environment provides the following tools and services for a user or an application:

- RPC (Remote Procedure Call), which makes it possible to call an application or function on any machine, just as if the resource were local or even part of the application.

- Threads (independently executable program segments), which can be distributed across different machines and executed simultaneously. Threads can speed work up considerably. The RSA encryption algorithm—which was expected to require over 15 years to crack—was cracked within months using threads.

- Security measures, which automatically apply to the entire network. This means that a user on a machine is protected automatically from a virus or unauthorized user on another machine, just as if the intruder on the other machine were an intruder on that machine.

In a DCE, all nodes can be synchronized to the DCE's clock, which effectively provides precise timing capabilities. DCE offers both global X.500 and also local CDS (cell directory services).

By making the entire network's resources available in a completely transparent manner, DCE helps make the fullest use of available resources and also makes it more likely that a resource will be available when needed.

D Channel

In an ISDN (Integrated Services Digital Network) system, the D channel is the "data," or signaling, channel. The D channel is used for control signals and for data about the call. This is in contrast to the B channel, which serves as a bearer for data and voice.

For BRI (Basic Rate Interface), the D channel has a data rate of 16Kbps; for PRI (Primary Rate Interface), the D channel has a data rate of 64Kbps. These two forms of the D channel are denoted as *D16* and *D64*, respectively.

→ **Broader Category** ISDN (Integrated Services Digital Network)

→ **See Also** BRI (Basic Rate Interface); PRI (Primary Rate Interface)

→ **Compare** B Channel; H Channel

DCOM (Distributed Component Object Model)

DCOM is Microsoft's Component Object Model (COM, also known as the Common Object Model) adapted for use on a network or internetwork. DCOM provides a distributed object architecture whose specifications define how objects (software components and resources) should behave and interact when distributed across a network or an internetwork.

Introduced in 1996, DCOM is an extended version of Microsoft's COM which is, itself, built on OLE (object linking and embedding) technology. DCOM's distributed operation is based on the remote procedure call (RPC) specification in the Open Software Foundation's (OSF) Distributed Computing Environment (DCE). Using RPCs, objects on one machine can call and use procedures on other machines.

DCOM uses this capability to enable COM elements (programs, users, and other objects) to communicate with and use the services of COM objects on another machine. DCOM can accomplish this directly—that is, as the application protocol. Or DCOM actions can be encapsulated in another protocol—for example, HTTP (Hypertext Transfer Protocol). "DCOM at work" shows an example of communication between two COM objects on different machines.

In this illustration, a COM object (1) that requires an object from another machine or network must use a DCOM service to mediate. The DCOM requests are sent down (2) the network's protocol stack—generally a TCP/IP-based stack. The communication makes its way across the network cloud (3) in an unspecified path. At the receiving network, the request travels up (4) the protocol stack, where it is handled by an appropriate DCOM service. The DCOM service passes (5) the transmitted request to the target COM object. This service will also begin the process of relaying the object response to the requesting object.

DCOM is also Microsoft's answer to the OMG's (Object Management Group) Common Object Request Broker Architecture (CORBA) specifications. DCOM and CORBA are currently vying to become *the* object architecture standard. CORBA has been around for several years, is an open, cross-platform architecture, and has the support of hundreds of companies; DCOM has been around for just a few years, is at least a semiproprietary architecture, is pretty much Microsoft's baby, and runs only in Windows environments. Of course, Windows machines account for over 80 percent of the PCs in operation, so DCOM's platform limitation is not as serious as it might appear at first glance.

Microsoft has submitted parts of the DCOM specifications to standards bodies—for adoption as open standards. However, some components remain proprietary. Furthermore, Microsoft continues to evolve DCOM and to add features that are also proprietary—at least initially. Microsoft has pledged, however, to support full interoperability between DCOM and CORBA.

→ *Compare* CORBA (Common Object Request Broker Architecture)

→ *See Also* ActiveX; COM (Component Object Model)

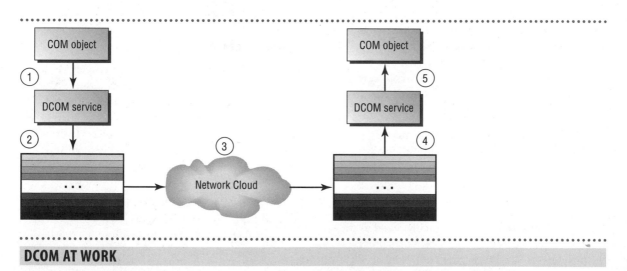

DCOM AT WORK

DCS (Defined Context Set)

In the CCITT's X.216 recommendations, an agreed-upon context for the delivery and use of presentation-level services.

DCS (Digital Cross-Connect System)

In digital telephony, a special-purpose switch for cross-connecting digital channels (for switching a digital channel from one piece of equipment to another). With a DCS, this cross-connect can take place at the rate supported by the slower of the two lines.

DDB (Distributed Database)

A database whose contents are stored on different hard disks or in different locations. Each disk or location may be managed by different machines. The Internet's domain name system (DNS) is an example of a distributed database.

→ See Also   Database

DDBMS (Distributed Database Management System)

Database management software that can handle a distributed database (DDB).

DDD (Direct Distance Dialing)

In telephony, the ability to dial a long-distance number without going through an operator.

DDE (Dynamic Data Exchange)

DDE is a technique for application-to-application communications. It is available in several operating systems, including Microsoft Windows, Macintosh System 7, and OS/2.

When two or more programs that support DDE are running at the same time, they can exchange data and commands, by means of *conversations*. A DDE conversation is a two-way connection between two different applications.

DDE is used for low-level communications that do not need user intervention. For example, a communications program might feed stock market information into a spreadsheet program, where that data can be displayed in a meaningful way and recalculated automatically as it changes.

DDE has largely been superseded by a more complex but more capable mechanism known as Object Linking and Embedding (OLE).

DDL (Data Definition Language)

Any of several languages for describing data and its relationships, as in a database.

DDM (Distributed Data Management)

In IBM's SNA (Systems Network Architecture), services that allow file sharing and remote file access in a network.

DDN NIC (Defense Data Network Network Information Center)

The DDN is a global network used by the U.S. Department of Defense (DoD) to connect military installations. Parts of the DDN are accessible from the Internet, and parts are classified.

The DDN NIC is a control center that provides information and services through the Internet. The DDN NIC does the following:

- Serves as a repository for the Requests for Comments (RFCs), which are used to define standards, report results, and suggest planning directions for the Internet community.

D

- Assigns IP (Internet Protocol) network addresses.

- Assigns numbers to domains (or *autonomous systems*, as they are called in the Internet jargon).

→ **See Also**   IR (Internet Registry)

DDP (Data Description Packet)

A DDP is used for synchronizing routing databases, or tables, with the OSPF (Open Shortest Path First) exchange protocol. When two routers need to exchange packets, one of them serves as the master router and the other as the slave router. The master router transmits DDPs, which contain information about the master router's routing table. The slave acknowledges each DDP and transmits back information about the slave's routing table. This exchange enables the two routers to update their tables, thereby ensuring that they are using the same routing map.

→ **Broader Category**   Routing

→ **See Also**   Protocol, OSPF (Open Shortest Path First)

DDP (Distributed Data Processing)

Data processing in which some or all of the processing and/or I/O (input/output) work is distributed over multiple machines.

DDS (Dataphone Digital Service)

DDS is an AT&T communications service that uses digital signal transmission over leased lines. Because data is transmitted digitally, no modem is required; however, a DSU/CSU (digital service unit/channel service unit) is needed at the interface between the digital lines and the customer's equipment. The customer equipment will generally be a remote bridge or router, because DDS is commonly used for providing point-to-point links in a wide area network (WAN).

DDS uses four wires, supports speeds between 2.4 and 56Kbps and is available through most LECs (local exchange carriers) and IXCs (interexchange carriers); that is, it is available through local or long-distance telephone companies.

DDS (Digital Data Service)

Leased lines that support transmission rates between 2.4 and 56Kbps.

DDS (Distributed Directory Service)

A DDS is one in which directory services (DSs) are located on two or more servers and is in contrast to a global centralized directory service. Such a global DS has two major limitations when faced with a very large (inter)network—one with millions of nodes, which may be arranged in a hierarchy of subnetworks.

First, a centralized DS can get bogged down dealing with the sheer volume of requests coming from so many nodes. This problem is made even worse by a second limitation: the fact that most of the requests are for local services, which really should not concern a global directory server. DDS helps ameliorate both of these problems by distributing the local directory service tasks while retaining a centralized global server for dealing with remote requests.

DE (Discard Eligibility)

In a frame-relay packet header, a bit that can be set to indicate that the packet can be discarded if network traffic warrants it. If network traffic gets too heavy, the network can discard packets that have this bit set.

D

DEA (Data Encryption Algorithm)

In general, an algorithm, or rule, for encrypting data. In the DES, the DEA is an algorithm for encrypting data in blocks of 64-bits each.

→ *See Also* DES (Data Encryption Standard)

Decibel (dB)

→ *See* dB (Decibel)

DEC Management Control Center (DECmcc)

→ *See* DECmcc (DEC Management Control Center)

DECmcc (DEC Management Control Center)

Network management software for Digital's DECnet networks. Products based on this core, such as DECmcc Director, are available for specific environments.

DECnet

DECnet is a proprietary network architecture from Digital Equipment Corporation (DEC). DECnet has gone through several major revisions during its lifetime. The two most recent versions, Phases IV and V, were released in 1982 and 1987, respectively. Both versions are still used.

Historically, DECnet networks consisted mainly of PDP-11s and VAXen, but the architecture can support a broad range of hardware, including PCs and Macintoshes. Gateways also exist for remote access and for access to SNA (System Network Architecture) networks.

DECnet Phase IV

The eight layers in the DECnet Phase IV model correspond roughly—sometimes very roughly—to the seven layers in the OSI reference model. The Phase IV layers are as follows:

Physical   Corresponds to the OSI Physical layer. This layer establishes a physical connection and manages the actual data transmission. This layer supports Blue Book (as opposed to IEEE 802.3) Ethernet protocols.

Data link   Corresponds to the OSI Data-Link layer. This layer supports Blue Book Ethernet, X.25, and DDCMP (Digital Data Communications Messaging Protocol) protocols.

Routing   Corresponds to the OSI Network layer. This layer routes packets to their destination and helps manage intra- and internetwork traffic. It permits adaptive routing, gathers network management data, and supports various routing protocols.

End-to-end communications   Corresponds roughly to the OSI Transport layer. This layer helps maintain network links, and segments and reassembles information (at sending and receiving ends, respectively). It supports the VAX OSI Transport Service (VOTS) protocol and DEC's own Network Services Protocol (NSP).

Session control   Corresponds roughly to the OSI session layer. This layer stores network name and address information, for use when establishing a connection. It is also responsible for breaking the network link when the transmission is finished. The session control layer supports both proprietary and OSI session protocols.

Network application   Corresponds roughly to the OSI Presentation layer. This layer enables local and remote file and terminal access. It supports OSI Presentation layer protocols and also DEC's Data Access Protocol (DAP).

Network management Corresponds very roughly to part of the OSI Application layer. This layer handles peer-to-peer network management. It supports DEC's Network Information and Control Exchange (NICE) protocol.

User Corresponds very roughly to part of the OSI Application layer—the part concerned with user applications.

DECnet Phase V

DECnet Phase V was designed to comply fully with the OSI reference model. This version has only seven layers, which correspond to the OSI layers. In general, DECnet Phase V supports OSI-compliant protocols at each level. It also supports DEC's own protocols (such as DDCMP and DAP) for backward-compatibility with Phase IV networks.

Designed to handle large networks, DECnet Phase V can use up to 20 bytes for address information. A network can be divided into domains for routing or administrative purposes. The address field includes an Initial Domain Part (IDP) value, which is unique for every network.

Decryption

Decryption refers to the process of decoding data that has been encoded (or encrypted) using a reversible algorithm. For example, a message can be encrypted using a sender's private key, a recipient's public key, and an encryption algorithm. This message can be decrypted using the sender's public key, the recipient's private key, and a decryption algorithm.

→ *See Also* Encryption

Dedicated Access Line (DAL)

→ *See* DAL (Dedicated Access Line)

Dedicated Circuit

A path that goes directly from a user location to a telephone company point of presence (POP); that is, it goes to the location at which a subscriber's leased or long-distance lines connect to the telephone company's lines.

→ *See Also* IXC (Interexchange Carrier); POP (Point of Presence)

Dedicated Line

In telecommunications, a dedicated line is a permanent connection—a connection that is always available—between two locations. That is, a dedicated line is a communications loop that is reserved for a single customer. This connection is provided on private, or leased, lines, rather than the public, dial-up lines, and so a dedicated line is also known as a *leased*, or *private, line*.

The bandwidth on a dedicated line depends on the type of service being used; it can range from 56Kbps to 1.544Mps—2.048Mbps in Europe—and even higher. Available dedicated-line services include the following:

DDS (Dataphone Digital Services) Provide synchronous transmission of digital signals at up to 56Kbps. Subrate (lower-speed) services are also available, at 2400 to 19,200bps.

56/64Kbps lines In Europe, these lines provide a full 64Kbps; in the United States and in Japan, 8Kbps are used for administrative and control overhead, leaving only 56Kbps for the subscriber. Such lines are also available through dial-up (nondedicated lines).

Fractional T1 lines Lines built up in increments of 64Kbps, to a maximum rate of 768Kbps.

T1/E1 lines   Provide 1.544Mbps for T1 (available in the United States and Japan) and 2.048Mbps for E1 (available in Mexico and Europe) service.

The availability and pricing of these dedicated-line services vary greatly in different geographical areas.

→ *Compare* Dial-Up Line

Dedicated Router

→ *See* Router, Dedicated

Dedicated Token Ring (DTR)

→ *See* DTR (Dedicated Token Ring)

De Facto Standard

A standard that results from widespread usage by the user community, rather than from the work of an official standards committee. This is in contrast to a *de jure standard*, which gets its legitimacy from a standards committee. De facto standards may be just as explicitly specified as de jure standards. De facto standards simply have not been given a "Good Standardizing" seal of approval. ARCnet is one of the best-known de facto standards.

Default Gateway

In a network routing situation, the default gateway for a router represents the location to which the router will forward a packet if it does not have an explicit path to the packet's destination. In short, the default gateway represents a router's fallback, or safety valve.

Default Path

In packet routing, a path used by a router to forward a packet when the packet itself contains no explicit routing instructions, and the router has no predefined path to the packet's ultimate destination. The default path is generally one to a router that is likely to have more detailed routing information.

Default Server

For a node, the default server is usually the server the node logs in to. If a user is logged in to more than one server, the default is the server that the user is currently accessing.

Default Value

A value used for a parameter or setting when no other value is specified by the user through a program or in a data file.

Default Zone

In an AppleTalk Phase 2 network, the zone to which a device or node belongs until it is assigned to a specific zone.

→ *See* AppleTalk

Defense Advanced Research Projects Agency (DARPA)

→ *See* DARPA (Defense Advanced Research Projects Agency)

Defense Data Network Network Information Center (DDN NIC)

→ *See* DDN NIC (Defense Data Network Network Information Center)

D

Deferral Time

In a CSMA (collision sense, multiple access) media access method, the amount of time a node waits before trying again to access the network after an unsuccessful attempt. The time depends on a random value and on the network's activity level.

→ **See** CSMA (Collision Sense, Multiple Access)

Deferred Procedure Call (DPC)

→ **See** DPC (Deferred Procedure Call)

Defined Context Set (DCS)

→ **See** DCS (Defined Context Set)

De Jure Standard

A standard that has been officially approved by a recognized standards committee, such as ANSI, CCITT, or IEEE. De jure standards may be national or international. Popular de jure standards include IEEE 802.3 (Ethernet) and IEEE 802.5 (Token Ring) for networks, and CCITT V.42bis (data compression) for modems.

→ **Compare** de Facto Standard

DEK (Data Encryption Key)

A value used to encrypt a message. The DEK is used by an encryption algorithm to encode the message and may be used by a decryption algorithm to decode the message. More sophisticated encryption strategies use different keys for encrypting and for decrypting.

→ **See Also** DES (Data Encryption Standard)

Delay

In an electrical circuit, a *delay* is a property that slows down high-frequency signals, causing signal distortion. An equalizer can be used to help deal with this problem.

In a network or communications connection, a delay is a lag before a signal is passed on or returned. More specifically, the delay in a communication is the amount of time that elapses from when a bit enters at the starting point to when the bit exits at the ending point. The total delay would be the amount of time it takes a bit to get from the source to the destination. However, delay can be measured between any two points in a communications path, and sometimes it is convenient or necessary to measure at intermediate points. This type of delay may be due to switching or to distances involved (for example, in satellite or cellular communications).

Some devices and connections will not tolerate delays longer than a predefined amount of time, and they may time-out if this time limit is exceeded. For example, a printer may time-out if there is too long a wait before the next instruction arrives. For some time-sensitive devices, you can change the default waiting time.

Delay is often used synonymously with *latency*, but this term has a specific meaning in ITU (International Telecommunications Union) recommendations.

There is often a trade-off in practical situations between delay and bandwidth. Specifically, companies must sometimes decide whether to tolerate a given level of delay or whether to shell out money for a higher bandwidth connection.

→ **Compare** Latency

Delay-Bound

In telecommunications, an application or transmission is said to be delay-bound if performance will not be improved by adding extra bandwidth. For example, a voice telephone call will not be improved by adding bandwidth. In contrast, the transmission of a large file can be improved by adding bandwidth. Such a transmission is said to be *bandwidth-bound*.

→ **Compare** Bandwidth-Bound

Demand Assigned Multiple Access (DAMA)

In telecommunications, a method for allocating access to communications channels. Idle channels are kept in a pool. When a channel capacity is requested, an idle channel is selected, allocated the requested bandwidth, and assigned to the requesting party.

→ **See** DAMA (Demand Assigned Multiple Access)

Demand Priority

Demand priority is a media-access method used in 100BaseVG, a 100Mbps Ethernet implementation proposed by Hewlett-Packard (HP) and AT&T Microelectronics. Demand priority shifts network access control from the workstation to a hub. This access method works with a star topology.

In this method, a node that wishes to transmit indicates this wish to the hub and also requests high- or regular-priority service for its transmission. After it obtains permission, the node begins transmitting to the hub.

The hub is responsible for passing the transmission on to the destination node; that is, the hub is responsible for providing access to the network. A hub will pass high-priority transmissions through immediately, and will pass regular-priority transmissions through as the opportunity arises.

By letting the hub manage access, the architecture is able to guarantee required bandwidths and requested service priority to particular applications or nodes. It also can guarantee that the network

can be scaled up (enlarged) without loss of bandwidth.

Demand priority helps increase bandwidth in the following ways:

- A node does not need to keep checking whether the network is idle before transmitting. In current Ethernet implementations, a wire pair is dedicated to this task. By making network checking unnecessary, demand priority frees a wire pair. This is fortunate, because the 100BaseVG specifications use quartet signaling, which needs four available wire pairs.

- Heavy traffic can effectively bring standard Ethernet networks to a standstill, because nodes spend most of their time trying to access the network. With demand priority, the hub needs to pass a transmission on only to its destination, so that overall network traffic is decreased. This means there is more bandwidth available for heavy network traffic.

By giving the hub control over a transmission, so that the message is passed to only its destination node or nodes, demand priority also makes it easier to prevent eavesdropping.

→ **Broader Categories** 100BaseVG; Media-Access Method

Demand Protocol Architecture (DPA)

→ **See** DPA (Demand Protocol Architecture)

Demarcation Point

In telephone communications, the point at which the customer's equipment and wiring ends and the telephone company's begins.

D

Demodulation

In communications, the process of removing and isolating the modulating signal that was added to a carrier signal for purposes of communication. For example, in serial communications involving computers and modems, the demodulation process converts the acoustic signal that has traveled over the telephone line into an electrical form from which the transmitted data can be determined.

Demultiplexer

A device that takes multiplexed material from a single input, and sends the individual input elements to several outputs.

DEN (Directory Enabled Network)

A DEN extends the resource management capabilities of a centralized directory service (such as Novell's Network Directory System or Microsoft's Active Directory) by adding such things as network and policy management information. In a DEN, the network directory can include elements that can control access on the basis of a corporate network policy or that can request a desired quality of service or a particular route for a connection.

DEN capabilities are intended primarily for use in enterprise and other large networks—mainly because the cost and effort required to create a DEN are too high for small networks. Furthermore, a DEN architecture would produce minimal—if any—performance gains for small networks.

The Distributed Management Task Force (DMTF) has assumed the task of developing the DEN specification. The information for DENs can be stored using the group's Common Information Format (CIM), which provides an object-oriented mechanism for representing information about managed network elements and about relationships among these elements.

While the concept and possibilities of directory-enabled networks are currently hot topics, nontrivial, real-world examples of such networks are still works in progress. There are several obstacles that must be resolved before DENs can become widely used:

- Specifying network policies for use in a DEN is a new undertaking and, as such, is still more of an arcane art than a science. More reliable and easier-to-use methods for specifying such policies must be developed.

- The cost of creating the infrastructure and information necessary for creating a successful DEN is substantial. For example, developing a network policy that is correct, consistent, usable, and extensible can cost over a million dollars for certain topics. Developing the directory that can implement the policy can cost another million or even more.

- More—possibly much more—must be learned about the full implications and the potential dangers of using DENs. Ignorance about these issues can lead to problems in network operations and security. For example, the importance and meaning of specific policy statements for a network can change over time as the network develops. Such changes must be reflected in the network rules by which the directory guides network operation; unfortunately, such changes may not even be recognized until they have been in effect for a period—in which case the network directory may not be updated quickly enough to avoid problems.

- A global directory is a central component for DENs. Currently, there are two plausible candidates that could become *the* standard global directory for such networks: Novell's Network Directory System (NDS) and Microsoft's Active Directory (AD). NDS is available, field tested, and highly regarded. In contrast, AD will be a component of Windows 2000, which has not been released as of this writing, but should be available by the time you read this. Despite the fact that AD currently exists only in beta software and on paper, Microsoft's clout in networking software is enough to make some system administrators wait before selecting a global directory.

- Appropriate protocols will need to be developed—either from scratch or by extending the capabilities of existing directory protocols (such as the X.500 Directory Access Protocol or its Lightweight offspring, the LDAP). Similarly, the capabilities of directory services must be enhanced to handle the more complex capabilities required of DENs.

While DENs offer the promise of very useful capabilities, it remains to be seen how soon—or even whether—this promise will be fulfilled.

Denial-of-Service Attack

In a denial-of-service attack, the invader overloads and crashes a server or PC by flooding it with phony messages. Such attacks can be launched against a single server or against multiple targets at the same time. Different variants of this attack strategy are developed—aimed at particular platforms or configurations. Such attacks generally try to take advantage of a particular weakness or loophole in the platform software.

Denial-of-service attacks are quite common and are often directed against government, corporate, or academic servers. For example, in early 1998, NASA was the victim of two variants—TearDrop2 and NewTear—which were aimed at Windows NT and Windows 95 platforms.

→ *Broader Category* Security

Dense Wave Division Multiplexing (DWDM)

→ *See* DWDM (Dense Wave Division Multiplexing)

De-osification

A term for the conversion of definitions that conform to OSI network management model to definitions that conform to the IP network management model. The term is used in TCP/IP environments that use SNMP (Simple Network Management Protocol).

Departmental-Area Network (DAN)

→ *See* DAN (Departmental-Area Network)

Departmental LAN

A small- to medium-sized network (up to about 30 users) whose nodes share local resources.

Deprecated

In the HTML (Hypertext Markup Language) 4.0 specifications, a deprecated feature (attribute or tag) is one that should not be used if it can be avoided. A deprecated feature is still supported in the current version of the specifications—for back compatibility. However, the specifications contain alternatives to deprecated features, and the deprecated features will eventually become obsolete.

DES (Data Encryption Standard)

DES is the official United States data encryption standard for nonclassified documents. DES uses a single, 64-bit value as a key and a *private*-key encryption strategy to convert ordinary text (*plaintext*) into encrypted form (*ciphertext*). (See the Encryption article for details on plaintext and ciphertext, as well as *private*- versus public-key encryption.)

In a *private*-key strategy, only the sender and the receiver are supposed to know the key (bit sequence) used to encrypt the data. The encryption *algorithm*, on the other hand, is publicly known.

D

Although it is relatively difficult to crack, DES cannot protect against fraud by the sender or the receiver. For example, there is no way to identify a sender who has learned the key and is pretending to be the legitimate sender.

An ardent early advocate for DES, the National Security Agency (NSA) has campaigned to remove DES as the official encryption standard. The NSA is advocating a classified algorithm (one under the NSA's control) as the basis for the encryption standard. To date, this suggestion has met with considerable resistance from the business and computing communities.

DEA (Data Encryption Algorithm)

When the DES is used for encryption, a message is divided into 64-bit blocks, and each block is encrypted separately, one character at a time. During the encryption of a block, the computer plays an electronic shell game: the characters in the block are scrambled 16 times during encryption, and the encryption method changes after each scrambling. The key determines the details of the scrambling and the character encryption. In short, each 64-bit block goes through over a dozen transformations during encryption.

Of the 64 bits used for the encryption key, 56 are used for encryption, and eight are used for error detection. The 56 bits yield about 70 quadrillion possible keys—almost 15 million possible keys for each person alive today. (Imagine the key chain you would need.)

The encryption algorithm involves several steps:

- Permuting (switching the order of) the bits in the block

- Repeating a computation that uses the data encryption key (DEK) and that involves substitution and transposition operations

- Permuting the bits in the block to restore the original order

DES Modes

DES can operate in any of four modes:

ECB (Electronic Cookbook) The simplest encryption method. The encryption process is the same for each block, and it is based on the encryption algorithm and the key. Repeated character patterns, such as names, are always encoded in the same way.

CBC (Cipher Block Chaining) A more involved encryption method in which the encryption for each block depends on the encryption for the preceding block, as well as on the algorithm and key. The same pattern is encoded differently in each block.

CFB (Cipher Feedback) A still more involved method in which ciphertext is used to generate pseudo-random values. These values are combined with plaintext and the results are then encrypted. CFB may encrypt an individual character differently each time it is encountered.

OFB (Output Feedback) Similar to CFB, except that actual DES output is used to generate the pseudo-random values that are combined with plaintext. This mode is used to encrypt communications via satellite.

→ *Primary Source* FIPS publication #46

→ *Broader Category* Encryption

Desktop

In the Macintosh and Windows environments, a desktop is a file server that provides access to applications and documents through the use of icons. On a workstation, the desktop provides a graphical representation of the files and programs located on that workstation. The term also refers to workstations that reside on user's desks (as opposed to laptops and palmtops, for example).

Desktop Management Interface (DMI)

→ *See* DMI (Desktop Management Interface)

Destination Address (DA)

→ *See* DA (Destination Address)

Destination ID (DID)

→ *See* DID (Destination ID)

DET (Directory Entry Table)

In Novell's NetWare, the DET is one of two tables used to keep track of directory information. The other table is the file allocation table (FAT). The DET is stored on a hard disk.

The DET contains information about a volume's file and directory names and properties. For example, an entry might contain the following:

- Filename
- File owner
- Date and time of last update
- Trustee assignments (or user rights)
- Location of the file's first block on the network hard disk

The DET also accesses the FAT, which is an index to the locations of the blocks that make up each file.

The contents of the DET are stored in special storage allocation units, called directory entry blocks (DEBs). Each DEB is 4 kilobytes, and NetWare can support up to 65,536 of these blocks.

To improve performance, NetWare can use directory caching or hashing. *Directory caching* keeps currently used directory blocks and the

FAT in a reserved area of RAM. Frequently used directory entries will be loaded into a cache memory. *Directory hashing* is the indexing of the directory entries, which speeds access to directory information.

Device Driver

A driver program designed to enable a PC to use or communicate with a particular device, such as a printer or monitor. A device driver generally has a more specific name, such as printer driver or screen driver, depending on the type of device involved.

Device Independent Backup Interface (DIBI)

→ *See* DIBI (Device Independent Backup Interface)

Device Numbering

Device numbering is a method for identifying a device, such as a hard disk, scanner, or floppy drive. Three numbers serve to define each device:

Hardware address The address associated with the board or controller for the device. This value is set either through software or by setting jumpers in the required configuration. Drivers that need to deal with the device can read the hardware address from the jumper settings.

Device code A value determined by the location of the device's board, the device itself, and possibly by auxiliary components (such as controllers) associated with the board. For example, a device code for a hard disk includes values for disk type, controller, board, and disk numbers.

Logical number A value based on the boards to which the devices are attached, on the controller, and on the order in which devices are loaded.

D

Device Sharing

Use of a centrally located device by multiple users or programs. For example, a printer or hard disk may be shared among several workstation users. Since most devices are idle a high proportion of the time, sharing them is a cost-effective way to make a resource more widely available and more likely to be used.

DFS (Distributed File System)

A file system with files located on multiple machines, but accessible to an end-user or a process as if the files were all in a single location.

DFT (Distributed Function Terminal)

In IBM's SNA (System Network Architecture), a terminal mode in which a terminal may support up to five different sessions, so that a user can access up to five applications through the same terminal.

→ *Compare* CUT (Control Unit Terminal)

DGM (Data-Grade Media)

→ *See* Cable, Data-Grade

DHCP (Dynamic Host Configuration Protocol)

→ *See* Protocol, DHCP (Dynamic Host Configuration Protocol)

DHTML (Dynamic HTML)

The name, Dynamic HTML (where HTML stands for Hypertext Markup Language), is used by both Microsoft and Netscape to refer to extensions and enhancements of HTML 4, as implemented in their respective browsers: Microsoft Internet Explorer 4 and Netscape's Navigator 4 and later. While these competitors differ in their approaches and their details, both versions of DHTML have several points in common.

Both browsers support cascading style sheets (CSS)—although support for the newer level 2 style sheets (CSS2) is still spotty in both browsers. Cascading style sheets make it possible to specify a default appearance for a document and also to override the default settings when desired.

Both browsers also provide much better support for positioning objects and for page layout. The manner in which the browsers do this is different, however.

Netscape uses layers. These can be positioned using either relative or absolute coordinates. They can be stacked in a specified order, using an attribute known as a z-order. Using z-order, a layer can be positioned immediately above or below another layer; or the layer can be positioned at a specified index location in the layer stack. Layers can be transparent or opaque.

Microsoft accomplishes the same kinds of things by using extensions to the CSS specifications. These extensions include a z-index, which is similar to Netscape's z-order, but which applies to page elements rather than to layers. Although Internet Explorer does not support layers, it does support essentially the same effects, but using different elements.

Both browsers take advantage of the fact that all elements on an HTML page are now accessible in script files. (In HTML versions prior to 4, script files could interact only with Java applets or ActiveX controls embedded in the HTML file.) The Document Object Model (DOM) for each browser includes mechanisms for working with page elements and also for handling events that might occur on a page. This event-handling capability makes DHTML better able to deal with interactive documents and even able to handle changes that are made to a page that is already being displayed.

The increased interactivity of Web pages and the complete accessibility of page elements has made it necessary to change the browser object model as well. Each browser has been completely revamped to handle the new tasks made possible by DHTML.

It remains to be seen which, if any, of the extensions introduced by Netscape and Microsoft will make it into the HTML standards.

→ *See Also* HTML (Hypertext Markup Language)

DIA (Document Interchange Architecture)

DIA is software and services defined by IBM, to make it easier to use documents in a variety of IBM environments. DIA includes the following services:

- APS (Application Processing Services)
- DDS (Document Distribution Services)
- DLS (Document Library Services)
- FTS (File Transfer Service)

→ *Compare* DCA (Document Content Architecture)

Diagnostic Program

A diagnostic program tests computer hardware and peripheral devices for correct operation. Some problems, known as *hard faults*, are relatively easy to find, and the diagnostic program will diagnose them correctly every time.

Other problems, called *soft faults*, can be difficult to find, because they occur sporadically or

only under specific circumstances, rather than every time the memory location is tested.

Most computers run a simple set of system checks when the computer is first turned on. The PC tests are stored in read-only memory (ROM) and are known as power-on self tests (POSTs). If a POST detects an error condition, the computer will stop and display an error message on the screen. Some computers will emit a beep signal to indicate the type of error.

Dial-Back

In network operations, dial-back (also known as *call-back*) is a security measure to prevent unauthorized dial-up access to a network. The networking software maintains a list of users and the numbers from which they might dial in.

When a user wants to dial into the network, the server takes the call, gets the user's login information, then breaks the connection. The software then looks up the user in the dial-up table and calls back the number listed for the user.

As an access control and security measure, dial-back works reasonably well. However, it can fail when the user needs to dial in from a different location, or when an unauthorized person has gained access to the location from which the user generally dials in (the network calls a number, not a person).

Dialed Number Identification Service (DNIS)

→ *See* DNIS (Dialed Number Identification Service)

Dial-Up Line

A dial-up line is a nondedicated communications line in which a connection can be established by dialing the number, or code, associated with the destination. A common example of a dial-up line, also called a *switched line* or *public line*, is the public telephone line. Dial-up lines generally support speeds of 2400 to 9600bps.

The connection is created at dial-up time, and it is destroyed when the call is finished. This is in contrast to a *leased line* (also called a *private* or *dedicated line*), in which a connection between two specific points is always available.

With a dial-up line, the same calling node can be connected with an arbitrary number of destinations. Costs accrue only for the duration of a particular connection.

→ **Compare** Dedicated Line

DIB (Directory Information Base)

In the CCITT X.500 Directory Services model, the body of directory-related information. Directory system agents (DSAs) access the DIB on behalf of directory user agents (DUAs).

→ **See Also** DIT (Directory Information Tree); X.500

DIBI (Device Independent Backup Interface)

An interface proposed by Novell to make it easier to move material between different environments on the network.

Dibit

A pair of bits treated as a single unit. For example, a dibit is used in certain modulation methods that can encode two bits in a single modulated value. The four possible dibits are 00, 01, 10, and 11.

Similarly, a *tribit* consists of three bit values treated together, and a *quadbit* is a four-bit sequence. Quadbits are used, for example, in quadrature amplitude modulation (QAM).

→ **See Also** Quadbit; Tribit

DID (Destination ID)

In an ARCnet packet, the address of the destination node.

DID (Direct Inward Dialing)

In telephone communications, a system in which an outside caller can reach a number in a private branch exchange (PBX) directly, without going through a switchboard.

Dielectric

A nonconducting material, such as rubber or certain types of plastic, used as an insulating layer around the conductive wire in coaxial and twisted-pair cable.

Diffusing Update Algorithm (DUAL)

→ **See** DUAL (Diffusing Update Algorithm)

Digital

In computing, telecommunications, and other endeavors that require the coding of data, a digital representation is one that uses discrete digits to represent data values. Digital values are generally contrasted with analog ones, which can take any values in a continuous range. Analog values can be represented—strictly speaking, approximated—in digital form by taking samples of the analog signal at regular intervals and by representing the values in these samples with a digital value. (Nyquist's Theorem demonstrates that—for an adequate digital representation—the analog signal must be sampled at a rate that is twice the maximum frequency range over which the analog signal ranges.)

While it is not a requirement, in practice most digital values are represented in binary form—that is in terms of values that use only the digits 0 and 1. The range of values that can be represented in a particular situation depends on the number of bits used to represent the digital values. For example, a representation that uses 8 bits (1 byte) can represent values between 0 and 255, inclusive; with 16 bits, values between 0 and 65,535 can be represented.

Digital Access and Cross-Connect System (DACS)

→ *See* DACS (Digital Access and Cross-Connect System)

Digital Audio Tape (DAT)

→ *See* DAT (Digital Audio Tape)

Digital Certificate

→ *See* Certificate

Digital Circuit

In communications, lines that transmit data as unmodulated square waves, which represent 0 or 1 values. Digital circuit lines are provided by common carriers, such as telephone companies.

Digital Communication

Digital communication is a telecommunications method that uses digital (discrete) signals, usually binary values, to represent information. The original information may be in analog or digital form.

A digital transmission uses digital, rather than analog, signals. Digital signals are encoded as discrete values, representing 0 or 1. These binary values may be encoded as different voltage or current levels, or as changes in voltage levels.

In an analog signal, information is represented as variations in a continuous waveform's amplitude or frequency. To transmit analog information, the analog signal passes through a codec (coder/decoder), which functions as an analog-to-digital converter (ADC). The codec samples the analog signal thousands of times a second, representing each sample value as a unique 8-bit digital value.

The codec's output is a sequence of discrete voltage levels, which represent the sample values. This sequence is transmitted over the appropriate lines, which may support speeds ranging from 2400bps to more than 200Mbps.

The received digital signal is cleaned to recover the signal information. A codec then converts the digital signal back to analog form. At this end, the codec serves as a digital-to-analog converter (DAC). The sampled values are used as reference points for synthesizing a continuous waveform that tries to reproduce the original analog signal.

The quality of the synthesized signal depends on the sampling frequency (usually 8000 times per second) and on the number of bits used to represent the possible signal levels (usually 8 bits).

The elements involved in the process are illustrated in "Digital communication of an analog signal."

Analog Signal: Information is represented as variations in a continuous waveform's amplitude or frequency.

Codec: The analog signal is converted to digital form.

Digital Signal: The codec's output is a sequence of discrete voltage levels, which represent the sampled values.

Transmission: The digital signal is transmitted over the appropriate lines.

Digital Signal: The received digital signal is cleaned, to recover the signal information.

Codec: The digital signal is converted back to analog form.

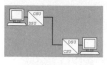

Analog Signal: The quality of the synthesized signal depends on the sampling frequency and on the number of bits used to represent the possible signal levels.

DIGITAL COMMUNICATION OF AN ANALOG SIGNAL

Compared with analog transmissions, digital transmissions are generally less susceptible to noise, are easier to work with for error detection and correction, and require somewhat less complex circuitry.

Digital Cross-Connect System (DCS)

→ *See* DCS (Digital Cross-Connect System)

Digital Data Service (DDS)

→ *See* DDS (Digital Data Service)

Digital ID

An element attached to an electronic message to authenticate the message and sender. The digital ID is assigned by a certification, or authentication, authority and is valid for only a limited period. A digital ID contains the following elements:

- The sender's name, address, and organization
- The sender's public key
- A digital signature from the certification authority
- A serial number for the digital ID
- Validity period for the digital ID

Digital Intel Xerox (DIX)

→ *See* DIX (Digital Intel Xerox)

Digital Line Carrier (DLC)

→ *See* DLC (Digital Loop Carrier)

Digital Loop Carrier (DLC)

→ *See* DLC (Digital Loop Carrier)

Digital Multiplexed Interface (DMI)

→ *See* DMI (Digital Multiplexed Interface)

Digital Network Architecture (DNA)

A layered architecture from Digital Equipment Corporation (DEC). DNA is implemented in the various incarnations of DECnet.

→ *See* DNA (Digital Network Architecture)

Digital Sense Multiple Access (DSMA) Protocol

→ *See* Protocol, DSMA (Digital Sense Multiple Access)

Digital Service (DS)

→ *See* DS (Digital Service)

Digital Signal Cross-Connect Between Levels 1 and 3 (DSX1/3)

→ *See* DSX1/3 (Digital Signal Cross-Connect Between Levels 1 and 3)

Digital Signal Processor (DSP)

→ *See* DSP (Digital Signal Processor)

Digital Signature

In network security, a digital signature is a unique value associated with a transaction. The signature is used to verify the identity of the sender and also the origin of the message. Digital signatures cannot be forged.

To illustrate how digital signatures can be used, suppose user A and user B are communicating using an encryption strategy, such as the RSA public-key encryption strategy. With the RSA strategy, user A has a public and a private key, and user B has a private and a public key, which differ from user A's keys.

"Communications using digital signatures and a public-key encryption method" shows what must happen for user A and user B to communicate using a digital signature.

→ *Broader Categories* Encryption; Security Management

Digital Speech Interpolation (DSI)

→ *See* DSI (Digital Speech Interpolation)

Digital Subscriber Line (DSL)

→ *See* DSL (Digital Subscriber Line)

Digital Subscriber Line Access Multiplexer (DSLAM)

→ *See* DSLAM (Digital Subscriber Line Access Multiplexer)

Digital Termination Service (DTS)

→ *See* DTS (Digital Termination Service)

Digital-to-Analog Converter (DAC)

→ *See* DAC (Digital-to-Analog Converter)

Digital Versatile Disc (DVD)

→ *See* DVD (Digital Versatile Disc)

To encrypt and sign a message, user A does the following:

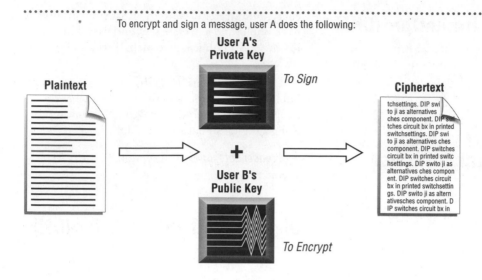

To decrypt and authenticate a message, user B does the following:

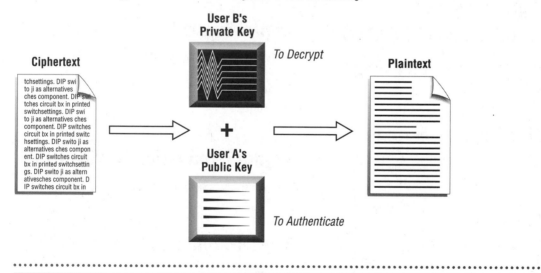

COMMUNICATIONS USING DIGITAL SIGNATURES AND A PUBLIC-KEY ENCRYPTION METHOD

Digital Versatile Disc—Random Access Memory (DVD-RAM)

→ *See* DVD (Digital Versatile Disc)

Digital Versatile Disc—Read-Only Memory (DVD-ROM)

→ *See* DVD (Digital Versatile Disc)

Digital Versatile Disc—Read/Write Memory (DVD-R/W)

→ *See* DVD (Digital Versatile Disc)

Digital Versatile Disc—Rewritable (DVD+RW)

→ *See* DVD (Digital Versatile Disc)

Digital Video Disc (DVD)

→ *See* DVD (Digital Versatile Disc)

Digital Wallet

A digital wallet is a software product that is used to store information about a customer—for example, name, shipping address, telephone number, and credit card number. This information is stored in encrypted form and can be accessed only if all parties involved in a transaction can produce the appropriate certificates to demonstrate their authenticity and have access to cryptographic keys needed to encrypt or decrypt the wallet's contents. The wallet's owner must also provide a password to open the wallet for the transaction.

Digital wallets may be client-side or server-side packages. A client-side digital wallet resides on the owner's PC. The consumer downloads and installs the software from a digital wallet vendor, fills in the required information, and then encrypts the wallet's contents. To make a purchase, the consumer opens the wallet to provide the information to the merchant.

A server-side digital wallet is stored on a server at a financial institution or at the wallet vendor. All parties involved in a wallet-based transaction must provide the appropriate certificates to demonstrate their authenticity. Transactions involving a digital wallet are generally brokered by the wallet vendor or by the financial institution, with the broker getting a percentage of each transaction's price or a flat fee for each transaction from the merchant. (A digital wallet costs the consumer nothing—except for the extra money spent because the wallet makes shopping online so very easy.)

Until now, the major obstacle to digital wallets has been the lack of a standard for collecting and representing information in a digital wallet. This meant that different merchants might support different wallet packages. The consumer had to support multiple wallets or else had to go through the tedious process of providing all the pertinent information for each online transaction.

Recently, the major players in e-commerce software announced support for a common standard for representing e-commerce information: the Electronic Commerce Modeling Language (ECML).

→ *Broader Category* E-Commerce

Digital Wrapper

A digital wrapper is software that can serve any of several roles for other files (such as e-mail, images, or programs). For example, a wrapper can encrypt the file contents or allow file access only to users who have the appropriate key. The wrapper is "wrapped" around a file—that is, the code for wrapper and file are combined in the appropriate manner to enable the wrapper to carry out its functions. Digital envelopes, which are used to encrypt e-mail, are probably the most common use for digital wrappers at this time.

In addition to encryption and access control, digital wrappers can be used to deliver software and to provide access to online sales or product information, product expiration warnings, and so forth. As the volume of Web commerce increases, digital wrappers are expected to get wider use. Also, new uses for digital wrappers will be developed.

DIP (Dual In-line Package) Switch

A DIP switch is a block with two or more switches, each of which can be in either of two settings. DIP switches are used as alternatives to jumper settings when configuring a component. "A DIP switch" illustrates an example of a rocker-type DIP switch.

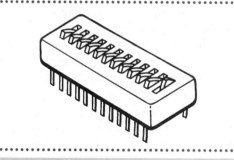

A DIP SWITCH

DIP switches are used in printed circuit boards, dot-matrix printers, modems, and many other peripheral devices.

Direct Broadcast Satellite (DBS)

→ *See* DBS (Direct Broadcast Satellite)

Direct Connection

In networking, a direct connection is an unmediated connection to the network. For example, a direct connection might be through a network cable attached to the network interface card (NIC).

In telecommunications and wide area networks (WANs), direct connection is a connection to long-distance lines that does not go through a local carrier. This type of connection is in contrast to the switched-digital access method, in which the connection does go through the local carrier.

Direct-Control Switching

In switching technology, a system in which the path is established directly, by signals in the network, rather than through a central controller.

Direct Current (DC)

→ *See* DC (Direct Current)

Direct Distance Dialing (DDD)

→ *See* DDD (Direct Distance Dialing)

Directed Transmission

In an AppleTalk network using the LocalTalk network architecture and its LocalTalk Link Access Protocol (LLAP), a directed transmission is one intended for a specific node. It is in contrast to a *broadcast transmission*, which is intended for all nodes.

In infrared communications, directed transmission is a method in which a signal is aimed at a central reflective target and read by receiving nodes as the signal bounces off the target. This is in contrast to a *diffuse transmission*, which travels in multiple directions, but is much weaker in each direction.

→ **Broader Categories** AppleTalk; Infrared Transmission LLAP

→ **Compare** Broadcast Transmission

Direct Inward Dialing (DID)

→ **See** DID (Direct Inward Dialing)

Directional Coupler

A coupler that can send a split signal in only one direction. This is in contrast to a bidirectional coupler, which can split a signal in more than one direction.

→ **See Also** Coupler

Direct Link

A connection, or circuit, that connects two stations directly, without any intervening stations.

Direct Memory Access (DMA)

→ **See** DMA (Direct Memory Access)

Director

A director is a system management entity that issues directives and commands to agents for performing a function.

Directory

A directory is an organizational concept that makes it possible to group files, so that files can be accessed

more easily. For example, all files related to a particular project or application may be grouped in a single directory. To further group files, they can be placed in subdirectories within directories.

Grouping files in a directory makes it possible to organize these files on a logical basis and at a logical level. Creating subdirectories makes it possible to impose a hierarchical structure on files. A subdirectory is said to be contained in a *parent directory*.

Grouping certain files distinguishes them implicitly from other files that are *not* in the directory. Because files in a directory are effectively partitioned from files outside, it's possible to use the same file names in different directories.

The Directory Hierarchy

Directories can contain other directories, which can contain still other directories, so that multiple levels of containment are possible. A directory structure looks like a tree. This tree has an infelicitously named *root directory* at the top of the tree, (sub)directories as branches, and files as individual leaves at the ends of the branches.

A file can be referred to or located by specifying a path to it. This path consists of a sequence of directory (or subdirectory) names that are passed in traversing the tree to the file. Such a path usually begins with the root and ends with the file name.

File Path

In a file path, directory names are separated by a special character, which differs from environment to environment. For example, in DOS, the separator character, or delimiter, is the backslash (\); in UNIX it is the forward slash (/). Some operating environments will accept either delimiter.

In crowded or complex environments, such as in a directory structure with many subdirectory levels, file paths can get quite long. Unfortunately, most operating systems limit the number of characters allowed in a path formulation. For example, DOS path names can be at most 127 characters; NetWare's can be up to 255 characters. Length limitations can be a problem when trying to pass material from one program to another.

To avoid problems with such limits, most operating environments provide mechanisms for specifying relative partial paths. For example, a *relative path* is one that "begins" at the current directory location (as opposed to beginning at the root).

Fake Root Directory

Versions 3.*x* and later of Novell's NetWare allow you to define a subdirectory as a *fake root* directory. To an application, this directory looks just like the root, and administrators can assign user rights from the fake root directory.

One advantage of a fake root is that the real root directory need not be cluttered because of an inflexible application. Also, the true root directory is not compromised because user rights must be assigned at that level.

Directory Structure

As stated, a directory structure is inherently hierarchical and can be represented as a tree with the root at the top. This hierarchical property can be used to keep a hard disk organized and easy to use. It can also help contribute to network security by making certain types of accidents much less likely.

Directory structure refers to the way in which directories and subdirectories are organized in relation to each other; that is, it refers to how they are laid out conceptually on a hard disk or partition.

Flat versus Deep Directory Structure

A directory structure can be *flat* or *deep*—depending on the number of subdirectories at the root and on the number of subdirectory levels.

A flat directory structure has lots of subdirectories under the root, but few, if any, sub-subdirectories. Such a structure is likely to arise if there are no commonalities in the kinds of directories being created (and, therefore, little or no need to create higher-level groupings). "A flat directory structure" shows an example of this structure.

A deep directory structure, on the other hand, may have many levels of subdirectories. For example, this type of structure might be used if there are a few categories of programs, with various possible activities for these programs. "A deep directory structure" illustrates this type of setup.

Network Directory Structures

In a networking context, much of the directory structure will be determined by how the networking software sets itself up and on the needs of users on the network. Networking packages try to isolate system-critical files and programs from general access. This means that the structure will have at least two directories: one for the system and one for users. In practice, directory structures for networks will be more complex than those for stand-alone machines.

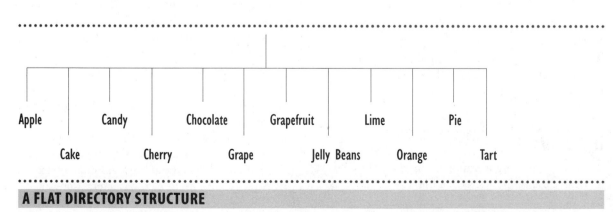

A FLAT DIRECTORY STRUCTURE

DIRECTORY STRUCTURE SUGGESTIONS

Various computer mavens and kibitzers have offered suggestions about what types of directory structures are best:

- In terms of accessibility, for example, structures with no more than four or five levels are recommended. With too many levels, paths can get unacceptably long.

- Groupings and structures should be "logical" or "reasonable"—terms whose definitions are generally left to the reader or the administrator.

- A directory should not contain "too many" files. In some environments, the operating system will provide at least an upper bound on what constitutes "too many." In other cases, the software will dictate how many files are to be included in the directory.

- In a network, it's often useful to structure directories so that one set of access rights at the top-level directory applies to all that directory's subdirectories and files. For example, you might put all applications in a PROGRAM directory and all working files in a WORK directory and assign the appropriate access rights to those two main directories.

For example, Novell's NetWare creates four predefined directories on its SYS volume: SYSTEM, PUBLIC, LOGIN, and MAIL. Administrators and users can build around this "proto-structure," by adding more directories on this volume, or by creating additional volumes with different directories.

UNIX-based networking software will be installed within the existing UNIX directory structure.

Administrators will build the files and directories needed to run the network around and under the predefined directories. For example, each user may get his or her own "home" directory, which will generally be a subdirectory in some "user" area. Applications should be placed in separate directories.

When creating a directory structure and naming directories, it is important to determine any restrictions that apply. In particular, you need to find out which application requires the shortest file/directory names and the shortest paths. The resulting directory structure must be accessible even with the most severe restrictions.

Higher-Level Grouping Concepts

Directories are created, in part, to deal with the proliferation of files. Similarly, partitions on a hard disk can be created to deal with the proliferation of directories and with the storage requirements imposed by thousands of files and directories.

A network file server may have to manage gigabytes of material—possibly more material than can fit on a single hard disk. To make it possible to deal with elements at this next level of storage requirements, higher-level grouping concepts are introduced. In fact, from an information management perspective, a file server is nothing more than a way of grouping a few megabytes of material.

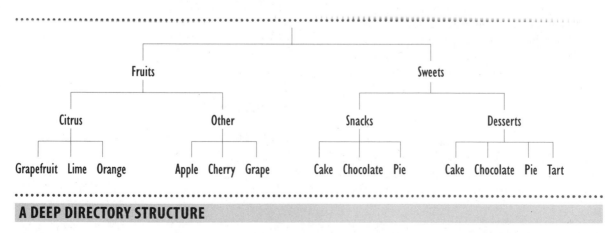

Within this framework, the concept of a directory is just a middle-level management element. For example, in the NetWare environment, a file is associated with:

- A file server
- A volume (which may encompass one or more hard disks)
- Directories and subdirectories

To specify a file path, all the elements are included, as in this example of a full NetWare path:

MYSERVER/SYS:PUBLIC/INFO/TECH/
CABLE.TEX

Do not confuse the NetWare Directory Services (NDS) Directory (which is written with an uppercase *D* in Novell's documentation) with the file system directory (lowercase *d*) structure maintained by the NetWare operating system. The Directory contains information about objects (resources, users, and so on); the directory contains information about files and subdirectories. See the NDS (NetWare Directory Services) article for information about the NDS Directory.

Directory Caching

Directory caching is a method that uses a fast storage area to help speed up the process of determining a file's location on disk. File allocation table (FAT) and directory entry table (DET) information about the most commonly used directory entries can be written to the directory cache memory, from which the information can be retrieved quickly. Directory caching is a feature of Novell NetWare.

The advantages of directory caching can be augmented if the file server uses a cache and if the requested file's contents happen to be in the server's cache. As the directory cache fills up, the least-used directory entries are eliminated from the cache.

Directory Enabled Network (DEN)

→ *See* DEN (Directory Enabled Network)

Directory Entry Table (DET)

→ *See* DET (Directory Entry Table)

Directory Hashing

A method for organizing directory entries to minimize the search time for an entry. The hashing provides guided access to the desired entry, so that fewer entries need to be checked along the way.

Directory ID

In an AppleTalk network, a unique value associated with a directory when the directory is created.

Directory Information Base (DIB)

→ *See* DIB (Directory Information Base)

Directory Information Shadowing Protocol (DISP)

→ *See* Protocol, DISP (Directory Information Shadowing Protocol)

Directory Information Tree (DIT)

→ *See* DIT (Directory Information Tree)

Directory Management Domain (DMD)

→ *See* DMD (Directory Management Domain)

Directory Operations Protocol (DOP)

→ *See* Protocol, DISP (Directory Information Shadowing Protocol)

Directory Rights

In various networking environments, restrictions and privileges that define which activities the *trustee* (the user or process) logged in to the network is allowed to perform.

→ *See Also* Access Rights

Directory Service (DS)

→ *See* DS (Directory Service)

Directory Service Area (DSA)

→ *See* DSA (Directory Service Area)

Directory Synchronization

In directory management, the task of maintaining multiple directories, and of avoiding or resolving inconsistencies by making sure all directories are updated properly.

Directory System Agent (DSA)

→ *See* DSA (Directory System Agent)

Directory User Agent (DUA)

→ *See* DUA (Directory User Agent)

Directory, Virtual

In Windows NT Server, virtual directories may be used in Web sites created using server packages such as Microsoft's Internet Information Server (IIS). Virtual directories can make directories appear—to a browser, for example—to be in a location other than their actual location in the directory structure. This capability can be useful because it allows different Web sites to use the same (virtual) directories for particular purposes. By being able to use the same directory names, script files can be used in the same manner for each Web site.

Direct Outward Dialing (DOD)

→ *See* DOD (Direct Outward Dialing)

Direct Wave

In wireless communications, an electromagnetic signal that is transmitted through the air, but low enough to reach the destination without being reflected off the earth or off the ionosphere. A direct wave requires a line of sight between sender and receiver.

Dirty Power

Dirty power refers to electrical power (AC or DC) that is subject to any of several common types of power disturbances, including spikes and surges, sags (or brownouts), and line noise. Dirty power is a major cause of computer and network failures.

→ *See* Power Disturbance

D

DIS (Draft International Standard)

For international standards committees, an early version of a proposed standard. The DIS is circulated to all committee members for consideration and comment.

DISA (Data Interchange Standards Association)

The DISA was created in 1987 to serve as the secretariat for ASC X12 (Accredited Standards Committee for X12), which is the committee charged by ANSI (American National Standards Institute) with formulating EDI (electronic data interchange) standards. Since then, the Association has taken on other responsibilities, including publication of the X12 documentation and providing support to other standards bodies about EDI.

Discard Eligibility (DE)

→ *See* DE (Discard Eligibility)

Discrete Multitone (DMT)

→ *See* DMT (Discrete Multitone)

Disk Array Subsystem (DAS)

→ *See* DAS (Disk Array Subsystem)

Disk Cache

→ *See* Cache

Disk Coprocessor Board (DCB)

→ *See* DCB (Disk Coprocessor Board)

Disk Driver

Software that serves as the interface between the operating system and the hard disk; also known as a *disk interface driver*. The network vendor usually includes drivers for the most common types of hard disks (ESDI, SCSI, and IDE), and the hard disk manufacturer may include drivers for specific network operating systems.

Disk Duplexing

Disk duplexing is a data-protection mechanism that uses two or more hard disks, with a separate channel from the PC to each disk. (A *channel* is the hard disk and the components that connect the drive to an operating environment.) A disk-duplexing system automatically writes everything to both disks, using the separate channels. "Disk duplexing" illustrates this process.

If one disk or channel fails, the networking software notifies the system administrator. The administrator should fix or replace the defective disk or channel, to get it back on line as quickly as possible. Until the disk is replaced, the disk duplexing software will continue writing to the working disk.

Some implementations of disk duplexing support *split seeks*, in which data are read from whichever disk finds the data first.

→ *Broader Category* Data Protection

→ *Compare* Disk Mirroring

Disk Mirroring

Disk mirroring is a data-protection strategy that uses two hard disks, which are accessed through a single disk channel. (A *channel* is the hard disk and the components that connect the drive to an operating environment.) All the data is written to both hard disks, but using the same channel. "Disk mirroring" illustrates this process. This is in contrast to disk duplexing, in which separate channels are used.

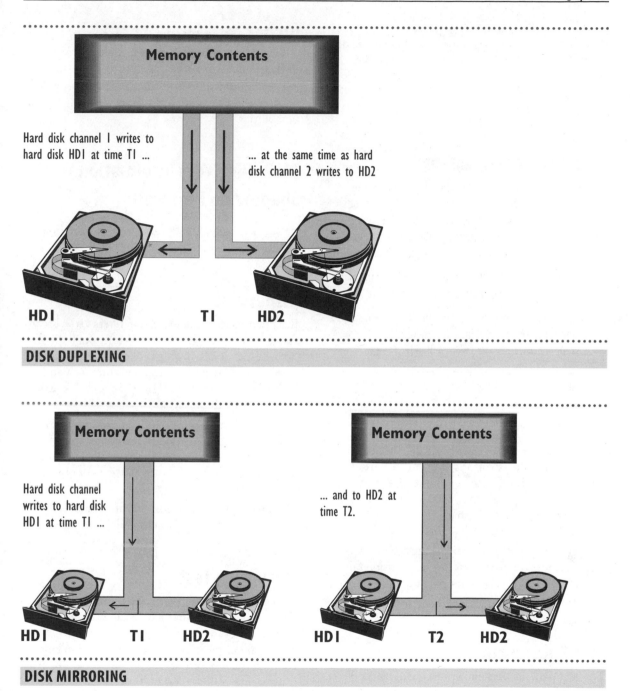

Memory Contents

Hard disk channel I writes to hard disk HDI at time TI ...

... at the same time as hard disk channel 2 writes to HD2

HDI TI HD2

DISK DUPLEXING

Memory Contents

Memory Contents

Hard disk channel writes to hard disk HDI at time TI ...

... and to HD2 at time T2.

HDI TI HD2

HDI T2 HD2

DISK MIRRORING

Note that all the data is written twice in succession with disk mirroring. Note also that failure of the disk channel makes both disks inaccessible.

→*Broader Category*   Data Protection

→*Compare*   Disk Duplexing

IDE DRIVES AND DISK MIRRORING

IDE drives are not suitable for disk mirroring, because one of the IDE drives is automatically designated master and the other slave. The master does diagnostics for both drives and controls the slave drive. This relationship has the following consequences, which limit the desirability of IDE drives for disk mirroring:

- If the master crashes, the slave is useless, since the master runs the show for both drives.

- If the slave crashes, the master won't find it. Rather, the master will keep searching when there is no response from the slave drive and will eventually time out.

Disk Striping

Disk striping is a data-storage strategy that combines comparable partitions on separate hard disks into a single volume. Data can be read from or written to multiple partitions at the same time, because each partition is on a separate disk, and each disk has its own read/write heads.

Disk striping with parity distributes parity information across the partitions. If one partition fails, the information on the other partitions can be used to reconstruct the missing data.

Disk Subsystem

The components that make up a hard disk drive: drive unit, hard disk, controller, interface card, and cable. When discussed as a separate entity, a disk subsystem is generally housed as an external drive.

DISOSS (Distributed Office Supported System)

An IBM mainframe-based package that provides document preparation and electronic mail (e-mail) capabilities.

DISP (Directory Information Shadowing Protocol)

→*See*   Protocol, DISP (Directory Information Shadowing Protocol)

Dispersion

In a fiber-optic signal, dispersion refers to the broadening of the light signal as it travels through the fiber. Dispersion is directly proportional to distance traveled. Dispersion also imposes a limit on bandwidth, because two light signals cannot become so dispersed that they overlap.

In a wireless (infrared, radio, or microwave) transmission, dispersion refers to the scattering of the signal, which is generally caused by the atmospheric conditions and by any particles or objects in the transmission path.

In an electrical transmission, dispersion is the distortion of the signal as it travels along the wire.

Disruptive Test

In network management, a diagnostic or performance test that requires a break in ordinary network activity in order to run. Some network management packages require verification before running the test, or make it possible to run such a test automatically at certain times, such as when there is little other network activity.

→*Compare*   Nondisruptive Test

Distance Vector

Distance vector refers to a class of routing algorithms. Distance vector algorithms compute distances from a node by finding paths to all adjacent nodes and by using the information these nodes have about continuing on the paths adjacent to them.

Distance vector algorithms can be computationally intensive. The computations are needed for convergence, which is the process of finding a stable route to a destination. The convergence problem can be alleviated somewhat by defining different routing levels.

Examples of distance vector algorithms are the ISO's Interdomain Routing Protocol (IDRP) and the routing information protocols (RIPs) supported in the TCP/IP suite and in Novell's IPX/SPX suite, and IGRP (Interior Gateway Routing Protocol).

→ *Broader Category* Routing

→ *See Also* Link State Algorithm

Distortion

Any change in a signal, particularly, in the signal's shape. The factors that can cause or contribute to distortion include attenuation, crosstalk, interference, and delay. *Nonlinear distortion* occurs because the signal's harmonics (multiples of the signal's fundamental frequency) are attenuated (weakened) by different amounts.

Distributed Application

A *distributed application* is one that executes on multiple machines in a network, generally, with specialized portions of the application executing on each machine.

For example, in a client/server network, an application front end may execute on the user's workstation to provide an interface for the user, and a back end for the application may execute on

a server to do the work requested through the front end. The back end will pass the results to the front end, and then to the user.

This is in contrast to a *centralized application*, which executes entirely on a single machine.

Distributed Architecture

A configuration in which processors are located in multiple devices, possibly in multiple locations. Each processor is capable of functioning independently or in cooperation with other elements in the architecture.

Distributed Authentication Security Service (DASS)

→ *See* DASS (Distributed Authentication Security Service)

Distributed Common Object Model (DCOM)

→ *See* DCOM (Distributed Component Object Model)

Distributed Component Object Model (DCOM)

→ *See* DCOM (Distributed Component Object Model)

Distributed Computing

In a distributed computing environment, both work and resources may be spread across different nodes in a network or even across different networks.

D

There is no necessary relationship between the location at which a task or resource is requested and the location at which this request is fulfilled. For example, a machine on network A may need something printed quickly and then sent to another location. In a distributed computing environment, this can be done by sending the materials to the destination machine and then printing them out at that location. Or the material may be printed at a second location and then sent to its destination.

The distributed dimension of the computing process should be transparent to the user. That is, the user should not need to be concerned with the fact that, for example, a particular task must be carried out by a specific machine or that a required resource is in a different office.

Distributed Computing Environment (DCE)

→ *See* DCE (Distributed Computing Environment)

Distributed Database (DDB)

→ *See* DDB (Distributed Database)

Distributed Database Management System (DDBMS)

→ *See* DDBMS (Distributed Database Management System)

Distributed Data Management (DDM)

→ *See* DDM (Distributed Data Management)

Distributed Data Processing (DDP)

→ *See* DDP (Distributed Data Processing)

Distributed Directory Service (DDS)

→ *See* DDS (Distributed Directory Service)

Distributed File System (DFS)

→ *See* DFS (Distributed File System)

Distributed Function Terminal (DFT)

→ *See* DFT (Distributed Function Terminal)

Distributed interNet Applications Architecture (DNA)

→ *See* DNA (Distributed interNet Applications Architecture)

Distributed Network Architecture (DNA)

→ *See* DNA (Distributed Network Architecture)

Distributed Office Applications Model (DOAM)

→ *See* DOAM (Distributed Office Applications Model)

Distributed Office Supported System (DISOSS)

→ *See* DISOSS (Distributed Office Supported System)

Distributed Processing

In networking, distributed processing describes a setup in which responsibilities and services are spread across different nodes or processes, so that particular tasks are performed by specialized nodes somewhere on a network. This is in contrast to *central processing*, in which multiple nodes share the computing power of a single server.

In distributed processing, a station that needs something done sends a request onto the network. The server responsible for the service takes on the task, does it, and returns the results to the station. The station need never know who actually did the work.

Distributed processing is much less susceptible to high activity levels, because the extra work can be spread out among many servers. On the other hand, distributed processing requires much more extensive bookkeeping and administration, and much more passing on of information.

→ *Compare* Central Processing

Distributed Queue Dual Bus (DQDB)

→ *See* DQDB (Distributed Queue Dual Bus)

Distributed Relational Data Architecture (DRDA)

→ *See* DRDA (Distributed Relational Data Architecture)

Distributed System

A distributed system consists of multiple autonomous computers that are linked and that can—through software—give the appearance of being a single, integrated computer system. The individual computers may be parts of a local, wide, or global area network. "A sample distributed system" shows an example of such a system.

Examples of distributed systems abound, including the Internet, various University computing centers, and ATM (automatic teller machine) networks.

Features of Distributed Systems

Several features and capabilities are considered desirable for distributed systems. These include the following:

Resource sharing This refers to the ability for users to share hardware (e.g., CPU time, peripherals), application software (for example, groupware), or data (e.g., reference materials). A resource manager can coordinate resource allocation and sharing. Two approaches to resource sharing are common: client-server and object-based. These are described more fully below.

Concurrency This refers to the fact that multiple users may be requesting or accessing system resources at the same time. Ideally, processors should be able to deal with multiple users simultaneously. A distributed system automatically demonstrates concurrency each time two or more users do things at the same time on their own machines.

Openness An open system is one for which specifications and interfaces have been made public, so that developers can create products for the system. An open system can more easily handle new hardware or software configurations because there are officially accepted specifications. Open systems also adhere to open principles for internal operations. For example, IPC (interprocess communication) calls provide a standard mechanism for processes or components to communicate with each other.

D

Transparency   This refers to the fact that a user doesn't need to know that different resources being used may be scattered all around the world. For the user, there should be no significant difference between requesting a local resource and one at some remote location.

Scalability   This refers to the ability of the system to grow—for example, through the addition of new computers or by the creation of internetworks. When a distributed system grows, certain information may need to be duplicated at multiple locations in order to maintain the efficiency of the original, smaller

system. Such *replicas* must be updated and corrected in a synchronized manner.

Fault tolerance   This refers to the system's ability to continue functioning after one or more components become unavailable either because of hardware or software failure. One way to handle hardware failure is to include redundant components in the system. This is an effective but expensive solution. In a fault-tolerant system, a software failure will affect only the process or processes that failed. Among other things, this means that a process should not be able to freeze another process or overwrite the memory or data for another process.

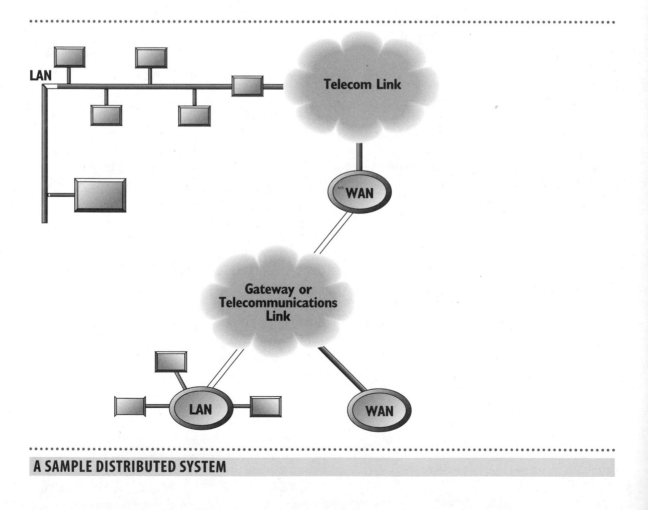

A SAMPLE DISTRIBUTED SYSTEM

In a client-server approach to resource sharing, each server process is a centralized resource manager—that is, transactions generally go through a server. Servers may provide only certain services and may complement each other with respect to the services they provide. A client-server approach works well for general-purpose sharing of information and resources.

In an object-based approach, each resource is regarded as an object, which can be moved anywhere in a distributed system while still remaining accessible. In an object-based approach, all shared resources can be viewed in the same way. An object manager can control access to objects or classes of objects.

An important task in a distributed system is the handling of the file and directory system. Various approaches have been developed for this task. These include the Network file system (NFS) from Sun and the Andrew File System (AFS) from Carnegie-Mellon University. Currently, distributed systems are most likely to use UNIX machines, partly because useful file systems have been developed for UNIX environments.

Distributed systems are in contrast to centralized systems in which multiple users may be connected via terminals or PCs to a single host machine, which may itself be a PC. Mainframe-based centralized systems are sometimes known as *monolithic systems*.

Distributed System Object Model (DSOM)

→ *See* DSOM (Distributed System Object Model)

Distributed Systems Architecture (DSA)

→ *See* DSA (Distributed Systems Architecture)

Distributed Transaction Coordinator (DTC)

→ *See* DTC (Distributed Transaction Coordinator)

Distribution Frame

A location at which wiring is concentrated. In a sub- or intermediate distribution frame (SDF or IDF), wiring from components (such as nodes in a network) is concentrated at a single location. A backbone cable runs from such SDFs to the main distribution frame (MDF), which serves as a wiring center for all the voice and data cable in a building, and which connects the building to the larger power structures in the outside world.

Distribution List (DL)

→ *See* DL (Distribution List)

DIT (Directory Information Tree)

In the CCITT's X.500 Directory Services (DS) model, a directory information tree (DIT) contains the information for a directory information base (DIB).

The information in a DIT will generally be distributed. This provides faster access to the information at the distributed locations. Since a DIT can get quite large, distributing it also helps keep down the size of the DIT materials at any single location.

Objects in a DIT

The objects in a DIT may represent intermediate categories, such as country, organization, or organizational unit, or they may represent specific objects, such as a device, a person, or an alias for

D

either of these. The root of the DIT is an imaginary entry with a null name. This serves as a base for naming elements in the tree.

An object gets its name from the path between the tree's root and the object. A particular object may be found in multiple locations in the tree; that is, the object may have multiple names. For example, a particular end-user might be found in the DIT as a CPA by day (on a path through the user's employer) or as a rock guitarist by night (on a path through a musician's union).

A DIT does not contain the actual objects, just information about them. Each location in the tree has predefined attributes associated with it. The attributes will depend on the object class to which the entry belongs. An *object class*, such as country or organization, determines which attributes are mandatory and which are optional for objects belonging to that class.

Objects in the tree will have specific values associated with these attributes. Although an object may appear at multiple locations in the DIT, each object will have only one body of information associated with it.

Operations on the DIT

Two general classes of operations are possible in a DIT: retrieval (reading) and modification (creating and writing). A given DIT operation may apply to a single entry or to a group of entries. The X.500 model supports three of the four possible operation classes:

- Retrieve a single entry
- Retrieve a group of entries
- Modify a single entry

The fourth operation class, Modify a group of entries, is not supported in X.500

Using the DIT

End-users or processes can access the information in the DIT as follows:

- A directory user agent (DUA) provides the user with access to the DIT through an *access point*. A particular access point may support one or more of the operation classes.

- A directory system agent (DSA) provides the requested services for the DUA, and can also provide services for other DSAs. Since the DIT can be large and may be distributed, more than one DSA may be involved. A particular DSA is generally responsible for a portion of the DIT. This portion is known as a *context*.

→ *Broader Category* X.500

Diversity

In microwave communications, diversity refers to either of two strategies for providing safeguards against equipment failure:

Frequency diversity   A separate frequency band is allocated for use in case the main band cannot be used (for example, because of noise or other interference).

Space diversity   Two receiving antennas are set up close—but not too close—to each other. If the primary target antenna malfunctions, the auxiliary antenna will be used to pull in the signals.

DIX (Digital Intel Xerox)

The three companies whose early work on networking eventually were eventually led to the development of the Blue Book Ethernet standard.

DL (Distribution List)

In the 1988 version of CCITT's X.400 Message Handling System (MHS), a tool for reaching multiple recipients with a single transmission. The DL includes all addresses to which a message is to be sent.

DLC (Data Link Control)

As a general term, DLC refers to the functions provided at the Data-Link layer of the OSI reference model. These functions are generally provided by a logical-link-control (LLC) sublayer. DLC is also a protocol, which is discussed in the Protocol, DLC article.

DLC (Digital Loop Carrier)

In telephone service, a DLC provides a way of multiplexing multiple calls onto a single digital line, or loop. For example, a T1 carrier (which operates at 1.544Mbps) provides access for 24 digital channels, which are combined on a single line using time division multiplexing (TDM). DLC is also expanded as *digital line carrier*.

DLCI (Data Link Connection Identifier)

In frame-relay communications, a field in the frame-relay header. The DLCI represents the virtual circuit number associated with a particular destination.

DLL (Dynamic Link Library)

A DLL is a precompiled collection of executable functions that can be called in programs. Instead of linking the code for called DLL functions into a program, the program merely gets a pointer to the DLL at runtime. The required DLL file must be accessible at runtime, however. Multiple programs can use the same DLL.

DLLs are used extensively in Microsoft Windows, OS/2, and in Windows NT. DLLs may have filename extensions of .DLL, .DRV, or .FON.

DLS (Data-Link Services)

The services provided at the Data-Link layer in the OSI reference model.

DMA (Direct Memory Access)

Direct memory access is a method for transferring data from a drive or other peripheral device directly to the computer's memory, without involving the CPU (central processing unit).

The DMA process is managed by a specialized DMA controller chip, which is generally faster than the processor. When the data transfer is finished, the controller chip informs the processor, which can then proceed as if the processor had managed the transfer. Each DMA controller can handle up to four devices.

DMD (Directory Management Domain)

In the CCITT's X.500 Directory Management Services, a collection of one or more directory system agents (DSAs), and possibly of some directory user agents (DUAs), all managed by a single organization.

→ *See Also* X.500

DMI (Desktop Management Interface)

DMI provides a standard method for identifying PC hardware and software components automatically, without intervention from the user. At a minimum, DMI identifies the following information about any component installed in a PC:

- Manufacturer
- Component name
- Version
- Serial number (if appropriate)
- Installation time and date

DMI is supported by Digital Equipment Corporation (DEC), IBM, Intel, Microsoft, Novell, Sun, and more than 300 other vendors.

DMI (Digital Multiplexed Interface)

In digital telecommunications, a T1 interface between a private branch exchange (PBX) and a computer.

DMT (Discrete Multitone)

DMT is the official ANSI standard line code for asymmetric digital subscriber line (ADSL) communications technology. The line code determines how 0s and 1s are represented electrically in a transmission.

DMT works by dividing a 1.1MHz bandwidth (ranging from 0 to 1.1MHz) into 256 equal-sized *subcarriers*, or *subchannels*. Each subcarrier gets 4.3125KHz. In practice, only about 250 of the subcarriers are actually used in a communication session. Usually, the subcarriers in the highest frequency ranges are not used, because these are most susceptible to attenuation and interference with increasing distance. Most of the subcarriers are used for transmitting information, but a few are reserved for special purposes. For example, subcarriers 1 through 6 (which use the lowest frequency bands) are used for analog voice transmissions.

Generally, 32 subchannels are used for receiving (also known as upstream communications, in this context), and 250 are used for sending (that is, for downstream communications). Since there are at most 256 available subchannels, it follows that some of the channels must be used for both sending and receiving. To make this double duty possible, DMT uses *echo cancellation* to remove, mathematically, any signals that bounce back, or echo, along a subcarrier. If echo cancellation is not possible in a given session, only 218 downstream transmission subchannels are allocated so that the remaining 32 subchannels can be used for upstream traffic.

DMT hardware chips try to distribute a transmission evenly across all available subchannels. Activity in every subchannel is monitored constantly during a session. If a subchannel has a high error rate—for example, because of echo or outside interference (such as a nearby AM radio station)—bytes to be transmitted are directed to other subchannels until the problem disappears. Because of this, DMT makes possible a rate-adaptive connection—known as *rate-adaptive asynchronous digital subscriber line (RADSL)*.

Because DMT is an open and an official standard, it is more widely supported in chip sets than either CAP (carrierless amplitude/phase modulation) or QAM (quadrature amplitude modulation). CAP and QAM, however, claim a larger user base, partly because the underlying technology has been available for much longer. DMT also offers certain other advantages over CAP and QAM, including broad support in the industry for the DMT chip set, greater flexibility, and somewhat better noise immunity than CAP or QAM.

→ *Broader Category* ADSL (Asymmetric Digital Subscriber Line); Encoding, Signal

→ *See Also* CAP (Carrierless Amplitude/Phase Modulation); Modulation

DNA (Digital Network Architecture)

A layered architecture from Digital Equipment Corporation (DEC). DNA is implemented in the various incarnations of DECnet.

→ *See Also* DECnet

DNA (Distributed interNet Applications Architecture)

DNA is Microsoft's newest packaging for the following technologies:

- An object model, as specified in Microsoft COM (Component Object Model) and DCOM (Distributed COM) and as instantiated through ActiveX controls.

- Web services and connections, as provided through Internet Information Server (IIS), Internet Explorer, SQL Server, Exchange Server, and Outlook.

- Programming and scripting capabilities, as provided in DHTML (Dynamic Hypertext Markup Language), VBScript, Jscript, and Microsoft Java Virtual Machine (JVM).

Microsoft's object model serves as the core of the DNA technology, and the common services all know how to use COM/DCOM to get things done.

DNA (Distributed Network Architecture)

A term for a network in which processing capabilities and services are distributed across the network, as opposed to being centralized in a single host or server.

DNIC (Data Network Identification Code)

A unique, four-digit value assigned to public networks and to services on those networks.

DNIS (Dialed Number Identification Service)

A telephony service that retrieves information about the number being called. This information can include the name of the number's owner and the number's location. DNIS is very commonly used with 800 and 900 lines. For example, when multiple lines—each with different numbers—all come into the same call distributor, DNIS can tell which number a caller used.

→ *Compare* ANI (Automatic Number Identification)

DNS (Domain Naming System)

DNS—also known as Domain Name Service—is the distributed naming service used on the Internet. The DNS can provide a machine's IP address, given domain names for the machine. Various products have been developed to provide DNS, such as the Berkeley Internet Name Domain (BIND). DNS is described in RFCs 1101, 1183, 1637, and on up through 2181, 2183, 2219, and 2230.

Internet Domains

The basis for the domains in the DNS may be geographical, such as an entire country, or organizational, such as a common group or activity. The top-level domains represent the most general groupings, and these domain names are standardized. There are currently 14 top-level organizational domains and 59 top-level geographical domains. See the tables "Internet Top-Level Organization Domains" and "Internet Top-Level Geographic Domains" for lists of these domains. Seven of the top-level names were added in 1997. These are listed in *italics*.

INTERNET TOP-LEVEL ORGANIZATIONAL DOMAINS

Domain Name	Interpretation
arts	Artistic and cultural sites
com	Commercial organization
edu	Educational institution
firm	Businesses
gov	Government agency or organization
info	Information and news services
int	International organization
mil	U.S. military
net	Networking organization
nom	Individuals
org	Nonprofit organization
rec	Recreation and entertainment sites
store	Merchants
web	Sites doing Web-related work

INTERNET TOP-LEVEL GEOGRAPHICAL DOMAINS

Domain Name	Interpretation	Domain Name	Interpretation
aq	Antarctica	it	Italy
ar	Argentina	jp	Japan
at	Austria	kr	South Korea
au	Australia	kw	Kuwait
be	Belgium	li	Liechtenstein
bg	Bulgaria	lt	Lithuania
br	Brazil	lu	Luxembourg
ca	Canada	lv	Latvia
ch	Switzerland	mx	Mexico
cl	Chile	my	Malaysia
cn	China	nl	Netherlands
cr	Cost Rica	no	Norway
cs	Czech and Slovak Republics	nz	New Zealand

INTERNET TOP-LEVEL GEOGRAPHICAL DOMAINS (continued)

Domain Name	Interpretation	Domain Name	Interpretation
de	Germany	pl	Poland
dk	Denmark	pr	Puerto Rico
ec	Ecuador	pt	Portugal
ee	Estonia	re	Reunion
eg	Egypt	se	Sweden
es	Spain	sg	Singapore
fi	Finland	si	Slovenia
fr	France	su	Soviet Union
gb	Great Britain	th	Thailand
gr	Greece	tn	Tunisia
hk	Hong Kong	tw	Taiwan
hr	Croatia	uk	United Kingdom
hu	Hungary	us	United States
ie	Ireland	ve	Venezuela
il	Israel	yu	Yugoslavia
in	India	za	South Africa
is	Iceland		

Domain Names in Internet Addresses

An Internet name consists of a *userid* followed by an at sign (@), which is followed by one or more names separated by dots. The most general of these names refer to domains. Domain names are found at the *end* of an Internet name.

A particular name may include references to one or more domains. The rightmost of these is a top-level domain. The ordering from specific to general in an Internet name is in contrast to the elements in an IP (Internet -Protocol) address, in which the first (leftmost) number represents the most general division.

DOAM (Distributed Office Applications Model)

DOAM is an overarching OSI (Open Systems Interconnection) model for several application-layer processes. The DOAM deals with document and data organization and transmission. Its functions include the following:

- Document Filing and Retrieval (DFR)
- Document Printing Application (DPA)
- Message-Oriented Text Interchange System (MOTIS)
- Referenced Data Transfer (RDT)

Document Content Architecture (DCA)

→ **See** DCA (Document Content Architecture)

Document Interchange Architecture (DIA)

→ **See** DIA (Document Interchange Architecture)

Document Management

Document management refers to the range of tasks and considerations that may arise in relation to the online creation, modification, and storage of simple, compound, or hypertext documents.

- A *simple document* contains text and possibly formatting commands, but no graphics, voice, etc.
- A *compound document* —also known as a *multimedia document* —can include graphics, sound or video, in addition to text.

- A *hypertext document* is one that contains links to other documents or other locations in the same document. With the appropriate software, a user can access the material associated with such links from within the document. Hypertext documents may be simple or compound. The materials accessible through a hypertext document may be located in different places. For example, the material accessible from a home page on the World Wide Web (WWW) might be located on machines scattered all around the world.

Tasks such as the following are considered part of document management. Note that in some cases the required tools are generic and are not tied to document management systems. For example, encryption or compression programs are used for purposes other than document management.

Creation Documents may be created in many different ways: by scanning existing documents for text (and possibly also for graphics), with an ordinary text editor, word processor, desktop publishing program, or hypertext (e.g., HTML) editor. Depending on the method used to create the document, the result may be a simple or a compound one.

Storage A document can be stored as one or more elements. The media on which a document is to be stored may be considered primary, secondary, or tertiary. Primary media are those that are almost always available and very frequently used. Hard disks are the best example of a primary medium. Secondary media are also almost always available, but have much slower access times than primary media. CD-ROM drives are a good example of secondary media. Tertiary media are available only upon request, and they usually have slower access times than primary media. Tapes or discs that must first be mounted are examples of tertiary media.

Retrieval Users must be able to call up and view documents. Ideally, the online view of a retrieved document should be comparable to a printed version. That is, formatting and layout information should be preserved. This requires the use of special viewers or browsers that can interpret the formatting and layout commands and translate them into the appropriate display instructions. Popular viewers include Acrobat from Adobe, WorldView from Interleaf, and DynaText from Electronic Book Technologies.

Transmission   To be truly useful, a document management system must be accessible to multiple users. These may be in different geographical locations. Consequently, it may be necessary to send a document from one location to another. The transmission should be as efficient and inexpensive as possible, but should be error-free and leave the document unchanged.

Reception   Just as it must be possible to send a document to specified locations, it must also be possible to receive the document at that location. Resources must be available to reconstruct the document (for example, if it was sent in packets) and to check its integrity.

Revision   Very few documents are perfect right from the start. As a result, users must be able to revise documents. For simple documents, this can be done using a text editor; for compound documents, more sophisticated editing capabilities are needed. Editors that can use markup languages such as HTML (Hypertext Markup Language) or its more general and powerful predecessor SGML (Standard Generalized Markup Language) are becoming increasingly popular.

Compression   Compression reduces a document's size by taking advantage of redundancy in the document. This saves storage and also saves money when the document is transmitted. Compression of compound documents can get complicated since different types of compression algorithms are most appropriate for text and images.

Encryption   Encryption makes a document more difficult to use if stolen—since the document will be gibberish to anyone who doesn't know the encryption method or key. Document encryption is particularly important with personal and financial data. Encryption and compression are often used together. In such cases, it's extremely important to do things in the correct order. For example, compressing and then encrypting is most effective for text documents. If such a document is transmitted, the algorithms must be applied in reverse order at the receiving end—that is, decryption then decompression.

Document management software can be grouped into three categories:

- *File managers*, which generally work with only a single or a limited number of file formats. During storage, documents may be converted to the supported format, which may be proprietary.

- *Library managers*, which handle documents in their native formats and which include security capabilities. Library managers can also track document versions.

- *Compound Document Managers*, which treat documents as virtual entities that are always subject to change. Instead of handling a document as a static object, a compound document manager sees a document more as a set of pointers to various elements, any of which may be revised between one viewing and the next.

Document Transfer and Manipulation (DTAM)

→ *See* DTAM (Document Transfer and Manipulation)

Document Type Definition (DTD)

→ *See* DTD (Document Type Definition)

DOD (Direct Outward Dialing)

In a Centrex or a private branch exchange (PBX), a service that makes it possible to get an outside line directly, without going through the system's switchboard.

Domain

In both the Internet and OSI (Open System Interconnection) communities, the term *domain* refers to an administrative unit. The details of such a unit, however, differ in the Internet and OSI environments.

In the Internet community, a domain is an element in the DNS (Domain Naming System), which is a naming hierarchy. See the DNS article for more information about Internet domains.

In the OSI community, a domain is also a division created for administrative purposes. In this context, the details are based on functional differences. The five management domains defined in the OSI model are accounting, configuration, fault, performance, and security. See the Network Management article for more information about these domains.

The term has several other meanings in different networking contexts:

- In IBM's SNA (Systems Network Architecture), a domain represents all the terminals and other resources controlled by a single processor or processor group.

- In Novell's NNS (NetWare Name Service), the collection of servers that share bindery information constitutes a domain.

- In NetWare 4.*x*, a domain is a special area in which an NLM (NetWare Loadable Module) can run.

- In Windows NT Server, a domain is a collection of clients and servers that use the same security permissions database and that use a common name.

NetWare 4.*x* actually has two domains for NLMs: OS_PROTECTED and OS. In the OS_PROTECTED domain, you can run untested NLMs to ensure that they do not corrupt the operating system memory. The OS domain is where NLMs that are proven reliable can run more efficiently.

Domain Model

In Windows NT Server, a domain model provides a structure for administering networks. Users, groups, and resources can be grouped logically into domains. Users log on to a domain, rather than to a specific server. Logon administration and authentication is handled by a primary domain controller (PDC), using the accounts database in a Security Accounts Manager (SAM).

The SAM database can be copied to other servers, which are designated as backup domain controllers (BDCs). Accounts on the BDCs are synchronized with the PDC so that users can log on through either the PDC or a BDC. The use of multiple domain controllers makes it possible to do load balancing, which can improve performance. A BDC can also be used as a fallback in case the PDC is down, which offers fault tolerance for the network.

If multiple domains are created, their administration can be simplified by establishing trust relationships between domains. Once such relationships have been established, the related domains can be administered as a single entity. Thus, if a trust relationship exists between domains, a user who needs to use resources or files in both domains does not need to log on to each domain separately.

NT Server supports four domain models: single domain, master domain, multiple master domain, and complete trust domain.

Single Domain

In the single domain model there is—you guessed it—just one domain that includes all the servers, clients, and resources for the network. Since everything is in a single domain, no trust relationships need to be managed, and the domain controller can handle authentication for all accounts. Both accounts and resources are centralized within the same domain. This model is most appropriate for small networks because it is easy to manage. Performance can suffer, however, if the domain controller(s) must handle a large number of accounts.

Master Domain Model

In the master domain model (shown in "Master domain model"), user accounts and authentication for all domains are centralized in a single master accounts domain. The master domain administers accounts and access privileges for any other domains (which may be departments, divisions, or whatever organizational unit warrants its own domain). Control over resources is decentralized and left to the administrators of the various domains.

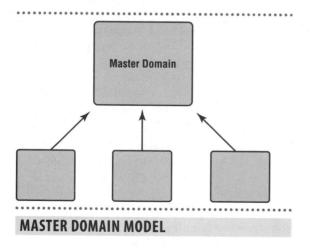

MASTER DOMAIN MODEL

Each of the domains must trust the master accounts domain, but there need not necessarily be trust relationships between the trusting domains.

Multiple Master Domain Model

The multiple master domain model is useful for large networks and is necessary for those with more than 40,000 accounts. In this model, there are multiple master accounts domains. The master controllers may each be responsible for separate divisions of an enterprise network—for example, for East Coast and West Coast or domestic and international operations.

While the master accounts controllers administer accounts and authentication for their respective fiefdoms, they are still part of the larger enterprise network. In a multiple master domain model, reciprocal trust relationships between the master accounts domains are necessary. In addition, each of the other (resource) domains must trust each of the master accounts domains. "Multiple master domain model" shows these relationships. Two or more master domains administer a network. Any other domains must be administered by all of the master domains. Each master domain must be able to communicate with all other master domains in the network.

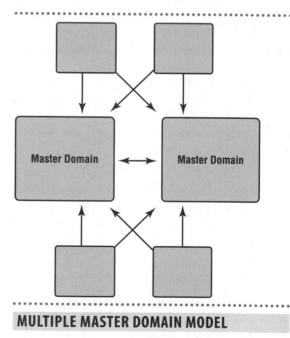

MULTIPLE MASTER DOMAIN MODEL

Complete Trust Domain Model

In a complete trust domain model, each domain is responsible for its own accounts and resources. This model is used if domain administrators want or need to keep control over accounts in their own domains. However, for these domains to work together in the same network, reciprocal trust relationships between the domains are needed. "Complete trust domain model" shows this arrangement. In a complete trust model, each domain is connected to every other domain, so that each domain can influence every other domain. Note that all the relationships are bidirectional.

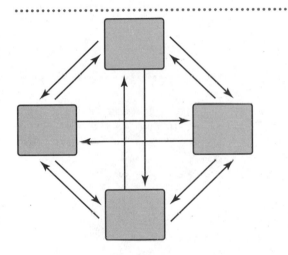

COMPLETE TRUST DOMAIN MODEL

→ *Broader Category* Windows NT

Domain Name Service (DNS)

→ *See* DNS (Domain Naming System)

Domain Naming System (DNS)

→ *See* DNS (Domain Naming System)

Domain Specific Part (DSP)

→ *See* DSP (Domain Specific Part)

Domino

→ *See* Lotus Domino

DOP (Directory Operations Protocol)

→ *See* Protocol, DISP (Directory Information Shadowing Protocol)

DOS Client

A workstation that boots DOS and gains access to the network using workstation software.

DOS Extender

Software that enables DOS programs to execute in protected mode and to make use of extended memory. Two widely used DOS extender specifications are VCPI (Virtual Control Program Interface) and DPMI (DOS Protected Mode Interface).

→ *See Also* DPMI; Protected Mode; VCPI

DOS Protected Mode Interface (DPMI)

→ *See* DPMI (DOS Protected Mode Interface)

DOS Requester

In Novell's NetWare 3.12 and 4.*x*, the DOS Requester is client software that runs on a workstation and mediates between applications, DOS, and NetWare. The DOS Requester replaces the NETX.COM network shell program used in earlier versions of NetWare.

The software actually consists of a terminate-and-stay resident (TSR) manager (VLM.EXE) and several Virtual Loadable Modules (VLMs), which can be loaded at startup or as needed. The software also includes modules for dealing with security, DOS redirection, transport-layer protocols, and NDS (NetWare Directory Services) or bindery commands. "Structure of NetWare's DOS Requester" illustrates the components.

VLM.EXE is the VLM manager and is responsible for loading the appropriate module at the appropriate time. VLM also controls memory usage and communication between relevant modules.

CONN.VLM is the *Connection Table Manager*, which allows clients to connect to a network (assuming, at least for now, that the user is authorized to do so).

The DOS Requester's components fit into a three-layer structure:

- The DOS Redirector, the REDIR.VLM module, resides at the *DOS Redirection Layer*. This module provides DOS file services and callouts. This is the topmost of the three layers.

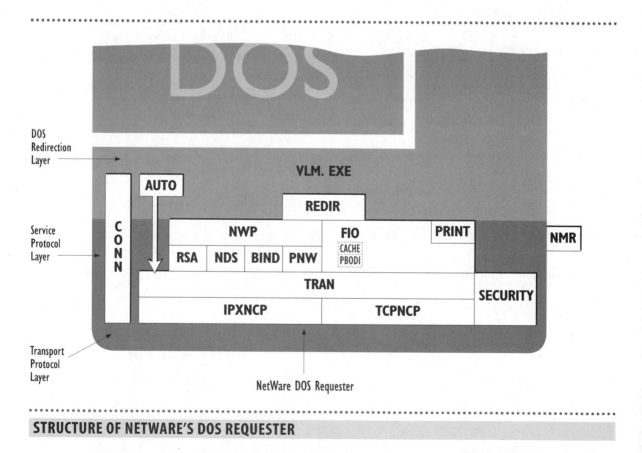

STRUCTURE OF NETWARE'S DOS REQUESTER

- The *Service Protocol Layer* has modules for providing NetWare-specific services and also file, print, and security services. The components that make up this layer are described below.

- The *Transport Protocol Layer* is the lowest of the three layers and is responsible for making sure packets are transmitted and that the connection is maintained. The TRAN.NLM module is the Transport protocol multiplexer and is responsible for enabling communications between the available protocols (IPX or TCP) and the resources at the service protocol layer. The IPX and TCP protocols are handled by IPXNCP.NLM or TCPNCP.NLM, respectively. If necessary, the AUTO.VLM module can be used to reconnect a workstation to a server automatically—for example, to re-establish a broken connection. AUTO.VLM will automatically reconfigure the system to its original state.

The following services are provided at the Service Protocol Layer:

- NetWare services are provided to handle the different flavors of NetWare: NetWare 2.x and 3.x (which use binderies), NetWare 4.x (which uses NetWare Directory Services, or NDS), and Personal NetWare. These flavors are handled, respectively, by BIND.VLM (for 2.x and 3.x), NDS.VLM (for 4.x), and PNW.VLM (for Personal NetWare). The module for the appropriate protocols is determined and called by NWP.VLM—the NetWare Protocol multiplexer.

- File services are handled by the FIO.VLM (file input/output) module. This module uses a basic file transfer protocol by default. If desirable or necessary, however, FIO can use special methods when reading or writing. These measures include using a cache (CACHE) or a packet-burst protocol

(PBODI), or transmitting large internet packets (LIP).

- Print services are provided by the PRINT .VLM module. Since PRINT.VLM uses the FIO capabilities, it can use any of the special measures listed for FIO.VLM. The print module's behavior depends on the settings it finds in the NET.CFG configuration file.

- Security services (both encryption and authentication) are provided through RSA.NLM, a module that implements the Rivest, Shamir, and Adleman public-key encryption algorithm.

Unlike the NetWare shell, the DOS Requester may be called by DOS to do a task that is network based and that DOS is, therefore, unable to perform. For example, DOS may use the DOS Requester to access file services on a remote machine.

The DOS Requester still processes NetWare requests to get them into the appropriate format and then sends the requests on to the server.

→ **Broader Category** Network Shell

→ **Compare** NETX

Dotted Decimal

Dotted decimal, also known as *dotted digit*, is the notation system used to represent the four-byte IP (Internet Protocol) addresses. An address in this format is called a *dot address*.

→ **See** IP Address

Double Buffering

The use of two buffers for input and output in order to improve performance and increase throughput. In a double-buffered environment, one buffer is processed while the other is filling.

DOV (Data over Voice)

In communications, a strategy for transmitting data over the voice channel at the same time as a voice transmission. A human listener would not hear the data being transmitted. DOV requires special equipment.

→ *Compare*   DUV (Data under Voice)

Downgrading

In the CCITT X.400 Message Handling System (MHS), the process of converting a message from the 1988 MHS version format to a format suitable for an MHS based on the 1984 version of X.400.

Downlink

In telecommunications, a downlink is a communications link between any of the following:

- A mobile base station to a PCS (Personal Communications Service) or other cellular communications end user

- The head end of a cable broadcasting network to a cable subscriber

- An ADSL (asymmetric digital subscriber line) or other *x*DSL service provider to a subscriber

- A satellite to one or more earth stations

→ *Compare*   Uplink

Download

To transfer data, such as a file, from a host computer to a remote machine. For example, the host may be a mainframe or a BBS (bulletin board system) computer. Downloading requires a communications protocol that both the host and recipient can understand and use.

→ *Compare*   Upload

Downsizing

Downsizing refers to the redesign of mainframe-based business applications to create applications capable of running on smaller, less expensive systems, often local area networks (LANs) of PCs. A client/server architecture is the model most often implemented during downsizing.

In moving applications from large computer systems to PCs, it is possible that security, integrity, and overall control will be compromised. Development and training costs for the new system can be high. However, a collection of appropriately configured PCs, networked together, can provide more than ten times the power for the same cost as a mainframe computer supporting remote terminals.

A more accurate term might be *rightsizing*, to match the application requirements of the corporation to the capabilities of the hardware and software systems available.

Downstream Physical Unit (DSPU)

In a ring topology, a DSPU is a device that lies in the direction of travel of packets.

Downtime

A machine or other device that is not functioning is said to be *down*. Downtime is a period during which a computer or other device is not functioning. This is in contrast to *uptime*, during which the machine *is* functioning.

Note that uptime and downtime are not synonymous with availability and unavailability. A device may be unavailable during uptime (for example, because of heavy activity).

DP (Draft Proposal)

For some standards committees, a preliminary version of specifications or standards. The DP is circulated for a limited time, during which comments and critiques are collected by the standards committee.

DPA (Demand Protocol Architecture)

In Microsoft's LAN Manager network operating system, DPA is a feature that makes it possible to load and unload protocol stacks dynamically. This capability makes it possible to support other network environments, such as VINES or NetWare, in the same machine.

DPA was originally added by 3Com to its implementation of LAN Manager, but it has since been added to versions supported by other vendors.

→ *Broader Category* LAN Manager

DPC (Deferred Procedure Call)

In Windows NT and NT Advanced Server, a called function whose task is less important than the currently executing function. As a result, execution of the called function is deferred until higher priority tasks are completed.

DPMI (DOS Protected Mode Interface)

DPMI is an interface specification from Microsoft. The interface is designed to provide DOS extension. By providing this capability, DPMI enables DOS programs to run in protected mode, so that they can make use of extended memory, take advantage of system safeguards afforded in protected mode, and so on.

The data and execution safeguards provided in protected mode allow most programs to run as DOS tasks on their own or under Windows 3.*x*.

DPMI provides enhanced capabilities for 80286 and higher processors.

DPMI was developed partly in response to the older VCPI (Virtual Control Program Interface). DPMI and VCPI are incompatible, so these two interfaces should not be mixed on a network.

→ *Compare* VCPI (Virtual Control Program-Interface)

→ *See Also* DOS Extender; Protected Mode

DQDB (Distributed Queue Dual Bus)

DQDB is a network architecture that has been recommended by the IEEE 802.6 committee for use in metropolitan-area networks (MANs). DQDB has the following characteristics:

- Operates at the bottom two layers of the OSI reference model: the physical and Data-Link layers. Actually, DQDB operates at the Physical layer and at the media-access-control (MAC) *sublayer*, as defined by the IEEE 802.2 committee.

- Uses two buses for the network. Each bus operates in a single direction, and the buses operate in opposite directions. A node on the network may transmit and receive on one or both buses, depending on where the node is located in relation to the bus ends.

- Generally uses fiber-optic cable as the physical medium. Copper cable is generally not used, because it has difficulty supporting both the distances and the bandwidth that may be required for a MAN. This may change, however, as higher-grade copper cable becomes available. (Note that copper cable *is* used in many MANs, but as access cable to connect individual nodes or subnetworks to the MAN bus.)

- Can support circuit-switched voice, data, and video, and can handle synchronous or asynchronous transmissions.

- Provides connection-oriented, connectionless, and isochronous communications services.

- Allocates bandwidth dynamically, using time slots.

- Supports transmission speeds of at least 50Mbps, and will eventually support speeds of about 600Mbps.

- Uses 53-octet slots for transmissions.

The performance of a DQDB configuration is independent of the number of nodes and of the distances involved, which makes DQDB ideal for high-speed transmissions.

DBMS Topology

DQDB uses a dual-bus topology, with the buses transmitting in opposite directions. The first node in each direction is the head of the bus. This node has special responsibilities for the bus, including the task of generating the slots in which data are transmitted.

Since the head node is at the starting end of the bus, all other nodes on the bus are *down the line*, or to move the metaphor (and the bus) to the water, *downstream* from the head node. Conversely, the head node is *up the line* or *upstream* from all the other nodes on the bus. Node positioning is important when controlling access to the network.

The DQDB architecture may use either the "traditional" open bus topology shown in "DQDB with open bus topology," or the looped bus shown in "DQDB with looped bus topology." Because the looped bus topology is easier to reconfigure if a node goes down, it is used more commonly. In fact, when a looped bus is reconfigured to compensate for a lost node, the result is an open bus.

In a looped bus topology, the head node is also the endpoint, or tail, for the bus. While this looks just like a ring topology, the looped bus differs because the head node does not pass on a transmission it receives as the tail. Note also that the same node serves as the head for both buses on a looped bus.

DQDB Structure

The DQDB architecture is described in terms of three layers in the 802.6 specifications, as illustrated in the "Layers in the DQDB architecture."

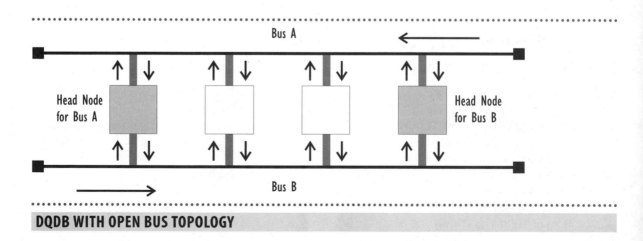

DQDB WITH OPEN BUS TOPOLOGY

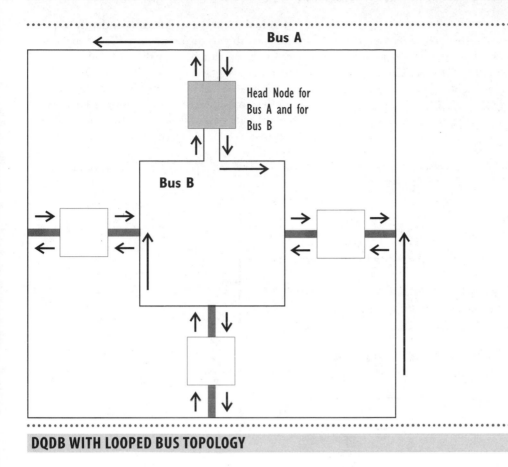

Bus A

Head Node for
Bus A and for
Bus B

Bus B

DQDB WITH LOOPED BUS TOPOLOGY

The DQDB layers are as follows:

Physical layer The lowest layer, which supports several transmission schemes. At its lower end, this layer interfaces to the physical medium; at the upper end, the layer uses a convergence function to get data from the upper layer and to prepare the data for transmission across the medium.

DQDB layer The workhorse layer of the DQDB architecture. It corresponds to the lower half of the OSI reference model's Data-Link layer, or the MAC sublayer as specified by the IEEE 802.2 committee. The DQDB layer can provide services for any of several types of connections. This layer is divided into three sublayers (described later in this article).

Outside layer The third "layer" is not really part of the DQDB architecture, nor is the layer's name official. This level is included in the specifications in order to specify the services that the DQDB layer must be able to provide. The description of required services is quite heterogeneous, largely because the DQDB architecture supports such a variety of connections and transmissions.

D

DQDB Layer Services

To accommodate the requirements of the layers above it, three types of services have been defined for the DQDB layer in the 802.6 specifications: connectionless, connection-oriented, and isochronous.

The connectionless services do not establish a fixed connection before transmitting data. Instead, individual packets are sent independently of each other, possibly by different paths. This type of service might be requested by the LLC sublayer, which makes up the upper half of the Data-Link layer. The MAC convergence function (MCF) does the translation and preparation needed to have the data passed down into the proper form for transmission.

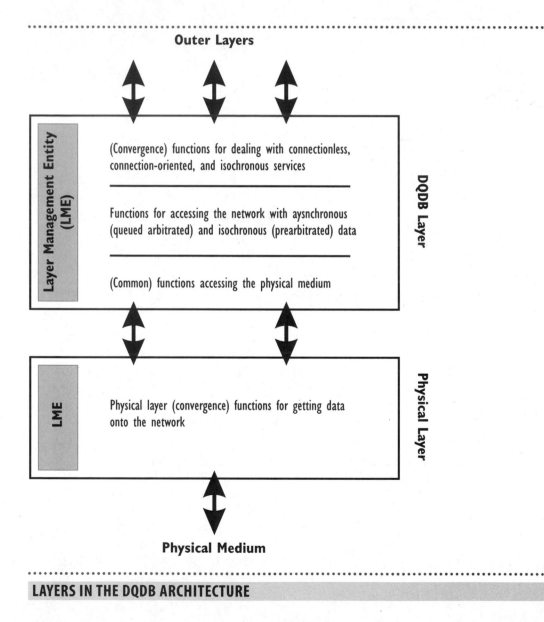

Outer Layers

Layer Management Entity (LME)

(Convergence) functions for dealing with connectionless, connection-oriented, and isochronous services

Functions for accessing the network with aysnchronous (queued arbitrated) and isochronous (prearbitrated) data

(Common) functions accessing the physical medium

DQDB Layer

LME

Physical layer (convergence) functions for getting data onto the network

Physical Layer

Physical Medium

LAYERS IN THE DQDB ARCHITECTURE

The connection-oriented services establish a connection first, then send the data and, finally, break the connection. Because a fixed (if temporary) connection is established, all the data takes the same path. This makes both the sender's and the receiver's jobs a bit easier.

The isochronous services assume a constant transmission pace. Such transmissions are often synchronous, but this is not required.

DQDB Sublayers

The DQDB layer is divided into three sublayers:

- The topmost layer interacts with the "outside" layer; that is, it interacts with the applications that want (or need) to use the DQDB. At this layer, functions are specified and/or defined for the three main types of services (connectionless, connection-oriented, and isochronous) provided by the DQDB layer.

- The middle layer provides functions for arbitrating access to the network. Two types of slots are used: queued arbitrated (QA) and prearbitrated (PA). The QA slots carry asynchronous data from either connectionless or connection-oriented services. The PA slots carry isochronous data.

- The bottom sublayer provides access to the physical medium for both asynchronous and isochronous data. This sublayer also includes functions for controlling the configuration and for serving as the head of the bus.

An MCF is defined for the top DQDB sublayer. This function does the preparations for data using connectionless services. A connection-oriented convergence function (COCF) has been proposed in the 802.6 documents, but has not yet been defined. Similarly, the function needed for handling isochronous data has been proposed but not defined.

DQDB Operation

Information moves around a DQDB network in 53-octet slots, and slots from different nodes are intermingled in the network traffic. This means that nodes need to be able to break higher-layer packets into 52-byte chunks before sending the information. Nodes also must be able to reconstruct a packet from the slots received in a transmission. The 52 bytes will contain pieces of a higher-level packet. The fifty-third byte in a slot is for access control information.

The head node is responsible for creating empty slots and sending these down the line, where the slots will be used by nodes to send their messages. By generating as many slots as needed, the head node can make sure that each node on the bus gets access.

To do this, the head node must know how many slots are needed by the nodes. Suppose a node (N) wants to transmit on one of the buses (let's say bus A). In order to get a slot on bus A, N must indicate—*on bus B*—that N needs a slot. This request will eventually reach the head node for bus A, which will increment a counter that indicates the number of slots A needs to create.

Bus A creates empty slots and sends these down the line. As the slots move down the line, they are taken by the nodes that have requested them. These nodes fill the slots and send them toward their destination. A node will take only the slot it has requested, even if that node needs additional slots since its last request.

There are restrictions built into the slot request and generation process to help ensure that the slots are being allocated fairly and that the architecture's bandwidth is being allocated in a balanced fashion.

Draft International Standard (DIS)

→ *See* DIS (Draft International Standard)

Draft Proposal (DP)

→ *See* DP (Draft Proposal)

DRAM (Dynamic Random Access Memory)

DRAM is a type of chip memory in which information is stored in capacitors, whose charge must be refreshed periodically. This is in contrast to SRAM (static random access memory) in which information is stored differently.

Dynamic RAM is slower but much cheaper than SRAM and is, therefore, much more widely used. Most of the chip memory in a PC (stand-alone machine or network-based workstation) is DRAM. If SRAM chips are used at all, they may be used for cache storage.

→ **Broader Category** Memory

→ **Compare** SRAM (Static Random Access Memory)

DRDA (Distributed Relational Data Architecture)

A distributed database architecture from IBM. DRDA forms the core of the database management capabilities in IBM's SystemView network management package.

Drive

A drive is a data storage location. Drives may be the following:

- Physical, such as floppy disk drives, hard disk drives, or tape drives.

- Logical, such as hard disk partitions or NetWare drives. Logical drives represent organizational entities.

- Virtual, such as RAM disks or virtual disks. These use physical resources to mimic physical drives, but their contents disappear when the computer is turned off.

In the DOS environment, drives are referenced by letters. For example, A: and B: represent floppy disk drives on a PC. In a NetWare network, drives A: through E: represent local drives on a workstation; drives F:, G:, and so on, are logical *network drives*.

→ **See Also** Directory; Drive Mapping

Drive Mapping

The process of assigning a hard disk volume or directories on this volume to a particular logical disk drive is called *drive mapping*, or simply *mapping*. For example, a workstation user might use drive mapping to designate the server's hard disk as logical drive H: (from the workstation's perspective).

Each user can have his or her own set of drive mappings, which can be loaded into the user's working environment when logging on to the network or specified during regular operation.

In NetWare and other operating systems, it is possible to map a drive letter to a particular directory on the server. In effect, this mapping makes the directory the root of the specified drive. Drive mapping gives a user immediate access to the directory and is one way of dealing with path name restrictions (as discussed in the Directory article).

NetWare supports four types of drive mappings:

- Local mappings, which are to local hard disks and floppy drives. By default, drives A: through E: may be used for local mappings.

- Network mappings, which are to volumes and directories on the network. By default, drives F: through Z: may be used for network mappings.

- Network search mappings, which are to directories that contain programs or data files. Users can specify conditions and rules under which search directories will be checked. See the Search Drives article for more information.

- Directory map objects mappings, which allow a Directory map object to reference the location of commonly used files or applications.

Drive mappings can be temporary or permanent in NetWare. Temporary mappings disappear when a session is ended.

Driver

A driver is a program that serves as an interface between two programs or between a program and a hardware component. For example, to ensure that a network interface card (NIC) will work with a network software package, drivers are used.

In Windows NT and NT Advanced Server (NTAS), the term *driver* is used more broadly and also encompasses file systems, such as the file allocation table (FAT) used by DOS and the high performance file system (HPFS) used by OS/2.

Types of Drivers

Drivers can be written for virtually any kind of device or interface, including the following:

- Printers, scanners, disks, monitors, recordable or rewritable CDs (compact discs) or DVDs (digital versatile discs), and other devices

- SCSI, RS-232, RS-422, IDE, and other interfaces

- NICs, such as for Ethernet and Token Ring

Drivers are often specialized; a particular driver may support a single device model for a particular program. However, rather than creating drivers for every model, manufacturers may create a more or less generic driver interface, and then encourage developers to adapt the interface for their products to this generic interface. Vendors may also adapt generic drivers to handle the special features of particular products.

UPDATING DRIVERS

Because the driver program is generally a small piece of software, it's relatively easy to change. For this reason, drivers tend to be updated fairly frequently. Vendors can generally tell you whether their drivers have been updated, and several magazines list driver updates as a regular feature.

Keep your drivers up to date, but make sure you can return to an older driver—in case incompatibilities develop with the newer version.

NIC Driver Interfaces

In local area networking, two generic driver interfaces are widely supported:

- NDIS (Network Driver Interface Specification), developed jointly by Microsoft and 3Com for LAN Manager, but now used for other network packages as well.

- ODI (Open Data-link Interface), an alternative to NDIS developed by Novell for its NetWare products. It is currently less widely used than NDIS, but is nonetheless widely supported.

Both of these represent efforts to provide a general interface between NICs and the higher-level protocols supported in a particular network.

NDIS and ODI provide generic interfaces, but specific drivers for particular adapters are also still used, partly because specific drivers can optimize the performance of the product. Most adapters ship with dozens of drivers.

→ *See Also* NDIS (Network Driver Interface Specification); ODI (Open Data-link Interface)

Drop

An attachment to a horizontal cabling system (for example, through a wallplate). This is generally the point through which a computer or other device is connected to the transmission medium on a network. A drop is also known as a *drop line*.

Drop Box

In an AppleShare server, a term for a folder for which write (Make Changes) but not read privileges are granted. Users can add items to the folder but cannot open the folder or see its contents.

Drop Cable

→ *See* Cable, Drop

Dropout

Temporary loss of the signal in a transmission, such as through malfunction, power loss, or interference.

Drop Set

All the components needed to connect a machine or other component to the horizontal cabling. At a minimum, this includes cable and an adapter or connector.

Drop Side

All the components needed to connect a machine or other component to the patch panel or punchdown block that connects to the distribution frame.

DS (Digital Service)

DS is a communications service that uses digital signaling methods. More specifically, DS represents a telecommunications service in North America, which defines a four-level transmission hierarchy, with increasing bandwidths.

DS uses pulse code modulation (PCM) to encode an analog signal in digital form. The signal is sampled 8000 times per second, and each sample value is encoded in an 8-bit value. The signal transmission uses time division multiplexing (TDM).

DS1–DS4 Levels

DS*x*, (Digital Signal, where *x* is 0, 1, 1C, 2, 3, or 4) represents a hierarchy of channel capacities for digital signals. The hierarchy defines protocols, framing format, and even the signal frequency used at the specified level.

The *DS* in DS0, DS1, and so on, is sometimes expanded to *digital service*. The terms are sometimes written as DS-0, DS-1, and so on.

The data signals are transmitted over T-carrier lines, such as T1 or T3. The higher-capacity channels are based on the 64Kbps DS0 channel. The DS0 channel is based on the 4KHz analog channel used for ordinary voice communications.

The 1.544Mbps DS1 channel is constructed of the smaller DS0 channels. Twenty-four DS0 channels are multiplexed into a single DS1 channel, yielding a 1.536Mbps bandwidth for data. An extra *framing bit* is added to each 192-bit (eight bits per channel × 24 channels) frame. This is known as the 193rd bit, and it represents the extra 8Kbps in the DS1 channel capacity.

Either of two techniques is commonly used to handle framing in DS1 channels: D4 or ESF. The signals in a DS1 channel can be transmitted over T1 lines.

Lower-capacity digital channels are also possible. These channels are also built up by combining DS0 channels, which can be transmitted over fractional T1 (FT1) lines. An FT1 line consists of one or more DS0 channels.

Higher-capacity channels are built by multiplexing lower-bandwidth channels, together with framing and administrative overhead. The overhead bits are transmitted in separate channels, which may have 8, 16, or even 64Kbps bandwidths.

"Digital signal hierarchy for North America" summarizes the digital signal hierarchy as it is defined in North America. The channel configurations are somewhat different in Europe and Asia.

To give you a sense of the relative sizes involved in the DS hierarchy, if a DS0 channel were represented as being an inch thick, a DS4 channel would be wider than a football field.

→ See Also D4 Framing; DACS (Digital Access and Cross-Connect System)

DS (Directory Service)

Directory-related services provide functions for naming, locating, and working with entities (machines, users, or other resources) on a network. Directory services (as defined in the CCITT X.500 specifications and in other models) are provided at the Application layer, as are naming services (as in Novell's NDS and Banyan's StreetTalk Directory).

D

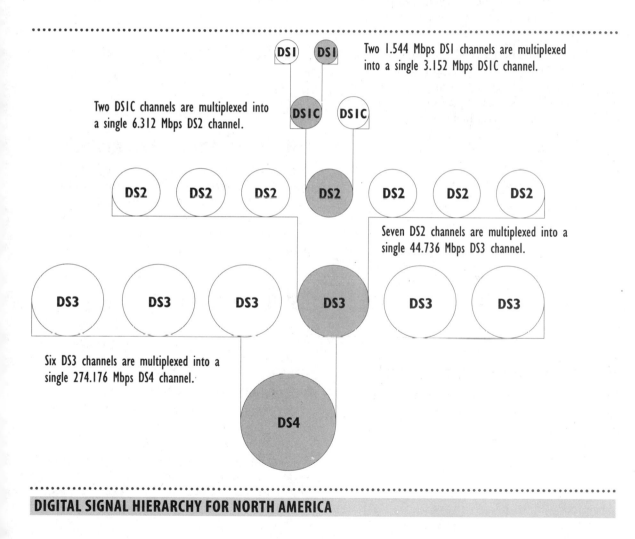

Two 1.544 Mbps DS1 channels are multiplexed into a single 3.152 Mbps DS1C channel.

Two DS1C channels are multiplexed into a single 6.312 Mbps DS2 channel.

Seven DS2 channels are multiplexed into a single 44.736 Mbps DS3 channel.

Six DS3 channels are multiplexed into a single 274.176 Mbps DS4 channel.

DIGITAL SIGNAL HIERARCHY FOR NORTH AMERICA

X.500 is the best-known open directory service. Proprietary directory services include Sun Network Information Service+ (NIS+), Novell Directory Services (NDS), Banyan StreetTalk Directory, and Microsoft Active Directory. These and other proprietary directory services provide either full compatibility with X.500 or at least some means of working with X.500 services.

In the X.500 standard, services are specified, provided, and controlled using the Directory Access Protocol (DAP). Because of the complexity of the functions and services involved, implementing the DAP completely has proven something of a challenge.

To allow the use of the X.500 directory services over the Internet, the Lightweight Directory Access Protocol (LDAP) has been developed. This provides at least basic reading and writing services and simple management functions. Similar functionality is provided by the appropriate protocols for the Domain Name System (DNS) and also for the uniform resource naming and addressing system used on the World Wide Web.

→ **See Also** Active Directory; NDS (Novell Directory Services); StreetTalk; X.500

DSA (Directory Service Area)

In telephony, a term used to describe the calling area covered by a directory service.

DSA (Directory System Agent)

In the CCITT X.500 Directory Services model, software that provides services for accessing, using and, possibly, for updating a directory information base (DIB) or tree (DIT), generally for a single organization.

→ **See Also** X.500

DSA (Distributed Systems Architecture)

An OSI-compliant architecture from Honeywell.

DSC (Data Stream Compatibility)

In IBM's SNA (Systems Network Architecture), a basic, bare-bones printing mode.

→ **Compare** SCS (SNA character string)

DSE (Data Switching Equipment)

Equipment used in a switching network, such as X.25.

DSI (Digital Speech Interpolation)

In digital telecommunications, a strategy for improving the efficiency of a communications channel. DSI works by transmitting during the "quiet" periods that occur in normal conversation. DSI can nearly double the number of voice signals that can be carried on the line.

DSL (Digital Subscriber Line)

DSL is the communications technology that underlies ISDN (Integrated Services Digital Network) and the several variants that make up the xDSL family of services. These include ADSL (asymmetric DSL), RADSL (rate-adaptive DSL), SDSL (symmetric DSL), and VDSL (very high speed DSL), to name just a few.

DSL does what its name suggests: it provides a digital connection for customers or other end users. By using digital signaling methods, both voice and data can be transmitted over the lines, and at much higher speeds than are possible with ordinary modems. For example, the digital subscriber lines for ISDN operate at 192Kbps. Of this bandwidth, 144Kbps are available to provide an ISDN Basic Rate Interface (BRI) for a user. The BRI consists of two 64Kbps B (for bearer) channels and one 16Kbps D (for data or delta) channel. The B channels are used for transmitting data, and the D channel is used for control and signaling purposes. *x*DSL implementations attain even higher speeds for DSL connections.

While direct digital connections between end users will—in all probability—eventually become common, DSL currently can be used only to connect to the Internet or to another network.

→ *See Also*   ADSL (Asymmetric Digital Subscriber Line)

DSLAM (Digital Subscriber Line Access Multiplexer)

In asymmetric digital subscriber line (ADSL) and its various *x*DSL cousins, a DSLAM is an access node that multiplexes many incoming ADSL lines at the service provider's central office (CO). An access node is the termination point—at the CO—of an ADSL local loop between a customer and the CO.

The DSLAM multiplexes these local loops. The multiplexed stream is passed on to a TCP/IP router or possibly to an ATM (Asynchronous Transfer Mode) switch, and is sent on from there to the appropriate service provider (for example, Internet, video-on-demand, and so forth).

→ *See Also*   ADSL (Asymmetric Digital Subscriber Line)

DSMA (Digital Sense Multiple Access) Protocol

→ *See*   Protocol, DSMA (Digital Sense Multiple Access)

DSOM (Distributed System Object Model)

IBM's implementation of the CORBA (Common Object Request Broker Architecture) model from the OMG (Object Management Group).

→ *See Also*   COM (Component Object Model); CORBA (Common Object Request Broker Architecture); DCOM (Distributed Component Object Model)

DSP (Digital Signal Processor)

A device that can extract and process elements from a stream of digital signals.

DSP (Domain Specific Part)

In the OSI reference model, part of the address for the network-layer service access point (NSAP). The DSP is the address within the *domain*, which is the part of the network under the control of a particular authority or organization.

→ *See Also*   SAP (Service Access Point)

DSPU (Downstream Physical Unit)

In a ring topology, a DSPU is a device that lies in the direction of travel of packets.

DSR (Data Set Ready)

A signal from a modem, sent when the modem is ready to operate. In the RS-232C interface, this signal is transmitted on pin 6.

→ *Compare*   DTR (Data Terminal Ready)

D

DSU/CSU (Data Service Unit/Channel Service Unit)

In digital telecommunications, the DSU and CSU are two components of a DCE (data-communications equipment) device. These components provide access to digital services over DDS, T1, and other types of lines.

The DSU performs the following tasks:

- Connects to the DTE (usually a router or remote bridge) through a synchronous serial interface, which is a V.35 or an RS-422 connection; RS-232 connections are also possible for subrate (low-speed) services.

- Formats data for transmission over the digital lines.

- Controls data flow between the network and a CSU.

The CSU, which must be certified by the FCC (Federal Communications Commission) does the following:

- Terminates the long-distance connection at the user's end.

- Processes digital signals for the digital lines.

- May test remote loopback on the lines.

- Serves as a buffer to keep faulty subscriber equipment from bringing down the digital service.

Functionally, the DSU/CSU component is comparable to a modem; each mediates between a digital computing element and a transmission medium. The medium is analog in the case of the modem and digital for the DSU/CSU.

"DSU/CSU devices provide access to digital lines" shows how this component fits into a networking scheme.

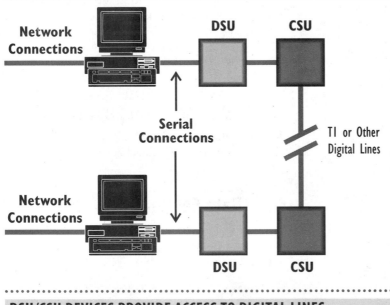

DSU/CSU DEVICES PROVIDE ACCESS TO DIGITAL LINES

DSX1/3 (Digital Signal Cross-Connect Between Levels 1 and 3)

In digital communications, DSX1/3 specifies the interfaces for connecting DS1 and DS3 signals (which entails connecting T-1 and T-3 lines).

DTAM (Document Transfer and Manipulation)

DTAM provides the communication functions for the ITU's (International Telecommunication Union) application-layer Telematic services. Telematic services are communications services other than telephony and telegraphy. These include teletex (basically, souped-up telex), fax transmission, and telewriting (transmission of hand drawing or writing, so that the resulting image is duplicated at the receiving end).

The DTAM specifications cover three *service classes*, which specify—at a very general level—the actions allowed on documents. The service classes are *bulk transfer* (BT), *document manipulation* (DM), and *bulk transfer and manipulation* (BTM). Each service class is defined by more primitive functional units and by communication support functions.

To transfer documents, DTAM uses either application level support functions or session layer services. In the latter case—known as *transparent mode bulk transfer*—DTAM bypasses the Presentation layer and sends the material directly to the session layer. This is allowed only in cases where the received document just needs to be sent on to another location. Since the recipient acts as an intermediary, no presentation of the document is necessary. Transparent mode is allowed only for Group 4 faxes, which are not yet widely used.

In *normal mode*, DTAM uses the services of the ACSE (Association Control Service Element), the RTSE (Reliable Transfer Service Element), or the ROSE (Remote Operation Service Element)—depending on the required task.

Documents that the DTAM can handle must conform to the *ODA* (Open Document Architecture) standard. This standard is used for the interchange of compound documents—that is, of documents that may contain graphics, video, or sound in addition to text.

The DTAM protocols provide the means by which two DTAM service elements (DTAM-SEs)—or rather two applications using DTAM—communicate. The communication support functions help pass packets (known as PDUs, or protocol data units) up or down in the OSI hierarchical model. "DTAM model" illustrates the hierarchical as well as the lateral relationships.

So far, the DTAM protocol supports over a dozen different types of PDUs. For example, the DINQ (D-initiate request) PDU is used for the Association use control functional unit. This unit is the one that controls whether there is any association between DTAM entities at either end of the connection.

Since several of the functional units have yet to be finalized, there's a good chance that more PDU types will be defined.

→ *Primary Sources* ITU recommendations T.431, T.432, and T.433. T.62bis provides guidelines for transmissions that bypass the Presentation layer and communicate directly with the session layer.

→ *See Also* ACSE; ODA; ROSE; RTSE

DTC (Distributed Transaction Coordinator)

The DTC is a component in Microsoft Internet Information Server (IIS). It is used by the transaction server to handle components that reside on or that use other machines.

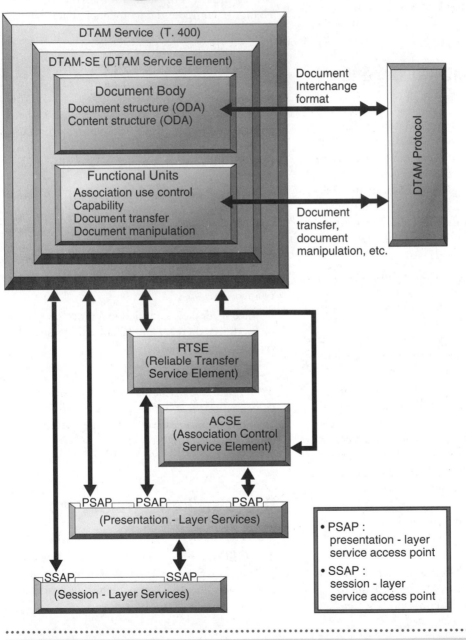

DTAM MODEL

DTD (Document Type Definition)

Various markup languages—for example, the venerable SGML (Standard Generalized Markup Language) and the upstart XML (eXtensible Markup Language)— use a DTD to describe the structure of a document and the elements used in that document. The DTD specifies each element that may appear in a document, attributes associated with each element, and the contexts in which an element may appear.

These elements may relate to document layout (headings, lists, etc.), appearance (fonts, margins, etc.), or structure (sections, subsections, etc.). DTDs can be written to specific document types (such as articles, books, catalogs, etc.); or they can be written for a generic document, which is designed to cover any kind of creation from a laundry list to a novel or to the IRS code.

The advantage of DTDs is that they provide a modular presentation of the elements allowed in a particular document. By separating the document definition from the contents it becomes much easier to change the document format by changing the DTD.

The specification for the widely used HTML (Hypertext Markup Language) is essentially a DTD for a Web document. The language specification defines what is allowed in an HTML file and when it is allowed.

DTDs are required for SGML files and are optional—but strongly recommended—for XML documents.

→ *See Also* HTML (Hypertext Markup Language); SGML (Standard Generalized Markup Language); XML (eXtensible Markup Language)

DTE (Data Terminal Equipment)

In telecommunications, a terminal, a PC, or another device that can communicate with a DCE (data communications equipment) device. For example, in analog telecommunications, a modem serves as a DCE and provides access to the telephone lines; in digital communications, a DSU/CSU provides access to the lines for a DTE.

DTMF (Dual Tone Multifrequency)

DTMF is a telephone technology that makes it possible to create 16 different tones using eight frequencies. These 16 tones suffice to provide a unique tone for each of the 12 base buttons on a Touch-Tone telephone, as well as for up to four additional keys.

Refer the illustration "Frequencies for buttons on a Touch-Tone telephone" shows how the frequencies are assigned to the buttons.

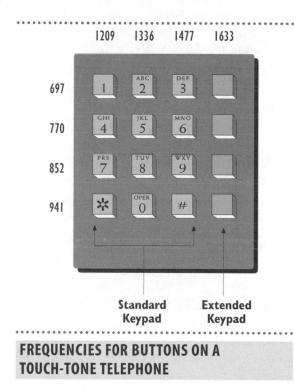

FREQUENCIES FOR BUTTONS ON A TOUCH-TONE TELEPHONE

DTR (Data Terminal Ready)

In the RS-232 interface, a control signal—generally from a modem—used to indicate that a device (for example, a computer) is ready to send and receive data. In an RS-232C, this signal is sent on pin 20.

→ *Compare* DSR (Data Set Ready)

DTR (Dedicated Token Ring)

DTR is a variant of the standard Token Ring technology. In DTR, a direct connection is possible between a node and the token ring switch. Such a node could then make use of the entire network bandwidth, since there are no other nodes that can share it. ASTRAL (Alliance for Strategic Token Ring Advancement and Leadership) is supporting both DTR and Token Ring switches. The IEEE 802.5 committee—which is the working group for Token Ring topology—will wait and see whether it proves viable and becomes widely used before committing to the new technology.

→ *Broader Category* Token Ring

DTS (Digital Termination Service)

In telecommunications, a service by which private networks can get access to carrier networks using digital microwave equipment within a frequency band allocated by the FCC (Federal Communications Commission) for this purpose.

DUA (Directory User Agent)

In the CCITT X.500 Directory Services model, a program that provides access to the directory services. The DUA mediates between an end user or a client program and a directory system agent (DSA), which provides the requested services.

→ *See Also* X.500

Dual-Attachment Concentrator (DAC)

→ *See* DAC (Dual-Attachment Concentrator)

Dual-Attachment Station (DAS)

→ *See* DAS (Dual-Attachment Station)

Dual Cable System

A broadband wiring arrangement in which separate cables are used for transmission and receiving. Such a wiring system may be used, for example, in a 10Broad36 broadband Ethernet or a broadband (IEEE 802.4) token-bus architecture.

→ *Compare* Split Cable System

DUAL (Diffusing Update Algorithm)

The Enhanced Interior Gateway Routing Protocol (E-IGRP) is used to route packets between intermediate routers—that is, between routers that are connected to other routers, rather than to clients. The E-IGRP uses the DUAL to eliminate or avoid routing loops and to update the routing tables of neighboring routers after sending a packet on the next hop of its journey.

The algorithm works by sending a packet to one of its neighbors and then evaluating the costs and potential consequences associated with this move. If the evaluation is favorable—has a lower cost than the previous state—the appropriate routers update their routing information to reflect the new path. These updates will then diffuse through the affected routers. If the selected path is higher cost, the router tries a different path until it finds a less costly one or until all the possibilities are exhausted and no better path has been found. In that case, the router will query its neighbors in an effort to find a cheaper path.

→ **Broader Category** Routing

Dual Homing

In networking, a configuration in which a node can be connected to the network through more than one physical link. If one link fails, the station can still communicate via the other link.

In FDDI (Fiber Distributed Data Interface), dual homing refers to the fact that an FDDI card can be connected to two FDDI concentrators. The card must be in a server, bridge, or router. This redundancy gives the FDDI connection a fault tolerance. One of the connections will be active, but the other will be ready if the first connection breaks.

Dual In-Line Package (DIP) Switch

→ **See** DIP (Dual In-Line Package) Switch

Dual Tone Multifrequency (DTMF)

→ **See** DTMF (Dual Tone Multifrequency)

Duplex

In telecommunications, the term duplex is used in two different ways:

- In most telecommunications-related contexts, the term is used to indicate bidirectional communications. Used in this way, the term is in contrast to *simplex*, which refers to one-directional communication. In *full-duplex* communications, transmissions can go in both directions simultaneously; in *half-duplex* mode, transmissions can go in

either direction, but in only one direction at a time. The term is also used in this way when speaking of communications in (Ethernet) networks.

- In the variants of digital subscriber line (DSL) technology—which are known collectively as *x*DSL—the term is used to indicate communications that are the same speed in both directions. Used in this way, the term is in contrast to *asymmetrical*.

→ **Broader Category** Telecommunications

Duration

→ **See** Call Duration

Duty Cycle

In an electrical signal, the proportion of a time period during which the signal is on, which is when it represents a bit value of 1.

DUV (Data under Voice)

In telecommunications, a strategy for transmitting voice and data over the same line.

→ **Compare** DOV (Data over Voice)

DVD (Digital Versatile Disc)

DVD—also known as digital video disc in some contexts—is a promising, up-and-coming storage and recording technology that has been up-and-coming for several years, and that has been making promises during that entire time. There are indications, however, that the technology may finally be getting on track—except, perhaps, for the format battle that is going on with respect to rewritable DVD discs.

Essentially, DVD technology is the upscale successor to CD (compact disc) technology. DVD uses a laser recording technique, like CD technology, but uses a laser with a shorter wavelength. This is one of the reasons why DVD technology supports storage capacities from 4 to 30 times the 660MB capacity of CDs.

DVDs can store 2.6GB or more on a single-sided disc, and twice that (or more) on a double-sided disc. Since the DVD surface is designed to allow two layers of recording, such discs will eventually be able to store over 10GB on a disc. (In fact, the expectation is that it will be possible to eke out some extra capacity, and DVD technology is eventually expected to support up to 17GB per disc—assuming, of course, that DVD is not leapfrogged by some newer technology.)

Because of its very high storage capacity, DVDs can deliver high-quality video and sound—provided the DVD player is supported by the proper accoutrements (top-notch speakers, high-resolution displays, fast MPEG decoder hardware, and a fast machine). Unfortunately, the many possibilities afforded by this rich technology also provide many opportunities for incompatibilities or for other things to go wrong. Furthermore, there is still a rather sparse selection of software available for controlling DVD players and getting the most out of them. As a result, most of the DVD-based products currently available are movies. Fortunately for PC users, however, DVD drives can read CDs.

DVD drives generally require a decoder card to convert the MPEG-2 video stream into an uncompressed form for viewing. Depending on how this stream gets to your PC, there may be incompatibilities between the DVD hardware and your graphics card.

If the video stream is merged with the graphics signal after the signal has gone through the graphics card, incompatibilities are unlikely, since the graphics card doesn't need to deal with the video stream. This type of merging is known as *video overlay*.

In contrast, if the video stream is fed into the graphics card for processing, incompatibilities can arise, particularly with older graphics cards. This is because *video inlay*, as this processing method is called, requires the graphics card to support the use of linear memory addressing. Most newer cards support this, but many older cards do not. In some cases, however, support for this addressing scheme can be added through drivers.

Similarly, DVDs can contain movie-theater quality audio, encoded in Dolby Digital (formerly known as AC-3 Surround Sound). To some extent, sound cards can try to approximate the 3-D effects of Surround Sound in software and over the speakers attached to your PC. Most sound cards can handle the digital AC-3 stream and can integrate this signal from the decoder card with the PC sound signals. However, to do this, the decoder card must be connected to the PC's sound card. For some DVD drives, the PC's speakers must also be connected to the decoder card in order to take full advantage of the 3-D quality of the AC-3 stream.

Many incompatibilities will disappear as specifications evolve and as hardware manufacturers respond to this evolution.

DVD Variants

The following variants on DVD technology are currently available or are expected to be available by 1999.

DVD-Video

This is primarily a consumer technology and is intended to deliver video with high-quality sound. The consumer DVD drives that are designed for these discs cannot read any of the PC-based DVD formats (in particular, DVD-ROM).

DVD-ROM

This is the basic DVD technology. It provides for read-only discs with a capacity of 4.7GB on each side. The DVD specification is in its third version (DVD-3). DVD-1 was mainly a source of frustration and confusion because of hardware incompatibilities with other PC components and, in some cases, between particular DVD discs and drives from particular vendors or from other countries. Also, the Media Control Interface (MCI) tools available for programming DVD devices were inadequate to the task, and developers were unable to create products that would run reliably in all configurations. In a somewhat rare occurrence, MCI capabilities were actually scaled back, and developers were asked to work with tools that were weaker, but that had the advantages of robustness and compatibility.

Many of the hardware problems were ironed out in DVD-2, although there were still difficulties. For one thing, the MCI programming interface was replaced by Microsoft's superior DirectShow multimedia programming tools. Also, DVD-2 drives included a second, yellow laser to read CD-ROM, CD-R, and CD-RW discs, which are recorded using a yellow laser.

DVD-3 drives offer mainly speed enhancement, with the greatest gains being in the speed at which the drive can read CDs. For example, a DVD-3 drive can read DVDs at a 4× rate (about 5.7MBs) and can read CDs at 24×. The CD speed sounds very impressive, but it actually leads to only minimal performance gains. One reason for this is that most programs on CD are written for 2× or 4× drives, and there is actually not much gained by speed beyond 8× or so.

Access times for DVD-ROM drives are comparable to those for CD-ROM drives—about 100—150 milliseconds. Transfer speeds for DVD-ROM drives are given in terms of a base rate (1×) of 1.385KBs. DVD-2 drives support 2× and DVD-3 drives support 4× transfer rates. A DVD-3 drive can read a CD at about 24× the CD rate of 150KBs, which is about 3.6MBs.

DVD-ROM drives can read CD-ROM, CD-R, CD-RW, DVD video, and DVD-ROM. DVD-ROM drives should be able to read discs in the DVD-R/W format being developed by Pioneer

and expected to be available by mid-1999. DVD-ROM drives *cannot* read DVD-RAM or DVD+RW discs.

DVD-R

DVD-R (for recordable) is a write-once technology that is intended for development and premastering use. DVD-R discs can hold 3.95GB on each side, and this capacity is eventually intended to be 4.7GB per side. DVD-R discs are laid out in the UDF (Universal Disc Format), just like their CD-R counterparts. Discs created using DVD-R can be read by DVD-ROM drives.

DVD-RAM

DVD-RAM (for DVD random access memory) is a technology for recording once onto a blank DVD. This technology uses a red laser in the 635 to 650nm range to burn tiny holes into the disc's surface. With a more powerful laser than a CD-ROM drive, DVD-RAM can write almost 2.7GB on each side of a disc. By the end of 1999, DVD-RAM manufacturers hope to increase the capacity of a DVD-RAM disc to 4.7GB per side, just like a standard DVD-ROM disc.

DVD-RAM drives use constant linear velocity (CLV) technology for recording and playback. This makes it possible to deliver data at a constant rate, which makes DVD-RAM well suited for delivering video.

However, DVD-RAM discs can only be read by another DVD-RAM drive, and sometimes even that doesn't work. The disc contents are quite fragile, and susceptible even to fingerprints and smudges. As a result, DVD-RAM discs must be kept in a nonremovable Type 1 case, or cartridge. This also makes them physically incompatible with ordinary DVD drives.

For this reason, and also because of the way data are written on DVD-RAM discs, a DVD-ROM drive cannot read discs created with DVD-RAM. The next generation of DVD-RAM technology is expected to support a Type 2 case, which allows removal of the disc. These discs will then be

D

playable in specially adapted DVD-ROM drives. (Only one-sided DVD-RAM discs will be removable, however, so the compatibility in this regard between the DVD-ROM and DVD-RAM technologies will still be limited.)

However, a DVD-RAM drive can read all the CD formats mentioned for DVD-ROM. The DVD-RAM drive can also read DVD video and DVD-ROM discs, as well as being able to read and write DVD-RAM discs.

DVD+RW

DVD+RW (for DVD rewritable) is an alternate rewritable DVD technology. Unlike DVD-RAM, which can do only a one-time write on a disc and which must write the entire disc in a single session, DVD+RW discs can be written a little at a time—for example, just by dragging files to the disc. Moreover, the discs can be reused because the material on the discs can be erased (actually, burned off with a laser). This is possible because the DVD+RW specifications support packet writes, which allows the disc to be filled in packet-sized chunks. DVD+RW technology supports up to 3GB on each side of the disc. Both DVD-RAM and DVD+RW use the Universal Disc Format (UDF) when writing discs. (In contrast, older CD technologies use the ISO 9660 file system. UDF-compatible drives, however, can read ISO 9660 discs.)

DVD+RW uses constant angular velocity (CAV) for data storage and retrieval. This means that the disc spins at a constant rate, which means that more data can be written to or read from the outer tracks than from the tracks near the inside of the disc. This makes DVD+RW technology suitable for data storage purposes.

Whereas DVD-RAM writes its content in a nonstandard tracking layout, DVD+RW writes material in the same way as DVD-ROM discs are written. Because of this, the next generation of DVD-ROM drives should be able to read DVD+RW discs. Currently, neither DVD-RAM nor DVD-ROM drives can read DVD+RW discs.

In contrast, a DVD+RW drive can read any of the CD formats, as well as DVD video and DVD-ROM discs. A DVD+RW drive cannot read a DVD-RAM disc. The proponents of DVD+RW technology hope to enable DVD+RW drives also to write CD-R discs.

DVD-R/W

DVD-R/W (for DVD-read/write) is a high-end rewritable DVD technology from Pioneer. Like DVD+RW, Pioneer's technology supports random access reading, writing, and erasing. DVD-R/W discs will hold 4.7GB on each side. The disc surfaces will have a higher reflectivity, which will make them easier for DVD-ROM drives to read. However, this will also make the discs less robust. Whereas DVD+RW discs can be rewritten up to 10,000 times, DVD-R/W discs will survive only about 1000 rewrites.

In fact, DVD-R/W will be compatible only with DVD-ROM drives. DVD-R/W drives will not be able to read or write discs for CD-ROM, DVD-RAM, or DVD+RW.

DVD-R/W is expected to be available by the second half of 1999. Since drives are expected to cost several thousand dollars, this technology will most likely be used for creating DVD-ROM discs in a manufacturing or distribution setting.

MMVF

The MMVF (for Multimedia Video Format) is a technology developed by NEC, and intended—as its name suggests—primarily for video data. MMVF discs will hold 5.2GB on each side. This capacity is desirable for certain markets because it will hold two full hours of video.

MMVF discs will be compatible with DVD-ROM drives, but little is known about compatibility with other DVD technologies or with CD technologies.

→ **Broader Category** Storage

→ **Compare** CD (Compact Disc)

DWDM (Dense Wave Division Multiplexing)

DWDM is an optical communications technology that multiplexes light signals of different wavelengths (and, hence, of different frequencies) along a single optical fiber. Each wavelength (also known as a lambda) is a separate communications channel and can support a bandwidth of up to 2.5Gbps. Currently, about two dozen channels can be multiplexed, for a throughput of up to 60Gbps. Eventually, this technology is expected to support up to 128 channels per fiber—for throughputs of several hundred Gbps.

DWDM is actually an extension of WDM (wave division multiplexing), although the demarcation point between WDM and DWDM has yet to be officially specified. DWDM is currently used mainly for long-distance connections and is expected to be used for medium-distance communications also.

Dynamic Addressing

In an AppleTalk network, dynamic addressing refers to a strategy by which nodes automatically pick unique addresses. A new node keeps trying addresses until it finds one that is not already claimed by another node. Dynamic addressing is also referred to as *dynamic node addressing*.

Dynamic addressing works as follows:

- The node selects a valid address at random and sends an *enquiry control packet* to that address.

- If the address belongs to a node, the node responds with an *acknowledge control packet*. The new node then selects another address at random and repeats the process.

- If the address does not belong to a node, the enquiring node takes it as the node's new address.

→ *Broader Category* AppleTalk

Dynamically Assigned Socket (DAS)

→ *See* DAS (Dynamically Assigned Socket)

Dynamic Configuration

In networking, a system capability in which the file server can allocate memory as needed, subject to availability, while the network is running. Dynamic reconfiguration enables the server to allocate more resources (such as buffers, tables, and so on) as necessary in order to avoid congestion or overload on the network.

Dynamic Data Exchange (DDE)

→ *See* DDE (Dynamic Data Exchange)

Dynamic HTML (DHTML)

→ *See* DHTML (Dynamic HTML)

Dynamic Link Library (DLL)

→ *See* DLL (Dynamic Link Library)

Dynamic Random Access Memory (DRAM)

→ *See* DRAM (Dynamic Random Access Memory)

Dynamic Routing

In various networking environments, automatic rerouting of data transmissions in order to maximize throughput or to balance traffic on transmission channels. Routing decisions are based on

D

available and acquired data about network traffic patterns. Dynamic routing is also known as *dynamic adaptive routing*.

Dynamic Web Page

A dynamic Web page is an HTML (Hypertext Markup Language) file that is created by a Web server when a browser or other program requests it. The instructions for creating a dynamic Web page may be specified in a CGI (Common Gateway Interface) program or by some other type of script file. In Windows-based machines, ASP (Active Server Pages) scripts or applications in the form of DLLs (dynamic-link libraries) using the ISAPI (Internet Server Application Programming Interface) can also be used to create dynamic Web pages.

A browser can request a dynamic Web page in any of the following ways:

- By activating a script directly from the browser. To do this, type the script's URL (Uniform Resource Locator) into the browser's address field, including values for any parameters the script will need.

- By activating a script through a hypertext link in an HTML document. This allows an HTML file to call another, dynamic one. This is arguably the most common way of requesting a dynamic Web page.

- By activating a script from an HTML form. This method lets you pass more complex parameters than a hypertext link could handle.

Dynamic Web pages are useful if the contents to be presented are likely to change or if the material to be included may vary, depending on the context or on the user requesting the page. For example, a Web site may show a customized Web page to a user. The contents will be geared to the user's special interests—as determined by past search or buying activities, by user responses to a survey, or by other information about the user.

In addition to parameters passed to it, the server building a dynamic Web page can get information from cookies (text stored on the user's machine during previous visits), surveys, or information brokers (companies that sell various types of information—both public and personal and, in some cases, illegally obtained).

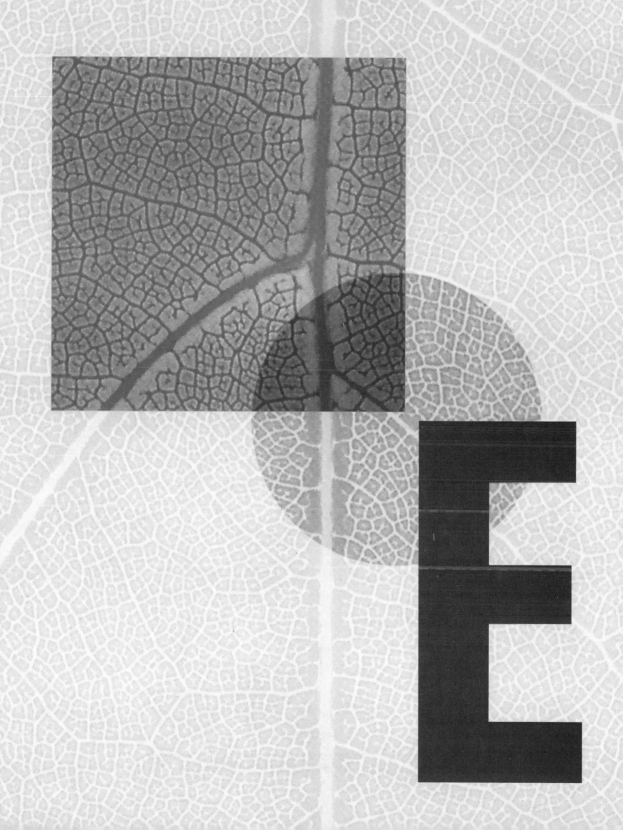

E

E1 Carrier

In digital telecommunications, E1 is a carrier channel configuration defined by the CCITT and used in Europe, Mexico, and South America. Like the T carrier channels (T1, T2, and so on) defined in North America, the E1 carrier channel is built up of 64Kbps voice channels. See the DS (Digital Service) article for a discussion of how the T-carrier channels are defined.

The E1 carrier is defined as 30 64Kbps voice channels and 2 64Kbps signaling channels. In ISDN B and D channel terminology, this type of carrier is known as 30B+2D. The E1 carrier has a bandwidth of 2.048Mbps.

E1 links can be multiplexed into higher-capacity carriers. The illustration "Hierarchy of E1-based digital carriers" shows the E1 carrier hierarchy, which is analogous to the T1 hierarchy defined for digital communications in North America, Australia, and Japan. Because the hierarchy also allocates channels for link management and signaling, the data rates are higher than the number of 64Kbps channels indicates.

→ **Broader Category** Digital Communication

→ **Compare** T1 Carrier

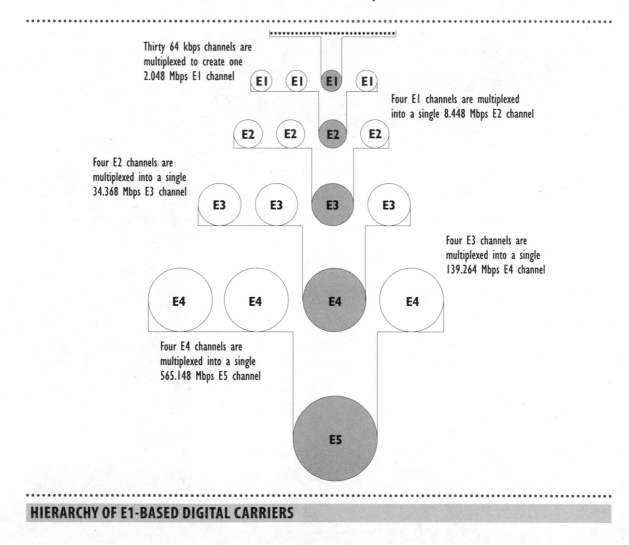

Thirty 64 kbps channels are multiplexed to create one 2.048 Mbps E1 channel

Four E1 channels are multiplexed into a single 8.448 Mbps E2 channel

Four E2 channels are multiplexed into a single 34.368 Mbps E3 channel

Four E3 channels are multiplexed into a single 139.264 Mbps E4 channel

Four E4 channels are multiplexed into a single 565.148 Mbps E5 channel

HIERARCHY OF E1-BASED DIGITAL CARRIERS

E3 Carrier

In digital telecommunications, E3 is a carrier channel configuration created by multiplexing 16 E1 channels—each with a 2.048Mbps bandwidth—and control channels. This yields an effective throughput of 34.368Mbps of combined data and overhead bits.

→ *See Also* E1 Carrier

Early Token Release (ETR)

→ *See* ETR (Early Token Release)

EARN (European Academic and Research Network)

A European network that provides file transfer and e-mail (electronic mail) services for universities and research institutions.

Earth Station

The ground-based portion of a satellite communications system is called an *earth station* or a *ground station*. The station consists of an antenna and receiver (or transceiver) that are in communication with a satellite in geosynchronous orbit, as in the illustration "Satellite and earth stations."

A satellite communicates with earth stations on the ground. Under certain conditions and with certain terrains, two earth stations may need to use a satellite to communicate with each other. Signals can be beamed from an earth station to the satellite and from there to the destination node (another earth station). These communications services can be leased from various companies. For long distances, the prices are competitive with earth-based connections (such as leased or public lines).

The size of the antenna required to receive signals at an earth station depends on the transmission frequency. For 19.2Kbps lines, an antenna of about 1.2 to 3 meters (4 to 10 feet) in diameter is sufficient. For faster speeds (such as the 1.544Mbps speed of T1 lines), larger antennas are required. These are harder to install and maintain, and may require special permits.

E

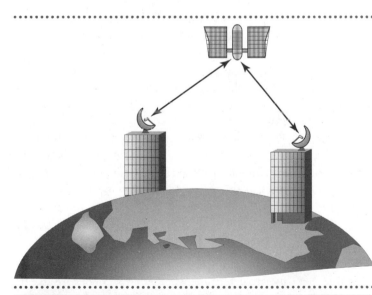

SATELLITE AND EARTH STATIONS

EBCDIC (Extended Binary Coded Decimal Interchange Code)

EBCDIC (pronounced "eb-se-dic") is an 8-bit character encoding scheme used on IBM-mainframes and minicomputers. EBCDIC is an alternative to the ASCII encoding scheme, which is used on PCs.

E-Business

→ *See* Electronic Commerce

ECB (Electronic Cookbook)

An operating mode for the Data Encryption Standard.

→ *See* DES (Data Encryption Standard)

ECC (Error Correction Code)

In digital communications, a term applied (sometimes incorrectly) to any of several types of codes used to detect or correct errors that may arise during transmission.

→ *See* Error Detection and Correction

Echo

As a verb, echo refers to the display of typed text on the screen. Other definitions discuss the term in particular contexts, such as electrical signaling.

Echo Cancellation

When a signal (let's call it *a2b*) is sent over electrical wire from one node (A) to another (B), that signal may bounce back from B toward A. This is known as an echo (let's call this *a2be*). Because of echo, a transmission from B to A (let's call this *b2a*) will

consist of both the information being sent from B to A (that is, the content of *b2a*) and also any echo from the previous *a2b* signal (that is, *a2be*). Echo cancellation is a process by which such a signal echo is subtracted out from a received digital signal. Subtracting out *a2b* from a received *b2a* signal effectively cancels the echo (*a2be*) so that only the content of B's transmission remains.

Echo cancellation is necessary if transmissions go in both directions over the same wires, and if the transmissions use the same frequency range. The use of frequency division multiplexing (FDM) will not eliminate echo, but it will make its effects more negligible.

Echo, Electrical

In electrical transmissions, an *echo* is a signal that "bounces off" the destination station (or an intermediate station) and is reflected back toward its source. The echo is a weaker version of the original signal, and it will interfere with any incoming signal, which can lead to noise and transmission errors.

An echo can occur if the transmission lines are not properly terminated or if there is an electrical mismatch (for example, in impedance levels) between the sending and receiving stations.

To eliminate the disruptive effect of an echo, a device called an *echo canceler* can be used. This device makes a copy of the echo and superimposes a displaced copy on the echo in order to cancel the echo signal and remove it from the transmission lines.

An echo suppressor can also be used to eliminate echo signals. An echo suppressor does the same thing as an echo canceler, but works differently.

Echo/Echo Reply

In networking environments, echo signals can be used to determine whether target nodes are able to receive and acknowledge transmissions. The echo signal is sent out, and the sender waits for an acknowledgment.

The method provides a simple mechanism for checking network connections. With this scheme, a node sends an Echo packet to a destination to determine whether the destination is connected. If the destination is connected and able to communicate, it responds with an Echo Reply packet.

This echoing strategy is quick and dirty, but only minimally informative. Furthermore, packet delivery may be unreliable, because most Echo/Echo Reply schemes are transmitted at the Network layer, which may not guarantee packet delivery. One way to increase reliability is to repeat the echo signal a number of times to test the connection. The proportion of trials that are successful will shed light on the reliability of the connection.

The error-signal strategy for simple network monitoring is used in several network protocols, including ICMP (Internet Control Message Protocol), AppleTalk, XNS (Xerox Network Services), and Novell's IPX (Internet Packet Exchange).

Most network management packages use more powerful protocols, such as SNMP or CMIS/CMIP for monitoring network activity. See the SNMP (Simple Network Management Protocol) and CMIS (Common Management Information Services) articles for more information about these protocols.

ECL (Emitter-Coupled Logic)

A logic scheme for very high-speed digital circuitry. Compare ECL with CMOS (complementary metal-oxide semiconductor) and TTL (transistor-transistor logic).

ECMA (European Computer Manufacturers Association)

An association that provides technical committees for other standards organizations, such as the ISO (International Standardization Organization) and the ITU (International Telecommunications Union), formerly named the CCITT (Consultative Committee for International Telegraphy and Telephony).

ECMAScript

ECMAScript is the name for the official scripting language adopted by the European Computer Manufacturers Association in 1997. ECMAScript is based primarily on Netscape's JavaScript, with more limited influence from Microsoft's JScript variant. However, ECMAScript has capabilities that extend beyond both variants.

→ *See Also* JavaScript; JScript

→ *Compare* VBScript

ECML (Electronic Commerce Modeling Language)

ECML provides an open format for representing information in electronic commerce, or e-commerce, transactions. The lack of a common representation method has been a major obstacle to the growth of e-commerce. This is one reason why many of the major players in e-commerce recently agreed to support ECML—even though many of these corporations have developed their own proprietary representations. ECML can be used to provide a common format for e-commerce data, which are often stored in data objects known as e-wallets (and also as electronic or digital wallets).

Currently, such e-commerce data may be in any of a dozen or so different formats—depending on which particular "standard" is used by the merchant with whom a customer is doing business. This means that potential customers may need to provide information in several different forms when doing business with different Web merchants. Format incompatibility may also make it infeasible for some merchants to exchange data.

E

ECML makes it possible for such merchants to communicate by providing a common set of fields and data representations. This also makes it easier for customers because they can enter their information once, and then use this information for any subsequent Web purchases from merchants who support ECML.

This is because a customer's e-wallet information can be stored—in encrypted form, naturally—on the customer's machine, on a machine at the customer's financial institution, or on some other trusted host. Any time the customer wants to make a purchase over the Internet, the customer merely has to make the information in the e-wallet available. ECML helps to ensure that merchants will be able to read this information.

→ **Broader Category** Electronic Commerce

→ **See Also** E-Wallet

ECN (Explicit Congestion Notification)

In frame-relay transmissions, ECN is a mechanism for indicating that there is traffic congestion on the network. Such congestion can be indicated in either or both of two bit values in a packet header:

- The BECN (Backward Explicit Congestion Notification) bit is set in frame-relay headers moving in the direction opposite the congestion, and serves to warn source nodes that congestion is occurring "down the line."

- The FECN (Forward Explicit Congestion Notification) bit is set in frame-relay headers to warn a destination node that there is congestion.

"Use of ECN bits to signal congestion" shows how these bits are used for signaling if there is congestion around node B.

→ **Broader Category** Frame Relay

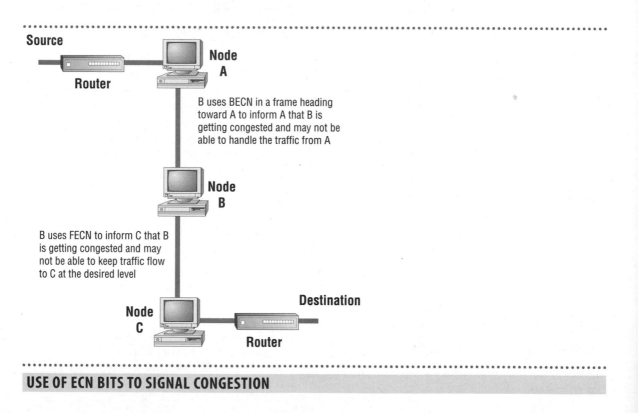

Source

Router

Node A

B uses BECN in a frame heading toward A to inform A that B is getting congested and may not be able to handle the traffic from A

Node B

B uses FECN to inform C that B is getting congested and may not be able to keep traffic flow to C at the desired level

Node C

Destination

Router

USE OF ECN BITS TO SIGNAL CONGESTION

ECNE (Enterprise Certified NetWare Engineer)

A title given to people who have successfully met the requirements for CNE (Certified NetWare Engineer) and who pass several additional courses and tests in order to be able to troubleshoot and operate enterprise-wide networks.

In addition to being a CNE, ECNE candidates must demonstrate mastery of advanced concepts related to the NetWare operating system (either version 3.11, 4.*x*, or 5.*x*—depending on the candidate's specialization) and of topics selected from various electives. Elective areas include such topics as Internetworking products, UnixWare, and NetWare programming.

→ *See Also* CNA, CNE, CNI

E-Commerce

→ *See* Electronic Commerce

ECTP (Ethernet Configuration Test Protocol)

→ *See* Protocol, ECTP (Ethernet Configuration Test Protocol)

ED (End Delimiter)

A field in a token-ring token or data frame. ED indicates the end of a token or data frame.

→ *See* Token Ring

Edge Device

An edge device is a network node (for example, a hub, switch, or router) with one or more user interfaces. That is, an edge device is connected to one or more end users and also to the network. Edge devices are in contrast to backbone devices, which are network nodes that are connected only to other network nodes.

The name is also used for a device that connects directly to an ATM (Asynchronous Transfer Mode) network.

→ *Compare* Backbone Device

EDI (Electronic Data Interchange)

EDI provides specifications for business transactions that are done electronically—for example, on a network or an internetwork. EDI standards specify the type of information that needs to be available or exchanged for various types of transactions. The standards also specify the format this information must have.

Originally developed for use in mainframe environments, EDI has long been quite expensive to implement. Despite this, there were almost 250,000 EDI subscribers—that is, companies that could create and use EDI-compliant forms and services—in 1998. That number is expected to reach over 650,000 by 2002.

One factor that will help fuel this growth rate is the increasing availability of EDI applications that are Internet enabled. This will help decrease the costs of implementing EDI capabilities, which will make EDI a feasible option for smaller businesses.

EDI Services

EDI services can translate data into the appropriate formats, and can send and receive such formats. EDI services and standards support multiple protocols and multiple platforms. For example, EDI services may run on mainframes, minicomputers, or PCSs; the services may run under VMS, MVS, UNIX, Windows, etc. Data can be transmitted using various protocols, including the ITU's (International Telecommunication Union, formerly the CCITT) X.400 message handling systems.

EDI activities are broken down into transaction sets and functional groups. A *transaction set* consists of data that is exchanged between parties to produce an interchange (of forms, funds, etc.). For example, the transmission of a purchase order, an insurance form, or an invoice can all be transaction sets. A *functional group* consists of several similar transaction sets (such as five invoices).

The transaction set is made up of segments. Each segment is either an administrative chunk (such as a header or trailer) or part of the data being exchanged (for example, an invoice, purchase order, or other type of form). With certain exceptions, segments are transmitted in a predefined sequence, and some segments may be repeated. Each segment in a transaction set is either mandatory, optional, or floating. Allowable data segments are defined and described in the *Data Segment Dictionary*.

Data segments are, in turn, made up of data elements. A *data element* is the smallest unit of information in EDI. The allowable data elements are described in the *Data Element Dictionary*. In their respective dictionaries, each data segment and data element are assigned unique identification numbers, and each will have one or more attributes and values associated with it. When reading articles about EDI, it's not uncommon to find references to particular forms or items by number.

The corpus of documents, forms, and other items in the world of EDI is enormous. This is so, in part, because standards have been developed for entire industries (transportation, health care, finance, etc.). Some of these industries are known for their bureaucratic excesses, and one of the goals of EDI is to help save time, work, paper, and money by automating much of the work and by maintaining records in electronic (as opposed to paper) form as much as possible.

Various surveys and studies have found that companies can save anywhere from a few percent to almost 90% on relevant transactions by switching to EDI. It's not uncommon for a company to report savings of $10 or more on each purchase order, for example.

Note that for such savings to be realized, both parties involved in a transaction must use EDI. In fact, one reason EDI continues to grow is that companies who are using EDI may require prospective suppliers or partners to use EDI in their dealings with the company. Once these suppliers have switched, they may, in turn, require that *their* clients use EDI.

EDI Standards and Variants

In the United States, most of the work on EDI specifications and standards has been done by ANSI X12 committees—actually, by subcommittees that address more specific topics. Over two dozen task and work groups from the various subcommittee areas have met or are meeting. For example, an Interactive EDI work group and a Data Security task group have been formed by the X12C subcommittee, which is concerned with communication and controls. That is, the X12C subcommittee is concerned with making sure information can move smoothly, quickly, and securely over electronic lines. Other subcommittees include X12E (product data), X12F (Finance), X12G (Government with, surprisingly, just two task groups), X12I (Transportation), and X12N (Insurance with, not surprisingly, a dozen Work Groups and ten task groups).

Other standards for EDI also exist. For example, continental Europe uses ODETTE (Organization for Data Exchange by TeleTransmission in Europe) and the United Kingdom uses TRADACOMS (Trading Data Communications Standards).

Internationally, the ISO's (International Standardization Organization) EDIFACT (EDI for Administration, Commerce, and Transport) standard is considered the official specification. This is sometimes also known as the UN/EDIFACT standard, where UN represents the United Nations.

The various national standards organizations all have the option of being represented in the EDIFACT committees—either directly or through another organization. For example, the United States and several South American countries comprise the PAEB (Pan American EDIFACT Board). Members of the PAEB represent US interests in EDIFACT—at least in part.

Eventually, EDI is expected to make up a large part of the traffic in X.400 systems—possibly as e-mail traffic—and also in CTI (computer-telephony integration) systems. The use of Web Information Systems (WISs)—together with XML (eXtensible Markup Language) forms—can potentially offer a less expensive way to create EDI forms and documents.

→ **Primary Sources** ISO recommendation 9735; various ANSI documents including X12.3 (Data Element Dictionary) and X12.22 (Data Segment Dictionary); CCITT recommendation x.435

EDO (Extended Data Out)

A variant of dynamic random access memory (DRAM) that helps improve memory speed and performance. By altering the timing and sequence of signals that activate the circuitry for accessing memory locations, EDO keeps data in currently accessed locations available even while beginning the next memory access. Not all processor chip sets support EDO RAM.

EEMA (European Electronic Mail Association)

A European association of developers and vendors of electronic mail products. The EMA (Electronic Mail Association) is the counterpart in the United States.

EFF (Electronic Frontier Foundation)

The EFF is an organization founded in 1990 to help ensure that the "electronic frontier" remains accessible and open to everyone. The EFF tries to accomplish its goals by providing a forum for the discussion of issues related to the use of electronic networks, and a voice for end-users in public policy and other debates.

On occasion, EFF also provides a legal-defense fund for Sysops and other computer-using individuals being prosecuted by the government.

GETTING IN TOUCH WITH EFF

To contact the EFF, write, phone, fax, or modem:

- Electronic Frontier Foundation
- 1001 G Street NW, Suite 950
- East Washington, DC 20001
- Telephone: (202) 347-5400 (voice)
- Fax: (202) 393-5509
- E-mail: eff@eff.org

Effective Bandwidth

The central part of the total bandwidth in a communications channel. This is the section in which the signal is strongest and clearest. The effective bandwidth is generally the area within which the total attenuation is less than 3 decibels (dB). (An attenuation of 3dB corresponds roughly to a 50 percent reduction in signal strength.)

Effective Isotropic Radiated Power (EIRP)

→ **See** EIRP (Effective Isotropic Radiated Power)

Effective Rights

In Novell's NetWare environment, *effective rights* refer to the rights a user can exercise in a particular directory or file (versions 2.x and later) or in the

E

Directory tree created by the NetWare Directory Services (NDS, in version 4.*x*).

Effective rights are defined with respect to the following:

Directory rights in the file system   Directory effective rights are determined by any trustee assignments. If no such assignments exist, the effective rights of a directory are determined by the user's effective rights in the parent directory and the directory's Inherited Rights Mask (in NetWare 3.*x*) or Maximum Rights Mask (NetWare 2.*x*).

File rights in the file system   File effective rights are determined by any trustee assignments for the file. Otherwise, the user's effective rights in the directory apply.

Object rights in the NDS   Object effective rights (in NetWare 4.*x* only) define what a user is allowed to do with an object entry in the NDS Directory tree. These rights apply to the object as a single structure in the tree, not to the properties associated with the object or to the object itself. For example, if a user has a Browse right for an object, the user does not automatically have access to property information.

Property rights in the NDS   Property effective rights (in NetWare 4.*x* only) define what kind of access a user has to the information associated with an object.

Effective rights for NDS objects and properties are determined by

- Inherited rights associated with the object or property, taking into account any Inherited Rights Filters (IRFs) that apply

- Trustee assignments associated with a user or group

- Applicable security restrictions

→ **Broader Category**   NetWare

Effective Throughput

The number of data bits transmitted within a given time (such as a second). This is in contrast to ordinary, or simple, throughput, which represents the total number of bits (both data and administrative) transmitted.

EFS (End Frame Sequence)

The EFS is the last field in a token-ring data packet.

→ **See**   Token Ring

EFS (Error Free Second)

One second of transmission without errors. The total or average number of EFS can be used as an index of transmission quality.

EGP (Exterior Gateway Protocol)

→ **See**   Protocol, EGP (Exterior Gateway Protocol)

EIA (Electronic Industries Association)

The EIA is an association that represents American manufacturers in standards organizations. The EIA has published several widely used standards, such as RS-232C, EIA-232D, RS-422, and RS-449. These standards govern the electrical characteristics of connections between computers and other electronic devices (such as modems or printers). The CCITT has created international versions of several EIA standards.

Reports that are concerned more directly with communications are produced jointly with the TIA (Telecommunications Industry Association). For example, EIA/TIA-568 defines five categories for unshielded twisted-pair (UTP) cable, and specifies the minimal performance requirements for each category.

EIB (Enterprise Information Base)

In enterprise networks, the EIB is an information base containing management and performance-related information about the network. The information in this type of database is used by network management or monitoring software.

EIDE (Enhanced Integrated Drive Electronics)

EIDE is Western Digital's extension of the specification for the IDE (Integrated Drive Electronics) hard disk interface. (IDE is the most common name for this interface standard, which was eventually codified as an ANSI standard named the AT Attachment, or ATA.)

EIDE was designed to overcome several shortcomings in the original interface. EIDE does the following:

- Increases the maximum transfer rate from 4 to 16Mbps. It does this by supporting two fast transfer modes. While bursts at 16Mbps are possible, the typical transfer speed is about 11Mbps.

- Increases the maximum storage capacity from 528MB to 8.4GB. It does this by using logical block addressing (LBA), which is a way of getting access to more actual sectors than are accessible through the DOS interrupts used to access the hard disk. Older BIOS versions may not support the translations necessary for LBA. (EIDE can actually support up to 138GB, but Windows-based environments are limited to 8GB because DOS is still such an integral part of Windows and because that's all DOS can support.

- Provides support for the ATAPI (ATA Packet Interface) standard, which allows the interface to communicate with devices other than just hard disks —for example, with CD-ROM or tape drives.

- Increases the maximum number of devices supported from two to four. It does this by allowing for two controllers, each of which can support two devices. One of the controllers will serve as the primary controller, and the other as a secondary controller. Generally, the primary controller is faster than the secondary controller and is used for hard disks; the secondary controller may be used for slower devices.

The enhancements added in EIDE were combined with those developed by Seagate Technology for their Fast ATA interface. The combined specification became the ATA-2 standard. This has since been superseded by the ATA-3 standard, which increases transfer speeds even higher, stabilizes the electrical behavior of the interface, and adds security features.

→ *Compare*   IDE (Integrated Drive Electronics)

EIGRP (Enhanced Interior Gateway Routing Protocol)

→ *See*   Protocol, EIGRP (Enhanced Interior Gateway Routing Protocol)

EIRP (Effective Isotropic Radiated Power)

The strength of a signal received at an earth station in a satellite communications system; that is, the strength of the satellite's signal by the time it reaches the ground. This value is generally measured in decibels (dB).

EISA (Extended Industry Standard Architecture)

EISA is an architecture for the PC expansion bus that provides 32-bit bus access, but that remains compatible with the 8- and 16-bit ISA (Industry Standard Architecture) that characterizes the IBM-PC and its descendants.

This architecture was developed by a consortium of hardware manufacturers in response to the 32-bit proprietary Micro-Channel architecture developed by IBM.

→ **Broader Category** Data Bus

→ **Compare** ISA; MicroChannel; PCI; VESA

EKTS (Electronic Key Telephone System)

In telephony, a key telephone system (KTS) that uses electrical switches. By shrinking the entire KTS down to electronic circuitry, it becomes easier to add features and to install the KTS in a telephone.

→ **See Also** KTS

ELAP (EtherTalk Link Access Protocol)

→ **See** Protocol, ELAP (EtherTalk Link Access Protocol)

Electrical Signal

Electrical energy (voltage or current) transmitted as a waveform. Signals are distinguished by their amplitude (strength), frequency or period (repetition rate), and phase (timing).

Communication occurs when a *modulating signal* (which represents information) is superimposed on a fixed *carrier signal* (which serves as a baseline) and is then transmitted, as in "Carrier and modulating signal." The information is represented by changing one or more of the modulating signal's distinguishing features.

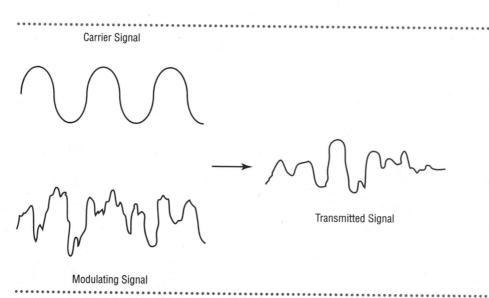

Carrier Signal

Transmitted Signal

Modulating Signal

CARRIER AND MODULATING SIGNALS

Electromagnetic Interference (EMI)

→ *See* EMI (Electromagnetic Interference)

Electronic Commerce

Electronic commerce, or *e-commerce*, refers to the buying and selling of products, services, or information over the Internet—in particular, over the World Wide Web. However, the term can also be used to describe the same or similar kinds of activities over corporate intranets or extranets.

The world of e-commerce is complex, constantly changing, and rapidly evolving. Because e-commerce standards are still in the process of development, vendors tend to go their own ways, with the result being that there are generally several possibilities for doing any of the tasks (ensuring security, making shopping choices, paying, and so forth) required for being an e-commerce operator or consumer. Within this chaos, a few main components can be identified.

The two main types of e-commerce are business-to-business (B2B) and business-to-consumer (B2C). Of these, B2B accounts for the great majority of e-commerce revenues. Included in B2B e-commerce are such things as supply-chain automation, advertising fees, and the selling and buying of mailing lists and customer profiles.

To work properly, e-commerce requires a considerable infrastructure—for security, transaction processing, and so forth. The major components for e-commerce are defined and operate within this infrastructure. Only some of the necessary components are used directly by the parties involved, however. Other elements play critical and necessary roles, but only behind the scenes.

The following are the main directly used components for e-commerce:

- A Web site from which the product or service can be purchased.

- A means of marketing the product to potential customers—for example, through advertising, mailings, push technology, etc.

- A way for the customer to search for, select, and buy the products or services.

- A currency that can be used for purchases.

- A way of completing the transaction using the necessary elements of the infrastructure—to do such things as transferring currency from the buyer's account to the seller's.

- A way of recording and completing the transaction in a secure manner. In this case security applies to both the financial and the personal aspects of the transaction.

Web Sites

If you have something to sell on the Internet, you must provide a potential customer with a Web site or other location from which the customer can purchase the desired product. You can set up your own Web site—for example, using any of the available e-commerce packages. These packages range in price from free to tens of thousands of dollars.

If you set up your own Web site, you'll be responsible for setting up the security for the site—which can be a complicated task. The e-commerce package you select may or may not provide the security you need. You'll also have to provide your own hardware for the Web site.

Another option is to rent a virtual storefront. For example, you may be able to lease e-commerce software and several megabytes of storage space from your Internet Service Provider (ISP) or from a Commerce Solution Provider (CSP). CSPs specialize in just such e-commerce-related services.

In the case of a virtual storefront, the service provider will generally be responsible for site security. In that case, of course, you will need to evaluate the quality of the service provider's security—and that can be a very difficult thing to do.

E

Marketing Resources and Strategies

To get someone to buy a product or service, a merchant needs some way of making potential customers aware of the product. On the Web, various strategies are available.

Advertising is the most obvious way to bring a product to the attention of potential customers. On the Web, this can take the form of *banner ads*, which are displayed when a user reaches a Web site on which the merchant has placed an ad. Generally, such ads will be displayed in Web portals or on frequently visited Web pages. The display may or may not be guided by personalized information about the user's preferences.

Interstitial ads are also becoming popular. Such ads are displayed while behind the scenes activity is taking place—for example, while a page is being assembled for display. Once the activity is completed, the ad disappears.

Content channels and push technology can also be used to deliver material of interest to potential customers. Content channels deliver information and updates about specific content—for example, news, financial reports, sports, entertainment, and so forth. *Push technology* provides a way of delivering information to customers who are likely to be interested in the products being pushed. This is because push technology uses information about previous visits to a Web site—such as the information stored in cookies—to decide what information to deliver to a site visitor.

Product brokering agents provide another way of delivering information of relevance and potential interest to a customer. These are agent programs that rely on customer profile information to determine what products will be of most interest to the user. For example, users who do business with sites such as Amazon.com will get information about new books in their areas of interest—based on their buying and browsing profile. Such information would be selected and delivered by a product brokering agent.

Customer Resources

The customer needs to be able to determine what merchants and products are available, to make comparisons between different online (or offline) merchants, and to make product selections. Some of these resources are made available at the merchant's site; others are available as utilities, plug-ins, or add-ons.

To find out what's available, a potential customer can use search engines (such as AltaVista, Lycos, and Yahoo!). Information received through subscriptions to the appropriate information or sales channels and from push technology also helps keep the customer abreast of new products and technologies. Product brokering agents at specific Web sites are also an important source of information in many cases because the information delivered by these agents is tailored to the customer's buying habits and (expressed or inferred) interests.

Once the customer has decided on a product or products, *shopbots* can do price comparisons by searching for the product(s) at various merchants' sites and then comparing prices for the product(s). (Shopbots are examples of a *merchant brokering agent*, which provide comparative information about merchants. A businessbot—a comparable comparison shopper agent for business-to-business commerce—is still in the design stages.)

The software for the actual shopping trip (so to speak) is provided by the merchant. Some form of this shopping software is included with just about every e-commerce package. Currently, this class of tools is generally limited to a shopping cart metaphor. The software lets the customer wander through the "store"—that is, through the database containing information about the available products—pushing along their shopping cart.

The customer can put any product of interest into the shopping cart, which they can eventually take to the checkout register. At that point the customer can either buy the product or discard it. The shopping cart metaphor is handy because everyone has some experience with these vehicles. However, it is not particularly flexible: items usually have to be added one at a time and specific items generally can be added only from certain locations.

Electronic Currency

Once the customer decides on something to buy over the Web, how are they to pay for it? There are several possibilities here, including credit cards or some type of electronic cash or *scrip*.

Credit Cards

To accept credit cards, the merchant needs a *merchant account*, which must be assigned by a financial institution, known as the *acquiring bank*. The acquiring bank will determine which types of credit cards the merchant can accept, and will accept payment from valid accounts on those credit cards.

The customer's side of the transaction is made possible by the *issuing bank*—that is, the bank that issued the customer's credit card. A *processing network*, such as Verifone or CyberCash, will get authorization for a purchase from the issuing bank. Once this authorization is obtained, the purchase can take place.

At some point after the purchase is made—generally within 24 hours—the acquiring bank will arrange for the amounts involved to be transferred from the issuing bank to the acquiring bank—that is, from the customer's to the merchant's account.

The actual transfer of credit card number information can be done in either of two ways: online or offline. In an *online transfer*, the customer's credit card information is transmitted over the Web. In this case, one of the security measures discussed in the next section should be used to safeguard the customer's credit card information.

In an *offline transfer*, the customer phones in the credit card number to the merchant's customer service representative. In such a transfer, the credit card information cannot be intercepted as it works its way between customer and merchant—unless, of course, either party's telephone is tapped. Of course, even if the customer safely telephones in the number, it may still get stolen once the merchant stores the information in a customer database. (The same danger may exist even with a merchant who uses all the proper encryption and other security measures when transmitting data, but who fails to properly encrypt or otherwise safeguard data stored in a corporate database.)

Regardless of whether the credit card number comes in over the Web or over a voice call, it will then be processed at the back end—to actually complete the transaction. The merchant will get authorization for the charge, and will then arrange for the acquiring bank to make the appropriate transfer from the issuing bank. The product will be delivered to the customer in whatever manner was specified in the conditions of sale.

Credit cards are arguably the most common method of payment for e-commerce purchases. In a sense, such commerce is a natural extension of catalog shopping by phone. Because of the overhead costs involved in credit card transactions (electronic transaction fees, bank cuts of the credit card charge, and so forth), credit cards are not practical for purchases costing less than about $10 or so.

Electronic Cash

An alternative payment method is to use some sort of electronic cash or scrip. Various e-cash or scrip systems are currently in use and are, effectively, duking it out to see which strategy or strategies will become the standard. Such payment methods are being used primarily for the emerging microcommerce market.

Microcommerce refers to a developing technology for carrying out transactions involving small charges. Such *micropayments* may be requested, for example, if someone wants to read or cite a particular paper, journal, or book. Since the charges involved here may amount to only a few cents—or even just fractions of a cent—credit cards are out of the question as payment tools.

Instead, the strategy in microcommerce is to lay in a supply of e-cash or a line of e-credit, and then draw from this to make any necessary micropayments. Essentially, the customer puts a limited amount of e-cash—which may have been purchased using a credit or debit card—into some sort of "e-wallet," and then pays with funds from the wallet.

E

Two main systems are used to handle such e-currency: a centrally controlled notational system and a locally controlled token system.

- In a *notational system*, the e-cash is kept in an account on behalf of the customer—much like the balance in your checking account is maintained for you by your bank. When the customer wants to use a service or access certain information, they just authorize a transfer of e-cash from their e-wallet to the merchant's. The "e-bank" holding the customer's e-wallet then makes the requested transfer. The customer can spend until the e-cash balance reaches the minimum level allowed. At that point, they must either stop spending or replenish the e-cash supply. The CyberCoin system from CyberCash is an example of such a model.

- In a *token system*, the customer buys a supply of tokens from a broker—just as you might buy a supply of ride tickets at a county fair or chips in a gambling casino. When the customer needs to pay for some information or service, they just need to give the merchant a token of the appropriate value. The merchant can take the token to the broker and redeem it for its monetary value. Like the tickets at the county fair, such tokens are anonymous currency. No one needs to know where the token comes from, since the token itself has value. By the same token (pun intended), if the token is lost or stolen, the money on which the token's value is based will also be lost. When the customer runs out of tokens, they either need to stop spending or buy some more from the broker. eCash from DigiCash and MilliCent from Digital Equipment Corporation are both token systems.

Electronic currency need not be monetary. Any kind of currency that can be assigned a value can be used. For example, a merchant might offer promotional tokens that can be redeemed for merchandise or services. The frequent flyer miles system works in this way. Note that multiple merchants can participate in the same currency or token plan.

Transaction Processing

Once the customer has selected what they want to buy, and the payment methods and details have been worked out, it's time to carry out the actual transaction. Various kinds of software can be used for this aspect of electronic commerce, which is a form of online transaction processing (OLTP). Depending on the platforms involved, the OLTP may be carried out using any of several models for online transactions.

For ordering, the customer may provide the information in a simple form. They might be able to complete the form merely by clicking on the items they want to purchase. In a business-to-business transaction, the forms involved are likely to be more complex, and they will probably conform to the Electronic Data Interchange (EDI) standard.

In any event, the merchant will need to have access to the appropriate infrastructure to be able to carry out such transactions online. In most cases, this access (or even the infrastructure) will be provided by the merchant's e-commerce software or by a transaction-processing package.

The customer's side of the transaction is much simpler, and is generally handled by the merchant's software as well. One reason it's simpler is because the customer generally doesn't need to save a permanent record of the transaction—except possibly for a simple receipt.

Security in Electronic Commerce

Surveys and polls consistently find that most people who hesitate to shop over the Internet do so because they have reservations about inadequate security for the transactions and about loss of privacy. The two main solutions that have been offered for security in electronic commerce are the Secure Socket Layer (SSL) Protocol and the Secure Electronic Transaction (SET) specification.

SSL was developed by Netscape to provide a way of encrypting the information provided by users when they fill out forms online. The information is encrypted before being sent out onto the network. This is designed to keep people with network sniffer software from simply intercepting and reading the information in the form. All e-commerce programs support at least some version of the SSL protocol.

SET was created by a consortium made up mainly of credit card companies, banks, and other financial institutions. It is a complex system that will require the creation of hundreds of thousands—more likely, millions—of digital signatures. It will also require the creation of a global public key infrastructure and will, essentially tie every credit card holder (as well as other groups) into that infrastructure—whether they like it or not. With SET, the customer will register their credit card for Internet shopping. They will be assigned a digital signature, which will be unique to their card ordering from their PC. Any Internet purchases attempted with this card from another PC—such as one belonging to someone who has stolen the card number—will be considered invalid.

Once the card is acknowledged as valid, the customer will get a message that verifies that they are actually dealing with the merchant they expected, and not with some rogue site. Once everyone has been authenticated, the credit card information is sent directly to the acquiring bank, which will get authorization for the purchase amount, and will then authorize the merchant to ship the merchandise. In an SET transaction, the merchant never actually sees the credit card number. In addition, all transmissions in SET are encrypted.

Currently, SET has been implemented only on a very limited scale, since a full implementation will be a major undertaking.

Both security approaches are adequate—as far as they go. That is, with respect to maintaining the security and integrity of the information as it passes between the parties, both SSL and SET are reasonably secure. SSL is perhaps more useful because it is more widely supported at this point.

However, transmission security is only one part of the entire security picture. Neither SSL nor SET has any control over what happens to the information once it reaches its destination. On the merchant's computer, the customer's private information is only as safe as the merchant's in-house security

measures make it. That means the information is subject to attack by intruders.

Unfortunately, in too many cases customer information is also subject to attack (of a different sort) from within. Many merchants will collect customer information and will then sell this information in mailing lists and to information brokers. Since surveys generally show that fewer than 20 percent of businesses state their privacy policies online, there is serious room for abuse in this area, and clear breaches of ethics (and, possibly, also of the law) are quite common.

The United States lags far behind most European countries and the European Union in its privacy protection laws. Every time a legislator or other government official begins talking about establishing privacy laws, the business community promises to police itself. However, details on how, specifically, this is to be done rarely appear. The limited legislation that exists in this area generally places the burden on the customer. That is, it's up to the customer to request that their name be removed from lists or that personal information should not be accessible to anyone. There is often no way of checking whether the businesses contacted actually complied with the request.

In contrast, most parts of Europe have strict privacy laws. These laws place the burden on the merchants, who must request the right to collect or release information.

Ultimately, inadequate privacy protection may turn out to be the biggest obstacle to the growth of electronic commerce—at least in its B2C variety.

→ **See Also** EDI (Electronic Data Interchange); OLTP (Online Transaction Processing)

Electronic Commerce Modeling Language (ECML)

→ **See** ECML (Electronic Commerce Modeling Language)

E

Electronic Cookbook (ECB)

→ *See* ECB (Electronic Cookbook)

Electronic Data Interchange (EDI)

→ *See* EDI (Electronic Data Interchange)

Electronic Frontier Foundation (EFF)

→ *See* EFF (Electronic Frontier Foundation)

Electronic Industries Association (EIA)

→ *See* EIA (Electronic Industries Association)

Electronic Key Telephone System (EKTS)

→ *See* EKTS (Electronic Key Telephone System), KTS

Electronic Mail (E-Mail)

→ *See* E-Mail (Electronic Mail)

Electronic Mail Association (EMA)

An association of developers and vendors of electronic mail products.

Electronic Mailbox

In an e-mail (electronic mail) system, a directory provided to store messages for a single user. Each e-mail user has a unique ID and a unique mailbox.

→ *See Also* E-Mail

Electronic Switched Network (ESN)

→ *See* ESN (Electronic Switched Network)

Electronic Switching

In circuit switching, hardware in which the connections are made electronically (rather than electromechanically).

Electronic Wallet

→ *See* E-Wallet

Elevator Seeking

Elevator seeking is a technique for optimizing the movement of the read/write heads in a file server's hard disk.

Requests for disk access from different nodes are queued on the basis of the heads' position; that is, requests for data from the same area of the disk are fulfilled together. The heads move in a sweeping motion from the outside of the disk to the inside. This strategy reduces read/write head activity and greatly increases the throughput.

The name *elevator seeking* comes from the fact that people going to a particular floor get off together, regardless of when each person got on the elevator. Similarly, the elevator stops at floors as they are reached, not in the order in which the floors were requested.

Elliptic Curve Encryption

Elliptic curves are a special class of functions that can be defined over certain mathematical fields. Such curves can be used to create public and private keys for encryption and for digital signatures.

While the use of such functions has only recently become feasible, there are indications that certain encryption algorithms using elliptic curves can offer advantages over more commonly used RSA algorithms. For example, a 160-bit public key created using elliptic curves offers a level of security that is comparable to a 1024-bit public key created with an RSA algorithm; similarly, the corresponding private keys are 160 bits and 2048 bits, respectively. (Actually, special bits must be added to help in the encryption and decryption processes. These make the elliptic curve private key 801 bits long and the RSA private key 2560 bits.)

The smaller key sizes translate into savings because some of the required computations are easier (and faster) as a result. While easier to encrypt, an elliptic code is currently as difficult to decrypt as the longer RSA key. However, the time savings are not as large as the relative key lengths would suggest. This is because suitable elliptic curves are harder to generate than the numbers and exponents that need to be computed for the RSA algorithm.

While they have been around for over 10 years, much less is known about the general properties of elliptic curves (and the encryption elements they generate) than about the properties of RSA algorithms. Elliptic curves will become much more interesting as the minimum key lengths required for secure encryption become ever longer.

→ **Broader Category** Encryption; Security

→ **See Also** RSA (Rivesi, Shamir, Adleman) Algorithm

ELS (Entry Level System) NetWare

ELS NetWare refers to low-end NetWare products that support a limited number of stations and a limited range of hardware. ELS NetWare comes in two configurations:

- ELS Level I supports up to four nodes, a few different network interface cards, and a limited set of operating environments.

- ELS Level II supports up to eight nodes and a much broader range of hardware and operating environments.

ELS products are no longer sold.

EMA (Electronic Mail Association)

An association of developers and vendors of electronic mail products.

EMA (Enterprise Management Architecture)

EMA is a network management model from Digital Equipment Corporation (DEC). With this model, DEC hopes to provide the tools needed to manage enterprise networks, regardless of the configurations that make up the network. The architecture is designed to conform to the ISO's CMIP (Common Management Information Protocol).

The DEC Management Control Center (DECmcc) Director implements the current version of the EMA model. This product is extended by several add-on products that are designed for specialized management tasks.

In order to achieve vendor and protocol independence, the EMA isolates the Director as much as possible from implementation details. The Director is in charge of managing network elements, and it uses several kinds of modules for its tasks.

- Access modules, to provide a path to the network elements being managed. Each access module supports a single type of network element, such as a bridge or a device belonging to a particular type of network. Access modules use widely supported protocols, such as the CMIP and the Internet community's SNMP, to communicate.

E

- Functional modules, to provide the capabilities for carrying out the performance, configuration, security, and other types of management tasks.

- Presentation modules, which provide an integrated, standardized interface for the Director.

The other major component of the EMA model is the Executive. This element contains the information about the network elements in a Management Information Repository.

→ *Broader Category* Network Management

E-Mail (Electronic Mail)

E-mail (also written as *email*) is an application that provides a message transfer and storage service for the nodes on a network or internetwork or for a stand-alone machine through a dial-up service. Each user has an electronic mailbox (a unique directory for storing electronic mail), and other users can send e-mail messages to the user at this mailbox.

The e-mail messages are sent to an *e-mail address*. For the end-user, an e-mail address is generally written as a sequence of names, separated by periods or other special characters, as in `fiddle@faddle.edu`.

Once the message is stored in the recipient's mailbox, the owner of the mailbox can retrieve whatever messages look important and/or interesting. E-mail packages differ in the ease with which such selections can be made and also in the services the packages provide.

All e-mail packages will send and deliver mail, and all can let users know when they have mail. Most packages allow you to create the message by using the e-mail software or by using your own resources. Many packages also allow recipients to reply to a message by simply annotating the original message. Some packages allow voice mail, which requires additional hardware.

Setting up a proprietary e-mail service on a single network is generally straightforward, but may be of little value in the long run. In order to exchange e-mail with users on other networks or in remote locations, more powerful software is needed.

E-mail services are also available through dial-up services such as CompuServe and MCI Mail.

If an e-mail message cannot be delivered, it may be stored temporarily in a *post office*. This is just a service with available storage and with the ability to check periodically whether the recipient is ready to take delivery. E-mail handling is an example of the more general store-and-forward strategy.

History and Overview of Electronic Mail

The first e-mail systems were developed in the late 1960s and early 1970s. These were mainly small-scale, departmental systems—although the ARPANET was a major factor in the development of electronic messaging. These systems were also mainly proprietary, with little effort being made to enable e-mail systems to communicate with each other—even within the same company. The first e-mail systems consisted of little more than file transfer capabilities.

In the late 1970s and early 1980s, public e-mail services became available through service providers such as AT&T Mail, MCI Mail, and CompuServe. For the most part, mail services on these providers were used by businesses and by individuals. Research and academic e-mail services developed on what was becoming the Internet.

At the same time, PCs appeared and quickly became extremely popular. By the mid- to late 1980s, e-mail packages for LANs were appearing and proliferating. As was the case with public and corporate e-mail services, each package had its own formats and protocols.

As mail and messaging services became more popular and more widely used, the need for interoperability grew. As a result, standards were developed:

- The X.400 series of recommendations from the CCITT (Consultative Committee for International Telegraphy and Telephony, now going under the name International Telecommunications Union, or ITU) provided standards for electronic messaging and mail. The first version of the X.400 standards appeared in 1984, and these are known as MHS 84 (for message handling system, 1984). X.400 systems commonly serve as a backbone for delivering mail between (possibly incompatible) e-mail systems.

- The SMTP (Simple Mail Transfer Protocol) in the IP (Internet protocol) suite provided e-mail standards and protocols for the Internet.

In the late 1980s and early 1990s, e-mail continued to grow rapidly in popularity. During this period, formats became more standardized, and even the LAN-based packages began to support either X.400 or SMTP or both.

Two other events have helped make electronic mail a truly international service:

- The appearance of the CCITT X.500 standards for directory naming and services helped make it possible to keep track of addresses and locations more easily and in a more consistent manner. During this same period, a new version of the X.400 MHS standards appeared—known as MHS 88.

- The appearance of gateways, which could serve as a transfer place between incompatible mail systems—sort of like the locks in the Panama canal provide a transfer between incompatible oceans.

The mid- to late 1990s promise to be an even more exciting period for electronic mail. Several kinds of developments are likely to take place during this period:

- Increasing bandwidth, so that even huge files can be sent quickly and easily via e-mail. The planning and work are already underway for gigabit-level bandwidths for such services, and even terabit-speed networks are beginning to be discussed.

- Support for video, audio, and graphics in a mail or message service. The Multi-purpose Internet

Mail Extensions (MIME) provide guidelines for how such materials should be handled. While these represent a start, it's likely that major developments will occur in this area.

- The appearance of intelligent agents to help in mail handling and delivery, and also to help users screen their mail.

- The development of wireless mail services will continue, helping to spur advances in wireless networking.

- The generalization of electronic mail and messaging to encompass electronic commerce—for example, through EDI (electronic data interchange).

- The use of e-mail as a medium for workflow messages and traffic. Workflow software is used to specify or manage the sequence of tasks needed to carry out and complete a project—particularly when the project requires the participation of multiple workers.

- The use of encryption, digital signatures, and other security techniques to keep the content of e-mail messages hidden from unauthorized eyes. This is an essential development if e-mail is to become a vehicle for electronic commerce. *PEM* (privacy enhanced mail) is an example of such a security measure. The more general *PGP* (pretty good privacy) algorithm may also be used for encryption). S/MIME, a secure version of the MIME specification also supports encryption.

- The ability to include video in e-mail is becoming increasingly feasible as bandwidth increases.

E-Mail System Components

The architecture of an e-mail system can vary, but all e-mail systems need to provide the following types of services:

- Terminal and/or node handling, so that the mail service can understand user requests and respond to those requests.

E

- File handling, so that electronic messages can be stored as files in the appropriate mailbox. These are general file handling abilities, with a few exceptions.

- Communications handling, so that a mail server (for example) can talk to and exchange messages with another server at a remote site. For the most part, these are general communications capabilities.

- Local mail services, so that a mail server can receive and deliver mail from local users.

- Mail transfer, so that a mail server can deliver electronic messages to another server, and can receive electronic messages from the other server.

Encryption and multicast capabilities are also common e-mail system features.

MHS (Message Handling Service) is Novell's e-mail system for NetWare. MHS is a store-and-forward system that also provides gateways into other messaging systems, most notably, into X.400 systems.

E-Mail Protocols

Until recently, the e-mail universe was filled with proprietary protocols, few of which could talk to each other. Fortunately, this has changed. Most e-mail products now support either or both of two widely used standards: the SMTP (Simple Mail Transfer Protocol) from the TCP/IP protocol suite, or protocols specified in the CCITT's X.400 series of standards.

→ *See Also* MHS (Message Handling System), MIME (Multipurpose Internet Mail Extensions), PEM (Privacy Enhanced Mail), PGP (Pretty Good Privacy); S/MIME (Secure Multipurpose Internet Mail Extensions)

Embedded SCSI

A hard disk with a SCSI interface and a controller built into the hard disk.

EMI (Electromagnetic Interference)

Random or periodic energy from external sources that can interfere with transmissions over copper cable. EMI sources can be artifacts (such as motors or lighting—particularly fluorescent lighting) or natural phenomena (such as atmospheric or solar activity). Compare this with RFI (radio frequency interference).

Emitter-Coupled Logic (ECL)

→ *See* ECL (Emitter-Coupled Logic)

EMM (Expanded Memory Manager)

An EMM is a program that provides access to expanded memory.

→ *See Also* Memory Management

Emotag

An emotag is the Web page, or HTML (Hypertext Markup Language), equivalent of an ASCII emoticon used in e-mail and other text communications. Emotags are fake HTML tags, which indicate the kinds of sentiments expressed in emoticons—for example, `<smirk>`, `<frown>`, `<just kidding>`, or `<flame>` and `</flame>`.

→ *See Also* Emoticon

Emoticon

In electronic communication, *emoticons* are special symbols that are used to convey emotions (elation, disappointment, and so on) or commentary (sarcasm, irony, and the like) related to the text. Emoticons are also known as *smileys*.

Emoticons are built using characters available on any keyboard. For example, the emoticon **;-)**

represents a wink, which can convey irony, sarcasm, or a conspiratorial "nudge-nudge, know what I mean." The following are examples of emoticons:

:-)	Smile; happiness; agreement; laughter
:-(	Frown; unhappiness; disagreement; anger
;-)	Half-smile; irony; sarcasm; joking
(@w@)	Amazement; incredulity
;-o	Shout
;-r	Disgust; displeasure (tongue sticking out)

→ *Primary Source* *Smileys* by David W. Sanderson (O'Reilly & Associates) includes more than 650 symbols.

→ *See Also* Emotag

EMS (Expanded Memory Specification)

In the DOS environment, the specification for expanded memory (a type of memory that is allocated on separate boards, and whose contents are paged into "ordinary" memory piecemeal). Although the EMS calls for expanded memory to have its own hardware, various memory managers and drivers can emulate expanded memory in extended memory.

→ *See Also* Memory

Emulation

A complete functional duplication of one machine or device by another. For example, a PC may emulate a 3270 terminal in order to communicate with an IBM mainframe. A hardware device or a software package that provides emulation is called an *emulator*.

→ *See Also* Terminal Emulation

Encapsulation

In a layered networking model, encapsulation refers to a process by which each layer subsumes the PDU (protocol data unit) from the layer above into a larger PDU by adding a header to the higher-layer PDU. (A PDU is a packet built at a particular layer, which is used for communicating with a program at the same layer on a different machine). For example, a Transport-layer protocol encapsulates a PDU from the session layer.

The layer is often indicated by adding an initial letter to *PDU*. for example, a presentation layer PDU would be written as PPDU or P-PDU.

Encapsulation is used by internetwork links, such as certain routers or gateways. *Encapsulating routers* operate at the Network layer, and *Transport-layer gateways* operate at the higher, Transport layer.

The inverse process—removing the lower-layer headers at the receiving end—is known as *decapsulation*. "Encapsulation and decapsulation" illustrates these processes.

The steps involved in encapsulation and decapsulation are as follows:

1. A packet is created at layer n. The packet consists of a payload (P) containing data and a header (H) containing addressing and other control information.

2. The layer-n packet is passed down to layer n-1, where the entire packet is encapsulated—as payload—by adding a layer n-1 header.

3. This layer n-1 packet is passed down to the next layer (n-2) and encapsulated—again by adding a header to the upper layer packet.

4. This encapsulation process continues down the layers until the bottom layer is reached. The packet at this layer is actually transmitted to another machine or network.

5. At the receiving end, the decapsulation process begins by stripping off the layer n-1 header

E

and passing the payload up to the next layer. Note that decapsulation frees the payload at a lower level to become the packet for the layer above.

6. Headers for the higher layers are peeled off as the materials are passed up the layers.

7. At the topmost layer of the receiving end, the original packet will once again be revealed, and the data in this packet will finally be delivered after their long journey.

Encoding

Encoding is a process by which information in one form or at one level of detail is represented in a different form or at a different level.

Encoding Contexts

The term is widely used, and encoding is practiced in many contexts. For example, encoding may be used in the following ways:

- In text processing, characters, digits, and other symbols are represented as decimal values between 0 and 128 or between 0 and 255. ASCII and EBCDIC are examples of character-encoding schemes.

- In telegraphy, characters and digits are represented as sequences of dots and dashes. Morse code is an example of this encoding scheme.

- In data translation schemes, which are commonly used before the data are encoded as electrical or optical signals, blocks of bits are translated into blocks in a different representation system. For example, in Gigabit Ethernet,

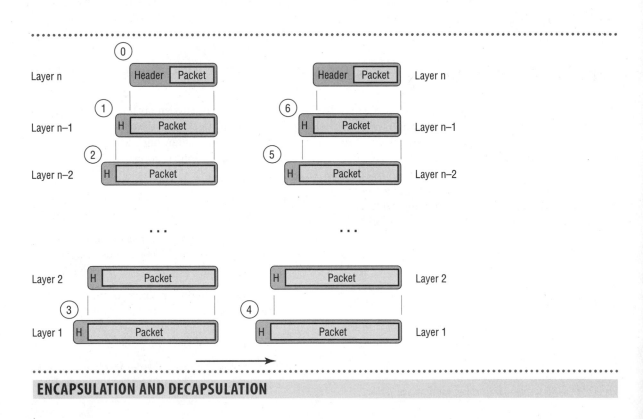

ENCAPSULATION AND DECAPSULATION

8-bit blocks are translated into 10-bit blocks before being encoded as signals. In 100BaseT4 Ethernet networks, 8-bit blocks are translated into 6-*trit* blocks—that is, into blocks using a ternary, or three-valued, representation. The purpose of such translation schemes is to get data into a representation in which possible values can be distinguished more easily. This decreases the chances of confusing two different values because their signal encodings are too similar.

- In the transmission of digital signals over networks, binary values (0 and 1) are represented as changes in voltage or current levels. Signal-encoding schemes include AMI (Alternate Mark Inversion), Manchester, Differential Manchester, and MLT-3.

Special Forms of Encoding

Special forms of encoding include translation and compression. In translation, one encoding scheme is converted to another, such as from EBCDIC to ASCII. In compression encoding, redundant information is represented in a more efficient manner.

In the X.400 Message Handling System (MHS), a distinction is made between two types of encoding for a packet: definite or indefinite. A definite encoding scheme includes explicit length information in a packet. This information is generally stored in a *length field*.

An indefinite encoding scheme uses a special character (EOC, for end of content) to indicate when the end of a packet is reached.

Note that encoding here refers to the form a packet takes, rather than to the form an electrical signal takes.

Encoding, Signal

Signal encoding is a set of rules for representing the possible values for an input signal in some other form. For example, in digital communications, the signal-encoding rule will determine what form an electrical signal will take to represent a 1 or a 0.

Dozens of rule sets have been proposed just for digital signals. Each has its advantages and disadvantages. In the simplest encoding scheme, a particular voltage level represents one value, and a different (or zero) voltage represents a different value. For binary inputs, just two different voltage levels are needed.

Note that the actual voltage levels and charges used to represent the bit values depend on the logic being used for the circuitry. TTL logic is used in situations where circuit speed is important; because of its lower voltage requirements, CMOS logic is used where low power consumption is more important (for example, in battery-powered computers).

It is possible to encode more than one bit in a digital signal. For example, by allowing four different voltages, you can represent two bits in each signal; with eight voltages, you can represent three bits at a time, and so on. The trade-off is that the components must be able to make finer discriminations, which makes them more expensive to manufacture or more error prone.

Signal Timing

Each signal has a predefined duration, so that the voltage for a single signal will be held for a specified amount of time. The shorter this time needs to be, the faster the potential transmission speed. The trade-off is that the faster signal allows less room for distortion by noise, so that the error rate may increase.

In order to distinguish the individual bits in a series of the same bit values, such as a series of 1 values in succession, sender and receiver may use clocking (a timing mechanism used to determine the start of a bit signal) to establish the duration of a signal for a single bit, which is called the *bit interval*. Each party in the communication uses its own clock to time the signal.

Since transmission speeds can be more than 1Gbps, the clocks must be very closely synchronized.

E

In practice, the clocks may need to be resynchronized millions of times per second.

To avoid the overhead of inserted clocking bits, most encoding schemes use actual bit values (generally a 1) as the clocking bit. This works fine unless there are long stretches without any 1 values. (At high speeds, a "long" stretch can be as short as a single byte.) For these cases, special, adaptive encoding schemes, such as B8ZS (bipolar with eight zero substitution), have been developed to make sure such a sequence never occurs.

Self-Clocking Encoding Schemes

Some encoding schemes are self-clocking, in that the clocking is built into the signal itself. This clocking usually takes the form of a voltage change at the middle of the bit interval.

Although self-clocking schemes make external clocks and adaptive encoding unnecessary, they cannot operate at more than half the speed of the system clock. This is because two clock cycles must be used to split a bit interval in half.

Transition Coding

Some encoding schemes use transition coding in which a value is encoded by a transition (from one voltage level to another) *during* the bit interval. For example, the representation of a 1 in a scheme with transition coding may consist of a positive voltage for half the bit interval and zero voltage for the other half. This type of encoding scheme is also self-clocking. Transition coding tends to be less susceptible to noise.

A Sampling of Encoding Schemes

The following general encoding schemes summarize a few of the strategies used to represent binary values.

Unfortunately, there is little consistency in signal-encoding terminology, so that the same term may

refer to two different encoding schemes. If the encoding method is important for your purposes, ask the vendor for sample timing diagrams, so that you can see the actual encoding.

Unipolar   Uses a positive or a negative voltage (but not both in the same scheme) to represent one value (for example, 1), and a zero voltage to represent the other. Unipolar encoding does not use transition coding, and it requires an external clock.

Polar   A positive voltage represents one value and a negative voltage represents the other. Polar encoding does not use transition coding, and it requires an external clock.

Bipolar   Uses positive, negative, *and* zero voltages, usually with zero voltage representing one value and a nonzero voltage representing the other. Bipolar encoding may use transition coding, and it may be self-clocking.

Biphase   Includes at least one transition per bit interval. In addition to making this scheme self-clocking, the transition coding also makes it easier to detect errors. Biphase schemes are often used for networks.

Of these schemes, variants on bipolar and biphase are the most widely used. The following sections describe some specific versions of bipolar and biphase strategies. In a specific communications context, a binary value may undergo several encoding schemes before actually being transmitted.

AMI (Alternate Mark Inversion)

AMI, also known as *ABP* (*alternate bipolar*) *encoding*, is a bipolar scheme. This signal-encoding method uses three possible values: +V, 0V, and –V (positive, zero, and negative voltage). All 0 bits are encoded as 0V (zero voltage); 1 bits are encoded as +V and –V (positive and negative voltage) in alternation. "AMI encoding for a bit sequence" shows an example of AMI encoding.

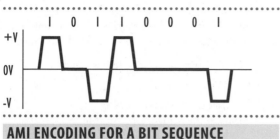

AMI ENCODING FOR A BIT SEQUENCE

AMI encoding is used in DSx-level transmissions, as in ISDN (Integrated Services Distributed Network), FDDI (Fiber Distributed Data Interface), and other high-speed network architectures.

AMI encoding is not self-clocking. This means that synchronous transmissions, such as those using digital signal methods, must use an external clock for timing. The positive and negative voltages associated with 1 bits are used for this timing.

In order to ensure that the transmission never gets out of synch, some environments require a minimum density of 1 values in any transmission. The minimum pulse density is generally set to at least one in every eight bits. To ensure that this pulse-density requirement is met, a variant encoding method, called B8ZS, is used.

B8ZS (Bipolar with 8 Zero Substitution)

Like AMI, B8ZS uses three possible values: +V, 0V, and -V (positive, zero, and negative voltage). All 0 bits are encoded as 0V (zero voltage); 1 bits are encoded as +V and -V (positive and negative voltage) in alternation. Unlike AMI, however, B8ZS requires that at least one bit out of every eight must be a 1; that is, eight consecutive 0 values will never occur in B8ZS.

If eight consecutive 0 bits are encountered, the encoding will insert a 1 before the eighth 0. This value will be removed at a later point. A minimal density of 1 values is needed because these values are used for timing. If the transmission contains too long a string of 0 values, the sender and receiver can get out of synch without knowing it. By ensuring there will be at least one opportunity to synchronize

every eight bits, the transmission can never get too far out of synch.

Differential Manchester

Differential Manchester is a biphase signal-encoding scheme used in Token Ring local-area networks (LANs). The presence or absence of a transition at the beginning of a bit interval indicates the value; the transition in mid-interval just provides the clocking.

For electrical signals, bit values will generally be represented by one of three possible voltage levels: positive (+V), zero (0V), or negative (-V). Any two of these levels are needed—for example, +V and -V.

There is a transition in the middle of each bit interval. This makes the encoding method self-clocking, and helps avoid signal distortion due to DC signal components.

For one of the possible bit values but not the other, there will be a transition at the start of any given bit interval. For example, in a particular implementation, there may be a signal transition for a 1 bit. "Differential Manchester encoding for a bit sequence" shows an example of a signal using +V and -V, with signal transition on 1 bits.

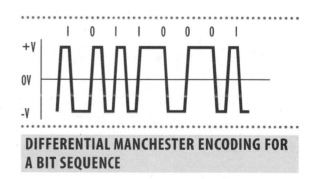

DIFFERENTIAL MANCHESTER ENCODING FOR A BIT SEQUENCE

In differential Manchester encoding, the presence or absence of a transition at the beginning of the bit interval determines the bit value. In effect, 1 bits produce vertical signal patterns; 0 bits produce horizontal patterns, as shown in the figure. The transition in the middle of the interval is just for timing.

Manchester

Manchester is a biphase signal-encoding scheme used in Ethernet LANs. The direction of the transition in mid-interval (negative to positive or positive to negative) indicates the value (1 or 0, respectively) and provides the clocking.

The Manchester scheme follows these rules:

- +V and -V voltage levels are used.

- There is a transition from one to the other voltage level halfway through each bit interval.

- There may or may not be a transition at that start of each bit interval, depending on whether the bit value is a 0 or 1.

- For a 1 bit, the transition is always from a -V to +V; for a 0 bit, the transition is always from a +V to a -V.

In Manchester encoding, the beginning of a bit interval is used merely to set the stage. The activity in the middle of each bit interval determines the bit value: upward transition for a 1 bit, downward for a 0 bit. "Manchester encoding for a bit sequence" shows the encoding for a sample bit sequence.

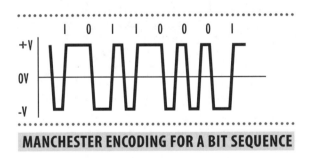

MANCHESTER ENCODING FOR A BIT SEQUENCE

MLT-3 Encoding

MLT-3 is a three-level encoding scheme that can also scramble data. This scheme is one proposed for use in FDDI networks. An alternative is the two-level NRZI.

The MLT-3 signal-encoding scheme uses three voltage levels (including a zero level) and changes levels only when a 1 occurs. It follows these rules:

- +V, 0V, and -V voltage levels are used.

- The voltage remains the same during an entire bit interval; that is, there are no transitions in the middle of a bit interval.

- The voltage level changes in succession: from +V to 0V to -V to 0V to +V, and so on.

- The voltage level changes only for a 1 bit.

MLT-3 is not self-clocking, so that a synchronization sequence is needed to make sure the sender and receiver are using the same timing. "MLT-3 encoding for a bit sequence" shows an example of this encoding.

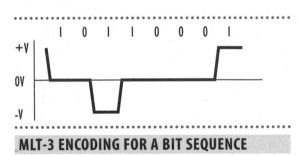

MLT-3 ENCODING FOR A BIT SEQUENCE

NRZ (Non-Return to Zero)

NRZ, also known as *differential encoding*, is a bipolar encoding scheme that changes voltages between bit intervals for 1 values but not for 0 values. This means that the encoding changes during a transmission. For example, 0 may be a positive voltage during one part, and a negative voltage during another part, depending on the last occurrence of a 1. The presence or absence of a transition indicates a bit value, not the voltage level.

NRZ is inexpensive to implement, but it is not self-clocking. It also does not use transition coding.

"NRZ encoding for a bit sequence" shows the encoding for a sample bit sequence.

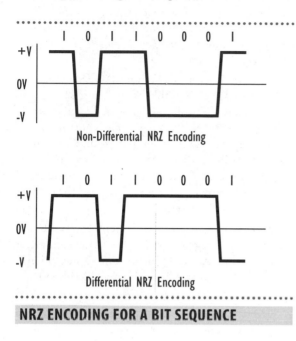

NRZ ENCODING FOR A BIT SEQUENCE

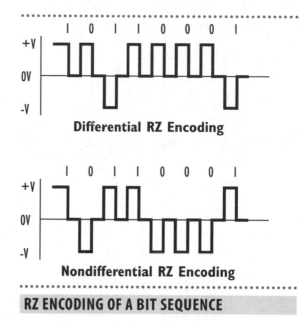

RZ ENCODING OF A BIT SEQUENCE

RZ (Return to Zero)

RZ is a bipolar signal-encoding scheme that uses transition coding to return the signal to a zero voltage during part of each bit interval. It is self-clocking.

"Differential and nondifferential RZ encoding of a bit sequence" shows both differential and nondifferential versions of the RZ encoding scheme. In the differential version, the defining voltage (the voltage associated with the first half of the bit interval) changes for each 1 bit, and remains unchanged for each 0 bit.

In the nondifferential version, the defining voltage changes only when the bit value changes, so that the same defining voltages are always associated with 0 and 1. For example, +5 volts may define a 1, and -5 volts may define a 0.

FM 0 Encoding

FM 0 (frequency modulation 0) is a signal-encoding method used for LocalTalk networks in Macintosh environments. FM 0 uses +V and -V voltage levels to represent bit values. The encoding rules are as follows:

- 1 bits are encoded alternately as +V and
- -V, depending on the previous voltage level. The voltage level remains constant for an entire bit interval for a 1 bit.
- 0 bits are encoded as +V or -V, depending on the immediately preceding voltage level. The voltage changes to the other value halfway through the bit interval.

"FM 0 encoding for a bit sequence" shows the encoding for a sample bit sequence.

FM 0 is self-clocking because the encoding for a 0 bit can be used to determine the length of a bit interval and to synchronize the sender and receiver.

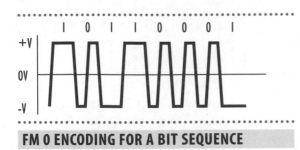

FM 0 ENCODING FOR A BIT SEQUENCE

Encryption

Most simply, encryption is a process in which ordinary text or numerical information (*plaintext*) is converted into an unintelligible form (called *ciphertext*, among other terms) using a well-defined (and reversible) conversion algorithm and a predefined bit value (known as a *key*). The key provides a starting value for the encryption algorithm.

For various reasons, some information must be kept encrypted. Because of the fervor with which this statement is believed, encryption has become an active area of research and study. Much computing and brain power has been expended in developing encryption algorithms that are impossible to crack and then cracking them.

Three broad strategies can be used for encryption: the traditional strategy, the private-key strategy, and the public-key strategy.

Traditional Encryption

The traditional encryption strategy is simply to devise and apply a conversion algorithm. The receiver must know the algorithm and the key in order to reverse the conversion and decrypt the information. This approach has two weaknesses:

- The algorithms and keys used tend, as a class, to be easier to crack than those used in the other strategies.

- The algorithm or key may be stolen or intercepted while being communicated to the receiver.

Secret-Key Encryption

Secret-key encryption strategies use a single key—known only to the sender and the receiver—and a public encryption algorithm. Private-key encryption is also known as *one-key key*, *single key*, or *symmetric key encryption*.

The Data Encryption Standard (DES), which was adapted in 1977 as the official United States encryption standard for nonclassified data, uses a secret-key strategy. The encryption algorithm is quite complex, and involves numerous permutations and transpositions of message elements. See the DES article for more information. Different levels of encryption can be used to make the ciphertext even more unintelligible.

As long as the secret keys are kept secret, this encryption strategy is very effective. For example, even though it uses only 56 bits for the encryption key, the DES has an extremely small likelihood of being cracked.

Secret-key strategies have one major disadvantage: it is not possible to protect a message against fraud by either the sender or the receiver.

Public-Key Encryption

Public-key encryption strategies use the two halves of a very long bit sequence as the basis for the encryption algorithm. Public-key encryption is also known as *double-key encryption* or *asymmetric key encryption*.

One key (one half of the bit sequence) is placed in a public-key library to which everyone has access. The other key is known only to a single party, and is this party's private key. Either half of the bit sequence can be used to encrypt the information; the *other half* is needed to decrypt it. Someone wishing to send a message can use the receiver's public key to encrypt the message; the receiver can use the private key to decrypt it. To reverse the process, the erstwhile receiver uses the private key to encrypt the message. The destination party can use the public key to decrypt the message.

This encryption strategy is simple to implement. It is also relatively easy to crack unless the initial bit sequence is quite long. The RSA algorithm is an exception to this weakness, and has the advantage of being able to protect against fraud by the sender or receiver. See the RSA Algorithm article for more information.

End Bracket

A circuit board with slots into which other boards can be plugged. The motherboard in a PC is a backplane. A *segmented backplane* is a backplane with two or more buses, each with its own slots for additional boards.

End Delimiter (ED)

→ *See* ED (End Delimiter)

End Frame Sequence (EFS)

The EFS is the last frame in a token-ring data packet.

→ *Broader Category* Token Ring

End Node

In a network, a station that serves as a source or a destination for a packet. An end node should be able to communicate through all the layers in the OSI Reference Model or an equivalent layered model.

→ *See Also* Node

End of Content (EOC)

In telecommunications, a special character used to indicate the end of a message or page.

End Office (EO)

→ *See* EO (End Office)

End System (ES)

In the OSI Reference Model, an end system (ES) is a network entity, such as a node, that uses or provides network services or resources. An end system is known as a *host* in Internet terminology.

Architecturally, an end system uses all seven layers of the OSI Reference Model. This is in contrast to an intermediate system (IS), or router, which uses only the bottom three layers (the subnet layers) of the model. "Communications involving intermediate and end systems" shows the relationship between intermediate and end systems.

→ *Broader Category* OSI Reference Model

→ *Compare* Intermediate System (IS)

End-to-End Routing

A routing strategy in which the entire route is determined before the message is sent. This is in contrast to node-to-node routing, in which the route is built step-by-step.

End-User

In a network, the ultimate consumer of a networking service.

Enhanced Integrated Drive Electronics (EIDE)

→ *See* EIDE (Enhanced Integrated Drive Electronics)

E

Enhanced Interior Gateway Routing Protocol (EIGRP)

→ See Protocol, EIGRP (Enhanced Interior Gateway Routing Protocol)

Enhanced Parallel Port (EPP)

→ See EPP (Enhanced Parallel Port)

Enhanced Small Device Interface (ESDI)

→ See ESDI (Enhanced Small Device Interface)

ENS (Enterprise Network Services)

ENS is an extension to Banyan's VINES network operating system (NOS). ENS enables StreetTalk to keep track of servers using NOSs other than

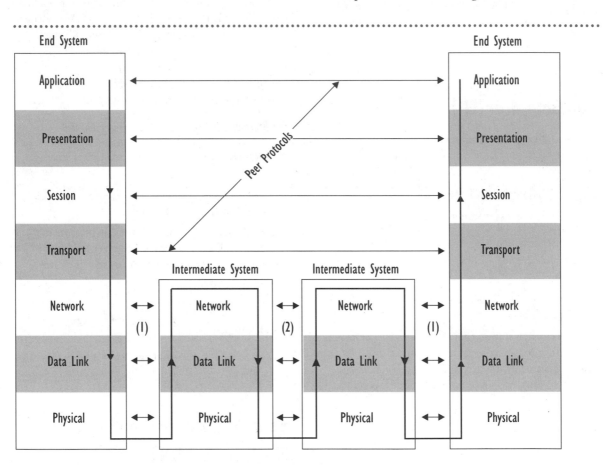

(1) Network Access Protocol
(2) Routing Protocol

COMMUNICATIONS INVOLVING INTERMEDIATE AND END SYSTEMS

VINES, such as any version of Novell's NetWare 2.x and later or of Apple's AppleTalk.

StreetTalk is the global naming service for VINES. A naming service keeps track of which nodes and devices are attached to the network and assigns a global name to each node. The name is independent of the particular network in which the node is located, and makes it possible for a user connected to one server to use resources attached to a different server, without knowing which specific server has the resources.

ENS for NetWare is a special version for use in NetWare versions 2.2 or later. Naming services are not needed in version 4.0, because this version provides global naming through the NetWare Directory Services (NDS).

ENS for NetWare includes four components:

- Server software, which runs the dedicated server that is needed to run ENS for NetWare

- A StreetTalk agent, which runs as a VAP (Value-Added Process, for NetWare 2.x) or as an NLM (NetWare Loadable Module, for NetWare 3.x)

- Client software, which must run on each workstation that wants to use ENS

- ENS utilities, which are used instead of Net-Ware utilities

Enterprise Certified NetWare Engineer (ECNE)

→ See   ECNE (Enterprise Certified NetWare Engineer)

Enterprise Computing

A term for networks that encompasses most or all of a company's computing resources. In most cases, an enterprise computing network will include a whole range of computers, which may be running different operating systems and belong to different types of networks. Consequently, one of the biggest challenges for enterprise computing is to achieve interoperability for all its components.

One way to do this is to use the protocols from the World Wide Web. With these protocols, the enterprise network can become an intranet—or even an extranet, if noncompany computers are also allowed access to the network.

→ See Also   Extranet; Intranet; Network, Enterprise

Enterprise Information Base (EIB)

→ See   EIB (Enterprise Information Base)

Enterprise Network Services (ENS)

→ See   ENS (Enterprise Network Services)

Enterprise System Connection Architecture (ESCON)

→ See   ESCON (Enterprise System Connection Architecture)

Entity

In networking models, *entity* refers to an abstract device, such as a program, function, or protocol, that implements the services for a particular layer on a single machine. An entity provides services for entities at the layer above it and requests services of the entities at the layers below it.

The term entity is also used to refer to a device on a network, at least when that device is running a program or providing a service.

E

Entrance Facilities

In a premises distribution system (PDS), the location at which the building's wiring and the external wiring meet.

Entry Point

For networking hardware, the point at which a node is connected to the network; for software, the point at which a program, module, or function begins executing. In IBM's NMA, *entry point* refers to the software through which an SNA-compliant device can communicate with the network management program.

→ *See Also* NMA (Network Management Architecture)

Entry State

In a routing table for an AppleTalk network, a value that indicates the status of a path. Such an entry may have the value good, suspect, or bad, depending on how recently the path was verified as being valid.

Envelope

In communications or electronic mail (e-mail) systems, *envelope* refers to information that is added to a data packet in order to make sure the packet reaches its destination and is received correctly. This information is generally appended as a header (and possibly also a trailer) for the data packet.

In relation to an electrical signal, envelope is used as a term for the signal's shape, such as sine, square, or trapezoidal.

The term *enveloping* refers to a process by which multiple faxes are included in a single transmission.

Envelope Delay Distortion

In an electrical signal, the amount of delay between different frequencies. The greater this delay, the greater the distortion.

EO (End Office)

In telephony, a central office, which is where a subscriber's lines are terminated and connected to other exchanges.

→ *See* CO (Central Office)

EOC (End of Content)

In telecommunications, a special character used to indicate the end of a message or page.

EPP (Enhanced Parallel Port)

A parallel port with a maximum signal rate of 16Mbps. The EPP specifications were developed jointly by Xircom and Zenith, and the developers plan to produce a 64Mbps version. The faster port makes external LAN cards (such as those produced by Xircom) more viable.

Equalization

The process by which a device's frequency-response is made uniform over a specified frequency range. This is done to eliminate, or at least decrease, distortion in a signal due to high-frequency signals being slowed to a greater degree than lower-frequency waves. It also helps to compensate for signal attenuation. A device that performs equalization is called an *equalizer*.

Modems and rate-adaptive technologies perform what essentially amounts to "self-equalization" when they adjust their transmission rates in response to line noise or error conditions.

Erlang

In communications, a measure of the degree to which a communications channel is being used to capacity. One Erlang is defined as 36 CCS (hundreds of call seconds), which amounts to an entire hour of channel usage at capacity.

Error Correction Code (ECC)

→ *See* ECC (Error Correction Code)

Error Detection and Correction

In communications, an *error* is a situation in which the received material does not match what was sent. Errors can arise for any of many reasons, including the following:

- Problems with the signal, such as noise, interference, or distortion

- Protocol problems, so that sender and receiver cannot understand each other

- Buffer overflow, such as when the capacity of a channel or a device is exceeded

Error correction is a term for any of several strategies for ensuring that the receiver ends up with the same message as the one originally sent. To accomplish this, two steps are necessary: detecting an error and correcting it. In digital communications, errors are at the level of individual bits, so the task becomes one of ensuring that the bit sequence received matches the one sent.

Various precautions and measures can be taken to identify and possibly even correct errors. These measures vary in how effective they are, and all impose a transmission penalty in the form of extra bits that must be sent.

Error-Detection Methods

Detecting errors involves the identification of an incorrect or invalid transmission element , such as an impossible character or a garbled (but not encrypted) message.

In general, error-detection strategies rely on a numerical value (based on the bytes transmitted in a packet) that is computed and included in the packet. The receiver computes the same type of value and compares the computed result with the transmitted value. Error-detection strategies differ in the complexity of the computed value and in their success rate.

Error-detection methods include cyclic or longitudinal redundancy checks and the use of parity bits. Parity bits, CRC (cyclic redundancy check), and LRC (longitudinal redundancy check) values are sometimes referred to as ECCs (error correction codes), even though, strictly speaking, they can only help *detect* errors. *Hamming codes*, on the other hand, are true ECCs, because they provide enough information to determine the nature of the error and to replace it with a correct value.

CRC (Cyclic Redundancy Check)

CRC is an error-detection method based on a transformation of the bit values in a data packet or frame. The transformation involves multiplying the bit pattern by a polynomial equation, whose order depends on the number of bits allocated for the computed value. The more bits, the better the error-detection capabilities.

The sender computes a CRC value and adds this to the data packet. The receiver computes a CRC value based on the data portion of the received packet and compares the result with the transmitted CRC value. If the two match, the receiver assumes the packet has been received without error. Note that a matching CRC value is no guarantee of an error-free transmission, although it does make it almost certain that any errors overlooked involved more than two bits in the packet.

The following are some of the CRC tests that have been developed and that are used in communications and networking contexts:

CRC-12   A 12-bit CRC check, used with older protocols, most notably, IBM's BSC (Binary Synchronous Communication) protocol.

CRC-16   A 16-bit CRC check, used in many file transfer protocols. CRC-16 can detect all single- and double-bit errors, all errors in which an odd number of bits are erroneous, and most error bursts (signals in which multiple bits in succession are erroneous, for example, because of some temporary glitch or interference in the power supply).

CRC-CCITT   A 16-bit CRC check, intended as an international standard.

CRC-32   A 32-bit CRC check, used in local area network (LAN) protocols because it can detect virtually all errors.

Parity, or Vertical Redundancy Checking (VRC)

Parity, also known as *vertical redundancy checking* (*VRC*), is a crude error-detection method, which is used in serial transmissions. With this method, an extra bit is added at regular locations, such as after seven or eight data bits. The value of the parity bit depends on the pattern of 0 and 1 values in the data byte and on the type of parity being used.

Bits 3, 4, and 5 in the UART (universal asynchronous receiver/transmitter) line control register (LCR) determine the parity setting in a serial communication. The following values are used (with bit values displayed in the order 345):

None (000)   The value of the parity bit is ignored.

Odd (100)   The parity bit is set to whatever value is required to ensure that the bit pattern (including parity bit) has an odd number of 1 values. For example, with 1010 1101, the parity bit would be set to 0.

Even (110)   The parity bit is set to whatever value is required to ensure that the bit pattern (including parity bit) has an even number of 1 values. For example, with 1010 1101, the parity bit would be set to 1.

Mark (101)   The parity bit is always set to the mark value (1).

Space (111)   The parity bit is always set to the space value (0).

Block Parity, or Longitudinal Redundancy Checking (LRC)

Another type of parity, called *block parity* or *longitudinal redundancy checking* (*LRC*), is computed for each bit place value in a block of bytes. For example, after every eight bytes, an additional byte is set. One of these extra bits corresponds to each place value for the preceding set of bytes. Block parity is always set to even (according to ISO standard 1155), so that each block parity bit is set to whatever value is required to give the column of bits an even number of 1 values.

"LRC and VRC Parity" shows these two types of parity in a single transmission.

```
1001    011-1       B
0011    111-0       l
1100    110-1       o   P
1001    000-1       c   a
1101    101-0       k   r
1010    101-1           i
0001    100-1           t
                        y
1001    110-1           B
                        i
                        t
                        s
```

Byte Parity Bits

LRC AND VRC PARITY

Error-Correction Methods

Once an error is detected, the most common correction scheme is to request a retransmission. The retransmission may consist of either just the erroneous material, or of the corrected material *and* all the material that was sent after the error but before the receiver alerted the sender. Needless to say, correcting errors can become expensive if there are a lot of them.

It is possible to develop automatic error-correction tools. For example, *forward error correction* (*FEC*) methods enable the receiver to correct an error without requiring a retransmission. Popular FEC methods include Hamming and HBC (Hagelberger, Bose-Chaudhuri) coding.

To do error-correction on the fly, many extra bits must be added to the message in order to locate and correct errors. (Once located, correcting a bit-level error is really not difficult: if 0 is wrong, then 1 must be the value). Such methods may be used in communications in which retransmissions are more disruptive and/or costly than the overhead of sending correctable information.

Error Correction Code (ECC)

In digital communications, a term applied (sometimes incorrectly) to any of several types of codes used to detect or correct errors that may arise during transmission.

→ *See Also* Error Detection and Correction

Error Rate

A measure of erroneous transmission elements in relation to the total transmission. This information can be conveyed in several ways. A widely used index is the BER, which specifies the number of erroneous bits per million (or billion or trillion) bits.

→ *See Also* BER (Bit Error Rate)

ES (End System)

→ *See* End System (ES)

ESCON (Enterprise System Connection Architecture)

ESCON is a fiber-optic communications channel. IBM developed this architecture for use as a back-end network for connecting its ES/9000 series (or compatible) mainframes and peripheral devices, such as controllers, channel extenders, and storage devices.

ESCON uses either 50/125 or 62.5/125 (core/cladding diameter) multimode fiber. The light source for ESCON is an LED (light-emitting diode), which sends signals at a wavelength of approximately 1325 nanometers (nm). This wavelength is popular because of its optical properties.

ESCON uses a 4B/8B signal-encoding scheme, in which groups of four or eight bits are encoded as 5- or 10-bit symbols, respectively. 4B/8B is more efficient than the Manchester or differential Manchester signal-encoding schemes used in most local-area networks (LANs). ESCON supports transmission speeds of up to 200Mbps.

The optical fiber runs from the mainframe's channel controllers to a copper-based (not optical), switched-star concentrator, which IBM calls a *director*. Control units for the mainframes are connected to the director. Concentrator and mainframe can be 2 or 3 kilometers (1 to 2 miles) apart, depending on whether the 50 or 62.5 nanometer fiber core is used.

The director keeps channel activity down by sending signals only to lines for which the signals are intended, as opposed to passing the signals on to all lines (as a passive concentrator would do).

→ *Broader Categories* Cable, Fiber-Optic; Network Architecture

ESDI (Enhanced Small Device Interface)

An interface and storage format for hard disks. ESDI can support relatively high-capacity (up to a gigabyte or so) drives and supports access times as low as about 10 milliseconds. Compare ESDI with IDE and SCSI.

ESF (Extended Superframe Format) Framing

In digital signaling, ESF is a method for framing a DS1 channel. *(Framing is identifying the individual channels in the DS1 channel).* ESF framing groups 24 (193-bit) frames into an ESF superframe, so that each DS1 channel consists of one ESF superframe.

In each ESF superframe, the values in every 193rd bit (in bits 193, 386, and so on) are used for any of three purposes:

- Framing, as originally intended (frames 4, 8, 12, …, 24).

- A 4Kbps link between endpoints (frames 1, 3, 5, …, 23).

- A 6-bit cyclic redundancy check (CRC) value (frames 2, 6, 10, …, 22)

The eighth bit in every channel of frames 6, 12, 18, and 24 is used for signaling between central offices. The signaling capabilities for ESF framing are more sophisticated than for D4 framing, because four frames provide signaling for ESF, compared with only two frames for D4. "Elements in ESF framing" illustrates this method.

→ *Compare* D4 Framing

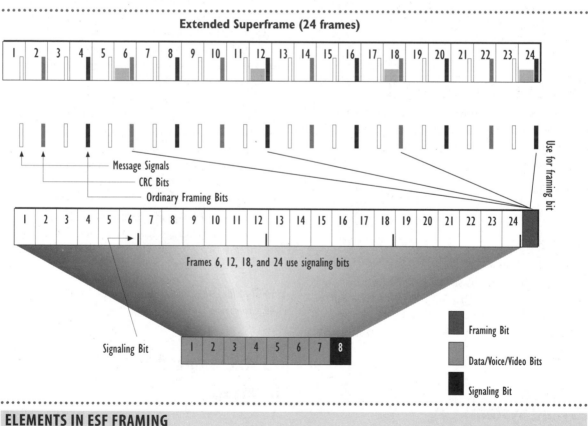

Extended Superframe (24 frames)

Message Signals
CRC Bits
Ordinary Framing Bits

Use for framing bit

Frames 6, 12, 18, and 24 use signaling bits

Signaling Bit

1 2 3 4 5 6 7 8

Framing Bit
Data/Voice/Video Bits
Signaling Bit

ELEMENTS IN ESF FRAMING

ESN (Electronic Switched Network)

An ESN is a telecommunications service for private networks. A *private network* is one consisting of multiple PBXs (private branch exchanges) at various locations. ESN provides automatic switching between PBXs, so that a PBX can be called from any other PBX in the network without the need for a dedicated connection between the two PBXs.

Because a private network is also known as a *tandem network*, an ESN is said to provide "electronic tandem switching."

Establishment Controller

In an IBM environment, an *establishment controller* can support multiple devices, such as IBM or ASCII terminals or token-ring nodes, for communication with a mainframe host. The controller communicates with the host's front-end processor (FEP). The IBM 3174 establishment controller is an example of this type of controller.

If local, the link between controller and device can be over a parallel line, an ESCON link, or through a token-ring network. Remote connections can use V.24, V.35, or X.21 interfaces, and SNA/SDLC, X.25, or BSC protocols.

In IBM's SNA (Systems Network Architecture) environment, an establishment controller is a type 2.0 PU (physical unit).

➡ *Broader Category* SNA (Systems Network Architecture)

➡ *See Also* Cluster Controller

Ethernet

Ethernet began as a shared-media network architecture, but it has since undergone some drastic changes. The elements of traditional Ethernet are the result of work by Xerox, Intel, and Digital Equipment Corporation. Ethernet, along with variants defined in the IEEE 802.3 standard, is currently the most widely used architecture for local-area networks (LANs). According to some estimates, there are more than 25 million Ethernet nodes around the world, with annual sales adding to this at the rate of 10 million nodes per year. Estimates of Ethernet's share of the LAN configurations range between 75 and 90 percent.

A great deal has happened in the Ethernet world in the past few years. For one thing, Ethernet has also become a switched-media architecture. For another, Ethernet network speeds have increased a hundredfold, from the 10Mbps of the original Ethernet to the 1Gbps of Gigabit Ethernet.

Before discussing these developments, I first summarize the general features of a "standard" (10Mbps) Ethernet network, noting differences where relevant. A 10Mbps Ethernet network has the following characteristics:

- Operates at the two lowest layers in the OSI Reference Model: the Physical and Data-Link layer.

- Uses a bus topology. Nodes are attached to the trunk segment, which is the main piece of cable in an Ethernet network. 10BaseT, a variant architecture based on the IEEE 802.3 standard, can use a star topology. 100BaseT networks must use a star topology, according to the IEEE 802.3u specifications. Other switched-media variants, including Gigabit Ethernet, also use a star topology.

- Can operate at a speed of up to 10Mbps. Several variants operate at slower speeds, and newer variants operate at 100Mbps and 1Gbps, respectively.

- Uses CSMA/CD, a media-access method based on collision detection. This access method is specified as part of the IEEE 802.3 document. 100VG-AnyLAN, an alternative 100Mbps variant, uses demand priority as the media-access method. Connections in Gigabit Ethernet networks almost always operate in full-duplex mode and nodes generally communicate directly through switches. These two factors—together with the use of buffered distributors to prevent overflow—make collision detection unnecessary for Gigabit Ethernet.

- Broadcasts transmissions, so that each node gets the transmission at the same time. A broadcast strategy is necessary for a collision detection type of media-access method.

- Uses Manchester encoding to represent the 0 and 1 values that make up the physical signal. This is a self-clocking encoding method that includes a voltage transition in the middle of each bit interval. To break a bit interval into two halves, the clock rate must be at least twice the maximum transmission speed, so that a 20MHz clock is required for 10Mbps Ethernet. (Implementations don't actually achieve the maximum transmission rate, so that you can get by with slower clocks.) 100BaseT4 and Gigabit Ethernet networks use different encoding methods.

- Uses 50-ohm coaxial cable. Variants can use 50- or 75-ohm coaxial, twisted-pair, and fiber-optic cable. Each type of cable has its characteristic add-ons (connectors and terminators).

- Is a baseband network, although variants also support broadband networks.

"Context and properties of Ethernet" summarizes this architecture.

Ethernet Versions

Ethernet's roots go back to Project ALOHA at the University of Hawaii in the 1960s. The CSMA/CD access method was developed for the ALOHA WAN.

Ethernet version 1.0 was superseded in 1982 by Ethernet 2.0, which is currently the official 10Mbps Ethernet standard. This is also known as DIX (for Digital, Intel, Xerox) Ethernet or Blue Book Ethernet. Standards for Ethernet variants at two higher speeds have also been developed—

specifically, two fast, 100Mbps Ethernet standards and a Gigabit Ethernet specification also have been ratified.

A variant on this Blue Book standard was formulated by the IEEE 802.3 working group. This variant is sometimes called Ethernet as well. However, although Ethernet and 802.3 are similar, there are differences in the way the Data-Link layer is handled and in the format of a packet. These differences are explained later in this article.

Context

Network Architecture
  Shared-Media
    ARCnet
    Ethernet ———
    Token Ring
  Switched-Media

Ethernet Properties	
Description	Shared-media, baseband network
Topology	Bus (Ethernet 1.0 or 2.0) Bus or Star (802.3-based Ethernet)
Access method	CSMA/CD
Speed	Up to 10 Mbps
Cable	50-ohm coaxial (Ethernet 1.0 or 2.0) 50-ohm coaxial, unshielded twisted-pair, Fiber-optic (802.3-based Ethernet)
Frame size	46-1500 data bytes
Variants	10Base5 (thick Ethernet) 10Base2 (thin Ethernet) 10BaseT (twisted-pair Ethernet) 10BaseF (fiber-optic Ethernet) 10Broad36 100 Mbps Ethernets (proposed)

CONTEXT AND PROPERTIES OF ETHERNET

Because of these differences, difficulties will arise if you try to mix different types of Ethernet on the same network. 802.3 and Ethernet 2 nodes cannot coexist on the same network. Fortunately, most implementations allow you to select which flavor of Ethernet you want to use on the network. Higher speed variants are based on the 802.3 flavor of Ethernet, and so they can communicate with 10Mbps 802.3 Ethernet nodes. (It's generally not a good idea, however, for a 1000Mbps node to communicate directly with a 10Mbps node. The faster node will spend most of its time doing absolutely nothing.

Some networking environments let you have different types of packets on the network under certain conditions. For example, NetWare allows both 802.2 and 802.3 packets to coexist on a network. (Packet types are discussed later in this article.)

Ethernet Groupings

Ethernet networks are grouped by their broadcast method, type of cable, and physical properties.

Baseband versus Broadband

In a baseband network, one node can broadcast at a time. In a broadband network, multiple nodes can broadcast at the same time.

Blue Book Ethernet operates only in baseband mode. Ethernet 802.3-based implementations can operate in either baseband or broadband mode.

Thick, Thin, and Twisted-Pair

Ethernet networks are also categorized according to the type of cable used. Thin and thick Ethernet use thin and thick coaxial cable, respectively. Twisted-pair Ethernet is actually an 802.3 architecture that uses unshielded twisted-pair (UTP) cable. The following are some of the synonyms for these Ethernet varieties:

Thick Ethernet   ThickNet, Standard Ethernet, 10Base5

Thin Ethernet   ThinNet, Cheapernet, 10Base2

Twisted-pair Ethernet   UTP Ethernet, 10BaseT

Physical Layer Properties

The IEEE 802.3 working group developed a simple notation system to characterize various Physical-layer properties of an Ethernet network. Ethernet networks are described using three elements related to the wiring and the physical signal. Each description has three elements:

Speed/Band/Length or *Cable-type*

as in

10Base5

The first element, *Speed*, specifies the approximate maximum transmission speed, or bandwidth, in megabits per second (Mbps) for the network. This will be a 1, 5, 10, 100, or 1000 (for newer, gigabit networks).

The second element, *Band*, is either Base or Broad, depending on whether the network is baseband or broadband. For example, 10Base5 specifies a baseband network; 10Broad36 specifies a broadband network.

The third element, *Length* or *Cable-type*, usually specifies the approximate maximum length of a network segment, in hundreds of meters. For example, 10Base5 can have network segments of up to 500 meters (1650 feet). In some cases, the length value is specified in 50-meter increments. For example, the 1Base5 network supports network segments up to 250 meters, not 500 meters.

In other cases, the third element is used to specify cable type. For example, 10BaseT and 10BaseF specify networks with twisted-pair and fiber-optic cable, respectively.

The table "Types of Ethernet Networks" summarizes the types of Ethernet networks that have been defined in IEEE 802.3 or by other groups. See the 10Base*x*, 10Broad36, 100BaseT, and Gigabit Ethernet articles for more details.

E

TYPES OF ETHERNET NETWORKS

Type	Description
10Base2	Thin Ethernet using thin (3/16-inch), 50-ohm coaxial cable. Maximum segment length is 185 meters, and there can be at most 30 nodes per segment. Also known as Cheapernet.
10Base5	Thick Ethernet using thick (3/8-inch), 50-ohm coaxial cable. Although it's the cabling for Blue Book Ethernet, this is not a very popular configuration because thick coaxial cable is difficult to handle and install. Maximum segment length is 500 meters, and there can be at most 100 nodes per segment.
10BaseT	Twisted-pair Ethernet using UTP cable. This configuration was adopted as the 802.3i standard in 1990, and it is becoming popular because UTP is inexpensive and easy to install and work with. Maximum cable segment length is 100 meters.
1Base5	The StarLAN network developed by AT&T. StarLAN uses UTP cable and a star topology, and was defined long before the 10BaseT standard was proposed.
10Broad36	The only broadband network defined in the 802.3 standard. This network uses 75-ohm coaxial cable (CATV cable).
10BaseF	The only network in the 802.3 standard that explicitly calls for fiber-optic cable. This type is actually divided into three variations: 10BaseFB, 10BaseFP, and 10BaseFL.
10BaseFB	This network uses optical fiber for the backbone, or trunk, cable. Trunk segments can be up to 2 kilometers (1.25 miles) in length.
10BaseFP	This specifies a network that uses optical fiber and a star topology. The coupler used to distribute the signal is passive (does not regenerate the signal before distributing). As a result, such a network needs no electronics except for those in the computer. Maximum length for a piece of such cable is 500 meters (1,650 feet).
10BaseFL	This specifies a network that uses optical fiber to connect a node to a hub, or concentrator. Cable segments can be up to 2 kilometers in length.
100VG-AnyLAN	A 100Mbps Ethernet network developed by Hewlett-Packard and AT&T Microelectronics.
100BaseT	A 100Mbps Ethernet network Physical-layer specification originally developed by Grand Junction Networks. This is a standard of the IEEE 802.3u study group. Variants include 100BaseT4, 100BaseT2, 100BaseTX, and 100BaseFX.
100BaseFX	A 100Mbps network Physical-layer specification that uses a pair of either 50/125µm or 62.5/125µm optical fibers.
100BaseT2	A 100Mbps network Physical-layer specification that uses two pairs of Category 3 or higher shielded or unshielded twisted-pair wire.
100BaseT4	A 100Mbps network Physical-layer specification that uses four pairs of Category 3 or higher shielded or unshielded twisted-pair wire. 100BaseT4 also uses an 8B/6T data-translation scheme.
100BaseTX	A 100Mbps network Physical-layer specification that uses two pairs of Category 5 shielded or unshielded twisted-pair wire.
1000BaseT	A Physical-layer specification for a 1Gbps network over four pairs of Category 5 unshielded twisted-pair wire.
1000BaseX	A Physical-layer specification for a 1Gbps Ethernet network. This is a standard of the IEEE 802.3z study group, with physical signaling based on the Fibre Channel specifications. Variants include 1000Base-CX, 1000Base-LX, and 1000Base-SX.
1000Base-CX	A 1Gbps network Physical-layer specification that uses two pairs of 150-ohm balanced copper cable (twinax). Used for short-distance connections (between rooms or between a room and a wiring closet). Maximum distance between nodes is 25 meters.
1000Base-LX	A 1Gbps network Physical-layer specification that uses long wavelength signals over a pair of optical fibers. Mainly used for horizontal cabling. Maximum distance between nodes is 3 kilometers with single-mode fiber; 440 or 550 meters with 62.5 or 50 micron multimode fiber, respectively.
1000Base-SX	A 1Gbps network Physical-layer specification that uses short wavelength signals over a pair of optical fibers. Mainly used for backbone cabling. Maximum distance between nodes is 260 or 525 meters for 62.5 and 50 micron multimode fiber, respectively.

Ethernet Hardware

Although the details differ, Ethernet networks all use a limited number of components, which include Ethernet network interface cards (NICs), cables, connectors, transceivers and receivers, hubs, punch-down blocks, and baluns.

Ethernet NICs

Each node must have an Ethernet NIC, which provides the computer with access to the network. An NIC converts, packetizes, and transmits data from the computer, and receives, unpacketizes, and converts data received over the network. NICs are architecture-specific. This means that you cannot use an Ethernet NIC for a Token Ring network. It also means that you may not be able to use an 802.3 card for an Ethernet network, or vice versa.

An Ethernet and an 802.3 card *can transmit* packets to each other, because the Ethernet and 802.3 packets have the same general structure. However, the variant cards *cannot read* each other's packets, because certain fields in the packets have different types of information. Some NICs support both Ethernet and 802.3 formats, and are therefore able to read and create both types of packets. Even if the cards cannot communicate directly, the networking software will generally be able to translate.

Ethernet NICs can have any or all of the following connectors: BNC, DIX, RJ-*xx*. On NICs with multiple connectors, you will generally need to set DIP switches or jumper settings on the board to indicate the type of connector you will be using.

Ethernet cards include a hardware address on a ROM chip. This address is assigned by the IEEE and the vendor and is unique to that particular NIC. Part of the address contains vendor information, and part identifies the board itself. This address can be used by bridges and routers to identify a particular node on a network.

The high cost of NICs was one early obstacle to Gigabit Ethernet adoption. These cards were expensive because the original Gigabit Ethernet specification supports only optical fiber. The transceivers for fiber-optic connections are considerably more expensive than the simpler transceivers for wire connections. This cost has gone down somewhat, as economies of scale have kicked in.

With the development of fast (100Mbps) and Gigabit Ethernet, dual-speed NICs have been developed. These will be either 10/100 or 100/1000Mbps varieties. With such a card, a node can operate at either of the two speeds supported—depending on the speed of the other node. Note that there are no 10/1000Mbps cards. Such a speed difference would be too painful to watch. Making a 1Gbps node work with, and wait for, 10Mbps nodes might be something like driving in a Porsche on an open highway from New York to San Francisco, but having to do it behind a turtle.

If all three node speeds are found in the same network, it will be in a three-tiered arrangement. There will be Gigabit Ethernet nodes at the top, using 100/1000Mbps NICs to communicate with 100Mbps nodes in the middle tier. Other 100Mbps nodes will use 10/100Mbps NICs to communicate with the 10Mbps nodes at the bottom.

Ethernet Cable

Blue Book Ethernet networks use coaxial cable. Networks based on the 802.3 architecture can use coaxial, fiber-optic, or twisted-pair cable. The cable in an Ethernet network may have any of several functional uses:

- Trunk cable is used for the main network segment, which is known as the *trunk segment*. Nodes are attached, directly or indirectly, to the trunk segment. This may also be known as the *backbone segment*, particularly if there are network segments attached—for example, through switches or hubs. Such segments often use optical fiber these days. One of the early uses of Gigabit Ethernet has been for such backbones.

- Drop cable is used to attach nodes indirectly to a trunk segment in a thick Ethernet network. This type of cable is also known as transceiver cable (because it connects the node to a transceiver) and as AUI cable (because of the type of connectors at either end of such a cable).

- Patch cable is used in 802.3 networks to connect any of the following: two hubs, a node from the wallplate to a punch-down block, or a wiring hub to a punch-down block.

See the Cable article for more information about network cabling.

Ethernet Connectors

Connectors are used to connect cable segments. An Ethernet (bus) network also needs terminators and grounded terminators, because network segments must be properly grounded and terminated to prevent signals from being reflected back over the network.

The following types of connectors are used:

- Thick Ethernet networks use N-series connectors and terminators on the trunk, and AUI, or DIX, connectors on the NIC.

- Thin Ethernet networks use BNC connectors and terminators on the trunk and on the NIC.

- Twisted-pair Ethernet networks use RJ-45 connectors or variants on these. These networks do not require separate terminators.

- Various types of fiber-optic connectors, including the BFOC (Bayonet Fiber Optic Connector, also known as the ST, or straight through, connector).

See the Connector; Connector, AUI; Connector, BNC; Connector, Fiber-Optic; and Connector, RJ-*xx* articles for more information.

Repeaters and Transceivers

Repeaters clean and regenerate a signal. Repeaters are used in the middle of a stretch of cable that is so long that the signal quality would deteriorate to an unacceptable level without regeneration. Hubs often act as repeaters.

Transceivers can transmit and receive signals. Transceivers provide the actual point at which the node makes contact with the network. Ethernet/802.3 transceivers may be internal (on the NIC) or external, depending on the type of Ethernet. External transceivers, which are used for thick Ethernet, are attached to the trunk cable with an N-series connector or with a vampire tap.

Transceivers are called *MAUs* (*medium attachment units*) in the IEEE 802.3 document.

Hubs

Hubs are wire collectors. They are used in 802.3 networks that use twisted-pair cable. Wires from nodes in a twisted-pair Ethernet network may be terminated at the hub. Hubs may be internal (boards installed in a machine) or external (stand-alone components). These components are also known as concentrators.

Hardware manufacturers have created special-purpose hubs that enhance the operation of an Ethernet network or that extend the capabilities of certain components. Examples of these are enhanced hubs and switched hubs.

Enhanced hubs for 10BaseT networks have been enhanced with various capabilities and features by different manufacturers. These enhancements include the following:

- Network monitoring and management capabilities.

- Nonvolatile memory, to save settings and performance information even during a power outage.

- Security features, such as the ability to send a packet only to its destination, while sending a busy signal to all other nodes. This helps increase the security on the system by preventing a meaningful message from being intercepted by an unauthorized node.

Switched-hub technology can increase the effective bandwidth of an Ethernet network by allowing multiple transmissions on the network at the same time. For this technology to work, the network must have multiple servers, and the hub must be able to switch to any of multiple network segments.

Ethernet Switches

An Ethernet switch connects a limited number of network segments. This is in contrast to a simple bridge, which connects two segments. Each network segment communicates over the switch through its own port on the switch, and each port can have its full bandwidth. Ethernet switches operate at the data link level (level two of the OSI hierarchy), and work in many ways like a multiport bridge.

Like a multiport bridge, an Ethernet switch can segment a larger network—for example, to help relieve traffic congestion by not allowing transmissions within a segment to leave that segment.

However, Ethernet switches have some additional features that help make them very popular. By placing switches intelligently in a large network, it's possible to produce more efficient network arrangements, thereby resulting in faster throughput. Some switches can even provide dedicated connections between two network segments.

Kalpana developed the first Ethernet switch just a few years ago. Since then, switches have become extremely popular as one solution to the increased traffic on Ethernet networks—with faster Ethernets being the other. Because of their popularity, numerous vendors now supply Ethernet switches.

Two basic classes of Ethernet switches are available:

- *Workgroup* switches communicate with only a single node on each port. Such a switch can provide dedicated services between segments. Because only a single machine can communicate at each port, a workgroup switch doesn't need to check for collisions at the port, and it only needs minimal resources for storing addresses. Such switches require simpler circuitry, and so are relatively inexpensive—often less than $300 per port. The use of such

devices on the network can effectively make it a switched-media architecture—at least for the pair of nodes involved in a communication.

- *Network*, or *segment*, switches are more sophisticated and more expensive. Such switches support multiple nodes at each port—and must, therefore, be able to store all the addresses and forwarding information. Network switches use the spanning tree algorithm to prevent redundant paths between segments.

Punch-Down Block

A punch-down block may be used in a twisted-pair network to provide a more convenient location to terminate wires from nodes in such a network. A punch-down block is a device for making physical contact with the wire inside a cable jacket, thereby establishing the necessary connection for electrical activity. Using such an intermediate connection makes it easier to change the wiring scheme.

Baluns

Baluns are used to connect coaxial cable segments (for example, an AUI cable attached to a node) and twisted-pair cable segments (for example, a cable attached to a hub).

Ethernet Layout

Ethernet uses a bus configuration. Ethernet 802.3 networks can also use a star topology, as can fast Ethernet and Gigabit Ethernet networks.

In a bus, nodes are attached to the network's backbone, or trunk segment. Nodes are attached directly in thin Ethernet and with a drop cable in thick Ethernet. "A thick Ethernet (bus) layout" shows an example of a layout of a bus network.

The number of nodes that can be attached to a trunk segment depends on the type of cabling: a 10Base5 (thick coaxial) segment can support up to 100 nodes; a 10Base2 (thin coaxial) segment can support no more than 30 nodes.

E

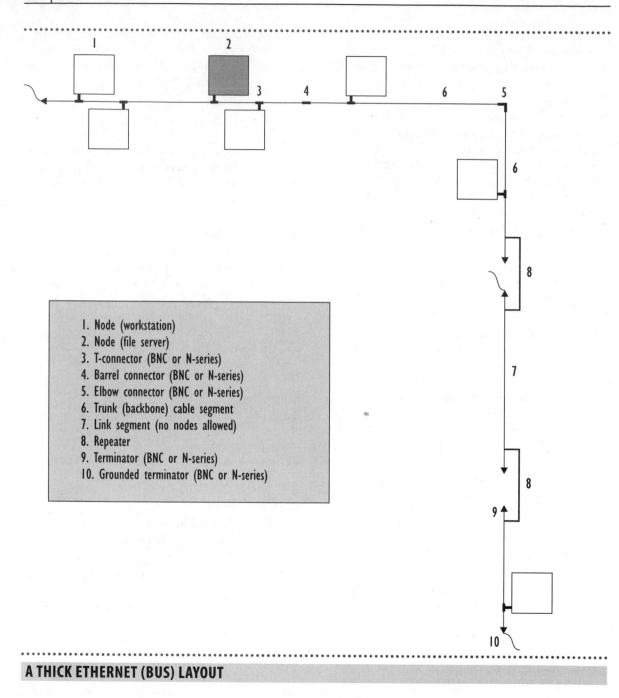

1. Node (workstation)
2. Node (file server)
3. T-connector (BNC or N-series)
4. Barrel connector (BNC or N-series)
5. Elbow connector (BNC or N-series)
6. Trunk (backbone) cable segment
7. Link segment (no nodes allowed)
8. Repeater
9. Terminator (BNC or N-series)
10. Grounded terminator (BNC or N-series)

A THICK ETHERNET (BUS) LAYOUT

A link segment connects two repeaters. A link segment is not treated as trunk segment. You cannot attach a node to link segment cable; you must attach the node to the trunk segment.

Both ends of *each* Ethernet trunk cable segment need to be terminated, and one of these ends need to be grounded. Depending on the type of cable, N-series or BNC terminators are used. If there are repeaters connecting trunk segments, each of the segments must be terminated separately at the repeater.

A fiber-optic inter-repeater link (FOIRL) uses special transceivers and fiber-optic cable for a link segment. With an FOIRL link, the segment between the transceivers can be up to 2 kilometers (1.25 miles).

In a star topology, such as in twisted-pair Ethernet, the nodes are attached to a central hub, rather than to a backbone cable. The hub serves to broadcast transmissions to the nodes and to any other hubs attached. "Layout of a twisted-pair (star) Ethernet network" shows the layout for a simple star network.

The gray area around the hub indicates that the connections to the hub may not be direct. A node or MAU may be connected directly to a wallplate, from there to a punchdown panel, and from there to the hub.

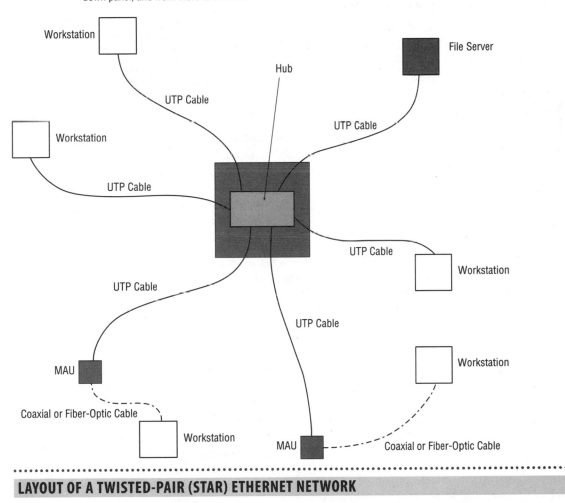

LAYOUT OF A TWISTED-PAIR (STAR) ETHERNET NETWORK

Ethernet Operation

An Ethernet network works as follows:

- Access: A node that wants to send a message listens for a signal on the network. If another node is transmitting, the node waits a randomly determined amount of time before trying again to access the network.

- Transmission: If there is no activity on the network, the node starts transmitting, and then listens for a collision. A collision occurs if another node also found the network idle and started transmitting at the same time. The two packets collide, and garbled fragments are transmitted across the network.

- Collision handling: If there is a collision, the first node to notice sends special jam packets to inform other nodes of the collision. The colliding nodes both retreat and wait a random amount of time before trying again to access the network.

- Reception: If there is no collision, the frame is broadcast onto the network. All nodes listen to each packet transmitted. Each node checks the packet's destination address to determine whether the packet was intended for that node. If so, the node processes the packet and takes whatever action is appropriate. If the node is not the recipient for the packet, the node ignores the packet. (This eavesdropping feature of Ethernet networks—actually, of bus topologies in general—makes it difficult to implement message-level security on an Ethernet network.)

Ethernet Frames

Ethernet frames, or packets, come in several flavors. However, all Ethernet frames consist of preamble, header, data, and trailer components.

Each of the Ethernet frame elements has a predefined structure:

Preamble (8 bytes) Consists of eight bytes, which are divided into seven preamble bytes and one start frame delimiter (SFD) byte for certain packet flavors. These bytes are used to mark the start of a packet and to enable the sender and receiver to synchronize.

Header (14 bytes) Consists of three fields: a 6-byte destination address, a 6-byte source address, and a 2-byte field whose value is interpreted as a length for some packet flavors and as information about the network-level protocol for other flavors. Interpreting this third field as length or type distinguishes the two main types of Ethernet packets (Ethernet 2 and 802.3-based packets).

Data (46–1500 bytes) Contains whatever packet was passed by the higher-level protocol. Ethernet 2 packets contain network-layer packets in the data component; 802.3-based packets get the data component from a sublayer that may add to the network-layer packet. The data component must be at least 46 bytes, so it may include padding bytes.

Trailer (4 bytes) Consists of a frame check sequence (FCS). These bytes represent a CRC (cyclic redundancy check) value, which provides information for detecting errors in a transmission. This component is the same in all packet flavors.

Not counting the preamble, the three remaining components yield Ethernet packets that are between 64 and 1518 bytes.

SQE SUPPORT

All Ethernet variants except version 1.0 expect a SQE (signal quality error) signal from transceivers. This signal, which is also known as a *heartbeat*, "proves" that the component is working and is, therefore, capable of detecting collisions.

Mixing components that do and don't support SQE on the same network is asking for trouble. If a component sends an SQE signal to a component (such as NIC) that doesn't support SQE, the receiver may assume the signal indicates a collision, and will send a jam signal (the signal used to stop transmission when a collision occurs).

Ethernet Packet Flavors

The major distinction in packets is between Ethernet 2 and 802.3-based flavors. This distinction depends on how the values in the third header field are interpreted. The Ethernet packet flavors include Ethernet 2, 802.3, 802.2, and Ethernet SNAP.

File servers for Ethernet networks will generally be able to handle multiple frame flavors, although you may need to run a utility to take advantage of this capability. With a multi-flavor server, nodes that use different Ethernet versions may be able to communicate with each other, but only through the server. For example, nodes using 802.3 and Ethernet 2 NICs may be able to pass packets, but they will not be able to communicate directly with each other.

Ethernet 2

This is the simplest of the packet flavors. The third header field is Type, and its value specifies the source of the Network-layer protocol being used. The table "Selected Ethernet Type Field Values" lists some of the possible values for this field. The data component is whatever was received by the Data-Link layer from the Network layer above it. (The other packet formats receive the data component from a Data-Link sublayer.)

802.3

This flavor has Length as the third header field. The field's value specifies the number of bytes in the data component. The 802.3 flavor is sometimes known as *802.3 raw*, because it does not include LLC (logical-link control) sublayer information in the data component (as does, for example, an 802.2 frame).

E

SELECTED ETHERNET TYPE FIELD VALUES

Value (Hexadecimal)	Source	Value (Hexadecimal)	Source
0x0600	Xerox XNS IDP	0x803f	DEC LAN Traffic monitor
0x0800	IP (Internet Protocol)	0x8046	AT&T
0x0801	X.75 Internet	0x8065	University of Massachusetts, Amherst
0x0805	X.25 Level 3	0x809b	EtherTalk (AppleTalk running on Ethernet)
0x0806	ARP (Address Resolution Protocol)		
0x0807	XNS Compatibility	0x809f	Spider Systems Ltd.
0x0a00	Xerox 802.3 PUP	0x80c0	Digital Communications Associates (DCA)
0x0bad	Banyan Systems		
		0x80d5	IBM SNA Services over Ethernet
0x6003	DEC DECnet Phase IV	0x80e0	Allen-Bradley
0x6004	DEC LAT	0x80f3	AARP (AppleTalk ARP)
0x6005	DEC DECnet diagnostics	0x80f7	Apollo Computer
0x6010	3Com Corporation	0x8137	Novell NetWare IPX/SPX
0x7030	Proteon	0x9000	Loopback (Configuration test protocol)
0x8008	AT&T	0x9001	Bridge Communications XNS Systems Management
0x8035	Reverse ARP		
0x8038	DEC LANBridge	0x9002	Bridge Communications TCP/IP Systems Management
0x803d	DEC Ethernet CSMA/CD Encryption Protocol		

802.2

This packet is similar to the 802.3 format in that it has a Length (rather than a Type) header field, but differs in that part of the data component is actually header information from the LLC sublayer defined above the MAC sublayer in the IEEE 802.2 standard. The first three or four bytes of an 802.2 packet's data component contain information of relevance to the LLC sublayer. The first two bytes contain values for the DSAP (Destination Service Access Point) and SSAP (Source Service Access Point). These values identify the protocols being used at the network level.

The third byte is the Control field, which contains information regarding the type of transmission (such as connectionless or connection-oriented) being used. The packet passed by the Network layer follows after these three values.

Ethernet_SNAP (Sub-Network Access Protocol)

This variant of an 802.2 packet contains LLC sublayer information as well as five additional bytes of information as part of the data component. Two of the five bytes specify the type of protocol being used at the Network layer. This is the same information as in the Type field for an Ethernet 2 packet, except that the field is in a different location in the packet. This Ethernet Type field is preceded by a three-byte Organization Code field, which specifies the organization that assigned the Ethernet Type field value.

The table "Selected Ethernet Type Field Values" shows a list of selected Ethernet Type field values.

"Structure of an Ethernet frame" shows the components of the different flavors of Ethernet frames.

Invalid Frames

A destination node checks for several types of errors that can creep into Ethernet packets (or frames). In particular, the node checks for each of the following types of invalid packets:

- Long (oversized) packets are longer than the allowed size (1518 bytes for Ethernet), but have a valid CRC value. These may be caused by a faulty LAN driver.

- Runt (undersized) packets are shorter than the minimum size (64 bytes), but have a valid CRC value. These may be caused by a faulty LAN driver.

- Jabber packets are longer than 1518 bytes and have an *invalid* CRC value. These may be caused by a faulty transceiver.

- Alignment errors are packets that have extra *bits*, which means that they do not end on byte-boundaries. Such packets will also have invalid CRC values. These may be caused by a faulty component (NIC, transceiver, or cable).

- CRC errors are packets that have a valid number of bytes and end on a byte-boundary, but that have an invalid CRC value. These may be caused by noise on the cable or because a cable segment was too long.

- Valid packets are packets that have none of the preceding problems. Only valid packets are passed on the higher-level protocols in a transmission. Valid packets are created by properly functioning networking software and hardware.

802.3 Differences

The IEEE 802.3 working group, whose task was to formulate a standard for CSMA/CD-based networks, came up with something that looks like Blue Book Ethernet, but that differs in several important ways. The Ethernet 802.3 standard was adopted in 1985, and the addition (802.3i) was adopted in 1990.

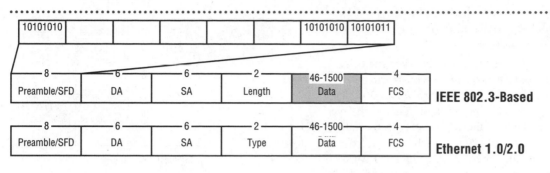

IEEE 802.3-Based

Ethernet 1.0/2.0

Preamble: 7 identical bytes; used for synchronization
SFD (Start Frame Delimiter): Indicates the frame is about to begin
DA (Destination Address): Contains the address of the frame's destination
SA (Source Address): Contains the address of the frame's sender

Length: Indicates the number of data bytes (IEEE 802.3-based variants)
Type: Indicates the upper-level protocol that is using the packet (Ethernet 1.0/2.0 variants)
Data: Contains the information being transmitted, which may consist of a higher-layer packet (may be padded)
FCS: A frame check sequence

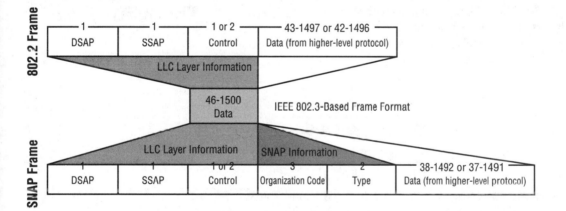

DSAP (Destination Service Access Point): Specifies the process receiving the packet at the destination's network layer
SSAP (Source Service Access Point): Specifies the process sending the packet from the source's network layer
Control: Specifies the type of LLC service requested

Organization Code: Specifies the organization that assigned the following Type field
Type: Indicates the upper-level protocol that is using the packet

STRUCTURE OF AN ETHERNET FRAME

The table "Differences between Ethernet 802.3 and Blue Book Ethernet" summarizes the distinctions between these variants.

Because 802.3 distinguishes between the LLC and MAC sublayers, the process of creating a packet for transmission goes through an extra level of handling. In 802.3 networking, a network-layer packet becomes the data for a PDU (protocol data unit) at the LLC sublayer. A PDU, in turn, becomes the data when an MAC sublayer packet is constructed for transmission over the physical connection. In Blue Book Ethernet networking, the network-layer packet becomes the data portion of a packet. "Layers involved in handling Blue Book and 802.3 Ethernet packets" illustrates the process.

Twisted-Pair Ethernet

A 10BaseT, or twisted-pair Ethernet, network uses unshielded twisted-pair (UTP) cable and a star topology, as opposed to the coaxial cable and bus topology of Blue Book Ethernet. In this architecture, each node is connected to a central wiring hub, which serves as the relay station for the network. This 802.3-based variant was officially adopted as IEEE standard 802.3i in 1990.

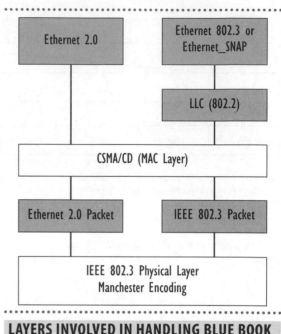

LAYERS INVOLVED IN HANDLING BLUE BOOK AND 802.3 ETHERNET PACKETS

DIFFERENCES BETWEEN ETHERNET 802.3 AND BLUE BOOK ETHERNET

802.3	Ethernet
Supports bus or star topologies.	Supports only a bus topology.
Supports baseband or broadband networks.	Supports only baseband networks.
Defines only the MAC sublayer of the Data-Link layer. Uses the LLC sublayer defined in the IEEE 802.2 standard for the rest of the Data-Link layer.	Does not divide the Data-Link layer into sublayers.
Uses 7 bytes for a preamble and 1 byte as a start of frame delimiter (SFD) for a packet.	Uses 8 bytes for a preamble; does not distinguish a separate SFD byte.
Uses the third header field to indicate the length of the frame's data component.	Uses the third header field to specify the type of higher-layer protocol using the data-link services.
Can use the SQE signal as a network management device.	Can use the SQE signal as a network management device only in version 2.0.

A twisted-pair Ethernet network needs the following components:

- NIC with on-board MAU (or transceiver), to mediate between the node and the network (one per node)

- External MAU, for mediating between the network and nodes that use coaxial or fiber-optic cable (optional)

- UTP cable, to connect nodes to a wiring hub

- Wiring hubs (stand-alone or peer)

- Punch-down block, to make wire termination more flexible and easier to change (optional)

- RJ-45 connectors, for connecting to wall plates and to NICs

In order to be sufficiently free of interference, UTP cable for a network should have enough twists in the wire. Some telephone cable may not be suitable, because it is too flat and has too few twists. The cable also must have enough conductors for the eight-wire RJ-45 connectors.

Each node in a 10-BaseT network is connected directly or indirectly to a wiring hub. Indirect connections can be through wall plates or by connecting the PC to an external MAU, which is connected to a wall plate or to a hub.

10BaseT networks can use either of two kinds of hubs:

- A stand-alone hub is an external component with RJ-45 connections to link the nodes. This type of hub has its own power supply.

- A peer hub is a card that can be installed in one of the machines on the network. This internal hub must be connected physically to the NIC in the machine, and it depends on the PC for its power.

Nodes are connected to one of these hubs—from a distance no greater than 100 meters (330 feet)—using UTP cable with RJ-45 connections at each end. A 10BaseT network can have up to four linked hubs.

Thick Ethernet

A 10Base5, or thick Ethernet, network uses thick ($^3/_8$-inch) coaxial cable (with 50-ohm impedance) for the network backbone. The 50-ohm cable is specially designed for this version of Ethernet, but standard thick coaxial cable can also be used.

Thick Ethernet Components

A thick Ethernet network uses the following components:

- Ethernet NICs to mediate between node and network (one per node)

- Thick coaxial cable for trunk cable segments (with nodes attached) or for link segments (between repeaters, and with no nodes attached)

- Transceivers to attach to the trunk segment, and to do the required conversions when the node transmits or receives (one per node)

- Transceiver, or drop, cable with DIX connectors on each end, to connect the NIC in the node to the transceiver attached to the trunk segment (one per node)

- N-series barrel connectors to connect pieces of cable in the trunk segments (the fewer the better)

- N-series terminators, to terminate one end of a trunk segment (one per trunk segment)

- N-series grounded terminators, to terminate *and ground* one end of a trunk segment (one per trunk segment)

- Repeaters (optional), to extend the network by regenerating the signal before passing it on

The thick cable is relatively difficult to manage and install. Most networks that use thick cable use it as the network backbone, which is not expected to change. The nodes in the network are attached using additional cable, called drop cable or transceiver cable.

Thick Ethernet Configuration

The following configuration rules and restrictions apply for thick Ethernet.

- The maximum length of a trunk segment is 500 meters (1640 feet).

- The network trunk can have at most five segments, for a total trunk of 2500 meters (8200 feet). Of these five cable segments, up to two can be link segments (without nodes attached) and up to three can be trunk segments (with nodes attached).

- Within a thick coaxial trunk segment, you can use N-series barrel connectors to link shorter pieces of cable. You can use repeaters to connect two segments into a longer network trunk. A repeater counts as a node on each of the segments the repeater connects.

- You can have at most 100 nodes (including repeaters) attached to each trunk cable segment.

- A thick Ethernet network can have at most 300 nodes, of which 8 will actually be repeaters.

- Each trunk segment must be terminated at one end; the segment must also be terminated and grounded at the other end. When using thick coaxial cable, this is accomplished using N-series terminators, which are connected to the male.

- N-series connectors at each end of the trunk segment.

- Nodes are connected to the trunk cable using a transceiver cable from an AUI, or DIX, connector on the NIC to an AUI connector on a transceiver. The male connector attaches to the NIC and the female connector to the transceiver.

- The transceiver is connected to the trunk cable with a vampire tap or with an N-series T-connector.

- Transceivers must be at least 2.5 meters (8 feet) apart on the trunk, although the machines themselves can be closer together.

- The transceiver cable can be at most 50 meters (165 feet) long, which is the maximum distance a node can be from the network cable trunk.

"Major components of a thick Ethernet network" shows an example of a thick Ethernet network.

Thin Ethernet

A 10Base2, or thin Ethernet, network uses thin (3/16 inch) coaxial cable (with 50-ohm impedance) for the network backbone. Thin coaxial cable is quite popular because the cable is much easier to prepare and install than thick Ethernet cable.

Thin Ethernet Components

A thin Ethernet network uses the following components:

- Ethernet NICs, containing a transceiver, to mediate between node and network (one per node)

- Thin coaxial cable for trunk cable segment

- BNC barrel connectors to connect pieces of cable in the trunk segments (the fewer the better)

- BNC T-connector to attach a node to the network (one per node)

- BNC terminators, to terminate one end of a trunk segment (one per trunk segment)

- BNC grounded terminators, to terminate *and ground* one end of a trunk segment (one per trunk segment)

- Repeaters (optional), to extend the network by regenerating the signal before passing it on

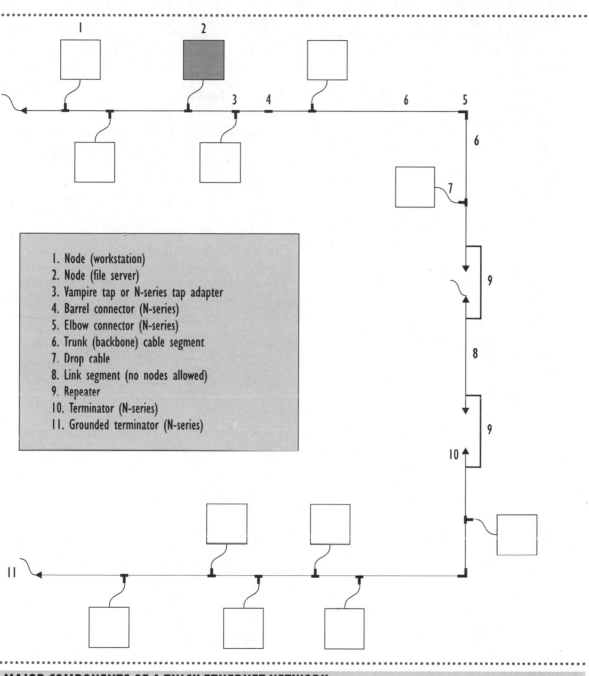

1. Node (workstation)
2. Node (file server)
3. Vampire tap or N-series tap adapter
4. Barrel connector (N-series)
5. Elbow connector (N-series)
6. Trunk (backbone) cable segment
7. Drop cable
8. Link segment (no nodes allowed)
9. Repeater
10. Terminator (N-series)
11. Grounded terminator (N-series)

E

MAJOR COMPONENTS OF A THICK ETHERNET NETWORK

Thin Ethernet Configuration

The following configuration rules and restrictions apply for thin Ethernet:

- Each trunk segment can be at most 185 meters (607 feet). Each trunk segment can consist of multiple pieces of cable, linked using BNC barrel connectors.

- The network trunk can have at most five segments, for a total trunk of 925 meters (3035 feet). Of these five cable segments, up to two can be link segments (those with no nodes attached) and up to three can be trunk segments (without nodes attached).

- You can use repeaters to connect two segments into a longer network trunk. A repeater counts as a node on each of the segments the repeater connects.

- You can have at most 30 nodes (including repeaters) attached to each trunk cable segment.

- A thin Ethernet network can have at most 90 nodes, of which 8 will actually be repeaters.

- Each trunk segment must be terminated at one end; the segment must also be terminated and grounded at the other end using BNC terminators, which are connected to the male BNC connectors at each end of the trunk segment.

- Nodes are connected to the trunk cable using a BNC T-connector that is attached to the NIC.

- T-connectors must be at least 0.5 meter (1.6 feet) apart on the trunk, although the machines themselves can be closer together.

"Major components of a thin Ethernet network" shows an example of a thin Ethernet network.

Hybrid Ethernet

You can combine thin and thick coaxial cable in the same Ethernet network, provided that the network elements meet the appropriate cable specifications. This approach can be less expensive than a pure thick Ethernet configuration, and more robust than a pure thin Ethernet configuration.

One approach is to combine thick and thin coaxial cable within a trunk segment. In this case, the connection is made using hybrid (BNC/N-series) adapters. One end of the adapter is a BNC connection and the other end is an N-series connection. Two versions of this adapter are available: one has female connections at either end, and the other has male connections.

When thin and thick coaxial cables are combined within the same segment, you need a formula to determine the amount of each type of cable you can use. The following formula assumes that no trunk segment is longer than 500 meters (1640 feet):

$$(1640 - Len)/3.28 = MaxThinCoax$$

where *Len* is the length of the trunk segment and *MaxThinCoax* represents the maximum length of thin coaxial cable you can use in the segment.

You can also build a network trunk using thin and thick trunk segments. In this case, the transition is made at the repeaters. Each segment must meet the specifications for that type of cable, just as if the entire trunk were made of the same type of cable.

As with thin or thick Ethernet segments, each end of a hybrid segment must be terminated. The terminator must match the type of cable at the end. Thus, if one end of the segment ends in thin coaxial and the other ends in thick coaxial, you need a BNC terminator at the first end and an N-series terminator at the second end. You can ground either of the ends.

Note that all the cable used in both thick and thin Ethernet networks has the same impedance: 50 ohms. This is one reason why it is relatively easy to combine thin and thick Ethernet segments.

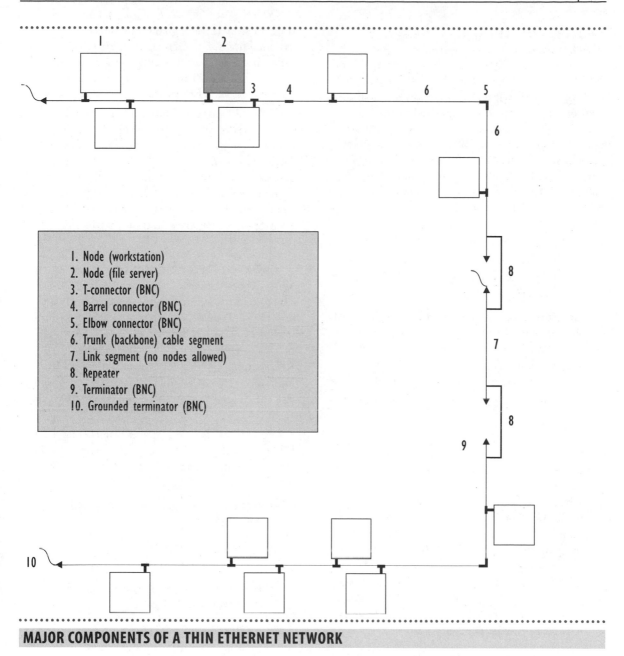

1. Node (workstation)
2. Node (file server)
3. T-connector (BNC)
4. Barrel connector (BNC)
5. Elbow connector (BNC)
6. Trunk (backbone) cable segment
7. Link segment (no nodes allowed)
8. Repeater
9. Terminator (BNC)
10. Grounded terminator (BNC)

MAJOR COMPONENTS OF A THIN ETHERNET NETWORK

Evolution: Fast Ethernet

Two fast Ethernet variants were accepted as official standards in June 1995. Both of these are capable of 100Mbps speeds over UTP cable. 100VG-AnyLAN, developed by Hewlett-Packard and several other vendors, was accepted as a standard by the IEEE 802.12 study group. On the same day, several variants of Grand Junction's 100BaseT were accepted as extensions of the 802.3 10BaseT standard. The variants are: 100BaseFX (for fiber-optic cable), 100BaseT4 (for connections with four available wire pairs), and 100BaseTX (for high-quality Category 5 cable). A 100BaseT2 variant (for two pairs of Category 3 or higher wire) was also accepted in 1997.

In order to achieve such high speeds, developers have found it necessary to take liberties with certain Ethernet features, as follows:

Access method   A major difference concerns the access method to be used. HP's 100VG-AnyLAN uses demand priority as its media-access method. This strategy involves packet switching and takes place in the hubs that serve to concentrate nodes on a twisted-pair network. 100BaseT uses CSMA/CD, as in traditional Ethernet.

Cable Type   Current versions of twisted-pair Ethernet run on cable that meets the TIA-568 standards for Category 3 cable or higher. Category 3 cable is rated for transmission speeds of up to 10Mbps, but it is often pushed to faster speeds. Standard Ethernet requires two pairs of cable—one pair for each direction. 100BaseT Ethernet variants require either two or four pairs of Category 3 cable or else two pairs of Category 5 cable (which *is* rated for 100Mbps speeds). 100VG-AnyLAN uses special signaling methods, and so it can use ordinary Category 3 cable.

NICs   Cards that support a 100Mbps Ethernet must be capable of switching to the slower 10Mbps speed, and must be able to detect when it is necessary to do so.

Fast Ethernet cards send a fast link pulse (FLP) signal to indicate that they are capable of 100Mbps transmission. If this signal is not detected, it is assumed that the node is an ordinary (10Mbps) one. Other proposed features, such as the frame format and configuration restrictions, are the same as for the current 802.3 Ethernet.

Of the fast variants, 100VG-AnyLAN has not proven as successful as its developers and proponents had hoped. In light of subsequent developments (see next section), 100Mbps Ethernet in general may prove to be a transitional architecture in the Ethernet world. However, the relatively small additional cost for 100Mbps may make 100Mbps the base speed for home networks.

...And Even Faster Ethernet

With Gigabit Ethernet, this popular LAN architecture also joins—in fact, moves toward the head of—the ranks of the very high speed communication architectures. Gigabit Ethernet supports transmission speeds of up to 1000Mbps. Gigabit Ethernet is actually a very clever hybrid of the high-speed Fibre Channel transmission technology and the Ethernet packet structure and networking architecture.

For its Physical layer, gigabit Ethernet uses the Fibre Channel specifications and data translation schemes. Three variants for the Physical layer are defined in the IEEE 802.3z specifications:

- 1000Base-CX uses two pairs of balanced copper cable.

- 1000Base-LX uses a pair of optical fibers and long wavelength light.

- 1000Base-SX uses a pair of optical fibers and short wavelength light.

At the Data-Link layer, Gigabit Ethernet is more or less standard—with a few extensions and modifications. These are needed to deal with some unacceptable consequences of increasing network performance by a factor of 10 over the fast Ethernet specs and by a factor of 100 over standard Ethernet specs—for example, a maximum network size of 20 meters.

The original Gigabit Ethernet standard—IEEE 802.3z—was ratified in June 1998. This standard was defined only for fiber-optic cabling and for balanced (twinaxial) copper cable. The specifications for the copper cabling allow a maximum distance of 25 meters between nodes—a solution clearly intended only for special connections. A supplement—IEEE 802.3ab—defines the operation for four pairs of Category 5 UTP wire, but this is still a proposed standard.

Gigabit Ethernet Features and Tricks

Gigabit Ethernet achieves its high bandwidth through a combination of several design considerations. First, the technology takes full advantage of the transformation of Ethernet into a switched-media architecture (with the introduction of Ethernet switches). Switches can be used to establish direct connections between communicating nodes. Since no other nodes will be using the same channel, there is no need to worry about collisions. Even though collisions are essentially nonexistent in such a configuration, it's still possible to use CSMA/CD as the media-access method. In practice, however, switched Ethernet does not use CSMA/CD.

Second, Gigabit Ethernet networks can—and generally do—operate in full-duplex mode. This allows communication in both directions at the same time. This is feasible because there is no need to worry about collisions.

Gigabit Ethernet makes several other extensions and modifications in order to achieve its high speeds. First, to help prevent bottlenecks or overflows in devices that may have trouble dealing with the high speeds, Gigabit Ethernet includes a component known as a *buffered distributor*. This is a full-duplex device that functions like a hub. It has multiple ports, and it can connect two or more Ethernet links at the full 1Gbps speed. The buffered distributor forwards all packets to every segment except to the one from which the packet came. More important, the distributor includes a buffer in which it can temporarily store frames to keep them from getting dropped by a slow device on the network.

Gigabit Ethernet also has two other modifications to increase the minimum network size, while still maintaining transmission efficiency. To keep the number of collisions down to an acceptable level, the maximum size of an Ethernet network is essentially determined by how long it takes to send the shortest valid Ethernet frame. The collision domain, as this maximum distance is called, is the distance over which a signal can make a round trip in the time it takes to send the shortest frame. Classically, such a frame is 64 bytes in size.

However, at 1Gbps, the collision domain is only about 20 meters—clearly not a useful size for a network whose components can cost thousands of dollars. To increase the collision domain, Gigabit Ethernet uses *carrier extension*, which essentially makes the minimum frame size 512 bytes. By padding shorter frames out to this size, a Gigabit Ethernet network gains extra time for the collision domain, but at the cost of possibly transmitting eight times as many bytes as necessary.

To decrease this potential inefficiency, Gigabit Ethernet allows *packet bursting*, which lets a node send up to 3KB of frames back to back—that is, without letting another node transmit anything. In such a burst, only the first frame needs to be padded using carrier extension.

Hardware Considerations

Gigabit Ethernet makes considerable demands on hardware, and performance bottlenecks are not uncommon. In fact a Gigabit Ethernet server must have some pretty strong specs. For example, the server needs at least 1MB of cache memory. Currently, most Windows-based machines come in a configuration with 512KB of cache. In effect, the cache requirement rules out most available hardware as potential servers.

Even if the cache requirements are met, there are still more potential problems. The general consensus is that Gigabit Ethernet pretty much stretches the PCI bus (currently found in most Windows-based machines) to its limits. Thus, the performance of a Gigabit Ethernet network may be server-bound—at least for the current generation of machines.

Gigabit Ethernet really expects optical fiber—the copper-based variants notwithstanding. Many companies have not yet installed such fiber. Or, companies may have the "wrong" kind of optical fiber installed. For example, if the network is supposed to extend for a mile or so, single-mode fiber is needed. If the existing wiring is multimode fiber, there's a problem. Performance issues aside, single-mode and multimode fiber are also physically incompatible.

Prospects for Gigabit Ethernet

Gigabit Ethernet's considerable hardware requirements are accepted as part of the cost of doing business, and Gigabit Ethernet is expected to become the dominant LAN technology within a few years. Until then, it is most likely to be used in the following ways:

- To provide a high-speed backbone for a network

- To allow a single 1Gbps switch to take over the work of several 100Mbps switches

- For research situations with high bandwidth requirements—for example, when working with huge data objects or giant databases

See the entry on Gigabit Ethernet for more details on this technology.

Isochronous Ethernet

An isochronous transmission is one that occurs at a constant rate. This is required, for example, when sending voice or video, since the information could become unintelligible if sent at varying speeds or with pauses in mid-transmission. Such time-dependent transmissions are not possible with ordinary Ethernet—largely because the media access method (MAC) is probabilistic, and is not designed for constant activity.

To make it possible to transmit voice and video over Ethernet networks, National Semiconductor submitted specifications for *isoENET*—an isochronous version of Ethernet—to the IEEE 802.9 committee. 802.9 is the committee that deals with the integration of voice and data (IVD). In 1995, the committee ratified IEEE 802.9a as the standard for what was officially named ISLAN16T, for Integrated Services Local Area Network. (The 16T indicates that the standard supports 16Mbps transmission over twisted-pair wire.)

The ISLAN16T specs support transmissions using ISDN (Integrated Services Digital Network) signaling methods—but running over Category 3 UTP (unshielded twisted pair) cable. ISLAN16T's 16Mbps bandwidth is broken into two major components. In addition to the 10Mbps bandwidth for ordinary Ethernet transmissions, ISLAN16T supports up to 96 B channels, each with a 64Kbps capacity—for a total throughput of about 6Mbps—for the isochronous part of the transmission.

See the entry for ISLAN16T for more information on this technology.

Advantages of Ethernet

Ethernet networks offer the following advantages:

- Good for networks in which traffic is heavy only occasionally or in which traffic consists of a few long transmissions.

- Easy to install.

- Technology is well-known and thoroughly tested.

- Moderate costs—although this is not yet true of gigabit Ethernet components.

- Flexible cabling, especially when using twisted-pair cable.

Disadvantages of Ethernet

Ethernet networks have the following disadvantages:

- Heavy traffic can slow down a network that uses a contention access system such as CSMA/CD. Such congestion is less likely to be a problem with the 100Mbps Ethernets—at least until the traffic catches up with the greater bandwidth. It is even less of a problem with gigabit Ethernet.

- Since all nodes are connected to the main cable in most Ethernet networks, a break in this cable can bring down the entire network. Star topologies, as in 100Mbs Ethernet and in gigabit Ethernet, are more forgiving in this regard.

- Troubleshooting is more difficult with a bus topology. Again, the star topologies are simpler to deal with in this regard.

- Room for incompatibilities because of frame structure (such as 802.3 versus Blue Book Ethernet).

→ *See Also* 100BaseT, 100VG-AnyLAN, Gigabit Ethernet, ISLAN16T

→ *Broader Category* Network Architecture

→ *Compare* ARCnet; ATM; FDDI; Token Ring

Ethernet Configuration Test Protocol (ECTP)

→ *See* Protocol, ECTP (Ethernet Configuration Test Protocol)

Ethernet Meltdown

A situation in which traffic on an Ethernet network approaches or reaches saturation (maximum capacity). This can happen, for example, if a packet is echoed repeatedly.

EtherTalk

EtherTalk is the driver used to communicate between the Macintosh and an Ethernet network

interface card. It is Apple's Ethernet implementation for the AppleTalk environment.

Two versions of EtherTalk have been developed:

- EtherTalk Phase 1 is based on the Ethernet 2 version, also known as Blue Book Ethernet.

- EtherTalk Phase 2 is based on the IEEE 802.3 Ethernet variant.

→ *Broader Categories* AppleTalk; Ethernet

→ *Compare* ARCTalk; LocalTalk; TokenTalk

EtherTalk Link Access Protocol (ELAP)

→ *See* Protocol, ELAP (EtherTalk Link Access Protocol)

ETR (Early Token Release)

ETR is a frame, or packet, control process used in 16Mbps Token Ring networks. ETR makes it possible for multiple packets to be moving in the ring at once, even with just a single token for packet control.

Ordinarily in a Token Ring network, only the node with the token can send a packet, so that only one packet is moving around the network at any one time. This packet travels around the ring. Each node passes the packet on, and the destination node reads the packet. When the packet returns to the sender (with acknowledgment and verification of its receipt), that node strips the packet, and passes the token to the next active node on the ring.

With ETR, the sender releases the token immediately after releasing its packet. The next node on the ring sends the packet on. Since this node now has the token, the node can send its own packet. Immediately after sending the packet, the node releases the token. Successive nodes pass on whatever packets they receive, and they send their own

E

packets (if they have any to send) when the token reaches them.

Note that ETR allows multiple packets on the network, but that there is only one token on the network at any time.

→ *Broader Categories* Token Passing; Token Ring

ETSI (European Telecommunications Standards Institute)

A European standards committee that has defined a subset of ISDN's proposed functionality for use in Europe. This variant is known as EuroISDN, and is analogous to the National ISDN versions (NI-1, NI-2, and a planned NI-3) developed in the United States. The ETSI is also looking into specifying guidelines for providing interoperability between EuroISDN and National ISDN.

European Academic and Research Network (EARN)

A European network that provides file transfer and e-mail (electronic mail) services for universities and research institutions.

European Computer Manufacturers Association (ECMA)

→ *See* ECMA (European Computer Manufacturers Association)

European Electronic Mail Association (EEMA)

A European association of developers and vendors of electronic mail products. The EMA (Electronic Mail Association) is the counterpart in the United States.

European Telecommunications Standards Institute (ETSI)

→ *See* ETSI (European Telecommunications Standards Institute)

European Workshop for Open Systems (EWOS)

→ *See* EWOS (European Workshop for Open Systems)

Event

In certain programming models—for example, the one underlying the Windows graphical user interface (GUI)—an event is generated in response to actions in the program or applet. For example, a mouse click event is generated when the user clicks the mouse button; similarly, a key press event is generated when the user presses a key.

Code in an application or applet can be associated with the events the program is able to handle. When a particular event is generated, the appropriate event-handling code is executed.

In a GUI (such as the one in Windows), most programs execute in an event-driven manner. That is, the flow of the program's elements will depend on the events that are generated in response to the user's (or the program's) actions. Such programs will continue executing until the user indicates they are done by exiting the program.

Event-Driven Program

An event-driven program is one whose execution sequence and duration depend on the actions of a user, rather than on a predefined program logic. Even an event-driven program has a predefined logic; however, at the most general level, this logic is very unobtrusive: "as long as there is something to do, do it."

At any given point in running an event-driven program, a user may have several possible actions they can take—for example, clicking on an active area of a Web page, opening a window on the screen, or selecting an element from a toolbar—to name just a few. Depending on the action taken, an appropriate event handler will be started to do its work.

Event-driven programs allow the kind of flexibility needed to surf the Web or to do other tasks that may include digressions along the way.

Event Reporting

In network management, a data-gathering method in which agents report on the status of the objects under the agents' purview. The agent generates a report containing the relevant information and sends this report to the management package. This is in contrast to *polling,* in which the management program periodically requests such reports from agents.

E-Wallet

An e-wallet—also known as a digital wallet—is a data object that contains the information necessary for a customer to make purchases and carry out other transactions online. The e-wallet will contain such information as the customer's name, address, credit card number, and purchase information.

The format in which this information is stored depends on the protocol being used for the e-wallet. Currently there are over a dozen different "standards" being used— which is one of the major obstacles preventing e-commerce from becoming the gazillion dollar industry everyone is expecting.

There are some indications that this may change for the better. Recently, many of the major players in e-commerce—most of whom have been competing with each other and producing the many conflicting standards—have announced support for a common standard: ECML (Electronic Commerce Modeling Language). It remains to be seen just how strong this support is.

→ *Broader Category* Electronic Commerce

→ *See Also* ECML (Electronic Commerce Modeling Language)

EWOS (European Workshop for Open Systems)

One of three regional workshops for implementers of the OSI Reference Model. The other two are AOW (Asia and Oceania Workshop) and OIW (OSI Implementers Workshop).

Exchange

In telephone communications, an exchange is an area serviced by a central office, or CO. An exchange consists of a sequential block of phone numbers, each associated with the same three-digit value (known as the *exchange ID*, or *XID*).

Each exchange in North America is characterized by an office class and a name. The table "North America Exchange Classes and Names" summarizes how the classes are defined.

NORTH AMERICA EXCHANGE CLASSES AND NAMES

Exchange Class	Name
1	Regional centers (RCs) or points (RPs). These have the largest domains: a dozen or so cover all of North America. The class 1 offices are all connected directly to each other.
2	Sectional centers (SCs) or points (SPs).
3	Primary centers (PCs) or points (PPs).
4	Toll centers (TCs).
4P	Toll points (TPs).

Continued on next page

NORTH AMERICA EXCHANGE CLASSES AND NAMES (continued)	
Exchange Class	Name
4X	Intermediate points (IPs). These are used only with digital exchanges, and are designed to connect to remote switching units (RSUs).
5	End offices. These are owned by local telephone companies. Ownership of the broader centers varies. Individual subscribers are connected to class 5 offices, of which there are many thousand in North America.
5R	End offices with remote switching capabilities.

Exchange Carrier

A *local exchange carrier* (LEC), which is a company that provides telecommunications services within an exchange, or LATA (local access and transport area).

Exchange Server

→ *See* Microsoft Exchange Server

Exclusion

In the Dynamic Host Configuration Protocol (DHCP), an exclusion is a way of specifying IP addresses or address ranges that the protocol may not assign when it is handing out addresses to machines that will be (temporarily) on the network. Addresses that are not excluded can be specified in a *scope*, which is merely a range of addresses that DHCP *is* allowed to assign.

Expanded Memory Manager (EMM)

→ *See* EMM (Expanded Memory Manager)

Expanded Memory Specification (EMS)

→ *See* EMS (Expanded Memory Specification)

Expansion Bus

A set of slots, such as those on a motherboard, into which expansion cards can be plugged in order to provide the computer with additional capabilities and access to external devices.

Expansion Chassis

A structure that includes a backplane (circuit board with slots for other boards) and a power supply. The chassis may be closed and self-standing, or it may be rack mountable for installation into a larger component.

Explicit Congestion Notification (ECN)

→ *See* ECN (Explicit Congestion Notification)

Explorer Frame

In networks that use source routing, such as IBM Token Ring networks, an explorer frame is used to determine a route from the source node to a destination. An explorer frame is also known as a *discovery packet*, particularly in the Internet community.

There are two types of explorer frames:

- An all-routes explorer frame explores all possible routes between source and destination

- A spanning-tree explorer frame follows only routes on the spanning tree for the network. (A spanning tree is an optimal set of paths for all possible connections in a network.)

Extended Addressing

In AppleTalk Phase 2, extended addressing is a scheme that assigns an 8-bit node number and a 16-bit network number to each station. Extended addressing allows for up to 16 million (2^{24}) nodes on a single network.

This is in contrast to the *nonextended addressing* used in AppleTalk Phase 1 networks, and also in networks that use a LocalTalk architecture. Nonextended addressing uses just the 8-bit node number, which limits networks to 254 nodes (not 256, because two of the node numbers are reserved).

Packets for extended networks use the *long DDP* packet format; packets for nonextended networks use the *short DDP* packet format, which omits network address bytes (since these are either undefined or 0).

Extended Binary Coded Decimal Interchange Code (EBCDIC)

→ *See* EBCDIC (Extended Binary Coded Decimal Interchange Code)

Extended Character Set

The term *extended character set* refers to characters with codes between 128 and 255 in the ASCII encoding system. Standard ASCII encoding uses seven bits to represent the 128 characters between 0 and 127. This standard ASCII character set is an international standard.

In contrast, the extra 128 characters available in an extended eight-bit ASCII encoding actually have several "standards" associated with them. Various vendors have created their own encoding for these extended characters. The extended characters are generally used to encode foreign characters, special symbols, or simple graphics elements.

→ *Broader Category* ASCII (American Standard Code for Information Interchange)

Extended Data Out (EDO)

→ *See* EDO (Extended Data Out)

Extended Industry Standard Architecture (EISA)

→ *See* EISA (Extended Industry Standard Architecture)

Extended Memory Specification (XMS)

→ *See* XMS (Extended Memory Specification)

Extended Superframe Format (ESF) Framing

→ *See* ESF (Extended Superframe Format) Framing

eXtensible Markup Language (XML)

→ *See* XML (eXtensible Markup Language)

Extensible MIB (Management Information Base)

In an SNMP environment, a MIB for which a vendor can define new variables when implementing the MIB.

→ *See Also* MIB (Management Information Base), SNMP (Simple Network Management Protocol)

E

Exterior Gateway Protocol (EGP)

→ *See* Protocol, EGP (Exterior Gateway Protocol)

External Data Representation (XDR)

→ *See* XDR (Extended Data Representation)

Extranet

An extranet is an intranet that allows access to at least some outside users or corporations. An intranet, in turn, is an organizational or corporate (inter)network that uses Internet protocols. By using the TCP/IP protocol stack, an intranet achieves seamless interoperability and a certain degree of platform independence—even if the organizational internetwork includes different architectures.

One goal in creating such an intranet is to make information resources directly accessible and

portable. That is, corporate users should be able to access such resources directly—without having to go through an MIS or IT department.

By extending this accessibility to users outside the corporate (fire)walls, so to speak, an extranet extends the interoperability and portability of information resources to noncorporate users and also to corporate users who might need to call in from the road or home. Regardless of the origin of such calls, the user—provided they have the appropriate access rights—will have the same transparent access to the extranet resources.

An intranet or extranet may, in fact, use the Internet as part of its communications cloud, as in the following illustration, "An example extranet." By encrypting communications over the Internet, a corporation can effectively create its own virtual private network (VPN).

→ *Compare* Intranet

→ *See Also* VPN (Virtual Private Network)

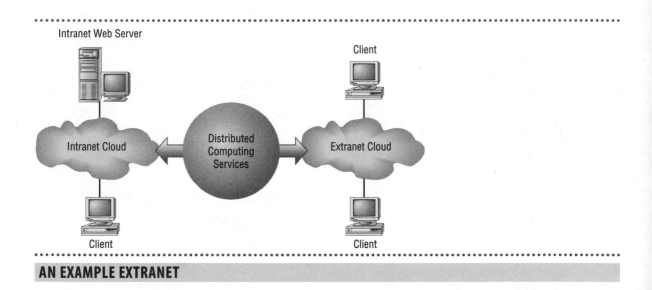

AN EXAMPLE EXTRANET

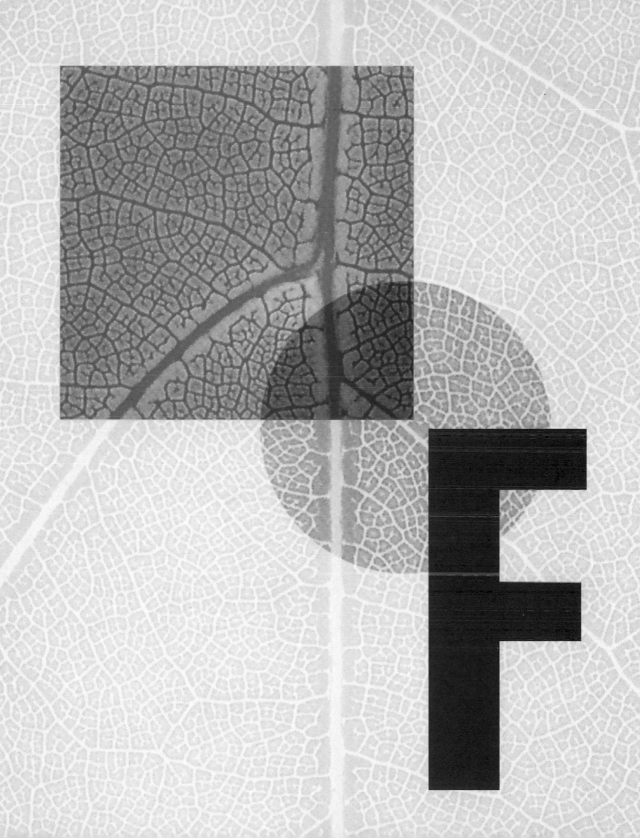

Fabric

In the Fibre Channel architecture, a fabric is a mechanism for interconnecting nodes in a fabric topology. In a fabric, each node is connected to a switch, and the switches are completely interconnected so that any node can be (more or less directly) connected to any other. Any necessary routing is done by the fabric itself, and multiple connections can exist at any given time.

Facility

In telephone communications, a facility is a transmission link between two locations, or stations. In an X.25 packet, a facility is a field through which users can request special services from the network.

Facility Bypass

In telecommunications, a facility bypass is a communication strategy that bypasses the telephone company's central office. For example, wireless transmissions might use facility bypass.

Facility Data Link (FDL)

→ *See* FDL (Facility Data Link)

Facsimile

→ *See* Fax

Fade Margin

The fade margin is essentially a measure of spare power in an electrical or wireless signaling context. Specifically, it refers to the amount of signal (in decibels) that can be lost before the signal becomes unintelligible.

Fading

In electrical or wireless signaling, *fading* is the decrease in the signal's strength because of any of the following:

- Obstruction of the transmitter's or the receiver's antenna

- Interference (from other signals or from atmospheric conditions)

- Increased distance from the transmission source

Fading is sometimes referred to as just *fade*, as in *fade margin*. The fade margin refers to the amount of signal (in decibels) that can be lost before the signal becomes unintelligible.

FADU (File Access Data Unit)

In the OSI's FTAM (File Transfer, Access, and Management) service, a file access data unit (FADU) is a packet that contains information about accessing a directory tree in the file system.

Fail-Safe System

A computer system that is designed to keep operating, without losing data, when part of the system seriously malfunctions or fails completely.

Fail-Soft System

A computer system that is designed to fail gracefully, with the minimum amount of data or program destruction, when part of the system malfunctions. Fail-soft systems close down nonessential functions and operate at a reduced capacity until the problem has been resolved.

Fake Root

In Novell's NetWare versions 3.*x* and later, a fake root is a drive mapping to a subdirectory that makes the subdirectory appear to be the root directory. For example, the following maps drive F: to look like the root of directory RADISH:

MAP ROOT F:=SYS:APPS\RADISH

A fake root allows you to install programs into subdirectories, even though they insist on executing in the root directory. With the programs in a subdirectory, administrators can be more specific about where they allow users to have rights, and avoid granting rights at the true root of the volume.

Fake roots are not allowed in all environments. For example, fake roots cannot be used with OS/2 clients. When a fake root is used, there are also restrictions on how certain commands work and on how certain actions—for example, returning to the original (non-fake) root—must be performed.

→ *Broader Category* NetWare

FAL (File Access Listener)

In Digital Equipment Company's DECnet environment, a program that implements the DAP (Data Access Protocol) and that can accept remote requests from processes that use DAP.

Fall Time

The amount of time it takes an electrical signal to go from 90 percent of its level down to 10 percent, as shown in "Rise and fall times." This value is important, because it helps set an upper limit on the maximum transmission speed that can be supported. Compare it with rise time.

Fanout

In communications and signaling, a fanout is a configuration in which there are more output lines than input lines.

FAQ (Frequently Asked Questions)

In the Internet community, a FAQ is a compilation of the most commonly asked questions, *with answers,* about any of dozens of topics. Many of these questions might be asked by newcomers, who may know little or nothing about a topic.

F

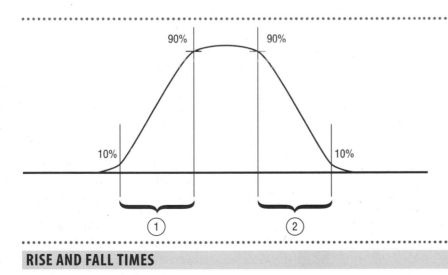

RISE AND FALL TIMES

FAQs are posted in order to minimize the number of users who actually do ask the questions. Users can download and read the answers at their leisure, rather than tying up the lines by mailing these questions across the Internet and waiting for the answers to come pouring in.

FAQs can be found in archives on the Internet, and will have names such as disney-faq/disneyland, audio-faq/part1, or usenet-faq/part1. In FAQ archives, you can find a variety of information, such as where to look for old, out-of-print Disney videos, what to listen for when evaluating speakers (the electronic kind), and so on.

Thomas Boutell maintains a list of FAQ files at

http://www.boutell.com/faq/

Far End Block Error (FEBE)

In broadband ISDN (BISDN) networks, an error reported to the sender by the receiver when the receiver's computed checksum result does not match the sender's checksum.

Far End Crosstalk (FEXT)

→ *See* FEXT (Far End Crosstalk)

Far End Receive Failure (FERF)

In broadband ISDN (BISDN) networks, a signal sent upstream to indicate that an error has been detected downstream. An FERF might be sent, for example, because a destination has reported an error.

Fast Busy

In telephony, a fast busy tone indicates that all circuits through a required trunk are busy. The fast busy tone operates at 120ipm (interruptions per minute), which is twice the rate of an ordinary busy signal. The latter is used to indicate that the phone number being called is in use.

Fastconnect Circuit Switching

The use of fast, electronic switching to establish a path (circuit) between two stations.

Fast Ethernet

Any of several Ethernet variants based on either an approach originally developed by Grand Junction or on one developed by Hewlett-Packard. The Grand Junction variant was ratified as IEEE 802.3u and is known as 100BaseT. The 100 refers to the network speed—100Mbps; the BaseT indicates that it is a baseband network using twisted-pair wire. There are actually three variants on this standard, as described in the 100BaseT entry.

The term is also used to refer to a 100Mbps Ethernet variant developed by Hewlett-Packard and ratified as IEEE 802.12. This variant is known as 100VG-AnyLAN, and it differs from standard Ethernet in that it uses the noncontentious demand priority as a media access method rather than CSMA/CD (Carrier Sense Multiple Access/Collision Detect).

→ *Broader Category* Ethernet

→ *See Also* 100BaseT; 100VG-AnyLAN

Fast Infrared

Infrared transmissions use a frequency range just below the visible light spectrum - from about 300GHz to 430THz (teraHertz). These waves require a line of sight connection between sender and receiver or between each of these and a common cell or target (which may be a wall or ceiling). Because of the line of sight restriction, infrared is limited to short-distance (that is, local area) communications.

Standards for infrared networks have been developed by the IrDA (for Infrared Data Association, a consortium of around 100 hardware and software companies) and the IEEE 802.11 working group. The IrDA has developed specifications for the bottom three layers of a network (physical, data link, and network) for speeds of 115.2kbps, 1.15Mbps, and 4Mbps. Of these, the 4Mbps version is known as fast infrared.

The IEEE 802.11 Wireless Standards groups have developed specifications for both radio wave and infrared wireless transmissions. The original 802.11 specifications provided a transmission speed of 1Mbps, and specifications for a fast have also been created.

In 1998, Hewlett Packard proposed an even higher-speed version of infrared that can transmit data at up to 16 MBps. This very fast infrared (VFIR) specification should be approved as an IrDA standard by the time you read this. VFIR is intended for transferring files between PCs and devices such as scanners or digital cameras.

In fact, such transfers are about the only use for which fast and very fast infrared protocols are feasible. This is because these high speeds can be supported only for distances of about one meter, and only within a very narrow orientation cone (about 15 degrees of the receiver). The IrDA is expected to approve another infrared standard - Advanced Infrared - that will allow speeds of 4Mbps over distances of up to 10 meters and within a 180 degree cone.

→ *Broader Category* Wireless communication

Fast Link Pulse (FLP)

→ *See* FLP (Fast Link Pulse)

Fast Packet Switching (FPS)

→ *See* FPS (Fast Packet Switching)

FastPath

A high-speed gateway between AppleTalk and Ethernet networks.

FAT (File Allocation Table)

The FAT (file allocation table) is where DOS keeps its information about all the files on a partition and about the disk location of all the blocks that make up each file. Because losing a FAT can be fatal in the PC world, DOS maintains a second copy of the FAT.

Some network operating systems, such as NetWare, also use FATs as part of their file handling. For example, NetWare uses a directory entry table (DET) and a FAT. Access to the FAT is through the DET.

The standard FAT is a 16-bit system and is referred to as FAT16. This means that there is room in a FAT for 64K pointers to disk locations. Thus, a FAT16 system can allocate storage for 64K blocks. The total storage a FAT can map depends on the size of each block (or cluster or allocation unit). Hard disk blocks, or clusters, can be 4, 8, 16, or 32KB each. This means that the largest amount of storage a FAT16 system can handle is 2GB.

This storage limitation is, of course, a problem, since PCs these days come with hard disks much larger than that. To overcome this storage limitation, you can use partition management software. Such packages let you define multiple partitions, each of which gets its own file allocation table.

The limited number of pointers in a FAT16 table has another drawback: it can lead to wasted space. The only way to cover a 2GB hard disk is by using 32K allocation units. This means that the smallest chunk of disk space that can be used is 32KB. A file containing the four-word sentence, "FAT16 can waste storage" will take up 32,768 bytes of storage. Partition managers can help reduce storage inefficiency by defining partitions that can use smaller cluster sizes. For example, for partitions with a capacity less than 512MB you only need clusters that are 8KB in size. Table "Cluster Sizes for FAT16 and FAT32" shows the relationship between partition size and cluster size in the two file allocation systems currently supported by Microsoft.

F

CLUSTER SIZES FOR FAT16 AND FAT32

Partition Size (in MB)	FAT16 Cluster Size (in KB)	FAT32 Cluster Size (in KB)
0–31	0.5	Not supported
32–63	1	Not supported
64–127	2	Not supported
128–255	4	Not supported
256–511	8	Not supported
512–1023	16	4
1024–2047	32	4
2048–8191	Not supported	4
8192–16,383	Not supported	8
16,384–32,767	Not supported	16
32,768–65,535	Not supported	32

FAT32

Microsoft introduced the FAT32 system in an OEM (Original Equipment Manufacturer) Service Release of Windows 95—one available only with new PCs— and in Windows 98. Microsoft also expects to use FAT32 for Windows 2000 (formerly known as NT 5). FAT32 provides a more efficient way to allocate disk space. However, it is incompatible with FAT16 file systems, as well as with other file systems such as NTFS and HPFS (High-Performance File System).

FAT32 files cannot yet be compressed. Furthermore, only utilities specifically developed for FAT32 will work on this file system; other utilities (anti-virus programs, disk maintenance programs, and so forth) will not work. Most applications that work with Windows 95 should also work with Windows 98 using FAT32 because these programs generally don't try to bypass the BIOS or hard disk controllers.

As you can see from the table "Cluster Sizes for FAT16 and FAT32," FAT32 can support disks up to 8GB in capacity using 4KB clusters. FAT32 requires at least a 512MB hard disk. So, the tradeoff with FAT32 is efficient storage against file system incompatibility.

Various tricks can be used to speed up access to the FAT, including caching and indexing the FAT. *Caching* the FAT involves storing it in chip memory (RAM) for faster access. Indexing information in a FAT can be accomplished by using a hashing function.

FAT32

→ *See* FAT

Fault

A fault is a break or other abnormal condition in a communications link. A fault generally requires immediate attention. The fault may be physical or logical.

Fault isolation

When anything goes wrong in a network or a stand-alone system, it's important to determine the cause of the problem before trying to fix it. Fault isolation refers to the process of tracking down a system or network anomaly. Depending on the type of error (for example, hardware or software, cabling or chips, and so forth) various tools may be available to assist in the fault isolation process.

Fault Management

One of five basic OSI network management tasks specified by the ISO and CCITT, fault management is used to detect, diagnose, and correct faults on a network.

Fault Detection and Assessment

A network management package can detect faults by having nodes report when a fault occurs, as well as by polling all nodes periodically. Both capabilities are necessary for thorough fault management. It may not be possible to get reliable reports about certain types of faults, such as one that causes an entire network to go down. For such cases, polling will provide at least the negative information of no response to a poll.

On the other hand, polling uses bandwidth that could be used for transmitting information. As in the real world, the more time spent on administrative work (polling), the less opportunity for doing real work (transmitting information). The value of the information obtained through polling must be weighed against the loss of bandwidth.

The bandwidth consumed by polling depends also on the complexity of the polling method. For example, a simple method sends a signal and waits for an echo to acknowledge that the channel is open. All network management environments include facilities for echo polling. More complex polling may check for more details, such as whether the node has something to send and whether a higher-priority level is requested.

When a fault is detected, the network management package must assess the fault to determine whether it is necessary to track it down and correct it immediately. Certain types of faults affect or shut down vital network services, and these faults must be dealt with as soon as possible. Other faults may involve only a path between locations, and they may not be crucial because alternate paths exist.

To determine the type of fault and its locations, the network management package may need to do some testing. For example, if a poll does not get the expected echo, the management package needs to determine whether the fault is in the poller, the pollee, or the link between them. This may require signal monitoring or loopback testing.

Fault Correction

Once the fault has been detected, identified, and located, measures must be taken to correct it. In some cases, such as when there is redundancy in the system, the management package may be able to correct the fault automatically. More likely, the

network administrator or engineer will need to intervene in order to correct the fault. The ease with which this happens depends on the reliability of the detection and diagnosis, and on the type of information provided about the fault.

The fault-management system must be able to trace faults through the network and to carry out diagnostic tests. Fault correction requires help from the configuration management domain.

Fault Reporting

To collect the information necessary to detect and report faults, fault-management systems use either of two families of protocols: the older SNMP (Simple Network Management Protocol) or the OSI standard CMIP (Common Management Information Protocol).

Faults can be reported in various ways. The simplest (and least informative) is an auditory alarm signal, which merely alerts the system administrator.

Actual information about the fault can be reported as text, or through a graphical interface that shows the network layout schematically, with the fault located in this diagram.

→ **Broader Category** Network Management

→ **See Also** Accounting Management; Configuration Management; Performance Management; Security Management

Fault Point

In networking, a location at which something can go wrong. Fault points often tend to be at connection locations.

Fault Tolerance

Fault tolerance is a strategy for ensuring continued operation of a network even when certain kinds of faults arise. Fault-tolerant networks require some sort of redundant storage medium, power supply, or system.

For example, a fault-tolerant cabling system will include extra cables, in case one cable is cut or otherwise damaged. A fault-tolerant disk subsystem will include multiple copies of data on separate disks and use separate channels to write each version.

In some configurations, it is possible to remove and replace the malfunctioning component (for example, a hard disk) without shutting down the system. See the SFT (System Fault Tolerance) article for information about Novell NetWare's fault-tolerant features.

→ **Broader Categories** Data Protection; Security

Fax

A fax, or facsimile, is a long-distance photocopy; it is a reproduction of a text or graphics document at a remote location. The document is scanned (or already available in digitized form), encoded into a standard format for faxes, transmitted over telephone or private lines, and printed (or stored) at the receiving end. *Telecopy* and *telefax* are other terms for fax. "The fax transmission process" illustrates how a fax is sent.

Fax images have resolutions that range from about 100×200 (vertical × horizontal) dots per inch (dpi) to about 400×400dpi.

The CCITT has formulated fax format and transmission standards, referred to as Groups 1–4, which represent a range of signaling methods and formats, as follows:

- Group 1 uses frequency modulation of analog signals, and supports only slow transmission speeds (6 minutes per page). Group 1 offers low (100dpi) resolution.

- Group 2 uses both frequency and amplitude modulation to achieve higher speeds (between 2 and 3 minutes per page). Group 2 also offers low (100dpi) resolution.

- Group 3 uses quadrature amplitude modulation (QAM) and data compression to increase transmission speeds to about one page per minute. Group 3 supports various automatic features and offers 200dpi resolution. Commercially available fax machines support at least the Group 3 format.

- Group 4 supports higher-speed digital transmissions, so that a page can be transmitted in about 20 seconds. Group 4 offers 200 or 400dpi resolution. Three classes are distinguished under the Group 4 format (which is not yet in wide use).

→ **See Also** Modulation

Fax Device

A fax device can be used to send and receive faxes on a network, under the control of a fax server. This may be a machine or a board. Machines may use thermal or plain paper.

In general, thermal paper comes in rolls, fades and cracks quickly, and must be cut as the fax leaves the machine. The main (and only) advantage of thermal paper fax machines is price.

Fax *boards* can generally accept text or graphics files (in the appropriate format), can convert these into fax format, and can transmit the resulting information. Fax boards can also receive faxes and convert them to the appropriate form for use. Because fax boards have no paper supply of their own, most boards can send their files to a printer for hard copy.

Although the speed and resolution capabilities for most fax machines are similar—thanks, in part, to the CCITT fax standards—there are certain considerations when selecting a fax device for use on a network.

For example, if your network receives many faxes daily, you will not want to use a thermal paper fax machine that insists on printing every fax received. On a busy day, there might be a 100-foot roll of faxes to wade through (literally) in order to find your fax.

For a network, you will probably want the fax device to suppress printing (if requested), and to pass an electronic version of the received fax to the appropriate program.

→ *Broader Category* Peripheral

→ *See Also* Modem, Server, Fax

FBE (Free Buffer Enquiry)

A field in an ARCnet frame.

→ *See Also* ARCnet

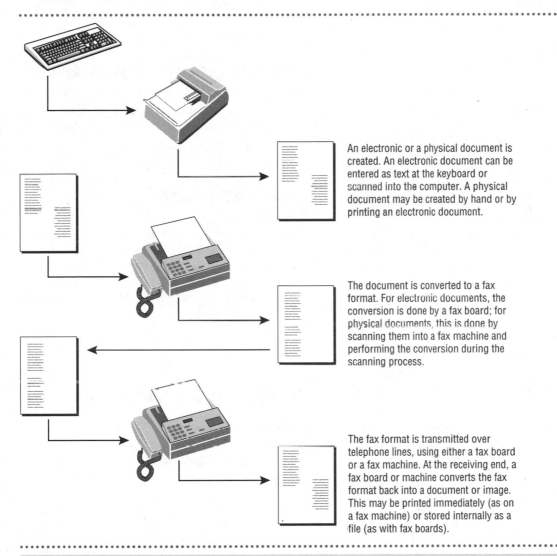

An electronic or a physical document is created. An electronic document can be entered as text at the keyboard or scanned into the computer. A physical document may be created by hand or by printing an electronic document.

The document is converted to a fax format. For electronic documents, the conversion is done by a fax board; for physical documents, this is done by scanning them into a fax machine and performing the conversion during the scanning process.

The fax format is transmitted over telephone lines, using either a fax board or a fax machine. At the receiving end, a fax board or machine converts the fax format back into a document or image. This may be printed immediately (as on a fax machine) or stored internally as a file (as with fax boards).

THE FAX TRANSMISSION PROCESS

FC (Frame Control)

A field in a token-ring data packet, or frame. The FC value tells whether the frame is a MAC-layer management packet or whether it is carrying LLC (logical-link control) data.

F Connector

→ *See* Connector, F

FCC (Federal Communications Commission)

A federal regulatory agency that develops and publishes guidelines to govern the operation of communications and other electrical equipment in the United States.

Perhaps the best-known FCC regulations are those that define and govern class A and class B devices, and those that allocate the electromagnetic spectrum. The device certifications are based on the amount of radio frequency interference (RFI) the device may cause for other devices in the vicinity.

Class A certification is less stringent, and it is assigned to equipment for use in business contexts. The more stringent class B certification applies to devices that are used in the home.

The FCC also allocates portions of the electromagnetic spectrum for particular uses such as the following:

- The frequency band between 88 and 108MHz is allocated for FM radio broadcasting.

- The bands between 54 and 88MHz and between 174 and 216MHz are allocated for VHF television.

- The band between 470 and 638MHz is allocated for UHF television.

- Bands in the 4, 6, and 11GHz ranges have been allocated for long-haul telecommunications using a common carrier.

- Bands in the 18 and 23GHz ranges have been allocated for short-haul transmissions, such as those in private networks.

The FCC also sets tariffs, which specify the rate categories that common carriers can use in setting their rates.

FCS (Fibre Channel Standard)

The FCS, is based on the high-speed Fibre Channel technology, and it provides the specifications for optical fiber in the FDDI (Fiber Distributed Data Interface) network architecture.

FCS (Frame Check Sequence)

In network or other transmissions, the FCS is a value that is used to check for errors in a transmitted message. The FCS value is determined before sending the message, and it is stored in the packet's FCS field. If the new FCS value computed from the received packet does not match the original, a transmission error has occurred.

→ *See Also* Error Detection and Correction

FDDI (Fiber Distributed Data Interface)

FDDI is an ANSI standard (X3T9.5) for a network architecture that is designed to use fiber-optic lines at very high speeds.

An FDDI network has the following characteristics:

- Uses multimode or single-mode fiber-optic cable.

- Supports transmission speeds of up to 100Mbps.

- Uses a ring topology. Actually, FDDI uses dual rings on which information can travel in opposite directions.

- Uses token-passing as the media-access method. However, in order to support a high transmission rate, FDDI can have multiple frames circulating the ring at a time, just as with ETR (early token release) in an ordinary Token Ring network.

- Uses light, rather than electricity, to encode signals.

- Uses a 4B/5B signal-encoding scheme. This scheme transmits 5 bits for every 4 bits of information. (This means that an FDDI network needs a clock speed of 125Mbps to support a 100Mbps transmission rate.) The actual bits are encoded using an NRZ-I strategy.

- Uses an LED (light-emitting diode) or a laser operating at a wavelength of roughly 1300 nanometers (nm). This wavelength was chosen because it provides suitable performance even with LEDs.

- Supports up to 1000 nodes on the network.

- Supports a network span of up to 100 kilometers (62 miles).

- Supports nodes up to 2 kilometers (1.25 miles) apart when using multimode cable and up to 40 kilometers (25 miles) when using single-mode cable.

- Supports a power budget (allowable power loss) of 11 decibels (dB) between nodes. This value means that about 92 percent of the signal's power can be lost between two nodes. (The signal is at least partially regenerated by the transceiver at each node.)

- Can handle packets from either the LLC (logical-link control) sublayer of the Data-Link layer or from the Network layer.

- Supports hybrid networks, which can be created by attaching a subnetwork (for example, a collection of stations arranged in a star or a tree) to the ring through a concentrator.

"Context and properties of FDDI" summarizes this architecture.

FDDI Applications

The FDDI architecture can be used for three types of networks:

- In a backbone network, in which the FDDI architecture connects multiple networks. Optical fiber's very high bandwidth makes FDDI ideal for such applications.

- As a back-end network to connect mainframes, minicomputers, and peripherals. Again, the high bandwidth makes FDDI attractive.

- As a front-end network to connect special-purpose workstations (such as graphics or engineering machines) for very high-speed data transfer.

FDDI Documents

The FDDI standard consists of four documents: PMD, PHY, MAC, and SMT. Each of these describes a different facet of the architecture.

PMD (Physical Medium Dependent)

PMD represents the lowest sublayer supported by FDDI. This document specifies the requirements for the optical power sources, photodetectors, transceivers, MIC (medium interface connector), and cabling. This is the only optic (as opposed to electrical) level and corresponds roughly to the lower parts of the Physical layer in the OSI Reference Model.

The power source must be able to send a signal of at least 25 microwatts (25 millionths of a watt) into the fiber. The photodetector, or light receptor, must be able to pick up a signal as weak as 2 microwatts.

F

The MIC for FDDI connections serves as the interface between the electrical and optical components of the architecture. This connector was specially designed by ANSI for FDDI, and is also known as the FDDI connector.

The cabling specified at this sublayer calls for two rings running in opposite directions. The primary ring is the main transmission medium. A secondary ring provides redundancy by making it possible to transmit the data in the opposite direction if necessary. When the primary ring is working properly, the secondary ring is generally idle.

PHY (Physical)

The PHY layer mediates between the MAC layer above it and the PMD layer below it. Unlike the PMD layer, this is an electronic layer. Signal-encoding and signal-decoding schemes are defined at the PHY layer. Functionally, this corresponds to the upper parts of the OSI Reference Model Physical layer.

Context

Network Architectures
    Electrical
        Ethernet, ARCnet, etc.
        Coaxial
    Optical
        FDDI ─────────────────┐

FDDI Properties	
Medium	Multimode or single-mode optical fiber
Light source	LED or laser operating at approximately 1300 nm wavelength
Encoding scheme	4B/5B + NRZI
Topology	Dual rings, traveling in opposite directions
Access method	Token passing, but with multiple frames allowed
Data frame size	Maximum of 4500 data bytes plus 8+ bytes for a preamble
Layers	PMD optical, PHY, MAC, SMT
Performance	Supports transmission speeds of up to 100 Mbps Can provide and maintain a guaranteed bandwidth Supports up to 1000 nodes on the network Supports a network span of up to 100 km Supports nodes up to 2 km apart with multimode cable; up to 40 km with single-mode cable
Variants	FDDI-I and FDDI-II

CONTEXT AND PROPERTIES OF FDDI

MAC (Media Access Control)

The MAC layer defines the frame formats and also the media-access method used by the network. This corresponds to the lower part of the OSI Reference Model data-link layer. The MAC and PHY layers are implemented directly in the FDDI chip set.

The MAC layer gets its data from the LLC sublayer above it.

SMT (Station Management)

The SMT component monitors and manages the node's activity. The SMT facility also allocates the architecture's bandwidth as required.

There are three elements to the SMT component:

- Frame services generate frames for diagnostics.

- Connection management (CMT) controls access to the network.

- Ring management (RMT) troubleshoots the network.

If there is a fault in the primary ring, the SMT facility redirects transmissions to use the secondary ring around the faulty section. This component can also use the secondary ring to transmit data under certain conditions, achieving a potential transmission rate of 200Mbps. This component has no counterpart in the OSI Reference Model. SMT capabilities may be implemented in hardware or software.

FDDI Versions

The original FDDI specification (retroactively named FDDI-I) called only for asynchronous communications using packet-switching. (Actually, there was a synchronous traffic class in FDDI-I, but this did not guarantee a uniform data stream as would be required, for example, for voice or certain video data.)

To handle voice, video, and multimedia applications in real-time, a uniform data-transmission capability was added in a revision that is generally known as FDDI-II, but that is officially named *hybrid ring control* (HRC) FDDI. This new capability uses circuit-switching, so that FDDI-II supports both packet- and circuit-switched services. "FDDI-I and FDDI-II organization" shows the major differences between the two versions.

The major structural additions to FDDI-II are a medium access control element capable of dealing with circuit-switched data, and a multiplexer capable of passing either packet- or circuit-switched (that is, data, voice, video, and so on) material to the Physical layer. This hybrid multiplexer (HMUX) gets frames from both the MAC connected to the LLC sublayer and from the isochronous MAC, or IMAC, added in FDDI-II.

The IMAC interacts with one or more circuit-switched multiplexers (CS-MUXs), which are capable of delivering voice, video, or any other kind of data that requires a continual connection and a constant rate. The IMAC and the HMUX together make up the HRC element that distinguishes FDDI-II.

An FDDI-II network can operate either in basic or hybrid mode, depending on whether circuit-switched services are needed. By default, FDDI networks operate in basic mode, which can handle only packet-switched data.

The standard has been broadened in several other ways to support a greater variety of components. For example, the original standard called for 62.5/125 micron multimode cable and for LEDs as the power source. Extensions have made other diameters of multimode cable and also single-mode cable acceptable, and have made lasers a possible power source.

FDDI Hardware

An FDDI network contains the following hardware elements: stations, NIC, cable, dual bypass switch, connectors, concentrators, and couplers.

FDDI Stations

A station, or node, on an FDDI network may be a single-attachment station (SAS) or a dual-attachment station (DAS).

A DAS node has two transceivers, which are connected to the primary and secondary rings,

F

respectively. This node can be connected directly to the network backbone. DAS nodes are also known as class A stations.

An SAS node has only one transceiver, which is connected to the primary ring. This node cannot be connected directly to the network backbone. Instead, it must be attached through a concentrator, which is connected to both rings. The advantage of this method is apparent when SAS transceivers fail, because the failure will be contained by the concentrator and will not bring down the entire network. SAS nodes are also known as class B stations.

NIC

The NIC contains either one or two transceivers that meet the PMD specifications. Not surprisingly, the one transceiver NICs are less expensive. An FDDI NIC has both a power source and a photodetector on the NIC.

Cable

Either single-mode cable or 62.5/125 micron multimode cable can be used. (The two values represent the diameter of the optical fiber's core and cladding components, respectively.) Often, cable with two core segments is used. One core is used for the primary ring, and the other is used for the secondary ring.

Even though only one multimode cable configuration is officially supported, in practice, FDDI networks may also support 50/125, 85/125, and 100/140 micron cables. The restriction depends on the power budget (allowable power loss) for the cable.

See the Cable, Fiber-Optic article for more information.

Dual Bypass Switch

A dual bypass switch is an optional component. It is often attached to nodes to make it easier to bypass the node in case of failure.

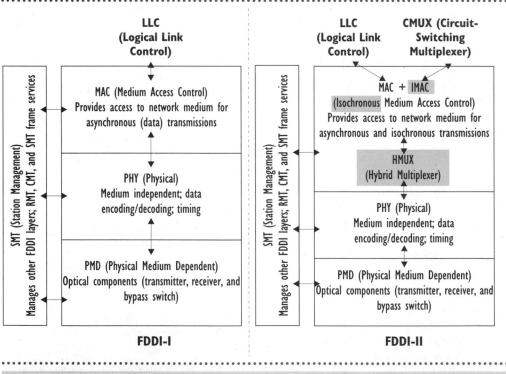

FDDI-I AND FDDI-II ORGANIZATION

Connectors

The FDDI standard calls for specially designed connectors: MIC connectors. The MIC was designed to protect the ferrules that hold the fiber for the actual connection. The MIC is also expected to provide a snug, robust fit and to minimize signal loss at the connection.

The connection ends are polarized (asymmetrically cut), so that it is not possible to inadvertently link primary or secondary cables to each other. The connectors are also keyed to make it impossible to connect the wrong components to each other. There are different keys for connecting cable segments and for connecting nodes to a concentrator or a concentrator to a backbone. The FDDI MIC is a duplex connector, so that cables for both rings can be connected simultaneously. Special adapters are available to enable an MIC to connect to two ST connectors or to a transceiver.

FDDI variants have been developed that support SC, ST, and other types of fiber-optic connectors, partly because these are less expensive than FDDI connectors. Within a stretch of cable (at locations other than interfaces) the FDDI standard actually allows any kind of connector, provided the total power loss for the entire stretch of cable does not exceed the 11 dB power budget.

If you plan to use non-MIC connections in your FDDI setup, be sure to do your research carefully. Make sure that all the components you will be using will support the nonstandard connectors.

See the Connector, Fiber Optic article for more information.

Concentrators

Concentrators serve as wiring centers for FDDI nodes. For example, concentrators may be used in a front-end network. Concentrators are connected to both the primary and secondary rings. Because of this, concentrators provide a link between the SAS and the secondary ring. As such, the concentrator assumes the function of secondary transceiver for each of the SASs attached to the concentrator.

Concentrators also come in single-attachment or dual-attachment forms (SAC and DAC, respectively). DACs can be connected to any of the four node types (SAS, DAS, SAC, and DAC) and can be used to attach stations or clusters of stations to the logical ring, even though these nodes are physically elsewhere.

SACs, in contrast, are used primarily for attaching SASs and other SACs. A SAC must connect to a DAC, which is part of the ring.

Couplers

A coupler serves to split a light signal into two or more signals. For example, a coupler may be used to transmit the signal to multiple nodes.

The efficiency of a coupler can be an important factor in a fiber-optic setup. Whereas an electrical signal retains its strength when split, the same is not true of light. Splitting a light beam into two equal beams is equivalent to a 3 dB loss for each beam.

See the Coupler, Fiber-Optic article for more information.

F

GETTING FDDI COMPONENTS

There are still enough complexities and variations in the world of fiber optics that you should seriously consider going with a single vendor for your fiber-optic needs. Get that vendor to guarantee that the components will work together, so that you won't have to worry about all those details. Make sure to give that vendor a list of performance specifications that the network must meet.

FDDI Ports

Stations on an FDDI network communicate through ports. Four types of ports are defined for FDDI stations:

- Port A is defined only for dual-attachment devices (DACs and DASs), and is connected to the incoming primary ring and the outgoing secondary ring.

- Port B is defined only for dual-attachment devices (DACs and DASs), and is connected to the incoming *secondary* ring and the outgoing primary ring.

- Port M (Master) is defined only for concentrators (DAC or SAC), and connects two concentrators. This port can also be used to communicate with both DASs and SASs.

- S (Slave) is defined only for single-attachment devices, and is used to connect two stations or a station to a concentrator.

FDDI Operation

In creating an FDDI network, the first task is to configure the ring. After each station on the network is identified, it is assigned a unique address, usage priorities, and so on.

Initially, the network operates in basic mode, and continues to do so until a station requests a switch to hybrid mode. If this is feasible, the stations go through a process to determine the cycle master, which essentially runs the hybrid mode by controlling the creation and transmission of the cycles (bit-filled time slots) that provide the structure for a network in hybrid mode.

In basic mode, a token circulates from node to node, as follows:

1. When an unused (available) token reaches a node (node A), the node grabs the token and transmits a frame. Then node A releases the token. First the frame and then the token reach the node's nearest downstream neighbor (node B).

2. If the frame is addressed to node B, the recipient copies the pertinent information (source address and data), sets the Frame Status field to an appropriate value, and sends the frame on to make its way back to the sender (node A). If node B is not the destination for the frame, the node simply passes the frame on unchanged.

3. Next, node B gets the token that node A released immediately after the frame. If node B has something to say, node B grabs the token, sends its frame, and follows this immediately with the token.

Note that there are now two frames circulating, but only one token. Allowing multiple frames to circulate simultaneously is one way to achieve a high-transmission speed in an FDDI network.

When things are working smoothly, the FDDI configuration is as illustrated in "An FDDI network with the primary ring working properly," with the secondary ring idle. When a connection between two stations is broken, the station with a frame but no destination information sends the frame onto the secondary ring, as shown in "An FDDI network with a break, forcing a switch over to the secondary ring." On that path, the frame reaches the station that was the next destination before the break.

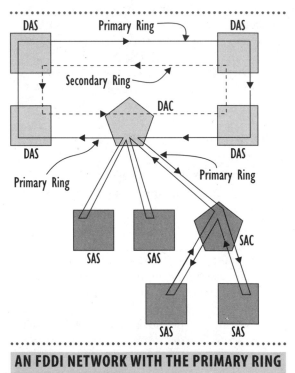

AN FDDI NETWORK WITH THE PRIMARY RING WORKING PROPERLY

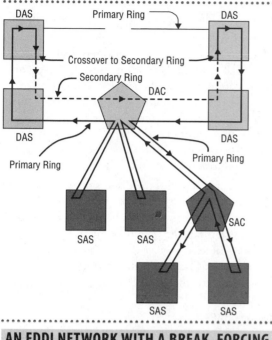

DAS

Primary Ring

DAS

Crossover to Secondary Ring

Secondary Ring

DAC

DAS

DAS

Primary Ring

Primary Ring

SAC

SAS

SAS

SAS

SAS

AN FDDI NETWORK WITH A BREAK, FORCING A SWITCH OVER TO THE SECONDARY RING

An FDDI network can have both synchronous and asynchronous transmissions occurring at the same time. These transmissions are controlled by the SMT facility. The SMT component can allocate a fixed portion of the bandwidth for synchronous transmissions, leaving the rest of the bandwidth available for asynchronous transmissions. Different priority schemes are used to control access to the synchronous and asynchronous portions of the bandwidth.

As is the case with any token-passing network, it is necessary to monitor the network to make sure the token does not get corrupted, lost, or trapped by a node that goes off line. The SMT is responsible for such monitoring.

All nodes monitor the ring to check for problems. If a node detects a token problem—a problem that might require the network to be reinitialized—the node initiates a claim token process. This is a contest

in which one node finally wins the right to reinitialize the ring and issue a new token.

If a node detects a serious error (such as a break in the ring), that node sends a beacon frame. As other nodes detect the error or receive a beacon frame, they also start sending beacon frames. A node stops sending beacon frames as soon as the node receives such a frame from its nearest upstream neighbor (NAUN).

The frame immediately downstream from the problem will be the last node transmitting beacon frames, and this node will stop as soon as it receives its own beacon frame back, because this will indicate that the problem has been resolved (usually by switching to the secondary ring to bypass the fault).

Once the problem has been resolved, the last beaconing node starts the claim token process.

Extended Dialogs

FDDI allows a node to seize control of the token temporarily, and to restrict its use in order to carry out an extended interaction with a specific other node. Only the nodes involved in the interaction can use this token. These two nodes will communicate with each other until the interaction is finished, at which point one of them will release an unrestricted token.

Note that a restricted token will not trigger a claim token process because each node gets to see the token. Nonprivileged nodes (those not involved in the extended interaction) simply are not allowed to use the token.

Station Management for FDDI

As stated, the SMT component has three major responsibilities: connection management, ring management, and frame services.

CMT (Connection Management)

CMT is concerned with the station's coordination with the network, the physical connection (PCM), and the station's configuration. The coordination task is known as entity-coordination management

F

(ECM), and it makes sure that all the required ports are working properly, with the network and with each other.

The PCM is responsible for the negotiations that determine the type of port associated with the station, availability of a MAC component for testing the link, and also for connecting the station. If these negotiations are successful, the CMT switches to the settings required to connect the station to the network and to enable it to communicate once connected.

RMT (Ring Management)

RMT is used to keep the ring in working order. Toward this end, RMT checks for duplicate addresses and for stuck beacons (a frame sent to indicate a major error on the ring, such as a break).

A stuck beacon arises when a station keeps sending beacon frames. This happens when the station never gets a beacon from another node (which would indicate that other nodes are also aware of the failure). In case of a stuck beacon, the RMT uses a trace function to help isolate the error and to recover from the stuck beacon.

Frame Services

Like all good management services, the SMT has its own communications facilities, which provide the required information independently of the data being transmitted across the network. The station management functions are implemented through several special-purpose frames, which are used to allocate and check resources, exchange information with stations, and so on. The SMT frames are described in the next section.

FDDI Frames

FDDI has three types of frames: tokens, command, and data frames. These are used in basic FDDI operation. When the system is operating in hybrid mode, transmissions are defined by cycles (125 microsecond intervals), with bit sequences defined within this framework. Cycles are discussed later in this article.

Frames consist of the preamble, header, contents, and trailer. The preamble is generally not included when determining the frame's length.

Discussions of FDDI frames can be confusing, because FDDI signal encoding uses a five-bits-for-four encoding scheme. When describing the size of frame elements, the number of bits involved before encoding will be based on octets, or more directly, on 4-bit nibbles; after encoding, 25 percent more bits will be floating around, because each nibble is encoded into a 5-bit symbol.

For consistency with the discussion of frames for other architectures, the following descriptions use the byte-based bit counts that hold prior to encoding. For example, the preamble for an FDDI frame consists of at least 8 bytes; that is, the preamble has 16 nibbles or 64 bits. In post-encoding terms, this amounts to 16 symbols, or 80 bits.

Token Frames

A token frame consists of three bytes plus the preamble, as follows:

Preamble (8+ bytes): Consists of 64 or more bits, each with a predefined value. The preamble serves as a pattern with which the receiver can set the signal clock.

Starting Delimiter (1 byte): Indicates the actual start of the frame.

Frame Control: Only the two most significant bits are used for the token frame. A byte value of 1000 0000 indicates an unrestricted token, which can be used without restrictions for both synchronous and asynchronous communication. A value of 1100 0000 indicates a restricted token, whose use in asynchronous transmissions has constraints.

Ending Delimiter (1 byte): Indicates the end of the frame.

"An FDDI token frame" shows the components of a token frame in FDDI.

64+ bits Preamble	8 bits SD	8 bits FC	8 bits ED

SD = Starting Delimiter
FC = Frame Control
ED = Ending Delimiter

AN FDDI TOKEN FRAME

Data Frame

A data frame contains packets that were received from higher-level protocols and that are being sent to another node. A data frame consists of at most 4500 bytes (9000 symbols), not counting the preamble.

Preamble (8+ bytes): Same as for a token frame.

Starting Delimiter (1 byte): Same as for a token frame.

Frame Control (1 byte): Provides the following information through four bit groupings: Whether the frame is part of a synchronous or an asynchronous transmission (1 bit), whether the frame is using 2- or 6-byte addresses (1 bit), whether the frame is a data (LLC-layer) or command (MAC-layer) frame (2 bits), and the type of command if the frame is a command (4 bits).

Destination Address (2 or 6 bytes): Contains the address of frame's recipient. The receiving

node saves the source address and the frame's data before passing the frame to the next node in the ring.

Source Address (2 or 6 bytes): Contains the address of frame's sender.

Information (at most 5601 nibbles): Contains the packet received from the higher protocol layer.

Frame Check Sequence (4 bytes): Contains the results of a CRC (cyclic redundancy check) to determine whether an error has crept into the frame.

Ending Delimiter (4 bits): Same value as in a token frame, but stored only once.

Frame Status (12+ bits): Used to indicate the result of the frame's trip around the ring. The recipient uses this field to indicate whether the frame was received correctly. An unchanged Frame Status field indicates that the destination node was not found on the ring.

"An FDDI data frame" shows the components of this frame.

Command Frames

Command frames have the same structure as data frames, except that the information field is always 0 bytes long. A command frame contains instructions for doing maintenance on the network ring. These instructions are contained in the Frame Control field.

F

64+ bits Preamble	8 bits SD	8 bits FC	16 or 48 bits DA	16 or 48 bits SA	0+ bits Info	32 bits FCS	4 bits ED	12 bits FS

SD = Starting Delimiter   **FCS = Frame Check Sequence**
FC = Frame Control   **ED = Ending Delimiter**
DA = Destination Address   **FS = Frame Status**
SA = Source Address

AN FDDI DATA FRAME

Command frames cannot have the same structure as token frames because the Frame Status field provides information about the results from carrying out the command.

SMT Frames

The SMT component uses various special-purpose frames to keep things running smoothly:

ECF (Echo Frame): Used for tests within the SMT operation.

ESF (Extended Services Frame): Provides a mechanism for user-defined frames.

NIF (Neighbor Information Frame): Used to contact the frame's downstream neighbor.

PMF (Parameter Management Frame): Makes remote management possible.

RAF (Resource Allocation Frame): Used to allocate the bandwidth as needed.

RDF (Request Denied Frame): Indicates that the SMT component has encountered an invalid frame or ID.

SIF (Station Information Frame): Used to pass information about a station's configuration and operation.

SRF (Status Report Frame): Used to keep other stations updated about a station's status.

Transmissions in Hybrid Mode

When an FDDI-II station operates in hybrid mode, the transmission is structured around a cycle, which is a packet that is repeated continuously during a session. Cycles are generated by a special node that functions as the cycle master.

Each cycle is 125 microseconds long and contains 12,500 bits. Each cycle has room for the following:

Preamble (5 nibbles): As usual, the preamble is used for synchronization.

Cycle Header (12 bytes): Provides information about the contents of the rest of the cycle.

DPG (Dedicated Packet Group, 12 bytes): Can be used for handling transmissions that involve packet transfers.

WBC (Wideband Channel, 96 bytes per channel per cycle): Provides multiple transmission channels, each with up to 6.144Mbps bandwidth.

This cycle arrangement helps ensure that every channel can get maximum use. Toward this end, each WBC can be divided into lower bandwidth channels, which enables traffic from a greater number of stations to travel simultaneously along the network. This would not increase the bandwidth, because each of the channels would have a smaller capacity. Since not all stations will have over 6 million bits of information to send every second, turning a WBC into a few dozen 64Kbps channels can actually help increase traffic on the network.

The cycle header is a crucial element in the hybrid mode of operation, because the contents of this header help ensure that each station is properly synchronized and also provide the information that enables stations to interpret the contents of the rest of the cycle. For example, the header might indicate whether the data is to be treated as packet-switched or isochronous (circuit-switched) data.

Variants

Some vendors are supporting an architecture similar to FDDI on electrical cable. This variant is known as CDDI (Copper Distributed Data Interface) or TPDDI (Twisted Pair Distributed Data Interface), and it is an effort to extend the FDDI specifications to copper shielded or unshielded twisted-pair wiring. There are as yet no official standards for CDDI, so there is little guarantee of interoperability with products from different vendors.

See the ESCON, Fibre Channel, and SONET articles for discussions of other variants.

→ *Broader Category* Network Architecture

→ *See Also* Cable, Fiber-Optic; Connector, Fiber-Optic; Coupler, Fiber-Optic

FDDITalk

Apple's implementation of FDDI (Fiber Distributed Data Interface) protocols and drivers for use in an AppleTalk network.

→ *See Also* EtherTalk, LocalTalk, TokenTalk

FDL (Facility Data Link)

In an extended superframe (ESF) format digital transmission, an FDL is a 4Kbps communications link between the sender's station and the telephone company's monitors. This 4Kbps band is created by taking half of the 24 framing bits in an ESF and using them for the link.

→ *See Also* ESF (Extended Superframe)

FDM (Frequency Division Multiplexing)

A multiplexing scheme in which the bandwidth of a medium is divided into distinct and mutually exclusive frequency ranges. FDM is generally used for analog transmissions, and is in contrast to TDM (time division multiplexing), which is generally used for digital transmissions.

→ *See Also* Multiplexing; TDM (Time Division Multiplexing)

FDMA (Frequency Division, Multiple Access)

In communications, a strategy for assigning multiple channels within a large bandwidth. Once channels are assigned, signals can be sent along these channels using a multiplexing strategy such as FDM (frequency division multiplexing).

→ *Compare* CDMA (Code Division Multiple Access); TDMA (Time Division Multiple Access).

→ *See Also* Multiplexing

FDX (Full Duplex)

A communication setup in which transmissions can go in both directions at the same time. This is in contrast to simplex and half-duplex connections.

Feature Group

A feature group refers to a set of services developed by the Bell Operating Companies, and designed to provide customers with access to Interexchange Carriers (IECs or IXCs) of their choice.

- Feature Group A gives customers access to an IEC by dialing a 7- or 10-digit number, followed by a personal identification number.

- Feature Group B provides access to an IEC using a 7-digit code of the form 950-10*xx*, where the *xx* identifies a particular IEC.

- Feature Group D provides access to an IEC, originally using a code of the form 10*xxx* to select the IEC before dialing a number. The *xxx* identifies the IEC. For example, under this system, 10288 would select AT&T as the IEC, 10333 selects Sprint, and so forth. Such a code is used to override the customer's Preferred Interexchange Carrier (PIC), which is the carrier the customer selected for long-distance service. Thus, if the customer just dials 1 for a long-distance call, that customer's PIC will be used. This feature group has been modified, so that it is now necessary to dial 1010*xxx*(*x*)—for example, 1010220, 1010321, 1010345, or 10109000.

FEBE (Far End Block Error)

In broadband ISDN (BISDN) networks, an error reported to the sender by the receiver when the receiver's computed checksum result does not match the sender's checksum.

FEC (Forward Error Correction)

A type of error correction in which a transmission includes enough additional information for the receiver to locate and correct any bit-level errors that arise during transmission.

→ *See Also* Error Detection and Correction

FECN (Forward Explicit Congestion Notification)

In Frame Relay networks, FECN refers to a bit that is set in a frame to notify the destination (or receiving) device that there is congestion on the network and that the receiving device should take any possible measures to avoid the congestion.

→ *See Also* BECN (Backward Explicit Congestion Notification); ECN (Explicit Congestion Notification)

Federal Communications Commission (FCC)

→ *See* FCC (Federal Communications Commission)

Federal Information Exchange (FIX)

→ *See* FIX (Federal Information Exchange)

Federal Networking Council (FNC)

→ *See* FNC (Federal Networking Council)

Feed

In telecommunications, a circuit through which data is sent to a central station or for transmission along a network backbone.

FEP (Front-End Processor)

In an IBM SNA (Systems Network Architecture) network, an FEP is a component that controls access to the host computer (the mainframe). The FEP, also known as a *communication controller*, is generally attached to the host by a fast, direct connection (often a fiber-optic link), and is controlled by the host through a network control program (NCP) loaded and executed on the FEP.

Through the NCP, the FEP relieves the host of tasks such as establishing connections and monitoring links. The FEP is also responsible for doing any data compression or translation as the data moves between host and remote device.

In IBM hardware terms, the FEP is a controller in the 37*xx* series; in SNA terms, the FEP is a Type 4 PU (physical unit). 37*xx* controllers vary in the number of lines they can handle and in the speed these lines can support.

→ *Broader Category* SNA (Systems Network Architecture)

FERF (Far End Receive Failure)

In broadband ISDN (BISDN) networks, a signal sent upstream to indicate that an error has been detected downstream. An FERF might be sent, for example, because a destination has reported an error.

Ferrule

In a fiber-optic connection, a component that serves to keep the optical core and cladding aligned and immobile. The fiber cladding may be glued to the ferrule with epoxy. Ferrules may be made of ceramic (the most reliable), plastic, or stainless steel.

→ *See Also* Connector, Fiber-Optic

FEXT (Far End Crosstalk)

In an electrical signal, interference, or leakage, of a transmitted signal from one wire into another wire. FEXT is measured at the *receiving* end, in contrast to NEXT (near end crosstalk).

Fiber Bandwidth

A measure of a fiber-optic cable's ability to carry information, usually expressed in terms of megahertz (MHz) or megabits per second (Mbps) per kilometer or some other distance.

Fiber, Blown

A location with blown fiber has everything in place for using optical fiber—except the fiber itself. In such a location, the casing for the optical fiber has been put into place, but has been left hollow. When the switch to fiber-optic cable finally occurs, the actual fibers will be blown through the tubes using compressed air.

The use of blown fiber is quite rare—in part because it is so expensive. Effectively, wiring by using blown fiber requires two wiring installations: one for the casing and one for the fiber. Conceivably, such an expensive wiring method can be worth it in installations where very high security is a necessity. If unauthorized interlopers must be allowed in, it's better if all they can do is lay an empty tube. It's much more difficult to include a tap in a cable that doesn't yet have any wiring. The actual fiber could be blown in by trusted, in-house staff operating a rented wind machine.

Fiber Bundle

In fiber optics, a collection of fibers that are routed together. Two types of bundles are distinguished:

- *Flexible bundle.* A collection of fibers that are grouped, or bundled, at either end of the cable, but that are free to move between these endpoints.

- *Rigid bundle.* A collection of fibers that are melted together to form a single rod that is bent into the desired shape during manufacture. Rigid, or *fused*, bundles are less expensive to manufacture than flexible ones.

→ *Broader Category* Cable

Fiber Channel

→ *See* Fibre Channel

Fiber Channel Standard (FCS)

→ *See* FCS (Fibre Channel Standard)

Fiber, Dark

A term for optical fiber that has been installed but is not being used. According to some estimates, over half of the installed fiber-optic cable is still dark fiber.

Fiber Distributed Data Interface (FDDI)

→ *See* FDDI (Fiber Distributed Data Interface)

Fiber-Optic Inter-Repeater Link (FIRL)

→ *See* FOIRL (Fiber-Optic Inter-Repeater Link)

Fiber-Optic Inter-Repeater Link (FOIRL)

→ *See* FOIRL (Fiber-Optic Inter-Repeater Link)

F

Fiber Optics

Fiber optics refers to a communications technology that uses light signals transmitted along special fibers, instead of electrical signals transmitted along copper wire.

Networks based on fiber optics offer numerous advantages over those based on copper wiring and electrical signals, including the following:

- Immunity to electromagnetic interference, eavesdropping, and jamming

- Higher bandwidth

- Greater distances allowed

Currently, fiber-optic networks also offer a major disadvantage: price.

→ *See Also* Cable, Fiber-Optic; FDDI (Fiber Distributed Data Interface)

Fibre Channel

Fibre Channel is a high-speed transmission technology, originally developed for connecting mainframe computers to various peripheral and storage devices. The bandwidth for a particular implementation depends on the type of cable, on the light source, and on the wavelength of light being used for signals. Bandwidths range from more than 100Mbps at the low end (with LEDs and multimode fiber) to about 1Gbps (with lasers and single-mode fiber-optic cable). Versions with speeds up to 4.25Gbps have been approved by ANSI committees, but products for these speeds are not yet on the market.

Fibre Channel actually offers features of both channel and network connections. A *channel connection* is essentially a (more or less) direct, end-to-end link between two devices. Often these are a master and a slave device. Since such closed connections generally don't need to worry about other traffic, channel connections tend to have low overhead. The connection is generally very high speed because of the hardware.

However, Fibre Channel can also handle network-type traffic, in which traffic can go to any of multiple nodes, and in which transmissions may need to cover short or long distances. Such connections generally have much higher overhead than channel transmissions because of framing and addressing requirements. In contrast to channel connections, network-type connections tend to be more software-intensive.

Fibre Channel Uses

As stated, Fibre Channel was originally developed to provide high-speed connections between a computer and a storage array or other peripheral device. This is still one of the main uses for the technology.

Another use has been in configurations in which processors are run together in clusters to create parallel processing capabilities. The Fibre Channel connection provides sufficient bandwidth to allow the processors to work together in this way.

Fibre Channel is actually suited to a very common task, but has not yet been widely used in this way. Fibre Channel supports the use of higher-level protocols and their commands over Fibre Channel connections. Thus, Fibre Channel could be used to provide the bandwidth for LAN (Local Area Network) backbones.

Fibre Channel Performance

The original Fibre Channel specifications define four transmission speeds: 133Mbps, 266Mbps, 531Mbps, and 1.062Gbps. Since the standard was adopted, the ANSI Fibre Channel workgroup has also defined specifications for 2.134Gbps and 4.25Gbps rates.

The original Fibre Channel specifications were only for optical fiber. However, the technology was eventually redefined to run on coaxial or shielded twisted-pair (STP) copper cable. (The Fibre in the name was introduced after nonoptical media were allowed. The European spelling of fiber was used to maintain a connection to the original specification—which now was no longer just for fiber—without explicitly limiting the technology to that medium.) Performance specifications covered media running at 25 and at 100Mbps. Table "Fibre Channel Media" shows the distances supported for various grades of media.

Fibre Channel can use either a light-emitting diode (LED) or a laser as the light source, and the light can have a wavelength between 780 and 1300 nanometers. Thus, the energy source can range from low to high level.

Two levels of optics are specified for Fibre Channel. One of these requires built-in safety measures. The optical fibre control (OFC) variant uses lasers that are sufficiently high energy to damage eyes. To make sure no one is injured by accidentally walking between the transmitting and receiving nodes, OFC configurations need to check for line of sight between sender and receiver. If the line of sight is broken, the laser immediately stops transmitting.

Non-OFC lasers use less power, and pose no danger to the eyes. No special safety precautions are needed for non-OFC configurations.

Fibre Channel uses 8B/10B encoding for its transmissions. In this data translation scheme, 8-bit blocks are translated into 10-bit symbols, and these are transmitted. The extra bits are used for error detection and correction, and sometimes for control purposes. This error checking method is known as *disparity control*.

Fibre Channel Frames

Fibre Channel transmissions are packaged into frames. These illustrate the small overhead involved in this technology. "A Fibre Channel frame" shows the elements included in a Fibre Channel frame.

F

FIBRE CHANNEL MEDIA

Media Type	Rated Bandwidth (Mbps)	Distance Supported (meters)
Single-mode optical fiber—long wavelength (LWL)	25	10,000
Single-mode optical fiber—short wavelength (SWL)	100	10,000
Multimode optical fiber (50 micron)—LWL or SWL	25	2000
Multimode optical fiber (50 micron)—SWL	100	500
Multimode optical fiber (62.5 micron)—LWL	25	1500
Multimode optical fiber (62.5 micron)—SWL	25	750
Multimode optical fiber (62.5 micron)—SWL	100	175
Shielded twisted-pair (STP) copper wire	25	50
Coaxial	25	75
Coaxial	100	25

SOF	Addressing, etc.	Header	Payload	CRC	EOF
①	②	⑤	⑥	③	④

A FIBRE CHANNEL FRAME

The core of such a frame is the data field, which can be up to 2112 bytes. Of this chunk, 64 bytes are used for a header (5), and the remaining 2048 bytes can be used for payload (6).

Preceding the data field in a transmission, Fibre Channel includes a 4-byte Start Frame element (1), and a 24-byte Frame Header (2). After the data field, the frame transmission closes with a 4-byte CRC (cyclic redundancy check) element (3) and a 4-byte End Frame indicator (4).

A Fibre Channel frame can have up to 2148 bytes, with either 36 or 100 bytes of overhead—depending on how the data field header is being used.

Fibre Channel Sessions

An entire Fibre Channel session is known as an *exchange*. For example, an exchange could consist of a session in which a computer requests and receives a particular large data object from a storage device.

An exchange consists of several *sequences*. For example, in the exchange described above, the following might be sequences: Finding out whether the storage device has the desired object; requesting the object; receiving transmission of the object.

Each of these sequences is made up of one or more frames.

Fibre Channel Topologies

Devices in a Fibre Channel environment are connected to each other through a *Fibre Channel cloud*. The details of the connections within this cloud are of no concern to the devices.

Fibre Channel supports three topologies for connecting devices: point-to-point, arbitrated loop, and fabric. All three topologies are interoperable, which means a particular configuration can include any combination of topologies. The topologies are also transparent, which means that a device doesn't need to know what kind of topology it is using to connect to the Fibre Channel cloud.

The devices in a Fibre Channel configuration are connected through ports, with an identifier based on the topology involved or on the purpose the device serves. Connections use two optical fibers or a pair of wires. One fiber or wire is used for communication in each direction. Thus, each fiber or wire has a transmitter at one end and a receiver at the other.

Point-to-Point

In a point-to-point topology, two devices are connected directly over a single, full-duplex link. This is the simplest topology, for example, for a server and a CD jukebox. The two ends of the connection need to be able to operate at a common speed and they need to use the same protocol.

Devices connected in a point-to-point topology are known as *N-ports* and are shown in the top of figure "Fibre Channel topologies."

Arbitrated Loop

An arbitrated loop topology is much like a token ring. Devices are arranged in a ring or other closed figure. Each device receives signals from one device and transmits to the next one in the loop. In this way, a transmission travels around the entire loop.

Up to 127 nodes—known as *NL-ports*—can be connected to the loop. If a port wants to communicate, it asks to use the loop. If the loop is available, the port establishes a connection with its destination port. During their session, only these two ports will be communicating; all the other ports in the loop will merely be passing frames on—that is, acting as repeaters.

Since only one session can be going on at a time, an arbitrated loop topology essentially makes the Fibre Channel configuration a shared-media technology. However, an arbitrated loop is an inexpensive configuration, since over 100 nodes can be connected without any repeaters, hubs, or switches.

"Fibre Channel topologies" shows how such a topology can fit in with the others supported in Fibre Channel. In an organizational network, the arbitrated loop component might represent a department or a workgroup. This group can be connected to the rest of the enterprise network through the fabric.

F

Fabric

A fabric—or, in the case of a Fibre Channel topology, *the* fabric—is an almost magical concept that essentially represents a richly connected configuration. As shown in "Fibre Channel topologies," the fabric makes up the entire Fibre Channel cloud. Think of the fabric as the equivalent of a giant switch, which can connect any node to any other.

In a fabric topology, every node is connected to an actual switch inside the fabric. Such nodes are known as *F-ports*. Inside the fabric, switches are connected to each other, sometimes with multiple paths to provide redundancy and extra bandwidth. These switches serve as intermediate-level nodes for establishing connections—much like routers, except that the fabric as a whole accomplishes any necessary routing.

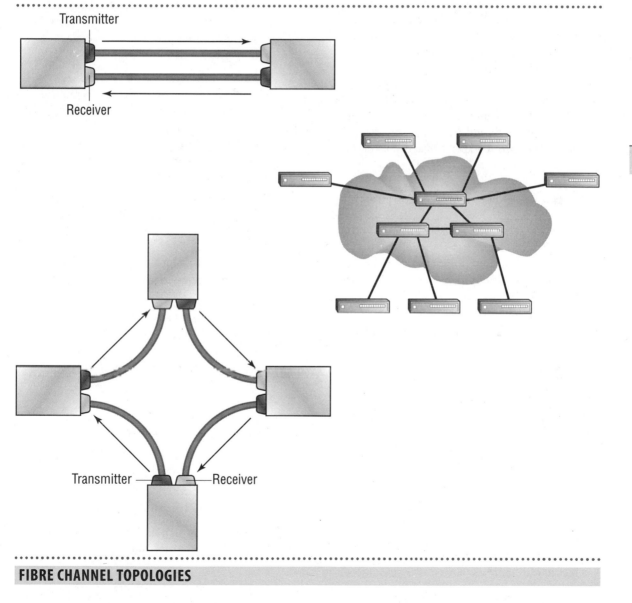

FIBRE CHANNEL TOPOLOGIES

Fibre Channel Layers

The Fibre Channel architecture is organized into five layers—FC-0, FC-1, FC-2, FC-3, and FC-4. The arrangement of these layers also provides a protocol stack over which Fibre Channel services can be used.

FC-0

FC-0 represents the Physical layer. The properties and parameters—electrical, mechanical, and optical—for the four supported transmission rates are specified at this layer. These rates are 133Mbps, 266Mbps, 531Mbps, and 1.062Gbps. Because of overhead due to data translation and other administrative functions, the actual data throughput is lower than the specified rates. Data rates are closer to 100Mbps, 200Mbps, 400Mbps, and 800Mbps. Details of the physical connections and also of the optics (OFC and non-OFC) are also specified at this layer.

FC-1

FC-1 is the layer at which transmission protocols are specified. Timing, line balance, serial encoding and decoding are all defined at this layer. The 8B/10B data translation scheme is defined and carried out at this layer. In this scheme, 8-bit blocks are encoded into 10-bit symbols before transmission. The extra two bits are for *disparity control*, which provides basic error detection and correction.

The FC-1 layer specifications were borrowed for use in Gigabit Ethernet.

FC-2

FC-2 is the layer at which signaling protocols are defined. This is where byte sequences are established, frames are created, and service classes and traffic management are defined. Traffic management functions include link management, flow control, buffer management, and error control.

The following five service classes are defined at this layer:

> **Class 1:** This defines a hard-wired or dedicated connection between two nodes. Maximum bandwidth for this connection is guaranteed, and frames are delivered in the same order they were sent. Since the connection is dedicated, Class 1 service is ideal for high-throughput transmissions—such as video. The receiving node must acknowledge each frame received.

> **Class 2:** This defines a connectionless, shared-bandwidth service. It makes no delivery guarantees, but uses frame switching to multiplex frames from different exchanges onto the same lines. As a result, frames may be received out of sequence. As is the case with Class 1, Class 2 receivers must send an acknowledgement for every frame received.

> **Class 3:** This class is just like Class 2 service, except that no acknowledgement is required—that is, there is no delivery confirmation. This time-saving actually makes Class 3 the fastest available class. As such, Class 3 service is handy for video or for any type of transmission that is being broadcast to many users.

> **Class 4:** This is a connection-oriented mode, with guaranteed performance. Unlike Class 1 service, the connection here is a virtual one, rather than a dedicated physical one. Specifications for constant bit rate (CBR), or isochronous, connections are still being developed.

> **Intermix:** This is actually a hybrid class in which elements of other classes—especially of Classes 1 and 2—are multiplexed into a Class 1 package and transmitted with the same guarantees that are offered for Class 1.

FC-3

The FC-3 layer is where common services are defined. These are services that affect multiple nodes—or at least both parties in a session. Services include the following:

- Multicast, in which a transmission is sent simultaneously to multiple nodes.

- Striping, in which multiple ports are used together to increase bandwidth.

FC-4

FC-4 is the layer at which high-level protocols and command sets come into contact with the Fibre Channel layers. This layer includes an application interface through which details of higher-level protocols (such as TCP/IP or SCSI) and commands are mapped into Fibre Channel terms. Supported protocols include the following:

- AAL5 (ATM Adaptation Layer, level 5)
- FC-LE (Fibre Channel Link Encapsulation Protocol)
- HIPPI (High Performance Parallel Interface)
- IEEE 802.2
- IP (Internet Protocol)
- IPI (Intelligent Peripheral Interface)
- SCSI (Small Computer System Interface)
- TCP/IP (Transmission Control Protocol/Internet Protocol)

The Fibre Channel Standard (FCS) provides the specifications for optical fiber in the FDDI (Fiber Distributed Data Interface) network architecture.

→ *Broader Category* Cable, Fiber-Optic

Fibre Channel Standard (FCS)

→ *See* FCS (Fibre Channel Standard)

Field

Most generally, a field is an element in a compound data structure, such as a packet database record, or form. In connection with networking packets, a field refers to a packet element that begins at a specific position in the bit block that makes up the packet. For example, in an Ethernet 2 packet, the source address field begins at the seventh byte in the packet.

Field-Replaceable Unit

A field-replaceable unit is any hardware that can be replaced from a field location and that does not require depot service.

FIFO (First In, First Out)

The processing strategy for the queue abstract data type. In this strategy, the element added least recently is the element removed first. For example, the single-line bank queues for the next available teller are FIFO queues. Compare FIFO with LIFO (last in first out).

File Access Data Unit (FADU)

→ *See* FADU (File Access Data Unit)

File Access Listener (FAL)

→ *See* FAL (File Access Listener)

File Allocation Table (FAT)

→ *See* FAT (File Allocation Table)

File Attribute

A value, or status, associated with a file. The value specifies, for example, the kinds of actions allowed with the file. Examples of file attributes include read-only, read/write, and archive. Files on a network will generally also have attributes that pertain to the access and usage rights and restrictions associated with the file.

→ *See Also* Attribute

F

File Caching

File caching is a scheme in which an area of RAM is reserved for use as fast-access *cache memory*. Frequently used files (or file chunks) are kept in this cache area for faster access.

When there is a request for a file, the operating system first checks whether the file is in the cache. If so, the file is retrieved from the cache rather than from its permanent storage, and the cache version will be modified if the file is changed. If the file is not in the cache, it is retrieved from disk (and may be written to the cache area).

There are various trade-offs and several strategies for deciding when to write the contents of a file in the cache to disk. These decisions are made when configuring (or possibly when creating) the cache program; they are not made by the end user.

The use of file caching can speed up performance, sometimes by a considerable amount. Other steps to improve performance include elevator seeking, which speeds up the storage and retrieval of data from the hard disk, and directory caching and hashing, which speed up the retrieval of information from the directory entry tables.

File Extension

In many operating systems, a file extension is a suffix added to a file name. In many cases, the extension identifies the type of file (text, program, graphics, and so on).

In DOS, a file extension can be at most three characters and must be separated from the file name (maximum eight characters) by a period. In the name PROGRAM.EXE, for example, *PROGRAM* is the name and *EXE* is the extension. It is not uncommon to include the leading period when specifying the extension, as in .EXE, for a program file.

The number of possible extensions is quite large, even if just letters are used.

The following are some examples of common file extensions and the types of files they represent:

- EXE, COM, and BAT indicate DOS files that can be executed. Files ending in BAT are batch files.
- NLM indicates a NetWare Loadable Module.
- DXF, GIF, PCX, PNG, and TIF indicate types of graphics files.
- C, CPP, ASM, and PAS indicate source files in particular programming languages: for C, C++, Assembler, and Pascal programs, respectively.
- ASC and TXT generally indicate files containing ordinary text.
- PS and EPS files are usually PostScript files, which may contain instructions for drawing a graphics image. PS files are text files; an EPS file can include a binary image.

Along with these, there are scores of other extensions. Some of these are listed in table "Common File Extensions."

File Indexing

In Novell's NetWare, file indexing is a strategy by which FAT (file allocation table) entries are indexed for faster access. This makes it possible to move directly to a particular block in a file, without needing to move through all the blocks that precede it.

NetWare versions 3.11 and later automatically index a FAT entry with more than 64 blocks, which is a file whose contents are scattered over more than 64 blocks on the disk.

A more powerful indexing strategy is used for files with more than 1023 blocks. Note that 4KB is the smallest block size supported by NetWare, which makes a file with 1024 blocks equal to 4MB, or almost twice the size of the original text files for this book.

COMMON FILE EXTENSIONS

Extension	Comments	Extension	Comments
ABF	Adobe Binary (Screen) font	C	C language source
ACT	(Microsoft Office Assistant) Actor file	CAB	Cabinet
ADB	Appointment database (HP 100LX)	CAL	Calendar schedule data file
ADI	AutoCAD Device-Independent plotter file	CAS	Comma-delimited ASCII
AFM	Adobe Font Metric	CB	(Microsoft) Clean Boot
AI	Adobe Illustrator	CCAD	ClarisCAD
AIF, AIFF	Audio Interchange File Format	CCH	Corel Chart
AIFC	AIF Compressed	CDA	CD Audio
AIM	AOL Instant Messenger	CDF	Channel Definition Format
ALB	(JASC Image Commander) Album	CDI	(Philips) Compact Disk Interactive
ANI	Windows animated cursor	CDR	Corel Draw
ANS	ANSI text	CDT	Corel Draw Template
APP	Appended	CDX	Corel Draw Compressed drawing
APR	Lotus Approach 97	CER	Certificate file
APS	Visual C++ file	CFG	Configuration
ARC	Archive compressed file	CFM	Cold Fusion template
ARJ	Archive (Robert Jung)	CGM	Computer Graphics Metafile
ART	Clip art format	CHK	Checkdisk (file fragment)
ASA	Microsoft Visual InterDev file	CHM	Compiled HTML
ASC	ASCII text file	CHR	Character set
ASF	(Microsoft) Advanced Streaming Format	CHT	ChartViewer / Harvard Graphic Vector
ASM	Assembler source file	CLASS	Java class
ASP	Active Server Pages	CLP	(Windows) Clipboard
ATT	AT&T Group 4 bitmap	CLS	Visual Basic Class module
AU	(Sun) Audio	CMD	Windows NT Command file
AVI	Audio Video Interleaved	CMF	Corel Metafile
AVR	Audio Visual Research file	CMP	Companion (Virus)
BAK	Backup	CMV	Corel Move (animation)
BAS	BASIC	COM	Command (program file)
BAT	Batch	CPP	C++ language source
BFC	Windows 95 Briefcase	CRD	Cardfile
BI / BIN	Binary	CRT	Certificate file
BMK	Bookmark	CSC	Corel Script
BMP	Bitmap	CSS	Cascading Style Sheet (for HTML and XML documents)
BOOK	FrameMaker Book file		
BPL	Borland (Delphi 4) Packed Library		

Continued on next page

F

COMMON FILE EXTENSIONS (continued)

Extension	Comments	Extension	Comments
CST	(Macromedia Director) Cast resource file	EMF	Enhanced Windows Metafile
CSV	Comma separated variable	EML	Microsoft Outlook Express Mail Message
CUR	(Windows) Cursor file	EPHTML	Enhanced Perl-Parsed HTML file
CV	Microsoft CodeView file	EPS / EPSF	Encapsulated PostScript Format
DAM	Damaged	EXC	Microsoft Word Exclusion Dictionary
DAT	Data / WordPerfect data merge	EXE	Executable file
DBF	DBase Format	F	FORTRAN file
DCR	Shockwave file	FAX	Group 3 fax file
DCU	Delphi Compiled Unit file	FDF	(Acrobat) Forms Definition File
DCX	Fax image (PCX-based)	FIF	Fractal Image File
DEF	C++ Definition	FITS	Flexible Image Transport System
DEM	USGS Map	FLA	Macromedia Flash movie file
DIB	Device Independent Bitmap	FLC / FLI	AutoDesk FLIC animation file
DIC	Dictionary file	FLT	Corel Filter file
DIF	Data Interchange Format (spreadsheet)	FM	FrameMaker document file
DIR	(Macromedia) Director	FNT	Font file
DLG	C++ Dialog Script	FON	System Font file
DLL	Dynamic Link Library	FOR	FORTRAN file
DLS	Downloadable Sound	FP	FileMaker Pro file
DOC	DOCument (FrameMaker, MS Word, WordPerfect, WordStar, et al)	FRM	(Visual Basic) Form file
		FT	(Lous Notes) Full Text index
DOT	Microsoft Word Document Template	FTS	(Windows) Full Text Search index file
DPL	(Borland) Delphi 3 Packed Library	FXP	FoxPro compiled file
DR	(Virus) Dropper	G / GEN	Generic (Virus) Detection
DRV	Driver file	GED	Graphic Environment Document file
DRW	Micrografx Designer Draw	GEM	Graphics Environment Manager
DSP	Microsoft Developer Studio Project	GID	(Windows 95) Global Index file
DSW	Microsoft Developer Studio Workspace	GIF	Graphics Interchange File (image file)
DTD	Document Type Definition (for SGML, HTML, and XML documents)	GR	Generic (Virus Detection and Removal)
		GRP	(Program Manager) Group file
DUN	Microsoft Dial-Up Networking (Export)	GZ	UNIX GNU Zip file
DV	Digital Video file	H	C program Header file
DVI	TeX DeVice Independent	HDF	Hierarchical Data Format file
DWG	AutoCAD DraWinG file	HEX	Macintosh BinHex file
DXF	AutoCAD Drawing Exchange Format	HLP	Help file
EDD	Element Definition Document		

Continued on next page

COMMON FILE EXTENSIONS (continued)

Extension	Comments
HPGL / HGL	Hewlett-Packard Graphics Language
HPJ	(Visual Basic) Help Project file
HPP	C++ program Header file
HST	History file
HT	HyperTerminal file
HTA	HTML Application
HTM / HTML	Hypertext Markup Language (Web documents)
HTT	Microsoft Hypertext Template file
HTX	HTML extension (for processing report from database query)
ICM	Image Color Matching (profile) file
ICO	(Windows) Icon
ID4	Infini-D
IDA	Internet Database Administration
IDC	Internet Database Connector (database queries)
IDD / IDF	(Windows 9x) MIDI Instrument Definition File
IDQ	Internet Data Query
IDX	Database Index file
IFF	Interchange File Format
IGES	Initial Graphics Exchange Specification file
IMA	Mirage / WinImage
IMG	Graphics Environment Manager Image
INC	Include file (Assembler, Active Server, etc)
INF	Information file
INI	Initialization file
INTD	Intended file
ISO	ISO 9660 CD-ROM file
JAR	Java Archive file
JAVA	Java source code
JBF	Paint Shop Pro image browser file
JFF / JFIF / JIF	JPEG files
JPE / JPG / JPEG	Joint Photographic Experts Group (compressed image file)
JS	JavaScript file
JTF	JPEG bitmap

Extension	Comments
KBD	Keyboard
LEG	Legacy document file
LHA / LZH	LH ARC (compressed file)
LIB	Library file
LLX	LapLink Exchange agent file
LNK	Windows shortcut file
LOG	Log file
LSP	LISP source file
LST	List(ing)
LWO / LWOB	Lightwave Object
LWP	Lotus Wordpro 96/97 file
LWS / LWSC	Lightwave Scene
LZH	LH ARC compressed file
M3D	(Corel) 3D Motion file
MAC	MacPaint Image
MAD	Microsoft Access Module
MAF	Microsoft Access File
MAK	(C, Visual Basic, or Visual C++) Make file
MAM	Microsoft Access Macro
MAN	UNIX Manual
MAP	Map file
MAQ	Microsoft Access Query
MAR	Microsoft Access Report
MAT	Microsoft Access Table
MDB	Microsoft Access Database
MID / MIDI	Musical Instrument Digital Interface
MIF / MIFF	Management Information Format File / Machine Independent Format File
MMF	Microsoft Mail File
MMM	Microsoft Multimedia Movie
MNG	Multi-Image Network Graphics
MOD	Amiga audio file
MOV	(QuickTime for Windows) Movie
MP2 / MP3	MPEG, Audio Layer II / Layer III
MPA	MPEG-related

F

Continued on next page

COMMON FILE EXTENSIONS (continued)

Extension	Comments
MPE / MPG / MPEG	MPEG animation
MPP	Microsoft Project file
MSC	Microsoft Management Console log files
MSG	Microsoft (Mail) Message
MSN	Microsoft Network file
MSP	Microsoft Paint bitmap
MUS	Music file
MWP	Lotus Wordpro 97 file
NCD	Norton Change Directory
NCF	Lotus Notes Internal Clipboard file
NFF	Neutral File Format
NLM	NetWare Loadable Module
NWS	Microsoft Outlook Express News Message (RFC822 MIME format)
OBJ	Compiled Object
OLB	OLE Object Library file
OLE	OLE Object file
OOGL	Object-Oriented Graphics Library
OPL	(Psion) Organizer Programming Language source file
OPO	OPL Output executable file
OPX	OPL Extension DLL
ORC	Oracel 7 Script file
ORG	Lotus Organizer file
OVL	Overlay
OW	Overwritten
PAS	Pascal source file
PAT	Corel Draw Pattern file
PBK	Micorsoft Phonebook file
PBM	Portable Bitmap
PCC	Z-Soft graphics file
PCD	(Kodak) Photo-CD file
PCL	Printer Control Language file
PCT	(Macintosh) Picture
PCX	Z-Soft Paintbrush bitmap file
PDB	Palm Pilot Database file

Extension	Comments
PDF	(Adobe) Portable Document Format / (Net-Ware) Printer Definition File
PFA	Adobe Type 1 Font (ASCII format)
PFB	Adobe Type 1 Font (binary format)
PFM	Printer Font Metric file
PGM	Portable Graymap
PGP	Pretty Good Privacy encrypted file
PHTML	Perl-parsed HTML file
PIC	Lotus 1-2-3 graphics file / PC Paint bitmap
PIC / PICT / PICT2	Macintosh picture
PIF	Program Information File
PIX	Inset Systems bitmap
PKR	(PGP) Public Keyring
PL	Perl source file
PLS	(MPEG) Playlist file
PLT	(HPGL) Plotter / AutoCAD Plot
PM5 / PM6	PageMaker 5 / PageMaker 6 file
PNG	Portable Network Graphics
PNT / PNTG	Macintosh paint
POT	Microsoft PowerPoint Template
PP4	Picture Publisher 4 bitmap file
PPA	Microsoft PowerPoint Add-In
PPF	Picture Publisher File
PPM	Portable Pixelmap bitmap file
PPS	Microsoft PowerPoint Slide Show
PRC	Palm Pilot Resource file
PRF	Windows System file
PRN	Print(er)
PS	PostScript
PSD	Photoshop Drawing
PUB	(Microsoft / Ventura) Publisher file
PWD	Microsoft Pocket Word
PWL	Microsoft (Windows 9x) Password List
PWZ	Microsoft PowerPoint Wizard file
PXL	Microsoft Pocket Excel (spreadsheet)
PY / PYC	Python Script file

Continued on next page

COMMON FILE EXTENSIONS (continued)

Extension	Comments
QBW	QuickBooks for Windows file
QIF	Quicken Import File
QIF	QuickTime-related Image File
QRY	Microsoft Query
QT / QTM	QuickTime movie
QTI / QTIF	QuickTime-related Image File
QTP	QuickTime Preferences file
QXD	Quark XPress Document file
RA	Real Audio sound file
RAM	RealAudio Metafile
RAW	Raw bitmap file
RDF	Resource Description Framework
RDS	Ray Dream Studio
REC	Recorder Macro
REG	Registration file
RES	Microsoft Visual C++ Resource file
RIF / RIFF	Raster Image File Format
RLE	Run Length Encoded bitmap
RMF	Rich Map Format
RPM	Red Hat Package Manager file
RPT	Microsoft Visual Basic Report file
RTF	Rich Text Format
SC2 / SCD	Microsoft Schedule+ 7 file
SCP	Dial-Up Networking Script file
SCR	Screen shot / Windows Screensaver
SDL	SmartDraw Library file
SDR	SmartDraw Drawing file
SDT	SmartDraw Template
SDV	Semicolon Divided Values file
SEA	Self-Expanding Archive
SGML	Standard Generalized Markup Language
SHTML	HTML with server-side include (Apache Web servers)
SHW	Corel Show
SIG	Signature file

Extension	Comments
SKA	PGP Secret Keyring
SPL	Splash / Shockwave Flash object
SQC	SQL (Structured Query Language) Common Code file
SQR	SQL Program file
SRC	Source text file
SSI	Server-side include (NetWare servers)
STM	HTML with server-side include (Microsoft IIS)
STY	(Ventura Publisher) Style sheet
SW	(Raw) Signed Word
SYS	System or Driver file
TAR	Tape Archive file
TAZ	UNIX Gzip Tape Archive file
TBK	(Asymetrix) Toolbook multimedia file
TCL	Tcl/Tk script file
TEX	TeX text file / texture file
TGA	Targa bitmap
TGZ	UNIX Gzip Tape Archive file
THEME	Windows 9x Desktop Theme file
TIF / TIFF	Tagged Image File Format
TLB	OLE Type Library file
TMP	Temporary file
TOC	Table of Contents file
TTF	True Type Font file
TUT	Tutorial
TXT	ASCII text
UDB	(Windows NT) Uniqueness Database file
UDW	Raw Unsigned Double Word data file
ULAW	US Telephony Audio format file
URL	Internet Shortcut File
UU / UUE	UU-Encoded file
UW	Raw Unsigned Word file
VBP	Visual Basic Project file
VBW	Visual Basic Workspace file
VCF	(Netscape) Virtual Card File

Continued on next page

COMMON FILE EXTENSIONS (continued)

Extension	Comments	Extension	Comments
VIR	Virus-infected file	WPG	WordPerfect Graphics (image file)
VLB	Corel Ventura Library	WPT	WordPerfect Template file
VOC	Sound Blaster audio file	WRI	Microsoft Write / Lotus Symphony
VP	Ventura Publisher document file	XAR	Corel Xara Drawing file
VRML	Virtual Reality Modeling Language file	XBM	MIME xbitmap image file
VSD	Visio Drawing file	XIF	Xerox Interchange Format
VSS	Visio Stencil file	XL	Excel
VSW	Visio Workspace file	XLA	Excel Add-In
VXD	Windows Virtual Device Driver file	XLB	Excel Toolbar
W6W	Microsoft Word	XLC	Excel Chart
WAV	Soundwave / Windows waveform	XLD	Excel Dialog
WBK	Microsoft Word Backup file	XLK	Excel Backup
WCM	WordPerfect Macro file	XLL	Excel Add-In file
WDB	Microsoft Works Database	XLM	Excel Macro file
WDD	Wright Design Drawing	XLS	Excel worksheet file
WEB	Corel Xara Web document file	XLT	Excel Template file
WIZ	Microsoft Word Wizard	XLW	Excel Workbook (or Workspace) file
WK1 / WK3 / WK4	Lotus 123 version 1 or 2 / 3 / 4 spreadsheet	XML	Extensible Markup Language
WKS	Lotus 123 Worksheet / Microsoft Works	XNK	Microsoft Exchange shortcut file
WMF	Windows Metafile	XWD	X Window Dump file
WORD	Microsoft Word file	Z	UNIX Gzip file
WP / WPD	WordPerfect document file	ZIP	(PKZIP) compressed file

File Name

A file name is the name of a file on a disk used so that both you and the operating system can find the file again. Every file in a directory must have a unique name, but files in different directories can share the same name.

In DOS, file and directory names have two parts. They can have up to eight characters in the name, and up to three characters in the optional file-name extension, separated from the name by a period. Many applications take over the extension part of the file name, using specific groups of characters to designate a particular file type.

In the Macintosh operating system, file names can be up to 31 characters and can contain any character except a colon (:), which is used to separate elements of a path name.

In the OS/2 HPFS, files can have names of 254 characters, including many characters that are illegal in DOS file names, such as spaces. The Windows NT File System allows 255-character file names and also provides some degree of security by including permissions when sharing files.

→ *See Also* File Extension

File Service Process (FSP)

→ *See* FSP (File Service Process)

File Sharing

An arrangement by which multiple users can access the same file(s) simultaneously. File access has restrictions, and it is generally controlled by both application and networking software. For example, certain parts of the file may be locked (made inaccessible) if a user is already accessing that file.

→ *See Also* Access Rights, Attribute, Security

File System

In an operating system, the file system is the structure used for file entries. The file system organizes information about files, such as their names, attributes, and locations.

Examples of file systems include the following:

CDFS (CD-ROM File System): Used to store information about files on a compact disk.

FAT (File Allocation Table): Used by various versions of DOS. Most versions use FAT16, but Windows 98 and a late OEM Service Release of Windows 95 use FAT32; Windows 2000 (formerly NT 5) is also expected to use FAT32.

HPFS (High Performance File System): Used in OS/2.

NTFS (NT File System): Used by Windows NT and NT Advanced File Server.

HFS (Hierarchical File System): Used by the MAC OS on the Macintosh.

NFS (Network File System): A distributed file system originally developed by Sun Microsystems to make it easier to handle files on remote systems, but now used widely on UNIX and other distributed systems—for example, on the Internet. NFS is a distributed *network* file system, which means that it also needs a local file system in place. This local file system may be operating system specific. For example, a UNIX environment may use a local file system such as ext2fs.

AFS (Andrew File System): Another network distributed file system, originally developed at Carnegie-Mellon University, and a major contender to become the file system of the future on large networks such as the Internet.

In Novell's NetWare 4.*x* and later, the term *file system* is used in preference to *directory structure* (the term in pre-4.0 NetWare versions) to describe the structure of the system and the user's files and directories. This revised usage is to avoid confusion between the file system information and the contents of Novell's Directory (the information tree created by the global naming service that replaced the NetWare bindery from earlier versions).

Novell's file system has three major levels:

- Volume, which is the highest level, and which refers to a partition created by the NetWare installation program. A volume may encompass any amount from as little as part of a hard disk to as much as multiple disks.

- Directory, which is an intermediate level that contains other directories or files.

- File, which is the most specific level. This is the level at which a user or a process generally works.

File Transfer

File transfer is the process of copying a file from one machine or location to another. File transfer is a common networking task.

When a file is transferred over a network, the file must first be divided into smaller packets for transmission. The details of this "packetization" depend on the transfer protocol (communications and packaging rules) being used. This protocol also determines how the transfer instructions are given.

In networking contexts, FTP (File Transfer Protocol) and FTAM (File Transfer, Access, and Management) are two popular protocols. For transfer over modems, Kermit, XMODEM, YMODEM, and ZMODEM are some of the available protocols.

If the file is being transferred between different operating environments, the file may also be reformatted during the transfer. For example, in transferring text files between UNIX and DOS environments, the ends of lines must be changed; in transferring from a Macintosh to a DOS environment, the Macintosh file's resource fork will be discarded, and the data fork may also need to be reformatted.

File Transfer Protocol (FTP)

→ *See* Protocol, FTP (File Transfer Protocol)

File Transfer Service (FTS)

→ *See* FTS (File Transfer Service)

Filter

In electrical signaling, a filter is a device used to allow certain frequency bands to pass, while blocking other bands.

More generally, a filter is any sort of device or algorithm that can be used to selectively discard or pass elements of a signal, symbol, or other type of stream.

Filtered Packet Service

A filtered packet service is a security measure in which access to a network (or to a particular user) can be limited to packets that satisfy predefined criteria. For example, any of the following types of packets can be filtered if desired:

- Packets transmitted using a specific protocol
- Packets coming from a particular address, network, or subnetwork
- All packets *except* those coming from a particular address, network, or subnetwork

Filtering

In hardware, filtering is a process of frequency selection and exclusion. Signals within one or more frequency bands are allowed to pass unmodified, but all other signals are blocked.

In network operations, filtering is a process for selecting and discarding packets in order to control access to a network or to resources, such as files and devices. The basis for the filtering can be addresses or protocols.

For example, bridges filter network traffic so that local packets stay on their networks, rather than being passed to another network. Various security measures can be used to filter user access to files.

Packets that are not filtered are generally forwarded to an intermediate or final destination.

The rate at which packets are checked and filtered is called the *filtering rate*. For a bridge, this is generally a better index of the bridge's performance than simple throughput.

Finder

In Apple's Macintosh environment, an application that provides access to applications and documents.

Finger

An Internet utility that can be used to determine whether a particular user is logged onto a particular machine, and also to find out something about the user. To use this command, type **finger** followed by the name of the user about whom you want information. If the user is on a machine different from yours, you also need to include the user's address.

If the specified user has an account on the specified machine, the finger command will display information such as the person's login and real-life names, office and phone number, and the person's last login. Finally, finger will display (or act upon the commands from) any plan or proj files found in the fingered person's files. The details that are shown depend in part on the fingered person's configuration. Finger is generally considered a point of vulnerability in network security, since the program can tell a would-be intruder quite a bit about the users—or, rather, the accounts—on a network. For example, knowing when users last logged on can help identify rarely-used accounts.

Firewall

A firewall is a network component that provides a security barrier between networks or network segments. Firewalls are generally set up to protect a particular network or network component from attack, or unauthorized penetration, by outside invaders. However, a firewall also may be set up to protect vital corporate or institutional data or resources from internal attacks or incompetence. Internal firewalls are generally placed between administrative, or security, domains in a corporate or institutional network. For example, a firewall might be set up between the network domain that houses the payroll and personnel information and other parts of the corporate network.

All traffic to or from the protected network must go through the firewall; the firewall is designed to allow only authorized traffic. If the firewall does its filtering job successfully, attacks will never even reach the protected network.

To be effective, the firewall must also be able to protect itself from penetration. To help ensure this, firewalls are generally designed to be special-purpose machines. That is, the firewall will not provide

services beyond those necessary to authenticate the user and to decide whether to allow the traffic through. If a received packet is legitimate, the firewall will pass on the traffic to the appropriate next machine.

Firewalls are not gateways, but they do often work in association with gateways. One reason for this is that both firewalls and gateways tend to sit between networks. The gateway's job is to translate packets as they move between different network environments; the firewall's job is to filter them.

In some cases, however, the gateway and firewall functions will be provided by the same network components. This can happen, for example, if a network is communicating with an alien network, so that the communication requires a gateway. In such a case, however, the filtering and gateway (i.e., translating) elements will still be distinct and will communicate with each other through an internal filter.

Three broad categories of firewall are distinguished, although a particular firewall installation may include more than one of these.

Packet-filtering: Such low-level filters pass or drop packets based on their source or destination addresses or ports. This level of filtering is already provided by routers. Such a firewall is easy and inexpensive to set up, but its capabilities are quite limited. A packet-filtering firewall can fail if its table of valid and invalid addresses is incorrect. Such a firewall is also susceptible to address-spoofing (making a filter believe that a packet is coming from a different address).

Application-filtering: These higher-level filters screen traffic involving specific applications or services (for example, ftp or e-mail). The advantage of such a filter is that it allows for more sophisticated evaluation and authentication measures. For example, such a firewall could be designed to protect against a gopher server moving a renegade file onto a machine or to check for an attack entering with an application. A major disadvantage of a filter operating at the application level is that such programs can be

F

very complex and have many possible action sequences. The large number of possibilities—for example, an application calling another application—makes it very difficult to build in safeguards against every possible attack.

Circuit-level: Such a filter looks not only at source and destination addresses but also at the circuits (temporary paths) that have been established for a connection. Such circuits are established—for example, when using TCP (transport control protocol)—during an initial handshaking session. Such a filter can detect address-spoofing, for example, because such a misleading packet would have no way of getting the circuit information that is set up during the handshaking. While very effective for certain protocols, circuit filters are of limited use with connectionless protocols (such as UDP), which may send packets over various paths.

Like all security measures, firewalls can be useful, but they are not foolproof. They have the advantage of concentrating security measures and issues, making it easier to set up and maintain them. Of course, such centralization also provides an Achilles heel—that is, a point of vulnerability. If an intruder can get around (or, more often, under) the firewall, then an attack is possible.

A firewall's effectiveness depends on all traffic going through the firewall. This is not a sufficient condition for security, however. In *tunneling*, one packet is encapsulated inside another. With this strategy, a packet from an untrusted machine or user could be placed into a packet from a trusted machine, and the latter packet could then be sent through a firewall. Unless the firewall actually takes each packet apart and examines its contents, there is no guaranteed effective protection against tunneling.

Firewire

Firewire is the popular name for a high-speed serial bus standard. Officially known as IEEE 1394-1995 (Standard for a High Performance Serial Bus),

Firewire offers an inexpensive, easy-to-use bus connection that can be used to attach up to 63 daisy-chained devices to a PC or just to each other—that is, without a PC.

Firewire's bandwidth makes it easy to provide full-motion video at 30 frames per second (fps), and also CD-quality audio. Two channels that can handle both video and audio are available even in the slowest Firewire variant.

A major attraction of Firewire is that it can connect consumer devices—such as camcorders or TVs—to a PC. With this capability, you can download a recorded 8-millimeter (mm) or VHS tape to a PC, edit the material, and then send it back to the original medium. In other words, Firewire makes it easy for you to edit your home movies on your PC. Since such materials are often digital, a direct connection between device and PC is possible—so you won't need a digitizer or other auxiliary devices.

The Firewire interface was originally developed at Apple, and was designed mainly for connecting devices to Macintoshes. Firewire was intended as a high-speed alternative to parallel interfaces such as SCSI (Small Computer Systems Interface); however, it also serves as a low-cost bus for peripherals and as a bus that can serve as a bridge between compatible 32-bit buses on different machines. Firewire has attractive features for each of its projected uses:

- As an alternative to the SCSI bus, Firewire has a throughput of 100, 200, 400, or 800Mbps, and versions supporting rates as high as 1.2Gbps are being designed. (The actual rates are 98.304, 196.608, 393.216, and 786.432Mbps, but these are generally rounded up to the easier-to-remember values.) This bandwidth is sufficient to carry full-motion video and CD-quality audio even at the lowest speed. Firewire has another advantage over SCSI: there's no need to assign IDs to each device because that's done automatically by the bus. Also, Firewire daisy chains don't need to be terminated electrically at each end, as SCSI chains do.

- As a low-cost bus for peripherals, Firewire is cheap enough to be used even in consumer devices. In fact, the first use of Firewire was in Sony digital camcorders. Firewire is also very easy to install, since no device IDs are needed. The Firewire cable can even provide up to about 1.5 amperes of DC juice to keep peripheral devices fed, even while they are turned off.

- As a bridge between other buses, Firewire can actually support thousands of peripherals or devices. Even though each connector can support only up to 63 devices, buses can also be connected. More specifically, up to 1022 buses can be connected, with each of these supporting up to 63 devices. With this many possible connections, Firewire can easily scale to whatever size you might need.

Firewire Cabling

Firewire cabling must provide both power and data. To accomplish this, the Firewire specification calls for six wires. Two of these supply power for the attached devices. The other four are grouped into two twisted-wire pairs. Each of the twisted pairs is shielded. In addition, there is shielding around the two shielded pairs and the power wires.

Firewire Protocol Layers

Firewire uses a three-layer protocol stack to provide the interface and to control packet handling and transmissions. The bottom two layers (physical and link) are hardware-based; the topmost layer (transaction) is implemented in firmware.

Physical Layer

The lowermost, physical layer defines connectors and the electrical characteristics of signals for each of the transmission media that the interface supports. This layer also includes logic for establishing an ordering for the devices (by making one device the root and ordering the other devices in relation

to this one) and also for arbitrating access by the devices that want to send or receive something.

If no devices are in a particular hurry, the physical layer gives access on the basis of natural priority. Devices get access to the bus in succession, in an order based on the devices' relative positions in the daisy chain.

Devices can also compete for access, by using either fair or urgent arbitration. When arbitration is used, bus access is divided into intervals. During an interval, multiple devices will get access to the bus. In *fair arbitration*, devices compete, on equal terms, for access to the bus. The device that gets access gets to send a packet. Once the action is completed, the device sets an internal flag and drops out of the access game for the rest of the interval. The remaining devices play another round of grab the bus. This process continues until the interval is over. During the interval, no device will get access to the bus more than once. Once the interval is over, a new one can begin, so all interested devices get to compete again for access.

Link Layer

The link layer above the physical one handles the packaging and transmission of packets for the devices that have something to send or receive. It supports asynchronous and isochronous transmissions. Packets in asynchronous transmissions can be of variable size and will contain various kinds of administrative information (including a destination address). Each packet transmitted asynchronously must be acknowledged. Ordinary data transmission is done this way.

In contrast, isochronous transmission uses fixed-size packets, which are transmitted at a constant rate, and which require no acknowledgement. Isochronous packets also use special, simplified addressing. Video and real-time data will often be sent in such packets. Because such materials often have stringent time constraints, such transmissions will use urgent arbitration, which gives the transmitting device priority in the bandwidth.

F

Transaction Layer

The transaction layer slices a session up into request-response units that can be used by higher layers. The layer makes sure the transmitted packages are actually received intact, and takes care of the timing and pacing needed to check this.

This layer works with *subactions*, each of which consists of a transmitted packet, together with an acknowledgement. A *transaction* can consist of a single such subaction. Or it may consist of a pair of subactions: a *request* subaction (packet plus acknowledgement) and a *response* subaction (packet plus acknowledgement). The subactions that make up such a transaction may be separated by time and also by other subactions (which are parts of different transactions).

Subactions

A subaction is made up of five elements, each of which occurs in a separate time interval.

- Arbitration sequence, during which devices negotiate to determine who gets control of the bus.

- Packet transmission, during which a single packet is transmitted.

- Acknowledgement gap, which is an idle period on the bus. This gap occurs in part because the receiver must get the packet, unpack it, and prepare an acknowledgement. Even though the bus is idle during this gap, no device can steal the bus.

- Acknowledgement, during which the receiving device returns an acknowledgement packet to indicate that it received the transmitted packet and to specify what the receiver will do with (or about) the packet.

- Subaction gap, which is an idle period designed to prevent other devices from grabbing the bus before the tasks in the subaction are completed. Specifically, this gap ensures that the acknowledgement packet can be sent before another device grabs the bus.

As you'll see below, under certain conditions the subaction gap may be omitted in a transaction. Under other conditions, the acknowledgement and acknowledgement gaps may be omitted.

Subactions for isochronous transmissions have only the arbitration sequence and the packet transmission in common with other types of subactions. In addition, isochronous subactions include an isochronous gap, in which the bus is idle until the same or another isochronous device grabs the bus and begins the next subaction.

Isochronous subactions continue until all the isochronous devices have finished sending their packets. Once this has been done, the isochronous sequence ends with a subaction gap, which is always longer than the isochronous gaps. The subaction gap indicates that the isochronous portion of the session is finished, and gives control of the remaining session bandwidth to non-isochronous devices—on a first-come, first-served basis.

Transactions

Firewire transactions may do any of three types of actions: read, write, and lock.

- A *read transaction* involves a request for specified information from the target device, and a response in which the requested data are returned to the requesting device.

- A *write transaction* involves a request whose packet is to be written to a location on the target device, and may include a response indicating whether the packet has, in fact, been written.

- A *lock transaction* includes both a request and a response. The file(s) involved in the transaction are locked—that is, made inaccessible to any devices except those involved in the transaction. This lock remains in effect until the transaction is completed.

Of the three transaction types, write is the most versatile. That is, it can be used with the greatest variety of transaction patterns.

Other Firewire Features

Firewire also does the following:

- Supports *hot swapping*, or *plugging*, which allows you to connect or disconnect a device without turning off your system. The bus will automatically reconfigure to reflect the changes.

- Allows the most widely separated devices to be up to 72 meters apart.

- Uses a three-layer protocol stack to provide the interface and to control transmissions.

- Supports transmissions using either an asynchronous or an isochronous format. Asynchronous transmissions send both data and information for the transaction layer to a specific address. Isochronous data are broadcast on channels.

FIRL (Fiber-Optic Inter-Repeater Link)

→ See FOIRL (Fiber-Optic Inter-Repeater Link)

Firmware

Instructions encoded permanently in ROM (read-only memory) on a chip. Certain operating system components or boot instructions are encoded as firmware.

First In, First Out (FIFO)

→ See FIFO (First In, First Out)

First-Level Interrupt Handler (FLIH)

→ See FLIH (First-Level Interrupt Handler)

FIX (Federal Information Exchange)

A connection point between the Internet and any of the federal government's internets.

Fixed Priority-Oriented Demand Assignment (FPODA)

In networking, an access protocol in which stations must reserve slots on the network. These slots are allocated according to the stations' priority levels.

Fixed Routing

A routing strategy in which packets or messages are transmitted between the source and destination over a well-defined and constant path.

Flag

A flag is a value that represents a setting or condition. Since a flag represents a yes or no, on or off, or similar choice, only a single bit is needed to represent a flag value. Because of this, multiple flags are generally combined into a byte or word. For example, in bit-oriented protocols, a flag byte is a bit sequence used to mark the start and/or the end of a frame.

To determine a flag setting, you can mask (screen out) all the bits except the flag bit of interest. The mask byte (word) would contain 0 bits everywhere except in the position corresponding to the flag bit. A mask has 0 bits at every location except at the desired flag bits, where it has a 1 bit. By taking the logical AND, which is 1 only if both the mask and flag bits are 1, of the bit sequence, it is possible to determine a flag setting.

In NetWare security, the attributes that determine the access and use rules for a file or directory are also known as *flags*.

F

Flag Byte

In bit-oriented protocols, a bit sequence used to mark the start and/or the end of a frame.

Flag Character

In X.25 packet-switching technology, a special character (0111 1110) that is included at the beginning and end of every LAPB frame to indicate a frame boundary. The protocol uses *bit stuffing* to ensure that this bit sequence never occurs elsewhere in the packet (for example, as part of the packet's data).

Flag Sequence

In serial data transmission, a flag sequence is a unique pattern of (usually eight) bits that is used to mark the start and end of a frame. Flag sequences are used in bit-oriented protocols, such as the Advanced Data Communication Control Procedure (ADCCP), Synchronous Data Link Control (SDLC), and High-Level Data Link Control (HDLC) protocols.

Flame

On the Internet, a flame is a nasty message usually aimed at the author(s) of particular postings or the perpetrator(s) of actions to which the flamer (the flame's author) has taken exception. Breaches of *netiquette* (unofficial rules of behavior on the Internet) often incur flames. The flame is sometimes used to express the flamer's anger and sometimes to insult the target (i.e., the flamee). The word can also be used as a verb.

Flamers generally warn of a flame by specifying "FLAME ON!" in the posting's subject header. Users have been known to deliberately provoke flames by posting *flame bait*, and simple flames have been fanned into long-running *flame wars*.

Flash Memory

Nonvolatile RAM, which retains its contents even when power is shut off. Flash memory can, however, be erased or reprogrammed. Flash memory is useful for storing configuration information, which must be retained between sessions but may change during any session.

Flat File Database

→ *See* Database

Flat Name Structure

A naming strategy in which each name is unique, and in which there is no logical, physical, or other relationship between names. For example, this strategy may be used for files or network nodes. Such names are accessible only through table lookup. Compare this with a hierarchical name structure.

Flattened Network

A flattened network is one that has a switched backbone—that is, a network backbone that is implemented in a switch. In such a backbone, all network-critical devices are plugged directly into ports in the switch.

FLIH (First-Level Interrupt Handler)

In a network, an interrupt handler whose job is to determine which device or channel generated the interrupt, and then to invoke a second-level interrupt handler to actually process the request behind the interrupt.

Floating Point Unit (FPU)

→ *See* FPU (Floating Point Unit)

Flooding

In a network, the uncontrolled propagation of discovery or other packets.

Flooding Protocol

→ *See* Protocol, Flooding

Flow

In communications contexts, a flow is a stream of symbols between two locations. Processing of the flow will depend on the content. However, a flow may need to be controlled at the receiving end—for example, if the transmission rate is too high for the receiver and there is danger that the flow will exceed the receiving buffer's capacity. In that case, the receiver will transmit some type of flow control signal in hardware or software.

In high-speed networks, such as Gigabit Ethernet, a flow is a stream of packets that should get handled in the same way by a routing function. For example, the packets in a flow might belong together because they are all being sent from a common source to a common destination and because all are being sent using the same quality of service (QoS). The presence of a flow can be used to help save time for routers—for example, by tagging the elements in the flow so that the router need not check the actual routing information.

Flow Control

In communications, flow control refers to an action used to regulate the transfer of information between two locations. Flow control is helpful if the device at one location is much faster than at the other. For example, flow-control may be necessary when a computer is communicating with a printer or modem.

Hardware flow-control methods use signals on the pins used for RTS (request to send) and CTS (clear to send); software methods send specific byte values (XON and XOFF) to control the transmission of data.

In internetworks, flow control is handled by a router, which is a device that sends transmissions in the appropriate direction and also reroutes transmissions around troubled or congested locations.

FLP (Fast Link Pulse)

One of a series of identical signals sent at startup by a fast or Gigabit Ethernet device—that is, by a device (Ethernet adapter, bridge, or switch) capable of supporting a transmission rate of up to 1000Mbps.

FLPs may contain only timing pulses, or they may also include control data in the pulses.

→ *See Also* Fast Ethernet

Flux Budget

In FDDI networks, the amount of light that can be lost between adjacent nodes without having the transmission become unintelligible.

FNC (Federal Networking Council)

A committee consisting of representatives from government agencies that are involved with networks that connect to the Internet.

Focal Point

In IBM's NMA (Network Management Architecture), *focal point* is a term for the node on which the network management software is running. This is generally a mainframe host in NMA.

Other nodes and devices communicate with the focal point either through entry points (in the case of SNA-compliant devices) or service points (in the case of non-IBM devices or networks).

F

→ *Broader Category* NMA (Network Management Architecture)

→ *See Also* Entry Point, Service Point

FOCC (Forward Control Channel)

In cellular communications, the FOCC allows communication from the base station (BS) to the mobile stattion (MS)—for example, a subscriber's phone. This channel uses frequency shift keying (FSK) to modulate the signal, operates at up to 10kbps, and is used for control and signaling, rather than for actual communication.

A forward control channel uses three discrete streams—stream A, stream B, and a busy-idle stream—which are multiplexed for transmission. Depending on a bit value in a mobile identification number (MIN), materials are sent through stream A or B. Bits in the busy-idle stream are used to indicate the status of the reverse control channel (RECC).

Communications on the FOCC use the EIA-553 standard for mobile station / land station communication. This is also true of the RECC, which provides for signaling from the MS to the BS. Adherence to EIA-553 makes components less dependent on specific manufacturers and suppliers, since any EIA-553 component should be able to communicate with any other compliant component—regardless of the manufacturers involved.

→ *Broader Category* Cellular Communications

→ *See Also* RECC (Reverse Control Channel)

Foil Shield

In some coaxial cable, a thin shield, usually made of aluminum bonded to both sides of a tape, that surrounds the dielectric and is, in turn, covered by a braid shield. Together, the foil and braid shields provide good protection against electrical interference.

→ *See Also* Cable, Coaxial

FOIRL (Fiber-Optic Inter-Repeater Link)

An FOIRL (sometimes written as *FIRL*) is a link segment that uses fiber-optic cable to connect two repeaters in a standard Ethernet or an 802.3-based Ethernet network. An FOIRL cannot have any nodes. The standard connector for such a link is the SMA connector (IEC 874-2).

Footprint

In satellite communications, a footprint refers to the earth area covered by a radio signal from the satellite. In networking, the term is used to refer to the amount of RAM (random-access memory) an application uses during execution.

Foreground Process

A process or program that gets the highest priority for execution. Other processes or programs get attention when the foreground process does not need the processor at a particular instant. These lower-priority processes are said to run in the *background*.

Foreign Exchange (FX)

→ *See* FX (Foreign Exchange)

Fork

In the Macintosh file system, a *fork* is either of two components for a file: the data fork, which contains the actual information in the file, or the resource fork, which contains application-specific data.

→ *See Also* Macintosh

Forum

A forum is common area—for example, a chat room—where users can communicate directly with each other. Forums are generally created for discussion of particular topics or products.

Forward Control Channel (FOCC)

→ **See** FOCC (Forward Control Channel)

Forward Error Correction (FEC)

→ **See** FEC (Forward Error Correction)

Forward Explicit Congestion Notification (FECN)

→ **See** FECN (Forward Explicit Congestion Notification)

Forwarding

In a network bridge, router, or gateway, or in a packet-switching node, *forwarding* is the process of passing a packet or message on to an intermediate or final destination. This is in contrast to *filtering*, in which a packet is discarded. The basis for the filtering or forwarding can be addresses or protocols.

Ordinarily, a bridge or another forwarding device does the following:

- Reads and buffers the entire packet.
- Checks the address or protocol.
- Filters or forwards the packet, depending on the value found and on the filtering criteria.

In *on-the-fly forwarding*, a device begins forwarding the packet as soon as the device determines that this is the appropriate action. This means that the packet can be on its way to a new destination while still being read by the bridge.

For Your Information (FYI)

→ **See** FYI (For Your Information)

Four-Wire Circuit

In telephone communications, a circuit made up of two pairs of conducting wires. One pair is used for transmitting and the other pair for receiving. This provides full-duplex (FDX) operation. A four-wire terminating circuit is a hybrid circuit in which four-wire circuits are connected to two-wire (one-pair) circuits.

FPODA (Fixed Priority-Oriented Demand Assignment)

In networking, an access protocol in which stations must reserve slots on the network. These slots are allocated according to the stations' priority levels.

FPS (Fast Packet Switching)

In certain packet-switching architectures, FPS is a switching strategy that achieves higher throughput by simplifying the switching process. Steps to accomplish this include the following:

- Leaving error-checking and acknowledgments to higher-level protocols.
- Using fixed-size packets.
- Using simplified addresses, where possible.
- Switching packets as they come in, rather than buffering the entire packet before sending it on.

F

Not all architectures use each of these techniques. FPS is used, for example, in frame- and cell-relay implementations. This strategy is feasible only when the communications lines are clean, so that all but a tiny fraction of transmissions are error-free.

FPU (Floating Point Unit)

A math coprocessor chip that specializes in doing floating-point arithmetic. Examples include the 80*x*87 family of processors from Intel, as well as third-party FPUs, such as those from Cyrix and AMD.

FQDN (Fully Qualified Domain Name)

In the naming system for the Internet, the complete name for a machine on the network. The FQDN includes both the machine's name (the hostname) and domain name(s). For example, if *sand* is a hostname and it is located at the University of Antarctica, the machine's FQDN might be *sand.antarcticau.edu*.

→ **See Also** DNS (Domain Naming Service)

Fractal Compression

Fractal compression is a lossy image compression method that relies on self-similarity—that is, patterns repeated at different levels of the image—as the basis for reducing the file's size. The method's proponents claim it is better at reducing file size while maintaining image quality than JPEG (Joint Photographic Experts Group), which is currently the most widely used lossy compression method. Not surprisingly, critics disagree.

Much of the mathematics underlying fractal compression—known as iterated function theory, or IFT—uses patented algorithms. This is one reason fractal compression has not caught on as widely as its proponents have hoped.

→ **Broader Category** Compression

→ **Compare** JPEG (Joint Photographic Experts Group)

Fractional T1 (FT1)

→ **See** FT1 (Fractional T1)

FRAD (Frame Relay Access Device)

A FRAD is a special device for connecting a workstation to the frame relay network cloud. Such FRADs are designed for data transmissions, but special versions can be created for carrying other content.

For example, special FRADs are used to provide voice over frame relay transmissions. Such voice-enabled FRADs can compress a voice conversation into 8Kbps channels, so that eight voice conversations could be handled over one 64Kbps connection.

Also known as a frame relay assembler/disassembler.

Fragment

A fragment is part of a packet, which may be created deliberately or by accident.

In the context of an Ethernet network, packet fragments may be created unintentionally by a collision between two packets transmitted at the same time. These fragments may circulate for a brief period, but will soon disappear. Until that happens, jam packets are sent along the network to ensure that one of the nodes does not try to do something with the fragments.

In the context of the IP (Internet Protocol), a packet is deliberately broken into fragments if the packet is too large for service from the lower layer.

This process is known as *fragmentation* in the Internet environment. The same process is known as *segmentation*, and the packet parts are known as *segments*, in environments that conform to the OSI reference model.

When a packet is fragmented, the data portion is broken in parts. Each part is combined with the header, and is passed down to the layer below for further processing, such as for encapsulation into the lower-layer packets.

The reverse process—removing redundant headers and recombining several fragments into the original packet—is known as *reassembly*.

Fragmentation

In disk storage, fragmentation refers to the tendency of file clusters to become spread across a disk as the file is modified. Fragmentation affects system performance because a file's components must be retrieved from all over the disk, which forces the read heads to move unnecessarily in order to retrieve the clusters.

Special programs can be used to defragment storage—that is, to move file components—so that the elements in a file are stored sequentially on the disk. Such an arrangement allows files to be accessed more quickly.

Frame

In some network architectures, such as Token Ring, X.25, and SNA (Systems Network Architecture), *frame* is a term for a data packet, particularly for a packet at the Data-Link layer of the OSI reference model.

In connection with non-multiplexed communications, the terms *frame* and *packet* have come to be used interchangeably. *Packet* was originally the broader term, with *frame* being restricted to packets only at the data-link level of particular protocols.

In the frame-relay network architecture, a frame is a fixed-size packet. See the Frame Relay article for more information about these frames.

The term *frame* is also used to refer to one or more bits that occur in a predefined location in a time interval, and that are used for control and synchronization purposes.

In transmissions that use TDM (time division multiplexing), a frame is a sequence of time slots, each of which contains a chunk from one of the channels being multiplexed. For example, in a DS1 signal, a frame contains 24 such chunks: one from each of the 64Kbps channels being multiplexed. Several such frames may, in turn, be grouped into larger frames, called *superframes*, as in the ESF (extended superframe) grouping strategy.

In HTML (Hypertext Markup Language), a frame provides a way of dividing the browser's window into separate sections, in which different content—for example different Web pages—can be displayed. Individual frames can be defined using the <FRAME> tag to specify each separate display section. These are defined inside a <FRAMESET> .. </FRAMESET> structure.

Inside the <FRAMESET> tag, you need to specify either column or row information. This is specified using either the COLS= or the ROWS= attribute, as in the following:

```
<FRAMESET COLS="50%,*,150">
```

This example creates three columns, and also shows the three ways to specify a column size:

- As a percentage of the screen width (50%)

- In terms of the number of pixels (150)

- To take any available space (*)

The frameset specifies three columns' worth of frames. The leftmost column will take half the window, the rightmost will be 150 pixels wide, and the middle column will take up any remaining width. Within the frameset, the individual frames will be defined. Each frame definition will have at least the following minimal form:

```
<FRAME SRC="srcfilename.html">
```

Other attributes may also be included, including scrolling behavior and margin sizes. The frameset structure also provides a way to specify the content to be displayed by a browser that does not support frames. This is done using the <NOFRAMES> .. </NOFRAMES> tag.

The following HTML file shows a simple example for displaying frames:

```
<HTML>
<HEAD>
<TITLE> Frame Test</TITLE>
</HEAD>
<BODY>
<FRAMESET COLS="50%,*,200" ROWS="70%,*">
<FRAME SRC="file1.html">
<FRAME SRC="file2.html">
<FRAME SRC="file3.html">
<FRAME SRC="file4.html">
<FRAME SRC="file5.html">
<FRAME SRC="file6.html">
<NOFRAMES>
Text for browsers that don't support
frames
</NOFRAMES>
</FRAMESET>
</BODY>
</HTML>
```

➞ *See Also* HTML (Hypertext Markup Language); Packet

Frame Alignment

In frame-based transmissions, frame alignment refers to the timing relationship between the boundary of a received frame and the receiver's clock.

➞ *Compare* Frame Slip

Frame Check Sequence (FCS)

➞ *See* FCS (Frame Check Sequence)

Frame Control (FC)

➞ *See* FC (Frame Control)

Frame Duration

The frame duration refers to the amount of time that elapses between transmission of the first bit in the frame and the last —that is, the frame duration represents the amount of time it takes to send an entire frame.

Frame Reject Response (FRMR)

➞ *See* FRMR (Frame Reject Response)

Frame Relay

Frame Relay is one of several contenders for a wide area networking standard. Other contenders include ATM, BISDN, and cell relay. Frame Relay was originally intended as a bearer service for ISDN (Integrated Services Digital Network). It is suitable for transmitting data only, not for transmitting voice or video, because these require constant transmission capabilities.

An Overview of Frame Relay

Frame Relay provides fast packet-switching by leaving various checking and monitoring to higher-level protocols. Frame Relay has a high throughput and low delays. It also is efficient, making maximum use of available bandwidth. Frame Relay can have a bandwidth as high as 2Mbps. In contrast, X.25, which also uses packet-switching, is much slower, because the X.25 protocol will ask for data to be retransmitted if packets are lost or garbled.

The standard is packet-oriented and well-suited to "bursty" data, which is data with very high traffic volume at some times, almost no traffic at others. In contrast, circuit-switched networks are inefficient with bursty data, because assigned circuits cannot be used for other transmissions when both parties on the circuit are idle.

Frame Relay discards any packets that cannot be delivered, either because their destination cannot be found or because there are too many packets coming in at once. Discarding packets is Frame Relay's way of telling its users that they are overdoing it. Discarding is a viable error-handling strategy, because transport-layer protocols (such as SPX, NetBIOS, and TCP) have their own error-detection mechanisms. Frame Relay relies on higher-level protocols to do error correction and to request retransmissions if packets are lost or discarded. This means that Frame Relay should be used over "clean" lines, so that there are not too many errors for the higher-level protocols to discover.

The standard can notify sources and/or destinations if there is heavy traffic (congestion) on the network. Notified nodes are expected (but not required) to adjust their transmissions in order to reduce the congestion.

Because it operates at the Physical layer and the lower part of the data-link layer of the OSI Reference Model, frame relay is protocol-independent, and it can transmit packets from TCP/IP, IPX/SPX, SNA, or other protocol families.

"Context and properties of Frame-Relay networks" summarizes the characteristics of this standard.

Frame Relay Operation

Frame Relay uses statistical multiplexing to move frames across the network. Actually, for the user, Frame Relay provides access to the network by getting whatever packets it can onto the network.

Context

WAN/Telecommunications Standards
   Circuit Switching
   Packet Switching
      Fixed-size Packets
         ATM
      Variable-size Packets
         Frame Relay ——
Message Switching

Frame Relay Properties

Uses digital telephone lines for wide-area transmissions

Fast, with high throughput and low delays

Efficient (makes use of any available bandwidth)

Transmission rates up to 2 Mbps

Packet-oriented and well-suited to "bursty" data

Suitable only for data, not for voice or video

Suitable for use over clean lines

Discards any packets it cannot route or deliver

Operates at physical and lower data-link layers

Protocol-independent (can transmit any higher-layer protocol)

Leaves error correction and retransmissions to higher-layer protocols

Routing is over virtual circuits

Can report network congestion to source and/or destination nodes

F

CONTEXT AND PROPERTIES OF FRAME RELAY NETWORKS

Frame Relay Packets

As illustrated in "A Frame-Relay packet," packets are variable-length, and the header can be as small as 2 bytes. Bit values in the header and flag fields are used for control and signaling.

The header for a Frame Relay packet includes a 10-bit DLCI (data link connection identifier) value, which is split over 2 bytes. This value represents the port to which the destination network is connected. When a packet reaches a node, the node sends it on to the appropriate port or else discards the packet. The routing algorithm used to determine paths can be a major factor in the network's performance.

The header also includes 2 bits for explicit congestion notification (ECN), which is to inform nodes in either direction of heavy traffic. (See the ECN article for information about how these bits are used.)

One bit is used to indicate whether the packet can be discarded, if necessary. The EA (extended address) bits are available if more header bytes might be needed, which may be the case if a network is so large that 1024 DLCI values will not suffice. (Actually, fewer than 1024 DLCI values are available; DLCI 1023 is reserved for passing information about the virtual circuits that have been established, and other DLCI values are reserved for internal use.)

Deciding If Packets Can Be Discarded

One way the network decides whether a packet can be discarded is by considering the network activity of the packet's source. Each node on a Frame Relay network has a committed information rate (CIR) associated with it. This rate represents the user's estimate of the node's average bandwidth requirements.

When network traffic starts approaching the congested stage, each user's traffic is compared against

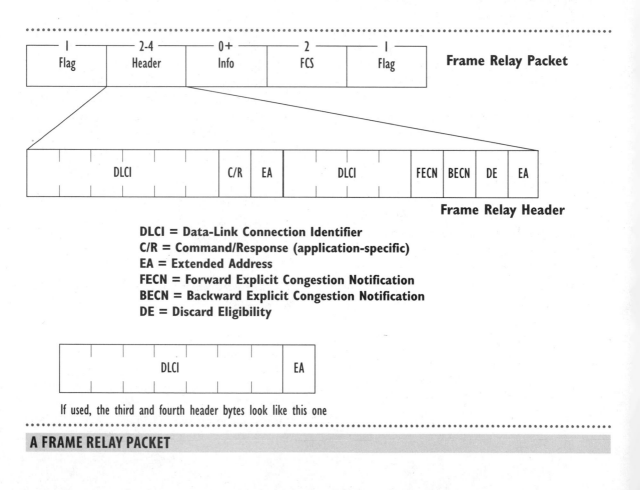

DLCI = Data-Link Connection Identifier
C/R = Command/Response (application-specific)
EA = Extended Address
FECN = Forward Explicit Congestion Notification
BECN = Backward Explicit Congestion Notification
DE = Discard Eligibility

If used, the third and fourth header bytes look like this one

A FRAME RELAY PACKET

the CIR for that user. If the node is below the node's CIR, packets from that node get through. When a node is slightly above its CIR, the network will try to deliver the node's packets if possible, but will discard them if necessary. If the node's activity is above its CIR by some predefined amount, the node's packets are automatically discarded.

Sender and receiver can exchange limited status information, provided that the two nodes both adhere to LMI (Local Management Interface) specifications. (Actually, the communication will be between the router and the network, standing in for the source and destination, respectively.)

→ **Primary Sources** CCITT publications I.233, I.370, Q.922 and Q.92; ANSI documents T1.606, T1.617, and T1.618. The ANSI and CCITT documents are very similar, showing good agreement on the part of the standards committees.

→ **Broader Category** Packet-Switching

Frame Relay Access Device (FRAD)

→ **See** FRAD (Frame Relay Access Device)

Frame Relay Assembler/ Disassembler (FRAD)

→ **See** FRAD (Frame Relay Access Device)

Frame Slip

In transmissions involving framed data—for example, data delimited by start and stop bits—a frame slip occurs when the receiver's clock and a received frame fall out of synchrony (alignment).

Frame Status (FS)

→ **See** FS (Frame Status)

Framing

In asynchronous communications, framing is the process of inserting start and stop signals before and after data being transmitted. These framing elements delimit the data by serving as borders for the data. They allow the receiver to determine the sender's timing, because the duration of the start bit indicates the bit interval size being used by the sender.

A *framing error* occurs in asynchronous communication when the receiver incorrectly identifies the start and stop signals, or the framing, in a transmission.

Framing Bit

In digital communications, a framing bit is sent to mark the boundary of a transmission unit, and is used to help the receiver with timing—so that sender and receiver remain in synchrony with each other. For example, start and stop bits in asynchronous serial communications are used for framing, as is the 193rd bit in a T1 communications channel.

Framing bits, which are also known as sync bits, do not carry data.

→ **See** 193rd Bit; Start Bit; Stop Bit

Framing Error

→ **See** Framing

Free Buffer Enquiry (FBE)

→ **See** FBE (Free Buffer Enquiry)

Free Software Foundation (FSF)

→ **See** FSF (Free Software Foundation)

F

Free Space Attenuation

In wireless communications, the amount of signal loss between the transmitting and the receiving stations.

Free Space Communication

Free space communication refers to any communications which use the air waves instead of a closed medium (such as fiber-optic cable or copper wire).

Freeware

The term freeware encompasses a range of software products whose main commonality is that users need not pay to use the software. If there are any costs involved, these will be to cover duplication, handling, and distribution.

Many freeware products do have restrictions on their use, however. For example, programs that use code from the Free Software Foundation's GNU (for GNU's Not UNIX) library must agree to abide by terms set out in a license—which include agreeing to make the program source code available. Some freeware products—for example, Linux—have allowed commercial implementations to be developed. These generally include added features or tools, and almost invariably sell for much less than more traditionally commercial software.

A surprisingly large proportion of Internet and other network infrastructures are built upon freeware. For example, consider the following:

- The TCP/IP protocol stack moves traffic across the Internet and across thousands of intranets and extranets.

- Apache servers are sitting in thousands and thousands of locations to receive this traffic and pass it on to their clients.

- Most of these clients are running browsers that are based on the freeware Mosaic browser.

- When browsers display any of the 850 million Web pages out there, chances are excellent that they are processing instructions in HTML (Hypertext Markup Language) or XML (eXtensible Markup Language) files. These files are, of course, transported using the HTTP (Hypertext Transfer Protocol) or a secure version (such as HTTPS) that encrypts transmission using a secure socket layer (SSL) protocol.

Recently, freeware has started moving into the corporate structure. For example, over a period of about two years, Linux went from a penetration of practically zero to 13 percent. That is, about 13 percent of corporations are running Linux systems for at least some of their corporate computers—and the projections are for even further inroads.

Other forces that are helping to increase the influence of freeware include

- The Open Source movement, which is attracting products from major corporations such as Netscape and IBM.

- The growing realization that the bazaar-style programming philosophy underlying much freeware actually can make good economic sense, and that it is not as bizarre as it might seem at first glance from a business perspective.

→ **See Also** Cathedral versus Bazaar; Open Source

Frequency

For periodic phenomena, such as sound or light waves, a measure of the number of times a cycle repeats within a given interval (such as a second). The cycle frequency is expressed in hertz (Hz). One hertz equals one cycle per second.

Frequency-Agile Modem

In a broadband system, a frequency-agile modem can switch frequencies in order to allow communications over different channels (different frequency bands) at different times.

Frequency Band

A range of frequencies within which a transmission occurs. For example, the frequency band for ordinary telephone signals is between about 300 and 4000 hertz.

Frequency Converter

A device that can be used to convert between the sender's and the receiver's frequency ranges in a broadband system. For example, in a broadband network (or in a cable TV system), the headend (main transmitter) may need to convert the incoming signals before sending them on to network nodes (or cable subscribers).

Frequency Delay

In signaling, a delay that may be caused by the fact that signals of different frequencies travel at slightly different speeds through a given medium and, therefore, reach the destination at slightly different times. This delay can result in signal distortion. Various devices, such as an equalizer, can correct the problem.

Frequency Division, Multiple Access (FDMA)

→ See FDMA (Frequency Division, Multiple Access)

Frequency Division Multiplexing (FDM)

→ See FDM (Frequency Division Multiplexing)

Frequency Shift Keying (FSK)

→ See Modulation

Frequency Translator

In a broadband cable system, an analog device that converts from one block of frequencies to another.

Frequently Asked Questions (FAQ)

→ See FAQ (Frequently Asked Questions)

FRMR (Frame Reject Response)

In a connection using the SDLC (Synchronous Data Link Control) protocol, a signal from the receiving station indicating that an invalid frame or packet has been received.

Frogging

In broadband communications, inversion of the signal frequencies in order to equalize the distortion and loss across the transmission's bandwidth. The incoming channel with the highest frequency will go out as the lowest frequency band, the second highest in will be the second lowest out, and so on.

Front-End Processor (FEP)

→ See FEP (Front-End Processor)

FrontPage

→ See Microsoft FrontPage

FS (Frame Status)

A field in a token-ring data packet.

→ See Also Token Ring

F

FSF (Free Software Foundation)

FSF is an organization, based in Cambridge, Massachusetts, dedicated to creating high-quality software and making both the executable and source code freely available. The foundation is headed by Richard Stallman, who is a well-known consultant and guru in the UNIX community.

Perhaps the best-known product from the foundation is the GNU (for GNU's Not UNIX) operating environment. GNU includes dozens of work-alike versions of popular applications. For example, Oleo is the GNU spreadsheet program.

FSK (Frequency Shift Keying)

→ *See* Modulation

FSP (File Service Process)

On a file server, a process that executes and responds to file-handling requests.

FT1 (Fractional T1)

In digital communications, a portion of a 1.544Mbps T1 carrier, or line. Fractional T1 lines are available from IXCs (interexchange carriers), and can have bandwidths of 384, 512, or 768Kbps, corresponding roughly to a quarter, a third, and half of a full T1 carrier.

FTP (File Transfer Protocol)

→ *See* Protocol, FTP (File Transfer Protocol)

FTS (File Transfer Service)

FTS refers to any of a broad class of application-layer services for handling files and moving them from one location to another. The following are just some of the services that have been developed within the OSI framework:

CGM (Computer Graphics Metafile)   A format for storing and exchanging graphics information. It is documented in ISO document 8632.

DFR (Document Filing and Retrieval)   A proposed ISO standard for allowing multiple users to work with documents on a remote server. DFR is part of the DOAM (Distributed Office Applications Model).

DPA (Document Printing Application)   Also part of the DOAM.

EDI (Electronic Data Interchange)   Any of several proposals for exchanging data electronically, using predefined formats. Several special-purpose "EDIfices" have been developed, including EDIME (EDI messaging environment), EDI-MS (EDI message store), and EDIFACT (EDI for administration, commerce, and transport). They are documented in ANSI document X.12.

ILL (Interlibrary Loan)   A proposed standard to allow the loan of books and other documents among libraries all over the world. It is documented in ISO documents 10160 and 10161.

JTM (Job Transfer and Manipulation)   A standard that specifies how jobs can be distributed for remote processing, and how reports and output can be sent wherever specified. It is documented in ISO documents 8831 and 8832.

MHS (Message Handling System)   As defined in the CCITT's X.500 series of specifications.

ODA/ODIF (Open Document Architecture/ Open Document Interchange Format)   Standards for the structure of a document and for the document's format during transmission. These standards are documented in CCITT documents T.411 through T.418 and ISO 8613.

RDA (Remote Database Access)   A standard for accessing data in remote databases.

RDT (Referenced Data Transfer)   Part of DOAM.

TP (Transaction Processing) A standard that specifies how data from online transactions is to be distributed. It is documented in ISO document 10026.

VT (Virtual Terminal) Specifications for a "generic terminal," which can be emulated in software and used to access any host.

FTS2000

FTS2000 is a long distance telecommunications service used by federal government agencies and offices. Use of FTS2000 for various government purposes is mandatory. FTS2000 supports several types of service, including the following:

- Switched voice service for voice or data up to 4.8 kb/s

- Switched data at 56 kb/s and 64 kb/s

- Switched digital integrated service for voice, data, image, and video up to 1.544 Mb/s

- Packet–switched service for packetized data

- Video transmission for both compressed and uncompressed video

- Dedicated point-to-point private line service for voice and data

Full Duplex (FDX)

→ *See* FDX (Full Duplex)

Fully Qualified Domain Name (FQDN)

→ *See* FQDN (Fully Qualified Domain Name)

Function Management Layer

The topmost layer in IBM's SNA. An end user deals directly with this layer which, in turn, deals with the data-flow control layer.

→ *See* SNA (Systems Network Architecture)

FX (Foreign Exchange)

In telephone communications, a line or service that connects a user's (subscriber's) telephone to a central office (CO) other than the one that provides basic service for the subscriber's exchange.

FYI (For Your Information)

The name for a series of Internet documents intended to provide basic information about the Internet, its services, and about certain topics related to the Internet. While they are published as *RFC (Request For Comments)* documents, FYI papers differ from most RFCs in that the FYI papers are generally (but not always) less technical, and FYIs do not specify standards. Example FYI titles include:

- FYI 30 : "A Primer on Internet and TCP/IP Tools and Utilities" (1997, RFC 1855)

- FYI 28 : "Netiquette Guidelines" (1995, RFC 2151)

- FYI 24 : "How to use Anonymous FTP" (1994, RFC 1635)

- FYI 23 : "Guide to Network Resource Tools" (1994, RFC 1580)

- FYI 18 : "Internet Users' Glossary" (1993, RFC 1392)

- FYI 10 : "There's Gold in them that Networks! or Searching for Treasure in all the Wrong Places" (1993, RFC 1402; 1991, RFC 1290)

- FYI 1 : "F.Y.I. on F.Y.I. : Introduction to the F.Y.I. Notes" (1990, RFC 1150)

FYI 10 illustrates a common occurrence in the FYI and RFC literature. The more recent version makes the older one obsolete. Thus, RFC 1402 is the newer (and, hence, more correct) version of FYI 10.

F

G

An abbreviation for the prefix *giga*, as in GHz (gigahertz) or Gbps (gigabits per second). This order of magnitude corresponds to 2^{30}, which is roughly 10^9, or billions (in the United States counting system).

→ *See Also* Orders of Magnitude

Gain

In electrical signaling, an increase in a signal's voltage, power, or current. This type of increase can occur only through amplification. Noise caused by a momentary increase in signal amplitude is called a *gain hit*.

Gatedaemon

In the Internet environment, a program that can be used for routing packets. Gatedaemon, or *gated* (pronounced "gate dee"), as it is called, supports multiple routing protocols, such as exterior gateway protocols, and protocol families.

→ *See Also* Protocol, Routing

Gateway

In the context of local-area networks (LANs) and mainframe connections, a gateway is a hardware and/or software package that connects two different network environments. For example, a gateway can be used to connect a PC-based network and an IBM mainframe, or a Token Ring network and an AppleTalk network. The figure "Context and properties of gateways" summarizes the characteristics of this type of internetwork link.

More generally, the term can refer to any device or software package that connects two different environments, regardless of whether networks are involved. As such, a gateway can also be considered a communications server or, in some cases, an access server.

Context

Internetwork Links
  Bridge
  Gateway ──────┐
  Router   │
                ▼

Gateway Properties

Connects dissimilar networks, such as different architectures, LAN to mainframe or WAN, . . .

Some provide access to special services, such as e-mail or fax

Operates at upper layers of the OSI Reference Model

Takes transmission capabilities for granted in order to focus on content and format

Often does data translation or conversion

Needs a network interface card for each architecture supported

CONTEXT AND PROPERTIES OF GATEWAYS

In the Internet community, the term *gateway* has been used to refer to anything that connects networks. The connecting device is generally a router, and this term has replaced gateway in Internet contexts.

Gateways in Networks

A gateway provides a LAN with access to a different type of network, an internetwork, a mainframe computer, or a particular type of operating environment. A gateway serves to connect networks with very different architectures, for example, an Ethernet LAN and an SNA network, or a LAN and an X.25 packet-switching service. Gateways are also used to provide access to special services, such as e-mail (electronic mail), fax, and Telex.

Gateways can operate at several of the higher OSI Reference Model levels, most notably at the session, presentation, and application layers. Gateways usually operate above the communications subnet (which comprises the bottom three layers in the OSI Reference Model). This means that gateways take transmission capabilities for granted and concentrate on the content of the transmission.

In the course of doing their work, gateways may very likely change the representation of data before passing it on. For example, a gateway may convert from ASCII to EBCDIC on the way to an IBM mainframe, encrypting or decrypting data between the source and destination environments. Gateways also must do protocol conversion, since the different environments connected by a gateway will generally use different protocol families.

The multilayer operation of gateways is in contrast to repeaters, bridges, and routers, which each operate at a single level (the physical, data-link, and network layers, respectively), and which do not change the data in any way.

Essentially, a gateway, which is generally a dedicated computer, must be able to support both of the environments it connects. To each of the connected network environments, the gateway looks like a node in that environment. To provide this support, the gateway needs an interface card and at least some shell software for both of the environments being connected. In addition, the gateway runs special software to provide the necessary conversion and translation services and to communicate with the two environments. Practically speaking, a gateway needs a considerable amount of storage and RAM (random-access memory). The operation of a network gateway is illustrated in "A gateway looks like a different environment to each of the networks it connects."

Some gateways are unidirectional, which means that they handle traffic in one direction only. In such cases, you may need to install two separate gateways for bidirectional communication.

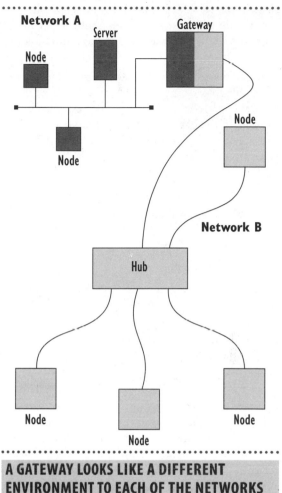

A GATEWAY LOOKS LIKE A DIFFERENT ENVIRONMENT TO EACH OF THE NETWORKS IT CONNECTS

Gateway Operation

The behavior of a gateway depends on the type of connection being established. For example, when connecting a PC to an IBM mainframe, the gateway may also provide terminal-emulation capabilities, in addition to translating between EBCDIC and ASCII character codes. Terminal-emulation capabilities make it unnecessary to install a terminal-emulation card in each node that wants to access the mainframe. In this type of connection, the mainframe will think it is talking to a controller that is channeling sessions from multiple terminals, and the workstation will behave and look like a terminal.

A gateway for message-handling services needs to be able to package and represent messages in whatever form is necessary for the destination. In particular, the gateway needs to be able to access remote networks through public or private data-transmission services (for example, X.25).

In general, a gateway may provide a variety of services, including the following:

- Packet format and/or size conversion

- Protocol conversion

- Data translation

- Multiplexing

Gateways as Bottlenecks

Gateways are often bottlenecks in network communications. For example, a gateway that connects remote locations may need to use a synchronous protocol (such as SDLC), which operates at a relatively slow 19,200 bits per second (bps). Even if gateways use faster transmission protocols, they may slow down a network because of all the data translation and other tasks (such as terminal emulation) they must perform.

Depending on the environments being connected, it may be possible to get around certain speed limitations, almost always at the expense of a few (or a few dozen) "kilobucks."

Gateway Categories

Gateways can be grouped in various ways. A common general grouping scheme uses the attributes on which the gateway services operate:

- An *address gateway* connects networks that have different directory spaces but that use the same protocols. This type of gateway is

common, for example, when dealing with a Message Handling Service (MHS).

- A *protocol gateway* connects networks that use different protocols. The gateway does the protocol translations.

- A *format gateway* connects networks that use different representation schemes (for example, ASCII versus EBCDIC). The gateway maps between the two formats.

Special-purpose gateways that provide access to specific services are becoming more widely used. As with servers, the terminology regarding gateways is quite variable and is extensible. Gateways are sometimes named after the devices to which they connect. You may also see some kinds of gateways, particularly those involving mainframes, marketed as access servers.

The following list contains just a sample of the types of gateways that have been developed. These types are not mutually exclusive.

X.25   Provides access to X.25 packet-switching services for remote communications. This type of gateway may be used by a wide-area network (WAN) or an enterprise network.

Fax   Provides access to fax machines at remote locations. The gateway will convert messages to fax format.

E-mail   Provides services (such as e-mail connections) between LANs. E-mail gateways often connect network-operating-system-specific MHSs to an X.400 mail service.

Internet   Provides access to the Internet backbone network. An Internet gateway is used by an intermediate-level network or by an outernet (a network that is not part of the Internet).

SAA   Provides access to machines using IBM's SAA (Systems Applications Architecture) environment.

SNA Provides access to machines using IBM's SNA (Systems Network Architecture) environment, which is the architecture for the entire IBM mainframe line.

Mainframe Connects a LAN to a network of one or more mainframes. These gateways require a PC, a (3270) emulation board, and the appropriate gateway software. By dedicating a single machine as a gateway, you can save the cost of outfitting all nodes with terminal-emulation cards and capabilities. An SNA gateway is a mainframe gateway.

→*Broader Category* Internetwork Link

→*See Also* Bridge; Brouter; Router; Switch

Gauge

A measure of electrical wire diameter. Under the American Wire Gauge (AWG) standards, higher gauge numbers indicate a thinner cable. See the AWG article for a table of some sample gauge values.

Gaussian Noise

In electrical signaling, noise resulting from the vibration of atoms or molecules. This noise occurs over all frequencies, and it increases with temperature.

G

WHAT TO LOOK FOR IN A GATEWAY

Because of the overwhelming number of combinations that might be connected by gateways, it's important to make sure you get a gateway that's suitable for your environment and needs. The following list contains just some of the things you need to determine when selecting a gateway.

- What specific networking environment(s) does the gateway support? What restrictions, if any, are there on this support?

- What protocols does the gateway support? This will be determined, in part, by the networking environments supported.

- If it's a special-purpose gateway, what particular implementations of the service does the gateway support? For example, which e-mail packages does an e-mail gateway support? Be aware that a gateway may support some packages for certain networking environments and other packages for other environments.

- If the gateway will provide access or communications capabilities, what interfaces are supported?

- What are the hardware requirements for the gateway? For example, does the gateway require a card for each end? Does the gateway require a stand-alone machine? If so, what capabilities does the machine need?

- Is the gateway bidirectional?

- Do nodes attached to the gateway need to run special software (for example, emulation packages) or does the gateway take care of that?

- How many nodes (or terminals or sessions) can the gateway support at a time?

- What's the gateway's throughput?

- What management capabilities does the gateway provide/support?

GDMO (Guidelines for the Definition of Managed Objects)

An ISO specification that provides notation for describing managed objects and actions involving such objects.

GDS (Generalized Data Stream)

The format for mapped data in the APPC (Advanced Program-to-Program Communications) extension of IBM's SNA (Systems Network Architecture). Data from high-level applications is converted to GDS format before transmission. This helps protect from format differences, such as when one application uses the ASCII character format and the other uses EBCDIC.

General Format Identifier (GFI)

→ *See* GFI (General Format Identifier)

Generalized Data Stream (GDS)

→ *See* GDS (Generalized Data Stream)

General-Purpose Interface Bus (GPIB)

→ *See* GPIB (General-Purpose Interface Bus)

General Switch Telephone Network (GSTN)

→ *See* GSTN (General Switch Telephone Network)

Generic Flow Control (GFC)

→ *See* GFC (Generic Flow Control)

GEO (Geosynchronous Earth Orbit) Satellite

GEO refers to a special orbit around the earth, such as the orbit of a communications satellite. A satellite in geosynchronous orbit is known as a *geosynchronous* or *geostationary satellite*. The orbit is "synchronous" because the satellite makes a revolution in about 24 hours—keeping pace with the earth's rotation. The satellites are about 36,000 kilometers (22,350 miles) above the earth, and they appear to be stationary over a location.

Even though a geostationary satellite has a footprint (reception and transmission range) of half the earth, it actually takes three geostationary satellites to get 24-hour total earth coverage.

GEO satellites are in contrast to other classes of satellites—some with lower earth orbits. These include LEO (low earth orbit), MEO (medium earth orbit), and HEO (high earth orbit and also highly elliptical orbit) varieties.

Geostationary Earth Orbit (GEO)

→ *See* GEO (Geosynchronous Earth Orbit)

Geosynchronous Earth Orbit (GEO)

→ *See* GEO (Geosynchronous Earth Orbit)

Geosynchronous Orbit

→ *See* GEO (Geosynchronous Earth Orbit)

GFC (Generic Flow Control)

In the ATM networking model, a protocol that is used to make sure all nodes get access to the transmission medium. This service is provided at the ATM layer in the model.

GFI (General Format Identifier)

In an X.25 packet, a field that indicates packet formats and several other features.

Gigabit Ethernet

On June 29, 1998, Ethernet joined a very elite club of technologies capable of transmitting a billion bits every second. With the ratification of the Gigabit Ethernet specification as the IEEE 802.3z standard, the world's most popular LAN architecture also became one of the fastest communications technologies—capable of transmitting the entire contents of the *Oxford English Dictionary* in a few seconds.

Gigabit Ethernet supports transmission speeds of up to 1000Mbps—a hundred times faster than the speed of the original 10Mbps Ethernet. Currently, there is official support for this transmission speed only over optical fiber; however, by the time you read this, there should also be a standard in place to support these speeds over multiple pairs of unshielded twisted-pair (UTP) copper wire.

The impressive thing is that Gigabit Ethernet manages to achieve such high speeds while staying largely compatible with both 10Mbps and 100Mbps Ethernet variants. Gigabit Ethernet does this by taking full advantage of recent developments in how nodes on Ethernet networks can communicate.

Something Old (Traditional Ethernet)

Traditional Ethernet—as defined in the IEEE 802.3 standard—is a shared-media LAN architecture that uses collision detection as the access

control mechanism. This means that the nodes in an Ethernet network share the same wires for their transmissions. Any node can broadcast as long as there is no one else talking. If two nodes try to access the network at the same time, their packets will collide, and this collision will be detected by both the sending parties and by other nodes on the network. Each of the colliding parties will wait a randomly determined amount of time before trying to transmit its packet again. See the entry for CSMA/CD (Carrier Sense Multiple Access with Collision Detection) for details on this access process.

Using this access method, traditional Ethernet supports packet transmission rates of up to 10Mbps. Ethernet networks can use cable (twisted pair or coaxial) or optical fiber as the transmission medium. The maximum size of a network and the number of nodes allowed on it depend on the medium being used. In general, optical fiber supports greater distances.

Gigabit Ethernet uses the 802.3 Ethernet frame format. This has a minimum size of 64 bytes and a maximum size of 1,518 bytes. As you'll see below, gigabit Ethernet does put its own twist on certain aspects of Ethernet frames. (Recently, there has been a move to develop standards for supporting 9,000-byte jumbo frames for Gigabit Ethernet. Several vendors already have products that can support these oversized frames.)

Something New (Gigabit Ethernet Operation)

Gigabit Ethernet achieves its high bandwidth through a combination of several design considerations. First, the technology takes full advantage of the transformation of Ethernet into a switched-media architecture (with the introduction of Ethernet switches). Switches can be used to establish direct connections between communicating nodes. Since no other nodes will be using the same channel, there is no need to worry about collisions.

Second, Gigabit Ethernet networks can, and generally do, operate in full-duplex mode. This

G

allows communication in both directions at the same time. Again, this is feasible because there is no need to worry about collisions.

To help prevent bottlenecks or overflows in devices that may have trouble dealing with the high speeds, Gigabit Ethernet includes a component known as a *buffered distributor*. This is a full duplex device that functions like a hub. It has multiple ports, and it can connect two or more Ethernet links at the full 1Gbps speed. The buffered distributor forwards all packets to every segment except the one from which the packet came. More important, the distributor includes a buffer in which it can temporarily store frames to keep them from getting dropped by a slow device on the network.

To keep the number of collisions down to an acceptable level, the maximum distance between nodes in an ordinary Ethernet network is determined essentially by how long it takes to send the shortest valid Ethernet frame. The *collision domain*, as this maximum distance is called, is the distance over which a signal can make a round trip in the time it takes to send the shortest frame. Classically, such a frame is 64 bytes in size.

However, at 1Gbps, the collision domain would be only about 20 meters—clearly not a useful size for a network whose components can cost thousands of dollars. To increase the collision domain, Gigabit Ethernet uses *carrier extension*, which essentially makes the minimum frame size 512 bytes. By padding shorter frames out to this size, a Gigabit Ethernet network gains extra time for the collision domain, but at the cost of possibly transmitting eight times as many bytes as necessary.

To decrease this potential inefficiency, Gigabit Ethernet also allows *packet bursting*, which lets a node send up to 3KB of frames back to back—that is, without letting another node transmit anything. In such a burst, only the first frame needs to be padded using carrier extension.

Something Borrowed (Gigabit Ethernet Layers)

Gigabit Ethernet is actually a hybrid construction. It borrows its physical layer from the high-speed Fibre Channel technology. The figure "Gigabit Ethernet layer structure" shows the layers and sublayers defined for Gigabit Ethernet, and also illustrates how these correspond to the Fibre Channel layers.

Gigabit Ethernet uses the same data-link layer structure as 802.3 Ethernet. Also as in 802.3 Ethernet, this layer is subdivided into the upper Logical Link Control sublayer and the lower Media Access Control sublayer. Gigabit Ethernet does provide a few extensions and modifications at the data-link layer. These are needed to deal with some unacceptable consequences of increasing network performance by a factor of 10 over the fast Ethernet specs and by a factor of 100 over standard Ethernet specs—for example, a maximum network size of 20 meters.

The physical layer, which is also subdivided, borrows from Fibre Channel technology. Specifically, the Physical Coding Sublayer (PCS) uses the 8B/10B encoding defined at layer FC-1 of the Fibre Channel specification. This data translation scheme encodes 8-bit blocks into 10-bit blocks, or symbols, with the extra bits being used for error correction and control purposes in what is known as *disparity control*. The PCS is responsible for data encoding and decoding, and it serves as the interface between the lower physical sublayers and the upper layers.

Below the PCS is the Physical Medium Attachment (PMA) sublayer. This component has the task of serializing the 10-bit symbols before sending them down for actual transmission. Conversely, the PMA deserializes incoming transmissions, and passes them to the PCS as 10-bit symbols.

The Physical Medium Dependent (PMD) sublayer is at the bottom. It takes the serial stream from the PMA and translates its elements into a form suitable for the medium to which the node is attached. For example, if the node has a fiber-optic connection, the serial stream is converted into optical signals; for a copper connection, the stream is translated into electrical signals. This sublayer borrows the interface and media specifications from the FC-0 Fibre Channel physical layer. The connection between the PMD and the actual media is defined by the Media Dependent Interface (MDI).

The IEEE 802.3z standard specifies three types of media:

- 1000Base-CX uses two pairs of 150-ohm balanced copper cable. This electrical medium can be at most 25 meters in length, and so is intended primarily for connections between rooms or between a room and a wiring closet.

- 1000Base-LX uses a pair of optical fibers— either multimode or single mode—and long wavelength light (LWL). For multimode fiber (either 50 or 62.5 micron), the maximum distance between nodes is 550 meters;

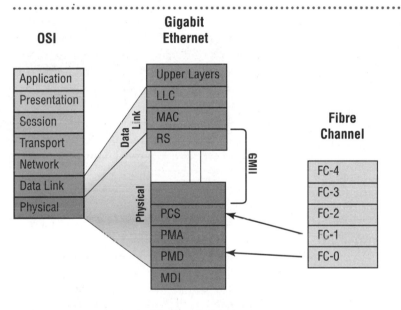

FC-0: Fibre Channel (Physical) Sublayer 0 - Interface and Link
FC-1: Fibre Channel (Physical) Sublayer 1 - Encoding/Decoding
FC-2: Fibre Channel (Physical) Sublayer 2 - Signaling
FC-3: Fibre Channel (Physical) Sublayer 3 - Common Services
FC-4: Fibre Channel (Physical) Sublayer 4 - Upper Layer and Mapping
GMII: Gigabit Medium-Independent Interface
LLC: Logical Link Control
MAC: Media Access Control
MDI: Media Dependent Interface
PCS: Physical Coding Sublayer
PMA: Physical Medium Attachment Sublayer
PMD: Physical Medium Dependent Sublayer
RS: Reconciliation Sublayer

GIGABIT ETHERNET LAYER STRUCTURE

G

for single-mode fiber, the maximum distance is about 3km.

- 1000Base-SX uses a pair of multimode optical fibers and short wavelength light (SWL). Maximum distance between nodes is 200 meters for 62.5 micron fiber and 450 meters for 50 micron fiber.

Specifications for a fourth type of medium have also been developed, but these were not ratified at the same time as the 802.3z specifications. By the time you read this, the 802.3ab specifications for Gigabit Ethernet over twisted-pair copper wire—known as 1000Base-T—should be a standard as well.

1000Base-T uses four pairs of category 5 unshielded twisted-pair (UTP) wire, and can support distances of up to 100 meters between nodes. Because the 1000Base-T specifications use different encoding schemes than the other Gigabit Ethernet variants, a special Gigabit Media-Independent Interface (GMII) must be used between the PCS and the Reconciliation Sublayer (RS) for the data-link layer above. The GMII provides a logical signal interface, and is designed to allow different media to be used. The GMII is not needed for any of the CX, LX, or SX variants, because these all use the same encoding scheme defined in FC-1.

Hardware Considerations

Gigabit Ethernet makes considerable demands on hardware, and performance bottlenecks are not uncommon. In fact, a Gigabit Ethernet server must have some pretty strong specs. For example, the server needs at least 1MB of cache memory. Currently, most Windows-based machines come in a configuration with 512KB of cache. In effect, the cache requirement rules out most available hardware as potential servers.

Even if the cache requirements are met, there are still more potential problems. The general consensus is that Gigabit Ethernet pretty much stretches the 32-bit PCI bus (currently found in most Windows machines) to its limits. Thus, the performance of a Gigabit Ethernet network may

be server-bound—at least for the current generation of machines.

Gigabit Ethernet really expects optical fiber—the copper-based variants notwithstanding. Many companies have not yet installed such fiber. Or, companies may have the "wrong" kind of optical fiber installed. For example, if the network is supposed to extend for a mile or so, single-mode fiber is needed. If the existing wiring is multimode fiber, there's a problem. Performance issues aside, single-mode and multimode fiber are physically incompatible.

Gigabit Ethernet Limitations

Gigabit Ethernet could replace other popular communications technologies, such as ATM (Asynchronous Transfer Mode), FDDI (Fiber Distributed Data Interface), and frame relay—at least for certain purposes. With its high speed, Gigabit Ethernet would seem ideal for transmitting such data as video or other kinds of materials with high bandwidth requirements.

The main problem is that Gigabit Ethernet has no quality of service (QoS) capabilities to speak of. That is, there is no way to reserve paths or to prioritize frames that might need guaranteed bandwidth or other special handling.

Proponents argue that Gigabit Ethernet supports the Resource Reservation Protocol (RSVP). This protocol is used to reserve resources required for a particular class of service. The protocol reserves the resource for an end-to-end connection between nodes. That means the resource is booked for intermediate points in the connection as well. This ensures that the traffic continues to flow without interruption between the endpoints. The ability to select a class of end-to-end service makes it possible to use RSVP to define QoS levels.

However, RSVP can only reserve whatever resources are available for the underlying network architecture. In the case of Gigabit Ethernet, there just aren't many resources. Also, RSVP's overhead can add up if there are lots of small flows.

One thing Gigabit Ethernet implementations do support is multilayer switching, which helps keep routers from getting overwhelmed by the high bandwidth traffic. In particular, layer-three switching helps simplify things most directly for routers. Various strategies are possible here, with most of them using some sort of tagging or labeling strategy to identify traffic in a particular flow.

A flow is essentially a stream of data that is going in the same direction—that is, data that will get the same treatment from a routing function. Since the stream is all going the same way, only the start of the flow needs routing instructions. The rest of the flow can simply be tagged for easy identification. Intermediate points in the path may also be used—for example, to ensure that the flow can cut through a node on its path. The path of such a flow, which may involve virtual circuits (VCs), is managed by an appropriate protocol. The Ipsilon Flow Management Protocol, or IFMP, is widely used.

Prospects for Gigabit Ethernet

Gigabit Ethernet is expected to become the dominant LAN technology within a few years. Until then, it is most likely to be used in the following ways:

- To provide a high-speed backbone for a network

- To allow a single Gbps switch to take over the work of several 100Mbps Ethernet or 155Mbps ATM (Asynchronous Transfer Mode) switches

- For cases with high bandwidth requirements—for example, when working with huge data objects or giant databases in research or other contexts

→ *Broader Category* Ethernet

→ *See Also* 100BaseT; 1000Base-T; 1000Base-X

GigaPOP

On the still experimental Internet2, a gigaPOP (for giga point-of-presence) is a high-speed network access provider capable of supporting transmission rates of up to 2.4Gbps.

Gigaserver

A gigaserver is the name given to a device with a massive storage capacity that is considered a key element in the home entertainment system of the future. The gigaserver will be connected, via very high bandwidth lines, to delivery services over which a home user can download movies, concerts, and so forth.

Glare

In certain bidirectional telephone circuits, such as private branch exchange (PBX) lines, a condition in which an incoming and outgoing call "meet," possibly causing crossed connections. One way to avoid this problem is to use a *ground start* signaling technique.

Global Group

In Windows NT, a global group is one whose users have access to servers and workstations in the users' own domains and also in other domains (provided that the other domains allow access from the user's group or domain). Global groups can affect the entire network, and so are stored on the primary domain controller (PDC).

Global groups are in contrast to local groups, which affect only the computer on which the group was created. Global and local groups are the two basic group types in Windows NT.

Global Name

In a network or an internetwork, a name known to all nodes and servers. This is in contrast to a local name (a name associated with a particular server). A global name is fully qualified; that is, it includes all the intermediate levels of membership associated with the name.

→ *See Also* Global Naming Service

G

Global Naming Service

A global naming service provides mechanisms for naming resources that may be attached to any of several file servers in a network. First developed in the StreetTalk service in Banyan's VINES software, these capabilities have been added to other network operating systems, such as version 4.0 of Novell's NetWare.

Names in a global naming service have a predefined format, which reflects the different levels of operations in the network. For example, StreetTalk names have the format:

```
Item@Group@Organization
```

Global naming services are in contrast to local naming services, such as those provided by the bindery in NetWare versions 3.*x* and earlier.

Global Positioning System (GPS)

→ *See* GPS (Global Positioning System)

Globalstar

Globalstar is a system of 48 satellites in low earth orbits (LEO). Developed by Loral and Qualcomm, Globalstar is intended to provide data, fax, and telephony services.

→ *Compare* Iridium Project; Teledesic

Global System for Mobile Communications (GSM)

→ *See* GSM (Global System for Mobile Communications)

Global Tree

Global tree is an unofficial term for a tree that uses Abstract Syntax Notation One (ASN.1) to represent objects related to networking, particularly to network management. The root of this tree is unnamed, and the tree's main subtrees are administered, respectively, by the CCITT, the ISO, and by a joint ISO-CCITT committee.

Most management and much Internet-related information is found in the iso(1) (sub)tree. Subtrees under iso(1) are administered by various groups and organizations. These organizations may, in turn, grant a subtree under theirs to other groups. For example, under its subtree, the ISO set up a branch for different organizations. For reasons that will be explained, this subtree is named *org(3)*. The illustration "Partial view of the global ASN.1 tree" shows some branches on this tree.

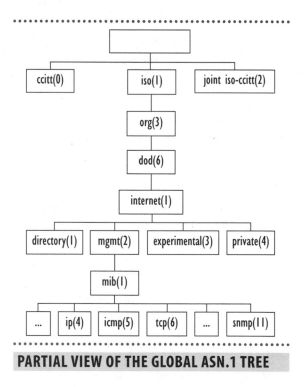

PARTIAL VIEW OF THE GLOBAL ASN.1 TREE

The global tree has appeared under various names, including the following:

- *MIB tree*, because the tree includes entries for a management information base (MIB)

- *ASN.1 tree*, because the tree's information is represented using the Abstract ASN.1 notation

- *SMI tree*, for structure of management information tree

Notation

Each node in the tree has a name and a number associated with it. Each of these values identifies an object (very loosely and broadly defined) for the tree. The numbers correspond, with some exceptions and restrictions, to the sequence in which subtrees were assigned.

Two ways of referencing elements in the tree are commonly used: global notation and local notation.

Global notation uses just the numbers associated with each node, with the values for the individual nodes on the path separated by decimal points. In this notation, the full name for the internet(1) node would be 1.3.6.1; the last 1 is the one for internet.

Local notation lists just the new node's parent and the new node's number. (The parent of node A is the node immediately above node A.) In this notation, internet(1) is named {dod 1}, because, as illustrated in the figure "Partial view of the global ASN.1 tree," dod is just above internet. The *dod* part represents internet subtree's parent, and the 1 indicates that *internet* is the subtree with index 1 under *dod*. This notation assumes that the application reading it will be able to determine the full name for *dod*.

Levels of Detail

At the higher levels of the tree, the nodes are quite "large" (international and national organizations or agencies). Further down in the tree, the topics are more specific. The global tree covers a huge range of detail, from international standards organizations at the highest level to the value for the setting on a particular model of network interface card.

Networking-related protocols and objects will have their own nodes somewhere in the tree. Each of these objects will have a unique path to it. For example, information relating to the TCP protocol begins at *tcp(6)*, which is found at location 1.3.6.1.2.1.2.1.6 in the tree; information about the IP protocol begins at 1.3.6.1.2.1.2.1.4 in the tree.

As part of the descriptions for these protocols, the subtrees will include nodes for particular functions and entities for the protocol. These can, in turn, be refined. By the time you get to the bottom of a subtree, the trail will have accumulated all there is to tell (as far as the network is concerned) about the object at that node.

In order to avoid conflicts, specific locations in the tree are reserved and allocated for particular purposes. The *internet(1)* subtree includes *experimental(3)* and *private(4)* subtrees. Within *private(4)*, for example, specific companies can be provided with "space" to define their extensions or variations for elements described elsewhere in the tree.

As standards are revised or updated, portions of the tree will change. For example, the *mib-2(1)* subtree under *mgmt(2)* replaced the *mib(1)* subtree when the revised management information base, MIB-II, was defined.

→ *Broader Categories* MIB (Management Information Base); Network Management

→ *See Also* Internet

Global User

In Windows NT, a global user is one whose account is created as part of the Windows NT Security Access Manager (SAM). This allows a global user to log on to any computer that is attached to the security domain for the network.

Global user accounts are in contrast to those for local users, who can access only the server for

G

which their account has been set up and only from the machine on which the user account has been set up. Whereas global users log onto a network domain, local users log onto a computer.

GMT (Greenwich Mean Time)

The time at the Greenwich observatory. This is generally used as the reference time when a standardized value is needed. This official name has been changed to UTC (a permuted acronym for Universal Coordinated Time).

Gopher

On the Internet, a gopher is a long-popular, but now obsolescent, distributed service that can organize, retrieve, and provide access to hierarchically related information. The information can be in various forms: library catalogs, databases, newsgroups, and so on. Gopher servers are available at various locations throughout the Internet, and are accessible through TELNET or through a gopher client. While gopher is still being used, support for this service is being dropped from newer software. For example, version 4 of Microsoft's Internet Information Server (IIS) no longer supports gopher. One reason for the decline in gopher's popularity is that it is largely text based, and its capabilities are far exceeded by those provided, using HTTP, over the Web.

A gopher client can make use of any accessible gopher servers. The details of a gopher session depend on which gopher server you use to access the Internet and on the information that you request.

In a gopher session, you can access the requested information through a single, dynamic menu system, regardless of where on the Internet the information is actually located. This is because a gopher, in essence, organizes and presents all the information within a single "gopherspace."

For retrieval, a gopher (which comes from the expression "go fer") server must know a file's type in order to determine how to handle the file when passing it on to the client. For example, plain text or HTML (Hypertext markup language) files are passed as stored, unless the file has been compressed. In that case, the server will uncompress the file before passing it to the client.

To make gopher easier and more efficient to use, two tools are often used:

- *Veronica* makes it easier to search for an item. Veronica will search all accessible gopher servers, check all their menus, and return information about those items that satisfy the specified search criteria. Veronica servers can search on substrings and can even handle Boolean (AND, OR, NOT) operators in the search strings. (The name comes from the *Archie* comic strip, which features a character named Veronica. The name is in recognition of the fact that Veronica does for gopher servers what the archie service does for FTP sites—namely, collect and search a summary of their contents.)

- *Jughead* makes it possible to limit searches to a specified set of gopher servers. (This time the name is in honor of Archie's other friend in the comic strip.)

In addition, gopher clients allow you to create bookmarks to mark a menu or directory. Once a bookmark has been created, you can jump immediately to the menu or directory at the bookmark. This saves the time of moving manually through a hierarchy of gopher menus. Using a variant of the bookmark, you can record a gopher search so you can repeat the search regularly, if desired.

→ *See Also* Internet; WAIS

GoS (Grade of Service)

In telephony, a general measure of performance with respect to a particular variable. Most commonly, GoS refers to the probability that a call will get a busy signal or a long delay before connection. For example, if 1 call in 500 gets a busy signal, the GoS probability would be 0.002.

GOSIP (Government OSI Profile)

The OSI Reference Model as defined by the United States government. Compliance with this standard is required for many types of purchases for government installations, and particularly for those purchases having to do with networking.

Government OSI Profile (GOSIP)

→ *See* GOSIP (Government OSI Profile)

GPIB (General-Purpose Interface Bus)

A parallel interface that is very popular for connecting scientific apparatus to computers. This interface was developed at Hewlett-Packard (HP) for in-house use, and is sometimes still known as the *HPIB*. GPIB has been standardized by the IEEE as IEEE-488.

GPS (Global Positioning System)

GPS is a satellite-based system that makes it possible to determine where on earth you are. GPS consists of 24 satellites orbiting the earth about every 12 hours, at an orbit distance of about 20,200 kilometers. Using signals from these satellites and a handheld receiver, you can determine your location to within about 100 feet. A military craft or vehicle can determine its location to within an even smaller distance—about 10 or 15 feet. To establish your location, the receiver must get signals from three of the GPS satellites.

The timing signals from GPS satellites are very accurate. In fact, they are so accurate that you could use them to synchronize operations on digital networks. Used this way, the timing signals replace the Primary Reference Sources (PRS) networks ordinarily used to synchronize devices and operations.

Grace Login

A login in which the user logs in with an expired password. In many networks, passwords are valid only for a limited time. After that time has elapsed, a user must change his or her password. Most networks allow a limited number of grace logins before the user must change the password.

Graded-Index Fiber

In fiber optics, cable in which the cladding, or cover, around the fiber core consists of multiple layers, each with a slightly different index of refraction. This provides a cleaner signal than single-step fiber.

→ *See Also* Cable, Fiber-Optic

Grade of Service (GoS)

→ *See* GoS (Grade of Service)

Graphical User Interface (GUI)

→ *See* GUI (Graphical User Interface)

Greenwich Mean Time (GMT)

→ *See* GMT (Greenwich Mean Time)

G

Ground

An electrical reference voltage for other voltages in a system. Any network must be grounded, as must network segments. In a circuit, a ground is a common return path for electric current. A ground and polarity checker is a tool for testing the grounding and polarity (direction of flow) of a circuit.

Ground Start

In telephone communications, a signaling technique in which a party gets a dial tone by grounding the circuit in a private branch exchange (PBX). This grounding helps to prevent a collision between incoming and outgoing calls, which is a condition known as *glare*. Pay telephones and phones in a PBX often use ground start.

Ground Wave

In wireless communications, a low-frequency radio signal that travels over the earth's surface.

Groupe Special Mobile (GSM)

→ *See* GSM (Global System for Mobile Communications)

Group, Network

In networking, a group is an organizational concept that can help make network administration easier. A group contains multiple members, all of whom share resources, files, or data. The network administrator can assign rights to an entire group, making these rights available to every member of that group.

Most network operating systems support the creation and use of groups, but these systems differ in the number of groups allowed and in the ease with which a group can be created, modified, or retrieved.

In Novell's NetWare versions 2.*x* and 3.*x*, the special group EVERYONE contains all users.

Group, Telecommunications

In telecommunications, a telecommunications group is a communications channel formed by combining 12, 4 kilohertz (kHz) voice channels, each using a different carrier frequency. This 48kHz "superchannel" is transmitted in broadband fashion, with all channels transmitted simultaneously, using frequency division multiplexing (FDM) with analog signals and time division multiplexing (TDM) with digital signals. A group in the telecommunications context is also known as a *group channel*. The frequency spectrum used by a group is known as a *group signal*.

Just as channels are combined into groups, groups are combined into supergroups, and so on up the hierarchy shown in the table "Telecommunications Groupings."

TELECOMMUNICATIONS GROUPINGS

# of 4kHz Voice Channels	Grouping Name
12	Group
60 (5 groups)	Supergroup
600 (10 supergroups)	Mastergroup
3,600 (6 mastergroups)	Jumbogroup

The hierarchy in the table is only one of several methods used for grouping channels. The groupings in the table represent the L-carrier systems used by the various baby Bells. In contrast, a grouping hierarchy developed by the International Telecommunications Union (ITU) combines five 60-channel supergroups into a single 300-channel master group. Three such master groups are combined into a 1500-channel supermastergroup. In the ITU hierarchy, there are no jumbogroups.

Group Object

In Novell's NetWare 4.0 Directory tree, a type of *leaf object* that has several user objects associated with it. Group objects allow administrators to grant several users rights at the same time, in the same way rights can be granted to network groups.

Groupware

Groupware is a client-server based software genre that shares features with several other types of applications, but that generally puts its own unique slant on these features.

Like a database, groupware allows multiple individuals to share a common pool of information. Unlike a database, however, each group member can view and handle the information in a manner tailored to that group member's needs.

In fact, groupware can be designed to enforce domain-specific views of the information. That is, particular group members may have limited views of the material. For example, personnel or customer information in a corporate database may be available to people in several departments, but each department may get a different view of the data. Thus, a technical support person may need to know a customer's configuration and software purchases, but that person doesn't need access to information about the customer's credit, occupation, or demographics.

Groupware also shares features with integrated software (for example, Lotus SmartSuite, Microsoft Office, or Corel's PerfectOffice) in that various types of tools are available within an integrated environment. Unlike such suites, however, groupware is designed for use by multiple individuals who need to exchange information and to update it in a synchronized manner. In contrast, a software suite is designed to provide a single individual with a variety of tools in an integrated, easy-to-switch environment. It's irrelevant whether the individual uses the different tools on a single body of material or on independent content. For example, the user of a software suite may decide to use a spreadsheet for sales data, presentation software for dealing with product information, and a document processor to create ad copy.

Like workflow software, groupware allows users to develop material and then pass it off to other project members. Unlike workflow software, however, groupware need not be restricted to time- or sequence-dependent exchanges.

Like document management software, groupware uses a document (rather than a database record) as its standard element. Document management packages are designed to provide archiving capabilities and to allow multiple users access to the documents. Such packages are generally designed to allow document users to communicate indirectly—through the document, so to speak. In contrast, groupware is designed to allow users to communicate directly with each other—either about or with documents. To make this possible, a groupware product will include some type of electronic mail service.

In addition to its application-based features, groupware also includes development tools. These are essential because the software's capabilities must be tailored to a group's particular needs. To make this possible, it is often necessary to create services that can handle the group's documents in the appropriate manner.

Lotus Notes is arguably the best-known example of groupware.

➞ *See Also* Integrated Software Suite; Lotus Notes; Workflow Software

GSM (Global System for Mobile Communications)

GSM was originally developed in the mid-1990s to provide a standard technology that would unify the confused and incompatible state of cellular communications in Europe. The Groupe Special Mobile (whence the abbreviation) was formed by the European Conference of Post and Telecommunications Administrations to create the desired standard.

The group's mandate was to develop a standard that would do the following:

- Support any type of mobile communications device.

- Allow roaming within any GSM country.

- Use digital technology to provide services (see below) of the sort available with ISDN (Integrated Services Digital Network) technology.

- Operate efficiently in two frequency ranges: 890–915MHz and 935–960MHz.

- Be able to coexist with existing systems in the same frequency bands.

A special variant operating in the 1800MHz range was developed for use in Britain, and it has also come to be widely used in densely populated areas. This variant is known as DCS1800, for Digital Communications Services 1800.

GSM Services

The GSM specifications drew heavily on the ISDN architecture and model. Like ISDN, GSM distinguishes between basic and supplementary services.

Basic Services

Two categories of basic services are defined:

- Bearer services are those that make communications between two parties possible. In networking terms, bearer services cover the lower three layers (physical, data link, and network) of the seven-layer OSI Reference Model. These services make it possible to establish a connection and to send signals across that connection.

- Teleservices are those that make it possible to exchange meaningful information—that is, to actually communicate over the connection. In the networking model, teleservices correspond to the upper four network layers (transport, session, presentation, and application). Telephony, fax services, and telex are all examples of teleservices.

Supplementary Services

Supplementary services provide added value to telecommunications by enhancing both bearer services and teleservices. Examples of supplementary services include caller identification, call forwarding, conference calling, and call blocking.

The Spread of GSM

Although developed originally for use in Europe, GSM was soon adopted in Africa, the Middle East, and the Pacific region. In contrast, the dominant cellular communications technology in North and South America was the analog AMPS (Advanced Mobile Phone Service). However, in the past year or so, GSM services have become available and Global System for Mobile Communications has come to be used as the expansion for GSM in English-speaking countries.

GSM's prospects as a dominant cellular technology are promising.

GSM (Groupe Special Mobile)

→ *See* GSM (Global System for Mobile Communications)

GSTN (General Switch Telephone Network)

A public telephone network.

Guaranteed Bandwidth

In networking or telecommunications, the capability for transmitting continuously and reliably at a specified transmission speed. The guarantee makes it possible to send time-dependent data (such as voice, video, or multimedia) over the line.

Guard Band

In telecommunications and electrical transmissions, a guard band (sometimes written guardband) is a thin frequency band used to separate bands (channels) above and below the guard band. By providing a gap between the two channels, the guard band helps prevent interference and signal leakage.

In cellular communications, a guard band is a 3MHz band that separates two voice channels, in order to keep the channels from interfering with each other.

In the never-ending quest to transmit more and more quickly, some vendors have developed products that transmit data along these guard bands.

Guard Time

In time division multiplexed (TDM) signaling, a brief interval of "silence" between transmissions. This period can be used for synchronization and for compensating for signal distortion. This is the temporal analog to a guard band.

Guest

In many networks, Guest is a special account or user name. This account is for the use of anyone who needs to log in to the network for public information. The access must be temporary, and the account is afforded only restricted access rights.

For example, in Windows NT, Guest is one of the two accounts created automatically by the operating system during installation—the other is the Administrator account. The Guest account gives one-time users access to a limited number of services or facilities on the network, presumably without giving the user access to any sensitive information or to any system services from which the user could gain administrator rights or other types of control over the network. When a Guest

user logs off, all the user's preferences and configuration changes are discarded so that there is no trace of the user after the session.

Experts advise against allowing anonymous users from the Internet to gain access to your network through a Guest account. Rather, such users should get access through another, IUSR_computername, account set up by the operating system for this purpose.

Guest Account

→ *See* Guest

GUI (Graphical User Interface)

A graphically based interface, such as a Microsoft Windows, Motif, or Macintosh interface. In GUIs (pronounced "gooeys"), information and commands are presented through icons, and the user gives commands by pointing to or manipulating the icons. GUIs are in contrast to character-based interfaces, such as the default interfaces for DOS or UNIX.

G

Guided Media

Transmission media that constrain the electromagnetic, acoustic, or optical signal because of physical properties of the medium. For example, in fiber-optic transmissions, the cladding reflects the signal back into the core. Similarly, coaxial or twisted-pair cable constrains the electrical signal, and telephone lines constrain an acoustic signal.

Guidelines for the Definition of Managed Objects (GDMO)

→ *See* GDMO (Guidelines for the Definition of Managed Objects)

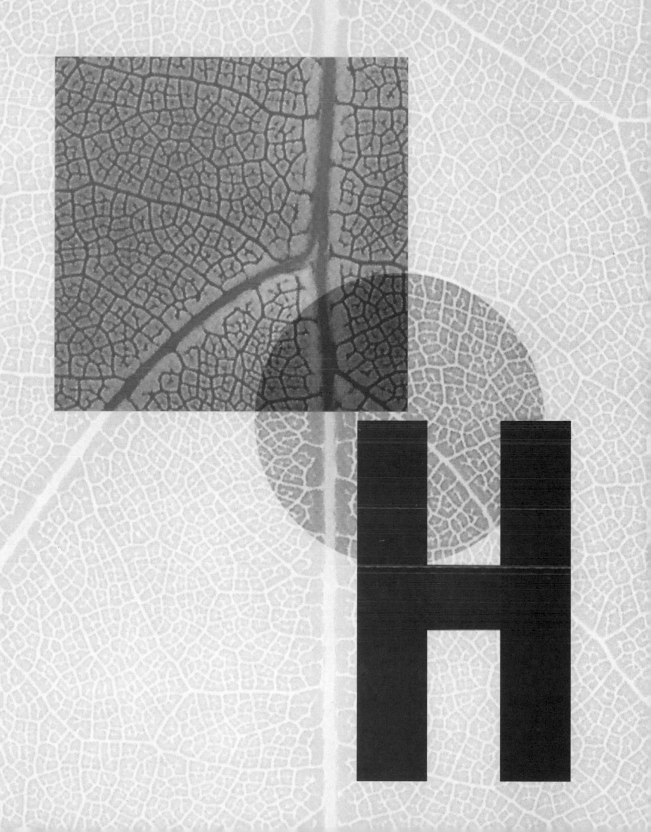

H.xxx

The H.xxx series of publications includes ITU-T (International Telecommunications Union—Telecommunication Standardization Sector) specifications and definitions related to the transmission of non-telephone signals. These include audiovisual content, data, fax, telegraphy, videoconferencing, and videophone. Table "Selected H-Series Recommendations" lists a few of the documents currently in force in this series.

SELECTED H-SERIES RECOMMENDATIONS

Recommendation	Description
H.21	Provides specifications and terminology for international voice-frequency telegraph systems.
H.34	Provides guidelines on subdividing the frequency band of a telephone-type circuit for use in telegraphy and other services.
H.43	Specifies standards for the transmission of document facsimiles over leased telephone lines.
H.51	Specifies power levels for data transmissions over telephone lines.
H.52	Specifies standards for the transmission of wide-spectrum signals (data, fax, etc.) over wideband group links.
H.100	Specifies standards for equipment related to visual telephone and videoconferencing systems.
H.120	Specifies standards for codecs for videoconferencing using primary digital group transmissions.
H.130	Specifies frame structures for use in international interconnections of codecs used for videoconferencing or visual telephony.
H.140	Describes a multipoint, international videoconferencing system.
H.221	Specifies a frame structure for audiovisual "teleservices" using a channel with a possible bandwidth ranging from 64 to 1920Kbps.
H.230	Defines various control and indication signals for audiovisual systems.
H.231	Describes a multipoint control unit for audiovisual systems using digital channels at speeds up to 2Mbps.
H.233	Specifies data encryption standards for real-time multimedia and other audiovisual services.
H.234	Specifies standards for encryption key management and authentication systems for audiovisual services.
H.242	Defines a system for establishing communications between audiovisual terminals using digital channels at speeds up to 2Mbps.
H.261	Specifies a standard for video-compression codecs for use with ISDN or other services that manage data in multiples of 64Kbps. H.261 supports CIF and QCIF images.
H.263	Extends and improves H.261 to increase efficiency and to provide support for SQCIF, 4CIF, and 16CIF images.
H.320	Defines narrowband visual telephone systems and terminal equipment for transmitting real-time multimedia over ISDN or other circuit-switched services. This specification uses voice signals based on the G.711 and G.728 standards.
H.321	Specifies standards for real-time multimedia transmitted over broadband multipoint systems and terminal equipment—as used in B-ISDN (Broadband ISDN) and in ATM (Asynchronous Transfer Mode).
H.322	Specifies standards for real-time multimedia transmitted over packet-switched networks and with a guaranteed bandwidth.
H.323	Extends H.320 to provide standards for real-time multimedia transmitted over packet-switched networks, such as intranets and LANs. H.323 is based on the RTP (Real-time Transport Protocol), and uses video based on the H.261 and H.263 standards, voice based on the G.711 and G.728 standards, encryption based on the H.233 and H.234 standards, and data based on the T.120 standard.
H.324	Extends H.320 to provide standards for real-time multimedia transmitted over analog POTS (Plain Old Telephone Service) lines. Such transmissions use V.34 or faster modems. H.324 relies on the same standards as H.320, but uses the G.723 standard for audio because it supports compressed audio signals.

Hacker

An avid computer user who enjoys exploring and testing the limits of computers, and who enjoys "hacking together" solutions to programming or other computing problems. Hackers often extend their zealous explorative tendencies to others' computers—breaking into networks, corporate or university computers, etc. Generally, however, these explorations don't have any malicious or destructive goals.

In contrast, the term cracker is used to describe users who do have destructive plans when they break into other computer systems. Unfortunately, in general parlance, hacker has come to be used for both of these sometimes intrusive types.

HAL (Hardware Abstraction Layer)

In Windows NT and NT Advanced Server, the HAL mediates between the operating system kernel and specific hardware. By implementing functions for interfaces, caches, interrupts, and so on, the HAL can make every piece of hardware look the same to the higher layers. This helps make NT more transportable to other machines.

Half Bridge

In wide area networks, either of a pair of bridges that are separated by a telecommunications link. Instead of connecting directly to another network, the half bridge is connected to another half bridge by telephone or other long-distance cable.

Half Duplex (HDX)

Half duplex refers to a communication setup in which transmissions can go in either direction, but in only one direction at a time. With half-duplex operation, the entire bandwidth can be used for the transmission.

In contrast, full-duplex operation must split the bandwidth between the two directions.

Half-Open Connection

A "wannabe" (that is, incomplete) connection, half of which is already established. The other half is still open (not connected). For example, a half-open connection exists after you finish dialing a telephone number but before the call starts ringing.

Half Router

Either of a pair of routers that are separated by a telecommunications link. The link is transparent to non-router stations, so that the two halves of the router together look like a single, full-function router.

Hamming Code

A Hamming code is a true error-correcting code, which works by inserting extra bits at predefined locations in a transmission. Mathematically, the spacing and values of these bits makes it possible to determine if an error has occurred, where the error is, and how to correct it.

→ *See Also* Error Detection and Correction

Handle

In an operating system, a pointer to a resource or a feature, such as a file or device. The supply of handles may be limited by the operating system or environment. For example, DOS allows up to 20 file handles by default.

In a networking context, handle refers to a user's name or nickname online. This may be a username or a name used to identify the user in online discussion or chat groups. The term nick is also used to refer to a discussion group member's name.

H

Hand-off

In cellular communications, hand-off refers to the transfer of a connection from one cell to another. Hand-off time is generally between 200 and 1200 milliseconds (msec), which accounts for the delay you will sometimes hear when talking to someone on a cellular telephone.

Such a delay can cause problems for devices that require frequent reassurance that a connection still exists. For example, some modems will disconnect if a long delay occurs in a connection.

You will see this term written as both hand-off and handoff. Hats off to the language coiners, because so far they have kept their hands off making it two separate words.

Handshaking

Handshaking is an exchange of signaling information between two communications systems. Handshaking establishes how the two systems will transmit data.

Two broad classes of handshaking are distinguished:

- Hardware handshaking uses the request to send (RTS) and clear to send (CTS) pins to control transmissions.

- Software handshaking uses the XON and XOFF characters to signal when to stop and start the transmission.

Hard Disk

A hard disk is a magnetic storage device consisting of multiple spinning platters (disks), each with its own read/write heads. Hard disk drives have a much higher storage capacity (up to 15GB or more) than floppy disks. They also have a much faster access time and higher transfer rate than floppy disk drives. The access times of hard disks are as low as 5 to 20 milliseconds (msec); floppy disk access times are 200 msec or more.

Hard disks differ from each other (and from floppy disk drives) in the interfaces and formats (encoding techniques and rules) they use, and also in the speed with which the disk spins. Faster spin rates generally mean higher throughput.

Hard Disk Interfaces

Interfaces differ in the capacities and transfer speeds they support. The following are some widely used hard disk interfaces:

- ESDI (Enhanced Small Device Interface), which supports medium- to high-capacity drives, with capacities of up to 2GB. Transfer speeds of 1 to 3MBps are typical.

- IDE (Integrated Drive Electronics), which combines controller and hard disk into a single integrated, and more intelligent, unit. The disadvantage is that you cannot format such a drive yourself. This interface is often used on laptops, partly because it is an integrated drive. It can support capacities of up to .5GB, but it is typically used for drives with capacities of a few hundred megabytes. Transfer rates can be as high as 2Mbps.

- EIDE (Enhanced Integrated Drive Electronics), which is a superset of the IDE interface. EIDE can handle 1GB and larger hard disks. Support for this enhanced interface is provided by a controller chip on the motherboard. While the EIDE (and the IDE) specifications were developed originally for the ISA (Industry Standard Architecture) bus architecture, the interface is also used with other bus standards, such as PCI (Peripheral Component Interconnect). The EIDE interface's popularity was somewhat tarnished recently when a silent, data-corrupting bug was found if certain EIDE controllers were used in a particular way. This flaw affects certain PCI motherboards that contain a particular EIDE controller chip. It was reported in August 1995 in the comp.os.os2.bugs newsgroup.

- IPI (Intelligent Peripheral Interface), which supports transfer rates of up to 25 MBps and storage capacities of several gigabytes.

- SCSI (Small Computer System Interface), which provides a generic interface for other devices (scanners, CD-ROM drives, other hard disks, and so on) and can support very high-capacity drives. SCSI can support up to eight devices in a single expansion slot. Two major versions of this interface have appeared: SCSI-1 and SCSI-2. SCSI-1, the slower, less capable of the pair, supports drives of up to 2GB and transfer rates as high as 5MBps. An ordinary SCSI-2 interface supports transfer rates of up to 10MBps. Wide SCSI, a 32-bit interface, can transfer up to 40MBps. SCSI-2 can support drives with capacities of 3GB or more.

- SMD (Storage Module Device), which is a medium speed (up to 4MBps) interface. SMD is commonly used with minicomputers and mainframes. SMD supports drives of up to 2GB.

Hard Disk Formats

Two encoding strategies provide the basic formats used on most hard drives: MFM and RLL. MFM (Modified Frequency Modulation) encoding is used for low-capacity disks of 50 MB or less and for floppy disks.

RLL (Run Length Limited) encoding can store twice as much in the same area as MFM, and can support very high-capacity drives. Because of this, RLL encoding is used with all the major hard disk interfaces.

Various flavors of RLL encoding can be defined. These differ in the fewest and most consecutive 0 values they can handle. For example, RLL 2,7 means a signal must receive at least two 0 values in succession but no more than seven. (MFM is actually a low-level version of RLL: RLL 1,3.)

Hard Error

In a token-ring network, a serious error that threatens the continued operation of the network. This is in contrast to a soft error, which will not bring down the network.

Hardware Abstraction Layer (HAL)

→ *See* HAL (Hardware Abstraction Layer)

Hardware, Network

The hardware for a network includes the following types of components: nodes, topology, connection elements, and auxiliary components. This article presents an overview of the hardware items. See the article about the specific component for more details on that component.

Nodes

The computers in a network may be used for workstations, servers, or both. A network can include PCs, Macintoshes, minicomputers, and even mainframes. PCs need a network interface card (NIC) installed for networking capabilities. Macintoshes and Sun workstations come with networking capabilities built in, so that a special card is not required to use the native network architecture for these machines.

The NICs mediate between the computer and the network by doing the necessary processing and translation to enable users to send or receive commands and data on the network. NICs are designed to support particular network architectures, such as Ethernet, ARCnet, or Token Ring.

Connection Elements

Network connection elements include the following:

Cable   Coaxial, twisted-pair, IBM type, or fiber-optic.

H

Wiring centers   Hubs, concentrators, or MAUs (multistation access units), as shown in "Wiring centers." Wiring centers gather multiple input lines and feed them into a smaller number of output lines—generally one. Centers differ in such details as what is at the other end of the lines and what is being carried over the lines. Lines coming into a wiring center (1) might include network nodes or telephone-line (voice or data) connections. Lines going out of the wiring center (2) may connect to a trunk that aggregates individual connections into a single outgoing channel or to a network server.

Intranetwork links   Connectors, repeaters, transceivers, switches, and so on, as shown in "Intranetwork links." Such links may connect component segments (as connectors or repeaters do, for example) or they may connect higher-level network elements (as switches do). Links that connect component segments (1) are (more or less) fixed. In contrast, switches (2) can connect different nodes at different times. With the appropriate switching components, a switch can connect any node to any other node when requested to do so.

Internetwork links   Bridges, routers, gateways, switches (sometimes), and so on, as shown in "Internetwork links." Routing tasks will play a role in any internetwork link—even if they are as simple as deciding whether or not to pass a packet to another network. Links such as bridges and gateways (1) often perform filtering tasks for the single network to which they provide access. Routers (2) work by filtering among multiple possible paths.

Wireless components   Transceivers, antennas, cells, satellites, and so on, as shown in "Wireless components." Each node on the network will have transmission capabilities (1)—for sending packets to other nodes. For some wireless networks (2), walls and ceilings are essential components as signal-relay elements. Each node will also be able to receive packets from other nodes (3). Generally, the transmission and receiving capabilities will be combined in a single transceiver.

Cable provides a transmission medium as well as a physical link between the nodes on the network. Connectors and repeaters attach cable sections to each other; connectors and transceivers attach NICs to a cable and thereby to the network. Switches allow you to connect different network nodes directly to each other (through the switch), which makes it possible to provide full bandwidth communication between the two nodes. Transceivers and baluns enable different types of cable to be connected to each other under certain conditions. Terminators absorb a transmission at the end of a network, thereby preventing the signal from traveling back in the other direction on the network. The types of intranetwork links allowed in a particular network will depend on the cable used and on the network topology.

Wiring Connector

WIRING CENTERS

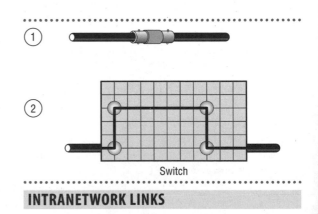

Switch

INTRANETWORK LINKS

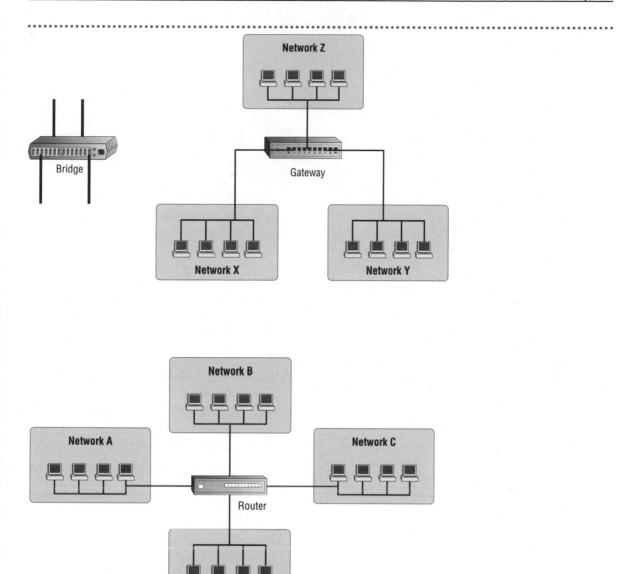

Bridge

Gateway

Router

INTERNETWORK LINKS

H

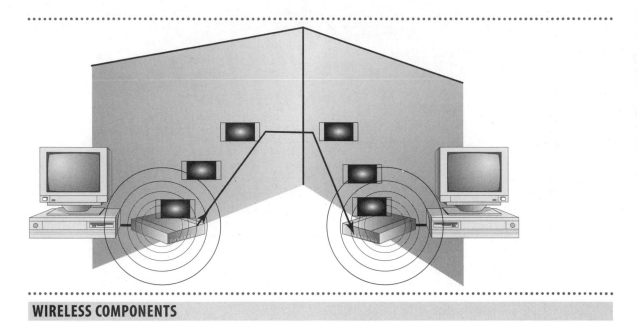

WIRELESS COMPONENTS

Wiring centers serve as focal points for network elements, and may also influence the logical arrangement of nodes on the network.

Internetwork links may be bridges, routers, gateways, and so on. In some cases, a switch can also connect two networks; switching and routing functions can also be combined in a switching router. Such components serve to connect networks to other networks. The type of internetwork connector used depends on whether the two networks are of the same type; that is, it depends on the type and amount of translation that is needed.

The details of wireless components and the conditions under which they can be used depend on the type of wireless connection (infrared, microwave, or radio wave transmission).

Auxiliary Components

Auxiliary components can include peripheral devices, safety devices, and tools.

Peripherals include printers, fax machines, modems, tape drives, CD-ROM drives, and so on. Such devices will generally be attached to a server machine, which will control access to the devices by the nodes on the network.

Safety devices include UPSs and SPSs (uninterruptible and standby power supplies), surge protectors, and line conditioners.

Tools include line analyzers, crimping tools, and so on. These tools are not part of the network itself, but should be available if needed.

Topology

The arrangement of cable and nodes in the network, known as the network topology, is also considered part of the hardware.

The physical topology represents the physical layout of the network, and is distinguished from the logical topology, which determines how communication takes place on the network. The logical topology may be bus or ring; the physical topology might be bus, ring, star, mesh, tree, and so on.

HARDWARE COMPATIBILITY

Check hardware compatibility very early in the network design and implementation process. The following are some tips on planning the hardware for your network:

- Several network vendors have certification programs, through which particular hardware combinations are tested and certified as compatible with each other and with the vendor's networking software. If you have the opportunity to do so, ask the vendors specific questions regarding compatibility.

- If a consultant or vendor is configuring your network for you, get a written guarantee that you will be provided with a working network. Note that this is not the same as a guarantee that you're getting a network that does what you need it to do.

When you're configuring a network, there are trade-offs with respect to the number of different vendors you deal with. Try to avoid buying all your equipment from a single source, because that makes you much too dependent on that source. If that source goes out of business, your own business could be threatened as the network components start breaking.

On the other hand, buying from too many different vendors is asking for compatibility and support problems. The greater the number of different components you have, the greater the likelihood that one or more of those components will have quirks that will cause difficulties when you least expect them. Keep in mind that support people tend to assume that the fault lies with a component other than theirs. Each vendor will try to get you to talk to the other vendors.

Harmonica

In cabling, a device than can convert a 25-pair cable into multiple 2-, 3-, or 4-pair cables.

Harmonica Block

In cabling, a wiring block that can be used to connect a limited number (up to a dozen) of RJ-11 plugs, each coming from different nodes, into a common wiring center.

Hashing

A process by which access to files or other information can be accelerated. This is accomplished through the use of an indexing function that decreases the number of elements that need to be searched. Hashing is commonly used for improving access to lists, such as dictionaries and directory lists.

HBA (Host Bus Adapter)

A special-purpose board designed to take over data storage and retrieval tasks, thereby saving the CPU (Central Processing Unit) some work. A disk channel consists of an HBA and the hard disk(s) associated with it. Novell's Disk Coprocessor board is a SCSI HBA adapter.

H Channel

In an ISDN (Integrated Services Digital Network) system, an H channel is any of several "higher-rate" channels that can be used for transmitting user data. An H channel can be leased as a single unit, and can then be subdivided into lower-bandwidth channels. These higher-speed channels are defined for situations where such high bandwidth is required, such as when transmitting video or other graphics information.

The following H channels are defined:

H0 A 384Kbps channel, which is equivalent to six B, or bearer, channels, each of which has a 64Kbps capacity.

H10 A 1.472Mbps channel, which represents just the 23 B channels for a PRI (Primary Rate Interface) line. This H channel is used only in the United States.

H11 A 1.536Mbps channel, which is equivalent to the PRI in the United States, Canada, and Japan. This 1.536 channel actually consists of 23 64Kbps B channels and one 64Kbps D channel.

The D channel is generally being used for signaling.

H12   A 1.92Mbps channel, which is equivalent to the 30 B channels in the European PRI.

→ *See Also*   B Channel; D Channel

HCSS (High-Capacity Storage System)

In Novell's NetWare 4.x and later, a storage system that includes optical disks as part of the file system. These provide slower, but much higher-capacity, storage for files. The HCSS oversees the use of these media, so that access to files on optical disks is transparent to the user.

The HCSS can move user data to and from the writable optical storage, as required. These processes are known as data migration (moving to) and demigration (moving from). Such migrations will be transparent to the user—even in directory listings.

Because the data migration and demigration processes are transparent, they must be able to start up automatically when required. Two criteria are used to determine when to migrate or demigrate data:

- Capacity threshold, which specifies the percentage of a hard disk that can be filled before the HCSS automatically moves some of the material to secondary storage.

- LRU, or least recently used selection criterion, which specifies that the file(s) with the oldest "last used" date will be the first to be moved to secondary storage; the second oldest will be stored second, and so forth.

HDLC (High-Level Data Link Control)

→ *See*   Protocol, HDLC (High-Level Data Link Control)

HDSL (High-Bit-Rate Digital Subscriber Line)

HDSL is a symmetric variant of digital subscriber line (DSL) technology. DSL connections make use of ordinary analog telephone lines to support high-speed transmission of digital signals. In particular, DSL technology uses the local loop—the lines going from a customer's premises (home or office) to the telephone company's central office (CO)—to get its signal to the digital environment and connections at the CO. The entry for the best known variant, ADSL (Asymmetric Digital Subscriber Line), describes the technology in greater detail.

HDSL achieves speeds of up to 1.544Mbps in North America and up to 2.048Mbps elsewhere. HDSL supports these speeds in both directions, which is where the technology gets its "symmetric" label. The bandwidth differences between North America and the rest of the world are due to standards, rather than technological limitations. In North America, the standard high-speed line—a T1—is built out of (multiplexed from) 24 64Kbps channels; in Europe and most other parts of the world, the standard high-speed line—an E1—is built out of 30 channels.

To attain its high throughput, HDSL uses two wire pairs. HDSL2, a newer variant, achieves the same speeds using only a single wire pair. HDSL2 will also provide more interoperability between products from different vendors.

These high communications speeds do come at a cost, however. First, DSL lines are currently available only in densely populated areas, where most premises are within 2 or 3 miles of a CO. This is because the high speeds attainable by DSL technology can only be sustained for distances of about 15,000 feet for HDSL, and about 18,000 feet in the best of cases (strong and clean signal, new and minimally bent wiring, no heavy machinery nearby).

HDSL also requires special equipment to handle the digital signal at either end of the local loop, as shown in "An HDSL configuration." HDSL

Terminal Units (HTUs) are required at the CO and also the customer, or remote, end. These are known as the HTU-C and HTU-R, respectively, and they provide the main DSL connection in HDSL configurations. At the customer end, the HTU-R (R for remote) connects to the customer premises equipment, which is likely to be a high-speed multiplexer—for example, with a T1 bandwidth of 1.544Mbps. (Even though the HTU-R is at the customer's end, it is still phone company equipment.) The two HTUs are connected by one or two copper wires—depending on the desired speeds, the distances involved, and the line quality. At the phone company's CO, the HTU-C receives transmissions and passes them to a cross-connect, where the connections can be routed to the appropriate wiring trunks for the destination.

These devices are comparable to DSUs (Data Service Units), which are used in digital communications. However, HTUs are not modems, because the transmission between the two HTUs is entirely digital. HTUs are sometimes also known as HDSL transceiver units.

Other DSL variants include ADSL (asymmetric DSL), CDSL (consumer DSL), IDSL (ISDN DSL), RADSL (rate-adaptive DSL), SDSL (symmetric or single-pair DSL), and VDSL (very high speed DSL).

→ *Broader Category* High-Speed Access Technologies

→ *Compare* ADSL (Asymmetric Digital Subscriber Line); DSL (Digital Subscriber Line); CDSL (Consumer Digital Subscriber Line); IDSL (ISDN Digital Subscriber Line); RADSL (Rate-Adaptive Digital Subscriber Line); SDSL (Symmetric Digital Subscriber Line); VDSL (Very High Speed Digital Subscriber Line)

HDSL2 (High-Bit-Rate Digital Subscriber Line 2)

→ *See* HDSL (High-Bit-Rate Digital Subscriber Line)

HDSL Terminal Unit (HTU)

→ *See* HTU (HDSL Terminal Unit)

H

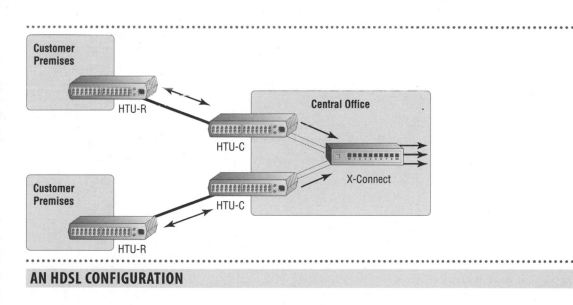

AN HDSL CONFIGURATION

HDSL Terminal Unit, Central Office (HTU-C)

→ *See* HTU (HDSL Terminal Unit)

HDSL Terminal Unit, Remote (HTU-R)

→ *See* HTU (HDSL Terminal Unit)

HDX (Half Duplex)

HDX refers to a communication setup in which transmissions can go in either direction, but in only one direction at a time. With half-duplex operation, the entire bandwidth can be used for the transmission. In contrast, full-duplex operation must split the bandwidth between the two directions.

Head End

In a broadband network, the starting point for transmissions to end users. For example, cable network's broadcast station is a head end. End-user stations can generally transmit control and error information, but no data, to the head end. The term is also used to refer to the base, or root, node in a tree topology, or a node on either of the buses in a DQDB (Distributed Queue, Dual Bus) architecture.

Header

In a transmission packet, the header contains control and other information that precedes the data in the packet. Header fields include source and destination addresses, packet type information, various types of identifier information, and so on.

In addition to header and data portions, a packet may also have a trailer section after the data. The trailer generally includes error-detection fields, such as cyclic redundancy checks (CRCs).

In an e-mail (electronic mail) message, the header is the information that precedes the actual message. The message header includes information such as the sender's address, message subject, date, and time.

Header Error Control (HEC)

→ *See* HEC (Header Error Control)

HEC (Header Error Control)

An 8-bit field in an ATM-cell header. Its value is calculated using the remaining 32 bits of the header in order to detect errors in the header. Because the HEC field is relatively large (compared with the cell size), this value can even be used to correct single-bit errors.

→ *See Also* ATM (Asynchronous Transfer Mode)

Helper Application

→ *See* Plug-In

Hertz (Hz)

A unit of frequency. Hertz is used, for example, to describe the periodic properties of acoustic, electrical, and optical signals. One hertz is equal to one cycle per second.

Heterogeneous Network

A network that is using multiple protocols at the network layer. In contrast, a homogeneous network uses a single protocol at the network layer.

Hexadecimal

Hexadecimal is a number system that uses 16, instead of the more common 10, as the base for place value holders. Each place value is 16 times the preceding place value. For example, 1, 16, and 256 represent the hexadecimal place values corresponding to the 1, 10, and 100 values in the decimal (base 10) system.

To supplement the ten digits (0 through 9), hexadecimal notation uses the letters a through f (in uppercase or lowercase) in order to represent the values 10 through 15, respectively. Thus, the hexadecimal value B9 represents 185: $11 \times 16 + 9$.

Hexadecimal values are written with a leading 0x (zero and x) or with a trailing H. For example, 0xb9 and B9H represent the same decimal value.

Each hexadecimal value takes four bits, so that a byte consists of two hexadecimal digits. The table "Binary, Decimal, and Hexadecimal Values" shows the decimal and hexadecimal values corresponding to the 16 possible 4-bit sequences, and to a few select byte values.

BINARY, DECIMAL, AND HEXADECIMAL VALUES

Bit Sequence	Hexadecimal	Decimal
0000	0H	0
0001	1H	1
0010	2H	2
0011	3H	3
0100	4H	4
0101	5H	5
0110	6H	6
0111	7H	7
1000	8H	8
1001	9H	9
1010	AH	10
1011	BH	11
1100	CH	12
1101	DH	13
1110	EH	14
1111	FH	15
1111 0000	F0H	240
1111 0111	F7H	247
1111 1111	FFH	255

HFC (Hybrid Fiber/Coax)

A configuration that uses HFC consists of both coaxial and fiber-optic cable. Such configurations are used, for example, by cable companies. While this can increase the bandwidth for the fiber-based segments, some of the throughput gains may be offset, in certain cases, by a need to convert a digital signal (traveling over fiber) into an analog one (for the coaxial section of the signal transmission). Cable TV providers used to send both data and TV signals in analog form, but are rapidly moving to digital transmission technologies for both. The conversion between digital and analog forms is made by a cable modem.

HFS (Hierarchical File System)

The file system for the Macintosh operating system.

Hiccup

A transmission error in which data is dropped and must be retransmitted. Hiccups may be caused by momentary line or port interference, buffer overflow, power losses or surges, or by simple computer or program perversity.

Hierarchical Database

→ *See* Database

Hierarchical File System (HFS)

→ *See* HFS (Hierarchical File System)

Hierarchical Name Structure

A naming strategy that relies on the hierarchical relationship between two entities. This strategy is used, for example, for files or network entities. In a network context, a node's name is based on the name of the parent node, which sits immediately above the node in a hierarchy. Compare this with a flat name structure.

Hierarchical Routing

In an internetwork, hierarchical routing is routing in which multiple levels of networks (or of routers) are distinguished.

For example, in the Internet, three routing levels may be used: backbone, midlevel, and stub. At the backbone level, routing among midlevel networks is supported; at the mid-level networks, routing between sites (stub networks) is supported. At a particular site, internal routing among the network's nodes is supported.

Hierarchical Storage Management (HSM)

→ *See* HSM (Hierarchical Storage Management)

High-Bit-Rate Digital Subscriber Line (HDSL)

→ *See* HDSL (High-Bit-Rate Digital Subscriber Line)

High-Bit-Rate Digital Subscriber Line 2 (HDSL2)

→ *See* HDSL (High-Bit-Rate Digital Subscriber Line)

High-Capacity Storage System (HCSS)

→ *See* HCSS (High-Capacity Storage System)

High-Level Data Link Control (HDLC)

→ *See* Protocol, HDLC (High-Level Data Link Control)

High Level Language Application Program Interface (HLLAPI)

→ *See* HLLAPI (High Level Language Application Program Interface)

High Memory Area (HMA)

→ *See* HMA (High Memory Area)

High-Performance File System (HPFS)

→ *See* HPFS (High-Performance File System)

High-Performance Parallel Interface (HiPPI)

→ *See* HiPPI (High-Performance Parallel Interface)

High-Speed Access Technologies

Although data can travel across a corporate (inter)network or the Internet at hundreds of megabits per second, and even faster in some cases, a user dialing in from home is likely to be communicating at less than one thousandth of that speed. Until recently, access technologies have been a major—if not the biggest—limiting factor in network access over long distances.

Modem technology is still, by far, the most popular way of dialing into a network or logging onto the Internet. However, modems have their limitations, which are becoming acutely felt.

Modem communications have improved steadily over the years, from their very humble 300bps beginnings. This improvement has come in a very short time period. Less than 10 years ago, computer users could get excited about a modem speed increase from 14.4 to 28.8Kbps. A file that took three hours to transmit at 14.4Kbps took only an hour and a half at the 28.8Kbps "superspeed." Their excitement might have been tempered a bit had they realized that, within a few years, they would be able to send the same material in a single second—over a 155Mbps ATM (Asynchronous Transfer Mode) connection.

With the recent entrenchment of 56Kbps modems, standard modem technology has pretty much reached its limit—it looks very much as if 56Kbps is the highest speed at which analog modems will communicate. Even the 56Kbps is an overstatement of the maximum speed possible with an analog modem. For reasons having to do with maximum power allowances, the fastest transmission possible with a 56K modem is really only about 53Kbps. And even this speed is rare because it requires squeaky—or, perhaps more accurately, squeakless—clean lines. In practice, speeds of 35 to 45Kbps are most likely.

An investment in ISDN (Integrated Services Digital Network)—that is, a switch from analog to digital telephone service—provides a modest increase in access speed at a fairly substantial financial cost. Without doing anything fancy (such as aggregating ISDN lines), access speeds of 64 and even 128Kbps are possible using ISDN.

While such access speeds are very fast compared to the original 300bps, they still pale in comparison to the speeds at which traffic moves across the Internet backbone. Over the past few years, however, several technologies have become available that offer access to the Internet or other networks at speeds approaching 1Mbps and higher—still only a fraction of online speeds, but a considerably larger fraction.

Four promising technologies are described briefly here. Separate entries for each of the technologies provide more detailed accounts. Each of the technologies has unique features, advantages, and drawbacks. Proponents for each of them are betting—in some cases, betting heavily—that their technology will become the high-speed access technology of the future (or at least until an even faster one comes around).

ADSL and the Other DSL Cousins

Asymmetric digital subscriber line (ADSL) is arguably the best-known variant of a technology that can deliver high bandwidth—at least in the downstream direction—using only ordinary analog telephone lines, but with some special equipment attached at either end, as shown in "An ADSL connection." Some DSL variants allow you to talk and send data simultaneously over these lines. Those that do, require special equipment that can split or combine the voice and data signals depending on which way the transmission is going and which side the splitter is on.

In an ADSL connection, a subscriber (1) can send both voice and data signals simultaneously. These are split into two channels in the sender's ADSL modem, and transmitted to the ADSL modem at the receiving end. Here (2)— usually the telephone company's central office (CO)—the signals are sent on to an appropriate device. Voice signals (3) are sent to the PSTN (Public Switched Telephone Network) and data signals to a multiplexing device known as a DSLAM (DSL Access Multiplexer). A subscriber's data signals are multiplexed with signals from other subscribers. They are then sent on (4) over high-speed lines to their destination—which is generally an access

H

provider. The high-speed transmission usually goes through an ATM switch.

The asymmetric in the name indicates that the technology supports different speeds in the upstream (subscriber to service provider) and downstream (service provider to subscriber) directions. In all cases, the downstream speeds are higher—which is as it should be because, presumably, most subscribers do much more downloading than uploading. The table "Example Asymmetric DSL Connections" shows supported upstream and downstream speeds for several asymmetric DSL variants.

RADSL is similar to ADSL, except that it can adjust the transmission rates according to line quality. CDSL is a low-end technology that works with simpler special equipment. This equipment can handle either voice or data, but not both at the same time. CDSL hardware is simple and inexpensive enough to make that manufacturers hope eventually to ship new PCs with such modems already included.

VDSL is still largely a technology of the future, but promises great things once it has arrived. It is intended for use in situations where a high-speed fiber-optic line—possibly an ATM connection—is available to move the data on its path.

The maximum distances in table "Example Asymmetric DSL Connections" refer to the longest stretch of wire over which the transmission speeds can be supported. Note that the extremely high speeds of VDSL can be supported for less than a mile. This means that a subscriber would need to live within about 1500 yards of a central exchange to take full advantage of VDSL's capabilities.

Symmetric variants support equal upstream and downstream speeds. The table "Example Symmetric DSL Connections" provides information about three symmetric variants.

HDSL and HDSL2 differ in that HDSL uses two pairs of wires for its transmissions, whereas HDSL2 uses only a single pair. SDSL also uses only a single wire pair, but supports only half the speed of HDSL2. IDSL is really just an ISDN BRI (Basic Rate Interface) (two 64Kbps bearer, or B, channels and one 16Kbps D channel) line, except that it travels over the analog local loop lines.

DSL connections—generally ADSL—are still only available in limited areas. Not surprisingly, these tend to be in more populous regions where there are lots of potential subscribers. This is also to be expected because rural telephone customers are more likely to be great distances from a central

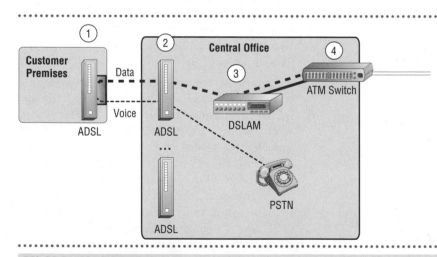

AN ADSL CONNECTION

exchange, which means they are more likely to exceed the maximum allowed distances for the DSL transmission.

Pricing for DSL services varies considerably. Subscribers in some areas can get ADSL service and a connection to an ISP (Internet Service Provider) for about $40–50 per month, and can also have equipment charges and installation fees waived. In contrast subscribers in other areas may have to pay over $100 per month, in addition to sizable equipment and installation fees.

For more details, see the entries for the individual variants listed in the tables, and also for DSL (Digital Subscriber Line).

Cable Modems

If you're like nearly 100 million other people in this country, your cable company already has a high-speed line running to your home. Attach a cable modem—that is, one designed for use with the broadband signals and coaxial cable used by the cable company—and voilà, you've got an instant high-speed connection to the Internet.

Proponents of cable modem technology claim that a downstream bandwidth of 20Mbps and even higher is possible. While this is true, a single subscriber is very unlikely ever to get this entire bandwidth. Rather, the bandwidth would be shared with other subscribers connected to the trunk over which the signal is coming. In practice, an individual subscriber may only get 2Mbps or so of this bandwidth—which still makes for a very fast connection.

There may be obstacles to such a high-speed cable modem connection. For example, it may not be a simple task to stretch that coaxial connection the extra distance to your PC—especially if your PC and TV are at opposite ends of the house. Additional cable may need to be run, which may create or add to installation costs.

Another problem arises from the fact that most of the cable running into subscribers' homes is one-directional. Since subscribers rarely have need to communicate upstream in a cable TV connection, the entire bandwidth is dedicated to transmissions from the head end—that is, from the cable company. (The connection is not entirely one-directional.

H

EXAMPLE ASYMMETRIC DSL CONNECTIONS

DSL Variant	Speeds (upstream/downstream)	Maximum distance
ADSL (asymmetric digital subscriber line)	16 to 640Kbps (u)/1.5 to 8Mbps (d)	18,000 feet
CDSL (consumer digital subscriber line)	16 to 128Kbps (u)/maximum of 1Mbps (d)	18,000 feet
RADSL (rate-adaptive digital subscriber line)	16 to 640Kbps (u)/1.5 to 8Mbps (d)	18,000 feet
VDSL (very high speed digital subscriber line)	1.5 to 6Mbps (u)/13 to 52Mbps (d)	4500 feet

EXAMPLE SYMMETRIC DSL CONNECTIONS

DSL Variant	Speed(s)	Maximum Distance
HDSL/HDSL2 (High-bit-rate digital subscriber line)	1.544Mbps (North America); 2.048Mbps (elsewhere)	12,000 to 15,000 feet
IDSL (ISDN digital subscriber line)	144Kbps	18,000
SDSL (symmetric, or single-pair, digital subscriber line)	768Kbps	10,000

It does allow the devices at the subscriber's end to send control and acknowledgement signals.)

It remains to be seen whether cable companies are willing to make the investments necessary to make the connection with individual subscribers more two-directional. One possibility is to use hybrid fiber/coax (HFC), which uses both coaxial cable and optical fiber in different stretches. Regardless of the method used, (re)wiring the cable population will be an expensive undertaking. To make things even more interesting, this expense comes at a time when cable business is stagnating or perhaps even declining due to the growing popularity of direct broadcast satellite (DBS) services. The expense also comes at a time when the cable industry is battling the communications industry for eventual control of what will become the home communications, entertainment, and information markets.

However, the payoffs could be even greater if broadband cable becomes the delivery medium of choice for what is sometimes known as the convergence of technologies for handling data, voice, and video. This technological convergence is paralleled by the accelerating corporate merging of the communications and entertainment industries—which is happening even as the industries battle each other.

ISDN

ISDN services have been available for many years, and have become moderately popular among businesses. ISDN uses digital lines for both voice and data communications. This means that special lines and other equipment are needed. Not surprisingly, the initial costs for ISDN can be considerable—often in the thousands of dollars. In addition, monthly line and access charges can help make ISDN too expensive for most individual users. Despite the expenses, ISDN can still be cost effective for businesses to which the high bandwidths can make a big difference.

Two service classes are available in ISDN: BRI (Basic Rate Interface) and PRI (Primary Rate Interface). BRI supports a data transmission speed of 128Kbps, provided as two 64Kbps B (or bearer)

channels. In addition, a 16Kbps D channel is provided for sending control and other signals between the endpoints in a connection. The bandwidth provided by BRI may be adequate for the needs of a home user, but it is doubtful whether—for an individual—the speed increase afforded is worth the installation and monthly costs.

The second service class—PRI (Primary Rate Interface)—is much more suitable for business needs. In North America, PRI service consists of 23 64Kbps B channels and 1 64Kbps D channel, which aggregate to 1.536Mbps. In addition, 8Kbps are included for line-management signals, bringing the throughput to 1.544Mbps, which corresponds to a T1 line in the digital signal (DS) hierarchy. In places other than North America, PRI consists of 30 B channels and 1 D channel. These 31 64Kbps channels aggregate to 1.984Mbps, to which 64Kbps are added for line-management signals. Thus, this PRI variant has a throughput of 2.048Mbps, which corresponds to an E1 line in the DS hierarchy.

ISDN continues to gain customers in the business world, but it is a long shot for the home communications and entertainment market. Even in business, there is a good chance that ISDN will eventually lose out to a DSL technology or to wireless delivery services.

Satellite and Other Wireless Services

A fourth high-speed access possibility is a wireless delivery service, most likely from a direct broadcast satellite (DBS). Currently, such satellites are used mainly to deliver digital television signals to homes. In fact, satellite TV services are making serious inroads into the customer base for cable TV. In addition to TV signal delivery, DBS currently offers downstream speeds of 400Kbps. (Satellites actually have a much higher bandwidth, but only deliver a limited part of that to individual subscribers.)

The signal is downloaded to an antenna on or near the subscriber's house, as in "A wireless connection." As the illustration shows, signals for a wireless connection are generally sent from the home base to a satellite or a relay station. From there, the signals are beamed in a broadcast fashion, to any antennas within the broadcast area. Any antennas tuned to specific frequency ranges—that is, to specific channels in the communication spectrum—will pick up signals in that range. Signals may be scrambled—so that only subscribers to a satellite service can decode them when they are received.

Just a few years ago, such antennas were huge—often close to 10 feet in diameter. Now, all you need is a minidish antenna (with a diameter of only 18 inches or so) with a clear line of sight to the appropriate section of the sky.

Upstream communication is possible, but only if you have an ordinary, analog modem. Because of the technology used, upstream speeds are limited to 56Kbps.

Currently, most DBS services use GEO (Geosynchronous Earth Orbit) satellites. These are in orbit at 22,500 miles above the earth, and they revolve around the earth at a speed that matches the earth's rotation. As a result, a given satellite remains stationary over a particular earth location. Because of their great distance, GEO satellites have a very large footprint (signal coverage area). However, their great distance means that there is always a delay (of about 700msec) in the signal.

GEO satellites are expensive to launch. They require a Titan-class rocket because they need to be pushed into a high orbit. From there, the signal needs to be powerful enough to reach earth with enough strength to be useful. However, once deployed, a GEO satellite has an easy orbit, and can be expected to last for up to 15 years.

DirecPC, a satellite Internet access service from Hughes Communications is a GEO satellite system. Hughes plans to deploy 8 more GEO satellites in its Spaceway project and 14 more in the Expressway project. Once these GEO satellites are deployed, DirecPC will be able to provide 1.5Mbps downstream.

Several projects are underway or planned to deploy LEO (low earth orbit) satellites. These satellites are deployed less than 1000 miles above the earth. They are very complex, much more intelligent than GEO

H

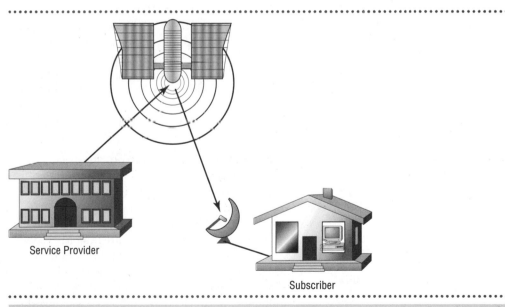

Service Provider

Subscriber

A WIRELESS CONNECTION

satellites, and can have up to 10 times as many circuits as a GEO satellite. LEO satellites have a tough orbit—between the Van Allen radiation belt and the atmosphere—and they tend to burn up within about 5 years. However, they are inexpensive to launch and don't need much power to transmit. As a result, they are economically feasible—at least in the eyes of the companies and consortia deploying LEO satellites. LEO satellites have only a 10msec delay, which will not be noticeable to humans.

Iridium is arguably the best-known LEO project. For Iridium, a consortium led by Motorola will deploy 66 LEO satellites to be used for cellular telephone service. (There were originally supposed to be 77 satellites. In fact, the project got its name because Iridium has atomic number 77.) Other LEO projects include Aries (54 satellites to be used for dual-mode telephony), Globalstar (48 satellites to be used for data, fax, and telephony services), LEOSAT (24 satellites to be used for mobile data services—for example, to automobiles), Skybridge (64 satellites), and Teledisc (288 satellites to be used for providing Internet access).

In addition, projects are underway to deploy MEO (medium earth orbit) satellites, which orbit 6000–10,000 miles above the earth, as well as hybrid projects that include combinations of satellites in different orbits or that augment GEO satellites already deployed.

Based on the billions of dollars being invested in satellite deployments, it is clear that important players in the telecommunications industry expect satellites to provide all types of services, including Internet access. See the entry for Satellite Systems for more information.

High-Speed Circuit

In telecommunications, circuits capable of faster transmission rates than are needed for voice communication. High-speed circuits generally support speeds of 20Kbps or more.

High-Speed Local Area Network (HSLAN)

→ *See* HSLAN (High-Speed Local Area Network)

High-Speed Serial Interface (HSSI)

→ *See* HSSI (High-Speed Serial Interface)

High-Usage Trunk Group

In telecommunications, a cable group that is intended as the primary path between two switching stations. As the primary path, this trunk will get the majority of the traffic between the two stations.

HiPPI (High-Performance Parallel Interface)

The High-Performance Parallel Interface (HiPPI) was developed in the late 1980s to provide a way to connect supercomputers at speeds befitting those state of the art machines (see connection 1 in the illustration entitled "A simple HiPPI connection"). Such a connection may be 25 meters with ordinary (copper) HiPPI, 200–300 meters with a serial (fiber-optic) HiPPI, or up to several kilometers with fiber extenders.

HiPPI was also intended to provide a very high speed channel over which a supercomputer or mainframe could communicate with storage or other peripheral devices as shown in part 2 of the illustration. Such connections are generally of the ordinary (parallel) variety, and are limited to about 25 meters. The switches for such connections cost $20,000 and more. But, of course, this was loose change compared to the millions or even tens of millions of dollars it cost to build the machines the switches were used to connect.

The goal was to move lots of data from one location to another, and to do this very quickly. The data was to be moved over a direct, short-distance connection between two endpoints, so there was little need for fancy protocols or address processing. The result is that HiPPI connections need only three commands: Request (source requests a connection), Connect (destination establishes the connection), and Ready (destination is ready to receive data).

Today, HiPPI is used in a great many ways, as described in the following "Uses for HiPPI" section. As a result, much work is being done on making HiPPI able to carry data using different protocols, and also to make HiPPI interoperable with other networking protocols.

Basic Facts

HiPPI is a very simple, very high speed, connection-oriented, circuit-switched, and protocol-independent interface. It plays well with others, supports flow control, and can use either copper or fiber media. The details of these features are as follows:

Very simple   As stated earlier, only three commands are needed to transmit between a point-to-point connection.

Very high speed   HiPPI supports speeds of 800Mbps or 1.6Gbps in either or both directions. HiPPI uses 50-pair, shielded copper cable, and operates in 32-bit parallel mode. One 50-pair cable is used for each unidirectional 800Mbps channel. With four cables, it's possible to get a total throughput of 3.2Gbps, with 1.6Gbps in each direction. In practice, however, 800Mbps in each direction is the maximum speed generally used—for the simple reason that there are very few devices capable of sustaining even a throughput of 800Mbps, much less a higher one. The electrical and mechanical details of the Physical-layer connection are specified in the ANSI X3.183 HiPPI-PH1 document.

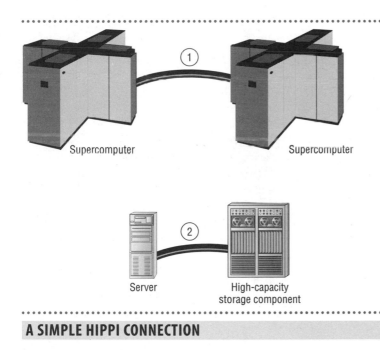

Supercomputer   Supercomputer

Server   High-capacity
storage component

A SIMPLE HIPPI CONNECTION

H

Connection-oriented   HiPPI connections are established in much the same way as a telephone call. A source device specifies the code for ("dials the number for") a destination device, with which the source wants to establish a connection. This connection must be established before the transmission can begin. Once established, no other devices can transmit across the connection—just as no one can simply join in an ongoing telephone conversation from a third line.

Circuit-switched   HiPPI configurations use crossbar switches (as in telephone company circuits) to route and establish a connection. These switches are nonblocking, which means that multiple connections can exist at the same time—provided each has a unique switch pattern (that is, path between source and destination through the crossbars). Because of this capability, the effective bandwidth of a HiPPI network can actually be several times 1.6Gbps. The operation of HiPPI switches is specified in the ANSI X3.222 HiPPI-SC4 (for switch control) document.

Protocol independent   A HiPPI channel can transmit either raw data, datagrams using the TCP/IP protocol, or IPI-3 packets. Raw data includes HiPPI framing elements, but no higher-layer protocols. IPI-3 is a protocol used to connect computers and RAID (Redundant Array of Inexpensive Disks) storage devices. The HiPPI framing protocol packages transmission elements into three components: Header, D1, and D2. The header contains information about the sizes and offsets for D1 and D2, D1 contains control information, and D2 contains data. Each component must start on a 64-bit boundary. The packets created by the framing protocol can be transmitted individually or they can be combined into bursts that may be up to 4GB in size. Specifications for how HiPPI handles packet framing are defined in the ANSI X3.210 HiPPI FP2 (for framing protocol) document.

Plays well with others   HiPPI already supports the transmission of protocols that are compliant with the IEEE 802.2 Logical Link Control specification—for example, protocol suites such as TCP/IP, lower-level network architectures such as Ethernet, Token Ring, and FDDI (Fiber Distributed Data Interface), as well as WAN architectures such as ATM, FDDI, and Frame Relay. Generally, such transmissions use encapsulation to get a particular protocol or packet type across a HiPPI connection. For example, ANSI document X3.218 (HiPPI LE3) defines how to encapsulate higher-level protocols such as TCP/IP within HiPPI packets. Efforts are also underway to develop standards for enabling HiPPI to interoperate with other popular network architectures, including ATM, Fibre Channel, and SONET.

Supports flow control   HiPPI uses a credit system to keep track of the Ready signals from the destination, and transmits data only when the destination is ready. In this way, a HiPPI device can keep from overflowing the receiving device's buffers. HiPPI does not, however, support quality of service guarantees, and so it is not intended for sending isochronous—or time-dependent—data. In practice, however, HiPPI is perfectly capable of handling such data because its bandwidth is high enough to avoid just about any sort of delay.

Can use either copper or fiber media   The original specifications called for the use of copper wire, and supported distances of up to 25 meters. By cascading switches, it is possible to extend this distance to about 200 meters. However, for any longer distances, optical fiber is needed, and the HiPPI-Serial specification (see below) provides for this. Using multimode fiber, HiPPI connections can extend to 2 kilometers; with single-mode fiber, this distance can be extended farther to 10 kilometers.

HiPPI provides error detection but not error correction. The next version, HiPPI-6400, is expected to provide both.

HiPPI does not currently support multiplexing or packet broadcasts. The latter is, of course, important in many networks. However, in some cases, HiPPI can effectively broadcast simply by transmitting the packets to the individual destinations in succession. Again, the tremendous bandwidth allows HiPPI to get away with this.

Currently, HiPPI provides little in the way of network administration tools. However, a HiPPI MIB (Management Information Base) specification is being developed. When completed, this will make it possible to monitor and administer HiPPI connections.

Interoperability Issues

As stated earlier, HiPPI supports 802.2-compliant network architectures and protocols. It also supports the Intelligent Peripheral Interface 3 (IPI-3) used for various types of storage devices, most notably for RAID storage. Standards also have been or are being developed to define how HiPPI can interact most effectively with other high-speed technologies, such as ATM, Fibre Channel, Gigabit Ethernet, and SONET.

HiPPI and Fibre Channel can interact in either of two ways—in part because they are both products of the same ANSI committee (X3T11). Standards have been developed to send upper-layer Fibre Channel data over lower-layer HiPPI media, and for sending upper-layer HiPPI protocols over lower-level Fibre Channel media.

For transmission over intermediate distances, HiPPI can be used with ATM. For example, a standards committee is working on defining a gateway and protocols to allow HiPPI data to be encapsulated and sent over an ATM connection to another HiPPI device or network at the other end. This process would use AAL 5 (ATM Adaptation Layer 5).

An analogous gateway has been defined to allow HiPPI transmissions to be sent over a SONET network to another HiPPI device or network. With such a gateway and SONET technology, data can be sent very quickly over very large distances. For example, researchers at Los Alamos National Lab-

oratories (where HiPPI was first created and where the HiPPI/SONET gateway was developed) have sent HiPPI data 70,000 kilometers—to a satellite and back to a receiving network—at 1Gbps speeds.

Uses for HiPPI

As stated earlier, HiPPI was originally developed as a simple but fast channel between powerful computers or between such a computer and a peripheral device. As price decreases have brought HiPPI components from their rarified origins down to high-end networking, human ingenuity has managed to find uses for a simple, high-bandwidth technology. The following list summarizes a few possible uses for HiPPI:

- In the film industry—for example, in creating special effects or for managing the data during film editing. Centropolis Effects LLC generated a terabyte—that is, 1000GB—of data for *Godzilla*, starring Matthew Broderick. These had to be merged with live-action footage, and HiPPI servers were used to merge animation with the live action.

- For the transmission of full-motion video or other high bandwidth content—for example, to trade shows as when, for example, scenes from *In the Line of Fire* (starring Clint Eastwood) were transmitted and played at a supercomputing conference.

- In network backbones—for example, to connect HiPPI clusters or Ethernet segments.

- As a controller (see "A HiPPI controller") for a cluster of servers or workstations. HiPPI can be used to connect the cluster members to peripherals, to each other, or to other clusters or networks.

- As a switching point in a tiered network—as, for example, when a HiPPI switch connects high-end computers or storage devices to servers which may, themselves, be connected to LANs or LAN segments.

H

The illustration shows both HiPPI connections (probably over copper wire) and also ordinary (copper) connections, as required by the network's basic architecture. The elements in the illustration are as follows:

- A server cluster, consisting of individual servers grouped together, and accessed as a single entity—so that an actual task goes to the next available server.

- A HiPPI controller, providing, in this case, access control.

- A high-capacity storage component.

- Workstations/clients connected to the server cluster.

- Individual servers in the cluster.

Development and Directions

The somewhat oxymoronically named HiPPI-Serial is not a standard for serial ports. Rather, it is an implementer's agreement (IA) that was developed to enable HiPPI to use fiber-optic media, which use a serial transmission scheme. Although developed to support fiber media, HiPPI-Serial has also been used to link switches directly via their serial ports, and it is able to deliver the full 800Mbps bandwidth. Nevertheless, HiPPI-Serial is generally used with fiber-optic media.

Once developed, the HiPPI-MIB (Management Information Base) will make it easier to monitor and administer HiPPI networks. It will enable self-discovery of switch addresses, and will also make it possible to resolve HiPPI and media access control (MAC) addresses.

HiPPI-6400

HiPPI-6400 is the even higher speed successor to HiPPI—if you can imagine that. HiPPI-6400, also known as SuperHiPPI, has the following features:

- Eight times the speed. Each simplex channel will support 6400Mbps (hence the name).

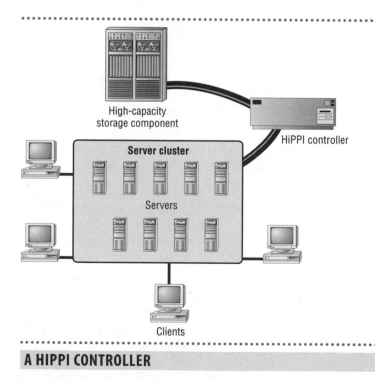

High-capacity storage component

HiPPI controller

Server cluster

Servers

Clients

A HiPPI CONTROLLER

With four cables, this means a total through-put of over 25Gbps!

- A latency (transmission delay) of less than one microsecond.

- End-to-end as well as link-to-link checksums for error detection and error correction in the form of retransmitted packets.

- Use of micropackets to automate ULA (Universal LAN MAC Address) assignment.

- Back-compatibility with earlier HiPPI standards.

- Simple multiplexing capabilities through the use of four virtual channels (VCs) in each physical channel. This allows time-sensitive data to use some of the VCs, while leaving others available for the remaining traffic.

- The use of fixed-size micropackets (32 bytes of data plus 8 bytes of control) for increased hardware efficiency.

- Ability to span multiple Physical-layer switches, which provides a simple multidrop capability.

- Bridging capabilities using 48-bit ULAs and the 802.1d standard.

- A MAC header that is similar to the header for Ethernet packets, making bridging and translation between the protocols easier.

- Credit-based flow control to prevent buffer overflow.

- A Scheduled Transfer (ST) Protocol which makes it possible to transfer material to and from memory or storage directly—bypassing the processor.

HiPPI-6400 should be an ANSI standard by the time you read this. Commercial products based on HiPPI-6400 are already available. A commercial version of HiPPI-6400 is available as GSN (Giga-byte System Network).

→ **Compare** Fibre Channel

Hit

A momentary change in the phase (timing) or amplitude (strength) of a signal. This produces signal distortion and can increase the error rate.

HLLAPI (High Level Language Application Program Interface)

In the IBM environment, a PC-based package used for creating interfaces between mainframes and PC applications. HLLAPI is designed for use with high-level programming languages, such as C, Pascal, and BASIC.

HMA (High Memory Area)

In extended memory (memory with addresses above 1MB), the first 64KB block of allocatable memory. More specifically, the HMA is the memory between addresses 100000H and 10ffffH.

→ **See Also** Memory

HMMP (Hypermedia Management Protocol)

→ **See** Protocol, HMMP (Hypermedia Management Protocol)

HMUX (Hybrid Multiplexer)

In the FDDI-II network architecture, a component at the media-access-control (MAC) layer. The HMUX multiplexes network data from the MAC layer and also isochronous (time-dependent) data, such as voice or video, from the isochronous MAC (IMAC) layer. The HMUX passes the multiplexed stream to the PHY (medium-independent physical) layer. "FDDI-I and FDDI-II Organization" in the FDDI entry.

H

Hogging

In network communications, hogging occurs when a transmitting node takes more than its share of the network's bandwidth for transmission. For example, in a slotted-ring network, hogging occurs when a node takes all available empty slots, leaving none for "upring" nodes.

Holding Time

In telecommunications, the holding time is the amount of time for which a call keeps control of a communications channel—that is, the call duration.

Home Directory

In various multiuser environments, such as UNIX or Novell NetWare systems, a directory created specifically for a user, and intended as the user's root directory on the network. The user's login script generally includes an instruction that maps a drive designation to the home directory after the user logs on to the network.

Home Page

A home page is the starting point for a hypertext document on the World Wide Web. The links from a home page may lead to other documents at the same site or to documents that belong to other people or corporations, and that may be scattered around the world. These linked Web pages may themselves be home pages.

Each home page is associated with a URL (Uniform Resource Locator), which specifies the page's location. For example, the following URL gets you to the home page for information about the best Web services—as determined by user votes—in various categories.

```
http://wings.buffalo.edu/contest/
awards/index.html
```

A URL provides three essential items of information:

- The protocol required to request the page. In most cases, this will be HTTP (Hypertext Transfer Protocol), but other protocols (such as FTP) are possible.

- The machine on which the document is found. In most cases, this information will be specified with domain names. In rare instances, this information will consist of the Internet addresses (that is, of four decimal values in succession).

- The path information for the file under discussion. This includes the file's name at the end.

Home pages have many uses. Corporations or organizations may use a home page to provide information to customers or others interested in the company's products. Individuals may use home pages to provide easy access to their favorite documents.

Some example home pages are shown in the following list. Keep in mind, however, that home pages may disappear or move, and frequently do so. After a home page moves, a message may be displayed for a limited period of time. some browsers can move immediately to the new location.

```
http://lycos.cs.cmu.edu
```
This document is the starting point for Lycos, a search engine for finding documents on the World Wide Web. This page is updated regularly.

```
http://www.godlike.com/muds/
```
This document contains links to various types of information about MUDs (Multiuser Dimensions) and related game environments. This page is updated regularly.

```
http://www.cs.colorado.edu/home/
mcbryan/WWWW.html
```
This document provides the starting point for the WWWW, the World Wide Web Worm search engine. This page is updated regularly.

```
http://www.ucc.ie/info/net/acronyms/
acro.html
```
This home page gives you access

to a regularly updated list of over 13,000 acronyms and abbreviations related to computing. The list is updated approximately weekly, and there is a provision for submitting new acronyms.

A home page makes up part of an HTML (Hypertext Markup Language) document, and can be stored as an ordinary ASCII file—albeit one containing HTML markup tags.

Home Run

In a wiring plan, a cable that runs from the wallplate to a distribution frame. This is generally two-, three-, or four-pair cable.

Homogeneous Network

A network that is using a single protocol at the network layer. In contrast, a heterogeneous network uses multiple protocols at the network layer.

Hop Count

In message or packet routing, a hop is a transmission between two machines, which may be nodes or routers, depending on the size of the network or internetwork across which transmissions must go.

In network routing, the number of nodes or routers through which a packet must (or may) pass in going from the source to the destination is called the hop count. Some protocols or services will keep track of the number of hops for a packet and will discard the packet and display an error message if the hop count exceeds a predefined value. For example, a hop count of 20 for an IP (Internet Protocol) packet means that a packet must reach its destination before it is passed through 20 routers.

In calculating the cost of a route, the number of nodes or routers the packet must pass through is used. In determining a packet-lifetime value, the number the packet may pass through is used.

Host

In the mainframe and minicomputer environments, a host or host computer is a machine that provides processing capabilities for attached terminals or nodes. Often, a front-end processor (FEP) or a controller (or host controller) mediates between the host and the terminals. PCs accessing such a host generally must run a terminal-emulation program in order to pretend they are terminals.

In the PC environment, the host is the computer to which a device is connected. For example, a PC can be the host for a network interface card (NIC), or a printer, or both.

On the Internet, a host is a machine through which users can communicate with other machines. For example, a minicomputer at a university may serve as a host for access to the Internet.

Host Bus Adapter (HBA)

→ See HBA (Host Bus Adapter)

Hostname

In the Internet environment, the name for a machine, such as thelma or henry. The hostname is part of the more complete fully qualified domain name (FQDN).

Host-to-Terminal

In communications and networking, a connection in which a central machine (the master) handles multiple terminals (the slaves).

Hot Fix

Hot Fix is a NetWare data-protection strategy in which data are redirected "on the fly" from defective to safe locations on a hard disk.

H

NetWare's Hot Fix capability verifies data by reading the newly written data and comparing it with the original data, which is stored in RAM until it is verified. If there is a discrepancy that can be attributed to defects in the media, the software writes the data in question to a specially allocated holding area and stores the address of the defective sector(s) in a table set aside for that purpose.

HotJava

HotJava is a browser (hypertext reader) program developed by Sun Microsystems in 1994—in part, to demonstrate the capabilities of its Java programming language, which was just being introduced. In addition to being able to display graphics, sound, and text, HotJava can display animation and can even distribute and execute applets (simple programs).

HotJava is written in Java, which is a high-level, object-oriented language designed to be architecture-independent and usable in distributed environments. Applets written in Java can be run on any machines for which a Java interpreter and run-time system are available. HotJava can dynamically link in the ability to handle new formats or protocols, provided Java applets for handling the new material are available on the server.

These applets will reside with the material so that the browser itself need not be changed. If a HotJava user requests a format or a protocol that HotJava doesn't understand, the browser simply asks the server for the support code, downloads it, and then downloads the requested material. This is all done in a manner that is completely transparent to the user.

HotJava can download and "display" programs with which the user can interact and work. For example, with a HotJava browser, a science class could download an interactive program illustrating concepts being studied; a math or accounting class could download calculators or special computation programs—for example, to generate sample data on the fly. When HotJava was first released, other browsers were unable to do such things. Over time, however, features have been added to HTML (Hypertext

Markup Language)—which is used to create Web documents—and to the browsers themselves. HotJava's capabilities are no longer as impressive as they were when the program was first released.

Because of the way Java is designed, downloaded applets are secure, so that users don't need to worry that a virus or other type of bug is being downloaded with it. There are ways around this security blanket statement, so it's important not to be too complacent about running applets.

HotJava has faded into the background over time, but it may be getting a second look—because of the availability of a new generation of Java tools and the inherent allure of platform independence.

→ *Primary Sources* http://java.sun.com

→ *Broader Concept* Browser

Hot Key

In general, a hot key is a keystroke or keystroke combination that causes a particular action or function to be executed, usually regardless of the current state of a program or process.

In PCs communicating with a mainframe, a hot key is a special keystroke or keystroke combination used to switch between using a PC as a terminal (connected to a mainframe) or a PC (as a stand-alone machine). Most terminal-emulation and communications packages provide this capability. The specific key sequence differs for different packages.

Hot Line Service

A private, point-to-point telephone connection. With such a connection, there is no need to dial; one telephone rings as soon as the other is picked up.

Hot Potato Algorithm

In networks, a routing algorithm in which a node routes a packet or message to the output line with the shortest queue.

Hot Spot

In an HTML (Hypertext Markup Language) document—that is, on a Web page—a hot spot is a section of the screen that is responsive to a mouse click. For example, clicking on a hot spot will move you to the document at the other end of the link and will display that document.

Hot Standby

In microwave communications, a strategy in which two transmitters and two receivers are connected to an antenna. At a given time, only one of these is doing any work. If that transceiver unit malfunctions, the hot standby immediately replaces it and takes over the transmission and receiving duties.

HPFS (High-Performance File System)

A file system developed for OS/2, versions 1.2 and later—including the newer OS/2 Warp. The HPFS was designed to overcome limitations of the DOS file system, including file name restrictions, inability to associate attributes with a file, and so on.

HPFS supports the following:

- File names of up to 255 characters

- Up to 64 kilobytes of extended attributes for each file

- Advanced caching methods for faster disk access

- Very high-capacity hard disks (up to 64 gigabytes)

- On-the-fly write-error recovery

DOS does not support the HPFS, but Windows NT does. HPFS cannot be used on a floppy disk.

HPPI (High-Performance Parallel Interface)

→ See HiPPI (High-Performance Parallel Interface)

HSLAN (High-Speed Local Area Network)

HSLAN is a term used to describe local area network (LAN) architectures with transmission speeds of 100Mbps or more. Most of the architectures that can feasibly serve as HSLANs are designed for larger networks, such as metropolitan-area networks (MANs) or wide area networks (WANs). The high- and higher-speed Ethernets (fast and Gigabit Ethernet) are major exceptions to this generalization, since Ethernet is the preeminent LAN architecture.

Architectures that can be used for HSLANs include the following:

- ATM (Asynchronous Transfer Mode), which is a broadband extension of the ISDN (Integrated Services Digital Network) architecture that has been poised for great things for many years now. ATM is most suitable for WANs.

- FDDI (Fiber Distributed Data Interface), which uses optical signals and media to achieve its high speeds. FDDI is already widely used for special-purpose networks, such as those connecting mainframes to controllers or connecting high-end workstations to each other.

- 100Mbps Ethernets, which includes two variants: 100BaseX and 100VG-AnyLAN. The former is the more direct successor to traditional 10Mbps Ethernet.

- Gigabit Ethernet, which supports speeds of up to 1Gbps.

H

HSM (Hierarchical Storage Management)

A data storage strategy in which data are distributed across three levels of storage media:

- Primary, or online, storage refers to disks that are immediately accessible. Active material will be stored in online storage.

- Secondary, or near-line, storage refers to devices that can be made accessible automatically—that is, without operator intervention. Material that is currently dormant (but that may need to be consulted or reactivated) is stored in secondary storage. CD-ROM or optical drive jukeboxes are commonly used for secondary storage.

- Tertiary, or off-line, storage refers to media and other hardware that must be requested and mounted or installed each time the material is needed. Material that is unlikely to be needed again is stored in such files.

HSSI (High-Speed Serial Interface)

A term applied to serial connections that transmit at more than 20Kbps.

HTML (Hypertext Markup Language)

HTML is the language used to create hypertext documents for the World Wide Web. HTML is used to describe various types of elements in the document—for example, section headings, subheadings, lists and list elements, tables, emphasized material, and so forth. With a few exceptions, the HTML tags have do not directly determine how the material will actually look when it is displayed.

Newer versions of the language allow you to specify even fancier things, such as the following:

- Forms that a user can complete and submit

- Java applets or ActiveX controls to carry out tasks or produce effects on the page

- Ways of making different areas of the screen behave differently when a user clicks on them or moves the mouse pointer over them

HTML is a markup language, which means that formatting commands, or tags, are written directly into the source file. Tags are interspersed with ordinary text, and are not interpreted until the file is displayed or printed by a browser program. The actual appearance when the document is displayed will depend on the browser being used.

The most recent version of HTML (and of the browsers that display it) also supports the use of style sheets, which make it possible to specify structural elements in separate files and then to refer to these elements in the document. Multiple style sheets can be used, or cascaded, in the same document. To date, two levels of style sheets have been developed: CSS1 and CSS2 (for cascading style sheets 1 and 2, respectively).

HTML Versions

HTML and HTTP (Hypertext Transport Protocol, the protocol that is used to request and deliver HTML pages) were both developed in the 1980s at CERN, a European scientific research center for particle physics. The goal was to make it possible to structure and distribute documents in a manner that would make it easy for researchers to share their work and to get access to information regardless of where that information was located. The first incarnation of what is now the World Wide Web was created during this process. URLs (Uniform Resource Locators) also were invented during this defining moment for the Web. Tim Berners-Lee was the person mainly responsible for these innovations. A sidebar discusses these innovations in their broader context.

BACKGROUND TO THE WEB

HTML, HTTP, and URLs, while ingenious inventions, were not created out of thin air. It doesn't diminish Berners-Lee's contribution to note that he wasn't working in an intellectual vacuum. In my opinion, it actually adds to the stature of the contribution to realize that Berners-Lee's creation synthesizes developments from three different areas.

The HTML language is actually based on SGML (Standard Generalized Markup Language), which was created by Charles Goldfarb and others during the 1970s. SGML is a language—actually, a metalanguage—for automating the process of marking up documents for publication. SGML is very powerful and complex, and for years its use was limited largely to large corporations with the resources to learn the language completely.

One of the capabilities of SGML is that it can provide generalized markup—that is, it can describe the general structure of a document. For example, a book might include front matter, chapters , and back matter. Chapters might include different level heads, paragraphs, lists, tables, and so forth. Some elements will be required, and others will be optional; some elements will be constrained with respect to the contexts in which they can appear, and others will be usable anywhere. Such features and qualifications can all be included in the document's description.

Such descriptions identify structural elements; they do not specify the appearance of those elements. The actual appearance will be determined when the document is displayed or printed. Note that, by separating the document's logical structure from its appearance, SGML makes it possible for the same document to be used in different ways. For example, the same document elements could be rendered in one way if going to a printer and in a different way if going to a screen display or to a machine that will read the material.

Document descriptions can be created in document type definition (DTD) files. The elements in a single DTD can then be used to mark up different books. Once the contents of a specific book are marked up, a computer program can be used to determine whether the book has all the required elements, and whether they appear in the correct ways and places. (The ability to automate such processes was one of the reasons SGML was developed in the first place.)

As it turns out, the HTML language is such a DTD file. HTML is officially an SGML application. HTML specifies a fixed set of document elements and markup tags for these elements. Because the set is fixed, you can't add your own tags by defining new ones. (This restriction in HTML is, in fact, one of the shortcomings that XML—for eXtensible Markup Language—overcomes. XML is generally regarded as the most likely successor to HTML for Web publishing.)

Berners-Lee took a complex construct—SGML—and created something simple and easily usable from it. He took a product that took over 10 years to create (and that probably takes almost as long to understand completely) and made from it something that you can learn in a day. The basic elements of HTML can be learned in a few hours, and using them is straightforward. Creating an HTML document is a tedious (and, consequently, error-prone) process. However, because it is a well-defined and structured language, HTML editors can be designed and used to automate the process of creating an HTML file. The decoding of an HTML file is just as straightforward—which is one reason why browsers and Web robots are possible.

HTTP, which is used to move HTML files as needed, is a transport protocol such as those developed for the TCP/IP Internet protocol suite. This suite of open protocols has been a major factor in allowing cross-platform communications. Just like the other protocols in the TCP/IP suite, HTTP is designed to be platform-independent, so that material can be retrieved from whatever platform contains it. (HTTP just transports. Other programs—either networking software or an application—must make sure that the retrieved material is usable in the current environment. In other words, HTTP will deliver material, but other programs need to worry about how to use it.)

The notion of a URL makes it possible to enrich a document by adding links to other documents. When the original document is displayed by a browser, the browser can retrieve the documents specified in URLs, and can display them as part of the local document. In fact, the reader may not even know that displayed material is not part of the actual document.

URLs help implement the concept of hypertext, which was first proposed by Vannevar Bush and popularized by Ted Nelson. Hypertext makes it possible to read (or otherwise explore information) in nonlinear ways. By jumping to text or other types of material linked to a document, it's possible to read a report whose elements may be located on dozens of different computers all over the world. (The term hypertext has come the be used to refer to any sorts of material that can be linked to a document—including text, images, video, audio, and the like. Strictly speaking, we should use the term hypermedia, but that just hasn't happened. Of course, the usage of hypertext isn't completely incorrect. After all, a picture is worth a thousand words and so could be regarded as being hypertext.)

A URL is actually just a special example—one of several—of a more general concept, known as a Uniform Resource Identifier (URI). This concept is still being developed and refined.

H

Berners-Lee's inventions became widely popular, and were a major factor in the sudden burgeoning of the Internet and, in particular, of the World Wide Web. Widespread use quickly exposed shortcomings in the design of Web languages and tools. This led to modifications and additions. The first widely used HTML version was 2.

The current official standard is version 3.2. However, just about all the interesting developments in the language have come since version 3.2. These have resulted from the competition between the leading browsers—Microsoft Internet Explorer and Netscape Navigator and Communicator. In their efforts to outdo each other, folks at Netscape and at Microsoft (and other people as well) keep extending HTML's features in order to give their browsers something to do.

Some language extensions were developed in common. Others arose from different features being added to competing browsers. Still others came about because Netscape and Microsoft developed different ways to accomplish essentially the same things—needless to say, these features and extensions are the messiest and the most confusing.

HTML 4—which is a recommendation, not a standard—is the product of a lot of careful technical evaluation and judgment, some behind-the-scenes jostling and lobbying, a bit of pragmatic accommodation and compromise, and perhaps even a coin toss or two. For the most part, HTML 4 is an extension and expansion of HTML 3.2. This means that any documents valid in HTML 3.2 will also be valid in HTML 4; however, there are also version 3.2 elements that are being phased out. In version 4, these elements are deprecated, which means that HTML 4–compliant browsers will accept the elements, but versions beyond HTML 4 may not. "HTML and related resources" tries to illustrate this state of affairs.

The illustration shows that a Web page—that is, an HTML file—can actually be built from various combinations of numerous components. These include the following:

- Markup language components and extensions—including the official HTML 3.2, the widely used HTML 4.0, DHTML (Dynamic HTML), and browser specific extensions (mainly from Microsoft and Netscape).

- Markup language add-ons—most notably, cascading style sheets (CSS1 and CSS2), but also elements such as frames and image maps.

- Programming elements, such as script files—created using any of several scripting languages.

- Executable elements, such as Java applets and ActiveX controls.

HTML 4 is the version all current browsers and HTML editors strive to comply with. The fact that it is a recommendation and not a standard quickly becomes clear when you realize that most HTML editors that claim to support both Microsoft and Netscape browsers do so by writing separate files. Browsers have unique features that are not included in HTML 4.

Despite these application dependencies, HTML 4 is still the version of choice because it includes elements that allow HTML documents to become interactive and dynamic—capable of accepting input from users or of being created on the fly, based on the latest available data. Features of the HTML language are discussed below.

The Structure of an HTML Document

HTML files are ordinary text files. They have two main components: a head and a body.

- The head contains administrative information—for example, the document title or reference locations for relative addressing. (In relative addressing, links, or references, are assumed to be in the same directory as the source file. The location of this directory must be specified). In general, the head contains information about the document.

- The body contains the materials (text, references to text, image, and other types of files, etc.) that make up your document—that is, the content along with markup tags.

In addition, some auxiliary files can also help make up an HTML document. In HTML 4, a document can have cascading style sheet files associated with it. Such files contain markup information and description details of document elements (in terms of HTML commands). This information can be used in the actual document file—once a reference has been made to the style sheet file in the HTML document. Multiple style sheet files can be used for a given HTML document. As a result, the same type of element can be used differently in different part of a document—simply by referring to different style sheet files.

HTML documents can also have scripts, Java applets, or ActiveX controls associated with them. Scripts can be included inline—that is, directly in the HTML file. Or they can be in a separate file, with a reference to the script file in the HTML file. Browsers don't all behave the same way in response to scripts, so there can sometimes be confusion surrounding such files. Another problem (or advantage, depending on how you look at it) is that browsers have different HTML extensions and special features.

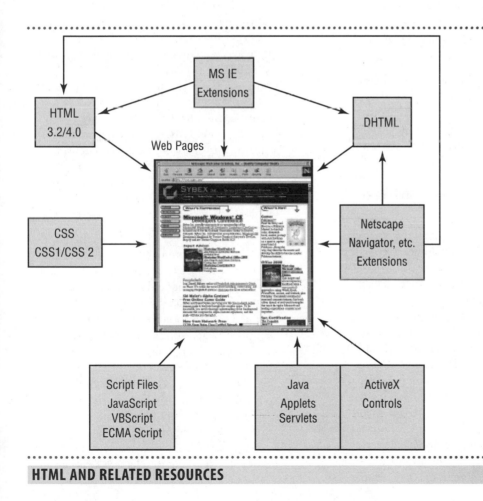

HTML AND RELATED RESOURCES

HTML Language Elements

At the most general level, the following types of HTML elements are defined:

- Character entities are special characters or symbols that aren't part of a minimal alphanumeric character set and that may not be available on a particular keyboard. Examples of character entities include angle brackets (< and >), ampersands (&), characters with cedillas (such as ???C), etc. HTML character entities begin with & and end with a semicolon. For example, <, >, &, and Ç are the codes for <, >, &, and ~,c, respectively.

- Empty markup tags are instructions that take no special arguments. For example, <P> and <HR> represent, respectively, a new paragraph indicator and a command to draw a horizontal line.

- Nonempty markup tags are instructions that include parameters, and that apply to a limited section of text or other material. Such tags generally come in pairs, with one member of the pair indicating the beginning and the other member the end of the material being affected. For example,

```
<B>In an HTML document, this text
will be in boldface</B>
```

produces something like: In an HTML document, this text will be in boldface. One of the most important elements in an HTML document—the anchor—is also indicated using nonempty markup tags. This element is discussed later in the entry. This nonempty markup tags category is quite high level in terms of the document elements it can affect. It also covers many variations and nuances in the way tags can be used. For example, anchors, tables, lists, forms, frames, objects, and image maps are all document elements that can be created using tags. They do very different things, however, and have very different effects on the way the document is used. For example, frames make it possible to define multiple browser windows, each of which can be used to display different HTML documents or different parts of the same document. Image maps are used to make different areas in a single window into hot spots—that is, into elements on which a mouse click will produce a response. (Many popular Web sites use image maps as a fancy, eye-catching way to let users select where on the site to go.) Forms are used to get input from the user. This input may influence the way in which the Web page is processed or even which Web pages are displayed. Tables can be used to display information in an organized and... well...tabular fashion. However, they can also be used to control the arrangement of material when displayed—for example, to ensure that certain elements are displayed in particular ways in relation to other elements. The <OBJECT>...</OBJECT> tag was created by Microsoft for including COM (Component Object Model) elements (such as ActiveX controls) in HTML files. The tag has been included in HTML 4, and will be used to include miscellaneous types of content, such as Java applets, ActiveX controls, plug-ins, etc. The tag is intended to replace certain deprecated tags, including <APPLET>, which had been used in earlier versions of HTML to incorporate multimedia files and applets.

- Style sheets are language elements that make it possible to specify document elements and layout in a manner (and in a location) independent of the content. These styles can then be applied to appropriate sections of a document simply by associating document elements with styles through the use of the required tags. Because styles can be named, the style elements can be associated more easily with document sections—simply by defining the association in a script file and then referring to the style element by name in the document. The appearance of the element can be changed simply by changing the element's definition in the style sheet.

- Attributes are features or properties associated with tags. Certain attributes can be used with just about any tag; other attributes are defined only for certain tags. Some attributes are like flags—they are either present or absent, set or not. Other attributes take values. For example, HREF in the anchor example in the next section is an attribute with a value; on the other hand, COMPACT, a now-deprecated attribute, works like a flag.

When displayed, the actual appearance of an HTML document depends on the browser controlling the display. Browsers differ in the way in which they interpret specific tags—to the extent allowed by the HTML specifications. In a way, tags represent suggestions, so that different browsers might produce different displays. For example, the <EM> and </EM> tags indicate the start and end of material that is to be emphasized. The way to do this (for example, using boldface or italic) is left up to the browser. Browsers can also differ in the basal typefaces and sizes they use, which can give a document very different appearances.

Example: Anchors

The anchor is one of the most important and most versatile elements in an HTML document. This element can indicate a cross-reference that can be reached at the click of a button. The anchor can also represent the name of a location to which readers might jump. Consider the following:

```
<A HREF= http://www.ncsa.uiuc.edu/
General/Internet/WWW/HTMLPrimer.html>
Introduction to HTML </A>
```

This anchor associates a link with the "Introduction to HTML" text. When displayed by a browser, this line will appear underlined (or will be made to look different by other means)—to indicate that there is more information available about this topic. (Note that only "Introduction to HTML" will be displayed. The other material in the anchor is administrative.) Clicking on the "Introduction to HTML" text (or selecting it by other means) will cause the browser to

retrieve and display the contents of the file HTML-Primer.html. The long piece of text following the HREF field is an example of a URL—essentially an address in Webspeak. The browser will retrieve information from this location.

The http indicates that the material is to be retrieved using the Hypertext transfer protocol. The www.ncsa.uiuc.edu portion specifies the machine on which this file is located. In this case, the URL indicates that the file is found on a specific computer (www.ncsa) at the University of Illinois at Urbana-Champaign (uiuc.edu). Note that the Web server names in the URL must be available (i.e., up and running) for this retrieval process to work. Finally, the /General/Internet/WWW/ HTMLPrimer.html portion specifies the path leading to the file on the www machine. (Note that the file name does not conform to DOS restrictions on file names. For historical reasons, most of the files on the Internet are, in fact, UNIX files. Such files can have multiple letter-extensions and long names—at least when presented by a UNIX file system.)

Ordinarily, the information in a URL takes the browser to the top of the specified Web page, or HTML document. It's also possible to jump to a particular section in the document specified by the URL; in fact, it's even possible to jump to a different location in the Web document being displayed—that is, in the same document. In other words, assuming all the proper tags are in place, you could jump immediately from a page you're reading to a particular word in a dictionary file or you could jump immediately to a specific chapter in the book you're reading. In practice, the first screen of many Web documents is nothing other than a list of topics from which you can select the one you want to display. When you click on a topic, this may take you to a different location in the current file, or it may take you to a different Web document.

The Future of HTML

There is no doubt that HTML's simplicity has been an important factor in the creation of the millions of Web pages currently accessible. There is also little doubt that there are limits to the kinds of things it's feasible to do with HTML.

One reason for this is that HTML is a closed language specification. There is no clean way to add new tags and attributes. A new tool—XML (eXtensible Markup Language)—is now available, and it may be able to help matters.

XML is actually a subset of SGML, and it can be used to create markup languages. With XML it is possible to create custom DTDs (document type definitions) for a particular purpose or content area. These DTDs are XML applications. Recall that HTML is actually an SGML DTD. In effect, this means you can use XML to create custom versions of HTML. That is, you can use XML to create DTDs to suit the particular needs of your problem.

Several XML applications have been developed, including Chemical Markup Language (CML), Mathematics Markup Language (MML), Open Transaction Protocol (OTP), Open Software Distribution (OSD), the Web Interface Definition Language (WIDL), and Microsoft Channel Definition Format (CDF), which is used to implement channels in push technology.

HTML will continue to be used for years. However, it will be increasingly supplemented with XML applications. There are even proposals circulating for creating XHTML (eXtensible HTML) as an XML application.

Lots of neat things will be happening with Web pages in the next few years, and HTML will continue to play a big part.

→ *Compare* XML (eXtensible Markup Language)

→ *Primary Sources* Many introductions to HTML exist on the Web. These include:

`http://www.ncsa.uiuc.edu/General/`
`Internet/WWW/HTMLPrimer.html`

`http://www.utoronto.ca/webdocs/`
`HTMLdocs/NewHTML/intro.html`

The document at the utoronto site has an extensive HTML bibliography accessible from it, in addition to lots of information about HTML.

However, probably the most fruitful place to begin any search for documents about HTML (or any other topics related to the Web) is at the WWW Consortium's Web site:

`http://www.w3.org`

In addition, books about HTML are appearing almost as quickly as new features in the browser wars.

→ *See Also* WWW (World Wide Web)

HTML (Hypertext Markup Language) Database

→ *See* Database

HTML Service Manager

Microsoft HTML Service Manager actually consists of several service managers that can be used to administer various Internet Information Server (IIS) services for a Web site created with IIS. In particular, the following service managers are available:

- Internet Service Manager for HTTP (Hypertext Transfer Protocol) and FTP (File Transfer Program) services

- Index Service Manager for indexing and summarizing the Web pages on a Web site

- NNTP (Network News Transfer Protocol) Service Manager for newsgroup-related services

- SMTP (Simple Mail Transfer Protocol) Service Manager for handling messaging and e-mail services

HTML Service Manager is only one of several tools that can be used to administer IIS services. Other methods include using Microsoft Management Console (MMC), scripting, and editing the metabase.

→ *Broader Categories* Microsoft IIS (Internet Information Server); Windows NT

HTTP (Hypertext Transfer Protocol)

→ **See** Protocol, HTTP (Hypertext Transfer Protocol)

HTTPD (Hypertext Transfer Protocol Daemon)

An HTTPD is a program that can recognize and respond to requests using HTTP (the Hypertext transfer protocol). HTTP is the primary protocol for requesting and providing documents on the Internet's World Wide Web (WWW). In essence, an HTTPD is the simplest form of Web server.

The first HTTPDs were written for UNIX systems (hence the "daemon" in the name). However, as other platforms (for example, Windows) have joined the WWW, Web servers have been created for these newer environments. As demands and capabilities have grown, the simple daemon program has given way to more sophisticated Web servers that are capable of more than just retrieving and sending hypertext documents: on-the-fly text searches, handling URL redirection (document address changes), etc.

HTTPS (Hypertext Transfer Protocol, Secure)

→ **See** Protocol, SHTTP (Secure Hypertext Transfer Protocol)

HTU (HDSL Terminal Unit)

An HTU is a special device that is required at either end of an HDSL (High-bit-rate digital subscriber line) connection. HDSL technology allows high-speed digital signals to be sent between a customer's premises (home or office) and the local telephone company central office (CO). HDSL uses the ordinary analog telephone lines—known as the local loop—for this transmission.

HTUs are required at either end to handle the digital signal. The device at the CO is known as the HTU-C, and the one at the user's end is the HTU-R (with R for remote). These devices are not modems. Rather, they are comparable to the DSUs (data service units) used in digital communications.

HTU-C (HDSL Terminal Unit, Central Office)

→ **See** HTU (HDSL Terminal Unit)

HTU-R (HDSL Terminal Unit, Remote)

→ **See** HTU (HDSL Terminal Unit)

Hub

A hub is a component that serves as a common termination point for multiple nodes and that can relay signals along the appropriate paths. Generally, a hub is a box with a number of connectors to which nodes are attached, as shown in "A stand-alone hub." Hubs usually accommodate four or eight nodes, and many hubs include connectors for linking to other hubs.

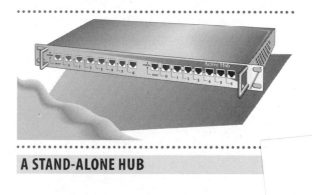

A STAND-ALONE HUB

H

A hub usually connects nodes that have a common architecture, such as Ethernet, ARCnet, FDDI, or Token Ring. This is in contrast to a concentrator, which can generally support multiple architectures. Although the boundary between concentrators and hubs is not always clear, hubs are generally simpler and cheaper than concentrators. Token Ring hubs are known as multistation access units (MAUs or MSAUs).

Hub-node connections for a particular network all use the same type of cable, which may be coaxial, twisted-pair, or fiber-optic. Regardless of the type of cabling used for hub-node connections, it is often advisable to use fiber-optic cable for hub-hub connections.

Hubs may be located in a wiring closet, and they may be connected to a higher-level wiring center, known as an intermediate distribution frame (IDF) or main distribution frame (MDF).

In light of its central role, you should seriously consider connecting a hub to a UPS (Uninterruptible Power Supply).

Hub Operation

All hubs provide connectivity; they pass on signals that come through. The simplest hub broadcasts incoming signals to all connected nodes; more intelligent hubs will selectively transmit signals. Any other services a hub provides will depend on the capabilities that have been built into the hub. For example, MAUs (Token Ring hubs) and active hubs (used in the ARCnet architecture) also boost a signal before passing it on. MAUs also do some internal routing of the node connections in order to create a ring arrangement for the nodes.

There are constraints on the distances that can separate a hub from a node or from another hub. These constraints depend on the type of hub (active or passive) and on the network architecture. In general, allowable node-hub distances are shorter than hub-hub distances.

Hub Features

In addition to connectivity, some hubs also provide management capabilities. Some hubs include an on-board processor which can monitor network activity and can store monitoring data in a MIB (management information base). A network management program—running on the hub or on a server—can use these data to fine-tune the network in order to improve the network's performance.

Just about all hubs have LEDs (Light-Emitting Diodes) to indicate the status of each port (node). Many hubs can also do partitioning, which is a way to isolate a nonfunctioning node.

Other capabilities can be built into hubs or can be provided through software. For example, hubs can be provided with nonvolatile memory, which can retain states and configuration values in case of a power outage.

Hubs can also be built or imbued with security capabilities. For example, with the help of software, certain high-end hubs can be made to send data packets to a destination node and garbage packets to all other nodes. This makes it much more difficult for a node to read packets not intended for that node.

Various types of special-purpose or enhanced hubs have been developed to incorporate some subset of these features. The hub variants are discussed in the following sections. In some cases, devices may be considered hubs or concentrators.

Peer versus Stand-Alone Hubs

A peer hub is implemented on a card that plugs into an expansion slot in a PC. Such a hub can use the computer's power supply. (The computer's power supply should be adequate, but is not guaranteed to be so.)

A stand-alone hub is an external hub that requires its own power supply. This type of hub is generally a box with connectors for the nodes that will be attached, and possibly with special connectors for linking two hubs.

Intelligent Hubs

An intelligent hub is a hub with special capabilities for configuration and/or management. For example, an intelligent hub may be able to partition nodes automatically in order to isolate a defective node. Similarly, an intelligent hub (such as in a 10BaseT network) can monitor network activity and report the data to a management program somewhere on the network. Some intelligent hubs can be controlled from a remote location.

The dividing line between intelligent hubs and concentrators is not always clear. In this gray area, vendors may use either hub or concentrator to refer to their product, presumably using whichever term is expected to generate more interest and sales.

Multi-Architecture Hubs

A device that that is capable of supporting multiple network architectures (for example, Ethernet and FDDI, or Ethernet and Token Ring) is sometimes called a multi-architecture hub, but is more likely to be called a concentrator. This flexibility is accomplished by having separate network interface cards for each architecture supported.

Active versus Passive Hubs

In ARCnet networks, an active hub, in addition to serving as a wiring and signal relay center, cleans (adjusts the timing of) and boosts a signal. To perform these tasks, an active hub needs its own power supply.

In contrast, a passive hub, used in low-impedance ARCnet networks, merely serves as a wiring and relay center. The signal is properly directed as it passes through, but it is not cleaned in any way. Because passive hubs do not change the signal in any way, they do not require a power supply.

Active hubs can be connected to nodes (servers or workstations), other active hubs, or passive hubs. Active hubs can be separated from each other by up to 610 meters (2000 feet) when using coaxial cable, and by up to 1.6 kilometers (1 mile) with fiber-optic cable.

A passive hub may be connected to a node or to an active hub, but not to a passive hub. Passive hubs generally support distances of only about 30 meters (100 feet).

→ **Broader Category** Intranetwork Link

→ **See Also** Concentrator; Wiring Center

Hub and Spoke

A term for an arrangement with a central component and multiple peripheral, or outlying, components. For example, a central office with connections to smaller branch offices would have a hub-and-spoke arrangement.

Hub Card

In 10BaseT networks, a multiport card that can be used in place of a hub.

Hundred Call Seconds (CCS)

In telephone communications, a measure of line activity. One CCS is equivalent to 100 seconds of conversation on a line, so that an hour of line usage is 36 CCS; 36 CCS is equal to one Erlang, and indicates continuous use of the line.

Hunt Group

In telephony, a group of lines which are tried (hunted) in succession, until an available one is found to make a call. If a selected line is busy, the next line is tried.

Hybrid Circuit

In telephone wiring, a circuit in a four-wire (two-pair) cable that can be used to divide these into two-wire (one-pair) paths.

H

Hybrid Fiber/Coax (HFC)

→ *See* HFC (Hybrid Fiber/Coax)

Hybrid Mode

In an FDDI-II network, a mode of operation that makes both packet- and circuit-switched services available, so that both data and voice can be transmitted on the network. This is in contrast to basic mode, which supports only packet-switching and can transmit only data (no voice).

→ *See Also* FDDI (Fiber Distributed Data Interface)

Hybrid Multiplexer (HMUX)

In the FDDI-II network architecture, a component at the media-access-control (MAC) layer. The HMUX multiplexes network data from the MAC layer and also isochronous (time-dependent) data, such as voice or video, from the isochronous MAC (IMAC) layer. The HMUX passes the multiplexed stream to the PHY (medium-independent physical) layer. See "FDDI-I and FDDI-II Organization" in the "FDDI" entry.

Hyperlink

A link or cross-reference in a hypertext or hypermedia document.

→ *See Also* Hypermedia, Hypertext

Hypermedia

Material that is arranged with hyperlinks—that is, directly accessible connections. With hyperlinks, the contents of the file or document can be examined in a non-linear sequence. A hypermedia document differs from a hypertext file in that the document can include sounds and pictures in addition to text. Thus, when "reading" a hypermedia document

about Mozart, a user might be able to click on hyperlinks to get descriptions of Mozart's contemporaries, a picture of Mozart, or perhaps even an excerpt from one of his musical compositions.

→ *Compare* Hypertext

Hypermedia Management Protocol (HMMP)

→ *See* Protocol, HMMP (Hypermedia Management Protocol)

Hypertext

Text that is arranged with hyperlinks—directly accessible connections—so that the contents of the document can be "read" in a non-linear fashion. By clicking on a hyperlink, the reader can jump around within the document, and even to other documents.

→ *Compare* Hypermedia

Hypertext Markup Language (HTML)

→ *See* HTML (Hypertext Markup Language)

Hypertext Transfer Protocol (HTTP)

→ *See* Protocol, HTTP (Hypertext Transfer Protocol)

Hypertext Transfer Protocol Daemon (HTTPD)

→ *See* HTTPD (Hypertext Transfer Protocol Daemon)

Hypertext Transfer Protocol, Secure (HTTPS)

→ *See* Protocol, SHTTP (Secure Hypertext Transfer Protocol)

HYTELNET

HYTELNET (also written Hytelnet or hytelnet) provides a menu-driven, hypertext front end for the Telnet remote terminal emulation program. Written by Peter Scott at the University of Saskatchewan, HYTELNET provides an index of all known Telnet servers, so you can use it to search for catalogs, databases, bulletin boards etc. Once you've used HYTELNET to access the desired Telnet server, however, you may still have to deal with that server's interface and constraints.

If HYTELNET is available on your system, you can start it by typing hytelnet. If not, you can access it through a HYTELNET gateway, such as the one provided by EINet (now known as TradeWave). To do this, use a browser (hypertext file reader), and set it to the following URL (uniform resource locator—essentially a Web address):

```
http://galaxy.einet.net/hytelnet/
HYTELNET.html
```

You can also try HYTELNET through the University of Saskatchewan. To do this, you need to Telnet to herald.usask.ca, and use hytelnet as the login ID.

HyTime

HyTime is an international standard (ISO 10744) for handling hypermedia documents and the objects in them using SGML (Standard Generalized Markup Language). In HyTime, an object is simply part of a document, and can have any form: text, audio, video, a program, an image, etc. In SGML terms, HyTime provides guidelines for creating document type definition (DTD) files. DTDs contain descriptions of what constitutes a valid document of a particular type. (HTML, or Hypertext Markup Language, which is used to create Web documents, is an example of a DTD.)

In particular, HyTime specifies how certain basic concepts can be represented in SGML. These include such things as associating document objects with hyperlinks, relating document objects in space and time, including nontext material in the document, and so forth. HyTime includes six modules to help do its work:

- Base module, which provides facilities used by other modules.

- Finite Coordinate Space (FCS) module, which makes it possible to schedule an object in time and/or space within a bounding box called an event. (Note that, for purposes of such scheduling, HyTime treats time and space as equivalent.)

- Location Address module, which specifies how to identify the locations of document objects by name, by coordinate location, or by semantic construct.

- Hyperlinks module, which provides five different types of hyperlinks.

- Event Projection module, which specifies how events in one Finite Coordinate Space (the source) are to be mapped onto a second FCS (the target).

- Object Modification module, which makes it possible to modify an object in an object-specific way before rendering the object.

→ *Broader Category* SGML (Standard Generalized Markup Language)

Hz (Hertz)

A unit of frequency. Hertz is used, for example, to describe the periodic properties of acoustic, electrical, and optical signals. One hertz is equal to one cycle per second.

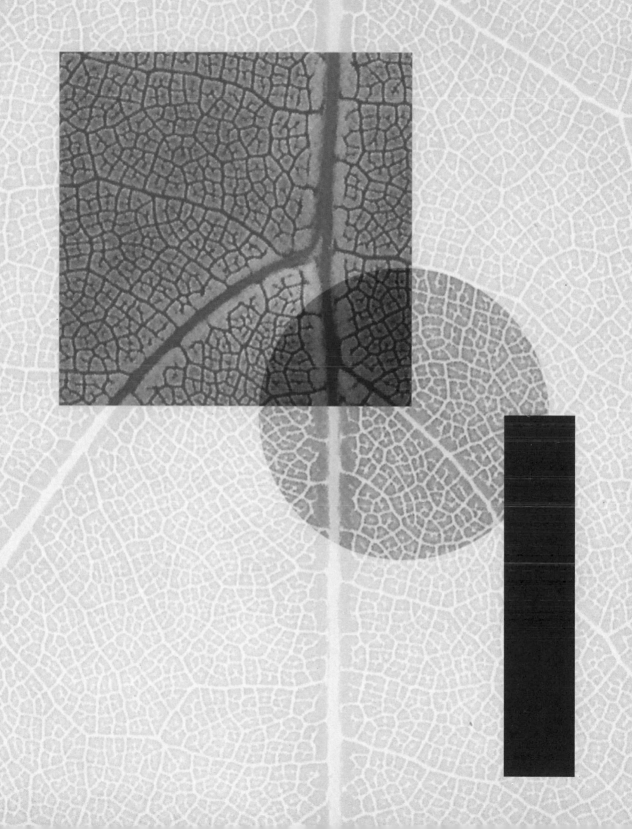

IA5 (International Alphabet 5)

IA5 is a seven-bit code that defines the character set used for message transfers, according to the CCITT X.400 Message Handling System (MHS) specifications.

In its default coding, IA5 is almost identical to the ASCII system. However, because certain character encodings can be changed, IA5 can take on a non-ASCII form. In particular, the following encodings may be redefined:

- Two possible representations can be used for each of the characters corresponding to codes 35 and 36 (decimal). The ASCII encoding uses # and $, respectively.

- Ten characters may be redefined according to national needs. For example, characters may be redefined to represent characters with diacritical marks (umlauts, accents, or tildes, depending on the country). These have codes 64, 91 through 94, 96, and 123 through 126.

You can create and register a particular variant of IA5 encoding, provided that your variant is defined according to these constraints. Various national alphabets have been registered with the ECMA (European Computer Manufacturers Association).

A different character set, defined for Teletex (an international electronic-mail service), uses eight bits, and so provides twice as many possible characters.

→ *Primary Sources* CCITT recommendation T.50; ISO document 646

IAB (Internet Architecture Board)

An organization (originally Internet Activities Board) that oversees standards and development for the Internet. This board also administrates, with the help of the IANA (Internet Assigned Numbers Authority), the internet(1) subtree in the global tree in which all networking knowledge is stored. The IAB has two task forces: IETF (Internet Engineering Task Force) and IRTF (Internet Research Task Force).

IAC (Inter-Application Communication)

In the System 7 operating system for the Macintosh, a process by which applications can communicate with each other and exchange data, IAC can take any of several forms, depending on what is being communicated and who is involved in the communication.

- Copy and paste provides the most perfunctory form of IAC. This type of communication uses a commonly accessible storage area, the Clipboard, as the communication point. Copy and paste is best suited for communicating or exchanging information that is not going to change or be updated, such as a list of the fields in a packet for a particular networking protocol.

- Publish-and-subscribe is used for information that may be revised and updated, such as spreadsheets or text files. A most recent version of the information is always stored in a file known as the edition. Applications that need this information subscribe to the edition, so that the application is always notified when the edition is updated. This makes it possible to create a document from materials drawn together from various sources, even as these sources are being created.

- Events are used to drive program execution and also to control the flow of data in a communications or other type of program. Apple events are lower level, and they adhere to a predefined protocol (the Apple Event Interprocess Messaging Protocol). Macintosh processes and servers use Apple events to get other processes to do their work. Higher-level events are requests from an application to the operating system or to another application. Either Apple or higher-level events can be used to enable one program to control or give orders to another.

- The Program to Program Communications (PPC) Toolbox provides low-level, but flexible and powerful, routines to enable applications to communicate with each other.

IANA (Internet Assigned Numbers Authority)

A group in the Internet community that is responsible for assigning values for networks, attributes, and so on. This service, which is operated by the University of Southern California Information Sciences Institute (USC-ISI), makes sure that the same identifier values are not assigned to two different entities.

IAP (Internet Access Provider)

→ *See* ISP (Internet Service Provider)

IBM Network Management (IBMNM)

A protocol used for network management in an IBM Token Ring network.

IBMNM (IBM Network Management)

A protocol used for network management in an IBM Token Ring network.

ICANN (Internet Corporation for Assigned Names and Numbers)

Until spring 1999, Network Solutions InterNIC Registration Services (NSI)—under government contract—was the only organization allowed to register and assign domain names for the DNS (Domain Name System) that is used to associate names with Internet addresses. The government decided to open up the domain registration process by allowing private companies to serve as registrars.

This was done in part to reflect the fact that the Internet is a global enterprise.

To facilitate this privatization process, ICANN was formed to develop criteria for screening potential domain name registrars and to select five registrars for an initial trial period. During this two-month period, these test registrars would be allowed to assign domain names—in coordination with NSI—in order to work out the details of having multiple registrars. After the test phase, ICANN was to use its criteria to select other companies as additional registrars.

So far, the project has been somewhat successful but has also been plagued with problems—partly due to the logistics of allowing multiple registrars and partly due to NSI's reluctance to give up total control of the registration process and to open its registry database to the new registrars.

ICMP (Internet Control Message Protocol)

→ *See* Protocol, ICMP (Internet Control Message Protocol)

IDA (Integrated Digital Access)

A facility that provides access to multiple digital channels, such as voice, video, and data channels.

IDAPI (Integrated Database Application Programming Interface)

A proposed standard for interfaces between applications that serve as user front-end programs and back-end programs that actually access databases. IDAPI was developed by Borland, IBM, Novell, and WordPerfect as an alternative to Microsoft's ODBC (Open Database Connectivity).

IDC (Insulation Displacement Contact)

In cabling, a type of wire termination in which the connector cuts the cable's insulating jacket when the connector is attached. Most unshielded twisted-pair cable is terminated at an IDC.

IDC (Internet Database Connector)

The IDC is a plug-in—for Microsoft Internet Information Server (IIS)—that makes it possible to publish databases as they are needed. An IDC file contains the queries and other instructions needed to create an HTML (Hypertext Markup Language) file from the database. To create this file, the results of the database queries are combined with formatting instructions contained in an .HTX (for HTML extension) file. (IDC can be used to query a database, but not to update it.)

This dynamic publication method ensures that the HTML file returned to the browser contains the most up-to-date information available from the database. Such dynamic publication is more informative and less expensive than the use of static Web pages that must be updated on a regular (and no doubt frequent) basis—perhaps even by a person.

IDC is actually an ISAPI (Internet Server Application Programming Interface) application. IDC's functionality has been largely superseded and improved on by newer technologies, such as Active Server Pages (ASPs), which can do more than IDC—for example, they are able to update a database.

→ *Broader Category* ISAPI (Internet Server Application Programming Interface); Plug-In

→ *Compare* ASP (Active Server Pages)

IDE (Integrated Drive Electronics)

IDE is a hard disk interface and technology in which the controller is on the hard disk. Because the controller circuitry is small enough to fit on the drive, IDE hard disks have long been popular for laptop and notebook computers. Transfer rates for IDE drives can be as high as 2MBps.

A more recent Enhanced IDE (EIDE) standard supports drives with a capacity of 1GB or more. These high-capacity IDE drives are becoming increasingly popular, and this enhanced technology may give SCSI (Small Computer Serial Interface) technology competition in the high-capacity storage market.

→ *Broader Category* Hard Disk

Identifier Variable

In NetWare login scripts, a variable used as a placeholder for special values, such as a user's login name. This makes it possible to create scripts that can be used by multiple users or in various contexts simply by changing the values associated with the script's identifier variables.

IDF (Intermediate Distribution Frame)

An intermediate location for routing wiring in a building. An IDF is connected to an MDF (main distribution frame) at one end and to end users at the other end. In a multi-floor building, each floor is likely to have an IDF, partly because of the difficulty in running multiple wires vertically in buildings. An IDF is generally located in a wiring closet.

IDG (Inter-Dialog Gap)

In the LocalTalk variant for AppleTalk, the minimum gap between dialogs. For LLAP (LocalTalk Link Access Protocol), this gap is about 400 microseconds.

IDI (Initial Domain Identifier)

In the OSI reference model, the part of a network address that represents the domain (an administrative unit).

IDL (Interface Definition Language)

In the Common Object Request Broker Architecture Object Model (CORBA/OM), the IDL is a special language used to define interfaces through which clients can issue requests. CORBA specifies a platform-independent and programming language-independent object model and an architecture that is designed to enable clients to issue requests to objects.

In a CORBA-compliant world, the client can be on any machine on any platform, the request can be made in any programming language, and the object of which the request is made can also reside on any machine on any platform. Interfaces determine what requests can be made, and also how a request must be formulated.

In order to support (programming) language independence, the IDL is used to describe interfaces in a language-neutral intermediate format. Note that IDL is a specification or definition language and not a programming language.

Once an interface has been specified in IDL, *mappings* can be created to translate the interfaces from IDL into a (programming) language-appropriate form. These mappings create *IDL stubs*, which are language-specific interfaces through which requests can be made. Also, the mappings are used to create *implementation skeletons*. These are programming structures from which it's possible to invoke the methods required to comply with a request. The skeleton contains no details of the methods calls—or of anything else, for that matter. That information must be added by the developer who created the implementation (definition and language-specific instantiation) for the object of interest.

Once an IDL stub and an implementation skeleton have been created, information about them can be stored in an interface repository (IR). The IR serves as a platform-specific location for the centralized management of IDL definitions and other request-related information. "IDL and object requests" shows how these elements are related.

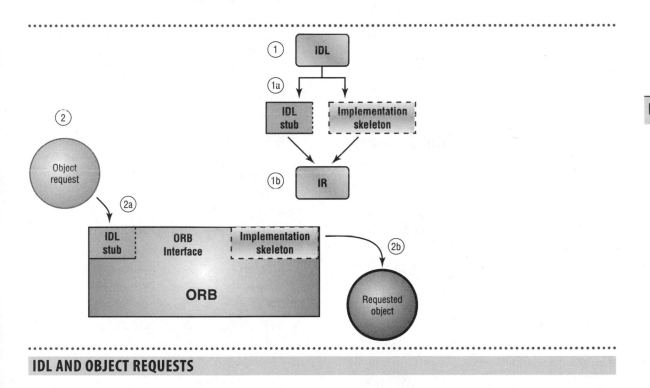

IDL AND OBJECT REQUESTS

In the object request process, the IDL is used (1a) to create a platform-specific IDL stub and also an implementation skeleton to actually perform a task. Once created, these elements are stored (1b) in the platform-specific IR. An element that makes an object request can do so through the IDL stub (2a), which is brought in to add to the ORB capabilities. The implementation skeleton interacts with the requested object.

→ **Broader Category** CORBA (Common Object Request Broker Architecture)

Idle Cell

In ATM, a cell that is transmitted when there is not enough other network traffic to keep the rate at a specified level. An idle cell can be discarded at any point in the transmission, such as when the network traffic reaches a level at which the idle cell is no longer needed.

→ **See Also** ATM (Asynchronous Transfer Mode)

IDN (Integrated Digital Network)

A network that uses digital signaling and circuitry.

IDS (Intrusion Detection System)

An IDS is software that can complement the security services provided by authentication and firewall software. A major limitation of both of these well-known security products is that they are one-shot security measures. The authentication and firewall packages perform their checks at specific points in the login or network access process; then, each makes a decision about whether to allow the user further access. Should an intruder manage to get by these screenings, neither product can provide any further security help.

Authentication software can verify a user's identity by requiring the user to provide a (supposedly) secret item of information—such as a password. However, if an intruder-to-be manages to steal a valid password and provide it during the login process, the authentication software has no reason to keep the intruder out.

Similarly, properly configured firewalls are good at screening against certain types of intruders—mainly those who try to break into a network directly. Firewalls can screen against packets from certain addresses or those using certain kinds of protocols, among other things. However, firewalls generally are unable to detect attack code hidden inside a packet or to protect against intruders that are already beyond the firewall (for example, employees already inside the company whose firewall is guarding against the outside world).

In contrast, intrusion detection software does its work during the user's (or the intruder's) session on the network. An IDS monitors network activity—continuously or at frequent intervals—looking for signs of known attack strategies and also checking CPU and/or network activity for statistical deviations from the usual, or expected, values. For example, the IDS might look for increased efforts to access sensitive areas (that is, those areas that might contain confidential information) or to install or modify files, or the IDS may monitor what kinds of packets are being transmitted and their destination.

IDS software comes in three main varieties:

- The older host-based software. Such products reside on individual machines and monitor the activity of applications and of the operating system.

- The newer network-based software. Such products monitor network activity and traffic in real time.

- Hybrid products that have features of both host-based and network-based software.

If the IDS sees something anomalous, it may block the action or inform the server of the anomaly. The software will also log all subsequent activity—in order to provide more information about the possible attack and also to provide details of the break-in (should it prove to be one).

Note that, unlike authentication and firewall software, intrusion detection packages can identify intruders after they have managed to get onto the network (whether from outside or from inside). This is important because it makes it more difficult for the intruder to accomplish anything or to cause any damage. The fact that the IDS can monitor aggregate activity using statistical criteria also makes it more difficult for an intruder to cover their tracks.

IDS packages are often discussed together with another security product—one that shares some of the elements and goals of IDS: risk-assessment software (also known as scanner software) works with a database of known attack strategies. The scanner software tries to use known strategies to access— that is, break into—the network. If any of them work, the network server and administrator are both notified.

IDSL (ISDN Digital Subscriber Line)

IDSL is an unusual member of the digital subscriber line (DSL) family of technologies. It is unusual because it is considerably slower than the other DSLs, which include ADSL (asymmetric DSL), HDSL (high-bit-rate DSL), RADSL (rate-adaptive DSL), SDSL (symmetric DSL), and VDSL (very high bit rate DSL). Except for IDSL, the various DSLs can all reach download speeds of 1Mps or better—as high as 52Mbps in the case of VDSL. In contrast, IDSL has a 144Kbps limit in each direction—and only 128Kbps of this is for data, with the remaining 16Kbps being for control and signaling.

It is also unusual in that it implements ISDN (Integrated Services Digital Network)—the original DSL—in a more versatile variant of the technology. One of the attractions of ADSL (arguably the best-known variant) and the other DSLs is that they allow you to send both data and voice simultaneously.

IDSL provides BRI (Basic Rate Interface) service over analog telephone lines. BRI provides two 64Kbps bearer, or B, channels plus a 16Kbps D channel for signaling. The technology does require special equipment—namely, a DSL terminal unit at either end of the connection. However, these expenses are much less than the costs of the special equipment needed for an actual ISDN line.

IDSL is a symmetric technology, which means that it supports the same speeds in both directions. Other, asymmetric, DSL variants support higher speeds downstream (provider to customer) than upstream.

→ See Also ADSL (Asymmetric Digital Subscriber Line); HDSL (High-Bit-Rate Digital Subscriber Line); ISDN (Integrated Services Digital Network); RADSL (Rate-Adaptive Digital Subscriber Line); SDSL (Symmetric Digital Subscriber Line); VDSL (Very High Bit Rate Digital Subscriber Line)

IDT (Interrupt Dispatch Table)

In Windows NT and NT Advanced Server (NTAS), a table used by the operating system kernel to determine and locate the routine for handling a particular interrupt. The kernel maintains a separate table for each processor, since the processors may use different interrupt handlers.

IDU (Interface Data Unit)

In the OSI reference model, a data structure that is passed between layers, as when an entity at one level provides a service for an entity at a higher level.

IEC (Interexchange Carrier)

→ See IXC (Interexchange Carrier)

IEC (International Electrotechnical Commission)

An international organization, with members from more than three dozen countries, that sets electrical standards. The acronym is sometimes also used for *interexchange carrier*, which is more commonly denoted by IXC.

IEEE 802.x

The IEEE (Institute of Electrical and Electronics Engineers) is an American professional organization that defines standards related to networking and other areas. The IEEE 802.x standards are perhaps the best-known IEEE standards in the area of networking. These are a series of standards, recommendations, and informational documents related to networks and communications.

The IEEE publications are the products of various technical, study, and working groups, some of which have been meeting for over a decade, others of which are just a few months old.

The recommendations are mainly concerned with the lower two layers in the OSI reference model: the Data-Link and Physical layers. The IEEE recommendations distinguish two sublayers in the OSI model's Data-Link layer: a lower, MAC (media access control) sublayer and an upper, LLC (logical-link-control) sublayer.

Note that several of the standards (802.1 through 802.11) have been adopted and superseded by newer versions (8802-1 through 8802-11, respectively) from the ISO (International Standardization Organization) and the IEC (International Electrotechnical Commission), whose standards are internationally accepted. The literature has not yet caught up with these revisions, so you will still see references to IEEE 802.3, for example, rather than to ISO/IEC 8802-3.

The following are the IEEE 802.x standards:

- 802.1 specifies standards for network management at the hardware level, including the spanning tree algorithm. This algorithm is used to ensure that only a single path is selected when using bridges or routers to pass messages between networks and to find a replacement path if the selected path breaks down. This document also addresses systems management and internetworking.

- 802.2 defines the operation of the LLC sublayer of the OSI model's Data-Link layer. LLC provides an interface between media-access methods and the Network layer. The functions provided by the LLC, which are to be transparent to upper layers, include framing, addressing, and error control. This sublayer is used by the 802.3 Ethernet specifications, but not by the Ethernet 2 specifications. It is also supported by high-speed interfaces such as HiPPI (High-performance Parallel Interface).

- 802.3 describes the Physical layer and the MAC sublayer for baseband networks that use a bus topology and CSMA/CD (Carrier Sense Multiple Access with Collision Detection) as their scheme for accessing the network. This standard was developed in conjunction with Digital, Intel, and Xerox, so that it matches the Ethernet standard very closely. Ethernet 2 and IEEE 802.3 are *not* identical, however, and special measures are required to allow both types of nodes to coexist on the same network. In June 1995, the 802.3u working group adopted a standard for several variants of 100BaseT Ethernet—that is, a version of Ethernet operating at up to 100Mbps over twisted pair wiring. (100VG-AnyLAN, the main competitor for 100BaseT was adopted as a standard the same day by the 802.12 working group.) In 1998, the 802.3z working group adopted the Gigabit Ethernet specification.

- 802.4 describes the Physical layer and the MAC sublayer for baseband or broadband networks that use a bus topology, token passing to access the network, and either CATV or fiber-optic cable. The specifications in this document are closely related to the MAP (Manufacturing Automation Protocol), which was developed by General Motors and which is widely accepted in industrial settings.

- 802.5 describes the Physical layer and the MAC sublayer for networks that use a ring topology and token passing to access the network. IBM's 4Mbps Token Ring product line conforms to this standard, as does IBM's faster (16Mbps) token-ring network.

- 802.6 defines standards for MANs (metropolitan area networks), whose nodes are scattered over distances of more than 5 kilometers (3 miles). Part of the 802.6 committee's goal was to find an acceptably fast and inexpensive technology for transmitting among nodes in a MAN. The document recommends the use of DQDB (Distributed Queue Dual Bus) technology for such networks, rather than more expensive leased lines or less expensive but slower public packet-switched networks.

- 802.7 is the report of a TAG (Technical Advisory Group) on broadband networks. The document specifies the minimal physical, electrical, and mechanical features of broadband cable, and also discusses issues related to installation and maintenance of such cable.

- 802.8 is the report of a TAG on fiber-optic networks. The document discusses the use of optical fiber in networks defined in 802.3 through 802.6, and also provides recommendations concerning the installation of fiber-optic cable.

- 802.9 is the report of a working group addressing the integration of voice and data (IVD). This document specifies architectures and interfaces for devices that can transmit both voice and data over the same lines. The 802.9 standard, which was accepted in 1993, is compatible with ISDN, uses the LLC sublayer specified in 802.2, and supports UTP (unshielded twisted-pair) cable. The 802.9a working group developed an IsoEthernet, or isoENET, specification, which attempts to provide bandwidth and protocol support for voice or other time-sensitive transmissions over Ethernet networks. This specification was officially adopted in late 1995 as Integrated Services Local Area Network 16T (ISLAN16T)—where the 16T indicates a 16Mbps speed over twisted-pair wires.

- 802.10 is the report of a working group addressing LAN (local area network) security issues, including data exchange and encryption, network management, and security in architectures that are compatible with the OSI reference model.

- 802.11 is the name for a working group addressing wireless networking standards.

- 802.12 was convened to study the 100VG-AnyLAN Ethernet proposal from Hewlett-Packard and other companies. This architecture supports speeds of up to 100Mbps, but uses a different media access scheme than the Ethernet versions defined by 802.3 committees. In fact, the demand priority media access method is the main focus of this working group. In June of 1995, the 802.12 committee adopted 100VG-AnyLAN as a standard. This is one of the two 100Mbps standards adopted at that time. The other was the 100BaseT, adopted by 802.3u.

"The IEEE 802 committees and working groups" shows the various committees. Note that the work of the 802.2 committee serves as a basis for several other standards (802.3 through 802.6, and 802.12). Several of the committees (802.7 through 802.11) serve primarily informational functions, in principle, for any of the architecture committees.

Note that different 802.*x* committees have specified different bit orders for transmissions. For example, 802.3 (CSMA/CD) and 802.4 (token bus) have specified LSB (least significant bit) first; 802.5 (token ring) has specified MSB (most significant bit) first, as has ANSI X3T9.5, the committee responsible for the FDDI architecture specifications. These two approaches are known as little-endian and big-endian, respectively.

This difference in bit ordering has consequences for bridges and routers, which must do bit switching when routing between networks, so that addresses and frames are interpreted correctly.

IEEE 1394

→ *See* Firewire

IESG (Internet Engineering Steering Group)

In the Internet community, the executive committee for the Internet Engineering Task Force (IETF).

IETF (Internet Engineering Task Force)

A committee that operates under the auspices of the Internet Activities Board (IAB) to help establish standards relating to the Internet. The IETF is largely responsible for formulating the Remote Network Monitoring Management Information Base (RMON MIB), which is expected to become the standard for monitoring and reporting network activity in the Internet environment.

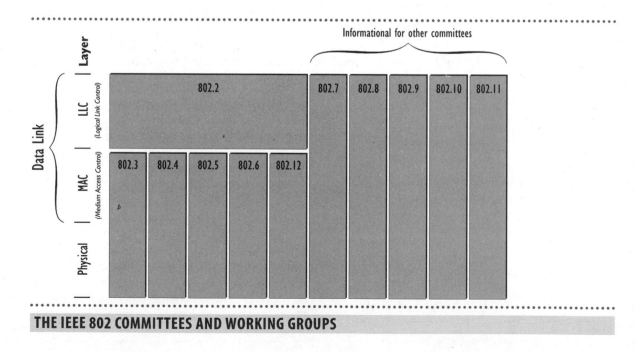

THE IEEE 802 COMMITTEES AND WORKING GROUPS

IFG (Interframe Gap)

The maximum amount of time between successive frames, or packets, in a network transmission. For example, in the LocalTalk variant of the AppleTalk software, an IFG of 200 microseconds is considered normal.

IFMP (Ipsilon Flow Management Protocol)

→ *See* Protocol, IFMP (Ipsilon Flow Management Protocol)

IFRB (International Frequency Registration Board)

An ITU (International Telecommunications Union) agency that is responsible for allocating frequency bands in the electromagnetic spectrum. Together with the *CCIR* (International Consultative Committee for Radiocommunication), the IFRB was replaced in 1993 by the ITU-R (International Telecommunication Union—Radiocommunication Standardization Sector).

→ *See Also* ITU

IFS (Installable File System)

An IFS is a file system that can be loaded dynamically into an operating system. Being able to treat an existing file system, such as the FAT (file allocation table) system used in DOS, as an IFS can help make newer operating systems or releases backward-compatible with earlier environments.

For example, Windows NT has an IFT, which can do the following:

- Read directories using FAT, CDFS (CD-ROM file system), or HPFS (high-performance file system, used in OS/2 formats).

- Read and write files using the formats appropriate for the file system.

Similarly, the IFS is a feature of Windows 95 that enables it, among other things, to provide 32-bit file access (32BFA), long file names, and built-in support for networks. The Windows 95 IFS services are provided by the IFSMgr VxD (IFS Manager virtual device driver).

IGRP (Interior Gateway Routing Protocol)

→ *See* Protocol, IGRP (Interior Gateway Routing Protocol)

IHL (Internet Header Length)

A field in an IP (Internet Protocol) datagram, or packet. The field's 4-bit value specifies the length of the datagram's header in 32-bit words.

IIOP (Internet Inter-ORB Protocol)

→ *See* Protocol, IIOP (Internet Inter-ORB Protocol)

IIS (Internet Information Server)

→ *See* Microsoft IIS (Internet Information Server)

ILEC (Incumbent Local Exchange Carrier)

The Telecommunications Act of 1996 decreed that competition to provide telephone services should be allowed at all levels of service. With respect to local telephone service, the existing service provider—known as the Local Exchange Carrier (LEC)—is known as the Incumbent LEC (ILEC). In most cases, this is a Regional Bell Operating Company (RBOC). Competing providers of local service are known as Competitive LECs (CLECs) or Other LECs (OLECs). These are independent carriers, in most cases.

→ *Broader Category* PSTN (Public Switched Telephone Network)

IM (Instant Messaging)

IM technology makes it possible for groups of users to establish online chat groups whose members can exchange electronic messages almost instantaneously. When a member of an IM group gets a message they are informed immediately if they are online. This is in contrast to ordinary e-mail management, in which users need to check their mail server for new messages.

Instant messaging is a fairly new technology, so there are currently only proprietary interfaces and standards. This technology—or, more precisely, access to it—is currently the focus of skirmishes between AOL (America Online) and MSN (Microsoft Network).

IMAC (Isochronous Media Access Control)

In the FDDI II architecture, an element in the architecture's media-access-control (MAC) layer that can handle time-dependent data, such as voice or video, received through a circuit-switched multiplexer (CS-MUX). This element is in contrast to the ordinary MAC component, which gets network data (packets) and processes them for transmission over the architecture's Physical layer.

Image Map

In an HTML (Hypertext Markup Language) file, an image map is an image whose area is responsive to mouse clicks. In other words, the image area is a hot spot that provides a link to another URL (Uniform Resource Locator—essentially, a Web page address).

However, unlike an ordinary image link, clicking on different parts of an image map will link to different URLs. Many corporate home pages use image maps. The different sections of the image map might send visitors to different divisions or product lines in the corporation.

Image maps can be server side or client side—depending on whether the image is created before the page is sent to the browser or while the browser is displaying the page. To create an image map, you need to specify the coordinates of each area, along with the URL to which the area links. This can be a tedious task, so various image map creation packages have been developed. These let you draw the area and identify the different sections. The program then determines the coordinates and generates the image map instructions.

→ *Broader Category* HTML (Hypertext Markup Language)

Impairment

Any of various types of degradation in electrical signals because of interference, loss, or distortion. Signal-to-noise ratio (SNR), echo, and response at different frequencies are examples of impairment measures.

Impedance

Impedance is the opposition alternating electrical current encounters as it moves along a circuit. Impedance is analogous to friction and is one cause of signal attenuation. Impedance represents the ratio of voltage to current along the transmission line, and it is measured in ohms.

Factors that determine the impedance of a cable segment include distance between conductors (such as between the signal wire and the conductive shield in coaxial cable), and the type of insulation surrounding the wire.

Most network architectures use cable with characteristic impedance. For example, Ethernet cabling is usually 50-ohm, and ARCnet uses 93-ohm cable.

Implicit Congestion Notification

A means of determining that there is congestion on a network. Certain transport protocols, such as TCP from the Internet TCP/IP protocol suite, can infer when network congestion is occurring. This notification is in contrast to explicit notification methods, such as the ECN (explicit congestion notification) method, used in frame-relay networks.

Improved Mobile Telephone Service (IMTS)

→ *See* IMTS (Improved Mobile Telephone Service)

IMR (Internet Monthly Report)

Notices of news and developments that are posted monthly on the Internet. You can get the report by joining the mailing list for the report or by downloading a copy whenever you feel curious.

IMS (Information Management Systems)

A mainframe-based database management and communications package from IBM for use in its SNA (Systems Network Architecture). IMS uses a hierarchical database model.

IMTS (Improved Mobile Telephone Service)

In mobile telephony, a type of service that allows direct dialing between a mobile telephone and an ordinary (wired) phone. (In this context, the ordinary telephone is known as a *wireline*.)

Incumbent Local Exchange Carrier (ILEC)

→ *See* ILEC (Incumbent Local Exchange Carrier)

Inband Signaling

Signaling and control information that is transmitted at frequencies that lie within the regular, data channel bandwidth, rather than using frequencies that lie outside this bandwidth (as in *out-of-band signaling*). A dial tone is an example of inband signaling. The term may also be written as *in-band signaling*.

Independent Telephone Company (ITC)

→ *See* ITC (Independent Telephone Company)

Index

In a database or other context, an index is a collection of keys, which provide access to records in the database. The keys in an index are generally organized in some type of data structure—such as a binary or B-tree or a hash table—that makes it easier to access a specific record in the database.

Index of Refraction

A measure of the degree to which light will travel at a different speed in a given medium, such as in water or in a fiber-optic core made of a particular type of material.

Index Server

→ *See* Microsoft Index Server

Index Service Manager

→ *See* HTML Service Manager

Inductance

Inductance is a property of an electrical circuit or device that can be used to counter the effects of capacitance on the electrical properties of a circuit. The power delivered in an electrical circuit is a function of both the voltage and the current, and is maximal when these two properties are in phase. Unfortunately, capacitance—the tendency for electrical charge to build up on a dielectric (nonconductor) between two conductors—gradually makes voltage and current fall out of phase, which reduces the power delivered in the circuit. Properly applied inductance can be used to bring voltage and current back into phase, thereby increasing the delivered power. Inductance coils with known properties are attached at specific locations to clean up and boost the power in an electrical connection. Such coils are essential elements in cabling for the telephone system.

→ *Compare* Capacitance

Inductor

An electrical component in line conditioners and surge protectors. Inductors help remove noise caused by electromagnetic and radio frequency interference. Compare this with a capacitor or MOV (metal oxide varistor)

Industrial, Scientific, and Medical (ISM)

→ *See* ISM (Industrial, Scientific, and Medical)

Industry Standard Architecture (ISA)

→ *See* ISA (Industry Standard Architecture)

Information Agent

A program that can search databases for information specified by the user. The information agent will search a predefined set of databases, or may allow the user to specify the database(s) to use.

Information Management Systems (IMS)

→ *See* IMS (Information Management Systems)

Information Systems Network (ISN)

→ *See* ISN (Information Systems Network)

Infrared Transmission

Infrared transmission is wireless communications, over a relatively small area, using infrared components to transmit and receive signals. Infrared transmissions use a frequency range just below the visible light spectrum. These waves are used in wireless networks, but require a line of sight connection between sender and receiver or between each of these and a common cell or target.

An infrared signal can be focused or diffuse. A focused signal is aimed directly at the target (receiver or cell); or the signal may be beamed at a surface and reflected off this to a receiver. A focused signal can travel over a greater range but only to a specific target. In contrast, a diffuse signal travels in multiple directions, but is much weaker in each direction. As a result, the range of a diffuse signal is much smaller than for a focused signal.

Transmissions that use reflection fall into two categories:

- *Directed transmissions* use a common central target, and all transceivers bounce and read signals off this target. A directed transmission is useful if the network configuration stays constant (if nodes do not move around). There are generally restrictions on the number of transceivers that can see the target and the range over which these transceivers are distributed.

- *Diffuse transmissions* use everyday objects, so that the target can change if necessary. This newer technology is useful if nodes are moved around a great deal.

In contrast to reflected transmissions, a point-to-point transmission aims the signal directly at the target.

Advantages of infrared transmissions include the following:

- Components are relatively inexpensive.

- Very high bandwidths, from about 400 gigahertz (GHz) to about 1 terahertz (THz) are possible.

- Signals can be reflected off surfaces (such as walls), so that direct line of sight is not necessary.

- Transmissions can be multidirectional.

Disadvantages of infrared transmissions include the following:

- Transmission distance is limited.

- Transmission cannot penetrate walls.

- Possible health risks from infrared radiation.

- Atmospheric conditions (such as rain or fog) can attenuate the signal.

Infrared transmissions are used in contrast to cable-based transmissions or to other types of wireless transmissions (such as those using microwaves).

No license is required for infrared networks.

→ **Broader Category** Network, Wireless

→ **Compare** Microwave Transmission; Radio Wave Transmission

Inheritance

In object-oriented programming (OOP), object classes are defined in terms of attributes and methods. The *methods* are the operations that individual examples of the object class can perform or that can be performed on the instances.

Once a class—C1—has been defined, other classes can be created and defined in terms of this class. Classes that are created in terms of another class are known as *descendants* of that class; the class that is the source of the descendant's definition is known as an *ancestor*.

A descendant's definition includes the definition of the ancestor class. This means, of course, that the attributes and methods of the ancestor class are already predefined for (inherited by) the descendant. *Inheritance* refers to this predefinition.

→ **Broader Category** OOP (Object-Oriented Programming)

Inherited Rights Mask/Inherited Rights Filter (IRM/IRF)

→*See* IRM/IRF (Inherited Rights Mask/Inherited Rights Filter)

Initial Domain Identifier (IDI)

→*See* IDI (Initial Domain Identifier)

In-Place Upgrade

An in-place upgrade is one that is installed over an earlier version. Because the previous version of files will be destroyed when you are using this type of upgrade, it is crucial to first back up the entire hard disk or partition and make sure you have a floppy boot disk.

If you have many files in the old format—*and* you can spare the space during installation—consider renaming the directory containing the old version, and then installing the new version in the directory structure that had been used.

Insertion Loss

The amount of signal loss at a connection in the cable or between the cable and a device, such as a transceiver or a node. This loss is measured in decibels (dB). With electrical cable, losses in the 10 dB range are not uncommon; with fiber-optic cable, losses are generally 2 dB or less.

Inside Wire

On a customer's premises, the wiring between an individual workstation and the demarcation point for the public wiring.

INSTALL

A Novell NetWare server utility used for managing, maintaining, and updating NetWare servers. INSTALL can be used for the following tasks:

- Creating, deleting, and managing hard-disk partitions and NetWare volumes on the server.

- Installing NetWare and other additional products, and updating the license or registration disk.

- Loading and unloading disk and LAN drivers.

- Adding, removing, repairing, checking, and unmirroring hard disks.

- Changing server startup and configuration files.

Installable File System (IFS)

→*See* IFS (Installable File System)

Instant Messaging (IM)

→*See* IM (Instant Messaging)

Insulation Displacement Contact (IDC)

→*See* IDC (Insulation Displacement Contact)

INT 14H

The PC interrupt used to reroute messages from the serial port to the network interface card. This interrupt is used by some terminal-emulation programs. The bit-oriented INT 14H is generally regarded as being badly documented, but it is widely used nonetheless. An alternative is to use INT 6BH. This is the approach taken, for example, in Novell's NASI (NetWare Asynchronous Services Interface). NASI is generally considered faster than the INT 14H approach, but it is not as widely supported.

Integral Controller

A controller built into a mainframe, as opposed to an external controller, which is a separate device.

Integrated Database Application Programming Interface (IDAPI)

→ *See* IDAPI (Integrated Database Application Programming Interface)

Integrated Digital Access (IDA)

→ *See* IDA (Integrated Digital Access)

Integrated Digital Network (IDN)

→ *See* IDN (Integrated Digital Network)

Integrated Drive Electronics (IDE)

→ *See* IDE (Integrated Drive Electronics)

Integrated Services Digital Network (ISDN)

→ *See* ISDN (Integrated Services Digital Network)

Integrated Services Local Area Network 16T (ISLAN16T)

→ *See* IsoEthernet

Integrated Service Unit (ISU)

→ *See* ISU (Integrated Service Unit)

Integrated Software

Software in which several applications are mutually accessible and able to exchange and update data in a consistent and transparent manner. While it is not required, the component applications are generally on a single machine—either a stand-alone computer or on a server. Arguably, office suites (such as Microsoft Office, Corel WordPerfect Suite, and Lotus SmartSuite) are among the best known and most widely used examples of integrated software.

Various techniques are available to enable programs to exchange data. These vary in their level of sophistication, power, and complexity. At the most basic level, IPC (interprocess communication) capabilities can be used to accomplish such exchanges—provided one is willing and able to write the necessary programs. Prefab capabilities include the Windows Clipboard, DDE (Dynamic Data Exchange), and OLE (Object Linking and Embedding). Of these, OLE is the most powerful. The office packages use Microsoft's OLE technology to make possible automatic updates in applications whenever data or documents are revised. Database and network access may be provided through other package components—generally add-on modules.

Generally, such integrated packages are controlled by a task management component, through which the user can get access to any of the applications in the suite. These components usually can also be configured to launch other Windows applications.

I

Integrated Terminal

A terminal capable of handling multiple streams, such as voice, video, and data.

Integrated Voice and Data (IVD)

→ *See* IVD (Integrated Voice and Data)

Intelligent Peripheral Interface (IPI)

→ *See* IPI (Intelligent Peripheral Interface)

Intelligent Printer Data Stream (IPDS)

→ *See* IPDS (Intelligent Printer Data Stream)

Interactive Voice Response (IVR)

→ *See* IVR (Interactive Voice Response)

Inter-Application Communication (IAC)

→ *See* IAC (Inter-Application Communication)

Interconnect Company

A company that supplies telecommunications equipment to connect to telephone lines. Such equipment must be registered with the telephone company before it can be connected to the telephone company's lines.

Inter-Dialog Gap (IDG)

→ *See* IDG (Inter-Dialog Gap)

Interdomain Routing Protocol

The ISO equivalent of an exterior gateway protocol (EGP) in the Internet vocabulary. This type of protocol routes packets between different domains (subnetworks under the control of a single organization) in an internetwork. IDRP is also the name of a specific interdomain routing protocol.

→ *See* IDRP, Protocol

Interexchange Carrier (IEC or IXC)

→ *See* IXC (Interexchange Carrier)

Interface Definition Language (IDL)

→ *See* IDL (Interface Definition Language)

Interface, Hardware

A hardware interface is a hardware connection between two devices. A hardware interface requires physical, electrical, and functional specifications that define how the two devices connect and communicate.

The physical interface specifies features such as the number of pins, wires, and so on, and the manner in which these are arranged and attached.

The electrical interface specifies the magnitude, duration, and sign of electrical signals. For example, it specifies the voltage level and duration for 0 and 1 values. Three types of electrical interface are commonly used: voltage, current loop, and contact closure.

The functional interface specifies the interpretation of the signals on each wire. For example, for the EIA-232D serial interface, pins 2 and 3 are for transmitting and receiving data, respectively; pins 4 and 5 are request to send (RTS) and clear to send (CTS), respectively.

Some common hardware interfaces include the following:

- EIA-232D, which specifies 25-pins, asynchronous or synchronous serial transmissions, at up to 19,200bps for up to 15 meters (50 feet). This revision has replaced the old, familiar RS-232C interface.

- EIA-530, which specifies 25-pins, asynchronous or synchronous serial transmissions at up to 2Mbps for up to 610 meters (2000 feet). This interface is getting considerable support from the United States government, and may eventually supplant EIA-232D.

- V.24/V.28, which is a CCITT standard that is functionally equivalent to EIA-232D.

- V.90, which is an ITU T standard for 56Kbps modems.

Interface, Software

A software interface is a software connection between two programs or two program elements, such as procedures or functions. Software interfaces are characterized by several features, including the following:

- Parameters, which are slots used to pass information between processes. Parameters may be typed (passed as characters, digits, or other pre-interpreted values, as in Pascal or C functions) or untyped (passed as bytes or blocks, as when streams are used).

- Parameter format, which determines how the bits in a byte are ordered, such as whether the least or most significant bit is passed first.

- Evaluation order, which determines whether parameters are evaluated from left to right or from right to left.

- Clean-up responsibilities, which determine whether the calling or the responding process is responsible for getting rid of parameters from the stack after the interaction is complete and the parameters are no longer needed.

Application program interfaces (APIs) provide a commonly used means of passing information between programs, in particular, between an application program and an operating system. APIs provide predefined calls for accomplishing this.

Interface Data Unit (IDU)

→ See IDU (Interface Data Unit)

Interference

Unanticipated input that affects the definition or quality of data being transmitted. The sources of interference depend on the type of signals involved and on the context. For example, electrical signals are susceptible to other electrical signals, magnetic fields, jamming, and atmospheric conditions. In contrast, optical signals are relatively impervious to these types of interference.

Interframe Gap (IFG)

→ See IFG (Interframe Gap)

Interior Gateway Routing Protocol (IGRP)

→ See Protocol, IGRP (Interior Gateway Routing Protocol)

InterLATA

In telephony, circuits or services that cross between two exchanges, which are known as local access and transport areas, or LATAs. InterLATA services are provided by interexchange carriers (IXCs).

INTERLNK

In MS DOS 6.x, INTERLNK is a program that makes it possible to connect two computers through serial or parallel ports, and to share drives and printer ports on the computers.

One of the computers (the client) can access the drives and printers on the other (the server). For the connection to work, the following conditions must be met:

- For serial connections: three-wire serial cable or seven-wire null-modem cable and a free serial port on each computer

- For parallel connections: a bidirectional parallel cable and free parallel ports on each computer

- DOS 6.x on one computer and DOS 3.3 or later on the other

- The INTERLNK.EXE program on client computers, and an entry in the client's CONFIG.SYS file to load this driver

- 16KB and 130 KB of available memory on the client and server, respectively

To start the server, the INTERSVR command is used.

Intermediate Cross-Connect

In a premises distribution system (PDS), a cross-connect (connection between blocks) between wiring closets.

Intermediate Distribution Frame (IDF)

➞ *See* IDF (Intermediate Distribution Frame)

Intermediate System (IS)

➞ *See* IS (Intermediate System)

Intermediate System (IS)

➞ *See* IS (Intermediate System)

Intermediate System to Intermediate System (IS-IS) Protocol

➞ *See* Protocol, IS-IS (Intermediate System to Intermediate System)

Internal Organization of the Network Layer (IONL)

➞ *See* IONL (Internal Organization of the Network Layer)

Internal PAD

In an X.25 or other packet-switching network, a packet assembler and disassembler (PAD) that is located within a packet-switching node.

Internal Routing

In networks using Novell's NetWare, internal routing provides access to multiple networks within a single file server. Each network is represented by a separate network interface card (NIC) in the server. The routing between cards (that is, between networks) is accomplished by using the file server's NetWare operating system to move material.

The use of internal routing increases flexibility because each NIC can be connected to its own physical network. In fact, these networks can use different protocols. For example, one NIC can be connected to an Ethernet network, and another to an ARCnet or Token Ring network, as shown in "Internal routing."

International Alphabet (IA5)

→ *See* IA5 (International Alphabet 5)

International Electrotechnical Commission (IEC)

→ *See* IEC (International Electrotechnical Commission)

International Frequency Registration Board (IFRB)

→ *See* IFRB (International Frequency Registration Board)

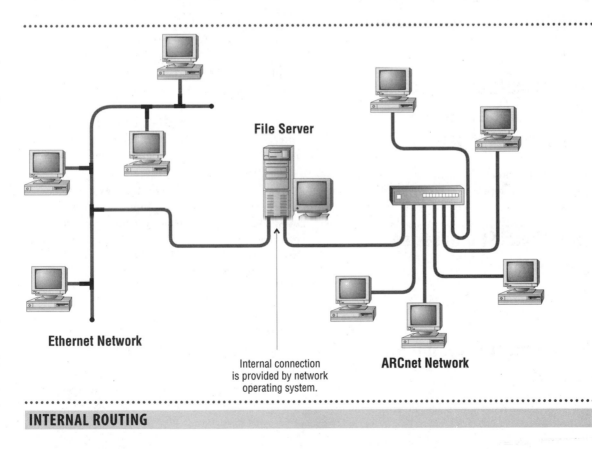

File Server

Ethernet Network

Internal connection
is provided by network
operating system.

ARCnet Network

INTERNAL ROUTING

International Numbering Plan

In telecommunications, a strategy developed by the CCITT for allocating telephone numbers around the world. There are several subplans, each for different regions of the world, including ones for North America and Europe.

International Reference Version (IRV)

→ *See* IRV (International Reference Version)

International Standardization Organization (ISO)

→ *See* ISO (International Standardization Organization)

International Standardization Organization Development Environment (ISODE)

→ *See* ISODE (International Standardization Organization Development Environment)

International Standardized Profile (ISP)

→ *See* ISP (International Standardized Profile)

International Telecommunications Union (ITU)

→ *See* ITU (International Telecommunications Union)

International Telecommunications Union—Telecommunications Standardization Section (ITU-T)

→ *See* ITU-T (International Telecommunications Union—Telecommunications Standardization Sector)

Internet

As a general term, an internet is an internetwork, which is a network consisting of two or more smaller networks that can communicate with each other. See the Internetwork article for a discussion of this type of networking.

As a specific reference, *the* Internet (note the uppercase *I*) is the giant internetwork created originally by linking various research and defense networks (such as NSFnet, MILnet, and CREN). Since then, various other networks—large and small, public and private—have become attached to the Internet. Depending on the definition we use for host, the Internet has anywhere from about 8 million to over 50 million hosts. Either way, the Internet is by far the largest network in the world. Just a list of all the nodes would be a book much larger than this one.

The Internet, its ancestors, and its subnetworks have been the developing grounds for many of the most commonly used protocols and networking principles. For example, the TCP/IP protocol suite was developed as part of the ARPAnet project, which was a predecessor to many of the subnetworks, and also to the Internet itself.

Internet Structure

The Internet has a three-tiered structure:

- The *backbone* is the highest level in the Internet hierarchy; it is the level that holds the entire Internet together. It consists of networks such as NSFNET and EBONE. The backbone will carry traffic and do routing for the intermediate (transit) level networks. Because this high-level traffic volume can get heavy, the backbone networks have a very high bandwidth. For example, the NSFNET runs over T3 lines, which have a bandwidth of about 45Mbps. Bandwidth problems already arise occasionally, and the general consensus is that a bandwidth crisis is quite likely.

- The *mid-level networks*—also known as *regional*, or *transit, networks*—lie below the backbone. These carry data and do routing for the lower-level (stub) networks and for their own hosts. A mid-level network must have paths to at least two other networks. Examples of transit networks include NEAR-NET, PSINet and SURANET. A mid-level computer is sometimes known as a rib site because it's an appendage off the backbone. (It just goes to show you that even as technical a

topic as networking can sometimes get a good ribbing ☺).

- The *stub networks* are basically local or metropolitan area networks. These carry packets only between hosts, but not between networks. This is the level with which most users communicate. A stub network may be connected to other networks, but will not carry traffic for them. Examples of stub networks include Bestweb and the Santa Cruz Community Internet.

This structure is sketched in the illustration "Three levels of Internet networks."

The Internet grows very rapidly: at the rate of 10 to 20 percent per *month*. The number of networks branching off the Internet backbone more than doubled within a 16-month period. There are now millions of nodes, and planning is already underway for managing a *billion*-node internetwork.

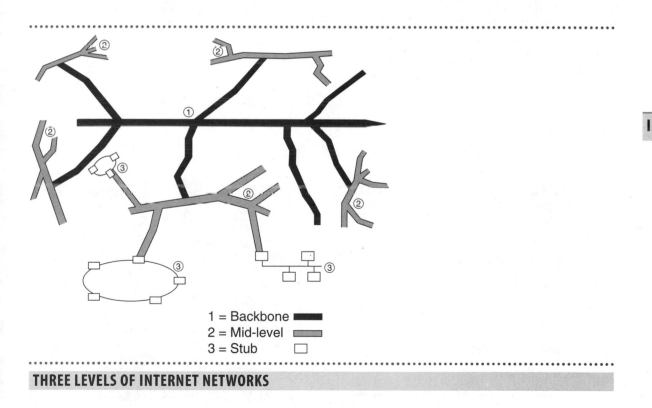

1 = Backbone ▬▬
2 = Mid-level ▬▬
3 = Stub ☐

THREE LEVELS OF INTERNET NETWORKS

Internet Organizations

The IAB (Internet Architecture Board, formerly Internet Activities Board) oversees standards and development for the Internet. This board also administers, with the help of the IANA (Internet Assigned Numbers Authority), the internet(1) subtree in the global tree in which all networking knowledge is stored.

The IANA is responsible for assigning values for networks, attributes, and so on. This service, which is operated by the University of Southern California Information Sciences Institute (USC-ISI) makes sure that the same identifier values are not assigned to two different entities.

The IAB has two task forces: IETF (Internet Engineering Task Force) and IRTF (Internet Research Task Force). The IETF is the committee largely responsible for formulating the Remote Network Monitoring Management Information Base (RMON MIB), which is expected to become the standard for monitoring and reporting network activity in the Internet environment.

The IRTF works on long-term research projects. These projects may have to do with any aspect of Internet operations, and some results have led or may lead to major changes in certain aspects of Internet activity. Topics on which the IRTF has worked include how to increase the privacy of electronic mail, and how to make services available to mutually suspicious participants.

The IESG (Internet Engineering Steering Group) is the executive committee for the IETF. The IRSG (Internet Research Steering Group) is the group that oversees the IRTF.

GETTING IN TOUCH WITH THE ISOC

You can write, phone, fax, or send e-mail to ISOC:

- The Internet Society; 11150 Sunset Hills Road, Suite 100; Reston, VA 20190-5321; USA

- Telephone: (703) 326-9880

- Fax: (703) 326-9881

The ISOC (Internet Society) is an international organization that promotes the use of the Internet for communication and collaboration. It provides a forum for the discussion of issues related to the administration and evolution of the Internet. The ISN (Internet Society News) is the official newsletter of ISOC. "Internet administrative layout" shows how these various committees and groups are related.

There are hundreds (possibly thousands) of services and resources available on the Internet. These include the following:

- Electronic mail (e-mail)

- Remote login services (Telnet)

- Special interest and other discussion groups and forums (Usenet)

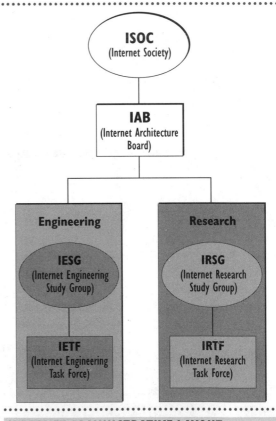

INTERNET ADMINISTRATIVE LAYOUT

- File retrieval and transfer services (FTP)

- Various services to find files, interest groups, and even individual users (including Archie, Veronica, Jughead, Gopher, Finger, and World Wide Web, or WWW)

- Magazines, news services, directories, and other information (including White Pages Directories and mailing lists)

- Real-time, node-to-node or conference communications (Talk and Internet Relay Chat, or IRC)

- Games, jokes, and other diversions for passing, enjoying, or wasting your time

The following is a very brief summary of some of the more commonly used services and resources on the Internet. Just a list of the close to 30,000 Usenet discussion groups runs longer than 50 pages in small print.

Archie   A service for gathering, indexing, and displaying information (such as a list of the files available through anonymous FTP). See the Archie entry for information about specific Archie clients and servers.

Browsers   Programs that can read hypertext files, such as those found on the World Wide Web (WWW). Various browsers are available, ranging from the line- and text-oriented Lynx to the graphics- and multimedia-browsers such as Microsoft Internet Explorer and Netscape Navigator. See the entry on browsers and entries for specific browsers for more information.

Finger   A service that can provide information about the person associated with a particular userid.

FTP   A program that allows you to transfer files between computers. Many Internet nodes contain files that are available to the general public through anonymous FTP. An FTP program is generally provided by Internet Access Providers as part of their basic software package.

Gopher   A distributed service that can organize and provide access to hierarchically related information. The information can be in various forms: library catalogs, databases, newsgroups, and so on. Very popular during the Internet's earlier—more text-oriented and less Web-dominated—days, Gopher services are used relatively rarely these days.

Internet Hunt   A monthly information scavenger hunt in which participants try to find the answers to 10 questions using only resources available on the Internet. The Internet hunt is an excellent, fun, and non-threatening way to learn about the Internet and its available services and resources.

IRC (Internet Relay Chat)   A service that extends Talk capabilities to allow multiparty conversations.

Jughead   A service that helps make certain Gopher searches easier and more manageable.

Lycos   A portal (see below) as well as a tool for searching for documents on the World Wide Web. Lycos is a search engine with information on a significant percentage of the estimated 350+ million Web documents. Go to http://www.lycos.com to see the Internet through Lycos.

Mail   A very basic mail service developed for UNIX systems, but also available on the Internet. Other mail programs are easier and/or more powerful. These include Elm and Pine (for UNIX) and Eudora and Outlook Express (for Windows).

MUDs   These Multiuser Dimensions (or Dungeons) are sophisticated descendants of earlier dungeons and dragons games. MUDs and related resources (MUSHes, MOOs, MUSEs, etc.) provide interactive game or virtual environments in which players can assume roles or characters, can manipulate simulated environments (labs, societies, etc), or just socialize. Each MUD environment has its own client and server programs.

News   Various newsreaders (programs for searching and reading news items) are available on the Internet. UNIX newsreaders include rn (read news), nn (no news, a more selective newsreader), and tin (threaded Internet newsreader). Windows newsreaders include News Xpress, WinTrumpet, and WinVN.

Ping   A simple program that can be used to determine whether a connection is available between your machine and a specified other machine. You can also use Ping to test whether you're connected properly to your Internet Access Provider.

Players   Programs for playing various kinds of audio or sound files. Players differ in the file formats they can handle, in the speakers and sound boards they support, and in the platforms on which they run. For Windows, RealAudio is probably the most widely used audio player.

Portal   A Web home page that strongly influences a Web surfer's view of the Internet because it is the first page the user sees when logging on to the Internet. The content and—perhaps even more important in the eyes of many—the advertisements that the user sees can have a considerable advantage over competitors whose materials are buried somewhere deep in the Web's 350+ million pages. Excite, Infoseek, Lycos, MSN (the Microsoft Network), and Yahoo! are among the most popular portals.

Readers   Programs for interpreting and displaying the contents of formatted documents (such as PostScript files). Such programs must be able to understand formatting and layout commands and must also be able to translate these into instructions for displaying the material on the screen. Arguably, the best known reader is the one for Adobe Acrobat. Readers are essentially viewers (see below) for documents.

Talk   A service that allows two users logged onto the Internet to communicate with each other in real time (subject to any transmission and routing delays).

Telnet   A program that provides terminal-emulation capabilities for logging in to a network from a remote location.

Usenet   A loose network of close to 30,000 discussion groups about various topics ranging from the mainstream and mundane to the esoteric and "out of this world," with some topics being even further out than that.

Veronica   A service that helps make Gopher searches easier and more manageable.

Viewers   Programs for displaying various types of graphics or video files. Viewers differ in the kinds of files they can handle, in whether they can handle compressed files (either on-the-fly or through preprocessing), and in whether they can handle animation or video formats. Viewers generally fall into one of three categories: those that can handle images (possibly compressed), those for displaying animation, and those for displaying video.

Wais   A service that can be used to gather information about a topic from various locations and provide easier access to the information.

White Pages Directories   Resources that provide electronic address listings for users on the Internet.

World Wide Web   A giant information network containing—according to one estimate—over 350 million hypertext documents that are accessible through Web server programs. To access and read or print such documents, users need a browser program that can request the documents from the server and display them for the user. The Web is currently the fastest growing segment of the Internet as individuals and corporations are discovering the advantages of putting their own Web pages (hypertext documents) on the Web.

WWWW (World Wide Web Worm)   A search engine for finding hypertext documents on the Web. WWWW can search for keywords or keyword combinations in titles, authors, or contents of the documents, and will display the addresses of documents that match your search criteria. WWWW has information about more than 3 million documents.

Yahoo!   An information locator service and also a portal, Yahoo! provides an excellent starting point for exploring all sorts of content areas. To start such a search at the top level, just go to `http://www.yahoo.com`.

internet(1)

In the global tree of network information, a subtree administered by the Internet Activities Board (IAB). The full name for this subtree is 1.3.6.1; the local name is {dod1}. Notable subtrees under this one include *mgmt(2)*, which contains the definitions for network management objects and packages.

→ *See Also*   Global Tree

Internet Access Provider (IAP)

→ *See*   ISP (Internet Service Provider)

Internet Architecture Board (IAB)

→ *See*   IAB (Internet Architecture Board)

Internet Assigned Numbers Authority (IANA)

→ *See*   IANA (Internet Assigned Numbers Authority)

Internet Control Message Protocol (ICMP)

→ *See*   Protocol, ICMP (Internet Control Message Protocol)

Internet Corporation for Assigned Names and Numbers (ICANN)

→ *See*   ICANN (Internet Corporation for Assigned Names and Numbers)

Internet Database

→ *See*   Database

Internet Database Connector (IDC)

→ *See*   IDC (Internet Database Connector)

Internet Domain

In Windows NT, an Internet domain is a network whose computers can all communicate with each other without the need of a router. That is, the domain provides a grouping of computers that requires no routing as long as communications are only between computers within the domain. A router would be necessary if a computer wanted to communicate with another one in a different domain.

Internet Engineering Steering Group (IESG)

→ *See*   IESG (Internet Engineering Steering Group)

Internet Engineering Task Force (IETF)

→ *See*   IETF (Internet Engineering Task Force)

Internet Explorer

→ *See* MSIE (Microsoft Internet Explorer)

Internet Header Length (IHL)

→ *See* IHL (Internet Header Length)

Internet Hunt

A monthly quiz that poses 10 questions. All the answers must be found using only the Internet and its resources. The hunt is both entertaining and enlightening. It provides an excellent, non-threatening way to learn about the Internet. To get the list of questions, point a gopher client to the `gopher.cic.net host`.

Internet Information Server (IIS)

→ *See* Microsoft IIS (Internet Information Server)

Internet Inter-ORB Protocol (IIOP)

→ *See* Protocol, IIOP (Internet Inter-ORB Protocol)

Internet Layer

In the TCP/IP protocol stack, the Internet layer is where packets move between source and destination in a network or between networks. In short, this is the layer at which routing decisions are made and carried out. The Internet layer corresponds roughly to the Network layer in the OSI reference model.

Protocols used at this layer include the following:

Address Resolution Protocol (ARP) This is used on a LAN to translate an Internet address into the corresponding physical hardware address. Compare DHCP and RARP below.

Dynamic Host Configuration Protocol (DHCP) This is used to assign an Internet address on the fly to a network node. Functionally, DHCP is equivalent to, but more versatile than, RARP. DHCP also is a functional inverse of ARP, in that it finds (actually, assigns) an Internet address, given a physical hardware address. (Microsoft uses DHCP—rather than RARP—for its TCP/IP stack.)

Internet Control Message Protocol (ICMP) This protocol controls data flow and reports congestion or other error conditions. ICMP uses IP to do its work.

Internet Protocol (IP) This provides a directionless, best-effort delivery of packets between nodes on the same or different networks. *Directionless* means that packets do not necessarily take the same path between source and destination. *Best-effort* means that there is no guarantee that the packets will be delivered in order—or even that they will be delivered at all.

Reverse Address Resolution Protocol (RARP) This does essentially the same thing as DHCP—namely, assign an Internet address given a physical hardware address—except that RARP is more restrictive and more tedious to use. Most implementations of TCP/IP currently use the newer DHCP. RARP is, as its name suggests, the opposite of ARP.

Internet Monthly Report (IMR)

→ *See* IMR (Internet Monthly Report)

Internet Packet Exchange Open Data-Link Interface (IPXODI)

→ *See* IPXODI (Internet Packet Exchange Open Data-Link Interface)

Internet Protocol (IP) Address

→*See* IP (Internet Protocol) Address

Internet Protocol (IP) Datagram

→*See* IP (Internet Protocol) Datagram

Internet Protocol (IP) Masquerade

→*See* IP (Internet Protocol) Masquerade

Internet Protocol (IP) Multicast

→*See* IP (Internet Protocol) Multicast

Internet Protocol, Secure (IPSEC)

→*See* Protocol, IPSEC (Internet Protocol, Secure)

Internet Protocol (IP) Spoofing

→*See* IP (Internet Protocol) Spoofing

Internet Protocol (IP) Switching

→*See* IP (Internet Protocol) Switching

Internet Protocol (IP) Tunneling

→*See* IP (Internet Protocol) Tunneling

Internet Registry (IR)

→*See* IR (Internet Registry)

Internet Relay Chat (IRC)

→*See* IRC (Internet Relay Chat)

Internet Research Steering Group (IRSG)

→*See* IRSG (Internet Research Steering Group)

Internet Research Task Force (IRTF)

→*See* IRTF (Internet Research Task Force)

Internet Router (IR)

→*See* IR (Internet Router)

Internet Server

→*See* Server, Internet

Internet Server Application Programming Interface (ISAPI)

→*See* ISAPI (Internet Server Application Programming Interface)

Internet Server Application Programming Interface (ISAPI) Application

→*See* ISAPI (Internet Server Application Programming Interface)

Internet Server Application Programming Interface (ISAPI) Filter

→ **See** ISAPI (Internet Server Application Programming Interface)

Internet Service Manager

→ **See** HTML Service Manager

Internet Service Provider (ISP)

→ **See** ISP (Internet Service Provider)

Internet Services List

A list of services available on the Internet. The list is maintained by Scott Yanoff and is updated regularly. You can use anonymous ftp to get the list from the /pub directory of the csd4.csd.uwm.edu FTP site.

Internet Society News (ISN)

→ **See** ISN (Internet Society News)

Internet Standard (IS)

→ **See** IS (Internet Standard)

Internet Talk Radio (ITR)

→ **See** ITR (Internet Talk Radio)

Internetwork

An internetwork is a network that consists of two or more smaller networks that can communicate with each other, usually over a bridge, router, or gateway.

Internetworking has long been one of the major buzzwords in the world of networking. Implementing the concepts behind the term is one of the major problems and sources of confusion in the world of networking. Cisco Systems has taken a major step toward taming the internetworking problems with their IOS (Internetworking Operating System), which is discussed in a separate entry.

Internetworking is the process of establishing and maintaining communications, and of sending data among multiple networks. The goal in an internetworking task is to get data from one user (the source) to another (the destination). This is known as end-to-end service.

Stating the goal is easy; accomplishing it is something else entirely. The details of how to provide the end-to-end service depend to a large extent on the ends, but also on the intermediaries: the nodes and other devices encountered along the way. The following types of connections are common:

LAN to LAN The local area networks (LANs) are assumed to be close enough so that such a connection does not need telecommunications capabilities. Difficulties can arise if the LANs use different network architectures.

LAN to mainframe A connection between a LAN and a mainframe may or may not require telephone communications. The task will almost certainly involve data translations (for example, on their way through a gateway), and will probably require terminal emulation on the part of the LAN's representative in the connection.

LAN to WAN A connection between a LAN and a wide area network (WAN) requires telecommunications capabilities. The distance-related phase can be either slow or expensive.

With ordinary telephone lines, the slow speeds (up to about 19,200 bits per second) create a bottleneck, since LAN speeds are several hundred times as fast. Fast lines, on the other hand, are still expensive. Once the telecommunications problems are resolved, network protocol compatibility remains a potential problem.

The details of how to accomplish internetwork connections have filled many thousands of pages, because internetworking can take many forms and may take place at any of several layers. For example, for relay systems such as X.25, the internetworking takes place through the three lowest layers of the OSI reference model. In particular, X.25 protocols operate at the Network layer.

In contrast, for Message Handling Systems such as the CCITT X.400 recommendations, communications between networks may take place at the application layer. In all cases, however, the lower layers eventually need to get involved in order to do the actual relaying of packets.

Connectionless and Connection-Oriented Services

One fundamental distinction has guided much of the work on internetworking: the distinction between connectionless and connection-oriented services.

Connection-Oriented Services

When the network services are connection-oriented, a temporary (for the duration of the communication) path is established, and data is relayed along this connection.

Because the path is pre-established, certain routing information can be assumed, which simplifies the packets that need to be constructed and sent. In all acceptable internetworking implementations, these details should be completely transparent to the users. As far as users are concerned, the connection between the endpoints is direct. Because connection-oriented services are so tidy, it is easier to do error-checking and flow control.

Various protocols have been developed to provide connection-oriented services. For example, the CCITT's X.25 is a connection-oriented Network layer protocol, as is CONP (Connection-Oriented Network Protocol). The X.25 protocol has been adapted for connection-oriented services by both the OSI and the Internet communities. COTP (Connection-Oriented Transport Protocol) is a protocol for the transport layer. The NetWare SPX (Sequenced Packet Exchange) protocol is connection-oriented.

Connectionless Services

In connectionless service, data transmission does not need to wait for a path to be established. Packets are routed independently to their destinations, so that two packets from the same message or transmission might take two different paths.

Because packets travel independently, they probably will not arrive in order. Consequently, the original sequence needs to be reconstructed at the destination end. This is generally done at the transport layer in the OSI reference model.

CLNP (Connectionless-mode Network Protocol), CLTP (Connectionless-mode Transport Protocol), and UDP (User Datagram Protocol) are connectionless service protocols. The first two are used in OSI environments; the UDP is used in TCP/IP-based environments. The IPX (Internetwork Packet Exchange) and the MHS (Message Handling Service) protocols are two examples of connectionless NetWare protocols.

Internetworking Features

Internetworking may involve only local networks, or there may be long-distance connections between networks, so that WAN connections come into play. Paths between endpoints can get quite long, particularly if there are many networks between the two end users.

Regardless of the layer under consideration or of the types of networks involved, the internetworking process always has the same type of structure:

- Any required internetworking services are supplied for a layer by the layer below it. For example, transport-layer protocols get routing (pathfinding) and relaying (data-movement) services from the Network layer.

- The services are requested and provided through well-defined service access points (SAPs). These SAPs not only provide interfaces, but they also provide unambiguous addresses by which to refer to the user of the network services.

- The actual data-transmission path may include one or more intermediate systems, which are usually routers. The routers will make use of the lower three OSI layers, known as the *subnet layers*, to move the data along to the next router or to the destination node.

"Layer-oriented view of an internetworking path" shows the elements involved in an internetworking process. Note that the service users need to know nothing about the details of the transmission path.

In addition, several features are *desirable* in any internetworking service:

- The use of the services should be completely transparent to the end users. Any required routing and relaying should be done by the service providers, and should be of no concern to the end users.

- The use of the services should not affect the transmitted data in any way. This means that the data that reaches the destination should be identical to the data that left the user, regardless of where the data has been during its journey. The exception is when a gateway is used to send data to a different type of network, so that the data may *need* to look different when it reach its destination.

- The end users should be able to expect a given quality of service when using the network services.

→ **Primary Sources** ISO documents 8208 and 8878 (X.25); ISO document 8208 (CONP); ISO document 8073 and CCITT recommendation X.224

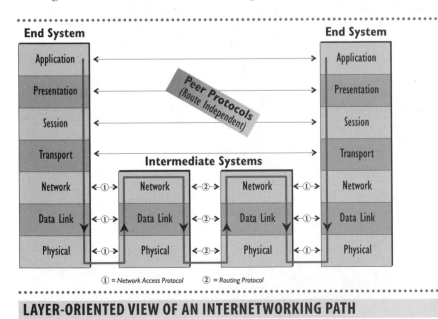

① = Network Access Protocol   ② = Routing Protocol

LAYER-ORIENTED VIEW OF AN INTERNETWORKING PATH

(COTP); ISO document 8348 (connectionless services); ISO documents 8473 and 8880-3 (CLNP); ISO 8602 (CLTP); RFC 768 (UDP).

→ **See Also**   Internetwork Link

→ **Compare**   Interoperability

Internetworking Unit (IWU)

→ **See**   IWU (Internetworking Unit)

Internetwork Link

An internetwork link serves to connect two or more networks. The networks may be identical, similar, or dissimilar. They may be located near each other or far apart. "Context of internetwork links" summarizes these types of connections.

Identical networks use the same PC and network architectures and the same or comparable cabling. For example, a bridge may link two token-ring networks or a thin (10Base2) Ethernet network to a

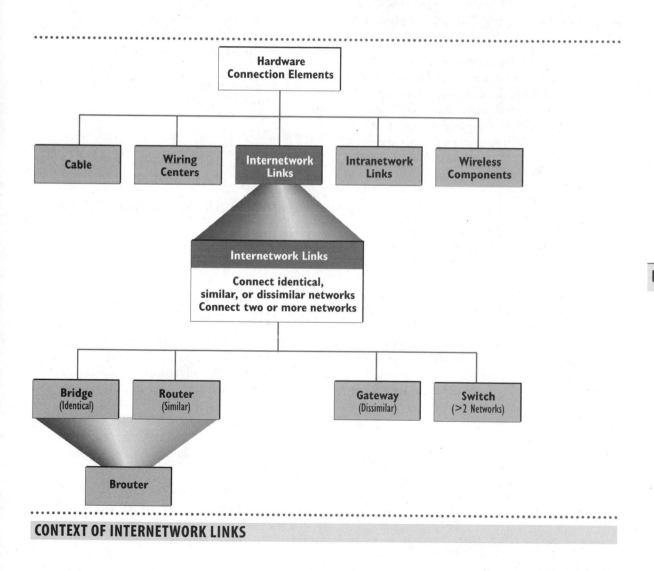

CONTEXT OF INTERNETWORK LINKS

twisted-pair (10BaseT) network. These types of networks are often created for convenience. For example, an internetwork may be created to turn a large network into two smaller ones, in order to reduce network traffic.

Similar networks use the same PC architecture (for example, Intel-based) but may use different network architectures, such as Ethernet and Token Ring. Dissimilar networks use different hardware and software, such as Ethernet and an IBM mainframe.

Internetwork links differ in the level at which they operate. This difference also affects the kinds of networks they can link. The following links may be used:

- A *bridge* provides connections at the Data-Link layer, and it is often used to connect networks that use the same architecture. A bridge serves both as a link and as a filter: passing messages from one network to the other, but discarding messages that are intended only for the local network. This filtering helps reduce traffic in each network.

- A *router* determines a path to a destination for a packet, and then starts the packet on its way. The destination may be in a network removed from the router by one or more intermediate networks. To determine a path, a router communicates with other routers in the larger (inter)network. Routers operate at the Network layer, and most are protocol-dependent; that is, each router generally can handle only a single network-layer protocol. Special multiprotocol routers, such as Novell's Multiprotocol Router, are available. Because they need to do much more work to get a packet to its destination, routers tend to be slower than bridges.

- A *brouter* combines the features of a bridge and a router. It has the forwarding capabilities of a router, and the protocol independence of a bridge. Brouters can process packets at either the data-link or network level.

- A *gateway* moves packets between two different computer environments, such as between a local area network and a mainframe environment or between Macintosh and PC networks. Gateways operate at the session layer and above. Because they connect dissimilar networks, gateways may need to do data translation (for example, between ASCII and EBCDIC), compression or expansion, encryption or decryption, and so on.

- A *switch* (in this context) is a multiport bridge or gateway. Whereas a gateway connects two environments (for example, two electronic-mail systems), a mail switch can connect several such systems. Similarly, an Ethernet switch can direct packets to any of several Ethernet subnetworks to which the switch is attached.

→ **See Also**   Bridge; Brouter; Gateway; Intranetwork Link; Router; Switch

Internetwork Operating System (IOS)

→ **See**   IOS (Internetwork Operating System)

InterNIC

The InterNIC is the domain name authority. That is, it is the root DNS (Domain Naming Service) source, and it assigns all the top-level domain names (for example, `.com`, `.org`, `.au`, `.fr`, and so forth) throughout the world. In the United States, the InterNIC also assigns most second-level domain names (for example, `microsoft`, `netscape`, and `sybex`. (The InterNIC does not assign `.mil` and `.us` domain names.)

The term InterNIC is sometimes used to refer more generally to any naming authority for top- and second-level domain names.

Interoffice Channel (IOC)

→ *See* IOC (Interoffice Channel)

Interoperability

The other great buzzword, along with *internet-working*, in the network world is *interoperability*. This term refers to the ability of two different networks to work together. For example, interoperability describes how networks can communicate or share data with each other, regardless of whether these networks use the same network architecture.

Interoperability is taken for granted when the networks are homogeneous; that is, when they use the same architecture. Even when the networks are heterogeneous, some degree of interoperability is almost always possible, although the costs in performance degradation or in required equipment may be unacceptably high.

One way to think of these terms is to regard interoperability as the capability for working together and internetworking as the actual cooperation.

The term interoperability is also used to refer to the ability of different software products to work together in the same environment.

→ *See Also* Internetwork

Interpersonal Messaging (IPM)

→ *See* IPM (Interpersonal Messaging)

Interpersonal Messaging Service (IPMS)

→ *See* IPMS (Interpersonal Messaging Service)

Interprocess Communication (IPC)

→ *See* IPC (Interprocess Communication)

Inter-Repeater Link (IRL)

In an Ethernet network, a cable segment between two repeaters. An IRL cannot have any nodes attached. If the cable is optical fiber, it is known as a FOIRL (fiber-optic inter-repeater link).

Interrupt

An interrupt is a mechanism by which one computing element, such as a drive or a program, can get the attention of another element, such as the CPU (central processing unit) or another program. Operating systems that use interrupts have a mechanism for weighting and dealing with the interrupts. Interrupts may be generated by hardware or software.

For hardware interrupts in a PC environment, there are 8 or 16 interrupt request lines (IRQs). Machines with an 80286 or higher processor have 16 lines. Each device attached to a computer can be assigned an IRQ. When it wants a service from the CPU, the device signals on this line and waits. In principle, each line may be assigned to a device; in practice, certain IRQ lines are reserved by the system for its own needs.

IRQs have different priority levels, and the higher priority lines are assigned to the most important functions on the PC. By doing this, an operating system or interrupt handler can be sure that no vital activities are interrupted.

IRQ values for a device may be set through software or by setting jumpers or DIP switches on the expansion board for the device. When configuring devices on your machine, it is important that you do not have two devices that use the same IRQ (at least if there is any chance that the two devices will be used at the same time).

I

Hardware Interrupts

Hardware interrupt signals are conveyed over specific interrupt request lines (IRQs).

The number of IRQs in a particular machine, 8 or 16, depends on the number of *interrupt controller chips* on the processor. In machines that conform to the ISA (Industry Standard Architecture), the Intel 8259A Programmable Interrupt Controller chip is used. Each 8259A has 8 IRQs. Machines with an 80286 or higher processor have two chips, and therefore have 16 IRQs. The second 8259A is controlled by the first, and must announce interrupts on its lines (IRQs 8 through 15) by signaling on the first chip's IRQ 2. "IRQ lines" shows these interrupt lines.

The illustration also shows the standard IRQ assignments for ISA machines. Note that there are some differences in the assignments for single- and double-chip processors. Note also that extensibility is built into both controller chips. The IRQ 2 on the primary interrupt controller chip makes it possible to cascade the IRQs from the second chip. In a similar manner, IRQ 9 on the second chip allows for additional signals. Network-related interrupts can be indicated through this IRQ.

Software Interrupts

Executing programs also use interrupts to get resources needed to perform some action. For example, there are software interrupts to access a monitor screen or disk drive, to handle a keystroke or a mouse click, and so on.

There are software interrupts for handling specific requests and for performing specific actions (for example, determining memory size). There are also interrupts that provide access to more functions

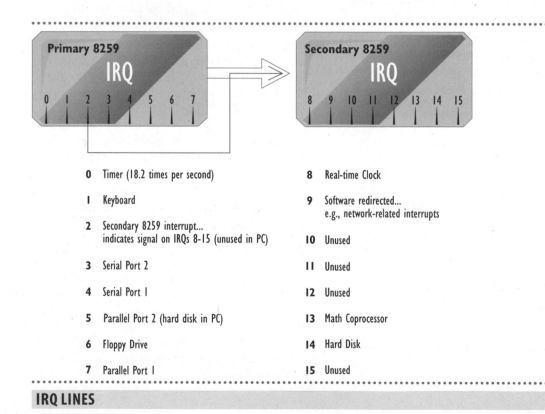

0	Timer (18.2 times per second)	8	Real-time Clock
1	Keyboard	9	Software redirected... e.g., network-related interrupts
2	Secondary 8259 interrupt... indicates signal on IRQs 8-15 (unused in PC)	10	Unused
3	Serial Port 2	11	Unused
4	Serial Port 1	12	Unused
5	Parallel Port 2 (hard disk in PC)	13	Math Coprocessor
6	Floppy Drive	14	Hard Disk
7	Parallel Port 1	15	Unused

IRQ LINES

(for example, DOS interrupt 21H, which provides a function dispatcher that can access any of several dozen different functions).

Handling Interrupts

Each type of interrupt invokes its own *interrupt handler*, which is a program designed to deal with the interrupt. The location of a specific interrupt handler is found in an *interrupt vector table*. DOS provides a 256-entry table for storing such addresses. Note that it is possible to preempt the default interrupt handlers by substituting the address of an alternate handler in the appropriate vector table cell.

Interrupt Dispatch Table (IDT)

→*See* IDT (Interrupt Dispatch Table)

Interrupt Request (IRQ)

→*See* IRQ (Interrupt Request)

Interrupt Request Level (IRQL)

→*See* IRQL (Interrupt Request Level)

Intraexchange Carrier

A local telephone company; that is, a carrier that handles calls within an exchange. These are known as *intraLATA* calls, because exchanges are known as local access and transport areas, or LATAs. An intraexchange carrier is also known as an *LEC* (local exchange carrier).

Intraframe Encoding

In video signal transmission, a compression strategy in which only those parts of a video frame that have changed are encoded for transmission.

IntraLATA

In telephony, circuits that lie within a single exchange (known as a local access and transport area, or LATA). IntraLATA service is provided by a local exchange carrier (LEC); that is, by a local telephone office.

Intranet

Most simply put, an intranet is a home-grown Internet. More specifically, an intranet is a network that uses Internet protocols and services to connect computers at a single location or at locations throughout the world. These machines may be of the same type and running on the same platform, or the network may consist of a heterogeneous collection of machines and platforms.

Corporate intranets can be created for all sorts of reasons and on all sorts of scales: departmental, regional, or international, to name just a few. It's also not uncommon for companies to have multiple intranets. The kinds of components an intranet will need depends on the use to which the intranet will be put. For example, a departmental intranet will have different software needs than an intranet set up to provide all employees with access to corporate product or policy documentation.

Many corporate intranets are set up primarily to make documentation of one sort or another more widely and more easily available. Such intranets, in the simplest cases, need just Web authoring tools and browsers, along with Web server software to deliver the materials, beyond the basic elements required in all intranets, which are discussed in the next section.

Intranet Components

Regardless of their purpose, all intranets have the same collection of components—although the details, configuration, and relative importance of the components may vary from intranet to intranet.

The following elements must be present, in some form, in any intranet:

- A network of some sort. The intranet can be built on just about any type of underlying network: campus, departmental, or other type of local area network (CAN, DAN, or LAN); metropolitan or other type of wide area network (MAN or WAN); enterprise or other type of global network. Really, the only requirements for the base network is that the architecture and any existing protocols should be able to support TCP/IP—either as an alternative protocol suite or as a protocol suite that can run on top of the network's native protocols.

- The TCP/IP protocol stack. Although strictly speaking, other protocol stacks could be used, the TCP/IP stack has become so widely used and so entrenched that you'll be hard-pressed to find any alternatives that appear in a significant number of intranets. (Vendors may create their own implementations of the TCP/IP stack, but they're still running those protocols.)

- Services for the intranet. While it's certainly possible to think of all sorts of services you could provide, any intranet worth its salt will provide at least the basic services available on the Internet. These include e-mail, FTP (File Transfer Protocol), news (using NNTP, or Network News Transfer Protocol), DNS (Domain Name Service), and so forth. And, of course, any intranet will make extensive use of Web services to search for and read HTML (Hypertext Markup Language) documents.

- Server software to provide the intranet services. An intranet may use several different intranet servers—for example, mail, Web, FTP, and so forth.

- Client software to make use of the intranet services.

- Software and possibly also hardware to provide security services for the intranet. Such services will include resources to provide authentication of users trying to access the intranet. There should also be resources to check for and to prevent efforts to subvert the normal operation of the intranet and gain access to restricted elements of the intranet software or hardware. Finally, security measures and resources should exist to guard against efforts by software to damage existing files or otherwise disrupt the contents or operation of the intranet.

Features and Advantages of Intranets

There are good reasons why intranets are fast becoming all the rage. They can be simple to set up, don't make heavy demands on the server, and are generally easy to maintain. The following points summarize some other attractions of intranets:

- As stated, all intranets will have a common software base—namely, the protocol suite and Web software. The TCP/IP suite is open (nonproprietary) and cross-platform. It provides a common communications and transport mechanism. The Web software—HTTP (Hypertext Transfer Protocol), browsers, HTML editors, other Web authoring tools, and Web server software—provides the common base for creating, delivering, and viewing Web pages.

- Most of the software needed for intranets is easily available—often from many different vendors. Availability means you won't be tied to the fortunes or abilities of a particular vendor.

- Much of the software is inexpensive, and some of it is even free. The free software is generally of high quality—in some cases, better than commercial versions.

- Both the protocol stack and the Web tools scale easily, so it makes little difference whether the intranet is set up for a dozen or a thousand users. Scalability is an important factor for both performance and cost.

- Everyone—at least everyone with the appropriate access rights—can use the same methods to access any content on the intranet. And, this access method is the same as the methods people use to access the Internet, so users are likely to be already familiar with it.

- Just as it's easy to edit Web pages on the Internet, intranet materials can also be updated easily. Using push technology, a channel containing information about changes in documentation—for example, product or policy updates—can be delivered automatically to those affected by the changes.

- Since much of the activity on most intranets consists of responding to browser requests for Web pages, you don't necessarily need an industrial-strength server. A processor with moderate speed and a good supply of memory should work just fine.

Disadvantages of Intranets

Intranets do have minor disadvantages, but no real major drawbacks. Many of the disadvantages are more on the level of annoyances than of major problems. Most of the problems involve the degree to which certain things can be done, and the ease with which they can be done.

For example, it's fairly easy to create static HTML documents—that is, Web pages that just present material. However, to create more complex pages—those with special effects, those that are created on the fly, or those that accept user input—it's necessary to (learn how to) use more complex tools, such as CGI (Common Gateway Interface) scripts, Perl programs, Java applets or applications, or ActiveX controls.

Conversion software can be used to create HTML files from other kinds of documents, such as text or database files—provided these files were created using widely available software for which

translation tools are available. Things get a bit more difficult, however, if legacy data—perhaps from old mainframe systems—need to be converted. The basic intranet tools don't really include anything for dealing with legacy systems. (XML, or eXtensible Markup Language, the purported successor to HTML, is much more useful for creating custom document definitions. With XML tools, it will be much easier to develop conversion software to handle legacy data.)

While intranet services make document sharing easy, they are not much help when it comes to resources for actually collaborating directly. That is, collaborators can send a document back and forth—with each collaborator making suggestions or changes and then sending it on. However, there is no simple way for them to simultaneously work on the same copy of the document or to use separate copies on which changes are synchronized automatically by software. (Where it is supported, such a paired-copy arrangement is created by *replication*, in which a document in progress is copied, and the copy is then sent to a coworker. Changes in either the document or its replicated copy are resynchronized as soon as the changes are detected.)

Despite such drawbacks, intranets are growing at an astounding pace—in both number and popularity. This trend is likely to continue for a while, although the details of intranets are almost certain to evolve.

→ *Compare* Extranet

Intranet Server

→ *See* Server, Intranet

Intranetwork Link

An intranetwork link is a component that serves to connect two elements in the same network. This link may be physical or electrical. "Context of intranetwork links" summarizes this type of connection.

Node-network and cable-cable links can be distinguished. Under node-network, we also include node-node links—as when a switch is used (see below) to connect two nodes for direct communication. The following components create these links:

- *Connectors* establish a physical link between two components. There are more than a dozen connector types, some of which come in several shapes and sizes. For a given network configuration, only a small number of connectors will be appropriate. For example, an ARCnet network will use either BNC or modular (RJ-*xx*) connectors. A connector is a passive component, and some signal loss (the insertion loss) is involved.

- *Transceivers* establish an electrical connection between a workstation and the network. The transceiver may be located on the network interface card or it may be attached to the workstation by a drop cable. In the latter case, the transceiver will include connectors to attach to both the drop and the network (trunk) cable.

- *Repeaters* establish an electrical connection between two cable segments. Repeaters clean and boost signals before passing them on to the next segment. Because signals are boosted, repeaters can be used to extend the maximum distance over which a signal can travel. In order to accomplish this task, repeaters need their own power supplies.

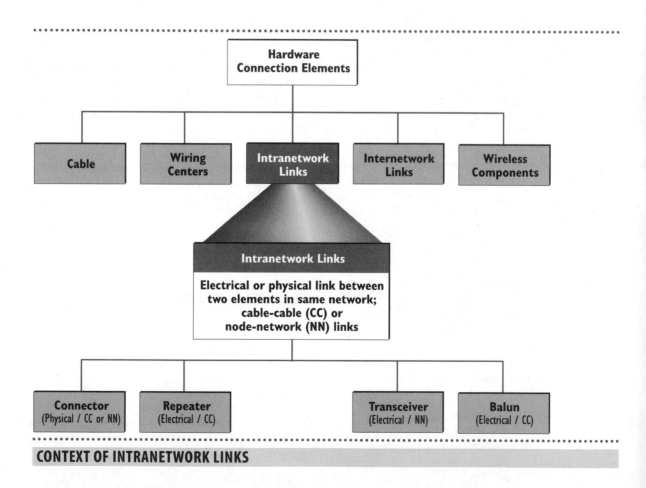

CONTEXT OF INTRANETWORK LINKS

- *Baluns* establish an electrical link between different types of cables, such as twisted-pair and coaxial. In particular, a balun connects cables that have different impedances, and it makes the necessary impedance conversions as signals pass through the balun.

- *Hubs* connect multiple nodes to a network. They have separate connections for each node on one side, and a shared connection to the network server (or to another hub) on the other. Because hubs divide up the total bandwidth among all connected nodes, the actual bandwidth of any single node may be only a tiny fraction of the total bandwidth. Because of this bandwidth dilution, hubs are rapidly being replaced by switches (see below), which can usually give communicating nodes total bandwidth.

- *Switches* establish a physical and a logical link between two nodes. The tremendous advantage of switches is that switches allow each pair of nodes connected in this way to use the full bandwidth available for the network. Unlike hubs, which dilute the bandwidth by dividing it among all the nodes connected to it, switches provide each connection with a complete bandwidth—assuming, of course, that a given switch is sufficiently powerful to do this.

→ **See Also** Balun; Connector; Connector, Fiber-Optic; Hub; Internetwork Link; Repeater; Switch; Transceiver

Intrusion Detection System (IDS)

→ **See** IDS (Intrusion Detection System)

Inverted-List Database

→ **See** Database

Invitation to Transmit (ITT)

In an ARCnet network architecture, the ITT is the token frame.

Inward Wide Area Telephone Service (INWATS)

→ **See** INWATS (Inward Wide Area Telephone Service)

INWATS (Inward Wide Area Telephone Service)

In telephone communications, an 800 service; that is, a service in which the called party pays for the call.

IOC (Interoffice Channel)

In digital telecommunications, a communications link between two carrier offices (for example, two local telephone offices) or between points-of-presence (POPs) for two interexchange carriers (IXCs). For high-speed lines (such as T1), the cost for such a channel is on a per-mile basis. This term is also written as *inter-office channel*.

IONL (Internal Organization of the Network Layer)

In the OSI reference model, IONL is a detailed specification for the Network layer. This specification was made in order to distinguish more clearly the levels of service provided by the Network layer.

In IONL, the Network layer is divided into three sublayers:

Subnetwork access At the bottom of the Network layer, the subnetwork access sublayer provides an interface over which to send data across a network or subnetwork. Services at this level are provided by a subnetwork access protocol (SNAcP). The X.25 packet-level protocol is an example of a subnetwork access protocol.

Subnetwork-dependent   Protocols operating at this sublayer assume a particular type of subnetwork, such as an Ethernet local area network. This type of subnetwork-dependent convergence protocol (SNDCP) has been defined by the ISO.

Subnetwork-independent   This sublayer provides *inter*networking capabilities for the layers above it. Protocols at this sublayer can work with multiple subnetworks. The services provided by a subnetwork-independent control protocol (SNICP) are independent of particular subnetworks. CLNP (Connectionless-mode Network Protocol) is an SNICP.

→ *Primary Source*   ISO document 8648

I/O Request Packet (IRP)

IRPs are used in Windows NT and NT Advanced Server for communications between drivers.

IOS (Internetwork Operating System)

The IOS is software that enables the Cisco family of routers to perform routing and bridging over an internetwork. The IOS can be configured to control the following:

- What networking protocols can be routed (using Network layer, or layer 3, addresses) or bridged (using Data-ink layer, or layer 2, addresses) on the router being configured. Routable protocols include AppleTalk, CLNS (Connectionless Network Service), DECnet, IP (Internet Protocol), IPX (Internetwork Packet Exchange), SNMP (Simple Network Management Protocol), VINES (Virtual Integrated

Network Services), and XNS (Xerox Network Systems). Layer 2 protocols, such as HDLC (High-Level Data-Link Control) and LAT (Local Area Transport), must be bridged since they do not support layer 3 addresses.

- What routing protocols will be used to do the actual routing. Certain routed protocols have default routing protocols associated with them, which will be used automatically. For example, the IPX RIP (IPX Routing Information Protocol) is used to route IPX packets; the RTMP (Routing Table Maintenance Protocol) is used to route AppleTalk packets. Other protocols do not have a default routing protocol, so it is necessary to select from available options. For example, either RIP or Cisco's proprietary IGRP (Interior Gateway Routing Protocol) can be used to route IP packets.

- What interfaces on the router will be used for which routed protocols. Cisco routers can support various interfaces, including Ethernet and Token Ring LAN (local area network) interfaces, fast and low-speed serial interfaces, and ISDN BRI (Integrated Services Digital Network Basic Rate Interface) interfaces. The number and type of interfaces supported by a particular router depend on the model.

- What processes will execute in a particular IOS configuration. IOS processes include those that route specific packet types, implement the various routing protocols, and control memory allocation, The number and types of processes available in a particular IOS configuration will depend, in part, on the router's processing power and available memory.

IOS is proprietary software but, given Cisco's dominance in the router market, this is not considered a problem. IOS is available in a number of flavors depending on what kinds of support are needed.

IP (Internet Protocol) Address

An IP address is an address for a station or other device on the Internet. This type of address consists of 4 bytes, which are represented as decimal values separated by periods, as in 123.45.67.89. In order to ensure uniqueness, IP addresses are assigned in part by the Internet Assigned Numbers Authority (IANA).

To deal with the rapid growth of the Internet, IP addresses have become hierarchical, and the address bits can be given any of several interpretations.

The bits in an IP address are allocated for Net and Host (*Node* in Internet terminology) fields, which specify a network and host number, respectively. Originally, 8 bits were allocated for networks and the remaining 24 bits for the host information. Since there are well over 255 networks now attached to the Internet, such an addressing scheme is no longer adequate.

To help handle the growth of the Internet, several classes of addresses have been defined. These differ in how they allocate bits for the Net and Host fields.

IP Address Classes

The following classes are defined for IP addresses:

- Class A is used for very large networks (networks with a large number of nodes). This class uses 7 bits for Net and 24 bits for Host. The high-order bit is 0 in such an address. There are 128 class A networks possible. The now-defunct ARPANET, which had a network address of 10, is an example of a network in this class.

- Class B is used for medium-size networks, such as networks that span a large college campus. This class uses 14 bits for Net and 16 bits for Host. The two high-order bits are

set to 10. This address class is also popular for local area networks (LANs), particularly if they use subnetting.

- Class C is used for small networks (those with no more than 255 nodes). This class allocates 21 bits for Net and only 8 bits for Host. The three high-order bits are 110.

- Class D allocates 28 bits for a special multicast address, which is an address in which a group of targets are specified. The first 4 bits of such an address are always 1110.

- Class E is a reserved address class. Addresses in this class are for experimental use, and cannot be guaranteed to be unique. The first 4 bits of this type of address are always 1111.

In summary, address classes are distinguished by the high-order bits: 0 for class A, 10 for class B, 110 for class C, 1110 for class D, and 1111 for class E. Two particular Net addresses—0 and those with all 1s—are reserved. Net address 0 is reserved for the originating entity (network or host), and address 255 is used for broadcasts. "IP address breakdown" shows how the bits are allocated for the different address classes.

IP Subnet Addresses

The use of subnetting provides additional flexibility in addressing. A subnet is a portion of a network or an internetwork that can be viewed, from the outside, as a single element.

An IP address that uses subnetting has three types of information: network, subnet, and host. Subnets are identified by combining an address with a mask, which is a bit pattern that cancels out unwanted bits, so that only the bits of interest remain.

→ *Primary Source* RFC 1349

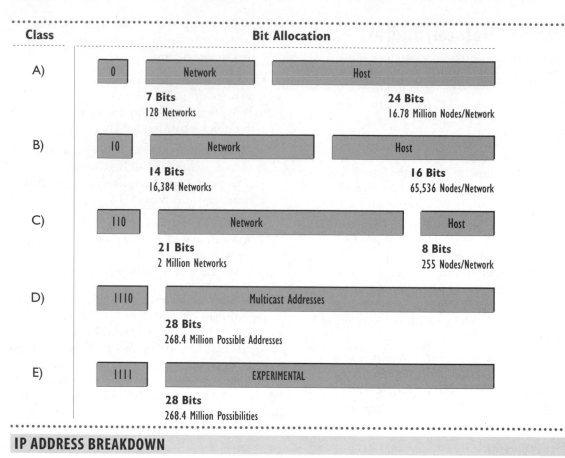

IP ADDRESS BREAKDOWN

IPC (Interprocess Communication)

IPC is a set of services for exchanging control information and data between separate processes or programs on the same or different hosts. OS/2 implements IPC as part of its multitasking capabilities.

IPC between processes on the same machine can use any of several mechanisms, including the following:

- Shared memory, in which the two processes both access a common area of memory.

- Named pipes, in which a two-way virtual circuit is established. For sharing on a network, named pipes (which allow two-way communications) must be used.

- Semaphores, in which the processes signal when there is something to communicate.

IPC capabilities are particularly important for applications that run in client/server computing environments.

IP (Internet Protocol) Datagram

The basic packet sent across the Internet. An IP datagram contains source and destination addresses, fields for various bookkeeping and tracking information, and data.

IP (Internet Protocol) Masquerade

In an IP masquerade, a host (the masquerader) communicates with a server on behalf of another host (the client). The masquerader will generally be a proxy server, and will pretend to be the origin of the requests made of the server. Likewise, the masquerading host will also accept responses from the server, and will pass them on to the appropriate client. A proxy host will generally carry out such masquerades for multiple clients.

An IP masquerade—also known as Network Address Translation (NAT)—offers several benefits. First, it protects the identity of clients making requests. Second, it allows a single network address to be multiplexed and used for an entire network. A related benefit is that it makes it possible to use any addresses one wishes for the network hosts, since only the proxy's address needs to be valid for the outside world. Also, by running the masquerader on a firewall, network traffic can be screened to prevent certain kinds of attacks at the network layer. IP masquerades cannot prevent attacks at higher levels in the protocol suite. To prevent against such attacks, application-level proxies must be included in the firewall.

IP (Internet Protocol) Multicast

An IP multicast is a transmission that is sent to multiple destinations. For example, a packet might be multicast to all subscribers on a mailing list or to participants in an interactive conference. Similarly, updated routing tables might be multicast to all the routers on an internetwork. Clients can also multicast—for example, to find a server that can carry out a specified task or provide a required resource.

A diskless workstation can send a multicast packet to find a server that can provide bootstrap code for the workstation. Finding boot code can also be done using a broadcast packet, which is sent to all destinations on a network. This is, in fact, the more common way of finding the boot, but it is less efficient than a multicast would be.

IP multicast addresses are class D addresses, which means they begin with 1110 in the leftmost (high-order) bits. The remaining 28 bits can be used for the multicast group ID. See the IP (Internet Protocol) Address entry for the class distinctions.) This means that multicast group IP addresses must be in the range 224.0.0.0 to 239.255.255.255 (1110 0000 0000 0000 0000 0000 0000 0000 to 1110 1111 1111 1111 1111 1111 1111 1111).

Certain addresses are set aside for special multicast groups. These are known as permanent host group addresses, and they are assigned by the IANA (Internet Assigned Numbers Authority). Permanent host group addresses are published in Assigned Numbers RFCs. The following are some example addresses:

- All systems on this subnet: 224.0.0.1
- All routers on this subnet: 224.0.0.2
- RIP-2 (Routing Information Protocol, 2): 224.0.0.9
- NTP (Network Time Protocol): 224.0.1.1

IP (Internet Protocol) Spoofing

IP spoofing is a network attack strategy in which the attacker uses the IP address of another host as the attacker's own—in order to gain access to the network under assault. This strategy can succeed only if the spoofed address is one that is recognized by the network and is allowed to access it.

IP (Internet Protocol) Switching

IP switching is a way of optimizing packet handling by mapping forwarding tasks directly to a hardware switch matrix or fabric. Effectively, IP switching turns a connectionless transmission into a connection-oriented one. IP switching was developed in 1996 by Ipsilon—largely to provide an alternative to MPOA (Multi-Protocol Over ATM). Because they go through a switch, connections get the full bandwidth, rather than having to share the media (as in an ordinary Ethernet network).

To accomplish this, a multiport bridge or router treats all the packets going to the same destination in the same way. A sequence of packets all going to the same destination is known as a flow, and any required routing and QoS (quality of service) information for the flow can be determined from the first packets in the flow. After that, the router can save time by not having to do a full lookup for the destination of the remaining packets in the flow. Special protocols—for example, the Ipsilon Flow Management Protocol (IFMP)—are used to identify the existence of a flow and to control the packets in such a flow.

IP switching is an example of layer 3 switching, and represents only one possible strategy. Others include Tag switching and Aggregate Route-based IP Switching (ARIS). An IETF (Internet Engineering Task Force) working group for Multi-Protocol Label Switching (MPLS) is currently at work developing a standard for layer 3 switching.

IP (Internet Protocol) Tunneling

IP tunneling refers to the use of encryption services for moving packets around the Internet. The *tunnels*—a term for the collection of available encryption services—help provide a secure channel over the Internet.

→ *Broader Category* Security

IPDS (Intelligent Printer Data Stream)

In an SNA (Systems Network Architecture) environment, a printing mode that provides access to advanced function printer (AFP) capabilities, such as the ability to output text, graphics, and color (if supported) simultaneously on a printer.

IPI (Intelligent Peripheral Interface)

A hard disk interface that supports transfer rates of up to 25Mbps and storage capacities of several gigabytes.

→ *See Also* Hard Disk

IPM (Interpersonal Messaging)

In the ITU X.400 series of recommendations for message handling systems (MHS), one of the two major categories of message handling, with the other being a message transfer system (MTS). IPM represents a type of message handling for use in ordinary business or private correspondence. The handled elements—interpersonal messages—consist of *heading* and *body* components. Headings are made up of fields (such as name, address, subject) and values for these fields. The actual content of a message makes up the body. The entire content can be broken into smaller chunks (*body parts*), each of which may be manipulated separately.

The interpersonal messaging process is assumed to take place in an IPME (Interpersonal Messaging Environment) under the control of an IPMS (Interpersonal Messaging System). In IPM, users exchange messages and replies over the IPMS, as shown in "IPM and its components").

As shown in the graphic, users in IPMEs have three main kinds of capabilities:

- *Originate*: in which the user initiates a message transmission or exchange. Various types of originate actions are possible—including a probe to determine whether anyone is listening, and transmitting the start of a message.

- *Receive*: in which the user receives a message or a probe through the IPMS.

- *Manage*: in which the user can change material associated with the user's headings (name, address, etc).

→ **Broader Category** MHS (Message Handling System)

→ **Compare** MTS (Message Transfer System)

→ **Primary Sources** ITU recommendations X.400, X.402, X.420

IPMS (Interpersonal Messaging Service, or System)

In the 1984 version of the X.400 Message Handling Services recommendations, a user-to-user service that provides electronic-mail capabilities. The other major class of services provided in the 1984 version was Message Transfer Service (MTS).

IPSEC (Internet Protocol, Secure)

→ **See** Protocol, IPSEC (Internet Protocol, Secure)

Ipsilon Flow Management Protocol (IFMP)

→ **See** Protocol, IFMP (Ipsilon Flow Management Protocol)

IPX Network Numbers and Internetwork Addresses

In Novell NetWare networks, IPX external and internal network numbers are assigned. The IPX external network number is a unique hexadecimal value associated with a network or network cable segment. The value may be from one to eight hexadecimal digits (up to 4 bytes), and is assigned arbitrarily.

The IPX internal network number is a hexadecimal number that uniquely identifies an individual file server. This value can also be from one to eight

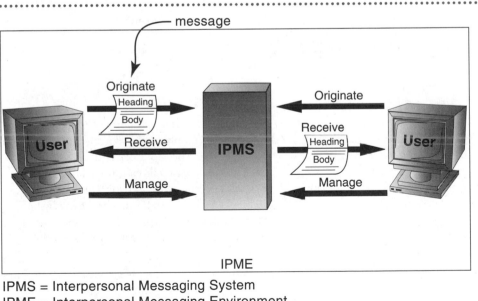

IPMS = Interpersonal Messaging System
IPME = Interpersonal Messaging Environment

IPM AND ITS COMPONENTS

hexadecimal digits, and it is assigned arbitrarily to the server during the installation of the networking software.

An IPX internetwork address in NetWare is a three-part, 12-byte address. The first part (4 bytes) is the IPX external network number. The middle part (6 bytes) is the node number. The third part (2 bytes) is the socket number, which is the number associated with a particular device or process.

IPX internetwork addresses are generally represented as hexadecimal values, so they can have as many as 24 digits associated with them. (And you thought that 10 telephone digits was too much trouble!)

→ See Also Address

IPXODI (Internet Packet Exchange Open Data-Link Interface)

In Novell NetWare 3.*x* and later, IPXODI is a protocol driver that can prepare workstation requests intended for the network. The preparation may involve attaching the appropriate header to the packet, packaging the packet in the appropriate manner, and passing the packet on to the link-support layer (LSL).

(The LSL mediates between the LAN driver for the network interface card and the protocol stack running on the network.)

Data sent using IPXODI is handled as datagrams, which means the packager makes a best effort but cannot guarantee delivery. The next higher layer, SPX (Sequenced Packet Exchange), makes sure the data was received correctly.

→ Broader Category NetWare

IR (Internet Registry)

A central database that contains the network addresses of machines and ID numbers of autonomous systems (domains) on the Internet.

The task of maintaining the IR is delegated by the Internet Assigned Numbers Authority (IANA) and is being carried out by the Defense Data Network Network Information Center (DDN NIC).

This process has become considerably more difficult as the corporate world joins the Internet, wanting to use its trademarked names, and willing to put its lawyers to work to get its way.

IR (Internet Router)

In an AppleTalk internetwork, a device that uses network numbering to filter and route packets.

IRC (Internet Relay Chat)

A protocol that provides access to a global talk network in which participants can communicate in real time to converse about topics of mutual interest. Different conversations take place over different channels. IRC is an extension and enhancement of the UNIX *talk* program to—among other things—allow more than two users to talk at a time. IRC can serve as an inexpensive conference call method.

→ Compare Avatar Chat

Iridium Project

Iridium (named after the chemical element, which has an atomic number of 77) is a telecommunications project, initiated by Motorola. Iridium's goal is to make worldwide mobile communications possible by blanketing the earth with low earth orbit (LEO) satellites. (An LEO satellite orbits the earth about 600 miles above the earth, and can be used for signal transmission and other communications tasks.)

The project originally called for 77 LEO satellites, but that number has since been reduced to 66. These satellites would allow point-to-point communications between any two locations on earth. With such coverage, you can use a handheld phone, with a single telephone number, anywhere on earth.

As this book was going into production, the Iridium consortium declared bankruptcy. After investing over a billion dollars, Iridium had garnered fewer than 200,000 subscribers. Clearly, the future of the Iridium satellites is in doubt.

→ *Compare* Project 21

IRL (Inter-Repeater Link)

In an Ethernet network, a cable segment between two repeaters. An IRL cannot have any nodes attached. If the cable is optical fiber, it is known as an FOIRL (fiber-optic inter-repeater link).

IRM/IRF (Inherited Rights Mask/Inherited Rights Filter)

In environments for Novell NetWare 3.*x*, the IRM is a security measure that determines which trustee rights a user can carry over (inherit) from a directory into a subdirectory in the NetWare file system.

The IRM does not grant any new rights (trustee rights the user does not already have). Rather, the IRM controls which of the trustee rights *already granted in a parent directory* can also be used in the current directory.

The IRM does not take away trustee rights granted in a particular subdirectory. For example, if the IRM for directory X filters out all but the File Scan right, then a user with a Modify right in directory X will not be able to carry that right over to subdirectories of X. If, however, the user is granted a Modify right for subdirectory Y, then the IRM for X has no effect on that right.

NetWare 4.*x*: Inherited Rights Filter

In NetWare 4.*x*, the inheritance mechanism is known as the Inherited Rights Filter (IRF). For files and directories, the IRF works the same way as the IRM.

In addition, the IRF controls access to objects and properties in containers on the NetWare Directory Services (NDS) tree. Because the IRF can block Supervisor rights under certain conditions, it is wise to grant a trustee all rights that are appropriate, rather than granting just the Supervisor right.

→ *Broader Category* Access Rights

IRP (I/O Request Packet)

IRPs are used in Windows NT and NT Advanced Server for communication between drivers.

IRQ (Interrupt Request)

An IRQ is a mechanism for signaling an interrupt in PC hardware. Each device attached to a computer is assigned an IRQ. When it wants a service from the CPU (central processing unit), the device signals on this line and waits.

IRQs have different priority levels. The higher priority lines are assigned to the most important functions on the PC. By doing this, an operating system or interrupt handler can be sure that no vital activities are interrupted.

When configuring devices on your machine, it is very important that you do not have two devices that use the same IRQ—at least if there is any chance that the two devices will be used at the same time.

IRQL (Interrupt Request Level)

In Windows NT and NT Advanced Server (NTAS), a measure of relative priority for interrupt request lines. During program or thread execution, a processor uses a cutoff interrupt request level. Interrupts below that level are blocked (masked), while interrupts at or above that level are handled. A thread can change the IRQL.

IRSG (Internet Research Steering Group)

In the Internet community, the group that oversees the Internet Research Task Force (IRTF).

→ *See Also*   Internet

IRTF (Internet Research Task Force)

A group within the Internet community that works on long-term research projects. These projects may concern any aspect of Internet operations, and some results have led or may lead to major changes in certain aspects of Internet activity.

IRV (International Reference Version)

A particular variant of the IA5 (International Alphabet 5) character-encoding scheme. IRV is identical to the ASCII encoding scheme.

IS (Intermediate System)

In the OSI reference model, an Intermediate System is a network entity that serves as a relay element between two or more subnetworks. For example, repeaters, bridges, routers, and X.25 circuits are all intermediate systems at the Physical, Data-Link, and Network layers, respectively.

Architecturally, an intermediate system uses at most the bottom three layers of the OSI reference model: Network, Data-Link, And Physical. These are the so-called subnet layers. This is in contrast to an end system (ES), which uses all seven layers of the model. A node is an end system.

An intermediate system is also known as a *relay open system* in the OSI reference model. You will

also see *internetworking unit*, or *IWU*, used to refer to an intermediate system.

→ *Broader Category*   OSI Reference Model

→ *Compare*   End System (ES)

IS (Internet Standard)

An Internet Standard is a specification that has undergone a formal evaluation and testing process, has proven stable and viable, and has been widely implemented. For example, an Internet Standard might be a specification for a protocol.

Internet Standard is the final level in a three-stage process:

Proposed Standard (PS)   A specification that appears robust is submitted for testing. This specification is sufficiently detailed and stable to warrant implementation.

Draft Standard (DS)   A specification that has been a Proposed Standard for at least six months and which has been tested in at least two implementations that have interacted with each other.

Internet Standard (IS)   A specification that has been a Draft Standard for at least four months and has general acceptance as worthy of implementation and use.

ISA (Industry Standard Architecture)

The architecture for the PC expansion bus used in the original IBM PC and in its descendants (including the XT, AT, and models based on the 386, 486 and higher chips). This architecture provides for 8- and 16-bit access to the PC and allows limited control of the bus. Compare it with EISA, MCA, PCI, and VESA.

ISAPI (Internet Server Application Programming Interface)

ISAPI is a collection of functions developed by Microsoft to make it easier to create interactive or dynamic Web pages—that is, for enabling a Web server to accept input from someone reading a Web page or to generate a Web page when needed. The reason for generating the page on demand is that the server can build the page using the most up-to-date version of the content that is to go on the page. ISAPI provides a proprietary programming interface for doing such server-side programming in a Windows-based environment

ISAPI was developed and released for use with Microsoft Internet Information Server (IIS), but the API also provides a general interface to any Windows-based Web server. As such, ISAPI is comparable to similar server-side programming tools, such as the CGI (Common Gateway Interface) and Netscape NSAPI (Netscape Services Application Programming Interface). CGI scripts are probably the most widely used server-side programming tools. This has been due more to lack of alternatives than to CGI's features, which include potential security risks, mediocre-to-slow performance, and poor scalability (as well as some more positive features, such as relative ease of use).

ISAPI files are generally stored as DLLs (dynamic link libraries) and are used as needed. Programs based on proprietary APIs, such as ISAPI and NSAPI offer several advantages over CGI scripts, including the following:

- Greater efficiency and scalability because the API needs to be initialized and loaded into memory only once. Multiple scripts can all use the same copy of the DLL. In contrast, a separate copy of a CGI script must be loaded for each script that uses it. Not surprisingly, a server can easily get overwhelmed if lots of clients are trying to do a task simultaneously—even if that task is a very simple one.

- Scripts using the APIs enable the server to maintain a connection with a browser until the interaction is over. Again, this is in contrast to normal server functioning, which is stateless. In a stateless connection, the server and browser break the connection after each request, and must reestablish a new connection for the next request. This means that the server has no memory of having communicated with the browser so that all the preliminaries to establishing a connection must be done anew for each request. Talk about unnecessary paperwork...

- Scripts based on the APIs make it easier to include plug-ins or other special components to do special tasks (such as authentication, logging, and so forth).

Two types of ISAPI DLLs are distinguished: ISAPI applications and ISAPI filters.

ISAPI Applications

ISAPI applications are similar to CGI programs in the kinds of things you can do with them. An ISAPI application begins executing if a Web server is asked to return a Web page that consists of or includes an ISAPI application. If such a page is encountered, control is passed to the page.

CGI programs and ISAPI applications can do the same kinds of things. Other things being equal, however, ISAPI applications can generally run faster than CGI programs because of the way the run-time environment is handled. On balance, however, ISAPI programs are more difficult to create because they require a Win32 SDK (Software Development Kit) and a programming environment such as Microsoft Visual C++.

Even though ISAPI applications have advantages over CGI scripts, there are still features of ISAPI that make it—potentially—just as dangerous as CGI. For example, ISAPI applications are not restricted in the data or files that the application can access. This means that a rogue or a clueless ISAPI application can cause file damage to the browser's system. (There are ways of restricting such access—essentially, by relying on the access privileges available to the user running the application.)

Microsoft has announced plans to create a wrapper for ISAPI applications. This wrapper can be used to make an ISAPI application CGI-compliant so that the application can be used wherever a CGI script could.

ISAPI Filters

ISAPI filters are designed to provide additional services through IIS—either by preprocessing the browser's HTTP requests on their way to the Web server or by postprocessing the HTML document on its way back to the browser. Once created, a filter can be applied globally—that is, for any requests and documents that come through. Or, if desired, the filter can be used for just specific requests or documents or even for just specific features of a document.

Filters can help with tasks such as the following:

- Providing security-related services such as authentication, encryption, or access restrictions.

- Extending IIS's capabilities by making it possible to implement new HTTP commands—that is, commands for which IIS does not have built-in support.

- Creating special-purpose activity logs or traffic analyses not normally provided by IIS.

→ *Compare* CGI (Common Gateway Interface); NSAPI (Netscape Services Application Programming Interface)

ISAPI (Internet Server Application Programming Interface) Application

→ *See* ISAPI (Internet Server Application Programming Interface)

ISAPI (Internet Server Application Programming Interface) Filter

→ *See* ISAPI (Internet Server Application Programming Interface)

ISDN (Integrated Services Digital Network)

ISDN is a potential telecommunications standard that is capable of sending digitally encoded voice, data, video, and other signals on the same lines. ISDN can also provide access to a variety of communications, information processing, and supplementary services. "Context and properties of ISDN" summarizes the characteristics of ISDN.

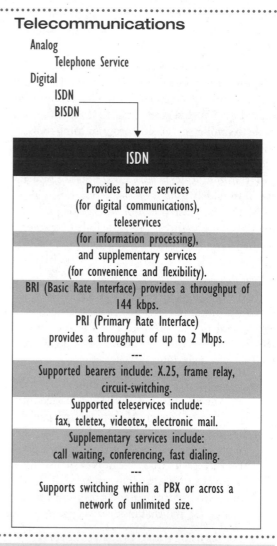

Telecommunications

Analog
  Telephone Service
Digital
  ISDN
  BISDN

ISDN

Provides bearer services (for digital communications), teleservices (for information processing), and supplementary services (for convenience and flexibility).

BRI (Basic Rate Interface) provides a throughput of 144 kbps.

PRI (Primary Rate Interface) provides a throughput of up to 2 Mbps.

Supported bearers include: X.25, frame relay, circuit-switching.

Supported teleservices include: fax, teletex, videotex, electronic mail.

Supplementary services include: call waiting, conferencing, fast dialing.

Supports switching within a PBX or across a network of unlimited size.

CONTEXT AND PROPERTIES OF ISDN

ISDN is a completely digital service. An ISDN implementation must provide any adapters needed to translate analog or non-ISDN compatible signals. ISDN has the following features:

- Supports bandwidths of about 2Mbps—enough to fill a European E1 transmission channel.

- Uses a single digital link to get the gamut of a user's communications devices (telephone, fax, computer, or video) onto the ISDN lines.

- Provides bearer services for communications, teleservices for information processing, and supplementary services.

- Allows for internal and external switching, so that calls can stay within a PBX (private branch exchange) or travel across a vast network to a destination that might be halfway around the world.

ISDN Services

ISDN provides access to a wide variety of services, as illustrated in "ISDN services."

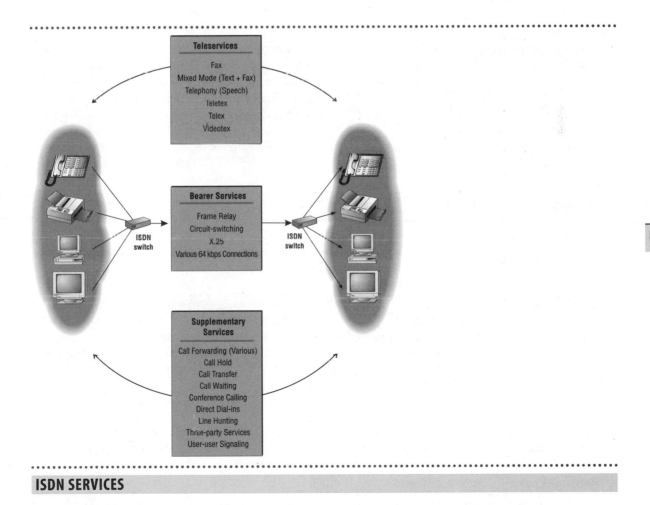

ISDN SERVICES

Bearer Services

Bearer services are concerned with moving information from one location to another. Several bearers are supported:

- Frame relay, which uses fast packet-switching and stripped down processing to provide 2Mbps throughput.

- X.25, which provides packet-switched services at modest speeds, but with good error handling and flexible routing services.

- Circuit-switched connections capable of carrying voice or data at up to 64Kbps, and even at multiples of this rate.

Teleservices

Teleservices are concerned with processing information in various ways. Teleservices include the following:

- Mixed mode, which allows a combination of text and image (facsimile) information to be sent together.

- Telefax, which provides fax transmission, store, and forward capabilities.

- Teletex, which provides text communication capabilities using a standardized alphabet.

- Telex, which provides interactive communication capabilities.

- Videotex, which includes capabilities for sending, storing, and retrieving text and graphics information.

Supplementary Services

The supplementary services are designed to make it easier to use the bearer and teleservices. Supplementary services include telephony's greatest hits, including caller ID, call forwarding and waiting, and conference calling.

ISDN Equipment

The CCITT has provided detailed recommendations concerning the types of equipment that can be used with ISDN and also how to accomplish this. Several categories of equipment are distinguished. The categories and their functions are summarized in the table "ISDN Equipment Categories." "ISDN hardware and interfaces" shows how these elements fit together.

ISDN EQUIPMENT CATEGORIES

Category	Description
TE2	Hardware that is not compatible with ISDN, such as telephones, computers, video devices, fax machines. TE2 equipment is connected over an R Interface to a terminal adapter, which makes the incoming signals ISDN-compatible.
TE1	Hardware that is compatible with ISDN.
TA (Terminal Adapter)	Mediates between a TE2 device and the ISDN network. The TA is connected to the NT2 (the user's switching exchange) over an S interface. The TA's output will conform to the appropriate one of four CCITT standards: V.110, V.120, X.30, or X.31.
NT2	Provides a switching exchange on the user's premises. Such an exchange can take supported input from the appropriate device, either directly or through a TA. The NT2 can then move the signal to an internal network (such as a PBX) or send it on to the service provider's lines. The NT2 is connected to the TE2 or TA components over an S interface; the NT2 is connected to the NT1 over a T interface.
NT1	The point at which the service provider's lines and switches terminate and the user's equipment (CPE) begins. There is a T interface between an NT1 and an NT2 at the customer's end. The NT1 is connected to a local carrier's central office over a U interface, which gets the 4-wire configuration on the user's premises down to the 2-wire configuration on the phone lines.
LT (Line Termination)	The point in the central office at which the lines from the user's NT1 terminates. This location communicates over a V interface with the analogous termination for exchanges (ET).
ET (Exchange Termination)	Also located at the central office.

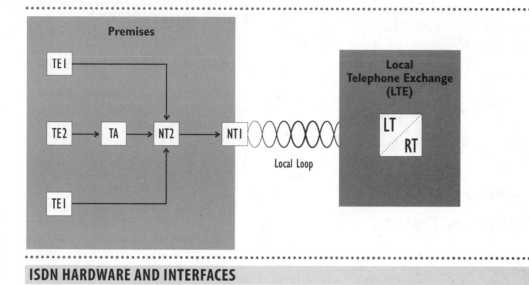

ISDN HARDWARE AND INTERFACES

ISDN Transmission Rates

ISDN supports either medium- or high-speed transmission rates. Rates are based on the number of B and D channels allocated.

D channels are used for signaling; B (for bearer) channels carry data. A D channel may be 16 or 64Kbps; a B channel is 64Kbps.

The BRI (Basic Rate Interface) rate consists of two B and one 16Kbps D channel (2B+D), which equal a bandwidth of 144Kbps.

The configuration for the PRI (Primary Rate Interface) rate depends on where the lines are. In the United States, Canada, and Japan, a PRI line consists of 23B+D. This D channel is 64Kbps, so the PRI rate is 1.536Mbps. In Europe, the PRI rate is 30B+D, for a bandwidth of 1.920Mbps.

ISDN transmission channels can also be grouped in other ways. The following H channels have been defined:

- H_0, which consists of six B channels, for a bandwidth of 384Kbps.

- H_10, which consists of the 23 B channels from the PRI, and has a transmission rate of 1.472Mbps. This channel is used only in the United States.

- H_11, which is just another name for the PRI and has a transmission rate of 1.472Mbps. It is used only in the United States.

- H_12, which again is just another name for the PRI and has a transmission rate of 1.920Mbps. It is used in Europe.

ISDN has long been popular in Europe, but was always an up-and-coming technology here—until recently. It has taken several years, but ISDN is finally getting established in North America. This growth is being spurred, in part, by the rapid drop in rates for individual subscribers and also by installation fee waivers being offered as incentives by providers. Its growing popularity is spurring developers and other workers in the field to revise or upgrade existing methods or protocols. For example, in the Internet community, a multi-link version of the PPP (Point-to-Point Protocol) has been developed.

Despite the healthy growth rate due to its new-found popularity, it's still not clear whether ISDN, its broadband big brother—broadband ISDN (BISDN)—or some other technology will become *the* digital technology.

→ *Primary Sources* The CCITT's I-series of recommendations are all concerned with ISDN in one form or another. Recommendations I.112, I.120, and I.200 provide general definitions and orientations.

ISDN Digital Subscriber Line (IDSL)

→ *See* IDSL (ISDN Digital Subscriber Line)

IS-IS (Intermediate System to Intermediate System) Protocol

→ *See* Protocol, IS-IS (Intermediate System to Intermediate System)

ISLAN16T (Integrated Services Local Area Network 16T)

→ *See* IsoEthernet

ISM (Industrial, Scientific, and Medical)

A term used to refer to three frequency ranges made available in 1985 by the FCC for unlicensed spread spectrum communication. Prior to this action, these ranges—902–928MHz, 2.4–2.5GHz, and 5.8–5.9GHz—had been allocated for industrial, scientific, and medical use, respectively.

ISN (Information Systems Network)

A high-speed switching network from AT&T. ISN can handle both voice and data transmission, and can connect to many popular networks, including Ethernet and SNA-based mainframes.

ISN (Internet Society News)

ISN is the official newsletter of the Internet Society (ISOC).

ISO (International Standardization Organization)

A worldwide body made up of representative groups from member nations. The ISO develops communications and other types of standards, including the seven-layer OSI reference model for connecting different types of computer systems. It is also sometimes called the International Standards Organization.

iso(1)

In the global tree of networking information, a top-level subtree administered by the ISO. Objects found under this subtree include the Internet, and network management topics.

→ *See Also* Global Tree

Isochronous

Isochronous means time-sensitive. In particular, an isochronous transmission or communication session is one whose operation is dependent on constant time intervals.

An isochronous connection ensures that there will always be an integral number of time intervals between any two transmissions, whether synchronous or asynchronous. This type of transmission capability is needed, for example, for digitized voice or video signals.

Isochronous Media Access Control (IMAC)

→ *See* IMAC (Isochronous Media Access Control)

ISOCON

A Novell NetWare tool for managing and monitoring the OSI-compliant protocol stack in a multiprotocol network. ISOCON provides data- and error-rate information for devices that use protocols based on the OSI reference model. Compare it with ATCON and TCPCON.

ISODE (International Standardization Organization Development Environment)

An implementation of the higher layers of the OSI reference model, to enable them to operate in a TCP/IP network. It is pronounced "I sew dee ee."

IsoEthernet

IsoEthernet (also known as IsoNet) is a variant of Ethernet designed for isochronous (constant rate) transmissions, which are required, for example, when sending video or voice. The IsoEthernet specifications were developed largely by National Semiconductor, and were then submitted to the IEEE 802.9 committee. The 809.2a working group's specifications were adopted as a standard in late 1995, under the official name of Integrated Services Local Area Network 16T (ISLAN16T). The 16T refers to the speed (16Mbps) and the medium (twisted-pair cable).

These specifications support transmissions using 10Mbps Ethernet and also ISDN (Integrated Services Digital Network) signaling methods—all running simultaneously over Category 3, 4, or 5 UTP (unshielded twisted-pair) cable. IsoEthernet effectively combines 10Mbps Ethernet and ISDN services.

IsoEthernet has a 16Mbps bandwidth, which is broken into two major components. In addition to the 10Mbps bandwidth for ordinary Ethernet transmissions, IsoEthernet supports up to 96 B channels, each with a 64Kbps capacity—for a total through-put of about 6.144Mbps—for the isochronous part of the transmission.

The Ethernet channel travels just as on an ordinary Ethernet network. The isochronous data is removed at a Hub/Switch, and is sent to a PBX (private branch exchange) or to a TDM (time division multiplexer). The isochronous channel's signaling is compatible with both ISDN and ATM networks.

→ *Broader Categories* Ethernet; Isochronous

→ *See Also* PACE (Priority Access Control Enabled)

ISP (International Standardized Profile)

A standardized subset of a not-yet-finalized specification—that is, one still under development. A *profile* (also known as a *functional standard*) is a clearly defined subset of an emerging standard—presumably a subset that provides enough of the specification to permit a working implementation of at least the subset.

In an effort to avoid, or at least minimize, the chaos that can result when vendors, countries, or areas implement different parts of a not-yet-standardized specification, the ISO (International Standardization Organization) published a set of guidelines for creating standardized subsets. These guidelines are published in ISO Technical Report 10000, and they provide a mechanism whereby the individual profiles created by regional working groups or standards committees can be coordinated by a Regional Workshop Coordinating Committee (RWCC).

ISP (Internet Service Provider)

An ISP is a service provider that provides some way to connect to the Internet. Several access methods are possible, and a particular ISP may allow any or all of these methods. ISPs—sometimes also known as IAPs (Internet Access Providers)—fall along a spectrum with respect to service: at one end, IAPs provide only Internet access; at the other end, online service providers have Internet access as only a small part of their business.

Most ISPs have at least some plan that allows unlimited access for a flat monthly fee, and they generally also have less expensive plans that allow a fixed number of access hours, with additional time charged at a fixed hourly rate. Smaller ISPs serve only a limited calling area, and provide access numbers only for certain area codes. Some do provide 800 numbers, but this access is generally not free. Even larger access providers, such as AOL (America Online) and AT&T provide local numbers in many areas, but they also provide 800 numbers in places not accessible over local numbers.

The following types of accounts are common:

UNIX shell account   With this type of account, the user is dialing into a UNIX server that allows public access. To the server, the user's computer looks like a dumb terminal. With such an account, the subscriber can use the server's Internet utilities. Since UNIX interfaces can be Spartan, many subscribers with such an account use The Internet Adapter (TIA) to give them a friendlier interface.

SLIP or PPP account   With this type of account, the user's computer becomes an Internet host—that is, a machine on the Internet. The subscriber's computer gets its own Internet address (although this may be different each time the user logs on), and Internet utilities (FTP, Telnet, etc.) must be available on the subscriber's machine. The subscriber accesses the Internet by using SLIP (Serial Line Internet Protocol), CSLIP (Compressed SLIP), or PPP (Point-to-Point Protocol) over a modem.

BBS account   With this type of account, the user is calling up the BBS, and is then using BBS software to access the Internet. Any file transfers, etc., must go through the BBS machine, and will incur any storage or transport fees for such storage.

ISPs usually provide at least the SLIP or PPP software, and may include some utilities for navigating the Internet. The ISP will also provide a script or other file to make it easier to log in. Almost all new PCs come with Internet access software already installed. In many cases, this will be preconfigured for an access provider that has paid the PC manufacturer or Microsoft some sort of licensing fee. However, the software will also have a way to allow users to sign up with an access provider of their choice.

ISU (Integrated Service Unit)

In digital telephone services, a device that consists of CSU (Channel Service Unit) and DSU (Digital Service Unit), and that replaces a modem on a DDS (Digital Data Service) line.

ITC (Independent Telephone Company)

A local exchange carrier (LEC) that is not a Bell operating company (BOC). There are currently more than 1500 such companies in the United States.

ITR (Internet Talk Radio)

Audio programs distributed over the MBONE (multicast backbone) attached to the regular Internet. For information about ITR, send an e-mail message to the infoserver at info@radio.com.

→ *See* MBONE

ITT (Invitation To Transmit)

In an ARCnet network architecture, the ITT is the token frame.

ITU (International Telecommunications Union)

ITU is a United Nations agency formed to help develop and standardize telecommunications around the world. The ITU had three subagencies:

- The ubiquitous CCITT (Consultative Committee for International Telephony and Telegraphy), which is responsible for dozens of communications, interface, and other types of standards. On March 1, 1993, the CCITT was officially replaced by the ITU-T (International Telecommunication Union—Telecommunication Standardization Sector). CCITT publications are now known as ITU-T publications.

- The IFRB (International Frequency Registration Board), which is responsible for allocating frequency bands in the electromagnetic spectrum for telecommunications. Together with the CCIR (next item), the IFRB has been replaced by the ITU-R (International Telecommunication Union—Radiocommunication Standardization Sector).

- The CCIR (Consultative Committee on International Radio), which is responsible for recommendations relating to radio communications. Together with the IFRB, the CCIR has been replaced by the ITU-R (International Telecommunication Union—Radiocommunication Standardization Sector).

ITU-T (International Telecommunications Union— Telecommunications Standardization Section)

The official designation for the committee that replaced the CCITT (Consultative Committee for International Telegraphy and Telephony) on March 1, 1993. Sometimes also written as *ITU-TS* or *ITU-TSS*.

IVD (Integrated Voice and Data)

The physical integration of voice and data in a single network is the primary focus of the working group for IEEE 802.9. In practice, this amounts to the integration of ISDN (Integrated Services Digital Network) and LAN (local area network) architectures and protocols. This has resulted in the Integrated Services for Local Area Networks 16T (ISLAN16T) standard, which was approved in 1993 as IEEE standard 802.9.

IEEE 802.9 specifies the interface between equipment that produces packetized or time-sensitive (isochronous) data and an access unit, which uses TDM (time division multiplexing) to combine the data for further transmission.

IVR (Interactive Voice Response)

A term for various computer telephony configurations that include voice processing technology. Generally, a user uses a touch tone phone to communicate with such a system, and the system uses digitized voice or voice synthesis to respond.

Examples of IVR systems include automated order entry lines, crossword puzzle answer services, and college registration lines (electronic rather than human ones). In an automated order entry system, the caller enters product codes by pressing buttons on the phone, the system confirms the item name, availability, and price by voice response, and the order is entered into the system.

IWU (Internetworking Unit)

An intermediate system.

→ *See* IS (Intermediate System)

IXC (Interexchange Carrier)

An interexchange carrier (or, sometimes, channel) is a telephone service company that provides long-distance connections between local exchange carriers (LECs), or local telephone companies. In particular, an IXC (sometimes also abbreviated as IEC) provides telephone services between local access and transport areas (LATAs).

IXCs are allowed to provide carrier service only from areas in which the IXC has a point of presence (POP), or a switching office. Currently, there are about 700 IXCs in the United States and Canada. The best known of these are AT&T, MCI, and Sprint.

→ *Broader Category* PSTN (Public Switched Telephone Network)

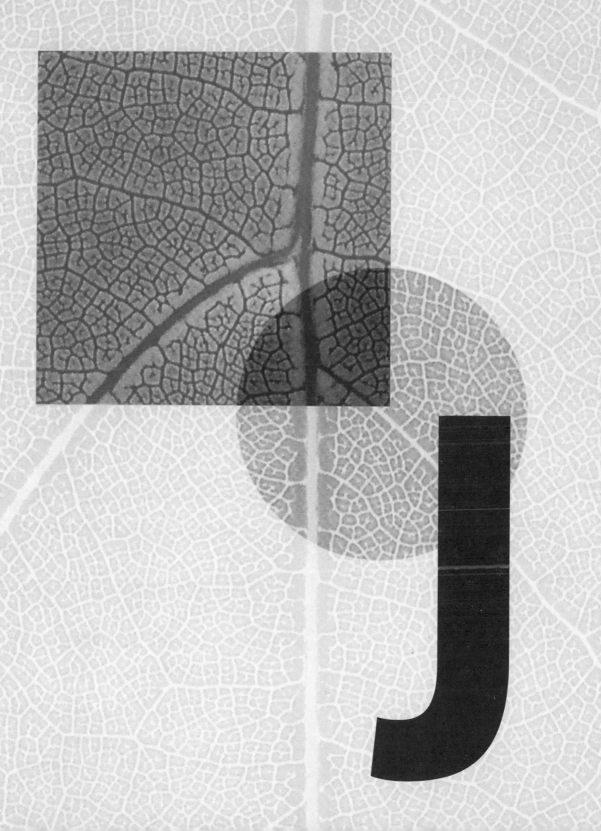

Jabber Detector

In a network that uses the CSMA/CD (Carrier Sense Multiple Access with Collision Detection) media access method, a jabber detector is a device that helps prevent a node from transmitting constantly (for example, if the node is malfunctioning).

Jabber Packet

In an Ethernet network, a jabber packet is a meaningless transmission generated by a network node because of a network malfunction (such as a faulty transceiver) or other error. A jabber packet is larger than the maximum size (1518 bytes for Ethernet) and contains a bad CRC value. In contrast, long frames exceed the maximum frame length, but have a valid CRC value.

Jack

A female connector; specifically, a connector with sockets, or slots. This is in contrast to a male connector, known as a plug.

→ *See Also* Connector

Jacket

The outer cover, or sheath, on a cable. The material of which the jacket is made will determine, in large part, the cable's safety properties. For example, a plenum cable jacket must be constructed from fire-resistant material such as Teflon.

→ *See Also* Cable

Jamming

Jamming refers to the radiation of a specific range of frequencies in order to make it more difficult or impossible to use signals in that frequency range

for communication. Jamming may be deliberate or accidental.

Active jamming—by far the most common type—is deliberate jamming.

In *passive jamming*, the interference arises as an incidental side effect of another action. For example, passive jamming may occur because someone in the vicinity happens to be using the same frequency range.

Jam Signal

In an Ethernet network, a signal sent to tell other nodes on the network that a packet collision has taken place.

→ *See Also* CSMA/CD; Ethernet

JANET (Joint Academic Network)

An electronic-mail (e-mail) network run by universities and other academic institutions in Great Britain. JANET is an X.25 network, and provides e-mail access to just about anywhere in the world through connections to other networks, such as BITNET and JUNET.

Japanese Standards Association (JSA)

→ *See* JSA (Japanese Standards Association)

Japanese UNIX Network (JUNET)

→ *See* JUNET (Japanese UNIX Network)

Jargon File

A file containing various informative, amusing, and enlightening terms related to computers and the computing culture. The file is available on the World Wide Web (WWW) through the following URLs (Uniform Resource Locators, which are essentially document addresses):

http://www.ccil.org

http://www.tuxedo.org/~esr/jargon_toc
.html

It is also available as a highly recommended book: *The New Hacker's Dictionary, 3rd edition*, edited by Eric Raymond (MIT Press).

Java

Java is an object-oriented programming language, developed in the early 1990's at Sun Microsystems. Java was designed for network programming— that is, for creating programs that can execute as needed across a network. Java is both an evolutionary and a revolutionary language. It has features that make it an excellent choice for just about any kind of programming project.

Java Features

Java has several features that make it an attractive programming language:

- It has a true object-oriented design. Because it is unencumbered by backward compatibility requirements, Java's object hierarchy is more cleanly and simply designed than is the hierarchy for C++.

- The language has numerous features designed to simplify development— including automatic garbage collection, a virtual machine that can be embedded in applications and other contexts to execute Java code, and programming tools that let the developer decide whether to opt for speed or portability.

- It has a syntax that is very similar to C++ syntax, which means C++ programmers will have a relatively easy time learning Java.

- It was designed to be platform independent. To accomplish this, Java programs are compiled to an intermediate bytecode, which can then be executed on any machine with an appropriate interpreter (a Java Virtual Machine, or JVM) or with a just-in-time (JIT) compiler that can compile the bytecode to native code on the fly. The latter produces faster-running code, but makes the code more platform dependent. Also the compilation time must be considered, although this will generally be negligible.

- It can be used to create both applications (free-standing executable programs) and applets (programs designed to execute within a Web page or even within another application). Applications and applets can execute only if there is an appropriate interpreter on the target machine. For applets, this interpreter will generally be embedded in the browser.

- It uses a sandbox security model to prevent applets from accessing any files or other resources on the machines on which the applets execute. Basically, all Java applets must execute within their sandbox.

Java Programs

To create Java programs, you need a version of the Java Developer's Kit (JDK). Currently, JDK 1.2 is the most recent official version, although version 2 is expected soon.

A Java source file is compiled to an intermediate format known as *bytecode*. This bytecode file can be moved to, and executed on, any machine with a Java interpreter. This interpreter, known as the Java Virtual Machine (JVM), must be written for the target machine. The JVM will interpret and execute the bytecode instructions in the target platform native code. Figure "Creating a Java program " illustrates this process.

In some implementations, the JVM will include a just-in-time (JIT) compiler, which monitors the code being generated and executed by the interpreter, with an (electronic) eye to caching code elements that can be optimized and then used the next time they are needed. This can speed up program execution by a factor of 100 in some—admittedly rare—cases. One drawback of Java is that interpreted code almost never executes as quickly as compiled code. Consequently, for some purposes, the standard Java runtime environment may not be satisfactory.

One possible way around this is to use a JIT compiler, which will translate the entire bytecode program into native code. The compiled and optimized program can then execute more quickly than an interpreted version.

Microsoft's version of Java—which is currently the subject of legal wrangling between JavaSoft and Microsoft—is known as Java++.

→ *See Also* JavaScript

Java Database Connectivity (JDBC)

→ *See* JDBC (Java Database Connectivity)

JavaScript

JavaScript is a scripting language that is based on Java, and that was developed to provide the Netscape Navigator browser program with more power, and also to give Web page designers a tool to spice up Web pages. JavaScript provides client-side scripting capabilities. JavaScript scripts are client-side programs. This means that the script will execute when the Web page is displayed on the client machine.

Scripts are programs in that they contain instructions that are carried out according to pre-defined rules. However, scripts differ from programs in that they are not compiled.

Scripts are inserted into HTML files and are interpreted by the browser whenever the appropriate section of the document is read. The effects possible with a JavaScript file are limited primarily by the Web designer's imagination, although there are limitations inherent in the design of the HTML language.

Scripts cannot access anything on a PC outside of the browser. That is, a JavaScript script file can execute only within the browser.

JavaScript is the main component in the recently standardized ECMAScript, which is the official scripting language for Web documents. Other ECMAScript features were taken from JScript, which is Microsoft's implementation of JavaScript.

→ *Compare* VBScript

JavaSpace

→ *See* Jini

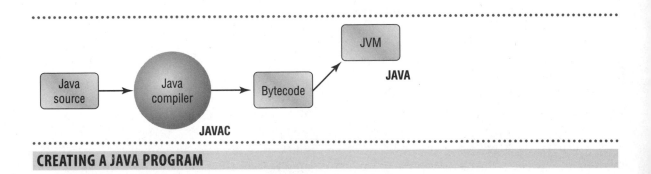

CREATING A JAVA PROGRAM

Java Virtual Machine (JVM)

→ *See* JVM (Java Virtual Machine)

JCL (Job Control Language)

A command language that provides the instructions for an operating system to run an application program.

JDA (Joint Development Agreement)

An agreement between IBM and Microsoft to develop various operating system technology, such as OS/2. The agreement has since been terminated. Each vendor went in its own development direction: OS/2 for IBM and Windows NT for Microsoft.

JDBC (Java Database Connectivity)

JDBC provides a Java-based interface between databases and program objects. For example, it can provide support for clients trying to access and search a database. JDBC is designed to be platform independent so that the same resources can be used on any Java-compliant platform—that is, on any platform with a Java interpreter, or Java Virtual Machine (JVM).

→ *Broader Category* Database

→ *Compare* ODBC (Open Database Connectivity)

JEDI (Joint Electronic Data Interchange)

A United Nations task force that represents the United Nations in meetings and events related to EDI (Electronic Data Interchange).

→ *See Also* EDI (Electronic Data Interchange)

Jini

Introduced in July 1998, Jini (pronounced like "genie") is a Java-based technology from Sun Microsystems. It provides a type of "Plug and Play" mechanism that enables various types of objects (devices and services) to communicate and make use of each other's resources and capabilities. Jini objects can work across platforms because Jini is built on the platform-independent Java programming environment and because each Jini object includes its own interfaces and any drivers or other components required to interact with the object.

Jini services and auxiliary tools are implemented as components in a series of layers built on top of the Java Virtual Machine (JVM) on which Java programs and applets execute. The Jini infrastructure is built directly on the JVM. The infrastructure consists of the Discover and Join services, which are administered by the Jini Lookup Service.

The Lookup Service functions as an intermediary between the Jini infrastructure and the transaction and object sharing services that are the ends for which Jini provides the means. These services operate at a layer above the Jini infrastructure and, together with the infrastructure, make up the Jini programming model.

Transaction services help ensure that any Jini services are carried out completely or not at all. Sun's JavaSpace technology provides the services necessary to migrate and share Jini objects across distributed networks. For example, client applications might communicate with a JavaSpace server to request a Jini object. To request a Jini resource through JavaSpace, a client sends a template of what the Jini object should look like to the JavaSpace server. This component finds the object that best fits the template by sending requests to Jini Lookup Service.

Java's Remote Method Invocation (RMI) provides the "glue" that holds all the services and elements together in a Jini network. RMI is Java's version of remote procedure calls (RPCs).

J

Creating a Jini Network

A network of Jini objects can be created on the fly. In fact, a Jini network is more like a connected federation (Sun's word) of devices and services in a distributed computing space. Jini devices and services can join or leave the federation as necessary.

To join a Jini network, a device or service simply needs to make its presence and capabilities known to the network. It does this by broadcasting a 512-byte discovery packet that announces the object's presence on the network and that provides a way of contacting the object.

Lookup services on the network will notice the discovery packet and will query the object as to its capabilities. The object will join the network by sending a proxy object containing the Jini object's interfaces and information about its resources and capabilities. Jini objects generally will use discovery and join protocols to connect to a Jini network, but other ways of doing this are allowed by the Jini specification.

The Lookup service will grant the object a limited-duration lease. This lease must be renewed at the end of the lease's duration interval. If the object does not rejoin the network, the lease will expire and the object will no longer be considered as part of the network.

Objects or other clients that want to use a Jini object will contact a Lookup Service that will connect client and service to each other. Once the contact between these is made, the Lookup Service no longer plays a role in the connection. Clients are granted leases to use Jini objects for a limited time, either on an exclusive or nonexclusive basis.

HENs and Other Jini Possibilities

Jini's technology makes it possible to add objects to a network or remove them as desired. Moreover, it's possible to do this in an automated fashion. Finally, the entire Jini environment fits into a 70KB JAR (Java Archive) file. This means that Jini can be implemented directly on devices—for example, printers, scanners, TVs, CD players, and even refrigerators and toasters.

These are highly desirable capabilities because they open up possibilities for all sorts of networks. Note that Jini networks do not require any computers. Because of this, you could create, for example, a home entertainment network (HEN) in which your TV, video, and audio equipment could be connected.

Jini is only one of several technologies that are trying to make it possible to carry out distributed computing across multiple platforms in a flexible and painless manner. Other technologies that provide one or more of the services made possible by Jini include CORBA (Common Object Request Broker Architecture), Microsoft Transaction Server (MTS), DCOM (Distributed Component Object Model), and Lucent Technology's Inferno environment.

→ *Broader Category*   Java

JIT (Just-in-Time) Compiler

In Java programming environments, a JIT is a compiler that runs on a target machine and that compiles a Java bytecode file on the fly into the platform's native code. The compiled program can then execute more quickly than a bytecode program that is interpreted and executed by a Java Virtual Machine (JVM).

→ *Broader Category*   Java

→ *Compare*   JVM (Java Virtual Machine)

Jitter

In signaling, a variation in the timing between the source's and receiver's clocks or in the constancy of the source clock rate. *Phase jitter* can cause the signal to be slightly out of phase. In *amplitude jitter*, the amplitude of a signal varies over time.

Job Control Language (JCL)

➡️ *See* JCL (Job Control Language)

Job Transfer and Manipulation (JTM)

➡️ *See* JTM (Job Transfer and Manipulation)

Join

A join combines records from two or more tables into an aggregate table. The term *join* is used to indicate both the record combination operator and the resulting aggregate table.

➡️ *Compare* Union

Join Protocol

➡️ *See* Protocol, Join

Joint Academic Network (JANET)

➡️ *See* JANET (Joint Academic Network)

Joint Development Agreement (JDA)

➡️ *See* JDA (Joint Development Agreement)

Joint Electronic Data Interchange (JEDI)

➡️ *See* JEDI (Joint Electronic Data Interchange)

Joint Photographic Experts Group (JPEG)

➡️ *See* JPEG (Joint Photographic Experts Group)

Joint Technical Committee (JTC)

➡️ *See* JTC (Joint Technical Committee)

Jonzy's Universal Gopher Hierarchy Excavation and Display (Jughead)

➡️ *See* Jughead (Jonzy's Universal Gopher Hierarchy Excavation and Display)

Journaling

In transaction processing, a strategy in which every transaction is recorded, so that a database or file can be recreated in case of failure or malfunction.

JPEG (Joint Photographic Experts Group)

An image compression standard that uses a discrete cosine transformation to achieve compression ratios as high as 100:1. JPEG, pronounced "jay peg," is an example of a lossy algorithm, which means that some image details will be lost at high compression ratios.

Originally implemented only in hardware, JPEG compression schemes are now available in many image viewing or handling packages. JPEG compression occurs in three steps:

1. Discrete cosine transformation (DCT), which converts image data into a breakdown based on frequencies.

J

2. Quantization, which adjusts the granularity (number of bits) used to represent various frequencies, so that little storage is wasted to represent rarely occurring frequencies. The coarser granularity for these infrequent frequencies introduces the loss during the compression. The degree of compression (and concomitant loss of information) depends on how the granularity is adjusted.

3. Lossless compression of the quantization data. Once the data have been reduced by dropping out details of rarely occurring information, the remaining information is reduced again by applying a common compression algorithm (such as Huffman or run length encoding).

JSA (Japanese Standards Association)

The Japanese counterpart to ANSI (American National Standards Institute) in the United States or to the CSA (Canadian Standards Association) in Canada.

JScript

JScript is Microsoft's implementation of JavaScript.

→ **See Also** JavaScript

JTC (Joint Technical Committee)

Any of several such committees formed by the ISO (International Standards Committee) and IEC (International Electrotechnical Commission). Perhaps the best known is JTC1, which is the committee that was largely responsible for the OSI Reference Model.

JTM (Job Transfer and Manipulation)

In the OSI Reference Model, one of several file transfer services (FTSs) defined at the application layer. JTM enables an application to do data processing on a remote machine.

→ **See Also** ASE (Application Service Element)

Jughead (Jonzy's Universal Gopher Hierarchy Excavation and Display)

In the world of gophers (file finders and fetchers) on the Internet, Jughead is a program that makes it possible to limit a search to a specified set of gopher servers. Jughead accomplishes this by searching only the higher-level menus of "Gopherspace"—which are more likely to be associated with particular servers.

To use Jughead, you must point a gopher client to a Jughead server—for example, the one at `gopher.utah.edu`. On many servers, you can also get Jughead by selecting a menu item that reads something like "Search Gopherspace by Top-level Menus." Such a menu may not mention Jughead at all.

→ **Broader Category** Gopher

→ **Compare** Archie, Veronica

Jukebox

An optical storage system that can hold multiple disks at the same time, allowing one of these to be selected at any given time.

Jumbo Frame

In Gigabit Ethernet, a jumbo frame represents a proposed increase in the maximum Ethernet frame size to 9000 bytes. This increase is being proposed by manufacturers of network interface cards (NICs) for Gigabit Ethernet networks. The advantage of allowing jumbo frames is simply that the NICs would have to process fewer frames. And, since much of frame processing involves checking headers, this time saving could be significant.

Currently, there are no standards related to jumbo frames. Instead, various NIC manufacturers are implementing support in their own ways.

→ *Broader Category* Gigabit Ethernet

Jumbo Group

In telecommunications, a jumbo group is a multichannel group consisting of six master groups. A *master group* is itself a conglomerate of a large number of channels. The jumbo group consists of 3600 voice channels, all transmitted simultaneously over a broadband connection. Each voice channel is 4kHz. The table "Jumbo Group Constituents" shows the way a jumbo group is built up in a hierarchy developed by the Bell System. A hierarchy from the ITU uses a somewhat different set of groupings and does not include a jumbo group.

JUMBO GROUP CONSTITUENTS

Name	Bandwidth	Number of Voice Channels
Channel	4KHz	1
Group	48KHz	12
Super Group	240KHz	60 (5 groups)
Master Group	2400KHz	600 (10 super groups)
Jumbo Group	14.4MHz	3600 (6 master groups)\

Jumper

A wire or metal bridge whose placement can be used to close a circuit. A jumper can establish electrical connections that indicate configuration settings. Jumpers are alternatives to DIP switches for storing configuration values. A group of jumpers is called a *jumper block*.

JUNET (Japanese UNIX Network)

A research network for noncommercial institutions and organizations.

Just-in-Time (JIT) Compiler

→ *See* JIT (Just-in-Time) Compiler

JVM (Java Virtual Machine)

The JVM is a Java language interpreter. Java programs are compiled into an intermediate bytecode format. This format is platform independent and can be executed on any machine for which a JVM has been written. When a Java program is to execute, it can be interpreted and simultaneously executed by the JVM.

The advantage of this approach is that Java code is platform independent. A disadvantage is that interpreted code almost always runs more slowly than compiled code. As a way around this problem, the Java environment also offers the possibility of trading in some of the platform independence for speed by using a just-in-time (JIT) compiler to translate the bytecode completely into native code prior to executing it.

→ *Broader Category* Java

→ *Compare* JIT (Just-in-Time) Compiler

J

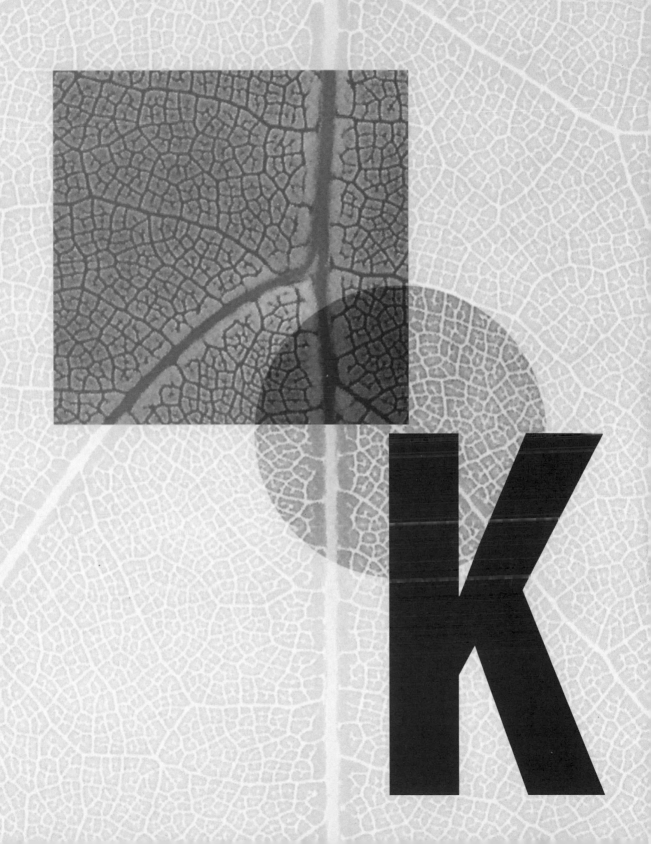

K

Used, generally in lowercase, as an abbreviation for the prefix *kilo*, as in kbps (kilobits per second). This order of magnitude corresponds to 2^{10}, which is 1,024, or roughly 10^3. A kilobyte (KB) is 1,024 bytes. A kilohertz (kHz) is 1,024 cycles per second.

→ *See Also* Orders of Magnitude

K56flex Technology

K56flex is one of the two technologies developed independently to push modem operation to 56kbps.

→ *See* 56K Modem

KA9Q

An implementation of the TCP/IP protocol suite for amateur packet radio systems. KA9Q is discussed in RFC 1208.

Kb, KB, Kbps, KBps

Abbreviations for various computing-related magnitudes expressed as multiples of 1,024. This value represents the quantity associated with the prefix *kilo* in a binary number system.

The lowercase *b* stands for *bits*, and the uppercase *B* stands for *bytes*. Each byte represents 8 bits. Thus, 3kb would be three kilobits (which equals 3,072 bits); in contrast, 3kB would be three kilobytes (which equals 3,072 bytes or 24,576 bits).

The following list summarizes the abbreviations:

- **Kb, kb:** kilobit, where each kb is 1,024 bits

- **KB, kB:** kilobyte, where each kB is 1,024 bytes or 8,192 bits

- **Kbps, kbps:** kilobits per second

- **KBps, kBps:** kilobytes per second

K-Band

The K-band is the portion of the electromagnetic spectrum that covers frequencies ranging from 10.9GHz (gigahertz) to 36GHz. This frequency band includes the Ku-Band (13GHz–18GHz), which is used in satellite communications. The Ka-Band (33GHz–40GHz) is sometimes also considered part of the K-band, even though part of its frequency range lies outside that of the K-band. Radar signals include the various K-bands in their frequency range.

KDC (Key Distribution Center)

In data-encryption terminology, a KDC is a center for storing, managing, and distributing ecncryption keys. The KDC distributes public encryption keys to the parties involved in a transmission. To verify the authenticity of the keys, the KDC signs the message in which the keys are distributed. The Kerberos authentication server, which will be used in the networking versions of Windows 2000, uses a KDC.

KDD (Kokusai Denshin Denwa)

A Japanese long-distance telephone service provider.

Keep Alive Message

Keep alive messages are exchanged between network devices to indicate that a virtual connection between the devices is still in existence. The message both indicates that the connection is active and also helps keep it that way by causing network traffic along the connection.

In some network configurations, a router may send keep alive messages on behalf of nodes on another network. This process is known as *spoofing*, and is used in part to keep network traffic down by reducing the amount of traffic that comes from administrative signaling.

Kerberos

Kerberos is a network security system originally developed for Project Athena at MIT (Massachusetts Institute of Technology). Kerberos is a *distributed authentication system*. It verifies that a user is legitimate when the user logs in, as well as every time the user requests a service. The system is designed to provide authentication for users who may be logging in to the network from an unattended workstation. Such stations must be regarded as suspect, or untrusted, because their physical security cannot be guaranteed.

Kerberos protects transmissions by using special keys, called *tickets*, to encrypt transmissions between Kerberos and a user. Kerberos uses private-key encryption methods. This is in contrast to a service such as Digital Equipment Corporation's (DEC's) DASS (Distributed Authentication Security Service), which uses public-key encryption.

→ *Broader Categories* Authentication; Security

→ *See Also* DASS (Distributed Authentication Security Service)

Kermit

A popular file transfer protocol. Kermit has been implemented on most types of hardware, and it is widely used, particularly when logging on to bulletin board systems (BBSs).

Kernel

The kernel is the core of an operating system. The kernel contains the most essential operating system services, such as task schedulers and interrupt handlers, and is always loaded whenever the operating system is active. It can call other operating system services (such as file or other input/output [I/O] services) when requested by a user, a function, or an application.

Key

In a database, a key is an element used to distinguish records in the database. Keys can be based on multiple fields in a record, and each record should have a unique key. Keys are stored in an index for more efficient search and manipulation.

In cryptography, a key is a bit sequence that is used to prime an encryption process and to enable a decryption process. The longer the key—that is, the more bits in the sequence—the more secure an encryption will be.

Keyboard Send and Receive (KSR)

→ *See* KSR (Keyboard Send and Receive)

Key Distribution Center (KDC)

→ *See* KDC (Key Distribution Center)

Keying

Keying refers to the process of entering text or other types of data. The term is also used to refer to the process of making components nonsymmetrical in order to make sure they are connected properly. Keying is important in situations in which incorrect connections can cause damage to circuitry and components. For example, modular telephone (RJ-*xx*) plugs and jacks may be keyed; MMJ connectors are a keyed variant of RJ-*xx* connectors. Cables connecting disk drives to power supplies may also be keyed.

Key Management Protocol (KMP)

→ *See* KMP (Key Management Protocol)

K

Key Manager

In Microsoft's Internet Information Server (IIS) the Key Manager is used to create encryption keys needed to use Secure Socket Layer (SSL) communications, and to install these keys at the appropriate Web site. Any keys that are created by the Key Manager must be verified—given a certificate—by a Certificate Authority. IIS includes a Certificate Authority that can be installed on the server. Or, the key needs to be certified by an outside Certificate Authority, such as VeriSign.

→ *Broader Category* Microsoft IIS (Internet Information Server

Keypad

A keypad is a small, often special-purpose, keyboard or key array. Keypads are used on small devices such as calculators or as supplements to a regular keyboard, such as the numeric keypad or the arrow keys arrayed on the side of some computer keyboards.

Key Pulse

A key pulse is a telephone signal system in which a calling digit is selected by pressing a key corresponding to the digit.

Key Telephone System (KTS)

→ *See* KTS (Key Telephone System)

kHz (Kilohertz)

A kilohertz is 1,000 hertz, or cycles per second. Each hertz (cycle) represents one occurrence of a periodic event, such as an electromagnetic signal.

Killer Channel

In digital telecommunications, a transmission channel whose timing is off, so that the channel overlaps and interferes with other channels.

Kill File

On the Internet, a data file that contains instructions to filter out ("kill") news postings and e-mail from certain persons or about certain topics. Also called a *bozo filter*.

Kilo

→ *See* K

Kilobit (Kb)

→ *See* Kb, KB, Kbps, KBps

Kilobyte (KB)

→ *See* Kb, KB, Kbps, KBps

Kilobits per Second (Kbps)

→ *See* Kb, KB, Kbps, KBps

Kilobytes per Second (KBps)

→ *See* Kb, KB, Kbps, KBps

Kilohertz (kHz)

→ *See* KHz (Kilohertz)

Kilowatt-Hour (KWH)

→ *See* KWH (Kilowatt-Hour)

KIS (Knowbot Information Service)

On the Internet, an experimental service that can query directory services in order to retrieve requested information. KIS uses knowbot programs to search the directory services for the information. Other services that provide directory-related information include whois and the White Pages Directory.

KMP (Key Management Protocol)

In a secure network, KMP is a protocol used for checking security keys.

Knowbot

A program that can track down information, even if it is in a remote location. Knowbots (from *knowledge robots*) are still mainly an experimental technology, although there is one well-known and widely used example: In the Internet environment, knowbots are used in the KIS (knowbot information service) to get directory service ("white pages") information.

Knowbot Information System (KIS)

→ *See* KIS (Knowbot Information System)

Kokusai Denshin Denwa (KDD)

→ *See* KDD (Kokusai Denshin Denwa)

KSR (Keyboard Send and Receive)

A KSR device is a telephoneless telephone—a communications device that consists of a keyboard and printer. Because the device has no storage, messages are printed as they are received, and are transmitted as they are typed at the keyboard.

KTS (Key Telephone System)

In telephony, a KTS is an arrangement of multi-line phones in which users can press keys to access lines to a central office or to a PBX (private branch exchange), or to access KTS features. KTS features include the following:

- Putting a caller on hold
- Calling or answering on a selected line
- Contacting a party over an intercom
- Transferring a call to another line

The KTS signals are sent to and processed by a *key service unit*, or KSU.

An EKTS is a KTS that uses electrical switches. By reducing the entire KTS down to electronic circuitry, it becomes easier to add features and to install the KTS in a telephone.

KWH (Kilowatt-Hour)

A KWH is a unit of work that represents 1,000 watts of energy delivered for one hour.

K

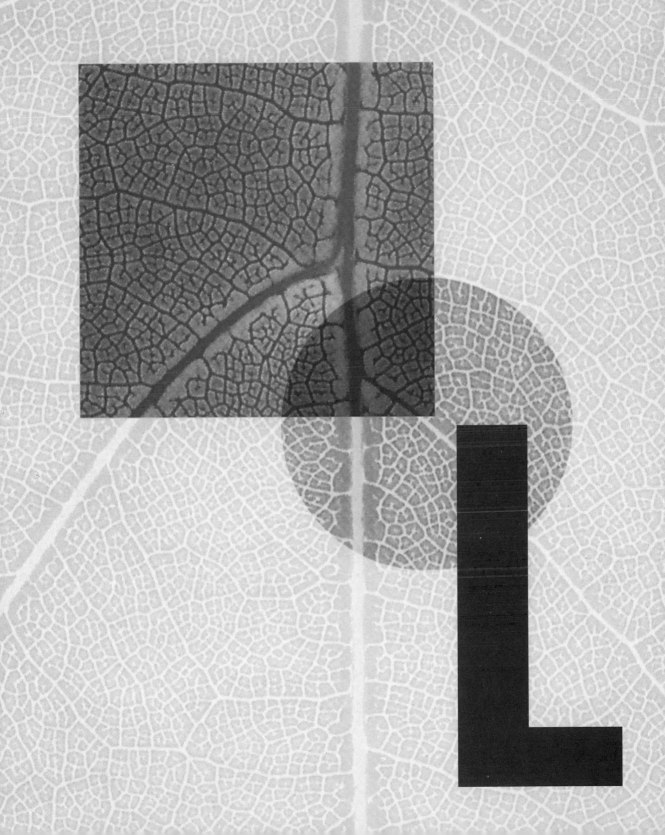

L3 Switching

→ *See* Layer 3 Switching

LAA (Locally Administered Address)

In a Token Ring network connected to a mainframe, the LAA is a parameter used by a 3174 controller to determine whether the node can access the mainframe.

LAM (Lobe Attachment Module)

In a Token Ring network, a LAM is a box with multiple interfaces to which new nodes (known as *lobes*) for the network can be attached. A LAM may have interfaces for up to 20 lobes. Functionally, a LAM is like a multistation access unit (MAU), but with a larger capacity: 20 nodes, as opposed to 8 for the MAU. The LAM interfaces may use either IBM connectors or RJ-45 plugs.

LAMs can be daisy-chained and connected to a hub, known as a *controlled access unit (CAU)* in token-ring terminology. Each CAU can handle up to four LAMs, for a total of 80 lobes.

LAMA (Local Automatic Message Accounting)

The process by which the local telephone company handles automatic billing for local and toll calls. This accounting method requires automatic number identification (ANI), a capability that has been adapted to provide caller ID services. An alternative accounting strategy, CAMA (Centralized Automatic Message Accounting), accomplishes the same thing but at a central office.

LAN (Local Area Network)

A LAN is a collection of two or more computers that are located within a limited distance of each other and that are connected to each other, directly or indirectly. LANs differ in the way the computers are connected, in how information moves around the network, and in what machine (if any) is in charge of the network. "Context and properties of a LAN" summarizes some of the features of LANs.

The computers in a LAN may be PCs, Macintoshes, minicomputers, mainframes, or machines with other architectures. However, there are restrictions on the combinations that are feasible and sensible. This article focuses on PC-based LANs, although other configurations are also mentioned.

LAN Terminology

The PCs in a LAN are called *nodes*, and nodes may be either *servers* or *workstations*. Workstations are sometimes known just as *stations*.

Minicomputers or mainframe computers in a LAN generally serve as *hosts* for PCs or terminals that are connected to the computer. Most computer-terminal connections are over telephone or dedicated lines, so that these configurations are generally considered *wide area networks*, or *WANs*.

Nodes are connected to a network by means of a *network interface card (NIC)*, which is also called a *network adapter card*, *network board*, and a dozen other names. The NIC is installed in an expansion slot in the node. This NIC is connected directly or indirectly to the network cable. Each node must have its own NIC. A server can have multiple NICs, which allow that server to be connected to multiple networks simultaneously.

Types of LANs

LANs differ in their configuration at two levels:

- In the administrative relationship between nodes. In this sense, LANs are divided into *server-based* and *peer-to-peer* (or just peer) varieties.

- In the physical and logical relationships among nodes. This has to do with the manner in which information moves around the network. LANs differ in the *architecture* (Ethernet, Token Ring, FDDI, and so on) and *topology* (bus, ring, or star) they use.

Server-Based LANs versus Peer-to-Peer LANs

In a *server-based network,* a server controls access to some resource (such as a hard disk or printer) and serves as a host for the workstations connected to the server. A workstation requests services, such as access to files or programs on the hard disk or use of a printer, from a server.

Servers run the network operating system (NOS) software; workstations run client software that manages the communication between the workstation and the network.

Servers may be dedicated or not. A *dedicated server* can be used only as a server; it cannot be used as a workstation as well. A *nondedicated server* can be used as a workstation, as needed, even when it continues to perform server duties.

A server-based LAN is in contrast to a *peer-to-peer network,* in which each node may be either a server or workstation as the need arises. In general, large networks—those with more than a few dozen nodes— are more likely to be server-based. This is because the reliability and security of server-based networks are easier to test than those of peer-to-peer networks.

Peer-to-peer LANs, also known simply as *peer LANs,* are more egalitarian in that each node can initiate actions, access other nodes, and provide services for other nodes without requiring a server's permission, although access or password restrictions may be in effect.

Context
Network Types
  CAN
  DAN
  Enterprise Network
  GAN
  MAN
  WAN
  LAN

LAN Properties

LANs can be PC-based (servers and workstations) or host-based (hosts and terminals).

Server-based LANs have a dedicated server. The NOS usually replaces the native OS, and security can be well-controlled. Such LANs are suited for a large range of network sizes.

On peer-to-peer LANs most machines can be server or workstation. The NOS often runs under the machine's native OS, and security is not well-controlled. Peer LANs are not suitable for large networks.

LAN architectures include ARCnet, Ethernet, FDDI, and Token Ring.

Architecture determines network size, distance limitations, and lower-level protocols.

NOS determines higher-level protocols and available services.

L

CONTEXT AND PROPERTIES OF A LAN

For example, in a peer-to-peer LAN, a given node (node A) may provide services for another node (node B) at one point; at another time, node B may provide similar or different services for node A.

Network software for peer LANs is more likely to work *with* the native operating system (for example, DOS). In contrast, the network software for server-based LANs generally replaces the native operating system. One reason for this is the server in a large network is kept very busy, and it becomes too inefficient to go through two layers of operating systems. In the case of DOS, there is another, more fundamental reason: DOS cannot do multitasking.

LAN Topologies

A topology describes the physical or logical layout of a LAN. The *physical topology* is concerned with how the cabling connects nodes. There are several physical topologies, including bus, ring, star, tree, and star-wired ring. Some of these are variants of others; some are hybrids.

A *logical topology* describes how information is passed among nodes. There are only two fundamental logical topologies:

- *Bus*, in which all information is broadcast, so that every node gets the information at (just about exactly) the same time. Since information is generally intended only for a single node, the other nodes discard the message as soon as they determine they are not the destination.

- *Ring*, in which information is passed around from node to node until it reaches its destination.

LAN Architectures

The definition of a LAN architecture includes cabling, topology, media (network) access method, and packet format. The architectures that are commonly used for LANs are based in electrical wiring, although some of these architectures also support optical fiber as an alternative transmission medium.

For the past several years, LAN architectures have been in a continuous state of transition. The traditional architectures, including ARCnet, Ethernet, and Token Ring, are being replaced by high-speed versions that are faster than their predecessors by a factor of 10 or more. It is not yet clear just how all these transitions will play out.

SERVER-BASED AND PEER-TO-PEER NETWORK OPERATING SYSTEMS

Examples of peer-to-peer NOSs include the following:

- 10net 5.1 from Tiara Systems
- Complete Network from Buffalo Products
- LANsmart from D-Link Systems
- LANstep from Hayes Microcomputer Products
- LANtastic from Artisoft
- Personal NetWare from Novell
- PC/NOS Plus from Actrix
- PowerLAN from Performance Technology
- Web from Webcorp
- Windows for Workgroups from Microsoft

All of these NOSs support peer-to-peer networking, but some—for example, Personal NetWare from Novell—also provide more of the capabilities (for example, security) expected of server-based NOSs. NOSs for server-based networks include the following:

- LAN Manager from Microsoft
- LAN Server from IBM
- NetWare from Novell
- PacerShare from Pacer Software
- PathWorks from Digital Equipment Corporation (DEC)
- StarGroup System from NCR
- TotalMac from Syntax
- VINES from Banyan Systems
- Windows NT Advanced Server (NTAS) from Microsoft

The traditional, but now pretty well obsolete, LAN architectures support transmission speeds ranging from about 2.5Mbps for ARCnet networks to 16Mbps for some Token Ring implementations. Traditional Ethernet supports speeds up to 10Mbps.

The replacement architectures are either high-speed variants of existing ones or fiber-based architectures, such as FDDI (Fiber Distributed Data Interface) or ATM (Asynchronous Transfer Mode). The fiber-based architectures have traditionally and more commonly been used for WANs. Examples of high-speed variants include several fast Ethernet versions (which support speeds of up to 100Mbps), the even faster Gigabit Ethernet (which supports speeds up to 1Gbps), and ARCnet Plus, which supports a 20Mbps rate. A 100Mbps Token Ring implementation has also been developed. However, this high-speed Token Ring (HSTR) has had little luck gaining momentum, due largely to the fact that many token ring operations—perhaps seeing the writing on the wall—are switching to fast or Gigabit Ethernet configurations.

Traditional (10Mbps) Ethernet networks are now being marketed for use in home networks.

LAN Hardware

The hardware for PC-based LANs includes computers, NICs, cables, connectors, wiring centers, safety devices, and tools.

Computer

For most PC-based networking packages, server machines officially must be at least 80486 models. In practice, however, servers really need to be Pentium-class models. Many LANs use servers with two (or, more rarely, four) processors. Workstations can be lower-level machines. See the Computer article for more information about computers used in networks.

NIC (Network Interface Card)

An NIC makes a PC network-capable. Each PC needs at least one NIC. NICs are designed for particular network architectures (Ethernet, Token Ring, and so on). Note that some computers (for example, Macintoshes) come with networking capabilities built-in, and do not need a special NIC as long as you use the native networking resources.

In some cases, NICs for higher-speed architectures can also support slower speeds. For example, 10/100 and 100/1000 Ethernet cards make it possible to mix nodes of two different speeds in a network. For a given speed/performance level, Ethernet cards tend to be least expensive compared to other LANs (such as Token Ring and ARCnet—due, in part, to economies of scale afforded by Ethernet's huge market share.

Cable

LAN cable can be coaxial, twisted-pair (possibly telephone cable), or fiber-optic, depending on the resources and on the network architecture. For certain network types, you need cable for both the main network trunk and also for attaching individual nodes to this trunk or to wiring centers (such as hubs or concentrators). This "attachment" cable is known in various contexts as *drop*, *patch*, *adapter*, or *transceiver cable*.

In some cases, the cost of the actual cable will be low compared with the cost of testing and installing the cable. In fact, the cable installation costs can sometimes be so high that it may be wise, economically, to install fiber-optic cable for the future while installing copper (twisted-pair or coaxial) cable for the present. See the Cable article for general information about network cabling and the Cable, Coaxial; Cable, Fiber-Optic; and Cable, Twisted-Pair articles for information about the specific cable types.

Connectors

The connectors must be suitable for the cable being used. Connectors are used to link cable segments, to attach nodes to a network trunk, and to connect a cable to a wiring center. Certain connectors are used to terminate a cable segment to prevent spurious signals on the network. Some of the terminators must have special grounding caps.

See the Connector and Connector, Fiber-Optic articles for more information about connectors.

L

Wiring Center

Wiring centers are components to which multiple nodes are connected in some network architectures. Wiring centers may simply collect connections and relay signals (as passive hubs do), or the centers may clean and regenerate the signal before directing and relaying it (as active or intelligent hubs do).

Depending on how big and how capable you need them, wiring centers may cost you anywhere from a few hundred to many thousands of dollars.

Switches

Switches are relatively recent additions to the LAN hardware armamentarium, but they have effected a major change in the nature and possibilities of Ethernet architectures. A LAN switch is a device that makes it possible to establish direct connections between two nodes (which are represented by ports at the switch). Because of the way switches are configured, multiple connections of this sort can be operating at the same time.

The switch circuitry is able to provide each of these connections with full bandwidth. Since each pair of connected nodes essentially has a full-speed network, the Ethernet architecture need not be a shared-media architecture anymore. This also makes it possible to use Ethernet in full-duplex mode. This, in turn, is an important element in the very high speed Gigabit Ethernet architecture.

Safety Devices

Safety devices protect the network from crashes or damage due to electrical irregularities or power loss. You should protect at least your servers with an uninterruptible power supply (UPS), and you should protect each workstation with at least a surge protector.

These components are mainly insurance purchases. Unlike many types of insurance, however, network insurance is always a good investment. Results of various studies show that network hardware malfunctions are disconcertingly common, and that the costs of malfunctions—in both repair expenses and in lost data and revenues—can be astronomical. On the other hand, limited protection

may cost as little as $50 per workstation for surge protectors to a few hundred dollars for a UPS for a server with a large hard disk.

Tools

The tools are partly insurance and partly convenience devices. Since networks are often most expensive when they are down or functioning incorrectly, it is important to be able to test components when things go wrong. You should also test components before installing them, to ensure that you do not install a faulty component, and then test them periodically to make sure they are functioning properly. Special tools are available for testing network components.

Network testers can be quite expensive (thousands of dollars). Convenience tools, such as wire crimpers and voltmeters, are quite inexpensive (from a few dollars to a few hundred). The amount you will need to spend on tools depends on the size of the network, the importance of the network's contents, and on who will be doing network maintenance. Of course, if you do not spend the money for these tools (and for training yourself or the other person who will use them), you may end up paying even more money to have an expert come in and repair your network.

Miscellaneous Hardware

Your network might include other special hardware. For example, special disk controller boards can speed up disk access and overall performance. Remote access boards can enable users to call into a network from a remote location.

Like automobile options, network add-ons can be expensive items.

LAN Software

The software for LANs includes drivers, NOSs, network shells or requestors, network applications, management programs, diagnostic programs, and backup software. Some or all of these software components may be included in the NOS package, or they may be available as add-on products.

NIC Drivers

Drivers mediate between the NIC and the networking software running on either a workstation or the server. Drivers are hardware-specific. However, two "generic" driver interfaces have been developed: ODI (Open Data-link Interface) and NDIS (Network Driver Interface Specification).

Drivers are usually included with the NIC or with the NOS. If neither is the case, you can almost certainly download whatever driver you need from a vendor's bulletin board. (Unfortunately, the drivers are just about the only free software when it comes to networking.)

NOS

The NOS runs on the server and is responsible for processing requests from workstations, for maintaining the network, and for controlling the services and devices available to users. An NOS may replace the native operating system, or run as a program on top of the native operating system. In addition, NOSs may use the native file system or introduce their own file system. For example, Novell's NetWare and Banyan VINES replace the existing operating system and use their own file systems. Novell's NetWare for OS/2 runs simultaneously with OS/2 in a different disk partition. NetWare for UNIX runs as a process within UNIX. Artisoft's LANtastic supplements DOS and uses the DOS file system for its own directories.

The NOS can be a considerable expense. NOS software is generally priced as a function of the number of nodes you plan to attach to the network. Most vendors give you packages for predefined network sizes, such as for 5-, 10-, 25-, and 100-node networks. This vendor-biased pricing scheme may mean extra up-front expense, since you may need to pay for nodes you do not need at the moment. However, your network will probably grow to use the extra available nodes, so the investment will not be wasted.

Workstation Software

Each workstation on a network needs software to handle the communication between the workstation and the network. This software is known by various names, such as *shell, redirector, requestor, or client.* Generally, this software works with the workstation's native operating system. Some tasks are performed by the operating system, and some are redirected to the network. How the task allocation decision is made depends on the type of network software being used.

Network-Aware Applications

Network-aware versions of applications are designed specifically to run on a network. Network-aware versions keep track of whether a file or application is already being accessed, and they may prevent additional users from accessing the same file or running the same program. Sophisticated programs designed for a client/server computing environment can run in multiple pieces on separate machines. For example, a database program may run a front end (an interface for the user) on the workstation, and a back end (to process and carry out user commands) on the server.

Network versions of software packages may not always be different from the stand-alone versions, but they will, however, almost always cost more. You may need to pay five or ten times as much for a network version as for a single copy. However, the network copy will include a license for use by multiple users, so that the cost of the network version will generally be comparable to the cost of buying multiple stand-alone versions of the software.

Network Management Software

Network management programs can monitor activity on the network and gather data on network performance. The information can be used to fine-tune and improve the performance of the network. Management software is optional and tends to be expensive, but it may help save lots of money at some later time.

Diagnostic and Backup Software

Diagnostic and backup programs can be used to help anticipate problems or to catch them early, and

L

also to help deal with the problems once they have arisen. As with management software, network versions of some packages may be expensive, but they can save your system (and *you*) under some circumstances. For example, virus detection can save you hours of grief and job hunting. Similarly, software for testing the hard disk can identify bad disk sectors (or sectors about to go bad) before data is written there and lost, and can move any data from bad sectors to safe locations.

Some networking software includes both diagnostic and backup capabilities. If this suits your needs, and if it works with the hardware you have, you can save yourself some money. Otherwise, you *need* to get backup software and you should also get diagnostic software.

LAN Costs

Just as with any large-scale project, the start-up costs for LANs tend to be the major share of the expenses.

Many of the costs are one-time expenses. These will become less painful with the passage of time. If a network runs successfully for even a year without major malfunction, the cost of a UPS will seem like small potatoes.

Depending on the network architecture you selected, the power you want, and the quality of components you intend to use, costs per node may range from a few hundred dollars (above the cost for the node itself) to many thousands of dollars (for example, for fiber-optic networks).

While you may be able to keep the price of your workstations down, you will probably need to count on a few thousand dollars (perhaps as high as $10,000 or $15,000) for each server, particularly for servers with hard disks. If you want built-in safety features (such as duplicate storage of information), this will cost even more. Again, such an additional expense may be advisable for servers, but is usually unnecessary for workstations.

LAN Development

The process of developing a LAN from a gleam in someone's eye (or a sentence in a memo) to a working network has four main phases:

Planning   There may be several rounds of planning. The early rounds should be mainly research and just a little planning; with time, the relative prominence of research and planning should invert. Later planning phases involve investigating what is feasible, given your resources and needs.

Design   During the LAN design phase, you need to select a network architecture and begin specifying the details for the network. Your choices depend on what you have discovered during the planning phases.

Implementation   During this phase, the network is actually put together, debugged, and set into action. Depending on what needs to be done, this phase will include tasks ranging from buying and installing cable to connecting the hardware, installing the software, and basically getting the network up and running. Make sure you have a plan for LAN implementation.

Operation   This phase overlaps with the implementation phase. These phases may last for weeks or even months. Major revisions to the network are not uncommon in the first few months of operation. After everything is installed and has been found to work, you are ready for the day-to-day network activity. Unfortunately for a LAN administrator, even ordinary operations may not provide any respite. This is the phase during which the tasks described in the LAN Administration section become relevant.

LAN Planning

In the early planning phases, you need to investigate whether there is a need for a LAN and also an interest in having one. The goal of the first planning phase—*assessing need and desirability*—is to decide whether there is any point in trying to design a network. If you decide a network is appropriate, you next need to investigate what approaches are feasible for developing a network in your specific situation.

Need and Desirability Planning

One of the most important steps in planning a network is to investigate as thoroughly as possible the pre-network context. Study current operations to determine working patterns, bottlenecks, and needs. This will also help determine likely future needs.

Talk to the people who will be affected to determine their needs and wants, and also their expectations and fears. You will need the cooperation of the users. Be aware of and take into account company, office, and interoffice politics.

Determine the needs or problems that make a LAN desirable or necessary. If the orders for a LAN came from higher up, there may be difficulty convincing the staff; if the impetus comes from the trenches, you will need to convince the money holders. These two different audiences may require very different strategies.

Although it may be necessary or desirable to create a LAN, there are often alternatives—for example, additional stand-alone machines or the use of switchboxes—and you need to consider these as well. One way to be sure of doing this is to evaluate different ways of fulfilling employees' or management's needs.

You will need to decide whether a network will fulfill the needs identified or if an alternative will fulfill the needs as effectively at a lower cost. Be sure to keep future plans in mind. For example, a network might be more expensive up front, but may be easier and cheaper to expand later on.

Determine particular resources and constraints that may influence the eventual LAN. For example, hardware and software, employee skills, and power and wiring constraints can affect your decision. Evaluate these with respect to the audience you will need to convince. For example, the front

office may assume that you will be using existing cable. This may have implications for your strategy.

Once you have gathered all your data, summarize and write up this information. Be sure to reference the source of each item, and also indicate what information is verified, verifiable, unverified, and questionable (or whatever categories make the most sense for your purposes). It is always easier to go back and verify something if you know where the information came from.

Feasibility Planning

After you have finished the background research and have established a need for a network (or at least for some type of change from the present situation), you need to start thinking about what is available and what can be done.

For example, you should determine which resources (machines, cabling, software, and so on) are available and which of these resources will be usable *and useful* for a network.

Next, determine the costs for a network. Make sure to remember both the obvious and less obvious sources of expenses. Obvious ones include the following:

- Cabling for both materials and installation (keep in mind that installation costs can be high)

- Hardware (computers, NICs, and so on)

- Safety devices (UPSs, surge protectors, and so on)

- Networking and application software

- Fees for consultants, designers, architects, and anyone else who can think of an excuse to bill you

- Ongoing costs, such as for those for line leasing, the system administrator's salary, maintenance contracts, technical support, upgrades, and so on

- Training costs, for network users and administrators

L

Less obvious costs include those for company downtime: for example, during the switch over to networked operation, and then when you need to do the switch again because something went wrong with the first installation. Then there will be downtime after you have installed and implemented the system and the network goes down. It is a good idea to include emergency resources in your initial planning, so that at least some work can be done.

And also consider the costs due to temporary productivity decreases while employees get used to working on a network.

LAN Design

By the end of the network design phase, you should have detailed descriptions of what the network will look like and how it will operate. You should also have a detailed list of the components, a timetable, and an implementation procedure.

The network design process is a mystic mixture of art, science, CPA and *spendthrift* mentalities (at the same time), luck (good or bad), and accident. The design process is a detailed planning phase, operating within the constraints imposed through the feasibility study.

As with any mysterious process, there are many ways to go about it. The following sections outline a few design strategies.

Counting Nodes and Assigning Tasks

Many planning issues and tasks are simplified if you can determine the exact number of nodes on the network. Once you have some numbers, and perhaps location information, you can begin assigning tasks and responsibilities to different nodes.

For example, if a network expects to have 500 nodes, you may want to assign tasks and capabilities in a way that minimizes the distance traveled to use those resources. One way to do this is with duplicate (or triplicate) function assignments. For example, you might define three separate print servers (each with its own printer) for three crowded areas.

Defining Network Operations

It is a good idea to begin formulating a network usage and resource statement. By sketching out how the network will function—including how information will flow, who will control its flow, and so on—you will get some insight into the most appropriate type of relationship between stations. This, in turn, will help you decide what kind of topology to use.

In some cases, the network operations may have implications for the kind of cable you will need to use. For example, if you decide to situate nodes from the same LAN on multiple floors, you may want to insist that the *riser cable* (which runs between floors) should be optical fiber.

Defining Network Administration and Security

The amount and type of security a network needs will depend on the kinds of data on the network and also on the kinds of users who are logging in to the network. For example, if it is better to destroy data than to let a competitor see it, there will be heavy emphasis on encryption and less concern with safeguarding.

In part, the security needs will help shape the type of administration the network will have. The type of network (for example, server-based or peer-to-peer) will also influence the way it will be administered.

Defining Administrative Policy

Part of the network design task includes defining a policy for how the network will be administered. It is important to have an explicit, written policy for LAN use that is ready when the LAN goes into operation.

An administrative policy will include guidelines for every important aspect of the network's operation, including the following:

- Backup and maintenance (when and how to do backups, maintenance schedules, and so on)

- Software monitoring or regulation, to ensure that licensing limits are not being violated

- Software upgrade procedures, to ensure that everyone is working with the same version of a software package

- Operating procedure for emergencies, such as virus attacks, power outages, or component malfunctions

- Security setup and enforcement, for example, to specify regulations concerning password format, required password changes, and so on

For example, you will need to decide how the use of applications will be managed. It is essential for each network user to be using the same version of application programs. Explicit procedures for ensuring this should be part of the LAN policy document.

Also, if a user's workstation becomes infected with a virus, the entire network is at risk. Therefore, if data integrity is crucial or if network downtime is unacceptably expensive, it may be necessary to set policies regarding the kinds of software users are allowed to install on a workstation. Such a policy will not be completely enforceable, but making the restrictions explicit will help emphasize the importance of the issue. Users may comply with the policy because they see the reasons for doing so.

It is also important to include in the administrative policy explicit plans for dealing with specific tasks or problems before you actually need to deal with them. While it is useful advice in general, it is crucial in relation to networks: When confronted with a problem or task, stop!

The policy should include measures for dealing carefully with the situation, to ensure that no irreversible actions are taken before the network is backed up in its current state (if possible).

The administrative policy should be updated regularly and modified as necessary.

Checklists and Worksheets

Lists represent one of the most useful general-purpose tools for just about any type of task. Because the individual items are distinct, lists are easy to expand, rearrange, and edit. They can even be organized into a more useful format, such as in a tree structure.

Two types of lists are common for network design planning:

- Checklists, usually consisting of tasks and/or questions. Task lists are useful for accomplishing something; question lists are useful for verifying or checking something. Because they can be open and freeform, task lists are useful for ill-structured tasks—those that do not have simple instructions but involve multiple steps.

- Worksheets, either property summaries or action charts, such as flow charts or Booch diagrams. Property summaries are handy for making comparisons. Action charts are useful for well-defined tasks of medium complexity.

A LAN DESIGN CHECKLIST

The following annotated list illustrates the kinds of questions you may find in LAN design checklists.

What services will be provided on the network? What machines will provide the services?

The answers to these questions will depend on your reasons for setting up a network in the first place, and also on the hardware you have or will make available for the network.

- Who will control access to these machines, and how will access be controlled?

The LAN administrator will "control" access by assigning user privileges and access rights. The actual security measures instituted will depend on how costly a security breach would be. The simplest measures used to introduce such controls include logins, passwords, user IDs, and so on.

- How will access to files and services be controlled?

As with access to machines, the LAN administrator can assign file or command privilege levels to network users.

- How will users be added and removed?

Continued on next page

L

A LAN DESIGN CHECKLIST (continued)

In most cases, the processes for managing users will be fairly mechanical and will be carried out by the LAN administrator. However, it's important to establish clearly from the outset how user accounts will be managed.

- How will new users be trained? How will current users be kept up to date? Who will be responsible for providing the required training?

Initial user training is crucial to the network's success, since inexperienced and ignorant (regarding the network) users will be unproductive, frustrated, and—eventually—stand-alone users. Depending on the situation, you may want users trained by in-house or outside staff.

- How will user operation be monitored?

The information from monitoring users can be useful, at least during early phases. However, monitoring can be tricky, because it's imperative that users feel they have privacy on the network and do not need to worry about being watched.

- How will new software be evaluated, tested, and installed? Once tested, who will be responsible for installing it on the network and making sure it works?

Testing software for a network can be a nightmare. Software testing may be done by an independent testing company. The advantage is that a good testing company will have a more comprehensive and systematic test suite than the more haphazard methods of most end-users. The disadvantage is that the testing will be aimed at the general network user, and may not include tests that are appropriate for specific users.

- How will application programs be managed? Who will be responsible for upgrades and for making sure all users are working with the same versions of applications and files? What kinds of restrictions, if any, will there be on applications that users can run on their workstations?

You need to ensure that network users are all using the same version of applications. Also, to avoid viruses, which can cause data loss and company downtime, you may need to set policies regarding the software that users can install on their workstations.

- How will file management and backup be managed?

Although this is generally the LAN administrator's responsibility, the question needs to be asked, because backups are so vital for a network.

- How will connections to other networks be managed, if applicable?

The answer to this will depend, in part, on the type of networks that are to be connected. For example, connecting two Ethernet networks is less of a task than connecting an Ethernet and an SNA network.

- How will the network be maintained? For example, who will be responsible for periodic hardware checks: testing the cable integrity, hard disk, and so on?

While it is important to be conscientious about doing maintenance on stand-alone hardware, it is essential to be compulsively so when it comes to networks. A hardware malfunction on a network can be much more costly than on a stand-alone machine. Regular and careful maintenance can help minimize the likelihood of such a malfunction.

- What provisions will be built in for network expansion?

Network expansion is more than just adding some extra machines. It may require additional network cabling or electrical wiring. There may also be tradeoffs (such as size versus performance) to be considered. Networking software and network-based applications may need to be upgraded to allow for more users. These and other possibilities make it important to build expansion into a network design.

Several of the books in the Novell Press series have useful checklists. Two recent ones include Logan Harbaugh's *Problem Solving Guide for NetWare Systems* and David Clarke's *CNA Study Guide*.

Maintenance Sheets

Make sure you set up an explicit, completely defined, and thorough hardware maintenance procedure. The maintenance should include not only event-driven troubleshooting and repair, but also preventative maintenance, such as diagnostics and cleaning to keep the hardware from failing in the first place.

Develop a checklist and a worksheet for this maintenance. These records will help ensure that maintenance tasks are done the same way every time.

LAN Implementation

The actual construction of the LAN and installation of the networking software takes place during an implementation phase. This process requires carrying out the installation plan slowly and systematically, testing each component before it is added to the network, and then again after it has been added to the network. The original installation *plan* may be revised several times during this phase, as a result of information derived from the actual installation *process*.

An implementation plan should outline on paper each phase of the installation process, and should describe what happens during each phase. The plan should also note what the prerequisites and results are for each phase. Finally, the plan should specify what tests are to be run to make sure that each phase has been carried out successfully.

The implementation phase should include frequent meetings to review the progress, deal with any unanticipated problems or findings, and make any modifications suggested or required by the progress to date. The first of these meetings should take place before you begin the installation, and should be to evaluate the "raw" implementation plan—the plan before any steps are actually carried out. After all the steps are done, a final review meeting should be held to evaluate and sign off on the implementation.

Network Installation

The following are some general considerations and suggestions to keep in mind during LAN installation:

- If possible, keep users informed of what is happening at all times.

- If possible, get a diagram of all existing cabling, whether you plan to use the cabling or not. If you are using it, you need to test it, and you may need to repair, update, or extend it. If you do not plan to use the cabling, you may be able to use any conduits already built for installing the cable that you *will* be using.

- Test components as early in the installation as possible. For example, test cable *before* it is installed. Then test it again after it is installed.

- Cable should be installed by people who know what they are doing.

- Do not proceed to the next step in the installation until you have confirmed that the previous step was successful.

- Actual hardware installation should always include an overseer or an oversight process, just to make sure there are no obvious mistakes or oversights.

- Detailed records of the exact type of cable and connectors, including source and part numbers are important. The same is true for components such as hubs, bridges, routers, NICs, and so on. Record this information as the components are added to the network.

- Also record *where* in the network each component is installed.

- All hardware to be used in the network should be run for an extended time before installation to give the machine's components an adequate burn-in time. Hardware should be checked very carefully after installation. Each piece should be tested as it is installed.

L

- Once all nodes are attached, test the entire system.

- If possible, test application software first on a non-network machine, to make sure it actually works and is free of viruses and of obvious bugs or defects.

- Install applications onto the network, and test each one carefully. Do not test software on actual data. Test only with data you can afford to lose. Back up your system before testing.

- Back up all machines before adding them to the network.

Network User and Administrator Manuals

Develop detailed manuals for all persons involved with the network, from supervisors and administrators to users. The manuals should be tailored for the audience, using a "need-to-know" criterion for deciding what to include.

User manuals need contain only information about such things as logging in to the network, accessing network services, and running applications.

Administrator manuals should include detailed information about the hardware configuration of each node, and also the basic software configuration (operating system version, RAM and storage capabilities, and so on) for all the application and network software. The administrator's manual should also include a cable map showing all cables, connectors, and NICs on the network.

Try to make the administrator manuals detailed and complete enough for a trained outsider to be able to maintain the system if necessary.

Training

The implementation plan should include training of users and of the administrator. Think very carefully about whether user training should be done by in-house or outside staff. There are advantages and disadvantages to each approach.

In-house people are more likely to know the exact needs and layout of the organization, as well as your personnel. If the LAN administrator is someone already experienced with networks *and* good at conveying this experience and knowledge, user instruction may be added to the list of administrative tasks.

If the administrator does not meet these standards, it is probably wiser to bring in an outside person to provide the necessary training. Keep in mind that someone who is doing a training course as a one-shot deal—whether it is the administrator or another person on your company's staff—will probably have much less experience in training than someone who is a professional trainer. The trainer must not only know the material, but must also be able to present it. Not all companies have such a person.

If you pick the proper outside trainers, you can be reasonably assured that they know their stuff and can present it. (Get recommendations and references for potential trainers.) Someone who does lots of training is more likely to know the kinds of problems and difficulties users typically encounter. The trainer may arrange for a portion of the training to be dedicated just to problems.

On the other hand, outsiders are generally (but not always) more expensive than in-house trainers, especially in a rapidly growing and changing field in which information is a premium commodity. Also, outsiders do not know your company or your staff as well (but this can also be an advantage in some cases). A presentation by someone who gives them all the time is more likely to be formulaic, rather than being tailored to your company's particular needs.

Whether you use in-house or outside trainers, the training costs may seem high. But keep in mind that the money you invest in training can save many times that amount through improved ability and accelerated learning (and, presumably, productivity) curves. In some touchy political situations, it may even be worthwhile paying for some training *before* installing a network. This can be helpful, for example, if the staff is resisting the network. Getting some exposure to a network may help the staff develop a more favorable attitude.

Implementing a LAN in a Working Environment

The discussion of the implementation process has assumed that the network was being created from fresh machines. In practice, this is rarely the case. Instead, you may need to implement a network with machines that already have their applications and operating environments. Even worse, you may need to do this while these machines are expected to conduct business as usual, so that there is pressure to get the network up as quickly and smoothly as possible.

The transition between old and new systems must be planned very carefully. The network developer should remain involved during such a transition. You should have a contingency plan if the transition fails.

Various changeover strategies are possible, including the following:

Cold conversion This is a complete and immediate changeover; it is the simplest and least expensive. However, cold conversion is not suited for operations with critical applications. Make sure you have a way of retrieving the last state of the old system and starting up from that state, in case the new system does not work.

Conversion with overlap In this strategy, the old system keeps operating as the new one is started, so that both systems operate simultaneously for a short period. If the resources are available, this method is clearly the most desirable. The longer you can afford to run both systems, the more opportunity you have to fine-tune the network.

Piecemeal conversion In this approach, the new system is implemented in phases. These phases must be planned, and a phase must begin only after the previous phase has been successfully completed. This strategy requires fewer resources (but more time) than conversion with overlap. Because of the time scales involved, piecemeal conversion makes it more difficult to retreat to the older method if something goes wrong.

Once the transition is complete and the network becomes the normal mode of operation, the system administrator and any developers or planners still involved must observe everything carefully and must talk to users to get as much information about network usage and user reaction as possible.

This information will enable you to identify the following types of problems:

- Bugs in the system, which may produce incorrect results or which may crash the system.

- Bottlenecks in the network, which lead to inefficiency and slow down network performance. These can be fixed or at least minimized by fine-tuning the network.

- User problems, which may indicate software problems or inadequate training.

LAN Access

LAN access refers to the process of getting commands or information onto a network. The access can be at either of two levels:

- Access to the network medium at the Physical layer. Physical access to the network medium is discussed in the Media-Access Method article.

- User access to the network by logging in. Logical access is discussed in the Login article.

LAN Administration

A LAN administrator, or supervisor, runs the network. The administrator is responsible for "doing whatever is necessary to make sure the network keeps working." More specifically, an administrator's duties include tasks such as assigning access and security levels to users, making sure the equipment is functioning, verifying that resources are not being used inappropriately, and checking that users are keeping their storage use in check.

The following sections describe some task areas that may be involved in LAN administration. Note that these are by no means the only types of tasks a

L

LAN administrator must handle. In fact, all but the simplest, most vanilla-flavored networks will introduce oddities and requirements of their own.

Security

Security and access control involve making sure the contents and components of the network are safe from corruption by user error or by attack from inside or outside. This will generally require taking measures to control user access to the network and its resources.

As a security guardian, the LAN administrator must allocate user access rights to the information and resources available on the network. By allowing users only into certain directories, the core of the operating environment is kept secure and safe from accidental damage.

Specifically, LAN security deals with the following types of concerns:

- Only authorized users can access the LAN and its components.

- Unauthorized users cannot accidentally or deliberately destroy files.

- Unauthorized users cannot copy or otherwise steal files or data.

- Files and data are not corrupted or destroyed by viruses, worms, or Trojan horses (all types of invasive programs that can cause direct or indirect damage to your files and/or your running programs).

- Files, data, and hardware components are not destroyed by power irregularities (surges, sags, and so on) or other electrical phenomena.

Security Measures

Administrators can take various types of measures to help increase network security, including the following:

- Exercise access control and user authentication through login procedures and password requirements. User IDs and passwords are important for maintaining system security.

Users should *not* use as passwords such items as nicknames, names of family members, telephone numbers, or other data associated directly with the user. Users should also change passwords regularly. Some administrators require periodic changes.

- Assign access privileges (or trustee rights) to users to control who has access to what, and to help keep vital files secure, at least from accidental and casual attack.

- Be vigilant about policing user IDs and accounts. Accounts should be closed and IDs invalidated immediately whenever users are removed from the network.

- Be aware of any back doors into the networking software. A *back door* is a special command or action that allows unrestricted access to the software and, usually, to the hardware on which the software is running. System developers often build such back doors into their creations to allow emergency access (and possibly for other reasons).

- Limit physical access to nodes, especially to a file server node, to help reduce security breaches. For example, only the LAN administrator should have access to the file server running the network. Ideally, this machine should be locked or have its keyboard removed when it is unattended.

- Protect the system from viruses and other invaders. Always install from write-protected disks, and keep master disks and boot disks write-protected. Never install a program whose provenance you do not know, and do not let users do so either. Virus-detection software should be installed on any bridges or other devices that communicate with other networks. This is because a different network is comparable to a disk of unknown provenance.

- Provide power protection, at least for network servers. For other nodes, surge suppressors might suffice.

- Use call-back modems to help protect against unauthorized access. When a user calls in to access the network, the modem takes the call and gets some required information from the caller. The caller hangs up, and the modem checks on the user and the information provided. If everything looks legitimate, the modem calls the user back, and the user is on the network.

- If LAN tapping is a concern, consider using fiber-optic cable, because this is the most difficult to tap.

- If sensitive data is involved, consider using encryption strategies. There are various methods for data encryption. See the DES (Data Encryption Standard) and Encryption articles for more information.

You can use special-purpose machines and boards to do complete audits of network access and use, and even to record all activity on the network. This information can help you identify security weaknesses and breaches (but can also give users the impression that they are being watched).

Programs exist to help with network security. Such programs can be instructed to watch for viruses, watch for changes or attempted changes to network or applications software, or allow only "approved" programs to execute on the network.

Configuration

The system administrator needs to be able to determine the configuration of a network at all times. To do this, the administrator should have the following information:

- An up-to-date list of every component on the network, with exact model number, location, and with information about factory and current settings

- A complete cabling diagram

- A complete list of all application software on the network, with version and default settings information

This information should be updated scrupulously, and checked obsessively for correctness. Having incorrect information that is believed correct is much, much worse than having no information at all.

In addition, the administrator should be able to get, if necessary, information about network activity (over time or at a given time), storage and memory usage, and ongoing user sessions.

It is important to keep configuration information on a non-networked PC or else make sure to print a copy of the most recent configuration information anytime you update the file. This way, you will have the necessary information if the network goes down.

User Support

User support entails answering user questions about applications on the network and about the network in general, resolving user problems with applications or with the network, training new users, and keeping users informed as the network changes.

Documentation

The LAN administrator should see that adequate documentation is available about using the hardware and software on the network. In some cases, the administrator may need to create local release notes, which are special additions to official documentation. These release notes will describe any unique features of the local installation or implementation.

Operations

To keep a network operating normally, it is useful to monitor the network during day-to-day operation. This involves making sure all components are working and resolving any user problems that arise.

Maintenance and Upgrades

In addition to making sure a network is operating smoothly, an administrator should try to ensure that the network will continue to do so. Regular maintenance checks on the equipment help keep

L

things running or at least help to ensure that problems will be caught before they become major. Regular backups help ensure that data loss is kept to a minimum in the event of network malfunction.

Make sure to keep at least one backup copy of all software and data. If possible, have one such copy off-site. Backups should be scrupulously done and carefully labeled, so that it is always possible to restore a relatively up-to-date version of the network in case of disaster.

As a network ages and evolves, equipment and software will need to be replaced. These processes open up several barrels of worms:

- As new software versions are released, they need to be installed. Older versions should be removed and should be replaced completely, if at all possible. Doing this is not always easy, and may not even be possible. For example, if some project is dependent on a particular version of a package, you will not be able to remove it.

- New software may not be an improvement over older versions, and it may need to be uninstalled and replaced with the older software. To avoid this nightmare, it is advisable to test new versions thoroughly before installing them. (A "baby" network, with just a few nodes, might be a good place to do this.) Before installing new software, make sure there is a way to uninstall it if necessary.

- New hardware may be incompatible with existing equipment, and may force a decision as to whether to replace more than anticipated or to forego whatever technological advances the new hardware promises.

- New hardware may be incompatible with existing software. This can happen, for example, if there is a lag before drivers appear for the new hardware.

In short, while advances in hardware and software may sound wonderful to end-users and "techweenies," these improvements are just more things to help make an administrator's life miserable.

To keep software maintenance and upgrades manageable, make sure to keep detailed information such as the following about all software on the network:

- Name, version, and serial number of each package

- Detailed installation and usage instructions

- A log of user reports of difficulties or problems with the software

Performance Monitoring

Performance monitoring and analysis involve tracking the network's behavior (counting packet collisions, measuring traffic and response times, and so on), with an eye toward identifying inefficiencies and bottlenecks so they can be eliminated. Various software and hardware products are available to help with this task.

While monitoring system performance, keep careful track of the following:

- Operating costs

- Threats to security

- User satisfaction

- User productivity

Track these indexes especially thoroughly during the first few weeks after network installation. Do not be surprised if some of the measures change quite drastically during this period. For example, costs may drop drastically after the startup period. In contrast, user satisfaction and productivity may rise after the initial problems and frustrations are resolved.

Network Accounting

Accounting involves overseeing costs incurred by users, charges to be paid by users, and so on. An administrator needs to make sure that the users do not exceed their usage allowances and that accounts are paid up.

Problems

Problem and fault handling involve identifying problems, failures, or bottlenecks in the hardware or software, determining their cause, deciding how to correct them, and taking whatever steps are necessary (including calling a service technician, if that is what the LAN administration plan calls for) to correct the problem.

Design

If he or she is lucky, an administrator's duties will include helping to design and implement the network. While both of these are major tasks, input during these initial phases can help make the later administrative tasks much easier. (Of course, this opportunity has been known to backfire on occasion, and an administrator may be "stuck" with the network he or she helped design.)

See the LAN Design section in this article for more information.

Other Task Groupings

Other task breakdowns have been proposed. For example, the OSI has specified five categories of network management tasks:

- Accounting management
- Configuration management
- Fault management
- Performance management
- Security management

These are discussed in separate articles, as well as in the Network Management article.

LANalyzer

A network monitoring and management product from Novell. LANalyzer (and other products of its type) can inventory network components and configurations, perform various types of network mapping, and monitor packet traffic. It also can do trend analyses on this traffic (in order to anticipate congestion, and warn the network administrator).

LAN ADMINISTRATION VERSUS LAN MANAGEMENT

The terms *LAN administration* and *LAN management* are often used interchangeably. However, there are some differences between the two tasks.

The functions defined for LAN management can at least be summarized officially by reference to the five management domains specified by the OSI network management model. In contrast, the duties of a LAN administrator are often vaguely defined, and may even be defined dynamically; as a new type of issue, problem, or crisis arises, the LAN administrator's duties are (re)defined to include its resolution.

LANAO (LAN Automation Option)

In IBM's NMA (Network Management Architecture), an optional add-on to the NetView package that implements the NMA. LANAO simplifies and, for certain data, automates the monitoring and management of one or more Token Ring networks.

→ *See Also* NetView

LAN Automation Option (LANAO)

→ *See* LANAO (LAN Automation Option)

LAN Bridge Server (LBS)

→ *See* LBS (LAN Bridge Server)

L

LAN Driver

A LAN driver is a hardware-specific driver program that mediates between a station's operating system and the network interface card (NIC). A LAN driver is also known as a *network driver*.

The LAN driver must be loaded in order to access the NIC, and the network protocols must be able to communicate with the NIC through this driver, as illustrated in the illustration "LAN drivers sit between the hardware and the network shell."

To make NICs accessible to any of multiple protocols that might be running on a network, generic interfaces for LAN drivers have been created. The best known of these interfaces are ODI (Open Data-link Interface) from Novell and Apple and NDIS (Network Driver Interface Specification) from Microsoft and 3Com.

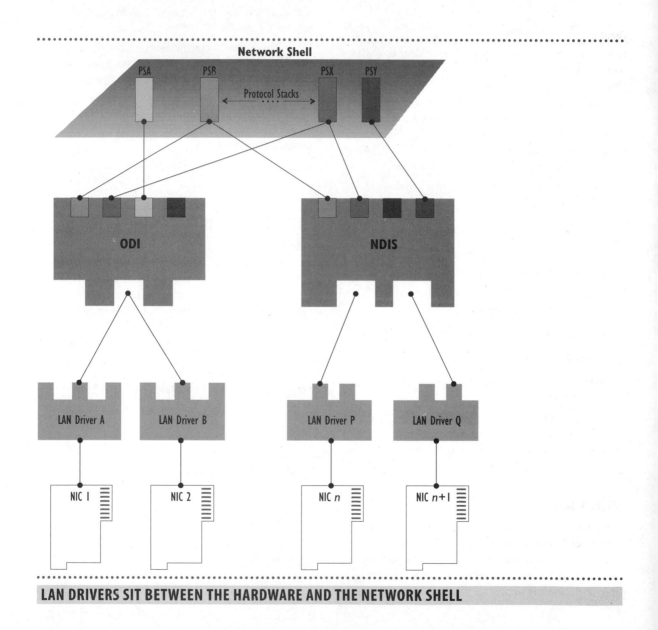

LAN DRIVERS SIT BETWEEN THE HARDWARE AND THE NETWORK SHELL

→ *Broader Category* Driver

→ *See Also* NDIS (Network Driver Interface Specification); ODI (Open Data-link Interface)

LANE (Local Area Network Emulation)

LANE is a service for Asynchronous Transfer Mode (ATM) networks. It enables Ethernet and Token Ring—the two most popular local area network architectures—to operate as emulations on top of the ATM architecture.

This means that machines connected using ATM can pretend to be, for example, Ethernet nodes. And they are, except that they are nodes on an *emulated LAN*, or *ELAN*. In LANE mode, the nodes will communicate using the usual LAN protocols. These protocols will be handled at the media access control (MAC) layer, just as in an ordinary (that is, nonemulated) LAN. The LAN emulation layer at which this MAC interface is provided hides the ATM cell relay network that is actually doing the work underneath. The nodes on this emulated LAN can be connected, via a bridge, to a standard LAN.

LAN applications can run over the ATM network, just as if they were running on a genuine LAN. Clients and servers communicate with each other over the LAN Emulation User-to-Network Interface (LUNI). This interface is located at the LAN emulation layer, and it is used to provide such emulated LAN services as the following:

- Initializing the network by determining available services and addresses for the services

- Registering nodes by recording their MAC addresses

- Relating these LAN addresses to the "true" ATM addresses of the nodes

LANEs consist of clients and several types of (logical) servers. The logical servers will generally all reside in the same physical server, but need not do so. The following are the main components of an ELAN:

LANE client (LEC)   This can be a workstation node or another connection device, such as a bridge, router, or switch.

LANE server (LES)   This node is responsible for maintaining the address registry and for responding to client requests.

LANE configuration server (LECS)   This server is responsible for initializing client nodes with LAN-specific information.

Broadcast and unknown server (BUS)   This server is responsible for handling broadcasts and multicasts—transmission schemes that are frequently used in LANs but that do not generally arise on ATM networks. The BUS also handles packets before the destination's ATM address has been resolved.

ELANs can also communicate with each other. Such interactions take place over the LAN Emulation Network-to-Network Interface (LNNI or, sometimes, LENNI).

LANE was developed by the ATM forum mainly for the purpose of making ATM technology more attractive to LAN administrators and for giving it more prominence in the local area networking community. A related product is MPOA (for Multi-Protocol over ATM), which is designed to enable other networking protocols—in particular, the Internet's TCP/IP stack and the platform-specific counterparts of vendors such as Novell or Microsoft—to run on top of ATM.

→ *Broader Category* ATM (Asynchronous Transfer Mode); Ethernet; Token Ring

→ *See Also* MPOA (Multi-Protocol over ATM)

LAN Emulation

→ *See* LANE (Local Area Network Emulation)

LAN Emulation Network-Network Interface (LNNI or L-NNI)

→ *See* LNNI (LAN Emulation Network-to-Network Interface)

LAN Emulation User-to-User Interface (LUNI or L-UNI)

→ *See* LUNI (LAN Emulation User-to-Network Interface)

LAN Inventory Package

A LAN inventory package is any of several products that can automatically create an inventory of the components and configuration on a local area network (LAN). This type of software is used to keep track of changes to the network configuration.

LAN inventory packages may also be able to do at least some monitoring of network activity or performance. You can find listings of LAN Inventory and other networking-related products in the Annual Buyers Guide issue of *LAN* magazine, which comes out in the fall.

LAN Manager

LAN Manager is a much-licensed, server-based network operating system (NOS) from Microsoft. The LAN Manager server capabilities have also been implemented as Windows NT Advanced Server (NTAS). LAN Manager supports various low-level network architectures, including ARCnet, Ethernet, and Token Ring cabling and protocols. With the introduction of Windows NT and Windows NT Advanced Server, LAN Manager is no longer being updated.

LAN Manager Servers and Clients

LAN Manager supports servers running under OS/2, UNIX, and certain Windows NT configurations. It supports clients running under various operating systems or environments, including DOS, Windows, OS/2, and System 7 (the Macintosh operating system).

The capabilities and hardware requirements for workstations depend on the operating environment. For example, DOS workstations can be anything from 8088-based PCs to the high-end machines, and can run any version of DOS from 3.3 onward. OS/2 workstations, in contrast, require at least an 80286 machine.

Windows and Windows for Workgroups machines can also be used as LAN Manager workstations. Machines in a Novell NetWare network can be workstations on both the LAN Manager and the NetWare networks. Macintosh machines must be able to use AppleShare to be LAN Manager workstations.

LAN Manager Protocol Support

LAN Manager uses NetBEUI (NetBIOS Extended User Interface) as its main transport- and session-layer protocol but includes support for the TCP/IP protocol stack used for the Internet and most UNIX systems. NetBEUI is an efficient protocol *within* a network, but is not well-suited for use across subnetworks. "LAN Manager architecture" shows LAN Manager's components.

The NOS supports other protocol stacks, including several proprietary ones developed by LAN Manager licensees, through add-on products. For example, it can support Microsoft's own MS-DLC protocol, which helps provide workstations with access to mainframes in an SNA (Systems Network Architecture) environment. This protocol is used by terminal-emulation products, such as IRMA Workstation for Windows and Rumba from Wall Data, for access to the Data-Link layer. It may access this layer through an NDIS (Network Driver Interface Specification) interface.

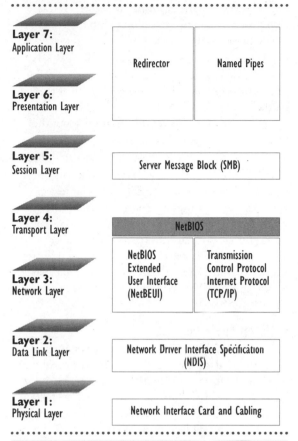

Layer 7: Application Layer	Redirector	Named Pipes
Layer 6: Presentation Layer		
Layer 5: Session Layer	Server Message Block (SMB)	
Layer 4: Transport Layer	NetBIOS	
Layer 3: Network Layer	NetBIOS Extended User Interface (NetBEUI)	Transmission Control Protocol Internet Protocol (TCP/IP)
Layer 2: Data Link Layer	Network Driver Interface Spécification (NDIS)	
Layer 1: Physical Layer	Network Interface Card and Cabling	

LAN MANAGER ARCHITECTURE

LAN Manager also supports various network management capabilities and protocols, including SNMP (Simple Network Management Protocol) developed for TCP/IP networks, and NetView, IBM's network management package for SNA networks.

Other LAN Manager Features

LAN Manager includes support for the following additional features:

- Server-based capabilities such as file and printer services.

- Distributed computing and communications capabilities, such as named pipes (two-way

communications channels between processes or machines) and mailslots (one-way channels).

- Peer-to-peer networking in Windows for Workgroups environments.

- Remote booting, access, and monitoring, as well as shared modems for dial-out capabilities.

- LAN security at both the user and share levels. User-level security is more stringent: a user must be able to log in to the network and have access privileges to the desired resource. With share-level security, the user requests access to a device rather than actually logging in to the network.

- The definition of *domains*, which are larger subnetworks that are managed by a single organization.

In addition, LAN Manager 2.2 includes several Windows-based utilities.

Both versions 1.0 and 2.0 have been licensed by Microsoft to other vendors, who have marketed the same basic product under different names. For example, IBM's LAN Server 1.x is based on LAN Manager 1.0, as is 3Com's 3+Open software. DEC PathWorks is based on LAN Manager 2.0.

LAN Manager for UNIX (LMU)

→ *See* LMU (LAN Manager for UNIX)

LAN Network Manager (LNM)

LNM is an SAA-compliant network management product from IBM. The product is used to help manage Token Ring networks. Because it can work with NetView (a mainframe-based network management program), LNM is particularly useful for managing networks that are part of larger, SNA (Systems Network Architecture) networks. The product can use both CMIP and SNMP network management protocols.

L

LAN Network Manager runs under OS/2 Presentation Manager. When running as a stand-alone product, it can function as a focal point (data gatherer) for a network. Running in conjunction with NetView, it can function as an entry point (an SNA-compliant reporter, or agent) for NetView.

LAN/RM (Local Area Networks Reference Model)

LAN/RM is a term used to refer to the IEEE 802.x series of specifications, most of which are related to local area networks (LANs).

→ **See Also** IEEE 802.x

LAN Server

A server-based network operating system (NOS) from IBM. The package is based on Microsoft's LAN Manager, and it supports servers running in the OS/2 environment.

→ **See Also** LAN Manager

LANstep

LANstep is a networking environment from Hayes Microcomputer Products. It supports up to 255 users on a peer-to-peer network that includes features usually associated with larger and server-based networks.

LANstep Services

Network services may be distributed over one or more nondedicated servers, and an authorized user anywhere on the network can access a service by name, without needing to specify the location of the server that provides the service. This transparent access is provided by LANstep's Smart Directory Services, which maintain a global resource directory and which can direct a user's request for a named service to the appropriate server. Access rights are also distributed, along with the resources to which the rights relate.

Just as the network can provide services, users can provide resources in the form of data or other files. The user owns the resource, and he or she can set the access rights for the resource. Only users with access rights will get information about the resource.

LANstep supports the "classic" network architectures: ARCnet, Ethernet, and Token Ring, and it supports the appropriate network adapters, provided these are compliant with the NDIS (Network Driver Interface Specification). LANstep uses NDIS to support multiple protocol stacks. This makes it possible to communicate with different networking and operating environments (such as Novell's NetWare or UNIX).

LANstep Environment

LANstep provides its own operating system and interface. It also allows DOS and Microsoft Windows applications to execute, and includes support for application software that uses NetBIOS protocols. LANstep can also provide access to network resources through Microsoft Windows.

LANstep allows users to map drive letters to specific drives or directories. In addition, the environment includes predefined mappings for certain drive letters to important or frequently used locations. For example, drive F: is mapped to the directory of the currently executing application. These predefined mappings can be changed.

LANstep Management

Although LANstep services and access rights can be distributed, LANstep management is centralized. Smart Directory Services provide a centralized database of available services.

Network security is centralized by having users log into the network, rather than into each server on the network or into each service. Once authenticated, the user can use any of the resources to which the user has access.

The menu-based interface displays references only to resources, files, and directories accessible to the user. If a user does not have access rights to the color printer, then this resource does not appear in the user's menus. This helps provide increased security by making it more difficult for users to get unauthorized access to any resource. The user's menus are updated dynamically if the system or user configuration changes.

Network management utilities are available to perform both service- and server-based tasks, such as version control or server activity monitoring, respectively.

Other Features

LANstep provides a proprietary electronic mail (e-mail) service, but can also use an optional mail gateway to allow access to other mail services. These services must support the ISO's MHS (Message Handling System) standard, however.

LANtastic

LANtastic is a term used loosely to refer to an extended family of products that provide various types of networking capabilities on proprietary and standard local area networks (LANs). The core product associated with the term is a network operating system (NOS) that provides flexible and efficient peer-to-peer networking capabilities. The LANtastic series of products is by Artisoft.

LANtastic Features

The LANtastic NOS has the following capabilities and features:

- Connects machines running any combination of DOS, Windows 3.x, Windows 9x, and Windows NT. This makes it an ideal NOS for small businesses that may not be able to

upgrade their workstations to every new release of Windows software.

- Runs on proprietary network interface cards (NICs) or on Ethernet cards.

- Supports networks ranging in size from two to a few hundred nodes. LANtastic is aimed at the small- to medium-sized network market, and it is on the low end of the price range.

- Supports peer-to-peer LANs (allows any node to serve as either a server or a workstation) or server-based LANs (with a dedicated server).

- Provides various types of servers, including file, print, CD-ROM, and access. Some of these capabilities require add-on hardware or software products. LANtastic is particularly efficient in providing CD-ROM services: only the machine that has the CD drive needs to load the Microsoft CD-ROM extensions driver. This saves memory on the other machines.

- Supports e-mail (electronic mail) and real-time chatting services.

- Supports a variant that runs over a NetBIOS protocol. This version is independent of particular NICs in that it will run (in principle) in any environment that supports NetBIOS, including Token Ring or ARCnet networks.

- Allows servers to control access to files, directories, and services, by requiring passwords for access and controlling access privileges.

- Allows network activity to be logged through an auditing feature. This log will include a record of any unsuccessful attempts to log in or to access forbidden services.

Information about LANtastic and ancillary products is available at Artisoft's Web site (www.artisoft.com).

L

LAN Traffic Monitor (LTM)

→ *See* LTM (LAN Traffic Monitor)

LAN, Transparent

A networking service that makes it possible for two LANs to communicate over telecommunications links without having to deal explicitly with the long distance connection. That is, a node on one LAN talking to a node on another one will not need to be concerned with the fact that the communication is going over telephone lines.

LAN, Virtual

A network configuration that can be created as needed by software and that can span physical LANs and topologies. Virtual LANs can be helpful when using workflow or other software that allows interaction on a larger project by multiple users.

LAN, Wireless

In a wireless LAN, communication is accomplished using infrared signals or radio waves. Although the actual transmission is through open air, the configuration is not always completely wireless. The PC may be connected via cable to a wireless transmitter.

Infrared LANs

Infrared LANs use a portion of the spectrum that goes from wavelengths of about 1mm down to about 0.7 microns (which corresponds to 700nm, or nanometers). This corresponds to frequency bandwidths ranging from about 300GHz to roughly 430THz (terahertz, where tera is the prefix for trillions). Although this fairly large bandwidth makes up the infrared spectrum, LANs generally use only the area around 820nm (which corresponds to a bandwidth of about 367THz) because this wavelength suffers the least signal attenuation in air as the medium.

An infrared LAN node needs an adapter card and a transducer to participate in the network. The adapter card plugs into a PC slot, and is used to handle the LAN protocols. The transducer plugs into the adapter via a cable, and is used to transmit and receive the infrared signals. Infrared signals do not go through walls or ceilings—rather, they bounce off these boundaries.

Diffused Transmission LANs

Infrared LANs can use either diffused or point-to-point transmission. In diffused transmission, a signal is beamed off a surface, such as a wall or ceiling. Receiving nodes catch the signals as they bounce off the surface. Diffused transmission LANs operate over distances of about 50 feet. Since they need a surface for bouncing the signal, diffused transmissions work only indoors. Such LANs can achieve speeds of 1–4MBps.

Point-to-Point LANs

Point-to-point LANs rely on a direct link between nodes. Such a link can take one of two forms. *Point and beam* connections are used to transfer files between PCs and peripherals—for example, printers.

True point-to-point LANs use an underlying Token Ring architecture, as defined in the IEEE 802.5 specifications. In a Token Ring LAN, only one node—the one with the token—can transmit at a time, and the transmission proceeds in a fixed sequence from one node to the next. Each node in a point-to-point LAN receives a signal from its upstream neighbor node and transmits to its downstream neighbor. In some point-to-point LAN products—for example, InfraLAN Technology's InfraLAN—each node actually has a separate transducer for sending and receiving. Such LANs can support the 4Mbps and 16Mbps speeds of traditional Token Ring networks.

Radio-Wave LANs

Radio-wave LANs operate in three narrow bands in the 900MHz to 6GHz frequency range. These three swaths are known collectively as the ISM band because they are used for industrial, scientific, and medical transmissions. However, the Federal Communications Commission (FCC) also allows unlicensed use of this spectrum for wireless communications, provided the transmission power of the devices is less than one watt. Other parts of this spectrum are also used, but these are licensed for specific purposes, such as mobile telephony.

Specifically, radio-wave LANs operate over one of the following bands:

Industrial (I-Band) The 26MHz band from 902MHz to 928MHz. Used in North and South America, this band is also used for cellular phones.

Scientific (S-Band) The 83.5MHz band from 2.4GHz to 2.4835GHz. Used worldwide, this band is also used for cellular phones.

Medical (M-Band) The 125MHz band from 5.725GHz to 5.850GHz. Used in North and South America.

Radio-wave signals will pass through walls and other solid objects. This makes them more versatile. However, it also makes it more difficult to control their reach.

Radio-wave LANs can be distinguished by the frequency range in which they operate and also by the manner in which they use that frequency range. Two main strategies for using a frequency range are narrowband and spread spectrum.

Narrowband LANs

In narrowband modulation, a transmission stays within a small frequency range. This is, for example, the way in which radio stations broadcast. Since all transmission power is concentrated on the band, the signal can be made very strong—which is desirable for radio stations, but not necessarily for LANs.

Because of the potential for interference with unregulated use, the FCC does require narrowband systems to be licensed. In this way, specific frequencies can be allocated over geographical

areas to minimize the potential for interference within a given frequency.

Spread-Spectrum LANs

LANs can also use spread-spectrum modulation. In this approach, a transmission is distributed over a wider range of frequencies, with tiny chunks of a transmission being sent at different frequencies. There are two ways of spreading a transmission over a spectrum:

Direct sequence In this approach, the bits in a transmission are combined with a special *chipping code* that moves the transmission to different frequencies in succession, and that ensures that the frequencies used remain within the allowable range. Multiple transmissions can take place on the same channels, simply by applying chipping codes in a manner that ensures that no two transmissions ever use the same frequency at the same time.

Frequency hopping In this approach, bits in a transmission are sent at frequencies selected in a predetermined sequence, known as a *hopping code*. The receiving node must know the hopping code in order to look for the transmission components in the correct sequence. The FCC requires frequency-hopping transmissions to use at least 75 different frequencies per channel, and to spend no more than 400 milliseconds (msec) at a time at any given frequency. As with direct sequence, multiple transmissions can take place at the same time—simply by making sure that each uses a different hopping code.

The effects of interference are minimal on spread-spectrum transmissions because interference during a transmission at a given frequency will only make it necessary to retransmit the same small packet at the next frequency. The odds of continued interference on each successive frequency are *very* small.

By the same token, spread-spectrum signals are virtually impossible to jam—unless, of course, the jammer knows the chipping or hopping code. Frequency-hopping spread-spectrum technology was actually developed by the actress Hedy Lamarr and George Antheil, a musician and colleague of the actress. In fact, the Hollywood inventors hold a patent on the technology, which they developed in order to make it possible to control torpedoes without having to worry about jamming or interference by enemy signals.

Depending on the product, radio-wave LANs can range in size from 100 feet or so to over 3000 feet. Transmission speeds range from about 250Kbps to over 5Mbps. In general, the higher the supported rate, the shorter the maximum distance, and vice versa—although there is considerable variation in the midrange of both performance and size.

Wireless LAN Standards

The IEEE 802.11 working group has developed specifications for wireless LAN transmissions. These specify the physical interface for three wireless variants: diffused infrared, direct-sequence spread spectrum, and frequency-hopping spread spectrum. These interfaces are for LANs operating in the 2.4GHz band—which is the only band supported internationally.

Note that the three bands discussed in this passage are not the only frequencies used for wireless networks. LANs in other ranges, however, will require special licenses, and this may affect the cost of the network.

Wireless LAN Products

The following are some examples of wireless LAN products:

- WaveLAN, which was originally developed by NCR but is now marketed by Lucent. One version of WaveLAN uses the 902 to 928MHz band, and can support open air LANs of up to about 250 meters (800 feet). A second version uses the 2.4GHz band, and can support LANs of up to 60 meters (about 200 feet).

- RangeLAN from Proxim offers several versions that use spread-spectrum technology in the 2.4GHz band. One version supports speeds of up to 1.6Mbps for distances of almost one kilometer.

- BICC Communications' InfraLAN, which uses infrared signals, has a range of only 25 meters (80 feet) or so.

- Motorola's Altair, which uses radio waves in the 18 to 19 gigahertz (GHz) range, works for only about 20 meters (70 feet) indoors and about twice that distance outdoors.

- FreePort from Windata supports speeds of up to 5.7Mbps over distances of about 80 meters (260 feet). It can serve as a wireless bridge for 802.3 Ethernet LANs.

Products are beginning to appear that make wireless LAN technology available to home users. It is very likely that this will be a burgeoning area in the next few years.

LAPB (Link Access Protocol, Balanced)

→ *See* Protocol, LAPB (Link Access Protocol, Balanced)

LAPD (Link Access Protocol, D-Channel)

→ *See* Protocol, LAPD (Link Access Protocol, D-Channel)

LAP-M (Link Access Protocol for Modems)

→ *See* Protocol, LAP-M (Link Access Protocol for Modems)

Large Internet Packet (LIP)

→ *See* LIP (Large Internet Packet)

Laser Transmission

A laser is a source of exceptionally coherent, or focused, light. The name comes from *light amplification by stimulated emission of radiation*.

The light is of a single wavelength or of a small spectrum around a single wavelength. The light source is used to read signals off a CD-ROM data or music disc, and may also be used as a signal source in a fiber-optic network. LEDs (Light-Emitting Diodes) are an alternative signal source in fiber-optic communications.

Laser line width, more commonly known as *spectral width*, refers to the range of light wavelengths (or frequencies) emitted by a laser.

Laser transmission refers to wireless communications using lasers. A laser sends the pulses (which can represent 0 and 1 values) over a narrow path to a receiver. Photodiodes at the receiving end convert the light pulses back into bits.

Advantages of laser transmissions include the following:

- Very high bandwidths, generally above 1 terahertz (THz) and even in the hundreds of THz range, are possible, even when infrared light is used.

- Light is impervious to interference and jamming.

Disadvantages of laser transmissions include the following:

- A line of sight is usually required between sender and receiver, which also limits the maximum distance between parties.

- Because the transmission uses a very narrow beam of extremely focused light, sender and receiver must be precisely aligned.

- Atmospheric conditions (such as rain or fog) can attenuate or distort the signal.

Laser transmissions are used in contrast to cable-based transmissions or to other types of wireless transmissions, such as those using microwaves.

→ *Related Articles* Cable, Fiber-Optic; Fiber Optics

Last In, First Out (LIFO)

→ *See* LIFO (Last In, First Out)

Last Mile

In telephony, a somewhat poignant term used to refer to the link between the customer's premises and the local telephone company's central office. For various reasons, this is the most expensive and least efficient stretch in the entire telephone network's cabling system.

LAT (Local Area Transport)

A Digital Equipment Corporation (DEC) protocol for high-speed asynchronous communication between hosts and terminal servers over Ethernet.

LATA (Local Access and Transport Area)

A LATA is a local telephone exchange—that is, a limited geographical and administrative area that is the responsibility of a local telephone company. Calls that cross LATA boundaries are handled by interexchange carriers (IXCs), or long-distance carriers.

The local telephone company is also known as a *local exchange carrier* (*LEC*). The Telecommunications Act of 1996 stipulates that any LATA must allow service to be provided by at least two LECs. The LEC in place when the act was passed is

L

known as the *incumbent LEC (ILEC)*. The act requires that the LATA also be open to one or more *competitor LECs (CLECs)*, or *other LECs (OLECs)*.

Latency

The term latency is used in several ways in relation to communications and networking. These definitions have some overlap, but also differ in certain ways. Part of the divergence has to do with the fact that the concept (and the definition) of latency is interwoven with the concepts of delay and bandwidth.

Most generally put, *delay* is a value associated with individual bits, whereas latency includes both time associated with the bits (delays) as well as time required in between bits. *Bandwidth*—which is defined as number of bits per unit time—is the concept that ties these two elements together.

More specifically, *delay* is the time elapsed between a bit going into one end of a transmission pipe and that same bit coming out at the other end. Thus, delay depends, in part, on the length of the transmission pipe. This means that the delay value will depend on where it is being measured. It's not uncommon to report delay values for end-to-end transmission and also for transmission between two intermediate points—for example, between two routers in an internetwork.

In contrast, *latency* is the time elapsed between the *first* bit going in and the *last* bit coming out. Thus, latency is based on the sum of the delays for all the bits involved *plus* the time required between bits. Latency may be measured for a packet or for an entire transmission. Latency is the product of delay and bandwidth. This is the official definition offered by the ITU-T (International Telecommunications Union—Telecommunications Sector).

For a network or communications channel or resource, latency thus represents the amount of time before the channel or network is available for a transmission. Thus, in shared-media networks (such as Ethernet), latency can refer to the amount of time a node must wait before it can transmit its packet. This duration will depend on the size of

the packet that is currently being transmitted on the network.

For example, in Ethernet switches, and other devices that store packets before forwarding them, latency can be defined as the amount of time it takes to store, check, and forward a packet. In traditional (that is, 10Mbps) Ethernet networks, the latency varies from about 90 microseconds for the shortest possible packet (64 bytes) to about 1254 microseconds for the largest possible packet (1518 bytes). As soon as the packet is forwarded, the switch is ready for another packet. These latency values include a constant 40-microsecond component for switching processes, and a variable component dependent on the number of bytes in the packet. Defined in this way, latency is a variable because its value is dependent in part on a variable packet size.

In contrast, networks that use fixed packet sizes (such as ATM cells or HiPPI packets) are in better positions to guarantee a constant latency. For example, ATM cell-relay networks can guarantee latencies of about 30 microseconds, Such constant values are important, for example, when transmitting video or other high-bandwidth materials in real time.

In data transmissions, latency is the amount of time required for a transmission to reach its destination. This is essentially the ITU-T definition expressed more informally.

Layer

In an operating, communications, or networking environment, layers are distinct levels of capabilities or services that build upon each other. A layer uses the services of the layer below it and provides services to the layer above it.

Layers communicate with layers above and below them through well-defined interfaces. As long as interfaces do not change, internal changes in a layer's implementation have no effect on the layers above or below. Such vertical communication generally takes place within a single machine. The process is illustrated in "Communications between and over layers."

A given layer on a machine uses a predefined protocol to communicate with the layer's counterpart on another machine. This horizontal communication generally takes place between different machines. However, the communication is direct only at the lowest, Physical layer. Horizontal communication between higher layers is indirect; it requires vertical communication in both machines.

A transmission from a particular layer on a particular machine needs to move down through the other layers to the first layer on that machine. At this level, the machine communicates directly with the first layer on the other machine. On the other machine, the transmission is then passed upward through its layers.

Layer Models

In the worlds of communications and networking, layers are used to distinguish the types of network- and application-based activities that are carried out. For example, perhaps the best-known layer model is the seven-layer OSI reference model for describing network activities. Its layers range from

the Physical layer, at which details of cable connections and electrical signaling are specified, to the application layer, at which details of the immediate interface between an application and network services are defined. Other layer models include IBM's SNA (Systems Network Architecture), Digital's DECnet, and the TCP/IP model used on the Internet.

Layered Architecture

A *layered architecture* is a hardware or software design in which operations or functions at one level (layer) build upon other operations or functions at a lower level. One of the best-known examples of such a design is the UNIX operating system.

In a layered architecture, each layer uses the layer immediately below it and provides services to the layer above it. For example, in the OSI reference model, the Data-Link layer uses the Physical layer below it to transmit bits across a cable link. The Data-Link layer, in turn, provides the Network layer above it with logical (and, indirectly, physical)

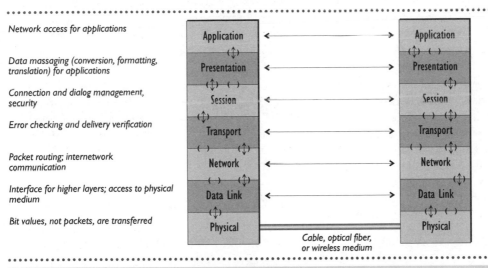

Network access for applications — Application
Data massaging (conversion, formatting, translation) for applications — Presentation
Connection and dialog management, security — Session
Error checking and delivery verification — Transport
Packet routing; internetwork communication — Network
Interface for higher layers; access to physical medium — Data Link
Bit values, not packets, are transferred — Physical

Cable, optical fiber, or wireless medium

COMMUNICATIONS BETWEEN AND OVER LAYERS

access to the network. In such a model, a Network layer packet becomes the data component of a Data-Link level packet, through a process known as *encapsulation*.

Layered architectures for networking environments generally distinguish at least two classes of layers:

- Transport-based layers, which are concerned with the problem of getting data from one location to the other.

- Application- or user-based layers, which are concerned with making sure the transmitted data is in a form suitable for the application that will use it.

These layer classes can be refined into smaller groups.

→ *See Also* OSI Reference Model

Layer 3 Switching

Switching is a connection technology that can connect pairs of nodes in a network or internetwork and that can enable each switched connection to use the full network bandwidth. This is in contrast to shared bandwidth, which is necessary for ordinary network connections and for network bridging or routing. In switching, connections are made in hardware—through the switch matrix, or fabric.

In layer 3 switching, connections are made—and packages are forwarded—on the basis of layer 3 network addresses. Layer 3 switching has been implemented in several different ways, including aggregate route-based IP (Internet Protocol) switching (ARIS), cell-switched routing (CSR), IP switching, tag switching, and even multilayer switching. The latter combines layer 2 (media access control, or MAC) and layer 3 switching.

→ *See Also* IP Switching; Tag Switching

Layer Management Entity (LME)

→ *See* LME (Layer Management Entity)

LBRV (Low Bit Rate Voice)

Digitized voice signals that are being transmitted at speeds lower than the 64Kbps channel capacity, generally either at 2400 or 4800bps. Voice data will either be compressed or will use sophisticated encoding methods.

LBS (LAN Bridge Server)

In an IBM Token Ring network, a server whose job is to keep track of and provide access to any bridges connected to the network.

LBT/LWT (Listen Before Talk/Listen While Talk)

LBT represents the fundamental rule for a CSMA/CD (Carrier Sense Multiple Access/ Collision Detection) media-access method. A node wishing to send a packet onto the network first listens for a special signal that indicates that the network is in use. If no such signal is heard, the node begins transmitting.

A related concept is called *LWT (listen while talk)*. LWT says that a node should keep listening for an "in use" signal even while transmitting. (By extension, the LBT and LWT rules could be applied to other aspects of life, no doubt with wonderful effects.)

LC (Local Channel)

In digital telecommunications, a link between a customer's premises and the central office.

LCC (Lost Calls Cleared)/LCD (Lost Calls Delayed)

In switching systems, LCC is a call-handling strategy in which blocked calls are lost, or discarded. This is in contrast to a LCD strategy, in which blocked calls are queued for later, or delayed, processing.

LCD (Liquid Crystal Display)

A veteran display technology that has been around since the early days of calculators and digital watches. This technology has long been taken for granted, and is now becoming very popular because of the thin-panel screens it makes possible. An LCD screen element is lit by passing voltage through the special liquid crystal at the element's location and then bending the light that the crystal emits.

The use of bent light makes the display dependent on the viewing angle and also on the amount of ambient light, with the latter being important for contrast. A constant internal light source can be used to produce fixed contrast, and thereby reduce the importance of ambient light. Such a light source is generally placed at the back of the screen and is known as backlighting. If placed at the edge, the light source is known as edgelighting or sidelighting.

LCD quality control has reached a level that makes large thin-panel LCD screens feasible. 17″ thin-panel monitors with 1280×1024 pixel resolution are now available for prices in the $1000 range.

LCI (Logical Channel Identifier)

In an X.25 (or other switching) packet, a field that indicates the virtual circuit (logical channel) being used for the packet.

LCR (Least Cost Routing)

In a PBX (Private Branch Exchange) telephone system, a feature that selects the most economical path to a destination.

LCR (Line Control Register)

In a UART (Universal Asynchronous Receiver/Transmitter), a register that is used to specify a parity type.

LDDS (Limited-Distance Data Service)

In telecommunications, a class of service offered by some carriers. LDDS provides digital transmission capabilities over short distances using line drivers instead of modems.

LDM (Limited-Distance Modem)

A short-haul modem, which is designed for very high-speed transmissions (more than 1Mbps) over short distances (less than 20 miles or so).

LE (Local Exchange)

→ See LATA (Local Access and Transport Area)

Leaf Object

In Novell's NetWare NDS, an object that represents an actual network entity, such as users or devices. Five types of leaf objects are defined: user-related, server-related, printer-related, informational, and miscellaneous. Each of these types includes several more specific object types.

→ See Also Container Object, NDS (NetWare Directory Services)

L

Leaf Site

On the Internet, a computer that receives *newsfeeds* from other Usenet sites, but does not pass these feeds on to other computers.

Leased Line

→ *See* Dedicated Line

Least Cost Routing (LCR)

→ *See* LCR (Least Cost Routing)

Least Significant Bit (LSB)

→ *See* LSB (Least Significant Bit)

LEC (Local Exchange Carrier)

A local telephone company; a company that provides telephone service within an exchange, or calling area. LECs are connected by IXCs (interexchange carriers). LECs are also known as *local carriers*. The Telecommunications Act of 1996 requires each calling area to be open to at least two LECs as follows:

- The incumbent LEC (ILEC), which was the local carrier when the act was passed.

- One or more competitor, or other, LECs (CLECs or OLECs, respectively), which will be alternate local carriers.

LED (Light-Emitting Diode)

A semiconductor device that can convert electrical energy into light. LEDs are used in calculator displays and for the lights on computers and modems. LEDs are also used as light sources in communications using fiber-optics. The more expensive alternative to this use is the laser.

Legacy Data

Legacy data generally refers to corporate data or other files stored on older systems—often mainframes. Such files often use outdated formats that may no longer be supported on the newer corporate networks. One of the goals of object models and object request broker architectures is to make it possible to get access to such legacy data—for example, to add the information to a corporate data warehouse.

→ *See Also* Data Mining; Data Warehousing

Legacy Wiring

Wiring that is already installed in a business or residence. Legacy wiring may or may not be suitable for networking purposes.

LEN (Low-Entry Networking)

An IBM term for peer-to-peer configurations in IBM's SNA (Systems Network Architecture).

LENNI (LAN Emulation Network-to-Network Interface)

→ *See* LNNI (LAN Emulation Network-to-Network Interface)

LEO (Low Earth Orbit) Satellite

Low earth orbit satellites circle at an altitude of about 600 miles above the earth. This is in contrast to *medium earth orbit (MEO) satellites)*, which are at altitudes ranging from about 2000 to 10,000 miles, and to *geosynchronous earth orbit (GEO) satellites*, which remain in an orbit that is stationary relative to the earth—at an altitude of 23,000 miles or so in space.

Because of their low orbits, LEO satellites have very short transmission latencies—only about 10msec. This means such satellites can be used for any type of communications, including real-time. (Satellites in higher orbits have longer delays—as high as 700msec for GEO satellites—which makes it difficult to use such satellites for certain tasks.) As a result, LEO satellites tend to be packed with much more complex circuitry than GEO satellites—sometimes with up to 10 times as many components.

LEO satellites are less expensive to launch that their higher-altitude counterparts, and they remain in their orbits for about five years. LEO satellite projects require multiple satellites to blanket the entire earth. For example, the Iridium Project led by Motorola will consist of 66 satellites in low earth orbit. (The project originally called for 77 satellites, but it has been scaled down.)

→**Compare** GEO (Geosynchronous Earth Orbit); MEO (Medium Earth Orbit) Satellite

LFN (Long Fat Network)

An LFN is a very high bandwidth, long-distance network. LFNs have bandwidths of several hundred megabits per second with proposed gigabit per second speeds. Because of the high bandwidths, LFNs can cause performance and packet-loss problems for TCP/IP protocols.

For example, some LFNs will have such high bandwidths that all the segment numbers possible under TCP/IP will be used in less than 30 seconds. Since TCP/IP segments may be allowed up to 120 seconds to reach their destination, packets with duplicate numbers may coexist.

Various fixes are currently being explored for these problems, but so far none has received general acceptance.

LID (Local Injection/Detection)

In fiber optics, a LID is a device used to align fibers when splicing them together.

Lifetime

In general, a value that represents the length of time a particular value, feature, or link should be considered valid. In Internet router advertisement messages, lifetime indicates the amount of time a router's information should be considered valid.

LIFO (Last In, First Out)

The processing strategy for a stack. In this strategy, the element added most recently is the element removed first. For example, in employment situations where seniority is observed, the most recently hired employee is the first one to be laid off if business gets slow. The FIFO (first in, first out) strategy takes the opposite approach.

Light-Emitting Diode (LED)

→**See** LED (Light-Emitting Diode)

Lightweight Protocol

→**See** Protocol, Lightweight

Limited-Distance Data Service (LDDS)

→**See** LDDS (Limited-Distance Data Service)

L

Limited-Distance Modem (LDM)

→ *See* LDM (Limited-Distance Modem)

LIMS (Lotus Intel Microsoft Specifications)

The acronym LIM refers to the members of the consortium that originally created the expanded memory standard.

LIMS refer to specifications developed for implementing expanded memory. This is memory allocated on special chips, and then mapped into 16KB pages allocated in the area of memory between 640KB and 1MB.

The memory specification was developed in order to make more memory available to 8086 processors, which cannot operate in protected mode, as is needed to access memory addresses above 1MB.

Line

A line refers to a circuit or link used in data or voice communication.

Line Control Register (LCR)

→ *See* LCR (Line Control Register)

Linear Predictive Coding (LPC)

→ *See* LPC (Linear Predictive Coding)

Line Card

In communications, a line card serves as the interface between a line and a device.

Line Circuit

In telephony, the circuit that detects whether a line is on- or off-hook, and that handles call origination and termination.

Line Conditioner

A line conditioner is a device for keeping the voltage supply to a device within a "normal" range.

Line conditioners are most useful in places where there are likely to be brownouts or power sags (lower than normal voltages). Over time, sags can damage systems just as badly as voltage spikes (excess voltage) can. Studies indicate that sags alone account for almost 90 percent of all electrical disturbances.

In addition to massaging the voltage supply, most line conditioners can also detect some common line anomalies: reversed polarity, missing ground, or an overloaded neutral wire. In some cases, these problems can also damage data or equipment.

Although a line conditioner is limited in the load it can handle, a typical conditioner can serve for multiple outlets. The power requirements of the devices connected to these outlets cannot exceed the line conditioner's capacity, however.

Line conditioners are known by several other names, including *voltage regulator*, *power conditioner*, *line stabilizer/line conditioner*, or *LS/LC*.

Line Conditioning

In analog data communications, line conditioning refers to any of several classes of services available through the telephone company for improving the quality of a transmission. Line conditioning tries to attenuate or eliminate the effects of certain types of distortions on the signal.

Line conditioning becomes more necessary as transmission speeds increase. For example, on ordinary telephone lines, transmissions at more than 9600 bits per second often require line conditioning.

Two types of line conditioning are available:

- C conditioning tries to minimize the effects of distortion related to signal amplitude and distortion due to *envelope delay*. Five levels of type C conditioning (C1, C2, through C5) are distinguished, with level C5 the most stringent.

- D conditioning tries to minimize the effects of *harmonic distortion* in addition to the amplitude and envelope delay distortions handled by type C conditioning.

Line Control Register (LCR)

→ *See* LCR (Line Control Register)

Line Driver

A component that includes a transmitter and a receiver, and is used to extend the transmission range between devices that are connected directly to each other. On some lines, line drivers can be used instead of modems, but only for short distances of up to 15 kilometers (10 miles) or so. Line drivers are used in limited-distance data services (*LDDS*) offered by some telephone companies.

Line Extender

In the PSTN (Public Switched Telephone Network)—that is, in ordinary analog telephone service—the *local loop* is the section of wire that runs from a customer's home or office to the central office (CO) of the local telephone company. For various reasons, this loop can be a maximum of 18,000 feet under ordinary circumstances. That is, the customer premises equipment (CPE) should be no further than about 3.5 miles from the CO. Beyond that, signal attenuation (weakening) and the effects of noise can make the connection too marginal for satisfactory use.

Unfortunately, only about 80 percent of telephone customers are within this magical limit. Two main strategies are used to boost or clean the signal: line extenders and loading.

A line extender is a special device that can be attached to the local loop to boost the signal. A line extender is essentially an amplifier that can be used to stretch the allowable length for the local loop to about 25,000 feet (4.75 miles). The line extender must be matched to the specific loop. Loading is discussed in a separate entry.

→ *Compare* Loading; Loading Coil

Line Group

In telephony, a line group represents multiple lines that can be activated or deactivated as a group.

Line Hit

In electrical transmissions, a brief burst of interference on a line.

Line Insulation Test (LIT)

→ *See* LIT (Line Insulation Test)

Line Level

In an electrical transmission, the line level represents the power of a signal at a particular point in the transmission path. This value is measured in decibels (dB).

Line Load

In telephony, the line load represents the amount of usage a line is getting at a particular time, expressed as a percentage of capacity.

Line Monitor

In telecommunications, a line monitor is a device for spying on a line. The device can be attached to the line and can record or display all transmissions on the line.

Line-of-Sight Communications

In line-of-sight communications, a signal from one location is transmitted to another through the open air, without reflection off a satellite or off the earth.

Line Printer Daemon (LPD)

→ **See** LPD (Line Printer Daemon)

Line-Sharing Device

A multiplexing device that allows two or more devices to share the same line.

Line Speed

In telephony, line speed refers to the transmission speed a line will support for a given grade of service (GoS).

Line Status

In telephony, line status refers to a setting that indicates whether a telephone is idle (on-hook) or in use (off-hook).

Line Termination Equipment

In telecommunications, any equipment that can be used to send signals. This type of equipment includes line cards, modems, multiplexers, hubs, and concentrators.

Line Trace

In networking, a service that logs all network activity, for later examination and analysis.

Line Turnaround (LTA)

→ **See** LTA (Line Turnaround)

Link

A link is a physical or logical connection between two points.

Details of a physical link are specified in terms of the electrical characteristics of a signal going across the link, the pin assignments for the connection, and the physical nature of the connector.

Details of a logical link are specified in terms of a transmission or service protocol.

Link Access Protocol, Balanced (LAPB)

→ **See** Protocol, LAPB (Link Access Protocol, Balanced)

Link Access Protocol, D-Channel (LAPD)

→ **See** Protocol, LAPD (Link Access Protocol, D-Channel)

Link Access Protocol for Modems (LAP-M)

→ **See** Protocol, LAP-M (Link Access Protocol for Modems)

Linkrot

Linkrot occurs when a URL (Uniform Resource Locator)—that is, a Web address—becomes invalid. This can occur when the document corresponding to the URL is moved, removed, or renamed, or if the Web site containing the document is no longer accessible.

Link Service Access Point (LSAP)

→ *See* LSAP (Link Service Access Point)

Link State Advertisement (LSA)

→ *See* LSA (Link State Advertisement)

Link State Algorithm

A class of routing algorithms in which each router broadcasts connection information to all other routers on an internetwork. This saves the routers from checking for available routes, but adds the memory requirement of storing all the routing information.

→ *Compare* Distance Vector

→ *See Also* Algorithm

Link State Packet (LSP)

→ *See* LSP (Link State Packet)

Link Station Address

In network communications, the sending and receiving addresses for a station, or node. The sending address must be unique, but there may be multiple receiving addresses associated with each node. Each receiving address beyond the first for a node represents a group address. This can be used to identify the recipients of a multicast, for example.

Link-Support Layer (LSL)

→ *See* LSL (Link-Support Layer)

Linux

Linux is a UNIX clone for Intel 386, 486, and Pentium systems. The first versions of the kernel were developed by Linus Torvalds at the University of Helsinki. After he had a somewhat stable version, Torvalds released the source code across the Internet, and soon programmers and wizards around the world were busy fixing, improving, and adding to the kernel, file systems, drivers, and so forth. Linux is often cited as the best example of the bazaar approach to software development, as distinguished from the cathedral style of software houses such as Microsoft. See the entry for Cathedral versus Bazaar for more information about this.

Linux is a complete multiuser, multitasking environment, and is compatible—at the source level—with the IEEE POSIX.1 standard for portable UNIX systems, as well with most features of other popular UNIX versions (System V, BSD, etc).

Linux implementations generally come with a full complement of utilities: word processors, compilers, applications, etc. Many of these were developed as part of the Free Software Foundation's GNU (which stands for GNU's Not UNIX) project. However, many applications written for "official UNIX" compile and run with no modification under Linux.

Linux supports the full complement of protocols in the TCP/IP stack, as well as the client and server programs associated with the Internet environment (Telnet, FTP, NNTP, etc). It also supports other telecommunications and BBS protocols and environments.

Linux can run the various UNIX shells—Bourne (sh), C (csh), Korn (ksh), and Bourne again (bash)—

L

as well as the X Window graphical user interface. Unlike other versions of UNIX, Linux can coexist with MS-DOS—even in the same partition, if necessary.

Linux is freely available even though it's neither shareware nor public domain software. It is covered by the GNU GPL (General Public License). Under the GPL, people can modify the source code and sell their own versions; however, the new versions must also be sold under the GPL. That is, the resulting software cannot be restricted; it must be available for modification and reselling.

As a result, numerous Linux implementations and developer's or administrator's packages are available. Linux makes an ideal and inexpensive operating system for setting up an Internet server. In fact, Linux is growing rapidly in popularity, and various pundits are predicting that it may end up giving Microsoft Windows a run for its money as the preferred platform for corporate networks.

One consequence of this popularity is increased competition among Linux VARs (Value Added Resellers), with each trying to outdo the others by adding special features or capabilities to the VAR's implementation. One consequence of this is that incompatibilities are appearing among versions— so that binaries developed for one implementation will not work on other versions. The Linux Standards Board (LSB) is currently trying to establish standards to avoid such problems. It remains to be seen whether the group will succeed.

→ *Primary Sources* The best and most complete all around source of information about Linux is *The Linux Bible: The GNU Testament*, 4th edition (Yggdrasil Computing). For information about this, visit Yggdrasil's Web site at http//:www .yggdrasil.com. The *Linux Journal* is another good source of information.

LIP (Large Internet Packet)

In Novell's NetWare, LIP represents a packet format that allows for packets larger than the normal

NetWare limit of 576 bytes. This feature is useful for transmissions over an internetwork, because the larger packets can help increase throughput over bridges and routers.

Liquid Crystal Display (LCD)

→ *See* LCD (Liquid Crystal Display)

Listen Before Talk/Listen While Talk (LBT/LWT)

→ *See* LBT/LWT (Listen Before Talk/Listen While Talk)

LIT (Line Insulation Test)

In telephony, a test that automatically checks lines for shorts, grounds, and interference.

Little-Endian

In data transmission and storage, little-endian is a term that describes the order in which bytes in a word are processed (stored or transmitted). The term comes from Jonathan Swift's *Gulliver's Travels*, in which a war is fought over which end of an egg should be cracked for eating.

In little-endian storage, the low-order byte is stored at the lower address. This arrangement is used in Intel processors (such as the $80x86$ family), in VAX and PDP-11 computer series, and also in various communications and networking contexts. Most notably, it is used in the IEEE 802.3 (Ethernet) and 802.4 (Token Bus) specifications. In contrast, the IEEE 802.5 (Token Ring) specification uses big-endian ordering.

The term is less commonly used to describe the order in which bits are stored in a byte.

→ *Compare* Big-Endian; Middle-Endian

LLC (Logical-Link Control)

In the IEEE's LAN/RM (local area network reference model) the LLC is a sublayer above the MAC (media-access control) sublayer. Together, MAC and LLC are equivalent to the Data-Link layer in the OSI reference model.

The LLC provides an interface and services for the network-layer protocols, and mediates between these higher-level protocols and any of the various media-access methods defined at the lower, MAC sublayer. "The layer and sublayer arrangement for a LAN" illustrates the arrangement.

The details of the LLC are provided in the IEEE 802.2 document. Details of the MAC sublayer protocols are specified in the IEEE 802.3, 802.4, and 802.5 documents. The IEEE 802.1 recommendations provide a broader context for the sublayers and protocols. LLC is modeled after the SDLC link-layer protocol.

SAPs

Requests to the LLC are communicated through SAPs (service access points). SAPs are locations where each party, for example, a network-layer protocol and an LLC layer service, can leave messages for the other. Each SAP has a 1-byte "address" associated with it.

The same LLC sublayer may need to provide services for more than one network-layer protocol. For example, it may work with IP and IPX. The use of SAPs makes this possible, since each of these protocols will have a different SAP address value. A SAP uniquely identifies a protocol.

Delivery Services

The LLC can provide three types of delivery services. Type 1 is a connectionless service without acknowledgment. This is the fastest but least reliable type of service offered at the LLC sublayer. In a connectionless service, there is neither a predefined path

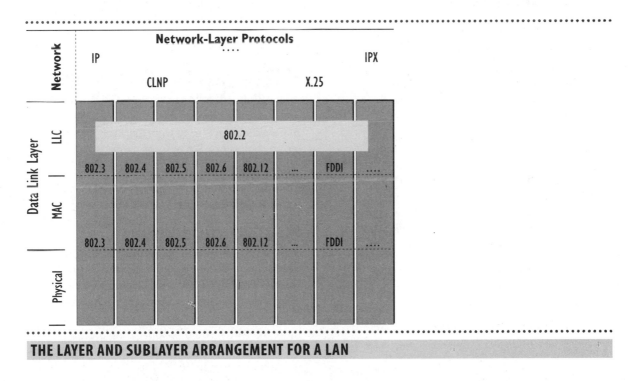

THE LAYER AND SUBLAYER ARRANGEMENT FOR A LAN

L

nor a permanent circuit between sender and receiver. Without acknowledgment, there is no way of knowing whether a packet reached its destination.

Despite its relative unreliability, Type 1 is the most popular service at this level, because most higher-level protocols *do* include delivery and error checking, so there is no need to duplicate this checking at the LLC layer. The Network layer IP protocol (of TCP/IP fame) is connectionless, as is NetWare's IPX protocol.

Type 2 is a connection-oriented service. In a connection-oriented service, a circuit is established before data transmission begins. The transport-layer TCP protocol, used on the Internet and on many other systems, is connection-oriented, as are the X.25 network-layer protocol and Netware's SPX protocol. With a connection—even if it is only virtual—the service can provide sequence control (so that message elements are assembled in the correct order by the receiver), flow and error control, and so on. Two flow control methods are commonly used at the LLC sublayer:

- Stop and wait, in which each LLC frame must be acknowledged before the next one is sent.

- Sliding window, in which *x* LLC frames can be sent before an acknowledgment is required. The value of *x* represents the window size.

Type 3 is a connectionless service, but with acknowledgment.

The LLC Frame

An LLC frame is known as a PDU (Protocol Data Unit). Its structure is defined in the IEEE 802.2 document. There are four major components to a PDU:

DSAP (destination service access point) An 8-bit value that identifies the higher-level protocol using the LLC services.

SSAP (source service access point) An 8-bit value that indicates the local user of the LLC

service. In many cases, this value will be the same as for the DSAP.

Control A 1- or 2-byte field that indicates the type of PDU. The contents of this field depend on whether the PDU is an information (I), supervisory (S), or unnumbered (U) frame. I frames, used for transmitting data, and S frames, used to oversee the transfer of I frames, are found only in type 2 (connection-oriented) services. U frames are used to set up and break the logical link between network nodes in either type 1 or type 2 services. They are also used to transmit data in connectionless (type 1 or type 3) services. Netware's IPX packets are unnumbered.

Data, or information A variable-length field that contains the packet received from the network-level protocol. The allowable length for this field depends on the type of access method being used (CSMA/CD or token passing). S frames do not have a data field.

"Examples of LLC frames" illustrates the frame components.

LLC2 (Logical-Link Control Type 2)

A protocol and packet format for use in SNA-based networks. This format is newer, more versatile, and more widely supported than the SDLC protocol also common in SNA environments.

LMDS (Local Multipoint Distribution Service)

Sometimes referred to as cellular TV, LMDS is a wireless distribution system that was originally intended to deliver TV signals. Despite being developed for distribution, LMDS does support two-way communications. In fact, the technology is more likely to be used for providing businesses with Internet access. LMDS is expected to support transmission speeds of up to 54Mbps.

LMDS is a multicell technology, which means it uses multiple cells, or transmitters, to cover an area. This helps avoid serious coverage problems because it minimizes the area that is not within line of site of a transmitter.

LMDS provides point-to-multipoint communications because signals from a transmitter can be received by any subscribers within the cell's two to three mile range. Adjacent transmitters use the same signal frequencies, but with different polarization (direction of the electric field carrying the signal).

The technology was originally designed to operate in certain sub-bands of the 2GHz frequency band located between 27.5GHz and 29.5GHz. However, the FCC has added a second, 300MHz, band between 31.0GHz and 31.3GHz. Two licenses will be granted in each area that will be covered by LMDS. A total of 1.15GHz will be provided for one license. This bandwidth will be assigned as three distinct bands within the two frequency ranges. The second license will be for a 150MHz bandwidth, which is provided as two segments of the band beginning at 31.0GHz.

Like its somewhat less efficient cousin, MMDS, LMDS is a new technology, and it remains to be seen how it fares when it must compete with the existing cable companies and with satellite cable distribution systems for cable TV customers, and with the various Internet access technologies (modem/PC, cable modem, satellite services, and DSL, or digital subscriber line, technology, among others) for Internet subscribers.

→ Broader Category Wireless Communications

→ See Also MMDS (Multichannel, Multipoint Distribution System)

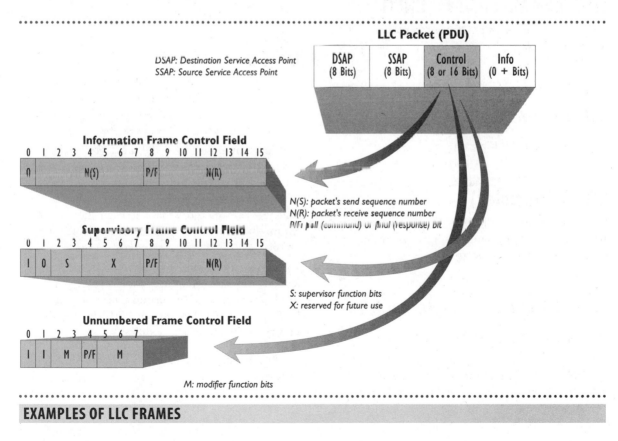

DSAP: Destination Service Access Point
SSAP: Source Service Access Point

LLC Packet (PDU)

| DSAP (8 Bits) | SSAP (8 Bits) | Control (8 or 16 Bits) | Info (0 + Bits) |

Information Frame Control Field

0 1 2 3 4 5 6 7 8 9 10 11 12 13 14 15

| 0 | N(S) | P/F | N(R) |

N(S): packet's send sequence number
N(R): packet's receive sequence number
P/F: poll (command) or final (response) bit

Supervisory Frame Control Field

0 1 2 3 4 5 6 7 8 9 10 11 12 13 14 15

| 1 0 | S | X | P/F | N(R) |

S: supervisor function bits
X: reserved for future use

Unnumbered Frame Control Field

0 1 2 3 4 5 6 7

| 1 1 | M | P/F | M |

M: modifier function bits

EXAMPLES OF LLC FRAMES

L

LME (Layer Management Entity)

In the OSI network management framework, a mechanism by which layers can communicate with each other to exchange information and also to access management elements at different layers. LMEs are also known as *hooks*.

→ *See Also* Network Management

LMI (Local Management Interface)

A specification regarding the exchange of management-related information between a network and any of various hardware devices (such as printers, storage devices, and so on).

LMU (LAN Manager for UNIX)

An implementation of LAN Manager, Microsoft's server-based network operating system, for UNIX servers.

L Multiplex

→ *See* LMX (L Multiplex)

LMX (L Multiplex)

In analog communications, LMX represents a hierarchy of channel groupings (group, super group, master group, and jumbo group).

LNNI (LAN Emulation Network-to-Network Interface)

LAN emulation, or LANE, is a service developed to enable an emulated Ethernet or Token Ring network to run on top of an Asynchronous Transfer Mode (ATM) network. The crucial activities for such an emulation take place at a LAN emulation layer, which presents a LAN-like media access control (MAC) layer to the emulated LAN (ELAN) and a different appearance to the ATM network beneath it—which is where all this LAN activity really is taking place.

In such an emulation, server and clients communicate through a LAN Emulation User-to-Network Interface (LUNI, or sometimes L-UNI), and ELANs communicate with each other through a LAN Emulation Network-to-Network Interface (LNNI, L-NNI, or LENNI).

→ *Broader Categories* ATM (Asynchronous Transfer Mode); Ethernet; LANE (Local Area Network Emulation); Token Ring

→ *See Also* LANE (Local Area Network Emulation)

LOAD and UNLOAD

In Novell's NetWare, the LOAD command is used to link modules or drivers to the network operating system (NOS). The UNLOAD command is used to unlink modules when they are no longer needed.

When a module is loaded, the NOS allocates a limited amount of memory for the module. The module may request more memory, temporarily, when actually doing work. When a module is unloaded, any memory that had been allocated to the module will be returned to the available memory pool.

NetWare Loadable Modules (NLMs) can be loaded and unloaded as needed. However, you need to be careful when unloading certain "low-level" modules (such as disk or LAN drivers) that may be needed by other modules.

→ *Broader Category* NetWare Loadable Module (NLM)

Load Balancing

In switching systems, load balancing is a strategy in which callers are distributed across all available channels. Load balancing makes the traffic on the channels as evenly distributed as possible.

In networking contexts, load balancing refers to a strategy in which network traffic is distributed in a fair way to any available servers, routers or other devices.

Loading

In the PSTN (Public Switched Telephone Network), the analog link between the local telephone company office (the CO) and the customer's home or office is known as the *local loop*. The wire running between the CO and the CPE (Customer Premises Equipment) cannot be too long, because both signal quality and strength decrease over distance. In practice, the local loop is limited to about 18,000 feet (roughly 3.5 miles). Beyond that, the signal quality can deteriorate to an unacceptable level.

One reason for this signal loss is *capacitance*, which is the tendency for electricity to build up on the wire. Capacitance buildup leads to signal deterioration by causing the voltage and current to get out of phase. Since power is the product of voltage and current, misalignment will decrease the power.

The effects of capacitance can be reversed or at least decreased by producing an appropriate amount of *inductance*, which is the tendency for electricity to *move* along the wire. The inductance can help bring voltage and current back into phase. Such inductance can be applied by *loading* the wire with appropriately spaced and sized *loading coils*. These are doughnut-shaped coils made of iron, and they are attached to the wires in a local loop. The iron in the coils is of a predefined level of purity and the coil is of a particular size. These standardization steps are to ensure that the proper amount of inductance is produced.

To keep things manageable, loading coils come in the following three standard sizes, with guidelines for spacing:

- B-44 loading adds 44 millihenrys of inductance to the wire. B-44 coils are placed 3000 feet apart.

- D-66 loading adds 66 millihenrys of inductance to the wire. D-66 coils are placed 4500 feet apart.

- H-88 loading adds 88 millihenrys of inductance to the wire. H-88 coils are placed 6000 feet apart.

With loading, the local loop can be extended to about 30,000 feet (5.7 miles).

→ **Compare** Line Extender

→ **See Also** Loading Coil

Loading Coil

In cabling, a device attached to copper wire to help reduce distortion of analog signals traveling across the cable. Loading coils make it impossible to transmit digital signals over the copper cables. This has consequences for premises that lie within a few miles of the telephone company office, because these very short connections generally use copper cable with loading coils.

→ **See Also** Loading

Load Sharing

In internetwork communications, load sharing refers to the ability of two or more bridges to divide network traffic between them. For example, the bridges might provide parallel paths to other networks.

L

Lobe

In a token-ring network architecture, lobe is a term for a node, or workstation.

Lobe Attachment Module (LAM)

→ *See* LAM (Lobe Attachment Module)

Local Access and Transport Area (LATA)

→ *See* LATA (Local Access and Transport Area)

Local Area Network (LAN)

→ *See* LAN (Local Area Network)

Local Area Network Emulation

→ *See* LANE (Local Area Network Emulation)

Local Area Networks Reference Model (LAN/RM)

→ *See* LAN/RM (Local-Area Networks Reference Model)

Local Area Transport (LAT)

→ *See* LAT (Local-Area Transport)

Local Automatic Message Accounting (LAMA)

→ *See* LAMA (Local Automatic Message Accounting)

Local Carrier

A local carrier refers to a local telephone company—that is, a company that provides telephone service within an exchange, or calling area. Such a calling area is known as a LATA (for local access and transport area). Local carriers are connected by IXCs (interexchange carriers), and are also known as local exchange carriers (LECs).

The Telecommunications Act of 1996 requires that each LATA have a least two LECs. The LEC that performed this service when the act was passed is known as the *incumbent LEC (ILEC)*. Any competing carriers are known as *competing LECs (CLECs)*, or *other LECs (OLECs)*.

Local Channel (LC)

→ *See* LC (Local Channel)

Local Exchange (LE)

→ *See* LATA (Local Access and Transport Area)

Local Exchange Carrier (LEC)

→ *See* LEC (Local Exchange Carrier)

Local Group

In Windows NT, a local group is one whose activities can affect only the computer on which the group was created. This is in contrast to a global group, which might have access to the entire network, and which might, therefore, affect the entire network.

→ *Compare* Global Group

Local Injection/Detection (LID)

In fiber optics, a LID is a device used to align fibers when splicing them together.

Local Loop

In telecommunications, a local loop is a connection between a home or business and the local telephone exchange, or central office. The local loop is also known as an *access line* or as *the last mile*.

Locally Administered Address (LAA)

→ *See* LAA (Locally Administered Address)

Local Management Interface (LMI)

→ *See* LMI (Local Management Interface)

Local Multichannel Distribution Service (LMDS)

→ *See* LMDS (Local Multipoint Distribution Service)

Local Multipoint Distribution Service (LMDS)

→ *See* LMDS (Local Multipoint Distribution Service)

Local Name

In a network or an internetwork, a local name is known only to a single server or domain in a network. Compare it with global name.

LocalTalk

LocalTalk is Apple's proprietary network architecture, for use in networks that run the AppleTalk networking software, such as Macintosh networks. LocalTalk operates at the Data-Link and Physical layers, which are the two lowest layers in the OSI reference model.

LocalTalk has the following characteristics:

- Uses twisted-pair cable.
- Uses an RS-422 interface.
- Uses either a DB-9 or a DIN-8 connector and two DIN-3 connectors. The DIN-3 connectors are designed so that a node can easily drop out of a network without disrupting the electrical activity of the now smaller network.
- Supports transmission speeds of up to 230.4Kbps.
- Uses operating system services, so that all Macintoshes come with built-in networking capabilities.
- Supports up to 255 nodes in a network.
- Allows nodes to be separated by up to 1000 feet.
- Uses the LocalTalk Link Access Procedure (LLAP) at the Data-Link layer to access the network.
- Uses the CSMA/CA (carrier sense multiple access/collision avoidance) method to access the network.
- Allows only one network number per network.

→ *See Also* AppleTalk

L

Local User

In Windows NT, a local user is one whose account is set up on a specific computer and for access through a specific server. Such a user must log onto the network from the computer on which the user's account is set up. Basically, a local user is allowed to log on to a single computer.

Local user accounts are in contrast to those for *global users*, who can access the network from any computer that is attached to the security domain for the network. Whereas local users log on to computers, global users log on to network domains.

Locking

Locking is a mechanism for ensuring that two network users or programs do not try to access the same data simultaneously. A lock may be advisory or physical. An *advisory* lock serves mainly as a warning, and it can be overridden. A *physical* lock serves as a control mechanism, and it cannot be overridden.

The following types of locks are distinguished:

File locking   A scheme in which a file server prevents a user from accessing any part of a file while another user is already accessing that file. This is the crudest and least efficient of the locking methods.

Record locking   A scheme in which a file server prevents a user from accessing a record in a file while another user is already accessing that same record. This is more efficient and less restrictive than file locking.

Logical locking   A scheme in which logical units (for example, records or strings) in a file are made inaccessible as required.

Physical   A scheme in which actual sectors or sector groups on a hard disk are made inaccessible as required. This is the standard locking scheme used by MS-DOS, and is in contrast to logical locking.

Files can also be locked to prevent or restrict general user access to files.

→ *Broader Category* Data Protection

Lockout

In networking, a lockout is an action or state in which a potential network user or application is denied access to particular services on the network or to the network itself.

Logical Address

In a network, a software-based value that is assigned during network installation or configuration, or when a workstation is added to a network. Network and node addresses are logical, and are in contrast to hardware addresses, which are fixed during the manufacturing process.

→ *See Also* Address

Logical Channel Identification (LCI)

→ *See* LCI (Logical Channel Identification)

Logical Link Control (LLC)

→ *See* LLC (Logical-Link Control)

Logical Link Control Type 2 (LLC2)

→ *See* LLC2 (Logical-Link Control Type 2)

Logical Number

A value assigned in a device-numbering scheme for a hardware device. The logical number is based on several factors and conditions, such as what other devices are attached, and the order in which these were attached and installed.

Logical Unit (LU)

→ See LU (Logical Unit)

Logical Unit to Logical Unit (LU-LU) Connection

→ See LU-LU (Logical Unit to Logical Unit) Connection

Logical versus Physical

Logical versus physical represents both a descriptive and functional distinction for several important concepts related to networks. In general, a logical configuration is based on function or on software; a physical configuration is based on hardware, possibly aided or enhanced by software.

For example, logical versus physical distinctions include the following:

- A PC may be physically attached to a network, but may be logically detached if the machine is operating in a stand-alone fashion (rather than as a workstation on the network).

- A network may be using a logical bus topology, which is implemented as a star in the physical wiring.

- A file server's hard disk may be logical drive H: in a workstation's configuration, and the physical drive may be in another room or building.

Login

A login is a process by which a workstation or terminal makes itself known to a server or host, and the workstation's user makes himself or herself known to the network, for authentication and security clearance.

The terms *login* and *logon* (or *log in* and *log on*) are used synonymously. In general, *logon* (or *log on*) is more likely to be used when discussing mainframe environments.

The Login Process

The login process generally involves booting or starting network software on the workstation to announce the machine's presence, and then providing a session through which a user can provide a valid ID and a password to prove that the user is allowed to be operating a workstation, or perhaps just *that* workstation, on the network.

The files and programs used to carry out the login process and validate a particular user logging in are stored in a *login directory*. This directory is created during the network operating system (NOS) installation process. The name and exact contents of a login directory may differ, depending on NOS. The login directory in Novell's NetWare is named SYS:LOGIN.

Once the network security is convinced of the user's authenticity, the user is given security clearance for access to the network and to some or all of the network's services. In NetWare, the network software runs a *login script* associated with the user. This script may contain commands to assign usage and access rights to the user, initialize the user's local environment on the network (load drivers, change directories, and so forth), map network drives for the user's environment, and execute programs or other commands.

Login Restrictions

The login restrictions that can be set to limit a user's ability to log in to a network fall into any of several management areas:

Security Requiring a user ID and a password helps control network access. The details surrounding password requirements may vary. For example, users may be allowed (or required) to change their passwords every so often. Users

L

may be limited in the number of incorrect passwords they can type before being shut out of the network.

Configuration   If memory usage or other system requirements are of concern, users may have limited access. For example, a login restriction may limit the amount of disk space a user is allowed to use.

Accounting   Various accounting restrictions can be imposed. For example, restrictions may apply to the account's total access time, amount of time open, range of hours during which it is accessible, or number and range of machines from which it is accessible.

Login Script

In Novell's NetWare, a login script is a sequence of commands executed when a user wants to log in to a network. These commands will initialize a node's and a user's operating environments, map directories, allocate resources for the user, and perform other startup tasks for the user.

Three classes of login scripts are distinguished:

Container, or System   The system script is created by the network administrator. It is used to set general parameters and mappings and to execute commands that are appropriate for all users. In NetWare 3.x, the system script is server-specific, which means that all users who log in to the server will have the server's system script executed. In NetWare 4.x, the system script is a property of a container object, so that all users in the container get the system script. The container, or system, login script is executed first.

User   The user script belongs to an individual user, and it does whatever remains to be done to initialize the environment for a particular user.

Profile   In the NetWare Name Service (NNS) and in NetWare 4.x, the profile script initializes the environment for all the users in a group. If defined, such a script executes between the system and user script.

If a configuration includes a system login script, this script is executed before either profile or user scripts.

Logins from Remote Locations

Remote access refers to logins from remote locations. These login procedures are accomplished by dialing into an *access server* (a special modem or computer) and logging in through this server.

The *network modems* that can be used as remote access servers must have an NIC-compatible with the network to which the modem is providing access.

Login Service

A login service is a tool for simplifying the login and authentication processes for users. The service consists of four main components, which reside on different machines.

- Client software, which runs on the client's workstation, and which the client can use to access the network and begin the login process.

- Server software, which runs on the target machine, and which will evaluate the user's authenticity and privileges before providing access to the requested services.

- Authentication service, which verifies that the user logging in is legitimate and is allowed on the network. If so, the authentication service gives the user a special ticket that serves as an ID. The authentication service should be running on a secure server.

- Privilege service, which ensures that the user is given access only to the applications and services for which the user has the required privileges. The privilege service should also be running on a secure server.

To use a login service, the user:

1. Checks in with the authentication service to get the validation ticket.

2. Checks in with the privilege service to get the user's PAC (Privilege Attribute Certificate).

Once the user has the PAC he or she can use the network's facilities—to the extent allowed in the PAC.

To increase security, any or all of the information can be encrypted at any or all of the login phases. The encryption methods can be different for each of the phases, if desired.

With the authentication and security possible when using a login service, SSO (single sign on) becomes a real possibility. In SSO, a user needs to have only a single user ID and password to access any part of a network allowed to the user.

Logout

A logout is a process by which a user's session on a network or a host is closed down and terminated in an orderly fashion. The user's workstation or terminal may be removed as an active node on a network. The workstation may remain physically attached, even though the logical connection between the node and the network is severed.

The terms *logout* and *logoff* (or *log out* and *log off*) are used synonymously; however there are some differences in usage. In general, *logoff* (or *log off*) is more likely to be used when discussing mainframe environments.

Long Fat Network (LFN)

→*See* LFN (Long Fat Network)

Long-Haul Carrier

A long-haul carrier is the carrier system for long-distance signals, which can range from hundreds of miles to transcontinental or international distances. The term encompasses cabling and signaling (including modulation) specifications. The currently used system was developed as the L carrier system just before World War II, but its capacity and reliability have been increased over the years.

For example, the first long-haul carrier L1 included 480 channels. This has since been increased to 13,200 channels in the L5E system. The end of the L carrier system may finally be in sight, however, as the switchover to digital communications progresses.

Long-haul carriers use mainly coaxial cable and analog signaling. Long-haul carriers are expensive, but this cost is offset by their tremendous capacity. This is in contrast to short-haul carriers.

A *short-haul carrier*, which is used for distances of a hundred miles or so, uses a less expensive technology because the shorter distances involved produce less signal loss. Short-haul carriers use less expensive (and less robust) modulation techniques and have much smaller capacities (usually no more than 24 channels or so) than long-haul carriers. This is because there are no provisions in the short-haul specifications for higher-order modulation. Short-haul carriers also have noisier channels than long-haul carriers.

Long-Haul Microwave Communications

Microwave (that is, gigahertz-level) transmissions over distances of 40 or 45 kilometers (about 25 or 30 miles).

Look-Ahead/Look-Back Queuing

In telephony, look-ahead queuing represents an automatic call distribution feature in which the secondary queue is checked for congestion before switching traffic to that queue. This is in contrast to look-back queuing, in which the secondary queue can check whether congestion on the primary queue has cleared up and, if so, return calls to that queue.

Loop

A circuit between a customer's premises and the central office (CO). This can take several forms, with the most common being a *line* (a pair of wires, in the simplest case).

Loopback

Loopback involves shorting together two wires in a connector, so that a signal returns to its source after traveling around the loop. The term is also used to refer to a test that relies on a loopback process. A *loopback plug* is a device for doing loopback testing.

Loopback Mode

An operating mode for certain devices, such as modems. Loopback mode is used for line testing: signals are sent back to their origin (hence, the *loopback*), rather than being sent on.

Loop Start

In analog telephone communications, a method by which a telephone can seize a line, or circuit. When a would-be caller picks up the telephone receiver, a circuit is closed and current flows, indicating that the telephone is off-hook and that the person wants to make a call.

Loop Timing

In digital communications, a synchronization method in which a clock signal (timing information) is extracted from incoming pulses.

Loose Source and Record Route (LSRR)

→ **See** LSRR (Loose Source and Record Route)

Loss

In electrical signals, a loss represents a decrease in signal level, or strength. In call or packet transmissions, loss is the disappearance of a packet or a call, which can occur if a packet is discarded because of heavy traffic or because of an addressing error.

Loss Budget

In electrical or optical signaling, the loss budget represents the combination of all the factors that cause signal loss between the source and destination.

Lost Calls Cleared (LCC)/Lost Calls Delayed (LDD)

→ **See** LCC (Lost Calls Cleared)/LDD (Lost Calls Delayed)

Lotus Domino

Lotus Domino is the name given to the Lotus Notes server in release 4.5 of Notes. While Domino began life as a Notes server, it has since been beefed up and enhanced to make it suitable as a Web or even an Enterprise server.

While it is still a Notes server, Domino now also provides native support for other protocols—in particular, for Internet and Web protocols. For example, Domino R5 supports the following:

- Internet messaging and directories. Domino R5 provides native support for mail, messaging, and directory-related protocols such as

SMTP (Simple Mail Transfer Protocol) and ESMTP (Extended SMTP), MIME (Multipurpose Internet Mail Extension) and S/MIMEv2 (Secure MIME), POP3 (Post Office Protocol) and IMAPv4, and LDAP (Lightweight Directory Access Protocol). Domino R5 also provides various special directory services, including the Directory Catalog (which makes quick lookups possible).

- Web application services. Domino R5 can handle Web applications created using any of the popular Web-based languages, including HTML (Hypertext Markup Language) 4.0, Java, JavaScript, or LotusScript, and even applications created using third-party Web design tools. R5 also includes support for CORBA (Common Object Request Broker Architecture) and IIOP (Internet Inter-ORB Protocol), which are so important for exchanging and using distributed objects. The server supports the standard security protocols and procedures, including SSL (Secure Sockets Layer), HTTPS (Hypertext Transfer Protocol Secure), and X.509 certificates.

- Database capabilities. Domino R5 can be connected to and can interact with various kinds of databases, including DB2, Oracle, ODBC (Open Database Connectivity), and Sybase.

- Domino Administrator. Domino R5 includes tools to help with network and server administration.

- Web development tools. The Domino product family includes Domino Designer, which makes it possible to design and create Web pages and Web sites.

Both server and client—that is, Domino and Notes—have developed nicely over successive releases, and both have become powerful products on their own as well as when working together.

→ *See Also* Lotus Notes

Lotus Intel Microsoft Specifications (LIMS)

→ *See* LIMS (Lotus Intel Microsoft Specifications)

Lotus Notes

Lotus Notes—or, simply, Notes—is arguably the best-known example of *groupware* in the PC-based networking world. Notes is, among other things, a distributed client-server database application for the Windows 3.x, 9x, and NT environments. The Notes server (which is not the same as a network file server) is responsible for running the Notes configuration at a particular installation. The Notes server is also responsible for enforcing access privileges when dealing with client requests. (The Notes server was renamed Domino in Release 4.5. It has since been extended into a more powerful and versatile product that can provide services for more than just Notes clients.)

Most fundamentally, Notes works with databases—albeit databases of a very flexible and free-form nature. The Notes database is built around documents, document groupings, and representations of document content. Documents can be form-oriented or unstructured.

Unlike standard database programs, Notes allows users to view the information in individualized ways, and to expand the database in just about any direction or manner desired. Thus, document contents can be organized and made available in different ways to different users or groups. Thus, Notes can be used for messaging, collaborative work, or even online instruction.

A view is a listing of documents available for a particular context or user. From a view, a user can select the specific document or documents of interest, and can access or use the documents as allowed by the user's access level.

Documents can contain links to other documents so that a user can switch quickly to the other end of

L

the link—regardless of whether the document at the end of the link is in the same database or even on the same machine. For example, a document might include links to elaborations, addenda, or tips. A customer's record in a vendor's database might include a link to technical support or complaint calls from the user.

Documents can also include buttons, which will cause predefined actions to be carried out when the button is pressed. For example, a document can include a button to forward material to other users or groups. Links or buttons built into forms become part of all documents based on that form; links and buttons built into a document appear only in that document (and any copies that might be made of it).

The presentation possibilities for a document's contents depend on whether the document is unstructured or whether it is based on a form. While early versions of Notes required a Notes administrator to configure the views available to users, the most recent release—Notes R5—allows users to configure their own versions. This release allows the user to set bookmarks for frequently used Web sites, select information and other channels to receive by default, and set tabs to make searches and Web page navigation easier.

In addition to its main functions, Notes provides useful auxiliary features—for example, electronic mail, a calendar, and scheduling capabilities. Development tools are available to create customized applications that can become accessible through Notes.

Electronic mail facilities form the basis for one of the *workflow automation* schemes supported by Notes: *routing applications*. In this approach, a project is passed along by mail from person to person as it is developed. Each person makes whatever additions or revisions are required from that user.

Shared applications are the other variant of workflow automation supported by Notes. In a shared application, a project is available at all phases to all relevant and authorized users. Each user contributes as required at the appropriate point, and each user can check on the project's status at any point.

Notes includes encryption capabilities, and a Notes server can require user authentication. Domestic and international versions of Notes use different encryption algorithms—in part because of export restrictions on encryption technology.

Notes R5 provides native support for various Internet standards and protocols, including those for e-mail (POP3, IMAP, SMTP), newsgroups (NNTP, MIME), security (SSL, S/MIME, X.509 certificates), directory services (LDAP), and Web pages (HTML, Java, JavaScript). Older versions of Notes required special plug-ins to provide such capabilities.

→ *See Also* Lotus Domino

Lotus SmartSuite

Lotus SmartSuite—or just SmartSuite—is a Windows (3*x*, 9*x*, and NT) product that integrates several applications into a single package. The components in Lotus SmartSuite Millenium 9.5—the most recent release as of this writing – are as follows:

- Lotus 1-2-3, which is the spreadsheet program that has produced fortunes and lawsuits galore. 1-2-3 is used for doing various types of charts and numerical worksheets. The Version Manager in 1- 2-3 allows users to do "what if" analyses—in which certain data values are changed or extrapolated in order to see how these changes would affect the rest of the financial or numerical picture.

- Lotus WordPro, which is the name for Lotus's word processing package beginning with version 4.0. Prior to 4.0, the word processor was known as Ami Pro. Along with the name change, the functionality of this application was also increased to make it easier for users to collaborate on shared documents. Also, WordPro uses a newer implementation of the Lotus-Script scripting language.

- Lotus Approach, which is a relational database program. Approach includes predefined templates for databases, and various other tools to make it easier to automate database creation and report generation.

- Lotus Freelance Graphics, which enables users to create slides, notes, and transparencies for presentations and other purposes. In addition to various chart and table templates, Freelance Graphics includes capabilities for adding sound, animation, and special transitions to presentations.

- Lotus ScreenCam is an application that lets users record activities on the screen and then play these back inside a Freelance Graphics presentation. With the appropriate hardware, you can also record audio.

- Lotus Organizer, which is a personal information manager (PIM)—that is, a program for setting appointments, reminders, and alarms, for storing address and phone book information, for keeping to-do lists, and for doing the kinds of things that can (but don't always) help make one more productive.

- IBM ViaVoice speech recognition software, which lets users dictate their documents and have (most of) their words converted directly into electronic form.

- Lotus FastSite Internet publishing tools, which enable users to create Web pages.

The various SmartSuite applications can be accessed from the SmartCenter. This is essentially a task manager designed to make it as easy as possible to use the included applications together. It's possible to add new applications to SmartCenter, to make these just as accessible as the included components.

- SmartSuite applications can use any of three ways to communicate and exchange data with each other. Of these three methods, only OLE—the most sophisticated—makes

it possible to update all versions of a document or project automatically: cutting and copying material to the Windows clipboard, and then retrieving the material in order to paste it in the new location. Using dynamic data exchange (DDE).

- Using object linking and embedding (OLE).

While not designed specifically for group or network use, SmartSuite can be licensed and used in such a context. In such a setting, working groups can take advantage of information exchange and application access capabilities.

Low Bit Rate Voice (LBRV)

→ *See* LBRV (Low Bit Rate Voice)

Low Earth Orbit (LEO) Satellite

→ *See* LEO (Low Earth Orbit) Satellite

Low-Entry Networking (LEN)

→ *See* LEN (Low-Entry Networking)

Low-Speed Modem

A low-speed modem is one operating at speeds of 600 bits per second or less.

LPC (Linear Predictive Coding)

A voice-encoding algorithm for use in narrowband transmissions, which can produce a digitized voice signal at 2400bps. LPC is used in secure telephone units (STU-III), which were developed by the National Security Agency. A variant, CELP (code excited linear predictive) coding can produce digitized voice output at 4800bps.

LPD (Line Printer Daemon)

In UNIX implementations, a daemon program that controls printing from a UNIX machine or network. The LPD program knows which printer or print queue it is printing to and so can make adjustments if necessary.

LPT1

The logical name for the primary parallel port. Additional parallel ports are LPT2 and LPT3. As a device, this port is also known as PRN. Compare it with COM1, the primary serial port.

LSA (Link State Advertisement)

In networks and internetworks that use link state algorithms for routing, an LSA is used to specify information about the links between a device (usually a router) and a network. The details of the LSA will depend on the devices involved and on the type of LSA being transmitted.

For example, a router link LSA is generated by each router for every network or area to which the router is connected. In contrast, a network link LSA is generated for every router attached to the network.

LSAs contain such information as a time stamp (to determine which LSA is more recent) and information about the cost of the link.

LSAP (Link Service Access Point)

Any of several SAPs at the logical-link control (LLC) sublayer of the OSI reference model's Data-Link layer. SAPs are addresses through which services are requested or provided.

→ *See Also* SAP (Service Access Point)

LSB (Least Significant Bit)

The bit corresponding to the lowest power of two (2^0) in a bit sequence. The actual location of this bit in a representation depends on the context (storing or transmitting) and on the ordering within a word. Compare it with MSB.

→ *See Also* Big-Endian, Little-Endian

LSL (Link-Support Layer)

In Novell's ODI (Open Data-link Interface), the LSL is an intermediate layer between the network interface card's LAN driver and the protocol stacks for various network and higher-level services, such as IPX and TCP/IP. This layer makes it possible for the same board to work with several types of protocols.

The LSL directs packets from the LAN driver to the appropriate protocol stack or from any of the available stacks to the LAN driver. To do its work, the LSL uses interrupt vectors INT 0x08 and INT 0x2F.

The LSL for DOS can support up to eight boards.

→ *Broader Category* ODI (Open Data-link Interface)

LSP (Link State Packet)

In a protocol that uses link state routing, an LSP contains information about all the connections for a router, including information about all the neighbors for that packet and the cost (in money, time, error rate, or other currency) of the link to each neighbor. This packet is broadcast to all other routers in the internetwork.

LSRR (Loose Source and Record Route)

In Internet transmissions, an IP (Internet Protocol) option that enables the source for a datagram to specify routing information and to record the route taken by the datagram. This option helps ensure that datagrams take only routes that have a level of security commensurate with the datagram's security classification.

LTA (Line Turnaround)

In half-duplex communications, the amount of time it takes to set the line to reverse the transmission direction.

LTM (LAN Traffic Monitor)

A device for monitoring the activity, or traffic, level in a network.

L-to-T Connector

In telecommunications, a component that connects two (analog) frequency division multiplexing (FDM) groups into a single (digital) time division multiplexing (TDM) group. This allows the analog channels to be sent over a digital signal 1 (DS1) line.

LU (Logical Unit)

In IBM's SNA (Systems Network Architecture), an LU is an entry point into a network. LUs are one of three types of addressable units in an SNA network. The other two units are PUs (physical units) and SSCPs (system services protocol units).

LUs differ in the types of communications possible with them and in the types of protocols used. The table "Logical Unit Types" lists the types of LUs defined.

LOGICAL UNIT TYPES

Type	Description
LU 0	Communication from program to device.
LU 1	Communication from program to device, with a master/slave relationship between the elements. Used for mainframe batch systems and printers that use the SNA character string (SCS) data format.
LU 2	Communication from program to device, with a master/slave relationship between the elements. Used for 3270 terminals.
LU 3	Communication from program to device, with a master/slave relationship between the elements. Used for 3270 Data Stream terminals.
LU 4	Communication from program to program or from program to device, with a master/slave or a peer-to-peer relationship between the elements. Used for printers using the SCS data format.
LU 6.0	Communication from program to program, with a peer-to-peer relationship between programs. Used for host-to-host communications using either CICS or IMS subsystems.
LU 6.1	Same as LU 6.0.
LU 6.2	Communications from program to program, with a peer-to-peer relationship between programs. Used for dialog-oriented connections that use the General Data Stream (GDS) format. Also known as APPC.
LU 7	Data Stream terminals used on AS/400, System 36, System 38, and so on.

LU-LU (Logical Unit to Logical Unit) Connection

In IBM's SNA (Systems Network Architecture), an LU is an entry point into a network—for example, a program. An LU-LU connection represents communication between two LUs. The relationship between the participants in the communication depends on the types of LUs involved. (Table "Logical Unit Types" in the entry for LU summarizes the main types of LUs and the types of communications they can have.)

L

When both LUs are programs, the main issue is whether the programs communicate as peers or whether they operate in a master-slave relationship. For example, LU 4 types may use either a peer-to-peer or a master-slave relationship; in contrast, LU 3 types communicate with devices and use a master-slave connection.

→ *Broader Category* SNA (Systems Network Architecture)

→ *See Also* LU (Logical Unit)

LUNI (LAN Emulation User-to-Network Interface)

LAN emulation, or LANE, is a service developed to enable an emulated Ethernet or Token Ring network to run on top of an Asynchronous Transfer Mode (ATM) network. The crucial activities for such an emulation take place at a LAN emulation layer, which presents a LAN-like media access control (MAC) layer to the emulated LAN (ELAN) and a different appearance to the ATM network below it—on which all this LAN activity is taking place.

In such an emulation, server and clients communicate through a LAN Emulation User-to-Network Interface (LUNI, or sometimes L-UNI), and ELANs communicate with each other through a LAN Emulation Network-to-Network Interface (LNNI, L-NNI, or LENNI).

→ *Broader Categories* ATM (Asynchronous Transfer Mode); Ethernet; LANE (Local Area Network Emulation); Token Ring

→ *See Also* LANE (Local Area Network Emulation)

Lurking

On a network or an internetwork, lurking is listening without participating in an interactive user forum, special interest group, or newsgroup.

Lycos

Lycos is many things to many people, and is very successful at all of them. Lycos is a portal, an information service, and a World Wide Web search engine.

As a portal, Lycos is the first site many users see when accessing the Web. This means that Lycos gets first crack at delivering information, financial, entertainment, or other channels (thematically selected information delivered automatically using push technology). More important, for many of the parties involved, it also means advertisements at the Lycos portal will be the first ones any users going through Lycos will see. In terms of advertising real estate, screen space in a portal is prime property. As one of the four major portals for the Web, Lycos gets its fair share of about a quarter of a billion hits per day.

As an information service, Lycos provides news and other channels to which users can subscribe, and through which they can get daily information updates about topics of interest. Most such services are free to the subscriber because the channels are financed by advertisements. Certain specialized subscriptions do have fees associated with them.

As a Web search engine, Lycos seeks out and returns URLs (Uniform Resource Locators, which are essentially addresses for objects on the Web) pertaining to a topic a user specifies. This means an information seeker can use Lycos to find references to hypertext documents or other materials that satisfy the search criteria the user specifies. Lycos has Web agents that regularly retrieve information about many of the more than 800 million or so articles on the Web. This information must be updated frequently to help keep up with the rapid pace of growth on the Web. To give you a sense of this growth, the last edition of this book mentioned the six million or so articles (that is, Web pages) on the Web. Over that time period, the Web has grown at an average rate of over 800,000 pages per day.

Lycos allows you to specify a search string or to fill out a form to set search criteria. You can search either a small or a large catalog of documents. To access Lycos, set a Web browser to the following URL:

`http://www.lycos.com`

"Lycos home page" shows what this URL looks like at the time of this writing.

→**Broader Category** Portal; Search Engine

→**Compare** WWWW (World Wide Web Worm); Yahoo!

Lynx

Lynx is a character-based browser (hypertext file reader) for UNIX and other platforms. While Lynx cannot display graphics, it does give you the option of saving images on disk for later examination with an appropriate viewer program.

To use Lynx, just type the program name at a UNIX prompt. On the same line, specify the Web server you want to use. Once started, Lynx will display the requested home page, but without graphics. Where a graphics-based browser would display an image, Lynx will simply have "[image]" or some other text designed into the page.

→**Broader Category** Browser

→**Compare** Mosaic; MSIE (Microsoft Internet Explorer); Netscape Navigator

LYCOS HOME PAGE

L

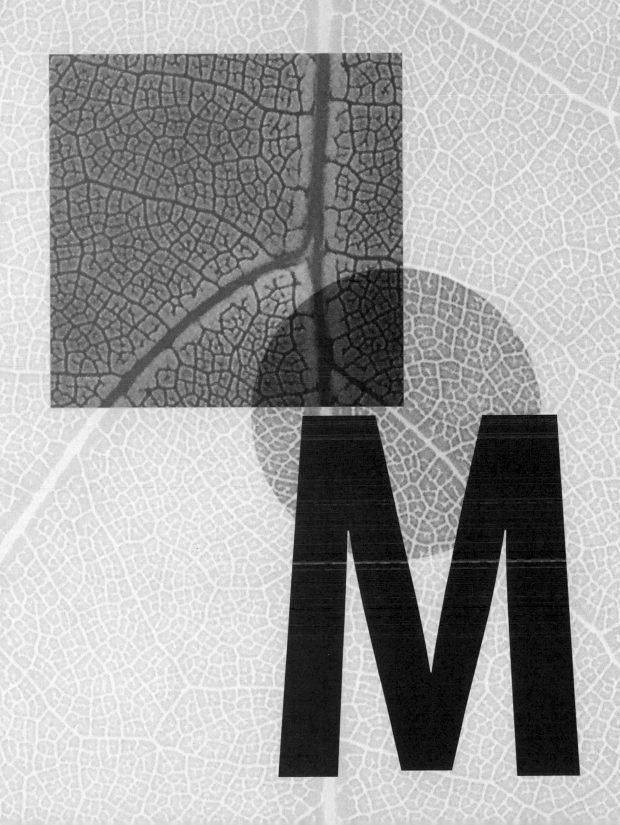

M

In uppercase, an abbreviation for the prefix *mega*, as in MHz (megahertz) or Mbps (megabits per second). This order of magnitude corresponds to millions, which is 10^6 or $2^{20,}$ when binary values are involved. In lowercase, *m* is used as an abbreviation for the prefix *milli*, as in msec (millisecond) or mA (milliampere). This order of magnitude corresponds to one thousandth, which is 10^{-3}, or 2^{-10} for binary values.

→ *See Also* Order of Magnitude

M13

In telecommunications, the method used to multiplex 28 T1 (1.544Mbps) channels into a T3 (44.736Mbps) channel.

→ *See Also* T1 Carrier

MAC (Media Access Control)

In the IEEE 802.*x* networking model, the lower sublayer of the OSI Data-Link layer. The MAC and the LLC (logical link control) sublayer above it provide higher-level protocols (such as TCP/IP or IPX/SPX) with access to the physical network medium.

→ *See Also* OSI Reference Model

MAC Convergence Function (MCF)

→ *See* MCF (MAC Convergence Function)

Mach

Mach is an operating system created at Carnegie-Mellon University. A UNIX variant, Mach is based on the BSD 4.3 version developed at UC Berkeley. Although it has UNIX roots, Mach was written from scratch, and it was designed to support advanced features such as multiprocessing (support for multiple processors, or CPUs) and multitasking (the ability to work on more than one task at a time).

Mach is also significant for introducing the microkernel as an alternative to the traditional operating system kernel, which is much larger and feature-filled. The NeXTSTEP operating system is a version of Mach implemented originally on NeXT computers and now ported to Intel processors.

Macintosh

Macintosh is the shared name for a family of graphics-based computers from Apple. These computers have been built around the Motorola 680*x*0 family of processors (for example, the 68030 or 68040) and, more recently, the PowerPC chip.

The rather large Macintosh family consists of several classes of computers, with high- and low-end models in most classes.

Models in the classic series look similar to the original Macintosh, released in 1984. Examples include the Classic and Classic II, as well as the LC (for low-cost color) and LC II. For both monochrome and color versions, the II versions are higher-end models than the others, but neither is very high-end when compared with other classes in the family.

Models in the desktop Mac II line look more streamlined than models from the classic line. These models also include one or more NuBus expansion slots. Compact versions have the screen and computer in a single unit. At the low end are the Mac II, MacIIx, and MacIIcx, which use 68030 or earlier versions of the processor. High-end desktop machines can be found in the Quadra series, whose members have a 68040 processor.

Models in the portable PowerBook lines are self-contained, lightweight machines. Low-end models include the PowerBook 100 and the PowerBook 140. Higher-end models include the PowerBook 180.

Models in the PowerPC series use a RISC (reduced instruction set computing) processor built through a joint effort of Apple, IBM, and Motorola. Models include the Power Macintosh 6100/60, 7100/66, 8100/80, and G3. These machines include emulation software that enables DOS and Microsoft Windows programs to run on the machine.

Macintosh Networking Capabilities

All but the earliest Macintoshes come with built-in networking capabilities, so these machines require no special network interface cards (NICs) or adapters. By default, Macintoshes use AppleTalk as their networking system, with support for several different network architectures at the data-link level. You will need a NIC if you intend to use something other than AppleTalk as the networking software and LocalTalk as the data-link architecture.

Macintosh File Format

A Macintosh file has two distinct types of information associated with it: data and resources. The contents are stored in *forks*.

The *data fork* contains the actual file information, such as the text that makes up a letter or the code that makes up a program. When a PC reads a Macintosh file, only the data fork is read.

In addition to a data fork, a Macintosh file has a *resource fork,* which contains the resources (applications, windows, drivers, and so on) that are used with the file. Non-Macintosh environments ordinarily are not designed to deal with the resource fork. However, under certain circumstances, non-Macintosh environments may store the resource forks. For example, a NetWare server can store both data and resource forks for Macintosh files if the Macintosh name space is loaded on the server. DOS workstations can access the Macintosh files through the appropriate applications, but they will not handle the files in the same way as on a Macintosh.

Despite the difference in format, most network operating systems have provisions for storing, or at least accessing, Macintosh files.

→ *Related Articles* AppleTalk, LocalTalk

WARNING: MANIPULATING ALIEN FILES

Be sure to use the *network* operating system commands (rather than DOS commands) when moving, copying, or otherwise manipulating files with an alien format on a network.

For example, don't use the DOS COPY command to copy a Macintosh file. If you do, only the data fork will be copied. Use Novell NetWare's NCOPY command instead.

Macintosh Client

A Macintosh computer connected to a network. For example, a Macintosh client may be connected to a Novell NetWare network. If a NetWare server is running NetWare for Macintosh modules, the Macintosh can retrieve files from that server. A Macintosh client can also run executable Macintosh files on the network.

Macintosh File System (MFS)

→ *See* MFS (Macintosh File System)

Macromedia Dreamweaver

Macromedia's Dreamweaver is among a growing group of products that provide total—or almost total—control over the design, creation, and maintenance of Web sites. This feature-rich tool provides a certain degree of product security by making it possible to control who gets access to what elements of a project and for what purposes. For example, only certain members of a development team will need access to the actual HTML (Hypertext Markup Language) or XML (eXtensible Markup Language) source code that contains most of the information for generating the actual Web pages on the site. Access to the source code can be controlled so that only those people who need to get to work with it. This is a project management feature that helps ensure the integrity of the final product—namely, the Web site.

M

Dreamweaver Operation

Dreamweaver—now in its second major version, as Dreamweaver 2—includes the components necessary to create a Web site built on HTML or XML documents. This might include cascading style sheets, script files, applets, image files, animation, sounds, and video. Dreamweaver distinguishes itself from all but the one or two other top-notch products in this genre by how well the product fulfills the usability requirement.

Specifically, Dreamweaver's development tools are designed to make it easy to create the content and layout for the Web site—without necessarily knowing anything about HTML or XML. In addition, however, the Dreamweaver environment also enables an advanced user to get considerable control over a Web page by making it possible and easy to work with the actual source code from which the Web pages will be built. In fact, Dreamweaver includes other features that enhance usability. These are discussed later in this section.

Using Dreamweaver's visual authoring environment, a Web designer can specify what components are needed for a Web page and also how these components are to fit together. On the first pass, this process can be as simple as selecting elements, dragging them to the required location, and dropping them there. Once this is done, the resulting product can be fine-tuned and edited to get it exactly the way the designer wants it.

Even much of the fine-tuning can be done without having to muck around in the source code. For example, Dreamweaver makes exact placement of page elements easy to do by using layers to hold and manipulate different content elements. This activity is functionally equivalent to doing design and layout for an ordinary (printed) page. Thus, someone familiar with standard desktop publishing tools such as Adobe PageMaker or Photoshop will feel comfortable working in Dreamweaver. (The results of the developer's work will be translated into frame- and table-based HTML code to make exact positioning easier. However a Web page developer can do a fine job without knowing how this is done—or without even being aware *that* it is done.)

Because it's possible to establish a relationship between table elements and layers, Dreamweaver actually provides a very handy feature—support for something known as a tracing image—that makes it much easier to turn a preliminary design sketch for the Web page into the actual page. The preliminary layout sketch may be created with a product such as Photoshop. Once created, the design sketch can be used as a background in Dreamweaver. The actual page can then be laid out simply by arranging the page elements over the background. The components in the tracing image can be treated as elements in a table; these elements can be associated with layers, and the layers can then be manipulated as necessary to get the desired layout exactly right.

With Dreamweaver, it's possible to create dynamic Web pages that can be updated on the fly—for example, with the most up-to-date information—when the page is actually to be delivered to a browser. You can also create interactive pages that can accept input from users sitting at the other end of a browser looking at your Web page.

As the site is designed, Dreamweaver generates the required (HTML or XML) code to provide the materials and layout instructions for the site. This code can be edited—by working directly with the source. Dreamweaver's Roundtrip HTML makes it possible to do this easily—by enabling the editor to see immediately what the effects of source changes will be. In fact, the user can make the changes in the visual environment, see what results they produce, and also see the modified HTML code.

Other Dreamweaver Features

As stated, Dreamweaver is rich in features, so we can list only some of the main ones here. The following is a list of some of the more important, useful, and interesting Dreamweaver features:

- Integrated tools, which include a platform-specific HTML editor (Allaire's HomeSite 4 for Windows environments and BBEdit from Bare Bones for the Macintosh platform), as well as tools for scripting, creating Java applets, and for dealing with XML elements.

- Site map generation. Dreamweaver can generate a site map—that is, a reference that provides an overview of the Web site. The site map shows what pages are connected to what other pages. From this information, you can determine something about both the content and the organization of the site.

- Support for both the established HTML and also the up-and-coming XML languages. In fact, Dreamweaver makes use of XML's ability to serve as a front end for accessing data elements to simplify the Web page editing process.

- Extensive editing functionality, including global search and replace, and support for regular expressions for editing Web content. You can use Dreamweaver's site map to edit the layout of the site—for example, by changing connections among the individual pages on the site.

- Dream templates, which provide predesigned layout elements, and which make it easier to separate the page's style from its content. Various developments in the past few years—most noticeably, the development of cascading style sheets (CSS), and the increasing use of document type definition (DTD) files and of XML—have shown the advantages of separating form and content.

- Special effects—such as rollovers—through the use of scripts or applets.

- WYSIWYS (What-You-See-Is-What-You-Serve), which makes it possible to create a dynamic Web page, and then see exactly how that page will look to a user through that user's browser.

- Playing well with others, which enables Dreamweaver to work smoothly with third-party products.

All in all, Dreamweaver provides a very useful collection of tools and capabilities for designing and building a Web site. Dreamweaver's most direct competition comes from products such as Elemental Software's DrumBeat (now DrumBeat 2000) and Fusion from NetObjects. See the Resources section in Appendix B for the URL listing Macromedia products.

→ *Broader Category*   Web Publishing

Macromedia Lingo

Lingo is a very powerful scripting language developed for use in products such as Macromedia Director 7 Shockwave Internet Studio. While Lingo is a proprietary language, Macromedia has tried to make it similar to more widely used "standard" languages such as JavaScript (or ECMAScript, as it is known in its official version).

→ *Broader Category*   Scripting Language

→ *See Also*   JavaScript; VBScript

Macromedia Shockwave

Shockwave is a product that can deliver multimedia content quickly and automatically. In particular, Shockwave can deliver audio, animation, or other bandwidth-heavy materials to any browser with access to a Shockwave plug-in. Shockwave can be delivered as a plug-in, or it can be integrated with a browser—as in release 5 of Microsoft Internet Explorer (MSIE5).

Shockwave can automatically update itself if it needs to deliver content to an older version. This makes it possible to have recent versions that will include the latest features and fixes.

Macro Virus

A macro virus is one that spreads within files created by applications that support macro languages—for example, Word documents or Excel spreadsheets. The first macro viruses began to

M

appear in 1994. They worked by simply masquerading as macros used in standard document styles. Since then, such viruses have become much more sophisticated—as was demonstrated in March 1999, by the Melissa virus and the variants that followed it.

Melissa disabled the macro protection that had been built into Word largely because of the threat of macro viruses. The virus also sent copies of itself in documents to the first 50 e-mail addresses in the infected user's address book. Beyond some insertions that occurred under special circumstances, Melissa did no actual damage directly to user files.

However, by turning off macro protection, Melissa did potentially open the door to other viruses. Also, by sending out multiple copies of itself from each infection site, the virus worked like a chain letter, and it quickly slowed down or completely crashed mail servers at more than 100 companies. By sending itself out in documents from the user's system, Melissa could conceivably have sent out confidential information just by chance. Also, while Melissa did no direct damage, there is no guarantee that variants won't do something more malicious.

Microsoft Word in its various versions is arguably the most popular target of macro viruses. However, similar types of attacks can be made on spreadsheet files and also on non-Microsoft applications. Because such viruses infect files that are often exchanged over networks or by e-mail, macro viruses can spread very quickly. This is especially true if the virus masquerades as a macro that is used by other documents of the same type.

→ *Broader Category* Virus

→ *See Also* Melissa Virus

MAFP (Multicast Attribute Framing Protocol)

→ *See* Protocol, MAFP (Multicast Attribute Framing Protocol)

Mailbomb

A very large file or a very large number of messages sent to an e-mail address as a prank or in an effort to crash the recipient's mail program.

Mailbot

An automated mail server—also known as an *infoserver*. A mailbot is a program that can automatically carry out actions specified in an e-mail message or reply to e-mail requesting specific information. The mailbot is activated by an incoming message addressed to the program. A common name for such a infoserver is *info* (surprise, surprise).

Mailbox

A file or directory used to store electronic mail messages.

Mail Bridge

A device that connects two networks and filters mail transmissions between them. Only mail that meets specified criteria will be passed from one network to the other. The two networks need not be using the same mail protocol. If they use different protocols, however, the mail bridge needs to be able to handle both protocols.

Mail Delivery System

A mail delivery system consists of the elements needed to get electronic mail (e-mail) from one location to another. The following elements may be used in a mail delivery system:

Mail server A program that manages delivery of mail or other information, upon request. Mail servers are generally implemented at the topmost layer (the applications layer) in the OSI reference model.

Mail directory   The directory for a network in which each user on a network has a unique electronic mailbox. This mailbox, which is usually a subdirectory, is used to store e-mail messages until the mailbox owner is ready to read them.

Mailbox   A directory provided to store messages for a single user. Each e-mail user has a unique ID and a unique mailbox. A mailbox is more commonly referred to as an *electronic mailbox*.

Mail exploder   A program used to deliver a message to all the addresses on a mailing list, which is a list containing addresses for all the destinations for a message. With a mail exploder available, a user just needs to send a message to a single address. The mail exploder will make sure that all names on the relevant mailing list get the message.

E-mail is not always intended for a local user, or even for someone using the same kind of mail server. Because of such complexities, there may be routing or translation difficulties. To help avoid or overcome these types of obstacles, a *mail gateway* can be used to connect two or more e-mail services. Mail gateways generally use a store-and-forward scheme to transfer mail between services.

The mail services connected by a gateway may be similar or dissimilar. Gateways that connect similar mail services are known as *mail bridges*. One reason for using a store-and-forward strategy is to give the gateway time to translate messages before passing them to a different mail service.

Another device that can be used to connect multiple e-mail environments to each other is a *mail switch*. A mail switch can route an input e-mail message to the appropriate output system. In addition to making the connection and passing the materials, a mail switch may also need to translate the messages from one e-mail format to another. In many cases, mail switches write the input to a standardized intermediate format, such as MHS or the X.400 format. The intermediate version is then translated into the output format.

In many ways, mail switches are coming to replace gateways. Most mail switches run on a minicomputer or a RISC (reduced instruction set computing) machine for better performance.

Mail Exchange (MX) Record

→ *See*   MX (Mail Exchange) Record

Mailing List

In a message-handling or an electronic mail (e-mail) service, a mailing list is a list of e-mail addresses. For example, a mailing list might contain the addresses of users interested in a specific topic. Messages about the topic can be sent automatically to all the addresses.

The delivery of messages to the addresses on a mailing list is handled by a *mail exploder*. On some networks, particularly those with heavy network traffic, a human may be asked first to determine whether the message should be transmitted to the entire mailing list. Manual filtering of messages can greatly reduce network traffic.

SUBSCRIBING TO MAILING LISTS

You can subscribe to, or join, special-interest mailing lists so that you will receive information about specific topics. When you do, it's important to observe the guidelines and etiquette associated with the list.

For example, you should adhere to these basic guidelines:

- Follow the local rules for joining or quitting a mailing list.

- Quit the list when you're no longer interested in the topic that binds the list members. This cuts down on the electronic junk mail traffic, and also saves you the chore of wading through the messages.

- Refrain from repeating messages that have already been distributed to the addresses on the mailing list.

M

Main Distribution Frame (MDF)

→ **See** MDF (Main Distribution Frame)

Major Resource

In a NetWare 4.*x* environment, a category of data used to guide backups. For example, a server or a volume might be categorized as a major resource. The data in a major resource can be backed up as a single group. Subdivisions within a major resource, such as directories or subdirectories, are known as *minor resources*.

MAN (Metropolitan Area Network)

A MAN is a network with a maximum range of about 75 kilometers (45 miles) or so, and with high-speed transmission capabilities. Most MANs include some type of telecommunications components and activity to handle long-distance transmissions. Because the distances are generally short enough to incur minimal telecommunications costs, the connections usually use very high-speed lines, such as T3, at almost 45Mbps.

MANs versus LANs and WANs

MANs have much in common with two other network categories: local area networks (LANs) and wide area networks (WANs). The following are the major differences:

- MANs generally involve higher speeds and greater distances than LANs.

- Unlike LANs, MANs generally include provisions for both voice and data transmissions.

- MANs generally involve higher speeds than WANs.

MANs often include several LANs connected to each other via telephone lines. "A MAN made up of several LANs connected by high-speed lines" shows such an arrangement.

MAN Architecture

Most MAN networks use either of two network architectures:

- FDDI (Fiber Distributed Data Interface), which supports transmission speeds of 100-plus Mbps, uses a dual-ring topology, and has optical fiber as the medium.

- DQDB (Distributed Queue Dual Bus), which is specified in IEEE 802.6. DQDB supports transmission speeds ranging from 50 to 600Mbps over distances as large as 50 kilometers (30 miles). As the name implies, DQDB uses a two-bus topology.

→ **Related Articles** DQDB (Distributed Queue Dual Bus); FDDI (Fiber Distributed Data Interface)

→ **See Also** LAN (Local Area Network); WAN (Wide Area Network)

Managed Object

In a network management model, any element in the network that can be managed (used or monitored). In addition to objects such as nodes, hubs, and so on, less tangible elements—services and protocols, files and programs, and even algorithms and connections—are also considered managed objects.

→ **See Also** Network Management

Management Domain (MD)

→ **See** MD (Management Domain)

Management Information Base (MIB)

→ **See** MIB (Management Information Base)

Managing Process

In network management, the managing process is the software that is in charge of management chores. The managing process initiates the requests for data and performs any supported and requested analyses on the data.

The managing process requests data and reports from *managing agents*. These agents are programs that monitor the activity of network stations with respect to whatever attributes are of interest and report the data from this monitoring to the managing process.

The programs for each managing agent (also known as a *management* agent) generally run on the node the agent is monitoring.

A managing process executes on the *managing station*, which is the machine collecting the performance data.

→ *See Also* Network Management

Manufacturing Automation Protocol (MAP)

→ *See* MAP (Manufacturing Automation Protocol)

Manufacturing Message Service (MMS)

→ *See* MMS (Manufacturing Message Service)

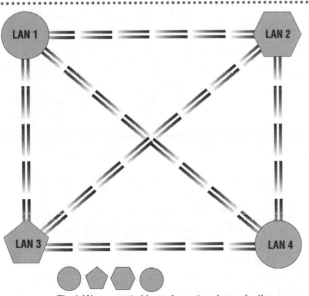

The LANs connected in such a network may be the same or different.

Because different types of LANs can be involved, connections to high-speed lines can take many forms. Bridges, routers, gateways, and switches are the most common connections.

A MAN MADE UP OF SEVERAL LANS CONNECTED BY HIGH-SPEED LINES

M

MAP (Manufacturing Automation Protocol)

MAP is a specification for how to automate tasks in computer integrated manufacturing (CIM) and other factory contexts. An early version of MAP was formulated by General Motors to guide its own procurement strategies. Subsequent development was expanded to include input from other companies as well as from technical organizations. By agreement, the MAP 3.0 specifications were left unchanged for a six-year period, which ended in 1994. These specifications were expected to undergo numerous revisions. However, the rapid development of the Internet, and of the World Wide Web in particular, have taken business processes, including manufacturing, in other directions. As a result, the manufacturing model underlying MAP has become more limited in its influence, and the MAP standard has become obsolescent.

MAP Network Types

Three types of networks are distinguished in the MAP model:

Type 1   These networks connect mainframes, minicomputers, and PCs operating at the highest levels in the automation hierarchy. The main tasks are information management, task scheduling, and resource allocation. Electronic mail (e-mail) and files are exchanged, and database operations may be carried out. This type of network does not involve time-critical activity.

Type 2   These networks connect work cells and workstations. The devices serve as process or machine controllers. They exchange programs, alarms, and synchronization signals. Certain exchanges are time-critical.

Type 3   These networks connect machines and their components, including individual sensors or actuators and the machine's controllers for these components. The components must operate in real-time, and must be able to operate in full-duplex mode; that is, being able to transmit in both directions at the same time. Commands and data are exchanged constantly but almost always in small chunks, because of the real-time restrictions.

The MAP network types differ in the following ways:

- The manufacturing hierarchy level at which the network is defined. The upper levels correspond to offices and shops. Intermediate levels correspond to work cells and stations (machines). The lowest levels correspond to individual pieces of equipment (components).

- The type of equipment involved. At the higher levels, mainframes and other large computers plod along at their own paces to process data destined to determine corporate destinies. At the lower levels, simple processors work in real-time to give specific commands and to pass simple data values.

- The kind of traffic on the network. This may be file transfers, database operations, e-mail, programs, data, commands, and so on. At the upper levels, information and general plans are exchanged; at the lower levels, data and specific commands are exchanged.

MAP Network Components

The MAP 3.0 specifications define three types of end systems in MAP networks: FullMAP, MiniMAP, and EPA.

FullMAP System

FullMAP stations are used in Type 1 networks, where time is not a factor. These stations use a full protocol suite for their activities, as shown in "Protocol suite for FullMAP stations."

MiniMAP System

MiniMAP stations are used in Type 2 and 3 networks, which may handle time-critical traffic. In order to speed things up sufficiently, these nodes communicate with a barebones protocol suite, as shown in "Protocol suite for MiniMAP stations."

The MiniMAP protocol suite includes only the top layer and the bottom two layers from the OSI hierarchy. The four middle layers are not used. This has important consequences in addition to speeding up communications:

- Only certain application level protocols are allowed.

- No routing is possible, so packets must stay within a network segment.

- Full-duplex communication is necessary, because there is no session control.

- No packet fragmentation is possible, since there is no Transport layer to do the fragmenting and reconstructing.

EPA System

In the EPA (Enhanced Performance Architecture) system, elements are defined in order to provide a mediator between the incompatible FullMAP and MiniMAP devices. EPA objects use a protocol suite that supports both the FullMAP and MiniMAP suites.

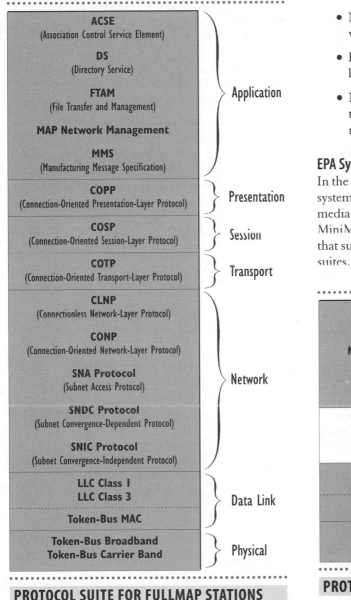

PROTOCOL SUITE FOR FULLMAP STATIONS

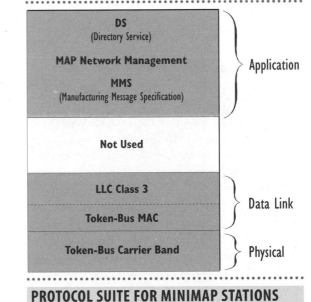

PROTOCOL SUITE FOR MINIMAP STATIONS

M

MAPI (Messaging Application Programming Interface)

An interface for messaging and mail services. Microsoft's MAPI provides functions for using Microsoft Mail within a Microsoft Windows application. Simple MAPI consists of 12 functions, such as *MapiDeleteMail(), MapiReadMail(), and MapiSendMail().* By calling these functions in the appropriate manner and combination, a Windows application can address, send, and receive mail messages while running.

Mapping

The process of assigning a drive letter to a particular logical disk drive.

→ *See* Drive Mapping and Search Drives

Margin

In a signal transmission, the allowance for a certain amount of signal loss, either through attenuation or over time.

Markup Language

A markup language is used to label sections of a file for special handling when the file is processed by an appropriate program. Markup elements are generally embedded in the file being marked up, although certain types of markups can be included in separate files, and can be read in prior to processing the document.

For example, markup labels could be embedded in a file to indicate sections of a document that should be in italics or boldface, or elements in a file could be identified as fields describing a purchase by a customer. In the first example, the markup instructions would be carried out when the document is displayed or printed by a browser. In the second example, the

file elements might be identified in order to generate a bill to send to the customer.

Markup languages may differ in their focus. Some—for example, HTML (Hypertext Markup Language)—are presentation-oriented, with commands that are used to specify document layout. Others—for example, XML (eXtensible Markup Language) applications—are oriented more toward identifying the document's structure, for indexing or processing by special-purpose programs. (XML is, in fact, a language for creating special-purpose markup languages, which are known as XML applications. HTML could have been created as an XML application.)

Examples of markup languages include CML (Chemical Markup Language), HTML, LaTeX, MathML (Mathematical Markup Language), and TeX. SGML (Standard Generalized Markup Languages) and XML are often also included as markup languages. They are, more accurately, languages for creating markup languages, which are known as applications. While HTML, CML, and MathML are all examples of markup languages, HTML is an SGML application, whereas CML and MathML are XML applications. (XML is a subset of SGML.)

Electronic markup languages—the actual focus of this entry—are not the only kind of markup languages. The rules and notation used by developmental and copy editors also comprise a markup language, whose rules are determined by a style or grammar guide. The instructions specified using such a language are carried out when the manuscript is put through production.

→ *See Also* CML (Chemical Markup Language); HTML (Hypertext Markup Language); MathML (Mathematical Markup Language); XML (eXtensible Markup Language).

Markup Tag

A markup tag is a formatting or inclusion command that is embedded as an annotation in a file being edited. The tag is an instruction for some type of processing or reading program—for example, a typesetting package or a Web browser (hypertext file reader).

Although the tags are visible in the original file, the effects of the tags are not. They are not visible to the user, or to anyone else, until the file is passed through the appropriate program. Such markup systems are in contrast to WYSIWYG (what you see is what you get) environments in which formatting commands are implemented immediately so that the user can see the effects right away.

Editing environments that use markup tags include such languages as TeX, SGML (Standard Generalized Markup Language), XML (eXtensible Markup Language), and HTML (Hypertext Markup Language). Of these, HTML is currently the language getting the most attention, because it is used to create hypertext pages for the World Wide Web (WWW).

In HTML, tags represent instructions about the document's structure and elements and about links to other documents or to other places in the file. Tags are denoted by placing them within angle brackets, or <> . HTML tags may be empty or nonempty.

- An *empty tag*—for example, <HR> or <P>—takes no arguments. Thus, the first tag (<HR>) is an instruction to draw a horizontal line at the location where the instruction was found. Similarly, <P> indicates a paragraph break.

- A *nonempty tag*—for example, <B>—applies only to certain elements or portions of text. This "scope" of influence is indicated by having a second version of a tag to indicate the end of the tag's influence. Ending tags are identical to their starting counterparts, except that they have a forward slash after the opening left angle bracket. For example, the tag </B> ends the section of text that began with <B>. All text between these two tags is written in boldface.

Masquerade

A security threat in which a user, process, or device pretends to be a different one. For example, a process may pretend to be the password-checking program in order to intercept user passwords; a user may pretend to be a different user (generally someone who rarely logs in or who has a very easy-to-guess password).

Master Domain Model

In Windows NT, the master domain model is one of four possible models for organizing and administering networks. In the master domain model, all user accounts are centralized in a single domain. Resources, however, may be decentralized and administered independently of each other. Thus, a master domain model has one accounts domain but may have multiple resource domains.

In trust relationships for this model, the trust flows toward the master domain. That is, the accounts domain is the trusted one, and the resource domains are the trusting ones.

The master domain model can be used only for networks with fewer than about 40,000 users. The other NT domain models are the complete trust domain model, the multiple master domain model, and the single domain model.

→ *Broader Categories* Domain Model; Windows NT

→ *Compare* Complete Trust Domain Model; Multiple Master Domain Model; Single Domain Model

Master Group

In PSTNs (Public Switched Telephone Networks), multiple calls are squeezed into a single wire pair using frequency division multiplexing (FDM). Such multiplexed signals are grouped into larger units in a hierarchy defined originally for the Bell Telephone System.

M

The FDM hierarchy is as follows:

Group   12 analog voice calls multiplexed onto a single wire pair.

Supergroup   5 groups—that is, 60 voice channels.

Master group   10 supergroups—that is, 600 voice channels.

Jumbo group   6 master groups—that is, 3600 voice channels.

Mathematical Markup Language (MML)

→ *See*   MathML (Mathematical Markup Language)

MathML (Mathematical Markup Language)

MathML is an XML (eXtensible Markup Language) application that was developed to make it easier to create and process documents with mathematical content. MathML consists mainly of a vocabulary for presenting various types of expressions and symbols.

You can find the official MathML recommendation at www.w3.org/TR/REC-MathML.

→ *Broader Category*   XML (eXtensible Markup Language)

Mating

The physical linking of two connectors to establish a connection. Since mechanical parts are involved in this linkage, there will be wear and tear on the connectors, and the quality of the connection may eventually deteriorate.

→ *See Also*   Connector; Connector, Fiber-Optic

MAU (Medium Attachment Unit)

In the IEEE 802.3 specifications, a MAU refers to a transceiver.

MAU (Multistation Access Unit)

MAU (sometimes abbreviated MSAU) is IBM's term for a wiring hub in its Token Ring architecture. This hub serves as the termination point for multiple nodes and can be connected to the network or to another hub, as illustrated in "MAUs in a Token Ring network."

Each MAU can have up to eight nodes (*lobes* in IBM's terminology) connected, and each MAU can be connected to other MAUs. The MAU has connectors for the lobes and two special connectors—ring in (RI) and ring out (RO)—for connecting MAUs to each other. A MAU organizes the nodes connected to it into an internal ring, and uses the RI and RO connectors to extend the ring across MAUs.

When MAUs are connected, it is possible to create a main and a secondary ring path. This redundancy can be helpful if the main ring path breaks. In that case, packets can be routed via the secondary ring path.

In the process of passing packets around the ring, a MAU can clean and boost a signal; that is, it can serve as a repeater. MAUs differ in the additional capabilities they provide.

The most widely supported MAU standard is that for IBM's MAU model 8228. You will often see references to "8228-compliant MAUs." This standard serves as a common denominator; it is a minimal set of capabilities that just about all MAUs support. Most MAUs have capabilities beyond those of the 8228. These capabilities can make a network more efficient, but can also increase the likelihood of compatibility problems.

Most MAUs have LEDs (light-emitting diodes) to indicate the status of each port (lobe) on the MAU. MAUs can automatically disconnect faulty lobes, without affecting the other lobes or disrupting the network.

Lobes are connected to MAUs using Type 1, 2, or 3 IBM cable. Because Type 3 cable is unshielded, you also need a media filter between the cable and the MAU, to clean certain noise from the signals before they reach the MAU. Type 6 cable is sometimes used to connect MAUs to each other, provided the distance between MAUs is just a few meters.

When using IBM Type 1 or 2 cable, more than 30 MAUs may be connected, supporting up to 260 nodes altogether. When using IBM Type 3 cable, up to 9 MAUs can be connected, supporting up to 72 nodes altogether.

→ **Broader Category** Token Ring

Maximum Burst Size (MBS)

→ **See** MBS (Maximum Burst Size)

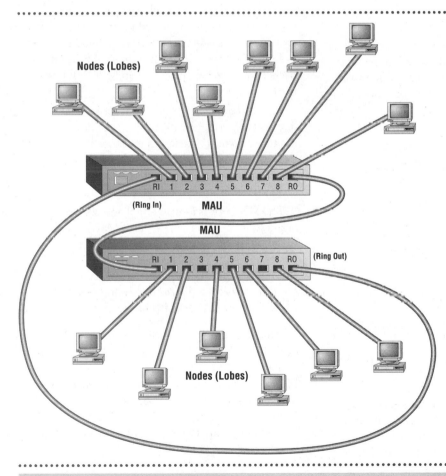

MAUS IN A TOKEN RING NETWORK

M

Maximum Receive Unit (MRU)

→ *See* MRU (Maximum Receive Unit)

Maximum Rights Mask (MRM)

→ *See* MRM (Maximum Rights Mask)

Maximum Transmission Unit (MTU)

→ *See* MTU (Maximum Transmission Unit)

M-Bit

In X.25 communications, an M-bit (for more data bit) is set in a data packet if the packet cannot fit all the data to be transmitted so that one or more additional data packets need to be sent.

MBONE (Multicast Backbone)

The MBONE is a multicast network that adds live audio and video capabilities to the Internet. A multicast network is one in which a packet is sent to all addresses on a subscriber or other type of list. This is in contrast to a unicast network (in which only a single user gets the packet at a time) and to a broadcast network (in which a packet is sent to all users, regardless of whether they are on lists or not).

The MBONE is a virtual network that sits on top of the Internet and provides multicast and real-time capabilities. The MBONE is organized as clusters ("islands") of networks that can support multicast IP (Internet Protocol) transmissions.

These islands are connected via *tunnels*, which are paths between endpoints that support multicast transmissions. Although the tunnel generally goes through ordinary (i.e., non-multicast) networks it does provide a virtual point-to-point connection between the endpoints. These are usually ordinary workstations that can run *mrouted* (multicast routing daemon) programs.

Because of its multicast capabilities, the MBONE can be used to reach large audiences, and can be used for two-way communications in real time. Real-time capabilities mean that voice or video data can be exchanged. In fact, the IETF (Internet Engineering Task Force) currently broadcasts its conferences over the MBONE. The MBONE requires special hardware, and it uses special protocols to handle the multicast packets quickly and efficiently.

The MBONE can cause potential security problems. One reason is that multicast packets are often encapsulated (stuffed) into ordinary Internet Protocol (IP) packets—so they can be transmitted through ordinary (i.e., non-MBONE) routers. The multicast packet will then be removed at an MBONE host for further processing.

This strategy causes a problem for security devices (such as firewalls) that check addresses, but not the contents of packages that travel through them. With such a setup, it would be possible to send a rogue packet past a firewall by putting it into an MBONE transmission.

The MBONE is international and considerably larger than most networks. As of May 1994, the MBONE spanned 20 countries and had over 900 routers. (You can get a PostScript graphic showing the high-level MBONE topology by using anonymous ftp to get the file /mbone/mbone-top.ps from the ftp.isi.edu ftp site.)

→ *Primary Sources* The most recent FAQ (frequently asked question) file is available by getting /mbone/faq.txt from the ftp.isi.edu ftp site. Hypertext documents are available from http://www.research.att.com/mbone-faq.html and from http://www.cl.cam.ac.uk/mbone/ in the United Kingdom. Other information sources are listed in the FAQ file.

MBS (Maximum Burst Size)

In traffic management for ATM (Asynchronous Transfer Mode), the MBS is a parameter that indicates how long the connection can sustain traffic at the peak cell rate (PCR)—that is, at maximum speed.

→ *Broader Category* ATM (Asynchronous Transfer Mode)

→ *Compare* MCR (Minimum Cell Rate); PCR (Peak Cell Rate); SCR (Sustainable Cell Rate)

MCF (MAC Convergence Function)

In the DQDB network architecture, a function that is responsible for preparing data from a connectionless service (a service in which each packet is sent independently of other packets, and different packets may take different routes to the same destination).

→ *See Also* DQDB (Distributed Queue Dual Bus)

MCR (Minimum Cell Rate)

In traffic management for ATM (Asynchronous Transfer Mode), the MCR is a parameter that specifies the minimum cell rate that must be provided in order for a connection to be deemed acceptable for a desired quality of service (QoS).

→ *Broader Category* ATM (Asynchronous Transfer Mode)

→ *Compare* MBS (Maximum Burst Size); PCR (Peak Cell Rate); SCR (Sustainable Cell Rate)

MCSE (Microsoft Certified Systems Engineer)

An MCSE is a computing professional who has demonstrated mastery of a range of core and elective topics relating to networking in general and to certain Microsoft products in particular. The topics are specified by Microsoft, and those who hope to become certified must do coursework and pass a set of exams.

Core topics for MCSE certification include networking essentials, Windows NT (Workstation, Server, and Enterprise versions), and Windows 9x. Elective topics include TCP/IP for NT, Microsoft Internet Information Server (IIS), Exchange, SQL Server, and Proxy Server.

Such certification programs have been created by several vendors, including Novell and Cisco, in addition to Microsoft. The programs are designed to ensure that consultants, administrators, and other computer professionals have the necessary training to work effectively with the vendors' products.

MD (Management Domain)

In the CCITT's X.400 Message Handling System (MHS), a limited, but not necessarily contiguous, area whose message-handling capabilities operate under the control of a single management authority. This authority can be the CCITT, a university, an organization, or other group. Two types of management domains are defined: ADMD (Administrative Management Domain) and PRMD (Private Management Domain).

MD5 (Message Digest 5) Algorithm

The MD5 algorithm is an encryption strategy for the Internet's SNMP (Simple Network Management Protocol (SNMP). The algorithm uses a message, an authentication key, and time information to compute a checksum value (the *digest*).

MDAC (Microsoft Data Access Component)

MDAC refers to a collection of add-ons for Windows NT 4. These are included to help in the

M

creation of Internet-based databases for use with database environments such as Oracle and SQL Server. The main MDAC components are the following:

- Microsoft OLE DB, which is middleware that translates OLE (object linking and embedding) function calls into database-specific calls that can be understood by a back-end database driver running on a Web server.

- ADO (ActiveX Data Objects), which are ActiveX components that can be used to communicate through OLE DB to manipulate (retrieve, edit, and restore) elements in an Internet-based database.

- RDS (Remote Data Service), which provides a client-side cache that clients can use to download data sets, manipulate them, and then return them.

MDF (Main Distribution Frame)

The MDF is the central distribution point for the wiring to a building. The wiring from an MDF may be routed to IDFs (intermediate distribution points) or directly to end-users. An MDF is generally located in a wiring closet.

→ *Compare* IDF (Intermediate Distribution Frame)

MDS (Multipoint Distribution Services)

MDS is a wireless distribution service developed in the early 1960s, and intended for video teleconferencing and other activities that can use closed-circuit communications. MDS originally was allowed to operate at a 10MHz bandwidth, but this was expanded to 12MHz (which is sufficient for two 6MHz channels).

The FCC regulates MDS as a common carrier, which makes it possible for MDS providers to rent out airtime or resell programming. In fact, once the bandwidth was increased, MDS became attractive to providers of entertainment video and pay-per-view services.

Mean Time between Failures (MTBF)

→ *See* MTBF (Mean Time between Failures)

Mean Time to Repair (MTTR)

→ *See* MTTR (Mean Time to Repair)

Media Access Control (MAC)

→ *See* MAC (Media Access Control)

Media-Access Method

The media-access method is the strategy used by a node, or station, on a network to access a network's transmission medium. Access methods are defined at the Data-Link layer in the OSI reference model. More specifically, they are defined at the MAC sublayer (as defined by the IEEE). "Media-access methods" shows how these methods fit into the network architecture.

Probabilistic versus Deterministic Access Methods

The two main classes of access methods are probabilistic and deterministic.

With a probabilistic media-access method, a node checks the line when the node wants to transmit. If the line is busy, or if the node's transmission collides with another transmission, the transmission is canceled. The node then waits a random amount of time before trying again.

Probabilistic access methods can be used only in networks in which transmissions are broadcast, so that each node gets a transmission at just about the same time. The best-known probabilistic access method is CSMA/CD (carrier sense multiple access/collision detect), which is used in Ethernet networks.

With a deterministic media-access method, nodes get access to the network in a predetermined sequence. Either a server or the arrangement of the nodes themselves determines the sequence. The two most widely used deterministic access methods are token-passing (used in ARCnet and in Token Ring networks) and polling (used in mainframe environments). Slots and registers are older access methods that have been superseded by token passing in most applications.

In general, probabilistic methods are most suitable for smaller networks with relatively light traffic. Deterministic networks are better suited to large networks and those with heavy traffic. Some network architectures, such as IBM's SNA (Systems Network Architecture), and some applications (real-time applications, such as process control) must use deterministic methods.

Media access may be determined at a station on a network or at a wiring center. The traditional media-access methods, such as CSMA/CD and token-passing, are determined at each node. As network traffic

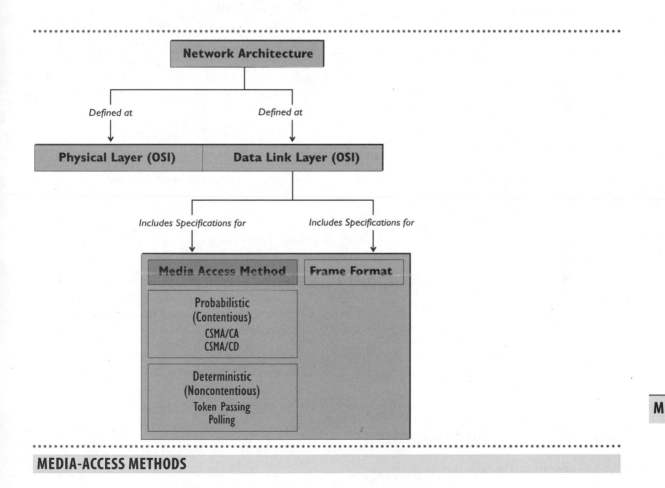

MEDIA-ACCESS METHODS

M

increases, stations (nodes) will spend more time waiting to access the network.

Other Access Methods

Higher bandwidth networks and networks with very heavy traffic require more efficient media-access methods. One way to accomplish this is to move access control to a wiring center (such as a hub). Then the nodes in the network do not need to worry about accessing the network. A node just transmits to the hub whenever the node has something to say. The hub then becomes responsible for getting each node's bits of wisdom onto the network.

Demand priority, which is used in Hewlett-Packard's highly-adapted high-speed 100BaseVG Ethernet standard, is an example of a media-access method that uses hub control.

→ *Broader Category* Network Architecture

Media Filter

A device for converting the output signal of a Token Ring network interface card to work with a particular type of wiring, such as unshielded twisted-pair (UTP) cable. Specifically, a device that can convert between UTP and shielded twisted-pair (STP) cables. A media filter is a passive device, designed mainly to eliminate undesirable high-frequency emissions.

Media Manager

In Novell's NetWare 4.*x* and later, a collection of resources for keeping track of and providing access to various types of storage devices (disk, compact disc, tape, jukebox, and so on), without requiring special device drivers.

Medium Attachment Unit (MAU)

→ *See* MAU (Medium Attachment Unit)

Medium Earth Orbit (MEO) Satellite

→ *See* MEO (Medium Earth Orbit) Satellite

Medium-Speed Digital Subscriber Line (MDSL)

→ *See* MDSL (Medium-Speed Digital Subscriber Line)

Melissa Virus

The Melissa macro virus was released in late March 1999 and fixes were made available almost immediately. Despite this, Melissa managed to spread more quickly than any previous virus and to shut down mail servers at numerous corporations and organizations.

Melissa was delivered as a Word attachment to an e-mail message apparently coming from someone known to the recipient. Once the attachment was opened, Melissa did the following:

- Lowered security settings and disabled access to Word's macro tool.

- Made changes in the machine's system Registry.

- Sent copies of itself to the first 50 entries in the victim's e-mail address book, which is how Melissa appeared to come from someone the (new) victim knows.

- Displayed various messages under certain specific conditions—for example, when the digits for time and date matched, as on June 17th (6/17) at 6:17.

By sending copies in e-mail messages to recipients who were almost certain to open them, Melissa managed to spread so very quickly. However, the most dangerous action is actually the last one described. Although these "surprise" actions were harmless in Melissa's case, a variant virus could use these surprises to deliver a harmful or even fatal payload—for example, instructions to format the disk or to destroy the Registry, file system, or CMOS information.

Since it was first discovered, Melissa has spawned various mutants, almost all of which are much more malicious than their inspiration. Many security experts warn that Melissa represents the first—and perhaps the most harmless—of a new breed of virus.

The virus was also a first for another reason. Melissa's creator was actually tracked down on the basis of a unique numerical code embedded in the virus file. The code was put in the file by one of the author's software packages, and was noticed by an alert computer expert.

→ *Broader Category* Virus

Memory

Memory is randomly addressable storage in a computer that is used to run programs, temporarily store data, and for other purposes. Memory is implemented in very fast access chips, which can be accessed several hundred times as quickly as a hard disk or a floppy disk drive.

Every location in a memory space has an address that identifies that particular location in the space. The form this address takes depends on the type of memory involved and also on the type of addressing used. For example, in IBM PC-based architectures, addresses in conventional memory are represented in terms of segment (16-byte paragraph) and offset components.

The chips used for the memory and the location of these chips depend on the type of memory. Four types of memory are commonly distinguished: conventional, upper, extended (including HMA), and expanded. "Memory layout" shows how these memory areas are related.

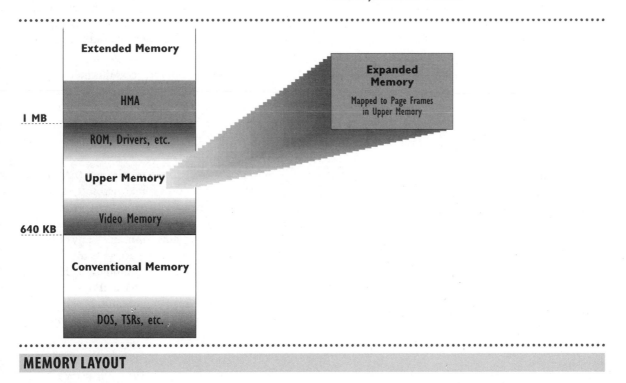

MEMORY LAYOUT

Conventional Memory

In IBM PCs, *conventional memory* is the first 640KB of memory. The architecture of the early Intel processors restricted the original IBM PC to accessing 1 MB of memory, 640KB of which was available for applications; the remaining 384KB was reserved for system use, the BIOS, and the video system. At that time, 640KB was more than ten times the amount of memory available in other personal computers. However, as both applications and DOS grew, they began to run out of room.

Conventional memory is generally represented in chips installed on the motherboard. The DOS kernel is loaded into conventional memory when you boot your computer. Most application programs execute in conventional memory.

Upper Memory

In IBM PCs, *upper memory* refers to the area of memory between 640KB and 1024KB, or 1MB. Traditionally, this area, also known as *system memory*, was accessible only to the system, not to user programs. Programs such as memory managers provide access to upper memory, and can store drivers, terminate-and-stay-resident (TSR) programs, and other necessary material in available locations in upper memory.

Upper memory is allocated in presized chunks called *upper memory blocks* (UMBs). Upper memory is allocated in the same chips as conventional memory.

Extended Memory

In IBM PCs, *extended memory* is memory above 1MB. This type of memory is available only in machines with 80286 and higher processors, because the machine must be in protected mode to access memory above 1MB.

Extended memory is defined by the Extended Memory Specification (XMS), and it is generally accessed through XMS drivers, such as HIMEM.SYS.

Extended memory is allocated in presized *extended memory blocks* (EMBs). Allocation for the EMBs begins at the location 64KB above the 1MB extended memory border; that is, above the high memory area (HMA). Extended memory is allocated on chips installed on the motherboard or in added memory banks.

HMA (High Memory Area)

The first 64KB of extended memory is called the *HMA*. In DOS versions 5.0 and later, the operating system kernel can be loaded into this area, freeing a considerable amount of conventional memory. In order to access the HMA, address line A20 must be enabled.

Expanded Memory

Expanded memory is a DOS mechanism by which applications can access more than the 640KB of memory normally available to them.

Expanded memory is provided in storage on a separate expansion board (or it is emulated in extended memory), and a special driver is used to map memory on these chips to 16KB pages allocated in upper memory.

Because programs cannot access this memory directly, the contents of expanded memory are moved piecemeal into pages that are allocated in the memory area between 640KB and 1MB. The more pages that are allocated, the larger the chunk of expanded memory that can be accessed at a given time.

The Expanded Memory Specification (EMS) LIM 4.0 (LIM is for Lotus Intel Microsoft, the companies that developed the specification) is the standard method of accessing expanded memory. This specification lets programs running on any of the Intel 8086 family of processors access as much as 32MB of expanded memory. Although the EMS calls for expanded memory to have its own hardware, various memory managers and drivers can emulate expanded memory in extended memory.

Memory Uses

Memory chips can also be categorized in terms of the manner in which the memory is used. In this regard, the two main categories are ROM (read-only memory) and RAM (random access memory). Each of these general classes comes in several variants, which are discussed in their own entries.

→ *See Also* RAM (Random Access Memory); ROM (Read-Only Memory)

Memory Managers

A *memory manager* is a program that controls access to available memory and that can manipulate available memory in order to make its use more efficient.

In particular, memory managers can do the following types of tasks:

- Provide access to expanded and/or extended memory.

- Emulate expanded memory (which assumes its own memory board) in extended memory.

- Move drivers and programs into upper and high memory, in order to make more conventional memory available.

For example, a memory manager can load drivers or certain programs into nonconventional memory areas. Because more conventional memory is available, users have greater flexibility in the kinds of programs they can run. Memory managers can also improve program performance because programs have more memory to work with.

Most programs support extended memory, but some older programs require expanded memory. Memory manager programs, such as 386MAX from Qualitas and QEMM-386 from Quarterdeck Systems, can simulate expanded memory in extended memory. This leads to the somewhat perverse situation in which information stored in one area of extended memory (the LIM simulation) is paged to another area of extended memory (the expanded memory pages allocated in upper memory) for use by a program most likely running in conventional memory.

Memory Dump

A displayed, saved, or printed copy of a specified area of internal memory, which should show the current values of the variables stored in the selected memory area. A memory dump provides "state-of-the-machine" (at that address) information.

Memory Pool

In Novell's NetWare, a memory pool of a finite supply of memory, not necessarily contiguous. Beginning with version 4, NetWare uses only a single memory pool, whose resources are allocated for whatever functions request them. NetWare version 3.x defines several memory pools, including a short-term and a file cache pool.

Memory Protection

In environments for NetWare 4 and later, memory protection is a memory management strategy that protects the server's memory from being corrupted by NetWare Loadable Modules (NLMs).

To accomplish its goals, NetWare's memory protection uses two different domains: OS and OS_PROTECTED. These domains are associated with two of the four privilege levels, or rings, managed by the Intel architecture. These privilege levels are protected from each other, so that programs or processes running in different levels cannot interfere with each other.

Novell recommends running third-party or untested NLMs in the OS_PROTECTED domain, at least until you are confident that the NLM is well-behaved. To do this, type the following commands at the server console before loading the NLM:

LOAD DOMAIN

DOMAIN=OS_PROTECTED

If you want to load the NLM from within the AUTOEXEC.NCF file, add these same two lines

M

to that file. To load an NLM in the OS domain, use the same commands, but change the second one to DOMAIN=OS.

MEO (Medium Earth Orbit) Satellite

MEO satellites circle at altitudes ranging from about 2000 to 10,000 miles above the earth. This is in contrast to low earth orbit (LEO) satellites, which are at an altitude of about 600 miles, and to geosynchronous earth orbit (GEO) satellites, which remain in an orbit that is stationary relative to the earth—at an altitude of 23,000 miles or so in space.

→ *Compare* GEO (Geosynchronous Earth Orbit) Satellite; LEO (Low Earth Orbit) Satellite

Message Digest 5 (MD5) Algorithm

→ *See* MD5 (Message Digest 5) Algorithm

Message Handling System (MHS), CCITT X.400

→ *See* MHS (Message Handling System), CCITT X.400

Message Handling System (MHS), NetWare

→ *See* MHS (Message Handling System), NetWare

Message ID (MID)

→ *See* MID (Message ID)

Message-Oriented Text Interchange System (MOTIS)

→ *See* MOTIS (Message-Oriented Text Interchange System)

Message Store (MS)

→ *See* MS (Message Store)

Message Switching

In message switching, a message makes its way from sender to receiver by being passed through intermediate nodes. Each node may store the entire message, and it will forward it to the next node when the opportunity arises.

Under certain types of connections, different parts of the message may take different routes to the destination during transmission. By using message switching and a store-and-forward method, a network operating system can make the most effective use of the available bandwidth.

Message Transfer Agent (MTA)

→ *See* MTA (Message Transfer Agent)

Message Transfer Layer (MTL)

→ *See* MTL (Message Transfer Layer)

Message Transfer Service (MTS)

→ *See* MTS (Message Transfer Service)

Messaging Application Programming Interface (MAPI)

→ See MAPI (Messaging Application Programming Interface)

Metabase

The metabase is used in version 4 and later of the Internet Information Server (IIS) component in Windows NT. The metabase is a hierarchical database used to store configuration parameter values for the following types of IIS objects:

- Files and directories
- Virtual directories
- Computers
- Web sites

The metabase is very similar to the Registry, which stores configuration information about your computer, the Windows environment, and the various objects in the environment. In a sense, the metabase is a streamlined (and, consequently, faster) registry. The IIS uses this faster version because Registry lookups might overwhelm the system when there is a lot of activity on the Web server created using IIS.

Configuration changes for the IIS environment and components are made in the metabase, rather than in the Registry. The Registry is also updated, however, if the changes affect other software.

Because the configuration information contained in the metabase largely determines how the IIS environment will look and operate, it's actually possible to administer IIS by editing the metabase. As always, making changes in such a file is fraught with danger, and should be done only if you really know what you're doing. Other, more straightforward, ways of administering IIS include the Microsoft Management Console (MMC), HTML Service Managers, and the use of scripts.

→ **Broader Categories** Microsoft IIS (Internet Information Server); Windows NT

→ **See Also** HTML Service Manager; MMC (Microsoft Management Console)

Metal Oxide Varistor (MOV)

→ See MOV (Metal Oxide Varistor)

Metering

The tracking of software availability and use on a network. One major goal of metering is to ensure that software licenses are not being violated. Some software products can meter themselves by using built-in metering concepts. More sophisticated products can do trend analyses of the metering data to help predict when new copies of a software product will need to be purchased or licensed.

Metropolitan Area Network (MAN)

→ See MAN (Metropolitan Area Network)

MFM (Modified Frequency Modulation)

An encoding method for floppy disks and low-capacity (50MB or less) hard disks. MFM hard disks can transfer more than 600KB per second.

MFS (Macintosh File System)

An older file system used in earlier Macintosh models. The MFS used a flat file structure, rather than the hierarchical file system used in more recent versions. Newer Macintoshes can read disks that use the MFS.

M

MHS (Message Handling System), CCITT X.400

An MHS is an application-level service element that enables applications to exchange messages. An electronic mail (e-mail) facility with store-and-forward capabilities is an example of an MHS.

In the CCITT's X.400 recommendations, an MHS can transfer messages between end-users, or between end-users and a variety of CCITT-defined services, such as fax, videotext, and so on.

MHS Components

The CCITT's X.400 MHS includes the following components:

- User agents (UAs) to provide interfaces for the end-users at one end and the Message Transfer System (MTS) at the other end.

- Access units (AUs) to provide interfaces for the CCITT services at one end and the MTS at the other end.

- A message store (MS) to provide temporary storage for messages before they are forwarded to their destination. The MS is a general archive in which mail can be held until the appropriate user retrieves it through a UA or until the allowable storage time for the message is exceeded. The MS is distinct from the mailboxes associated with individual users. UAs and other services use the MSAP (Message Store Access Protocol) to access the message store.

- An MTS, complete with message transfer agents (MTAs), to perform the actual transfer of the message from one end to the other. The MTAs are responsible for storing and/or forwarding messages to another MTA, to a user agent (UA), or to another authorized recipient. (An MTA is comparable to a mail agent in the TCP/IP environment.)

The MTS is a connectionless but reliable transfer capability. *Connectionless* means that parts of the message are transported independently of each other, and may take different paths. *Reliable* means that a message part will be delivered correctly or the sender will be informed that this was not possible.

Message Handling Layers

In the 1984 version of the X.400 MHS recommendations, the message transfer layer (MTL) is the lower sublayer of the OSI application layer. This sublayer provides access to the transfer services. Message transfer agent entities (MTAEs) carry out the functions at this sublayer. The 1984 version defines a protocol known as P1 for communications between MTAEs.

The user agent layer (UAL) is the sublayer above the MTL. The services for this sublayer may be implemented on a different machine than the one containing the MTL. For example, in a local area network (LAN) workstations may run the UAL to communicate with a server that provides the actual message transfer server. For configurations in which the MTL and UAL are on different machines, the recommendations provide a submission and delivery entity (SDE) to carry out the functions of the MTL.

MHS Management Domains

In the CCITT's X.400 MHS, a management domain (MD) is a limited, but not necessarily contiguous, area whose message-handling capabilities operate under the control of a single management authority. This authority can be the CCITT, a university, an organization, or other group.

Two types of management domains are defined:

ADMD (Administrative Management Domain)   A domain which is always run by the CCITT, such as national PTT (Postal, Telegraph, and Telephone) systems

PRMD (Private Management Domain)   A domain created by a local organization, such as a store, together with all its branches in the state, or a university campus

→ *Broader Category* X.400

→ *Related Articles* E-Mail; IPMS (Interpersonal Messaging Service)

MHS (Message Handling System), NetWare

In the Novell NetWare environment, MHS refers both to a protocol for mail handling and routing and to mail delivery service products for NetWare 2.x and later.

NetWare Global MHS

NetWare Global MHS is a collection of NetWare Loadable Modules (NLMs) that provide mail delivery service for networks using NetWare 3.x or later. MHS provides store-and-forward capabilities for various types of messaging services, including electronic mail, fax services, calendar and scheduling services, and also workflow automation.

Optional modules provide capabilities for accessing different messaging environments, including the following:

- UNIX and other TCP/IP-based networks, by using a module that supports the SMTP (Simple Mail Transfer Protocol).

- OSI environments, by using a module that provides support for X.400 protocols and services.

- IBM mainframes and AS/400 systems, by using the SNADS (SNA Distribution Services) module.

- Macintosh, OS/2, and other environments over gateways.

The related products NetWare MHS 1.5N and NetWare MHS 1.5P provide services for other environments. NetWare MHS 1.5N provides support for NetWare 2.x networks. MHS 1.5P supports laptops and remote PCs.

MIB (Management Information Base)

An MIB contains data available to a network management program. MIBs are created by management agents, so that each machine with an agent will have an associated MIB. The network manager will query these MIBs and may use an MIB of its own. The management MIB has more general information; the individual MIBs have machine-specific information.

The details of the MIB's format and the communication between manager and agents depend on the networking and network management model being used. For example, the Internet, OSI-compliant networks, and IBM SNA-based networks are based on different models, and so they have different MIBs. Translation capabilities are available for many environment combinations.

In the IP (Internet Protocol) network management model, the SNMP (Simple Network Management Protocol) contains *MIB views* (also known as *SNMP MIB views*), which are selective subsets of the information available in an agent's MIB. An MIB view can be created for a single station or for all the stations in an SNMP community.

MIB-II, which is described in RFC 2213, is the most recent standard. MIB-II information is delivered using the SNMPv2 protocol. However, the entire view of MIBs is undergoing major revision thanks, largely, to the phenomenally rapid growth of the World Wide Web and to the way its technology and philosophy have engulfed computing at all levels.

The contents of MIBs have traditionally been concerned with the performance of the technology (access, throughput, etc.). However, such information is of much more limited use when dealing

M

with management of or over an intranet. One reason is that the actual work for a task worthy of management attention may be distributed over multiple machines or even multiple networks. These networks may be real or they may be virtual networks.

Instead of filling MIBs with the traditional types of management information, various proposals are being developed for finding more interesting and useful information to provide. The general consensus is that more attention should be paid to collecting information about the network's functionality, rather than about its structure. For example, more attention must be paid to a network's scalability, degree and ease of integration with other networks or environments, and so forth. Web-based management tools and philosophies have sprung up to provide help with such changes.

Microbend/Microcrack

In fiber optics, microbends are tiny bends in fiber, and microcracks are microscopic cracks in fiber. Both of these flaws can affect a transmission.

→ *See Also* Cable, Fiber-Optic

MicroChannel

MicroChannel is a proprietary bus architecture developed by IBM for its PS/2 series of computers. Expansion boards for MicroChannel machines may have up to 32-bit data channels, but they are incompatible with machines that conform to ISA (Industry Standard Architecture) or EISA (Extended Industry Standard Architecture).

A MicroChannel environment allows you to use software to set addresses and interrupts for hardware devices. This means you do not need to adjust jumpers or dip switches on the boards. This also helps reduce the number of address and interrupt conflicts. MicroChannel was formerly known as *MCA*, but this name was dropped after a lawsuit

filed by the Music Corporation of America.

→ *Broader Category* Data Bus

→ *Compare* EISA (Extended Industry Standard Architecture); ISA (Industry Standard Architecture); PCI (Peripheral Component Interconnect); VL Bus

Microcom Networking Protocol (MNP)

→ *See* MNP (Microcom Networking Protocol)

Microkernel

A streamlined and stripped-down operating system kernel. A microkernel handles only the scheduling, loading, and running of tasks. All other operating system functions (such as input/output and virtual memory management) are handled by modules that run on top of this microkernel. The concept of a microkernel was developed at Carnegie-Mellon University and was implemented in the Mach operating system developed there.

Micron

A unit of measurement corresponding to one millionth of a meter (roughly $1/25,000$ inch), also called a *micrometer*. Units of this magnitude are used in networking to specify the diameter of optical fibers, as in 62.5 or 100 micron fibers.

Microsoft BackOffice

BackOffice is Microsoft's family of NT-based server products. The BackOffice Server 4 suite is intended to provide a complete line of servers for managing any type of network or intranet.

The core element in the suite is the Microsoft Windows NT Server, which includes the following special-purpose servers and other resources in the NT Option Pack:

- Microsoft Internet Information Server (IIS), which is used to administer Web sites on an intranet or an extranet.

- Microsoft Index Server, which is used to create indexes for the documents stored at Web sites on the server.

- Microsoft Internet Explorer (IE), which provides browser capabilities. Currently, BackOffice ships with IE4, but this will undoubtedly be 5 by the time you are reading this.

- Microsoft Certificate Server, which is used to create and verify certificates that can be used for authentication of users and also of software.

- Microsoft Transaction Server, which is used to manage actions on a Web server as transactions. This makes it possible to restore a state if an action cannot be completed.

- Microsoft Message Queue Server, which is used to provide message queuing and handling for applications. This enables the applications to use messaging for data exchange.

- Internet Connection Services for Remote Access Service (RAS), which enables users to connect to the Internet or to their corporate network even while on the road.

- Microsoft FrontPage, which is used for creating Web pages.

- Other programming and Web publishing tools, such as a Java Virtual Machine (JVM) for interpreting and running Java applets or applications, a Script Debugger, and various components to ease or enable various types of access.

In addition to the NT Server and Options Pack, the BackOffice suite includes several other components to provide capabilities and protection. Note

that these components are generally compliant with standards relating to the component's functions. In some cases, Microsoft also provides its own protocols for certain tasks or services. Other BackOffice components include the following:

- Microsoft Exchange Server, which is used to enable users to work collaboratively and securely online. Exchange Server supports security protocols such as Secure Socket Layer (SSL), the ITU-T's X.509 authentication specification and also Microsoft's own NTDS (New Technology Directory Service).

- Microsoft Proxy Server, which is used to provide firewalls and other resources for hiding and protecting data.

- Microsoft SQL Server, which is used to manage database creation, maintenance, and query—using SQL (Structured Query Language) or SQL-like instructions.

- Microsoft SNA Server, which is used to provide connectivity to older, non-Windows systems and platforms.

- Microsoft Site Server, which is used to manage intranets or e-commerce sites. The latter function is actually performed by a special, Commerce Edition of Site Server.

- Microsoft Systems Management Server, which is used to provide centralized control of the various network clients and resources.

- An Intranet Starter Site, which provides a finished template of an intranet site. An administrator could pour configuration and other information related to the local intranet into the Starter Site template.

Microsoft Certified Systems Engineer (MCSE)

→ See MCSE (Microsoft Certified Systems Engineer)

M

Microsoft Challenge Handshake Authentication Protocol (MS-CHAP)

→ *See* Protocol, MS-CHAP (Microsoft Challenge Handshake Authentication Protocol)

Microsoft Data Access Component (MDAC)

→ *See* MDAC (Microsoft Data Access Component)

Microsoft Exchange Server

Microsoft Exchange Server provides a back end for electronic messaging (e-messaging), and also represents one part of a client/server system. Such messaging goes beyond e-mail to provide an infrastructure for message routing to facilitate document exchange and other forms of collaboration. To provide such services, Exchange Server runs on Windows NT and supports various types of client applications—for example, Microsoft Outlook, which provides both e-mail and scheduling capabilities.

Exchange Server features and components include the following:

- Support for attachment links (as opposed to simple attachments) in e-mail. This makes it possible to include a link that can always point to the most recent version of the document.

- Support for public and private, or personal, folders. Folders can hold documents, messages, and even applications. A personal folder is accessible only by the folder's owner. In contrast, a public folder can be accessed by anyone with the appropriate permissions. In this way, public folders can be used to share information in collaborative projects—as an alternative to sending the document around to each project member. Access to folders is made using Exchange clients.

- Support for various application programming interfaces (APIs), including both the Simple and Extended Mail API (MAPI) from Microsoft and the ITU-T's Common Mail Call API (CMCAPI). These APIs can be used to create various types of mail or messaging-based applications.

- Supports NT security models, as well as additional security measures for specific purposes. These include the X.409 authentication standard and encryption protocols (such as SSL).

Exchange Server Structure

Microsoft Exchange Server has four main components that it must use, and about a dozen other components that are useful, but not required for basic operation:

Directory This is both a database of available resources and nodes, and also a service for providing access to these. The *directory service (DS)* functions as the access point to the directory database—for both Exchange clients on the network and also for DSs on other Exchange servers. The DS exchanges directory information with DSs on other Exchange servers. If these servers are at the same site, the information is exchanged directly; if the servers are at different sites, the exchange uses message transfer agents (see below).

Information store (IS) This also is both database and service. As a database—actually, as two databases—the IS saves materials (messages or other content) in either its public or private information stores. The IS service mediates between its two databases and other Exchange Server components. For example, it receives incoming mail and stores it in the appropriate mailboxes, notifies clients that they have new mail, and passes outgoing mail to an appropriate message transfer agent (see below). The IS also creates directory entries for new public folders.

Message transfer agent (MTA) The MTA is responsible for routing messages between the IS on the MTA's Exchange server and other servers. If the communication is between servers at the same site, the MTA handles the routing and transfer to the destination's MTA. If servers on different sites are involved, the MTA uses special components known as *connectors*. These are used to provide routing assistance and also conversion help, if needed. For example, if an Exchange server needs to exchange messages with a system that uses the ITU-T's X.400 messaging services, the MTA first converts Exchange Server messages from their native MAPI (Mail API) to an X.400 format. Connectors for other messaging systems include ones for Dynamic Remote Access Services (DRAS), Internet Mail Service (for using SMTP protocols), cc:Mail, and legacy systems using Microsoft Mail.

System attendant (SA) The SA is an attendant in two senses of the word: First, it pays attention to the server environment—that is, the SA monitors the server and its connections to other servers. Second, the SA tends to the server's needs—that is, it carries out necessary housekeeping and administrative tasks on behalf of the server. As a monitor, the SA checks on the quality and integrity of connections to other servers. The SA replies to regular queries that other servers send to make sure the connection is still established. It also monitors the server's directory, on the lookout for inconsistencies. When such discrepancies are found, the SA tries to fix them. Other functions the SA performs for the server include enabling and disabling encryption and digital signatures as security measures for Exchange, collecting data for tracking messages, generating foreign addresses (that is, addresses on different servers or platforms) for clients, and generating routing tables for the server. As the first Exchange component to start, and the last to shut down, the SA serves as a container for the rest of the Exchange Server components.

The optional components include the following:

- Exchange administrator program, which serves as a sort of home page for a particular Exchange server or for all the servers in an organization.

- Directory synchronization agent (DXA), which makes it possible to include foreign addresses—that is, addresses from outside the Exchange system—in an address book.

- Key management component, which provides support for encryption and digital signatures.

- Various Internet protocol servers, including IMAP (Internet Message Access Protocol), LDAP (Lightweight Directory Access Protocol), NNTP (Network News Transfer Protocol), OWA (Outlook Web Access), and POP3 (Post Office Protocol 3).

- Exchange connectors, such as those mentioned in relation to MTAs.

- Exchange gateways, which provide access to messaging environments such as Novell's GroupWise or IBM's SNADS (Systems Network Architecture Distribution Services).

Exchange Clients

Exchange Server provides the components and the resources (including APIs) for creating messaging-based applications using a variety of tools—including existing applications such as Microsoft Word or Excel. Clients for various types of services are provided as part of the Exchange Server environment. These include the following:

- Exchange Client, which provides access to a user's mailbox and folders (public and private). A separate Exchange Client is needed for each platform (Macintosh, Windows 3.*x*, NT, 9*x*, etc.).

M

- Forms designers for Exchange or Outlook. These can be used to create forms for collecting data or getting input from users.

- Forms collections for Exchange and Outlook. Forms created with the forms designers can be saved in libraries, and used by clients who need to perform tasks that particular forms make possible or easier.

- Outlook Client, which can integrate electronic messaging, contact management, scheduling, and task management with each other and also with other tasks.

- Schedule+, which provides planning, scheduling, and contact management, as well as messaging capabilities.

Note that the capabilities of the provided clients overlap—sometimes to a large degree. This is not unusual, since there are many ways of providing services. The existence of such clients also indicates that it is feasible to create clients with the particular configuration of capabilities and features that a user or organization needs.

→ *See Also* Lotus Notes

Microsoft FrontPage

FrontPage is Microsoft's highly regarded tool for creating and editing Web pages. With FrontPage you can create HTML (Hypertext Markup Language) files without necessarily knowing anything about HTML. Web pages created with FrontPage can even include Active Server Pages (ASPs)—additional instructions that are interpreted and executed by the server before the Web page is sent to the browser.

The ASP code will generate HTML markups for the browser to use when displaying the page. Active Server Pages thus make it possible to gener-

ate dynamic Web pages—that is, Web pages that are customized and generated as they are needed. Web pages that include ASP can also be interactive—that is, they can accept user input, and can display content based on that input.

FrontPage Modes

FrontPage can work in any of three modes: Normal, HTML, and Preview. In Normal mode, you can create the content and elements (images and other links) just as if you were creating a word processing file. Behind the scenes, FrontPage will generate HTML code for a browser to interpret.

In HTML mode, you can see the raw markup code that FrontPage has generated in response to your instructions in the file. Since this code is in a text file, you can edit it.

In Preview mode, FrontPage will display your document as it will appear to a browser. Actually, FrontPage will display only the static HTML portions—that is, the non-ASP elements. FrontPage will not execute the ASP instructions.

FrontPage exists in several versions, including FrontPage 98, FrontPage 2000, and FrontPage Express. The last is a pared-down version that is available with Internet Explorer. Other products that do similar kinds of things include Drumbeat 2.0 from Elemental Software as well as ColdFusion and Homesite from Allaire.

Microsoft IIS (Internet Information Server)

IIS is server software included as part of Windows NT Server 4, in the Windows NT Option Pack. IIS allows you to set up and operate a Web site as part of a Windows NT network, as well as providing other Internet-related services. IIS goes beyond being a mere Web server package, however, because it also provides support for other higher-level Internet protocols.

The created Web site and other services can be made accessible over the Internet, or access can be limited to an intranet or an extranet. Different types of hardware and different security measures may be advisable, depending on how the Web services will be used (that is, Internet, intranet, or extranet). Simply put, the more potential users, the faster and more powerful the server hardware should be; the greater the variety of potential users, the more stringent and comprehensive the security measures should be.

A site administered through IIS supports the following protocols and services:

- HTTP (Hypertext Transfer Protocol), which is used to transfer Web documents and inserts (HTML, or Hypertext Markup Language, files; image, sound, or video files, etc.). IIS 4 supports HTTP version 1.1.

- FTP (File Transfer Protocol), which is used for transferring text or binary files between servers or between a server and an end user.

- SMTP (Simple Mail Transfer Protocol), which is used for providing Internet mail services. (Supported only in version 4 and later.)

- NNTP (Network News Transfer Protocol), which is used for accessing news and user groups that might be supported on the Web site. (Supported only in version 4 and later.)

- Security services, which are provided mainly by the underlying NT operating system. Services include control of site, file, and directory access permissions, user authentication, Secure Socket Layer (SSL) communications, and transaction logging.

- Support for scripts, server-side includes, ASPs, and other ActiveX components, all of which make it possible to automate or carry out various kinds of tasks having to do with Web page handling.

- Support for multiple Web sites, so that different clients or departments can each set up their own Web pages and services. The same materials can be cross-linked to different Web sites, using virtual directories and Web sites, as described in the next item.

- Support for virtual Web sites and virtual directories, both of which make it possible to present the materials at a site in different ways. For example, the contents of a Web site might be presented in a different structure to in-house workers and to outsiders looking for information at the site. Or, a Web server may actually be hosting multiple Web sites—for example, for different departments or customers. By creating virtual Web sites or directories, the materials can be made available to (or protected from) specific groups of users.

- Database access, using an Open Database Connector (ODBC) to communicate with the appropriate database server software (for example, Microsoft SQL Server). IIS also supports the use of ActiveX Data Objects (ADOs) and Remote Data Service (RDS) for incorporating database information into Web pages. The database may be at the same or a different location as the Web site.

Beginning with version 4, IIS has dropped support for the Gopher protocol, which has become largely obsolete, as the World Wide Web has rocketed to prominence.

IIS runs as a Windows NT service, and can be administered from the NT command line, the Microsoft Management Console (MMC), or the Internet Services Manager Web pages. The Internet Services Manager program from IIS version 3 can also be used, but can only administer a single Web site and a single ftp site at a time.

In addition, other Windows NT services and components can be used with IIS. For example, Desktop Explorer and User Manager (or User Manager for Domains) can help set up security for the Web site; Windows Scripting Host can be used to automate many of the tasks when administering IIS from the command line.

M

→ *See Also* Server, Web; Windows NT

Microsoft Index Server

Microsoft Index Server is an extension to the Internet Information Server (IIS) component included with Windows NT. The Index Server is used to create indexes of the Web pages on a site and of their interconnections.

These indexes can be used to search for specific content in the Web pages. A user can specify search criteria—that is, content to find—and the Index Server will retrieve a list of documents that match the specified criteria.

→ *Broader Category* Windows NT

→ *See Also* Microsoft IIS (Internet Information Server)

Microsoft Internet Explorer (MSIE)

→ *See* MSIE (Microsoft Internet Explorer)

Microsoft Internet Information Server (IIS)

→ *See* Microsoft IIS (Internet Information Server)

Microsoft Mail

Microsoft's electronic mail package. Client software for Mail is available as a part of Microsoft Office and Office Professional, Windows for Workgroups, and Windows 95. Windows 95 also includes a post office (temporary message storage area). Mail *servers* are part of the Microsoft BackOffice suite and the Windows NT server.

Mail is compatible with Microsoft's Messaging Application Program Interface (MAPI) and is one of the messaging services supported by Microsoft Exchange in Windows 95. In Windows 98, however, e-mail services are provided by Outlook Express, which is tailored more toward handling Internet mail.

→ *See Also* Microsoft Exchange; Microsoft Office; Windows 95

Microsoft Management Console (MMC)

→ *See* MMC (Microsoft Management Console)

Microsoft Network (MSN)

→ *See* MSN (Microsoft Network)

Microsoft Office

Microsoft Office—or just Office for simplicity—is an integrated suite of applications, with implementations for Windows 3.*x*, Windows NT, Windows 9*x,* and Windows 2000, which should be available by the time you read this. Office has gone through several versions, with the two most recent being Office 97 and the newly released Office 2000.

Office also comes packaged in several different ways, with the following editions available in some or all of the Office versions: Standard, Professional, Small Business, Premium, and Developer. The editions differ in what programs are included, with the Premium and Developer editions having the most components.

The Developer Edition is available only for Office 97 and Office 2000. This includes all the programs in the Professional Edition, some smaller programs, and programming tools. Finally, only Office 2000 also comes in a Premium Edition, which has everything in the Developer's Edition except the programming tools.

Office includes the applications in the following list. *Excel*, which is Microsoft's entry in the electronic spreadsheet world. Excel provides all the standard features of a spreadsheet program. You can enter numerical or text data, can create and apply formulas where appropriate, can call functions to modify the data, and can format and modify the spreadsheet's content as you need. Excel allows you to create charts and graphs based on the numbers in your spreadsheets, and it allows you to print your numbers or graphs.

- *Outlook*, which provides electronic mail, calendar, and scheduling services. You can use Outlook to correspond electronically with others on a local area network or even across long-distance telephone lines. Within Outlook, you can compose, read, print, and forward messages. You can attach images or other files to mail messages. Versions prior to Office 97 used Mail as their e-mail service.

- *PowerPoint*, which is a presentation program. You can use PowerPoint to create slides, transparencies, handouts, speaker notes, etc. PowerPoint supports text and graphics in the presentation elements, and it allows you to use any of various transitions between slides. PowerPoint allows you to leave a predefined sequence and branch to specific slides in mid-presentation; you can also jump from a slide to any material (Excel spreadsheets, Word documents, etc) that may be linked to the slide. The application includes several wizards, which are programs that help accomplish certain tasks (such as specifying the format of slides or other elements).

- *Word*, which is a widely used word processing program. In addition to the usual word processing capabilities, Word includes over a dozen predefined templates to help you create certain types of documents, and each template comes in as many as four different "flavors" for creating different kinds of looks. Example templates include: brochure, fax cover sheet, letter, memo, press release, and purchase order.

Word also has wizards, which help you create specific documents by asking you questions about what you want to do, and then creating a document style based on your answers. Example wizards include: Calendar, Directory, Invoice, and Letter. Add-on products (ranging from freeware to buyware) expand Word's capabilities. Generally these add-ons take advantage of the fact that you can define macros to perform new actions. For example, one type of add-on enables Word to create HTML (hypertext markup language) documents, which are documents found on the World Wide Web (WWW). You can also get free macros to convert an existing Word file to HTML format, which can save you the work of creating new files. Word also includes spelling, style, and grammar checkers.

- *Access*, which is a relational database management program and is included only in Office Professional and in the Developer and Premium Editions. (You can, however, buy it separately and then add it to the regular Office environment.) You can use Access to create, query, and generate reports from databases containing just about whatever information you want. Access comes with 30 predefined database templates, including book inventories, personal or business contact lists, expense trackers, mailing lists, recipe collections, and wine inventories. Access also has wizards—special programs to help you do such things as setting up queries, creating tables, reports, mailing labels, and even controls and buttons. Access supports both macros and a programming language (Access Basic), which makes it possible to create modules that can perform tasks that are too difficult to accomplish with just macros.

- *Internet Explorer*, which is Microsoft's browser, and which, in many ways, serves as the central coordinator for the Office environment. Explorer has been part of the Office environment since Office 97.

M

- Miscellaneous programs, including Publisher, Front Page, Small Business Tools, and Photo-Draw. Each version of Office except the Standard Edition includes one or more of these programs. Only the Premium and Developer Editions of Office 2000 have all the programs.

Microsoft Site Server Express

Site Server Express is a component in Microsoft's Internet Information Server (IIS) environment. It is used to analyze Web sites in order to perform content analyses on the Web pages and to generate reports about the pages. Site Server Express analyses can determine such information as the number of links on each page, the amount of space required for the pages, and the number of times each page has been accessed.

Microsoft Transaction Server (MTS)

→ **See** MTS (Microsoft Transaction Server)

Microwave Transmission

Microwave transmission is unbounded or wireless network communication that makes use of microwaves to transmit the signals. Microwaves are in the 1 gigahertz (GHz) and higher region of the electromagnetic spectrum. Various sources put the upper frequency limit for microwaves at 30GHz, 300GHz, and 1 terahertz (THz). Whichever limit is used, microwaves still offer a potentially very high bandwidth; in practice, most microwave connections are in the low gigahertz range.

Microwave transmissions are used in wireless networks, but require a line of sight between sender and receiver.

This type of transmission is in contrast to cable-based transmission and to transmission using radio or infrared waves or laser signals. Like radio waves, the microwave spectrum requires licensing from the FCC (Federal Communications Commission). Microwave transmissions are very susceptible to eavesdropping, jamming, and interference (from natural or electrical sources).

Microwave transmissions can be broadband or baseband, and they can use earth-based or satellite receivers.

Earth-Based versus Satellite Receivers

With earth-based receivers, the microwave signal is beamed over a line-of-sight path to a parabolic antenna. The signal may be passed from antenna to antenna (with each of these functioning as a repeater). These antennas cannot be more than about 30 or 40 kilometers (20 or 25 miles) apart (because of the earth's curvature). In practice, earth-based microwave connections are rarely this large. Rather, the transmissions are usually just between buildings (less than 100 meters, or a few hundred feet).

With satellite-based receivers, the signal is beamed between an earth-based parabolic antenna and a satellite in geosynchronous orbit over the earth. The signal is then beamed from the satellite to other locations, possibly over thousands of miles. The signal from the satellite can be broadcast or focused, and the receiving antennas can be fixed or mobile.

Advantages of Microwave Transmission

Advantages of microwave transmission include the following:

- They have a very high bandwidth.

- Repeater antennas may be much less expensive to build over terrain where cable is inadvisable.

- The transmissions can reach remote locations, even if these are in hostile terrain.

- With satellite-based communications, long distances can be covered without intervening repeaters.

- Both transmitter and receiver can be mobile if necessary.

- The signals can be sent to a narrow or wide area.

Disadvantages of Microwave Transmission

Disadvantages of microwave transmissions include the following:

- Line of sight is required between stations or intermediate antennas.

- FCC licensing and approval for equipment are required.

- Microwave transmissions are very susceptible to eavesdropping, interference, and jamming.

- Microwave signals are also susceptible to atmospheric conditions. For example, rain and fog will attenuate the signals. More important, higher frequencies will be attenuated more, which distorts a transmission.

- Equipment is still expensive.

→ *Broader Category* Network, Wireless

→ *Compare* Infrared Transmission; Radio Wave Transmission

MID (Message ID)

In electronic mail (e-mail) or message handling, the MID represents a unique value associated with a particular message.

Middle-Endian

On 32-bit systems, a middle-endian byte representation strategy is one that is neither little-endian

(low-order byte at lower address) or big-endian (high-order byte first).

The bytes in a 16-bit word are stored 1-2 or 2-1 (for little- and big-endian representations, respectively). In proper 32-bit systems, these representations extend to 1-2-3-4 or 4-3-2-1. In contrast, middle-endian systems use representations such as 2-1-4-3 (big-endian bytes in little-endian words) or 3-4-1-2 (little-endian bytes in big-endian words).

Such ambiguous representations give rise to what is known as the *NUXI problem*: how to represent the letters of the word "UNIX" in a 32-bit word. The two "proper-endian" solutions are "UNIX" and "XINU." The middle-endian representations are "NUXI" and "IXUN."

→ *Compare* Big-Endian; Byte-Sex; Little-Endian

Middleware

Middleware refers to a level of hardware or, more commonly, software that sits between an application program and its operating environment—that is, its operating system (OS) or network operating system (NOS). A network shell is an example of middleware, as are object broker programs such as those used for the Common Object Request Broker Architecture (CORBA) or for Microsoft Distributed Component Object Model (DCOM).

The term is used particularly in reference to distributed application software. Communication between application software and middleware is generally through APIs (Application Program Interfaces). Middleware can help make it possible to achieve communication between incompatible environments or protocols.

The term is also used to refer to a class of development tools. Middleware of this type allows users to build simple products for performing specific tasks by linking together available services using a scripting language.

M

Migration

In networking and other computing contexts, migration is the process of moving operations from one technology to another. For example, a company might migrate from electrical to optical media. Migration is an important way of keeping up with emerging technologies.

A *migration path* specifies the details of the migration. The more clearly the path is defined, the smoother the migration should be.

In NetWare environments, migration refers to the conversion of a server and its contents from an earlier version of NetWare or from a different network operating system (NOS) to NetWare version 4.*x*.

The term is also used to refer to the progress of data from the primary storage area, such as the server's hard disk, to a secondary storage area, such as a tape or an erasable optical disk.

MILnet

One of the networks that make up the Internet. This network was originally used for unclassified military information.

MIME (Multipurpose Internet Mail Extension)

MIME is a mail handling standard developed by the IETF (Internet Engineering Task Force) to provide support for multimedia and multipart messages. MIME makes it possible to encode and transmit sound, video, and formatted data in a single message, and also to receive and handle (read, see, or hear) the message.

MIME User Agents

MIME capabilities are provided by MIME user agents (UAs), which can create, transmit, receive, and parse multimedia or multipart messages. "MIME agents in composition" and "MIME agents in display" show the UA's role in these processes.

To create a multimedia message, the MIME UA uses separate composition agents for each message type supported. These agents are used to create the message in an appropriate format. A UA might have agents for specific text or word processors (to handle formatting and other commands correctly), for audio, and for video. To help create audio or video messages, the respective agents might provide support for a microphone or camera, respectively. Because the MIME standard and UAs are extensible, new composition agents can be added.

A MIME UA also uses a MIME Message Designer and a MIME Message Builder. The Message Designer calls the appropriate composition agents to create the desired message. This component is also extensible and can be modified to use newly added composition agents. The Message Builder does the conversions needed to send the message using a mail delivery service. The Message Builder mediates between the Message Designer and the mail service, and it provides the interface between the MIME UA and the mail service.

At the receiving end, the MIME UA uses a MIME Format Message Parser to identify the different parts in a message. The Parser then passes the message parts to a Dispatcher, which calls Viewers designed specifically for a particular type of message.

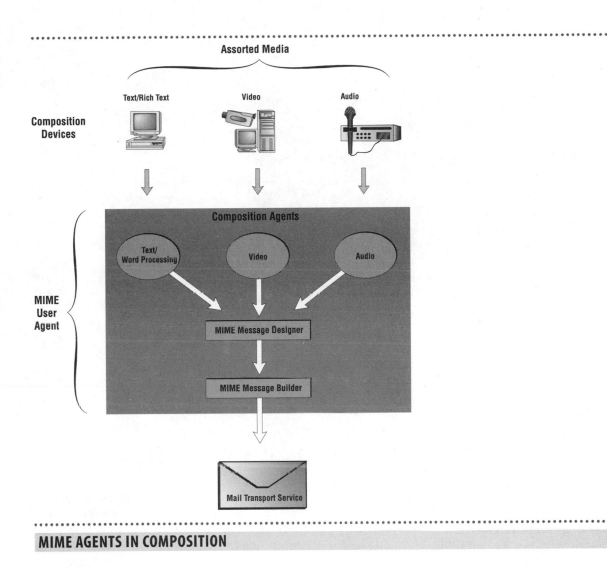

MIME AGENTS IN COMPOSITION

M

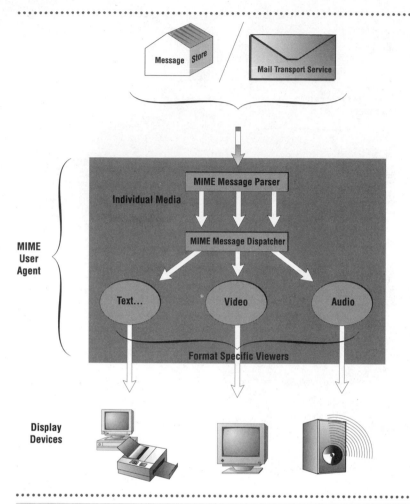

MIME Capabilities

Originally developed for the Internet, MIME was designed as an open and extensible standard. It is independent of specific platforms, and can (in principle) be used to send multimedia messages across different platforms and operating environments. Support for MIME has been built into several e-mail packages.

Because of its flexibility and extensibility, MIME opens many possibilities for making messaging services much more powerful. For example, a message might contain a program that can execute as part of the message, to do a demonstration or a calculation.

However, these possibilities also raise unresolved issues relating to security and compatibility. For example, it is important to be able to keep a message from doing damage to the recipient's files or system. It is also useful to be able to select which parts of a message to read, so that a laptop with minimal graphics capabilities does not need to receive the multi-megabyte animation component in a message.

S/MIME—for secure MIME—has been developed to deal with security issues. This variant is discussed in its own entry.

→ *Primary Sources* RFCs 1521, 1522, 1343, and 1344; approved as draft standards in RFCs 1590 and 1522

→ *See Also* S/MIME (Secure Multipurpose Internet Mail Extension)

Minicomputer

A computer that historically has been smaller than a mainframe, bigger than a breadbox, and (traditionally) more powerful than a PC. Minicomputers, particularly VAX machines from Digital Equipment Corporation (DEC), were popular as components in distributed networks, such as the ARPAnet. However, in recent years, this class of computers has largely disappeared as a separate category. High-end workstations and multiprocessor servers have taken over many of these functions.

Minimum Cell Rate (MCR)

→ *See* MCR (Minimum Cell Rate)

Minimum Spanning Tree (MST)

→ *See* MST (Minimum Spanning Tree)

Mirror

Also known as a *mirror site* or an *FTP mirror site*. An Internet site that contains a copy of the contents of an archive site. A mirror site is created in order to take some of the workload off a heavily-accessed archive. Mirror sites are updated on a regular basis from the archive. Two well-known archives that have mirrors are the SimTel archive of DOS programs and the CICA archive of Windows programs.

MLHG (Multiline Hunt Group)

In telephony, a multiline hunt group is a switching system in which a call can be switched automatically to a different line in the group if the line being called is busy.

MLI (Multiple Link Interface)

Part of the ODI generic network driver interface. Specifically, the MLI sits under the link-support layer (LSL). The latter deals with the protocol stacks, and the MLID (MLI driver) deals with the various network interface cards, or adapters, that support ODI.

→ *See Also* ODI (Open Data-link Interface)

MLT (Multiple Logical Terminals)

In an SNA environment, a feature of an IBM 3174 establishment controller. With MLT, even CUT (control user terminal) components can support multiple sessions simultaneously.

→ *See Also* SNA (Systems Network Architecture)

M

MMC (Microsoft Management Console)

MMC is a Windows NT component that makes it possible to manage various services—for example, those provided by the Microsoft Internet Information Server (IIS). MMC provides a common front end for managing any service that provides a *snap-in* object—a special ActiveX control—through which MMC can work. Essentially, MMC controls the snap-ins; the snap-ins, in turn, control the services of interest.

With MMC it is possible to save customized consoles to manage specific administrative tasks. Such consoles are saved in .MSC files, which contain window and snap-in configuration settings. These files are used to execute a task the same way each time. Because the files are quite small, it's even possible to exchange files with administrators on other networks.

MMDS (Multichannel Multipoint Distribution Service)

MMDS is a wireless digital distribution system for video and other materials. It can also be used to provide high-speed Internet access. An MMDS provider broadcasts its programming in all directions from a central location. Subscribers need an appropriate antenna and a line of sight to the broadcast tower, which can be up to 30 miles away.

An MMDS provider can currently provide up to 33 channels, which can come from various sources. An MMDS license provides 11 channels. Beyond that, up to 20 channels can be leased from the spectrum licensed for Instructional Television Fixed Service (ITFS). ITFS is licensed for use by educational institutions, which can broadcast instructional or other programming. Beginning in 1983, the FCC allowed such institutions to rent any excess capacity to outside parties—for example, to MMDS providers. In addition, two multipoint distribution service (MDS) channels can also be leased.

With appropriate data compression and technology advances, MMDS providers hope to be able to squeeze bandwidth for up to 200 channels out of the allocated spectrum. While MMDS is a relatively new service, it is built out of a combination of existing and state of the art technology, and it offers considerable freedom on how services can be configured.

→ *Compare* LMDS (Local Multipoint Distribution Service)

MMF (Multimode Fiber)

In fiber-optical signaling, multimode fibers can support multiple light paths at once. Multimode fibers are less expensive to make than single-mode fibers, but they are also noisier. The two most common MMF sizes are 50/125 and 62.5/125. The first number in each pair refers to the diameter of the fiber's core, and is measured in microns (millionths of a meter). The second value refers to the diameter of the cladding, or the cover around the core that is used to bounce the light signal back into the core as it travels down the fiber.

→ *See Also* Cable, Fiber-Optic

MMJ (Modified Modular Jack)

A variant on the RJ-*xx* jacks. The MMJ was developed by Digital Equipment Corporation (DEC) for use in its premises cabling. The wiring (and sequencing) is compatible with the RJ-*xx* wiring, but the MMJ is keyed to make it impossible to use with an ordinary RJ-*xx* connector.

MML (Mathematical Markup Language)

→**See** MathML (Mathematical Markup Language)

MMS (Manufacturing Message Service)

In the OSI reference model, the MMS enables an application on a control computer to communicate with an application on a slave machine. For example, MMS can be used in a production line or other automated operation context.

MMT (Multimedia Multiparty Teleconferencing)

MMT allows the transmission of data, voice, and/or video in a teleconferencing context.

MNP (Microcom Networking Protocol)

MNP refers to a family of protocols, developed by Microcom but licensed for use by third parties, for facilitating telecommunications. Some of the protocols are concerned with error correction; others are concerned with data compression.

Mobile Telephone Switching Office (MTSO)

→**See** MTSO (Mobile Telephone Switching Office)

Mobitex

A collection of wireless networks, operated by RAM Mobile Data. Mobitex connects more than 6000 cities in the United States, and is also found in Canada, the United Kingdom, and Scandinavia.

Modal Dispersion

In fiber optics, modal dispersion refers to the gradual spreading of an optical signal with increasing distance. A *mode* is a path for light to take through a fiber.

→**See** Cable, Fiber-Optic

Modem

A modem (from *mod*ulation-*dem*odulation) is a communications device that converts binary electrical signals into acoustic signals for transmission over telephone lines and converts these acoustic signals back into binary form at the receiving end. Conversion to acoustic form is known as *modulation*; conversion back to binary form is known as *demodulation*. The process is illustrated in "Modem operation."

In the terminology used in the RS-232C communications standard, modems are DCEs (data circuit-terminating equipment), which means they are connected at one end to a DTE (data terminal equipment) device. The DTE (a PC) sends instructions and data to the DCE for processing and further transmission.

Modems differ in the modulation methods they use and in the communications and transmission standards with which they comply. Modems are grouped in the following ways:

- Class: Narrowband, voice-grade, wideband, or short-haul.

M

- Modulation method: Frequency, amplitude, phase, quadrature amplitude, or trellis coded modulation.

- Signaling method: Any of several methods defined in Bell and CCITT standards.

- Error-correction method: None, trellis coded modulation, Microcom Networking Protocol, Link Access Protocol D (LAPD), or V.42.

- Location: Internal or external

Modem Class

The following classes of modems are currently used:

- V-series modems, which can operate at speeds up to 56Kbps.

- Wideband, which are high bandwidth, up to 64Kbps, modems used for computer-to-computer transmissions over a dedicated channel.

- Short-haul, which are very high bandwidth, up to 1.5Mbps, modems used for short distances (up to 20 miles). These are also known as *limited-distance modems* (*LDMs*).

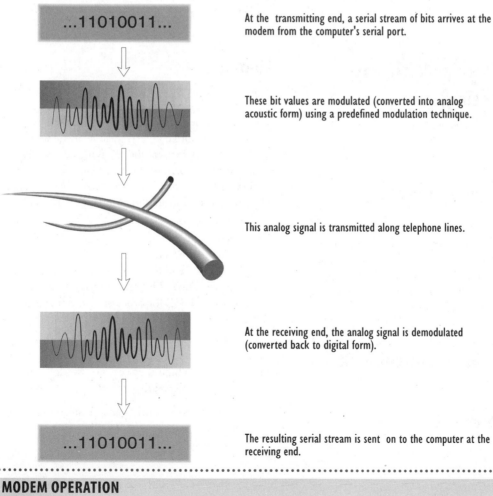

At the transmitting end, a serial stream of bits arrives at the modem from the computer's serial port.

These bit values are modulated (converted into analog acoustic form) using a predefined modulation technique.

This analog signal is transmitted along telephone lines.

At the receiving end, the analog signal is demodulated (converted back to digital form).

The resulting serial stream is sent on to the computer at the receiving end.

MODEM OPERATION

Modulation Method

Modems can encode the 0 and 1 values that come from the computer (the DTE) in any of several ways. This encoding process is known as *modulation*, and it entails making some change to the electrical wave that is being used to transmit the message. Modulation techniques involve signal frequency (pitch), amplitude (strength), phase (timing), or some combination of these.

Modulation methods include the following:

- Frequency modulation (FM) or frequency shift keying (FSK), which uses different frequencies for 0 and 1 values. The exact frequencies used depend on the modem's compatibility. FSK can encode 1 bit per baud (signal transition), so that the maximum transmission speed with FSK is 2400bps.

- Amplitude modulation (AM) or amplitude shift keying (ASK), which uses different amplitudes for 0 and 1 values. AM can encode 1 bit per baud.

- Phase modulation (PM) or phase shift keying (PSK), in which each value is encoded as a signal wave beginning at different points in the wave's cycle. PSK can encode up to 3 bits per baud (which requires eight unique offsets). For example, the bit pattern 000 might be encoded as a signal 45 degrees out of phase, 001 might be 90 degrees, and so on.

- Quadrature amplitude modulation (QAM), which combines AM and PSK, and can encode between 4 and 7 bits per baud.

- Trellis coded modulation (TCM), which uses an encoding scheme similar to the one used for QAM, but adds extra bits for its error-correction work.

The various shift keying methods may involve absolute values or they may involve differential values. For example, an FSK method may use specific frequencies to encode the binary 1s and 0s, or it may use a change in frequency to encode one value and a constant frequency to encode the other. This is a DFSK (with D for differential) method, which is less expensive and less error-prone, because it is easier to recognize a change in value than to recognize a specific value. See the Modulation article for more information about these methods.

Signaling Methods

Modems have been designed to two families of signaling specifications. One feature of the specifications concerns the allowed signal or transmission speeds. The other feature determines the kind of interaction possible between the two machines involved in a communication. The following types of connections are possible:

- Simplex, which is one-directional. For example, a connection to a tickertape machine or from a cable head end to a subscriber's box is a simplex connection.

- Half-duplex, which is two-directional, but not simultaneously.

- Full-duplex, which is two-directional at any time.

Specifications from Bell provide the signaling guidelines for lower-speed modems. The table "Bell Modem Specifications" lists these standards.

BELL MODEM SPECIFICATIONS

Bell Specification	Use
103/113	00bps half-duplex (used rarely, if at all)
201C	2400bps half-duplex
202S	1200bps half-duplex
202T	Up to 1800bps half-duplex on dial-up lines and full-duplex on leased lines
208A	4800bps half- or full-duplex over leased lines
208B	4800bps half-duplex over dial-up lines
212A	300 or 1200bps half- or full-duplex

M

The CCITT family provides the specifications for higher-speed modems and for modems that do error correction. The table "CCITT Modem Specifications" lists these standards.

CCITT MODEM SPECIFICATIONS

CCITT Specification	Use
V.21	300bps half-duplex over 2-wire lines (like its Bell counterpart, nearly obsolete)
V.22	1200bps full-duplex over 2-wire lines
V.22bis	2400 or 1200bps full-duplex over 2-wire lines
V.23	600 or 1200bps full-duplex over 2-wire lines
V.26	2400bps full-duplex over 4-wire leased lines
V.26bis	2400bps half-duplex over 4-wire dial-up lines
V.26ter	2400bps full-duplex over 2-wire dial-up or leased lines
V.27	4800bps full-duplex over 4-wire leased lines
V.27bis	2400 or 4800bps full-duplex over leased lines
V.27ter	2400 or 4800bps half-duplex over dial-up lines
V.29	9600bps on 4-wire leased lines
V.32	9600bps full-duplex over 2-wire lines; uses an error correction scheme specified by V.42
V.32bis	V.32 at up to 14,400bps
V.32ter	V.32 at up to 19,200bps
V.33	14,400bps on 4-wire leased lines
V.FAST	19,200bps over dial-up lines
V.34	28,800bps over dial-up lines (up to 115,200bps possible when using V.42bis compression)
V.90	57,600bps (theoretically) over dial-up lines, but only 53,000bps officially. (115,200bps with V.42bis compression)

Any standard that supports dial-up lines also supports leased lines; the converse is not true.

Hayes Command Set

Virtually all modems support the Hayes AT command set, which is a modem command format developed by Hayes Microcomputing for use in its modems.

The command format uses special signals and timing to distinguish commands from data in a modem session. Since its inception, the AT command set has been extended and updated to work with the more powerful modems as they have appeared.

Error Correction

Error-correction capabilities save on retransmissions, which can help increase throughput. Protocols with error-correction capabilities include the following:

- Link Access Protocol D (LAPD), which is based on the High-level Data Link Control (HDLC) synchronous protocol.

- Microcom Networking Protocol (MNP), which is actually a family of several protocols. MNP 5 and MNP 6 are used with high-speed, voice-grade modems. MNP 10 is still proprietary to Microcom, and is used in applications where error correction is crucial (for example, in wireless modems).

- Trellis Coded Modulation (TCM), which is used primarily with modems on leased lines.

- V.42, which provides error detection and correction; V.42bis also provides data compression.

Internal versus External Modems

A modem may be internal, so that it is implemented on a card that plugs into your computer, or external, so that it is contained in a separate box connected to your computer by a cable.

Internal modems are less expensive, take up less space on your desk, and can use the computer's power supply. However, they do not provide a convenient way of signaling modem activity (such as the use of lights on the modem's panel). An internal modem also requires an interrupt request line (IRQ) and a serial port address. Internal modems are now included as standard equipment in new PCs.

External modems take up more space on your desk but less inside your computer. Because they use a serial port (which is included on most computers), they do not take up one of your expansion slots. External modems will generally have lights to indicate various types of information during operation. External modems need their own power supply.

Modem Variants

A modem is nothing but a conversion machine. This basic capability has been packaged in a variety of ways: as cellular, fax, PCMCIA, portable, and wireless modems, to name just some of the ways. Some of these modem variants really are simply packaging differences. Others, however, work with different technologies—for example, an ADSL modem.

ADSL Modem

Asymmetric digital subscriber line (ADSL) technology provides high-speed connections using ordinary telephone wire. To accomplish this, however, the technology requires some special equipment. Such modems can support speeds as high as 8Mbps.

Cable Modem

A cable modem uses the cable TV company's wiring—rather than telephone lines—to achieve download transfer speeds as high as 10Mbps. Cable modems transmit and receive packets using radio-frequency cable channels. The connection from the user's PC and modem goes over the cable company's coaxial cable, and eventually reaches the cable company's head end—that is, the main transmission point, from which all cable transmissions begin. At the head end, a connection to the Internet can be made.

Cellular Modem

A cellular modem is one designed for use with cellular telephones. In order to deal with the uncertain world of wireless transmissions, cellular modems differ from their generic counterparts in several ways:

- They do not expect to hear a dial tone from a modem at the other end.

- They generally come with very advanced error-correction capabilities, such as the MNP 10 protocol from Microcom.

- They are more tolerant of timing fluctuations, which can arise, for example, when a transmission is handed off from one cell to another.

- They are more expensive, with prices that can go well over $1000.

It is possible to use a regular modem with a cellular telephone. This requires special adapters, however. The adapter must be able to fool the modem with a dial tone.

Fax Modem

A fax modem is a device that combines the capabilities of a fax machine and a modem. Fax modems can be distinguished by the fax format(s) they support and also by the type of interface they use.

Virtually all fax modems support the CCITT group 3 fax format. This standard calls for fax transmission at 9600 or 14,400bps, and for a fax resolution of 200×100 dots per inch (dpi) (horizontal $\times$ vertical) or 200×200 dpi in fine mode. (Groups 1 and 2, which preceded the group 3 standard by over a decade, are obsolete.)

The EIA is developing a class hierarchy to define the interface between a fax modem and the computer, and also to divide the work between these two devices. This hierarchy includes three classes:

- Class 1: Defines six commands which a fax modem must be able to understand. This class leaves most of the work (creating the fax and so on) up to the computer. Currently, only class 1 is widely supported and (more or less) finalized.

- Class 2: In this class, the modem does more of the work. Modems that support this interface understand about 40 commands. This is not yet an official standard, and is likely to be revised. Some fax modems support this class *as currently defined*.

M

- Class 3: This class will turn over the entire task of creating and transmitting the fax to the modem. This standard is far from completion.

In addition to this hierarchy, Intel and DCA have proposed a standard, called the Communicating Application Specification (CAS). The CAS is supported on all Intel fax modems and on models from several other vendors.

In addition to differing in the interfaces supported, fax modems differ in their capabilities. Some can send and receive faxes (called S/R fax modems); others can only send.

PCMCIA Modem

A PCMCIA modem is one that can be implemented on a Type II PCMCIA card. This card can be plugged into any notebook or palmtop computer that is compatible with this generation of PCMCIA card.

Portable Modem

A portable modem is compact and external. This type of modem can be transported easily and can be plugged into the appropriate port on any computer.

As technology progresses, components get smaller, faster, and more powerful. Portable modems are about the size of a deck of cards. To say such modems can be transported easily in a pocket would be stretching both the truth and the pocket. Although portable modems are bulkier than the PCMCIA modems, they have the advantage of being external and, therefore, more maneuverable.

Wireless Modem

A wireless modem is wireless when it is communicating with another modem, not with the computer. A wireless modem plugs into the computer's RS-232 port, but broadcasts over a wireless data network, such as the Mobitex networks run by Mobile Data.

Modem Bonding

In modem bonding, two modems—generally on a single board—are used together. In effect all the components are doubled. To use bonded modems, a user must have two phone connections.

Modem Pooling

Many networks, especially larger ones and those with a lot of dial-in activity, have multiple modems through which users can connect to the network. These will generally be handled as a pool of available resources, with each incoming call being passed to the next available modem.

Such modem pooling is commonly used, for example, by Internet access providers (IAPs). Users dial into a general access number, at which calls are handled in the order received. Each call is assigned to the next available modem. A user will then be assigned to a port for the session. This means that a user may not know what port or address will be assigned until the call and the connection are actually made. It also means that the details of a user's connection may be different each time the user calls in.

Multiport serial boards, which have two or more serial ports, can be used to handle multiple modems through a single board or card.

→ *Broader Category* Peripheral

Modem, 56K

→ *See* 56K Modem

Modem, Cable

A cable modem uses the cable TV company's wiring—rather than telephone lines—to achieve download transfer speeds as high as 10Mbps. A cable modem is considered to be a broadband device—most simply, because it operates in a bandwidth larger than 2Mbps.

Cable modems transmit and receive packets using radio frequency cable channels. The connection from the user's PC and modem goes over the cable company's coaxial cable, and eventually reaches the cable company's head end—that is, the main transmission point, from which all cable transmissions begin. At the head end, a connection to the Internet can be made. The illustration labeled "Example configuration using cable modems" provides an overview of a cable modem system. The cable coming from the user's home is coaxial. For some cable modem companies, the cabling over the entire route (that is, from home or office to the cable company head end) is coaxial; others have replaced the coaxial with fiber optic cable, which has greatly reduced errors and other messes.

High download speeds are no problem for cable modems, since cable TV services can have bandwidths as high as 1000MHz. In fact, the bandwidth allocated for even a single cable TV channel— 6MHz—can provide a transfer speed over 100 times faster than the fastest PC modems currently available. (These "fastest" modems are the 56K modems that are becoming increasingly popular.)

These high download speeds make cable modems ideally suited for retrieving files from a network. In contrast, such modems may be able to manage only the simplest upstream communications in some configurations. This is because the frequency range—5 to 50MHz—allocated by the FCC (Federal Communications Commission) for upstream communications happens to be a bandwidth in which lots of electrical devices—including refrigerators, freezers, and other appliances—emit noise. In other words, the upstream channel often has lots of garbage, which would have to be filtered out at the cable head end (that is, at the cable office). To make matters even worse, other cable modems use the same bandwidth for upstream communication, which means that the modems will also be competing with each other amid all the garbage in this frequency range.

High upstream speeds—up to 768Kbps—are possible with cable modems connected to cable providers that use hybrid fiber/coaxial cable. Such configurations use fiber-optic cable from the head end (that is, from the cable office) to a remote fiber unit, and use coaxial cabling from this point to the end users.

Additional drop cable may be needed when first setting up a cable modem—to connect the modem or to continue the wiring on the premises to the PC's location. This may be necessary because many users will have their TVs and PCs in different parts of the house.

Unlike modems that use the telephone lines, cable modems are generally always on.

→ **Broader Category**   Modem

Modified Frequency Modulation (MFM)

→ **See**   MFM (Modified Frequency Modulation)

Modified Modular Jack (MMJ)

→ **See**   MMJ (Modified Modular Jack)

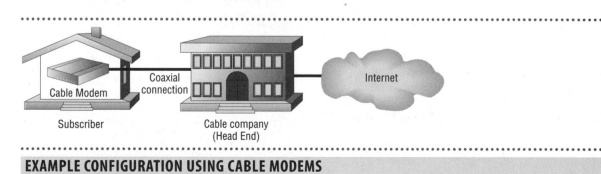

EXAMPLE CONFIGURATION USING CABLE MODEMS

M

Modulation

Modulation refers to the process of converting an informational signal (the modulating signal) into a form suitable for transmission using another (carrier) signal. This is accomplished by superimposing the information onto the (constant) carrier signal. The superimposed signal represents the information to be transmitted.

For example, a modem converts a binary value (communicated as an electrical signal) into acoustic form for transmission over a telephone line.

Modulation can involve either analog signals, digital signals, or both.

Analog Modulation

Analog modulation converts an analog signal (the information) into another analog signal (the carrier). The type of modulation depends on the feature of the carrier signal that is used to represent the information. Analog modulation can be of the following types:

Amplitude modulation (AM)   Varies the amplitude (strength) of the carrier signal. AM is used in radio and television broadcasting.

Frequency modulation (FM)   Varies the frequency (pitch) of the carrier signal. FM is used in radio and television broadcasting and in satellite communications.

Phase modulation (PM)   Varies the phase (time displacement) of the signal. PM is used in radio and television broadcasting and in satellite communications.

RF Modulation

RF modulation converts a digital signal to analog form (as is done in a modem, for example). The type of modulation and the amount of information that can be represented at a time depend on the features of the carrier signal that are modified. RF modulation can be of the following types:

Amplitude shift keying (ASK)   Varies the amplitude (strength) of the carrier signal. This method is used in low-speed (300bps) modems. This type of modulation is also known as *on-off keying (OOK)*.

Frequency shift keying (FSK)   Varies the frequency (pitch) of the carrier signal. This method is used in medium-speed (1200 and 2400bps) modems.

Phase shift keying (PSK)   Varies the phase (time displacement) of the carrier signal. Depending on how many different displacements are used, more than 1 bit can be represented in a single modulated signal. For example, by using four shift amounts (such as 0, 90, 180, and 270 degrees), 2 bits can be represented at a time. This method is used in medium- and high-speed (2400 and 4800bps) modems, and is also known as *binary phase shift keying (BPSK)*.

Quadrature amplitude modulation (QAM) Varies both the phase and the amplitude of the carrier signal. This makes it possible to encode as many as four bits in a single signal. QAM is used in high-speed (4800bps and faster) modems.

Quadrature phase shift keying (QPSK)   This method uses part of each cycle to indicate 0 or 1. It is similar to QAM.

Trellis coded modulation (TCM)   This is equivalent to QAM or QPSK, but includes extra bits for error correction.

"Quadrature amplitude modulation encoding" shows a QAM modulation scheme that encodes four bits in each signal, by using eight phase values, with two amplitudes at each value.

The shift keying modulation methods come in plain and differential forms. The differential versions encode different values simply as *changes* in the relevant signal feature, for example, as a change in frequency rather than as a change to a specific frequency. The following are the differential versions:

Differential amplitude shift keying (DASK)
Different digital values are encoded as changes in signal *amplitude*. This is in contrast to ASK.

Differential frequency shift keying (DFSK)
Different digital values are encoded as changes in signal *frequency*. This is in contrast to FSK.

Differential phase shift keying (DPSK) Different digital values are encoded as changes in signal *phase* (timing offset). This is in contrast to PSK.

Duobinary AM/PSK A digital signal is represented in analog form by varying both the amplitude and the phase (timing offset) of an analog carrier signal. The PSK element is used to reduce the bandwidth required for the transmission, not to encode a signal value. This modulation method is used in broadband versions of the IEEE 802.4 Token Bus architecture.

Differential modulation methods are easier to implement and are more robust than ordinary shift keying methods because the differential forms just look for differences, rather than for specific values.

Digital Modulation

Digital modulation converts an analog signal into a digital carrier (as in compact discs and digital

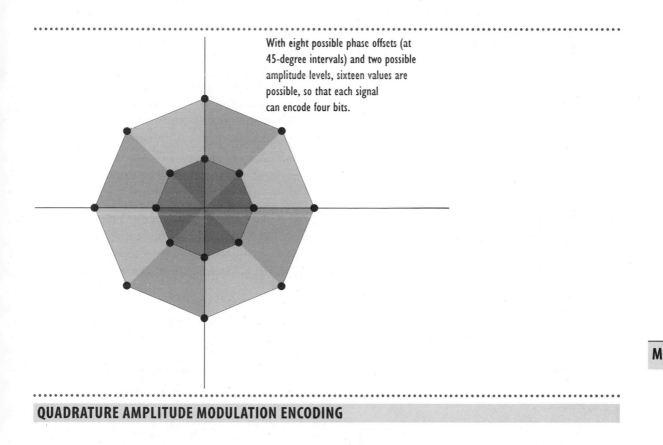

With eight possible phase offsets (at 45-degree intervals) and two possible amplitude levels, sixteen values are possible, so that each signal can encode four bits.

QUADRATURE AMPLITUDE MODULATION ENCODING

M

telephone lines, for example). The basic strategy is to convert an analog wave into discrete pulses by taking multiple samples of the analog signal and converting each sample into a corresponding discrete signal.

It has been demonstrated mathematically that the conversion can be made without any loss of information if enough samples are taken. The type of modulation used depends on what aspect of the pulse is modified to convey a value.

For example, pulse time modulation refers to a class of digital modulation methods in which a time-dependent feature of a pulse (for example, width, duration, or position) is varied to encode an analog signal that is being converted to digital form.

Digital modulation can be any of the following types:

Delta modulation (DM)   Represents the analog signal as a series of bits, whose values depend on the level of the analog signal relative to the previous level. If the signal is going up (increasing), the method sets a 1; otherwise, it sets a 0. This modulation method discards information on the rate at which the analog signal is changing.

Adaptive delta modulation (ADM)   Represents the analog signal as a weighted train of digital pulses. ADM differs from delta modulation in weighting the signal, which means that it takes into account the rate of change in the analog signal.

Adaptive differential pulse code modulation (ADPCM)   Amplitudes are represented using 4-bit values (rather than the 8 bits used in PCM), and a 32Kbps data-transfer rate is used (rather than 64Kbps, as for PCM).

Pulse amplitude modulation (PAM)   Represents the amplitude of the analog signal at sampling time with a carrier pulse of comparable amplitude. In short, PAM simply chops a continuous analog signal into a series of discrete signals.

Pulse code modulation (PCM)   Converts a signal into a serial stream of bit values. The signal is based on an analog signal that has already been modulated (generally by using PAM, but possibly using PDM, PPM, or PWM). The pulses are grouped into any of a predefined number of different levels using a quantizer, and each of the possible levels is represented by a unique bit stream. The number of possible values in this stream determines the granularity of the modulation. In most applications, 127 different levels are used, so that 7 bits are needed for each pulse. More sophisticated multimedia applications may use as many as 24 bits to represent pulses.

Pulse duration modulation (PDM)   Represents an analog signal by varying the duration, or width, of a discrete pulse. The dots and dashes used for Morse code represent such a modulation. This type of modulation is also known as pulse width modulation (PWM).

Pulse position modulation (PPM)   A pulse time method that represents an analog signal by varying the positioning (the time displacement) of a discrete pulse within a bit interval. The position is varied in accordance with the sampled value of an analog signal.

Pulse width modulation (PWM)   Represents an analog signal by varying the width (the duration) of a discrete pulse. This method is also known as *pulse duration modulation* (*PDM*).

Digital modulation methods differ in their goals. Waveform coding methods try to provide as complete a representation of the analog signal as possible; that is, they try to represent the original waveform in the output signal. The methods summarized above use waveform coding.

Source coding methods try to minimize the number of bits needed to provide an acceptable (but not necessarily identical) representation of the analog signal. Source coding methods are quite complex.

→ *See Also* Pulse Modulation

Monitor-Contention

→ *See* Token-Claiming

MONITOR.NLM

A Novell NetWare Loadable Module (NLM) for monitoring the status and performance of the NetWare server and network activity. The monitor also observes memory and processor use, and can do garbage collecting to clear memory when necessary.

Monitor, Standby

A standby monitor is a reserve device that can be put into operation as soon as the main monitor malfunctions.

Mosaic

Mosaic is the original name for a Web browser (hypertext file reader) developed at the NCSA (National Center for Supercomputing Applications) at the University of Illinois at Urbana-Champaign. The NCSA version of Mosaic was developed largely with federal funds, and is freely available for downloading and use. Like most freeware, however, NCSA Mosaic has not undergone the testing expected of a commercial product. Similarly, its features are more a reflection of its developers' needs and preferences than of the needs of a general audience.

While releasing *its* version as freeware, the NCSA also licensed the Mosaic software to third parties. These companies were free to enhance and develop Mosaic as they chose. Several companies released commercial versions of Mosaic as parts of more comprehensive Internet access software packages. Other companies have developed browsers based on Mosaic. For example, Microsoft's Internet Explorer is based on Mosaic.

→ *Broader Categories* Browser, WWW (World Wide Web)

→ *Compare* Lynx; Netscape Navigator

Most Significant Bit (MSB)

→ *See* MSB (Most Significant Bit)

Motherboard

The main circuit board in a computer. This board will hold the CPU (central processing unit), and may include a math coprocessor, various other controller chips, and RAM chips. In its role as a backplane, the motherboard provides slots for expansion. In recent years, motherboards have been in a state of active development. The main developments have been to put faster chips and bus circuitry on the board (while still managing to avoid damage due to heat buildup without adequate opportunity to dissipate) and changes in the way in which the central processing unit (CPU)—the main chip—is attached to the board. Traditionally, CPUs have been plugged into sockets right on the motherboard; however, Intel developed technology to allow the CPU to be put on a single edge connector (SEC) that plugs into one of the expansion slots. It is arguable whether this move provides true technological advance and performance improvements or whether it simply slows down the competition in the race to remain compatible with the Intel architecture.

→ *See Also* Backplane

MOTIS (Message-Oriented Text Interchange System)

A message-handling system developed by the ISO. The basic elements of this system are compatible with the model in the CCITT's X.400 specifications.

→ *See Also* MHS (Message Handling System)

M

MOV (Metal Oxide Varistor)

An electrical component in a line conditioner or surge protector. MOVs help clip high-energy spikes from an incoming supply. Compare MOV with capacitor and inductor.

MP3 (Motion Picture Experts Group—Layer 3) Encoding

MP3 is a scheme for encoding audio information in a highly compressed form and with high fidelity. With MP3 encoding, a WAV audio file can be compressed down to about 5–10 percent of its original size. Because MP3 compression discards mainly frequencies that are beyond the audible range, the resulting file generally shows little loss of quality.

MP3 encoding has become very popular because it can be used to exchange music files over the Internet in an efficient manner. As a result, MP3 sites are springing up to distribute both legitimate and illicit files. Needless to say, the recording industry is frightened, indignant, threatening all sorts of legal action, and frantically searching for a way to undermine MP3's popularity in order to regain control of music distribution.

MPI (Multiple Protocol Interface)

The top part of the link-support layer (LSL) in the generic ODI (Open Data-link Interface) for LAN drivers.

MPLS (Multiprotocol Label Switching)

The MPLS working group was formed by the IETF (Internet Engineering Task Force) to develop a strategy for layer 3 switching that could serve as an acceptable standard to replace the vendor-specific solutions that have been developed. Such switching makes it possible to save overhead by treating a sequence of

packets in a connection-oriented manner. Because the packets all need to go to the same location, the destination address only needs to be checked for the first packets. See the entry on Layer 3 Switching for information on what this means.

Ad hoc solutions to this task include Cisco's tag switching, IBM's ARIS (Aggregate Router-based IP Switching), Ipsilon's IFMP (Ipsilon Flow Management Protocol), and Toshiba's CSR (Cell-Switched Router).

→ **Broader Category** Layer 3 Switching

MPOA (Multiprotocol Over ATM)

MPOA is a service that makes internetworking over ATM (Asynchronous Transfer Mode) networks possible. It enables two clients to establish a switched virtual connection (SVC) over an ATM network—even if these clients are on different networks and use layer 3 addressing. By doing address resolution, MPOA components can convert layer 3 addresses to ATM addresses, which allows packets to move across the ATM network.

MPOA clients can be edge devices, which can move packets between emulated or legacy LANs (local area networks) and the ATM network. Or they can be ATM hosts, which can query MPOA servers and can forward packets using either layer 2 or layer 3 addresses.

MPOA server elements are distributed across the network. A route server works on address resolution, responds to client queries, and handles the routing protocols needed to communicate with legacy LANs. The MPOA server environment also includes packet forwarders and elements known as IASG Coordination Function Groups (ICFGs). ICFGs are responsible for dealing with subnets whose elements may be connected to different physical ports. (IASG stands for internetwork address subgroup, which is essentially a subnet—that is, a networking construct consisting of network nodes with the same layer 3 address prefix.)

MPOA services rely on a virtual router, which distributes the functionality (for example, path computation and packet forwarding) of a router across the ATM network. Specifically, a virtual router distributes the packet forwarding functions over the ATM network, but centralizes the path computation, address resolution, and routing table maintenance tasks in a route server. A virtual router is in contrast to a unified router, which has all the hardware elements in a single box, but which can be a bottleneck in high-speed networks (such as the 150Mbps and faster ATM networks and Gigabit Ethernet networks).

The complete MPOA service carries out several tasks:

- Configuring the devices involved. This is done by establishing a VCC (virtual channel connection) between a client and a server to allow the exchange of configuration information.

- Registering clients and locating legacy networks. This is also done using the VCC between clients and servers.

- Resolving destination addresses. This is done by a route server, and the information is provided upon request to a client or to an ICFG. Route servers also exchange information with each other to maintain their routing information and keep everything synchronized. For connections within the same subnet, clients can get the required information from an ICFG.

- Transferring data. This is generally done over a VCC (virtual channel connection) directly connecting the two clients, but it may also use default or remote forwarders.

- Communicating with legacy networks. This is done using routing protocols—or spanning trees if the LANs involved use bridging.

- Replicating certain MPOA components. This helps improve availability.

- Handling distributed subnets. This is done using the ICFGs, which exchange information about the subnet topologies in order to remain synchronized.

MPOA, which is still being developed by the ATM Forum, was developed as an effort to integrate the different solutions that have been created for internetworking over ATM. Existing solutions include ATMARP (ATM Address Resolution Protocol, for intra-subnet address resolution) and NHRP (Next Hop Routing Protocol, for inter-subnet address resolution), MARS (multicast address resolution server, for IP multicast), and LANE (LAN emulation, for Ethernet and Token Ring networks).

→ *Broader Category* ATM (Asynchronous Transfer Mode)

MPR (Multiport Repeater)

In an Ethernet network, an MPR is a repeater that connects multiple network segments in parallel. MPRs are generally used in thin Ethernet networks.

MRM (Maximum Rights Mask)

In Novell's NetWare 2.2, the MRM is a list of the trustee rights that users are allowed to exercise in a directory. An MRM is assigned to every directory. The MRM can block both inherited rights and specific trustee assignments. This means that, even if a user has been given all trustee rights to a directory, the directory's MRM can prevent the user from exercising some or all of those rights.

NetWare 2.2 uses the following rights to control file access and use:

- R (Read), which allows the user to open and read a file.

- W (Write), which allows the user to open and write to an existing file.

- C (Create), which allows a user to create a new file or directory.

- E (Erase), which allows a user to delete a file or a directory, including its files and subdirectories.

M

- M (Modify), which allows a user to change a file's or a directory's names and attributes, but not content.

- F (File Scan), which allows a user to see files in directory listings.

- A (Access Control), which allows a user to change trustee assignments and also the MRM.

The MRM was replaced by the Inherited Rights Mask (IRM) in NetWare 3.x, and by the Inherited Rights Filter (IRF) in NetWare 4.x.

→ **Compare** IRM (Inherited Rights Mask)/IRF (Inherited Rights Filter)

MRU (Maximum Receive Unit)

In network communications, the MRU represents the size of the largest packet that can be received over a physical link between two nodes. The MRU will generally depend on several factors, including the channel bandwidth and any timing constraints or considerations associated with the network architecture.

Under certain circumstances—in particular, when there are multiple links between two devices—it's possible to get throughput that exceeds the MRU. This is accomplished by combining several channels into a larger logical channel that can accommodate faster (combined) traffic than any of the individual physical channels. To actually accomplish this increased throughput, however, special protocols must be used, otherwise packets may not be reassembled correctly at the receiving end.

MS (Message Store)

In the 1988 version of CCITT's X.400 Message Handling Service (MHS), an MS is a general archive in which mail can be held until the appropriate user retrieves it through a User Agent (UA) or until the allowable storage time for the message

is exceeded. The MS is distinct from the mailboxes associated with individual users.

UAs and other services use the MSAP (Message store access protocol) to access the message store.

MSB (Most Significant Bit)

In a bit sequence, the MSB is the bit corresponding to the highest power of 2 for the sequence. In a byte, this would be the 128s digit (corresponding to 2^7); in a 16-bit word, the bit would correspond to the 2^{15} place value.

The actual location of this bit in a representation depends on the context (storing or transmitting) and on the ordering within a word. See the "Big-Endian" and "Little-Endian" articles for a discussion of these issues.

→ **Compare** LSB (Least Significant Bit)

MS-CHAP (Microsoft Challenge Handshake Authentication Protocol)

→ **See** Protocol, MS-CHAP (Microsoft Challenge Handshake Authentication Protocol)

MSIE (Microsoft Internet Explorer)

MSIE is Microsoft's entry in the browser wars. This browser's integration into Windows 98 was one of the factors that led to the Justice Department's suit against Microsoft.

Like its competition—most notably Netscape Navigator—MSIE supports the HTML (Hypertext Markup Language) 3.2 standard as well as most (but not all) of the HTML 4.0 and DHTML (Dynamic HTML) constructs. In addition, MSIE supports certain extensions that are unique to Microsoft's product. Explorer and Navigator do not implement all supported HTML (and DHTML) constructs in exactly the same way.

In addition to HTML support, MSIE 5—the most recent version—includes support for scripting languages (JavaScript and VBScript) and Web programming tools (such as Java and ActiveX), and even some support for the up and coming XML (eXtensible Markup Language).

→ *Compare* Netscape Navigator

MSN (Microsoft Network)

MSN is Microsoft's online service and ISP (Internet Service Provider). MSN originally debuted (as an online service with Internet access) around the same time as Windows 95—to a lukewarm response. The priority given to the online service—with Internet access as an option reflected Microsoft's belief at the time that the Internet was not where the real action was.

It soon became clear that this was not the correct call, and MSN was revamped as an ISP. Because Microsoft could make sure it appeared on the Windows desktop, MSN's subscription list continued to grow.

MSN has recently been retooled and repackaged as a Web portal—that is, as an access site to the Web for Internet access subscribers. This move has been quite successful, and MSN is now one of the most popular Internet access points.

MST (Minimum Spanning Tree)

In bridged networks or in an internetwork, the MST is the "shortest" set of connections that includes all the possible connections and that does not contain any loops (closed paths, in which a packet could get trapped).

→ *See Also* Bridge

MTA (Message Transfer Agent)

In an X.400 model, a component of a Message Handling System (MHS) that is responsible for storing and/or forwarding messages to another MTA, to a user agent (UA), or to another authorized recipient. The MTA is comparable to a mail agent in the TCP/IP environment.

MTBF (Mean Time Between Failures)

A measure of the durability of an electronic component. This value, also known as mean time before failure, represents the average amount of time that elapses between breakdowns.

→ *See Also* MTTR (Mean Time To Repair)

MTL (Message Transfer Layer)

In the 1984 version of the X.400 MHS (Message Handling System) recommendations, the MTL is the lower sublayer of the OSI reference model's application layer. This sublayer provides access to the transfer services. Message transfer agent entities (MTAEs) carry out the functions at this sublayer. The 1984 version defines a protocol known as P1 for communications between MTAEs.

The user agent layer (UAL) is the sublayer above the MTL. The services for this sublayer may be implemented on a different machine than the one containing the MTL. For example, in a LAN, workstations may run the user agent sublayer to communicate with a server that provides the actual message transfer server. For configurations in which the MTL and UAL are on different machines, the recommendations provide a submission and delivery entity (SDE) to carry out the functions of the MTL.

→ *Broader Category:* X.400

M

MTS (Message Transfer Service)

In the 1984 version of the CCITT's X.400 Message Handling System (MHS), the MTS is a connectionless but reliable transfer capability. (*Connectionless* means that parts of the message are transported independently of each other, and may take different paths; *reliable* means that a message part will be delivered correctly or the sender will be informed that this was not possible.)

The 1988 and 1992 versions of the MHS elaborated on the MTS. In the revised standards, the MTS is a worldwide, application-independent store-and-forward service for message transfers. This means that the MTS will deliver messages from one user to another, regardless of the relative locations of sender and recipient. Such actions assume, of course, that it is possible to deliver messages to the recipient.

The general-purpose MTS is distinguished from the more specialized IPMS (Interpersonal Messaging System)—the other major component of the MHS. The IPMS is used for personal or simple business correspondence. The MTS, on the other hand, is intended more for EDI (Electronic Data Interchange) documents. Such documents represent a cost-effective and environmentally sound (i.e., paperless) way of exchanging business forms, invoices, etc.

The MTS deals with requests from:

- User agents (UAs), which generally just front for ordinary users. UAs are abstract service elements, and each active UA will be associated with a real user at some level.

- Message stores (MSs), which hold messages until they are picked up by the user (agent).

- Access units (AUs), which serve as gateways between user requirements and low-level demands.

- Message transfer agents (MTAs), which work within the MTS and which—effectively—bind the MTS together. MTAs may connect to each other or to an end user. MTAs also deal with the message store and with access units.

→ *Primary Sources* The MHS model is covered in the X.400 series of ITU (formerly CCITT) recommendations. The MTS specifically is the subject of recommendation X.411.

MTS (Microsoft Transaction Server)

MTS is a middleware product that mediates between an Internet-based client and a backend for a database. MTS provides the functions needed to ensure that any transactions that take place are treated as atomic—that is, indivisible—elements. Saying that a transaction is atomic means that either of two things can happen:

- The transaction succeeds, and is executed to completion.

- The transaction fails, in which case no part of the transaction will remain and the environment will be restored to its state before the transaction was attempted.

MTSO (Mobile Telephone Switching Office)

In cellular communications, an MTSO is a central computer that monitors all transmissions. If a connection is too noisy, the MTSO searches for a less noisy channel, and does a hand-off by transferring the connection to another channel in the next cell.

The hand-off takes between 200 and 1200 milliseconds, which is quite a long time for some devices to wait. For example, some modems will disconnect if there is such a long break in the connection.

MTTR (Mean Time To Repair)

The average amount of time required to repair an electrical or other component. For many types of equipment, this value is in the 15- to 45-minute range.

MTU (Maximum Transmission Unit)

The largest packet that can be sent over a given medium. If a packet is larger than an MTU, the packet must be fragmented (or segmented), sent as two (or more) properly sized packets, and then repackaged at the receiving end.

The MTU between any two nodes in a single network is the same. However, for a connection that goes through several networks, the MTU for the entire connection—known as the *path MTU*—is determined by the shortest MTU anywhere in the path. (The Path MTU is abbreviated PMTU.)

MUD (Multiuser Dimension)

Also known as a Multiuser Dungeon, a MUD is an online environment for doing role playing and other types of interactions in adventure games or simulations. MUD activities are interactive, and in most of them players can take on roles or personalities of their own choosing. The laws that govern a particular MUD have either been defined in advance by the MUD's creator or they can be created as the game develops.

Players cooperate with or compete against each other. Some games provide tests of mental skill; others involve warfare. Still others may call for interpersonal (or societal or even global) planning and action. Many of the games are text-based, but some of the more sophisticated ones involve virtual reality. Players may prosper, wither, or even die—figuratively, of course.

Variants include MOOs (MUDs, Object-Oriented), MUSEs (Multiuser Simulated Environments), and

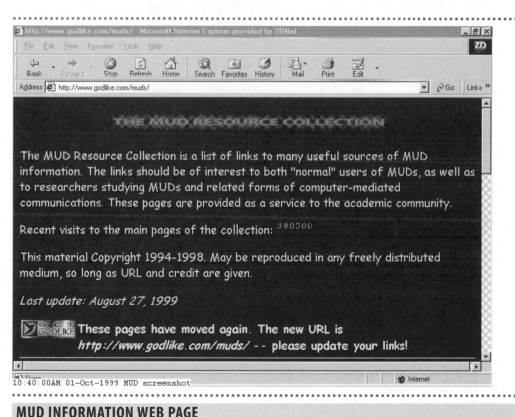

MUD INFORMATION WEB PAGE

M

MUSHes (Multiuser Shared Hallucinations). Of these, MUSEs are most likely to be educational—for example, in the form of science labs or other types of experimental or empirical endeavors.

→ *Primary Sources* The Web page at http://www .godlike.com/muds/ provides a rich set of resources about MUDs. "MUD information Web page" shows one browser's (Cello's) view of the home page for this file. While this page is updated at irregular intervals, the pages to which this document has links may be updated more frequently.

Multibyte Character

In encoding, a character represented by 2 or more bytes. These characters arise in languages whose alphabet contains more than 256 characters, as is the case with ideographic languages such as Chinese and Japanese.

Multicast

A transmission method in which one source node communicates with one or more destination nodes with a single transmission. However, in contrast to a *broadcast*, which is sent to all connected nodes, a multicast message is transmitted only to some of the possible recipients.

Multicast Attribute Framing Protocol (MAFP)

→ *See* Protocol, MAFP (Multicast Attribute Framing Protocol)

Multichannel Multipoint Distribution Services (MMDS)

→ *See* MMDS (Multichannel Multipoint Distribution Services)

Multi-CPU Architecture

A computer architecture that uses multiple processors, either to work together on the same tasks or separately on different tasks. This type of architecture can be used in local area networking contexts, such as in super-servers. However, in many cases, the extra processor is included for redundancy, rather than for efficiency.

Multidrop Connection

In networking, a connection in which multiple nodes are connected by a single line. For example, an Ethernet bus topology provides a multidrop connection.

Multi-homed Host

In the Internet environment, a single machine connected to multiple data links, which may be on different networks.

Multihomed Server

→ *See* Server, Multihomed

Multiline Hunt Group (MLHG)

→ *See* MLHG (Multiline Hunt Group)

Multimedia Multiparty Teleconferencing (MMT)

→ *See* MMT (Multimedia Multiparty Teleconferencing)

Multimode

In fiber optics, a class of fibers with a core thick enough for light to take several paths (known as *modes*) through the core. This is in contrast to a single mode fiber, whose core is thin enough so that light can take only a single path through the core.

→ *See Also* Cable, Fiber-Optic

Multimode Fiber (MMF)

→ *See* MMF (Multimode Fiber)

Multipath

In radio communications, a multipath refers to signals that are reflected back and that are out of phase with each other. Multipaths can arise in areas with lots of communications traffic, for example.

Multiple Access

Simultaneous access to the same file for multiple users. Multiple access is generally allowed only for reading files. If users are allowed to make changes to a file, some sort of locking mechanism is required to prevent users from interfering with each other's work.

Multiple Link Interface (MLI)

→ *See* MLI (Multiple Link Interface)

Multiple Logical Terminals (MLT)

→ *See* MLT (Multiple Logical Terminals)

Multiple Master Domain Model

In Windows NT, the multiple master domain model is one of four possible models for organizing and administering networks. This model is an extension of the master domain model. It allows multiple master domains, which, among them, control all user accounts. As in the master domain model, resources may be decentralized and administered independently of each other.

In trust relationships for this model, all accounts domains—that is, master domains—must trust each other. Thus, trust relationships among master domains are two directional. Each resource domain must trust every accounts domain.

The multiple master domain model makes it possible to scale enterprise networks up to handle hundreds of thousands of users. (The master domain model can support only about 40,000 users.) The other NT domain models are the complete trust domain model, the master domain model, and the single domain model.

→ *Broader Categories* Domain Model; Windows NT

→ *Compare* Complete Trust Domain Model; Master Domain Model; Single Domain Model

Multiple Protocol Interface (MPI)

→ *See* MPI (Multiple Protocol Interface)

Multiple UNC Provider (MUP)

→ *See* MUP (Multiple UNC Provider)

Multiple Virtual Storage (MVS)

→ *See* MVS (Multiple Virtual Storage)

M

Multiplexing

In communications or signaling, multiplexing is a technique for allowing multiple messages or signals to share a transmission channel. The two main ways of sharing a channel are time division multiplexing (TDM) and frequency division multiplexing (FDM).

Time Division Multiplexing (TDM)

In TDM, small slices from each input channel are sent in sequence, so that each input channel has some of the time on the output channel. If each of *n* input channels is given an equal time slice, then each channel gets only *1/n* of the time on the output channel. This multiplexing process is illustrated in "Time division multiplexing strategy."

TDM is sometimes used to create a secondary channel that operates at the limits of the main channel's bandwidth—which is generally not used for transmission.

The following variants on TDM are distinguished:

- ATDM (asynchronous time division multiplexing): Multiplexing in which the data is transmitted asynchronously.

- STDM (statistical time division multiplexing): A multiplexing method that polls nodes and immediately skips any nodes that have nothing to send.

- STM (synchronous transfer mode): Designed for use in BISDN (broadband ISDN) and also supported in the SONET (Synchronous Optical Network) architecture.

Frequency Division Multiplexing (FDM)

In FDM, the output channel is divided into multiple, smaller bandwidth channels. Each of these output "channelettes" is defined in a different frequency range, and each is allocated for transmitting one of the input channels. The output channels all have a capacity that is inversely proportional to the number of input channels. "Frequency division multiplexing strategy" shows this process.

Wavelength Division Multiplexing (WDM)

Since frequency and wavelength are inversely related for electromagnetic and optical signals, WDM is analogous to FDM, except that different signals are transmitted at different wavelengths along the same wire or fiber.

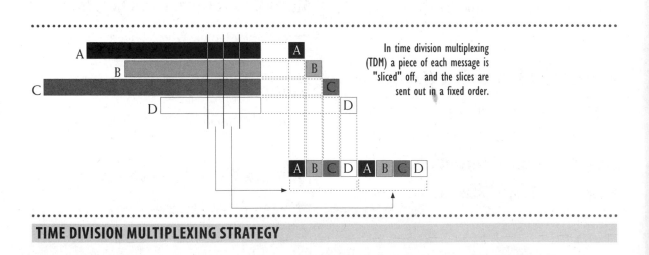

In time division multiplexing (TDM) a piece of each message is "sliced" off, and the slices are sent out in a fixed order.

TIME DIVISION MULTIPLEXING STRATEGY

Multiplexers

A *multiplexer* (or *multiplexor*) is a device for selecting a single output from among several inputs or for channeling several data streams into a single communications channel. The input channels are generally low-speed, while the single output channel is high-speed, with enough bandwidth to accommodate the multiple slower channels. This term is often abbreviated as *MUX*.

The multiplexer uses a predetermined strategy for combining multiple streams. For example, in TDM, the multiplexer gives each stream a time slice in the transmission. At the other end of such a transmission, another multiplexer (known as a *demultiplexer*) reverses the process, to extract the individual channels from the multiplexed stream.

Multipoint Connection

In networking, a connection in which multiple nodes are connected by a single line. For example, an Ethernet bus topology provides a multipoint connection.

Multipoint Distribution Services (MDS)

→ *See* MDS (Multipoint Distribution Services)

Multiport Repeater (MPR)

→ *See* MPR (Multiport Repeater)

Multiprocessing

A computing strategy in which multiple processors work on the same task. This is in contrast to *multitasking*, in which the same processor works on multiple tasks, apparently at the same time.

Multiprotocol Label Switching (MPLS)

→ *See* MPLS (Multiprotocol Label Switching)

Multiprotocol Over ATM (MPOA)

→ *See* MPOA (Multiprotocol Over ATM)

Multipurpose Internet Mail Extension (MIME)

→ *See* MIME (Multipurpose Internet Mail Extension)

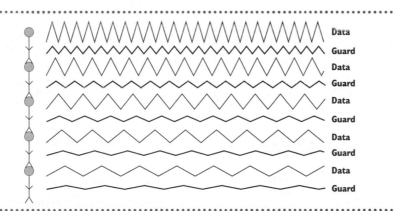

In frequency division multiplexing (FDM) each channel gets its own frequency band. Each of these is part of the total bandwidth. The data bands are separated from each other by guard bands.

Data
Guard
Data
Guard
Data
Guard
Data
Guard
Data
Guard

FREQUENCY DIVISION MULTIPLEXING STRATEGY

Multiserver Network

A multiserver network has two or more file servers on a single network. As with a single-server network, the nodes can access each server in accordance with their access rights. However, some nodes may not be able to communicate with every server, because the node and server may have different architectures (or be of different types), such as a Macintosh on a NetWare network.

The servers in a multiserver network have the same physical network number, but are distinguished by different node numbers within that physical network. For example, on physical network AAA3, the servers might be nodes 1 and 2.

Each server also has a unique internal network number, such as FFFA and FFFD for the two servers.

Multiserver networks involve only a single physical network address. This means that all network traffic flows across the entire network. The manner in which it flows—broadcast or sequentially—depends on the network architecture. Each server may generate its own network traffic, which will traverse the entire network. On the other hand, no special routing or filtering processes are necessary on a multiserver network.

In contrast, an internetwork includes at least two different physical network addresses. There must be a device that links the two networks. This will generally be either a bridge or a router, but may also be a gateway. If more than two networks are being linked, the connection is likely to be a switch. Because they can filter, network links can help reduce the traffic on the component networks. These links must do work—to check an address, find a route, or translate and route a packet.

Multistation Access Unit (MAU)

→ **See** MAU (Multistation Access Unit)

Multitasking

In multitasking, a single processor seems to be running two or more programs at the same time (concurrently). Actually, only one of these tasks gets the processor's attention at any given moment, so that the concurrency is only apparent. The currently running task is said to be in the *foreground*; the other tasks are running in the *background*.

Multitasking is different from *multiprocessing*, in which multiple processors work on the same task.

Preemptive versus Non-Preemptive Multitasking

Multitasking may be preemptive or non-preemptive. In *preemptive multitasking*, the operating system (or whatever program is controlling the multitasking) controls switching between tasks, and every task gets its turn in a predictable fashion. Windows NT and UNIX support preemptive multitasking.

In *non-preemptive multitasking*, an application or process gets to execute until it stops itself. The application cannot be interrupted, and it must be trusted to give up control. Novell's NetWare does non-preemptive multitasking.

Although non-preemptive environments run the risk of greedy or runaway applications that will not give up the chip, non-preemptive multitasking has certain advantages for server-based arrangements such as a NetWare network. An important one is that there is less need for synchronization of shared data and memory, because no other application or process is competing with the application that is executing.

Non-preemptive environments also have resources available to prevent an application from hogging the CPU (central processing unit), including direct intervention by the operating system itself.

Types of Multitasking

The following types of multitasking are distinguished:

   Context-switching   This is the simplest form of multitasking. Two or more processes, or tasks, are loaded, each with its own data and execution environment, or context. Only one task at a time gets the processor's attention. The operating system switches between tasks, usually when it wants to run another program. Task managers, which can be part of an operating system or of a shell, provide context-switching capabilities. Among other things, a task manager must provide and manage storage for each of the loaded tasks.

Cooperative   In cooperative multitasking, a background process is allowed to get the processor's attention during moments when a foreground process is temporarily idle. For example, a data analysis program may be running in the background while you are doing text editing. While you are thinking, the operating system will let the data analysis program do a bit of work. System 7, the Macintosh operating system, supports cooperative multitasking, which is non-preemptive.

Time-slice   In time-slice multitasking, each process gets a slice of the processor's time. All tasks may get equal time slices, or each will get a time slice whose size is proportionate to the task's priority. The operating system runs each of the tasks in succession, for the duration of the task's time slice. OS/2 and various mainframe operating systems support time-slice multitasking, which is preemptive.

Multithreading

A thread is an executable object, which belongs to a single process or program. Each thread comes with its own stacks, registers, and instruction counter.

Multithreading is a special form of multitasking in which all the tasks come from the same program. In multithreading, multiple processes from a single program execute, seemingly at the same time. This concurrency is only apparent because, as with multitasking, the processor is actually switching its attention very rapidly among all the threads.

Multiuser

Multiuser refers to an environment or operating system that supports more than one user at a time. UNIX is an example of a multiuser operating system; DOS and OS/2 are single-user systems.

Multiuser Dimension (MUD)

→ *See*   MUD (Multiuser Dimension)

MUP (Multiple UNC Provider)

In Windows NT, MUP (Multiple UNC provider, where UNC stands for *uniform naming convention*) refers to a driver that can determine which network to access when an application wants to open a remote file.

MVS (Multiple Virtual Storage)

MVS is an operating system used by IBM in many of its mainframes. MVS is basically a batch-oriented system that can manage large amounts of memory or storage.

Originally introduced in 1974, MVS has been modified and extended as the need has arisen. For example, MVS/XA (Extended Architecture) and MVS/ESA (Enterprise Systems Architecture) were introduced in the 1980s to handle IBM's newer mainframes, such as the ESA/370 product line and the ES/9000 models in the System/390 line.

MX (Mail Exchange) Record

In the Internet's DNS, a record is a data structure that indicates which machine(s) can handle electronic mail (e-mail) for a domain (particular portion or region of the Internet).

→ *See Also*   DNS (Domain Naming System)

M

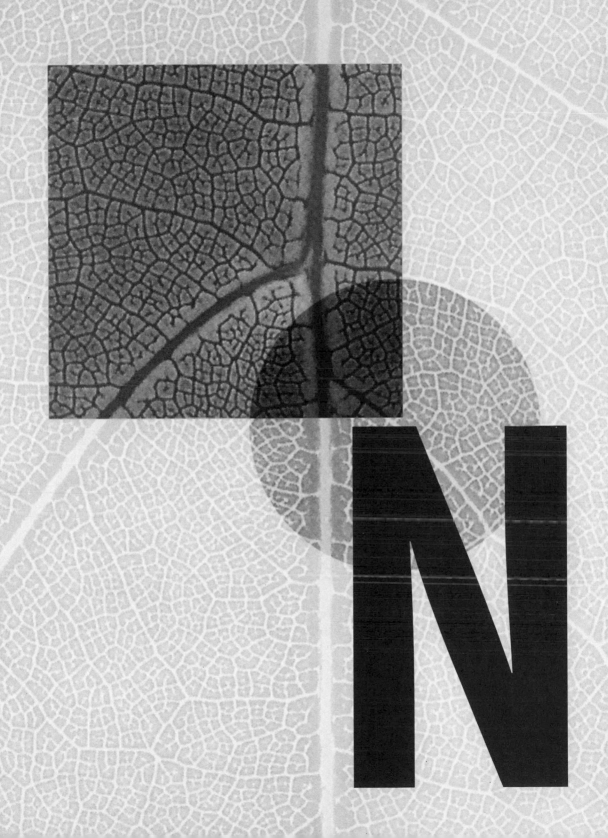

N

Used, usually in lowercase, as an abbreviation for the prefix *nano*, as in nsec (nanoseconds) or nm (nanometers). This order of magnitude is known as one billionth (in the United States counting system). It corresponds to 10^{-9}, or 2^{-30} if binary values are involved.

→ *See Also* Order of Magnitude

NA (Numerical Aperture)

In fiber optics, the NA indicates the range of angles over which a fiber core can receive incoming light.

NAC (Network Access Controller)

An NAC is a device that provides access to a network, for remote callers or for another network.

NAK (Negative Acknowledgment)

A signal used to indicate that an error has been detected in a transmission. In the ASCII encoding system, character 21 is used for NAK.

Named Pipe

In many operating environments, a stream that can be used for the exchange of information between two processes. The pipe can be referred to by name, and the storage allocated for the pipe can be accessed and used for reading and writing, much like a file, except that the storage and the pipe disappear when the programs involved finish executing.

Name Resolution

In a network or internetwork, name resolution refers to the process of mapping the name of a device or node to an address.

Name Server

→ *See* Server, Name

Name Space

A name space is a NetWare Loadable Module (NLM) that makes it possible to store non-DOS files on a Novell NetWare file server. You can store Macintosh, UNIX, OS/2, or other types of files on a NetWare 3.*x* or later server by linking the appropriate name space NLM to the operating system. You also must use the ADD NAME SPACE utility to add configuration information for the name space.

The volume to which the alien file is being added will create two directory entries for the file: a DOS entry and an entry with the information for the file's native format.

Adding a name space to a volume has its costs:

- More cache memory is needed to store the additional directory entries.

- Removing the name space is a major chore.

→ *Broader Category* NetWare

Naming Service

A naming service is a mechanism that makes it possible to name resources on the network and to access them through those names. This service associates a more easily remembered name with a network entity, and that name can then be used instead of the resource's network address. Naming services are available in most network operating systems.

A naming service can be either of two types:

- A *local naming service*, which is associated with a single server

or

- A *global naming service*, which is associated with a network or an internetwork

For example, Novell's NetWare versions prior to 4.0 use a local naming service; information about the resources associated with a server is stored in a resource database known as the *bindery*. The Novell Directory Services (NDS) used in NetWare 4.*x* and later is an example of a global naming service. Another example is StreetTalk, the global naming service for Banyan's VINES. With a global naming service, each object on the internetwork has a unique name, so you do not need to know the name of a server to find an object associated with that server.

→ *See Also* Bindery, NDS (Novell Directory Services), StreetTalk

NAP (Network Access Point)

In the context of the Internet, this term is generally used to refer to one of the four locations at which the top-level Internet Service Providers (ISPs) connect to the Internet backbone. These NAPs were originally created by the National Science Foundation but are now operated by major communications providers. The four original NAPs are located in Chicago (Ameritech), New York (Sprint), San Francisco (PacBell), and near Washington, DC (MCI WorldCom).

The term has also come to be used for several other major access points. These include Big East (operated by ICS Network Systems) and MAE West (operated in Silicon Valley by MCI World-Com). MAE West is actually the West Coast counterpart to WorldCom's MAE East, which is the name of the Washington, DC, NAP.

Since the NAPs are actually on the Internet backbone, they are at the top of the access hierarchy. The first-tier (national) ISPs each connect to at least one of the NAPs—with some connecting to all four. Second-tier (regional) ISPs can, in turn, connect to the first-tier ISPs. Third-tier ISPs connect to the second-tiers, and so on down the line. Only the top-tier ISPs are connected to NAPs.

Narrowband ISDN (NISDN)

→ *See* NISDN (Narrowband ISDN)

NAS (Network Application Support)

NAS is Digital Equipment Corporation's (DEC's) attempt to provide a uniform environment for software running on different platforms (such as VAXen and PCs), so that applications can be integrated with each other, regardless of the platforms involved.

NAS is designed to use international standards to support the multiple platforms. This is in contrast to the strategy used with SAA (Systems Application Architecture), which is IBM's counterpart to NAS. SAA relies on proprietary protocols to provide support for multiple platforms.

When completed, NAS will be incorporated into DEC's EMA (Enterprise Management Architecture).

NASI (NetWare Asynchronous Services Interface)

NASI provides specifications for accessing communications servers across a Novell NetWare network. The NASI SDK (software developer's kit) can be used to create applications that use the interface.

NAT (Network Address Translation)

→ *See* IP (Internet Protocol) Masquerade

National Center for Supercomputer Applications (NCSA)

→ *See* NCSA (National Center for Supercomputer Applications)

N

National Computer Center (NCC)

→ *See* NCC (National Computer Center)

National Information Infrastructure (NII)

→ *See* NII (National Information Infrastructure)

National Voluntary Laboratory Accreditation Program (NVLAP)

→ *See* NVLAP (National Voluntary Laboratory Accreditation Program)

NAU (Network Addressable Unit)

In IBM's SNA networks, an NAU is any location with one or more ports for communicating over the network. The three types of NAUs are PUs (physical units), LUs (logical units), and SSCPs (system service control points).

→ *See Also* SNA (Systems Network Architecture)

NAUN (Nearest Addressable Upstream Neighbor)

In a token-ring network, the NAUN for a particular node (A) is the node (B) from which A receives packets and the token. Each node in a token-ring network receives transmissions only from its NAUN.

→ *See Also* Token Ring

Navigator

→ *See* Netscape Navigator

NCC (National Computer Center)

The NCC in Britain is one of the centers that has developed automated software for testing compliance with X.400 and X.500 standards. These centers develop test engines based on the abstract test suites specified by the ITU (International Telecommunication Union). Other centers include the NVLAP (National Voluntary Laboratory Accreditation Program) in the US, Alcatel in France, and Danet GmbH in Germany.

NCC (Network Control Center)

In a network, the NCC is a designated node that runs the managing process for a network management package. This process is in charge of the network management task, and receives reports from the agent processes running on workstations.

→ *See Also* Network Management

NCCF (Network Communications Control Facility)

NCCF is a component of IBM's NetView network management software. It can be used to monitor and control the operation of a network.

→ *See Also* NetView

NCP (Network Control Protocol)

→ *See* Protocol, NCP (Network Control Protocol)

NCP Packet Signature

In Novell's NetWare 4.*x* and later, the NCP packet signature is a security feature that helps prevent a workstation from forging an NCP (NetWare Core Protocol) request packet and using it to get

SUPERVISOR rights on the network. (NCP is the protocol used in NetWare to encode requests to the server and responses to the workstation.)

Each NCP packet must be signed by the server or workstation sending the packet. The signature is different for each packet. If an invalid NCP packet is received, an alert is entered into the error log and sent to both server and workstation. This alert specifies the workstation and its address.

Four packet signature levels are possible for the server and also for the workstation, or client. The table "Server and Workstation Packet and Signature Levels" shows the levels and their meanings for server and client.

Server levels are set using the SET parameter; client levels are set in the NET.CFG file.

The four possible levels for each party yield 16 possible effective packet signature combinations, only some of which actually result in signatures. Some of these levels can slow down performance considerably, and others make it impossible to log in to the network. For example, if either the server or workstation is set to 3 and the other party's level is set to 0, log in will not be possible. There is a packet signature only if both server and client are set to 2 or higher or if either is set to 1 and the other to 2.

→ **Broader Category** Security

→ **Related Article** Digital Signature

NCS (Network Control System)

A software tool used to monitor and modify network activity. NCS is generally used to refer to older systems, which were run in a low-speed, secondary data channel created using time-division multiplexing. These components have been replaced by the more sophisticated network management systems (NMSs).

NCSA (National Center for Supercomputer Applications)

A computing center at the University of Illinois at Urbana-Champaign (UIUC). The NCSA is active in providing information and developing resources for the World Wide Web (WWW). In fact, the widely-used Mosaic browser (hypertext file reader) was originally developed at NCSA. The NCSA version of Mosaic is freeware and is available for downloading from many FTP or Web sites. Commercial versions—developed by companies who licensed the original Mosaic technology from NCSA—are also available.

The NCSA's Web server provides links to lots of interesting places. The "Starting Points for Internet Exploration" home page is at the following URL

SERVER AND WORKSTATION PACKET AND SIGNATURE LEVELS

Level	Server	Client
0	Server does not sign packets.	Client does not sign packets.
1	Server signs packets only if client requests it (if client level is 2 or 3).	Client signs packets only if server requests it (if server level is 2 or 3). This is the default.
2	Server signs packets if client can sign (if client level is 1 or higher). This is the default.	Client signs packets if server can sign (if server level is 1 or higher).
3	Server signs packets and requires clients to sign (or else login will fail).	Client signs packets and requires server to sign (or else login will fail).

N

(Uniform Resource Locator, which is essentially a Web page address):

```
http://www.ncsa.uiuc.edu/SDG/Software/
Mosaic/StartingPoints/NetworkStarting-
Points.html
```

Note that this entire beast is a single "gigaword" and should all be on a single line, with no spaces. The URL is also case sensitive.

NDIS (Network Driver Interface Specification)

NDIS provides a standard interface for network interface card (NIC) drivers. The NDIS standard was developed by Microsoft and 3Com, and it is supported by many NIC manufacturers. Because it allows multiple transport protocols to use the same NIC, this interface helps ensure the NIC's compatibility with multiple network operating systems.

NDIS matches a packet from the NIC's driver with the proper protocol stack by polling each stack until one claims the packet. This is in contrast to the competing ODI (Open Data-link Interface) standard from Novell and Apple. In ODI, the LSL (link-support layer) matches the packet with the appropriate protocol.

If the NIC can buffer a received packet, only the packet's header is checked to determine the protocol. If the NIC cannot buffer the packet, the entire packet is checked. Buffering saves work and can actually improve performance.

→ *Broader Categories* Driver, LAN Driver

→ *Compare* ODI (Open Data-link Interface), ODINSUP (ODI/NDIS Support)

NDS (Novell Directory Services)

NDS is a global naming service or, as Novell characterizes it, "a distributed computing infrastructure." First available in NetWare 4, this service provides and manages a global directory containing information about all the objects (users, resources, devices, and so forth) in a network, regardless of their location or the network's size and range.

This directory is not like a simple file directory, however; and it does not provide information about the files on a network. The global directory is more like a database with information about every object on the network. For each object in the directory, the NDS will have a collection of attributes, or properties, that describe the object: its features, allowable actions (or methods), access permissions, and so forth.

NDS was originally named NetWare Directory Services, but this name has been changed to reflect the fact that the directory services NDS provides are not limited to NetWare networks. Rather, NDS can be used as a directory service even in other environments. You may still see NDS referred to as NetWare Directory Services in some literature, however.

NDS makes it possible for a user to log in from any location on the network, get authenticated during this login, and then—for the rest of the session—use any resource or device without having to be authenticated for that resource.

Because NDS is based on the ITU-T X.500 specification for directory services, it can get along with any services that supports X.500. In fact, NDS supports a whole range of standards, most of them open, including LDAP (Lightweight Directory Access Protocol), RADIUS (Remote Authentication Dial-In User Service), DNS/DHCP (Domain Name System/Dynamic Host Configuration Protocol), and SMB (Server Message Block).

The Global Directory

The global directory for the NDS is organized as a tree, and it contains information about the following types of objects:

- Physical objects, such as users, nodes, and devices

- Logical objects, such as groups, queues, and partitions

- Objects that help to organize other objects in the Directory, such as Organization and Organizational Unit objects

The details of this tree structure are determined by a *schema*, which essentially defines the selection, contents, and location of objects in the tree. NDS comes with a *Base schema*, which specifies a collection of fundamental objects, attributes for these, and relationships among objects. The base schema may vary for different versions of NetWare. The objects mentioned in Table "NDS Leaf Objects" are generally included in a base schema—as are several other kinds of objects, known as container objects.

Specifically, the base schema establishes attribute restrictions and requirements—for example, which attributes must be associated with an object, the form or range that an attribute's values take, and so forth. It also specifies inheritance rules among objects. In object-oriented structures, inheritance means that a descendant object comes with (inherits) all the properties of its parent. The descendant object may have additional attributes, or it may modify the inherited attributes. Because the base schema determines the basic structure of the directory tree, it indirectly determines the complete, hierarchically based name for each object. This complete name is known as the object's distinguished name, and it is used for identification purposes.

A network administrator can modify the tree defined by the base schema to make it more suitable to the administrator's network. There are several ways of doing this—both automated and manual

Portions of the Directory tree will be copied to other locations where the information can be used by a server. Changes made to the Directory or to the tree must be updated at any locations at which a relevant portion of the tree has been replicated.

Note that while the Directory contains information about network objects, it does not contain information about the network's file system. The files and directories on a file server are not represented in the Directory at all. However, certain utilities, such as NetWare Administrator, display both NDS objects and files in what looks like a uniform manner, which makes it easier for a network administrator to manipulate both objects and files.

Objects in NDS

An object in NDS consists of *properties* and the values, or data, for those properties. For example, a User object includes address and telephone number properties; individual users will be distinguished in part by the information stored in these slots.

In the Directory structure, two categories of objects are distinguished: container and leaf objects. A third object, called the root object, is also recognized. This object is created during installation as the parent directory for any other objects. Once created, the root object cannot be deleted or changed.

Container Objects

Container objects are intermediate elements in the Directory tree. These help provide a logical organization for other objects in the Directory tree. A container can include other containers, leaf objects, or both.

Two main kinds of container objects are defined: Organization and Organizational Unit.

An Organization (O) object represents the first level of grouping for most networks. Depending on the scope of a corporate network, this level could represent a company, division, or department. At least one Organization object is required in each NDS Directory tree. An Organization object can contain Organizational Unit or leaf objects.

An Organizational Unit (OU) object can be used as a secondary grouping level. For example, Organizational Unit objects may be created for networks in which the contents of each Organization container are still too large. In a large network, Organizational Unit objects might be departments or project groups. These objects are optional, but they must be below an Organization or another Organizational Unit object if they are included. An Organizational Unit object can contain Organizational Unit or leaf objects.

N

The other two kinds of container objects are Country (C) and Locality (L). These objects are defined for compatibility with X.500 Directory Services, but are rarely used and are not required for compliance with the X.500 specifications.

Leaf Objects

Leaf objects represent information about actual network entities, such as users, devices, and lists. The table "NDS Leaf Objects" lists the types of leaf objects defined.

Object Rights

Object rights apply to the objects contained in the NDS global database. Trustee rights may be assigned for an object or they may be inherited from the object above it. The database objects provide information about the actual objects on the network. The following object rights are defined:

Supervisor   Grants all access privileges to the object and to its properties.

NDS LEAF OBJECTS

Leaf Object	Description
AFP Server	A NetWare node that supports the AppleTalk Filing Protocol and that is probably functioning as a server in an AppleTalk network.
Alias	Refers, or points, to a different location. An alias can be used to help simplify access to a particular object (for example, by using a local object to point to the object entry in a different part of the Directory).
Bindery Object	Included for backward-compatibility with earlier NetWare versions. Bindery objects are placed in the Directory by the migration (network upgrade) utilities, so the binderies from version 3.x servers have something to access in the Directory.
Bindery Queue	Included for backward-compatibility with earlier NetWare versions.
Computer	Represents a network node that is neither a file nor a print server.
Directory Map	Contains information about the network's file system, which is *not* encompassed by the NDS Directory. The information in a Directory Map provides path information, rather than actually showing the structure of the file system's directory. This information is useful for login scripts.
Group	Represents a list of User objects. The network supervisor can assign rights to all the users on this list simply by assigning the rights to the group.
NetWare Server (also NCP Server)	Represents any server running any version of NetWare.
Organizational Role	Represents a function or position within an organization, such as Leader, Consultant, or Moderator.
Printer	Represents a network printer.
Print Queue	Represents a network print queue.
Print Server	Represents a network print server.
Profile	Represents a shared login script. The script might be shared, for example, by users who need to do similar things during the login process but who are located in different containers.
User	Represents an individual who can log in to the network and use resources. Properties associated with User objects include those concerned with the actual person as an individual (name, telephone number, address, and so on) and as a network entity (password and account information, access rights, and so on).
Unknown	Used for an object that cannot be identified as belonging to any other object type, possibly because the object has become corrupted in some way.
Volume	Represents a physical volume on the network.

Browse Grants the right to see an object in the Directory tree that contains the global database.

Create Grants the right to create an object *below* the current one in the Directory tree.

Delete Grants the right to delete an object from the Directory tree.

Rename Grants the right to change an object's name.

Property Rights

Property rights apply to the properties of an NDS object. Note that object rights do not affect property rights. The following property rights are defined:

Supervisor Grants all rights to the property, but can be nullified by a specific object's Inherited Rights Filter (IRF).

Compare Grants the right to compare the property value to any other value. This right shows only how the two values compare; it *does not* allow seeing the property values.

Read Grants the right to see a property's value.

Write Grants the right to add, change, or even remove the values of a property.

Add or Delete Self Grants a trustee the right to remove only the trustee as one of the property's values.

Partitions and Replicas

To help keep things manageable, NetWare divides the Directory into partitions. A *partition* is a grouping of related or nearby container objects and their contents. In particular, a partition consists of a container object, the objects contained in it, and data about those objects. It does not contain information about the network's file system.

A partition might consist of a server and the stations and resources associated with it. A particular object belongs to only one partition, although the object can be accessed from anywhere on the network.

This grouping is then used as the basis for creating *replicas* for each partition. A replica is simply a copy of a partition, and it is created in order to make the information in the partition more easily available by copying the information to a local source. Replicas also ensure that there is no single point of failure for the Directory, This means that if a server that contains a partition goes down, but another server contains a replica of that partition, users can still access the Directory. The replicas are stored on servers throughout the network. This replication across the network has two purposes:

- It speeds up access to Directory information, since an object can be found by checking a smaller partition tree on a local server instead of searching the entire Directory tree at a central location (which every other query would also be pestering).

- It provides redundancy that, in turn, provides fault tolerance and a measure of network protection.

Replicas distribute Directory information across the network. In some cases, a replica may be updated, and this change will eventually be incorporated into the partition from which the replica was created. This makes it possible to change the Directory from anywhere on the network (provided the appropriate resources are available).

In order to help make such changes more manageable and better-controlled, a replica may be designated as read only. A read-only replica cannot be changed and need not be checked when updating the partition. In contrast, changes made to replicas with read and write properties are incorporated into the partition when updating. The synchronization of this updating process involves the use of time servers, as explained in the following section.

Using Time Servers to Coordinate Changes

Information about objects changes, such as a print queue grows or shrinks, a user changes a password, or an application is executed. Since these changes

N

may be recorded in replicas, it is essential to keep track of the timing and sequence of events when updating the Directory. That way, if two people change the same object from different replicas, the Directory can ensure that the changes occur in the correct order.

NetWare 4.x uses time synchronization for this purpose. In time synchronization, the NDS marks each event that occurs, along with the exact time of its occurrence, with a unique value, known as a *time stamp*.

To make time stamps useful, the network must ensure that all servers are keeping the same time. To accomplish this, special time servers are designated. These time servers provide the correct time to other time servers or to workstations. Three types of time-providing servers are distinguished in NetWare 4.x: Single Reference, Reference, and Primary. All other servers that accept time information from any of these servers are called *secondary* time servers.

In any network with more than one time server, the time servers work together to achieve a network time. The time servers influence each other until a kind of "average" time is achieved, and the servers deliver that time to the secondary servers. See the article on Time Synchronization for more information about time servers.

Other NDS Components

NDS includes several components designed to make certain tasks possible or easier:

- Z.E.N.works (for Zero Effort Networks) to automate application and desktop management, software distribution, and workstation maintenance

- ManageWise for network management, virus detection, remote and inventory control, file transfer, and configuration change management

- GroupWise for messaging, scheduling, and document management

Backward-Compatibility with Earlier NetWare Versions

NetWare 4 was the first major version of this network operating system to use a global and hierarchical naming service. Previous versions included a *bindery*, which uses a flat database associated with a single, local server. The NDS replaces the bindery.

To make it possible for bindery-based NetWare servers to access information in the Directory, the NDS includes a *bindery-emulation* feature that can present the Directory information in flat database form for the server's bindery.

→ **Broader Categories** Global Naming Service; NetWare

→ **Related Article** StreetTalk

STRUCTURING YOUR DIRECTORY TREE

All Directory trees have the root object and at least one organization object. If there are multiple organization objects, all of them are at the same level. Beyond this, the details of a Directory tree are completely open-ended.

The final configuration of your Directory tree can have profound effects on the ease with which users can access information in the tree, on the amount of traffic on the network, and on network administration. Your tree needs to be good as a data structure (to make searches efficient); it also needs to work as a representation of the available information.

Despite the importance of the Directory tree structure, finding the best one is more art than science. And modifying the Directory structure after it's set up is currently not simple, although tools to simplify Directory tree management are available.

Near End Crosstalk (NEXT)

→ **See** NEXT (Near End Crosstalk)

Nearest Addressable Upstream Neighbor (NAUN)

→ *See* NAUN (Nearest Addressable Upstream Neighbor)

Near Video on Demand (NVoD)

→ *See* NVoD (Near Video on Demand)

Negative Acknowledgment (NAK)

→ *See* NAK (Negative Acknowledgment)

NEP (Noise-Equivalent Power)

In a fiber-optic receiver, NEP represents the amount of optical power needed to produce an electric current as strong as the receiver's base noise level.

NetBEUI (NetBIOS Extended User Interface)

An implementation and extension of IBM's NetBIOS transport protocol. NetBEUI (pronounced "net-boo-ee") is used in Microsoft's LAN Manager and LAN Server. NetBEUI communicates with a network through Microsoft's NDIS interface for the network interface card.

→ *See Also* Protocol, NetBIOS

NETBIOS.EXE

A NetBIOS emulator program used in Novell's NetWare network operating system. This emulator makes it possible to run applications that use NetBIOS-based peer-to-peer or distributed communications (as opposed to using a server-based communications model, as in NetWare).

→ *See Also* Protocol, NetBIOS

NetBIOS Extended User Interface (NetBEUI)

→ *See* NetBEUI (NetBIOS Extended User Interface)

NetPartner

A network management system from AT&T. NetPartner can monitor voice and data links for wide area networks.

Netscape Communicator

Communicator is an integrated package from Netscape. Currently in version 4.7, it provides browsing, e-mail and instant messaging, word processing, and scheduling capabilities in a single package. Communicator includes the following components: Netscape Navigator (browser), Netscape Messenger (e-mail), Netscape AOL Instant Messenger (instant messaging), Netscape Composer (word processor), and Netscape Calendar (scheduling).

Netscape Navigator

Netscape Navigator was, arguably, the most widely used browser. Among other things, Navigator supports the following:

- Smart browsing, which enables it to suggest related Web sites when you're using it to surf particular Web locations.
- NetWatch, which can screen offensive content, using the PICS (Platform for Internet Content Selection) standard.

N

- HTML 3.2 (Hypertext Markup Language 3.2, which is the most recent standard) as well as most HTML 4 extensions, cascading style sheets (CSSs), and Dynamic HTML (DHTML) features such as absolute positioning. Many of the HTML 4 extensions are actually there because of Netscape and Microsoft. These two browser developers have created many of the features in their efforts to leapfrog each other in browser features and capabilities.

- Tools for Java development.

- The JavaScript scripting language.

- Encrypted communications and transactions using Secure Sockets Layer 3 (SSL3)encryption and authentication services.

See the entry for Netscape Navigator for more details about the browser.

Netscape Messenger

This is Communicator's mail client. It provides the following:

- User and address book interfaces designed for ease of use and flexibility

- Mail services using IMAP (Internet Message Access Protocol)

- Support for multiple address books, as well as the ability to search for e-mail addresses in these multiple books

- Support for importing messages, mail folders, and address books from the Eudora and Outlook Express mail clients

- The ability to synchronize e-mail and address books with 3Com's PalmPilot PDA (Personal Digital Assistant)

- Support for participating in secure discussion groups, using NNTP SSL (Network News Transport Protocol Secure Sockets Layer)

- Integration with desktop applications using MAPI (Messaging Application Programming Interface) support

- Support for roaming access—so that users can access their e-mail from anywhere in the world

Netscape AOL Instant Messenger

This component makes it possible for people to communicate in real time over the Internet or an intranet. Special features make it possible to communicate one-on-one or with a group instantly. AOL Instant Messenger also supports the use of Rich Text Format and of hyperlinks in messages.

Netscape Composer

Composer is a word processor that is Web-based and that has been designed for use on the Internet or on an intranet. Composer provides the following:

- Support for creating either HTML or plain text files. HTML files can make full use of the language features, including style sheets, tables, lists, page alignment, and even Java applets.

- Support for one-button publishing to a Web server, and for the use of FTP (File Transfer Protocol) or HTTP (Hypertext Transfer Protocol) to publish documents.

- Support for plug-ins to extend Composer's functionality.

Netscape Calendar

Calendar provides real-time scheduling of groups and resources. To accomplish these tasks, Calendar provides the following:

- The ability to search for free time slots on either local or remote servers.

- An enterprise-wide calendar for use in scheduling.

- The ability to delegate control of the schedule to another person, for example an assistant. The delegatee can then manage the calendar for the delegator.

- The ability to synchronize calendar and to do lists with 3Com's PalmPilot.

- An interface that is integrated with Netscape Messenger.

Communicator—or, more specifically, Navigator—has been in a seesaw battle with Microsoft Internet Explorer (MSIE, or simply IE) to provide the fastest and most feature-rich browser. Currently, MSIE has leapfrogged Navigator with version 5. Netscape, in the meantime, is working on moving version 4.7 of Communicator to version 5, which promises to leapfrog MSIE.

Netscape Navigator

Navigator, from Netscape Communications, was arguably the most widely used browser (hypertext reader)—until Microsoft pulled the rug out from under it by giving away its Internet Explorer (IE) browser beginning with Windows 95, and then integrating it into the operating system for Windows 98 . Microsoft's actions have had dramatic consequences: The bundling of browser and operating system was one of the actions that led to an antitrust suit by the Justice Department and the attorneys-general of 28 states. Microsoft's actions were also a factor in Netscape' decision to release the source code to Navigator as part of an Open Source program inspired, in part, by the success of Linus Torvald's Linux operating system and also by the force of the arguments in Eric Raymond's paper on the cathedral and the bazaar as models for software development.

The program was designed and cowritten by Marc Andreessen—the leader of the team that created the NCSA (National Center for Supercomputer Applications) Mosaic browser. While it can claim Mosaic as an inspiration, Navigator was designed from scratch to improve on, and add features not available in, the NCSA version of that browser.

Navigator is available for free—as a stand-alone browser and is also bundled in the Netscape Communicator package. "Navigator home page" shows the opening screen for the Communicator version in a Windows 98 environment. Versions are also available for UNIX and Linux (various flavors), and for Macintosh environments.

Navigator can do the following:

- Retrieve and display Web pages from any accessible Web site.

- Search the Web using hypertext-oriented Web crawlers (worms, spiders, etc.) or the more linearly oriented tools such as Gopher, Archie, Veronica, and WAIS (Wide Area Information Service). Users can type common words (instead of URLs) into the browser's Location field—using the Internet Keywords feature—to specify searches. In fact, Navigator's Smart Browsing takes proactive steps to help find relevant content—in the What's Related feature.

- Display images in any of several common formats (for example, GIF, JPEG, and XBM, in Navigator's case)

- Allow plug-ins to be installed—for example, viewers to display other graphics file formats or players for audio or video files. Dozens of such plug-ins have been created to extend Navigator's capabilities.

- Filter out offensive content using the Net-Watch feature, which uses filters based on the PICS (Platform for Internet Content Selection) standard.

- Download hypermedia (text, image, video, or sound) files using Navigator, or text and binary files using FTP

- Support HTML 3.2 (Hypertext Markup Language 3.2, the most recent official standard) as well as most HTML 4 extensions, cascading style sheets (CSSs), and DHTML

N

(Dynamic HTML) features such as absolute positioning.

- Support development tools such as the Java Development Kit (JDK) 1.1, the Abstract Windowing Toolkit (AWT) 1.1.5, the Java-Beans component library, and the Java Native Interface (JNI). Navigator also supports Java-Script 1.3, which complies with the ECMA-252 (European Computer Manufacturing Association) specification for a JavaScript scripting language.

- Encrypt communications if necessary or desirable, and if the contacted server supports it. This feature uses the Secure Socket Layer 3 (SSL3) specification developed by Netscape for just this purpose.

Navigator comes in 16- and 32-bit versions. The latter are for Windows NT and Windows 9*x* environments; the 16-bit version is for Windows 3.1. In the 32-bit version, Navigator is available as part of the Netscape Communicator integrated environment.

Netscape Communications is dedicated to supporting open standards and to making its own protocols (such as SSL) available for use by other parties. In keeping with this strategy, Navigator (and other Netscape products) supports over a dozen protocols and formats, including TCP/IP, HTML, HTTP, NNTP, URLs, CGI, SOCKS, MIME, Gopher, FTP, SMTP, and the RFC822 format for e-mail over the Internet.

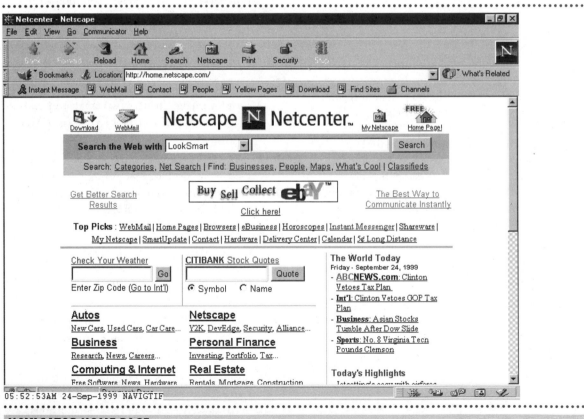

NAVIGATOR HOME PAGE

→ **Primary Sources** Information about Navigator, as well as about Netscape Communicator and other Netscape products is available through the company's home page:

```
http://home.netscape.com
```

From there, you can move all around Netscape's world; you can also explore a generous and wide-ranging slice of the Web's offerings. This is the Web page to which Navigator will move by default. There's a very good chance that a high proportion of the millions of copies of Navigator in use have this as their default home page.

→ **Broader Category** Browser

→ **Compare** MSIE (Microsoft Internet Explorer)

→ **See Also** Netscape Communicator

Netscape Services API (NSAPI)

→ **See** NSAPI (Netscape Services API)

NetView

NetView is a mainframe network management product from IBM. It is used for monitoring SNA (Systems Network Architecture)-compliant networks. NetView runs as a VTAM (Virtual Telecommunications Access Method) application on the mainframe that is serving as network manager.

NetView Components

NetView includes the following components:

- Access services
- Performance monitor
- Session monitor
- Hardware monitor
- Status monitor
- Distribution manager
- Host command facility
- Help desk facility
- Customization facilities

NetView uses the NMVT (Network Management Vector Transport) protocol to communicate with management agents operating at entry points (which connect SNA-compliant devices to NetView) and service points (which connect non-IBM devices or networks).

Many of NetView's features have been incorporated into IBM's LAN Network Manager, which is used to manage token-ring networks. LAN Network Manager can work together with NetView, such as when the LAN is part of a larger, SNA network. Novell's NetWare Management Agent for NetView also provides NetView support for NetWare servers running a Token Ring network. This product consists of several NetWare Loadable Modules (NLMs) that can forward NetView alerts to a NetView host machine and can also respond to requests from a NetView host for maintenance statistics.

NetView/PC

A related product, NetView/PC, provides an API (Application Program Interface) that enables developers to interface NetView with new hardware or software.

NetView/PC can be used as a manager for its own network. As such, the program can gather performance, usage, and billing information. NetView/PC also makes it possible for non-IBM devices, LANs, or even certain types of PBXs (private branch exchanges) to connect to an IBM NMA (Network Management Architecture) network.

→ **Broader Categories** Network Management; NMA (Network Management Architecture)

N

NetWare

NetWare is a network operating system (NOS) from Novell. Several different versions of NetWare are currently (or have been) available. These versions differ in the hardware they support, in the default protocol stack they use, in the networking services they provide, and in special features (such as fault tolerance).

Besides refinements and performance improvements, successive versions of NetWare have changed most dramatically in the following ways:

- Moved from being primarily a NOS for local area networks with at most a few hundred users to being able to handle enterprise networks and intranets that may be using several different platforms and that may have thousands or even millions of users and resources. For example, NetWare 5—the newest version—can handle networks with up to a billion objects and can handle files up to 8 *tera*bytes—large enough to store thousands of copies of the entire *Encyclopedia Britannica*.

- Moved from relying on a flat-file database (the bindery) for its network directory service to the much more sophisticated, versatile, scalable, and global Novell Directory Services (originally named NetWare Directory Services, but NDS in either case). NDS was first introduced in NetWare 4. The version in NetWare 5 is a much improved NDS, and hundreds of applications have been or are being developed that make use of NDS.

- Improved its ability to run clients smoothly on multiple platforms, and to connect to alien networks. With NetWare 5—and with the improvements in the NDS—the NOS can run clients with no problem on other platforms, such as UNIX, Windows (3.1, 9.*x*, and NT), and so forth. NDS can also manage directory services for these platforms so that machines running on other networks on that platform can be connected to a NetWare

network. With the switch to open protocol, NetWare can truly be said to play well with just about all others.

- Improved and streamlined its protocol suites, and generally moved from a suite consisting almost entirely of proprietary protocols to a suite consisting of the ultimate in open protocols: the Internet's own TCP/IP protocol suite. Early versions of the operating system ran proprietary protocols and offered other stacks in emulation modes; now NetWare runs open protocols and offers support for Novell's own proprietary protocols in a compatibility mode. Novell has constantly striven to improve the performance of its protocols—even the proprietary ones. For example, lightweight protocols (which have less overhead than ordinary protocols) have been developed and used whenever possible.

- Become an ideal operating system for intranets—networks that use the TCP/IP protocol suite and that use Web technology for their interface—because of the move to open standards. With the addition of a Web server (from Netscape) and a huge collection of development tools (for creating Web pages as well as for networking utilities) NetWare 5 has shown itself to be well suited to the task of running Web sites.

- Moved toward improving and integrating network administration and management tasks. With NetWare 5, desktop and client management tasks have been integrated in the form of Novell's Z.E.N.works (for Zero Effort Networks) package. The actual task of network management is done by Manage-Wise, and messaging and document management services are provided by Novell's GroupWise middleware package.

- Improved the performance of the NOS itself. NetWare 5 has a completely redesigned kernel, which is much more efficient and which can handle multiple processes at a time.

NetWare Versions

Valuable features (for example, fault-tolerant capabilities such as disk mirroring) from the earlier NetWare versions were incorporated into NetWare 2.2, which was released in 1991. Since then, NetWare versions 3.*x*, 4.*x*, and 5 have been released. While each version has introduced its own innovations, perhaps the most radical departure from the NetWare philosophy and product line comes in NetWare 5, which uses a completely different protocol stack than the one that NetWare versions have traditionally used. In discussions for this entry, I use the term *classic NetWare* to refer to NetWare versions prior to 5.

The table "NetWare Versions and Features" lists several NetWare versions and summarizes some of their features. Not all the versions summarized are still available.

NETWARE VERSIONS AND FEATURES

Version	Features
NetWare Lite	Maximum of 25 nodes per server
	Peer-to-peer network only (no dedicated server)
	Limited file, printer sharing
	Limited security features
	Runs as a DOS process
	No SFT features
	Can coexist with other NetWare versions
	Replaced by Personal NetWare
NetWare 2.2	Maximum of 100 nodes per server
	Use of dedicated or nondedicated server
	Full file, printer sharing
	SFT capabilities: disk mirroring, disk duplexing, and transaction tracking system (TTS)
	Security features
	Supports Macintosh file system
	Optional support for Macintosh clients
	Extensible through VAPs (Value Added Processes)
NetWare 3.*x*	Maximum of 250 nodes per server
	Supports only dedicated servers
	Supports multiple protocol stacks
	Supports multiple file systems (DOS, Macintosh, OS/2, UNIX)
	Optional support for multiple clients (DOS, Macintosh, OS/2, UNIX)
	Extensible through NLMs (NetWare Loadable Modules)
NetWare 4.*x*	Maximum of 1000 nodes per server
	Supports global resource, global naming (NDS)
	Supports up to 12 NetWare 3.x servers as part of NDS (NetWare 4.1)
	Supports on-disk file compression
	More stringent security, including auditing of network activity

Continued on next page

N

Version	Features
NetWare 4.x	Extensive network management capabilities
	Improved storage management (SMS) and message handling (MHS) capabilities
	E-mail capabilities
	Supports High Capacity Storage Systems (HCSS), such as optical drives
	Supports multiple drives in a jukebox for optical discs
	Special protocols and packet formats to speed up WAN connections
	Better routing protocols (NLSP)
	Supports data migration from earlier NetWare versions
NetWare for Small Business 4.2	Same core as NetWare 4.1, with additional components that are useful for businesses
	Includes QuickStart for network setup and Novell Easy Administration Tool (NEAT) for network administration; also includes Z.E.N. work (Zero Effort Networks) Starter Pack for managing client workstations
	Includes GroupWise for scheduling, messaging, and task management; also includes NetWare Connect for network access from remote locations, and Internet Connection Wizard for Internet access
	Includes a Web server (Netscape FastTrack Server), a browser (Netscape Communicator), and a browser accelerator (BorderManager FastCache)
	Includes Oracle 8 for designing and managing databases; also includes NetObjects Fusion for designing and creating Web pages
	Fully interoperable with other NetWare versions, and allows easy migration to newer versions or more powerful network support
NetWare 5	Includes an improved Novell Directory Service (NDS), which is based on the X.500 directory specifications and supports the Lightweight Directory Access Protocol version 3 (LDAP3)
	Has a new and improved kernel that can do multiprocessing
	Runs the Internet's TCP/IP protocol stack in native mode; includes support for the Domain Name Service (DNS) and for the Dynamic Host Configuration Protocol (DHCP); replaces Novell's Service Advertising Protocol (SAP) with the Internet's Services Location Protocol (SLP), which has less overhead
	Supports Novell's IPX/SPX protocol stack in a compatibility mode, and provides a bridge between IPX and IP suites; also supports multiprotocol routing—with IPX/SPX, TCP/IP, and AppleTalk
	Back compatible with NetWare versions from 2 through 4; includes support for the bindery, which was used prior to introduction of the NDS in NetWare 4
	Includes Web server and Web publishing tools; also includes tools for other types of development, including Java applets and plug-in modules
	Includes various Java-based utilities, a Java Virtual Machine (JVM), and various Java development tools
	Supports SAS authentication services for user authentication and PKIS (Public Key Infrastructure Services) for managing encryption and certificates in NDS.
	Includes Novell Storage Services (NSS), which supports files up to 8 terabytes in size, billions of volumes and files, and fast loading of volumes
	Supports Hot Plug PCI, which allows you to replace NICs while NetWare is running
	Includes the Z.E.N.works (Zero Effort Networks) desktop management tools; also has more sophisticated network management capabilities, including remote server management

Continued on next page

NETWARE VERSIONS AND FEATURES (continued)

Version	Features
Personal NetWare	Up to 50 nodes per server
	Up to 50 interconnected servers
	Distributed, replicated, object database allows a single login to entire network
	Fully compatible with other NetWare versions
	Supports NMS and SNMP management standards
	Built-in security, including access restrictions, password encryption, and audit trails
	Automatic reconnection if a server goes down
	Supports Client VLMs (Virtual Loadable Modules) for configuration flexibility

Note that later versions of NetWare generally inherit the features of earlier versions—or at least retain support for them in order to provide back compatibility. Thus, a NetWare 3.x server can do anything a NetWare 2.x server can, a NetWare 4.x server can do whatever a NetWare 3.x server can and so on. Also note that the NetWare versions have many more specific features along with the ones included in the table's summary.

NetWare Components

Server-based versions of NetWare (NetWare 2.x, 3.x, 4.x, and 5.x) consist of two components:

- The operating system software for the server. This component manages the network's files and resources, communicates with workstations, and deals with workstation requests.

- Workstation software, which is a network shell or redirector program. This component provides the workstation with access to the network and, therefore, to the resources and files on the server or on another workstation.

Server Software

The NetWare program running on the server is an NOS. NetWare has its own partition on the hard disk, and it may replace the native operating system (for example, DOS) as the program with which applications and other processes deal. In other cases,

NetWare may run as a process under the operating system, as does NetWare for UNIX. Even when it becomes the primary operating system, NetWare may still rely on the native operating system. For example, NetWare for DOS uses some DOS services as well as the DOS file system.

The capabilities of the NOS running on a server depend on several things, including the following:

- The version of NetWare running

- For version 2.x, the combination of Value-Added Processes (VAPs) loaded with the NOS

- For versions 3.x and later, the combination of NetWare Loadable Modules (NLMs) loaded with the NOS kernel

- Any auxiliary programs or modules being used to supplement the networking services

- The network size and resources

- The traffic load and patterns for the network

- The configuration of the hardware on which the NOS is running. Early versions of the operating system could run on fairly modest machines—even 80386-based machines. However, NetWare 5 is much beefier—it insists on at least a Pentium processor, with 64MB or more of RAM (128MB for certain configurations) and at least a gigabyte (GB) of storage.

N

Several core capabilities are available with any NetWare version:

- Controlled file and directory access. NetWare provides access controls and file and record locking. Of course, the newer versions, which have NDS, can do a much better job of controlling such access.

- Shared access to printing resources. The NOS (or a process controlled by the NOS) makes sure that print jobs are added to the appropriate queue and are printed. In NetWare 5, the Novell Distributed Print Services (NDPS) make it much easier to find, configure, administer, and use, printers anywhere on the network.

- Electronic mail (e-mail) capabilities. In versions prior to NetWare 5, these were provided through Novell's MHS (Message Handling Service) protocol, which third-party e-mail packages can use. Beginning with NetWare 5, e-mail and other types of messaging services are provided through GroupWise 5.5. This package provides a Universal Mailbox into which any kind of messages, appointments, or documents can be placed. Because GroupWise supports a range of protocols and command sets, users can access the contents of their mailbox in any of several ways: over the Internet or an intranet using any e-mail client that supports either the Post Office Protocol 3 (POP3) or Internet Message Access Protocol 4 (IMAP4), by using a browser to get access to one's mailbox, or by using applications that use the Messaging Application Programming Interface (MAPI).

- Security controls. For example, NetWare can require user log in and authentication procedures and limit user access rights. Here also, NetWare versions have kept up with developments in encryption and other security measures. NetWare 5 uses Safe Authentication Services (SAS) to authenticate user logins, and also Public Key Infrastructure Services (PKIS) for public key cryptography and for digital signatures. With digital signatures, NetWare can also support Secure Socket Layer (SSL) connections. For e-mail services, NetWare 5 supports both Pretty Good Privacy (PGP) and Secure Multipurpose Internet Mail Extensions (S/MIME) for protecting the contents of electronic messages.

- Interprocess Communication (IPC), which enables processes on the network to communicate with each other.

Client Software

The software on the workstation, or client, in a NetWare network must be able to communicate with the network and also with the workstation's operating system. Separate client software packages are needed for each platform that is to be connected to the network. This section describes an example of DOS client software for NetWare 4.x to illustrate the kinds of components that may be needed in processing a network request on a client machine. Because NetWare 5 uses the TCP/IP protocol suite, clients are much easier to create and support—especially on 32-bit Windows environments, which include DLLs (dynamic-link libraries) for the TCP/IP protocols.

The workstation software determines whether a request from a program or user is intended for the workstation operating system (for example, for DOS, Windows, or UNIX) or for the network. If the request is for the workstation, the software passes it on to whatever operating system is running on the client's workstation. If it is a network request, the software does the following:

- Converts the request into the appropriate format.

- Packs the request into a packet, together with routing and other administrative information. NetWare uses the NCP (NetWare Core Protocol) to formulate (and respond to) the requests and the IPX (Internetwork Packet Exchange) protocol to create the packet to be transmitted. Because NetWare 5 uses the TCP/IP protocol stack as its native protocol, IP is used instead of IPX.

- Passes this packet on to a network interface card (NIC) for packaging in a format suitable for the actual network architecture.

- Verifies that the packet was received correctly, and requests a retransmission if an error occurred.

Once the packet is passed to the NIC, the workstation component of the NOS is finished with its task. The software running the NIC does further processing and makes sure the packet gets onto the network.

For DOS workstations, the program that does these things is called the *NetWare shell* in versions preceding 4.*x*. In NetWare 4.*x*, this software is known as the *NetWare DOS Requester*. The DOS Requester software runs as a DOS process, but takes considerable control by intercepting certain key DOS interrupts. This is done so that network-related requests go on to the network.

The workstation software consists of several utilities, each responsible for one of the shell's tasks. These utilities include NET*x*.COM, SPX.COM, and IPX.COM. NET*x* does the intercepting, redirecting, and the first round of processing (into NCP form); SPX and IPX create packets designed for their counterpart programs at the destination.

The DOS Requester (NetWare 4.*x*) consists of a collection of Virtual Loadable Modules (VLMs), which are modules running on a workstation. The VLMs accomplish generally the same kinds of tasks as the shell utilities, but do so in different ways.

Classic NetWare Protocols

Because not everyone will upgrade to NetWare 5, and not all NetWare 5 users will immediately want to switch to the TCP/IP protocol stack, it's useful here to discuss the protocol suite that has been so successful for Novell prior to the release of NetWare 5. This section summarizes Novell's proprietary protocols. The various Internet protocols used in NetWare 5 are described in individual entries under Protocol. See, for example, Protocol, IP (Internet Protocol) for information on the Internet protocol that corresponds to Novell's IPX.

The traditional, or classic, NetWare NOS software corresponds roughly to the layers defined in the OSI reference model. The protocols supported within this framework are listed in the table " Classic NetWare Protocol Suite."

CLASSIC NETWARE PROTOCOL SUITE

Protocol	Description
Burst mode	Used instead of NCP for situations in which large amounts of data need to be transmitted.
IPX (Internetwork Packet Exchange)	Classic NetWare's standard network-layer protocol. IPX is used to route data packets from the Transport layer across a network.
NCP (NetWare Core Protocol)	The protocol NetWare uses to formulate and respond to workstation requests. It includes procedures for dealing with any service a workstation might request (such as file or directory handling, printing, and so on). Burst mode can be used to make NCP more efficient when transmitting large blocks of data (such as entire files) over slower WAN links.
NLSP (NetWare Link State Protocol)	A routing protocol that improves upon and has largely replaced RIP and SAP. NLSP is more efficient and more reliable than these older protocols. It also supports multiple paths between NLSP nodes, which affords a measure of fault tolerance in addition to improving performance.
RIP (Routing Information Protocol)	Used by routers and servers to exchange routing information on an internetwork. RIP packets can use NetWare's IPX protocol to move between stations. This variant of RIP is generally known as IPX RIP to distinguish Novell's classic version from the RIP protocol in the TCP/IP protocol suite. RIP has largely been replaced by NLSP.
SAP (Service Advertising Protocol)	Formerly used by NetWare services to broadcast their availability across the network. The protocol supports broadcast, query, and response packets. SAP has largely been replaced by NLSP in classic (that is, pre-NetWare 5) NetWare. NetWare 5 uses SLP (Services Location Protocol).
SPX (Sequenced Packet Exchange)	Classic NetWare's standard transport-layer protocol. It is used to ensure that data packets have been delivered successfully by the IPX services. SPX requests and receives acknowledgments from its counterpart on the receiving node, and also keeps track of fragmented messages consisting of multiple packets.
Watchdog	Used for maintenance purposes. It can determine whether the NetWare shell is still running on workstations that have been idle for a long time.

N

By default, classic NetWare uses the protocol stack shown in the "Classic NetWare and NetWare 5 protocol stacks." In addition to these protocols, NetWare supports frame formats for different network architectures (Ethernet, Token Ring, ARCnet, and so on) at the Physical and Data-Link layers. In classic NetWare, add-on modules also provide support for other protocol suites, such as the TCP/IP (used in UNIX systems) and AppleTalk protocol families.

The classic NetWare protocol collection also includes a NetBIOS emulation that provides access from peer-to-peer networks and from networks that support IBM's APPC (Advanced Program-to-Program Communication) protocols.

In contrast, the default NetWare 5 protocol stack is also shown in "Classic NetWare and NetWare 5 protocol stacks." Note that the stack breakdowns are quite similar in relation to the Open System Interconnect (OSI) 7-layer reference model—just the actual protocols are different.

Until NetWare 5, the SPX and IPX protocols were the ones most characteristically identified with NetWare. In the future, however, NetWare will join the growing ranks of network software providers providing native support for TCP/IP and for Web services. Access to the NIC and to the actual physical network depends on the network architecture and also on the LAN drivers being used.

→ See Also NDS (Novell Directory Services); Personal NetWare

NetWare Access Server

NetWare Access Server is a software product that enables up to 16 users to dial into a network from remote locations at the same time. The product works with Novell's NetWare version 2.1 and later.

The NetWare Access Server software is installed on a dedicated 386 (or higher) computer with a communications board installed. Users at remote workstations can use asynchronous modems, public or private X.25 packet-switching services, or ISDN services to connect to the access server. Once connected, remote users can access network resources or run DOS and Microsoft Windows programs.

→ Broader Category NetWare

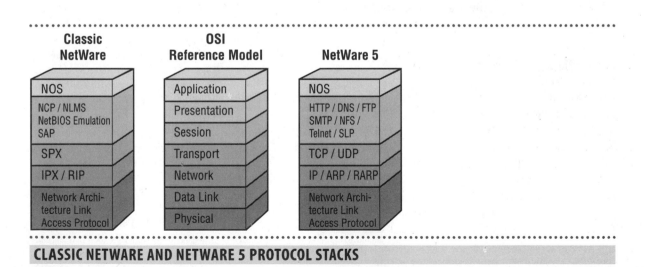

CLASSIC NETWARE AND NETWARE 5 PROTOCOL STACKS

NetWare Asynchronous Services Interface (NASI)

→ *See* NASI (NetWare Asynchronous Services Interface)

NetWare Directory Database (NDD)

→ *See* NDD (NetWare Directory Database)

NetWare Directory Services (NDS)

→ *See* NDS (Novell Directory Services)

NetWare for Macintosh

A collection of NetWare Loadable Modules (NLMs) that provide various NetWare services, including file handling, printing, network administration, and AppleTalk routing, for Macintosh clients on a Novell NetWare network. With NetWare for Macintosh, Macintosh users can access network resources, files, and applications, send print jobs to network printers, and take advantage of NetWare features, such as network security.

Users also get access to the Novell Directory Services (with version 4.*x* of the product), as well as access to AppleTalk print services. Thus, by running NetWare for Macintosh, users can get the benefits and resources accessible through a NetWare network, while keeping their familiar Macintosh interface.

→ *Broader Category* NetWare

NetWare for SAA

Novell's gateway package for connecting NetWare networks to various machines that support IBM's SNA (Systems Network Architecture), including AS/400s, 3090s, and 370s. NetWare for SAA is installed as a series of NetWare Loadable Modules (NLMs) in NetWare 3.*x* or 4.*x*, and it supports up to several hundred sessions for each gateway.

Once NetWare for SAA is loaded, a client on a NetWare network can get access to the applications and data on the IBM mainframe or midrange system—assuming, of course, that the user has the required access privileges. The client can be running any of the operating systems supported by NetWare: DOS, Macintosh, OS/2, UNIX, or Windows.

NetWare for SAA emulates PU2.0 and PU2.1 devices, which are both peripheral devices with access only through a communications controller or a front end processor. NetWare for SAA also supports 3270 and TN3270 (a Telnet variant) terminal emulation.

→ *Broader Category* NetWare

NetWare for UNIX

A program that provides NetWare support on machines running general-purpose operating systems, such as UNIX. NetWare for UNIX (formerly Portable NetWare) runs as a set of applications on the host. The software enables the host to provide file handling, printing, and backup services to clients, regardless of whether clients are running DOS, Microsoft Windows, or the Macintosh operating system. NetWare for UNIX is sold by the host system vendors.

NetWare/IP

NetWare Loadable Modules (NLMs) that provide support for the IP (Internet Protocol) as a routing protocol for NetWare 3.*x* and 4.*x* servers. With NetWare/IP, a NetWare server can function as a gateway between NetWare and TCP/IP networks. NetWare/IP is not needed with NetWare 5, because this version uses the TCP/IP protocol suite as its native stack.

N

NetWare Loadable Module (NLM)

→ *See* NLM (NetWare Loadable Module)

NetWare Management Agents

NetWare Management Agents are NetWare Loadable Modules (NLMs) that enable communication between a NetWare 3.x or 4.x server and external management software. If the external software is Novell's NetWare Management System, then the agent will carry out commands for the management software.

NetWare Management Agents can provide statistical information about the server and its performance: configuration, disk, memory and CPU usage, file activity, protocols and frames passed across the network, etc. The agents can also send alarms in case a server goes down or has exceeded threshold on a parameter. The agents support standard management and networking protocols—SNMP (Simple Network Management Protocol), IP (Internet Protocol), and IPX (Internetwork Packet Exchange).

Once a NetWare Management Agent has been installed, it can be used by multiple administrators at multiple locations. That is, more than one administrator can request statistics and information from the agent—provided, as always, that the administrator has the appropriate privileges.

NetWare 5 includes ManageWise 2.6, which is part of Novell Directory Services (NDS) included with NetWare. ManageWise offers network management using the Simple Network Management Protocol (SNMP). Because ManageWise is SNMP compliant, it can accept reports from such management agents.

→ *Broader Categories* NetWare; Network Management

NetWare Management System (NMS)

→ *See* NMS (NetWare Management System)

NetWare Multiprotocol Router (MPR)

The MPR is a collection of software routing products. These products can route protocols from the IPX/SPX, TCP/IP, SNA, and AppleTalk stacks concurrently. MPR can use a variety of network architectures and topologies, and supports long distance communications at speeds ranging from 1200bps to 2.048Mbps.

MPR also supports *dial on demand routing*, in which a server—for example, at a branch office—may ask for a line only when there's something to be sent or communicated. This is more cost effective than keeping a permanent connection with outlying offices or areas.

MPR consists of four main products:

- A two-port *branch-link router*
- A multiple-port (up to 16) *enterprise router*
- An SNA*Extensions package, which provides access to IBM SNA communications
- A WAN*Extensions package, which provides access to X.25 and frame relay networks

MPR (version 3.0) supports the following protocols:

IPX RIP   NetWare's routing information protocol

(IPX) NLSP   NetWare Link Services Protocol, which has largely replaced IPX RIP and SAP protocols, because it's more efficient

TCP/IP RIP   The Internet's slightly different routing information protocol

TCP/IP OSPF The Internet's Open Shortest Path First protocol for trading packets among routes within an autonomous system.

SNA IBM's System Network Architecture

AppleTalk AURP The AppleTalk Update Routing Protocol

AppleTalk RTMP The Routing Table Maintenance Protocol

In addition, MPR supports many WAN configurations, including ISDN, SMDS, PPP, and—with the WAN*Extension—frame relay and X.25. MPR also supports data compression and packet filtering to help keep WAN traffic to a minimum.

MPR supports the Internet's Simple Network Management Protocol (SNMP) for monitoring and managing routers.

→ Broader Categories NetWare; Protocol, Routing; Router

NetWare NFS

A collection of NetWare Loadable Modules (NLMs) that provide file handling and printing services for UNIX clients in a NetWare network. NetWare NFS uses the Network File System (NFS) application-layer protocol from Sun Microsystems.

NetWare NFS Gateway

The software that is installed on a Novell NetWare server and allows NetWare clients (using DOS or Microsoft Windows) to access files on an NFS (Network File System) server. To the client, the files on the NFS server appear to be on the NetWare server.

NetWare Peripheral Architecture (NPA)

→ See NPA (NetWare Peripheral Architecture)

NetWare Requester for OS/2

Software that runs on an OS/2 workstation and enables the workstation to connect to a Novell NetWare network. In addition to providing the necessary redirection services, this Requester allows application servers to communicate with the workstations without involving NetWare.

NetWare Runtime

NetWare Runtime is a version of the Novell NetWare operating system designed for use by one or two users. This version can be used as an application server, with applications based on NetWare Loadable Modules (NLMs) installed on it. This frees the regular NetWare server for other network tasks, such as file and print services.

NetWare Runtime can provide basic services, such as electronic mail (e-mail) and communications, and database services. The database capabilities are particularly important for applications that may have front- and back-end components (programs that run in part on a client and in part on a server).

Applications running with the NetWare Runtime system can use the NetWare protocol stack (SPX and IP) or other protocols (such as TCP/IP or AppleTalk).

→ Broader Category NetWare

NetWare Shell

In NetWare versions prior to 4.0, a terminate-and-stay-resident (TSR) program loaded on a workstation. The shell sits between the application environment and DOS.

→ See Also NetWare

NetWare TCP/IP

A collection of NetWare Loadable Modules (NLMs) that implement the TCP/IP protocol suite

N

in order to provide routing services for stations using the TCP/IP format. NetWare 5 does not need this NLM, because this version of NetWare uses the TCP/IP protocol suite as its native stack.

NetWare Telephony Services

NetWare Telephony Services is a software/hardware product from Novell that makes it possible to integrate a Novell NetWare network with a telephone PBX (private branch exchange). The product includes a hardware link between the NetWare server and the PBX. This link is administered through the server, and it is used for all the communications between network and PBX. Workstations that want access to the PBX must be running the appropriate part of the software and must communicate with the PBX through the network server.

The hardware link between the network and PBX consists of a PBX-specific board (installed in the server) and cabling. Details of the link (whether it is serial, ISDN, TCP/IP, or another type) and of the board will depend on the board's manufacturer, which is likely to be the PBX vendor. Fortunately, just about every board manufacturer supports the telephony services standard used in the Novell product. An appropriate PBX driver will make the board and the PBX accessible to the network.

In addition to board and driver, NetWare Telephony Services includes a NetWare Loadable Module (NLM) that enables and controls the communications between the network and the PBX. Actual telephony services, such as call forwarding or unified messaging of fax, voice, electronic mail, and other transmissions, are provided through applications. A Telephony Service Application Program Interface (TSAPI) is available for developers who want to provide such services in their products.

NetWare Telephony Services is eventually expected to encompass voice processing and speech synthesis, in addition to the call-control capabilities currently provided. For example, instead of clicking on an icon to dial a number or transfer a call, a user may be able to give the required commands verbally.

NetWare Tools

A collection of basic end-user utilities for NetWare version 4.x. The NetWare Tools utilities are installed separately from the NetWare server installation program. They can be used to accomplish various tasks on the network, such as mapping drives, sending messages, and setting up printing. NetWare tools are designed for end-user tasks. In contrast, administrative tasks are performed using utilities such as the NetWare Administrator.

NetWare Utilities

NetWare utilities are programs that can be used to accomplish specific tasks.

Utilities can be grouped in various ways, including graphics- versus text-based and server- versus workstation-based. Server-based utilities execute on the server, and they are generally used to manipulate the server. Some server-based utilities are NetWare Loadable Modules (NLMs). These are loaded using the LOAD command.

The NLMs actually hook into the operating system and execute until they are unloaded. Other server-based utilities are simply commands that the user types at the server console.

Workstation-based utilities execute on the workstation, even though they are installed on the server. These utilities are generally used to manipulate the networking environment: files, users, print queues, and so on. Some workstation-based utilities can be used by any legitimate user; others can be used only by administrators.

Graphics-based, or GUI, utilities use icons, dialog boxes, and so on, just as in Microsoft Windows or OS/2.

Text-based utilities run under DOS, and they can be command lines (for example, at the DOS prompt) or menus.

Utilities are added, dropped, consolidated, and divided as NetWare evolves. For example, NetWare 3.x has more than 120 utilities, whereas one counting method yields fewer than 75 utilities in NetWare 4.*x*. One reason for this is that some NetWare 4.*x* utilities consolidate several 3.*x* utilities.

GETTING INFORMATION ABOUT NETWARE UTILITIES

It is not possible to summarize all the NetWare utilities without adding a medium-length book to this encyclopedia. For more information about these utilities, you can read the following:

- The Utilities manuals and the *Quick Access Guides* for NetWare versions 3.*x* and later provide detailed and terse summaries, respectively, of the utilities for these versions.

- *Mastering NetWare 5*, by James Gaskin, is a comprehensive source.

Network

A network consists of computers, called *nodes* or *stations*. The computers are connected to, or can communicate with, each other in some way. Nodes run special software for initiating and managing network interactions. With the help of networking software, nodes can share files and resources, and tasks can be distributed over multiple machines on some networks.

Network Components

The following are the main hardware components of a network:

Nodes   Computers and network interface cards (NICs)

Topology   Logical and physical

Connection elements   Cabling, wiring centers, links, and so on

Auxiliary components   Peripheral devices, safety devices, and tools

See the Hardware, Network for more information about the hardware components.

The software components include the following:

Networking systems   Network operating system (NOS) and workstation software

Resources   Drivers and various types of server software. In the past few years, all sorts of servers have come into common use—for example, authentication, intranet, and Web servers.

Tools   Utilities, LAN analyzers, network monitoring software, and configuration managers

Applications   Network-aware software

The component groupings, particularly for the software, are not mutually exclusive. The same software may be viewed as belonging in multiple categories. For example, a NOS can include various network resources and tools.

Because of the connection and the software, nodes on the network can communicate and interact with each other. The interaction may be directly between two nodes, via one or more intermediate nodes, or through a server node. The interaction can be over a physical medium (such as electrical or fiber-optic cable) or by wireless means (using radio waves, microwaves, or infrared waves).

Users working on a network node can make use of available files and resources on other nodes as well. Each user generally has a limited range of access and usage privileges, which are monitored and controlled by the NOS. A (human) network administrator, or manager, oversees the NOS's configuration and operations. The administrator sets the user privileges.

Network Categories

Networks come in all shapes and sizes, and can be categorized using a variety of features and functions. These categorizations are neither exclusive nor exhaustive, but they do yield a rich crop of terminology, as summarized in the table "Network Groupings."

N

NETWORK GROUPINGS

Category	Description
Message Capacity	Whether the network can transmit one or more messages at a time. Networks may be baseband, carrierband, or broadband.
Range	The geographical or bureaucratic range over which the nodes are distributed. Networks can be categorized as LANs, WANs, MANs, CANs, DANs, SANs, and GANs, which are local, wide, metropolitan, campus, departmental, storage, and global area networks, respectively.
Node Types	Nodes in a network may be PCs, minicomputers, mainframes, or even other networks. Networks used for general-purpose computing and operations are most likely to be PC-based. MIS departments and universities are most likely to have networks that include minicomputers or mainframes. Backbone networks are networks whose "nodes" are actually smaller networks, known as access networks.
Node Relationships	The relationship among the nodes that make up the network. Networks categorized along these lines are known as distributed, peer-to-peer, server-based, and client/server.
Topology	Topology refers to both the network's logical topology (logical layout of nodes in the network) and physical topology (physical layout, including the wiring scheme by which nodes are connected). The main logical topologies are bus and ring. Physical topologies include bus, star, ring, and star-wired ring.
Architecture	The network architecture, which is defined by the cabling used, by the method used to access the network, and by the format of a data packet on the network. Common LAN architectures include Ethernet (in 10, 100, and 1000Mbps varieties), Token Ring, ARCnet, and FDDI.
Access Possibilities	At one extreme are shared-media networks, in which exactly one node can have access to the network medium at a given time. In contrast to this, switching networks allow multiple nodes to use the network at the same time. Switching networks accomplish this by multiplexing.

The various grouping are described in the following sections. Keep in mind that networking categories and terminology may overlap, complement, or be independent. For example, one person's local area network (LAN) may be another's campus-area network (CAN).

Networks Classified by Message Capacity

A network may be able to transmit one or more messages at a time. A *baseband* network can transmit exactly one message at a time. Most LANs are baseband networks. A *carrierband* network is a special case of a baseband network. In this type of network, the channel's entire bandwidth is used for a single transmission, and the signal is modulated before being transmitted.

A *broadband* network can transmit more than one message at a time by using a different frequency range for each message and then multiplexing these multiple channels (sending all the messages out on a single channel).

Networks Classified by Transmission Rate

In general, broadband networks support higher transmission rates. However, there is considerable variation in transmission rates for baseband networks, and there is considerable overlap in transmission rates. That is, there are lots of baseband networks that are faster than some broadband networks, even though broadband networks tend to support higher rates.

Very roughly, we can distinguish four generations of networks:

- The earliest networks operated at kilobit per second (Kbps) speeds, anywhere from fewer than ten to a few hundred kilobits per second.

- The second generation encompasses the transmission speeds for the "traditional" LAN architectures: Ethernet, Token Ring, and ARCnet. These have speeds in the 1 to 20Mbps range. The traditional speeds are 10Mbps or slower; the 16Mbps Token Ring and 20Mbps ARCnet Plus are improvements on the original designs.

- The current, third, generation supports transmissions in the 100+Mbps range. This includes FDDI (100Mbps), ATM (up to 600+Mbps), and fast Ethernet (100Mbps).

- The up-and-coming generation of networks supports transmissions at 1Gbps. At these speeds, the entire *Oxford English Dictionary* could be transmitted several times in a single second. These rates can be obtained only through multiplexing, since hardware devices (such as disk or tape drives) cannot supply data fast enough.

- The next generation of networks is expected to support speeds of 10Gbps and higher.

Networks Classified by Range

Networks are distinguished by the range over which the nodes are distributed. Interestingly, the *number* of nodes is not used as a major distinction (except by network software vendors when they sell packages to end-users). The table "Network Range Categories" summarizes the types of networks in this classification. See the article about the specific network type for a more detailed discussion.

The most common categories are LANs, WANs (wide area networks), and MANs (metropolitan area networks), but GANs (global area networks) will become increasingly popular—particularly in the form of intranets and extranets—as multinational corporations connect all their operations.

NETWORK RANGE CATEGORIES

Range Category	Description
LAN (local area network)	Consists of machines that are connected within a relatively small geographical radius (for example, within an office, floor, or a building) and by a particular type of medium. Functionally, a LAN consists of a group of computers interconnected so that users can share files, printers, and other resources. A LAWN (local-area wireless network) is a special type of LAN that uses microwave, infrared, or radio transmissions instead of cabling.
CAN (campus area network)	Connects nodes (or possibly departmental LANs) from multiple locations, which may be separated by a considerable distance. Unlike a WAN, however, a campus network does not require remote communications facilities, such as modems and telephones.
DAN (departmental area network)	A small network, which may connect up to 20 or 30 nodes so that they can share common resources. DANs are typically used in government agencies.
WAN (wide area network)	Consists of machines that may be spread out over larger areas, such as across a college campus, an industrial park, a city, or a state. WANs usually include some type of remote bridges or routers, which are used to connect groups of nodes by telephone or other dedicated lines. Because of this, the bandwidth for WANs tends to be considerably smaller than for LANs. A SWAN is a satellite-based WAN.
MAN (metropolitan area network)	Generally defined as a network that covers a radius of up to 50 or 75 miles. These types of networks use fast data transmission rates (over 100Mbps) and are capable of handling voice transmission.
GAN (global area network)	Usually an internetwork that extends across national boundaries and that may connect nodes on opposite sides of the world. As with very widely distributed WANs, most GANs are likely to be internetworks in disguise.
Enterprise	Connects machines for an entire corporate operation. The network may connect very diverse machines from different parts of the company. These machines may be in different rooms, buildings, cities, or even countries. Enterprise networks are increasingly likely to cross national boundaries in this age of multinational corporations. For various reasons, many enterprise networks are being revamped as intranets or extranets.
Intranet	Are networks—often corporate or organizational—that use the Internet's TCP/IP protocol suite to communicate and use Web technology as an interface for users. The advantage of intranets is that all accesses have the same structure and interface and that this interface is widely used and easy to learn. Arguably, the most popular place for intranets is in corporate networks.
Extranet	Are essentially intranets that allow at least some outside nodes—for example, noncorporate users—to access the network. That is, extranets are intranets that are open to some segments of the public.

N

LANs generally include only PCs. WANs generally include some type of remote connection. Enterprise networks typically require gateways to access the mainframe-based networks.

Networks Classified by Types of Nodes

PC-based networks are the fastest growing segment of the networking world. Such networks offer the greatest flexibility in where to put servers and how to divide the services among nodes on the network. References to "LANs" generally assume a PC-based network.

Most PC-based networks use either Macintoshes or IBM PC and compatible machines. Macintoshes come with networking capabilities built in; PCs require extra hardware (an NIC) to join a network.

The whole gamut of PCs may be used in networks. For example, an IBM-based network may have machines ranging from an XT to a machine with an 80486 or a Pentium processor. Of course, key functions may be restricted to certain classes of machines. For example, some networking software allows only Pentium-level machines as file servers; older machines can be used only as workstations or "smaller" servers (such as print or tape servers).

Use of *superservers*, which are souped-up PCs specially designed to be used as file servers, is becoming more popular. This is because hardware capabilities have reached a level at which it is feasible for a single machine to serve dozens of nodes, and possibly to serve nodes with different network architectures at the same time. To manage multiple architectures, a superserver needs the appropriate hardware for each architecture. (See the articles about servers, NICs, and the individual network architectures for more information.)

Networks that include minicomputers or mainframes are usually located in either business or university environments. In the business world, such networks are generally run by an MIS department. Historically, these network environments have been dominated for several decades by IBM mainframes. Minicomputers, produced by companies such as Digital Equipment Corporation (DEC) or Wang (and even IBM), made inroads only slowly in the business world. In the early days, minicomputers were used as front-end processors (FEPs) for mainframes.

Mainframe-based networks generally consist mainly of terminals, which communicate directly with the mainframe or through FEPs. PCs can be used in the place of terminals, but the PCs must run terminal-emulation software and may need to "play dumb" (pretend to be nothing more than a terminal) to communicate with the mainframe.

Mainframe-based networks generally use software that complies with IBM's SNA (Systems Network Architecture) and, if PCs are to be included as more than dumb terminals, SAA (Systems Applications Architecture). SNA and SAA provide comprehensive models (comparable to the seven-layer OSI reference model) for controlling the details of network operation and communication at several levels.

DEC's alternative to SNA is DNA (Digital Network Architecture), which provides a framework for networks built around minicomputers (such as DEC's VAX machines). DECnet is one example of networking software based on the DNA framework.

In university settings, distributed networks are quite common. In such networks, there is no centralized controller. Instead, nodes are more or less comparable, except that certain nodes provide the services available on the network. UNIX environments are particularly likely to use a distributed network architecture.

Minicomputer- and mainframe-based networks often provide services to LANs. Nodes on the LAN get access to the mainframe-based network through gateways. The real advantages of layered architectures become particularly clear in such interactions between the very different worlds of the LAN and an SNA-based network.

Backbone networks are designed with smaller, access networks as nodes. Such networks are able to provide the advantages of very large, heterogeneous networks while also allowing the simplicity of a

LAN. The access networks can operate as independent networks for the most part, but can get access to resources in any of the other networks linked to the backbone, provided, of course, that the access network has the appropriate usage privileges.

Networks Classified by Relationships among Nodes

Nodes on a network can be servers or workstations. A workstation makes requests, and a server fulfills them. The "server" actually controls the network, by providing the user at the workstation with only the resources the server sees fit.

With the introduction of products such as NetWare Lite, Personal NetWare, LANTastic, and Microsoft Windows for Workgroups, peer-to-peer networks have been gaining in popularity.

The following terms are used to describe the relationship between nodes in a network:

Peer-to-peer   Every node can be both client and server; that is, all nodes are equal. Peer-to-peer (or just peer) networks are useful if you need to connect only a few machines (generally, fewer than 10) and if no one will be running programs that push available resources to the limit.

Distributed   A network with no leader; that is, one in which any node can talk to any other. An example of a distributed network is Usenet, which is popular in the UNIX community. In a distributed network, servers are just that— machines, devices, or programs that provide services, as opposed to controlling network activity. Recently, a popular form of distributed network has been one that uses a server cluster—that is, multiple servers among which network tasks are distributed so that tasks are assigned to the first server available at the time the task starts. Another kind of distributed services network that has become popular recently is a storage area network (SAN), which distributes corporate data among multiple storage components.

Intranet/Extranet   In the past few years, intranets and extranets have become popular.

These are distributed networks that use the Internet's TCP/IP protocol stack and use Web technology for their interfaces. For the most part, such networks are built around Web servers, which deliver corporate or other materials as Web pages. Many corporate and enterprise networks are being revamped as intranets. Consequently, many intranets are closed networks that happen to use open protocols. Extranets, in contrast, are intranets that also allow access to certain outsiders—for example, clients or customers.

Server-based   A network with a dedicated file server. The server runs the network, granting other nodes access to resources. Most middle- to large-sized networks are server-based, and the most popular PC-based network operating systems (Novell's NetWare, Microsoft's LAN Manager, IBM's LAN Server, and Banyan's VINES) assume a server-based network.

Client/server   A sophisticated version of a server-based network. While workstations in server-based networks can get access to all sorts of resources through the server, the workstation must do most of the work. The server doles out the resources (downloads files and, possibly, applications to the workstation), and then lets the workstation run the programs.

In the most general form of client/server computing, the workstation makes a query or request, and the server processes the query or request and returns the results to the workstation. In a commonly used form, a front-end process running on the client sends a query or request to the back end running on the server. The back end does the requested work and returns the results to the client.

Networks Classified by Topology

There are thousands of ways you can connect computers into a network. Fortunately, these possibilities all reduce to a few fundamental types (just as all the possible wallpaper patterns reduce to about two dozen basic patterns).

N

When discussing network layouts, or topologies, it is useful to distinguish between the physical and logical layouts. The logical topology specifies the flow of information and communication in the network. The physical topology specifies the wiring that links the nodes in the network.

Logical Topologies

The two main logical topologies are bus and ring. In a bus topology, information is broadcast along a single cable, called the *trunk* cable. All nodes attached to the network can hear the information, and at roughly the same time. Only nodes for which the information is intended actually read and process the transmitted packets. The information broadcast and simultaneous access characterize a bus topology.

Because all nodes hear a transmission at the same time, contentious network-access methods, such as CSMA/CD, can be used. In contentious media-access methods, nodes get transmission rights by being the first to request them when there is no network activity.

"A linear bus topology" illustrates this logical topology.

In a ring topology, information is passed from node to node in a loop. Each node gets information from exactly one node and transmits it to exactly one node. Nodes gain access to the message sequentially (in a predetermined sequence), generally based on network addresses. As with all networks, a node is expected to process only those packets with the node as a destination.

Because all nodes do not hear a transmission at the same time, network-access methods cannot be based on contention for transmission rights. Instead, deterministic-access methods, such as token passing, are used. "A ring topology" illustrates this logical topology.

Physical Topologies

Whereas the logical topology controls how information moves across a network, the physical topology, or wiring scheme, controls how electrical signals move across the network. This has consequences for the status of a network if a node breaks down.

For example, a bus wiring scheme requires minimal cable, but can make troubleshooting more difficult than with, for example, a star wiring scheme.

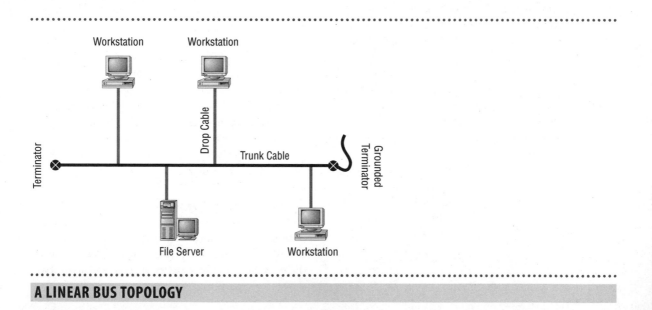

A LINEAR BUS TOPOLOGY

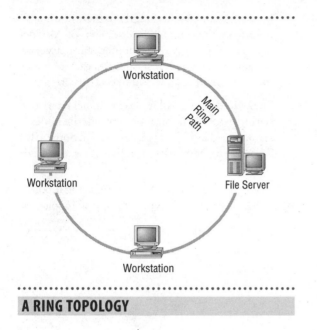

A RING TOPOLOGY

If a node attached to the bus over a drop cable goes down, there may be no way for the server to know this until the server tries to send the node a message and gets no response. In contrast, a star wiring scheme uses lots of cable, since each node may be a considerable distance from the central node or hub, but it is easy to determine when a node goes down because the central node can communicate directly with each node.

Although there are dozens of ways to label network wiring schemes, most of these fall into the following major groups:

Bus A central cable forms the backbone of the network, and individual nodes are attached to this bus, either directly or by means of a shorter piece of cable. Signals travel along the bus, and each node eavesdrops on all messages, reading only those addressed to the node. Ethernet and certain versions of ARCnet use a bus topology. Variants on a bus topology include tree and branching tree. "Bus networks" shows a bus network and two common variants.

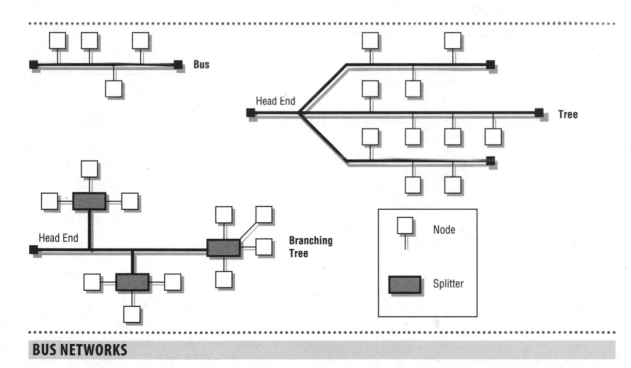

BUS NETWORKS

N

Ring The nodes are arranged in a (more or less imaginary) circle. Each node is connected to the node immediately before and immediately after. Messages are passed around the ring (more or less) in sequence. Again, a node takes the message if the node is the recipient, and passes the message on otherwise. FDDI and IBM Token Ring networks use a ring topology. Variants on the basic ring wiring scheme include slotted-ring, backbone, and multiple-ring topologies.

Star All nodes are connected to a central machine or to a wiring center (such as a hub).

Messages can be sent directly to their destinations from the center. Some versions of ARCnet use a star topology. A distributed star network is a variant in which several hubs, each of which forms a star, are connected to each other.

Star-wired ring All nodes are attached to a wiring center in a star topology, but the nodes are accessed as if they were in a ring. Some IBM Token Ring networks actually use a star-wired ring topology.

"A star topology" and "A star-wired ring topology" illustrate these two types of physical topologies.

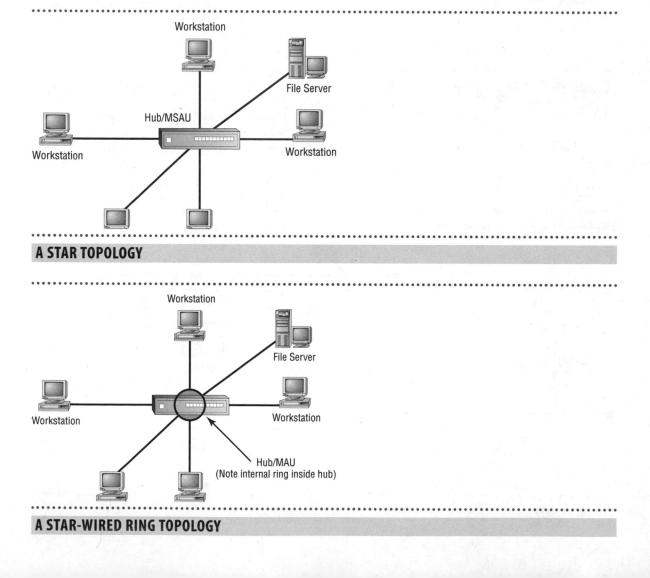

A STAR TOPOLOGY

A STAR-WIRED RING TOPOLOGY

These four schemes capture most of the network wiring configurations, but there are other ways of categorizing the network layout. For example, in a *mesh topology,* a node may be connected to one or more other nodes. In the extreme case, every node is connected directly to every other node. The advantage of direct access to each node is more than offset by the wires that will be running everywhere and by the fact that each node will need a port for connecting to every other node.

Networks Classified by Architecture

Network architectures differ in the cabling used (coaxial, twisted-pair, fiber-optic), the methods used to access the network (CSMA/CD, token passing, polling), the format of data packets sent across the network, and the network topology.

In general, different network architectures need translators in order to talk to each other. Routers and multiarchitecture hubs help to make such cross-architecture communications transparent to users.

The most commonly used network architectures are Ethernet/IEEE 802.3, ARCnet, Token Ring, and FDDI. See the Network Architecture article for more information.

Networks Classified by Access Possibilities

Networks can be shared-media or switched. In standard, shared-media network architectures (such as Ethernet or Token Ring), only one node can transmit at a time. That is, access to the network medium is exclusive. How a node gets access to the medium depends on the access method used (for example, CSMA/CD versus token passing versus polling).

Switched networks, in contrast, establish temporary connections as needed between parties. Such networks use multiplexing to enable multiple nodes to transmit at the same time. The basis used for the switching distinguishes such networks. Networks can be packet-switched, circuit-switched, or message-switched. High-speed variants of traditional networks may be switched networks—for example, fast (100Mbps) Ethernet and Gigabit (1000Mbps) Ethernet. See the Network, Circuit-Switched; Network, Message-Switched; and Network, Packet-Switched articles for details.

ALTERNATIVES TO NETWORKS

The following alternatives to networks have been used and should be considered before you go to the trouble and expense of creating your own network, especially if your main needs are for file sharing:

- SneakerNet: This involves the use of removable media—usually floppy disks—whose contents are transferred by carrying them from machine to machine, as needed. As befits this age of commercialization, SneakerNet has also been referred to as Adidasnet, Nikenet, and Reeboknet.

- Portable Drives: Portable hard disks and erasable optical drives are available, and at affordable prices. Portable drive interfaces allow such drives to be plugged into a parallel port for easy access. Erasable optical drives have capacities of over 200MB per disk.

- File Transfer Programs: These set up fast, short-distance links for rapid file or other data transfer between two machines. Such programs usually use the parallel port, and many use special cables for fast transmissions. In this context fast means only about 100Kbps or so.

- Switch Boxes: These allow two or more users to switch a resource (for example, a printer) from one machine to another. This technique isn't convenient, but it is inexpensive.

- Multiuser Systems: In these, a single processor does work for multiple users who are logged in through separate terminals. UNIX is a popular operating system for multiuser systems; DOS is not.

Planning a Network

If you are planning to set up a network, you should seriously consider hiring a professional consultant to help you. Be sure to make the prospective consultant prove to you that he or she is competent.

Before investing in a network, planning is essential. Always make sure you have all available information to guide your planning. There are some

N

guidelines to follow when you begin planning for a network:

- Formulate your needs as completely and clearly as possible. This will help you decide what components and services the network (or other solution) will need to include.

- Determine what resources (financial, equipment, and expertise) are available for planning, implementing, and running a network. This information will determine whether you are in a position to create and operate a network.

- Determine who will need access to the network and where these people are located. This information will help determine whether a network is a necessary or feasible solution for your needs. It will also give you information regarding possible cabling requirements. The cabling details will depend on the type of network (if any) you end up creating.

- Get to know your current usage and needs *in detail*. This will mean convincing the people using the (currently, stand-alone) PCs to start paying attention to what they do, how often, and for how long. This information will also help you decide whether a network is the best solution for your needs.

- Get detailed drawings of existing wiring. Once you have designed the network, you will be able to determine whether it is feasible to use some or all of the existing wiring, assuming that the wiring meets your performance requirements and that enough of the wiring is available to meet your cabling needs.

Chances are only moderate (at best) that you will be able to use the wiring—except, possibly, for short-hauls and special-purpose connections. On the other hand, if you can do it, this can save a considerable amount of money, since cable installation is a major chunk of network cabling expenses.

CALCULATING AVAILABLE RESOURCES

To play it safe, after you've determined the available resources, use only a portion of these for your working calculations. This downgrading will protect you against the inevitable resource losses and sags due to people leaving, becoming involved in other projects, and so forth.

The amount by which you need to decrease your estimates depends on the possible costs if your network is a failure and also on how stable the resources are. As a general rule of thumb, assume your available resources will be anywhere from 10 to 50 percent less than you estimated.

The converse of this coin concerns *cost* calculations. When you decide how much time and money things will cost, it's a good idea to *add* an amount or a percentage—as a hedge against Murphy's laws.

Once you've decided that a network is the appropriate solution for your needs, a second phase of planning begins. In this phase, the components and details of the network are designed. Later phases include implementing and actually running the network. See the LAN article for a more detailed discussion of LAN planning.

Network Access Controller (NAC)

→ *See* NAC (Network Access Controller)

Network Access Point (NAP)

→ *See* NAP (Network Access Point)

Network Addressable Unit (NAU)

→ *See* NAU (Network Addressable Unit)

Network Address Translation (NAT)

→ *See* IP (Internet Protocol) Masquerade

Network Administration

Network administration refers to the task of managing and maintaining a network, to make sure all programs are up to date, all hardware is functioning properly, and all authorized users are able to access and work on the network.

A network administrator, or manager, must do tasks such as the following:

- Setting up new accounts

- Assigning user privileges, permissions, and so on

- Doing billing and other accounting chores

- Testing and installing new software or hardware

- Troubleshooting existing hardware and software

- Backup and file management

→ *See Also* LAN (Local Area Network)

Network Analyzer

A network analyzer is a product that can be used to monitor the activity of a network and the stations on it, and to provide daily summaries or long-term trends of network usage and performance. A network analyzer can do tasks such as the following:

- Count or filter network traffic. For example, a network analyzer may count the total number of packets processed or count just the packets between specific nodes.

- Analyze network activity involving specified protocols or frame structures.

- Generate, display, and print statistics about network activity, either as they are being generated or in summary form (at the end of a shift or a day, for example).

- Send alarms to a network supervisor or network management program if any of the statistics being monitored exceeds predetermined thresholds. For example, if the program detects too many discarded or lost packets, it may send an alarm.

- Do trend or pattern analyses of network activity. For example, a network analyzer may identify network bottlenecks or find statistics whose average behavior is approaching a threshold. If the network analyzer program cannot do the trend analyses, it will at least allow you to export the data in a format that another program can use to do the desired analyses.

Network analyzers may be software only or may consist of both software and hardware. The latter may include an interface card for testing the network directly. This card may even include an on-board processor. Because of their greater capabilities, hardware/software analyzers are considerably more expensive than software only products. Prices for the hardware/software packages can be several times as high as for software-only products.

Network Application Support (NAS)

→ *See* NAS (Network Application Support)

Network Architecture

Depending on the scope of the discussion, a network architecture may refer to a model that encompasses an entire computing environment or to one that specifies just low-level features (cabling, packet structure, and media access) of a network.

Examples of global (encompassing) architectures include IBM's SNA (Systems Network Architecture), DEC's DNA (Network Architecture), and the ISO's OSI reference model. Such architectures are used for wide area networks (WANs) as well as local area networks (LANs). See the articles about

N

the specific architectures for more information about global architectures.

This article focuses on the more circumscribed PC-based architectures that specify a smaller range of features. PC-based architectures are most often used for LANs.

Architecture Functions

A PC-based network architecture encompasses the physical and Data-Link layers (the bottom two) of the OSI reference model. As such, the architecture specifies cabling, signal encoding, performance (such as transmission speed), packet structure, and the strategy used to access the network (media-access method). "Context and properties of network architectures" (below) illustrates the role of an architecture.

In turn, a network architecture determines the selection of various networking components, including network interface cards (NICs), wiring centers, cables, and connectors.

Network architectures are also built around particular topologies, although variant topologies exist for the electrically based architectures. For example, an Ethernet architecture uses a bus topology, but variants that use a star topology have been developed.

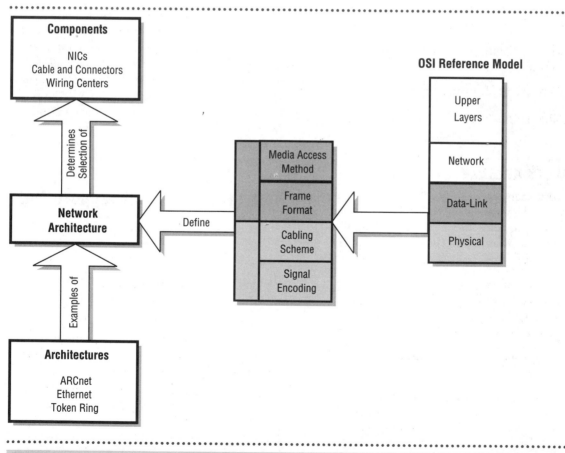

CONTEXT AND PROPERTIES OF NETWORK ARCHITECTURES

Generations of Architectures

Architectures for LANs can be split into several generations. The first generation saw the development of low- to medium-bandwidth architectures: LocalTalk (230Kbps), Ethernet (10Mbps), Token Ring (16Mbps), and ARCnet (2.5Mbps). These architectures are exclusively copper-based, at least in their original formulations.

The second generation consists of higher-bandwidth architectures: FDDI (100Mbps), ATM (155Mbps and higher), and higher-speed versions of first-generation architectures, such as 100Mbps Ethernet and 20Mbps ARCnet Plus. The fast variants are copper-based, and are an effort to speed up networks using existing cable resources. The new architectures are fiber-based, and are designed to carry multiple types of data (voice, video, and digital).

The third generation consists of very high bandwidth architectures. For example, Gigabit Ethernet is a 1000Mbps variant of traditional Ethernet that runs primarily on optical fiber. A copper-based variant is also expected to become a standard. Fibre Channel and HiPPI (High-performance Parallel Interface) are older, related technologies that have moved into the PC-based networking arena. HiPPI was originally developed to connect supercomputers; Fibre Channel was developed to connect mainframes to their storage components. Both support speeds of 1Gbps and higher. HiPPI runs on copper wire; Fibre Channel was originally developed to run on optical media. Many of these very high speed networks are switch based. Switches make it possible for multiple nodes to use full bandwidth at the same time. Another approach to achieving gigabit speeds is by aggregating several slower channels. This is done on telecommunications channels—for example, when multiple 64Kbps lines are aggregated into a 1.544Mbps T1 line.

The table "Common Network Architectures" summarizes the main types of architectures. See the article about the specific architecture for a detailed discussion.

→ *See Also* ARCnet; ATM; Ethernet; FDDI; Token Ring

Network Backbone

The main cabling for a network. This is the common cable to which servers and workstations are attached. For example, in a bus topology, each node on the network is attached either directly or over a shorter cable to the main network cable (the backbone).

Network, Back-End

A network that connects mainframes, minicomputers, and peripherals. A back-end network needs a very high bandwidth, so optical fiber is generally used as the transmission medium. FDDI is a popular architecture for this type of network.

Network, Baseband

A baseband network is one in which only a single channel is used for the entire network traffic. Unless specified otherwise, networks use baseband architectures.

A baseband network may actually use two channels, one in each direction, with each sharing part of the bandwidth. Even with just a single channel, it is possible for more than one packet to be on the network path at a given time. The two packets must be separated from each other by a time amount whose magnitude depends on the size of the network.

→ *Compare* Network, Broadband

Network Board

An expansion board that makes a computer network-capable, also called *network adapter*, *LAN card*, *network interface card*, *NIC*, along with other names.

→ *See* NIC (Network Interface Card)

N

COMMON NETWORK ARCHITECTURES

Architecture	Variants	Description
ARCnet	ARCnet Plus; TCNS	A widely used, easy-to-implement, architecture for small- to medium-size networks (maximum, 255 nodes). Uses coaxial, twisted-pair, or fiber-optic cable and can transmit at a maximum of 2.5Mbps. Its media-access method is token-passing.
Ethernet	Blue Book Ethernet (Ethernet 2.0); 802.3 Ethernet; 1Base5; 10Base2; 10Base5; 10BaseF; 10BaseT; 10Broad36	Blue Book Ethernet uses coaxial cable; 802.3-based variants can use coaxial, unshielded twisted-pair, or fiber-optic cable. Both types specify transmission speeds of up to 10Mbps, and both use CSMA/CD as their media-access method.
Fast Ethernet	100BaseT; 100VG-AnyLAN	Two 100Mbps variant standards. 100BaseT is a high-speed version of 802.3 Ethernet; 100VG-AnyLAN uses demand priority as its access method—as opposed to CSMA/CD.
Gigabit Ethernet	1000Base-CX; 1000Base-LX, 1000Base-SX	Very high speed variants that were designed originally to run on optical fiber. A copper-based variant has been developed, and should be a standard by the time you are reading this.
LocalTalk		A proprietary architecture developed by Apple, and used in networks that run the AppleTalk networking software. LocalTalk supports data-transfer rates of 230.4Kbps for up to 32 nodes in a network. This architecture usually uses coaxial cable, but also supports twisted-pair cable.
Token Ring	1, 4, 16Mbps	Usually associated with IBM. Token Ring is becoming increasingly popular as a network choice, despite its higher cost compared with Ethernet or ARCnet. Token Ring nodes are connected into a logical ring, regardless of the physical arrangement of the nodes in the network. Token Ring networks generally use special IBM cable, but fiber-optic cable can also be used. Token Ring architectures transmit at 4 or 16Mbps. Token Ring networks use a token-passing media-access method.
ATM (Asynchronous Transfer Mode)		A packet-switched network architecture that can be used for both LANs and WANs. ATM uses either Category 5 unshielded twisted-pair (UTP) or fiber-optic cable. ATM networks have a very high potential bandwidth: initially 155Mbps, but eventually reaching gigabit per second speeds. ATM uses a switching technology, so that multiple transmissions are possible at the same time.
FDDI (Fiber Distributed Data Interface)	FDDI-I, FDDI-II (HRC), CDDI, TPDDI	Uses light rather than electrical signals, and requires special optical fiber. FDDI networks can transmit at up to 100Mbps. The architecture actually uses two rings, which carry the signal in opposite directions. FDDI networks also use a token-passing scheme to control media access. Several companies have implemented electrically-based versions of FDDI. These "copper" variants are sometimes known as CDDI or TPDDI (for twisted-pair distributed data interface).

Network, Broadband

A broadband network is one that either uses multiple channels simultaneously or that shares a total bandwidth with transmissions that are not part of the network activity. In either case, a single channel in a broadband network represents only part of the total bandwidth supported by the cable and the transmission scheme.

Broadband networks use special cable that is capable of supporting multiple channels. For example, CATV cable (the sort used for cable television connections) may be used for a network.

Filters

Because signals in a broadband network must be confined to a portion of the total bandwidth, filtering and other signal-cleaning measures are necessary. This confinement makes the signal more delicate and subject to distortion (for example, because some of the signal's harmonics, and therefore, some of its power, are lost).

Several types of filtering may be used to help clean a broadband transmission. The filters are distinguished by the filtering technique they use, as well as by where in the transmission process they are applied.

For example, filters applied early in the transmission, prior to modulation, are known as *baseband*, or *premodulation*, filters. Those applied after the modulation are known as *passband*, or *postmodulation*, filters. More complex filters, such as the raised cosine type, operate in a more sophisticated manner.

Packet Padding

To compensate for the transmission errors that can arise because of distortion through filtering, broadband network architectures generally add additional header and trailer elements around the standard network packet.

For example, in a broadband Ethernet network, the Ethernet packet is framed with preambles and postambles. (The preamble actually uses some of the bits from the standard Ethernet packet, but encodes them differently to make the information more useful for a broadband transmission.)

Another way to reduce signal distortion is to use a more robust encoding method. For example, baseband Ethernet networks, along with most electrically based networks, use Manchester encoding to represent a bit value electrically. For various reasons, broadband Ethernet networks generally use NRZ (non-return to zero) encoding over parts of the transmission path.

Amplifiers

Amplifiers for broadband networks must perform to more stringent specifications and must produce much less distortion than amplifiers for baseband networks. Specifically, an amplifier for a broadband network must not have different amounts of distortion at different frequencies, because different channels would be affected differently in that case.

The amplifiers must also deal with much smaller voltages than in baseband networks. For example, whereas a signal in a baseband network may use two or more volts to represent a 1, the same value in a baseband network might be encoded with less than 100 millivolts (mV), and sometimes as low as 5 or 10 mV.

Collision Detection

Broadband networks cannot rely on the same methods as baseband networks to detect collisions. For example, a broadband Ethernet network must use a separate 4 megahertz (MHz) channel for collision detection. In contrast, a baseband Ethernet network simply needs to check the DC voltage on the wire.

→ *Compare* Network, Baseband

Network, Campus

A network that connects nodes, or possibly departmental local area networks, from multiple locations, which may be separated by a considerable distance.

N

Unlike a wide area network, a campus network does not require remote communications facilities, such as modems and telephones. This type of network is also known as a *campus-area network* (*CAN*).

Network, Cell-Switched

A network that combines the guaranteed bandwidth of a circuit-switched network with the efficiency of a packet-switched network. ATM is an example of a cell-switched network. Compare this with circuit-switched, message-switched, and packet-switched networks.

Network, Cellular

A cellular network is an example of a wireless network. A cellular network uses frequencies in the 825 to 890 megahertz (MHz) range, and special stations (cells) for passing a signal from sender to receiver. The information is transmitted through the open air between the sender's antenna and transceivers in cells surrounding the sender.

To transmit data, the networks compete with cellular voice channels in the bandwidth. Various strategies have been developed for maximizing the amount of data that can be sent over cellular channels, even while those channels are used for voice transmissions.

Cellular networks can be an attractive alternative for corporations in which a few nodes may be scattered over several nearby buildings. The cost of cabling between those nodes may be prohibitive.

Because of the transmission medium, transceivers must be in the line of sight. This means that transmissions will often be noisy, and the range of the cellular network may be limited in cities where tall buildings can interfere.

One way to improve the performance of cellular systems is to digitize the voice signal, then compress the data before transmission. Another method is to use multiplexing methods for digital transmissions, such as TDMA (time division multiplexing access).

Radio frequency (RF), infrared, and microwave networks offer alternatives to the cellular approach.

Cellular Network Advantages

Cellular networks have the following advantages:

- Nodes can be mobile.

- Frequency ranges being used have a large potential bandwidth.

- There are cells in just about all the major metropolitan areas in the United States.

Cellular Network Disadvantages

Cellular networks have the following disadvantages:

- Line of sight is required between transceivers and nodes.

- Because transmissions are through open air, they are susceptible to eavesdropping and interference.

- Components and services are still relatively expensive.

- Because signals may need to be passed from cell to cell, there may be delays in the transmission. Some software and some devices (for example, modems) get upset by such time-outs, and may stop working properly.

→ *Compare* Network, Radio Wave; Network, Infrared; Network, Microwave

Network, Centralized

A network in which control of the network is concentrated in a single machine, known as the *host* (mainframe) or the *server* (PC). This is in contrast to a *distributed network*, in which control is shared by several or all of the nodes on a network. Mainframe-based networks are generally centralized; PC-based networks may be centralized (server-based) or distributed (peer-to-peer).

Network, Circuit-Switched

A circuit-switched network is one in which a dedicated circuit, or connection, is established temporarily between two parties on the network. This circuit remains in effect until the communication between the parties is completed. Each connection that is established gets a limited but guaranteed bandwidth for the duration of the connection.

The best example of circuit switching is the telephone system, which uses this method to route calls to the appropriate telephone exchange. Since a telephone conversation takes place in real time, it is important that the connection remain established until the parties are ready to hang up.

A circuit-switched network has a low latency (time before the network is ready for the transmission). Circuit-switched networks are most useful for constant bit rate data (such as voice), and are wasteful for data that comes in bursts.

→ *Compare* Network, Cell-Switched; Network, Message-Switched; Network, Packet-Switched

Network Cloud

A network cloud (see the illustration "Communicating through a cloud") is used as both an image and a metaphor to represent an undefined network or network segment through which a communication between two end points passes. This intermediate network is represented as a cloud in diagrams to indicate that the details (elements and connections) within this network are not relevant to the topic of the illustration. As a metaphor, a network cloud again indicates that the details of a connection can remain numinous—that is, the endpoints don't need to know the details of their connection.

It is fortunate that these details need not be known—since there is no practical way in which they *can* be known for any given network. Since there is no way of knowing in advance just how much traffic there will be on all the possible paths at the time a message is actually sent, there is no way of knowing completely which of the possible and available paths will actually be used for a particular packet.

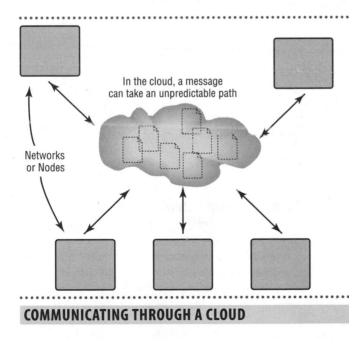

In the cloud, a message can take an unpredictable path

Networks or Nodes

COMMUNICATING THROUGH A CLOUD

N

Network Communications Control Facility (NCCF)

→ *See* NCCF (Network Communications Control Facility)

Network Control Center (NCC)

→ *See* NCC (Network Control Center)

Network Control Protocol (NCP)

→ *See* Protocol, NCP (Network Control Protocol)

Network Control System (NCS)

→ *See* NCS (Network Control System)

Network Database

→ *See* Database

Network, Departmental

A small- to medium-sized network (generally up to about 30 users) whose nodes share local resources, also known as a *departmental LAN* or a *departmental-area LAN* (*DAN*).

Network Diameter

The network diameter is the length of a network segment after it has been extended using up to four repeaters. Thus, if the maximum length of a segment in an Ethernet variant is 100 meters, for example, the network diameter for this variant would be 500 meters.

→ *Broader Category* Ethernet

Network, Distributed

A network in which control of the network is shared among some or all of the nodes on a network. The best examples of distributed networks are peer-to-peer local area networks (LANs) and UNIX-based networks. Distributed networks are in contrast to *centralized networks*, which may be host- or server-based, depending on whether the control is in a mainframe or a PC.

Network Driver Interface Specification (NDIS)

→ *See* NDIS (Network Driver Interface Specification)

Network, Enterprise

An enterprise network is one that connects an entire organization. For example, an enterprise network may connect all branches of a bank or a corporation with a chain of factories and stores. This type of network will often cover a wide area, and may even transcend national boundaries. In recent years, many enterprise networks have been revamped as intranets or extranets. These use the Internet's open TCP/IP protocol stack, and World Wide Web technology as a standard interface. Information—of whatever sort—is delivered using this standard interface, and is transported using the Internet protocols.

→ *See Also* Extranet; Intranet

Components of Enterprise Networks

An enterprise network is likely to consist of multiple local area networks (LANs), and may involve diverse hardware, network architectures, and operating environments. For example, an enterprise network may include everything from mainframes to palmtop (or at least subnotebook) computers. As a consequence, enterprise networks usually require routers or gateways.

Enterprise networks are both an attraction and a challenge. The challenge is to make very different and incompatible environments compatible with each other, or at least able to communicate. Existing environments were created without any thought to networking or integrating beyond the local group or department. The attraction is to succeed in unifying all the various means of communicating and computing.

Achieving Interoperability in Enterprise Networks

Interoperability refers to the ability of two different networks to communicate and work together, regardless of whether these networks use the same network architecture. This is vital to the success of enterprise networks.

In most cases, the difficulties arise when trying to connect the PC-based departmental and local area networks (LANs) with the centralized and mainframe-based MIS (management information system), or "corporate," networks. This is because these two computing environments were created for different purposes and, as a result, the architectures and communications protocols are very different in these two worlds.

LANs and PC-based networks have been developed largely to assist personal and group productivity—by sharing files, data, and resources. Until recently, DOS-based PCs have been limited to 16-bit operation, with true 32-bit programming and operating environments appearing only recently in the DOS world. This processing bottleneck has imposed limitations on the kinds of tasks that are feasible in PC networking environments. Mainframe-based environments have been used for heavy-duty processing, such as processing of large databases, and for providing centralized access to computing resources. Fortunately, 32-bit technology is now firmly entrenched with the move to Windows 95 and 98 in the PC world. As a result, it is now feasible to bring many of

these mainframe-level tasks down to PC-based networks—particularly networks in which processing tasks are shared among multiple processors or servers.

The use of open protocol stacks—such as the Internet's TCP/IP suite—makes it easier to support a common object model over the different types of environments. With such a model in place, information can be exchanged between different clients even though they represent information in incompatible ways. This is one of the reasons intranets have become so popular.

Allowing LANs and Mainframes to Communicate

Network operating systems (NOSs) have various strategies available to enable LANs and mainframe networks to work together. The approach taken depends partly on whether the NOS is primarily a LAN- or a mainframe-based system.

LAN-based operating systems (for example, Novell's NetWare or Banyan's VINES) generally use their native protocol stack to communicate with the LAN end of the enterprise network. For example, a NetWare server might use NCP (NetWare Core Protocol) and the IPX/SPX protocols to communicate with stations on an Ethernet network and to provide file and print services to these workstations. Lower-level communications can be accomplished through ODI (Open Data-link Interface) drivers. This allows the server to support other protocol stacks (for example, the AppleTalk or TCP/IP stacks) when communicating with Macintosh or UNIX-based clients.

To communicate with the mainframe end of the enterprise network, NOSs may use a gateway that supports a protocol stack and networking architecture compatible with the mainframe environment. Because the mainframe will often be an IBM, the gateway will generally use the SNA (Systems Network Architecture) protocols.

With this approach, the server (with its gateway) sits between the LAN and the mainframe. The server provides the usual file and printing services to the LAN; the mainframe may provide processing for

N

larger tasks. Workstations generally run their own applications.

Mainframe-based operating systems (such as MVS, VSE, or VMS) generally use a module that makes it possible to treat the LAN as just another session for the mainframe. For example in IBM environments, the SNA's APPC (Advanced Program to Program Communication) component allows a LAN (for example, a Token Ring network) to communicate with the mainframe as if the LAN were just another device on the mainframe's network. In this approach, the LAN is just another node on the mainframe's network. The mainframe provides print, file, and application services for its nodes.

→ *Broader Category* Network

Network, Flattened

A flattened network is one that supports a switched backbone. In such a backbone, the network backbone is implemented in a switch, with servers, routers, and other critical devices connected directly to ports on the switch. This replaces the backbone cable in more traditional network layouts. Network, Front-End.

A network of high-performance, special-purpose workstations (such as graphics or engineering machines). For maximum bandwidth, such machines will be connected using optical fiber.

Network, Heterogeneous

A network that is using multiple protocols at the Network layer. In contrast, a homogeneous network uses a single protocol at the Network layer.

Network, Homogeneous

A network that is using a single protocol at the Network layer. In contrast, a heterogeneous network uses multiple protocols at the Network layer.

Network, Host-Based

A network in which control of the network is concentrated or centralized in a mainframe. If the controller node is a PC, the network is said to be *server-based*. Host-based networks are examples of centralized networks, and are in contrast to distributed networks in which no single node has control of the network.

Network, Hybrid

A network that includes a mixture of topologies, such as both bus and star.

Network, Infrared

An infrared network is a type of a wireless network. An infrared network uses signals in the infrared range of the electromagnetic spectrum, in which the frequencies are in the hundreds of terahertz (THz).

Infrared networks work only over relatively short distances. They require either a line of sight between sender and receiver or a surface off which the signal can be reflected to the receiver.

No license is required for infrared networks. InfraLAN from BICC Communications is an infrared network that operates like a Token Ring network.

→ *See Also* Infrared Transmission

Network Interface Card (NIC)

→ *See* NIC (Network Interface Card)

Network Interface Layer

In the Internet's TCP/IP protocol stack, the Network Interface layer handles the low-level activity: the hardware dependent functions at the Physical layer, and the logical link components that provides an interface with the Internet layer above it.

The Network Interface layer is where the network architecture (Ethernet, Token Ring, and so forth) meets the TCP/IP protocol stack. Data coming into this lower level from the TCP/IP levels must be packaged for the network architecture and then for the physical medium over which the data must be transmitted.

Protocols that may be used at this layer include the Serial Line Internet Protocol (SLIP) or the Point-to-Point Protocol (PPP). "Layer structure for Internet protocols" shows where the Network Interface layer fits in the stack.

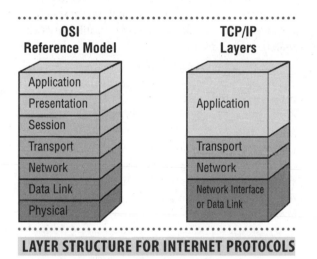

OSI Reference Model	TCP/IP Layers
Application	Application
Presentation	
Session	
Transport	Transport
Network	Network
Data Link	Network Interface or Data Link
Physical	

LAYER STRUCTURE FOR INTERNET PROTOCOLS

Network Interface Module (NIM)

→ *See* NIM (Network Interface Module)

Network Interface Unit (NIU)

→ *See* NIU (Network Interface Unit)

Network Management

The purpose of network management is to automate the processes of monitoring and adjusting the performance of a network, as well as providing reports about network activity. Network management models are built around managed objects, which are any network elements that can be used or monitored. These models generally specify the kinds of attributes managed objects must have and the kinds of functions associated with them.

A network management configuration generally involves a *managing process*, which runs on a *managing station*. The managing process collects performance and other data about the network or about particular nodes on the network. This information is actually gathered by *managing agents*, which are programs that monitor workstations and that can report this information to a managing process. The details of this monitoring and reporting process help distinguish different network management models.

Network management is generally implemented as a high-level application, so that the management software uses well-established protocol suites, such as the TCP/IP protocols, to do its work and to move its information around.

Various models have been proposed for network management. The two most comprehensive proposals are the models developed for the Internet Protocol (IP, or TCP/IP) and for the ISO's seven-layer OSI (Open Systems Interconnection) model. In addition, major network management packages still rely on mainframe-based management models, such as those developed by IBM, DEC, and AT&T.

The IP Management Model

The IP management model was developed for the Internet community in a series of RFC (Request For Comment) documents. The model's simplicity and portability have made it popular even outside the Internet community; it is arguably the most widely implemented network management model available. Most network management packages support it.

N

The components of the IP model have been updated and improved (as MIB-II and SNMP version 2). The effort and improvements indicate clearly that this "interim" network management solution is not going away.

The major components within this model are SMI (structure of management information), MIB (management information base), and SNMP (Simple Network Management Protocol).

SMI

The SMI component specifies how information about managed objects is to be represented. This representation uses a restricted version of the ISO's Abstract Syntax Notation One (ASN.1) system.

SMI relies heavily on ASN.1 notation, and represents a flexible way to organize and represent information—a method that is, for all practical purposes, infinitely extendible.

Information about management and other network elements is represented as properties associated with the element (object), along with values for some or all of these properties. To help organize or group this object information, additional elements are introduced.

The body of such information can be represented as a tree. Each managed object (network, station, application, function, setting, and so on) has a unique location in the tree. A tree can have branches, called *subtrees*, and these subtrees can have branches of their own. Each subtree is anchored by a root element. The intermediate root elements are generally organizational elements (as opposed to managed objects).

Leaf elements are those at the ends of branches; that is, they are the elements with no branches extending from them. These elements contain information about objects, often about specific objects.

Each managed network can provide content for a local information tree. In order to help provide order and common references, a global information tree is being constructed. This tree contains information about the objects defined in specifications for networking and other computer- and communications-related projects.

One of the branches on this global tree is administered by the ISO. This branch, which is named iso(1), contains the information used by network management packages. The administrator for a branch can grant branches on the subtree to particular organizations or vendors who can, in turn grant branches on their branches to other organizations, etc. For example, the ISO administers a branch, org(3), under which nonprofit organizations can grow subtrees. "Management information in the global information tree" illustrates this relationship.

Of most relevance for network management is the fact that special-purpose objects or MIBs can be defined and added to the global tree. Specific products can thus draw on a large standardized body of management information, which makes it much easier to create standardized and portable network management products.

The syntax for defining objects in this way is discussed in several RFCs, which are available through the Internet.

MIB

In the IP management model, the MIB contains the definitions and values for the managed objects relevant to a particular network. The information for the MIB component is acquired and updated by a *management agent*, which is a program whose task is to determine and report the information desired by a network management program. Each agent has an information base for the agent's network element; the management station can get information from this MIB through the agent.

The original version of this database was released in May 1990. The intent was to release successive versions of MIB, with each being a back-compatible extension. In this spirit, MIB-II (or MIB-2) was released in March of 1991.

For various reasons, the continued expansion of a generic MIB has been abandoned in favor of a scheme that allows extensions (such as those for a specific network or networking product) to be defined as separate nodes.

SNMP

SNMP is the protocol used to represent management information for transmission. Originally conceived as an interim protocol, to be replaced by the ISO's CMIS/CMIP model, SNMP has proven remarkably durable. In fact, a new and improved version, SNMP version 2, was proposed in 1992.

SNMP provides communications at the applications layer in the OSI reference model. This protocol is simple but powerful enough to accomplish its task. SNMP uses a management station and management agents who communicate with this station. The station is located at the node that is running the network management program.

SNMP agents monitor the desired objects in their environment, package this information in the appropriate manner, and ship it to the management station, either immediately or upon request.

In the global tree, there is a branch for SNMP under the MIB-2 node. (This branch was not defined in MIB-I.) There are also entries for SNMPv2 (an extended implementation that includes security features) in other parts of the global tree.

In addition to packets for processing requests and moving packets in and out of a node, the SNMP includes traps. A *trap* is a special packet that is sent from an agent to a station to indicate that something unusual has occurred. Novell's management products, including NetWare Management System (NMS) Runtime, NetWare Management Agent, NetWare Hub Services, and LANalyzer for Windows, support SNMP.

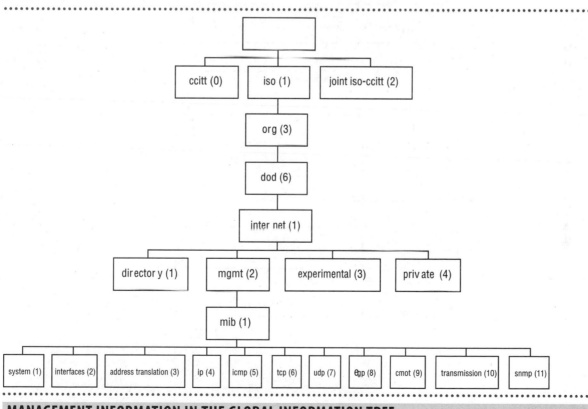

MANAGEMENT INFORMATION IN THE GLOBAL INFORMATION TREE

N

The OSI Management Model

The open systems-based management model from the OSI is arguably the most widely *discussed* network management model (the IP model is almost certainly more widely *implemented*).

With its emphasis on open systems, the OSI model is designed to operate in any -conceivable environment. By building on the seven-layer OSI model, the OSI system is guaranteed to have at least functional portability at each of the layers.

The OSI model has several important components:

- SMAP (systems management application process), which carries out the network management functions on a single machine. The SMAP may serve as a network manager or as an agent.

- SMAE (systems management application entity), which communicates with other nodes, including with the network manager, which is the machine that is in charge of the network management tasks. SMAEs use CMIP (Common Management Information Protocol) packets to communicate.

- LME (layer management entity), which provides network management functions that are specific to a particular layer. Each layer has its own LME.

- MIB (management information base), which contains the network management information received from each node.

The relationship of these elements is summarized in "Major components in the OSI network management model."

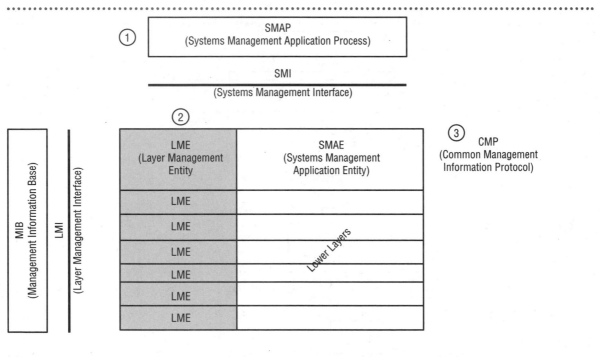

1. The SMAP is responsible for vertical management. It uses and possibly changes the MIB and communicates with SMAEs through the SMI.

2. The layer-specific LMEs are responsible for horizontal management. They manage the interaction between each layer and MIB. The LMEs communicate with the MIB through the LMI.

3. The SMAEs communicate vertically with the SMAP and horizontally with SMAEs on other nodes. This peer-level communication uses the CMIP.

MAJOR COMPONENTS IN THE OSI NETWORK MANAGEMENT MODEL

SMAE

An SMAE must do a lot of work to process management information and to communicate with other nodes. Functionally, an SMAE is organized as shown in the "The internal structure of an SMAE."

The SMASE (systems management application service element) represents the working element in the SMAE. This element relies on both a management service element, called CMISE (common management information service element), and a nonmanagement service element, called ASE (application service element).

Both SMASE and CMISE have well-defined packet formats, and may exchange information with their counterparts in other nodes. Such communications use management application protocol data units (MAPDUs) or common management protocol data units (CMIPDUs).

Management Levels

The components operate at either of two levels of network management specified in the ISO model: systems management or layer management.

Systems management encompasses five major areas and more than a dozen function classes. This is what is generally meant when network management is discussed. The SMAP and SMAE together make up the systems management capabilities.

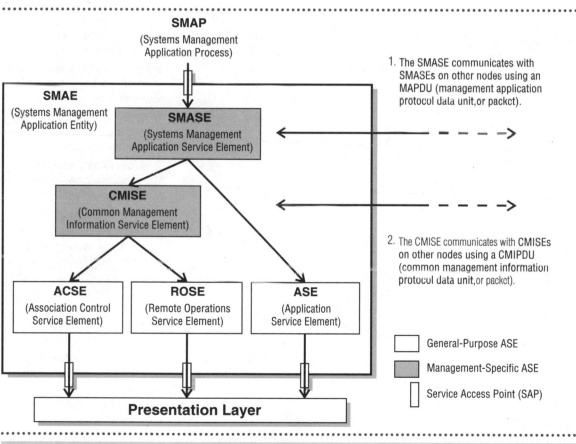

1. The SMASE communicates with SMASEs on other nodes using an MAPDU (management application protocol data unit, or packet).

2. The CMISE communicates with CMISEs on other nodes using a CMIPDU (common management information protocol data unit, or packet).

☐ General-Purpose ASE

▨ Management-Specific ASE

▯ Service Access Point (SAP)

THE INTERNAL STRUCTURE OF AN SMAE

N

Layer management encompasses the objects and functions that provide network management services at specific layers in the OSI reference model. These capabilities are needed to ensure that the network management package can communicate at whatever level is necessary.

In addition to these levels of management, the OSI model describes services and protocols that can be used to carry out network management tasks, as well as the format in which management information can be stored and retrieved.

CMIS and CMIP

Network management tasks are accomplished using CMIS (common management information services), which rely on CMIP to transfer information. Together, the services and protocol can provide all the capabilities needed to accomplish the network management tasks.

MIB

Storage format is specified through a MIB, which determines the representation, storage, and retrieval of management information.

The MIB for the OSI model is much richer and more flexible than the information base for the IP model. For example, whereas functions using SNMP can manipulate only attribute values for existing objects, CMIP-based functions can create or delete managed objects if necessary. Both models rely on the global information tree created by the ISO and CCITT to represent networking and other information.

Systems Management Domains

The OSI management model describes five major systems management domains, as well as the functions used by these domains. The domains, known as systems management functional areas (SMFAs), are accounting management, configuration management, fault management, performance management, and security management. Each of these areas is discussed in its own article.

The SMFAs use the lower-level systems management functions (SMFs) listed in the table "Systems Management Functions" to accomplish their work.

SYSTEMS MANAGEMENT FUNCTIONS

SMF	Description
Object management	Create, delete, examine, and update objects; report that such manipulations have taken place
State management	Monitor objects' management states; report when these states are changed
Relationship management	Establish, monitor, and view the relationships among objects
Alarm reporting	Provide notice of and information about faults, errors, or other abnormalities in network operation
Event reporting	Select events to be reported; specify the destinations for such reports
Log control	Specify how to handle event logs, such as what to add, when to add events, and how often to create new logs
Security alarm reporting	Provide notice of and information about faults, errors, or other abnormalities related to network security
Security audit trail	Specify the events and event formats to be used for a security log
Access control	Control access to management information and operations
Account metering	Specify a model for the objects and measures needed to keep track of resource usage, generate accounting and billing for such use, and enforce any accounting limits associated with a particular user
Workload monitoring	Specify a model for the objects and attributes needed to monitor; report on the performance of network components
Summarization	Specify a model for objects used to analyze and summarize network management information
Test management	Specify a model for objects that are used to test network components and services

Each node being monitored will have an agent (an SMAE) whose job is to monitor the node's performance in the functional areas of interest. The information collected by the agent is passed to a managing process and stored in a MIB.

CMISE

SMFs rely on CMISEs to do the necessary work. "Components and their relationships in systems management in the OSI model" shows the chain of commands used to perform systems management.

A CMISE consists of two components: CMIS and CMIP. The CMIS provides an interface through which a user can access the available services. The CMIP provides a way to package the data and service requests.

A CMISE provides three types of service:

- Management association services, which are necessary to enable applications to establish connections with each other. Using these services

(which are actually provided for the CMISE by the ACSE), two applications can establish the ground rules for their connection, the types of information they can exchange, and the types of application service elements and common management information services allowed in the communication. These ground rules form an application context.

- Management notification services, which report events involving managed objects to an authorized user (that is, client). Actually, this category consists of only a single action. The management notification service is analogous, in some ways, to the SNMP trap messages, which also serve to report about a particular state in an object.

- Management operation services, which carry out the tasks necessary to manage the network. These tasks include creating or deleting objects, reading or changing attribute values, and so on.

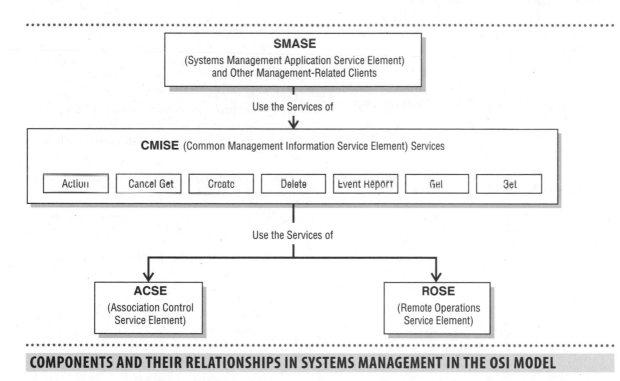

SMASE
(Systems Management Application Service Element)
and Other Management-Related Clients

Use the Services of

CMISE (Common Management Information Service Element) Services

| Action | Cancel Get | Create | Delete | Event Report | Get | Set |

Use the Services of

ACSE
(Association Control
Service Element)

ROSE
(Remote Operations
Service Element)

COMPONENTS AND THEIR RELATIONSHIPS IN SYSTEMS MANAGEMENT IN THE OSI MODEL

Certain services (for example, those that create or delete an object) require confirmation from the process involved that the service was carried out. Other services, such as changing attribute values, do not require such confirmation. (To determine whether an unconfirmed action was carried out, a process needs to check the new value.)

Actions can be performed on multiple objects, which can be specified using special parameters. In addition, CMIS provides sophisticated filtering capabilities, which can be used to select just the attributes (or attribute values) to be selected or changed.

These powerful selection capabilities, along with the ability to create or delete managed objects, make the OSI management model more complex than the IP model, and also make the two models relatively incompatible. Converting from OSI to IP format, known in the IP community as *de-osifying*, is not a simple task.

Note that the CMISE relies on lower-level and more specialized service elements, the application control service element (ACSE) and the remote operations service element (ROSE), to accomplish some of its tasks. CMIP also uses ROSE to transfer CMPIDUs.

ROSE operations may be synchronous or asynchronous; they may be confirmed, unconfirmed, or partially confirmed (report success or failure, but not both). Applications that use ROSE to work together may do so under any of three relationships (association classes):

- Association class 1: Only the application that initiates the association can invoke operations.

- Association class 2: Only the application that responds to the association can invoke operations.

- Association class 3: Either the initiating or responding application can invoke operations.

CMISE always uses association class 3, so that either application can invoke any required operations.

Mainframe-Based Management Models

Network management models based on mainframe networks operate from a central host. The most widely used mainframe model is IBM's NMA (Network Management Architecture), which is an extension of SNA (Systems Network Architecture).

NMA is concerned with four types of management: configuration management, problem management, performance and accounting management, and change management.

NMA is implemented through NetView, which has long been IBM's premier management package for SNA-based networks. The management software will run on the host, which is the focal point for the network management. This host will request various types of data from SNA-compliant devices at entry points and from non-IBM devices at service points. NetView uses the NMVT (Network Management Vector Transport) protocol to transmit management information. See the NMA article for more information.

Other Models

Although they are not as comprehensive as the ISO management model, other network management models have been proposed. Two of the more comprehensive are AT&T's UNMA (Unified Network Management Architecture) and Digital Equipment Corporation's EMA (Enterprise Management Architecture). Both models are discussed in their own articles.

These models can be distinguished on the basis of a few fundamental features:

- Whether the model is centralized, distributed, or both.

- Whether the model is concerned primarily with applications or with hardware.

- Whether the model is limited to LANs or WANs or whether it is independent of network size.

Location of Management Components

In a centralized model, all the management work is carried out by a single process or node. Such models tend to be CPU-based, and are similar to the host-centric models that have prevailed for so long in the mainframe world.

In a distributed model, each node has certain network management capabilities. The monitoring and data gathering are done independently by each node, and the results are reported to the central processing node, which will do the data analyses.

Some models may include both centralized and distributed features. For example, nodes on a network may be able to gather data, but may need to do so at the command of a central machine.

Focus of Model

Some network management models are concerned primarily with monitoring applications and transmissions; others are concerned with monitoring the state of the hardware during network activity.

A software-based model will provide usage, availability, and performance data about the applications on the network. In contrast, a hardware-based model will provide information about how hardware resources are used.

Scope of Model

While LAN and WAN management share many features, there are some important differences, including the following:

- Much LAN traffic is broadcast, which means a management package can collect at least some data passively. In contrast, the telecommunications link used in a WAN forces the management package to take an active part in the transmission.

- LAN networks are generally homogeneous; WAN networks may be heterogeneous.

- Because WAN transmissions may need to go through multiple switching networks, response times become much less reliable as indicators of network activity than in LANs.

Network Management Tools

The network management capabilities are usually implemented in software. The management tools may be specialized (for example, collecting just performance data) or comprehensive.

Tools must have monitoring, reporting, and analysis capabilities. Those tools that will serve as managing processes—as the control programs for the network management—also need control capabilities.

In general the management models do not specify the details of how these capabilities are to be implemented. For example, programs may report data in text or graphics form. Programs will also differ in their monitoring capabilities.

The tools may be designed for LAN or WAN management or both. Although many of the tasks are the same for managing both LANs and WANs, there are some important differences, mainly with respect to reporting and timing.

Management tools that are designed to manage both LANs and WANs are sometimes known as SuperManagers, and they are part of even more comprehensive architectures. Examples of Super-Managers include the following:

- IBM's NetView, which operates within IBM's SNA.

- AT&T's Accumaster Integrator, which operates within AT&T's UNMA (Universal Network Management Architecture).

- DEC's DECmcc Director, which operates within Digital's EMA (Enterprise Management Architecture).

Management tools may use text, graphics, sound, or some combination of these, to report data and analyses.

A comprehensive catalog of network management tools is published occasionally as an RFC. The most recent of these is RFC 1470, published in June 1993.

N

→ *Primary sources* IP management model: RFC 1155 (SMI), RFCs 1156, 1213, and 2011–2013 (MIB-I and II), RFC 1157 (SNMP); RFCs 1441, 1445–1447, 1451, and 1902–1908 (SNMPv2)

OSI network management model: ISO documents 10733 and 10737 (layer management), CCITT X.73x and X.74x series and the ISO 10164-x series (systems management), CCITT X.71x series and ISO 9595-x and 9596-x series (CMIS and CMIP), CCITT X.72x series and ISO 10165-x series (MIB)

→ *See Also* Accounting Management; Configuration Management; EMA (Enterprise Management Architecture); Fault Management; Global Tree; MIB (Management Information Base); NetView; NMA (Network Management Architecture); Performance Management; Protocol, SNMP; Security Management; SMI (Structure of Management Information); UNMA (Unified Network Management Architecture)

Network Management Architecture (NMA)

→ *See* NMA (Network Management Architecture)

Network Management Entity (NME)

→ *See* NME (Network Management Entity)

Network Management Vector Transport (NMVT)

→ *See* NMVT (Network Management Vector Transport)

Network, Message-Switched

A message-switched network is one in which messages from multiple users can travel along the network at the same time. The messages may be stored temporarily, and then forwarded to the destination by routing, or switching, the message through intermediate nodes until the message reaches its destination. Because of this message handling technique, message-switched networks are also known as store-and-forward networks. Electronic mail (e-mail) handling services are examples of message switching.

This method collects an entire message and then passes the message to its destination. This is in contrast to packet switching, in which the individual packets that make up a message are passed from source to destination (possibly in a haphazard order), and are then reassembled at the destination.

→ *Compare* Network, Circuit-Switched; Network, Packet-Switched

Network, Microwave

A microwave network is an example of a wireless network. A microwave network uses signals in the gigahertz (GHz) range of the electromagnetic spectrum. Such networks beam signals at antennas, from which the signal is broadcast to other nodes.

Networks use either an earth-based antenna or a satellite in geosynchronous orbit as the retransmission point. With a satellite, the signal can be transmitted thousands of miles; with earth-based antennas, the signal is limited to a few kilometers.

Microwave technology uses transmissions in the gigabit per second range, so that this technology begins at the upper limit of radio waves.

Like radio waves, the microwave spectrum requires licensing from the FCC (Federal Communications Commission). Microwave transmissions are very susceptible to eavesdropping, jamming, and interference (from natural or electrical sources).

→ *See Also* Microwave Transmission

Network Modem

A modem that is also a separate station on a network. This modem has its own network interface card, and it is connected directly to the network, as a node. A remote caller accesses the network through this node. A network modem can work as an access server.

Network News Transfer Protocol (NNTP)

→ *See* Protocol, NNTP (Network News Transfer Protocol)

Network Number

In a Novell NetWare environment, a hexadecimal value that uniquely identifies a network or a network cable segment. It is also known as the *IPX external network number*.

→ *See Also* IPX Network Numbers and Internetwork Addresses

Network Operating System (NOS)

→ *See* NOS (Network Operating System)

Network, Packet-Switched

A packet-switched network is one in which packets from multiple transmissions can travel along the network at the same time. The packets are simply routed, or switched, from source to destination using whatever temporary path is appropriate. A packet contains source and destination addresses (and also sequence information), so that packets can be passed from node to node until they reach their destination, and reassembled there.

For packet switching to work, the receiver must be able to reconstitute the transmission from the individual packets. This chore generally is the responsibility of a component or program that operates at the Transport layer of the OSI reference model.

Networks that involve large-scale data transmissions for many users at the same time (for example, private or public data lines) use packet switching. Many of these services comply with the X.25 standard, which provides an interface between a user and the packet-switched network. This interface includes PADs (packet assemblers/disassemblers) to make sure that a transmission is in packets before being sent onto the network and that the transmitted packets are reassembled before being passed to the receiver.

The performance of a packet-switched network depends in part on the protocol preparing the packets for the network. In some cases, packets are quite small (for example, 128 bytes in the XMODEM communications protocol), which can slow down the transmission. On the other hand, if packets are too large, the likelihood of an erroneous bit in the packet increases, as does the cost of retransmission if that happens.

Packet-switched networks are most useful for data that come in bursts. Such networks are unsuited for voice transmission (which requires a constant data rate) because delays can occur in transmission, packets can reach their destination "out of order," and the network may not be available immediately for transmission.

→ *Compare* Network, Circuit-Switched; Network, Message-Switched

Network Packet Switch Interface (NPSI)

An interface used in IBM's SNA (Systems Network Architecture).

→ *See Also* SNA (Systems Network Architecture)

N

Network, Peer-to-Peer

A network in which each node is assumed to have processing capabilities, and in which nodes can be servers or workstations as required, so that nodes are functionally equal. In a peer-to-peer network, nodes can use each other's resources and can provide available resources to other nodes. This is in contrast to a server-based network, in which one or more machines have special status as dedicated servers. Novell's Personal NetWare, Microsoft's Windows for Workgroups, and Artisoft's LAN-Tastic are examples of peer-to-peer networks.

→ *See Also* LAN (Local Area Network)

Network, Premises

A premises network is confined to a single building, but covers that building completely.

Network Printing Alliance Protocol (NPAP)

→ *See* NPAP (Network Printing Alliance Protocol)

Network Protocol

→ *See* Protocol, Network

Network, Radio

A radio network is an example of a wireless network. In such a network, communication is accomplished using radio wave transmissions. In such a transmission strategy, radio waves are broadcast in all directions, and can be picked up by any station with a suitable receiver. This makes radio waves suitable for broadcast situations in which security is not an issue.

Radio waves can penetrate walls, and do not require a line-of-sight connection between sender and receiver, which makes radio networks more flexible than wireless networks based on infrared or microwave transmissions.

Radio waves may be used for single-frequency or spread-spectrum transmissions. In single-frequency transmissions, the signal is encoded within a narrow frequency range. With such a signal, all the energy is concentrated at a particular frequency range. This signal is susceptible to jamming and eavesdropping. Depending on the frequency range being used, you may need a license to operate a single-frequency network.

Motorola's Altair system is an example of a single-frequency network. These networks operate within a frequency range that requires licensing, but the vendor takes care of that. Motorola must also assign you a frequency within which to operate, to ensure that your network does not interfere with another such network in the area. The Altair system operates as an Ethernet network.

In spread-spectrum transmissions, the signal is distributed over a broad frequency range, or spectrum. Spread-spectrum signals are extremely unlikely to interfere with other transmissions, since the other transmission would need to be using the same spreading algorithm. Spread-spectrum networks do not require licensing, at least not within the frequency range covered by such products (see ISM).

WaveLAN from NCR is an example of a spread-spectrum network. The hardware comes on an adapter card, and includes a transmitter and an antenna. The transmitter is capable of sending a 250 milliwatt signal for up to 245 meters (800 feet), under ideal outdoor conditions, or about a third of that distance under ordinary indoor conditions.

→ *See Also* Radio Wave Transmission

Network, Server-Based

A network in which one or more nodes have special status as dedicated servers. Other nodes must go through a server for resources on other machines. This is in contrast to a peer-to-peer network, in which each node may be either server or workstation as the need arises. Larger networks are more likely to be server-based, as are networks with sensitive or critical information. NetWare from Novell, VINES from Banyan Systems, and AppleTalk from Apple can each be used to create server-based networks.

→ **See Also** LAN (Local Area Network)

Network Service Access Point (NSAP)

→ **See** NSAP (Network Service Access Point)

Network, Shared-Media

A shared-media network is one in which all nodes share the same line, so that only a single transmission is possible at one time. This is in contrast to a switched network, in which multiple lines can be active at a time. Adding nodes to a shared-media network merely increases the traffic; it does not increase the capacity.

The standard network architectures—Ethernet, ARCnet, and Token Ring—create shared-media networks, at least in the architectures' basic forms.

In contrast, up-and-coming architectures, such as ATM (Asynchronous Transfer Mode), are switched networks. These architectures can support multiple channels at a time. In the case of ATM architectures, these channels can have very high bandwidths.

Enhancements for standard architectures can also provide limited switching capabilities. For example, switched-hub technology can enable multiple transmissions at the same time over an Ethernet network. Similarly, ETR (early token release) makes it possible to have multiple packets moving around a Token Ring network at the same time.

→ **Compare** Network, Switched

Network Station

A machine that is linked to a network. The network station can be either a workstation or a server.

Network, Switched

A switched network is one in which temporary connections between two nodes are established when needed. Routing a transmission through such temporary connections is known as *switching*. Switching is used for networks on which many nodes, or parties, may be accessing the network at the same time.

Three types of switched networks are in common use:

- Circuit-switched. The telephone system is the best example of a circuit-switched network.

- Message-switched. Electronic mail (e-mail) handling services that store messages and then forward them to their destination are examples of message-switched networks.

- Packet-switched: Networks designed for large-scale data transmission. For example, public or private phone services using the X.25 standard or the proposed Data Highway, generally use packet switching.

Each of these types of networks is discussed in a separate article.

Because connections are established as needed, switched networks can handle transmissions from multiple nodes at the same time. This is in contrast to a shared-media network (such as an Ethernet network), in which only a single transmission can be traveling at a time.

→ **Compare** Network, Shared-Media

Network-to-Network Interface (NNI)

→ **See** NNI (Network-to-Network Interface)

N

Network-to-Node Interface (NNI)

→ *See* NNI (Network-to-Network Interface)

Network Visible Entity (NVE)

→ *See* NVE (Network Visible Entity)

Network, Wireless

A wireless network is one that does not rely on cable as the communications medium. Such networks are also known as LAWNs (local area wireless networks). The IEEE 802.11 workgroup is responsible for developing a standard for wireless networking.

Wireless networks are used for purposes such as the following:

- Connecting machines within a building

- Connecting portable or mobile machines to a network

- Keeping a mobile machine in contact with a database

- Ad hoc networks (for example, in committee or business meetings)

Wireless networks use signals that cover a broad frequency range, from a few megahertz to a few terahertz. Depending on the frequencies involved, the network is known as a radio wave, microwave, or infrared network.

Wireless Network Groupings

Radio wave networks operate at frequencies anywhere from a few megahertz (MHz) to about 3 gigahertz (GHz), and they use either a single-frequency or spread-spectrum transmission strategy. Radio frequencies must be licensed from the FCC (Federal Communications Commission).

A single-frequency strategy transmits within a single, generally small, frequency band. This is susceptible to eavesdropping, interference, and jamming. In contrast, a spread-spectrum strategy distributes the transmission across a broader frequency range. The "spreading" sequence may be determined at random, and must be known to the receiver. This strategy is difficult to intercept without knowing the spreading sequence, and is unlikely to interfere with other transmissions.

Microwave networks use frequencies in the gigahertz range. At the low end, microwave overlaps with radio wave, since these terms are not associated with explicit boundaries. In fact, only some sources distinguish a separate microwave category. Others use radio wave to refer to the spectrum up to about 6GHz.

Microwave networks use either an earth-based antenna or a satellite in geosynchronous orbit as the retransmission point. With a satellite, the signal can be transmitted thousands of miles; with earth-based antennas, the signal is limited to a few kilometers.

The microwave spectrum requires licensing from the FCC. Microwave transmissions are very susceptible to eavesdropping, jamming, and interference (from natural or electrical sources).

Infrared networks use frequencies ranging from a few hundred GHz to about 1 terahertz (THz), just below the visible light spectrum. These waves require a line-of-sight connection between sender and receiver or between each of these and a common cell. An infrared signal can be focused or diffuse.

A focused signal is aimed directly at the target (receiver or cell), or the signal may be beamed at a surface and reflected off this to a receiver. This type of signal can travel over a greater range but only to a specific target. In contrast, a diffuse signal travels in multiple directions, but is much weaker in each direction. As a result, the range of a diffuse signal is much smaller than for a focused signal.

No license is required for infrared networks.

Wireless Network Standards

The IEEE 802.11 working group on wireless networking has published comprehensive specifications for wireless network architectures. Separate specifications have been developed for infrared networks and for two types of spread-spectrum radio networks. Separate protocols are needed for the Data-Link and the Physical layers.

The DFWMAC (Distributed Foundation Wireless Media Access Control) protocol was adopted in 1993 as the standard MAC protocol. DFWMAC supports transmissions of at least 1Mbps, and uses the CSMA/CA (carrier sense multiple access/collision avoidance) medium-access method, but requires acknowledgment that a transmitted packet was received.

The DFWMAC protocol can work with any of multiple Physical layer protocols. These protocols are distinguished in part by the frequency band in which they are being used. The table "Frequency Band Allocations" shows the frequency bands that have been allocated (or freed) by the FCC for the specified uses.

FREQUENCY BAND ALLOCATIONS

Bandwidth	Use
824–849MHz, 869–894MHz	Cellular communications.
896–901MHz, 930–931MHz	Private, land-based mobile communications (for example, radio and mobile data services).
902–928MHz	Unlicensed commercial use (for example, cordless phones and wireless LANs). Formerly allocated for industrial, scientific, and medical (ISM) usage.
931–932MHz	Common-carrier paging services.
932–935MHz, 941–944MHz	Point-to-point or point-to-multipoint communications.
1.85–1.97GHz, 2.13–2.15GHz, 2.18–2.2GHz	Commercial and noncommercial PCS (personal communications services).
2.4–2.5GHz, 5.8–5.9GHz	Unlicensed commercial use.

With the help of a PCF (point coordination function), DFWMAC can even handle time-sensitive transmissions such as video. This is possible because the PCF helps grab the transmission for enough time to transmit a superframe, which contains the time-sensitive information.

NETX.COM

NETX.COM is a network shell program for workstations in pre-4.*x* versions of Novell's NetWare. NETX is used to establish a connection with the NetWare operating system running on the server. Earlier versions of this program are DOS version-specific, and are named NET3, 4, 5, or 6, depending on the major DOS version. For example, NET5.COM was for DOS version 5.*x*. NETX.COM was developed to be DOS version-independent, effectively replacing these earlier versions.

NETX runs on top of DOS, and takes over certain critical DOS interrupts:

- 21H (the standard function dispatcher)
- 17H (used to send data to printer ports)
- 24H (the critical error handler vector)

With control of these interrupts, NETX intercepts user or application requests. If these are intended for the network, NETX encodes the requests or commands using the NCP (NetWare Control Protocol), and passes the constructed packet down through the IPX and Data-Link layers for transmission on the network. NETX communicates with the network driver either through Novell's ODI (Open Data-link Interface) or through a hardware-specific driver.

In NetWare version 4.*x*, NETX.COM has been replaced by the NetWare DOS Requester.

→ *Broader Category* NetWare

→ *Compare* DOS Requester

→ *Related Articles* IPX.COM, SPX.COM

N

NETx.VLM

In Novell's NetWare 4*x*, NETx.VLM is a Virtual Loadable Module (VLM) that runs as part of the NetWare DOS Requester and that serves to provide backward-compatibility with earlier NetWare versions, which use a network shell (NETx.COM) to direct user and application requests to DOS or to the network.

News

On the Internet, News is an information-sharing service that enables users to exchange messages about topics of mutual interest or just to look in and see what messages others are contributing to the exchange. In short, network news provides an interactive forum in which users can discuss ideas about particular or general topics. News is also known as *Net News*, *Network News* and *Usenet News*.

This open forum, in which messages are available for public viewing and reaction, is in contrast to the more personal mail service. In fact, one of the reasons a news service was developed on UNIX systems was to provide a more convenient way to exchange ideas and to hold conferences.

News messages are *posted* to a *newsgroup*, which is a collection of messages about a topic. Newsgroups are organized hierarchically, using subgroupings under seven general newsgroup categories. The newsgroups in these categories—or the network locations that distribute these newsgroups—make up the Usenet. As of early 1999, there were over 30,000 newsgroups.

Usenet sites mirror (maintain copies of) or distribute the messages for the following top-level categories, and possibly more.

comp computer science and related topics

news announcements and information about Usenet and news-related software

rec hobbies, arts, crafts, music, and other recreational activities

sci scientific research, advances, and applications for scientific fields other than computer science

soc topics of social relevance—with "social" defined just about any way you want it to be

talk debate and heated (or long-winded) discussion about controversial topics

misc categories that don't fit into any of the others in the list

The first of the following categories is not officially one of the high-level categories handled by Usenet machines. It is, however, distributed by most of them. The other categories may not be as easily accessible.

alt groups that haven't been officially accepted as official by the Usenet community or groups that don't (want to) fit into any of the categories (including **misc**)

bix business-related topics and announcements—including advertisements

gnu the GNU (GNU's Not UNIX) development project and the works of the Free Software Foundation (FSF)

k12 teaching-related topics for grades kindergarten through high school

de and **fj** discussions in German and Japanese, respectively

Within the high-level categories, there are subcategories, which have their own subcategories. This process can go through several levels. For example, *rec.sport.football.australian*, *rec.sport.football.canadian*, *rec.sport.football.college, rec.sport.football.fantasy*, and *rec.sport.football.pro* can all be found under the rec category. Similarly, you can find newsgroups such as alt.gopher (Gopher internet utility), *comp.lang.perl.misc* (Perl programming language), *at.astronomie* (astronomy in Austria), and *scruz.poetry* (poetry readings in Santa Cruz, CA). Note that the highest level in the hierarchy is the leftmost part of the name, with deeper levels being further to the right.

Newsreader programs generally keep a list of available newsgroups, and update this list each time you connect to the news server. Many newsreaders keep this list in text format. It's sometimes more convenient to just read this file to determine what newsgroups are available. It's possible to configure most newsreaders so that they report any newsgroups formed since the user last logged on.

Certain newsgroups—those in the *alt.binaries.** hierarchy—deal almost entirely in image files. While many of these are sexually-oriented, others contain computer art, graphs of fractal equations, etc. Files containing binary images must be processed in a special manner.

Getting the News

The news materials—that is, the messages posted to the various newsgroups—are delivered to news servers. Such deliveries are known as *feeds*; servers agree to deliver, exchange, or distribute feeds for each other.

The servers use Network News Transfer Protocol (NNTP) as their protocol when doing newsfeeds. One reason is that NNTP is interactive, so servers can select which newsgroups and articles they want. This can save many megabytes of transmissions and many hundreds of file deletions.

Users can read the news articles by getting them from a news server or by downloading them and reading them off-line. A *newsreader* program is used to connect to a news server and then to retrieve and read the news articles. Newsreaders are generally text-based programs that can display a list of articles in a particular newsgroup, and that can display at least the text portion of the articles.

Newsreaders can download, and usually upload, article files, and keep track of which articles the user has read or downloaded, which articles are new, etc. Newsreaders may include or support viewers for various graphics or other formats. They may also include or support special utilities for encoding or decoding a file, or for converting a file from one format to another.

In this context, file encoding and decoding refer to the conversion of 8-bit data chunks, which might produce bizarre or destructive effects during transmission, into safe ASCII characters. This is done by recoding three bytes from the source as four bytes in the converted version. Utilities such as BinHex and the UNIX environment's uuencode make such conversions.

The rapidly growing ability to include various types of information in a mail or news message has led to the development of the MIME (Multipurpose internet mail extension) specifications. These provide a notation and syntax for including various types of material in a file, and even include provisions for attaching required viewers or other simple programs to a message. MIME messages use Base64 encoding, which is another four-bytes-for-three encoding scheme.

Reading the News

A newsreader must be configured before use. The first time the newsreader is used, it will retrieve a list of all the newsgroups available on the connected news server, and will give the user an opportunity to subscribe to any or all of them. There are currently over 30,000 newsgroups, and news servers will typically accept feeds from at least several thousand of them. Not surprisingly, downloading the list for the first time will take a while.

You can subscribe to any or all of the newsgroups. If you subscribe, your newsreader will automatically retrieve information about the newsgroups whenever you connect to the news server. Depending on your configuration settings, the newsreader may deliver information only about new postings.

Finding the News

Pick just about any topic, and there's a good chance that you'll find a newsgroup that discusses it. To find out what newsgroups are available, subscribe to the *news.lists* newsgroup. You'll generally find an article containing a list of active newsgroups. Other

N

useful newsgroups for new news users include: *news.newusers.questions* and *news.announce.newusers*.

Newsgroup

On the Internet, a newsgroup is any of the more than 30,000 (and counting) article (posting, or message) collections that have been created. These collections are named and organized by topic, then subtopic, and so forth. Seven of the top-level groupings are carried over the Usenet; other newsgroups fall into the *alt* category or into any of the several dozen special interest categories. See the "News" article for more details and specific examples. News servers may carry and distribute some or all of the available newsgroups.

Newsreader

A newsreader is a program that can retrieve, organize, display, and send *postings* (messages, or articles) from newsgroups (named message collections, which may contain news, opinions, or just drivel). A series of articles that are part of a single discussion is known as a *thread*.

With a newsreader, you can perform actions such as the following:

- Select newsgroups to which you want to subscribe. This is a task for which there is considerable variation with respect to how they let you accomplish this. Some newsreaders start off by assuming you want to subscribe to all available newsgroups—all 14,500+ of them (if your news server carries them all); others let you specify to which newsgroups you want to subscribe.

NEWSGROUPS LIST

- Select the newsgroup articles that you actually want to read.

- Read the articles. Most newsreaders will keep track of the articles you've read from that newsgroup. Read articles won't reappear on your list of available articles for the newsgroup.

- Follow threads of a discussion over multiple articles. Some newsreaders are threaded (see below), which means that they will determine links between articles so that you can read them in the proper sequence if you like. If your newsreader isn't a threaded one, you can still do this, except that you'll have to find the thread yourself.

- Save articles to disk.

- Use e-mail to reply directly to the writer of an article.

- Post a response to an article, in which case your response will become part of the thread for the original article.

- Post an article of your own, in which case your article will become the start of a new thread.

- Create a file in which you can specify posters (that is, article writers) or topics you want to exclude (or, more rarely, include) automatically when the newsreaders retrieves news for you. The file containing the selection criteria is called a *killfile*, or a "bozo filter" because it's generally used to screen out rather than to include.

Newsreaders may be grouped in several ways:

- Newsreaders may be *character-based* or *windowed*, with the latter being more sophisticated.

- *Threaded* newsreaders arrange articles so that you can read the entire "conversation" (article series) without having to determine the sequence yourself. This is in contrast to *unthreaded* newsreaders, which make you determine the proper sequence yourself.

- *Online* newsreaders let you look at articles while you're connected to the Internet, whereas *offline* versions download the articles so you can read them at your leisure. The latter can save telephone and connect time, but they can also download a lot of useless postings.

Many browsers include newsreaders, or at least some limited capabilities for reading news articles. You won't necessarily be able to post things yourself, however.

Unix newsreaders include *rn* (read news), *trn* (threaded rn), *tin* (threaded internet newsreader), and *nn* (no news). Windows-based newsreaders include News Xpress, WinVN, and Free Agent. Newswatcher is a widely used Macintosh-based newsreader. You can also find other newsreader programs in software libraries such as the one operated at ZDNet. Start at `http://www.zdnet.com/swlib/`and explore the library.

Handling Newsgroup Subscriptions

In some environments, the most convenient way to handle newsgroup subscriptions is to edit the newsgroup list that the newsreader maintains. This file will be named something like *newsrc* (or *.newsrc* in UNIX environments), and will generally be an ASCII file.

Each available newsgroup will be listed in this file. Newsgroups to which you subscribe will contain a special character to distinguish them from the newsgroups to which you don't subscribe. For example, in UNIX environments (and in certain Windows newsreaders, such as News Xpress), newsgroup names will end in either a colon (:) or an exclamation point (!))—also known as a *bang sign* in UNIXese. The colon indicates a newsgroup to which you subscribe; the bang sign a newsgroup to which you don't.

Your most effective editing strategy will depend on how your newsreader starts you out—that is, with all bang signs (unsubscribed) or all colons (oversubscribed). In the former case, it's probably easiest to change only the newsgroups to which you want to subscribe. For newsreaders that start out by having you subscribe to all the newsgroups, it will probably be easier to change all the colons to bang signs, and then proceed as in the previous case. This assumes, of course, that you don't actually want to subscribe to all 14,500+ newsgroups.

Next Generation Digital Loop Carrier (NGDLC)

→ *See* NGDLC (Next Generation Digital Loop Carrier)

Next Generation I/O (NGIO)

→ *See* NGIO (Next Generation I/O)

Next Hop Routing Protocol (NHRP)

→ *See* Protocol, NHRP (Next Hop Routing Protocol)

Next ID (NID)

→ *See* NID (Next ID)

NEXT (Near End Crosstalk)

In a cable containing multiple wires, such as twisted-pair cable, NEXT (for near end crosstalk or near end differential crosstalk) refers to the leakage of a signal from one wire pair to an adjacent one. This interference is measured at the transmitting end, in contrast to FEXT (far end crosstalk). In analog systems, this can take the form of an echo, or a second signal. For example, when you can hear other voices on a telephone line, this may be caused by NEXT.

In digital systems, the crosstalk is much more likely to take the form of random noise. As such, it can be filtered out easily, so that the disruptive effects of NEXT are generally minimal in digital systems.

NEXT is generally measured in decibels per 100 or 1000 feet, and is usually denoted by a *positive* numerical value. For reasons having to do with the notation conventions, a high positive value is better; that is, the higher the value, the lower the effect of crosstalk. You will often see this figure reported as a minimum value.

→ *Broader Category* Crosstalk

→ *Compare* FEXT (Far End Crosstalk)

Next Station Addressing (NSA)

→ *See* NSA (Next Station Addressing)

NeXTSTEP

NeXTSTEP is a no-longer-supported object-oriented variant of the UNIX operating system. It is based most immediately on the Mach variant developed at Carnegie-Mellon University. Like Mach and Windows NT, NeXTSTEP uses a microkernel architecture in which only a barebones operating system core (the microkernel) stays loaded; other services are provided in modules that can be loaded as needed.

NeXTSTEP machines come with built-in support for thin and twisted-pair Ethernet. As a UNIX variant, NeXTSTEP supports the TCP/IP protocol suite, and NeXTSTEP machines can be either servers or clients on a TCP/IP network. They can also be NetWare or Macintosh clients; NeXTSTEP includes software that allows a NeXT machine to access file and print services on NetWare or AppleTalk networks.

Optional add-ons provide support for ISDN (Integrated Services Digital Network) and terminal-emulation capabilities for communications with IBM mainframes.

NeXTSTEP can support file servers and services, using the NFS (Network File System) popular in certain UNIX networks. The operating system also supports NetInfo databases and provides servers for these databases. In addition, NeXTSTEP can provide mail, printing, and fax modem services.

NeXTSTEP was designed originally as the native operating system for NeXT's hardware line. However, following the disappointing sales of NeXT machines, NeXT dropped out of the hardware business and has ported NeXTSTEP to Intel processors. With the demise of NeXT Computers, the operating system has been left adrift.

NGDLC (Next Generation Digital Loop Carrier)

Digital loop, or line, carriers (DLCs) multiplex several calls onto a single digital line, or loop. For example, a T1 carrier (which operates at 1.544Mbps) provides access for 24 digital channels, which are combined on a single line using time division multiplexing (TDM). The current generation of DLCs use point-to-point links (generally between a remote terminal, or RT, at the customer's end and a central office terminal, or COT, at the phone company's end).

NGDLC, which will eventually replace the current DLC, will support much higher speeds, easier access to broadband services, greater use of fiber-optic connections and technology, and more distributed control, or intelligence. For example, the use of SONET (Synchronous Optical Network) technology will supplant the current electrical T1, T3, and so forth, connections.

NGIO (Next Generation I/O)

NGIO is a proposed input/output architecture for moving data between server and storage more quickly. Originally developed by Intel, NGIO also has the backing of over 70 companies, including major computer vendors such as Dell and Sun Microsystems.

NGIO is expected to provide serial transfer at speeds of up to 2.5Gbps in each direction, using two wires for input and two for output. It will accomplish this by performing I/O without the processor's help, using I/O engines to allow communications between storage devices and memory.

To increase reliability, NGIO uses multiple I/O channels instead of a single pathway. This provides an opportunity for redundant channels in noisy environments or simply for faster throughput by simultaneously using multiple channels. NGIO will also use a switch fabric, which will allow data to take multiple paths between source and destination. This also will improve reliability because noisy paths could be avoided while cleaner connections could be exploited.

Version 1.0 of the NGIO specifications was released in July 1999, but it is unlikely that NGIO products will be available before 2001or even later. It also remains to be seen whether NGIO or a competing high-speed I/O standard will eventually be used. One potential alternative is Future I/O, which has the support of several networking giants such as Cisco, 3Com, and Adaptec, as well as hardware biggies such as IBM, Hewlett-Packard, and Compaq. Future I/O promises speeds of 10Gbps, but will require 40 wires instead of just 4.

NHRP (Next Hop Routing Protocol)

→ See Protocol, NHRP (Next Hop Routing Protocol)

NIC (Network Interface Card)

The NIC is the network component with a thousand names, including LAN adapter, LAN card, NIU (network interface unit), network adapter, and network board.

An NIC enables a PC to connect to and access a network. The NIC communicates through drivers with the node's networking software (shell or

N

operating system) at one end, and with the network (the cabling to the other nodes) at the other end.

NICs usually fit into expansion slots in a PC.

NICs and Network Architectures

NICs differ in the network architectures they support. This support is implemented in chips on the board. A network adapter might have Ethernet or Token Ring or FDDI chips, for example. (Chips and Technologies has developed ChipsLAN, a chip set that supports both Ethernet and Token Ring architectures, although not at the same time.)

There are dozens of NIC manufacturers and vendors, with hundreds of models. In practice, network operating systems officially support anywhere from a small number (usually fewer than a dozen) to several dozen specific cards. Other cards actually get their compatibility by emulating one or more of the officially supported cards.

Fortunately, these emulations are good enough, because NICs from different vendors are generally compatible, provided they support the same architecture. Thus, an Ethernet card from one vendor can communicate perfectly well with an Ethernet card from another vendor. However, an Ethernet NIC cannot communicate with a Token Ring NIC, even if both cards are from the same vendor, unless there is a translation component (such as a router) between the networks that are home to the two NICs.

The network architecture supported determines various performance features and restrictions for the NIC and, therefore, for the network. The architecture may constrain the cabling possibilities. For example, an Ethernet NIC may have only a BNC connector or only a DIX connector. However, if necessary, you can use a transceiver (for Ethernet) or a media filter (for Token Ring) to mediate between the NIC and the network cabling.

NIC Operation

The NIC mediates between the computer (and its user) and the network. For the sender, the NIC is responsible for getting the user's commands onto the network; for the receiver, the NIC is responsible for getting a transmission off the network and to the networking software running on the receiving machine.

Outgoing Network Activity

At the transmitting end, the NIC in a workstation translates user requests into a form suitable for transmission across the network. The NIC in a server translates system responses into the appropriate form to send them over the network. This translation process involves the following:

- Converting a parallel data chunk into a serial stream of bits.

- Dividing the bit stream into packets, whose form is determined by the network architecture the NIC supports. Some higher-end cards have multiarchitecture chip sets, so that a single NIC can support two different network architectures.

- Converting the bit values into electrical signals, using the encoding scheme appropriate for the architecture.

After the transmission is converted, the NIC accesses the network—using whatever media-access method the supported architecture specifies—and transmits the user's message in the appropriate packets.

Incoming Network Activity

At the receiving end, the NIC monitors the network, checking the current transmission to determine if the NIC's node fits the destination address. Any of the following are considered a "fit":

- The packet's destination address matches the address of the NIC's node.

- The packet's destination address indicates the packet is being broadcast to all nodes on the network.

- The packet's destination address indicates the packet is being multicast to a group of nodes, including the NIC's node.

After capturing a packet addressed to the node, the NIC translates the packet into a form suitable for the networking software. Part of this translation process strips off any overhead bits from the serial bit stream, and converts the remaining bits into a parallel data chunk. When the transmission is in an appropriate form, the NIC passes it to the application running on the node.

In addition to checking the network on their own, NICs also do various administrative tasks independently of the networking software running on the node. For example, the token-passing process, which controls media access for certain types of networks, is done entirely by the NICs. Similarly, some NICs include components for monitoring the network and the NIC, and for reporting any errors.

NICs and LAN Drivers

NICs communicate with the networking software through LAN drivers. The driver provides a crucial link between network and software.

In the ordinary world, a separate driver is needed for each operating system, card, and networking protocol combination. In order to save programming time and effort, and to avoid a driver population explosion, several efforts have been made to create generic interfaces, so that a single driver can handle multiple protocols for a given adapter and operating system combination.

Microsoft and 3Com developed the NDIS (Network Driver Interface Specification) standard, and Novell and Apple developed the ODI (Open Datalink Interface) standard. These generic interfaces differ in how they route a packet to the appropriate protocol stack, but both help reduce the number of drivers needed. With an NDIS- or ODI-compliant card, a single driver will handle packets for the DoD's TCI/IP, Novell's IPX/SPX, Apple's AARP, and even IBM's NetBIOS protocols.

Keep in mind that an NIC driver is involved in much activity, and can be a performance bottleneck if not properly written.

Card Sizes and Features

NICs differ in the following features:

- The size of the card's data bus. NICs come in 8-, 16-, and 32-bit versions. In general, 8-bit cards are adequate for workstations, but servers should get more powerful 16- or 32-bit cards.

- Whether the NIC supports *bus mastering*, a bus access method in which the card takes control of the bus directly, so that the card can bypass the CPU and send data onto the bus. In general, MCA and EISA machines support bus mastering, but ISA machines do not. PCI (Peripheral Component Interconnect) cards, which have become the standard, support bus mastering. Several types of transfer modes are possible with bus mastering, including burst mode, streaming data mode, and data duplexing. A particular bus-mastering scheme may support some or all of them.

- The board speed. Regardless of whether a NIC uses bus mastering, it needs to interact with the bus. Like other operations on the computer, interactions rely heavily on the timing (and speed) afforded by the computer's clock. In general, the bus speed will be one-third of the clock's speed, and the processor will operate at half the clock speed.

- The network architecture supported. The most widely used architectures include ARCnet, Ethernet, FDDI, and Token Ring. Newly available chip sets support both Ethernet and Token Ring architectures.

- Whether the NIC includes a processor. Some NICs include a processor (generally in the 80186 or 80286 class) to make the board more "intelligent." This intelligence will enable the board to do more of the work, freeing the node's processor for other duties. This is particularly important for the file server, since that processor gets requests from multiple sources.

- Whether the NIC has on-board RAM. Optional on-board RAM can serve as a buffer

N

when necessary. That is, any available RAM on the NIC can be used to store parts of a transmission, such as while the NIC waits to pass the received material to the node's networking software or to send the packets onto the network. For certain types of checking, the NIC may store a packet in RAM, passing only required fields to the networking software. If no RAM is available, the NIC must pass the entire packet to the software, which will slow down performance.

- Whether the NIC supports boot ROM. Most NICs include a socket for an optional diskless boot ROM. When this chip is installed, boot information is read from the ROM instead of from a boot disk (which becomes unnecessary). Such a chip is necessary for diskless workstations, which enable users to access network files and resources while working, but do not allow the user to take files off the network or to copy files to the network, since the workstation has neither a floppy nor a hard disk.

- Whether the NIC has LEDs (light-emitting diodes). Some of the fancier NICs may include LEDs at the interface. These LEDs will indicate board state or network activity.

Other things being equal, and assuming any network or other restrictions are met:

- 32-bit NICs are faster than 16-bit NICs, which are faster than 8-bit NICs.

- NICs with on-board RAM will generally work faster. The RAM is used as a buffer, so that the NIC is never the bottleneck in communication between the PC and the network.

- NICs with an on-board processor will be able to do more of the work. These NICs will also, of course, cost more.

Installing NICs

Standard NICs are snapped into an available expansion slot of your computer, just like a board

for any other add-on. When installed in a PC expansion slot, each NIC must get an I/O address and an IRQ, and the card may also be assigned a DMA channel. For some boards you also need to specify a memory address, which specifies a location used as a buffer for board-related operations. These settings become part of the system configuration for your computer. Usually, the vendor's default settings will work, unless you already have multiple add-on cards in your computer. If there is a conflict, you may need to assign different values.

NIC Addresses

NICs and nodes have several types of addresses associated with them. NICs have hardware addresses, whose values are "wired" into or set on the board.

For Ethernet and Token Ring cards, the hardware address is assigned by the manufacturer and is built into the card. The hardware address is completely independent of the network in which the board is ultimately used. Rather, the hardware address identifies the card's manufacturer and includes a unique "serial" number for that manufacturer's products. Part of this address is assigned according to guidelines specified by the IEEE.

For ARCnet cards, the network address is a value between 1 and 255, recorded in jumper or DIP switch settings. The system administrator must set this address manually. It is the administrator's responsibility to make sure that each card has a unique address. Failure to keep good records in this regard could lead to lots of frustrating trial and error until the machines with the duplicate addresses are identified.

As representative of a node in a particular network, an NIC also has network and node (or station) addresses.

As the network address, each physical network is assigned an eight hexadecimal-digit (four-byte) value between 0x1 and 0xFFFFFFFF. This network address value must be unique if the network is connected to other networks (via a router, bridge, or gateway). In an internetwork, each network can have only one network address.

WHAT TO LOOK FOR IN AN NIC

When you're shopping for NICs, find out about the product's reliability and the vendor's faith in that reliability. First, ask about the manufacturer's warranty. Five-year warranties are not uncommon for NICs, and some vendors even offer lifetime warranties.

One index of a product's reliability is the mean time before failure (MTBF). This value represents the amount of time before about half the units have broken down. For NICs, manufacturers quote times of 10 or 20 years. Such reliability is essential, since the costs of downtime will be several times the cost of an NIC.

The drivers included with a NIC are very important. An adapter should support either the NDIS or the ODI interface standard for NIC drivers (preferably both), because these two driver interfaces provide generic driver services. Having both these driver interfaces available makes the adapter considerably more portable and flexible. Above all, however, make certain the board includes a driver that will support your particular configuration.

Make sure any NIC you plan to buy is compatible with the PC architecture of your machines. The PCI bus is the de facto standard these days, so any NIC you buy will almost certainly need to use this bus.

If you're purchasing a NIC that supports bus mastering, you also need to know if its bus-mastering method is compatible with the method your computer uses. Bus mastering can improve throughput considerably, but only if the board and the computer support the same bus-mastering method, *and* if the bus mastering doesn't conflict with the hard disk controller. Since incompatibilities in this area can lead to lots of complaints and support calls, vendors do extensive product compatibility testing. Your particular configuration may be in their database, so check with the vendors involved before you buy and assemble the hardware.

You can sometimes save considerable money if you're in a position to buy multiple adapters at a time from a vendor. Many vendors feature 5- or 10-packs of a particular adapter at a reduced price.

Although speed enhances performance, you could end up paying extra for speed but not getting it. Vendors and users are constantly trying to get components to go faster—for example, to speed up interactions with the bus—and sometimes they succeed. The developed products may include superfast boards, which can operate at half or even full clock speed. These boards may work with a particular configuration created by the vendor, but are very likely to be incompatible with other products, at least in fast mode. To have the superfast board work with a generic computer, it may be necessary to operate the board at a slower speed, so the higher price for the extra speed might be wasted.

Individual nodes in a network also get node, or station, addresses. A node address uniquely identifies the node *within* the network. A file server that is attached to two different networks will have two network and two node addresses. Routers, bridges, and gateways have addresses in both of the networks they connect.

In Novell's NetWare 3.*x* and later, each *server* also has a unique IPX internal network number. This logical address is an eight-digit value between 1 and FFFFFFFF, and must differ from any other internal or network address associated with any network associated with the server.

Alternatives to Plug-In NICs

A node on a network needs some component that will mediate between the network and the computer's software. Usually, this capability is provided by an NIC that plugs into an expansion slot in the computer.

There are other ways of providing a mediating component. The variants are useful for -attaching non-desktop machines, such as laptops, notebooks, and palmtops, to a network. Alternatives include docking stations, external adapters, and PCMCIA cards.

External LAN drivers are generally available from the adapter's vendor. Before buying an external NIC, make sure this is the case and also make sure the driver supports your networking software. (Since a docking station will be using an ordinary NIC, special drivers are not necessary.)

Docking Station

A docking station is essentially an expansion box that turns a laptop, notebook, or palmtop computer into a desktop machine. The docking station has expansion slots, into which you can put whatever types of cards you want. To use the attached laptop (for example) on a LAN, you need to plug an NIC into one of the expansion slots.

Docking stations are hardware-dependent, and generally work with only a single model computer

N

from a single manufacturer. Docking stations can cost several hundred dollars. Note that you still need an NIC with a docking station.

External Adapter

An external adapter, or NIC, attaches to the laptop's parallel port. This adapter is just an NIC in a different case. External adapters can be pocket size (a.k.a. portable) or desk size. The desk-size version may support multiple types of cable in the same unit; the pocket-size adapter will have room for only a single type of connector.

External NICs generally include a pass-through parallel port, which provides an additional parallel port to replace the one bound to the external adapter. Note, however, that this additional port will be accessible only if it can be assigned a valid and accessible address.

The pocket-size adapter does not include a parallel port, but the adapter can be used with a parallel port multiplexer. Prices depend in part on the architecture being supported: ARCnet is cheapest, Token Ring most expensive.

Unlike docking stations, external adapters are hardware-independent (as is the case for ordinary NICs). This makes it possible to use these adapters with just about any laptop. Newer laptops have the EPP (enhanced parallel port), which supports burst speeds of up to 16Mbps.

External adapters are portable, hardware-independent, and easy to install. Because they communicate through the parallel port, such adapters do not need an address and IRQ line, which make setup much easier. External adapters use the IEEE hardware addressing algorithm (just like other types of NICs).

External adapters are slower because the parallel port is slower. Fortunately, these adapters will not slow down other network activity, because such tasks as token passing are handled right on board, without going to the port.

TIPS ON CONFIGURING NICS

The following are some tips and considerations for configuring NICs:

- Before changing any NIC settings, record the factory settings (or find these settings in the documentation), so you can restore them if necessary.

- If the default settings won't work, try the alternatives recommended by the vendor. Vendors will usually have two or three alternative settings.

- To change settings, you may need to move jumpers or change DIP switch settings. (On MCA and EISA machines you can make such changes through software.)

- If you change the board settings, make sure to change the values in any software configuration files.

- Most cards will want the DMA setting turned off, since this access method has outlived its usefulness and is often slower than ordinary CPU-controlled data transfer methods. (If DMA lines *are* used, line 3 is generally used.)

- If you change the IRQ, try to avoid certain values that are likely to cause conflict. These include IRQ 5 and IRQ 2.

- If you need to specify memory addresses, and you use memory management software, you may need to exclude the memory range the NIC uses from the memory manager's purview. To do this, most memory managers have an exclude command.

Even if the settings for an NIC seem to work, check them explicitly anyway. It may be that a conflict will arise only under relatively unlikely conditions. To check for such rare interactions, find out all the IRQ and I/O address assignments for the boards in your machine, and see whether any of these match the NIC's settings. If so, you may encounter conflicts at some point when both functions are used at the same time.

For example, if your NIC settings match those for the floppy disk controller, you'll run into problems if you try to access the floppy drive while accessing the network.

It's a good idea in general to have a record of the internal settings for your computer. Having this information easily accessible makes technical support and troubleshooting much easier. It will also save you time on technical support calls.

PCMCIA Cards

PCMCIA cards are very small (about the size of a credit card) and are designed to plug into small computers, such as notebooks and palmtops, and some peripherals. The PCMCIA interface standard is still relatively new (with PCMCIA 2 being the current major version), so these products are just beginning to appear.

ARCnet NIC

An ARCnet NIC has chips to handle the ARCnet network architecture. ARCnet NICs come with either a low- or high-impedance transceiver. A low-impedance card is generally used in ARCnet networks that use a star -topology; high-impedance cards are used in networks that use a bus topology. ARCnet cards generally have a BNC connector (since ARCnet typically uses coaxial cable).

ARCnet cards do not come with hardware addresses in a ROM chip. Instead, these cards have jumpers that can be set to specify an address for the node in which the card is installed. The network administrator needs to set this address (which must be between 1 and 255) for each card in the network. Each node must have a unique address. The administrator also needs to set the IRQ and I/O address on the card.

ARCnet cards are arguably the least expensive of the major architectures (such as Ethernet and Token Ring), with Ethernet adapters right down there as well.

Ethernet NIC

An Ethernet NIC supports the Ethernet network architecture. NICs that support the slightly different IEEE 802.3 standard are sometimes loosely called Ethernet NICs as well. Many boards support both Ethernet and 802.3.

Ethernet NICs can have BNC, DIX, and/or RJ-*xx* connectors. On boards with multiple connectors, you will generally need to set DIP switches or jumper settings on the board to indicate the type of connector you will be using. Some of the higher-end boards can sense automatically which interface you are using, or they will let you specify this in software.

Ethernet cards include a hardware address on a ROM chip. This address is assigned by the IEEE and the vendor and is unique to that particular board. Part of the address contains vendor information, and part identifies the board itself. This address can be used by bridges and routers to identify a particular node on a network.

With the advent of 100Mbps fast Ethernet and the even faster 1Gbps Gigabit Ethernet, the Ethernet network card market has become much more interesting. 10Mbps Ethernet cards have quickly fallen to the low end of the market. Hybrid cards, which can support either of two speeds, are currently very popular—in 10/100Mbs and in 100/1000Mbps versions. It's also possible to get just 100Mbps or 1000Mbps cards.

Token Ring NIC

A Token Ring NIC supports IBM's Token Ring network architecture. Token Ring NICs can have DB-9 and/or RJ-*xx* connectors.

Either shielded twisted-pair (STP) or unshielded twisted-pair (UTP) cable can be attached to the board using the proper types of connectors. On most Token Ring cards, you will need to set jumpers or DIP switches in the hardware to specify the type of connector being used. Other values that may need to be set using jumpers or DIP switches include the IRQ, I/O address, and operating mode, or speed, to either 4- or 16-Mbps. Not all cards will support both speeds.

Token Ring NICs are considerably more expensive than ARCnet or Ethernet cards.

One reason Token Ring cards cost more is that they include more complex circuitry. For example, each Token Ring NIC includes an agent, which can report node activity and NIC states to network management nodes.

The proliferation of Token Ring chip sets in the past few years will help bring prices down. Chip manufacturers include Texas Instruments, IBM, Western Digital, Chips & Technologies, and National Semiconductor.

N

Token Ring NIC Enhancements

Because Token Ring NICs have the most complex requirements and capabilities, they also offer the most opportunity for ingenuity and enhancements. Various enhancements have been added to Token Ring cards to make them more attractive, including the following:

- ETR (early token release) capabilities. ETR is a token-passing strategy that makes it possible to have more than one data packet circulating at a time around the ring.

- Interface sensing. Some NICs can automatically determine which of the available interfaces is being used for the network.

- Dual protocol chips. Several chip manufacturers, including Texas Instruments and Chips & Technologies, have developed chip sets that support both Token Ring and Ethernet architectures on the same board. This makes the board considerably more flexible and portable.

- Tools. Since Token Ring controllers are essentially processors, it is possible to program them to do new things. Adapter manufacturers are using a set of tools, developed by Proteon, for adding capabilities to the controller chip.

- On-chip protocols: Madge Networks has built adapters with the ability to run network protocols (such as Novell's IPX protocol) right on the adapter, which can help speed up performance.

NID (Next ID)

In an ARCnet frame, the NID is the address of the next node to receive the token.

NII (National Information Infrastructure)

A government term for the Internet and other public networks, which will form a seamless communications Web that will make huge amounts of information easily accessible to users.

The term is intended to encompass more than just the equipment and the connections between networks. It also includes the protocols—transmission, and network standards—the access and applications software, the information, and even the service providers.

→ *Primary sources* Documents related to the government's plans and pontifications about this infrastructure are generally available at `http://nii.nist.gov/nii/whatnii.html`.

NIM (Network Interface Module)

A network interface card, or network adapter.

→ *See Also* NIC (Network Interface Card)

NISDN (Narrowband ISDN)

A term sometimes used for the ordinary ISDN (Integrated Services Digital Network) architecture, to distinguish it from BISDN (Broadband ISDN).

→ *See Also* ISDN (Integrated Services Digital Network)

Nitwork

Nitwork refers to the kind of work that means the difference between a network and a notwork. In order to get and keep a network running, there are dozens, possibly hundreds, of details that need to be considered and dealt with. Overlooking or failing to resolve such details can cause frustrating problems that may be expensive and time-consuming to correct.

NIU (Network Interface Unit)

A business customer with multiple phone or data lines might multiplex them into a single high-speed trunk to the service provider—for example, into a T1 connection. For access to the digital trunk, the customer's equipment includes a Channel Service Unit/Digital Service Unit (CSU/DSU). This component multiplexes the customer's multiple lines, and packages the data or voice stream for transmission over the trunk. The CSU/DSU, which is at the end of the customer's equipment, connects to a network interface unit. The NIU thus represents the boundary between an end user's customer premises equipment (CPE) and the telephone company or other service provider's digital lines.

NIU is also used loosely to refer to a network interface card, or network adapter.

→ **See Also** NIC (Network Interface Card)

NLM (NetWare Loadable Module)

In Novell's NetWare 3.x and later, an NLM is a program that can be loaded and linked to function as part of the network operating-system (NOS). These modules can be loaded and unloaded as needed.

NLMs can be used to link different types of resources or services into the NOS, to make these available temporarily or for the entire time the network is running. When an NLM is loaded, NetWare allocates memory for the NLM to use. This memory and any resources used are returned for reuse when the NLM is unloaded.

NLMs help make network operation more efficient because services can be loaded more selectively. With the availability of NLMs, servers only need to load the core of the NOS. The core capabilities can be extended by adding only the modules that are likely to be needed.

NLM Classes in NetWare 4.x

NetWare 3.x and 4.x distinguish four classes of NLMs:

- Disk drivers, which enable communication between the NOS and the hard disks on the server. Such drivers have a DSK extension.

- LAN drivers, which control communication between the NOS and the network interface cards (NICs) in the server. Such drivers have a LAN extension.

- Management utilities and server applications modules, which make it possible to monitor and change the network configuration and activity. Such modules have an NLM extension.

- Name space modules, which allow non-DOS files and naming conventions to be used in the directory and file systems. Such modules have an NAM extension.

Some NLMs, such as LAN and disk drivers, will be loaded every time the network server is booted. These can be specified in the STARTUP.NCF and AUTOEXEC.NCF files, along with any options or commands for the NLMs.

With an open interface, the NOS's capabilities can also be extended or modified by creating new or different NLMs. Since these NLMs may not be tested as thoroughly as those included with NetWare (or they may be tested during network operation), it is important to protect the core NOS and NLMs from corruption by errant NLMs.

In order to increase network security, and also to protect the NOS from uncertified NLMs, which may be unreliable, NetWare takes advantage of *privilege levels* supported by the Intel processor architecture. This feature establishes a hierarchy of four rings (numbered 0, 1, 2, and 3). Of these, ring 0 is the most privileged. Any application or module can execute in a specified ring, and the application's operations are confined to the application's ring or to rings further out (with lower privilege levels).

Novell uses rings 0 and 3. By default, NetWare and any NLMs execute in ring 0, in the OS domain. However, in NetWare 4.x you can specify that an NLM should run in an OS_PROTECTED domain. In that case, the NLM will execute in ring 3, and will not be able to tamper with or corrupt the contents of ring 0.

→ **Broader Category** NetWare

→ **Compare** VAP (Value-Added Process)

N

NMA (Network Management Architecture)

NMA is IBM's network management model. This model is mainframe-oriented and centralized. It is used in IBM's NetView network management package and, more recently, in the more flexible SystemView.

In the NMA model, network management tasks fall into four categories:

- Configuration management, which is concerned with identifying the network elements and the relationships among them.

- Problem management, which is concerned with identifying, diagnosing, tracking, and resolving problems that arise.

- Performance and accounting management, which is concerned with monitoring the availability and use of the network's elements, and also with managing the billing for use of these resources.

- Change management, which is concerned with changes in hardware, software, or microcode.

These tasks are carried out by (or under the control of) the central host, which serves as the network manager. Under the NMA model, the network manager is the focal point for the network. Devices from IBM (that is, SNA-based) and non-IBM networks may be connected to the focal point in two different ways.

- Devices that support IBM's SNA (Systems Network Architecture) can connect through entry points. Such entry points serve as agents in reporting to the network manager at the focal point.

- Non-IBM devices must be connected through service points, which are nodes running special software (for example, NetView/PC) that can communicate with the NMA package. Such devices can also be connected if they can function as LU 6.2 (logical unit 6.2) devices.

The NetView/PC software can be used to connect a wide range of devices and networks to an NMA network. For example, NetView/PC can connect one or more Ethernet or Token Ring LANs, a PBX, or a single machine to a network using NetView. NetView itself runs as a VTAM application on the host machine.

Novell's NetWare Management Agent for NetView allows a NetWare server to function as a Token Ring network agent for a NetView host. The NetWare server can report alarms from the Token Ring network to the host, and it can also respond to requests from the host for maintenance statistics.

The NMVT (Network Management Vector Transport) protocol is used to exchange management data. This protocol uses management service request units to request and return information about the status or performance of elements on the network.

→ *Broader Category* Network Management

NME (Network Management Entity)

In the OSI network management model, the NME is the software and/or hardware that gives a network node the ability to collect, store, and report data about the node's activities.

→ *See Also* Network Management

NMS (NetWare Management System)

Novell's NMS is a software product that provides centralized management and monitoring of a local-area or enterprise network. NMS runs on a dedicated, Microsoft Windows-based machine. It provides a Windows-based interface and uses NetWare Management Agents, NetWare LANalyzer Agent, and NetWare Hub Services for data gathering and reporting. NMS monitors resource usage, configuration and traffic changes, and so forth, and can reconfigure the network, if necessary.

NMS Features

NMS provides monitoring and management capabilities in the following domains:

Asset management   NMS can identify, monitor, and protect network components. For example, NMS can automatically discover and map the configuration of a network. It can even help configure the network. NMS can also use password protection to prevent unauthorized changes to the configuration.

Fault management   NMS monitors devices, checking for changes that might indicate trouble; it constantly checks the network's connectivity, and will issue a real-time alarm if necessary. It can execute programs in response to alarms. NMS can keep a log of faults and alarms, and it can be used to test the connectivity of IPX and IP devices.

Address management   NMS can automatically determine and store all IP and IPX addresses on the network. It can search for duplicate addresses (so these can be eliminated), and it continues to monitor for duplicates during network operation.

Router management   NMS can monitor and report on routers that support the MIB II (Management Information Base II) standard. It can supply routers with either IP or IPX addresses, and can also monitor port usage.

NetWare server management   NMS works with a NetWare Management Agent to monitor and manage multiple NetWare servers.

Critical device monitoring   NMS will monitor any devices the system administrator specifies as critical, will track their performance, and will raise an alarm if a device is going to have or cause problems. NMS can also monitor and analyze traffic on a distributed network, even from a remote location.

Data storage and reporting   NMS will store data in a central Btrieve database, so that the data can be used for analyses or summaries. NMS can summarize and report on the information provided up to the time the report is generated.

NMS supports SNMP (Simple Network Management Protocol) as its management protocol, and provides an SNMP Browser to monitor and control SNMP devices.

NMS Agents

NMS uses several types of agents to get information or suggestions about network operation. Each is appropriate for a different type of task.

A NetWare Management Agent (NMA) is installed on a server and provides statistics about the server's configuration, memory allocation and central processing unit (CPU) usage. NMAs can also send alarms. An NMA makes it possible for the same network to be managed from multiple locations, provided each of the managing administrators has the appropriate access rights.

A NetWare LANalyzer Agent provides information about the interactions among devices and workstations, and it can also do analyses of the collected data.

The NetWare Hub Services Agent can be used to provide information about the network activity of its hub, which must conform to the Hub Management Interface (HMI).

In NetWare 5, network management tasks are handled by ManageWise 2.6, which is built into the Novell Directory Service (NDS).

→ *Broader Categories*   NetWare; Network Management

NMVT (Network Management Vector Transport)

In IBM's NMA, NMVT is the protocol used to exchange management data.

→ *See Also*   NMA (Network Management Architecture)

N

NNI (Network-to-Network Interface)

NNI can be expanded in following three different ways, depending on whether the two Ns stand for *network* or *node*:

- Network-to-network interface, for example, the interface between routers on two different networks or between Frame Relay networks.

- Network-to-node interface, for example, the interface between a client and a server.

- Node-to-node interface, for example, the interface between two machines on a peer LAN.

These types of interfaces represent general concepts, but certain interfaces also have specific meanings in particular technologies. For example, in the phone company's PSTN (Public Switched Telephone Network), a trunk (which combines multiple wires on a single line) is considered a network-to-network interface.

Similarly, NNI represents a network-to-network interface for Frame Relay technology. The device that would provide a network-to-node interface for frame relay is known as a Frame Relay access device (FRAD).

The ATM (Asynchronous Transfer Mode) architecture also includes network-to-network interfaces (connecting network switches) and network-to-node interfaces (connecting a user device to an ATM switch). The latter is also known as a user-to-network interface (UNI).

NNI (Network-to-Node Interface)

→ *See* NNI (Network-to-Network Interface)

NNI (Node-to-Node Interface)

→ *See* NNI (Network-to-Network Interface)

NNTP (Network News Transfer Protocol)

→ *See* Protocol, NNTP (Network News Transfer Protocol)

Node

On a network, an element with a network interface card (NIC) installed is called a node. A node is generally a computer (a workstation or a server), but may be another type of device, such as a printer or modem. Nodes that are not computers may have an NIC preinstalled.

Node Address

A node address is a unique numerical value associated with a specific node in a particular network. In general, this value is assigned to the network interface card (NIC) installed in the node.

This value may be assigned through software or in the hardware. For example, an NIC for an Ethernet network has a unique address assigned by the manufacturer. In contrast, boards for an ARCnet network or a Token Ring network are assigned addresses through jumper or switch settings.

A complete address for a node will include a network address that is common to all nodes in the same physical network, as well as the node address that is unique to the node within its physical network.

A node address is also known as a *node number*, a *physical node address*, or as a *station address*.

Node-to-Node Routing

A routing method used to get a packet from its source node to its destination, as opposed to simply routing a packet to the router nearest to the destination node.

Noise, Electrical

Noise is the term for random electrical signals that become part of a transmission, and that serve to make the signal (information) component of the transmission more difficult to identify. Noise can take various forms, including the following:

Impulse noise Voltage increases that last for just a short period, on the order of a few milliseconds. Examples include power surges or spikes, lightning, and switching on the line.

Gaussian, or white, noise Random background noise.

Crosstalk Interference on one wire from another.

There are limits set on the allowable levels for each of these types of noise.

To remove random noise from a signal, a *noise filter* can be used.

Noise-Equivalent Power (NEP)

→ *See* NEP (Noise-Equivalent Power)

Nominal Velocity of Propagation (NVP)

→ *See* NVP (Nominal Velocity of Propagation)

Nonce

In encrypted transmissions, a nonce is a number used in the cryptographic protocol being used to encrypt. The nonce value must—with very high probability—be different each time the protocol is used. This is necessary to make it impossible for someone to use material recorded from previously encrypted sessions to crack an encryption code.

→ *Broader Categories* Encryption; Security

Nondisruptive Test

In network management, a nondisruptive test is a diagnostic or performance test that can be run in the background, and that has little or no effect on ordinary network activity. Compare this with a disruptive test.

Non-Repudiation

A network security measure that makes it impossible for a sender to deny having sent a message (*origin nonrepudiation*) and for a recipient to deny having received the message (*destination nonrepudiation*).

Non-Return to Zero (NRZ)

NRZ is a signaling method in which the voltage does not necessarily return to a zero, or neutral, state after each bit is transmitted. Therefore, the signal remains at the same level for the entire bit interval, and may remain at this level for several bit intervals if the same value is transmitted multiple times in succession. Such a signal method is not self-clocking.

→ *See Also* Encoding, Signal

Nonshareable

A nonshareable file, device, or process is available to only one user at a time.

NOS (Network Operating System)

A NOS is a software package that makes it possible to implement and control a network and that enables users to make use of resources and services on that network. Examples of NOSs include Novell's NetWare, Banyan's VINES, Artisoft's LANtastic, and Microsoft's LAN Manager.

N

A NOS's responsibilities include the following:

- Providing access to files and resources (for example, printers) on the network

- Providing messaging and/or electronic mail (e-mail) services

- Enabling nodes on the network to communicate with each other

- Interprocess Communications (IPC); that is, enabling processes on the network to communicate with each other

- Responding to requests from applications or users on the network

- Mapping requests and paths to the appropriate places on the network

Server-Based versus Peer-Based NOSs

A NOS may be server- or peer-based. Server-based NOSs are considerably more complex (and usually more powerful) than NOSs for peer-to-peer networks. In the former case, the NOS and the server run the show. The NOS becomes the server's native operating system.

For example, Novell's NetWare requires its own hard disk partition, and the computer boots to this, rather than to DOS. NetWare does use some DOS services and also retains the DOS file structure. Most NOSs at least support the file structure from the native operating system; many use this file system as if it were the NOS's own native file system.

In peer-to-peer networks, any station can function as file server or as a client (consumer) for network services. Peer-to-peer NOSs are generally simpler than NOSs for server-based networks. Such NOSs often run simply as an ordinary process. In such a case, the NOS generally will run on top of the computer's native operating system (DOS, OS/2 or UNIX, for example). Even for a peer-to-peer network, however, the NOS takes over at least those operating system functions that relate to the network.

In server-based networks, workstations will generally run a network shell, or redirection, program,

rather than the entire NOS. The station's native operating system (for example, DOS, OS/2, or UNIX) will still be running and will share the workload with the networking software.

The networking shell may intercept user requests to determine whether the request is for the station's operating system or for the network. In the latter case, the shell redirects the request to the network interface card (NIC), through which the request will be passed to the NOS on the server. This is how the shell program for Novell's NetWare versions 3.*x* and earlier works.

In other arrangements, the native operating system does the screening, and the networking module is called only when necessary. This is how the DOS Requester used in NetWare 4.*x* workstations works.

Built-In NOSs

Some operating systems have networking capabilities built-in, including the following:

- The operating system used on Macintoshes

- The NeXTSTEP operating system from NeXT Computers, now available for Intel platforms

- UNIX

- Windows NT

- Novell DOS 7

In most such cases, the operating system's networking capabilities can be greatly enhanced through the use of utilities or other third-party programs.

→ *Related Articles* LAN Manager; LANtastic; NetWare; VINES

Notarization

In network security, notarization is the use of a trusted third party, called a *notary*, to verify that a communication between two entities is legitimate.

The "notary" has information that is used to verify the identity of the sender and receiver and also of the time and origin of a message.

Notwork

Notwork is a term used to describe a network that is operating unreliably or not at all.

Novell AppWare

AppWare is an abandoned architecture for making it easier to develop network-based software. App-Ware tools and philosophy have been replaced to a large extent by Java development tools.

Novell Directory Services (NDS)

→ *See* NDS (Novell Directory Services)

Novell Groupwise

Novell's Groupwise 5.5 is an integrated messaging and collaboration package that combines the functionality of e-mail, personal appointment management, group scheduling, workflow routing, and message, document, and task management. The task management capabilities can help with workflow routing because it's possible to move tasks around a network (that is, assign tasks to specific users) on a timed basis. For example, depending on the command, a task from a project can be moved (assigned) to a different user manually or automatically, according to a schedule.

Groupwise consists of client and server components, and also includes an integrated administrator component (NWAdmin) and gateways. The client provides an interface to give users access to the messaging system. Client programs are available for Windows NT 4, Windows 9x, Windows 3.1, Macintosh, and UNIX. The NWAdmin element is used to configure and maintain the messaging

capabilities for a network, as well as to support post offices and gateways.

The gateways allow Groupwise networks to exchange messages with other, alien messaging systems. Over a dozen different gateway modules are available, including APIs for DOS and OS/2 programs, DOS or OS/2 modules for Lotus Notes, cc:Mail, VMS Mail, X.25 and X.400.

GroupWise provides a universal mailbox, into which any sort of content—e-mail, faxes and other images, documents, even applications—can be stored. It also supports a wide range of protocols and standards, including : IMAP 4 (Internet Message Access Protocol 4), POP3 (Post Office Protocol 3), LDAP (Lightweight Directory Access Protocol), HTML 3.2 (Hypertext Markup Language, version 3.2), and Java.

NPA (NetWare Peripheral Architecture)

A Novell driver architecture in which NetWare drivers are built out of two components:

- HAM (Host Adaptor Module), which controls a server's adapter card for a particular peripheral.
- CDM (Custom Device Module), which controls the specific device attached to the adapter.

In addition to these modules, the NPA also has APIs that provide the hooks necessary for these components to communicate with other components. The HAI (Host Adapter Interface) and the CDI (Custom Device Interface) allow the HAM and CDM, respectively, to deal with the Media Manager.

This architecture makes it easier to provide support for new hardware as it appears, because only part of the driver software—the CDW—needs to be rewritten when the hardware attached to a server is upgraded.

N

NPAP (Network Printing Alliance Protocol)

A proposed standard for a bidirectional protocol to be used for communication among printers on a network. The protocol allows exchange of configuration and other data—independent of the printer-control or page-description language being used.

NPSI (Network Packet Switch Interface)

An interface used in IBM's SNA.

→ **See Also** SNA (Systems Network Architecture)

NRZ (Non-Return to Zero)

NRZ is a signaling method in which the voltage does not necessarily return to a zero, or neutral, state after each bit is transmitted. Therefore, the signal remains at the same level for the entire bit interval, and may remain at this level for several bit intervals if the same value is transmitted multiple times in succession. Such a signal method is not self-clocking.

→ **See Also** Encoding, Signal

NSA (Next Station Addressing)

In FDDI, NSA is an addressing mode by which a station can send a packet, or frame, to the next station in the ring, without knowing that station's address.

→ **See Also** FDDI (Fiber Distributed Data Interface)

NSAP (Network Service Access Point)

In the OSI reference model, the NSAP represents the location through which a Transport layer entity can get access to Network layer services. Each NSAP has a unique OSI network address.

→ **See Also** SAP (Service Access Point)

NSAPI (Netscape Services API)

NSAPI refers to a collection of programming functions—an applications programming interface, or API—to help when developing applications for use with a Netscape server. NSAPI is just one example of several such API packages created by vendors to work with their servers. Perhaps the best known alternative to NSAPI is Microsoft's ISAPI (Internet Server API), which was released to work with their Internet Information Server (IIS) software.

Back-end server applications developed using such APIs are becoming increasingly popular as alternatives to CGI (Common Gateway Interface) scripts for communicating with Web servers. While not as portable as CGI scripts, API-based applications have several runtime advantages (for example, memory for previous states and actions, and more efficient use of runtime environment) that make them attractive for use with today's busy servers.

→ **Compare** ISAPI (Internet Server API)

NTFS (NT File System)

NTFS is the native file system for Windows NT. NTFS features include the following:

- File names of up to 255 characters. Because NTFS supports the 16-bit Unicode character representation scheme, it is possible to include foreign characters in file names.

- Automatic creation of a DOS-compatible file name. NTFS automatically creates a version of the file name that is compatible with the 8.3 (name.extension) rule for DOS file names.

- Support for both the FAT (file allocation table) from DOS and HPFS (High-Performance File System) from OS/2.

- Special storage methods to help increase file access speed. For example, NTFS can actually store the contents of small files in its master file table (the table that contains file name, attribute, and location information). This provides almost immediate access.

- The ability to assign permissions for using and sharing files and directories.

- The use of a log to keep track of file transactions, to aid in recovery in case of malfunction.

- The ability to recover from disk crashes or errors. In some cases, the recovery can be done on the fly.

NuBus

NuBus is a bus specification that provides expansion capabilities for later Macintosh models. Based on a Texas Instruments design, the NuBus is a general-purpose bus that supports 32-bit data and address transfer. This bus connects to the Macintosh using a 96-pin DIN connector.

NuBus slots can be used to provide video capabilities (for example, color), extra memory, or networking capabilities. NuBus cards are self-configuring, and all NuBus expansion slots map to different internal addresses. To communicate with an expansion board, an application or process writes to a memory location associated with the board.

Null Modem

A serial cable and connector with a modified pin configuration, compared to an ordinary RS-232 cable. The null modem enables two computers to communicate directly (without modems as intermediaries). A null modem cable is also known as an *asynchronous modem eliminator* (*AME*). "Null modem pin assignments" shows the pin assignments for the various 9- and 25-pin combinations used on PCs.

Numerical Aperture (NA)

→ *See* NA (Numerical Aperture)

NVE (Network Visible Entity)

In an AppleTalk network, NVE refers to a resource that can be addressed through the network. An NVE is identified by name, type, and zone. The *entity type* specifies the generic class (such as LaserWriter or AFPServer) to which the resource belongs. Apple maintains a registry of entity types.

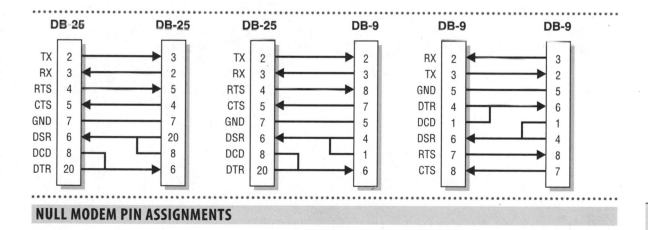

NULL MODEM PIN ASSIGNMENTS

NVLAP (National Voluntary Laboratory Accreditation Program)

The NVLAP in the United States is one of the centers that has developed automated software for testing compliance with X.400 and X.500 standards. These centers develop test engines based on the abstract test suites specified by the ITU (International Telecommunications Union). Other centers include the NCC (National Computer Center) in the UK, Alcatel in France, and Danet GmbH in Germany.

NVoD (Near Video on Demand)

Near video on demand refers to a digital video delivery service under which requested materials are not necessarily available immediately (as with video on demand, or VoD). Rather, the materials may be broadcast or made available at regular intervals—for example, every 15 or 30 minutes.

NVoD is expected to be the successor to the currently used pay-per-view (PPV) programming, under which the content provider makes a limited number of offerings available at predetermined times, for a fee. Eventually, even NVoD is expected to be replaced by VoD, under which any requested materials will be available immediately.

NVP (Nominal Velocity of Propagation)

In a network, NVP is a value indicating the signal speed, as a proportion of the maximum speed theoretically possible. This value varies with cable and with architecture. Values for electrically based local area networks range from about 60 to 85 percent of maximum. This value is also known as *VOP* (*velocity of propagation*).

Nyquist Theorem

Also known as the Nyquist Sampling Theorem., the Nyquist Theorem establishes the minimal requirements for sampling an analog signal in order to reproduce it in digital form with sufficient fidelity. The theorem says that the number of samples per second must be at least twice the highest frequency in the signal. For example, voice signals are sampled 8000 times per second. This value is derived from rounding the maximum frequency used in analog voice lines (3400Hz) up to 4000 Hz.

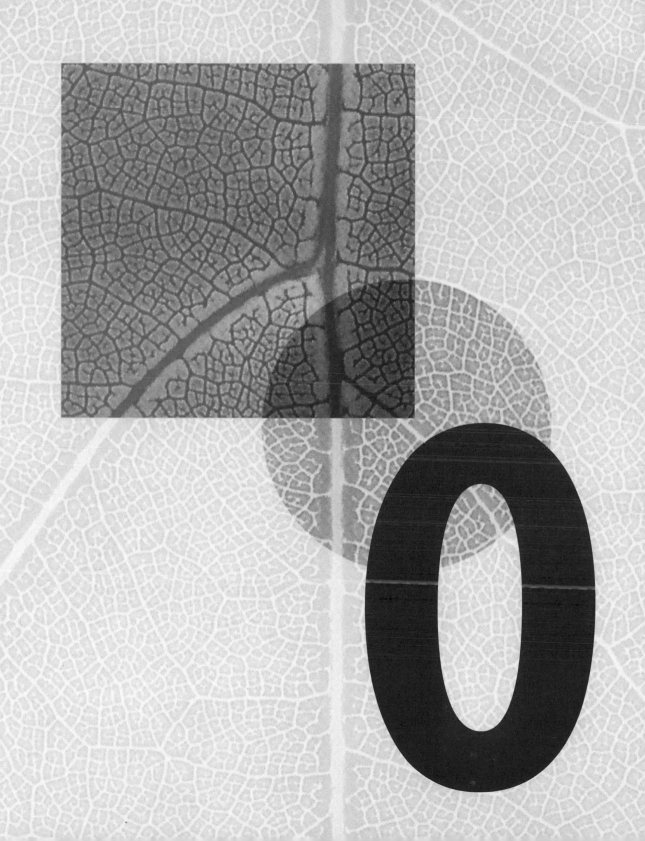

OAI (Open Application Interface)

In telecommunications, OAI refers to an interface that can be used to program and change the operation of a PBX (Private Branch Exchange).

OAM (Operations, Administration, and Maintenance) Functions

The OAM functions are a set of functions defined by the CCITT for managing the lower layers in an ATM (Asynchronous Transfer Mode) network, or more generally, a broadband ISDN (BISDN) network. The functions are implemented in a bidirectional flow of information between corresponding sublayers.

The functions fall into the following categories:

- Performance monitoring: These functions check that the network is functioning at the required level. They also generate information that can be used for maintenance.

- Defect detection: These functions identify defects or malfunctions in the network.

- System protection: These functions are responsible for isolating a malfunctioning element and switching over to other elements in order to keep the system running properly.

- Failure reporting: These functions inform other management entities (such as network management software or the other party) of a malfunction.

- Fault localization: These functions determine *where* a detected malfunction occurred, in order to enable the system to take the appropriate protection and failure-reporting measures.

Object

In its role as a current computing buzzword, the term *object* may refer to any type of entity that can have properties and actions (or methods) associated with it. Each property represents a slot into which specific information (a value for the property) can be filled. A particular combination of properties defines an object or object type, and a particular combination of values for the properties defines a specific instance of that object type.

In networking, the term *object* refers to an entity in some type of grouping, listing, or definition. For example, users, machines, devices, and servers are considered network-related objects. Abstract entities, such as groups, queues, and functions, can also be treated as objects. In short, an object is a network element.

Objects are mainly of interest in relation to specific networking contexts or models. For example, *managed objects* are elements that can be used to accomplish a task or monitored to get a performance overview and summary. These objects are important because they provide the data for the network management programs that network supervisors may be running.

In a Novell NetWare network, an object is any entity that is defined in a file server's bindery in NetWare versions $2.x$ and $3.x$, or in the NetWare Directory Services (NDS) in versions $4.x$. *NDS objects* are the objects contained in the database for the NDS. These are discussed in the NDS article.

The global information tree contains definitions of many of the objects used in network management and other network-related activities.

In *object-oriented programming* (*OOP*), an object is a self-contained component that consists of both data (properties) and code (actions). Programming objects may be defined in terms of other objects, in which case the derived object may inherit properties and methods from the parent object. An actual instance of an object type will contain specific data values and methods that can distinguish it from other instances of that object type.

Inheritance and polymorphism, which enable a single object type to look and behave differently (but appropriately) in different instances, are two features that help give OOP the power and flexibility for which it is noted.

→ *Related Articles* Global Information Tree; NDS (NetWare Directory Services)

ObjectBroker

ObjectBroker, from Digital Equipment Corporation (DEC), is a package that allows applications running in object-oriented environments, but on different hardware, to communicate with each other in a transparent manner. It also enables developers to create object-oriented applications and services that are distributed across a network.

ObjectBroker runs on a variety of platforms, including DEC's own OpenVMS, ULTRIX, and OSF/1 environments, several other UNIX variants, Macintosh System 7, Microsoft Windows, and Windows NT.

→ *Compare* OLE (Object Linking and Embedding)

Object Linking and Embedding (OLE)

→ *See* OLE (Object Linking and Embedding)

Object Linking and Embedding for Databases (OLE-DB)

→ *See* OLE-DB (Object Linking and Embedding for Databases)

Object-Oriented Database (OODB)

→ *See* Database

Object-Oriented Programming (OOP)

→ *See* OOP (Object-Oriented Programming)

Object Request Broker (ORB)

→ *See* ORB (Object Request Broker)

Octet

An octet is a group of eight bits. The term is generally used when describing frame, or packet, formats. Octet is used in preference to the more common term, *byte,* because not all machine architectures are byte oriented.

OC-x (Optical Carrier Level x)

The OC, or optical carrier, hierarchy designates bandwidths for signaling over optical fiber. These levels are used in the Synchronous Optical Network (SONET) specifications, and are generally paired with the equivalent bandwidths for the electrical signals. These synchronous transport signal (STS) values represent the bandwidths of the signals at either end of the optical fiber—where the signals must be in electrical form. OC levels are based on the 51.84Mbps transmission rate of an OC-1 channel, which also corresponds to STS-1 (or synchronous transport signal level 1).

Thus, OC-3/STS-3 channels have a 155.52Mbps bandwidth, OC-12/STS-12 channels have a bandwidth of 622.08Mbps, and so forth, up to OC-48/STS-48, which can carry 2.488Gbps.

A related specification, the ITU's SDH (Synchronous Digital Hierarchy), uses synchronous transfer mode (STM) transmission rates to specify channels. This hierarchy is based on a fundamental bandwidth of 155.52Mbps, which corresponds to OC-3. The table "Optical Carrier Channel Capacities" shows the relationships among these various channels. Note that the basic bandwidth for the SDH also corresponds to the speed of a basic ATM (Asynchronous Transfer Mode) network.

OPTICAL CARRIER CHANNEL CAPACITIES

OC Level	Transmission Rate	STM Level
STS-1/OC-1	51.84Mbps	—
STS-3/OC-3	155.52Mbps	STM-1
STS-9/OC-9	466.56Mbps	STM-3
STS-12/OC-12	622.08Mbps	STM-4
STS-18/OC-18	933.12Mbps	STM-6
STS-24/OC-24	1.244Gbps	STM-8
STS-36/OC-36	1.866Gbps	STM-12
STS-48/OC-48	2.488Gbps	STM-16

→ **See Also** SONET (Synchronous Optical Network)

ODA (Open Document Architecture)

The ODA is an ISO standard for the interchange of *compound documents*, which are documents that may contain fonts and graphics in addition to text.

The ISO 8613 standard specifies three levels of document representation:

- Level 1: Text-only data
- Level 2: Text and graphical data from a word processing environment
- Level 3: Text and graphical data from a desktop publishing environment

The standard is mainly concerned with preserving the layout and graphics information in the document. That is, a physical connection is taken for granted; it is the logical connection that is being standardized.

→ **Primary Source** ISO document 8613

ODBC (Open Database Connectivity)

An API (Application Programming Interface) developed by Microsoft for accessing databases under Windows. By providing a (more or less) generic interface for applications to use when dealing with databases, ODBC makes it possible for applications to access any type of database that is compliant with the interface. The application merely needs to speak "ODBCese." The ODBC routines will translate the client's requests into a form appropriate for the data supplier. Thus, an application can request information from customer records without having to worry about whether these are stored in an Access, Oracle, or other type of database. Because of this generalizability, ODBC has become a de facto standard.

Alternatives to ODBC include IDAPI (Integrated Database Application Programming Interface), which is a standard proposed by Borland, IBM, and Novell (among others), and JDBC (Java Database Connectivity) which provides a Java-based interface. Microsoft has developed OLE-DB (Object Linking and Embedding for Databases) as a further abstraction for handling not only ODBC but potentially also other interfaces to databases and to other types of data stores, such as e-mail post offices, spreadsheets, and so forth.

ODI (Open Data-Link Interface)

ODI is an architecture developed jointly by Novell and Apple that provides a standard interface for network interface cards (NICs) or device drivers. This makes it possible to use multiple protocols and multiple LAN drivers with a single NIC. For example, ODI can give a single workstation access to a Novell NetWare network through one protocol stack and to a UNIX-based or an AppleTalk network through another. In effect, ODI can make communications (partially) independent of both protocols and media.

ODI sits between LAN drivers (which talk to the NIC) and the protocol stacks. By providing separate interfaces to the protocols and the NICs, ODI allows these two levels to be mixed and matched in a transparent manner. "ODI sits between protocol stacks and network interface cards" shows this arrangement.

The interface for ODI actually consists of two main components: LSL and MLI. The LSL (Link-Support Layer) mediates between the protocols and the drivers. The LSL checks an incoming packet and sends it to the appropriate protocol stack. Outgoing packets are directed in an analogous manner to the appropriate MLID (Multiple Link Interface Driver).

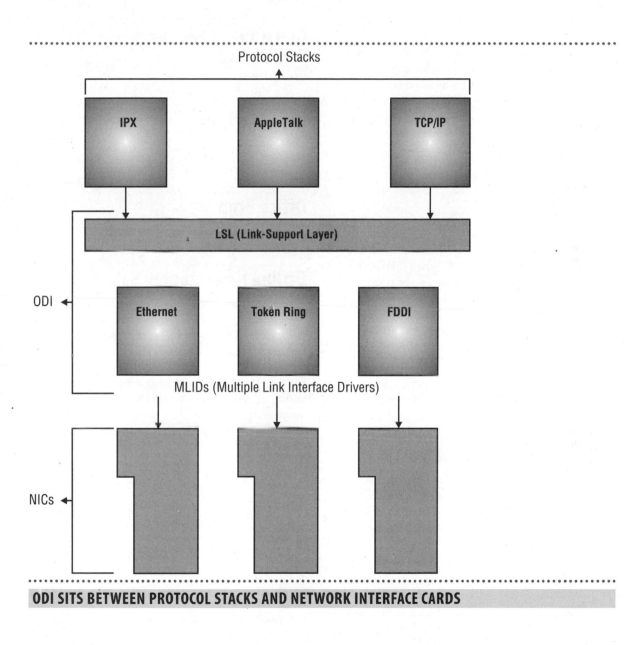

ODI SITS BETWEEN PROTOCOL STACKS AND NETWORK INTERFACE CARDS

The MLI (Multiple Link Interface) communicates with the NICs through an MLID. The MLI itself has three main components, each with a special focus:

- MSM (Media-Support Module) provides the interface to the LSL. This ODI component is relatively stable.

- TSM (Topology-Specific Module) provides the functions needed to deal with a particular network topology, such as Ethernet, Token Ring, or ARCnet. This component comes in several flavors, each of which is relatively stable. The module for a particular topology (such as Ethernet) handles all the variants for that topology (for example, Blue Book 802.3).

- HSM (Hardware-Specific Module) provides the interface to a particular NIC. This is the element that is most subject to change.

Novell also provides ODINSUP, a driver that serves as an interface between ODI and NDIS (Network Driver Interface Specification), which is Microsoft's counterpart to ODI. When ODINSUP is available, the LSL will pass any unrecognized packets to ODINSUP. This driver will, in turn, pass the packet to NDIS, on the assumption that the NDIS driver will be able to deal with it.

→ **Broader Categories** Driver; LAN Driver

→ **Compare** NDIS (Network Driver Interface Specification)

ODINSUP (ODI/NDIS Support)

ODINSUP is a Novell driver that can mediate between Novell's ODI (Open Data-Link Interface) and Microsoft's NDIS (Network Driver Interface Specifications) interfaces for connecting protocol stacks and LAN drivers.

With ODINSUP, it is possible for protocol stacks supported by NDIS to communicate through the ODI's interfaces, so that a workstation can load both ODI and NDIS drivers and stack managers at the same time. The workstation can then log into

different networks with a single network interface card (NIC).

→ **Broader Category** LAN Driver; NDIS (Network Driver Interface Specification); ODI (Open Data-Link Interface)

OFB (Output Feedback)

An operating mode for the Data Encryption Standard (DES).

Off Hook (OH)

→ **See** OH (Off Hook)

Office Drop

The network cable that goes to a node.

Offline Newsreader

An offline newsreader is one that can download files from a newsgroup so that a user can look at the postings at a later time. (A newsreader is a program for accessing, retrieving, and reading newsgroup postings.) Such a program can save in connect time charges, but may end up using a lot of storage and, in the end, taking just as much time as doing things online. Creating a useful *killfile* (news posting filter and selector) can help make an offline newsreader more effective.

→ **Broader Category** Newsreader

OFNP (Optical Fiber, Nonconductive Plenum)

A UL (Underwriters Laboratory) designation for optical fiber that meets certain fire-safety criteria.

→ **See Also** Cable, Fiber-Optic; Cable Standards

OFNR (Optical Fiber, Nonconductive Riser)

A UL (Underwriters Laboratory) designation for optical fiber that meets certain fire-safety criteria.

→ *See Also* Cable, Fiber-Optic; Cable Standards

OH (Off Hook)

In telephony, OH is used to indicate that a telephone line is in use.

Ohm

An ohm is the unit of resistance; the electrical counterpart to friction. This unit is symbolized by the uppercase Greek omega (Ω).

OIW (OSI Implementers Workshop)

OIW is one of three regional workshops for implementers of the OSI Reference Model. This workshop is for the North American region. The other workshops are EWOS (European Workshop for Open Systems) and AOW (Asia and Oceania Workshop).

OLE (Object Linking and Embedding)

OLE (pronounced "olay") is a mechanism by which Microsoft Windows applications can include each other's creations in files. For example, a graphics image or a spreadsheet can be incorporated into a document under the appropriate conditions. Once incorporated, this object can be modified or edited using the program that created it; the user can invoke this program by double-clicking on the object incorporated in the document file.

Currently, OLE is application-based, which means that OLE support must be written into the applications (as opposed to being available automatically as part of the Microsoft Windows environment). Any applications involved in an OLE transaction must explicitly support OLE. Two major versions of the OLE specifications, 1.0 and 2.0, have been released, and these have different capabilities. The possibilities in a given exchange are determined by the lowest version of OLE involved.

The *linking* and *embedding* in the name are actually alternatives. That is, you can do either of the following:

- *Link* a reference to the actual object into the document file. Before you can print the document or access the object through the document, the object needs to be loaded from disk. By retrieving the object only when needed, you ensure that the latest version of the object will be retrieved.

- *Embed* an object into a document file by making a copy of the object at the desired location. You can invoke the creating program from the embedded object; however, the embedded object is no longer affected by changes to the original object. That is, after embedding an image into a document, you can invoke the image-creation program from the embedded copy, but editing the original image does not change the embedded copy.

Many of OLE's features and capabilities have been streamlined and incorporated into Microsoft's more generic and more network-based ActiveX and COM/DCOM (Component Object Model/ Distributed COM) technologies. These are, in turn, being reworked into the even more general DNA (Distributed interNetworking Applications Architecture).

→ *Compare* DDE (Dynamic Data Exchange)

OLEC (Other Local Exchange Carrier)

→ *See* CLEC (Competitive Local Exchange Carrier)

OLE-DB (Object Linking and Embedding for Databases)

Microsoft's OLE-DB is middleware that mediates between a Web client (such as an application) and a data provider (for example, a server with a database, a spreadsheet, or an e-mail post office). OLE-DB provides a way to translate between the OLE (object linking and embedding) functions used by the client—usually through an ActiveX Data Object (ADO)—and the database-specific functions used on the data provider's end. Currently, a data provider is most likely to use Open Database Connectivity (ODBC) functions to access the provider's data store. (A *data store* is any entity that contains data, whether organized into a database or not. For example, a database, a spreadsheet, or an e-mail post office are all examples of data stores, since each has

information that may be requested or required by an application.) Thus, even though a different OLE-DB provider is needed for each type of database interface, the ODBC provider will be used unless the client specifies otherwise.

Since OLE-DB providers can use ODBC functions, OLE-DB operates at a higher level of abstraction than ODBC. This means both that an extra layer of processing is required and also that OLE-DB can be used for interacting with a broader range of data stores, as shown in "OLE-DB as middleware."

The process works as follows:

1. A program uses ADOs to request something from a database.

2. The ADO calls the appropriate OLE-DB provider.

3. The OLE-DB provider deals with the database interface.

4. In some cases—for example, with ODBC—the provider will actually deal with a separate front end for the database interface.

→ *Compare* ODBC (Open Database Connectivity)

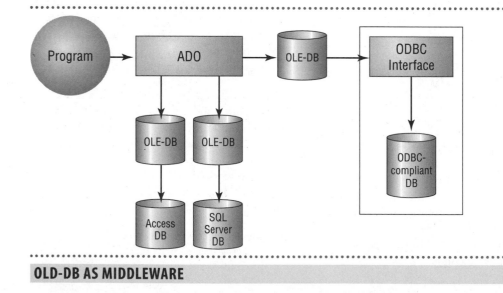

OLD-DB AS MIDDLEWARE

OLTP (Online Transaction Processing)

OLTP refers to business activities that are carried out electronically. Examples of OLTP include making withdrawals or deposits at an ATM (automatic teller machine), registering for courses electronically, or purchasing something over the Internet.

Special safeguards must be built into such transactions to ensure that there are no effects if something goes wrong and the transaction is not completed. For example, someone trying to get cash from their account through an ATM should not have the requested amount deducted from their account balance if the machine is unable to actually provide the cash.

The integrity of transactions is (virtually) ensured by adherence to the ACID (atomicity, consistency, isolation, and durability) principles, which have been formulated for just this purpose.

→ **Broader Category** Electronic Commerce

→ **See Also** ACID (Atomicity, Consistency, Isolation, and Durability)

ONC (Open Network Computing)

A model for distributed computing, originally developed by Sun Microsystems but now supported in most UNIX implementations, including Novell's UnixWare. The ONC model uses Sun's NFS (Network File System) for handling files distributed over remote locations. Communication with remote servers and devices is through RPCs (Remote Procedure Calls). The ONC model supports the TCP/IP protocol stack.

Online Transaction Processing (OLTP)

→ **See** OLTP (Online Transaction Processing)

OODB (Object-Oriented Database)

→ **See** Database

OOP (Object-Oriented Programming)

OOP represents a programming philosophy first developed in the CLU programming language and initially popularized in the Smalltalk language and development environment. In a sense, OOP represents a major departure from the traditional procedural orientation of structured programming (introduced by Edsger Dijkstra and others in the 1960s), which helped create the discipline of software engineering and (arguably) reached its peak in the Pascal and C programming languages.

Characterized by an explicit and fairly complete separation of function and content, structured programming is well summarized by the phrase "Data Structures + Algorithms = Programs," which is the title of a book by Niklaus Wirth, the developer of Pascal, Modula-2, and Oberon.

In structured programming, tasks are refined by breaking the problem down conceptually into smaller and more doable subtasks to represent the actions required by the problem and then selecting the most appropriate data structures to represent the problem elements. Programs built in this way are best suited for tasks with well-defined solution paths; they are not very good at dealing with less predictable, event-driven problems in which actions and problem elements depend on the events that occur.

In contrast, OOP is particularly suited to such types of tasks, and multitasking, multithreaded environments such as the Macintosh operating system and Windows NT are built using object technology. OOP is built around the concept of an object, which consists of attributes, or features, and of actions, or methods, associated with the object. The attributes define an object's properties; the methods enable the object to do things and also provide an interface through which other objects can access and possibly modify an object's properties. In essence, an object in an OOP program is a self-contained worker. An object is defined to have everything it needs to perform the task for which the object was defined. This truism actually does contain a truth: objects are designed to be able to do whatever they have to—that is, whatever is appropriate for the object.

An object-oriented program's execution generally consists of various objects communicating with other objects for purposes that are determined by the events that occur. For example, the execution of a session with a Web browser such as Navigator or Internet Explorer will depend on the actions the user takes at each point in the session. If the user clicks on a menu item or another hot spot on the screen, the mouse click is essentially a message—from the mouse pointer object to the object associated with that screen area. The screen object will know what the message means and will know how to perform the required action. This action may require the screen object to send a message to another object to get certain information (such as a URL, or Uniform Resource Locator) or to do something else that is required for the screen object to do its work. This message passing process will continue until the user has had enough and decides to end the session. At that point, a message will be sent to whatever object or objects are responsible for cleaning up, saving or purging whatever is necessary, and generally leaving things in order for whatever program will need to execute next in the environment.

Several features make OOP a very powerful and versatile programming philosophy. Two of the most important are inheritance and polymorphism, which are described next.

Inheritance

Inheritance refers to the fact that objects can be defined in terms of other objects—thereby acquiring an already defined set of attributes and methods to which a programmer can add features and methods that are unique to the derived object.

Objects defined in terms of other objects can be arranged in a hierarchical organization. An object (Chi) defined in terms of another object (Par) is known as a descendant, or child, object. The source object—in this case, Par—is known as the ancestor, or parent, object.

The child object will inherit the attributes and methods of the parent object, and will generally have additional attributes and methods associated with it. Some of the parent's attributes and methods may be changed for the child object. An object can serve as the ancestor for several different child objects. Child objects can, in turn, be parents for other objects.

For example, a Game object can serve as a parent for Card Game, Board Game, and Guessing Game objects. Card Game can serve as parent for Gin Rummy, Blackjack, Poker, Pinochle, and Go Fish games. Attributes for card games will include features of the "playing pieces" (in this case, a deck of cards), number of players, card values, and so forth. Methods will include dealing and playing hands, scoring points, and so forth.

In some programming languages, multiple inheritance is allowed. In such cases, an object can be defined in terms of more than one parent object, and can inherit features and methods from each parent. The C++ language allows true multiple inheritance, whereas Java allows a more limited form.

Polymorphism

Polymorphism is the OOP feature that enables a program to invoke the appropriate form of a method when necessary—even if the program has no way of knowing in advance which version will be needed. To use a trivial example, polymorphism would allow a card-playing program to deal a hand for the correct type of game when necessary. Polymorphism also allows the correct context menu to be displayed—for example, when you click on the right mouse button in a Windows environment.

One thing that helps make polymorphism possible is the use of dynamic binding in object-oriented programs. In a programming context, *binding* refers to the creation of a connection between a program element and a specific area of memory in the working environment.

In structured programming environments, which generally use static binding, such associations are made during the linking phase of program creation. A reference to a procedure or function in a program is translated into a reference to the starting location for that routine in the program's compiled code or in a dynamic link library accessible to the program. In static binding, this is done while the executable file is being created.

In contrast, in dynamic binding, such a connection is not made until the program actually executes. When the program encounters a reference to a routine—for example, DealHand in a card game—the program determines, *at run time*, whether to deal a hand of poker, blackjack, pinochle, or some other card game. The context in which the routine is encountered will tell the program which version is needed.

The selected method will work correctly because of a benefit of inheritance—namely, the ability to modify methods inherited from a parent. Thus, a generic DealHand routine will be modified for each child Card Game object that is defined. When appropriate, the child's method will override the method defined for the parent, and an OOP environment will know how to do this.

Code Reusability

A very handy consequence of the inheritance and polymorphism made possible in OOP environments is the fact that code can be reused very easily. As long as a programmer has access to the library containing predefined objects and to information about the names of public object elements (attributes and methods), the programmer can create derived objects based on objects in the library. Moreover, the programmer does not need access to source code or any other proprietary information about the object. In short, the programmer can extend the object hierarchy created by the developers of the available libraries.

Note the reference to "public object elements" in the preceding paragraph. Most OOP languages allow you to define at least two types of object elements: public and private. Public elements are those that are accessible to other program elements; private elements are those that are defined for internal use only—that is, for use by the object when doing its work or setting up its environment. Some languages allow refinements of this dichotomy—for example, by making certain elements available to some other elements but not to all.

The Price of Power

All of the power and convenience of OOP comes at a price, however. In order to enable the versatility that is possible with event-driven programs, object-oriented environments need to do a lot of busywork to set up and maintain its object world. Fortunately, the details of this work—which include garbage collection (reclaiming memory no longer being used), creation of space for the appropriate object type, and removing references to objects no longer in use—are, for the most part, done automatically by the environment. In the simplest cases, the programmer is responsible only for specifying when objects need to be created, which is done using a special function known as a Constructor. Sometimes the programmer will also need to indicate that an object is no longer needed, which can be done using another special function known as a Destructor.

Such open-ended administration is possible partly because object definitions must adhere to strict rules that ensure that each object fits the pattern for the object's type, or class. An object's class represents an abstract definition that is instantiated by an object.

Open

In a cable, an *open* refers to a gap or separation in the conductive material somewhere along the cable's path, such as in one wire in a pair. Depending on the gap, this may impede or preclude the transmission of data along the cable.

In networking and other computer-related contexts, *open* is used as an adjective to refer to elements or interfaces whose specifications have been made public so they can be used by third parties to create compatible (or competing) products. This is in contrast to *closed*, or *proprietary*, environments.

Open Application Interface (OAI)

→*See* OAI (Open Application Interface)

Open Database Connectivity (ODBC)

→*See* ODBC (Open Database Connectivity)

Open Data-Link Interface (ODI)

→*See* ODI (Open Data-Link Interface)

Open Document Architecture (ODA)

→*See* ODA (Open Document Architecture)

Open Network Computing (ONC)

→*See* ONC (Open Network Computing)

Open Pipe

A term used to describe the path between sender and receiver in circuit-switched and leased-line communications. The intent is to indicate that the data flows directly between the two locations (through the open pipe), rather than needing to be broken into packets and routed by various paths.

Open Shortest Path First (OSPF) Protocol

→*See* Protocol, OSPF (Open Shortest Path First)

Open Software Description (OSD)

→*See* OSD (Open Software Description)

Open System

Generally, a system whose specifications are published and made available for use, in order to make it easier to establish a connection or to communicate with the system. This is in contrast to a closed, or proprietary, system. Within the context of the OSI Reference Model, an open system is one that supports this model for connecting systems and networks.

→*See Also* OSI Reference Model

Open Systems Interconnection (OSI)

→*See* OSI (Open Systems Interconnection)

Open Systems Message Exchange (OSME)

→*See* OSME (Open Systems Message Exchange)

Open System Testing Consortium (OSTC)

→*See* OSTC (Open System Testing Consortium)

Operations, Administration, and Maintenance (OAM) Functions

→ *See* OAM (Operations, Administration, and Maintenance) Functions

Operating System (OS)

→ *See* OS (Operating System)

Optical Carrier Level-*x* (OC-*x*)

→ *See* OC-*x* (Optical Carrier Level *x*)

Optical Drive

An optical drive provides mass storage using optical or magneto-optical encoding. Optical drives are becoming more popular for networks because of their large storage capacity, which ranges from hundreds of megabytes to several gigabytes.

Optical drives are not yet supported directly in most network operating systems. One problem is the relatively slow access times for CD-ROM drives (200 to 350 milliseconds, or up to 30 times as long as hard disk access). This can cause network processes to time out (assume the device is not available and to return with an error condition). In some cases, however, the drive manufacturers can provide drivers and possibly other software to enable you to use the drive on a network.

Currently the following types of optical drives are available:

CD-ROM (compact disc–read-only memory) A read-only drive for a medium with a huge storage capacity of 660 megabytes (MB). CD-ROM drives cannot be used for recording data, only for reading. Compact discs can be useful as data, documentation, or software sources. Jukebox versions of CD-ROM drives can hold from 5 to 100 discs, and can provide access to any one of these discs within a few seconds.

WORM (Write Once, Read Many) A WORM drive can record on its medium, but can write only once to each location on the disk. Once written, the information can be read as often as desired. Like compact discs, WORM disks have a very high storage capacity.

EO (Erasable Optical) An EO drive uses a medium similar to a compact disc, but encased in its own cartridge. This is a read/write medium on which information is stored in optical form. Novell's NetWare version 4*x* supports a high capacity storage system (HCSS), which allows infrequently used network files to be stored on EO disks instead of on the hard disk.

OROM (Optical Read-Only Memory) This storage method uses a storage format similar to that of CD-ROM, but an OROM disk can be read by a magneto-optical drive.

MO (magneto-optical) This is a general term for drives that use optical means to store data.

→ *Broader Category* Peripheral

ADVANTAGES OF EO DRIVES

For all practical purposes, EO drives are mass storage devices, and they may soon be the storage device of choice. The medium has several significant advantages:

- Capacity: A disk the size of a 3.5 inch floppy disk can hold over 200 MB; a disk not much larger than a 5.25 inch floppy disk can hold a gigabyte of information.

- Security: The storage capacities are high enough to make it feasible to store entire working environments on a single disk, so that everyone can have his or her own working environments.

- Access Time: Access times of under 20 milliseconds are already possible, making EO drives competitive with hard disk drives.

Continued on next page

- **Data Integrity:** Data is stored optically rather than magnetically. This makes the data impervious to corruption or accidental erasure by electrical or magnetic disturbances.

- **Life Expectancy:** Since the read/write components never actually touch the medium, there is minimal wear and tear. EO discs have an expected lifetime of 30 to 40 years.

- **Price:** Street prices for such disks are already competitive with floppy disk prices and considerably better than hard disk prices. With economies of scale that can be expected as the market grows, these prices will fall even more.

- **Portability:** Portable EO drives, for example, the Tahoe and Tahoe-230 from Pinnacle Micro, make it easy and convenient to take your working environment when moving from place to place.

Fujitsu Computer Products (800-626-4686) offers 128 MB and 230 MB EO drives: the DynaMO and the DynaMO-230.

Pinnacle Micro (800-533-7070) has a whole line of EO drives, with capacities ranging from 128 MB to over 10 GB. The latter is actually a jukebox device, capable of holding several disks and of switching between them.

Optical Fiber, Nonconductive Plenum (OFNP)

→ **See** OFNP (Optical Fiber, Nonconductive Plenum)

Optical Fiber, Nonconductive Riser (OFNR)

→ **See** OFNR (Optical Fiber, Nonconductive Riser)

Optical Switch

An optical switch uses light to carry out a switching function, such as to connect an input stream to an output channel. Optical switches are much faster than electromechanical or electrical switches, and they are needed for the very high-speed communications technologies beginning to arrive.

Optical Time Domain Reflectometer (OTDR)

→ **See** OTDR (Optical Time Domain Reflectometer)

Optimistic Security

Optimistic security operates on a philosophy that can be described as "let them see and do everything, except what they shouldn't see and do." In other words, optimistic security takes the approach of allowing maximum permissions for accessing information, blocking access only to the materials for which the user or group should not have permissions. This is in contrast to pessimistic security, which takes a much more restrictive approach.

→ **Broader Category** Security

→ **Compare** Pessimistic Security

ORB (Object Request Broker)

An object request broker is a service that can enable existing applications to communicate with object-oriented applications or front-ends. This makes it possible for an application to request a service without knowing the directory structure of the environment from which the service is being requested. Once a request has been made, the ORB will find the requested object, if possible, and will apply the appropriate method—all in a manner that should be transparent to the requester.

The ORB is a central part of the CORBA (Common Object Request Broker Architecture) that has been developed by the OMG (Object Management Group).

→ **See Also** CORBA

Order of Magnitude

An order of magnitude refers to a change in a numerical value that is a multiple of the original, or reference, value. In decimal systems, changes that are powers of 10 are commonly used as orders of magnitude. Thus, A and B differ by one order of magnitude if one is 10 times the other; they differ by two orders of magnitude if one is 100 times the other. Note that A and B are still said to differ by an order of magnitude even if one is 90 times the other. For some computations, powers of 1000 (10^3) are used as (decimal) orders of magnitude.

The order of magnitude is determined by the base being used. Thus, in a binary system, powers of two determine orders of magnitude. The table "Prefixes for Selected Orders of Magnitude" lists some of the prefixes used.

PREFIXES FOR SELECTED ORDERS OF MAGNITUDE

Prefix	Name	2^x	10^y	Term
Y	Yotta	$x = 80$	$y = 24$	Septillions
B	Bronto	$x = 70$	$y = 21$	Sextillions
E	Exa	$x = 60$	$y = 18$	Quintillions
P	Peta	$x = 50$	$y = 15$	Quadrillions
T	Tera	$x = 40$	$y = 12$	Trillions
G	Giga	$x = 30$	$y = 9$	Billions
M	Mega	$x = 20$	$y = 6$	Millions
k	Kilo	$x = 10$	$y = 3$	Thousands
m	Milli	$x = {\sim}\text{-}10$	$y = {\sim}\text{-}3$	Thousandths
&m	Micro	$x = {\sim}\text{-}20$	$y = {\sim}\text{-}6$	Millionths
n	Nano	$x = {\sim}\text{-}30$	$y = {\sim}\text{-}9$	Billionths
p	Pico	$x = {\sim}\text{-}40$	$y = {\sim}\text{-}12$	Trillionths
f	Femto	$x = {\sim}\text{-}50$	$y = {\sim}\text{-}15$	Quadrillionths
a	Atta	$x = {\sim}\text{-}60$	$y = {\sim}\text{-}18$	Quintillionths

Note that the orders of magnitude are referenced to powers of two. That is, a "mega" is defined as 2^{20} (1,048,576), rather than as 10^6 (1,000,000 exactly). Both binary and decimal references can be used.

The context will determine which is more appropriate. For example, binary values are more meaningful when speaking of storage or memory quantities; decimal values are more meaningful when speaking of time or frequency values.

Originate Mode

In communications, the originate mode is the mode of the device that initiates the call and that waits for the remote device to respond. Compare this with response mode.

OS (Operating System)

The operating system is the software that runs a computer. DOS, OS/2, Windows NT, UNIX, and LINUX are examples of widely used operating systems.

An operating system does the following:

- Deals with the computer's hardware.

- Provides an environment and an interface for users.

- Carries out (executes) user commands or program instructions.

- Provides input and output, memory and storage, file and directory management capabilities.

An operating system generally provides a generic interface and command set for users. This interface can be replaced with a different operating system shell or enhanced in its functionality by means of APIs (application programming interfaces). Shells may also include additional commands you can use while running a particular shell. Microsoft Windows provides a graphics-oriented shell for DOS-based environments; the Thompson shell (from Thompson Automation) or the mks Toolkit (from Mortice Kern Systems) provide UNIX-like shells for DOS.

A computer's "native" (built-in or default) operating system may be supplemented or replaced by a different operating system, such as a network operating system (NOS).

In addition to the responsibilities of an ordinary operating system, a NOS must be able to do the following:

- Provide access to files and resources (for example, printers) on the network.

- Provide messaging and/or electronic-mail (e-mail) services.

- Enable nodes on the network to communicate with each other.

- Support interprocess communications (IPC), which enable processes on the network to communicate with each other.

- Respond to requests from applications or users on the network.

- Map requests and paths to the appropriate places on the network.

The NOS may actually perform the regular operating system's duties, or it may rely on the native operating system to carry these out.

OS/2

OS/2—or OS/2 Warp, as the latest version is called—is a 32-bit operating system for Intel-based machines. The system was originally developed jointly by IBM and Microsoft, but is now being developed completely by IBM. In this entry, "OS/2" refers to any version of the operating system. The "Warp" was added to the product name with version 3, and this word will be included only where that specific version of the operating system is under discussion.

OS/2 supports true preemptive multitasking, multiple threads, flat (i.e., non-segmented) memory addressing, an object-oriented graphical user interface (GUI), various types of networking, and installable file systems. A major benefit of true multitasking is that crashing an application will crash only that one application, and will not freeze the entire machine. Other tasks will continue executing.

File System Support

Support for the file allocation table (FAT) based system used in DOS, and OS/2's own HPFS (High-Performance File System) is built into OS/2. The system can also support add-on file systems, such as a CDFS (CD-ROM file system).

The HPFS has two particularly useful features: long names and extended attributes. HPFS names can be up to 254 characters and can include spaces. The extended attributes feature can be used to associate whatever information or properties are appropriate for a file. For example, icons, version or other special information, and resources used for the file can be stored in the extended attributes. An extended attribute can even be another file. These attractive features can cause compatibility problems, however. DOS and Microsoft Windows programs won't be able to use HPFS files.

OS/2's Workplace Shell provides a powerful object-oriented GUI that integrates the capabilities of both the Microsoft Windows Program and File Manager. Being object-based, the Workplace Shell knows how to manipulate various types of elements (such as text or data files, icons, applications, and devices), and can be taught to handle others. REXX is a command and macro programming language, which can be used to write scripts and enhance the Workplace Shell.

OS/2 Interfaces and Resources

REXX is a command and macro language that is included with OS/2. In fact, REXX is a full-fledged programming language, so you can use it to write scripts that are much more complex and sophisticated than the batch files that DOS supports. Such scripts can help enhance the Workplace Shell or make the user's work easier in other ways.

Version 3—that is, OS/2 Warp—also includes a Bonus Pak of resources that help make the OS/2 environment more intelligent and more capable. Properly used, such features can also make the user more useful and more capable. For example, the Bonus Pak includes a Personal Information Manager (PIM), which provides many of the elements you need to organize your life—at least on disk. The PIM includes a phone book, a calendar, and an appointment scheduler; it has a daily planner, note pad, and a to-do list. There is even a program, called Event Monitor, that will sound alarms and even carry out automated tasks for you.

IBM Works is an integrated software suite that provides several of the most commonly used applications—word processing, spreadsheet, database, and charting programs, and a report generator—in a single package. Collectively, the applications may not be as powerful as those included in the integrated office packages by Lotus (Smart Suite), Microsoft (Office and Office Professional), and Novell (PerfectOffice). Nevertheless, each application is a full-featured and fully-functional example of its genre.

The Bonus Pak also includes a multimedia viewer, which can handle image, video, and sound files. The viewer will call the appropriate component to display or play non-text material that appears in a program or file.

Several of the added resources have to do with networking or other forms of telecommunication. These resources include the following:

- HyperACCESS Lite, which is a general communications program that can serve as a front end for connections to online services or bulletin board systems (BBSs).

- FaxWorks for OS/2, which provides the ability to send, receive, view, manipulate, and print... (surprise, surprise) faxes.

- CIM (CompuServe Information Manager) for OS/2, which can provide access to CompuServe's online services.

- Internet Connection Services, which provide the software needed to connect to the Internet over a modem (using a SLIP connection), and which also includes programs for using the Internet. This package provides Gopher, FTP, and Telnet programs, as well as a newsreader, e-mail client, and a browser (hypertext file reader) for viewing World Wide Web (WWW) files. You can use this package

to connect to an Internet Access Provider. The program is preconfigured to connect you to the IBM Global Network, but you can sign up with a different provider if you wish.

OS/2 Versions

Version 1 of OS/2 was actually a 16-bit operating system. Current versions of OS/2 can, however, run these 16-bit programs by using a readdressing scheme. OS/2 2.0, which was released in 1992, was a major revision, but it could still run OS/2 1.x and DOS programs. Microsoft Windows support was limited to Windows 3.0, and programs running in enhanced mode were not supported.

Version 2.1, released in 1993, added support for Microsoft Windows 3.1 enhanced-mode programs. This version also added support for PCMCIA cards and improved support for other devices, such as CD-ROMs and monitors. OS/2 for Windows made OS/2 available to users who have Microsoft Windows 3.1 installed.

OS/2 Warp

With version 3.0, IBM added the word Warp to the name. It also simplified many of the system's networking capabilities and added a few. Version 3 packages come in either of two configurations:

- Those that include WIN-OS/2, which is IBM's emulation of Microsoft Windows 3.1. This form is more expensive but does not require you to have Microsoft Windows installed on your system. Once WIN-OS/2 is installed, it can run most Windows programs. It's possible to install this version even if Microsoft Windows is installed, although it's not clear why you would want to pay the extra money and use up extra storage, unless you need to run a 16-bit Windows application that can't run under WIN-OS/2, but can run under Windows.

- Those that don't include a Windows emulator. In this configuration, OS/2 can use Microsoft Windows to run Windows programs, provided Microsoft Windows is installed on your system.

OS/2 Warp Connect

OS/2 Warp Connect adds support for local area networks to the telecommunications and internetworking capabilities of plain OS/2 Warp. Warp Connect provides the software needed to support your machine as a network node—either at home or from a remote location. The additional networking support comes from the following:

- IBM Peer for OS/2, which enables users to share information and resources—that is, to function as peers in a network. These machines can also connect to PCs running Windows for Workgroups or other networking software.

- LAN Client solution, which makes the node a client machine for either a LAN Server or a NetWare network

- TCP/IP for OS/2, which provides a TCP/IP protocol stack and access to the Internet (after subscribing to an Internet Access Provider)

- LAN Distance Remote, which lets you connect a remote PC to the PC, and to get onto the network from the remote location

Warp Connect also includes Lotus Notes Express, which enables users on the network to collaborate on projects. Finally, Warp Connect comes with or without a Win-OS/2 component. These versions come in blue and red boxes, respectively.

OS/2 for SMP

In the past few years, machines with multiple processors have become increasingly popular. In Symmetric Multiprocessing (SMP), all the processors are equals, and a task can always be passed on to the next available processor.

OS/2 for SMP can support machines with between 2 and 16 processors, and provides the same multitasking and multiple thread support to a multiple processor system as regular OS/2 provides for a single processor. OS/2 for SMP conforms to version 1.1 of the Multiprocessor System Specification.

OS/2 for SMP must be pre-installed, and both pricing and configuration depend on the number of processors in the machine.

OS/2 LAN Server

This is actually a version of IBM's LAN Server network operating system built on OS/2. It provides support for a network server running DOS, Windows, and OS/2 clients or applications. An entry-level version supports up to 100 nodes, and an Advanced version supports up to 1000.

LAN Server 4.0 includes all of OS/2's features and capabilities, and adds its own enhancements and improvements—for example, fault tolerance and disk mirroring for extra data protection. Extensions to OS/2's HPFS make file access much faster.

LAN Server provides peer-to-peer capabilities so that machines—even DOS clients—can communicate with each other. Interestingly, IBM has made TCP/IP the default protocol stack in LAN Server 4.0. LAN Server can communicate with servers from other environments—including NetWare, Solaris, LAN Manager, Windows NT, MVS, and VM.

OS/2 and Networking

OS/2 is networking-friendly, and IBM is marketing OS/2 in part as an operating environment that can integrate various environments. In fact, both Microsoft's LAN Manager and IBM's LAN Server network operating systems are built on OS/2. LAN Manager runs on top of OS/2 1.3, but OS/2 2.0 and 2.1 machines can be clients on a LAN Manager network. LAN Manager is unlikely to be ported to newer versions, however since Microsoft has built its capabilities into Windows NT.

LAN Server also runs on top of OS/2, and it does support the newer versions as well. LAN Server 3.0 includes all of OS/2's features and capabilities and adds its own enhancements and improvements, such as fault tolerance and disk mirroring, which help provide data protection. Extensions to OS/2's HPFS provide more features and also make file access much faster.

OS/2 machines can be either servers or clients in a Novell NetWare network. With OS/2 machines, NetWare runs alongside OS/2. OS/2 systems can be clients in UNIX and VINES networks.

OS/2 and Windows

OS/2's influence is probably greater than its market share might suggest. While OS/2 has only a small share of the market when compared to DOS and Windows, this operating system is found in some mission-critical and widely-used applications. For example, ATM machines are almost all controlled by OS/2.

OSD (Open Software Description)

OSD is an XML (eXtensible Markup Language) application developed jointly by Microsoft and Marimba. It is used to mark up software packages with descriptions that will make it possible to deliver the packages or upgrades over the Internet or over an intranet. OSD is used to describe the software. Actual delivery is done using other mechanisms—for example, Microsoft's Channel Definition Format (CDF).

→ *See Also* XML (eXtensible Markup Language)

OSI (Open Systems Interconnection)

In networking and telecommunications, OSI is used to express the main concept of the ISO's seven-layered model. In this context, an open system is a computer (with software and peripherals) that supports this model for connecting systems on a network and for transmitting information among these systems.

→ *See Also* OSI Reference Model

OSI Implementers Workshop (OIW)

→ *See* OIW (OSI Implementers Workshop)

OSI Network Management Model

A network management model that provides a set of concepts and guidelines for various aspects of network management. The model does not provide standards or specifications; rather, it is intended as the conceptual basis for such specifications. Also known as the ISO network management model, for the International Standardization Organization, which developed the model.

→ *See* Network Management

OSI Network Address

In the OSI Reference Model, an address associated with an entity at the transport layer. This address may be up to 20 bytes long. OSI network addresses have two components: a standardized initial domain part, and a domain-specific part, which is under the control of the network administrator.

OSI Presentation Address

In the OSI Reference Model, an address associated with an entity at the application layer. This address consists of an OSI network address and of selectors that identify service access points (SAPs) for the presentation, session, and transport layers. The selector values provide layer-specific addresses.

OSI Reference Model

The OSI (Open Systems Interconnection) Reference Model is a seven-layer model developed by the ISO (International Standardization Organization) to describe how to connect any combination of devices for purposes of communications.

This model describes the task in terms of seven functional layers, and specifies the functions that must be available at each layer. The seven layers form a hierarchy from the applications at the top to the physical communications medium at the bottom. The functions and capabilities expected at each layer are specified in the reference model; however, the model does not prescribe how this functionality must be implemented.

The focus in this model is on the "interconnection" and on the information that can be passed over this connection. The OSI model does not concern itself with the internal operations of the systems involved.

Communications Models

The OSI Reference Model incorporates two communications models:

- A horizontal, protocol-based model by which programs or processes on different machines communicate

- A vertical, service-based model by which layers on a single machine communicate

These are illustrated in "Communications in the OSI Reference Model."

A program or protocol (P) on a particular machine (A) communicates with a counterpart program or protocol (Q) operating at the same layer on another machine (B). In order to do this, the program on each machine must rely on the services of the layer below the program's.

The sending program on machine A must rely on its service layer to encapsulate P's information properly, so that P's packets reach their destination. The receiving program (Q) on machine B must rely on its service layer to deliver a packet from P correctly. Q's service layer may, in turn, rely on *its* service layer to verify that the delivered material is error-free.

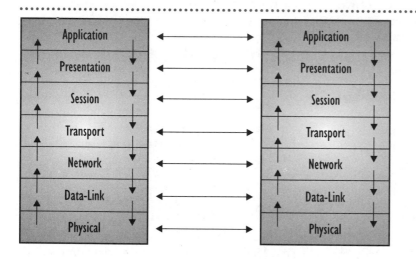

↓ **Service Calls and Packet Passing**

↑ **Packet Delivery**

↔ **Peer Protocol-Based Communication**

COMMUNICATIONS IN THE OSI REFERENCE MODEL

Communications Elements

In order to communicate, the following elements are needed:

- At least two parties wishing to communicate. These can be the same or different programs on each machine, or they can be two layers on the same machine.

- A common language, or protocol, with which these parties can communicate. Horizontally (that is, between machines) the two programs need a common protocol or an interpreter to translate for each program. Vertically, layers communicate through APIs (Application Program Interfaces). The APIs define the available functions for a layer and provide the mechanisms for invoking these functions.

OSI Layers

The OSI Reference Model uses seven functional layers to define the communication capabilities needed to enable any two machines to communicate with each other.

The seven layers range from the application layer at the top to the physical layer at the bottom. The top layer is where users and application programs communicate with a network. The bottom layer is where the actual transmissions take place. Services at one layer communicate with and make use of services at adjacent layers.

The middle layer (transport) is pivotal. It separates the application- and service-oriented upper layers from the network- and communication-oriented lower layers, which are known as the *subnet layers*. "OSI layer groupings" shows this division.

The individual layers are discussed in the sections that follow, from highest to lowest layer. The discussion includes examples of programs and protocols, but be aware that many programs have capabilities that span or straddle two or more OSI layers. This is particularly true of programs developed in other (non-OSI) communications frameworks (IBM

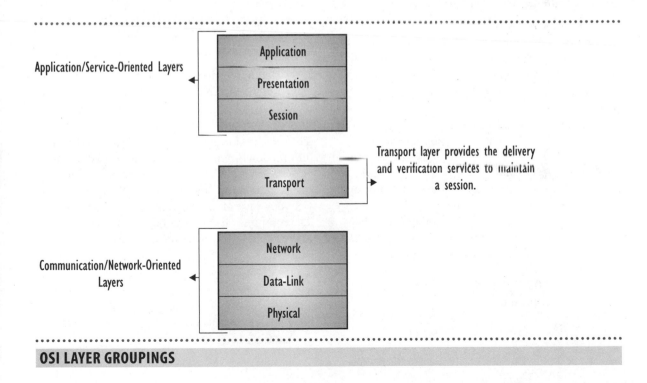

OSI LAYER GROUPINGS

mainframe, UNIX/Internet, and on). It is also more likely to be true with upper-layer programs.

For example, it is not unusual for a "hyperthyroid" application to include data translation capabilities (conversions, encryption, or compression), which are assigned to the presentation layer in the OSI model. Such a program can fit as an example in either layer.

Application Layer

The application layer is the topmost layer in the OSI Reference Model. This layer is responsible for giving applications access to the network. Examples of application-layer tasks include file transfer, electronic mail (e-mail) services, and network management.

Application-layer services are much more varied than the services in lower layers, because the entire gamut of application and task possibilities is available here. The specific details depend on the framework or model being used. For example, there are several network management applications. Each of these provides services and functions specified in a different framework for network management.

Programs can get access to the application-layer services through application service elements (ASEs). There are a variety of such ASEs, each designed for class of tasks. See the ASE article for details.

To accomplish its tasks, the application layer passes program requests and data to the presentation layer, which is responsible for encoding the application layer's data in the appropriate form.

Application Layer Protocols

Not surprisingly, application programs are found at this layer. Also found here are network shells, which are the programs that run on workstations and that enable the workstation to join the network. Actually, programs such as network shells often provide functions that span or are found at multiple layers. For example, NETX, the Novell NetWare shell program, spans the top three layers.

Programs and protocols that provide application-layer services include the following:

- NICE (Network Information and Control Exchange), which provides network monitoring and management capabilities.

- FTAM (File Transfer, Access, and Management), which provides capabilities for remote file handling.

- FTP (File Transfer Protocol), which provides file transfer capabilities.

- X.400, which specifies protocols and functions for message handling and e-mail services.

- CMIP, which provides network management capabilities based on a framework formulated by the ISO.

- SNMP, which provides network management within a non-OSI framework. This protocol does not conform to the OSI model, but does provide functionality that is specified within the OSI model.

- Telnet, which provides terminal emulation and remote login capabilities. Telnet's capabilities go beyond the application layer.

- rlogin, which provides remote login capabilities for UNIX environments.

Presentation Layer

The presentation layer is responsible for presenting information in a manner suitable for the applications or users dealing with the information. Functions such as data conversion from EBCDIC to ASCII (or vice versa), use of special graphics or character sets, data compression or expansion, and data encryption or decryption are carried out at this layer.

The presentation layer provides services for the application layer above it, and uses the session layer below it. In practice, the presentation layer rarely appears in pure form. Rather, application- or session-layer programs will encompass some or all of the presentation-layer functions.

Session Layer

The session layer is responsible for synchronizing and sequencing the dialog and packets in a network connection. This layer is also responsible for making sure that the connection is maintained until the transmission is complete, and ensuring that appropriate security measures are taken during a session (that is, a connection). Functions defined at the session layer include those for network gateway communications.

The session layer is used by the presentation layer above it, and uses the transport layer below it.

Session Layer Protocols

Session-layer capabilities are often part of other configurations (for example, those that include the presentation layer). The following protocols encompass many of the session-layer functions:

- ADSP (AppleTalk Data Stream Protocol), which enables two nodes to establish a reliable connection for data transfer.

- NetBEUI, which is an implementation and extension of NetBIOS.

- NetBIOS, which actually spans layers 5, 6, and 7, but which includes capabilities for monitoring sessions to make sure they are running smoothly.

- PAP (Printer Access Protocol), which provides access to a PostScript printer in an AppleTalk network.

Transport Layer

In the OSI Reference Model, the transport layer is responsible for providing data transfer at an agreed-upon level of quality, such as at specified transmission speeds and error rates.

To ensure delivery, outgoing packets are assigned numbers in sequence. The numbers are included in the packets that are transmitted by lower layers. The transport layer at the receiving end checks the packet numbers to make sure all have been delivered and to put the packet contents into the proper sequence for the recipient.

The transport layer provides services for the session layer above it, and uses the network layer below it to find a route between source and destination. The transport layer is crucial in many ways, because it sits between the upper layers (which are strongly application-dependent) and the lower ones (which are network-based).

Subnet Layers and Transmission Quality

In the OSI model, the three layers below the transport layer are known as the *subnet* layers. These layers are responsible for getting packets from the source to the destination. In fact, relay devices (such as bridges, routers, or X.25 circuits) use only these three layers, since their job is actually just to pass on a signal or a packet. Such devices are known as intermediate systems (ISs). In contrast, components that *do* use the upper layers as well are known as *end systems* (ESs). See the End System and Intermediate System articles for more information.

The transmission services provided by the subnet layers may or may not be reliable. In this context, a *reliable service* is one that will either deliver a packet without error or inform the sender if such error-free transmission was not possible.

Similarly, the subnet layer transmission services may or may not be connection-oriented. In connection-oriented communications, a connection between sender and receiver is established first. If the connection is successful, all the data is transmitted in sequence along this connection. When the transmission is finished, the connection is broken. Packets in such a transmission do not need to be assigned sequence numbers because each packet is transmitted immediately after its predecessor and along the same path.

In contrast, in connectionless communications, packets are sent independently of each other, and may take different paths to the destination. With such a communications mode, packets may get there in random order, and packets may get lost, discarded, or duplicated. Before transmission, each packet must be numbered to indicate the packet's position in the transmission, so that the message can be reassembled at the destination.

Since the transport layer must be able to get packets between applications, the services needed at this layer depend on what the subnet layers do. The more work the subnet layers do, the less the transport layer must do.

Subnet Service Classes

Three types of subnet service are distinguished in the OSI model:

- Type A: Very reliable, connection-oriented service

- Type B: Unreliable, connection-oriented service

- Type C: Unreliable, possibly connectionless service

Transport Layer Protocols

To provide the capabilities required for whichever service type applies, several classes of transport layer protocols have been defined in the OSI model:

- TP0 (Transfer Protocol Class 0), which is the simplest protocol. It assumes type A service; that is, a subnet that does most of the work for the transport layer. Because the subnet is reliable, TP0 requires neither error detection nor error correction; because the connection is connection-oriented, packets do not need to be numbered before transmission. X.25 is an example of a relay service that is connection-oriented and sufficiently reliable for TP0.

- TP1 (Transfer Protocol Class 1), which assumes a type B subnet; that is, one that may be unreliable. To deal with this, TP1 provides its own error detection, along with facilities for getting the sender to retransmit any errone-ous packets.

- TP2 (Transfer Protocol Class 2), which also assumes a type A subnet. However, TP2 can multiplex transmissions, so that multiple transport connections can be sustained over the single network connection.

- TP3 (Transfer Protocol Class 3), which also assumes a type B subnet. TP3 can also multi-plex transmissions, so that this protocol has the capabilities of TP1 and TP2.

- TP4 (Transfer Protocol Class 4), which is the most powerful protocol, in that it makes min-imal assumptions about the capabilities or reliability of the subnet. TP4 is the only one of the OSI transport-layer protocols that sup-ports connectionless service.

Other transport layer protocols include the following:

- TCP and UDP, which provide connection-oriented and connectionless transport services, respectively. These protocols are used in most UNIX-based networks.

- SPX, which is used in Novell's NetWare environments.

- PEP, which is part of the XNS protocol suite from Xerox.

- VOTS, which is used in Digital Equipment Corporation networks.

- AEP, ATP, NBP, and RTMP, which are part of the AppleTalk protocol suite.

Network Layer

The network layer (also known as the *packet layer*) is the third lowest layer, or the uppermost subnet layer. It is responsible for the following tasks:

- Determining addresses or translating from hardware to network addresses. These addresses may be on a local network or they may refer to networks located elsewhere on an internetwork. One of the functions of the net-work layer is, in fact, to provide capabilities needed to communicate on an internetwork.

- Finding a route between a source and a desti-nation node or between two intermediate devices.

- Establishing and maintaining a logical connection between these two nodes, to establish either a connectionless or a connection-oriented communication.

The data is processed and transmitted using the data-link layer below the network layer. Responsibility for guaranteeing proper delivery of the packets lies with the transport layer, which uses network-layer services.

Network Layer Protocols

Two important classes of network layer protocols are address resolution protocols and routing protocols. Address resolution protocols are concerned with determining a unique network address for a source or destination node.

Routing protocols are concerned with getting packets from a local network to another network. After finding the destination network, it is necessary to determine a path to the destination network. This path will usually involve just routers, except for the first and last parts of the path.

Protocols at the network layer include the following:

- ARP (Address Resolution Protocol), which converts from hardware to network addresses.

- CLNP (Connectionless Network Protocol), which is an ISO-designed protocol.

- DDP (Datagram Delivery Protocol), which provides connectionless service in AppleTalk networks.

- ICMP (Internet Control Message Protocol), which is an error-handling protocol.

- IGP (Interior Gateway Protocol), which is used to connect routers within an administrative domain. This is also the name for a class of protocols.

- Integrated IS-IS, which is a specific IGP.

- IPX (Internetwork Packet Exchange), which is part of Novell's protocol suite.

- IP (Internet Protocol), which is one of the UNIX environment protocols.

- X.25 PLP (Packet Layer Protocol), which is used in an X.25 switching network.

Data-Link Layer

The data-link layer is responsible for creating, transmitting, and receiving data packets. The data-link layer provides services for the various protocols at the network layer, and uses the physical layer to transmit or receive material.

The data-link layer creates packets appropriate for the network architecture being used. Requests and data from the network layer are part of the data in these packets (or *frames*, as they are often called at this layer). These packets are passed down to the physical layer; from there, the data is transmitted to the physical layer on the destination machine.

Network architectures (such as Ethernet, ARCnet, Token Ring, and FDDI) encompass the data-link and physical layers, which is why these architectures support services at the data-link level. These architectures also represent the most common protocols used at the data-link level.

The IEEE's (802.x) networking working groups have refined the data-link layer into two sublayers: the logical-link control (LLC) sublayer at the top and the media-access control (MAC) sublayer at the bottom. The LLC sublayer must provide an interface for the network layer protocols. The MAC sublayer must provide access to a particular physical encoding and transport scheme.

Data-Link Layer Protocols

Link access or data-link control protocols are used to label, package, and send network-layer (properly addressed) packets. The following protocols are used at the data-link layer:

- ELAP (EtherTalk Link Access Protocol), which provides a Macintosh with access to an Ethernet network.

- HDLC (High-level Data Link Control), which is based on IBM's SDLC and which has been standardized by the ISO. HDLC is a very flexible protocol for accessing data-link services.

- LAPB (Link Access Protocol, Balanced), which is used in X.25 networks.

- LAPD (Link Access Protocol, D channel), which is used in ISDN (Integrated Services Digital Network).

- LLAP (LocalTalk Link Access Protocol), which provides a Macintosh with access to a LocalTalk network.

- PPP (Point-to-Point Protocol), which provides direct medium-speed communication between two machines. PPP operates over serial lines.

- SLIP (Serial Line Interface Protocol), which provides access to an Internet protocol network over serial lines. This protocol can be used to access the Internet.

- TLAP (TokenTalk Link Access Protocol), which provides a Macintosh with access to a Token Ring network.

Physical Layer

The physical is the lowest layer in the OSI Reference Model. This layer gets data packets from the data-link layer above it, and converts the contents of these packets into a series of electrical signals that represent 0 and 1 values in a digital transmission.

These signals are sent across a transmission medium to the physical layer at the receiving end. At the destination, the physical layer converts the electrical signals into a series of bit values. These values are grouped into packets and passed up to the data-link layer.

Transmission Properties Defined

The mechanical and electrical properties of the transmission medium are defined at this level. These include the following:

- The type of cable and connectors used. Cable may be coaxial, twisted-pair, or fiber-optic.

The types of connectors depend on the type of cable.

- The pin assignments for the cable and connectors. Pin assignments depend on the type of cable and also on the network architecture being used.

- Format for the electrical signals. The encoding scheme used to signal 0 and 1 values in a digital transmission or particular values in an analog transmission depend on the network architecture being used. Most networks use digital signaling, and most use some form of Manchester encoding for the signal.

Physical Layer Specifications

Examples of specifications for this layer include the following:

- EIA-232D, which specifies both the interface and electrical signal characteristics for a serial connection between a DTE (data terminal equipment) and DCE (data circuit terminating). This standard is a revision and extension of the more familiar RS-232C standard that has connected so many computers to modems and printers over the years. Equivalent to CCITT V.24 (interface) and V.28 (electrical characteristics) standards.

- RS-422A and RS-423A, which specify the electrical characteristics of balanced and unbalanced voltage circuits for a digital interface. Equivalent to CCITT standards V.10 and V.11, respectively.

- RS-449, which specifies general-purpose serial interfaces for 37- and 9-pin connectors.

- RS-530, which specifies the interface for a high-speed 25-pin serial connection between a DTE and a DCE.

- ISO 2110, which defines the connector pin assignments for 25-pin serial connectors. These assignments correspond to those defined in CCITT V.24 and RS-232D.

- IEEE 802.3, which defines various flavors of Ethernet, including the physical connections and signaling methods.

- IEEE 802.5, which defines the physical connections and signaling rules for Token Ring networks.

Model Operation

The ultimate goal of the activity in the OSI Reference Model is peer communication: that is, to allow comparable layers on two different machines to communicate. Thus, an application on machine A wants to communicate with the same or a different application on machine B. Similarly, the transport layer on machine A is communicating with its counterpart on machine B.

Since there is no direct connection between peer layers, the communication must take an indirect course: down the layer hierarchy on one machine and up the hierarchy on the other machine. Thus, in order to communicate, the application layer on A must first communicate with A's presentation layer. This layer must, in turn, communicate with the session layer below it.

SAPs (Service Access Points)

The actual interfaces between layers are through service access points (SAPs). These are unique addresses that the layers involved can use to exchange requests, replies, and data. Because multiple programs may be running at a given layer, each needs its own SAPs for communicating with the layers above and below it.

SAPs represent the generic communications slots between layers. To identify the layer under discussion, it is common practice to include a letter identifying the lower layer in the pair. For example, a SAP linking a presentation layer process to the session layer below it would be known as an SSAP.

PDUs (Protocol Data Units) and SDUs (Service Data Units)

Information is passed between layers in the form of packets, known as PDUs (protocol data units). The packet size and definition depends on the protocol suite involved in the horizontal communications. The basic strategy for passing PDUs is as follows:

- Packets are padded as they make their way down the layers on the sending machine, and are stripped as they make their way up the layers on the receiving machine.

- Once passed to the lower layer (layer Y), a data packet from the layer above (layer X), known as an XPDU or X-PDU (after the layer) is padded by adding Y-specific header and trailer material. Once padded, the XPDU is passed as layer Y's data—as a YPDU—down to layer Z, where the padding process is repeated with different information. For example, in going from the presentation to the network layer, a packet is padded at the session and transport layers before being passed to the network layer.

- The header materials in a PDU provide handling and delivery information for the process that receives the packet. Trailer materials typically provide error-checking information.

PDUs are sometimes known as SDUs (Service Data Units) when being passed vertically, which is when the services of an adjacent layer are used to process or deliver the packet. Thus, a TPDU (a transport layer packet) may be considered an SDU when the packet is passed down to the network layer for routing. The literature is inconsistent as to whether this would be a TSDU or an NSDU—whether an SDU is named after the source or target layer.

As packets are padded, they may get too big to pass downward as single packets. When this happens, the packets must be segmented (divided into smaller packets), numbered, and sent on as properly sized PDUs. Segmented packets will need to be reconstructed on the receiving end.

PCI (Protocol Control Information)

Each sending layer gets material received from the layer above it, adds new material (which contains the layer's communication with its peer on the other machine), and passes this to the layer below for further processing.

At the sending station, this information is passed down until it reaches the physical layer. At this layer, the material is transmitted over an electrical or optical connection as a bit sequence. At the receiving station, the bit sequence is converted to bytes and is passed up the layers.

As it reaches each layer on the receiving machine, the layer removes the material included for the layer, takes whatever actions are appropriate for the message and the request, and then passes the stripped packet on to the next higher layer.

The header information that is added and stripped is known as the PCI (Protocol Control Information) component. Depending on the protocols involved, this may contain information such as source and destination addresses and control settings.

Each layer adds its own PCI as the packet is passed down to the layer. By the time a packet from an application reaches the data-link layer, it will have five PCIs attached: from the application, presentation, session, transport, and network layers.

In summary, the following is added and created at each layer:

APCI + data = APDU

PPCI + APDU = PPDU

SPCI + PPDU = SPDU

TPCI + SPDU = TPDU

NPCI + TPDU = NPDU

DPCI + NPDU = DPDU

→ *See Also* End System (ES); Intermediate System (IS); Network Management

OS Kernel

The core portion of an operating system. The kernel provides the most essential and basic system services (such as process and memory management).

OSME (Open Systems Message Exchange)

OSME refers to an IBM application for exchanging X.400 messages.

OSPF (Open Shortest Path First) Protocol

→ *See* Protocol, OSPF (Open Shortest Path First)

OSTC (Open System Testing Consortium)

A European consortium that developed a suite for testing conformance to the 1984 ITU X.400 series of recommendations about MHS (Message Handling System). This suite is used, for example, in the United States to assess conformance to the MHS requirements for GOSIP (Government Open Systems Interconnection Profile) certification. The Corporation for Open Systems (COS) in the US has developed a similar test suite.

OTDR (Optical Time Domain Reflectometer)

In fiber optics, an OTDR is a tool for testing the light signal. An OTDR can analyze a cable by sending out a light signal and then checking the amount and type of light reflected back.

Other Local Exchange Carrier (OLEC)

→ *See* CLEC (Competitive Local Exchange Carrier)

0

Out-of-Band Communication

A type of communication that uses frequencies outside the range being used for data or message communication. Because it does not use the frequency range in which the actual communication is taking place, out-of-band communication does not eat up bandwidth. Out-of-band communication is generally done for diagnostic or management purposes. This is in contrast to in-band communication, which includes its control and diagnostic signals in the communication frequency range, thereby taking bandwidth from the information or voice being transmitted.

Output Feedback (OFB)

→ *See* OFB (Output Feedback)

Overhead Bit

Overhead bits are transmission elements that are used by a network for routing or other purposes. Overhead bits can be used to provide such things as congestion indicators, addresses, TTL (Time to Live) indicators, and so forth.

P

PABX (Private Automatic Branch Exchange)

A telephone exchange that provides automatic switching and other communication capabilities. Since almost all exchanges are automatic these days, the term has come to be used almost synonymously with PBX (Private Branch Exchange).

PAC (Privilege Attribute Certificate)

In a login service, a note given to a user by the privilege service. This certificate, which cannot be forged, specifies the privileges accorded to the certificate's holder. When a user wants to access an application or a service, the PAC is checked to determine whether the user should be given the requested access.

PACE (Priority Access Control Enabled)

A proprietary variant of the Ethernet architecture developed by 3Com and collaborators for transmitting time-sensitive data, such as digitized video or audio, over Ethernet networks.

The strategy behind PACE is to prioritize the materials being transmitted, giving highest priority to data that must be sent at a constant rate to be comprehensible.

→ *Compare* isoENET

Pacing

In communications, the temporary use of a lower transmission speed. For example, pacing may be used to give the receiver time to catch up and process the data that has already been sent.

Packet

A packet is a well-defined block of bytes, which consists of header, data, and trailer. In a layered network architecture, packets created at one level may be inserted into another header/trailer envelope at a lower level.

Packets can be transmitted across networks or over telephone lines. In fact, network protocols and several communications protocols use packet switching to establish a connection and route information.

The format of a packet depends on the protocol that creates the packet. Various communications standards and protocols use special-purpose or specially defined packets to control or monitor a communications session. For example, the X.25 standard uses diagnostic, call clear, and reset packets (among others), as well as data packets.

Packets are sometimes also known as frames, although that term originally referred specifically to a packet at the Data-Link layer in the OSI reference model.

Packet Assembler/Disassembler (PAD)

→ *See* PAD (Packet Assembler/Disassembler)

Packet, Dribble

A packet that ends on an odd byte.

Packet, Jabber

A meaningless transmission generated by a network node because of a network malfunction, such as a faulty transceiver or other error. A jabber packet is larger than the maximum size (1518 bytes for Ethernet) and contains a bad CRC (Cyclic Redundancy Check) value. In contrast, long frames exceed the maximum frame length, but have a valid CRC value.

Packet, Ping

In an Ethernet network, a diagnostic packet sent by the NODEVIEW (or SERVERVU) applications in Novell's LANalyzer. The packet is used to test whether workstations or servers on the network are working correctly (are capable of receiving packets).

Packet Radio Network

A network which uses radio waves to transmit packets. Timing considerations aside, this approach may be the most plausible for long-distance wireless communications.

Packet Receive Buffer

RAM (random-access memory) set aside on a file server for holding packets temporarily, until they can be processed by the server or sent onto the network. The RAM is allocated as a number of buffers, each of a predetermined size. This is also known as a routing buffer or a communication buffer.

Packet, Runt

A packet with too few bits. Compare this with a dribble packet, which is a packet that ends on an odd byte.

Packet Switching

Packet switching is a transmission method in which packets are sent across a shared medium from source to destination. The transmission may use any available path, or circuit, and the circuit is available as soon as the packet has been sent. The next packet in the transmission may take a different path.

With packet switching, multiple packets from the same transmission can be on their way to the destination at the same time. Because of the switching, the packets may not all take the same paths, and they may not arrive in the order in which they were sent.

The X.25 telecommunications standard uses packet switching, as do many local and wide area networks.

→ **Compare** Circuit Switching; Message Switching

Packet-Switching Service

Any of several commercial enterprises that offer packet-switching capabilities to subscribers. CompuServe, SprintNet, and Tymnet are a few of the available services.

Packet Switch Node (PSN)

→ **See** PSN (Packet Switch Node)

PAD (Packet Assembler/ Disassembler)

A hardware or software component that mediates between a packet-switching network and a PC or other asynchronous device (such as a bridge or router). For example, PADs are essential components of an X.25 connection.

The PAD's function is to assemble the PC's data into packets suitable for transmission on the network, and to disassemble packets received from the network into a form suitable for the application running on the PC. The PAD can also create certain predefined administrative packets, such as call request and call clear in an X.25 network.

Paging

Paging is a memory-allocation strategy that effectively increases memory or allows more flexible use of available memory. A page is a contiguous chunk of memory of predefined size. Pages may be allocated as needed, usually in some area of RAM (random-access memory), such as the upper memory area between 640KB and 1MB. The original location of a page's contents may vary, depending on implementation.

The details of paging strategies can differ quite drastically. For example, a common use of paging is to create virtual memory on disk. When portions of working memory need to be removed temporarily, those portions can be stored on disk to make room.

In contrast, Novell's NetWare assigns 4KB memory pages to processes for use as needed. Page tables map between the physical memory associated with the page and the logical address space (for the process) provided by the pages.

PAM (Pulse Amplitude Modulation)

PAM is a method for representing a continuous analog signal by taking a sufficient number of discrete samples. While the information is still in analog form, the individual samples can be multiplexed over the same line with comparable samples from other signals.

PAM is not a true digital switching system, so there are limits to the fidelity with which signal samples can be multiplexed. However, it can be used as a first step in a more stable encoding strategy—known as

Pulse Code Modulation (PCM)—that truly does convert an analog signal to a digital form.

For PCM, the first step is to get an analog signal sample through PAM. After getting the sample, PCM assigns it a digital value based on the analog sample's value. Once quantized in this way, the digital value can be sent—instead of the actual analog sample. The digital value can be transmitted with much less loss and a lower error rate than is likely when sending an analog signal.

PAP (Password Authentication Protocol)

→ **See** Protocol, PAP (Password Authentication Protocol)

Parameter

A variable that can be assigned a value in order to change a configuration or to provide input for an instruction. In most instances, a parameter will have or get a default value if neither the user nor the application specify such a value.

Parameter RAM (PRAM)

→ **See** PRAM (Parameter RAM)

Parity

An error-detection method in which an extra bit is added at regular locations in a serial transmission (for example, after seven or eight data bits). The value of the parity bit depends on the pattern of 0 and 1 values in the byte and on the type of parity being used. Parity is also known as Vertical Redundancy Checking (VRC).

→ **See Also** Error Detection and Correction

Parity, Block

A type of parity that is computed for each bit place value in a block of bytes. For example, after every 8 bytes, an additional byte is set. One of these extra bits corresponds to each place value for the preceding set of bytes. Block parity is also called Longitudinal Redundancy Checking (LRC).

→ **See Also** Error Detection and Correction

Partition, Disk

In hard disk storage, a partition is a logical division of a physical hard disk. Partitions may be created to divide a large storage region into smaller, more manageable regions, or to store different operating systems.

Disk partitions were essential in earlier versions of DOS, which could not support more than 32MB of storage on a single "disk." Partitions are still common on high-capacity hard disks, because the FAT (file allocation table) DOS uses to store file and directory information can hold only a limited number of entries.

Each FAT entry represents a single, contiguous region of storage, called a cluster, or allocation unit. For a given configuration, all clusters are the same size, which may be 2, 4, or 8KB, or even larger. Under DOS, the smallest unit of storage that can be allocated is a single cluster. This means that a file containing a single character will still need an entire cluster. Large clusters are wasteful if you have many small files. Since each partition gets its own FAT, breaking a large-capacity hard disk into multiple partitions can make storage more efficient, because smaller clusters can be used.

In Novell's NetWare, a partition is a logical subdivision of a server hard disk, or volume. For example, a NetWare server may have a DOS and a NetWare partition on the same hard disk.

Passband

In electrical transmissions, filters can be designed to block certain frequencies from getting through. A passband represents a frequency range that can pass through such a filter.

Passband Filter

In telephony and other contexts involving electrical signaling, a passband filter is used to block signals in predefined frequency ranges. The frequencies outside the blocked ranges are known as the passband, and they are allowed to pass through the filter. Thus, a passband filter blocks everything but the passband.

Passive Coupler

In fiber-optic communication, a coupler that simply splits a signal as requested, and passes the weakened signals on to all fibers. There is always signal loss with a passive coupler.

→ *See Also* Coupler, Fiber-Optic

Passive Hub

A component in low-impedance ARCnet networks. A passive hub merely serves as a wiring and relay center. It merely passes the signal on, without changing it in any way. Passive hubs do not require a power supply.

→ *See Also* ARCnet; Hub

Passive Interface

In a dynamic, or adaptive, routing context, a passive interface receives updates for routing tables, but does not send updates of its own table. This is likely to be the case, for example, in a stub router—that is, a router connected to only one other router.

Passive Star

A network configuration in which the central node of a star topology passes a signal on, but does not process the signal in any way. This is in contrast to an active star configuration, in which signals are processed before being passed on.

→ *See Also* Topology, Star

Passive Star Coupler

A fiber-optic coupler (optical signal redirector) created by fusing multiple optical fibers together at their meeting point. This coupler serves as the center of a star configuration. This type of coupler is used for an optical (IEEE 802.4) Token Bus network that uses a passive star topology.

→ *See Also* Coupler, Fiber-Optic

Password

Many networks require users to enter a password as part of the login process, to verify that they are authorized to access the network. The characters in a password do not appear on the monitor as the user types them in, to keep the password from being observed by others.

Assigning Passwords

A password will generally be some letter or alphanumeric sequence. The network administrator usually assigns a password to a user when first creating that user's account. In most cases, the user should change the assigned password to one that he or she can remember easily. Only the user should know the password and be able to provide it during logging in.

Users can change their passwords when they wish, and should do so frequently. Some networks require users to change their passwords periodically. Passwords should not be based on letters or numbers significant in the user's life (address, birthday, nickname, first and/or last name, and so on).

Dynamic Passwords

Dynamic passwords provide a special type of password scheme in which a user's password is changed every time the user logs in to a network. In this type of system, the user uses a special device, called a Remote Password Generator (RPG), to generate a new password. When the user wants to log in to the network, the network responds with a special number, which the user must type into the RPG, together with the user's own personal identification number (PIN). The RPG then generates the password to use for the session.

Networks that use dynamic passwords need special software to generate the numbers used for generating the passwords. Each user must be provided with an RPG.

→ *Broader Category* Security

→ *Related article* Authentication

Password Authentication Protocol (PAP)

→ *See* Protocol, PAP (Password Authentication Protocol)

Patch Cable

Cable used to connect two hubs (or MAUs). IBM Type 1 or Type 6 patch cables can be used for Token Ring networks. These cables will have special IBM data connectors at each end.

→ *See Also* Cable

Patch Panel

A centralized wiring location in which twisted-pair or coaxial cables can be interconnected without connecting the cable to punch-down blocks. Using a patch cord, the cable is plugged into a modular outlet, which is linked to the desired location. This makes it easier to switch connections, in order to test or work around certain circuits.

Path Information Unit (PIU)

→ *See* PIU (Path Information Unit)

Path Vector Algorithm

The path vector algorithm is used in the BGP (border gateway protocol) routing protocol. The algorithm enables routers to process router connections and to exchange information about links more efficiently, and also to prevent loops from being introduced into routing computations.

PathWorks

A network operating system (NOS) from Digital Equipment Corporation (DEC). DEC's PathWorks is based on Microsoft's LAN Manager.

Payload

In ATM network terminology, the payload is the data portion of an ATM cell, or packet. This cell consists of a five-octet header and a 48-octet payload. More generally, payload refers to the data portion of a packet (for example, of an IP packet, or datagram).

PBX (Private Branch Exchange)

A telephone switching system configured for communications in a private network, but with possible access to a public telephone system. A PBX may use analog or digital signaling, and the switching may be done automatically or manually (for example, through an operator).

PC (Physical Contact)

A term applied to indicate that the cable or fiber elements involved in a connection are actually touching. The term is used mainly in connection with optical fiber.

PCI (Peripheral Component Interconnect)

PCI is a local-bus design from Intel. A local bus is one that is connected directly to the central processing unit (CPU).

The PCI design supports 64-bit data paths, arbitrated bus mastering (interrupt handling based on priority levels), and secondary caches to help speed up operations. The PCI bus is designed to accommodate increases in processor speeds.

This bus design is one of two main candidates to replace ISA and EISA as the next PC bus standard. The other contender is the VL (VESA local) bus design.

PCI (Protocol Control Information)

In the OSI reference model, protocol-dependent information added to a data packet before the packet is passed to a lower layer for further processing.

→ See Also OSI Reference Model

PCI-X (Peripheral Component Interconnect-X)

PCI-X is a bus design that provides a faster I/O technology and better performance than the PCI (Peripheral Component Interconnect) bus design that dominates today's PC hardware. PCI-X is championed by Compaq, Hewlett-Packard, and IBM, and it is basically an extension of existing PCI technology, which is largely an Intel creation. However, PCI-X promises considerable performance improvements over current standards.

The current PCI bus is a 32-bit design, uses a 33MHz clock speed, and can move data at 132MBps. In contrast, PCI-X will use a 64-bit bus design, running at 133MHz, and will deliver a throughput of about 1GBps.

Although PCI-X products should be available by the time you read this, it's unclear how long PCI-X is expected to serve as the I/O standard. Most experts expect the PCI-X architecture to be replaced by one of two even higher-speed technologies that will not be available until about 2001 at the earliest. These are NGIO (for next generation I/O) and Future I/O. The former is largely an Intel product, but already has the support of over 70 vendors. It promises speeds of up to 2.5GBps in each direction. Future I/O is being designed by a consortium consisting of the vendors who have created PCI-X, as well as several networking hardware vendors such as Cisco and 3Com. Future I/O claims it will be able to support a 10GBps throughput (but will require 40 wires to do this).

PCM (Pulse Code Modulation)

PCM is a technique for converting an analog signal into digital form. Once converted, the information in the original signal can be transmitted in digital form, often at very high rates of speed.

Getting the analog information into a digital form is a two-step process:

PAM (Pulse Amplitude Modulation) In the first phase, the continuous analog signal is sampled by taking discrete slices of the signal at a sufficiently high rate. These samples are analog representations of the signal at the moments when the samples were taken.

Quantization In the second phase, a digital value is assigned to each sample. The assigned value will be based on and will represent the sample's analog value.

Once in digital form, the information from the original analog signal can be multiplexed over digital (or analog) transmission lines.

→ *See Also* PAM (Pulse Amplitude Modulation)

PCMCIA (Personal Computer Memory Card International Association)

PCMCIA is an I/O standard that supports services or devices provided on boards the size of a credit card. PCMCIA specifies a 68-pin connection, which is used for all three of the cards described below. Originally developed for use in palmtop computers, the PCMCIA is being included in printers, laptops, and even larger computers.

The PCMCIA version 1.0 specifications were released in 1990. These support Type I cards, which are 3.3 millimeters (mm) thick, and which can provide volatile or nonvolatile storage (RAM, ROM, or flash memory).

The PCMCIA version 2.01 specifications were released in 1991. These support Type II cards, which are 5 mm thick, and which can be network interface cards (NICs), fax/modem cards, and so on. These also support a 10.5 mm thick Type III card. This card can actually provide a miniature hard drive. Type III cards are also used for wireless networks.

Socket Services software provides a standard interface to PCMCIA hardware, and Card Services software coordinates access to the actual cards. In theory, up to 4080 cards can be supported on a single computer.

PCMCIA Modem

A modem on a Type II PCMCIA card.

PCR (Peak Cell Rate)

In an ATM (Asynchronous Transfer Mode) networking architecture, the PCR is a parameter indicating the maximum traffic rate (in cells per second) that a particular data source on the network can sustain. The PCR is specified by a value indicating the maximum acceptable explicit rate (ER) in the Resource Management (RM) cell header. The PCR can be computed by taking the reciprocal of the minimum time between cells over the specified virtual connection (VC).

→ *Compare* SCR (Sustainable Cell Rate)

PCS (Personal Communications Services)

In telecommunications, a term used to describe the intended use for three sections of the electromagnetic spectrum that the FCC (Federal Communications Commission) is setting aside for unrestricted use by individuals and organizations.

In PCS, each subscriber will get a Personal Telephone Number (PTN) through which that person can be reached no matter where they might be. The PTN will be stored in a Signaling System 7 (SS7) database, which keeps track of where the PTN can be found at any time. When a call arrives for a particular PTN, an Artificial Intelligence Network (AIN) associated with the database will determine where the PTN is currently located, and will route the call appropriately.

A particular variant of PCS—PCS 1900—uses radio frequencies in the 1900MHz range. PCS 1900 systems can use either Code Division Multiple Access (CDMA) or Time Division Multiple Access (TDMA) technology.

PCS (Plastic-Clad Silica)

A type of optical fiber, with a glass core and plastic cladding. The performance of such fiber is inferior to all-glass fiber.

→ *See Also* Cable, Fiber-Optic

PDAU (Physical Delivery Access Unit)

In the 1988 version of the CCITT's X.400 Message Handling System (MHS), an application process that provides a letter mail service with access to a Message Transfer System (MTS). The MTS can deliver an image of the letter to any location accessible through the MHS.

→ *See Also* X.400

PDC (Primary Domain Controller)

In the Windows NT domain model, the PDC is in charge of the Security Accounts Manager (SAM), which contains the directory database used for managing the accounts for the entire domain. (A synchronized copy of the SAM is also kept on the Backup Domain Controller, or BDC). Only the PDC can make changes in the SAM.

Both the PDC and the BDC have global directory databases. In contrast, a member server—which has only a local directory database—does not need to handle the administrative tasks, and so is free to function as an application or other type of server.

→ *See Also* BDC (Backup Domain Controller)

PDH (Plesiochronous Digital Hierarchy)

The levels in the ITU's PDH correspond to those in the digital signal (or service) hierarchy (DS-0, DS-1, and so forth). The PDH was originally developed for carrying digitized voice over twisted-pair wire.

→ *See Also* DS (Digital Service)

PDN (Public Data Network)

In communications, a PDN is a circuit- or packet-switched network that is available to the public and that can transmit data in digital form.

A PDN provider is a company that provides access to a PDN, and that provides any of X.25, frame relay, or cell relay (ATM) services.

Access to a PDN generally includes a guaranteed bandwidth, known as the Committed Information Rate (CIR). Costs for the access depend on the guaranteed rate. PDN providers differ in how they charge for temporary increases in required bandwidth (known as surges). Some use the amount of overrun; others use the surge duration.

PDS (Premises Distribution System)

A cabling system that covers an entire building or campus. Also, the name of a premises wiring system from AT&T.

PDS (Processor-Direct Slots)

In the Macintosh environment, a general-purpose expansion slot. A PDS card is hardware-specific because the card is connected directly to the computer's processor, rather than being connected indirectly via a bus. The other expansion architecture used in Macintoshes is the NuBus.

PDU (Protocol Data Unit)

In the OSI reference model, a packet. Specifically, a PDU is a packet created at a particular layer in an open system. The PDU is used to communicate with the same layer on another machine.

→ *See* OSI Reference Model

PDU Lifetime

A value that indicates the number of routers a PDU (protocol data unit) can use before it must reach its destination or be discarded. Such a pruning measure is necessary to keep packets (PDUs) from traveling around and around on the network.

Peak Cell Rate (PCR)

→ *See* PCR (Peak Cell Rate)

Peak Load

For a network, the maximum load that can be (or is) placed on a network. This value may be expressed in any of several performance measures, including transactions, packets, or bits per second.

Peer

In communications, a device that is considered equal to another device with respect to communication capabilities.

Peer Hub

A hub that is implemented on a card that plugs into an expansion slot in a PC. A peer hub can use the computer's power supply. (The computer's power supply should be adequate, but is not guaranteed to be so.)

→ *See Also* Hub

Peer Layers

In a layered network architecture, corresponding layers on two stations. Communication between nodes at a particular layer uses a protocol supported at that layer. For example, nodes on a Novell NetWare network could communicate with each other at the Transport layer by using the SPX protocol.

PEM (Privacy Enhanced Mail)

PEM is one of the two major enhancements to the Internet mail message format defined in RFC 822. PEM provides mechanisms for encrypting, signing, and authenticating messages so that users can send e-mail that is reasonably secure against prying eyes, modems, or daemons.

PEM provides any or all of four types of "privacy enhancement services:"

Message confidentiality: by encrypting the message. PEM supports either public-key (asymmetric) or secret-key (symmetric) encryption. The data encryption key (DEK) that provides the basis for the encryption is, itself, encrypted during transmission. The DEK is encrypted using an interchange key (IK). DEKs may be generated by the appropriate user agent (UA) or obtained from a key distribution center.

Authentication of sender: by using, e.g., a digital signature

Non-repudiation of message origin: provided public key encryption methods are being used

Content integrity: when sending a message that includes a digital signature and an MIC (Message Integrity Check): to help determine whether there has been any tampering

PEM Messages

PEM messages are actually encapsulated in ordinary mail messages. The beginning of the PEM portion is indicated by a specific string. PEM message types are distinguished from each other by values in the message's PEM header. The following three types of messages are defined:

- ENCRYPTED, which means that all four PEM services have been implemented—that is, confidentiality, authentication, data integrity, and (if appropriate) non-repudiation.

- MIC-ONLY, which means that authentication, data integrity, and (if appropriate) non-repudiation are in effect. The message is still encoded in order to protect it from alteration by message transfer agents (MTAs) along the way. The encoding makes the message unreadable by user agents (UAs) that comply with the RFC

822 encoding format, but that are not PEM-compliant.

- MIC-CLEAR, which is like MIC-ONLY except that the message is not encoded. Such messages can be read by UAs that are RFC 822-compliant but not PEM-compliant.

To ensure everything will work, PEM takes the following steps:

- Transforms the data into a version that is so vanilla-flavored it won't crash anyone en route to the destination.

- Takes all necessary steps to get an encryption key (the DEK) for the recipient. The sender must first get a Certificate from a Certification Authority (CA) for each recipient using a public key algorithm for encryption. The sender checks the Certificate to make sure that its validity period has not expired, and also to make sure that the Certificate is not on a Certificate Revocation List (CRL), for example, because it has been reported stolen or compromised. The sender also needs to check the authenticity of the CA. With the public key found in the certificate, the sender encrypts the DEK.

- Uses the DEK to encrypt the message.

- Encapsulates the PEM message inside an ordinary mail message. The encrypted material is between lines that read "---BEGIN PRIVACY-ENHANCED MESSAGE---" at the start, and "---END PRIVACY-ENHANCED MESSAGE---" at the end. "Encapsulated PEM message" shows this. This encapsulation helps ensure that the encrypted message won't choke any device at an intermediate location. PEM is designed as an end-to-end service. As a well-behaved one, the encapsulation helps keep the encrypted material away from address checkers, such as routers or bridges. Since no intermediate node needs to fiddle with the encrypted portion, PEM can "ensure" content integrity.

For several reasons, PEM has not caught on as quickly as its developers hoped. One of these is the current incompatibility between PEM and MIME (Multipurpose Internet Mail Extensions), which is the other major enhancement of the RFC 822 format.

→ *Primary Sources* Various aspects and issues related to PEM are covered in RFCs 1421 through 1424.

→ *Compare* PGP (Pretty Good Privacy)

RFC 822 Message

RFC 822 Header

To:
From:
Subject:

RFC 822 Body

Blah, Blah, Blah

...

It's supposed to be a secret, but ...

Encapsulated PEM package

-----BEGIN PRIVACY-ENHANCED MESSAGE-----

PEM Header

Proc-type : 4, ENCRYPTED
Content-Domain: RFC822
...
...

PEM message body

... RW5jcnpwdGVkIFRleHRz ...
... Enc ryp ted Te xts ...

-----END PRIVACY-ENHANCED MESSAGE-----

Now remember, PEM's the word...

ENCAPSULATED PEM MESSAGE

PerfectOffice

PerfectOffice and PerfectOffice Professional were Novell's entries in the integrated office suite for Windows sweepstakes. When Novell sold this package to Corel Systems, the core package was renamed for its main product: WordPerfect Suite.

The following entries describe the features and components of PerfectOffice before it became WordPerfect Suite.

Common Features

The features and tools common to the various applications in PerfectOffice helped give the package its integrated feel. Some of the features were shared by all the applications; others were common to only some of them. For those of you who still have Perfect Office or would like to see the components of Perfect Office, see the following.

DAD (Desktop Application Director) This is the suite's control center, since all the Applications in PerfectOffice can be launched from here. DAD has three customizable toolbars: PerfectOffice, Control Panel, and Data Sharing. You can add new programs to the DAD bar, and you can also create a DAD bar for each of your program groups.

Common interface This helps make it easier to work within the different applications. As far as possible, applications use the same interface elements and provide at least the same general layout. The toolbar and other bars also use the same elements wherever possible, and use the same icons when appropriate.

Coaches These are interactive tutorials on specific tasks, resources, or topics. For example, there are WordPerfect coaches to help out with Columns, Graphics, and Footnotes; a Paradox coach provides a quick overview of Paradox. All the applications except Envoy and AppWare support coaches, and all have at least one coach for the application.

Experts Experts are applets that help you perform an entire task. For example, there is a Create Letter expert in WordPerfect; the Slide Show Expert in Presentation provides help with a central task for this application. WordPerfect and Presentation also work with some special experts—Upgrade Experts—which will take a user through the task of upgrading from an earlier version of the software or from a competitor's product.

QuickTasks These provide another way to get the program to do your work for you. Any of the 60+ QuickTasks will carry out the task for which it has been defined. You can invoke a QuickTask from within an application or from the PerfectOffice desktop. That is, you don't need to be in any of the applications to invoke a QuickTask. When you invoke one, you'll need to provide some information and answer some questions. The QuickTask will then go off and complete the task—for example, creating a fax, checking mail, scheduling an appointment—on its own. The QuickTask can even start multiple applications while doing its work. So with a few keystrokes and a few items of information, you can Create a Newsletter or a Budget or you can compute a loan amortization. Other predefined QuickTasks include Find File, Create Calendar, Create Agenda, Send File, Finish Document, etc. You can also define your own QuickTasks with the help of a QuickTask Expert! You can even create two special QuickTasks: "start my day" and "end my day." You could define these to execute your startup and shutdown procedures, for example. These QuickTasks can run any documents, macros, or programs you want, and in whatever order you want.

QuickFiles This component can be used in place of the Windows File Manager for managing files and directories. With QuickFiles you can launch programs, use QuickFinder to look for files based on word patterns in the name or contents, and create an index of files you need often.

QuickRun and QuickOpen These utilities keep track of programs and files used recently. When you call these utilities, you'll get a list of the last 10 programs (for QuickRun) or files (for Quick-Open) used. You can launch any of these with a click of the mouse. You must be running DAD to use these utilities.

"How Do I ..." Help This part of the online help provides information on how to accomplish various tasks. This focus on tasks and how to accomplish them is consistent with the use of Experts and Coaches, and also with the Quick-xxx (QuickRun, QuickOpen, etc) series of capabilities built into PerfectOffice.

Drawing Tools Several of the PerfectOffice applications have their own drawing tools. Of these, the tool included with Presentations has the most features and capabilities. This tool is accessible from any of the other applications in PerfectOffice and from any program that can create OLE objects. You can draw using either vectors or bitmaps.

PerfectOffice Features and Components

When it was available, version 3.0 of the Perfect-Office Professional suite included the following programs:

- QuattroPro 6.0 (spreadsheet)
- WordPerfect 6.1 (word processor)
- Envoy 1.0a (document manager)
- Presentations 3.0 (slide show and presentation graphics)
- InfoCentral 1.1 (information manager)
- Paradox 5.0 (database management system)
- AppWare 1.1 (visual application development tools)

The regular version of PerfectOffice had all the applications except Paradox and AppWare.

QuattroPro

QuattroPro 6.0 is the spreadsheet package. In addition to the "standard" number crunching capabilities for a spreadsheet program—entering, manipulating, and analyzing rows and columns of values—QuattroPro had some features that make it both easier to use and more powerful than your run-of-the-mill spreadsheet program.

QuattroPro included extensive help about the program, its commands, and objects. The application also included Coaches and Experts, both of which provided help accomplishing tasks. QuattroPro included over a dozen preprogrammed QuickTasks as well as predefined templates (spreadsheet formats). Users could modify both QuickTasks and templates to suit their needs. In addition, users could edit the properties of QuattroPro objects. Objects included spreadsheet cells or blocks, notebook pages, an entire notebook, or even the entire application. The ObjectInspector let you edit object properties.

WordPerfect

WordPerfect 6.1 is the suite's word processing program. This widely used and well-respected application is powerful, flexible, and comes with resources to make the user's life simpler and more productive. WordPerfect includes a tutorial and an Upgrade Expert to help make it easier to get started.

Once you're working, WordPerfect's QuickCorrect and QuickSelect features make your editing job much easier. With QuickCorrect, you can have the program automatically correct certain kinds of errors—for example, MUltiple Capitals or Capitalizing first letters of each sentence, etc.

QuickSelect makes it easy to mark portions of text—for example, for cutting and pasting. With QuickSelect, you can specify easily whether you want to work with letters, words, sentences, or paragraphs.

Experts such as Make It Fit (for forms) and Table (for document tables), templates such as Calendar, and coaches such as Bookmarks or Endnotes make word processing much easier.

Envoy

Envoy 1.0a is a document manager. This means Envoy can help you view documents, annotate them if you want, and then distribute them on a network. For example, you can create a report or article with WordPerfect and use Envoy to distribute it electronically for comment. Your readers can use Envoy to view the file and to comment on it. Comments can take any of several handy forms: highlighting text, inserting "sticky" notes or bookmarks, using OLE to embed other material, or creating hyperlinks between two sections of the document. After they've gotten their bytes in, your readers can spit the document right back at you—electronically, of course.

Presentations

Presentations 3.0 enables you to create and present slide shows—even interactive ones. You begin with masters, which are predesigned slides. By beginning with a master, it ensures that your slides are consistent with respect to backgrounds, colors, and fonts. Individual slides are created by specifying variations on template slides. Templates for various types of slides—titles, bullet lists, organizational charts, etc.—are available.

Presentations also includes an Expert to help you create the slide show, if you wish. Once you have designed and created the basic slide show, there are various resources and coaches available for editing and revising the slides, and for creating the transitions between slides. You can run your slide show when done, or you can print the slides to a file or printer.

Like WordPerfect, Presentations included an Upgrade Expert to help you get started with Presentations 3.0, if you've come from an earlier version or if you've defected from a competitor's presentation graphics package. One available QuickTask lets you create a slide show from a WordPerfect outline.

Presentations offers several views on the slides in a collection:

- Slide Editor View, in which slides appear in WYSIWYG (What-You-See-Is-What-You-Get)

format. This is the view for doing detailed editing.

- Slide List View, in which you get a list of all the slides, along with information about each slide. This view provides an administrative perspective, showing the details in verbal form.

- Outline View, in which you see just the text of the presentation, in outline form. This view lets you evaluate the clarity and coherence of your ideas and their presentation.

- Slide Sorter View, in which you see thumbnails of each slide. This view is helpful for evaluating the sequence, and for possibly rearranging the order of the slides.

Presentations allows you to add speaker notes to a presentation. These elements do not appear on the slides, but you could print out a version for yourself before you begin the show. When you print this, you get a small image of the slide, with the speaker notes alongside it.

InfoCentral

InfoCentral 1.1 lets you keep track of and make connections between files, and even between items within those files. The elements being organized are known as objects. An object can be anything that has a name, which leaves it pretty open-ended. Objects can be linked with each other by specifying a connection between them. This connection indicates the relationship between the objects.

Information about objects and connections is stored in an iBase (for information base) file. Within InfoCentral, it's easy to see, modify, or delete connections, and it's easy to add, view, edit, or delete objects. InfoCentral's FastFind lets you search for an item of information quickly and easily through a dialog box.

InfoCentral has half a dozen QuickTasks (including Schedule Appointment in InfoCentral and Create an InfoCentral phone list in WordPerfect) and three coaches (for QuickStart, FastFind, and Import) associated with it. This information manager also includes a QuickTour to provide an overview of the application.

Paradox

Paradox 5.0 is a Relational Database Management System (RDBMS). The "database management" part means that Paradox allow you to store, modify, and retrieve information. The "relational database" part says that this information's format and organization will be influenced (or constrained) by a particular model of how information should be organized.

In a relational database, data is organized into tables. Each row is a record—for example, a person, company, book. The database is made up of the information in a collection of such records.

The information consists of values for some or all of the table's columns. Each column is a field—for example, last name, company name, or title. It's assumed that the fields are meaningful for the types of records involved. There must also be some field or combination of fields that produces a unique value for every record. This simple or composite field is known as the key for the table. The key is used to sort and store the elements of a table.

An RDBMS lets you get information you specify from the database. If information about the same records appears in different tables, Paradox can merge the fields (in pretty much any combination) and provide information about just the fields and records you want. The RDBMS can retrieve the appropriate records, and can get the requested fields from whichever table contains them.

To accomplish things in Paradox, you can manipulate objects of various sorts. Paradox lets you create and use several types of objects, including

- Tables that contain actual data.

- Forms that you can use to display and enter data.

- Reports that can display selected data in a specified format.

- Queries, which enable you to retrieve data according to the query. Query by example (QBE) is used in Paradox.

- Scripts, which carry out specified actions under the appropriate conditions. Paradox's Object-PAL language is used to create script files.

- SQL (Structured Query Language) files, which enable you to write code using SQL.

- Libraries, which serve as repositories for code segments, and from which required functions or objects can be borrowed.

- Project Viewer, which provides a more graphical interface for users.

As is true of the other applications, Paradox includes several coaches and experts to help you master important tasks and to get a better overview of the Paradox environment.

AppWare

AppWare 1.1 lets you create programs without programming. By combining and manipulating any of a few dozen objects, and by specifying the behavior of these objects under various conditions, you provided AppWare with enough information to figure out how to generate the code to carry out your instructions.

The objects you manipulate are actually AppWare Loadable Modules (ALMs)—that is, pre-existing chunks of code. AppWare uses the AppWare Bus (which is included) to connect the modules you've specified and to compile them into an executable program. The AppWare Bus is essentially an engine that manages and coordinates the component ALMs.

The AppWare component in PerfectOffice comes with several ALMs which, together, contain hundreds of objects and functions. Other special-purpose ALMs are also available from third-party sources. The AppWare ALMs can be grouped into the following:

- Essentials, which contains objects and functions related to the Windows environment—for example, objects related to windows, menus, dialog boxes, etc. This ALM collection also contains general programming constructs such as arrays and subroutines.

- Multimedia, which provides objects and functions for handling video and sound.

- Communications, which provides objects and functions for serial connection and communication, file transfers, and terminal emulation.

- Application Linking, which provides the elements required for communications between objects or processes. Support for data exchange methods such as OLE and DDE are included in this group of ALMs.

AppWare also includes ALM Builder resources for creating new ALMs. Once created, you can use these ALMs along with the others. Be sure any sort of program or module is tested thoroughly before you start using it in other work.

Data Exchange

PerfectOffice offers several ways for applications and users to exchange data or other material. For communications between applications, PerfectOffice offers the tried, sometimes trying, and much derided Clipboard. In addition, PerfectOffice supports OLE (Object Linking and Embedding), which provides a much more sophisticated way to link an element into another one. By linking rather than copying, the insert can be updated if the original changes.

For communications between coworkers, Perfect-Office has Envoy, which could be used as an electronic distribution center. Similarly, OBEX (Object Exchange) offers a publish-and-subscribe solution. Users with information to share can publish it; anyone interested can subscribe to the publication. Subscribers were updated whenever there is a new version of the publication.

Performance Management

Performance management is one of five OSI network management domains specified by the ISO

and CCITT. This domain is concerned with the following:

- Monitoring the day-to-day network activity.

- Gathering and logging data based on this activity, such as utilization, throughput, and delay values.

- Storing performance data as historical archives, to serve as a database for planning network optimization and expansion.

- Analyzing performance data to identify actual and potential bottlenecks.

- Changing configuration settings in order to help optimize network performance.

The first two points address the data-collection capabilities expected of a performance-management package. The next two points concern data-analysis capabilities that are used to plan interventions. The last point relates to the control that such a package can exert to change a network's performance. Sophisticated packages can exert control directly; simpler packages require the system administrator to make the actual changes.

Data Gathering

Data is generally gathered by agents, which are associated with particular devices or network segments. These components are designed to monitor their devices, and to store or send the observed values to a database from which the network management component can get the information it needs.

Data pertaining to network performance must be gathered over time, and time must be taken into account when examining the information provided. Both the nature and level of network activity change over time, and some data will be tied to specific times. For example, on many networks, the activity level has peaks near the beginning and end of the work day, because those are the times when people log in and out.

Data-Gathering Methods

There are many ways in which data can be gathered, and careful thought must be given to selecting the most appropriate methods for your needs. For example, data collection may use one of the following methods

- In a snapshot approach, values are taken at a single instant in time. This approach is used most commonly when troubleshooting or when gathering "quick and dirty" statistics.

- In a statistical approach, the management component looks at network activity at periodic or random intervals. For example, data may be gathered for 30-second periods every 5 minutes.

- In an exhaustive approach, the network's activity is monitored constantly.

For more reliable, long-term performance information, a statistical or exhaustive approach is needed. Exhaustive data gathering produces more reliable data, but requires a larger chunk of the network's bandwidth. With statistical data gathering, more bandwidth is available for transmitting network material but less reliable performance data will be collected.

When you are gathering statistical performance data, it is important to examine assumptions about the data. In particular, many analysis techniques require that sample data points be independent of each other.

Type of Performance Data

The following types of data can be gathered easily and used to help improve network performance:

- Availability, which indicates the amount or proportion of the time that a device or other network object (such as a program or circuit) is available.

- Workload, which can indicate how close to capacity your network is operating. Workload may change quite drastically as a function of time. For example, a network may have a generally low workload, but may reach capacity at certain times of day.

- Response, or responsivity, which provides a measure of how quickly the network can respond to requests. In general, as workload goes up, responsivity goes down.

- Throughput, which provides a measure of how much information (or, at least, how many bytes) can get across the network. Throughput can be measured in various ways, such as by the number of packets or number of sessions.

- Errors, or failed transmissions, which provide a measure of noise and/or competition on the network. For example, if lots of nodes are clamoring to get transmission rights in an Ethernet network, a significant part of a network's traffic may be error or busy signals. The complement of error measures concern transmission accuracy; that is, the amount or proportion of time that no errors occur in a transmission.

Many performance indicators may be viewed from multiple perspectives and using different measures. Commonly used measures include frequency, relative frequency, duration, or delay. Note that the values on such measures may depend on more than just network activity; for example, the values may also depend on the processing power of the device in question.

For certain types of performance analyses, a management program may actually generate dummy network traffic in order to observe the effects of various levels of network activity on performance indicators.

NETWORK AVERAGE RESPONSE TIMES

For some networks, the average response (how quickly the network responds to requests) may be slow but roughly constant; for other networks, there may be large variations in response time. In extreme cases, users may get dropped from the network if some protocol or device times out because the delay was too long.

Absolute response times depend strongly on the types of devices involved. For example, some types of communications may involve response times of 10 seconds or more—a value that is generally too long for meaningful real-time transactions, but that may be perfectly fine for automated activity. Other connections may require response times of less than a second in order to establish or maintain a connection.

Data Presentation

Depending on the management package and its capabilities, performance data may presented in text or graphics form. Graphics may be histograms or frequency polygons that present the information.

Data may be presented in real-time, using either raw or normalized values, or after the fact, in either raw or summary form. Various types of data analyses and transformations may also be supported. High-end tools allow a user (who has the appropriate permissions) to query the performance database, usually by using a standardized method such as SQL (Structured Query Language).

Some performance-monitoring packages may present data only if certain threshold values are being approached or exceeded, to warn the system administrator of a potential fault.

Data Analysis

Performance data can be used to fine-tune a network as well as to do troubleshooting. Different types of data analyses may be appropriate, depending on your goal. For example, comparisons over time can provide information that will help you allocate network resources more effectively. In contrast, to find a problem area in a network, you may want to compare performance data from different segments of the network.

Such analyses are not always easy, since you will often need to rely on indirect or inferred information. For example, response time bottlenecks may be difficult to measure because there are several places in which bottlenecks might arise.

Performance-Management Package Actions

If a performance indicator approaches or exceeds a threshold value, the performance-management package may take action. This action may be as simple as giving an alarm to call the indicator level to the system administrator's attention. At the other extreme, the management package may change one or more configuration settings. For example, the software may change settings in order to allocate more buffer space or more processing power to the bottleneck point.

In general, interventions and changes in configuration values are more likely to be made through the configuration management component.

→ **Broader Category** Network Management

→ **See Also** Accounting Management; Configuration Management; Fault Management; Security Management

Peripheral

Networks can provide multiple computers with shared access to various peripheral devices, such as modems, faxes, and printers. The table "Common Networking Peripherals" lists the devices commonly connected to networks.

Devices may be attached to the following:

- A file server, which provides access to the peripheral device as a secondary service.

- A workstation used as a special-purpose server specifically to provide access to the peripheral.

- A stand-alone server, such as a printer server or a network modem. These servers are not installed in a computer. Rather, they have their own processor and NIC (network interface card).

- The network, such as a printer with an NIC installed, so that the printer can become a network node and can, effectively, be its own server.

COMMON NETWORKING PERIPHERALS

Peripheral	Description
CD-ROM drive	Provides read-only access to the contents of a huge (660MB) storage area. Such drives are becoming increasingly important as vendors move their software and documentation to compact discs.
Fax machine	Provide fax transmission and reception capabilities for multiple stations. Depending on the particular model, the fax may be able to store faxes, send them to a printer or a print queue (for output as soon as possible), and print them.
Hard disk	Generally internal, and controlled by the file server. External hard disks may be attached to supplement storage capacities, particularly if there is no available drive bay in the server. RAID drive systems are a special type of external disk configuration, used to provide fault tolerance and additional data protection. RAID systems may contain up to five hard disks.
Modem	Provides access to telecommunications services by first converting digital signals to acoustic analog form (modulation), then transmitting this information over public or leased telephone lines.
Optical drive	Provides access to WORM (Write Once, Read Many) or EO (Erasable Optical) disks, which store information using light rather than electricity. Such drives may eventually replace tape drives as the backup medium of choice.
Printer	Provides a medium for hard copy output. Print jobs are queued by the print server, and are delivered to the printer whenever the printer is ready.
Tape drive	Provide a sequential access medium for storing data that will not need to be retrieved often. Because the tape cartridges can hold considerable storage (over 250MB), such drives are currently the medium of choice for backing up large hard disk systems.

For devices in which real-time response is not necessary, user requests for the peripheral device are generally queued up by the server. The requests are then processed as they are encountered in the queue.

Because certain services, such as printing, can demand frequent attention from the CPU (central processing unit), queues may slow down server performance considerably. In such cases, there are advantages to attaching the peripheral to a workstation or to a stand-alone server.

For devices such as tape drives for backups, in which power stability and line quality are essential, the main consideration may be to make sure the device is connected to a machine with a backup power supply or with a line conditioner and surge protector. Another way to ensure that a peripheral is adequately protected against electrical problems is to attach an appropriate protection device (such as a UPS) directly to the peripheral.

WHAT TO LOOK FOR IN A PERIPHERAL

It's important to keep sight of the fact that a peripheral device is being attached to a network, as opposed to being connected to a single-user machine. This fact may influence your product selection.

For example, peripherals that can get overworked (such as printers) will need to be able to handle the workload afforded by the users on a network. Don't try to get away with attaching a printer that's designed to print about 3000 pages a month to a network with 250 users. If you do, the printer isn't the only thing that's going to be feeling the heat.

Similarly, make sure peripherals on a network have a capacity or speed appropriate for the demands of the network. If you plan to attach a tape backup system to your network, and you hope to do automated backups, then you need to install a system whose tapes can fit the capacity of the hard disks you plan to back up.

Finally, make sure there's no license violation when using devices (such as CD-ROM drives) that may be running products with usage restrictions.

Peripheral Component Interconnect (PCI)

→ *See* PCI (Peripheral Component Interconnect)

Peripheral Component Interconnect-X (PCI-X)

→ *See* PCI-X (peripheral Component Inerconnect-X)

Peripheral Router

A router that serves primarily to connect a network to a larger internetwork. This is in contrast to a central router, which serves as a transfer point for multiple networks.

→ *See Also* Router

Permanent Virtual Circuit (PVC)

→ *See* PVC (Permanent Virtual Circuit)

Permissions

A term used to describe access rights, or privileges, in some networking environments or operating systems. For example, in AppleTalk networks, permissions specify file and folder access rights.

In Windows NT, two important classes of permissions are share and file system permissions. *Share permissions* are used to control access to shared resources on the part of users and groups. Shared permissions include the following:

No Access Denies access to a shared directory.

Read Allows viewing of files and directories, loading of files, and executing them if appropriate.

Change Allows reading, creating, deleting, and modifying files and directories.

Full Control Allows changing files and directories, and also grants permissions for file systems.

File system permissions, which are defined only for configurations using the NTFS (New Technology File System), control access to files and directories on the network. Permissions—particularly those relating to files and directories—are used to increase security for the network.

→ *See Also* Access Rights

Per-Seat Licensing

Per-seat-licensing is one of the two main pricing modes by which Windows NT Server can be licensed. In per-seat licensing, the customer purchases a Client Access License (CAL) for each client that will be accessing a server.

Once licensed, a client can access any server for which the system administrator has granted the client access rights. No further access fees must be paid to Microsoft for use of the software. The server software is essentially licensed for general use—without regard to the number of clients expected to access it. In other words, client seats pay for access to any available servers, and servers are simply expected to respond to any clients that request access (always assuming, of course, that the client has network access privileges).

Such a licensing scheme is most cost effective for enterprise networks, since it potentially gives client seats access to any part of the network that they need.

In contrast, the more traditional per-server licensing lets a customer buy the right to have a specified number of clients access a server. For example, one might buy a 5- or 10- or 100-user license for a server. This would mean that the server software would be authorized to respond to at most the specified number of clients.

The per-server licensing scheme has worked fairly well until now. However, as networks grow and as users may need access for all sorts of remote locations, the per-server licensing scheme is proving ineffective for many configurations.

Per-Server Licensing

→ *See* Per-Seat Licensing

Personal Communications Services (PCS)

→ *See* PCS (Personal Communications Services)

Personal Computer Memory Card International Association (PCMCIA)

→ *See* PCMCIA (Personal Computer Memory Card International Association)

Personal Identification Number (PIN)

→ *See* PIN (Personal Identification Number)

Personal NetWare

Novell's Personal NetWare is peer-to-peer networking software with added features that make the product easier to manage and more secure than ordinary peer networks. This product is compatible with NetWare versions 2.2 and higher, so that Personal NetWare can be used as a network operating system for its own network.

Personal NetWare, which is included in the Novell DOS 7 package, provides support for the following:

- As many as 50 workstations per server, and up to 50 servers per network, to make 2500 node networks possible.

- Security measures, such as audit trails and encryption.

- Named pipes as an interprocess communication API (Application Program Interface). This makes it possible to access OS/2 application servers.

- Both the NMS (NetWare Management System) and the SNMP (Simple Network Management Protocol). A Personal NetWare network can be managed either as a stand-alone network or as part of an enterprise network.

- The use of client VLMs (Virtual Loadable Modules) for customizing workstations (that is, clients).

Personal NetWare uses Single Network View, a distributed and replicated database of information about all objects (stations, resources, and so on) on each server. Because there is a single database for the entire network, only a single login to the network is needed. In other peer networks, users usually need to log in to every server they want to use. A single login makes security and access rights easier to check and enforce.

Personal NetWare also has an Auto-Reconnect feature that automatically logs stations back in to a server that went down and has subsequently been put back into service.

Pervasive Computing

Pervasive computing is a central concept in Novell's strategic and product planning. Much of the research and development at Novell is based on the assumption that the future development of computing and networking will be strongly influenced by pervasive computing. In fact, Novell has created a model of pervasive computing.

Most simply, pervasive computing says that eventually computing will be everywhere and that any computer will be able to get in touch with any other computer anytime. A pervasive computing environment provides all users with access to other users or information any time, and from anywhere. Clearly, pervasive computing must rely on networking—actually, on very large-scale internetworking—to make this access possible.

For this environment, networking must become ubiquitous and as easy to use as the telephone. Network applications can help to provide this ease of use.

For pervasive computing to become a reality, computing and networking technology must be universally reliable. This can be accomplished through the combination of fault-tolerant and self-diagnosing hardware and software.

In Novell's model, a successful pervasive computing environment requires at least the following:

- Network Infrastructure, through which users will get access to services, applications, and communication tools. Programs such as networking operating systems help create and support this infrastructure.

- Network Services, which enable connections and provide information. Such services must be widely distributed, must support multiple platforms, and must be available to both users and programs. Users in this context may be consumers, administrators, or developers.

- Network Access, which enables a computer— at home, at work, or on the road—to make a connection with an access provider. Services provided by or through the access provider will actually enable the user to communicate on the network.

- Network Applications, which must perform their tasks just as they always have, except that these programs may have to perform them on a distributed system. Applications are expected to do their work in a transparent manner, so that the user doesn't need to worry about or even know how things are being done.

- Tools and APIs, which enable developers to add to the available tools and resources, and also to change the entire working environment.

- Network Management, which must be able to oversee activities and management on lower levels.

In terms of technology, the change to pervasive computing is evolutionary, because people will be able to use what they already have. In terms of the impact it will have on users, the change is revolutionary, because it will affect the way people work, play, buy, and sell.

People use operating systems in order to run stand-alone applications. Users can accomplish a great deal without knowing how the operating system works. In the same way, people can use networks to run network-aware programs, and do their work without knowing any of the technicalities of networking.

Novell believes computing is moving from a system-centric world to a user-centric one, with applications as the driving force behind the change—just as they have been behind other changes in the past. Applications involving business automation drove technology in the 1960s, business applications were the force in the 1970s, and personal productivity applications boosted changes in the 1980s. Now, in a time of explosive growth in the availability of computing devices, network applications are redefining the way we use computing technology.

Pessimistic Security

Pessimistic security operates on a philosophy of "let them see and do only what they have to see and do." That is, pessimistic security takes the approach of restricting permissions—giving users or groups access only to those files and resources they need to be able to use.

This is in contrast to optimistic security, which takes a much more permissive approach. Because it takes a more cautious approach, pessimistic security makes no assumptions about users taking protective measures on their own. Rather, pessimistic security takes whatever steps are necessary to protect user files and resources. Because it is more proactive than optimistic security, the pessimistic variant is much more difficult to administer; however, it is much more secure.

→ **Broader Category** Security

→ **Compare** Optimistic Security

Peta

An order of magnitude that corresponds to a quadrillion (10^{15} or 2^{50}).

→ **See Also** Order of Magnitude

PGP (Pretty Good Privacy)

PGP is an encryption program—and more—developed by Phil Zimmermann. It is easy to use, widely available, and generally free for non-commercial use. However, there are certain export and usage restrictions. PGP can

- Encrypt files using a private key encryption algorithm (IDEA),

- Send and receive encrypted mail,

- Create and verify digital signatures,

and

- Create, manage, certify, and revoke keys.

Using PGP

PGP actually uses three keys when doing its work:

- A public key, which is associated with a single party (individual or company), but which is publicly known. To be effective for encryption, such a key must be paired with a secret key known only to the owner of the public key. In a public-key encryption strategy, every person who needs to do encryption needs both a public and a secret key.

- A private key, which is known only to the key's owner. This key must be kept secret. It

is used for decrypting messages from others and also for making digital signatures.

- A session key, which is generated at random every time there is a message to encrypt. For reasons of efficiency, PGP actually uses the session key to encrypt the message, and then uses the recipient's public key to encrypt the session key. The session key is also secret, but is associated with a message rather than with a person.

Ordinarily, when A wants to send an encrypted message to B, A uses B's public key to encrypt it; B uses B's private key to decrypt it. When done in software, this strategy can be quite slow—almost a thousand times slower than a method that uses only a secret key. PGP does things somewhat differently. It uses the recipient's public key only to encrypt a single item—the session key. The rest of the message is encrypted using the secret session key.

Encrypting a Message

During the actual encryption process, PGP does four things:

- Generates a random session key. This is a 128-bit key.

- Uses the International Data Encryption Algorithm (IDEA) and the session key to encrypt the message.

- Uses the RSA encryption algorithm and the recipient's public key to encrypt the session key.

- Bundles the message and the encrypted session key to get the message ready for mailing.

Digital Signatures with PGP

A digital signature is a very powerful device for protecting the integrity, and demonstrating the authenticity, of messages. With a digital signature, you can prove that you wrote a message, check whether anyone has changed or tampered with the message, and keep others from signing your name to messages you didn't write.

PGP supports digital signatures, and uses a message digest function and your private key to create the signature. The message digest function is a 128-bit value computed from the contents of the message. This same value can be used by the recipient to verify the signature and the integrity of the message.

Key Handling in PGP

PGP asks users to create and enter a pass phrase any time they create a public key. Whenever the user wants to use that key, he or she must enter the pass phrase. PGP will use this phrase to decrypt the key from disk. PGP will also require the pass phrase if the user wants to sign a message with a secret key.

Public keys are stored in key certificates, with each key getting a separate certificate. A key certificate contains the following kind of information about a key:

- The key itself
- The key's creation date
- User ID(s) for the key's creator
- Possibly a list of digital signatures to vouch for the person

PGP supports key rings, which are files containing the public keys of people with whom you might communicate regularly. These files make it easier to keep track of keys. Your private key is not kept in the public key files.

Implementations and Distribution

PGP is available for a range of platforms, such as UNIX (various flavors, including Linux and Solaris), Windows, DOS, OS/2, Macintosh, and Amiga.

While the program itself is easy to use, determining what version to use can be quite a chore. This problem is made even more difficult because there are patent, licensing, and even import/export restrictions. Despite this, the program is available from many sites

on the Internet. Most of these versions carry licensing restrictions on usage and distribution.

For licensing reasons, version 2.3a was updated and revised. In fact, by the time you're reading this, version 2.3 will be incompatible with any of these later versions. Three variants were spawned:

- PGP 2.4 from ViaCrypt. This is actually a commercial version, and has given rise to PGP 2.7.

- PGP 2.6ui and 2.61.ui, which are the "unofficial international" versions. These versions can be used outside of the United States and Canada. Using these versions within those areas might make you guilty of a license violation.

- PGP 2.5, 2.6, 2.6.1, and 2.6.2, which are revised versions created to comply with restrictions.

As of September 1, 1995, version 2.3 files can no longer be read by newer versions of PGP.

→ *Primary Sources* PGP documentation and code are available from several locations. A good starting point is http://www.mantis.co.uk/pgp/pgp.html, since this provides home page addresses and other information about getting more material. An excellent source of general information about PGP is Simson Garfinkel's PGP: Pretty Good Privacy (O'Reilly and Associates, 1995).

Phase

In periodic signaling, a phase is a portion of the entire period. The phase is commonly used as a reference to offset the start of a signal. The phase is generally expressed in degrees or radians. For example, a 90 degree (or ~p/2) phase would be off by one-fourth of the entire period. The phase angle represents the phase difference between two signals. For example, two signals with a phase angle of 180 degrees will be complementary.

Phase Jitter

A distortion of a signal's phase caused by random fluctuations in signal frequency. This distortion makes it difficult to synchronize the signal.

Photodetector

In fiber-optic communications, a component that registers incoming light. The quality and sensitivity of such a detector can have a great influence on the transmission properties in a connection.

→ See Also Cable, Fiber-Optic

Photodiode

A component that converts light signals into electrical ones. Photodiodes are used in receivers for fiber-optic communications.

→ See Also Cable, Fiber-Optic

PHY

PHY is short for physical, and is used to refer to any of the following

- A physical sublayer, as in the physical layer of the FDDI (Fiber Distributed Data Interface) communications architecture, in which PHY is above the PMD (Physical Medium Dependent) sublayer.

- A physical layer, as in the ATM (Asynchronous Transfer Mode) technology, in which this layer itself has two sublayers: PMD (Physical Medium Dependent, also known simply as Physical Medium, or PM) and TC (Transmission Convergence).

- Either of two physical layers for Gigabit Ethernet, in which there are three sublayers: PCS (Physical Coding Sublayer), PMA (Physical Medium Attachment), and PMD

(physical medium dependent). One of the PHYs is defined for optical fiber and the other for Category 5 unshielded twisted-pair (UTP) copper wire.

Physical Contact (PC)

→ See PC (Physical Contact)

Physical Delivery Access Unit (PDAU)

→ See PDAU (Physical Delivery Access Unit)

Physical Layer Convergence Procedure (PLCP)

→ See PLCP (Physical Layer Convergence Procedure)

→ See Also Protocol, PLCP (Physical Layer Convergence Protocol)

Physical Layer Signaling (PLS)

→ See PLS (Physical Layer Signaling)

Physical Media

In the OSI reference model, any physical means for transmitting data. The bottom of the OSI model's Physical layer provides an interface to such media. Specifications for the physical media themselves are not part of the OSI model.

Physical Media Dependent (PMD)

→ See PMD (Physical Media Dependent)

Physical Network Management (PNM)

→ **See** PNM (Physical Network Management)

Physical Unit (PU)

→ **See** PU (Physical Unit)

PIC (Plastic Insulated Cable)

The wires in a plastic insulated cable are each wrapped in plastic insulation, which shields the wires from each other—thereby preventing (or at least minimizing) electrical interference.

PIC (Primary Interexchange Carrier)

The IEC (InterExchange Carrier, or long-distance carrier) that a subscriber uses. Also known as the preferred interexchange carrier.

Piggybacking

A transmission method in which acknowledgments for packets received are included in (piggybacked on) an ordinary data packet.

Pin

In some types of cable connectors, a male lead. This lead is generally only one of several (most commonly 9 or 25) that run through a cable.

PIN (Personal Identification Number)

A unique code, assigned to an individual for use in transactions on certain types of networks; for example, to do banking transactions through an ATM or to log in to networks that use dynamic passwords.

Ping

In Internet protocol networks, ping is an application used to test whether a remote device is properly connected to a network. Although ping is an acronym (for packet internet groper) that refers to an application, it has achieved word status, and the term is generally used as a verb. For example, "To test whether nodes X and Y can communicate, either X or Y can ping the other."

Ping uses an Echo/Echo Reply exchange, which provides one of the simplest network monitoring schemes. It sends an Echo message using ICMP (Internet Control Message Protocol). If properly connected, the device must respond with an Echo Reply message. The receipt of an Echo Reply indicates a viable connection.

Some versions of ping can also report how long it took to receive the Echo Reply and also the proportion of replies that were lost in transmission. These values can provide information about the traffic and noise levels on the network.

→ **Broader Category** Network Management

Pinout

The term pinout refers to the description of the function associated with each pin in a cable. "RS-232C pin assignments" shows the pinout for an RS-232C connection.

Pipe

In many operating environments, a stream that can be shared and, therefore, used to redirect data. For example, output may be redirected from one program through the pipe to become input for another program.

PIR (Protocol-Independent Routing)

Packet routing that is handled independently of the packet format and protocol being used. Such routing provides an alternative to tunneling, in which a packet is wrapped in another format in order to facilitate routing.

PIU (Path Information Unit)

In IBM's SNA network communications, a packet created when the path-control layer adds a transmission header to a Basic Information Unit (BIU) from the transmission-control layer above.

→ *See Also* SNA (Systems Network Architecture)

PKI (Public Key Infrastructure)

A PKI makes it possible for secure communications and business transactions to take place even over public networks—most notably over the Internet. Because they allow general access, such networks are inherently insecure.

A public key infrastructure provides several essential elements for authenticating parties and encrypting content, and also provides the required mechanisms for carrying out tasks at the appropriate times.

In particular, participants in a secure interaction using a PKI will have digital certificates to authenticate themselves—so that each party will know for certain that they are dealing with the parties with whom they expect to be dealing. The necessary certificates will be issued and verified by a Certificate Authority (CA)—that is, a trusted third party who verifies the identity and "acceptability" of the applicants prior to issuing a certificate. This certificate—a digital file that cannot be tampered with successfully—can be used anytime the certificate owner needs to validate his or her identity.

When someone wants to authenticate a certificate owner, the CA checks the certificate to make sure no one has tried to modify it prior to presenting it as proof of identity. VeriSign is arguably the best-known CA, but other major organizations (such as the Post Office) also issue certificates or plan to do so.

Signal	Pin Number	Pin Number	Signal
Secondary Transmitted Data	14	1	Protective Ground
DCE Transmitter Signal Element Timing	15	2	Transmitted Data
Secondary Received Data	16	3	Received Data
Receiver Signal Element Timing	17	4	Request to Send
No Defined Signal Designation	18	5	Clear to Send
Secondary Request to Send	19	6	Data Set Ready
Data Terminal Ready	20	7	Signal Ground/Common Return
Signal Quality Detector	21	8	Received Line Signal Detector
Ring Indicator	22	9	+ Voltage
Data Signal Rate Selector	23	10	- Voltage
DTE Transmitter Signal Element Timing	24	11	No Defined Signal Designation
No Defined Signal Designation	25	12	Secondary Received Line Signal Detector
		13	Secondary Clear to Send

RS-232C PIN ASSIGNMENTS

Digital certificates and a CA to issue them are two of the essential elements of a PKI. The CA vouches for the certificate's holder with its own reputation. However, to ensure that the CA has a reputation to stake, the CA must, itself, be verified by a Registration Authority (RA). The RA is a third PKI component.

In addition to the certificates, the CA, and the RA, a PKI also requires a safe place to store the certificates. For this purpose, one or more directories are needed. Generally, these will be directories that support the X.500 directory standard and the X.509 certificate structure.

A digital certificate will include a public key—a bit sequence of a predefined length—that is unique to the owner of the certificate, but that is accessible to anyone who wants to interact electronically with the key's owner. This key is part of a Public Key Cryptographic System (PKCS), which can be used to encrypt and decrypt any data being transmitted between two parties. An appropriate PKCS is the final essential component for a PKI.

In addition to the public key, a PKCS includes an encryption algorithm (such as the date encryption standard, or DES, or the proprietary RSA algorithm) and a private key (another bit sequence, but one that is related to the public key). Associated with each public key in a PKCS is a unique private key that is—or at least should be—known only to the key's owner.

This private key can be used to create a digital signature on documents or other types of files. This signature guarantees the authenticity of the message source and also ensures that no one tampers with the file en route. (Any tampering would change the file, so that the private key would no longer work for validating the file.)

The sender will encrypt the actual contents of a file with the recipient's public key (to which the sender will have access). A file encrypted in this way will be readable only by someone with the appropriate private key—which should be only the recipient.

Together, the components of a PKI offer the best materials currently available for keeping content and transactions safe on public networks. No element of the PKI is unbreakable; however, with sufficiently long keys and sufficiently careful screening of CAs and of applicants for certificates, a PKI can make data quite safe going across the Internet.

Unfortunately, the PKI does not completely cover the machines at either end of a connection. That is, the PKI can guarantee the safety and integrity of data as it moves between the parties in a connection. However, no element of the PKI has any control over what happens to the data at the destination—that is, once all the secret messages are decrypted and are sitting on a hard disk as ordinary files or as files in a PC's recycle bin.

Plaintext

Ordinary, unencoded text, which is in contrast to encrypted ciphertext.

→ **See Also** Encryption

Plastic-Clad Silica (PCS)

→ **See** PCS (Plastic-Clad Silica)

Plastic Insulated Cable (PIC)

→ **See** PIC (Plastic Insulated Cable)

PLCP (Physical Layer Convergence Procedure)

In the DQDB network architecture, a function that maps higher-level packets into a uniform format for transmission in a particular configuration. An example of a PLCP is the one for the DS3 services. This line is not a simple extension of the DS1 and DS2 lines below it in the power hierarchy. Instead, the services provide different timing and a different level of tolerance.

PLCP is also translated as Physical Layer Convergence Protocol, as in the ATM (Asynchronous Transfer Mode) network architecture. In that context, PLCP is a protocol used to map ATM cells through the Transmission Convergence (TC) sublayer to frames for a DS-3 line.

→ *See Also* DQDB (Distributed Queue, Dual Bus)

PLCP (Physical Layer Convergence Protocol)

→ *See* Protocol, PLCP (Physical Layer Convergence Protocol)

→ *See Also* PLCP (Physical Layer Convergence Procedure)

Plenum

An air shaft or duct in a building. This term has given its name to a type of cable—plenum cable—that is run through such a shaft. This cable must meet stringent fire-safety standards, so its jacket is made of material that will not burn easily and will not exude toxic fumes when exposed to heat.

Plesiochronous

In timing synchronization of digital signals, a situation in which corresponding events happen at the same rate in two systems (such as a sender and a receiver), but not necessarily at the same time. The clocks on these two systems run at the same speed, but they are not synchronized to the same reference time.

Plesiochronous Digital Hierarchy (PDH)

→ *See* PDH (Plesiochronous Digital Hierarchy)

PLS (Physical Layer Signaling)

The topmost component of the Physical layer in the OSI and IEEE 802.x layer models. This element serves as the interface between the Physical layer and the media-access-control (MAC) sublayer above it.

PLS (Primary Link Station)

In environments that use IBM's SDLC (Synchronous Data Link Control) protocol, a primary link station (or just a primary) is a node that initiates communications, either with another primary or with a secondary link station (SLS).

Plug

A male connector. Specifically, a connector with pins, which plug into the sockets on a female connector (known as a jack).

Plug-In

A plug-in is a self-contained chunk of code that can be added to another application or module to perform a particular task or to enhance the operation of the "plugged" application. For example, plug-ins are frequently added to Web browsers such as Netscape Navigator. These elements add to the browser's functionality—for example, by enabling the browser to handle certain types of image files, code elements, or commands. For example, Navigator acquires support for ActiveX controls through a plug-in. Other plug-ins make browsers able to understand commands or other elements that were designed for a competing browser.

Plug-ins are also known as *add-ins* or *snap-ins*.

PMD (Physical Media Dependent)

In various networking architectures, most notably FDDI, a Physical layer. This layer is responsible for the actual connection between two locations.

PNM (Physical Network Management)

Physical Network Management deals with the maintenance and management of the physical infrastructure of a network. This encompasses the cabling, connectors, power supply, etc. This aspect of network management has received relatively little attention, but is becoming more important as computers and networks become integrated with telephones, fax machines, and other devices.

PNNI (Private Network-to-Network Interface)

PNNI is a switch-to-switch protocol developed by the ATM Forum for use in ATM internetworks. The protocol was developed in anticipation of ever-larger ATM internetworks, with hundreds or even thousands of component networks. Such giant internetworks would make considerable demands on ATM switches—for available routes that will satisfy quality of service (QoS) needs for a connection. The protocol was designed to be easy to install and configure, efficient, scalable, and usable in multivendor environments.

PNNI has two main components: PNNI routing and PNNI signaling. The purpose of the routing component is to distribute information about the connections and topology of the networks. This information is distributed to the ATM switches that will need it.

To accomplish its work in an efficient manner, PNNI routing uses several tested strategies for keeping distribution elements (usually routers, but switches in the case of ATM networks) updated on the available paths. In particular, PNNI routing uses the following types of strategies:

- Link-state routing algorithms that have proven successful in non-ATM networks.

- Hierarchical routing strategies that can be used for internetworks with multiple levels.

A hierarchical routing approach summarizes path information about lower tiers, and then passes on only the summary information to upper level switches.

- Source routing, in which the sender in a communication can specify the path to be taken.

The information distributed by PNNI routing makes it possible to create a topology of the network. This topology is stored at every switch, and is updated as required.

PNNI signaling uses the network topology information to actually define a path for a connection, and to reserve the intermediate switches—in order to establish the desired connection. Once this is done, the actual communication can begin.

This summary provides only a very general overview of PNNI—which can also be expanded as Private Network-to-Node Interface, because the same protocols would apply for such a connection. As is usual for an ATM-related topic, the details are complex and filled with acronyms.

PNNI actually does a very good job of solving a very difficult task. The number of possible connections grows rapidly as the number of switches increases, which makes the routing computations potentially more formidable. Also, the fact that ATM connections can request a particular QoS desired or required adds an additional constraint on the routing task.

→ **Broader Category**   ATM (Asynchronous Transfer Mode)

Point of Presence (POP)

→ **See**   POP (Point of Presence)

Point-to-Multipoint Connection

A point-to-multipoint connection is a unidirectional connection in which information is transmitted from a single node to multiple targets—for example, as in cable transmission from the station to customers. In such connections, the transmitter is known as the *root* or the *head*.

→ *Compare* Point-to-Point Connection

Point-to-Point Connection

In a network, a direct connection between two nodes; that is, a connection without any intervening nodes or switches. In an internetwork, the term refers to a direct connection between two networks.

→ *Compare* Point-to-Multipoint Connection

Point-to-Point Protocol (PPP)

→ *See* Protocol, PPP (Point-to-Point Protocol)

Point-to-Point Tunneling Protocol (PPTP)

→ *See* Protocol, PPTP (Point-to-Point Tunneling Protocol)

Polarization

For connectors, the shape or form the connector takes. For example, with Unshielded Twisted-Pair (UTP) wire, the RJ11, RJ45, and MMJ connectors each have a different polarization.

Polling

Polling refers to a process of checking elements, such as computers or queues, in some defined order, to see whether the polled element needs attention (wants to transmit, contains jobs, and so on). In roll-call polling, the polling sequence is based on a list of elements available to the controller, or poller. In contrast, in hub polling, each element simply polls the next element in the sequence. Polling is used in various computing contexts to control the execution or transmission sequence of the elements involved.

In multitasking operating systems, polling can be used to allocate resources and time to the tasks currently executing. System performance and stability can depend on the way elements are organized. For example, the operating system may maintain a single queue for all the tasks (as in OS/2); or it may use a separate queue for each task (as in Windows NT). In the former case, a task that is hanging or has crashed may affect the performance of other tasks. In the latter case, such tasks will not affect each other's behavior.

In LANs, polling provides a deterministic media-access method in which the server polls each node in succession to determine whether that node wants to access the network. While polling is not very popular for PCs, it is still commonly used in networks that include mainframes and minicomputers.

Being deterministic, such polling is similar to token passing, and differs from probabilistic access methods such as CSMA/CD. In a deterministic approach, there is a fixed sequence in which tasks are done, which ensures that everyone gets a turn. In a probabilistic approach, the sequence depends on some random or pseudorandom process, so that it is not possible to determine which element will be selected next.

→ *Broader Category* Media-Access Method

→ *Compare* CSMA/CA; CSMA/CD; Token Passing

Polyvinylchloride (PVC)

→ *See* PVC (Polyvinylchloride)

POP (Point of Presence)

In telephone communications, the location at which a subscriber's leased or long-distance lines connect to the phone company's lines; that is, the point in a Local Access Transport Area (LATA) at which the subscriber's lines connect to an interexchange carrier (IXC). This is usually a central office.

Portable Modem

A compact, external modem that can be transported easily and that can be plugged into the appropriate port on any computer.

Portable Operating System Interface (POSIX)

→ **See** POSIX (Portable Operating System Interface)

Portable Operating System Interface for UNIX (POSIX)

→ **See** POSIX (Portable Operating System Interface)

Portal

A portal is an (advertisement-filled) access point to the Internet. Because they provide access to such a huge potential audience—over 250 million Internet accesses per day—portals represent prime space for Web advertisements, and competition among portals—which include America Online (AOL), Lycos, the Microsoft Network (MSN), ZDNet, and Netscape—is fierce.

Port, Hardware

In general, a hardware port is an access point to a computer, peripheral, network, circuit, switch, or other device. A port provides an electrical and physical interface between a component and the world. There are two fundamental types of ports:

Parallel port A hardware connection in which there are separate pins defined for all 8 data bits in a character. This means that an entire byte of information can be sent at a time.

Serial port A hardware connection in which only one pin is available for data transmission in a given direction, so that bits must be transmitted in sequence.

The wiring for a port is almost always associated with a particular physical interface. For example, both Centronics and GPIB ports are associated with interfaces of the same name. There are also numerous standard variants on these port types. For example, RS-232 is a serial port, and SCSI provides a parallel port.

Communication across a port can be established when the appropriate type of device is connected to the port, and when there is a compatible device at the other end of the connection.

Port Address or Name

A port address is a bus or memory address associated with a particular hardware port. There will generally be at least enough storage allocated at the port address to handle data being written or read at the port.

A port name can be used instead of an address to refer to a port. The port name is presumably easier to remember than an address. Operating systems sometimes have predefined names associated with certain ports. For example, DOS reserves the names COM1 and LPT1 to refer to the first serial and parallel ports, respectively.

P

Sharing a Port

A hardware device can be used to allow devices to share a port. Although port-sharing devices makes it possible for two or more devices to share a single port, they cannot use the port simultaneously.

→ *See Also* EPP (Enhanced Parallel Port); SCSI (Small Computer System Interface)

Port, IBM Type 3

An IBM Type 3 port is an enhanced serial port that uses direct memory access (DMA). This port can use an 11.0592 megahertz (MHz) clock, instead of the 1.8432MHz clock that is used for ordinary serial ports. This gives a maximum serial rate of 691,200bps, although IBM's ports support only up to 345,600bps.

The enhanced port is backward-compatible with 8250 UART (Universal Asynchronous Receiver/Transmitter) data registers, but includes additional registers. The port is used in IBM PS/2 models 90 and 95.

Port Selector

The hardware or software that selects a particular port for a communications session. The selection may be made at random or on the basis of a selection criterion.

Port, Software

A memory location that is associated with a hardware port or with a communications channel, and that provides storage for information moving between the memory location and the channel. In connection with the Internet, a port is a value at the Transport layer, used to distinguish among the multiple applications that may have connections with a single host.

While many port assignments can be arbitrary, certain ports are associated—either by fiat or by convention—with particular applications or services. In fact, the IANA (Internet Assigned Numbers Authority) determines the assignments of port numbers 0 through 1023. (Until recently, the IANA controlled only numbers between 0 and 255.) For example, the telnet remote login service on the Internet is associated with port 23. The table "Selected Port Assignments" shows other preassigned ports in this range. The services and applications listed in the table are each described in their own articles or glosses.

SELECTED PORT ASSIGNMENTS

Port Number	Service/Application (decimal)
7	Echo
9	Discard
13	Daytime
17	Quote of the day
19	Character generator
21	FTP (File Transfer Protocol)
23	Telnet (remote login service)
25	Simple Mail Transfer Protocol (SMTP)
37	Time
53	DNS (Domain Name Server)
67	BootP Server
70	Gopher (file search service)
80	WWW (World Wide Web)
88	Kerberos (authentication server)
110	POP3 (Post Office Protocol, version 3)
119	NNTP (Network News Transfer Protocol)
135	Locator Services
137	NetBIOS Name Services
138	NetBIOS Datagram Services
139	NetBIOS Sessions
191	Prospero
194	IRC (Internet Relay Chat)
515	LPR (Line Printer)
530	RPC (Remote Procedure Call)

Similarly, previously unassigned port numbers in the range 1024 through 65,535 can be registered with the IANA by vendors and organizations. For example, port 1352 is assigned to Lotus Notes.

→**Primary Sources** RFC 1700

Port Switching

In a communications session, the process of switching from one port to another, either because the port is malfunctioning or because it is overloaded. Such a switch should be transparent to the parties involved.

POSIX (Portable Operating System Interface

An IEEE standard that defines the interface between applications and an operating system. Originally developed to provide a common interface for UNIX implementations, POSIX has become more widely adopted, and operating environments ranging from DOS to IBM's MVS (Multiple Virtual Storage) support various parts of the POSIX standard.

POSIX is sometimes expanded as Portable Operating System Interface for UNIX.

Postamble

In a packet or message, a sequence of bits or fields that follows the actual data, or contents. The postamble, also known as a trailer, generally contains a Frame Check Sequence (FCS) or another error-checking field, and may include one or more flags or a predefined bit sequence to indicate the end of a packet. Compare this with the preamble.

Post, Telephone and Telegraph (PTT)

→**See** PTT (Post, Telephone and Telegraph)

Post Office

A Message Handling System (MHS) is another term for a message store for an intermediate storage location where messages can be held until they are retrieved by a recipient or sent on their way to a destination.

While storage is the main function of a post office, a useful post office will also be able to keep accounting information about the messages being stored and should even be able to provide summaries of the messages. Users should also be able to selectively retrieve mail from the post office.

On LANs, the post office will generally be accessed using file-sharing or remote-procedure-calling capabilities provided by the (network) operating system. Such methods may be proprietary. In contrast, POP3 (Post Office Protocol, version 3) is used to communicate with a Post Office on the Internet. Similarly, the P7 protocol allows communication with post offices in networks that use the X.400 Message Handling System.

→**Broader Categories** MHS (Message Handling System)

Power Budget

In a transmission context, the power budget is the difference between the transmitter's power and the receiver's sensitivity. This difference determines the amount of signal loss that can be allowed. The loss restriction, in turn, can determine the maximum distance the signal can travel without cleaning and boosting, and may also restrict the number of elements allowed to receive the signal.

For example, if a transmitter can send a 10 decibel (dB) signal, and the receiver is capable of detecting a -20 dB signal, the transmission has a power budget of 30 dB.

Power Disturbance

The supply of electrical power can be disrupted by several types of electrical activity. Power disturbances can cause data loss, and may also damage equipment. For example, if a hard disk read/write head is close to a surface when a brownout occurs, the head may dip enough to bounce along the surface, possibly damaging the surface and destroying data.

Types of Power Disturbances

Power disturbances can range from a brief surge in power to a total blackout.

Blackout

A blackout is a total loss of electrical power. Blackouts can be caused by lightning, broken power lines, and other natural and man-made disasters.

Brownout

A brownout is a short-term decrease in voltage level. Specifically, a brownout, also known as a sag, occurs when the voltage is more than 20 percent below the nominal RMS (Root Mean Square) voltage.

Brownouts can occur when a piece of heavy machinery is turned on and temporarily drains the available power, or when everyone feels the need to run their air conditioners at the same time. According to some sources, brownouts account for almost 90 percent of all power disturbances.

Power companies will sometimes create "rolling brownouts" during peak demand periods. In these planned brownouts, the voltage will be lowered temporarily in different areas for a period of time.

Spike

A spike is a very brief, very large increase in voltage. Specifically, a spike occurs when the voltage is more than twice the nominal peak voltage. Spikes, which are also known as impulses, are most often caused by lightning strikes.

Surge

A surge is a short-term increase in voltage. The duration of a surge is longer than for a spike, but the voltage increase is much lower than for a spike. Specifically, a surge occurs if the voltage is more than 10 percent above the nominal RMS voltage for more than $1/120$ second.

Surges are typically caused when the heavy machinery that caused a sag is turned off. Such power disturbances can cause data loss and can impose extra wear and tear on components. Surges account for a small proportion of power disturbances.

Noise

Noise is electrical activity that disrupts or distorts the sine wave pattern on which power is delivered. Noise is typically known as ElectroMagnetic Interference (EMI) or Radio Frequency Interference (RFI).

Noise can be caused by any of several factors, including other electrical activity and atmospheric conditions. Noise harms signals and information, not physical components.

Protection Against Power Disturbances

There are three general types of protection against power disturbances:

- Isolation, which tries to contain the disturbance before it reaches the protected device. Isolation protects against noise or interference, and also against voltage fluctuations.

- Regulation, which tries to maintain a constant power supply, through brownouts, surges, and even blackouts. A UPS (Uninterruptible Power Supply) is arguably the most effective regulation tool.

- Suppression, which tries to guard against unexpected or massive power surges. Surge protectors are the most commonly used suppression tool.

PPP (Point-to-Point Protocol)

In the Internet protocol environment, a protocol for direct communication between two nodes over serial point-to-point links, such as between routers in an internet or between a node and a router. PPP is used as a medium-speed access protocol for the Internet. The protocol replaces the older SLIP (Serial Line Internet Protocol).

PPTP (Point-to-Point Tunneling Protocol)

→**See** Protocol, PPTP (Point-to-Point Tunneling Protocol)

PRAM (Parameter RAM)

In an AppleTalk network, an area of volatile memory that is used to store important configuration information (such as the node's network address).

Preamble

Material, in a packet or message, that precedes the actual data, or contents. The preamble generally contains various administrative fields, such as fields with source and destination addresses, information about packet type or size, special signals, or bit sequences to indicate the start of a packet.

Preferred Interexchange Carrier (PIC)

→**See** PIC (Primary Interexchange Carrier)

Premises Distribution System (PDS)

→**See** PDS (Premises Distribution System)

Premises Network

A network confined to a single building, but that covers that building completely.

Pretty Good Privacy (PGP)

→**See** PGP (Pretty Good Privacy)

PRI (Primary Rate Interface)

PRI, also known as primary access interface, is one of two service categories provided for ISDN (Integrated Services Digital Network) networks. The PRI specifies either a 1.536Mbps bandwidth in North America and Japan, or a 1.984Mbps bandwidth in Europe.

These bandwidths correspond to T-1 and E-1 lines, respectively. Note that the T-1 and E-1 bandwidths are 1.544 and 2.048Mbps, respectively. The extra bandwidth covers 8Kbps and 64Kbps, respectively, for line-management transmissions.

The PRI bandwidth can be allocated in any of several combinations, depending on whether B or H channels are used. B (bearer) channels are used for data transmissions. H channels are groupings of B and D channels, which are channels used for control and other signaling between sender and receiver.

For T-1 lines, a common split uses 23 B channels and one 64Kbps D channel; for European lines, the corresponding E-1 channel consists of 30 B channels and 1 D channel. These breakdowns are denoted as 23B+D and 30B+D, respectively.

→**Compare** BRI (Basic Rate Interface)

Primary Domain Controller (PDC)

→**See** PDC (Primary Domain Controller)

Primary Interexchange Carrier (PIC)

→ *See* PIC (Primary Interexchange Carrier)

Primary Link Station (PLS)

→ *See* PLS (Primary Link Station)

Primary Rate Interface (PRI)

→ *See* PRI (Primary Rate Interface)

Private Branch Exchange (PBX)

→ *See* PBX (Private Branch Exchange)

Primary Interexchange Carrier (PIC)

→ *See* PIC (Primary Interexchange Carrier)

Print Device

A printer or other output device on a network, and seen as a network object from the perspective of the network. A network print device is configured by loading a Printer Definition File (PDF) into the appropriate print services environment on the network.

Printer, Network

A printer is one of the peripheral devices that can be shared on a network. The printer may be attached to the file server, to a workstation, or to a stand-alone print server device. Or the printer may have a network interface card (NIC) and run its own print server software. This type of printer can connect directly to the network and function as a regular node.

PRINTER ETIQUETTE

A network printer is a shared device. This means that each sharer has a certain responsibility for the care and feeding of the shared device. The rules of etiquette for network printers are to a large extent just common sense and good manners.

- Always restore the printer to its former state after your print job finishes. This includes flushing whatever fonts or macros you download.

- When you pick up your long print job, put into the paper bins one and a half times the paper your job used.

- If your printout is light, indicating that the toner might be nearing the end, inform the system administrator or whoever is responsible for the printer.

The following features are important for a network printer:

Duty cycle The workload the printer is able to handle, and is generally expressed in pages per month (ppm or ppmo). Network printers should have at least 20,000 ppm duty cycles.

Automatic switching The ability to switch automatically to whatever printing mode or language the current print job requires. For example, one job in a print queue may be in PostScript and the next may be using Hewlett-Packard's PCL. The printer should be able to handle these jobs without special intervention.

Automatic flushing The ability to flush any job that contains an error. Without this capability, the printer may hang if it encounters such a job, which will, in turn, stop the printing and cause the print queue to grow.

Paper bins A network-worthy printer should have a large paper bin—preferably two large bins, with the ability to switch automatically when one bin is empty. If the paper bins are too small, someone will need to keep replenishing the supply, or else the print queue will simply keep growing.

Speed The ability to print quickly enough to keep up with average demand on the network.

→ *Broader Category* Peripheral

→ *See Also* Server

Print Queue

On a network, a print queue is a directory that stores print jobs waiting to be printed. The jobs are printed in a first-in-first-out (FIFO) sequence. In Novell's NetWare 4.x, the print queue directory is in the QUEUES directory; in earlier versions, the directory is in the SYS:SYSTEM directory.

When a NetWare print queue is created, user ADMIN is assigned as a print queue operator. A print queue operator can change the status of print jobs or delete them from the queue.

Print Spooler

A program or process that can queue print jobs and submit these jobs to the printer when possible. Having a spooler program manage the queue relieves the processor of the task.

Priority Access Control Enabled (PACE)

→ *See* PACE (Priority Access Control Enabled)

Privacy Enhanced Mail (PEM)

→ *See* PEM (Privacy Enhanced Mail)

Private Automatic Branch Exchange (PABX)

→ *See* PABX (Private Automatic Branch Exchange)

Private Branch Exchange (PBX)

→ *See* PBX (Private Branch Exchange)

Private Leased Circuit

A leased communication line that provides a permanently available connection between locations.

Private Management Domain (PRMD)

→ *See* PRMD (Private Management Domain)

Private Network-to-Network Interface (PNNI)

→ *See* PNNI (Private Network-to-Network Interface)

Privilege Attribute Certificate (PAC)

→ *See* PAC (Privilege Attribute Certificate)

Privilege Level

In the Intel architecture, any of four rankings (0, 1, 2, or 3) that can be assigned to memory segments to create memory domains. Privilege levels, which are also known as protection rings, can be used to keep processes from damaging each other.

Novell's NetWare 4.x can use either of two levels: 0 or 3. Novell recommends running the NetWare operating system in level 0 (the OS domain), and running any untested third-party NetWare Loadable Modules (NLMs) in level 3 (the OS_PROTECTED domain) to protect the system. Once an NLM has been proven reliable, it can then be run in the OS domain to improve performance.

PRMD (Private Management Domain)

In the CCITT's X.400 model, a message handling system (MHS) or an electronic-mail system operated by a private organization, such as a corporation, a university campus, or a state university system.

→ *See Also* X.400

Probe

In an AppleTalk network, a packet sent to the remote end of the network. The probe requests an acknowledgment from the node at the end, which serves to indicate the end of the network and also to acknowledge that the node is functioning.

Process

A program or program portion that is executing on a host computer.

Processing, Centralized

A networking arrangement in which the processing is done by a central server or host node, which also controls the network. This arrangement is suitable for networks in which there is a great disparity in processing power between workstation and server. Mainframe-based networks generally use centralized processing.

Processing, Cooperative

A program-execution technology that allows different tasks in a program to be carried out on different machines. Cooperative processing is important for client/server computing, in which an application front end executes on a client (workstation) and a back end executes on the server.

Processing, Distributed

A networking arrangement in which processing is carried out in multiple and separate locations. Along with the work, control is also decentralized in such a network. There is no central manager, but there may be central monitors or repositories that have information about all relevant network activity.

Processor-Direct Slots (PDS)

→ *See* PDS (Processor-Direct Slots)

Profile

In the world of standards and specifications, a profile refers to a subset of a specification or standard. Profiles are created in order to speed product development and implementation. Parts of a specification may be sufficiently stable and practical to warrant implementation—often just for testing. Sometimes, however, profiles are implemented as strategic moves: to establish a presence in an up-and-coming market, or to grab a market share as early as possible.

Specifications often have to be implemented in phases for many reasons. A profile implementation can happen, for example, if a technology isn't advanced enough to support a complete specification.

Project 21

A project, initiated by the 64-country International Maritime Satellite Organization, for making worldwide mobile communications possible. The project calls for 30 to 40 satellites to blanket the earth. These would make possible point-to-point communications between any two locations on earth. Compare this with the Iridium Project.

Promiscuous Mode

For a network interface card (NIC) driver, an operating mode in which the NIC passes all packets that arrive to higher layers, regardless of whether the packet is addressed to the node. This operating mode makes it possible to pass everything that happens at a NIC on to a network analyzer.

Propagation Delay

The time required for a signal to pass through a component (such as a single device or an entire network) or from one component on a circuit to another. This value is important because the total propagation delay on a network may determine maximum network configurations.

Proprietary Server

A network server that runs a proprietary operating system and that is designed to be used with a particular vendor's hardware and software. Although they were popular as recently as a few years ago, such servers are no longer in vogue. The move is toward generic servers and open systems, which are vendor-independent.

Prospero

On the Internet, a tool for accessing, organizing, and using files that may be located in diverse remote locations. By running a Prospero client on the local machine, a user can get access to Prospero's capabilities. Information about Prospero is available via FTP from `prospero.isi.edu`.

Protected Mode

The default operating mode for memory allocation and usage for 80286, 80386, and higher processors. In protected mode, multiple processes can execute at the same time. Each process is assigned its own memory area, and no two memory areas overlap, so that programs cannot overwrite each other's work. The 8086 processor operates in real mode, which does not afford either multitasking or memory protection.

Protocol

A protocol is a set of predefined rules that govern how two or more processes communicate and interact to exchange data. The processes can be on the same machine or on different machines. For example, a transport-layer program on one machine uses a protocol to talk to the program's counterpart on another machine.

Protocols are generally associated with particular services or tasks, such as data packaging or packet routing. A protocol specifies rules for setting up, carrying out, and terminating a communications connection, and also specifies the format the information packets must have when traveling across this connection.

Some protocols require acknowledgment that an action has been successfully carried out, such as when a packet has been received. Under some circumstances, as in the case of a router going over modem-speed lines, such acknowledgments can slow down a transmission enough to throw off timing requirements for some protocols.

Protocols can be distinguished by several types of properties:

- The level, or layer, at which the protocol operates.

- The network architecture for which the protocol is designed. For example, bus-oriented protocols look and behave differently (in their details) than do protocols associated with ring-based networks.

- Whether the protocol is synchronous or asynchronous.

- Whether the protocol is connection-oriented or connectionless.

- Whether the protocol is character- or bit-oriented.

This entry discusses these distinctions. Individual protocols and types of protocols are covered in separate entries.

Protocols and Layers

A protocol stack, which consists of the protocols for a particular network architecture, includes protocols at different layers. Details of the protocols reflect the functions and services available at each layer.

Application Layer Protocols

An application layer protocol is any of various protocols that provide services for applications. These protocols are the primary interface between applications and a network. In general, application layer protocols provide some type of access or handling (directory, file, or message) services for a process accessing a network.

The application layer is defined as the topmost in both the seven-layer OSI (Open System Interconnect) reference model and the five-layer Internet layer model. However, the top Internet layer actually corresponds to the top three OSI model layers, so that an Internet-based application layer protocol may have a broader range or a different set of tasks than an OSI application layer protocol.

Examples of application layer protocols include the following:

CMIP (common management information protocol) and SNMP (simple network management protocol) OSI and Internet protocols, respectively, for network management and monitoring.

FTAM (file transfer, access, and management) and FTP (file transfer protocol) OSI and Internet protocols, respectively, for file transfer and handling. Sun's NFS (Network File System) and AT&T's RFS (Remote File System) protocols are comparable.

X.400 and SMTP (simple mail transfer protocol) OSI and Internet protocols, respectively, for e-mail or message handling and transfer.

Telnet Internet protocol for terminal emulation or for providing remote login capabilities.

Presentation Layer Protocols

Presentation layer protocols are responsible for providing any conversion, compression, or formatting needed to make data suitable for transmission or use. Practically speaking, the presentation layer and presentation layer protocols rarely appear in pure form. Generally, the presentation layer merges with either the application layer above or the session layer below, or with both.

For example, PostScript may be regarded as a presentation layer protocol—one that provides a format for graphics pages. However, PostScript can also be regarded as an application—a tool for creating page layouts.

Other examples of presentation layer protocols include the following:

- AFP (AppleTalk Filing Protocol), which is the top-level protocol in the AppleTalk protocol suite. As such, AFP also combines application- and presentation-layer services.

- Various TCP/IP protocols, such as FTP (File Transfer Protocol) and SMTP (Simple Mail Transfer Protocol). Note that these protocols are also considered Application layer protocols—because the TCP/IP layer model combines the top three OSI layers, including the Application and Presentation layers.

Session Layer Protocols

Session layer protocols are responsible for maintaining, synchronizing, and sequencing the dialog in a network connection. As with the presentation layer, session-layer capabilities are often part of other configurations (for example, those that include the presentation layer).

Examples of protocols that provide session-layer services include the following

- ADSP (AppleTalk Data Stream Protocol), which enables two nodes to establish a reliable connection for data transfer.

- NetBEUI (NetBIOS Extended User Interface), which is an implementation and extension of NetBIOS. This protocol actually merges into the presentation layer.

- NetBIOS, which actually spans the fifth, sixth, and seventh layers, but which includes capabilities for monitoring sessions to make sure they are running smoothly.

- PAP (Printer Access Protocol), which provides access to a PostScript printer in an AppleTalk network.

Transport Layer Protocols

In the OSI reference model, Transport layer protocols operate at the fourth, or transport, layer. This layer, or one very similar to it in other models, is important because it sits between the upper layers (which are strongly application-dependent) and the lower ones (which are network-dependent). Depending on whether the packets are being passed down the layers at the sender's end or up the layers at the receiver's end, the Transport layer is responsible for ensuring that the packets are sent off or received in the proper sequence and format.

To provide the capabilities required, several classes of Transport layer protocols have been defined in the OSI reference model. See the OSI Reference Model article for information about these protocols.

Transport layer protocols include the following

TCP (transmission control protocol) and UDP (user datagram protocol) Internet environment and most UNIX-based networks (connection-oriented and connectionless transport services, respectively)

SPX (sequenced packet exchange) Novell NetWare environments

PEP (packet exchange protocol) XNS (Xerox network services) protocol suite from Xerox

VOTS (VAX OSI transport service) DEC networks

AEP (AppleTalk echo protocol), ATP (AppleTalk transaction protocol), NBP (name binding protocol), and RTMP (routing table maintenance protocol) AppleTalk protocol suite

Network Layer Protocols

Network layer protocols are responsible for controlling the flow of data from end to end on the network, from the sender to the receiver. However, these protocols are not guaranteed to deliver the data successfully. To accomplish their tasks, Network layer protocols rely on the services of the underlying Data-Link layer protocols. Network layer protocols can be connection-oriented or connectionless.

Examples of Network layer protocols include the following

CLNP (Connectionless Network-Layer Protocol) and IP (Internet protocol) OSI and Internet protocols, respectively

DDP (Datagram Delivery Protocol) AppleTalk protocol

IPX (Internetwork Packet Exchange) Novell NetWare protocol

Data-Link Layer Protocols

Data-link layer protocols are any of various protocols that provide network access for users or applications. These protocols are the interface between application programs and a physical network. In general, Data-Link layer protocols provide the network interface card (NIC) with the bytes to be transmitted onto the network.

Examples of Data-Link layer protocols include the following

- Link-Access Protocols (LAPs) for various network architectures or configurations. For example, ELAP (EtherTalk LAP), FLAP (FDDITalk LAP), LLAP (LocalTalk LAP), and TLAP (TokenTalk LAP) are the Data-Link layer protocols in an AppleTalk network. Other commonly used link-access protocols include LAPB (Link-Access Procedure, Balanced) and LAPD (Link-Access Procedure, D channel).

- SDLC (Synchronous Data Link Control) from the ISO (International Standardization Organization) and the earlier HDLC (High-Level Data Link Control), from IBM).

- ARAP (AppleTalk remote access protocol), PPP (point-to-point protocol), and SLIP (serial line Internet protocol) for remote access or for communications over telephone lines.

Synchronous versus Asynchronous Protocols

Synchronous protocols rely on timing to identify transmission elements, and are most suited for transmissions that occur at a relatively constant rate. Asynchronous protocols, which are more suitable for transmissions that may occur in bursts, rely on special signals (start and stop bits) to mark the individual transmission elements. Both synchronous and asynchronous protocols are Data-Link layer protocols for transmitting bytes between a DTE (computer) and DCE (modem) or between two computers.

Early synchronous protocols were byte- or character-oriented. For example, the character-oriented Bisync from IBM or the byte-oriented DDCMP (Digital Data Communications Messaging Protocol) from DEC are synchronous protocols. Since

timing requires the use of special signals, characters that were used for link control could not be used as data characters. Newer, bit-oriented protocols avoid this problem, and are more efficient as a result. Examples of such bit-oriented protocols include SDLC, HDLC, and LAPB.

Most network protocols are asynchronous; most mainframe and terminal-handling protocols are synchronous.

Connectionless versus Connection-Protocols

Connection-oriented transmissions take place over a single path, so that a destination address is needed only while the path is being determined. After that, the transmission proceeds along the same path.

In connectionless service, data transmissions do not require an established connection between sender and receiver. Instead, packets are sent independently of each other, and may take different paths to the destination. Each packet must include the source and destination addresses, however.

Bit-Oriented versus Byte-Oriented Protocols

Character-, or byte-oriented protocols use bytes or characters to manage the communications link and for timing. A disadvantage of this method is that the bytes or characters used for the link control cannot be used as ordinary data bytes.

Most early synchronous protocols, such as IBM's Bisync or Digital Equipment Corporation's DDCMP, were byte-oriented. These have been superseded by more efficient bit-oriented protocols, which can establish timing and manage link controls with individual bits.

Bit-oriented protocols transmit individual bits, without regard to their interpretation. Such protocols can establish timing and manage data links using bit signals. Individual bits are used for timing (so that sender and receiver stay in synchrony) and also for link control. Examples of bit-oriented protocols include HDLC, SDLC, and LAPB.

Protocol, AARP (AppleTalk Address Resolution Protocol)

A protocol that maps AppleTalk (network) addresses to Ethernet or Token Ring (physical) addresses. This protocol is based on the widely used ARP (address protocol resolution) that forms part of the TCP/IP protocol suite. It is generally included in the definition for the network's link-access protocol (LAP) rather than functioning as a separate protocol.

Protocol, ADCCP (Advanced Data Communications Control Procedure)

An ANSI-standard (X3.66) communications protocol. ADCCP is bit-oriented, operates at the Data-Link layer, and is identical to ISO's HDLC (High-level Data Link Control) protocol. Both ADCCP and HDLC are extensions of the older SDLC (Synchronous Data Link Control) developed by IBM in the 1970s.

Protocol, ADSP (AppleTalk Data Stream Protocol)

A session-layer protocol that allows two AppleTalk nodes, usually two Macintoshes, to establish a reliable connection through which data can be transmitted. Once a session is established, the data is transmitted over a single path.

Protocol, AEP (AppleTalk Echo Protocol)

An AppleTalk Transport layer protocol used to determine whether two nodes are connected and both available. In general, echo protocols are used to determine whether a particular node is available.

They can also be used to get an estimate of the roundtrip time on the network.

Protocol, AFP (AppleTalk Filing Protocol)

An application/presentation layer protocol used between file servers and clients in an AppleShare network and for remote access to an AppleTalk network. AFP is also supported by most non-Macintosh network operating systems. For example, Novell's NetWare for the Macintosh provides AFP support for NetWare file servers.

Protocol, AFS (Andrew File System)

The AFS is a set of file handling protocols that makes it possible to access and use files on a network just as if these files were on your local system. The AFS is generally considered faster and more efficient than the NFS (Network File System), which is currently the most widely used protocol of this sort.

The general consensus is that AFS will eventually replace NFS as the dominant protocol for remote file handling—even though NFS is so strongly entrenched. (The popularity of NFS arises partly because NFS was released at a time when its capabilities were first in demand and partly because NFS supports the TCP/IP protocol suite, which rules on the Internet.)

→ *See Also*   Protocol, NFS (Network File System)

Protocol, ARAP (AppleTalk Remote Access Protocol)

A Data-Link layer protocol that allows a Macintosh node to access a network from a remote location, so that the node can work just as if connected physically to the network.

Protocol, ARP (Address Resolution Protocol)

In the TCP/IP protocol suite, a protocol for mapping between (4-byte) IP addresses and (6-byte) data-link addresses. Given an IP address, ARP will determine the appropriate data link address. The IP addresses are network-based; the data-link addresses are hardware-based and are associated with a machine. ARP variants have been developed for a variety of networking environments, including the AppleTalk environment(which supports AARP as the equivalent mapping protocol) and ATM networks (which use ATMARP as a mapping protocol).

ARP finds a hardware address corresponding to a network one. A related protocol—InARP (for inverse ARP)—works in the other direction. That is, given a data link address, InARP will find the corresponding IP address.

Protocol, ASDSP (AppleTalk Secure Data Stream Protocol)

ASDSP is a secure version of the AppleTalk Data Stream Protocol (ADSP), which is a session-layer protocol that enables two Macintoshes to establish a reliable connection.

Protocol, ASP (AppleTalk Session Protocol)

A session layer protocol in the AppleTalk protocol suite. ASP is used to begin and end a session, send commands from the client to the server, send replies from the latter, and send tickler packets between server and workstation (so that each machine knows that the other is still functioning).

Protocol, ATMARP (Asynchronous Transfer Mode Address Resolution Protocol)

ATMARP is an address resolution protocol—that is, a protocol that maps between network layer addresses and hardware addresses at the data link layer—that is, between layer 3 and layer 2 addresses. However, ATMARP includes extensions that make it suitable for use with ATM networks—for example, it maps between IP (Internet protocol) and ATM addresses. Specifically, given an IP address, an ATMARP server can find the ATM address corresponding to it. A client can, for example, use ATMARP to query an ATMARP server for the ATM address of another client for whom the IP address is known.

Inverse ATMARP, or InATMARP, is the protocol's counterpart for finding an IP address, given the ATM address. For example, an ATMARP server might query a client (with a known ATM address) to find out the client's IP address.

→ *Broader Category* ATM (Asynchronous Transfer Mode)

Protocol, ATP (AppleTalk Transaction Protocol)

In Macintosh-based AppleTalk networks, a Transport layer protocol that can provide reliable packet transmission. Packets are transported within the framework of a transaction, which is an interaction between a requesting and a responding entity (program or node).

Protocol, AURP (AppleTalk Update Routing Protocol)

In the AppleTalk protocol suite, a routing protocol that uses a link-state algorithm to determine routes through an internetwork. As is characteristic of link-state protocols, AURP reports only changes in the available connections in an internetwork.

Protocol, Authentication

An authentication protocol is used when a user needs to be authenticated before getting access to the network or to resources on it. Examples of authentication protocols for PPP (Point-to-Point Protocol) connections include PAP (Password Authentication Protocol), CHAP (Challenge Handshake Authentication Protocol), and EAP (Extensible Authentication Protocol).

→ *Primary Sources* These protocols are described in RFCs 1334, 1994, 2284, and 2484.

Protocol, BACP (Bandwidth Allocation Control Protocol)

BACP is included in Cisco's IOS (Internetworking Operating System)—beginning with release 11.3—and is used for negotiations between routers configured for Multilink PPP (Point-to-Point Protocol). Multilink connections involve the simultaneous use of multiple channels between communicating nodes to increase the bandwidth for the communication.

For various reasons, only one router in such a connection should be allowed to add or remove links during a connection. In IOS, the BACP is used to negotiate which router should be responsible for this task.

→ *Primary Sources* Multilink PPP is discussed in RFC 1990, and BACP is discussed in Cisco publications.

Protocol, BGP (Border Gateway Protocol)

In the Internet TCP/IP protocol suite, a protocol for routing packets between networks that use

different protocols. This type of protocol is known as an Exterior Gateway Protocol (EGP). BGP is an improved version of an older protocol (actually named EGP), and serves as the basis for the ISO's IDRP (Interdomain Routing Protocol).

→ *Primary Sources* BGP was originally defined in RFC 163, and updated to BGP-3 in RFC 1267. RFCs 1265, 1266, 1268, and 1269 discuss various topics related to BGP protocols.

Protocol, Bit-Oriented (BOP)

→ *See* Protocol, BOP (Bit-Oriented Protocol)

Protocol, BLAST (Blocked Asynchronous/Synchronous Transmission)

A protocol in which data is transmitted in blocks of a fixed number of bits, rather than as characters or in line-by-line mode. The BLAST protocol is useful in multiplexing situations because it can simplify framing.

Protocol, BOP (Bit-Oriented Protocol)

Bit-oriented protocols operate with individual bits as their basic unit of information—for both data and timing. BOPs transmit individual bits, without regard to their interpretation within larger units.

Such protocols can establish timing and manage data links using bit signals. That is, individual bits are used for timing (so that sender and receiver stay in synchrony) and also for link control. Content—that is, data—bits are sent in the same manner. The only thing that distinguishes data and timing or control bits is their position within the bit stream (for example, every xth bit is a timing bit) or their location in a bit pattern (e.g., after a sequence of y zeros, always send a one bit).

Bit-oriented protocols are an alternative and successor to the older byte-oriented protocols. The latter use bytes or characters to manage the communications link and for timing. A disadvantage of this method is that the bytes or characters used for the link control cannot be used as ordinary data bytes.

Examples of bit-oriented protocols include HDLC (High-Level Data Link Control), SDLC (Synchronous Data Link Control), and LAPB (Link Access Protocol, Balanced).

→ *Compare* Protocol, Byte-Oriented

Protocol, BOOTP (Bootstrap Protocol)

In the Internet community, a protocol for enabling a diskless workstation to boot and to determine necessary information (such as the node's IP address).

Protocol, Bracket

In IBM's SNA (Systems Network Architecture) and APPN (Advanced Peer-to-Peer Networking) environments, a bracket consists of one or more sequences of response units (RUs, which are essentially packets) that are exchanged by participants in a session. The bracket includes both the RUs and the responses to them.

The elements of a bracket make up a transaction, so the entire bracket must be completed before the next bracket can begin. A database query, together with the response, is an example of a bracket.

A bracket protocol is one that uses brackets to exchange information between participants in a session. Because a bracket protocol uses data flow control, one participant in the session must be designated as the initiator and the other as the respondent. With these roles, the participants can use rules guiding bracket operation to control the session.

→ *Broader Categories* APPN (Advanced Peer-to-Peer Networking); SNA (Systems Network Architecture)

Protocol, BSC (Bisynchronous Communication)

A character-oriented, synchronous protocol for controlling communications at the Data-Link layer. BSC was developed by IBM in the early 1960s to make communication with its mainframes easier. The BSC protocol supports ASCII and EBCDIC character codes, as well as a special 6-bit transcode (SBT) used only in BSC.

Protocol, Byte-Control

→ *See* Protocol, Byte-Oriented

Protocol, Byte-Oriented

Character-, or byte-oriented protocols use characters or bytes to manage the communications link and for timing. A disadvantage of this method is that the bytes or characters used for the link control cannot be used as ordinary data bytes.

Most early synchronous protocols, such as IBM's Bisync or Digital Equipment Corporation's DDCMP (Digital Data Communications Messaging Protocol), were byte-oriented. These have been superseded by more efficient bit-oriented protocols, which can establish timing and manage link controls with individual bits.

→ *Compare* Protocol, BOP (Bit-Oriented Protocol)

Protocol, CCP (Compression Control Protocol)

The Compression Control Protocol (CCP) is used with PPP (Point-to-Point Protocol) to configure, enable, and disable data compression algorithms on both ends of the point-to-point link. It is also used to signal in case of a failure of the compression/ decompression mechanism. CCP can support different compression algorithms in each direction in the connection.

CCP is similar to the Link Control Protocol (LCP), which is also used by the PPP. In fact, CCP and LCP both use the same package exchange mechanism. However, the LCP must do its work—establishing a reliable connection at the data link layer—before CCP packets can be exchanged.

→ **Primary Sources** The CCP is described in RFC 1962.

→ **See Also** Protocol, PPP (Point-to-Point Protocol)

Protocol, CHAP (Challenge Handshake Authentication Protocol)

CHAP is a protocol that can be used when a remote node needs to authenticate itself to a network server or when two routers need to authenticate themselves to each other in order to begin a PPP (Point-to-Point Protocol) session. CHAP is the strongest form of authentication used by NT servers—compared to PAP (Password Authentication Protocol) and Allow Anonymous (which requires no authentication). (Actually, Microsoft has added extensions to CHAP that make it even more stringent. This MS-CHAP protocol works with other Microsoft products as well, and can be used over a Remote Access Server (RAS). With MS-CHAP as the authentication protocol, the authentication process requires that Microsoft's encryption be used.)

The weaker PAP uses a two-way handshake and sends authentication strings (username, password, and so forth) in cleartext (that is, in unencrypted form). In contrast, CHAP encrypts these strings and uses a three-way handshake to authenticate users or hosts.

→ **Primary Sources** CHAP is discussed in RFC 1994, and other authentication protocols are discussed in RFCs 1334, 2284, and 2484.

→ **See Also** Protocol, MS-CHAP (Microsoft Challenge Handshake Authentication Protocol)

Protocol, CIDR (Classless Interdomain Routing)

CIDR was developed to deal with the rapid pace at which class C addresses were being used up because of inefficiencies in the way they were being assigned. CIDR makes it possible to allocate a contiguous chunk of class C addresses while using only a single class C address in a routing table for every 256 addresses assigned.

The CIDR protocol is used when routing between nodes at which such CIDR addresses have been assigned.

→ **Primary Sources** CIDR is described in RFCs 1519 and 1520.

Protocol, CIPX (Compressed IPX)

CIPX is a variant of Novell's IPX (Internetwork Package Exchange) protocol. CIPX uses a compressed header instead of the 30-octet header characteristic of IPX packets. The compressed header is between one and seven octets if just the IPX header is compressed.

For IPX packets that contain NCP (NetWare Core Protocol) data, it's possible to compress both the IPX and NCP headers simultaneously. Instead of a 36-octet NCP/IPX header, the CIPX header is between one and eight octets.

Such compression is useful when transmitting over relatively slow WAN (Wide Area Network) lines. The actual compression algorithm to be used must be negotiated between sender and receiver. It's also possible to use header compression in conjunction with a data compression algorithm, which can help further reduce the number of octets that must be transmitted. When both header and data compression are used, the order in which the applications are applied is important. The sender must first use header compression and then data compression; at the receiving end, the algorithms must be applied in reverse order.

→ **Primary Sources** RFC 1553

Protocol, Clearinghouse

A presentation-level protocol in the XNS protocol collection from Xerox. Banyan's StreetTalk naming service is a variant of Xerox's Clearinghouse protocol.

Protocol, CLNP (Connectionless Network Protocol)

In the OSI reference model, CLNP is the Network layer protocol for providing connectionless datagram service. As a provider of connectionless services at the Network layer, CLNP is comparable to the IP protocol in the Internet's TCP/IP suite, so it is also known as ISO IP.

Protocol, CLTP (Connectionless Transport Protocol)

In the OSI reference model, the Transport layer protocol for providing connectionless service. As a provider of connectionless services at the Transport layer, CLTP is comparable to the UDP protocol in the Internet's TCP/IP suite.

Protocol, Communication

A communication protocol, or set of guidelines, is used to regulate how two or more endpoints communicate with each other in any legal combination. Communication protocols can be defined at any of several layers in a Network layer model. The number and definition of the layers depend on the communications models being used.

In a network, both workstations and servers need to support communication protocols. In most local area networks (LANs), the server must be able to support protocols at several layers. Some servers support multiple protocol suites, so that the server may support more than one communication protocol at each of several layers.

Protocol Control Information (PCI)

→ **See** PCI (Protocol Control Information)

Protocol Converter

A device or a program that translates between two or more protocols, thereby enabling the devices or programs that use the respective protocols to communicate. The term is most commonly applied to devices (such as emulation cards) that provide protocol translations to enable a PC to communicate with a mainframe.

Protocol, CSLIP (Compressed Serial Line Interface Protocol)

CSLIP is a variant of the Serial Line Interface Protocol (SLIP), which is used when transmitting IP (Internet Protocol) packets over serial connections such as phone lines. SLIP and CSLIP are used to encapsulate the IP packets when accessing the Internet over a serial line.

CSLIP uses a compressed packet header, and so has less overhead than ordinary SLIP. The compression strategy—known as Van Jacobson compression, after its developer—works by transmitting only differences between successive packets. This makes it possible, in the case of a CSLIP packet, to reduce the header from 24 bytes to 5. While this overhead savings may be only a small percentage of the entire file, it can save a considerable number of bytes when a long document is being transmitted—particularly if the document contains many small packets.

→ *Primary Sources* The SLIP protocol is discussed in RFC 1055. Van Jacobson compression is described in RFC 1141.

Protocol, DAP (Directory Access Protocol)

In the CCITT's X.500 Directory Services model, a protocol used for communications between a DUA (directory user agent) and a DSA (directory system agent). These agents represent the user or program and the directory, respectively. The DAP is in contrast to the DSP (Directory Service Protocol), which is used by DSAs when communicating with each other.

Protocol, Data-Compression

In telecommunications, a data-compression protocol is any of several schemes used to compress data before transmission. These differ from data-compression programs in that the compression at the sending end and the decompression at the receiving end are automatic and completely transparent to the user. In fact, users may not even know the data is being compressed.

Two commonly used compression schemes are the CCITT's V.42bis, which supports transmission rates of up to 38,400bps, and Microcom's MNP 5, which supports rates up to 19,200bps.

Protocol Data Unit (PDU)

→ *See* PDU (Protocol Data Unit)

Protocol, DDCMP (Digital Data Communications Messaging Protocol)

A proprietary, byte-oriented protocol used at the Data-Link layer in DECnet networks. DDCMP can be used for synchronous or asynchronous transmissions.

Protocol, DDP (Datagram Delivery Protocol)

In an internetwork based on Apple's AppleTalk network software, DDP is a protocol for delivering packets between nodes on different subnetworks. This protocol is responsible for actually getting data from end to end, from the source to the destination.

The packets are actually delivered to sockets, which are addresses associated with particular processes on the node. Thus, a node might receive datagrams intended for different programs. While all delivered to the same machine, the datagrams would go to different processes running on that machine.

Either of two main forms of the DDP packet is used, depending on whether the datagram is being delivered within a network or is going across a router:

- Short DDP is used for datagrams being sent within a network.

- Long DDP is used for datagrams traveling between networks.

Protocol, DECP (Digital Equipment Corporation Protocol)

The DECP was the first spanning tree algorithm for transparent bridging, and it served as the basis for the spanning tree algorithm defined in the IEEE 802.1d specification. A spanning tree algorithm is used to find a valid path between network elements by locating a path with no loops in it.

Protocol-Dependent

Describes a process or component that is tied to a particular Network layer protocol, such as IP or IPX, and is therefore limited in the types of packets it can process. Simple routers, for example, are protocol-dependent, which means that the router can handle only packets that support a particular protocol. Multiprotocol routers, which can handle any of several protocols, are protocol-independent.

Protocol, DFWMAC (Distributed Foundation Wireless Media Access Control)

A Data-Link layer protocol for wireless local area networks, adopted by the IEEE 802.11 committee on wireless networks and designed to provide a common interface between various types of wireless and wired networks.

→ *See Also* Network, Wireless

Protocol, DHCP (Dynamic Host Configuration Protocol)

On a TCP/IP-based network, DHCP is used to get information about a client host's (i.e., a network node's) configuration from a DHCP server, which is a specially-designated network node. This is useful, for example, in situations where clients are assigned IP addresses dynamically, and where these addresses disappear after a session or after the host relinquishes the address.

This is common with Internet Access Providers that assign IP addresses as subscribers connect for a session. The configuration information may not exist until the client requests it. This helps keep down administrative chores.

DHCP is similar—and partially equivalent—to the BOOTP protocol, which is used by diskless hosts to get their predefined address when the host connects to the network. DHCP also has similarities with other configuration transmission or retrieval protocols, including RARP (Reverse Address Resolution Protocol), which is used in diskless workstations from Sun Microsystems. However, DHCP goes beyond both of these protocols in that it can handle more than just fixed addresses.

In addition to being a protocol, DHCP also provides a mechanism for allocating network addresses. In fact, DHCP provides three mechanisms:

- Automatic allocation, in which a permanent IP address is assigned to the host.

- Dynamic allocation, in which DHCP assigns a temporary IP address. This mechanism is what distinguishes DHCP from earlier protocols.

- Manual allocation, in which the network administrator assigns the address, and DHCP merely transfers the address.

A client may request a configuration from any available server by broadcasting a DHCPDISCOVER message to accessible servers. After getting any replies (DHCPOFFER messages), the client selects a server. The selected server's address is included in the DHCPREQUEST message the client sends to all the servers contacted originally. The selected server then begins creating the message with the requested configuration information; the other servers take the request message as an indication that they have been rejected and that they need not concern themselves with the client any longer.

The modified version of DHCP is being developed for use with the new version of the Internet Protocol (IPv6). The revised DHCP will provide dynamic addressing capabilities for the new 128-bit addressing scheme—just as the current version does for nodes in the 32-bit address space. A separate mechanism—stateless autoconfiguration—will be used to provide predefined addresses, such as those used in local links.

→ *Primary Sources* DHCP is discussed in RFCs 1541 (which defines DHCP), 1534 and 1533 (which discuss the relationship between DHCP and BOOTP).

Protocol, DISP (Directory Information Shadowing Protocol)

In Novell's NDS (Novell Directory Structure), directory information is replicated at multiple sites—so that the information will not be lost if the primary copy is corrupted or destroyed. Such "spare" copies are known as shadowed copies, and they are maintained and exchanged by Directory Service Agents (DSAs). Two DSAs that need or wish to exchange such shadow information will use the DISP to do so. Prior to doing so, however, the DSAs must establish a shadow operational binding that will connect the DSAs. This binding is established using the Directory Operations Protocol, or DOP.

Protocol, Distance-Vector

A distance-vector protocol is any of several routing protocols that use a distance-vector algorithm to determine available connections. With a distance-vector protocol, each router transmits information about the cost of reaching accessible destinations to each of the router's neighbors. Examples of distance-vector protocols include the following:

- RIP (Routing Information Protocol) from the TCP/IP protocol suite, but also used in other suites
- RTMP (Routing Table Maintenance Protocol) from the AppleTalk suite
- IDRP (Interdomain Routing Protocol) from the OSI suite

Distance-vector protocols are in contrast to link-state protocols, which use a different strategy for getting routing information. Distance-vector protocols provide information about the costs of reaching all possible destinations, whereas link-state strategies provide information only about the distances from a router to all its immediate neighbor routers. The distance-vector strategy requires more work when setting up or updating the routing information. In contrast, link-state protocols need to do more work during the actual routing.

→ *Broader Category*   Protocol, Routing

→ *Compare*   Protocol, Link-State

Protocol, DLC (Data Link Control)

A protocol used in IBM's SNA architecture to manage the physical connection and to ensure that messages reach their destination.

Protocol, DOP (Directory Operations Protocol)

→ *See*   Protocol, DISP (Directory Information Shadowing Protocol)

Protocol, DSP (Directory System Protocol)

In the CCITT X.500 Directory Services model, a protocol used by DSAs (directory system agents) when communicating with each other. This is in contrast to the DAP (Directory Access Protocol), which is used for communications between a DSA and a DUA (directory user agent). The latter represents a user or application hoping to use a directory service.

Protocol, ECTP (Ethernet Configuration Test Protocol)

A protocol used to test whether a particular LAN configuration conforms to the requirements for the Blue Book Ethernet (as opposed to the variant defined in IEEE 802.3 documents).

Protocol, EGP (Exterior Gateway Protocol)

In the Internet TCP/IP protocol suite, a class of protocols used for communications between autonomous systems. The two most widely supported EGPs are the Exterior Gateway Protocol (also known as EGP) and the Border Gateway Protocol (BGP). EGP is also a specific exterior gateway protocol (defined in RFC 904), which has since been replaced by the BGP—for which the most recent version, BGP-3, is defined in RFC 1267.

Protocol, EIGRP (Enhanced Interior Gateway Routing Protocol)

EIGRP is a proprietary link-state routing protocol developed by Cisco Systems. EIGRP gets improved performance by also using features and information based on distance-vector protocols and by operating with a built-in algorithm (the diffusing update algorithm, or DUAL) for removing transient loops in potential routes. Eliminating such loops decreases the amount of computation required.

→ *Compare* Protocol, IGRP (Interior Gateway Routing Protocol)

→ *See Also* Protocol, Distance-Vector; Protocol, Link-State

Protocol, ELAP (EtherTalk Link Access Protocol)

In the AppleTalk network protocol suite, the Data-Link layer protocol for EtherTalk (Apple's implementation of the Ethernet architecture).

Protocol, Error-Correcting

An error-correcting protocol is any of several communications protocols that is capable of both detecting and correcting simple transmission errors. The error detection and correction require the insertion of additional information at predefined points in the transmission. The sender and receiver compute a value using the transmitted data and compare the results.

Commonly used error-correcting protocols include Microcom's MNP 4 and MNP 10, which support rates of up to 9600bps, and CCITT's v.42, which supports rates of up to 9600bps.

Protocol, ES-IS (End System to Intermediate System)

In the OSI network management model, the type of protocol used by a node (an end system) to communicate with a router (an intermediate system).

Protocol, ESMTP (Extended Simple Mail Transfer Protocol)

ESMTP is a version of the Simple Mail Transfer Protocol (SMTP) that has been enhanced through the addition of several services and options, and that is designed to be extensible. ESMTP's added services were actually defined in RFC 821, the document in which SMTP was described. However, these services were not included among those required for a minimal SMTP implementation.

The added services include SOML (send or mail, which sends the message to the user's terminal if possible or to the user's mailbox if not), SAML (send and mail, which sends the message to the user's mailbox in every case and tries to deliver it to the user's terminal if possible), VRFY (which verifies a user's identity), and EXPN (which expands a mailing list by returning the email addresses of everyone on the list).

Since ESMTP is extensible, it is possible to define additional services. However, any new services must be registered with and approved by the IANA (Internet Assigned Numbers Authority)—in order to ensure that each new service has a unique code associated with it.

ESMTP works in the same way as SMTP, except that it begins session negotiations with an EHLO command instead of the HELO—to indicate that the sending host is using ESMTP. If the receiving host also supports ESMTP it will send an appropriate response.

ESMTP is sometimes known as SMTPE

→ **Primary Sources** ESMTP's services are defined in RFC 821, and are discussed in RFCs 1869 and 1870.

Protocol, File Transfer

Any of several protocols for transferring files between machines. File transfer is an application-layer service. The file transfer protocol used depends on the type of networks involved. For example, FTAM provides file transfer services for networks that use the OSI reference model, and FTP provides these services for TCP/IP protocols.

Protocol, FLAP (FDDITalk Link Access Protocol)

In the AppleTalk network protocol suite, the Data-Link layer protocol for FDDITalk (Apple's implementation of the FDDI network architecture).

Protocol, FLIP (Fast Local Internet Protocol)

FLIP is an Internet protocol that was developed as an alternative to TCP and IP for internetworks made up of large-scale distributed systems. FLIP was developed because it offered better security and network management capabilities for distributed systems than did TCP (Transfer Control Protocol) and IP (Internet Protocol).

FLIP was written at the Vrije University in Holland, and was originally designed for internetworks using the Amoeba distributed operating system.

Protocol, Flooding

A flooding protocol is used to inform routers of changes in link states in a network or Internetwork. When a router learns of a change in link state, it determines whether the information is newer than the information in its link state database. If so, the router sends a packet informing the Designated Routers (DRs) on the network of the new link state.

If the information is also new to the DR, it floods other routers with the Link State Update (LSU) information. Once all routers have received the LSU, they recompute their routing tables to update them.

Protocol, FTAM (File Transfer, Access, and Management)

In the OSI reference model, an application layer protocol and service for remote file access. FTAM enables an application to read, write, or otherwise manage files on a remote machine.

Protocol, FTP (File Transfer Protocol)

In the TCP/IP (or Internet) protocol suite, a file transfer protocol. FTP is an application layer protocol that uses the services of the TCP protocol at the Transport layer to move the files. anonymous FTP is an example of this protocol.

Anonymous FTP is used to download files from public directories. This provides a generic download mechanism. To use anonymous FTP, the user proceeds as follows:

- Run FTP to connect to the host needed.

- Respond with anonymous to the request for a user name.

- Respond with the user's electronic-mail (e-mail) address to the password prompt.

As Anonymous, the user will be allowed access to the directory containing the file or files desired. The system will send the requested files to the address specified as the password.

Protocol, HDLC (High-level Data Link Control)

HDLC is a bit-oriented, Data-Link layer protocol that has been standardized in several ISO documents (3309, 4335, and 7809), and that can support any of the following:

- Half- or full-duplex communications

- Circuit- or packet-switched networks

- Point-to-point or multipoint network topologies

- Transmission over cable or wireless media

HDLC was derived by the ISO from IBM's SDLC protocol in the late 1970s. HDLC uses essentially the same frame structure as SDLC. Also like SDLC, the HDLC protocol is concerned with primary and secondary nodes. A primary, or master, node controls a communication; a secondary node functions in response to a primary's commands. In addition to primaries and secondaries, HDLC supports combined components, which can serve as primary or secondary nodes, depending on the situation.

HDLC Transfer Modes

A major difference between HDLC and SDLC is the fact that HDLC can work using any of three different transfer modes and can function at multiple levels. HDLC can work in the following modes:

- NRM (Normal Response Mode), which uses one primary and at least one secondary. Before it can communicate, a secondary

must be given permission by the primary. SDLC uses this mode.

- ARM (Asynchronous Response Mode), which uses one primary and at least one secondary. Secondaries do not need permission to communicate with a primary.

- ABM (Asynchronous Balanced Mode), which uses one or more combined nodes. Since each node can be either a primary or a secondary, nodes can communicate without first getting permission. This is the mode that underlies most Data-Link layer protocols on LANs.

HDLC Operation

A session involving HDLC occurs in three phases:

- One node initiates an interaction, by requesting an initialization process, which involves the exchange of packets to establish the type of connection and transfer mode requested.

- The parties exchange information and control packets, known as DPDUs (data-link protocol data units) or frames.

- One node initiates a disconnect operation.

HDLC Frames

A session involves the exchange of three types of frames:

I (Information) frame Contains data, generally in the form of packets from higher-level protocols. I frames may also contain error-checking and flow-control information. I frames have both a sending and a receiving sequence number.

S (Supervisory) frame Provides a separate way to give commands and exert control in a session.

U (Unnumbered) frame Provides additional functions for link control.

"HDLC frame format" shows the format of an HDLC frame.

Basic Frame Format

Flag 8 Bits	Address 8*(1+) Bits	Control 8 or 16 Bits	Info 0+ Bits	FCS 16 or 32 Bits	Flag 8 Bits

I Frame Control Field

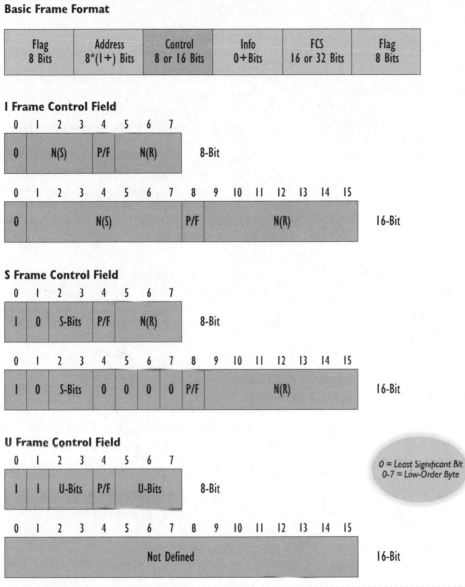

S Frame Control Field

U Frame Control Field

0 = Least Significant Bit
0-7 = Low-Order Byte

HDLC FRAME FORMAT

Protocol, Hello

In the ATM (Asynchronous Transfer Mode) network architecture, the Hello protocol is used as part of the broader PNNI protocol, which can provide routing and signaling on a switch-to-switch basis—that is between a node and a network or between two networks. (PNNI stands for either Private Network-to-Node Interface or Private Network-to-Network Interface.) More specifically, the Hello protocol is a link state protocol that nodes can use to determine where and who their neighbor nodes are.

→ *Broader Categories* ATM (Asynchronous Transfer Mode); Protocol, Link-State

Protocol, HMMP (Hypermedia Management Protocol)

HMMP is a communications protocol that extends HTTP (Hypertext Transfer Protocol) to enable management of network objects (such as servers, clients, and other network resources) over the Web. HMMP is essentially a network management protocol (such as the Simple Network Management Protocol, or SNMP) running over HTTP. However, HMMP can also be configured to work with other management interfaces, such as the Desktop Management Interface (DMI) which is used to manage PCs. Thus, HMMP helps to extend the capabilities of web-based programs (most notably, browsers) to enable them to manage network objects (such as routers or server) or PCs over the Web.

HMMP actually is part of an architecture that represents a new type of network management strategy—namely, a Web-based one. The WBEM (Web-based enterprise management) proposal defines a Hypermedia Management Architecture (HMMA) which provides an object-oriented and Web-based approach to managing network objects and events. HMMA consists of two major components: HMMS (Hypermedia Management Schema) and HMMP.

HMMS provides the management model, or schema. Because this management model is object-oriented, the managed objects can be handled in terms of their relationships with each other—which may include such object-based features as property inheritance and polymorphism. As is the case in other object-oriented contexts, objects communicate by passing events among themselves, and HMMP is used to accomplish this. The events that pass between a browser and the managed devices on the network (which are known as hypermedia managed objects, or HMMOs) are particularly important. For example, the browser may need to query a managed device about its state—in order to make decisions about subsequent actions.

The first implementation of such an architecture should be available by the time you are reading this. This implementation is known as the Hypermedia Object Model (HMOM).

Protocol, HTTP (Hypertext Transfer Protocol)

HTTP is a fast, stateless (amnesiac), and object-oriented protocol used most notably on the World Wide Web. HTTP is used to allow Web clients and servers to negotiate and interact with each other.

Because it is fast, HTTP is ideal for retrieving and transferring hypermedia materials across distributed systems. Because it is stateless, HTTP does not have any memory of transactions. This is handy for the network traffic patterns found on the Web—constant connections and disconnections. Because it is object-oriented, it can be used to send generic methods, such as GET and POST, to operate on a variety of data types (http, ftp, gopher, etc). In fact, new data types can be created and added to HTTP's capabilities.

HTTP Messages

HTTP messages have a Header and possibly a Body. The Header can contain three types of fields:

- General-Header fields, in which the sender can include information such as the date, or MIME-version, if applicable.

- Request-Header fields, in which the client can qualify the request. For example, If-Modified-Since is a request field that specifies a cutoff date—ignore the request if the object hasn't been modified since the specified date. Note that only clients will include this type of field.

- Entity-Header fields, in which the sender can provide specific information about the object being transferred.

HTTP supports two types of messages: Request (by the client) and Response (by the server). Either of these may be qualified by using the appropriate header fields.

Request Messages

A request message generally takes the form:

```
method object {header fields} {body}
```

A method is a function that can be associated with multiple objects and that may take different forms for some or all of these objects. HTTP request methods include GET, HEAD, and POST.

The object should refer to some type of file or resource. This object is specified by its URI (Universal Resource Identifier). Perhaps the best known examples of URIs are the URLs (Universal Resource Locators) that represent the addresses of pages on the Web.

Header fields are optional, as is a message body, but they can't both be left out of a message. GET and HEAD requests don't have bodies, because the client doesn't want to send anything other than the request. On the other hand, POST commands will generally have a message body, which consists of the material to be posted.

POST is defined in a way that makes it possible to use the same protocol for all the of the following:

- Annotating existing objects

- Posting a message to a mailing list, newsgroup, or bulletin board

- Passing data (from a user-completed form, for example) to a data-processing program

- Adding to a database

Response Messages

In the response message, the server sends back either the requested material or an error message. Actually, the server also sends some type of return code. This will be a three digit integer beginning with one of the following digits:

1xx (Information) Reserved for future use

2xxx (Success) The action was completed successfully

3xx (Redirection) Further action is needed before the request will be done

4xx (Client error) There may be a possible syntax error in the request or a non-defined request

5xx (Server error) The server was unable to carry out a valid request.

HTTP Variants

Because of the unbelievable growth of the Web, HTTP has been a busy little protocol. With heavy use, various weaknesses and problems with HTTP have appeared. An important shortcoming is HTTP's minimal security features. HTTP can do basic authentication, but not encryption. SHTTP (Secure HTTP) was developed by EIT to add security features to HTTP. SHTTP supports encryption and security checks.

Another way to improve security when using HTTP is to also use SSL (Secure Socket Layer) from Netscape Communications Corporation. SSL provides security and authentication capabilities by

P

mediating between the TCP/IP transport protocols and service-based protocols (such as HTTP).

→ *Primary Sources* Drafts of the HTTP specifications are available through the IETF home page, which is located at `http://www.ietf.cnri.reston.va.us/`.

In particular, documents relating to HTTP and other topics under consideration by the ietf will generally be available from the/ietf-online-proceedings directory of the `ftp.ietf.cnri.reston.va.us` FTP site.

A PostScript version of an August 1995 draft of the HTTP specifications has the following forbidding title:

`draft-ietf-http-v10-spec-02.ps`

Protocol, HTTPS (Hypertext Transfer Protocol, Secure)

HTTPS is a variant of the hypertext transfer protocol (HTTP) used by a server that is SSL-enabled. (SSL is the secure socket layer protocol developed by Netscape to provide encryption and autenthication for transactions.)

→ *See Also* Protocol, SSL (Secure Socket Layer)

Protocol, ICMP (Internet Control Message Protocol)

In the TCP/IP protocol suite, a protocol used to handle errors at the Network layer. ICMP is actually part of the IP, which is the Network layer protocol in the TCP/IP suite.

Protocol, IDP (Internet Datagram Packet)

A network-level routing protocol in the XNS protocol suite from Xerox. IDP can be used to route data or packets from any of several Transport layer protocols, including RIP (Routing Information Protocol), Echo, PEP (Packet Exchange Protocol), or SPP (Sequenced Packet Protocol). IDP was the basis for the NetWare IPX (Internetwork Packet Exchange) protocol.

Protocol, IDRP (Interdomain Routing Protocol)

An ISO protocol for routing transmissions between different administrative domains. This protocol uses a distance-vector algorithm and is based on the Border Gateway Protocol (BGP), which is used in the TCP/IP suite.

Protocol, IFMP (Ipsilon Flow Management Protocol)

IFMP is a protocol developed by Ipsilon to enable data to move more efficiently across a network or between networks. Specifically, IFMP makes it possible to attach a label to a flow at the data link level (layer 2). (A flow is a sequence of packets all going to the same destination address.)

Once a packet is identified as belonging to the flow, its destination address information need not be checked, which saves time.

This makes it possible to move packets across or between networks on the basis of layer 2 information—that is, without having to check (layer 3) network addresses for every packet.

IFMP is one of several solutions to the problem of routing packets as efficiently as possible. Others include Cisco's tag switching and efforts by IBM and Toshiba. The IETF (Internet Engineering Task Force) has set up a working group to develop an integrated solution that can be used by all vendors. The entry on MPLS (Multiprotocol Label Switching) describes this effort.

→ *See Also* Layer 3 Switching; MPLS (Multiprotocol Label Switching)

Protocol, IGP (Interior Gateway Protocol)

In the Internet TCP/IP protocol suite, a term for a protocol used by routers within an autonomous system to communicate with each other. Within the Internet community, the three most widely supported IGPs are RIP (Routing Information Protocol), OSPF (Open Shortest Path First), and Cisco's proprietary IGRP (Interior Gateway Routing Protocol). Integrated IS-IS is also an IGP, designed originally for OSI environments.

→ **Broader Category**   Protocol, Routing

→ **Compare**   Protocol, EGP (Exterior Gateway Protocol)

Protocol, IGRP (Interior Gateway Routing Protocol)

IGRP is Cisco's proprietary improvement on the Routing Information Protocol (RIP) that for a long time was the main protocol for routing within a domain. RIP has several shortcomings, with one of the most serious being its inability to scale well to larger networks or internetworks. Like RIP, IGRP uses a distance-vector algorithm to identify and evaluate possible routes between specified locations.

Whereas RIP uses only hop count as a metric for distance-vector computations, IGRP adds several other metrics, including delay, bandwidth, reliability, and load:

- Delay refers to the total amount of time a packet takes to get from the source to its destination.

- Bandwidth refers to the number of bits that can be transmitted over a connection within a specified time period (usually one second).

- Reliability indicates the probability that a packet will reach its destination.

- Load specifies the percentage of a connection's bandwidth that is actually being used. This is expressed as a fraction with 255 in the denominator, where 200/255 represents about 80 percent usage.

IGRP sends out updated routing tables to adjacent routers so that those can update their own routing information. Similarly, those routers send out their own routing tables. Once everyone is updated, routing can begin or continue. IGRP can use any of several methods to maintain a connection, but will generally default to a path hold-down technique for older implementations of the protocol and to route poisoning in the newest versions.

→ **Broader Categories**   Protocol, Routing; Protocol, IGP (Interior Gateway Protocol)

→ **See Also**   Protocol, RIP (Routing Information Protocol)

Protocol, IIOP (Internet Inter-ORB Protocol)

IIOP is a protocol developed to make it possible to request data objects over distributed systems—specifically, over the Internet. The protocol provides a way for clients to find, request, and use data objects when necessary. Such requests are made through an ORB (object request broker), which mediates between clients and a back end database application or a server managing access to such a database.

IIOP is used in CORBA (common object request broker architecture), which is a platform-independent specification that allows clients to interact across distributed networks—both with each other and with objects that are located in remote locations.

IIOP is based on GIOP (General Inter-ORB Protocol), but has been optimized for use on the Internet. Microsoft's protocols for COM+ (Component Object model) and DCOM (Distributed COM) represent a different way to deal with distributed objects. These protocols have the same functionality as IIOP, but have been developed and optimized primarily for use on a Windows—mainly Windows NT or Windows 2000-platform. WebBroker, another, more recent effort—and one still in development—is designed for use over the Web, and is optimized for that environment.

→ Broader Category CORBA (Common Object Request Broker Architecture)

Protocol, IMAP (Internet Message Access Protocol)

IMAP is a recently introduced protocol for communicating with a post office (temporary e-mail store) in order to store and retrieve e-mail messages in the post office. IMAP runs on top of TCP/IP. It is not a protocol for actually sending e-mail.

Introduced in December of 1994, IMAP is actually version 4—that is, it is known as IMAP4. Previous protocols to accomplish the same tasks had the same acronym, but a different expansion: IMAP2 and IMAP3 were known as "Interactive Mail Access Protocols."

→ Primary Sources IMAP4 is introduced in RFC 1730, and various aspects are discussed in RFCs 1731, 1732, and 1733. IMAP2 and IMAP3 are discussed in RFCs 1176 and 1203, respectively.

Protocol, InARP (Inverse Address Resolution Protocol)

→ See Protocol, ARP (Address Resolution Protocol)

Protocol, InATMARP (Inverse Asynchronous Transfer Mode Address Resolution Protocol)

→ See Protocol, ATMARP (Asynchronous Transfer Mode Address Resolution Protocol)

Protocol, InFlexion

InFlexion is a messaging protocol from Motorola. InFlexion is designed for use in narrowband PCS (Personal Communication Services). The protocol supports transfer rates of up to 112Kbps and it is two-way. This makes is possible to send messages in both directions in paging networks.

Protocol-Independent

Describes a process or device that is not tied to a particular Network layer protocol (such as DDP, IP, or IPX). For example, a bridge, which operates at the Data-Link layer, is protocol-independent. In contrast, older, single-protocol routers are protocol-dependent. This type of router is being replaced by the protocol-independent multiprotocol router.

Protocol-Independent Routing (PIR)

→ See PIR (Protocol-Independent Routing)

Protocol, Integrated IS-IS

The Integrated IS-IS protocol is used for communications among routers within an autonomous system (AS), or a routing domain. AS and routing domain are Internet and OSI terms, respectively. An AS consists of a collection of routers that are administered by the same organization and use the same protocol to communicate with each other.

This type of protocol is known as an Interior Gateway Protocol (IGP) or an intradomain routing protocol, in Internet and OSI terminology, respectively. The Integrated IS-IS protocol can be used in both TCP/IP (Internet) and OSI environments. Another example of an IGP protocol in the TCP/IP suite is the OSPF (Open Shortest Path First) protocol.

Protocol, Interdomain

To manage the increasing complexity of the Internet—as it grew from a few dozen to hundreds and then thousands of connected subnetworks—it was divided into autonomous systems, which were organizationally self-contained subnetworks. (Autonomous systems are known as domains in the Open System Interconnect, or OSI, reference model.) Each autonomous system (AS) is administered by a single organization. These autonomous systems can connect to the Internet over routers known as exterior gateways, and can communicate over the Internet backbone. Autonomous systems need not use the same platforms to communicate. Communication is possible as long as both systems in a communication support the IP (Internet Protocol) protocol stack.

Over this stack, the exterior gateways communicate with each other using interdomain protocols. These are also known as exterior gateway protocols (EGPs), but this term also refers to a specific example of such an interdomain protocol—defined in RFC 904. This EGP has been replaced by the Border Gateway Protocol (BGP-4), which is defined in RFC 1267.

→ *Broader Category* Protocol, Routing

→ *Compare* Protocol, IGP (Interior Gateway Protocol)

Protocol, IP (Internet Protocol)

IP is the widely supported Network layer protocol for the Internet. IP is one of the protocols in the TCP/IP protocol suite.

This protocol defines and routes datagrams across the Internet and provides connectionless transport service. The IP protocol uses packet switching and makes a best effort to deliver its packets. The IP protocol uses the services of the Data-Link layer to accomplish the actual transmission along the path.

IP Packet Header Fields

An IP packet consists of a header and data, known as a payload. The payload can be up to 64KB, and must be at least 512 bytes. The header consists of the following:

Version The version of IP being used. Version 4 is currently standard. Values of 5 or 6 indicate that special stream protocols are being used.

IHL (Internet header length) The number of 32-bit words used in the header. Padding is used to make sure the header ends on a 32-bit boundary.

ToS (Type of Service) The type of handling and delays that are allowed for the packet. The details of this field are currently in flux.

Total length The number of bytes in the entire packet, including the header. This value must be between 576 and 65536, inclusive.

ID A value created by the sender to identify the packet, so its components can be found and reassembled if the packet must be fragmented during its travels. This field is closely tied to the next 2-byte area.

Flags Three bits that are used to indicate whether the original IP packet has been fragmented and, if so, whether the current packet is the last fragment. The high-order bit is always 0. The middle bit is 0 if the packet may be fragmented and 1 otherwise. The low-order bit is 0 if the packet is the last fragment and 1 otherwise.

Fragment offset Thirteen bits that specify the location of the fragment in the original packet.

TTL (Time To Live) Originally, this field indicated the number of seconds the packet was allowed to travel in a network before being destroyed. Now it is interpreted as a hop count value, and is generally assigned a default value of 32. The contents of this field are decreased at each router to which the packet is passed.

Protocol This value specifies the higher-level protocol contained in the packet's data field. The table "Assignments for an IP Packet's Protocol Field" lists some of the values that have been assigned to specific protocols or organizations. Note that this list is subject to change. The Internet Assigned Numbers Authority (IANA) is the keeper of the protocol assignments. Official lists are published in the "Assigned Numbers" RFCs. The most recent of these is 1700. Many of the values not listed are still unassigned.

ASSIGNMENTS FOR AN IP PACKET'S PROTOCOL FIELD

Value	Protocol
0	Reserved
1	ICMP Internet Control Message Protocol
2	IGMP (Internet Group Management Protocol)
3	GGP (Gateway-to-Gateway Protocol)
5	ST (Stream Protocol)
6	TCP (Transmission Control Protocol)
8	EGP (Exterior Gateway Protocol)
11	NVP-II (Network Voice Protocol)
17	UDP (User Datagram Protocol)
80	CLNP (ISO Connectionless Protocol)
83	VINES
85	NSFNET-IGP (Internal Gateway Protocol)
88	IGRP (Internet Gateway Routing Protocol)
89	OSPF(Open Shortest Path First)
255	Reserved

Checksum This value is used to make sure the header has not been corrupted or changed during its travels. The value must be updated at each stopover point because certain fields are changed.

SA (Source Address) The IP address of the sender. This is not the same as an Ethernet or Token Ring address.

DA (Destination Address) The IP address of the destination node.

Options There may be up to three Option fields. The interpretations for these fields may be defined by the user of the protocol.

Padding This field is used to make sure the header ends on a 32-bit boundary.

Data This field contains material from a higher-level protocol.

The header is shown in "IP datagram header."

→ *Primary Source* RFC 791

→ *Broader Categories* TCP/IP Protocol Suite

Protocol, IPng/IPv6 (Internet Protocol, next generation/version 6)

IPng refers to the successor to IPv4 (Internet Protocol version 4) as the network-layer protocol in the Internet's TCP/IP protocol suite. This is the protocol responsible for routing or delivering packets to their destination.

The phenomenal growth of the Internet has begun to push IP to its limits. Because of this, an IETF (Internet Engineering Task Force) working group was formed to plan the next generation of protocols. In late 1993, an RFC (1550) was released on behalf of this working group. This document asked for white papers from anyone with suggestions for requirements that the new protocol should or must fulfill.

The document also listed 16 issues considered relevant when designing and creating the new protocol. These issues are a combination of technical issues relating to features and (current or imminent) shortcomings in IPv4, policy and administrative issues, and practical issues having to do with implementation and transition. Example issues include

Scalability The next version should be able to provide addresses for up to 10^{12} (that's right, a trillion) hosts!

Transition and deployment The details and considerations of how to switch from one protocol to the next must be planned out.

Mobile hosts Whether to make it easier for hosts to connect from mobile locations. If so, how to do it?

Robustness and Fault Tolerance How to ensure that the new version is at least as robust and fault tolerant as the current one.

The solicitation garnered almost 20 RFCs in response—mostly from representatives of different industries or organizations who might be affected by the new protocol. Respondents came from high-tech companies, universities, research centers, consortia, telecommunications, and entertainment industries, etc.

Based on this and other feedback, the IETF working group released a draft specification in June of 1995. In this document, the protocol is called IPv6 (IP version 6). A more recent version of the specification—still just a draft standard—is to be found in RFC2460, which appeared in December, 1998. While there is increased consensus for Ipv6, people and groups are still working on alternatives to the IETF specifications, and one of those may actually end up becoming the actual next version of IP.

IPv6 differs from the current version in the following areas:

Addressing capabilities IPv6 uses 16 octets (128 bits) for addresses (as opposed to 4 octets, or 32 bits, in IPv4). This is more than enough address space for a trillion hosts, and even enough to use different addressing schemes and hierarchies. To allay any fears of another address shortage threatening IPv6, note that 128 bits are enough for almost a trillion trillion nonhierarchical addresses for every square meter of surface area on our planet. This ratio

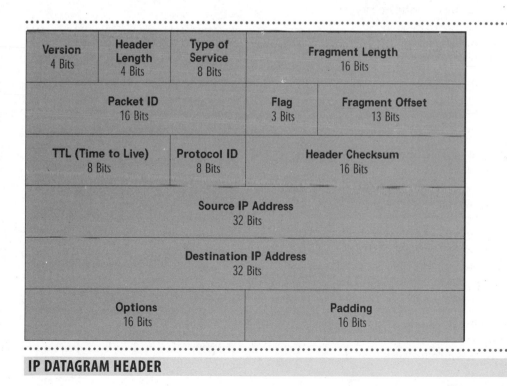

IP DATAGRAM HEADER

drops to about just a few thousand per square meter once bits are allocated for hierarchical groupings—still more than ample room for growth. IPv6 addresses actually identify interfaces rather than network nodes. A single node can have multiple interfaces, so can be reached through any of multiple addresses. IPv6 also supports a new type of address—an anycast address. Such an address is used when sending a packet to any of a group of interfaces, and it ensures that only one copy of the packet is sent to a node that is associated with multiple addresses on the anycast list.

Address notation 128 bits provide a lot of possibilities for addresses. IPv6 will, in fact, support several addressing schemes—for back compatibility and to increase the likelihood of a smooth transition to IPv6. The notation for specifying addresses will change, however. IPv6 will use colons (:) instead of periods to separate address elements. Special notation will make it easy to represent addresses that are encapsulated in the longer format—for example, current (32-bit) addresses which will have many leading zeros when represented as IPv6 addresses.

Header format The header format has been simplified by dropping some fields or making them optional. This is to reduce the overhead from the packet headers.

Header extensions and options IPv6 provides for several types of optional extension headers, which can provide special instructions for handling a packet. Currently, six extensions are supported: Hop-by-hop, routing, fragment, destination options, authentication, and encapsulating security payload. All extensions except hop-by-hop are processed only at the final destination. A hop-by-hop extension is processed at every stop.

Flow labeling capability IPv6 packets can be labeled as belonging to a particular packet sequence (traffic flow), which may be receiving special processing or which may require a particular type or quality of service.

Authentication and privacy IPv6 includes extensions that make it possible to provide some security measures with this protocol.

IPv6 Packets

An IPv6 packet consists of header(s) + payload. Between the IP header and the payload, the packet may include up to seven optional headers. (Any of the six extension headers listed earlier—hop-by-hop, routing, etc—can appear up to one time; the Destination Options header can appear twice.) The presence of such an optional header is indicated by a value in the Next Header field found in the packet (or optional) header. "IPv6 packet" shows the format of such a packet.

The value in the priority field specifies what kind of traffic is in the packet. The table "Priority Values" shows the possible types of traffic.

PRIORITY VALUES

Value	Meaning
0	Uncharacterized traffic
1	Filler traffic (e.g., news)
2	Unattended data transfer (e.g., e-mail)
3	Reserved
4	Attended bulk transfer (e.g., ftp, nfs)
5	Reserved
6	Interactive traffic (e.g., telnet, X)
7	Internet control traffic (e.g., routing protocols, SNMP)

The flow label is used to group packets that are to be given the same handling or type of service.

Payload length specifies the number of octets in the payload portion of the packet. A value of 0 means that the payload is actually being carried as part of a Jumbo payload in the hop-by-hop option. This payload must be larger than 65,535 octets.

The Next header field identifies the type of header that follows the IPv6 header. The value will determine whether there are any optional headers before the payload. If this value is zero in the IPv6 header, then the next header is a Hop-by-hop header. Otherwise, IPv6 uses the values used in the IPv4 Protocol field. The values associated with various protocols are listed in the "Assigned Numbers" RFC, the most recent of which is 1700. (See the table "Assignments for an IP Packet's Protocol Field" in the "Protocol, IP" entry for examples of such values.)

Hop limit is the maximum number of nodes through which the packet can be passed. Each node that passes the packet on will decrement the hop limit value by 1. If this value reaches 0 before the packet reaches its destination, the packet will be discarded. In IPv4, the lifetime of a packet is specified by the TTL (time to live) field. This was originally an actual time limit, but later became a hop count. In IPv6, a packet's lifetime is shortened only by hops between nodes, not by the mere passage of time.

The 128-bit Source Address field contains the address of the packet's originator. The details of the addressing scheme to be used with IPv6 are still being worked out.

The 128-bit Destination Address field contains the address of the packet's intended recipient. If the packet includes a Routing header, then the destination address may be only an intermediate stop.

The IETF specifications impose constraints and restrictions on the sequence in which certain headers can appear, and make strong recommendations about others. There are also restrictions on the address boundaries for the header fields.

IPv6 is only a draft, and may change—possibly several times—before it is finalized. Nonetheless, it represents a major departure from the current protocol, and is designed to enable modification up the line if this seems advisable.

→ *Primary Sources* Comments and discussions of IPng can be found in several RFCs, including 1550

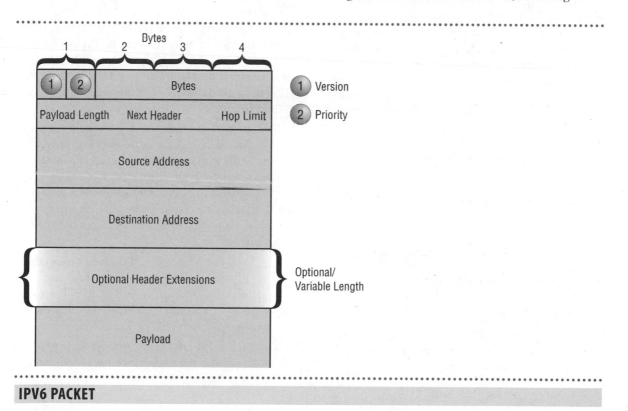

IPV6 PACKET

(the original solicitation for comments), most of the RFCs in the 1667 through 1688 range, 1705, 1726, and 1753. The Ipv6 draft specification is presented in RFC2460.

Protocol, IPSec (Internet Protocol Security)

IPSec refers to specifications being developed by an IETF (Internet Engineering Task Force) work group to add security services to IP transmissions. In particular, IPSec will provide authentication, integrity-checking, and encryption services for IP packets.

The security services provided by IPSec form the basis for secure communications using any of the following: encapsulated tunnels, host-to-host pipes, or VPNs (virtual private networks).

IPSec provides authentication services by adding an authentication header (AH) to IP packets, and by wrapping the packet's contents in an encapsulating security payload (ESP). Both of these are defined to be independent of the encryption algorithms being used; however, specific algorithms may be required to ensure interoperability in particular situations. IPSec supports multiple algorithms for key management (that is, for establishing session keys for traffic protection).

→ **Primary Source** IPSec is described in `http://www.ietf.org/html.charters/ipsec-charter.html`

→ **See Also** IP (Internet Protocol)

Protocol, IPX/SPX (Internetwork Packet Exchange/Sequenced Packet Exchange)

In Novell's NetWare, IPX and SPX are the network protocols responsible for ensuring successful internetwork communications.

IPX

IPX is a Network layer protocol, and it is responsible for addressing and routing packets to nodes on other networks. IPX assigns and works with Network layer addresses, as opposed to Physical layer addresses, which are assigned by the network interface card (NIC) manufacturers. The IPX protocol uses the services of the Data-Link layer, and it provides services to the SPX (Sequenced Packet Exchange) protocol in the next higher layer.

The IPX protocol is a connectionless protocol. This means that it doesn't need a fixed connection between source and destination. The protocol can send different packets along different routes, and doesn't need to worry about the sequencing.

IPX is also a datagram protocol. This means that each packet comes with everything you wanted to know about it. With this information, a higher level protocol at the receiving end can reassemble the packets in sequence.

IPX Packets

The IPX protocol is based on the IDP (Internet Datagram Packet) protocol from the XNS (Xerox Network System) model. The IPX and IDP packet structures are identical. This structure is shown in "IPX packet structure." Note that the packet has a 30-byte header.

The Length field indicates the total number of bytes in the entire IPX packet. This value must be at least 30 for the header. Note that an IPX packet can be at most 576 bytes if the packet is being routed, which allows for at most 546 bytes of data. The LIP (Large Internet Packet) enhancement allows larger packet sizes to be transmitted across IPX routers.

The Transport Control field is used to count the number of routers through which the packet passes, known as the hop count. The RIP (Routing information Protocol) is used to monitor this value. If the value reaches 16, the packet is discarded.

The Packet Type field indicates the higher-level protocol to which the packet is being passed.

Although 8 bits are allocated for this field, IPX uses just the following values:

- 0 for Unknown packet type

- 4 for PEP (Packet Exchange Protocol)

- 5 for SPX (Sequenced Packet Exchange)

- 17 for NCP (NetWare Core Protocol)

The Destination Address field specifies the 4-byte network address of the destination node. If the sender and destination are on the same network, this value is 0.

The Destination Node field contains the physical address of the destination node. The number of bytes needed for this address depends on the network architecture. For example, Ethernet and Token Ring network nodes use all 6 bytes; ARCnet nodes use only a single byte. For broadcasts, which are packets sent to every node, this field contains only F (hexadecimal) values.

The Destination Socket field contains the address value associated with the higher-layer process. This value is used to specify the location of the interface between the two layers. Values are assigned by Xerox, and vendors can register a

value range with Xerox for use in the vendor's products. The following values are of relevance for NetWare networks:

- 1 for RIP (Routing Information Packet)

- 2 for Echo Packet

- 3 for Error Handling

- 451H for NCP File Service Packet

- 452H for SAP (Service Advertising Protocol)

- 453H for Novell RIP, or IPX RIP

- 455H for NetBIOS

- 456H for Diagnostics

The multidigit values, which are in hexadecimal form as indicated by the H, have been assigned for use with NetWare.

The Source Network field contains the network address of the packet's source. If the network is unknown, this value is 0.

The Source Node field contains the physical address of the packet's source. This field is analogous to the Destination Node field, and the same information about physical addresses applies here.

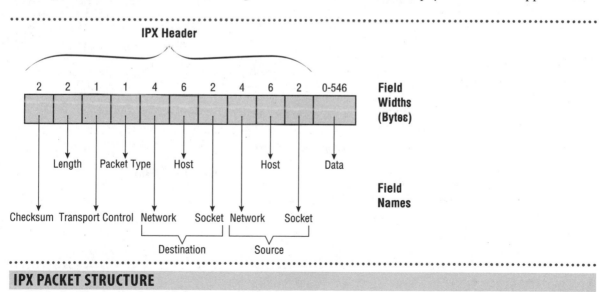

IPX PACKET STRUCTURE

The Source Socket field is analogous to the Destination Socket field in that it contains the address through which the source and destination communicate.

The Data field contains higher-level information being passed up or down in the protocol-layer hierarchy.

SPX

NetWare's Transport layer SPX protocol provides a connection-oriented link between nodes. A connection-oriented protocol is one that first establishes a connection between sender and receiver, then transmits the data, and finally breaks the connection. All packets in the transmission are sent in order, and all take the same path. This is in contrast to a connectionless service, in which packets may use different paths.

The SPX protocol ensures that packets arrive at their destination with enough sequence information to reconstruct the message at the receiving end, and also to maintain a connection at a specified level of quality. To accomplish this, SPX is responsible for flow control, packet acknowledgment, and similar activities.

An unfortunate disadvantage of a connection-oriented protocol arises when a broadcast packet is to be handled. The protocol must establish a connection with every destination before the packets can be sent. This can be a major undertaking, consuming time and resources.

To avoid such a situation, higher-level NetWare protocols such as NCP (NetWare Core Protocol) can bypass SPX and communicate directly with IPX.

SPX Packets

An SPX packet includes the same header fields as an IPX packet, and adds a 12-byte SPX header at the end. These 12 bytes come at the expense of the Data field, so that an SPX packet (without LIP) can contain at most 534 bytes of data. "SPX packet structure" shows the details of the SPX header.

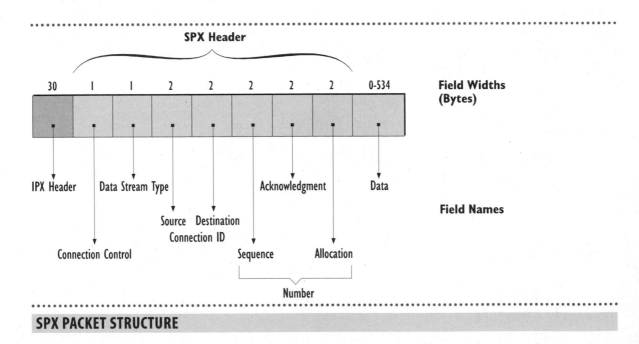

SPX PACKET STRUCTURE

The Connection Control field contains flags to control the flow of data between sender and receiver. Although eight flags are available, only the four high-order bits are defined:

- 10H to mark the last packet in the message
- 20H to signal for attention
- 40H to indicate that an acknowledgment is required
- 80H to identify a system packet

The Datastream Type field indicates whether the packet's Data field contains control information or a packet. If the Data field contains a packet, the Datastream Type will indicate which sort of packet (IPX, IP, and so on).

The Source Connection ID and the Destination Connection ID identify virtual circuits. The source ID is assigned by the sender of the SPX packet. The destination ID is used to demultiplex multiple virtual circuits from a single connection, as for a server.

The Sequence Number is used to number each packet in a message as the packet is sent.

The Acknowledgment Number indicates the sequence number of the packet the receiver expects to receive next. This value implicitly acknowledges any unacknowledged packets with lower sequence numbers. For example, an Acknowledgment Number of 20 indicates that the destination has received and at least implicitly acknowledges 19 packets.

The Allocation Number indicates the number of receive buffers available for a connection. This value is used for end-to-end flow control.

The Data field contains higher-level information being passed up or down in the protocol-layer hierarchy.

Protocol, IS-IS (Intermediate System to Intermediate System)

In the OSI network management model, IS-IS refers to a routing protocol that routers (intermedi-
ate systems) use to communicate with each other. Such a protocol is in contrast to an ES-IS protocol, which is for communication between a node and a router. An IS-IS protocol may be used within an Autonomous System (AS, also known as a domain) or between ASs. These two cases require IGP and EGP (interior and exterior gateway protocols).

IS-IS is an example of a link state protocol. Such protocols can be very efficient because routers exchange routing information only when something has changed. This cuts down on extraneous network traffic.

IS-IS refers both to a class of protocols (that is, those for communications between routers) and also to a specific protocol in this class. The IS-IS protocol (specific variant) is the ISO's standard protocol for routing CLNP (Connectionless Network protocol) packets.

→ *Compare* Protocol, ES-IS (End System to Intermediate System)

Protocol, KMP (Key Management Protocol)

KMP is used to check security keys for a network. It is part of the SILS (Standard for Interoperable LAN/MAN Security) specifications developed by an IEEE 802.10 working group.

Protocol, LAPB (Link Access Protocol, Balanced)

A bit-oriented, Data-Link layer protocol that is used in X.25 connections, such as to connect a terminal or node to a packet-switched network. LAPB is based on the HDLC protocol, and it can support half- or full-duplex communications in a point-to-point link. LAPB supports only the asynchronous balanced mode (ABM) of data transfer.

→ *See Also* Protocol, HDLC

Protocol, LAPD (Link Access Protocol, D Channel)

A data-link protocol for use on ISDN D channels.

Protocol, LAP-M (Link Access Protocol for Modems)

LAP-M is an error-correcting protocol, like MNP4, and is used in modem connections. LAP-M supports selective ARQ (Automatic Retransmission Request which means that in case of error only the erroneous packet is retransmitted. (This is in contrast to other versions of ARQ, some of which require retransmission of all packets that followed the erroneous one.)

Protocol, LAT (Local Area Transport)

LAT is a nonroutable, virtual-terminal protocol developed by Digital Equipment Corporation, and used only within a network. The protocol is non-routable because it does not use network-layer addresses, which are necessary for routing a packet between networks. Instead, LAT packets use only the six-byte hardware, or physical, address, which must be unique for each device on the network.

Because it has no network addresses, LAT packets can only be bridged between different segments on the same network. Other nonroutable protocols include the Maintenance Operation Protocol (MOP) and the NetBIOS Protocol.

➞ *Broader Category* Protocol, Nonroutable

Protocol, LCP (Link Control Protocol)

LCP is one of the three main components of the Point-to-Point protocol (PPP). PPP is mainly used to provide a way to encapsulate the IP packets while going over serial lines—that is, to get the IP packets over the serial connection and onto the network. LCP is used to set up, handle, and terminate the data link between the two points.

LCP is responsible for tasks such as the following:

- Establishing the link (through an exchange of Configure packets)

- Deciding on the options for encapsulating the (IP) packets

- Dealing with packet size limits or restrictions

- Possibly authenticating the identity of its counterpart (peer) at the other end of the link

- Testing to detect configuration errors such as a link that is looped back

- Testing to make sure the link is operating correctly

- Terminating the link—by exchanging Terminate packets—when finished or when necessary

LCP Packets

LCP uses three kinds of packets: Link Configure, Link Terminate, and Link Maintenance. Each of these comes in variants. For example, the Link Configure packet has four versions: Configure-Request, Reject, Ack (acknowledge), and Nak (negative acknowledge).

- The packet type information is stored in Code, the first field of the LCP packet, as shown in "LCP packet." This 8-bit field can take on values that are specified in the most recent "Assigned Numbers" RFC (currently RFC 1700).

- The Identifier field is also 8-bit. This value is used when matching requests and replies during an interaction.

- The 16-bit Length field indicates the total length of the LCP packet, including the four-octet header.

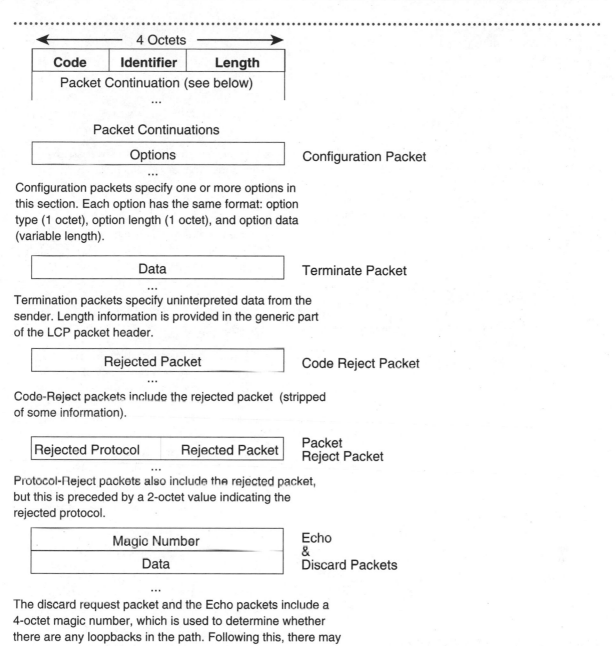

Configuration packets specify one or more options in this section. Each option has the same format: option type (1 octet), option length (1 octet), and option data (variable length).

Termination packets specify uninterpreted data from the sender. Length information is provided in the generic part of the LCP packet header.

Code-Reject packets include the rejected packet (stripped of some information).

Protocol-Reject packets also include the rejected packet, but this is preceded by a 2-octet value indicating the rejected protocol.

The discard request packet and the Echo packets include a 4-octet magic number, which is used to determine whether there are any loopbacks in the path. Following this, there may be zero or more octets of uninterpreted data.

LCP PACKET

- The Data label for the remainder of the packet serves as a generic term for a variety of contents, depending on the type of LCP packet. Structurally, this field consists of zero or more octets; semantically, the field's interpretation depends on the value of Code. Some of the possibilities are discussed below.

For a Configure-Request packet (Code = 1), this field consists of zero or more Configuration Options that the LCP wants to negotiate. Each option included has the same (type-length-value, or TLV) format: option type, option length, option details. The table "Configuration Options" lists currently defined options.

CONFIGURATION OPTIONS

Type	Option
1	Maximum-receive unit (MRU)
2	Async-Control-Character-Map
3	Protocol
4	Protocol
5	Magic Number
6	—Reserved—
7	Protocol field compression
8	Address and control field compression

The format and details of the data field for the options will be determined in part by the option's type.

→ *Primary Sources* The LCP is described in RFC 1661, and updates are described in RFC 2153.

Protocol, LDAPEXT (LDAP Extensions)

LDAPEXT refers to several types of extensions to the LDAPv3 (Lightweight Directory Access Protocol, version 3) that are planned or have already been implemented. The task of formulating and standardizing these extensions has fallen to one of several IETF (Internet Engineering Task Force) work groups involved with LDAP. These extensions have become desirable or necessary for a variety of reasons, including

- The need to search (ever-larger) directories more efficiently and to return search results in a more effective and flexible manner.

- The need to deal more effectively with dynamic directories, which are updated as configurations change during network operation. (This is in contrast to static directories, whose content is determined at the start of a session and remains unchanged throughout the remainder of the session.) The availability of hot plug technologies (such as the Universal Serial Bus, or USB) will make dyanmic directories essential. (A hot plug technology is one that can be added while a network is up and running.)

- The need for more reliable and effective authentication and access control—particularly as single-sign on capabilities (in which a user logs on once to a network or internetwork, is authenticated, and is then granted access to any allowed resources without requiring further authentication along the way) become more widely available.

- The need for more effective ways to do resource discovery on very large networks.

- The need for APIs (application programming interfaces) that can enable programs to make full use of the available directory services.

The LDAPEXT work group is addressing changes in the following areas:

- Access control and authentication.

- Sorting and paged retrieval of search results.

- Dynamic directories.

- Schema, referral, and knowledge reference maintenance.

- Server discovery using LDAP.

- APIs for LDAP.

Another IETF work group—LDUP—is dealing with issues related to duplication and replication of directories and directory services, and a third—LSD—has the task of working out how best to deploy the enhanced LDAP that will result from all these modifications.

→ **Primary Sources** The LDAPEXT work is described in http://www.ietf.org/html .charters/ldapext-charter.html

→ **See Also** Protocol, LDAP (Lightweight Directory Access Protocol); Protocol, LDUP (LDAP Duplication/Replication/Updating Protocol)

Protocol, LDUP (LDAP Duplication/Replication/Updating Protocol)

The IETF (Internet Engineering Task Force) LDUP work group is dealing with issues relating to the replication and duplication of directories and directory services across a network or Internetwork. The LDAPv3 (lightweight directory access protocol version 3) is used to give clients access to directory services. However, in its standard form, this protocol offers little help in dealing with the replication of directory information in order to provide more efficient access to the available services. Because of the growing size of networks, and the increasing demands made on servers to provide rapid access to available services, the protocol's performance suffers if the directory gets too large.

To help remedy this, the LDUP and two other IETF work groups have been formed. The LDUP work group is charged with developing an object-oriented model of the directory information and with formulating schemas to make it possible to make the appropriate portions of a directory available where needed. In particular, the directory schema is being extended to define object classes and subclasses which can be related and manipulated

using features that make object-oriented approaches so attractive—for example, property inheritance and polymorphism.

The LDUP work group is focusing on two main types of replication and is exploring six areas related to such replication. The replication types are multi-master replication and single-master, or master-slave, replication.

Multi-master replication provides a model in which a network or Internetwork may have several replicas of the directory services. and where any of these replicas can be updated without having to clear the update with a particular master. In single master replication, only one server functions as a master, and this server must give permission to update the replicas.

The LDUP work group is addressing such replication issues with respect to the following topics:

- Creating a LDAPv3 replication architecture that will define key concepts, specify what their functions are and how these can interact.

- Formulating a LDAPv3 replication information model (RIM) that will specify the schemas and the semantics of the information needed for carrying out, administering, and maintaining replications between LDAPv3 servers—particularly between servers running on different platforms. This model will provide guidelines for how different implementations will handle issues such as maintaining consistency across the replicas, dealing with deleted objects, and ensuring the equivalence of the topologies of replicas on the different platforms.

- Developing an LDAPv3 replication information transport protocol and managing the specifications to allow LDAPv3 to be used as the transport protocol or information being replicated.

- Creating specifications for mandatory replica management—to make possible the administration, maintenance, and provisioning of replicas. In some cases, these specifications will entail extensions to LDAPv3—which is actually the task of another work group—LDAPEXT.

- Developing LDAPv3 procedures for update reconciliation—so that conflicts between the states of different replicas can be detected and resolved.

- Developing LDAPv3 profiles that will include the information in this list (replication architecture, information model, and so forth) for both single and multiple-master replication.

Besides the LDUP work group, the LDAPEXT work group is formulating extensions to LDAPv3 and the LSD work group is determining how best to deploy the fortified LDAP protocol.

→ Primary Sources The work of the LDUP work group is described in `http://www.ietf.org/html .charters/ldup-charter.html`

→ See Also Protocol, LDAP (Lightweight Directory Access Protocol); Protocol, LDAPEXT (LDAP Extensions)

Protocol, Lightweight

A lightweight protocol is any of a class of protocols designed for use on high-speed internetworks. HSTP (High-Speed Transport Protocol) and XTP (Xpress Transfer Protocol) are examples of lightweight protocols. Lightweight versions of other common protocols have also been developed, with LDAP (lightweight directory access protocol) being, arguably, the most widely used of these.

Lightweight protocols combine routing and transport services in a more streamlined fashion than do traditional network and Transport layer protocols. This makes it possible to transmit more efficiently over high-speed networks, such as ATM or FDDI, and media, such as fiber-optic cable.

Lightweight protocols use various measures and refinements to streamline and speed up transmissions, including the following:

- Use of fixed header and trailer sizes. For example, XTP uses identical 40-byte headers and 4-byte trailers for both control and information packets. All the fields in the header are the same size (4 bytes), which also makes packet manipulation easier.

- More efficient use of checksum and error-correction. Checksums for XTP are located at the end of the header and at the end of the packet. This makes it possible to compute the checksums while transmitting the packets and to insert the computed value at the appropriate point. In traditional protocols (such as TCP), the packet checksum in the header, so the packet must be processed twice: first to compute the checksum and then to transmit.

- Error-checking is done only at the endpoints, rather than after each transmission, which can save considerable time. Such a cavalier attitude toward error checking is possible because transmission lines are much "cleaner" than they were when the traditional protocols were developed. Also, lightweight protocols make it easy to retransmit only erroneous packets. Traditional protocols demand the retransmission of an erroneous packet and all packets that followed it.

- Use of connection-oriented transmissions to save the overhead of transmitting a destination address with each packet. (A connection-oriented transmission is one in which a path is first established and then used for the duration of the transmission, so that all packets take the same path.)

By using a simple indexing scheme to identify packets for a message, lightweight protocols can use the same path for multiple messages at a time. This approach saves the time required to make routing decisions for each packet and also saves the overhead of address information in each packet and of hop counts (which are used to ensure that a packet is discarded if it does not reach its destination within a predefined number of stops).

Protocol, Link-State

A link-state protocol is any of several routing protocols that use a link-state algorithm to determine available connections. Examples of this type of protocol include the following:

- NLSP (NetWare Link Services Protocol) from Novell's IPX/SPX protocol suite.

- OSPF (Open Shortest Path First) from the TCP/IP suite.

- AURP (AppleTalk Update Routing Protocol) from the AppleTalk suite.

- IS-IS (Intermediate System to Intermediate System) from the OSI suite.

Link-state protocols are in contrast to distance-vector protocols, which use a different strategy for getting routing information. Distance-vector protocols provide information about the costs of reaching all possible destinations. Link-state approaches provide information only about the distances from a router to all its immediate neighbor routers. The former strategy is more computationally intensive when setting up or updating the routing information; link-state protocols need to do more work during the actual routing.

Link-state protocols send updates only when the network changes, whereas distance-vector protocols send periodic updates. The smaller resulting overhead for link-state protocols makes them better suited for routing over wide area internetworks. Link-state protocols are also better at dealing with changes to the network.

→ *Broader Category* Protocol, Routing

→ *Compare* Protocol, Distance-Vector

Protocol, LLAP (LocalTalk Link Access Protocol)

In the AppleTalk network protocol suite, the Data-Link layer protocol for LocalTalk, Apple's 235Kbps network architecture.

Protocol, LLC (Logical Link Control)

A protocol developed by the IEEE 802.2 committee, which defined the MAC (medium access control) and LLC sublayers of the OSI reference model Data-Link layer. The 802.2 specifications have been replaced by the ISO 8802-2 specifications. An LLC frame is based on the HDLC frame, except that the LLC frame uses different addresses and does not include a CRC field.

Protocol, LMMP (LAN/MAN Management Protocol)

A protocol for network management on local area networks. LMMP provides the OSI's CMIS/CMIP network management services, but implements them directly on the logical-link-control (LLC) sublayer of the Data-Link layer. LMMP provides application-level services and then bypasses the intervening four layers in order to use the LLC services. This makes it easier to implement LMMP but impossible to use routers. Because of its original name, CMIS/CMIP over LLC, LMMP is also known as CMOL.

Protocol, Low-level

A protocol below the Network layer in the OSI reference model. Specifically, a protocol at the Physical or Data-Link layer.

Protocol, LPP (Lightweight Presentation Protocol)

A presentation layer protocol defined for use in the CMOT (CMIP over TCP/IP) network management effort (which was never completed).

Protocol, LU 6.2 (Logical unit 6.2)

In IBM's SNA (System Network Architecture), LU 6.2 devices support peer-to-peer communications between programs. Such devices use the LU 6.2 protocol to set up and configure a communication session.

→ *Broader Category* SNA (System Network Architecture)

Protocol, MAFP (Multicast Attribute Framing Protocol)

MAFP provides a generic mechanism for setting up multicast distributions of content over the Internet. The protocol is used to describe one or more objects that are being transmitted (announced) over the Internet. These objects are referred to as "programs," and such an announcement takes the form of a set of attributes (name-value pairs) and a directory (to which the program is being announced).

In certain cases, the announcement may include other information such as IP addresses, ports, and TTL (time-to-live) parameters. Such additional parameters are distinguished from attributes so that firewalls or proxy servers can use this information and act on it without having to understand what the attributes mean.

MAFP is similar to the Session Description Protocol (SDP), which is used to announce multimedia objects or sessions. MAFP is independent of the transport protocol that will be used to deliver the programs.

Protocol, MLP (Multilink Procedures)

A protocol designed for use with multiple network connections running in parallel. MLP oversees the process of using a point-to-point protocol (such as LAPB or HDLC) in each of the connections. MLP can be used to balance the loads on the connections.

Protocol, MMIP (Media Manager Interchange Protocol)

The MMIP is an application-layer protocol that is used to enable media managers to exchange information. Media managers are servers with audio, video, and multimedia materials for viewing, and for (possibly) using and downloading.

Protocol, Modulation

Modulation protocols are designed for modulating digital signals for transmission over telephone lines. The protocols differ in the rates they support. The following protocols are widely supported:

- Bell 103A and 212A, which support speeds of 300 and 1200bps, respectively.

- V.21, which supports speeds of 300bps and which are used by group III fax machines to negotiate.

- V.22 and V.22bis, which support speeds of 600 to 1200bps and 2440 to 4800bps, respectively.

- V.32 and V.32bis, which support speeds of 9600bps and 7200 to 14,400bps, respectively.

- V.FAST, which supports rates between 19,200 and 24,000bps.

Protocol, MOP (Maintenance Operation Protocol)

The maintenance operation protocol is part of the DNA (Digital Network Architecture) Phase IV protocol suite. Like the local area transport (LAT) protocol, which is part of the same suite, MOP neither needs nor uses network (layer 3) addresses. As a result, it is considered a nonrouting protocol.

Protocol, MP (Multilink Point-to-Point Protocol)

MP is a protocol for splitting a signal, sending it along multiple channels, and then reassembling and sequencing it at the common destination for the channels. MP is actually an extension of the Point-to-Point protocol (PPP), and the MP packets are actually handled by PPP as if they belonged to a particular protocol (namely, MP).

MP is a proposed standard from the IETF (Internet Engineering Task Force), and it is generally regarded as more popular than an alternative standard created by BONDING (Bandwidth on Demand Interoperability Group).

→ *Primary Sources* RFC 1717

→ *See Also* Protocol, PPP (Point-to-Point protocol)

Protocol, MS-CHAP (Microsoft Challenge Handshake Authentication Protocol)

The CHAP protocol can be used when a remote node needs to authenticate itself to a network server or when two routers need to authenticate themselves to each other in order to begin a PPP (point-to-point protocol) session. While CHAP is a strong authentication protocol, Microsoft's MS-CHAP includes extensions that make it even more stringent.

MS-CHAP works with Windows NT as well as with Windows 9x Microsoft products, and it can be used over a Remote Access Server (RAS). In fact, the need for a remote authentication capability was the main reason Microsoft developed the extensions. With MS-CHAP as the authentication protocol, the authentication process requires that Microsoft's encryption methods be used.

→ *Primary Sources* MS-CHAP is described in RFC 2433

→ *Compare* Protocol, CHAP (Challenge Handshake Authentication Protocol)

Protocol, NBP (Name Binding Protocol)

An AppleTalk Transport layer protocol for mapping logical names to physical addresses.

Protocol, NCP (NetWare Core Protocol)

In Novell's NetWare, NCP is an upper-layer protocol that a NetWare file server uses to deal with workstation requests. NCP actually spans the top three OSI reference model layers: application, presentation, and session. The protocol provides capabilities such as the following

- Creating or breaking a connection for service
- File and directory handling
- Printing
- Security
- Changing drive mappings

When a workstation makes a request that its software will redirect to the server, the workstation software puts the request into the appropriate NCP format and passes the request to the IPX protocol. This protocol passes the packet to the server, which decapsulates (removes the headers and trailers from) the packet, finds the NCP request, and responds to it.

NCP can also be used to communicate directly with the Network layer IPX (Internetwork Packet Exchange) protocol under certain conditions. For example, when broadcasting a message (sending the message to all stations on a network), NCP can be used to avoid needing to establish explicit connections with each destination node. The connection-oriented SPX protocol at the Transport layer would need to do this, requiring extra time and resources.

→ *Broader Category* NetWare

Protocol, NCP (Network Control Protocol)

A network control protocol can be used to mediate between network-layer protocols and underlying data link protocols. Such protocols are generally used in conjunction with other protocols whose functions require communication between data link and network layers.

For example, PPP (point-to-point protocol), which is used to transmit TCP/IP packets over telephone lines, includes a collection of Network Control Protocols (NCPs) to deal with the various network-layer protocols that might be encountered. Once a connection has been established and the two parties have agreed to a working configuration, PPP uses NCP packets to select and configure the Network layer protocol(s) being used.

→ *See Also* Protocol, PPP (Point-to-Point Protocol)

Protocol, NetBEUI (Network Basic Extended User Interface)

A protocol developed originally for use on IBM Token Ring networks. Unlike IBM's original NetBIOS implementation, which used proprietary lower-layer protocols, NetBEUI was designed to communicate with standard (IEEE 802.2 logical-link-control) protocols at the lower layers. NetBEUI protocols are used in Microsoft's LAN Manager and in IBM's LAN Server networks.

Protocol, NetBIOS (Network Basic Input/Output System)

NetBIOS is an interface and an upper-level protocol developed by IBM for use with a proprietary adapter for its PC Network product. NetBIOS provides a standard interface to the lower networking layers. The protocol's functionality actually ranges over the top three layers (session, presentation, and application) in the OSI reference model.

Essentially, the protocol provides higher-layer programs with access to the network. The program has been adapted by other network packages (most notably, Microsoft's LAN Manager), and is now widely emulated. Note that not all NetBIOS implementations are equivalent, so you may encounter some incompatibilities.

NetBIOS can also serve as an API (Application Program Interface) for data exchange. As such, it provides programmers with access to resources for establishing a connection between two machines or between two applications on the same machine.

NetBIOS provides four types of services:

- Naming, for creating and checking group and individual names, and for deleting individual names. These names can be either hardware names or symbolic names.

- Datagram support, for connectionless transmissions that make a best effort to deliver packets, but that do not guarantee successful delivery. Packets in this mode are usually no larger than 512 bytes.

- Session support, for transmissions in which a temporary virtual circuit is established for the duration of a session so that delivery of packets can be monitored and verified. In this mode, NetBIOS will guarantee delivery of messages of up to 64KB.

- General services: for resetting adapter states, canceling application commands when possible, and so on.

→ *See Also* Protocol, NetBEUI

Protocol, Network

The name network protocol is often applied to any of the network layer (that is, layer) 3 protocols that can be used to forward packets between networks. These include IP (Internet Protocol) and IPX (Internetwork Packet Exchange).

→ *Compare* Protocol, Transport

Protocol, Network Management

A network management protocol is used for monitoring the performance and components of a network. This monitoring is generally performed by special programs, called agents. Each agent gathers data about particular functions or components on a single node.

Agent handlers organize, analyze, and filter this information before passing it on a network manager, which is a special program running (generally) on a dedicated machine.

The following are the two most widely used management protocols:

- SNMP (Simple Network Management Protocol), which was developed for networks that use TCP/IP

- CMIP (Common Management Information Protocol), a protocol from the ISO, for use in the OSI reference model.

Protocol, NFS (Network File System)

NFS is a protocol developed by Sun Microsystems for sharing remote files across UNIX or other networks.

This protocol makes accessing files on remote machines transparent for the user, so that the user's ordinary commands will work with these remote files; that is, the user will not even know that the files are anywhere but on the user's local machine.

Similarly, the user's ID will automatically be translated to ensure that it is unique on the network that contains the files. The user's ID must be translated, because the user must have access rights to the file. In many cases, files accessible over NFS will have minimal restrictions and will be generally available.

The NFS protocol works at the application level. As such, it is comparable to the FTAM (File Transfer, Access, and Management) protocol in the OSI reference model, and to AT&T's RFS (Remote File System) protocol in UNIX environments.

To communicate with and give commands on the remote server, NFS relies on Remote Procedure Calls (RPCs). These, in turn, use a generic External Data Representation (XDR) to move information around. This representation is environment-independent, so that files can be passed between operating systems. The information can be translated to the target system's format from the XDR form.

UDP (User Data Protocol) is most generally used as the actual transport protocol. This protocol is connectionless and unreliable. Packet sequencing and error detection are handled by the NFS protocol.

Because each transaction is considered independent of those that preceded it, NFS is considered a stateless protocol. This is convenient because it makes it unnecessary for sender and receiver to remain synchronized throughout. This, in turn, makes error recovery easier.

NFS also refers to a distributed file system developed by Sun Microsystems for use under its SunOS operating system.

→ *Compare* Protocol, FTAM; Protocol, RFS

Protocol, NHRP (Next Hop Routing Protocol)

Various protocols and solutions have been created to make it possible to transmit IP packets over ATM networks. In some cases different protocols are needed or used—depending on whether the IP addresses involved in the communications come from a single subnet (known as a logical IP subnet, or LIS) or from multiple subnets.

One task that must be handled when sending IP over ATM is address resolution—that is, mapping between IP and ATM addresses. If a single subnet is involved, ATMARP (asynchronous transfer mode address resolution protocol) and InATMARP (for inverse ATMARP) are used. (ATMARP will find the ATM address corresponding to a given IP, and InATMARP will find the IP address corresponding to a given ATM address.)

For cases in which connections may involve multiple subnets, the NHRP (pronounced "nurp") protocol is used. The protocol's job is to find an ATM address corresponding to a destination IP address along the path. The selected destination address will be on a route between the two ends of a connection, and will be selected in such a way that sending the packets along the ATM network will save hops (intermediate stops) at the IP (that is, network) layer. In other words, NHRP will try to find an ATM path that will require fewer stops than a path to the same destination that used only the layer 3 addresses.

NHRP was deevloped originally for use in IP environments, but it is able to handle other network layer internetworking protocols—for example, Novell's IPX (internetwork packet exchange). In fact, NHRP will even work if layer 3 protocols are sent over other switched networks (such as frame relay or X.25).

In fact, NHRP has been reworked to support layer 3 communications over any NBMA (nonbroadcast multiaccess network). Behind this imposing name hides a network that

- Does not have any built-in provisions for sending packets to everyone or even to large groups in a single transmission (nonbroadcast). This is the case with network architectures such as ATM because they are primarily connection-oriented. That is, a path is determined and reserved before any ackets are transmitted.

- Makes it possible to establish a direct path (through switches) between any two nodes on the network (the NBMA network, not the layer 3 network being carried). This is possible because of the connection-oriented operation of network architectures such as ATM, frame relay, and X.25.

NHRP will also be used in the MPOA (multiprotocol over ATM), which is an effort to provide an integrated solution that will be accepted by the various parties that have created solutions (such as IP over ATM).

Protocol, NICE (Network Information and Control Exchange)

A proprietary application layer protocol from Digital Equipment Corporation (DEC). The protocol is used in DECnet networks for testing the network and for getting information about node configurations.

Protocol, NLSP (NetWare Link State Protocol)

NLSP is a routing protocol in the NetWare IPX/SPX protocol suite. NLSP is an example of a link-state protocol, which is particularly well-suited for wide area routing. This is because link-state protocols broadcast only when something changes, which helps keep network traffic lower. This is in contrast to distance-vector protocols, which broadcast periodically.

NLSP is designed to replace the less efficient, higher overhead RIP (Routing Information Protocol) and SAP (Services Advertising Protocol). The newer protocol has numerous advantages over RIP and SAP:

Routing NLSP-based routers know more about the network's layout than RIP-based routers, so that routers can make more intelligent decisions.

Overhead NLSP has less overhead than RIP or SAP because it broadcasts only when something changes, whereas RIP and SAP broadcast their materials periodically.

Transfer Speed NLSP supports parallel paths (which makes it possible to split the network load). NLSP also reduces packet sizes by using IPX header compression.

Reliability Because it supports parallel paths, NLSP can keep network traffic flowing even when a path is down. NLSP checks the integrity of all links regularly.

Network Support Because it supports up to 127 hops for a packet, NLSP can be used on larger networks than RIP, which supported only up to 15 hops.

Protocol and Media Support NLSP is back-compatible with RIP, and can communicate with RIP-based routers. RIP- and NLSP-based routers can coexist on the same network, although communications must be at a level that the RIP-based router can handle. Similarly, NLSP is also compatible with various network types, including Ethernet, Token Ring, and point-to-point links.

Protocol, NNTP (Network News Transfer Protocol)

NNTP is the protocol used to distribute news article collections (newsfeeds) on the Internet. NNTP is also used to query a news server, which maintains a central database of articles and newsgroups, and to retrieve and post articles to a newsgroup. This database will consist of the Usenet news system and

probably some alternative newsgroups that have not found or have not even sought a place in the Usenet newsgroup family.

NNTP uses a reliable data stream (for example, TCP) to distribute and receive articles and also for communications between sender and receiver. NNTP allows interaction between sender and receiver—for example, between two servers with newsfeeds to exchange, or between a client host and a news server.

Because of its interactive capabilities, NNTP has advantages over other transfer methods—such as UUCP (UNIX-to-UNIX copy program). For example, if one server has a large newsfeed (newsgroup file collection) to pass to another server, the simplest thing—with UUCP—would be simply to transfer the entire contents. Because UUCP sends an article regardless of whether the receiving machine already has it, the receiving machine is left to delete any duplicates.

With NNTP, the receiving machine can specify easily which newsgroups and articles it wants—avoiding the unnecessary transmission of what could be dozens of megabytes. This selective capability also comes in handy for clients, who can select just the articles they want to read, and skip over anything else.

Although it was proposed almost 10 years ago, NNTP is still just a proposed standard. It is considered an elective protocol, which means that servers need not support it. Nevertheless, it is so widely used on the Internet that, for all practical purposes, it is the news transfer protocol.

→ *Primary Sources* The original proposal for NNTP is in RFC 977.

Protocol, Nonroutable

A nonroutable protocol is one that does not include any network-layer addressing—generally because the protocol deals only with nodes in a single network. Because they are all in the same network, individual nodes can be identified by the six-byte address in the Media Access Control (MAC) sub-layer, which is part of the Data-Link layer in the OSI (Open Systems Interconnect) reference model. (This address is also known as a hardware address or a physical address. Every node on a LAN must have a unique physical address.)

Packets sent using a nonroutable protocol only need MAC addresses, which cannot be used for routing the packet between networks. As a result, packets using such protocols can only be bridged—that is, passed between segments on the same network. Examples of nonroutable protocols include the Local Area Transport (LAT) Protocol, the Maintenance Operation Protocol (MOP), and the NetBIOS Protocol.

Protocol, NSP (Network Services Protocol)

A proprietary transport-layer protocol from Digital Equipment Corporation (DEC). NSP is used in DECnet networks.

Protocol, NTP (Network time protocol)

NTP is used to synchronize computer clocks on the Internet. This draft standard protocol makes it possible for a server to get the time from a national time source, and to distribute the time information to other nodes, so that these nodes can adjust their clocks using the primary server as a reference. Hosts can get their time from one of these secondary servers.

NTP is a very complex protocol, because it deals with the entire synchronization process—from physical measurement and clocking to dissemination. It also considers algorithms and strategies for improving accuracy—or at least minimizing loss of accuracy—during the multistep process. Depending on the host's location in relation to a time server, NTP is accurate to within 1–50 milliseconds.

Servers can disseminate the time information by unicasts (point-to-point transmissions) or by multicasts (transmission to all parties on a multicast list). The group address and memberships are determined by the Internet Group Management Protocol (IGMP).

→ *Primary Sources* NTP version 3 is described in RFC 1305. A simpler, less accurate, variant—SNTP, or Simple network time protocol—is proposed in RFC 2030.

Protocol, OSPF (Open Shortest Path First)

In internetworks that use the TCP/IP protocol suite, a routing protocol for passing packets between routers in networks within a given domain. (The open in the name is an adjective, not a verb, and is in contrast to proprietary.) OSPF is an example of a link state protocol, in which routers provide updated information only when there is something new to report. OSPF is also an example of an Interior Gateway Protocol (IGP).

Protocol, OSPF (Open Shortest Path First) Exchange

In networks that use the OPSF (open shortest path first) routing protocol, the OSPF Exchange protocol is used to synchronize the routing information databases that need to be exchanged among routers.

Protocol, Packet Burst

In Novell's NetWare, the Packet Burst protocol can be used on top of IPX (Internetwork Exchange Protocol) to send multiple NCP (NetWare Control Protocol) packets. It can send an entire burst, without waiting for an acknowledgment after each packet.

Because the protocol monitors the transmission, only lost or erroneous packets need to be retransmitted, not the entire burst. "Communications with and without packet burst" illustrates how Packet Burst works in contrast to other methods. Use of this protocol is sometimes known as operating in burst mode.

Without Packet Burst Mode

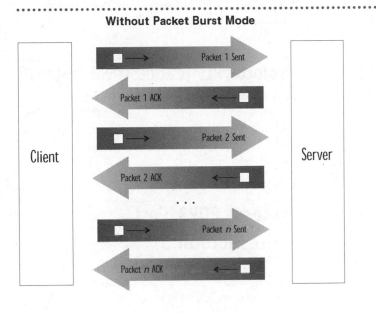

With Packet Burst Mode

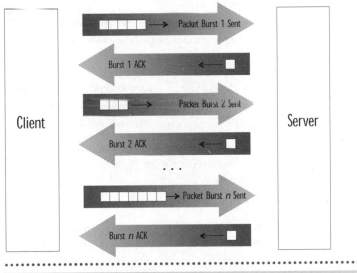

COMMUNICATIONS WITH AND WITHOUT PACKET BURST

Protocol, PAP (Password Authentication Protocol)

PAP is an authentication protocol that can be used when two routers—peers in a PPP (Point-to-Point Protocol) connection—need to provide authentication to each other or when a remote node needs to authenticate itself to a network server. PAP is a simple (and weak) authentication protocol that uses a two-way handshake to provide authentication.

Unlike CHAP (Challenge Handshake Authentication Protocol), PAP does not encrypt the authentication information (password and username), and the protocol is susceptible to various types of attacks.

→ **Primary Sources** PAP and other authentication protocols are discussed in RFCs 1334, 1994, 2284, and 2484.

Protocol, PAP (Printer Access Protocol)

In the AppleTalk protocol suite, the protocol used for communication between nodes (Macintoshes) and printers. PAP is used to set up, maintain, and terminate the connection between node and printer, and also to transfer the data.

Protocol, PEP (Packet Exchange Protocol)

A transport level protocol in the XNS protocol suite from Xerox.

Protocol, PLCP (Physical Layer Convergence Protocol)

In an ATM (Asynchronous Transfer Mode) networking architecture, the PLCP is used at the transmission convergence (TC) sublayer to map ATM cells to frames suitable for transmission over DS-3 (digital services, or signal, level 3) lines. DS-3 lines can support transmission rates of up to 155.52Mbps.

→ **See Also** PLCP (Physical Layer Convergence Procedure)

Protocol, PLP (Packet Level Protocol)

A protocol that specifies the details of data transfer between sender and receiver in an X.25 connection. PLP is full-duplex, and supports error detection and correction, packet sequencing, and transfer-rate adjustment.

Protocol, POP3 (Post Office Protocol, 3)

POP3 is the most recent version of the Post Office Protocol used to provide clients with access to a maildrop (post office) in which messages for the user may be stored. With POP3, users can retrieve any e-mail messages being held in temporary storage on a POP3 server.

By default, POP3 service is provided on Port 110. POP3 sessions involve the exchange of messages between the client and server. Messages passing between them conform to the message format specified in RFC 822. The session consists of two kinds of messages: commands and responses.

A POP3 session proceeds through several phases:

Connection The client opens a connection, and the server replies with a positive greeting—for example,

```
S:+OK POP3 server ready
```

Authorization Once a connection is established, the server requires the client to provide authentication. Two mechanisms are available for doing this. One of these involves encryption, and is used when a user doesn't want to be sending passwords.

Transaction During this phase, the user can check, retrieve, and delete messages. This stage can last for an indefinite period.

Update When the user gives the QUIT command, the server enters the update stage. All file updates (for example, deletions) requested by the user are actually carried out. Should the connection be lost before the user gives the QUIT command, the server skips the update phase, leaving files as they were before the user began the session.

→ *Primary Sources* POP3 is described in RFC 1939, with updates in RFCs 1957 and 2449.

Protocol, PPP (Point-to-Point Protocol)

PPP is used to transmit TCP/IP packets over telephone lines. The protocol provides a way of encapsulating datagrams so that they can be transmitted over a serial connection. In addition to the encapsulation mechanisms, PPP includes a Link Control Protocol (LCP) component that is used to establish, configure, maintain, and terminate the connection. Finally, PPP includes a collection of Network Control Protocols (NCPs) to deal with the various network-layer protocols that might be encountered.

To establish point-to-point communications,

- PPP first uses LCP to establish and test a link, and to agree on a configuration (for example, what packet framing method to use). The LCP may require authentication from its peer at the other end.

- PPP then uses NCP packets to select and configure the Network layer protocol(s) being used. Once the protocol information has been established, communications can begin, and PPP can begin transferring packets between the two endpoints.

In a sense, PPP really doesn't do anything but package datagrams and get them from a computer to the other end of a serial connection. Any negotiations or adjustments are made by having PPP send LCP or NCP packets. In its simplest form, the PPP packet consists of a 16-bit Protocol field, an Information field of variable size, and possibly some padding to round the packet out to an appropriate storage boundary.

The possible values for the Protocol field are specified in the most recent "Assigned Numbers" RFC—1700 as of this writing. There are certain restrictions on the values that can be assigned, but in some cases these create groupings that make it easier to categorize the protocol under consideration as being link control, network-layer, or network control, for example.

The Information field contains the packet being encapsulated. This may be, for example, an IP or an LCP packet. It is assumed that the encapsulated packet will be understood when it is unwrapped at the receiving end.

Note that the Protocol field is the entire PPP header. Since this header doesn't provide any packet length information, the packet needs framing to mark the start and end of the packet. PPP supports standard framing methods such as those provided by HDLC (High-Level Data Link Control).

With the growing popularity of the Internet, PPP has become widely used as one of the two main ways for users to get onto the Internet through an Internet Access Provider (IAP). PPP or SLIP (Serial Line Internet Protocol) provide the mechanism for getting packets from the TCP/IP services running on the PC to the IAP and onto the Internet. Of SLIP and PPP, the latter is generally considered the more intelligent and efficient, although objective evidence is hard to come by.

→ *See Also* IAP (Internet Access Provider); Protocol, SLIP (Serial Line Internet Protocol)

→ *Primary Sources* PPP is described in RFC 1661, with updates in RFC 2153.

Protocol, PPTP (Point-to-Point Tunneling Protocol)

The PPTP makes it possible to establish secure connections over the Internet using Microsoft's Remote Access Service (RAS). This is accomplished by first connecting the client to the Internet—usually through an Internet Service Provider (ISP). After this connection is established, the protocol establishes an encrypted link between the client and the RAS on the destination network. This encryption creates the tunnel for the connection.

Once the connection is established, it is possible to use the tunnel to communicate in a secure fashion across the Internet.

Protocol, Proxy

On the World Wide Web, this protocol is used when a proxy server communicates with information servers through a firewall. A proxy server is one that acts on behalf of another server—for security, efficiency, or other reasons.

For example, if your server is inside a firewall (a protective gateway that filters traffic in order to provide increased security), it won't be able to communicate directly with a Web server in the outside world. Instead, a special server—perhaps part of the gateway itself—will act instead of, or as a proxy for, your server. Your server will pass its request to the proxy. The proxy server will communicate with the Web server, make your requests, and pass the response back to your server—after filtering it, of course.

Protocol, QLLC (Qualified Link Level Control)

A protocol that allows IBM's SNA (Systems Network Architecture) packets to be routed over X.25 links. SNA by itself does not support a Network layer protocol and, hence, does not support routing.

Protocol, RARP (Reverse Address Resolution Protocol)

In the Internet TCP/IP protocol suite, a protocol that maps a hardware address to an Internet address. This protocol is important for diskless workstations, which need to determine their network addresses when the workstations log in to the network.

Protocol, RFS (Remote File System)

AT&T's application layer protocol for handling files on remote machines in a UNIX network. As an application layer protocol, it competes with the FTAM protocol developed for the OSI reference model and the NFS protocol developed by Sun Microsystems.

Protocol, RIP (Routing Information Protocol)

A routing protocol in the Novell NetWare protocol suite, RIP is generally known as IPX RIP to distinguish it from the RIP protocol associated with the TCP/IP protocol stack. RIP is a distance-vector protocol, which means it keeps a database of routing information that the protocol broadcasts at intervals. In the same manner, other protocols broadcast theirs, so that each router can update its routing information.

In the Internet TCP/IP protocol suite, RIP is an Interior Gateway Protocol (IGP), which is a protocol used by certain routers to communicate with each other and to determine routes. Like its IPX RIP counterpart, Internet RIP is a distance-vector protocol.

Protocol, RIPng (Routing Information Protocol, Next Generation)

RIPng is a version of the widely used distance vector RIP (Routing Information Protocol) modified for use with IPv6 (Internet protocol version 6). It is designed to be used as an interior gateway protocol (IGP) for a medium-sized autonomous systems (AS)—that is, for exchanging routing information within a network that is administered by a single organization.

While RIPing does represent an advance over the original RIP, it suffers from many of the same limitations as its predecessor—for example, being limited to 15 hops, or steps in the routing process. In general, distance vector protocols have been replaced by protocols based on a link state algorithm.

→ **Primary Sources** RIP is defined in RFC 1058, and its revision, RIP-2, is defined in RFC 1723. RIPng is described in RFCs 2080 and 2081.

→ **Broader Categories** Protocol, Distance Vector; Protocol, IGP (Interior Gateway Protocol); Protocol, Routing

→ **See Also** Protocol, RIP (Routing Information Protocol)

Protocol, Routing

A routing protocol is any of a class of protocols for determining a path between two nodes. The term is generally reserved for internetworking situations in which the two nodes are in different networks, so that routers or bridges are involved.

In an internetwork, the routing elements are known as intermediate systems (IS) and the user stations are known as end systems (ES). ISs use only the three lowest OSI reference model layers (Physical, Data-Link, and Network); ESs use all seven layers.

Two levels of stations (ES and IS) are sufficient to characterize small internetworks. As the internetwork grows, administration becomes more complex, so additional levels are needed.

For large internetworks, a single organization (corporation, state, or country, for example) may be responsible for multiple routers, or ISs. A group of routers under a common administrator is known as an autonomous system (AS) in Internet terminology, or a routing domain in the OSI network management model.

The three levels of ES, IS, and AS yield several types of arrangements, each of which may require a different protocol:

- ES-IS communication between workstation and router. This communication generally uses the workstation's native network level protocol, such as IP or IPX.

- IS-IS communication within an AS (or routing domain). This communication uses an interior gateway protocol (IGP). In OSI terminology, this is called an intradomain routing protocol.

- IS-IS communication between ASs. This communication uses an exterior gateway protocol (EGP). In OSI terminology, this is an interdomain routing protocol.

"Types of routing arrangements and protocols" shows some of these concepts and how they relate to each other.

Routing protocols may be either static, which means that the route is predetermined and fixed, or dynamic, which means that the route is determined at runtime and may be changed.

Examples of routing protocols include the following:

- BGP (Border Gateway Protocol)
- EGP (Exterior Gateway Protocol)
- Integrated IS-IS (Integrated Intermediate System to Intermediate System)
- OSPF (Open Shortest Path First)
- RIP (Routing Information Protocol)
- RTMP (Routing Table Maintenance Protocol)
- SPF (Shortest Path First)

Protocol, RSVP (Reservation Protocol)

→ **See** Protocol, RSVP (Resource Reservation Protocol)

Protocol, RSVP (Resource Reservation Protocol)

RSVP is a transport-layer protocol for requesting resources that can provide a particular quality of service (QoS) for application-level data in a flow (that is, in a sequence of packets all going to the same destination address). RSVP can also be used by routers to pass QoS requests to nodes along the

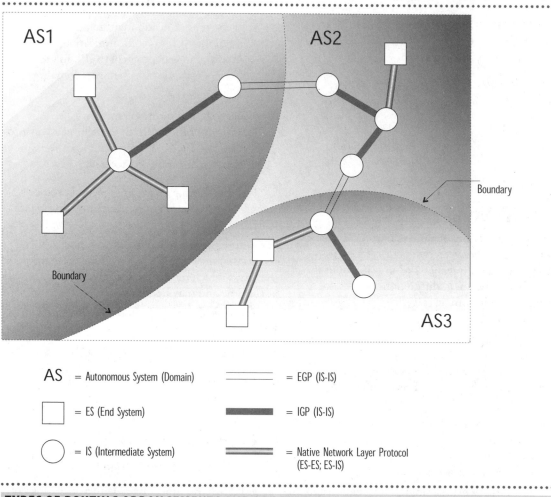

AS = Autonomous System (Domain)

▢ = ES (End System)

◯ = IS (Intermediate System)

═══ = EGP (IS-IS)

▬▬▬ = IGP (IS-IS)

═══ = Native Network Layer Protocol (ES-ES; ES-IS)

TYPES OF ROUTING ARRANGEMENTS AND PROTOCOLS

desired path. While RSVP is a transport layer protocol, it does not actually transport data. Rather, it is merely responsible for making sure the path for the data will satisfy the requested service criteria.

RSVP is a simplex protocol in that is sets up the QoS in only one direction. If the parties involved require a special QoS in both directions, then the RSVP protocol at either end must arrange for these separately. The receiving end must make the request.

RSVP is a very important protocol because it represents a first—even if somewhat simple and limited—effort to add QoS to the TCP/IP protocol stack. This stack was developed as a best-effort delivery service—that is, one with no QoS options—and it still functions in that manner for the most part.

RSVP is sometimes also expanded as resource reservation setup protocol or simply as reservation protocol.

Protocol, RSVP (Resource Reservation Setup Protocol)

→ *See* Protocol, RSVP (Resource Reservation Protocol)

Protocol, RTMP (Routing Table Maintenance Protocol)

In the AppleTalk protocol suite, a Transport layer protocol for tracking and updating the information in the routing table for an internetwork. RTMP is similar to the RIP (Routing Information Protocol) in the TCP/IP protocol suite and the RIP (Router Information Protocol) used in Novell's NetWare.

Protocol, RTP (Rapid Transit Protocol)

In IBM's Advanced Peer-to-Peer Networking (APPN) architecture, the RTP is used to avoid

congestion by performing flow control and error recovery end-to-end, rather than at each node in between. This greatly reduces the overhead on a network, which can help prevent congestion due to a filled buffer somewhere along the path.

→ *Broader Category* APPN (Advanced Peer-to-Peer Networking)

Protocol, RTP (Real-time Transport Protocol)

The Real-time Routing Protocol is one of the protocols in the new Ipv6 protocol stack, which is officially expected to replace the current IP stack in 1999. The Ipv6 RTP is designed for transporting data—such as audio, video, and real-time simulations—that must travel in real-time. RTP will provide end-to-end transport for either unicast or multicast transmissions.

Currently, users wishing to transport in real-time over IP networks must rely on the less satisfactory Resource Reservation Protocol (RSVP).

→ *Primary Sources* RTP is described in RFC 1889.

→ *See Also* Protocol, RSVP (Resource Reservation Protocol)

Protocol, RTP (Routing Table Protocol)

RTP is a routing protocol for the VINES networking operating system from Banyan Systems. The VINES RTP is based on the more widely used Routing Information Protocol (RIP), and is used to enable VINES routers to find each other and also servers and clients.

→ *Broader Category* Protocol, Routing

→ *See Also* Protocol, RIP (Routing Information Protocol)

Protocol, RTSP (Real-Time Streaming Protocol)

RTSP is an application-layer protocol that is used to control the distribution of material that must be delivered in real time—for example, continuous video or audio streams. The protocol can handle multiple streams at a time, and can use either connection-oriented (for example, TCP) or connectionless (for example, UDP) transport protocols to deliver the data.

The protocol can be used to

- Ask a media server to join an existing session—for example to play back or record material in the session.

- Retrieve materials from a media server. These materials can then be multicast or sent to a single client.

- Add material to an existing presentation—for example, adding a soundtrack to a video presentation.

Protocol, Scalable

A scalable protocol is one that can be used even if the number of nodes or routers on a network grows by a significant amount. It's particularly important to use scalable routing protocols because networks may be connected to any number of other networks—particularly if the connection is over the Internet.

Scalable protocols should use metrics that allow a packet to reach its destination even if a large amount of travel time or many intermediate stops are required. This is the reachability criterion, and it also requires scalable protocols to be able to find alternate paths, if necessary.

Scalable protocols should converge quickly on a path—that is, such protocols must be able to eliminate unpromising routes very quickly, and then be able to select quickly from the available paths. A fast convergence time is particularly important as

an internetwork grows, since the number or possible paths grows very rapidly as the size of an internetwork or a network increases.

EIGRP (Enhanced Interior Gateway Routing Protocol), NLSP (NetWare Link Services Protocol), and OSPF (Open Shortest Path First) are examples of scalable protocols.

→ **See Also**   Protocol, EIGRP (Enhanced Interior Gateway Routing Protocol); Protocol, NLSP (NetWare Link State Protocol); Protocol, OSPF (Open Shortest Path first)

Protocol, SCSP (Server Cache Synchronization Protocol)

SCSP can be used with various network architectures (such as ATM) to synchronize the database caches of MARS (Multicast Address Resolution Subgroup) or other address resolution elements within a subnet (known as a logical Internet subnet, or LIS).

Protocol, SDLC (Synchronous Data Link Control)

SDLC is a bit-oriented, Data-Link layer protocol that can support any of the following:

- Half- or full-duplex communications

- Circuit- or packet-switched networks

- Point-to-point or multipoint network topologies

- Transmission over cable or wireless transmission

SDLC Operation

SDLC was developed in the mid 1970s by IBM for use in IBM's SNA (Systems Network Administration) architecture. Because IBM was interested in facilitating connections between mainframes and terminals, SDLC is more effective for communications between unequal partners, such as a server and a workstation, but not between peers.

These two types of components are known as primaries and secondaries. Primaries give commands, and secondaries respond. Protocols derived from SDLC also support a third type of component: a combined node can function as either a primary or a secondary, depending on the situation.

Primaries and secondaries can be connected in any of several ways when using SDLC:

- Point-to-point, in which a single primary and a single secondary communicate.

- Multipoint, in which a single primary communicates with multiple secondaries.

- Loop, in which the primary is one node in a ring of secondaries. Each node is connected to the node immediately in front and in back. Transmissions begin at the primary, and are passed from node to node around the loop until the transmission again reaches the primary.

- Hub go-ahead, in which a primary communicates with multiple secondaries using an outbound channel, and secondaries communicate with the primary using an inbound channel. The inbound channel may be daisy-chained through each secondary.

An expanded version of SDLC was standardized by ANSI as ADCCP (Advanced Data Communications Control Procedure) and by the ISO as HDLC (High-level Data Link Control).

SDLC Frames

SDLC uses three types of frames: Information, Supervisory, and Unnumbered. Each frame type can occur within the same basic frame structure. "SDLC frame structure" shows these frames.

The frames have the following fields:

Flag Each SDLC frame begins and ends with an 8-bit flag. These flags always have the same value: 01111110. To ensure that such a bit sequence cannot be encountered anywhere else in an SDLC frame, the sender must insert a 0 after every string of five consecutive 1s. The receiver automatically removes these 0s before passing on the transmitted data. To improve efficiency, the ending flag for one frame can double as the starting flag for the next flag when multiple frames are transmitted in succession.

Address This 8-bit value contains the address of the secondary that will receive or send the frame. Since all transmissions involve the primary in SDLC, this address is never needed in a frame. SDLC includes provisions for multibyte address fields, and also for special addresses to indicate multicasts (in which some secondaries get the frame) or broadcasts (in which all secondaries get the frame).

Control This 8- or 16-bit field can contain any of three types of values: Information, Supervisory, or Unnumbered. These types are discussed below. Note that Information is used as both a frame type and as a field name.

Information This variable-length field contains the actual data being transmitted. Only certain types of frames have an Information field. Information-type frames include an Information field, as do two types of Unnumbered frames. Supervisory frames do not have Information fields, so they cannot be used for data transmission.

CRC This 2 byte field contains a cyclical redundancy check (CRC) value based on the Address, Control, and Information fields.

Each of the three frame types includes a poll/find (P/F) bit. This value is set to 1 if the primary wants the secondary to acknowledge receipt of the frame, and 0 otherwise. If the primary sets this bit to 1, the receiver will set the bit to a value that depends on other information in the Control field.

P

Basic Frame Format

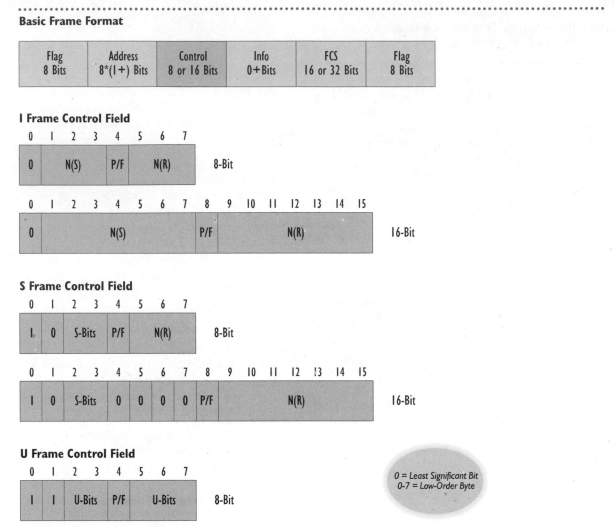

Flag 8 Bits	Address 8*(1+) Bits	Control 8 or 16 Bits	Info 0+ Bits	FCS 16 or 32 Bits	Flag 8 Bits

I Frame Control Field

```
0   1   2   3   4   5   6   7

0   N(S)    P/F   N(R)           8-Bit


0   1   2   3   4   5   6   7   8   9   10  11  12  13  14  15

0        N(S)              P/F         N(R)            16-Bit
```

S Frame Control Field

```
0   1   2   3   4   5   6   7

1   0   S-Bits  P/F   N(R)           8-Bit


0   1   2   3   4   5   6   7   8   9   10  11  12  13  14  15

1   0   S-Bits  0   0   0   0   P/F       N(R)            16-Bit
```

U Frame Control Field

```
0   1   2   3   4   5   6   7

1   1   U-Bits  P/F   U-Bits           8-Bit


0   1   2   3   4   5   6   7   8   9   10  11  12  13  14  15

1   1   U-Bits  R    U-Bits   P/F            R            16-Bit
```

0 = Least Significant Bit
0-7 = Low-Order Byte

SDLC FRAME STRUCTURE

Information-type Frame

An Information-type frame includes a 3-bit send sequence and a 3-bit receive sequence. (These are 7-bit values when 2 bytes are used for the Control field.) The send sequence represents the number of the next frame the primary will send. The receive sequence represents the number of the next frame the secondary expects to receive.

In case of error, the secondary stops updating the receive sequence value. The primary can use this value to determine the frame with which to begin retransmitting. Note that the primary must ask for an acknowledgment after every 7 (or 127) frames.

All information-type frames have a Control field that begins with a 0 bit. Such frames generally have 1 or more bytes in the Information field.

Supervisory Frame

A Supervisory frame is used to respond to information frames. The Control field for such frames begins with a bit pattern 10. In addition to the 10 and the P/F bit, the Control field for a Supervisory frame contains a 2-bit function code and a receive sequence value. The function bits specify the purpose of the frame, which can be to indicate any of the following:

- RR (Receiver Ready), when a secondary is ready to receive a frame.

- RNR (Receiver Not Ready), when a secondary is not ready to receive a frame.

- REJ (Reject Frame), when an error was detected in a frame.

Supervisory frames do not include an Information field.

Unnumbered Frame

An Unnumbered frame usually serves an administrative purpose, and it is usually sent on its own (rather than as part of a frame sequence). The Control field for such frames begins with a 11 bit pattern. Because Unnumbered frames are not grouped for any reason, there is no need for either send or receive sequence values.

Instead, an Unnumbered frame allocates 5 bits in the Control field to specify a function. the function can specify actions such as initializing or terminating a link, specifying whether the Control field is 1 or 2 bytes, and so on.

Two types of Unnumbered frames can also include an Information field. This field is used to send information relevant to the function being requested.

Protocol, SDP (Session Description Protocol)

SDP is used for describing multimedia sessions for the purpose of announcing a session, inviting participants to join it, or otherwise initiating a session. SDP is used only for description, and not for transport. Thus, it is independent of the transport protocol used.

An SDP description includes the following:

- Session name and purpose.

- Schedule for the session—that is, the time or times when the session will take place.

- The media comprising the session

- Information needed to receive the media (addresses, ports, formats, and so forth)

- Information about the bandwidth available for the session (optional)

- Contact information for the person responsible for the session (optional)

→ See Also   Protocol, SIP (Session Initiation Protocol)

Protocol, SGMP (Simple Gateway Monitoring Protocol)

In the Internet community, a now obsolete network management protocol. SGMP was a precursor to the SNMP (Simple Network Monitoring Protocol) that has become the most widely used network management protocol for TCP/IP environments.

Protocol, SHTTP (Secure Hypertext Transfer Protocol)

SHTTP is a secure version of the HTTP protocol, which is used to process and transport documents (Web pages) on the World Wide Web. (Web pages are hypertext files, and are generally created using the HTML, or hypertext markup language.)

SHTTP provides three major types of security services:

- Encryption, which means that the content of messages can be encrypted into what is gibberish for anyone but the person(s) with the mathematical key to decrypt the gibberish back to meaningful text. That is, encryption will ensure that only the person(s) authorized to receive the message—the "key personnel," so to speak—will be able to read it. SHTTP supports any of the popularly used encryption methods, including PEM (Privacy Enhanced Mail) and PGP (Pretty Good Privacy).

- Digital Signature, which is one way to prevent message forgery or tampering, and to verify the message source

- Authentication, which provides other mechanisms for testing the integrity of the file (i.e., determining whether anyone has changed it or tampered with it), and verifying that the sender is actually the author

SHTTP provides end-to-end secure communications, which means it must also be able to ensure the security along the way. SHTTP servers can communicate with both secure and non-secure (i.e., ordinary HTTP) servers. They will not provide secure information to a non-secure server, however.

SHTTP was originally developed at Enterprise Integration Technologies, and is currently under consideration by an Internet Engineering Task Force working group. SHTTP represents one strategy for providing security for activity and transactions on the Web. Another approach currently in use is Netscape's Secure Socket Layer (SSL).

→ *Primary Sources* The most current version of the Internet draft documents can be downloaded through the IETF home page,

```
http://www.ietf.cnri.reston.va.us/
```

or from the/ietf-online-proceedings directory of the `ftp.ietf.cnri.reston.va.us` FTP site.

Protocol, SIP (Session Initiation Protocol)

SIP is an application layer signaling protocol that is used to establish, modify, and terminate sessions involving one or more participants. An SIP session may be a multimedia conference or presentation (for example, a telecourse); it can also be a communication such as an Internet telephone call.

To establish a session the protocol sends out invitations—to either users or "robots" (for example, storage servers). These invitations contain descriptions of the session that enable participants to negotiate the media that will be used.

As part of its session control, SIP supports the following:

- Determining user location

- Determining user capabilities (for example, media and media parameters)

- Determining user availability for participating in the session.

- Call setup—that is, contacting the participants and establishing call parameters at both ends of the connection.

- Call handling, including transfer and termination of calls.

SIP is actually a very versatile protocol. It is independent of underlying protocols for transport and for conference control. It supports name mapping and redirection, which make it usable with ISDN (Integrated Services Digital Network) and with intelligent networking technology. The protocol is even extensible, so that new capabilities can be built in.

Protocol, SIP (Simple Internet Protocol)

This is a name used for IPv4, the successor to the original Internet Protocol (IP) and the predecessor to the newer IPv6, which is expected to become the new standard Internet Protocol.

→ **See** Protocol, IPng/IPv6

Protocol, SIPP (Simple Internet Protocol Plus)

→ **See** Protocol, IPng/IPv6

Protocol, SLIP (Serial Line Internet Protocol)

SLIP is a very simple protocol that is used solely for encapsulating and framing IP (Internet Protocol) packets that are being transmitted over serial lines—for example, via modem. Since it is used only in point-to-point connections, SLIP does no packet addressing or error checking.

SLIP is a de facto standard, and is used widely by users wishing to connect to the Internet from home through an Internet Access Provider (IAP). Despite its widespread use, SLIP is explicitly not an Internet standard.

A variant protocol—CSLIP, for compressed SLIP—uses a compression scheme (Van Jacobson compression) developed for TCP/IP-based networks. This scheme compresses the packet header from 24 to 5 bytes.

Because it lacks error-correction capabilities and because serial connections can sometimes be quite noisy, SLIP has largely been replaced by the somewhat more capable PPP (Point-to-Point Protocol).

→ **Primary Sources** SLIP is discussed in RFC 1055.

Protocol, SLP (Service Location Protocol)

The SLP provides a way to determine what network services are available and makes it possible to select a desired service. With the SLP, a user does not need to know which host on a LAN can provide the service. Instead, a user just needs to specify the service and a set of attributes, and the SLP can be used to find the service in a local area.

Protocol, S/MIME (Secure Multimedia Internet Mail Extension)

The S/MIME protocol makes the transmission of MIME messages secure by including digital signatures and encryption in the message body. S/MIME performs the same functions as the PGP (Pretty Good Privacy) encryption and authentication tool, but the two measures differ in their details and are not interoperable.

S/MIME uses a binary digital certificate based on the X.509v3 certificate standard, and it uses a triple DES encryption algorithm. This encryption uses the syntax specified in the Public-Key Cryptography Standard (PKCS) format #7.

S/MIME has been endorsed by several major networking and messaging vendors, including Banyan, ConnectSoft, Frontier, FTP Software,

Lotus, Microsoft, Netscape, Novell, Qualcomm, SecureWare, and VeriSign.

→ *Broader Categories* Encryption; Security

→ *Compare* PGP (Pretty Good Privacy)

→ *See Also* MIME (Multimedia Internet Mail Extension)

Protocol, SMTP (Simple Mail Transfer Protocol)

In the TCP/IP protocol suite, an application layer protocol that provides a simple electronic-mail service. SMTP uses the services of the TCP protocol at the Transport layer to send and receive messages.

Protocol, SNAcP (Subnetwork Access Protocol)

In the OSI specifications for the Internal Organization of the Network Layer (IONL), the type of protocol used at the lowest of the three sublayers into which the layer has been subdivided. Such a protocol must provide access to the subnetwork and must be able to transfer data to the subnetwork. The X.25 packet layer protocol is an example of a SNAcP.

Protocol, SNDCP (Subnetwork-Dependent Convergence Protocol)

In the OSI specifications for the Internal Organization of the Network Layer (IONL), the type of protocol used at the middle of the three sublayers into which the layer has been subdivided. Such a protocol must handle any details or problems relating to the subnetwork to which the data is being transferred.

Protocol, SNICP (Subnetwork-Independent Convergence Protocol)

In the OSI specifications for the Internal Organization of the Network Layer (IONL), the type of protocol used at the highest of the three sublayers into which the layer has been subdivided. Such a protocol must provide the routing and relaying capabilities needed to get data to its destination. The OSI's CLNP (Connectionless-mode Network Protocol) is an example of an SNICP.

Protocol, SNMP (Simple Network Management Protocol)

SNMP is a component of the IP (Internet Protocol) management model. It is the protocol used to represent network management information for transmission. Originally conceived as an interim protocol, to be replaced by the ISO's CMIS/CMIP model, SNMP has proven remarkably durable. In fact, a new and improved version, SNMP version 2, was proposed in 1992.

Two of the authors of SNMPv2, which is just about to be standardized, have asked for an extension from the IETF in order to get a formal evaluation of a stripped down alternative to SNMPv2.

SNMP Operation

SNMP provides communications at the applications layer in the OSI reference model. It was developed for networks that use TCP/IP. This protocol is simple but powerful enough to accomplish its task. SNMP uses a management station and management agents, which communicate with this station. The station is located at the node that is running the network management program.

SNMP agents monitor the desired objects in their environment, package this information in the appropriate manner, and ship it to the management station, either immediately or upon request.

In addition to packets for processing requests and moving packets in and out of a node, the SNMP includes traps. A trap is a special packet that is sent from an agent to a station to indicate that something unusual has occurred.

SNMP Community

The SNMP community is the component of the IP network management model that uses management stations and agents. A management agent may be polled by one or more management stations. An SNMP community is a way of grouping selected stations with a particular agent, in order to simplify the authentication process the agent must go through when polled. Each community is given a name that is unique for the agent.

The community name is associated with each station included, and it is stored by the agent. All members of an SNMP community share the same authentication code and access rights. They may also share the same SNMP MIB view, which is a selective subset of the information available in the agent's MIB (management information base). Stations in such a community can work only with the attributes included in the MIB view. An MIB view can be created for a single station or for all the stations in an SNMP community.

An agent may have multiple communities, stations may be in more than one community for a single agent, and a station may be part of communities associated with different agents.

By creating and using SNMP communities and MIB views, agents can simplify their work, thereby speeding up network response.

Protocol, SNTP (Simple Network Time Protocol)

SNTP is a variant of the draft standard NTP (Network Time Protocol), which is used to get the correct time from an official source, and then disseminate this time information to a subnet of servers. The protocol also enables servers to synchronize their clocks with that of the primary reference server, which gets the time directly from a source.

Whereas NTP is accurate to between 1 and 50 milliseconds at any location on the Internet, SNTP is accurate only to within several hundred milliseconds. SNTP trades off accuracy for simplicity. The authors suggest that SNTP be used only at the outskirts of the Internet—that is, in locations where hosts are unlikely to be providing time information to other hosts. Any host that is disseminating timestamps should use the more accurate NTP.

→ *Primary Sources* SNTP is discussed in RFC 2030. The complete NTP is discussed in RFC 1305.

Protocol, SPF (Shortest Path First) Flooding

In networks and internetworks that use the open shortest path first (OSPF) routing protocol, the SPF flooding protocol is used to send out link state advertisements. These provide neighboring routers with information about the type of links available through the advertising router.

A router will advertise one or more of different types of links, depending on the router's location and function. The five types of links are

- **Type 1 link (Router)** Sent by all routers, these links indicate the links for each adjacent router, including the type of service the router can provide.

- **Type 2 link (Network)** Sent by all routers, these links indicate all the routers that have a link to the designated router in a network area. (The OSPF protocol partitions large networks into smaller subnetworks, named areas. Much of the activity of routers in OSPF networks relates to the area in which the router is located.)

- **Type 3 link (IP summary)** Sent by area border routers (that is, by routers that connect in two areas), these links provide information about the network.

- **Type 4 link (Border router summary)** Sent by area border routers, these links indicate the connections to other border routers.

- **Type 5 link (External)** Sent by AS, or domain, routers (in this case, routers that connect the OSPF network to networks beyond it), these links indicate connections to the outside world, so to speak.

→ *Broader Category* Protocol, Router

→ *See Also* AS (Autonomous System); Protocol, OSPF (Open Shortest Path First)

Protocol, SPP (Sequenced Packet Protocol)

A transport level protocol in the XNS protocol suite from Xerox.

Protocol, SPX (Sequenced Packet Exchange)

→ *See* Protocol, IPX/SPX (Internetwork Packet Exchange/Sequenced Packet Exchange)

Protocol, SSCOP (Service Specific Connection-Oriented Protocol)

In the ATM (Asynchronous Transfer Mode) network architecture, the SSCOP is a data-link protocol used at the Signaling ATM Adaptation Layer (SAAL). SSCOP is a connection-oriented protocol that can provide reliable transport for signaling messages. SSCOP supports frame sequencing and end-to-end error recovery.

→ *Broader Category* ATM (Asynchronous Transfer Mode)

Protocol, SSL (Secure Sockets Layer)

SSL is a session level protocol that can be used to encrypt transmissions on the World Wide Web. SSL and a competing protocol, SHTTP (Secure Hypertext Transfer Protocol), can be used for sensitive transactions or for communications that must be kept secure. SSL provides assurance of privacy by encrypting data; it also provides message and server authentication, and can demand client authentication.

SSL is protocol independent, so it can encapsulate any of the application level protocols—FTP, HTTP, etc.—that might need to use SSL. SSL requires reliable transport, such as that provided by TCP.

SSL was developed at Netscape, and is now under consideration by an IETF (Internet Engineering Task Force).

SSL actually uses two different protocols:

- The SSL Record Protocol, which encapsulates everything that comes through, including SSL Handshake Protocol packets.

- The SSL Handshake Protocol, which is used to negotiate and establish security methods and parameters.

SSL Record Protocol

The data stream is encapsulated in records, which consist of a header and data. The data may be encrypted or not, and the record may be padded or not.

The data section of an encrypted packet has three parts:

- MAC-DATA, which is a message authentication code that is used to ensure that no one has tampered with the message. This field is 16 bytes when using some of the common authentication algorithms.

- ACTUAL DATA, which is the message that's being sent, and for which all the encryption overhead and work are being carried out

- PADDING-DATA, which is used to fill out packets—for example, to a boundary value required by the encryption key

A non-encrypted message contains only the actual data. Both padding and message authentication code are left out.

SSL Handshake Protocol

The SSL handshake protocol is used to set up the security measures that will be used. To do this, the protocol goes through the following phases of negotiation and testing:

- Hello, which is used to determine the capabilities of the parties involved and to select the algorithms that will be used for encryption and authentication.

- Key Exchange, during which the parties exchange material so that both agree on a master key (which will usually be one party's public key).

- Session Key Production, during which the session key or keys are created. These are the keys that will be used to encrypt the current messages. For various reasons, using such a session key to encrypt the message is much faster than using either party's public key. The session key is then encrypted using the master key and included in the message.

- Server Verify, during which the server must prove its authenticity. If the server fails this test, the master key and the session key(s) generated from it are considered untrustworthy, and the session is terminated.

- Client Verify, which is used only if the key exchange algorithm doesn't have such authentication built in. If used, the server requests a certificate from the client.

- Finished, during which the session is terminated.

The most recent complete version of SSL is version 3, but neither this or earlier versions are yet a standard, so much of the model is still tentative and is subject to change.

→ *Primary Sources* A draft of the most recent version of the specifications is generally available through the Netscape home page:

`http://home.netscape.com`

Protocol Stack

In networking, a protocol stack is a collection of related protocols used in a particular network. Together, the protocols in a protocol stack cover enough or all of the layers in the communications model being used. Widely used protocol stacks include the following:

- AppleTalk stack, used in Macintosh-based networks

- IPX/SPX stack, used in Novell NetWare networks

- TCP/IP stack, used in UNIX environments, such as the Internet

Protocol stacks are sometimes, loosely, known as a protocol suite. Strictly speaking, however, a protocol stack is a particular implementation of a protocol suite.

Protocol, Stateless

A protocol in which each transaction is independent of its predecessor and its successor, so that individual transactions may be repeated without affecting prior or future transactions. HTTP (Hypertext Transfer Protocol) I an example of a stateless protocol.

Protocol Suite

In networking, a protocol suite is a collection of related protocols. Together, the protocols in such a suite cover enough or all of the layers in the communications model being used. Widely used protocol suites include the following:

- AppleTalk suite, used in Macintosh-based networks.

- IPX suite, used in Novell NetWare networks.

- TCP/IP suite, used in UNIX environments, such as the Internet.

Protocol, SWAP (Simple Workflow Access Protocol)

SWAP is designed to enable an application to initiate, monitor, control, and manage a workflow process—for example, an application that needs to be fed data during execution. The protocol can also be used to enable two workflows to communicate with each other.

Protocol, Talk

The talk protocol is used for real-time communication on the Internet. It works only if both parties who intend to communicate are logged on at the same time.

Protocol, TCP (Transmission Control Protocol)

In the Internet TCP/IP protocol suite, a connection- and stream-oriented, Transport layer protocol. TCP uses IP (Internet Protocol) at the Network layer to deliver packets. TCP's byte stream performs the same kinds of services as Novell's SPX protocol and as the OSI TP4 protocol. In the TCP/IP suite,

the UDP (User Datagram Protocol) provides connectionless Transport layer service.

Protocol, TDP (Tag Distribution Protocol)

In a network that supports tag switching (a form of layer 3 switching that allows more efficient forwarding of packets) a TDP is used to distribute tag information to switches around a network. These tag switches can use this information to forward packets without having to check the destination network address for each packet.

→ *Broader Category*   Layer 3 Switching

→ *See Also*   Tag Switching

Protocol, Telnet

In the TCP/IP protocol suite, an application layer protocol that provides terminal-emulation capabilities. Telnet's services allow users to log in to a remote network from their computer.

Protocol, TFTP (Trivial File Transfer Protocol)

TFTP is a very simple file transfer protocol created for use on the Internet. This protocol is designed for use on top of the connectionless User Datagram Protocol (UDP). TFTP uses a lock-step approach to packet delivery—requiring an acknowledgement for each packet before sending the next one.

TFTP supports just a few types of packets:

- **Read Request (RRQ)** opcode = 1. Sent when the client wants to download a file.

- **Write Request (WRQ)** opcode = 2. Sent when the client wants to upload a file or when the packet begins "mail" mode.

- **Data (DATA)** opcode = 3. Contains up to 512 bytes of actual content. Data fields in data packets are regularly 512 bytes long, but the last packet in a transmission can be shorter.

- **Acknowledgement (ACK)** opcode = 4. Sent in response to each packet received correctly.

- **Error (ERROR)** opcode = 5. Sent if something did not work as expected—for example, if a packet was lost or there was an I/O error, etc. Error packets may be sent in reply—instead of an ACK packet—when things do not go as planned.

The only field that all five packet types have in common is their first one: Opcode, which is used to identify the type of packet. "TFTP packets" shows that this 16-bit field begins all TFTP packets. Note that only ACK packets are a fixed size. The following list describes the other fields, which are used in one or more of the packet types.

- Filename contains the name of the file to be written or read. This is a string variable in netASCII format, and is terminated by a zero byte. (Netascii is an 8-bit format that is based on a version specified in a USA Standard Code for Information Interchange document, together with modifications based on RFC 764 (Telnet protocol specification).

- Mode specifies the data format. This string can be any of three values: "netascii" or "octet" or "mail" in upper, lower, or mixed case. Netascii format uses the 8-bit ascii format mentioned in the previous item; mail is just like netascii except that a username is placed in the filename field and each mail transmission begins with a WRQ packet. Octet mode is used to transfer a file using the "native" 8-bit format of the source machine.

- Block # provides a way to identify the successive packets. Block numbers are assigned consecutively, beginning with 1.

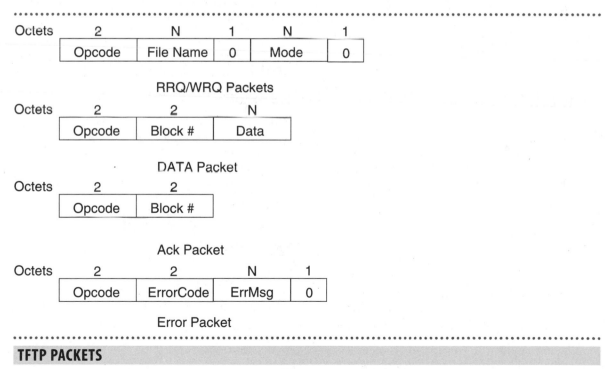

TFTP PACKETS

- Data provides the storage for actual information or content being sent using TFTP. This field can be between 0 and 512 bytes long. Since TFTP uses 512-byte packets, a packet less than 512 bytes is considered the end of the file.

- The 16-bit ErrorCode field contains an integer that indicates the type of error. Example error codes include: File not found (1), Disk full or allocation exceeded (3), Illegal TFTP operation (4), and No such user (7).

- ErrMsg is a string associated with a particular error code.

TFTP can transfer files, and that's just about it. TFTP really can't do much else—for example, give you a directory listing. The protocol is likely to quit under the slightest of problems. It is, however, very easy to implement, is not resource intensive, and has built-in rate and error-control (in the ACK required for each packet).

→ **Primary Sources** TFTP is described in RFC 1350, with several updates in RFCs 1782 through 1785 and RFCs 2347 through 2349.

Protocol, TLAP (TokenTalk Link Access Protocol)

In the AppleTalk protocol suite, the Data-Link layer protocol for TokenTalk, Apple's implementation of the Token Ring architecture.

Protocol, Transport

The term *transport protocol* refers to any of a class of protocols that provide connection services, error correction, and flow control for packets. Examples of transport protocols include TCP (Transmission Control Protocol) in the TCP/IP protocol suite and SPX (Sequenced Packet Exchange) in Novell's IPX/SPX suite.

In Microsoft's literature, the term is also used to refer to any protocol suite that provides these services and also the routing services of a network protocol. For example, in this usage, the term would refer to both TCP and IP (Internet Protocol) or to both IPX (Internetwork Exchange Protocol) and SPX.

→ **Compare** Protocol, Network

Protocol, UDP (User Datagram Protocol)

In the Internet TCP/IP protocol suite, a Transport layer protocol. UDP provides connectionless service and it uses IP (Internet Protocol) services at the Network layer. As a connectionless protocol, UDP is in contrast to the Internet's TCP (Transport Control Protocol), which provides connection-oriented service. The counterpart to UDP in the OSI protocol collection is TP4 (Transport Protocol Class 4).

Protocol, VOTS (VAX OSI Transport Service)

In the OSI reference model, a transport level protocol used on Digital Equipment Corporation (DEC) machines. VOTS can be used in local area or wide area networks.

Protocol, VTP (Virtual Terminal Protocol)

In Novell networking environments, VTP is a presentation- and application-layer protocol that provides a model of a general terminal for applications to use.

Protocol, XNS (Xerox Network Services)

XNS is a group of protocols that cover the layers in the OSI reference model. The Xerox model uses only five layers, but there is a close relationship between the Xerox and OSI models.

XNS Levels

The XNS levels are as follows:

- Xerox level 0 corresponds to OSI levels 1 and 2 (Physical and Data-Link).

- Xerox level 1 corresponds to OSI level 3 (Network).

- Xerox level 2 corresponds to OSI level 4 (Transport).

- Xerox level 3 corresponds to OSI levels 5 and 6 (Session and Presentation).

- Xerox level 4 corresponds to OSI level 7 (Application).

XNS Protocols

XNS includes the following protocols, several of which have been adopted or adapted by other network vendors:

- IDP (Internet Datagram Protocol), which serves OSI level 3.

- Echo, Error, SPP (Sequenced Packet Protocol), PEP (Packet Exchange Protocol), and RIP (Routing Information Protocol), which serve OSI level 4.

- Courier, which serves OSI level 5.

- Clearinghouse, which serves OSI level 6.

Protocol, XTP (Xpress Transfer Protocol)

A lightweight protocol developed for use on high-speed networks, as a replacement for traditional routing and transport protocols, such as TCP/IP. XTP's packet structure and transmission, error-correction, and control strategies streamline the protocol, saving transmission time and overhead.

→ *See Also* Protocol, Lightweight

Protocol, ZIP (Zone Information Protocol)

In the AppleTalk protocol suite, a Network layer protocol for maintaining a mapping of node names to zones (logical subnetworks). The protocol is used primarily by routers.

Proxy

A proxy, also known as a proxy agent, is an element that responds on behalf of another element to a request using a particular protocol. A proxy arrangement is used, for example, when an element does not support a particular protocol and it is not worth the trouble of implementing a protocol stack on that element so that it can support the protocol.

As an example, in the SNMP (Simple Network Management Protocol) component of the IP (Internet Protocol) management model, a management agent can respond on behalf of a network element that does not support SNMP or that is otherwise unable to communicate with the SNMP station. The proxy agent must support SNMP and must also be able to communicate with the represented element.

P

A proxy can also be used for security purposes—to shield users against attack from outside through material downloaded by or sent to the user. In such a context, a proxy server running on a firewall might accept messages or requests from users, change the label or source address on the requests, and then send them to their destination. The user is interacting with the proxy server, and is a client to this server. The proxy server, on the other hand, is interacting with the external server to which the message or request is being sent. The proxy server pretends to be the client requesting the service of interest. When a response is received from the external server, the proxy server relabels the material and passes it on to the actual client.

→ *See Also* Application-Level Proxy; Circuit-Level Proxy; Server, Proxy

Proxy ARP

A proxy arrangement in which one device (usually a router) answers address resolution requests on behalf of another device. The proxy agent (the router) is responsible for making sure that packets get to their real destination.

PSN (Packet Switch Node)

In a packet-switching network, a dedicated machine that accepts and routes packets.

PSTN (Public Switched Telephone Network)

A public network that provides circuit switching for users.

PTM (Pulse Time Modulation)

A class of digital modulation methods in which a time-dependent feature of a pulse (for example, width, duration, or position) is varied to encode an analog signal that is being converted to digital form.

PTT (Post, Telephone and Telegraph)

In most countries, a government agency that provides the named services.

PU (Physical Unit)

In SNA (Systems Network Architecture) networks, a term for a physical device and its resources on a network.

Public Data Network (PDN)

→ *See* PDN (Public Data Network)

Public-Key Encryption

A data-encryption strategy in which the encryption details depend on two keys: one public and one private. Each person's public key is stored in a key library, from which it will be available to anyone with the appropriate security clearance.

→ *See Also* Encryption

Public Key Infrastructure (PKI)

→ *See* PKI (Public Key Infrastructure)

Public Switched Telephone Network (PSTN)

→ *See* PSTN (Public Switched Telephone Network)

Pulse

Pulse refers to a brief and rapidly attained variation in the voltage or current level. Pulses are used, for example, to indicate a binary value. A pulse is characterized by the following:

- Amplitude of change.

- Rise and fall times, which represent the amount of time needed to change the level from 10 to 90 percent (rise) of maximum and from 90 percent back down to 10 percent (fall). In an ideal pulse, these values are both zero.

- Duration, or pulse width. The shorter the duration, the faster the transmission speed.

Pulse Amplitude Modulation (PAM)

→ *See* PAM (Pulse Amplitude Modulation)

Pulse Carrier

A signal consisting of a series of rapid, constant pulses that is used as the basis for pulse modulation (for example, when converting an analog signal into digital form).

Pulse Code Modulation (PCM)

→ *See* PCM (Pulse Code Modulation)

Pulse Time Modulation (PTM)

→ *See* PTM (Pulse Time Modulation)

Punch-Down Block

A punch-down block is a device containing metal tabs that puncture the jacket, or casing, on a twisted-pair cable. After puncturing the jacket, these tabs make electrical contact with the wires in the cable. This contact establishes a connection between the block and other blocks or specific devices. The block is connected to other blocks by a cross-connect. By making the appropriate cross-connections, it is possible to link nodes as necessary.

There are punch-down blocks specifically designed for data transmission, as opposed to the telephone company's original 66 punch-down block, which was used for dealing with analog signals. The 66 block is not suitable for use in networks because it is not designed to be disconnected and reconnected over and over (which is likely to happen when configuring a network).

In networking contexts, patch panels are more commonly used as an alternative to punch-down blocks for making cross-connections.

Push Technology

Push technology provides a mechanism for the distribution and delivery of information over the Web. The technology uses channels—essentially, potential connections—over which the content of interest can be "pushed" to the subscriber. For example, a subscriber might sign up for sports or business information, which can be delivered automatically once the channel is set up. The content provider will control what content (including advertisements) will be delivered.

Once a user has signed up for a channel, any new material can be delivered automatically any time the user starts their PC. (In most cases, the channel can be configured to ask before logging on to the Internet and delivering the material.)

Not surprisingly, push technology has a great deal that advertisers will find attractive—most notably, a captive audience consisting of anyone willing to accept the channel's delivery. For this reason, most new machines come with predefined channels (for which the content providers have paid a fee) to which the user is automatically subscribed.

PVC (Permanent Virtual Circuit)

In packet-switching networks, a logical path (a virtual circuit) established between two locations. Since the path is fixed, a PVC is the equivalent of a dedicated line, but over a packet-switched network.

→ *See Also* Virtual Circuit (VC)

PVC (Polyvinylchloride)

A material used in making cable jackets.

Python

Python is an interpreted, interactive scripting language developed by Guido van Rossum. It is object-oriented and platform-independent. Python is becoming quite popular for various web-related and other programming tasks.

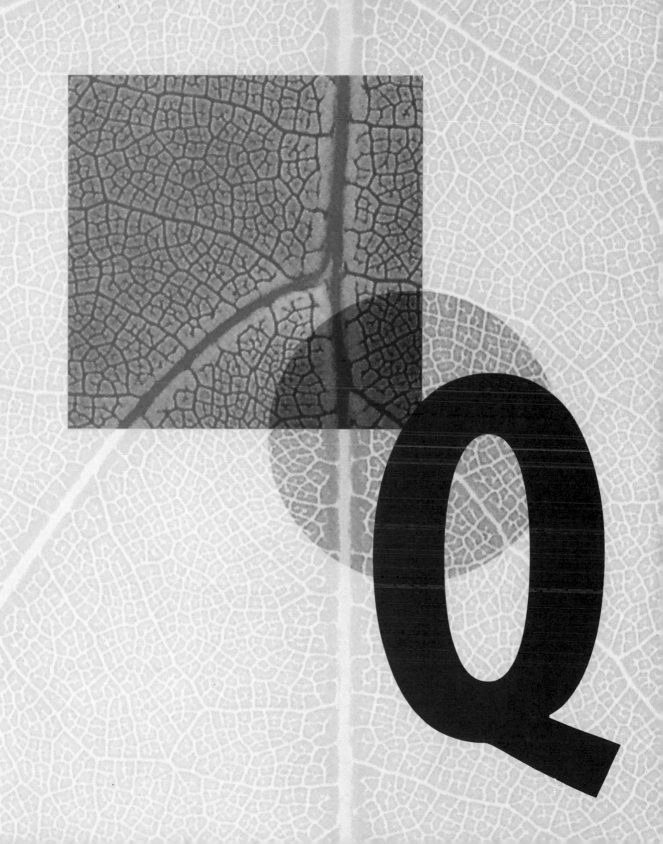

Q.###

The Q.### series of recommendations from the ITU-T (International Telecommunication Union-Telecommunication Standardization Sector) deals with telephone signaling and switching. Included in this series are several specifications for ISDN (Integrated Services Digital Network) and BISDN (broadband ISDN) signaling.

Specifications for certain interfaces for ATM (Asynchronous Transfer Mode) networks have also been created to make these interfaces compliant with the appropriate ITU specifications.

The following table lists some of the Q.### series of recommendations that are currently relevant.

QAM (Quadrature Amplitude Modulation)

→ See Modulation

Q-Bus

Q-Bus is a bus architecture used in the PDP-11 and MicroVAX machines from Digital Equipment Corporation (DEC).

Q.### SERIES OF RECOMMENDATIONS

Standard	Description
Q.700	General introduction to Signaling System 7 (SS7).
Q.701	Specifies functional description for Message Transfer Part (MTP) of SS7.
Q.711	Specifies functional description for the Signaling Connection Control Part (SCCP) of SS7.
Q.721	Specifies functional description for the Telephone User's Part (TUP) of SS7.
Q.730	Describes ISDN supplementary services (Call Waiting, Caller ID, and so forth) under SS7.
Q.731	Provides a description of number identification supplementary services using SS7.
Q.741	Specifies functional description for data user part of SS7.
Q.761	Specifies functional description for ISDN user part of SS7.
Q.771	Specifies functional description for transactional capabilities of SS7.
Q.920	General description of ISDN User-Network Interface (UNI) data-link layer interface for Digital subscriber Signaling System 1 (DSS1). Identical to ITU document I.440.
Q.921	Provides a specification of the ISDN UNI data-link layer interface. Identical to ITU document I.441.
Q.930	General description of ISDN UNI layer 3 interface for DSS1. Identical to ITU document I.450.
Q.931	Provides a specification of the ISDN UNI layer 3 interface for DSS1.
Q.2100	Provides an overview of the BISDN Signaling ATM Adaptation Layer (SAAL).
Q.2110	Specifies a service specific connection oriented protocol (SSCOP) for Broadband ISDN (BISDN) ATM Adaptation Layer (AAL).
Q.2120	Specifies a meta-signaling protocol for BISDN.
Q.2130	Specifies a service specific coordination function (SSCF) to support signaling at the UNI for a BISDN SAAL—or, in other words, Q.2130 specifies SSCF at UNI for BISDN SAAL.
Q.2140	Equivalent to Q.2140, except that it is for Network Network Interfaces (NNI).
Q.2931	Provides specification for a BISDN UNI layer 3 interface that provides basic call/connection control under DSS2. This specification was created to make ATM signaling at the UNI compatible with the signaling defined for ISDN in Q.931.

QCIF (Quarter Common Intermediate Format)

The Common Intermediate Format (CIF) is the de facto standard for videoconferencing images. This standard specifies a resolution of 352 × 288 pixels. CIF is defined in ITU-T standard H.261.

QCIF (for quarter CIF) is one of two lower-resolution variants that are sometimes used. QCIF has half the resolution in each dimension (176×144), which yields one-fourth the number of pixels compared to CIF. The lowest-resolution variant is SQCIF (for sub-quarter CIF), which has an 88×72 resolution. The lower resolution variants are defined in ITU-T standard H.263.

→ *Broader Category* Videoconferencing

→ *See Also* 4CIF (4× Common Intermediate Format); 16CIF (16× Common Intermediate Format); CIF (Common Intermediate Format); H.###; SQCIF (Sub-Quarter Common Intermediate Format)

QIC (Quarter-Inch Cartridge)

QIC is a set of tape standards defined by the Quarter-Inch Cartridge Drive Standards Organization, a trade association established in 1987.

Two standards are in common use: QIC 40 and QIC 80. Both use the DC-2000 series of mini-cartridges. QIC 40 writes 10,000 bits per inch on 20 tracks. QIC 80 writes 14,700 bits per inch on 28 tracks. QIC 80 can read QIC 40 tapes, but the reverse is not true. QIC 40 and QIC 80 format tapes are often used to back up small to medium hard-disk systems. Up to about 250MB will fit on a single tape using data compression. Most device drivers shipped with operating systems or with tape devices can handle both the QIC 40 and QIC 80 standards.

Other higher-density QIC formats allow for higher capacities. QIC 1350 handles up to 1.35GB of tape storage, and QIC 2100 handles up to 2.1GB.

QoS (Quality of Service)

QoS is a concept used in various communications and networking contexts to refer to how well a logical or physical connection is performing. Various measures can be (and have been) used to determine a value for this concept, including error rate, signal-to-noise ratio (SNR), delay, and latency.

Originally developed as a way to indicate how well telephone circuits were performing, the QoS concept is now used widely as a measure of network performance—particularly in switching networks, such as those provided by ATM (Asynchronous Transfer Mode) or X.25 architectures.

In ATM networks, QoS refers to a set of parameters for describing a transmission. These parameters include values such as allowable delay variation in cell transmission and allowable cell loss (in relation to total cells transmitted). The parameters apply to virtual channel connections (VCCs) and virtual path connections (VPCs), which specify paths between two entities.

Quad

As a general term, quad refers to something having four parts (sides, components, and so forth). In network-related contexts, quad is often used to refer to a cable with four wires, consisting of two twisted pairs, each insulated separately.

Quadbit

A quadbit consists of four bits treated (transmitted, processed, or interpreted) as a single unit. Quadbits are used, for example, in quadrature amplitude modulation (QAM), which encodes four bits into a single modulated value. There are 16 possible quadbit values, as shown in the table "Quadbit Values."

QUADBIT VALUES

Quadbit Value	Bit 3	Bit 2	Bit 1	Bit 0
0	0	0	0	0
1	0	0	0	1
2	0	0	1	0
3	0	0	1	1
4	0	1	0	0
5	0	1	0	1
6	0	1	1	0
7	0	1	1	1
8	1	0	0	0
9	1	0	0	1
10	1	0	1	0
11	1	0	1	1
12	1	1	0	0
13	1	1	0	1
14	1	1	1	0
15	1	1	1	1

→ *See Also* Dibit; Tribit

Quadrature Amplitude Modulation (QAM)

→ *See* Modulation

Quality of Service (QoS)

→ *See* QoS (Quality of Service)

Quantization

In digital-signal processing, quantization is the process of converting a PAM (pulse amplitude modulation) signal into PCM (pulse code modulation) form. This converts a signal from a level to a digital bit sequence.

Quarter Common Intermediate Format (QCIF)

→ *See* QCIF (Quarter Common Intermediate Format)

Quarter-Inch Cartridge (QIC)

→ *See* QIC (Quarter-Inch Cartridge)

Quartet Signaling

Quartet signaling is a strategy used in the 100VG-AnyLAN Ethernet implementation developed by Hewlett-Packard (HP) and AT&T Microelectronics. The strategy uses four wire pairs simultaneously, and relies on the fact that the wire pairs need not be used for sending and receiving at the same time.

The wire availability is guaranteed because demand priority, the media-access method used in 100VG-AnyLAN, enables hubs to handle network access for the nodes. Thus, quartet signaling provides four times as many channels as ordinary (10Mbps) Ethernet. It also uses a more efficient encoding scheme, 5B/6B encoding, as opposed to the Manchester encoding used by ordinary Ethernet.

The more efficient encoding, together with the four channels and a slightly higher signal frequency, make it possible to increase the bandwidth for an Ethernet network by a factor of 10 (from 10Mbps to 100Mbps).

Quartz Crystal

Quartz crystals are used for timing in PCs and other electronic devices. Such crystals are used because they can be made to resonate at a specific frequency, which can then be used to provide the timing needed for clock cycles.

Quat

A quat (for quaternary digit) is an element in a four-symbol representational system—for example, a value in a base-4 number system. This is analogous to a bit, which is a value in a base-2 number system.

→ See Also Trit

Query

Most simply, a query is a question. In a more specific context, a query is a request to a database management program or to an object request broker for some type of information or service. Queries are generally formulated in a query language (such as the widely used Structured Query Language, or SQL), and may be entered through scripts or in interactive sessions.

→ See Also Query Language

Query Language

In a database management system, a programming language that allows a user to extract and display specific information from the database. For example, SQL is an international database query language that allows the user to create or modify data or the database structure.

→ See Also SQL (Structured Query Language)

Queue

In data handling, a temporary holding structure in which values can be stored until needed. A queue is organized in such a way that the first item added to the queue is also the first item out of the queue. This processing is known as FIFO, for first-in, first-out. Job and print queues are perhaps the best known for those who work with computers.

In networking, a queue refers to a backlog of packets waiting to be processed.

Queuing

In a router or other networking component in which transmission elements can (or must) be sequenced, queuing refers to the reordering of the transmission elements (for example, packets) in order to meet some quality of service (QoS) criteria or in order to improve performance sufficiently to eliminate or reduce congestion.

As bandwidth demands increase, the throughput gains from queuing become more important, and effective queuing strategies become essential. To help find such strategies, an area of mathematics known as queuing theory has been developed.

Queuing Theory

Queuing theory is a branch of mathematics that studies how best to arrange elements for processing. This question is particularly important in network switching and routing—that is, in sequencing packets or calls for transmission. Queuing theory is an important tool for traffic management in a network.

One of the major accomplishments of queuing theory was determining that a single line in a bank will move customers through more quickly than if each teller has a separate line of customers.

Q

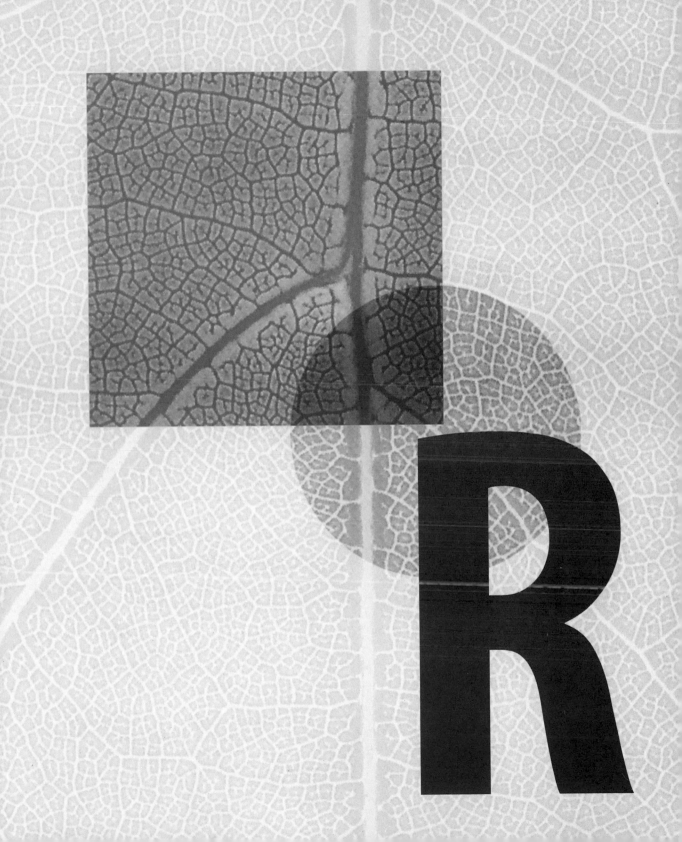

R

Radial Hierarchical Wiring

→ *See* Topology, Star-Wired Ring

Radio Frequency Interference (RFI)

→ *See* RFI (Radio Frequency Interference)

Radio Paging

A remote signaling method that uses radio waves to contact and activate a paging device, or beeper. This receiver beeps when contacted.

RADSL (Rate-Adaptive Digital Subscriber Line)

RADSL is a variant of the up-and-coming DSL (digital subscriber line) technology. Using the analog local loop that connects a subscriber to the local telephone company's central office (CO), this technology can support downstream speeds—that is, from service provider to customer—ranging from 128Kbps to over 8Mbps, depending on the DSL variant and the lines over which the signals must travel.

Briefly, DSL technology works as follows. Special technology at both ends of the connection—CO and customer premises—makes it possible to soup-up the performance of ordinary telephone lines over limited distances. Supported distances range from about 4500 feet to 22,000 feet, with most variants operating in the 12,000 to 18,000 foot range.

Arguably, the most common variant is asymmetric DSL (ADSL), which supports speeds of up to 8.192Mbps downstream, but only up to 640Kbps upstream. While different ADSL installations will support different speeds, a given installation's operating speed will be determined and fixed at initial setup. Like those of other DSL variants, ADSL's speeds will remain fixed after setup. This means

that two ADSL installations just a few hundred yards apart can have different speeds—simply because of differences in line quality.

RADSL helps minimize the long-term consequences of such differences in line quality by being able to adjust the connection rate to the highest levels supported given the line quality at the time a connection is made. Thus, RADSL is an ADSL implementation that can adjust the rates at which it operates. Most implementations of RADSL select their speed at start-up and then maintain that speed as long as the connection lasts; other implementations can adjust speeds dynamically—that is, during a session.

Most DSL implementations use either of two methods for encoding signals: CAP (carrierless amplitude/phase) modulation or DMT (discrete multitone). The details of these technologies are of no concern here except to note that DMT encoding is inherently rate adaptive, whereas CAP requires additional circuitry to become capable of rate-adaptive operation.

→ *Broader Category* DSL (Digital Subscriber Line)

→ *See Also* ADSL (Asymmetric Digital Subscriber Line)

RAID (Redundant Array of InexpensiveDisks)

RAID refers to a system setup that uses multiple drives and writes data across all the disks in a predefined order. Typically, RAID uses four or five drives, but more are not uncommon. The disk array is seen as a single drive by the user. Internally, the multiple drives can be accessed in parallel. RAID is also known as *drive array,* and is sometimes expanded as Redundant Array of Independent Disks.

The rules for reading and writing depend on which of the various RAID levels the system supports. These levels are designated by numerical values, with the most common levels numbered from

0 through 5, and with several less common levels having numbers above this range. Each value represents a different way of dealing with the data (not increasing power or speed). RAID levels include:

Level 0: Data striping or disk spanning; block interleaving. In data striping, data is written block by block across each drive, with one block to each drive. An alternative to data striping is disk spanning, in which data blocks are written to the next available disk. If a disk is full or busy, it may be skipped in a particular turn. This RAID level provides no fault tolerance, since the loss of a hard disk can mean a complete loss of data.

Level 1: Disk mirroring or duplexing. In disk mirroring, a single channel is used to write the same data to two different hard disks. If one drive is damaged, the data is still accessible from the other drive. On the other hand, if the channel fails, both drives are lost. In disk duplexing, data is written to two hard disks using two different channels, which protects the data, unless *both* channels or *both* drives fail.

Level 2: Data striping, bit interleaving. Each bit is written to a different drive, and checksum information is written to special checksum drives. This level is very slow, disk-intensive, and remarkably unreliable (since any of the multiple checksum disks can fail).

Level 3: Data striping, bit interleaving, parity checking. This is the same as level 2, except that a single parity bit is written to a parity drive instead of checksums to checksum drives. It is more reliable than level 2, because there is only one parity drive that can fail.

Level 4: Data striping, block interleaving, parity checking. This is like level 3, except that an entire block (sector) is written to each hard disk each time. Level 4 supports parallel reads—that is, reads from multiple disks at he same time—but does not support parallel writes.

Level 5: Data striping, block interleaving, distributed parity. This is like level 4 except that the parity or checksum information is distributed across the regular disks, rather than being written to special disks. Level 5 allows overlapping writes, and a disk is accessed only if necessary. This level is faster and also more reliable than the other levels.

Level 6: Data striping, block interleaving, distributed and multiple parity. This is like level 5 except that it uses a second parity scheme that is distributed across different drives from the first. This level is extremely reliable, but also expensive and difficult to implement.

Level 10: Data striping, disk mirroring or duplexing. This level uses data striping, with each stripe consisting of an array of mirrored or duplexed drives. This is more effective but also much more expensive than level 1.

Level 53: Data striping, bit interleaving, parity checking. This level uses data striping, with each stripe consisting of an array of level 3 drives. This is more effective but also much more expensive than level 1.

In summary, level 0 provides no fault tolerance, since all data is lost if a disk fails. Level 1 provides some fault tolerance if disk duplexing is used. Levels 2 through 5 provide fault tolerance in that a single disk can fail without loss of data. Of these, levels 1 and 5 are most commonly used.

In addition to the cost of the disk drives, a RAID configuration requires a special hard drive controller.

It is arguable whether the amount of increased reliability provided by RAID technology is worth the cost (which is about the same as for an external duplex system). In tests, disk duplexing generally outperformed RAID levels 3 through 5.

→ *Compare* SLED (Single Large Expensive Disk)

RAM (Random-Access Memory)

RAM is chip-based working memory, which is the memory used by programs and drivers to execute instructions and to hold data temporarily. RAM chips are distinguished by their access speed, which is on the order of about 70 nanoseconds, and by their capacity, which is currently between 1 and 4 megabytes (MB) per chip set.

Various types of RAM are distinguished in the literature:

- DRAM (dynamic RAM), which must be refreshed periodically in order to retain its information. Refresh periods are every few milliseconds or so.

- SRAM (static RAM), which retains its contents as long as power is supplied.

- VRAM (video RAM), which is used to provide memory for graphics processing or temporary image storage.

For a discussion of the different classes of RAM (conventional, upper, extended, and expanded), see the Memory article.

Rapid Transport Protocol (RTP)

→ See Protocol, RTP (Rapid Transport Protocol)

RARP (Reverse Address Resolution Protocol)

→ See Protocol, RARP (Reverse Address Resolution Protocol)

RAS (Remote Access Services)

RAS is a Windows NT service that provides limited wide area networking (WAN) capabilities.

For example, RAS allows remote access to a Windows NT network and provides packet-routing capabilities.

Windows NT includes a single-user version of RAS, which allows one user to access the network at a time. Windows NT Advanced Server (NTAS) includes a multiuser version, which allows up to 64 remote users. The RAS supports various types of WAN connections, including ISDN (Integrated Services Digital Network), modems, and X.25 links.

RAS can route packets using any of several popular protocol stacks, provided these stacks include support for Windows NT NetBIOS.

Rate-Adaptive Digital Subscriber Line (RADSL)

→ See RADSL (Rate-Adaptive Digital Subscriber Line)

RBOC (Regional Bell Operating Company)

In telephony, RBOC is a term for any of the seven companies originally formed as a result of the divestiture of AT&T. The RBOCs are Ameritech, Bell Atlantic, Bell South, NYNEX, Pacific Telesis, Southwestern Bell Corporation, and US West.

These RBOCs were created from the 23 BOCs (Bell Operating Companies) that existed before the divestiture. The table "Original RBOC Information" lists the original RBOCs, their domains, and the BOCs from which they were created. The RBOCs provide local telephone service, and are known as Local Exchange Carriers, or LECs.

Since the RBOCs were created, things have changed greatly in the telecommunications industry. Other, independent service providers have appeared, and the RBOCs have become only a handful among over 100 LECs. In addition to these competitors, a

1996 decree opened the market even further to competitive LECs (CLECs). However, this decree also allowed the RBOCs and other LECs to compete for long-distance customers.

ORIGINAL RBOC INFORMATION

RBOC	States Covered	Member BOCs
Ameritech	IL, IN, MI, OH, WI	IL Bell, IN Bell, MI Bell, OH Bell, WI Bell
Bell Atlantic	CT, DE, MD, NJ, PA, WV, VA	Bell of PA, Chesapeake and Potomac of MD, Chesapeake and Potomac of VA, Chesapeake and Potomac of Washington, DC, Chesapeake and Potomac of WV, Diamond State Telephone, NJ Bell
Bell South	AL, FL, GA, KY, LA, MS, NC, SC, TN	South Central Bell, Southern Bell
NYNEX	MA, ME, NH, NY, RI, VT	New England Telephone, New York Telephone, Southern New England Telephone
Pacific Telesis	CA, NV	NV Bell, Pacific Bell
Southwestern Bell	AR, KS, MO, OK, TX	Southwestern Bell
US West	AZ, CO, ID, MN	Mountain Bell
	MT, NB, NM, ND	Northwestern Bell
	SD, UT, WA, WY	Pacific NW Bell

To deal with this changing market, the RBOCs have done some consolidation among themselves, and more mergers are contemplated or in the works. RBOCs have also merged with other service providers. By mid-1998, only five of the original RBOCs were left:

- Ameritech, which covers the upper midwestern U.S.

- Bell Atlantic, which covers the northeastern U.S. and which now owns NYNEX

- Bell South, which covers the southeastern U.S.

- SBC Communications (formerly Southwestern Bell), which covers the southwestern U.S. and which now owns Pacific Telesis

- US WEST Communications, which covers the western U.S.

RC5 Encryption Algorithm

RC5 is a secret key encryption algorithm that uses a variable length key and that relies heavily on data-dependent rotations of bit values. The RC5 actually includes separate algorithms for expanding the secret key, doing encryption, and doing decryption.

RC5 can be implemented in many different ways, only some of which are likely to be secure. The algorithm's performance and level of security depend on three parameters:

W: word size (in bits). This may be 16, 32, or 64.

R: Number of rotation rounds. This may be any whole number between 0 and 255.

B: Number of bytes in the key. This may be any whole number between 0 and 255.

Different implementations of the algorithm are distinguished by their values on these parameters: RC5-w/r/b. For example, RC5-32/1/1 uses a 32-bit word, but does only one rotation and has only a single byte as the key. This algorithm is *not* secure.

In contrast, RC5-32/16/7 has a 56-bit key and does 16 rotations. These values are comparable to the values for the DES (Data Encryption Standard) algorithm that is currently in use.

Since RC5 is a recently developed algorithm, its behavior for many parameter combinations is still unknown.

→ *Broader Categories* Encryption

→ *See Also* DES (Data Encryption Standard)

R

RCONSOLE

A Novell NetWare 3.*x* and 4.*x* utility that allows a network supervisor to manage a server from a workstation. The supervisor can give commands and accomplish tasks, just as if the commands were being given directly at the server. In NetWare 4.*x*, RCONSOLE also includes asynchronous capabilities, allowing the supervisor to access the server via modem. In NetWare 3.*x*, the ACONSOLE utility provides asynchronous connections.

RDA (Remote Database Access)

An OSI specification to allow remote access to databases across a network.

RDS (Remote Data Service)

RDS is one of the Microsoft Data Access Components (MDACs) included in the Windows NT 4 Option Pack. RDS enables a client to retrieve a complete data set from a server, manipulate it locally, and then return it to the server when done. This saves bandwidth because the client doesn't need to exchange information on a continuous basis with the server.

Other MDAC elements include OLE-DB (Object Linking and Embedding for Databases) and ADO (ActiveX Data Objects), which sit between a client and a server with a data store (database, e-mail message center, spreadsheet, and so forth) that the client wants to access. OLE-DB serves as an interface to database access functions such as those in the ODBC (Open Database Connectivity) API (application programming interface). ADOs essentially serve as friendly front ends to OLE-DB.

→ *Broader Category* MDAC (Microsoft Data Access Component)

Read-after-Write Verification

A Novell NetWare data-verification measure in which the information written to disk is compared with the information in memory. If the two match, the information in memory is released. If they do not match, NetWare's Hot Fix feature assumes the storage location is bad, and redirects the information to a safe location in the Hot Fix redirection area.

Read-Only Memory (ROM)

→ *See* ROM (Read-Only Memory)

RealAudio

RealAudio provides support for audio in real-time over the Internet or over a corporate Intranet or extranet. RealAudio functions as a plug-in for a browser or server.

→ *Broader category* Plug-In

Real Mode

The operating mode for memory allocation and usage for an 8086 processor. This mode can use up to 1 megabyte of memory, and only one process can execute at a time. This is in contrast to the protected mode available in 80286 and later processors. In protected mode, multiple processes can run at the same time, and each process has its own (protected) memory area.

Real-Time Transport Protocol (RTP)

→ *See* Protocol, RTP (Real-Time Transport Protocol

RECC (ReverseControl Channel)

In cellular communications, the RECC allows communication from the mobile station (MS)—for example, the subscriber's phone— to the base station (BS). This channel operates at up to 10Kbps and is used for control and signaling, rather than for actual communication between the subscriber and whomever the subscriber is calling.

Communications on the RECC use the EIA-553 standard for mobile station/land station communication. This is also true of the FOCC (Forward Control Channel), which provides for signaling from the BS to the MS. Adherence to EIA-553 makes components less dependent on specific manufacturers and suppliers because any EIA-553 component should be able to communicate with any other compliant component—regardless of the manufacturers involved.

→ **Broader Category** Cellular Communications

→ **See Also** FOCC (Forward Control Channel)

Receive Only (RO)

→ **See** RO (Receive Only)

Receiver

One of the three essential components of a communications system. The other two are a transmitter and a communications channel. The receiver's job is to capture or store the transmission, and then convert it to visual or acoustic form.

Reconfiguration Burst

In ARCnet networks, a special bit pattern that is transmitted repeatedly whenever a node wants to force the creation of a new token or when a new node joins a network. Essentially, a reconfiguration burst resets the network.

Rectifier

A device that converts AC (alternating current) into DC (direct current).

Red Book

This term refers to the volumes of telecommunications standards published in 1985 by the CCITT.

Redirection

Redirection is the diversion of data or other signals from a default or intended destination to a new one. In most networking contexts, redirection is transparent to the user. For example, a print request may be redirected from the printer port to a spooler, or a workstation's request for access to a (supposedly) local drive is redirected to the server's disk.

In other contexts, the redirection may be explicit. For example, redirection can be accomplished by using the DOS redirection operators > and >> or the pipe (|) operator.

Redirection Area

In Novell NetWare's Hot Fix feature, an area of the hard disk set aside for storing data that would otherwise be written to bad disk sectors.

Redirector

A redirector is a program that intercepts program or user requests and directs them to the appropriate environment. A networking redirector can direct requests to DOS or to the network interface card (for transmission to the network server).

Similarly, DOS may redirect requests or calls to a network operating system while processing local operating system requests itself. The DOS Requester in Novell NetWare 4.x receives redirected commands

R

from DOS and sends them to the network for processing.

→ *See Also* DOS Requester

Reduced Instruction Set Computing (RISC)

→ *See* RISC (Reduced Instruction Set Computing)

Redundancy

Redundancy refers to a configuration or state with extra components or information. The redundant elements are included to make it possible to detect or compensate for malfunctions or errors. Redundancy may be applied to hardware, software, or information.

Hardware: Duplicate hard disks, servers, or cables are examples of hardware redundancy. Disk mirroring and disk duplexing are two ways to use duplicate hard disks; RAID (redundant array of inexpensive disks) systems provide for up to five hard disks. These types of redundant configurations increase a system's fault tolerance.

Software: The generation of extra copies of critical code segments helps prevent programs from accidentally corrupting the code. For example, copies may be created when the code is needed by different processes.

Information: Redundancy (parity) checks on information being transmitted can detect simple errors. More sophisticated use of information redundancy (such as Hamming coding) can actually correct such transmission errors. (Natural language actually has considerable redundancy. For example, with English, it turns out that you can lose, on average, almost half of the content of a message and still have a reasonable chance of determining the message content. This information must be lost at random spots in the message.

Losing the first or second half of the message would clearly leave you in a poor position for deciphering the message.)

Refractive Index

A measure of the degree to which light will travel at a different speed in a given medium, such as water or a fiber-optic core constructed of a particular type of material. It is also known as *index of refraction*.

Registered Resource

In Novell's NetWare, a resource (such as a disk drive) that can communicate with and provide data for the NetWare Management Agent. When a resource registers, it makes itself, its domain, and its capabilities known to the NetWare Management Agent.

Register Insertion

Register insertion is a media-access method used in some older ring topologies. In register insertion, a node that wants to transmit simply inserts a register (a buffer) into the ring's data stream at an appropriate point in the stream. The inserted register contains the packet to be transmitted (including data, addressing, and error-handling components).

Depending on restrictions, the node may be able to insert its register only during a break in the data stream, or the node may be able to insert its packets before passing a received packet on to the next node. Inserting a register effectively lengthens the logical ring, which means nodes must wait slightly longer for their packets to reach a destination.

The advantage of an insertion strategy is that multiple nodes can be transmitting at the same time. This is in contrast to simple token passing, in which only the node with the token gets access to the network.

The disadvantage of this method is that the ring can become overloaded if many nodes want to transmit at the same time. There is no way to control this, since register insertion does not have any provisions for preventing a node from trying to access the ring.

Register insertion was used in several experimental networks in the 1970s and 1980s, but has been superseded by token passing as the access method of choice for ring networks.

→ **Broader Category** Media-Access Method

→ **See Also** CSMA/CA (Carrier Sense Multiple Access with Collision Avoidance); CSMA/CD (Carrier Sense Multiple Access with Collision Detection); Polling; Token Passing

Registry

The Registry serves as a front end for configuration data in Windows 9.x and NT environments. Information about virtually everything related to the computer, network, or users is stored in huge data files accessible through the Registry. These data files can be several megabytes in size.

The Registry maintains separate data files for individual users (USER.DAT) and for the system hardware and software (SYSTEM.DAT). Separating user and system information makes it possible for users on networks to log on from different machines while still using the same configuration.

A third file—CONFIG.POL—may also be present. This file contains information about network or system policies. These may include restrictions on how users can configure their desktops, use resources, and so forth. If the file is present, CONFIG.POL settings override settings in both the user and system configurations.

Information in the registry's databases is organized hierarchically as values for various keys, and is stored in a form not readable by humans. Registry editor programs are available to translate the information into readable form and to enable users (or programs) to make changes directly in the Registry database. Any discussion of the Registry and how to use it will generally include warnings—every paragraph or two—about how dangerous it is to make changes to the Registry, and how it's essential to backup the Registry before making any changes. In short, it is incredibly easy to mess something up when dealing with the Registry.

During startup, the operating system gets information from the Registry files. If one of these files is found to be corrupt, Windows switches to a backup copy of the Registry. (The Registry is saved to a backup file everytime the system is shut down, and several—usually 5—generations of backups are kept.)

While Windows 9x, NT, and 2000 all use a Registry, these are not the same in the three environments. In general, the Registry for Windows NT and 2000 has greater functionality than the Windows 9x Registry. This is due mainly to the fact that the Registry had to be crippled to enable Windows 95 to operate in 4Mb of memory. Another major difference between the Win9x and WinNT/Win2000 Registries is that the former uses ASCII to encode characters, while the latter uses the newer and more versatile Unicode encoding scheme.

→ **Broader Category** Windows 9x; Windows NT

Relational Database

→ **See** Database

Relay

In telephony and other forms of telecommunications, a relay is an electromagnet that produces the contacts necessary for switching signals through a circuit, calls through a switchboard, and so forth.

The relay consists of a soft iron core with wire wrapped around it. When a current passes through the wire, the core becomes magnetized and attracts a small component (called an armature) to make physical contact with the relay. This produces the contact necessary for switching.

Relaying

The process of actually moving data along a path determined by a routing process. The data is relayed between a source and a destination. Relaying is one of the two major functions of the network layer in the OSI Reference Model (another is routing).

Relay Point

In a switching network or system, a point at which packets or messages are switched to other circuits or channels.

Reliable Transfer

In the OSI Reference Model, a transfer mode that guarantees that *either* of the following will happen when a message is transmitted: the message will be transmitted without error, or the sender will be informed if the message could not be transmitted without error.

Reliable Transfer Service Element (RTSE)

→ *See* RTSE (Reliable Transfer Service Element)

Remote Access

The ability to access a network or switching system from a long distance, using telephone lines or other channels.

Remote Boot

A process by which a workstation boots using instructions in ROM (read-only memory) and from a server, rather than from a workstation disk. Code for doing this is generally stored in a ROM chip on the workstation.

Remote Computing

Remote computing refers generally to computing done from a distant location. There are two main ways to accomplish this:

Remote node: You dial in through an access server, and become another node on the network. All communications must travel over phone lines between your remote node and the network. This is fine for tasks such as e-mail that don't require large amounts of data to be transferred back and forth. Using a computer as a remote node is also effective when applications are loaded and executed on the remote client. For example, the remote client might have a word processor and other office applications installed. With such a configuration, the work could be done offline, and the remote connection could be used for transferring files. As the remote client, you can be connecting to anything from a stand-alone PC to a communications server (that is, you can communicate in this way with your computer at home or with the corporate network).

Remote control: You dial from a remote location into your own computer , for example on the network, and you essentially become the keyboard and screen for your computer. The work is done on the host machine (i.e., the one at home); you just see the output. This method is better for working with large databases because the work can be done on the server, and only the results need to be shipped out to your screen. As the remote client, you control the host's keyboard from the remote site. For example, you would not need an executable version of your word processor to edit a file under this type of connection. Instead, you would use the word processor residing on the host—which can, again, be anything from your stand-alone home PC to a machine on the corporate network.

Remote computing is becoming increasingly popular, but is bringing its own share of logistical problems. For example, a working group—Mobile IP (Internet Protocol)—of the IETF (Internet Engineering Task Force) is trying to determine the best way to allow remote machines to log into the Internet. Among these issues is how to assign Internet addresses.

Remote Connection

A long-distance connection between a workstation and a network; a connection that involves telephone lines and that may require modems. Remote connections often require special timing considerations because many network transactions must happen within a very limited time period.

Remote Console

A networking utility that enables a network supervisor to manage a server from a workstation or from a remote location using a modem. The supervisor can give commands and accomplish tasks just as if all the commands were being given directly at the server.

→ *See Also* ACONSOLE; RCONSOLE

Remote Control

→ *See* Remote Computing

Remote Data Service (RDS)

→ *See* RDS (Remote Data Service)

Remote File System (RFS) Protocol

→ *See* Protocol, RFS (Remote File System)

Remote Job Entry (RJE)

→ *See* RJE (Remote Job Entry)

Remote Network Monitoring (RMON)

→ *See* RMON (Remote Network Monitoring)

Remote Operations Service Element (ROSE)

→ *See* ROSE (Remote Operations Service Element)

Remote Password Generator (RPG)

→ *See* RPG (Remote Password Generator)

Remote Procedure Call (RPC)

→ *See* RPC (Remote Procedure Call)

Remote Terminal (RT)

A remote terminal is one located far enough from a host or network to require a connection over telephone or special-purpose lines.

Repeater

A repeater is a hardware device that functions at the physical layer of the OSI Reference Model and that is used to connect two segments of the same network. The "Repeaters connect network segments" shows an example of a network with repeaters. This is in contrast to bridges, routers, and gateways, which connect different networks.

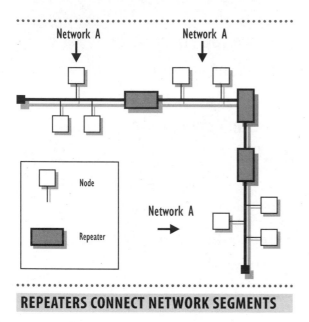

REPEATERS CONNECT NETWORK SEGMENTS

A repeater receives a signal from one segment, cleans and boosts the signal, and then sends it on to the other segment. Functionally, a repeater includes both a receiver and a transmitter, with a signal-cleaning component in between. (Compare this to a transceiver, which has the receiver and transmitter as independent components, so that the transceiver can either receive or transmit.)

A repeater may be incorporated into another device, such as a hub or even a node. In that case, the repeater may not be a distinct component, but its function is the same as that of a stand-alone device.

Repeaters can sometimes be used to extend a network beyond the limitations placed on the network's architecture. It is important to note, however, that a repeater can increase segment length only to overcome electrical restrictions; the repeater cannot be used to increase the time limitations inherent in the network's layout. For example, a repeater cannot stretch the network so that a transmission could take more than the allowable slot time to reach all the nodes in an Ethernet network.

Repeaters and Network Architectures

In general, a particular repeater works with only a specific type of network architecture. This has to do with the fact that different architectures use different cabling (for example, coaxial versus twisted-pair) or use cabling with different electrical characteristics (for example, 50-ohm versus 93-ohm resistance).

Note that in an ARCnet network, there is no need for special repeater devices, because active ARCnet hubs serve as repeaters.

Ethernet/802.3

For Ethernet networks, several types of repeaters are used. Repeaters for networks using twisted-pair cabling (10BaseT networks) are generally found in a wiring closet. Repeaters for thick (10Base5) or thin (10Base2) coaxial cable are likely to be found in the ceiling or wall where the cabling is run. IEEE specifications allow no more than four repeaters in a series between two nodes in an Ethernet network.

A repeater counts as a node on each Ethernet trunk segment it connects. The cable must be terminated independently of the repeater, which does not, in general, serve as a terminator.

In an Ethernet network, repeaters that connect to coaxial cable may be connected to a transceiver. IEEE 802.3 specifications specify that repeaters cannot be connected to transceivers that generate a SQE (signal quality error) test signal. This signal must be absent or disabled on the transceiver.

Multiport repeaters connect several segments. These repeaters generally have an autopartitioning capability, which allows them to disconnect any faulty segments automatically. This effectively quarantines the segment with the faulty node.

Token Ring

For Token Ring architectures, individual nodes serve as repeaters. In addition to "generic" repeaters, *main ring* and *lobe* types of repeaters are distinguished.

Main ring repeaters must be installed in pairs, on the main and the secondary ring, respectively. These repeaters are used when there is more than one MAU (multistation access unit) on the network. Electrical repeaters (such as the IBM 8218 repeater) can extend a ring path by as much as 750 meters (about 2500 feet); fiber-optic repeaters (such as the IBM 8219 and 8220 repeaters) can extend a fiber-optic ring path by as much as 2 kilometers (about 1.25 miles).

A lobe repeater boosts the signal for only a single lobe (a Token Ring node) attached to the MAU. A lobe repeater also extends the distance the lobe can be from the MAU. Each lobe may have its own repeater, although lobe repeaters are not common.

Repeater-Repeater Connections

Repeaters may be connected to other repeaters using IRLs (Inter-repeater links), which are just stretches of cable connecting two repeaters, without any nodes attached. FOIRLs (fiber-optic inter-repeater links) are commonly used to connect network segments on different floors. One reason for this is that fiber-optic cable is impervious to interference from strong electrical or magnetic sources. This is important because cabling between floors is sometimes run through the elevator shaft, and elevator motors can cause considerable interference with electrical signals.

→ *Broader Category* Intranetwork Link

→ *Compare* Transceiver

Replica

A replica is a copy of a partition from a directory service—for example, from the NDS (Novell Directory Services) used with NetWare 4.*x*. Replicas can be distributed across a network to allow faster and easier access to the information in the partition. Having copies of a partition in several locations also provides data protection. In Windows NT/2000, replicas of the Security Account Manager (SAM) and other crucial system files are stored on a backup domain controller (BDC), so they can be used if the primary domain controller (PDC) should fail.

A replica may be read-only or read-write. In the former case, the server can access and use the partition information, but cannot change it in the replica. Such a replica cannot be used to update the partition information. In contrast, the contents of a read-write replica can be changed by the server. Such changes will eventually be incorporated into changes in the partition information.

→ *Broader Categories* NDS (NetWare Directory Services); Partition

Repudiation

In network transmissions, denial by a sending node that the message was sent (*origin repudiation*) or by the recipient that the message was received (*destination repudiation*). One security measure that may be used in a network is non-repudiation, which makes it impossible for a sender or receiver to make such denials.

Request for Comments (RFC)

→ *See* RFC (Request for Comments)

Request/Response Header (RH)

→ *See* RH (Request/Response Header)

Request/Response Unit (RU)

→ *See* RU (Request/Response Unit)

Request to Send (RTS)

→ **See** RTS (Request to Send)

Reservation Protocol

A protocol that allows a node to take exclusive control of a communications channel for a limited period. Such control is needed in certain types of communications, such as communications between a satellite and a receiving station or when real-time data is being transmitted.

→ **See Also** Protocol, RSVP (Resource Reservation Protocol)

Residual Error

In communications, an error that occurs or survives despite the system's error detection and correction mechanisms. For example, a transmission error that does not violate parity might get through if a communication system does not use checksums to test the transmission.

Resistance

In an electrical circuit, the opposition to the flow of electricity.

Resource Fork

The portion of a Macintosh file containing information about the resources (windows, applications, drivers, and so on) used by the file. This information is environment-specific, and is generally meaningless in non-Macintosh implementations (such as DOS).

→ **See Also** Macintosh

Resource Reservation Protocol (RSVP)

→ **See** Protocol, RSVP (Resource Reservation Protocol)

Resources, Network

Resources are the manageable components of a network, including the following:

- Networking hardware, such as servers, workstations, cables, repeaters, hubs, concentrators, and network interface cards (NICs).

- Devices, such as hard disks, printers, modems, and optical drives.

- Networking software, such as network operating systems, and networking services (communications, print queues, file services, and so on).

- Auxiliary software, such as drivers, protocols, bridging, routing, and gateway software, monitoring and management software, and applications.

- Miscellaneous items, such as processes, security, data structures, users, and volumes.

In most network operating systems, resources must be registered in order to be installed or become available through the network. For example, in Novell NetWare environments, a resource such as a gateway package can be registered and installed by loading a NetWare Loadable Module (NLM) containing the gateway's services and functions. In other environments, such resources can be added permanently as plug-in or snap-in models, or the functionality can be added as needed in the form of Java applets and servlets or Microsoft's ActiveX controls.

Response Mode

In communications, the mode of the device that receives a call and must respond to it. Compare response mode with originate mode.

Response Time

In networking contexts, response time is the time required for a request at a workstation to reach the server and for the server's response to return to the workstation. Response time is inversely proportional to transmission speed for the network architecture being used.

The minimum return time value is increased by several other factors, including the following:

- Delays introduced by the network interface cards (NICs) in the workstation and the server.

- Delays in the server's response (for example, because the CPU is otherwise occupied when the request comes in or as the response is about to go out).

- Delays in accessing the server's hard disk and writing or reading any required data.

Restore

To install data and software that has previously been backed up. The restoration process uses the backup media. You will need to restore files if the originals are corrupted. When doing a total restoration, you first need to restore the most recent complete backup, and then restore each of the incremental or differential backups that followed the complete one.

→ *See Also* Backup

Return Band

In communications using FDM (frequency division multiplexing), a one-directional (simplex) channel over which remote devices respond to a central controller.

Return (Reflection) Loss

In signaling, the amount of a signal that is lost because it is reflected back toward the sender. This value is expressed as a ratio and is measured in decibels (dB).

Return to Zero (RZ)

→ *See* RZ (Return to Zero)

Return to Zero Inverted (RZI)

→ *See* RZ (Return to Zero Inverted)

Reverse Address Resolution Protocol (RARP)

→ *See* Protocol, RARP (Reverse Address Resolution Protocol)

Reverse Control Channel (RECC)

→ *See* RECC (Reverse Control Channel)

Reverse Lookup

A reverse lookup is a DNS (Domain Name Service) resolution task in which the server has an IP (Internet Protocol) address, and must determine the domain name that goes with the address. This is in contrast to ordinary name lookup, or resolution, in which the server has a domain name and must return an IP address.

RFC (Request for Comments)

In the Internet community, a series of documents that contain protocol and model descriptions, experimental results, and reviews. All Internet standard protocols are written up as RFCs.

RFI (Radio-Frequency Interference)

Noise in the radio frequency range that interferes with transmissions over copper wire. RFI comes from radio and television transmissions. A stretch of cable (for example, in a network) acts as an antenna for this type of interference.

RFS (Remote File System) Protocol

→ **See** Protocol, RFS (Remote File System)

RH (Request/Response Header)

In SNA (Systems Network Architecture) network communications, a 3-byte element added to a request/response unit (RU) at the transmission control layer, to create a basic information unit (BIU).

RI (Ring Indicator)

In the RS-232C specifications, a signal that indicates an incoming call.

RI (Ring In)/RO (Ring Out)

In Token Ring multistation access units (MAUs), RI is a port through which another MAU can be connected. The MAU also has a ring out (RO) port, through which the MAU can be connected to another MAU. "A small ring network" shows how MAUs can be connected.

→ **See Also** Token Ring

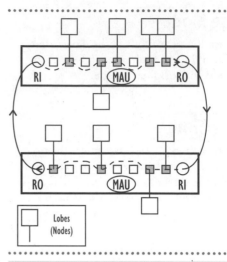

A SMALL RING NETWORK

Rights

In networking environments, rights are values, or settings, assigned to an object. These settings determine what the object (such as a user) can do with files, directories, and other resources.

→ **See Also** Access Rights, NDS (NetWare Directory Services)

Ring

In cabling, one of a twisted-wire pair, with the other wire being known as a tip. A four-pair unshielded twisted-pair cable has four tip/ring pairs. In networking, ring is a logical (and physical) network topology.

→ **See Also** Topology, Ring

Ring In (RI)/Ring Out (RO)

→ **See** RI (Ring In)/RO (Ring Out)

Ring Indicator (RI)

→ *See* RI (Ring Indicator)

RIP (Routing Information Protocol)

→ *See* Protocol, RIP (Routing Information Protocol)

RISC (Reduced Instruction Set Computing)

RISC is a computer-design strategy in which the machine logic is based on a small number of simple, general-purpose operations, each of which can be executed very quickly.

The RISC computer architecture was originally limited to high-end workstations, which were expensive but very fast. With technological and other progress, the architecture has become more widely used, and it now can be found even in ordinary computers for personal use. For example, several Macintosh models include a RISC processor.

→ *See Also* CISC (Complex Instruction Set Computing)

Riser Cable

Cable that runs vertically; for example, between floors in a building. Riser cable often runs through shafts (such as for the elevator). In some cases, such areas can be a source of electrical interference. Consequently, optical fiber (which is impervious to electromagnetic interference) is generally used for riser cable.

Rise Time

The amount of time it takes an electrical signal to go from 10 percent of its level to 90 percent. This value is important because it helps set an upper limit on the maximum transmission speed that can be supported. Compare this with fall time.

RJE (Remote Job Entry)

RJE is a method in which data and commands are transmitted from a remote location, to a centralized (mainframe) host computer, which does the processing. Although this method was popular in the mainframe heyday of the 1970s and early 1980s, centralized processing is rapidly being replaced by distributed processing, in which computing power is distributed over a network or internetwork.

RJ-xx

RJ-*xx* is a modular connection mechanism originally developed by the telephone company. (RJ stands for registered jack.) The connection allows for up to eight wires (used as four pairs). In RJ-*xx* connections, the jack is the female component and the plug is the male component.

Various RJ configurations are available. These are distinguished by the following:

- Number of wire pairs used (generally two, three, or four).

- Which wire pairs are used (known as the wiring sequence).

- Keying or other modifications to the plug and jack, designed to make correct connections easier and incorrect connections less likely.

For example, the telephone company commonly uses two-pair wire in an unkeyed connection. The first wire pair, which uses the two middle positions, carries the voice signal for the primary line.

Strictly speaking, the *RJ* designation applies only to cable that uses a particular wiring scheme (USOC, as described in the Wiring Sequence article). Other wiring sequences have different designations. However, RJ has become a generic designation to describe any type of modular connection.

The following are some commonly used RJ connections:

RJ-11: Four-wire (two-pair) connection. The telephone company version is used for ordinary single-line residential and business telephone lines. The two central wires (green and red) are tip and ring lines, respectively.

RJ-12: Six-wire (three-pair) connection. RJ-11 and RJ-12 connections use the same-sized plug and jack.

RJ-45: Eight-wire (four-pair) connection. The telephone company version is used for connections with multiple lines in the same location. If there is no competition for wires, such a connection can also be used for 10BaseT networks.

An RJ-45 connection uses a larger plug and jack than for RJ-11 or RJ-12. For unkeyed connections, you can connect an RJ-11 or RJ-12 plug to an RJ-45 jack, but you cannot fit an RJ-45 plug into an RJ-11/12 jack.

Although the "user-ends" of RJ-*xx* jacks all look alike, there are two ways of attaching this type of connector to the cable itself. One type of connector has prongs that wrap around the wire when the connector is crimped onto the cable. This type is used with solid, or single-strand, wire. The other type has prongs that pierce the wire when the connector is attached, and it is used for multistrand wire.

RLL (Run-Length Limited)

An encoding scheme for storing data on a disk. RLL uses codes based on the runs of 0 and 1 values, rather than on the individual bit values. This allows data to be stored more efficiently, which increases the effective capacity of the disk. RLL is in contrast to older encoding schemes, such as FM (frequency modulation) and MFM (modified frequency modulation).

rlogin

A remote login service provided as part of the Berkeley UNIX environment. This is an application-layer service, and it is comparable to the Internet's Telnet service.

RMON (Remote Network Monitoring)

RMON—now in its second incarnation as RMON-2—is a proposed standard for monitoring and reporting network activity using remote monitors. RMON is designed to supplement the management information obtained and used by the SNMP (Simple Network Management Protocol). The original RMON specification called for reporting about fairly low-level activity (packet and error rates, utilization percentages, and so forth) on network segments. RMON-2 was released in early 1997, and it includes provisions for taking a higher-level look at end-to-end performance as well. In particular, RMON-2 provides functions for getting information about the operation and performance of entire networks or of subnetworks in an internetwork.

Remote monitors are expected to do their work in a way that is minimally disruptive to network activity and that makes minimal demands on the available resources. Much of the information that remote monitors provide is summary information, some of which can be obtained passively (by counting packets, error signals, and so on).

As a supplement to the SNMP management functions and to the data in the MIB-II (management information base, version 2), RMON is included in the global tree under MIB-II. In the notation used to describe elements in the tree, RMON is mib-2 16.

RMON provides MIB elements of its own. The table "Subtrees of the RMON Entry in the Global Tree" lists these MIB elements.

SUBTREES OF THE RMON ENTRY IN THE GLOBAL TREE

Subtree	Description
Statistics	Performance and summary statistics about an entire subnetwork or network, not just a single node.
History	Sample statistics gathered at separate time intervals.
Alarms	Allows the management supervisor to specify when and how alarms are to be used. For example, a monitor may simply gather error information passively, but alert the network manager if the error level reaches a predefined threshold.
Hosts	Statistics about activity between a host and the network or subnetwork.
Host Top N	Summary statistics about the N hosts who are highest in each of several variables.
Traffic Matrix	Provides summary traffic and error information in the form of a matrix, which makes it much easier to find information about particular combinations.
Filters	Used to specify packets or packet types for the monitor to capture. For example, a filter might be specified to look only for packets going to a particular node or host.
Packet Capture	Specifies how the command console can get data from and about network activity.
Events	Contains a list of all the events, or activities, created by the monitor.

→ **Primary Source** RMON is described in RFCs 1757 and 2021, and some definitions are to be found in RFC 2074.

RMS (Root Mean Square)

The value of an AC voltage as it is actually measured (for example, by a voltmeter). Empirically, this value is 0.70707~MB times the peak voltage in the circuit.

RO (Receive Only)

In communications, a setting to indicate that a device can receive a transmission but cannot transmit it. Printers are probably the most widely used receive-only device.

Roamer

In telephony, a cellular telephone user who uses services in multiple cells (calling areas). For example, the user and telephone may move between coverage regions. Such roaming behavior can be costly. However, many service providers are now offering flat rates, with no roaming charges on some of their plans. This is possible because of the increased consolidation in the telecommunications industry and also the progress that has been made in covering the country with cells for handling calls.

Rollback

In database management or transaction processing, rollback refers to the process of returning a database to an earlier state—for example, if a transaction cannot be completed.

ROM (Read-Only Memory)

ROM is chip-based memory whose contents can execute and be read, but cannot be changed. Programs are put into ROM in order to save storage and working memory. Many notebook and special-purpose computers have operating systems and special applications in ROM. Diskless workstations have a ROM chip that enables the workstation to boot from a network server.

The following types of ROM are distinguished in the literature:

- EEPROM (electronically erasable, programmable ROM), which allows old data to be erased simply by writing over it.

R

- EPROM (erasable, programmable ROM), which allows old data to be erased by shining UV (ultraviolet) light on the chip in order to "deprogram" it.

- PROM (programmable ROM), which can be programmed once, even by the user, but cannot be changed once programmed.

- MROM (mask ROM), which is programmed during the manufacturing process and cannot be modified or reprogrammed.

Root Directory

In a hierarchical file system, the highest directory. All other directories are subdirectories of the root.

Root Mean Square (RMS)

→ *See* RMS (Root Mean Square)

Root Object

In the NDS global tree, the highest-level object. All country and organization objects are contained in the root object. Granting a user access rights to the root object effectively grants the user rights to the entire Directory tree.

→ *See Also* NDS (NetWare Directory Services)

ROSE (Remote Operations Service Element)

In the OSI Reference Model, ROSE is a general-purpose ASE (application layer service element) that supports interactive cooperation between two applications. For example, ROSE is used for remote procedure calls or for tasks that require cooperation between a client and a server.

The application requesting the association is known as the *initiator*. The application responding to it is the *responder*. The application that requests an operation is known as the *invoker*. The other application, called the *performer*, carries out the requested operation. An application association provides the context for the cooperation between the two application entities (AEs).

When an application association is established, the AEs involved must agree on an operation class and an association class for the interaction. The following five operation classes are defined, based on the type of reply the performer provided and on whether the interaction is synchronous or asynchronous:

- Class 1 (synchronous) reports both success and failure.

- Class 2 (asynchronous) reports both success and failure.

- Class 3 (asynchronous) reports only in case of failure.

- Class 4 (asynchronous) reports only in case of success.

- Class 5 (asynchronous) reports neither success nor failure.

The three association classes are as follows:

Association class 1: Only the initiator can invoke operations.

Association class 2: Only the responder can invoke operations.

Association class 3: Either the initiator or the responder can invoke operations.

The ROSE provides a mechanism for enabling applications to cooperate; however, ROSE does not know how to carry out the actual operations. The details of the operations must be agreed upon by the applications independently of ROSE. Similarly, the processes necessary to carry out the operation must be available once the association is established.

→ *Primary Sources* CCITT recommendations X.219 and X.229; ISO document 9072

→ *Broader Category* ASE (Application Service Element)

Route Discovery

In network architectures that use source routing, such as token-ring networks, the process of determining possible routes from a source to a destination node.

Route Poisoning

Routers must consider possibilities before selecting a path for a packet moving to another router or network. Since the number of possible paths can be huge, the more possibilities a router can eliminate in advance the better. And once a router has found a reasonable path to a particular destination, only paths that improve on the selected one should need to be considered.

Route poisoning is one way to help accomplish these goals. Once a router has found a usable path, the router will generally employ some type of technique to maintain that path until a better one comes along. In route poisoning, a router examines routes suggested by neighboring routers. If the suggested route is longer or more costly, the router marks it as unusable. This eliminates it as a possible path and also avoids the need to examine the route again—at least until conditions change in the routing picture. (In practice this may only be until the next update from the neighbor, which may occur just a minute or two later.)

Route poisoning is, in fact, an explicit technique used by newer versions of the Interior Gateway Routing Protocol (IGRP). (Interior gateway refers to the fact that this protocol is used for routing packets within an autonomous system, or domain.)

Router

The function of a router is to provide a path from a node on one network to a node on another network. The two networks may be separated by several intervening networks and, possibly, by many miles. "Routers connect nodes on different networks" shows an example of networks with routers. The router provides the path by first determining a route and then providing the initial connection for the path.

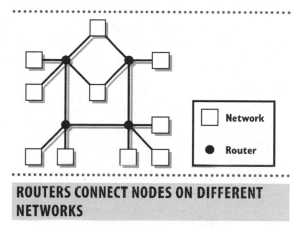

ROUTERS CONNECT NODES ON DIFFERENT NETWORKS

In practice, the routing is provided by a hardware device that operates at the network layer. The router may be internal or a stand-alone unit that has its own power supply. An internal router is implemented on a card that plugs into an expansion slot in a computer. This router uses the computer's power supply (which should be adequate, but is not guaranteed to be so).

The router can find a path for a packet from the router to the packet's destination, and it can forward this packet onto that path. Because it operates at the network layer, a router is dependent on the protocol being used, because this protocol will determine the address format in the packets. Thus, an IP (Internet Protocol) router will not be able to handle packets with addresses in ISO format. A router can work with different data-link layer protocols, but older ones can handle only a single network protocol. Newer, multiprotocol, routers can handle several protocols at the same time.

As a result, a router can be used as a packet filter based on network protocols (as well as addresses). Because it is independent of data-link layer protocols, a router can connect networks using different architectures (for example, Ethernet to Token Ring or Ethernet to FDDI).

Router Operation

A router gets a packet from a node or from another router and passes this packet on to a destination specified in an embedded (network layer) packet, which is known as an NPDU (network-layer protocol data unit). To determine the packet's ultimate destination, the router must strip off the data-link frame and determine the destination network address by looking at the NPDU.

The router must then determine the path to this destination, pack the NPDU into a data-link layer packet, and send the packet to the next router or directly to the destination node (if possible and appropriate). This destination is specified in the data-link layer envelope. The envelope may be for a different architecture than the one that sent the packet to the router. In that case, the router must use a data-link layer envelope that differs from the one that delivered the packet.

If the next destination for the packet happens to use a smaller packet size than the router received, the router must break the packet into suitably sized "subpackets" and ship the multiple smaller packets to the next destination. At the receiving end, the smaller packets may need to be reconstituted into the larger packet.

Interpreting Network Addresses

A network address differs from the physical address used by a bridge in that the network address is a logical address that locates a node as part of a (sub)network and also as an individual node within that network.

That network may, in turn, be part of a larger collection of networks. In fact, if the span of the entire conglomeration is large enough, there may be a whole hierarchy of networks, each organized at different levels. For example, the Internet consists of a backbone network whose nodes feed (route to) intermediate-level networks. These may, in turn, feed still more local networks, and so on, down to the destination node.

A network address may be interpreted as a hierarchical description of a node's location. For example, a node may be the twelfth one in a network on the tenth floor of a building. The building may have 15 floors, each with its own network. The building may be one of 30 in a single city, each with the same network hierarchy. The city's 30-building network may be only one of a dozen cities, each with similar network structures. The entire conglomerate network can be viewed as consisting of 12 city subnetworks, each of which consists of a number of building subnetworks, made up of floor subnetworks, which consist of nodes.

Levels of Routing

Several levels of routers can be defined. For example, a particular city might have building-level routers. Each router knows how to find a path from a node in its building to a node in another building. Basically, the router has the task of getting a packet to the router for the destination building.

When a building-level router receives a packet, the router checks whether it is intended for that building. If so, the router, passes it through to the floor for which the packet is intended. If not, the router determines a path to the destination building. (Note that building-level routers are not concerned with the city portion of an address.)

The conglomerate network might include city-level routers, whose job is to get packets to the destination cities. City-level routers are not concerned with the details of routing a packet to particular buildings in a city.

In this example, level 1 (building-level) routers communicate with other level 1 routers in their own (city) subnetwork. Similarly, level 2 (city-level) routers communicate with each other. In addition, each level 2 router communicates with the level 1 routers in its subnetwork, and each level 1 router communicates with the level 2 router for that city. "Multilevel routers" shows an arrangement with different levels of routers.

Organizing a network universe into levels simplifies the routing task. Routers need to find paths only for the levels they must deal with. The use of levels in this way also increases the number of nodes that can ultimately be part of a conglomerate network. In practice, the levels generally are determined by location (rather than numerical) constraints.

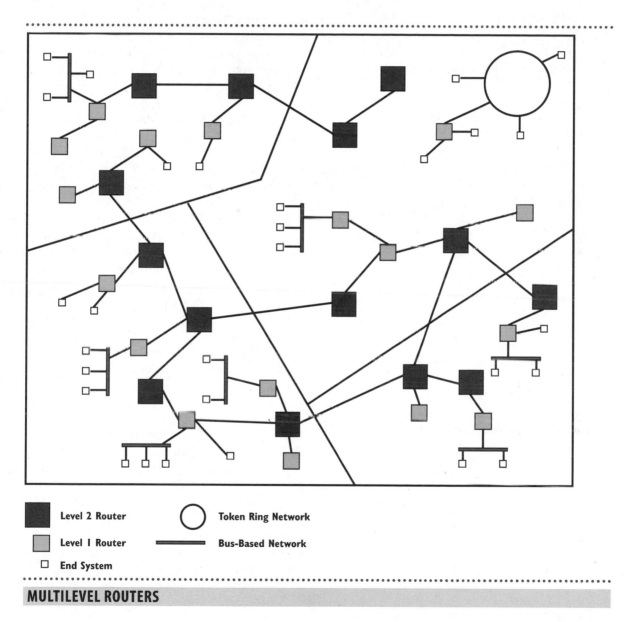

	Level 2 Router	◯	Token Ring Network
	Level 1 Router	——	Bus-Based Network
□	End System		

MULTILEVEL ROUTERS

Finding a Path

The router determines how to get to the specified network by communicating with other routers on the network. Because describing a node's location in a very large network can be complicated, locations are generally specified in terms of subnetworks.

Routes are computed using either of two classes of algorithms: distance-vector or link-state.

When using distance-vector algorithms (also known as *Bellman-Ford* or *old ARPAnet routing* algorithms), each router computes the distance between itself and each possible destination. This is accomplished by computing the distance between a router and all its immediate router neighbors, and by taking each neighboring router's computations for the distances between that neighbor and all *its* immediate neighbors. This information must be checked constantly and updated any time there are changes anywhere in the router network. This computational intensity is one drawback of distance-vector algorithms.

When using link-state algorithms, each router knows the location of and distance to each of its immediately neighboring routers, and can broadcast this information to all other routers in a link state packet (LSP). Every router transmits its LSP to every other router on the larger network, and each router keeps this information about every other router. If a router updates its LSP, the new version is broadcast and replaces the older versions at each other router.

Selection of an algorithm for a particular application depends on various factors. In general, routing algorithms can be compared in the following terms:

Convergence: How quickly the algorithm yields a route.

Robustness: How drastically the algorithm is affected by incorrect or missing information.

Memory requirements: How much memory will be needed to store all the distance-vector or link-state information.

Load splitting: How easily the algorithm can be extended to include load splitting, in which traffic between the same two routers may be sent across different paths in order to split the traffic more evenly (which can, in turn, increase throughput).

Router Groupings

Several categories of routers are distinguished: single-protocol or multiprotocol, central or peripheral, and local area network (LAN) or wide area network (WAN).

Single-Protocol versus Multiprotocol Routers

Because they operate at the network layer, routers are sensitive to the protocol being used. Thus, a router that can handle IP packets cannot handle IPX packets without the addition of special capabilities. Single-protocol routers were the rule for many years.

In the natural course of technological evolution, routers expanded their capabilities with respect to the network level protocols supported. High-end routers can process packets from more than one type of protocol. For example, a router might be able to handle IP, X.25, and IPX protocols. Multiprotocol routers are becoming much more widely used.

The cost of the increased capability is possibly decreased bandwidth in traffic for a particular protocol. That is, if a router needs to process both IP and IPX packets, it will need to split its available time and capacity between the two protocols.

Central Routers versus Peripheral Routers

A router may serve as the transfer point for multiple networks. For example, each network may be connected to a different board in a server or hub. These central routers are at the high end of the price and capability range, and they are usually multiprotocol routers.

In contrast, a peripheral, or branch office, router serves primarily to connect a network to a larger internetwork. These routers are more likely to be at the low end for price and performance. A peripheral router may be limited to a single protocol, particularly if the peripheral router can communicate with a multiprotocol router on the internetwork.

LAN versus WAN Routers

Another common course of technological evolution is to extend the reach of a device over greater distances. In this context, WAN routers, whose job is to find paths over widely distributed networks, are extensions of LAN routers, which connect LANs that are distributed over areas small enough to allow connections without requiring telephone lines. LAN and WAN routers do the same things, but the details of how these tasks are done vary considerably. Most notably, a WAN router needs to support protocols suitable for long-distance access and service (for example, protocols that support X.25). Partly, the development of WAN routers has been waiting for telecommunications lines with a sufficiently large bandwidth to make such routing feasible.

WHAT TO LOOK FOR IN A ROUTER

As with other hardware products, a main source of information about a particular router is the vendor. Useful information about routers includes the following:

- Type of router, such as whether it is a single-protocol or multiprotocol router, a LAN or WAN router, a bridging router (brouter), and so on.

- Types of networks connected.

- Protocol(s) supported.

- Transmission speeds (which may range from a few thousand bits per second to several megabits per second).

- Number of ports.

- Interfaces supported (for LANs or WANs).

- Network monitoring and management capabilities

Router Protocols

Like all network components, great and small, routers use protocols to accomplish their work. Router protocols may be concerned with providing a service, greeting neighbors, or routing.

Service protocols provide the packet format used to transmit information across the network layer. IP is the network-layer service for the TCP/IP protocol suite developed for the ARPAnet and still used on the Internet and in many other distributed networks. Other network-layer service protocols include Novell's IPX from the IPX/SPX suite, IDP (Internet Datagram Protocol) from the XNS suite, and the X.25 protocol.

Neighbor-greeting protocols enable nodes and routers to find each other, so that the range of connections can be determined. This information lets nodes know which other nodes and routers are accessible. Neighbor-greeting protocols also provide address-translation capabilities.

ES-IS (End System to Intermediate System) is a neighbor-greeting protocol defined by ISO document 9542. ICMP (Internet Control Message Protocol) and ARP (Address Resolution Protocol) are network-layer routing protocols that also include neighbor-greeting capabilities.

With routing protocols, routers determine paths for packets by communicating with neighboring routers at their level. Routers can request and obtain information about paths from the neighbor to still other routers. IS-IS (Intermediate System to Intermediate System) is a routing protocol specified by the ISO (DP 10589). RIP (Routing Information Protocol) and OPSF (Open Shortest Path First) are routing protocols in the TCP/IP suite.

Common Protocol Areas

As networks grow larger, it becomes increasingly likely that not all parts of the network will use the same protocols. This is particularly true if the network has multiple levels or is spread out, with smaller clusters.

These heterogeneous networks will, however, have areas that use a common protocol. Such areas are known as *routing domains* in OSI terminology, or *autonomous systems* (AS) in TC/IP specification terminology. See the table "Terminology for Routing Concepts" for a summary of the terms related to routing protocols in the IP and OSI environments.

TERMINOLOGY FOR ROUTING CONCEPTS

ISO	Concept	IP
Intermediate system (IS)	Router	Gateway
End system (ES)	Node	Host
Routing domain	Common protocol area	Autonomous system (AS)
Intradomain routing protocol	Protocol used within a domain	Interior Gateway Protocol (IGP)
Interdomain routing protocol	Protocol used between common protocol areas	Exterior Gateway Protocol (EGP)

Intradomain Routing Protocols

Protocols for use within a domain are known as *intra*domain routing protocols. RIP, OSPF, IGRP (Interior Gateway Routing Protocol), E-IGRP (Enhanced IGRP), and other protocols operate within a domain. In addition, there are protocols for routing multiple protocols at the same time. Examples are "ships in the night" (SIN) and integrated routing.

Interdomain Routing Protocols

A domain may be next to domains that use a different protocol. In this case, it may be necessary to route packets between domains, using *inter*domain protocols. The following interdomain routing protocols (IDRPs) serve this purpose.

- EGP (Exterior Gateway Protocol), which is the IP name for a specific protocol that connects different domains. The protocol has flaws, but has been around in the TCP/IP world for a long time.

- BGP (Border Gateway Protocol), which is a revision and improvement of EGP. In addition to being a TCP/IP protocol, BGP is also the basis for the ISO's IDRP protocol.

- IDRP, which is also the name of a specific interdomain routing protocol. It is based on the BGP protocol.

To do their work, routers can use connectionless or connection-oriented network layer protocols. A connection-oriented protocol first establishes a route and the connection (a virtual circuit, or VC), and then starts transmitting packets along this route. Packets are transmitted in order, and delivery can be guaranteed, since a protocol may require acknowledgment. With connection-oriented protocols, transport-layer services may not be required. The routing algorithm for such protocols is generally proprietary.

The X.25 protocol is a connection-oriented protocol. It specifies the interface between a node (known as a DTE in X.25 terminology) and a router (known as a DCE).

A connectionless protocol, which is also known as a datagram protocol, agrees to make its best effort to transmit a packet to its destination, but does not guarantee to do so. Moreover, packets may get to the same destination by different routes, and they may arrive in a jumbled order. Packets are assembled in the correct order by a transport layer protocol. The routing algorithms for connectionless protocols are generally open (publicly available). IP and CLNP (Connectionless Network Protocol) are two connectionless protocols.

→ **Broader Category**   Internetwork Link

→ **Compare**   Bridge; Gateway

→ **See Also**   NetWare Multiprotocol Router; Protocol, Routing

Router, ASB (Autonomous System Border)

Among routers that use the IETF's OSPF (Open Shortest Path First) link state routing protocol, an ASB router, or ASBR, is one that has a link to at least router in an external network. That is, an ASBR has at least one link to a router in a different autonomous system (AS). (An autonomous system is a network that is under the control of a single organization.)

Often, such external networks will be non-OSPF networks - that is, they will use different protocols. In such a case, the ASBR will serve as an interface for importing information (directory and resource lists, router links, and so forth) from the external network and exporting information to it.

Router, Area Border

In internetworks that use link state routing protocols - for example, IS-IS (Intermediate System to Intermediate System) or OSPF (Open Shortest Path First) protocols - an area is a portion of the internetwork. Areas are divisions created to make it easier for routers to manage their link state information. An area border router (ABR) - also known simply as a border router - is one that has at least one link to a router in a different area. Routers within an area that do not have links to routers in other areas are known as internal routers.

An area border router must keep separate link state tables for each area to which the router is connected.

Router, Border

→ *See* Router, Area Border

Router, Dedicated

A dedicated router is a computer that is optimized for performing the functions of a router, and that performs only these functions. A dedicated router does not perform any other general-purpose functions.

For such dedicated service, a computer can be pretty minimal. It requires none of the common peripherals—for example, keyboards, displays, or hard disks. Despite such minimal configurations, dedicated routers can still be expensive because they may use special-purpose RISC (reduced instruction set computing) processors or other optimized hardware.

The functions of a dedicated router can also be carried out by a multihomed server.

Router, Designated

In internetworks that use link state protocols, the designated router (or DR) serves as the contact point for link state information from routers within the DR's area and also from routers in oher areas with which the DR can exchange link state information. (An area refers to a collection of networks and routers that all have the same area identifier and the same link state information.)

The DR collects link state information from each router in the DR's area, and communicates this information to all routers to any external routers (that is, routers in other areas) with which the router may be connected. All routers within an area must be connected to the DR.

The DR and a backup DR, or BDR, are elected by all the routers in an area. This selection process uses the Router Priority information in the Hello packets that routers exchange with their neighbors. The DR simplifies the handling and disemination of link state information, and also keeps this information synchronized for all routers in the area. The BDR maintains the same link state information as the DR but does nothing until the DR becomes inoperative.

R

Router, Exterior

In an AppleTalk environment, a router that routes packets to a non-AppleTalk protocol (from which the packets may be transmitted by tunneling). In contrast, an interior router routes packets between AppleTalk networks.

Router, Interior

In an AppleTalk environment, a router that routes packets between AppleTalk networks. In contrast, an exterior router routes packets to a non-Apple-Talk protocol.

Router, Internal

→ *See*   Router, Intra-Area

Router, Intra-Area (IA)

In internetworks that use link state protocols, an area refers to a collection of networks and routers. The elements in an area have the same area identifier, and all routers within an area have identical link state information.

Routers in an area may either connect only to routers within the area or they may also connect to one or more routers in a different area. The former type of routers are known as *intra-area*, or internal routers; the routers with links to other areas are known as *area boundary routers* (ABRs), or simply as boundary routers.

Routing

Routing is the process of determining an end-to-end path between the sender and the receiver for a packet. This is one of the major functions of the network layer in the OSI Reference Model. Another function is relaying, which is actually passing packets along the path.

Types of Routing

The routing task can be performed by the source node (generally an end system) or by the intermediate nodes (generally a router) in the path. These two approaches give rise to two general types of routing: *source routing* and *hop-by-hop routing*.

Source Routing

In source routing, the source node determines the route and includes it in special fields in the packet being sent. This is also known as *end-to-end routing*, since the entire route to the destination is determined before the packet is sent.

For source routing, the source first needs to determine the route. This is accomplished by sending a discovery, or explorer, packet along each possible path. Once a suitable route has been determined, the intermediate destinations are added to the packet in 2-byte fields. Of these 16 bits, 12 are used to designate the (intermediate) destination network and four are used to designate the bridge (that is, the link) to the network. The bridge information is included for two reasons:

- If two networks are linked by more than one bridge, the packet might be sent over all possible links. This would lead to unnecessary network traffic and could eventually lead to network overload as copies of enough packets circulate.

- If a designated link is backed up or moving too slowly, an alternate link to the same destination network can be specified simply by changing the bridge value.

With a source-routing packet, the intermediate routers do not need to do any work finding routes. They just need to pass the packet to be specified intermediate routers. However, the success of a source-routing approach depends on the efficiency of the route, and it also requires each intermediate link to be open. For example, if a link is broken between the time the discovery packet and the actual source-routed packet are sent, the packet will be lost.

Source routing is used in Token-Ring networks, and this ability must be built into bridges for such networks, according to the IEEE 802.5 specifications.

Hop-by-Hop Routing

In hop-by-hop routing, the route between source and destination is determined along the way. Each node on the route makes a decision as to where the packet will be sent next. The packet being sent does not contain any special routing information, just the source and destination address. This is also known as *node-to-node routing*, *border routing*, and sometimes as *intermediate-node routing*. The different names come from different networking environments.

In hop-by-hop routing, each intermediate node needs to know how to reach the next node on a path. The efficiency of the routing depends on the quality of the information available to the intermediate nodes, but this approach is only minimally affected by unforeseen problems such as broken links. Since a router expects to be selecting a route anyway, having a broken link has little effect as long as there are other possible links.

A hop-by-hop approach can also adjust easily to traffic conditions along specific links and can select any available faster link. Internet routing generally uses a hop-by-hop approach.

Fixed versus Adaptive Routing

Routers differ with respect to when and how often they update their routing tables, or directories, for a session. Fixed, or static, routers take the routing table as it is at the start of a session and use the same table for the entire session—regardless of whether things change during the session. In contrast, adaptive, or dynamic, routers update their routing tables, and may incorporate the revised routes into a session so that two different packets in the same session may take two different routes to the same destination.

Computing Routing Information

Two general strategies are available for computing the information used to determine or select routes: *distance-vector* and *link-state*.

A distance-vector strategy gets information about the costs of reaching all possible destinations from a router and sends this information to each of the router's neighbors. In contrast, a link-state strategy gets only information about the costs of reaching each of a router's immediate neighbor routers. Commonly used algorithms are available for both of these strategies.

Routing Compared to Other Linkages

Besides routers, switches, bridges and gateways also provide hardware links between networks. Bridges connect similar or identical networks. Gateways connect dissimilar networks.

Bridging functions really just need to know whether the destination is on the local or a remote network. If it is on the local network, the packet is dropped at the bridge; if it is on a different network, the bridge passes the packet over to its other network. The bridging functions do not need to know actual path information.

Gateway functions are more concerned with making sure the packets are in the appropriate formats than with determining the destination. A gateway generally links just a small number of networks or environments. In contrast to packet format, paths are generally simple and fixed, so that routing is not a major issue.

→ *See Also* Algorithm; Protocol, Distance-Vector; Protocol, Link-State; Protocol, Routing; Router

Routing Buffer

RAM set aside on a Novell NetWare file server for temporarily holding packets until they can be processed by the server or sent onto the network. This is also known as a *communication buffer*.

R

Routing Domain

In the OSI Reference Model, routing domain is a term for a collection of routers that are part of a larger network but that are under the control of a single organization. The routers *within* a routing domain communicate with each other using a common *intra*domain routing protocol, such as the Integrated IS-IS (Intermediate System to Intermediate System) protocol.

Communication *between* routing domains uses an *inter*domain routing protocol, such as the proposed IDRP (Interdomain Routing Protocol).

In Internet terminology, a routing domain is known as an *autonomous system* (AS). An intradomain routing protocol is known as an *interior gateway protocol* (*IGP*), and an interdomain routing protocol is known as an *exterior gateway protocol* (*EGP*).

Routing Information Protocol (RIP)

→ *See*   Protocol, RIP (Routing Information Protocol)

Routing, Interdomain

In the OSI (Open Systems Interconnection) Reference Model, a domain refers to a network or subnetwork that is under the control of a single administration. Depending on the scale involved, a domain may be a department, a company, or even a country. For various reasons, routing within a domain has different requirements than routing across domains. Consequently, a distinction is made between intradomain and interdomain routing.

Interdomain routing—that is, routing across domains—uses interdomain routing protocols, also known as *Exterior Gateway Protocols*. This class of protocols includes the Exterior Gateway Protocol (EGP), Border Gateway Protocol (BGP), and Interdomain Routing Protocol (IDRP). EGP is actually a specific protocol, which shares its name with the

class of protocols. EGP is the basis for BGP, which replaced it; BGP, in turn, forms the basis for IDRP.

In contrast, intradomain routing—that is, routing within a domain—uses intradomain routing protocols, also known as Interior Gateway Routing Protocols (IGRP). This class of protocols includes the Routing Information Protocol (RIP), Open Shortest Path First (OSPF), Interior Gateway Routing Protocol (IGRP), and the Enhanced IGRP (E-IGRP).

→ *Broader Category*   Routing

Routing, Intradomain

→ *See*   Routing, Interdomain

Routing Protocol

→ *See*   Protocol, Routing

Routing Table

A table maintained for part of an internetwork. The table contains paths and distances between routers on the internetwork. Distances are generally measured in hops, and they may change. As a result, routing tables may be updated frequently.

Routing Table Maintenance Protocol (RTMP)

→ *See*   Protocol, RTMP (Routing Table Maintenance Protocol)

Routing Table Protocol (RTP)

→ *See*   Protocol, RTP (Routing Table Protocol)

RPC (Remote Procedure Call)

A mechanism by which a procedure on one computer can be used in a transparent manner by a program running on another machine. This mechanism provides an easy way to implement a client-server relationship. Although the general strategy is similar in different implementations, there are many variants on the RPC model.

RPG (Remote Password Generator)

A device that can be used to generate a unique password every time a user wants to log in to a network. The device uses a special number, which is generated by the network, and the user's personal identification number (PIN) to generate the password.

RSA (Rivesi, Shamir, Adleman) Algorithm

A patented public-key encryption algorithm (named for its inventors). This algorithm is used for encrypting messages and for creating digital signatures and certificates.

The algorithm could not be cracked for many years, but not for as long as expected. Using the processing capabilities of hundreds of computers and the intelligence of hundreds of colleagues, researchers have determined the keys (prime factors of a very large number) used in this encryption scheme.

➝ *See Also* Encryption

RSVP (Resource Reservation Protocol)

➝ *See* Protocol, RSVP (Resource Reservation Protocol)

RT (Remote Terminal)

A remote terminal is one located far enough from a host or network to require a connection over telephone or special-purpose lines.

RTMP (Routing Table Maintenance Protocol)

➝ *See* Protocol, RTMP (Routing Table Maintenance Protocol)

RTP (Rapid Transport Protocol)

➝ *See* Protocol, RTP (Rapid Transport Protocol)

RTP (Real-Time Transport Protocol)

➝ *See* Protocol, RTP (Real-Time Transport Protocol)

RTP (Routing Table Protocol)

➝ *See* Protocol, RTP (Routing Table Protocol)

RTS (Request to Send)

A hardware signal sent from a potential transmitter to a destination to indicate that the transmitter wishes to begin a transmission. If the receiver is ready, it sends a clear to send (CTS) signal in return. The RTS/CTS combination is used in the CSMA/CA media-access method used in Apple's LocalTalk network architecture.

R

RTSE (Reliable Transfer Service Element)

In the OSI Reference Model, an ALSE (application layer service element) that helps ensure that PDUs (protocol data units), or packets, are transferred reliably between applications. RTSE services can sometimes survive an equipment failure, because they use transport layer services. In the United States, other sources are usually used instead of RTSE to provide these services.

RU (Request/Response Unit)

In SNA (Systems Network Architecture) network communications, the type of packet exchanged by network addressable units (NAUs), which are network elements with associated ports (or addresses).

Run-Length Limited (RLL)

→ *See* RLL (Run-Length Limited)

RZ (Return to Zero)

A signal-encoding method in which the voltage returns to a zero, or neutral, state halfway through each bit interval. This method is self-clocking.

→ *See Also* Encoding, Signal

RZI (Return to Zero Inverted)

The inverted counterpart of the RZ signal-encoding method. RZI exchanges 1 and 0 in the descriptions. For example, a differential RZI has a signal transition for 0, and no transition for a 1; similarly, a non-differential RZI uses +5 volts for 0 and −5 volts for 1.

→ *See Also* Encoding, Signal

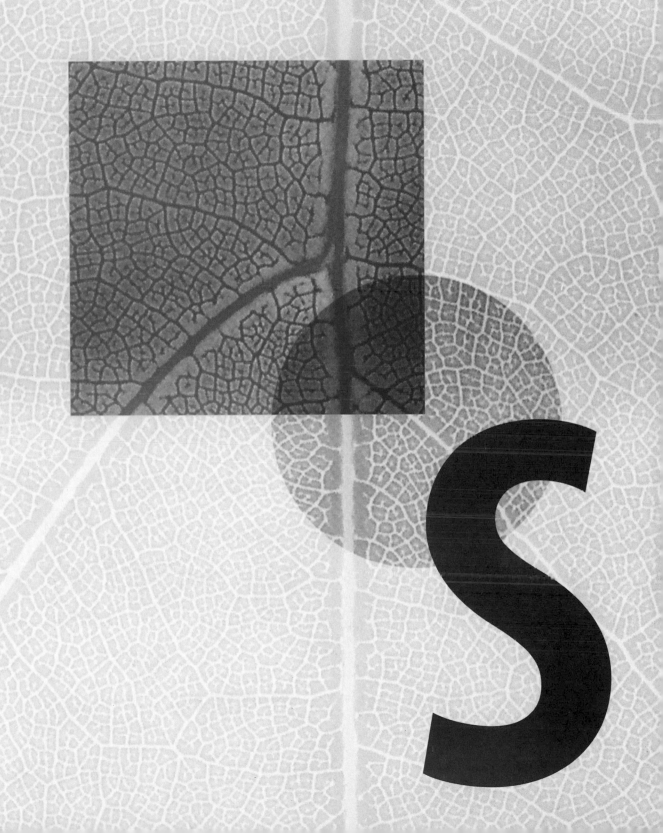

SA (Source Address)

A header field in many types of packets. This value represents the address of the node sending the packet. Depending on the type of address, this field may be four or six bytes or even longer.

→ *Compare* DA (Destination Address)

SA (Stub Area)

In a large network or internetwork, a stub area, or SA, is generally a small section on the fringes of the internetwork. SAs usually have only one or two routers connecting them to the network backbone. This makes routing information for these areas very simple because the routing database for a stub area will contain a default route to all network sections external to the stub area.

SAA (Systems Application Architecture)

SAA is an effort on the part of IBM to standardize the conventions, interfaces, and protocols used by applications in all IBM operating environments. The intent was to provide a unified, logical architecture for applications running on machines ranging from a PS/2 up to a System/370.

SAA has four main components:

CUA (Common User Access)   This component defines standard interfaces for applications that are window- or character-based. The user will interact with this interface. CUA includes specifications for screen and keyboard layout, and for selection methods using either a keyboard or mouse.

CPI (Common Program Interface)   This element defines APIs (Application Program Interfaces) that are consistent across all systems.

These are used by developers in their applications. The CPI standards relating to languages and databases follow ANSI specifications.

CCS (Common Communications Support) CCS defines a collection of communications protocols that machines can use to communicate with each other. The most commonly used protocols are LU 6.2 and HLLAPI.

Common Applications   This is concerned with developing common frameworks for the same kinds of applications running in different environments. This component is largely product-oriented, and is more for marketing and appearance than a substantive part of SAA. In fact, some armchair architects do not regard it as part of SAA.

The illustration "SAA components" shows how these components fit together with an operating system in a particular environment.

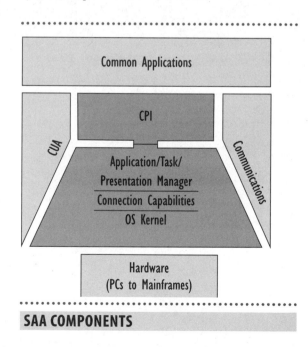

SAA COMPONENTS

SAC (Simplified Access Control)

In the CCITT X.500 Directory Services model, the more restricted of two sets of access control guidelines. The other set is BAC (Basic Access Control).

→ *See Also* X.500

SAC (Single-Attachment Concentrator)

In FDDI, a concentrator that serves as a termination point for single-attachment stations (SASs) and that attaches to the FDDI ring through a dual-attachment connector (DAC).

→ *See Also* FDDI (Fiber Distributed Data Interface)

Safety Device

Safety devices are designed to keep a file server or other piece of hardware running smoothly, regardless of power fluctuations or loss. The protection devices buffer, or shield, the hardware from the harsh world of the electrical power line.

Safety devices operate between the power line and the hardware's circuitry. For a network, the biggest natural threat to the hardware comes from the electrical lines. Drastic deviations or fluctuations in the electrical power supply can cause various types of damage, from minimal data loss to fried hardware.

Electrical Threats

As in other areas of life, electrical dangers can come from having too much or too little. Collectively, such disturbances are known as *overvoltages* and *undervoltages*, respectively.

Overvoltages include spikes and surges. Undervoltages include blackouts and brownouts (or sags). According to studies by IBM and by AT&T Bell Labs, undervoltages account for over 90 percent

of electrical disturbances, with brownouts accounting for about 87 percent and blackouts for about 5 percent of the total. Overvoltages account for the remaining 8 percent, with spikes accounting for 7 percent and surges for only about 1 percent of all electrical disturbances. See the Power Disturbances article for more information about these types of electrical disturbances.

In most cases, such disturbances occur sporadically. In some areas, voltage variations may be unnervingly frequent. This can be the case if the power supply passes through old lines or if there are malfunctioning components along the line. In some cases, your power company may be able to clean up the power supply.

In addition to these variations in the power supply, several types of noise, or random elements in the power supply, also exist in an electrical system:

- Common mode noise is noise arising because of voltage differences between the neutral and ground wires in a system. This type of noise is relatively rare for computer systems, and is almost completely eliminated by noise filters.

- Normal mode noise is noise arising because of voltage differences between the hot and neutral wires in a system. This type of noise has various sources (other electrical activity on the line, motors being turned on or off, and so on). Some of this noise is handled by noise filters, some is eliminated by various tricks and offsets (such as twisting wire pairs), and some gets through.

- Intersystem ground noise is noise that can arise when systems connected to different ground wires communicate. Each ground wire will try to serve as the reference level for both components. This type of noise can be minimized by connecting equipment to a common distribution panel, or frame, because this makes it more likely that the ground values will be the same. In general, noise filters do not help with this kind of noise.

S

Electrical Safety Devices

Various safety devices have been developed to deal with the most common and the most serious electrical threats:

- Surge protectors, or suppressors, protect a system from excess voltages, such as spikes and surges, and do some noise filtering.

- Line conditioners, or voltage regulators, protect a system from low voltages, such as sags. Some line conditioners also provide surge protection.

- UPS (uninterruptible power supply) devices protect a system when there is *no* voltage at all—during blackouts. Most UPSs also provide at least some protection against surges, spikes, and sags. During an outage, the connected device runs off the UPS's battery.

- SPS (standby power supply) devices are similar to UPSs, except that the power does not go through the SPS battery during normal operations. When there is a blackout, the SPS will switch to the emergency battery within a few milliseconds.

UPSs and SPSs provide the same protection but use a different method to do so. A UPS delivers power by sending it through a DC battery and then through an inverter to convert back to AC from DC. For a UPS, the *secondary* path is from the power lines to the device being powered, usually after going through a surge suppressor and a noise filter.

An SPS uses the battery and inverter as the secondary path, and the "direct" route from power lines to machine as the primary path. Only if the primary path is blocked does the power come from batteries.

Hybrid devices that combine features of UPS and SPS have been developed.

For more information about a particular safety device, see the separate article about the device.

Testing Safety Devices

Server maintenance should also include regular tests of the UPS or SPS, every six months or so, at the longest. Before starting such a test, you should log everyone off the network, so that no one inadvertently loses any data.

Next, run a batch program that does some busy work but whose actions will not destroy any of your data. For example, you can have your test program read and write a dummy file.

Next, unplug the UPS or SPS from the wall outlet. The network should be running solely on the battery power provided by the UPS or SPS. Depending on the configuration with your UPS, a message may be broadcast informing users that the network will be shut down soon. At the same time, the network software should be writing anything still in its cache, and should be preparing for a system shutdown. The amount of time available before shutdown depends on the network demands and on the performance rating of the UPS.

It is a good idea to drain the battery completely and then recharge it, since such batteries lose their power if they are continually drained a bit, then recharged, drained a bit, recharged, and so on, as happens during everyday functioning in a UPS.

Keep in mind that a UPS's battery lasts only about 5 years. After that time, the battery loses its ability to store charge efficiently.

Be aware that testing a UPS or SPS by disconnecting from the electrical power supply is helpful, but it is not the same as a real power disturbance. Studies have shown that the electrical activity when you unplug the UPS or SPS is different from the activity if there is a true power outage.

Determining Power Needs

Rating the power needs for a system is not always an easy task for several reasons. It is sometimes difficult to determine how much power a component draws, and it is easy to forget a component when adding up the power requirements. Also, some devices discuss power in terms of watts (W) and some in terms of volt amps (VA).

WHAT TO LOOK FOR IN A SAFETY DEVICE

Although safety devices can help with your peace of mind, be aware that no device is completely foolproof. If an electrical disturbance happens once, there is always the chance it will happen again. Just because your surge protector saved you the first time doesn't mean it will save you again.

Surge suppressors, line conditioners, and UPSs vary in the quality of their components. They also vary in the magnitude and number of attacks they can withstand.

You need to have four types of information about a safety device in order to evaluate the device properly and to compare it with similar devices:

- What's the minimum disturbance that will trigger the device?

- What's the maximum disturbance the device can withstand?

- How quickly can the device respond when there is a disturbance?

- How many high-level and low-level disturbances can the device withstand?

For example, some inexpensive surge suppressors are designed to protect your system against a single attack, perhaps two. Such suppressors are intended for use with ordinary appliances (such as toasters), rather than with computer equipment.

When shopping for safety devices, ask for the specifications sheets to find out the magnitude of damage the device can withstand. Make sure any devices you consider are UL-listed.

The relationship between watts and volt amps is a simple formula. To determine one value from the other, just multiply the starting value by a constant. The problem is that the constant is different for different devices. (For PCs, a volt amp is about 1.5 watts.)

To determine the power requirements for your system, you need to do the following:

- Identify all the components that draw power.

- Determine the power requirements for each component, using the same units when possible, and making any necessary conversions when not.

- Add the values for the individual components.

To be safe, round upwards, so that your estimate will be high, rather than low. The few dollars you save by buying a safety device with less capacity may be lost very quickly if the device is inadequate. Also, you should take expansion into account when computing power requirements.

Sag

A short-term decrease in voltage level. Specifically, a sag occurs when the voltage is more than 20 percent below the nominal RMS voltage, and lasts for a few seconds or longer.

→ *See Also* Power Disturbance

Salvageable File

In Novell's NetWare, a file deleted but not purged by the user. Salvageable files can be recovered if necessary, because NetWare actually saves the file in a special directory rather than deleting it. In contrast, purged files cannot be recovered.

SAM (Security Accounts Manager)

In Windows NT networks, the SAM contains the user account and security information that is used to authenticate users during the login process. Based on the results of the authentication, the SAM will issue an access token that contains the user's permissions. The SAM resides on the primary domain controller (PDC) and a synchronized copy is kept on the backup domain controller (BDC).

→ *Broader Category* Windows NT

S

Sampled Servo (SS)

→ *See* SS (Sampled Servo)

SAN (Storage Area Network)

As Web designers have added more and more multimedia materials to Web pages, the demands on network storage facilities—and also on network servers—have increased dramatically. SANs offer a way of dealing with increased storage demands and their effects on network operation.

As its name indicates, a SAN is a network. It provides a way to physically interconnect various kinds of storage devices and provide central administration for this storage facility. The SAN has its own server, which relieves the server for the main network (usually a LAN, or local area network) of the chore of administering and providing access to the storage devices.

If the SAN server has the appropriate capabilities and interfaces, the storage facilities can be made accessible to multiple networks—each of which may be running on a different platform and with a different protocol stack. In addition to providing network interfaces, the server could also provide interfaces for various database platforms.

The SAN is connected to the main network over a high-speed pipeline. Fortunately, there are several excellent transmission standards to choose from, including SCSI (Small Computer Systems Interface), Fibre Channel, and HiPPI (High-Performance Parallel Interface).

Sandbox Model

In Java programming, the sandbox model refers to the security mechanism for Java applets. These applets are allowed to operate only within their sandbox, or working area. They are not allowed to

call any processes on the target machine and are not allowed to alter files.

→ *Broader Categories*   Applet; Java

SAP (Service Access Point)

In the OSI reference model, a SAP is a well-defined location through which an entity at a particular layer can provide services to processes at the layer above.

To indicate the layering, the first letter of the specific layer being discussed is often added before the SAP. For example, a Transport layer entity provides services to the session layer through a TSAP (or a T-SAP). The illustration "SAPs and OSI layers" shows how SAPs relate to OSI layers.

SAP Addresses

Each SAP will have a unique address. This address can also be used as an access point to the service's user, which is the entity at the next higher layer. SAPs are assigned by the IEEE standards office. The table "SAP Addresses for Common Protocols" shows some examples of SAP address values associated with protocols. Addresses are in hexadecimal form.

SAP ADDRESSES FOR COMMON PROTOCOLS

Protocol	SAP Address Value (Hexadecimal)
IP (ARPAnet)	06
IPX (Novell NetWare)	E0
ISO Network Layer	F5
NetBIOS (IBM)	F0
SNA Group Path Control (IBM)	05
SNA Individual Path Control (IBM)	04
TCP/IP SNAP	AA
XNS (3Com)	80

DSAPs and SSAPs

The IEEE 802.2 specifications refer to SAPs through which network layer processes can request services from the logical-link-control (LLC) sublayer defined by the IEEE. The documents distinguish between source and destination access points. A DSAP (destination service access point) is the address to which the LLC passes information for a network-layer process. An SSAP (source service access point) is the address through which a network-layer process requests LLC services.

The DSAP and SSAP values are included as fields in packets for local area network (LAN) architectures that conform to IEEE specifications. In practice, these addresses are usually the same, since the process requesting a service is almost always the one that wants the results of that service.

→ **See Also** OSI Reference Model

SAP (Service Advertising Protocol)

In Novell's NetWare, a Transport layer protocol that servers can use to make their services known on a network. Servers advertise their services using SAP packets. These packets are retrieved and stored by routers. Each router maintains a database of all the servers within "wireshot," and each router broadcasts this information to other routers, typically every 60 seconds or whenever something changes.

Stations that need a service can broadcast SAP request packets. These packets will be answered by the nearest router with information about the requested service. In NetWare 5, SAP has been replaced by the Internet's Services Location Protocol (SLP), which has less overhead.

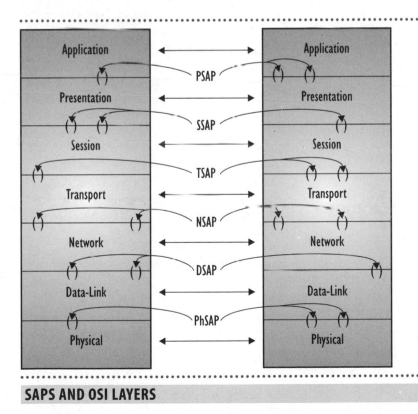

SAPS AND OSI LAYERS

SAS (Single-Attachment Station)

In FDDI, a station, or node, that lacks the physical ports to attach directly to both the primary and secondary rings. Instead, the SAS attaches to a concentrator (which may be single- or dual-attachment).

→ *See Also* FDDI (Fiber Distributed Data Interface)

SATAN (Security Analysis Tool for Auditing Networks)

SATAN is a very controversial set of network security tools. It consists of HTML files, shell scripts, and programs written in C, Perl, and Expect. These programs generate additional HTML files that are used to probe networks in order to:

- Determine the network's configuration and weak points.

- Probe these weaknesses to determine how vulnerable they make the network.

- Generate a report summarizing the network's configuration and weaknesses, and also SATAN's success during its probes.

Working with a browser and a World Wide Web client, users can have SATAN launch a light, normal, or heavy attack at a target machine or domain. In a light attack, the HTML documents, scripts, and programs are used to report about available host machines and remote procedure call (RPC) services. A Normal attack also finds out about the Finger, FTP, Gopher, SMTP, Telnet, and Web capabilities on the network, since certain features of these services—especially Finger and FTP—make networks particularly vulnerable. A heavy attack will look for other common vulnerabilities, such as trusted hosts or anonymous FTP directories with write permissions.

If vulnerabilities are found, SATAN can make use of expert system tools to investigate further. It can also provide a report of the vulnerabilities.

SATAN is extensible, and users can add their own attack or analysis tools.

SATAN's creators—Dan Farmer and Wietse Venema—claim that SATAN finds weaknesses a frighteningly high proportion of the time. Since it was "released" in April 1995, SATAN has apparently been so effective that manufacturers of security products have been known to issue press releases when one of their systems detects or withstands an attack by SATAN.

The release of SATAN has also led to the development of new security products—some of which check for SATAN attacks. In keeping with the terminology, these products have names such as Gabriel.

SATAN on the Loose

SATAN's developers have decided to make the package freely available to anyone interested. Because this includes both sides—security experts and administrators on one side, and crackers on the other—the decision has raised a considerable furor.

SATAN can be a benefit in that it gives system administrators and security specialists a very powerful tool for testing the adequacy of their network security. Once they find weaknesses, presumably they can fix them. SATAN can be a threat, however, because individuals or organizations trying to gain illegal access to corporate, government, or other sensitive networks get a big helping hand.

A more subtle problem—and possibly more damaging in the long run—is the potential for introducing weaknesses into a network just by using SATAN. The Computer Emergency Response Team (CERT) has issued advisories about SATAN, because certain ways of using the program may lead to security breaches.

It remains to be seen whether SATAN helps improve network security or whether it just makes the network administrator's life more difficult.

→ *Primary Sources* The documentation for SATAN is available from the following Web site:

```
ftp://ftp.win.tue.nl/pub/security/
satan_doc.tar.Z
```

This documentation has several obstacles that "protect" it from readers. First, it is a compressed archive (tar) file. Second, it requires a Web browser (such as Netscape or Mosaic), and version 5 of the Perl language. The documentation actually includes sample data from early trials. (In fact, the documentation consists of the SATAN package with the probing and data retrieval tools removed.) To view the sample data, the developers recommend a fast workstation with 32MB of memory and at least 64MB of swap space.

Satellite System

A satellite system refers to any of several classes of delivery or communications systems—most notably, direct broadcast satellite (DBS) systems. Satellite systems currently are used mainly for delivering digital television signals, but they also are becoming a factor in interactive service delivery. Moreover, they will play a central role in the ever-expanding wireless communications market and will be the centerpieces for personal communication systems (PCSs).

Until now, DBSs have largely used geosynchronous earth orbit (GEO) satellites to deliver the TV programming. Such satellites orbit at an altitude of about 22,000 miles. Their orbital velocity is equal to the earth's rotational velocity so that such satellites maintain a stationary position above a fixed point on the earth. Because of their huge footprints (coverage areas), only three GEO satellites are needed to cover the entire earth, which makes them appealing for delivery systems such as direct TV. However, their great distance from the earth, and the delays this engenders, make them less attractive for use in interactive communications.

Nevertheless, DirecPC, operated by Hughes Communications, uses GEO satellites to provide Internet access at a rate of up to 400Kbps downstream (from provider to subscriber). Plans are in place to add eight more GEO satellites to increase the downstream speeds to as much as 6Mbps. (For upstream communication, such implementations

use an ordinary telephone modem.) CyberStar—another GEO project, developed jointly by Loral and Alcatel—will deploy three GEO satellites, and will support 6.5Mbps downstream. Perhaps more important, this satellite system will also support a whopping 2.5Mbps upstream.

An alternative approach is to use satellites in lower orbits. Several low earth orbit (LEO) satellite projects are being deployed, developed, or planned. These satellites orbit at a much smaller distance from the earth—usually about 2000 miles. They have advantages and disadvantages over the higher GEO satellites.

On the plus side, launching an LEO is much easier and less expensive—requiring something on the order of a space shuttle as opposed to a Saturn rocket. Second, transmission delays are negligible—a few milliseconds (msecs), as opposed to the 700 msec for a GEO satellite.

On the down side, LEO orbits take much more punishment and are much more difficult to maintain—because of the effects of the atmosphere and space debris. This means LEO satellites have an expected lifetime of about five years—compared to about 15 years for a GEO satellite. Also, LEO satellites have much smaller footprints because they are not so far above the earth. As a result, LEO coverage requires more satellites.

Most LEO projects use several dozen satellites. For example, the Iridium project—from a consortium headed by Motorola—will deploy 66 LEO satellites. Even this number is down from the 77 originally planned for the project. An LEO project from Telediscec will use 288 satellites.

The LEO projects are mainly intended for communications and Internet access services. Satellite delivery of digital TV is likely to remain in the GEO—at least for the near future.

There are several other classes of earth orbit satellites, but these have been used primarily in other countries or for military purposes.

→ *See Also* GEO (Geosynchronous Earth Orbit) Satellite; LEO (Low Earth Orbit) Satellite

Scalable Protocol

A scalable protocol is one that can be used even if the number of nodes or routers on a network grows by a significant amount. It's particularly important to use scalable routing protocols because networks may be connected to any number of other networks—particularly if the connection is over the Internet.

Scalable protocols should use metrics that allow a packet to reach its destination even if a large amount of travel time or many intermediate stops are required. This is the reachability criterion, and it also requires scalable protocols to be able to find alternate paths, if necessary.

Scalable protocols should converge quickly on a path—that is, such protocols must be able to eliminate unpromising routes very quickly, and then be able to select quickly from the available paths. A fast convergence time is particularly important as an internetwork grows because the number or possible paths grows very rapidly as the size of an internetwork or a network increases.

EIGRP (Enhanced Interior Gateway Routing Protocol), NLSP (NetWare Link Services Protocol), and OSPF (Open Shortest Path First) are examples of scalable protocols.

→ *See Also* Protocol, EIGRP (Enhanced Interior Gateway Routing Protocol); Protocol, NLSP (NetWare Link-State Protocol); Protocol, OSPF (Open Shortest Path first)

Scaling

Expansion of a network by the addition of more nodes. The scalability of a network architecture or operating system should be a major factor in selecting network components.

Scattering

In communications over fiber-optic cable, signal loss that occurs when the light waves in the fiber core strike molecules or slight indentations in the cladding (material surrounding the fiber core).

Scope

A scope is a range of IP (Internet Protocol) addresses that may be used by a DHCP (Dynamic Host Configuration Protocol) server when it assigns IP addresses dynamically to computers that will be (temporarily) on the network.

Addresses that may *not* be used must be specified in an *exclusion*, which is simply a list of forbidden addresses.

SCR (Signal-to-Crosstalk Ratio)

In transmissions involving twisted-pair cable, a value that represents the decibel level of a signal in relation to the noise in the cable. Specifically, SCR is calculated as the ratio between the NEXT (near end crosstalk) and the attenuation on a cable. The SCR for an active hub is generally higher than for a passive hub.

SCR (Sustainable Cell Rate)

In the ATM (Asynchronous Transfer Mode) networking architecture, SCR is a network traffic parameter that represents the maximum *average* cell rate that can be sustained over a specified virtual connection (VC). This is in contrast to the peak and minimum cell rates (PCR and MCR, respectively). The former represents the maximum cell rate possible over the VC; the latter represents the minimum cell rate that the network must be able to guarantee in order for the virtual connection to be established.

→ *Broader Category* ATM (Asynchronous Transfer Mode)

→ *See Also* MCR (Minimum Cell Rate); PCR (Peak Cell Rate)

Scripting Language

A scripting language is both "higher-level" than a programming language and much more limited than it. A scripting language is higher-level in that you get much more work out of much less coding; however, it is more limited in that you generally cannot draw on resources such as DLL (dynamic-link library) or other library files, and you often have less control over the operating environment with scripting languages.

All the hedging in the preceding paragraph is necessary for two reasons:

- Individual scripting languages manage to overcome particular limitations or to do an end run around specific obstacles.

- Scripting can be used in the context of two very different operating modes. In the world of the Internet and, in particular, the World Wide Web, scripting refers to a mechanism for exerting control over elements in Web documents. Such scripting tends to be event driven and can be regarded as object based. In the world of operating system shells, scripting refers to the creation of procedural, or command, sequences that can be played when needed. Languages for such scripting tend to be programming languages dressed up to look like scripting languages—with Perl being perhaps the best example of this. Such languages are full-fledged programming languages that can also—in the right context—get the high work-to-code ratios that scripting languages achieve. This entry will focus on languages that fit the Web-based sense of the term.

The Web-based form of scripting includes several well-known languages, such as HTML (Hypertext Markup Language), JavaScript, and VBScript. Of these, HTML is by far the least powerful. In fact, both JavaScript and VBScript are designed to augment and extend the capabilities of HTML "scripts."

HTML as Scripting Language

While HTML is better known as a markup language, it serves as a scripting language for a browser—specifying how each element of a Web page is to be interpreted and providing guidelines for layout and display. By itself, HTML is quite a poor scripting language because it cannot handle any run-time contingencies other than those that have been written into the file—for example, links to other files. A server delivers an HTML file as a static document to a browser. Without enhancements, all the browser can do is display what has been delivered.

Cascading style sheets have helped to extend HTML's capabilities somewhat by making it possible to introduce selective effects through such style sheets. However, even these effects are limited to display time—that is, they can be introduced by the browser but not by a user.

Even greater possibilities were introduced with Dynamic HTML, an extension of HTML that comes with a document object model (DOM). Whereas basic HTML allows access only to certain tagged elements in a document, the object model underlying DHTML makes it possible—in principle—to access *any* element on an HTML page. However, because DHTML itself does not provide anything that you actually *can* do with a given element, it adds possibilities rather than capabilities. These possibilities are made real by the use of more powerful scripting languages that augment HTML and that take advantage of the DOM behind DHTML.

JavaScript and VBScript

JavaScript and VBScript are scripting languages developed by Netscape and Microsoft, respectively. (JavaScript has been adopted, with some modifications and extensions, as ECMAScript, which is a scripting language standard.) These languages can access—particularly with the DHTML DOM—any elements in a DHTML file.

Once accessed, these elements can essentially be "rewritten"—to produce special effects or contingency actions. The rewrite rules are stated in the script file, and many of them will take the form: "if this happens, do this"—for example, "if the user clicks with the left mouse button, display a message." Scripted actions depend on events, and the action taken depends on the element involved in the event—that is, on the object affected. The execution of a script file will basically consist of a series of sequences such as the following:

1. Determine what event has occurred;

2. Identify the object to which the event has occurred;

3. Determine the action associated with that object for that event;

4. Perform the appropriate action;

5. Wait until an event occurs.

The details of an actual session will be determined by the user. Depending on the events the user initiates—clicking on hot areas or filling in forms, for example—and the page elements on which the user initiates these, the document will be recreated as specified in the script files. Because of the way this process works, Web-based scripting languages are sometimes known as event-driven or object-based languages. (Note object-based is not the same as object-oriented; object-based languages use a weaker definition of object, and therefore lack many of the features of true object-oriented languages.)

Capabilities such as those afforded by scripting languages and an HTML page built on a document object model make a Web page truly interactive and dynamic in the sense of being modifiable on the fly.

The JavaScript and VBScript languages have different roots—Java for JavaScript and Visual Basic for VBScript—and their syntax differs accordingly. However, the languages are both quite flexible and capable, and it's possible to achieve the same kinds of things in both languages—although not necessarily in the same way.

Other, proprietary, scripting languages also exist. In the Web-related sense, Macromedia's Lingo scripting language is perhaps the best known. Lingo is used in Macromedia's Director software.

SCS (SNA Character String)

In IBM's SNA environment, a printing mode that provides various printing and formatting capabilities.

→ **Compare** DSC (Data Stream Compatibility)

→ **See Also** SNA (Systems Network Architecture)

SCSI (Small Computer System Interface)

SCSI is a high-speed, parallel interface standard that provides a generic interface for devices, such as scanners, CD-ROM drives, and hard disks. The original SCSI-1 specification was created in 1981 and was based on a proprietary interface: the Shugart Associates System Interface (SASI). It was not adopted as an official ANSI standard until 1986.

The SCSI-2 standard was adopted in 1991, and since then SCSI-3 has established itself. Both SCSI-2 and SCSI-3 come in several flavors that vary in bus width and speed and also in maximum transfer rate.

SCSI-1

SCSI-1 was originally developed to provide an interface between computers and hard disks. It uses an eight-bit bus with a 5MHz clock speed, and supports a maximum rate of 5 megabytes per second (MBps).

Specifications for SCSI-1 connections are quite complex because the standard provides for several combinations of electrical characteristics and pin assignments. With older components, some combinations can be harmful or even fatal to hardware.

Some—mostly older—components use an arrangement known as *single-ended (SE) SCSI pinout*. SE limits the maximum length of all the SCSI cable in a configuration to about 6 meters. Faster bus speeds—as in SCSI-2, described below—require even shorter distances. At the fastest speeds, some SCSI configurations could extend only about four or five feet.

An alternative with more robust electrical properties was developed. The *differential (DIFF) SCSI pinout* increased the maximum allowable cable length to a total of 25 meters. Moreover, this distance is not dependent on bus speed. DIFF pinouts use both a positive (+) and a negative (−) signal for each data bit, and for most of the control and signal bits (such as carrier detect, acknowledge, and so forth). This means that two pins are assigned for each of these components. While it is only one of several possible connector configurations, the table "Pin Assignments for Differential SCSI Pinout A-Cable" shows the pin assignments for what is arguably the most commonly used SCSI-1 connection. Pins are numbered from 1 to 50.

PIN ASSIGNMENTS FOR DIFFERENTIAL SCSI PINOUT A-CABLE

Pin(s)	Definition
1,2,22,31,32,49,50	Ground
3,5,7,9,11,13,15,17	+ signal component for data bits 0–7, respectively
4,6,8,10,12,14,16,18	− signal component for data bits 0–7, respectively
19	+ signal component for parity bit
20	− signal component for parity bit
21	DIFFSENS—detects invalid (i.e., SE) pinouts
23,24,27,28	Reserved
25,26	TERMPWR
29,30	+/− signal components for ATN (attention)
33,34	+/− signal components for BSY (busy)
35,36	+/− signal components for ACK (acknowledge)
37,38	+/− signal components for RST (reset)
39,40	+/− signal components for MSG (message)
41,42	+/− signal components for SEL (select)
43,44	+/− signal components for C/D (carrier detect)
45,46	+/− signal components for REQ (request)
47,48	+/− signal components for I/O (input/output)

As stated, the SCSI cable picture is quite messy, and there are several other cables that can be, and are, used for SCSI connections. Despite its well-deserved reputation for being difficult to set up, people were willing to put up with these problems and expenses in order to get the benefits of SCSI's high speeds and large storage capabilities—back in the days when 5MBps was considered fast and 1 or 2GB of storage were expected to last you a lifetime.

A SCSI-1 interface can support up to eight devices in a single expansion slot, and SCSI devices can be daisy-chained so that a single adapter can support a variety of devices. This type of configuration is illustrated in the illustration "SCSI chain." In a daisy-chain configuration, it is essential to make sure that every device in the chain has a different address and that the last device in the (electrical) chain is properly terminated.

While the newer standards offer higher speeds, SCSI-1 interfaces are still used to save costs, particularly for peripherals. However, this can be a disadvantage for an end user because the maximum speed of a SCSI chain is determined by its slowest component.

SCSI-2

SCSI-2, adopted in 1991, extended the command set and gave a more important role to something known as the Common Command Set (CCS), which was created to make the SCSI interface applicable to more types of devices than the hard disks for which it was originally developed.

SCSI-2 also introduced two mechanisms for increasing transfer rates: faster timing and wider bus. SCSI-2 implementations could use either, both, or neither of these mechanisms. Based on these mechanisms, it's possible to define the following SCSI-2 flavors:

- *Fast* SCSI variants double the bus clock speed to 10MHz.

- *Wide* SCSI variants extend the bus to 16 or 32 bits.

- *Fast Wide* SCSI variants increase both clock speed and bus width.

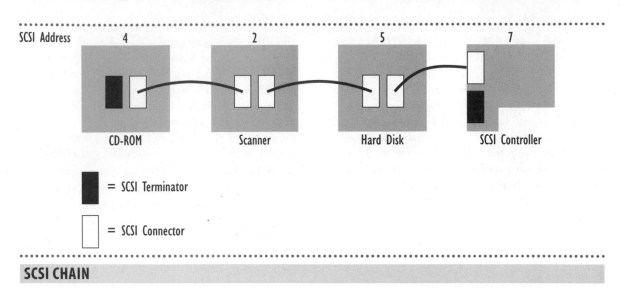

SCSI Address 4   2   5   7

CD-ROM   Scanner   Hard Disk   SCSI Controller

= SCSI Terminator

= SCSI Connector

SCSI CHAIN

Table "Properties of SCSI Variants" summarizes the SCSI-2 flavors, and includes SCSI-1 specs for comparison. Note that the table includes a variant, SCSI-2, whose specs look identical to those for SCSI-1. In fact, the performance specs are identical. The underlying command set is the only thing that distinguishes some SCSI-2 implementations from SCSI-1. Needless to say, this has caused considerable confusion and grief over the years.

PROPERTIES OF SCSI VARIANTS

SCSI Variant	Bus width	Bus speed	Maximum Transfer Rate
SCSI-1	8 bits	5MHz	5MBps
SCSI-2	8 bits	5MHz	5MBps
Fast SCSI-2	8 bits	10MHz	10MBps
Wide SCSI-2	16 (32) bits	5MHz	10 (20) MBps
Fast Wide SCSI-2	16 (32) bits	10MHz	20 (40) MBps

Widening the bus made it necessary to add a second cable. This B cable has 68 pins, whose assignments are shown in the table "Pin Assignments for Differential SCSI Pinout B-Cable."

PIN ASSIGNMENTS FOR DIFFERENTIAL SCSI PINOUT B-CABLE

Pin(s)	Definition
1,12,34,35,68	Ground
2–9	+ signal component for data bits 8–15, respectively
10	+ signal component for parity bit 1
11,45	+/– signal components for ACKB (Acknowledgement B)
13,47	+/– signal components for REQB (request B)
14–16	+ signal component for data bits 16–18, respectively
17,18,51,52	TERMPWRB
19–23	+ signal component for data bits 19–23, respectively
24	+ signal component for parity bit 2
25–32	+ signal component for data bits 24–31, respectively
33	+ signal component for parity bit 3
36–43	– signal component for data bits 8–15, respectively
44	– signal component for parity bit 1
46	DIFFSENS—detects invalid (i.e., SE) pinouts
48–50	– signal component for data bits 16–18, respectively
53–57	– signal component for data bits 19–23, respectively
58	– signal component for parity bit 2
59–66	– signal component for data bits 24–31, respectively
67	– signal component for parity bit 3

In addition to faster transfer rates, the wider SCSI-2 buses also provide support for more devices. Thus, a 16-bit bus can support up to 16 devices, and a 32-bit bus can support up to 32.

SCSI-3

SCSI-3 is both an extension of previous versions and also a radical departure. Like its predecessors, it provides support for parallel connections, higher bus speeds, and also higher maximum transfer rates. However, SCSI-3 also includes support for three serial interfaces. This moves SCSI from being solely a parallel interface, and also enables it to connect to

three high-speed interfaces that are rapidly expanding their presence in the networking world.

In fact, the SCSI-3 architecture is actually based on a collection of specifications. An upper level is built of a half dozen different command sets—for different device and data categories. The lower levels are built of protocol and physical interface specifications for the four different interfaces (one parallel and three serial) that SCSI-3 supports. Communication between these two levels is through a middle layer made up of the SCSI-3 Primary Commands (SPC). The various specifications and how they fit together are shown in the illustration "SCSI-3 building blocks."

S

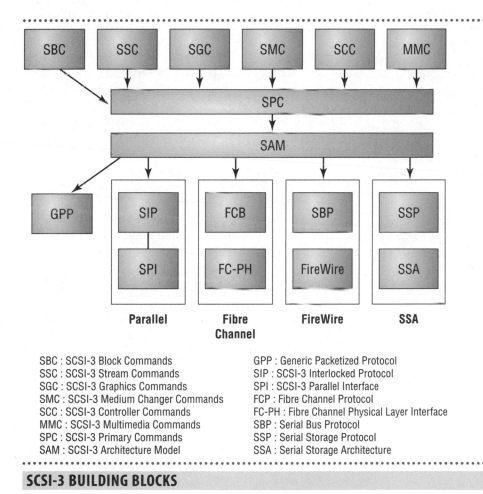

SBC : SCSI-3 Block Commands
SSC : SCSI-3 Stream Commands
SGC : SCSI-3 Graphics Commands
SMC : SCSI-3 Medium Changer Commands
SCC : SCSI-3 Controller Commands
MMC : SCSI-3 Multimedia Commands
SPC : SCSI-3 Primary Commands
SAM : SCSI-3 Architecture Model

GPP : Generic Packetized Protocol
SIP : SCSI-3 Interlocked Protocol
SPI : SCSI-3 Parallel Interface
FCP : Fibre Channel Protocol
FC-PH : Fibre Channel Physical Layer Interface
SBP : Serial Bus Protocol
SSP : Serial Storage Protocol
SSA : Serial Storage Architecture

SCSI-3 BUILDING BLOCKS

SCSI-3, which should be adopted as a standard by the time you read this, offers the variants shown in the table "SCSI-3 Variants."

SCSI-3 VARIANTS

SCSI Variant	Bus width	Bus speed	Maximum Transfer Rate
Ultra SCSI-3	8 bits	20MHz	20MBps
Wide Ultra SCSI-3	16 bits	20MHz	40MBps
Ultra2 SCSI-3	8 bits	40MHz	40MBps
Wide Ultra2 SCSI-3	16 bits	40MHz	80MBps

SCSI-3 also contributes to the cabling mess—introducing P- and Q-cable as the primary and secondary cables. These are 68-pin cables and, as with cables for earlier versions, come in either SE or DIFF versions. In addition, SCSI-3 also provides support for 110-pin cables and—because of the addition of Serial SCSI—a whole new family of cables also comes into play.

It remains to be seen how well SCSI will fare in today's market. As an interface for storage controllers (such as for hard disks), SCSI is getting competition from increasingly turbo-charged variants of the EIDE (Enhanced Integrated Drive Electronics) interface (also known as the ATA, for AT Attachment, interface). As a high-speed transfer interface, SCSI is seriously outperformed by such really high speed interfaces as Fibre Channel and its cousin, HiPPI (High-Performance Parallel Interface).

SD (Start Delimiter)

A field in a Token Ring data or token packet.

→ See Also Token Ring

SDDI (Shielded Distributed Data Interface)

A networking configuration that implements the FDDI architecture and protocols on shielded twisted-pair (STP) cable. A related implementation is CDDI (copper distributed data interface), which uses unshielded twisted pair (UTP) cable.

SDF (Sub-Distribution Frame)

An intermediate wiring center. For example, an SDF may be used for all the equipment on a particular floor. This type of frame is connected by backbone cable to a main distribution frame (MDF).

SDH (Synchronous Digital Hierarchy)

In North America, SONET (for Synchronous Optical Network) is the name given to a network transport technology that uses synchronous transmission of digital signals over fiber-optic lines. This technology offers several performance levels, which are built up by aggregating multiple channels to create the hierarchy. The ITU-T (International Telecommunications Union—Telecommunications Sector) name for this standard is SDH.

This high-speed technology offers many superior features, including speeds ranging from 51.84Mbps to 9.953Gbps, efficient transport, low overhead, superior management and administration resources, ability to handle any kind of data, back compatibility with current transport technologies, and topologies with redundancy and self-healing properties.

→ See Also SONET (Synchronous Optical Network)

SDSL (Symmetric Digital Subscriber Line)

SDSL is a variant of digital subscriber line (DSL) technology that uses the same speeds for upstream and downstream communication. DSL technology squeezes high digital transmission speeds out of ordinary analog telephone lines—provided these lines are within a limited distance of a telephone company central office (CO).

Most of the DSL variants are asymmetric in that the downstream channels are much faster than the upstream ones. This bias reflects the reality that most Internet sessions involve more downloading than uploading.

→ *Broader Category* DSL (Digital Subscriber Line)

→ *See Also* ADSL (Asymmetric Digital Subscriber Line)

SDU (Service Data Unit)

In the OSI reference model, a term for a packet that is passed as a service request parameter from one layer to the layer below it. For example, a Transport layer process may pass a packet down to the Network layer for transmission. The Transport layer's packet is an SDU for the Network layer.

→ *See Also* OSI Reference Model

Search Drive

In Novell's NetWare, a drive that is searched if a file is not found in the current directory. A search drive enables a user to work in one directory but access files, such as applications, in other directories, without needing to specify those other directories.

→ *See Also* Search Mode

Search Engine

A search engine is a program that is designed to traverse some type of search space. In relation to networking, the term is generally applied to a program used to find items—usually documents known as Web pages—on the World Wide Web.

Web search engines work in a variety of ways. Some use Web robots—automated server-based programs—to search through and index the hypertext documents available on the Web. Others simply gather information from available indexes.

Since the Web's inception, search engines have become much more sophisticated—both in the abilities of the engine and in the level of complexity of the material with which they can work. In fact, there are now dozens of "metasearch" engines—programs that submit queries to multiple search engines.

Examples of search engines include WebCrawler, World Wide Web Worm (WWWW), and Lycos.

S

Search Mode

In Novell's NetWare, search mode is a setting that specifies which search drives should be checked when a program is looking for a data file. The search mode is associated with an executable (EXE or COM) file.

NetWare allows the search mode for each file to be set individually. Alternatively, an entry in the NET.CFG file can set the search mode for entire groups of files. The table "NetWare Search Mode Values" shows the modes that are defined.

NETWARE SEARCH MODE VALUES

Mode	Description
0	The program checks NET.CFG for instructions. This is the default value.
1	The program checks the path specified in the file. If none is specified, the program checks the default directory and then all search drives.

Continued on next page

NETWARE SEARCH MODE VALUES (continued)	
Mode	**Description**
2	The program checks the path specified in the file. If none is specified, the program checks only the default directory.
3	The program checks the path specified in the file. If none is specified, the program checks the default directory. If the file open request is read-only, the program also checks the search drives.
4	Reserved for future use.
5	The program searches the specified path and then all search drives. If no path is set, the program searches the default directory and then all search drives.
6	Reserved for future use.
7	The program checks the path specified in the file. If the file open request is read-only, the program checks the search drives. If no path is specified, the program checks the default directory, and then all search drives.

Seat

In computer telephony, a term used to describe an aggregate configuration consisting of a phone line, port, and telephone. As computers and telephones become more integrated, equipment is becoming bundled and priced "per seat" rather than for the individual items.

Secondary Link Station (SLS)

→ **See** SLS (Secondary Link Station)

Secure Socket Layer (SSL) Protocol

→ **See** Protocol, SSL (Secure Socket Layer)

Secret-Key Encryption

A data-encryption strategy that uses a single key, known only to sender and receiver, to encrypt and decrypt transmissions.

→ **See** Encryption

Security

Security is an aspect of network administration concerned with ensuring that the data, circuits, and equipment on a network are used only by authorized users and in authorized ways. More fundamentally, security is concerned with ensuring the following:

Availability Network components, information, and services are available whenever needed.

Confidentiality Services and information are available only to those authorized to use them. This availability may differ for different users; that is, certain users may have more privileges and access than others.

Integrity Components and information are not destroyed, corrupted, or stolen, either through outside intervention or through in-house incompetence.

Threats to Security

The security of a network can be threatened, compromised, or breached with respect to hardware, software, information, and even network operation. In this context, a threat may be defined as a scenario that violates one or more of the security goals. For example, losses of hardware or data are threats to a network's security, as are thefts of passwords or user IDs.

A particular type of threat may or may not be avoidable, and may or may not ever happen. For example, if an unauthorized person has managed to learn a valid user ID and password, the threat is unavoidable, and the network's security is compromised. A compromised network is no longer secure, even though it may not be damaged. If that person uses the stolen information to access the network, the network's security actually will be breached.

To implement effective security measures, it is necessary to determine the possible threats and their consequences, and to develop effective measures against each of these threats.

Threats to network security may be categorized in terms of the network element that is threatened (for example, hardware or software) or in terms of the manner in which the threat affects the network if carried out. The following are some of the ways threats can be categorized:

- Internal or external. An internal threat derives from hardware or software on the network itself. For example, a malfunctioning or inadequate fan may cause a computer to overheat, damaging its circuits. An external threat derives from a person or from an element outside the network. For example, a disgruntled employee or user with a hammer or a strong magnet could provide a serious external threat.

- Intentional or accidental. An intentional threat has damage to the network as a primary or secondary goal. For example, an industrial or political spy trying to steal or corrupt information represents an intentional threat. In contrast, a power surge or a lightning strike that damages circuitry can be unfortunate, but can hardly be called intentional.

- Active or passive. In an active threat, damage to the network is a main effect. For example, a virus program may format a hard disk on the network, or an industrial spy may delete important network files. In a passive threat, damage to the network is a side effect or an unanticipated result of some other action. For example, the radiation and other signals that emanate from a network during a transmission may be picked up by an unauthorized user and used to obtain information about the network.

Anticipation of all passive threats requires a truly paranoid mind, since some passive threats can be far removed from actual information on the network. For example, a "listener" might be able to draw testable inferences about a network simply by observing transmission traffic patterns on the network.

Threats to Hardware

In this context, hardware refers to a range of objects, including computers, peripherals, cables, telecommunications lines, circuits, and just about any other device or component that someone manages to attach to a network, and through which energy can be sent into the network and information sent from it. Any of these objects may be threatened with destruction, damage, or theft; the object may be rendered temporarily or permanently unusable.

Some of the threats to hardware include the following:

- Theft, as when a computer or another piece of equipment is stolen. In some cases, such as when a hard or floppy disk is stolen, other aspects are also breached.

- Tampering, as when a cable is cut, or jumpers are set to unexpected or incorrect values.

- Destruction, as when a computer's circuitry is fried through an electrical power surge. More subtle forms of destruction can arise through temporary but frequent power decreases or outages or through inadequate ventilation around the computer.

- Damage, as when a cable loses its protection and properties because of humidity and other environmental conditions.

- Unauthorized use, as when someone taps into a cable or a telecommunications line in order to eavesdrop, steal secrets, or send in false information. Similarly, unauthorized access to and use of a node or terminal can also compromise a network.

- Ordinary equipment wear and tear, which is inevitable, but whose progress can be slowed by proper treatment and regular maintenance.

The specific threats to hardware are almost unlimited. Under the proper circumstances, just about anything can pose a threat to a hardware component.

Measures can be taken to avoid (or at least decrease the likelihood of) certain hardware threats. For example, theft or damage by outsiders can be avoided by locking the hardware in a room that is (ideally) inaccessible to all but the system administrator. Similarly, damage through external accidents (such as power disturbances) can be avoided by using surge protectors and other safety devices.

Threats to Software

In this context, software refers to the applications, shells, operating systems, and other programs that execute on and for the network. Data and work files are included in another section, as examples of information.

Threats to software include the following:

- Deletion, as when a program is deliberately or accidentally erased from a hard disk.

- Theft, as when a program is copied by unauthorized users.

- Corruption, as when software is infested by a virus, Trojan horse, or worm. Software can also be corrupted in other ways, such as by having a program send a copy of the program's output to an unauthorized file or location.

- Bugs, which may not manifest themselves immediately or which may be very subtle, arising only for certain values or conditions.

Network management programs may be able to watch for efforts to delete or corrupt a program. Management software cannot detect a program bug, but it may be able to recognize the bug's effects.

Threats to Information

In this context, information refers to configurations, files, transmissions, and other data representations.

In general, information is used or transformed by the programs discussed as software.

Threats to information include the following:

- Deletion, as when a database is deliberately or inadvertently erased.

- Theft, as when the information in a network transmission is overheard and saved by nodes other than the destination. The information may be intercepted, rather than taken away, so that it is still passed on to its original destination, just as in a normal network transmission. Information theft can also occur as a side effect of hardware theft, such as when a hard disk is stolen.

- Loss, as when data is lost during a network crash, because of a program bug, or because of user error.

- Corruption, as when data is garbled or partially lost. Another form of corruption is data replacement, as when the original data is intercepted and replaced with a modified version.

Some types of information corruption will be detected through cyclic redundancy checks (CRCs) or other error-detection measures. Efforts to delete a data file may be detected by some network management or virus-detection programs. Successful deletions will be detected the next time the file or database is accessed. (Of course, at that point it probably will be too late to do anything about the deletion.)

Threats to Network Operation

Network operation includes both ordinary network activity, such as transmissions, and meta-activity, such as network monitoring and management.

Threats to network operation include the following:

- Interruption, as when a cable connection is broken or a node on certain types of networks goes down.

- Interference, including jamming, as when electrical noise is introduced deliberately or by random external causes.

- Overload, as when network traffic becomes heavy because of too much ordinary activity or because a virus has been introduced and has replicated itself. When the network is overloaded, data packets may be lost or corrupted.

Networks that use optical signaling are much less susceptible to interference and overload.

Causes of Security Threats and Breaches

The following are the main causes of damage to network components or files:

- Unauthorized access to the network, which can result in theft of the hardware, software, or information.

- Unauthorized use of network information, as in the case of data interception.

- Random events, such as disasters or power anomalies.

Random external events generally threaten hardware directly and the contents of the hardware secondarily. Unauthorized access or use generally threatens software and data directly, while threatening hardware mainly as a means to this end (if at all).

Network operation may be disrupted by random external forces (rats, climate, or chemicals destroying a cable section, for example) or by user carelessness or maliciousness.

Security Goals

The most immediate goal of network security efforts is protect networks from all the types of threats; to make sure that the threatening events do not occur, or at least that they happen as rarely as possible. A second, but equally important, goal is to minimize the effects of security breaches once they have occurred.

As stated, a secure network is one that meets these requirements:

- That is always available to authorized users when needed.

- Whose contents and resources can be modified only by authorized users.

- Whose contents can be read or otherwise displayed only by authorized users.

More specifically, network security measures have the following goals, which together help make for a secure network:

- Prevent malicious damage to network hardware or files; prevent malicious misuse of hardware and software.

- Prevent theft of network components or information.

- Limit accidental damage or destruction of hardware or software, either through user carelessness or environmental events.

- Protect data confidentiality and integrity.

- Prevent unauthorized access to a network and unauthorized use of its resources. This goal includes the more specific one of preventing interception or theft of network files or transmissions.

- Provide for recovery from disasters (fire, flood, theft, and so on). There must be provisions for restoring the network data and getting the network back into service.

Security Measures

To accomplish these goals, measures such as the following are taken when implementing and running the network:

- Physically securing hardware from theft, as well as from fire, flood, and other threats.

- Logically securing hardware, such as by using encryption chips on network interface cards.

Encryption information must be stored in a separate location, in memory that is not directly accessible to the computer. Hardware security measures are necessary for networks that comply with moderate security levels (such as C2) as specified by the National Security Agency (these levels are listed later in this article).

- Use of power-protection devices, such as line conditioners to clean the electrical signals coming into the network components, and uninterruptible or standby power supplies (UPSs or SPSs) to keep the network running long enough to shut down properly in case of a power outage. Depending on the size of the network, only servers and other crucial components (such as hubs or routers) may have UPSs; "secondary" components may have just line conditioners or surge protectors.

- Use of system fault-tolerant servers, which contain redundant components. If the primary component fails, the secondary one immediately takes over. Networks with the highest degree of system-fault tolerance include auxiliary servers, which can take over if the main server fails.

- Use of redundant cabling, which often complements system fault-tolerant measures, provides a secondary set of connections for the network. Each node has two network interface cards, with connectors and cables coming off both.

- Doing regular *and frequent* backups onto tape, disk, or optical media. There are numerous backup strategies, ranging from periodic backups of the entire disk contents, incremental or differential backups, and continuous backups. Backup media should *not* be stored at the same location as the original material. Some tape backup systems allow password protection for tapes, so that only authorized persons can restore the backed up material.

- Use of redundant storage, in which multiple copies of information are stored. Again, various strategies are possible, including measures such as disk mirroring, disk duplexing, or the use of RAID (redundant array of inexpensive disks) technology.

- Use of diskless workstations, to prevent users from copying files or logging transmissions to disk.

- Use of callback modems to prevent unauthorized logins from remote locations. This type of modem takes login calls from users, gets the user's access information, then breaks the connection. If the user's login information and telephone number are valid, the modem will call the user back at a predetermined number to allow the user onto the network.

- Writing data to disk only after the targeted disk area is checked. If this area is defective, the material is redirected on the fly to a safe location. To support this feature, an area of the hard disk, usually about 2 percent of the total storage, is set aside.

- Transaction tracking, in which all the materials related to a transaction are kept in memory (or in temporary buffers on disk) and are written only once the transaction is completed. This scheme protects against data loss if the network goes down in the middle of a transaction.

- Use of audit trails, in which all user actions are recorded and stored.

- Controlling access to certain files or directories (for example, the user account and password data).

- Controlling uploading privileges to minimize the likelihood that someone can deliberately or inadvertently load a virus or other damaging program onto the network. Even if such privileges are strictly controlled, virus-detection software should still be used.

- Use of passwords and other user IDs to control access to the network. With dynamic passwords, users get new passwords (generated by a special device) every time they log in to the network.

- Use of host and key authentication in addition to passwords to ensure that all parties involved in a network connection are allowed to be there.

- Allowing users privileges based on the users' status and needs. For example, general users may have access to only files and applications in public directories and perhaps in their own work directories. Similarly, users may be allowed to access the network only at certain times or from certain nodes.

- Encryption of transmissions to prevent (or at least make more difficult) unauthorized theft of information transmitted across the network. Encryption strategies can use public- or secret-key encryption systems. (See the Encryption article for a discussion of the differences among these strategies.) Encryption cannot prevent interception of transmission; it can only make the contents of the transmission more difficult to read.

- Traffic padding, to make the level of network traffic more constant, thus making it more difficult for an eavesdropper to infer network contents.

- Use of various verification activities, such as message authentication codes (MACs) to determine whether a message has been received as sent. These codes are more sophisticated than ordinary CRCs, because the checksum that is attached is also encrypted. MACs make it much more difficult to intercept and modify a message (including its error-detection fields). Other verification activities include the use of digital signatures, notarization, and origin and destination non-repudiation.

- Recording and reporting efforts to access a network by an unauthorized user (for exam-
ple, by someone trying to guess a password or trying to log in at an unauthorized time). Such attempts should be reported to the system administrator and the network management facilities, through the use of alarms or other means. (See the Security Management article for more information about security-related alarms.)

- Packet filtering, or transmission of packets only to the destination node. For example, sophisticated hubs and concentrators can determine the destination for a packet, then transmit the packet to that node and transmit gibberish to the other nodes. This makes eavesdropping more difficult, if not impossible.

Most of the preceding security measures can be taken to several levels. Networks that need to conform to government security guidelines must implement particularly stringent and costly security measures. In general, the more security measures and redundancy built into a network, the more expensive the network will be.

Similarly, many of the security measures mentioned may be implemented at any of several functional levels in the OSI reference model.

Although the general form of security goals may not change significantly over time, security measures must evolve and change constantly, to keep up with the new methods that are developed to gain unauthorized access to networks and to steal their contents.

Government Security Levels

Four general security classes are defined in a government publication called the *Trusted Computer System Evaluation Criteria* but more commonly known as the Orange Book. The four classes are, in order of increasing security, as follows:

- Class D (minimal security)

- Class C (discretionary protection)

- Class B (mandatory protection)

- Class A (verified protection)

Class D Security

Class D includes all systems that cannot meet any of the higher security criteria. Systems in this class cannot be considered secure. Examples of class D systems include PC operating systems such as MS-DOS or System 7 for the Macintosh.

Class C Security

Class C is divided into C1 and the somewhat more secure C2. Operating systems such as UNIX or network operating systems that provide password protection and access rights might fall into either of these classes (most likely into C1).

C1 security features include the use of passwords or other authentication measures, the ability to restrict access to files and resources, and the ability to prevent accidental destruction of system programs.

In addition to the C1 features, C2 systems include the ability to audit or track all user activity, restrict operations for individual users, and make sure that data left in memory cannot be used by other programs or users.

Class B Security

Class B is divided into three levels. In general, class B systems must be able to provide mathematical documentation of security, actively seek out threats to security, and be able to maintain security even during system failure.

B1 systems must have all the security capabilities of a C2 system and then some. B1 systems must take all available security measures and separate the security-related system components from the ones that are not related to security. B1 documentation must include discussions of the security measures.

B2 systems must have the same as B1, as well as be able to provide a mathematical description of the security system, manage all configuration changes (software updates, and so on) in a secure manner, and check explicitly to make sure new software does not have any backdoors or other ways through which an outsider might try to access the secure system.

B3 systems must have a system administrator in charge of security, and must remain secure even if the system goes down.

Class A Security

A1 systems must be able to verify mathematically that their security system and policy match the security design specifications.

Security Accounts Manager (SAM)

→ *See* SAM (Security Accounts Manager)

Security Analysis Tool for Auditing Networks (SATAN)

→ *See* SATAN (Security Analysis Tool for Auditing Networks)

Security Management

Security management is one of five OSI network management domains specified by the ISO and CCITT. The purpose of security management in the OSI network management model is to provide a secure network as defined in the entry on security and to notify the system administrator of any efforts to compromise or breach this secure network. Very generally, a secure network is one that is always accessible when needed and whose contents can be accessed—read and modified—only by authorized users.

To accomplish these goals, the security management component needs to be able to determine all (actual and potential) access points to the network, and to make sure these points cannot be breached or compromised. If an unauthorized access occurs, the component must be able to provide the system administrator with the information needed to identify and locate the security threat.

Identifying Access Points

The most common access points to a network are the network's nodes, both local and remote. Less obvious access points include cables, air waves, and programs. For example, a potential thief can tap into a transmission line or simply pick a wireless transmission out of the air.

Programs can also be used to get illicit access to a network. For example, a program might be able to log in to network activity in secret or redirect program output to an unauthorized location. Many breaches of large networks (such as the Internet) occur because someone manages to sneak in a program that captures passwords as they move across the network.

In certain network architectures, notably Ethernet and Token Ring networks, all packets pass through every node. In these types of networks, it is easy to steal information from the network just by reading all packets that pass through one's node, regardless of whether the node is the packet's destination. In fact, network monitors operate by simply reading everything that goes by.

Some access points are extremely subtle. These provide information about the network activity through indirect measures, such as analysis of network traffic patterns. Although these measures may not immediately provide information about the contents of the network traffic, the patterns observed may provide enough of an entry to enable an eavesdropper eventually to decipher the contents.

For example, if a large company regularly sends a long transmission from the payroll computer to a bank the evening before every payday, an industrial spy might reasonably infer that funds are being transferred, and might eventually be able to extract account numbers or other useful information from this transmission, even if the transmission is encrypted.

Securing Access Points

The simplest way to secure an access point is to deny access to unauthorized users or listeners. Depending on the type of access point involved, there are many ways to do this. Some of the most common measures involve an authentication process of the machines, users, message, and/or encryption keys. Other security measures are described in the Security article.

The OSI network management model does not specify how such authentication is to be carried out. As yet, the model does not provide protocols for accomplishing authentication.

Security Alarms

An alarm is a signal used to indicate that something is not functioning as it should. The OSI network management model includes several types of alarms, which are used to indicate fault, performance, and security problems.

Alarms may refer to any of several facets of a network connection, and they should indicate how serious the problem is; that is, they should let the administrator know how quickly something needs to be done about the problem. Five types of security alarms are distinguished, each of which is used for a different network violation:

- Integrity violation, which indicates that network contents or objects have been illegally modified, deleted, or added.

- Operational violation, which indicates that a desired object or service could not be used.

- Physical violation, which indicates that a physical part of the network (such as a cable) has been damaged or modified without authorization.

- Security-mechanism violation, which indicates that the network's security system has been compromised or breached.

- Time-domain violation, which indicates that an event has happened outside its allowed or typical time slot.

Alarms may be at any of half a dozen severity levels. *Critical* and *major* alarms are given when a condition that affects service has arisen. For a critical alarm, steps must be taken immediately in order to restore the service. For a major alarm, steps must be taken as soon as possible, because the affected service has degraded drastically and is in danger of being lost completely.

Minor alarms indicate a problem that does not yet affect service, but that may do so if the problem is not corrected. *Warning* alarms are used to signal a potential problem that may affect service. Depending on the specific case, more diagnostic work may be needed before it makes sense to do something about the potential problem.

Indeterminate alarms are given if it is not possible to determine how serious the problem is. The system administrator will need to make a judgment about the problems that lead to alarms, and may need to decide how to proceed.

A *cleared* alarm is given when a problem has been taken care of. Such an alarm is needed in order to make it possible to automate (much of) the alarm-reporting process.

→ **Broader Category** Network Management

→ **See Also** Accounting Management; Configuration Management; Fault Management; Performance Management

Seed Router

In an AppleTalk internetwork, a router that defines the network number ranges for all other routers in the network and that makes it possible to assign node addresses in AppleTalk networks. Each AppleTalk internetwork needs at least one seed router.

Seek Time

The amount of time needed to move the read/write heads in a hard disk to a specified sector and track.

→ **Compare** Access Time

Segmentation

In networks that conform to the OSI reference model, segmentation is the process by which a packet is broken into parts and packed into several packets at a lower layer. Segmentation may be necessary because of packet-size restrictions at certain layers.

When a packet is segmented, the data portion is broken in parts, each part is combined with the header and with segment sequence information. The packet is passed down to the layer below for further processing (for example, for encapsulation into the lower-layer packets).

The reverse process, removing redundant headers and recombining several segments into the original packet, is known as *reassembly*.

At a larger level, segmentation is also used to describe the situation in which a large local area network (LAN) is divided into smaller, more manageable ones.

In the Internet community, segmentation refers to the process of breaking a TCP (Transmission Control Protocol) message into smaller parts before passing it down to the IP (Internet Protocol) layer. The term *fragmentation* is used to refer to the process of breaking down IP packets into smaller parts (known as IP datagrams) to be passed down to the Data-Link layer.

Selector

In the OSI reference model, a value used at a specific layer to distinguish each of the multiple service access points (SAPs) through which the entity at that level provides services to the layer above it.

Sequenced Packet Protocol (SPP)

→ **See** SPP (Sequenced Packet Protocol)

Serial Line Internet Protocol (SLIP)

→ *See* Protocol, SLIP (Serial Line Internet Protocol)

Serial Port

A hardware port in which only one pin is available for data transmission in a given direction, so that bits must be transmitted in sequence. The wiring for a port is almost always associated with a particular physical interface (for example, RS-232). A serial port is also known as a COM, or communications, port, and is used most commonly for a modem, printer, or mouse.

Server

Most generally, a server is an entity that provides some type of network service. The server may be hardware, such as a file server in a network, or software, such as network level protocol for a transport level client. The services may be access to files or devices, transport or translation facilities, and so on.

The server provides its service to other machines (workstations) on the network or to other processes. The illustration "Context of servers in networks" shows how hardware servers fit into the larger networking scheme.

In a server-based network, the most important hardware server is the *file server*, which controls access to the files and data stored on one or more hard disks. In most cases, local area networks (LANs) have PC-sized machines as file servers, although minicomputers and mainframes can also be file servers in networks. See the Server, File article for a detailed discussion of file servers.

At the PC level, the architectural choices for workstations and servers include the following:

- Machines using a segmented architecture, based on Intel's 80*x*86 chip series. This chip architecture is also used in clone chips from AMD, Cyrix, and other companies, and in the Pentium, Intel's successor to the 80*x*86 family.

- Machines based on Motorola's 68000 family of chips, such as Macintosh or NeXT.

- Machines based on a RISC (reduced instruction set computing) chip set, such as Sun SPARCstations.

Servers are usually personal computers or machines such as SPARCstations, but they could also be mainframes. Special-purpose servers, such as network modems, can have their own network interface cards (NICs) and can be connected directly to a network. Once connected, the modems can serve as access, or communications, servers.

Dedicated versus Nondedicated Servers

A server may be dedicated or nondedicated. Dedicated servers are used only as a server, not as a workstation. Nondedicated servers are used as both a server and workstation. Networks with a dedicated server are known as *server-based networks*; those with nondedicated servers are known as *peer-to-peer*, or just *peer, networks*.

Dedicated Servers

Dedicated servers cannot be used for ordinary work. In fact, access to the server itself is often limited. In the most security-conscious environments, the server's keyboard is removed, and the server is locked away to prevent any access by unauthorized users.

Most high-end network packages assume a dedicated server. If a network has a dedicated server, this is most likely a file server. In the networking literature, when you see references to *servers*, without any qualifier, the discussion usually concerns dedicated file servers.

A dedicated file server runs the network operating system (NOS) software, and workstations run smaller programs whose job is to direct user commands to the workstation's operating system or to the server, as appropriate. Both servers and workstations need NICs to function on the network, at least in PC environments.

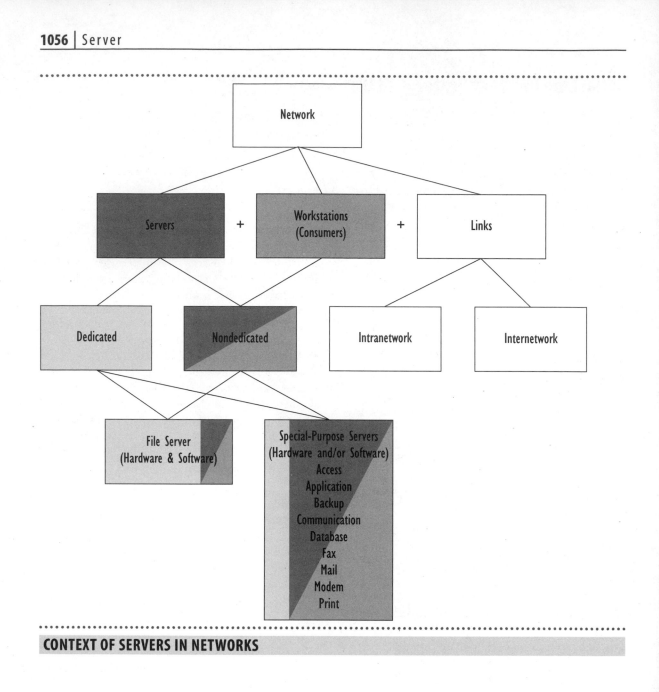

CONTEXT OF SERVERS IN NETWORKS

LOCKING UP THE SERVER

It's not a bad idea to put a dedicated server in a location to which access can be controlled. Removing the keyboard is not an adequate solution if any degree of security is required, since a potential interloper can bring a keyboard.

If the server is locked in a room, make sure the room has adequate ventilation and a clean enough power supply for the hardware. Also be sure to keep a tight rein on the keys to the room.

Nondedicated Servers

A nondedicated server can also be used as a workstation. Using a server as a workstation has several serious disadvantages, however, and is not advised for larger networks.

The following are some of the disadvantages of nondedicated servers compared with dedicated servers:

- Many of the NOSs that allow nondedicated servers run on top of DOS, which makes them extremely slow and clumsy. In contrast, most dedicated servers have software that replaces DOS, at least while the network is up and running. Such systems may also require a separate, non-DOS partition on your hard disk. Since this partition is under the direct control of the NOS (as opposed to being controlled indirectly through DOS), the NOS can arrange and deal with the contents of the partition in a way that optimizes performance.

- Running applications on a DOS machine while it is also supposed to be running a network can lead to a deadly performance degradation.

- Certain tasks will tie up a DOS-based machine, effectively stopping the network until the task is finished. For some devices that expect responses within a fixed amount of time, such as with modems or fax machines, this can lead to an error or fault condition because of the

time-out. This is less of a danger on machines that are capable of true multitasking.

- Adequate security is more difficult to maintain on a nondedicated server.

Generic versus Proprietary Servers

A generic server is one that is designed for use with vendor-independent networking software and hardware components, provided these components conform to industry standards (either official or de facto).

In contrast, a proprietary server runs a proprietary operating system and is designed to be used with a particular vendor's hardware and software. Not too many years ago, several of the major network vendors, such as 3Com, sold proprietary servers. These types of servers are no longer in vogue; the move is toward generic servers. These days, almost all LANs can be made of generic components.

Server Maintenance

It is important to set up a maintenance schedule for your server and strictly adhere to that schedule. To check the hardware, you should do at least the following things every few weeks (at the very longest interval):

- Clean the server carefully but thoroughly. Cleaning should include removing the dust balls that have accumulated around the fan and inside the machine since the last cleaning.

- Check cabling and connections for tightness and for signs of bending or stress. Do not disconnect connectors unless necessary, since many connectors are rated for a limited number of matings (attachment to another connector).

- If possible, check the cabling with a line analyzer.

- Run thorough diagnostics on the storage medium and on other system components to identify the components that are likely to fail and to deal with these before they actually do fail. Make sure the diagnostic program you plan to use is compatible with the hard disk format and with the networking software you are running.

- Check the quality of your power line by using a line tester. If the line shows lots of surges and/or sags during the testing, you are putting your network (and possibly your net worth) in danger, even if you use line conditioners, surge protectors, or UPSs. These safety devices can protect your system, but not forever. In fact, some surge protectors are designed to withstand only a single large surge.

The tricky part of server maintenance is finding the time to do it, since the network will need to be down, possibly for an extended period. In many cases, server maintenance will need to be done during those early morning hours when other servers all over the country are also being maintained.

Server Backups

Any adequate maintenance work should include regular backups onto tape or perhaps to optical media. Depending on how much work gets done on the network in a day and on how important the work is, backups may need to be done daily or every couple of days. The longer you wait between backups, the more work you can potentially lose.

Superservers

Several manufacturers have developed special-purpose machines that are specifically designed to be file servers. These superserver machines are souped up in one or more ways, including the following:

- Additional RAM, which may be used for whatever purpose the NOS deems most appropriate.

- Multiple processors, which can be used in whatever manner makes the most sense for the network. Although the current generation of networking software does not take

advantage of the processing power, the next generation of NOSs is expected to be able to do so.

- Extra expansion slots, to hold bridges, routers, or NICs.

- Redundant hard drive systems, to speed up disk access and throughput and also for data security.

Special-Purpose Servers

As long as there are developers and users, new services will be provided on networks. As long as services are provided, new types of servers will be specified. The same server machine can perform several of these roles simultaneously. For example, the file server can also serve as a print and fax server. In general, giving the file server double duty is a mixed blessing, and should be given careful consideration before you implement it.

The various special-purpose servers are discussed in separate articles. For example, see the Server, Access article for information about access servers.

→ *Broader Category*   Hardware

→ *Compare*   Workstation

→ *See Also*   Server, Access; Server, ACS (Asynchronous Communications Server); Server, Application; Server, ART (Asynchronous Remote Takeover); Server, Backup; Server, Communication; Server, Database; Server, Fax; Server, File; Server, Modem; Server, Print

Server, Access

An access server is a special type of communications server, designed for handling calls to the network from remote locations. A user dials into the access server, and the user's session appears as if it were running locally. Access servers are generally, but not necessarily, dedicated machines with special hardware for providing access services.

The access server hardware can include multiple cards, housed in a separate box or plugged into a node in the network. Each card has its own processor and may have multiple ports to handle multiple calls simultaneously. When there are multiple cards with CPUs (central processing units), the access server is said to be using a multi-CPU architecture. The processor that provides access to the network is known as the host.

Another way to configure an access server is to use a single card with a multitasking CPU capable of time-sharing. Multiple CPUs cost more but are more reliable, since failure of a single processor will not shut down the access server.

Networked modems have also been used as access servers.

In the mainframe world, an access server, or access hub, provides a way for users at terminals to communicate with a network that has a mainframe or minicomputer as the host machine.

→ **See Also** Server, Communication

Server, ACS (Asynchronous Communications Server)

An ACS is usually a dedicated PC that provides nodes with access to any of several serial ports or modems. The ports may be connected to mainframes or minicomputers.

When a user on a workstation wants access to a modem or a port, the user simply runs an ordinary communications program in a transparent manner. In order for this to work, one of the following must be the case:

- The communications program must include a redirector (to route the communication process to the appropriate server).

- The workstation must have a special hardware port emulation board installed. In that case, the communications package does not

require any special rerouting capabilities (but each workstation does lose an expansion slot).

- You must run a redirection program before starting the communications package. To work with such a software-based redirector, the communications package must be able to use DOS interrupt INT 0x14. Unfortunately, many communications programs bypass this interrupt to access the UART (universal asynchronous receiver/transmitter) directly for faster operation.

→ **See Also** Server, Communication

Server, Application

An application server is generally a dedicated machine that runs applications for workstations. Client-based applications execute on the workstation, and they require any necessary data files to be transferred from the server to the workstation. Using application servers can improve a file server's performance by offloading some of the file server's processing tasks.

Server-based applications run in two chunks: the front end runs on the workstation, and the back end runs on the server. In this way, the workstation can give commands and make requests through the front end, but the actual work and retrieval is done at the back end (on the server). Because of this, only the data processed or returned by the application needs to be sent to the workstation. When working with databases or spreadsheets, this can save considerable time. The tradeoff is that the server is busier because it may have to deal with several application back ends at a time.

Server-based applications are also known as *network-intrinsic*, because they are designed to run in a network environment. In contrast, client-based applications are either *network-aware* or *network-ignorant*. A network-aware application knows that more than one user may be working at the same time and takes any necessary precautions to ensure the users cannot accidentally destroy each other's work by working on the same part of the same file simultaneously.

To avoid problems, do not run network-ignorant applications over a network, because you risk corrupting your files. Also, you may be violating the software license.

Server, Archive

An archive server consists of software to keep track of file usage, to identify files that have not been used in a while (and that are, therefore, candidates for storage on a removable medium). Archiving services are often included with a backup or tape server.

Server, ART (Asynchronous Remote Takeover)

An ART server consists of software to provide a remote caller with access to resources of the local machine or network. The ARTS server receives input from the remote user and passes it to the local node, as if the input had come from the local keyboard. The server then captures any output at the local node and sends it to the remote location.

The result of all this remote user and server activity is that a keyboard in Kansas, running at an ARTT (Asynchronous Remote Takeover Terminal), can operate a stand-alone or networked computer in Chicago. The ART server will send Chicago's screen output to Kansas for display on the ARTT screen.

Server, Asynchronous Connection Transport

An asynchronous connection transport server consists of software to provide access to resources, such as electronic mail (e-mail) services, over telephone lines. This type of server does not require a dedicated machine.

Server, Authentication

An authentication server has the task of verifying that users logging onto a network are allowed to do so. Authentication servers can use any of several methods to check this.

In the simplest case, the server may not require any authentication. Users may simply be able to log in anonymously or under their own user name. However, in such cases, the server should allow access only to public areas of the network.

More stringent authentication checks include passwords or some sort of challenge authentication process—for example, CHAP (Challenge Handshake Authentication Protocol) or Microsoft's extension of this (MS-CHAP).

→ **Broader Category** Security

→ **See Also** Protocol, CHAP (Challenge Handshake Authentication Protocol); Protocol, MS-CHAP (Microsoft CHAP).

Server, Backup

A backup server can carry out system shutdowns and backups at regular or specified intervals. The server runs the backup software, which generally can notify all nodes of the impending backup, enable all nodes to end their sessions, and perform the required backup. Software for backups is usually included with the network software. There are also many good backup packages provided by third-party vendors.

Backup servers do not require dedicated machines. Backup services are often provided together with an archive server to keep track of file usage.

Backups may be to disk, tape, or to an optical medium such as WORM (write once, read memory) or EO (erasable optical) disks. In practice, backup to floppy disks is rarely done for networks, because the number of disks and the time required would be prohibitive. Backups to hard disk cartridges are much more common.

In practice, backups must be accompanied by regular and scrupulous disk cleaning and purging. Any files that are no longer used or needed should be removed, to increase the available storage and also decrease the amount of material that must be backed up. (DOS also gets very slow when directories have a large number of files.)

Make sure that the network software you intend to use supports any backup media you intend to use on the network. For example, if you intend to use a WORM drive for backup, make sure the network software's backup utilities support such drives. You may need special drivers in order to make this support possible.

Server-Based Network

A network in which one or more nodes have special status as dedicated servers. Other nodes (workstations) must go through a server for resources on other machines. This is in contrast to a peer-to-peer network, in which each node may be either server or workstation as the need arises.

→ *See Also* LAN (Local Area Network)

Server, Batch-Processing

A batch-processing server consists of software to carry out the tasks specified in batch files. This makes it possible to offload mechanical but time-consuming tasks, such as report generation, to an idle workstation. Batch-processing services are provided by third-party software. A batch-processing server does not require a dedicated machine.

Server, Communication

The term communication server applies to any of several types of servers that provide access to one or more modems and telephone lines. The server also runs the programs needed to establish connections with other machines, prepares files as needed, and sends or receives data. A communications server may be a dedicated machine or it may reside on a workstation.

A communication server may also provide access for remote control programs, which allow users to dial into the network from remote locations. For remote capabilities, special boards are usually required. For heavy remote traffic, you may need to dedicate a machine, known as an *access server*, to this service.

Some communications servers can provide terminal emulation for access to mainframes and minicomputers. Some can also provide connections to remote systems or networks.

Commonly used communications servers include the following:

- Gateways for access to mainframes.

- Asynchronous communications servers for access to dial-out modems.

- Remote access servers for access *from* remote locations.

Communications servers are also known as *dial-in/dial-out* servers.

Server Console

In Novell's NetWare, the console (monitor and keyboard) at which the network supervisor controls and views the activity of the server. From this console, the supervisor can do the following tasks:

- Load and unload NetWare Loadable Modules (NLMs), to change the network's capabilities.

- Configure the network.

- Send messages.

- View network activity.

- Shut down the server.

When not in use, the server console should always be secured from access. For example, the keyboard and monitor might be locked up in a room.

S

It is also possible to use a remote keyboard and monitor as a server console. A remote console allows a workstation to serve as the server console at another location.

Server, Content

An ISP (Internet Service Provider) uses a content server to present the ISP's home page to subscribers who log on through the provider. The content server will use a Web server to display this page and other pages at the site. The content server may also use other servers for specific purposes—for example, a terminal server (to receive subscribers' calls over their modems) or an authentication server (to make sure the caller is a subscriber in good standing).

Server, DAL (Data Access Language)

A DAL server consists of software to provide access to databases using DAL, which is Apple's extension of the SQL (Structured Query Language) database-manipulation language developed originally for use on IBM mainframes.

DAL servers are available for a variety of platforms, ranging from PCs to minicomputers and mainframes. On each platform, the server can provide transparent access to the major database management systems (DBMSs) available on that platform.

A DAL server does not require a dedicated machine.

Server, Database

A database server consists of software to provide access to database records for programs running on other nodes. A database server often runs on the network's file server, but does not require a dedicated machine.

This type of server is useful only if it can do the actual record retrieval and storage on the server, so

that it is not necessary to send entire databases between the server and workstation (client). Because of this, database servers are used mainly in client/server local area networks (LANs), in conjunction with special programs that can run a back-end component to do the work on the server and a front-end interface for a user on the workstation.

An SQL (Structured Query Language) server is a special type of database server designed for use with the SQL, which is probably the most commonly used database language.

Server, Directory

Software that provides access to directory information and directory services (DS) for other nodes on the network. A directory server does not require a dedicated machine.

Server, Disk

A disk server consists of a machine and software to control access to one or more hard disks and to any programs and data files stored there. This term has fallen into disuse because of the advent of file servers, which provide disk access as well as other types of services. Disk servers are often, but not necessarily, dedicated machines.

Server, Display

In the X Window graphics environment for UNIX, a display server (also known as an *X server*) is a hardware-dependent program that runs on the user's machine and that is responsible for controlling the display for whatever work is being done for the user.

A display server is not a server in the same sense as network-related servers are. The terminology for X Window (or X, as it is called) is in contrast to standard networking terminology. In this case, the server is actually the program that is fed data from another process or device, which is usually the role of a client.

In X, the *client* program is actually the one doing whatever task has been requested by the user. The client is a hardware-independent process whose job is to do the requested work and to feed the results to the user's workstation. It is the job of the display server to determine what to do with the results.

The details of the interface for the X window used by the display server are determined by a window manager program. Open Look from Sun Microsystems and Motif from the Open Software Foundation are examples of window managers.

Server, Fax

With a fax server (also known as a *facsimile server*), you can send a fax directly from your workstation, even if the fax machine is attached to a computer in another room or building. A fax server consists of software to provide access to one or more fax machines, and it runs the programs needed to prepare and send a fax or to receive one.

A fax server saves paper, since it is no longer necessary to print a file in order to fax it. The server will take the file, make any required conversions, attach a cover page, queue, and send the fax. A user can accomplish all this without leaving the workstation. Similarly, the fax server will receive faxes, make any required conversions, and store the fax on the file server until the recipient is ready to deal with the fax.

Fax servers do not require dedicated machines.

Server, File

A file server exerts considerable control over a network since all transactions go through this component. The illustration "File server processing a workstation request" shows one conception of the steps involved when a node (workstation) requests something from a file server.

A file server has one or more network interface cards (NICs), through which it runs the network.

Multiple NICs are needed if the server is working with more than one network architecture.

File Server Functions

In addition to controlling access to file and disk resources on a network, a file server is responsible for security and synchronization on the network. Security measures taken are designed to ensure that only authorized users can access a particular file. Synchronization measures, such as file or record locking, help ensure that two users cannot do incompatible things to the same file or record simultaneously.

File services are generally implemented in software, and they are a central part of the network operating system (NOS). Depending on the NOS, these services may run on top of the "standard" operating system (for example, DOS, OS/2, or UNIX), rather than being run in a network-based operating system.

File servers for a particular NOS are often named after the NOS. For example, you will see references to an AppleShare or a NetWare server, when the discussion concerns Apple's or Novell's NOSs.

File Server Requirements

An effective file server must be fast, reliable, and provide sufficient storage for all the data and programs users need. The server also needs enough memory to load whatever drivers and other programs are needed to run the network. (Note that other types of servers, such as print or fax servers, may not need heavy-duty hardware.) These needs can be at least partly fulfilled by configuring a file server with the appropriate hardware and software, which are discussed in the following sections.

The system components for the file server should be robust and reliable. The hardware components should be thoroughly tested, and they should have a long mean time before failure (MTBF): several hundred thousands of hours, at least. Some file servers actually have redundant components, so that a backup component can be put into service if the main component fails.

S

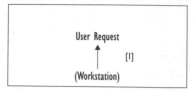

[1] The user at a workstation makes a request, either at the command line or through an application.

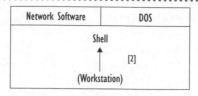

[2] This request is intercepted by the network shell running on the workstation to determine whether the request is for DOS or for the network. If it is for DOS, the request is passed on to DOS and the shell's job is finished (for the moment).

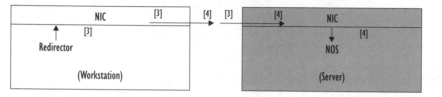

[3] Requests passed to the redirector are passed to the NIC, where they are packaged and sent onto the network, using whatever packet format and media-access method are supported by the NIC.

[4] The request is received by an NIC on the server, and it is unpackaged and passed to the network-level protocol being used on the server.

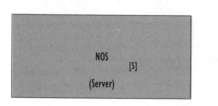

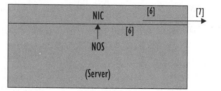

[5] The server processes the request to determine whether the user is allowed to make such a request and, if so, to take whatever steps are necessary to carry it out. This may require sending a response, some data, or even a program to the workstation.

[6] To respond, the server's NOS passes the response to the server's NIC. (The server knows the source of the request and will pass the response to the appropriate NIC in cases where there are multiple NICs in the server.) The NIC packages the response and sends it onto the network.

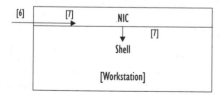

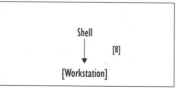

[7] The workstation's NIC catches the response and does whatever unpackaging is necessary to pass the response to the workstation's shell.

[8] The shell passes the response to the destination application, going through any required protocols or protocol levels to do this.

FILE SERVER PROCESSING A WORKSTATION REQUEST

To compensate for all the special requirements for a good file server, you can take a tiny bit of comfort in the fact that you do not need a fancy keyboard or graphics capabilities for your file server. In fact, many file servers have a simple monochrome VGA monitor. If your funds are limited, use the money for RAM (random-access memory) or other server components.

When you are shopping for a file server, it pays to investigate the track record of potential vendors. Also, you should check on the speed and quality of customer support and service. If the server goes down, you will need to get it up and running as quickly as possible.

File Server Processor

A fast Pentium processor is essential for a file server. Although some NOSs allow 80486 machines as servers, the greater memory flexibility afforded by the 80386 and 80486 is crucial for bringing the server's performance up to an acceptable level. Similarly, since the file server will spend a great deal of its time moving data between memory and storage and across the network, you need to make sure the processor can manipulate data in big chunks. For this reason, avoid using the half-width SL processors, which must do their work on "half a bus," as file servers.

Another processor consideration is clock speed, which specifies the number of cycles in a second. Since all actions in ordinary processors take at least a cycle, the shorter this period is, the faster a processor can work.

The original PC had a 4.77 megahertz (MHz) clock speed; high-end machines today have processors with clock speeds of 450MHz and higher. Again, faster is better only up to a point. Beyond that, other considerations come into play. For example, heat dissipation becomes more difficult, which makes the processor more susceptible to overheating and breakdown.

Also, speeding up the processor does not speed up any other components, so that the processor may need to spend its time waiting. The periods during which the processor waits for other components to catch up are called *wait states*. Each wait state is a cycle on the CPU (central processing unit) clock. In general, a processor with one or more wait states will be slower than a comparable processor without wait states.

File Server Memory

Several megabytes of RAM—64MB at the very least, preferably 128MB or more—are also crucial in a file server. Since caching can greatly improve performance, you should use some of the server's memory to create such a cache.

The optimum amount of memory to use for a cache must be determined by empirical means. Larger is better up to a point. When a cache is too small, it will be less likely that the required data is already in the cache area. However, when a cache is too large, the caching software may have too much material to administrate, so that the software spends too much time checking whether something is already in the cache. Different NOSs have different memory requirements.

File Server Storage

A good file server needs at least several hundred megabytes of fast-access hard disk storage. The desirable storage capacity depends on the size of the network. Some experts suggest 50MB of storage per user as a rough rule of thumb. Smaller allotments are probably fine for most networks, but larger estimates are advisable if future expansion would be a problem. Other considerations regarding hard disks on a file server are discussed later in this article.

Storage becomes even more of an issue with special technologies, such as RAID (redundant array of inexpensive disks), which can provide fault-tolerant storage, at the cost of much greater storage demands.

File Server Power Supply

A properly running server needs a *more than adequate* power supply and a good fan to make sure the working conditions for system components include sufficient power and proper air circulation.

S

File Server Safety Devices

A UPS (uninterruptible power supply) or SPS (standby power supply), along with surge-suppression and line-conditioning capabilities, are essential for protecting a network from power supply problems. Surge suppression and line conditioning are built into most backup power supplies. See the UPS and SPS articles for a discussion of the criteria and features to consider when selecting and installing these devices.

File Server NICs

Because the file server interacts most heavily with the network, responding to the requests of all the other nodes, it is important to provide this server with the most powerful NIC. Factors that can improve the performance of an NIC include the following:

- Dedicated processor on the NIC, to make the board more capable and more intelligent, thereby enabling the NIC to take over some of the chores that would ordinarily tie up the server's CPU.

- Amount of RAM on the NIC, to serve as a buffer or cache for material moving between the server and the network. The more checking and temporary storage that can be left to the NIC, the less work the server needs to do.

- Size of data bus (8-, 16-, or 32-bit). For the file server, get the widest data bus possible.

- Whether the NIC supports bus mastering, which allows the NIC to seize the system bus when necessary, without bothering the CPU. If so, make sure the bus-mastering schemes used by the computer and the NIC are compatible.

Hard Disks as File Server Components

Since much of a file server's activity involves sending or receiving data files, disk access can easily become a performance bottleneck. Network analyzer and diagnostic programs can provide statistics to help you decide whether the hard disk is being a bottleneck. For example, the statistic for average

disk I/O (input/output) operations pending gives a rough idea of how far the hard disk and controller have fallen behind because of demands from the nodes. While there are no hard and fast values, a level of 20 to 25 pending I/O actions is sometimes used as a cut-off point. If there are typically more than this many requests waiting, the hard disk is responsible for at least part of the slow performance.

One way to improve matters is to add a second hard disk controller and associate one or more of the hard drives with this controller. Then the hard disk access can be split over two disks, so that the controllers can work independently of each other.

Once you get a second controller, you can switch from disk mirroring to disk duplexing as a data-protection strategy. The former uses a single controller to write the same data to two different disks; the latter uses separate controllers to do this writing, thereby speeding things up considerably.

With a fast-access hard disk and a suitably sized cache, performance can be improved greatly. A hard disk's speed is reflected in three types of data:

- Access time, which is the average amount of time it takes to move the read/write heads to a specified location and to retrieve the data at that location. The lower the value, the better. Currently, hard disks with average access times of less than 15 milliseconds (msec) are common.

- Seek time, which is the amount of time it takes to move the read heads a track and then to wait until the appropriate sector on the target track is under the read head.

- Transfer rate, which represents the amount of data that can be transferred between the disk and memory in a second. This rate ranges from a few hundred kilobytes per second to 10Mbps for high-end hard disks.

Another hard disk feature that affects server performance is called *sector interleave*. This ratio reflects the ordering of sectors within a track. An interleave of 1:1 indicates that the sectors are arranged consecutively in a track. Other things being equal, this interleave will give the fastest transfer rate. A 2:1 ratio means there is one sector between sectors *x* and *x+1*; a 3:1 ratio indicates that there are *two* sectors between sectors *x* and *x+1*, and so on.

For some hard disks it is possible to arrange this ordering—to change the interleave—in order to speed up access to the data in a track. Not all hard disks take kindly to interleave changes. Do not adjust the interleave without making sure your hard disk controller will allow it, and without being fairly sure the new interleave will speed up hard disk performance.

The hard disk controller is another performance factor. This controller mediates between the hard disk and the computer's BIOS and bus. The controller makes the hard disk's read/write heads do what is needed and passes data between the hard disk and BIOS.

Some hard disk controllers have caches of their own to speed up performance, which may or may not conflict with software caches. Even if hardware and software caches do not conflict, adding a software cache may not improve performance significantly. In that case, dropping or decreasing the size of the software cache can free memory that can be put to better use. Determining the optimal cache setup will be an empirical question. Note that 16-bit controllers can transfer twice as much data at a time as 8-bit controllers.

SCSI DRIVES FOR FILE SERVERS

SCSI drives provide the best expansion capability and potential performance for a network file server. You can have up to seven drives on a SCSI host adapter, and the NOS may be able to handle multiple adapters. For example, Novell's NetWare allows up to five SCSI host adapters.

The more intelligent SCSI adapters have a connect/disconnect feature that allows the adapter to connect to a drive when that drive needs service, disconnect when done to provide service to another drive, and then reconnect when necessary to the earlier drive. In this way, each drive gets the adapter's attention when the drive needs it, so there is no time lost during waiting.

Allocating and Controlling Storage on the File Server

Unfortunately, the storage capacity of a file server cannot be unlimited. Consequently, you may quickly run into storage problems, in the form of limited available space or extremely large numbers of files.

To avoid storage problems, it is important to estimate storage requirements as accurately as possible when planning the network. As stated, a basic rule of thumb is to allocate about 50MB of storage per user.

Once you have your estimate, double it, and use this as a starting point for your storage requirements. If the network is expected to grow, either arrange for the additional storage right away or make sure that the storage capabilities of the server can be expanded.

To keep the file numbers from getting out of hand (and also to limit the amount of storage space being used), you can use the following measures:

- Do not allow users to store games and other "non-network" materials on the server's hard disk. This restriction also helps decrease the likelihood of virus attacks.

- Clean up the directories regularly, removing files that are no longer needed or that have not been used in a long time. The latter files may be allowed to stay unless the storage problems are severe. Before doing file cleaning, warn users so that they can save whichever files they want.

→ *See Also* Server

Server, Gateway

A gateway server provides a network or an application with access to resources on mainframes or in other remote environments, such as electronic mail (e-mail) services. Gateway servers include software and may also include hardware; and they generally use dedicated machines.

Server, Internet

An Internet server is configured to handle client requests coming in over the Internet. The majority of these requests will probably be from browsers belonging to clients calling from remote locations unknown. The needs for such a server are likely to be different from those for a LAN (local area network) server, for example.

An Internet server will probably have a greater need for memory and processing ability than for storage. This is because the server is likely to have a limited amount of material, but that material may potentially be accessed by hundreds of clients at a time. (There are numerous stories of servers getting thousands or even tens of thousands of requests— for example, after a favorable article or other media exposure.)

Most of these clients will be accessing the server's content over low-to-medium speed lines. Because the materials returned by the server will also be delivered over these lines, it is important to give consideration to bandwidth and location limitations when designing Web pages.

The number of potential clients is in the millions, and there is no way of knowing who these clients are or what their intentions might be. Because of this, security must be a very high priority for an Internet server. In fact, several kinds of security must be taken into account, including the following:

System and file integrity, which essentially refers to attacks on the server and its contents, must be protected. Use of anti-virus programs, login monitors, and so forth can help with this aspect of security. The NTFS (New Technology File System) includes security features to help protect files. Also, the use of firewalls can help prevent undesired access. And, of course, sensitive files should never be stored on such a server or in a location where they are accessible from the server. Ideally, an Internet server should be isolated from the rest of the corporate network—either physically or by a firewall.

Transaction integrity, which concerns the security of information—possibly personal information—moving between a client and the server, must also be ensured. To ensure that such information is not compromised, encryption can be used. For example, Secure Sockets Layer (SSL) offers such protection.

Server, Internet Message

An Internet message server consists of software to provide access to Internet resources over network bridges. This type of server is in contrast to an asynchronous connection transport server, which provides access over telephone lines. This type of server does not require a dedicated machine.

Server, Intranet

An intranet server is used to run a corporate or other type of intranet—that is, a network that uses the Internet's TCP/IP protocol stack and that relies on the Web browser interface to provide access to corporate information. Beyond managing the protocol stack, such a server will be concerned primarily with delivering Web pages in response to client requests—that is, it will function mainly as a Web server.

In most network operating systems—for example, Windows NT and Novell's NetWare—intranet servers can operate within the NOS, and can rely on NOS services for such tasks as authentication and access management. This is in contrast to an Internet server, which should be handled differently.

→ *Compare* Server, Internet

Server, Job

A job server consists of software to manage the tasks queued up in a network or in a special-purpose queue, such as a print or fax queue. Job servers do not require dedicated machines.

Server, LBS (LAN Bridge Server)

In an IBM Token Ring network, a server that consists of software to keep track of and provide access to any bridges connected to the network. An LBS server does not require a dedicated machine.

Server, Mail

A program that manages delivery of mail or other information, upon request. Mail servers are generally implemented at the topmost layer, the applications layer, in the OSI reference model. A mail server does not require a dedicated machine.

Server, Modem

A modem server is a type of communication server that provides access to one or more modems. The modem server is a node, which is usually a dedicated machine, on the network. This node has one or more modems attached.

Each other node that wants to use the modem server must have a redirector that can send the communications session and data to the server. Hardware redirectors take up an expansion slot in the workstation, but will work with any communications program. Software redirectors are tied to a specific network operating system (NOS) and will work only with communications programs that are capable of working with the redirector.

Server, Multihomed

A multihomed server is one that is connected to two or more different networks, using multiple network adapters. Because it is connected to multiple networks, such a server often serves as a router. It can generally perform the same functions as a dedicated router—performing these less efficiently,

but sometimes more cost effectively, than a dedicated machine.

A multihomed server will have an IP address for each network to which the server is connected. It's also possible to have logical multihoming, in which multiple addresses are defined using only a single network interface card.

Server, Name

A name server looks up an Internet host name and translates this into an IP address. Two kinds of name services may be used, depending on whether the hosts have NetBIOS names (for example, \\netbiosname) or Internet domain names (for example, www.internetname.com).

- *Windows Internet Name Service* (WINS) is used for NetBIOS names. The service gets name and address information from network browsers—programs that record names used on the network, along with any address information associated with the name.

- *Domain Name Service* (DNS) is used for Internet domain names. The DNS uses a table of names and addresses to resolve a request. If the service can't find the name in its table, the service sends the task up the hierarchy to the DNS server for that DNS. The BIND (for Berkeley Internet Name Domain) server is arguably the most commonly used DNS. This server is called *named*.

Server, Origin

On the World Wide Web, an origin server is one on which a particular resource resides or will be created.

Server, Print

A print server provides access to printers and runs the programs needed to create and operate print queues for jobs sent to the printers from the various nodes. Software needed to create a print server is included with the networking software.

Print servers, which may include special hardware, generally support multiple higher-level protocols, and they can usually support multiple printers through serial or parallel connections (or both). For example, the same print server might be able to queue files coming from machines running any of TCP/IP, AppleTalk, or NetWare's IPX/SPX protocols.

In order to use the printer managed by a print server, a workstation must associate an unused port on the workstation with the server's printer, and it must redirect print jobs to this port.

On many networks, file and print services are combined in the same machine, often for simple reasons of economy. There are advantages and disadvantages to this arrangement. The main advantage is that files need not be sent from the file server to the print server machine, and from there to the printer. The main disadvantage is that even the minimal overhead required to control the print queue and the printing activity will take away CPU (central processing unit) time from other network activity.

Some hardware print servers can also provide terminal services, with the connection to the host through a serial port.

Although it requires frequent CPU access, a print server's effect may not even be noticeable, even if the server is running on the file server.

Print servers sometimes run on dedicated workstations, but this is not allowed under all network operating systems. For example, Novell's NetWare 2.x and 3.x support print servers on dedicated workstations, but NetWare 4.x does not. Instead, the printer server under NetWare 4.x must be run on either the file server or an application server.

PRINT SERVER TIPS

When you're picking a printer to use with a print server, if at all possible, use a fast printer, since there may be several people waiting for their printouts. Keep in mind, however, that your print server must be able to feed the fast printer.

Also, if you have more than a few nodes that might use print services, make sure the printer's duty cycle can handle the load. Don't try to print 30,000 pages a month on a printer with a 3000 copy duty cycle.

On a peer-to-peer network, try to connect the printer to a workstation that is seldom used heavily, because the extra printing work may slow down the workstation's performance.

Server, Proxy

A proxy server is a program that serves as an intermediary between a client and a server. The proxy is a server from the user's point of view, but is a client as far as the target server is concerned.

Proxy servers are used in situations where filtering or shielding is desirable—for example, if a client computer is inside a firewall (protective program) and wants to communicate with a server outside the firewall. In such a situation, the client's request is passed to the proxy server, which communicates with the other side of the firewall. By forcing traffic to go through the proxy server, the firewall software has an easier time filtering.

Once the target server has responded, the proxy server checks the reply and does any required filtering. Then the proxy server passes the reply to the client. As far as the client is concerned, the interaction took place directly between client and target server.

→ *See Also* Application-Level Proxy; Circuit-Level Proxy; Proxy

Server Session Socket (SSS)

→ *See* SSS (Server Session Socket)

Server-Side Include (SSI)

→ *See* SSI (Server-Side Include)

Server, SQL (Structured Query Language)

A SQL server functions as a database server for systems that use the SQL database manipulation language developed by IBM for use on its mainframes, and then ported to minicomputers and PCs. SQL server software does not require a dedicated machine.

SQL Server is also the name of a relational database management system (RDBMS) developed by Sybase, Inc. This database system is available for several PC and minicomputer platforms, from Sybase as well as from third-party vendors. For example, Microsoft offers SQL Server for OS/2.

Server, Tape

A tape server consists of software to provide capabilities for backing files up to and restoring them from a tape drive. This type of server may also include archiving capabilities to identify files that have not been used for a specified amount of time and that might therefore be backed up to a removable medium. A tape server does not require a dedicated machine.

Server, TENNIS (Typical Example of a Needlessly Named Interface Standard)

A component whose job is actually to prevent services from being captured by the network, thereby leading to a net fault. The TENNIS server monitor keeps track of the number of consecutive net faults. If this number exceeds a predefined limit, the local service is temporarily discontinued, and service access goes to the next component.

Server, Terminal

A terminal server consists of software to provide a transparent connection between a terminal and one or more host computers. At the host end, this connection is through an asynchronous (serial) port. Because the connection is to be transparent, the host needs a separate asynchronous port for each terminal.

To avoid this hardware glut, the host's interface to the terminals may be equipped with a packet assembler/disassembler (PAD). This device provides multiplexing capabilities, so that multiple terminals can be processed through a single input line. Each terminal is associated with a unique virtual circuit (VC), and the PAD uses the VC identity to keep the input from the terminals separate.

A terminal server may provide multiple terminals with access to a host, or it may provide terminals with the ability to switch between sessions on different host machines.

Since each terminal can have settings and features, the PAD must keep a separate configuration file for each VC. The parameter values for terminals used in this way are defined in the CCITT X.3 standard.

Server, Transaction

A transaction server mediates between a client and a server in such interactions as electronic commerce, online banking, and stock trading. Besides requiring security, such interactions all demand that the transactions taking place should either be completed successfully or not be carried out at all. That is, the transaction server must make sure that all traces of any unsuccessful transaction are deleted—so that both parties in the transaction are restored to their pretransaction state.

Server, Web

A Web server generally delivers Web pages to clients (usually browsers) that request them, and administers the contents of its Web site. Web servers are generally used for intranets—that is, corporate networks that use TCP/IP protocol stacks and Web-based browser interfaces for requesting and delivering corporate information.

Setting up and operating a Web server is getting easier all the time—due, in part, to the many excellent Web server packages that are available.

Service

A service is a task or operation that is made available through an application or systems program. Operating systems (such as DOS), network operating systems (such as Novell's NetWare), and applications can provide services.

The services that can be provided are limited only by the ability of users and developers to think up new ones. Nevertheless, it is possible to distinguish different classes of service. For example, network services include file services (which control file access and storage), print services, communication services, fax services, archive services, and backup service packages.

A good network operating system (NOS) can provide the entire range of services, either as part of the NOS core or in the form of add-on modules, libraries, or APIs (Application Program Interfaces). The move currently is toward providing highly modular service packages.

According to some analysts, the ultimate outcome will be to make these services independent of particular NOSs, so that developers and possibly even users can create customized service packages.

The concepts of protocol and service are often found together. Specifically, for a given service, there is likely to be a protocol. Standards committees generally create separate specifications for services and protocols.

Service Access Point (SAP)

→ **See** SAP (Service Access Point)

Service Advertising Protocol (SAP)

→ **See** SAP (Service Advertising Protocol)

Service Data Unit (SDU)

→ **See** SDU (Service Data Unit)

Service Manager

Microsoft's IIS Service Manager—better known as the HTML Service Manager— actually consists of several service managers, which are provided as add-ons for Windows NT. These can be used to administer various services for a Web site created with Microsoft Internet Information Server (IIS). In particular, the following service managers are available:

- Internet Service Manager for HTTP (Hypertext Transfer Protocol) and FTP (File Transfer Program) services

- Index Service Manager for indexing and summarizing the Web pages on a Web site

- NNTP (Network News Transfer Protocol) Service Manager for newsgroup-related services

- SMTP (Simple Mail Transfer Protocol) Service Manager for handling messaging and e-mail services

HTML Service Managers are only one of several tools that can be used to administer IIS services. Others include Microsoft Management Console (MMC), Scripting, and editing the Metabase.

→ **Broader Categories** Microsoft IIS (Internet Information Server); Windows NT

Service Point

In IBM's NMA (Network Management Architecture), software through which a non-IBM device or a network can communicate with the NMA network manager. NetView is IBM's NMA management program, and NetView/PC is a service point.

→ *See Also* NMA (Network Management Architecture)

Service Provider

A service provider, also known as an access provider, is a company or individual that provides telephone access to a network or to another service—for example, to the Internet. For either a flat monthly fee or for an hourly charge, an Internet access provider (an IAP) will provide a telephone number and server through which subscribers can get onto the Internet.

Service providers differ in such features as:

* The modem speeds they can handle. Commonly, the issue is whether the provider can handle 28.8Kbps access; higher speeds are possible, as are ISDN connections.

* Whether the access number is a local or 800 number, or whether the access may be a toll call (which would add extra costs).

* The access protocols supported. Some providers let users access the server using ordinary communications software, and then provide network access protocols through the server; other providers support more direct protocols such as SLIP (Serial line Internet Protocol) or PPP (Point-to-Point Protocol).

* The range of Internet usage capabilities supported. At one extreme, providers may support only electronic mail, or e-mail, services. At the other extreme are providers that support any allowable type of access and usage.

* Cost—both startup and monthly costs.

Service Provider Identification (SPID)

→ *See* SPID (Service Provider Identification).

Servlet

Whereas an applet is a Java program that executes on the client side (generally within a Web page, as it is being displayed), a servlet is a comparable program but on the server side. Servlets can be used to do processing on the server before sending database records or other information to the client. Traditionally, server-side programs of this sort have been created using such tools as Perl or a CGI (Common Gateway Interface) script.

→ *Broader Category* Java

→ *Compare* Applet

Session

In networking, a logical connection between two nodes, generally a workstation and a server. This connection remains in effect until the task that necessitated the session is completed or some other constraint forces an end to the connection. Depending on the network architectures involved, any of several session layer protocols may be used to establish, maintain, and break a connection.

Session ID (Session Identifier)

In an AppleTalk network, a unique number associated with each session. The ID is used to identify the session and to distinguish it from other sessions.

SFT (System Fault Tolerance)

Novell's strategy for protecting network data. Novell's NetWare supports three levels of SFT.

Level 1 includes Hot Fix, read-after-write verify, and duplicate directory entry tables (DETs). With the Hot Fix feature, NetWare sets aside a certain amount of the available disk space as a reserved storage area. If a program tries to write data to a bad sector, the Hot Fix feature automatically redirects the output to the special storage area. Hot Fix mode is the default in NetWare. In read-after-write verify, NetWare compares the written material on disk with the material in memory before reusing the memory. The DETs contain information about the server's files and directories, so duplicating them ensures that this important information is available, even if one table becomes corrupted.

Level 2 includes disk mirroring or duplexing. In disk mirroring, data is written to two different hard disks, but over the same channel. Mirroring duplicates data in case one hard disk fails, but does not provide any protection if the hard disk channel fails. Disk duplexing uses two separate channels to write the identical data to two disks. Duplexing thus provides security against either hard disk or disk channel failure.

Level 3 uses duplicate servers, so that all transactions are recorded on both servers. If one server fails, the other will have an identical state, and will, therefore, be able to take over.

SGML (Standard Generalized Markup Language)

SGML is both a markup language and a tool for creating markup languages. SGML is a very powerful markup language that can be used for structuring documents and for summarizing this structure for easy access and display in a variety of ways. Because of its power and complexity, SGML tends to be implemented on large, expensive machines and to be used for publishing projects with lots of pages or with very complex material. For example, SGML is used to structure technical manuals and other documents in the aviation and automotive industries, where such documentation can fill thousands or even millions of pages. (The specifications for the SGML language actually run to over 500 pages—a possible candidate for processing with SGML?)

SGML tags and attributes can be used to define the structure of a document. The details of this structure are specified in a Document Type Definition (DTD) file. The actual document is marked up to indicate the different document elements in the document. Once marked, the SGML file is parsed—compared against the DTD for validity, and processed for display or for other use.

SGML is the source of both HTML (Hypertext Markup Language), which currently rules the World Wide Web, and of XML (eXtensible Markup Language), which is poised to dethrone HTML. However, these two languages are derived from SGML in different ways.

HTML is actually an SGML application. More specifically, it is a markup language created from SGML. HTML includes a limited set of tags, attributes, and other markup elements. Web developers have long stretched HTML to its limits—even as the language has been extended and augmented with new tags and with external elements such as cascading style sheets (CSS).

Such limitations are unavoidable, however, because HTML—no matter what the version—is inherently a closed language. That is, there is no way to add to the language while still staying within the specification. The only way to extend the language is to tack on new elements—which is what browser developers do. This is done at the cost of making the resulting document compatible only with a browser that supports the new elements.

In contrast, XML is a subset of SGML. It has been streamlined (to only about 50 pages of specifications) for use with the kinds of documents and information that are found on the Web. XML is an extensible language that can be used to create markup languages—just as SGML can be used. In fact, XML has already been used to create over a dozen special-purpose markup languages. Among the best known of these is Microsoft's Channel Definition Format (CDF).

→ *Compare* HTML (Hypertext Markup Language); XML (eXtensible Markup Language)

Shareable

A shareable file, device, or process is available to multiple users and can be used simultaneously if requested.

Shared Processing

A network configuration in which a single server processes tasks for multiple stations, all of which can communicate with the server. The nodes must share the computing power of the central processor, so the busier the network, the slower tasks will get done.

→ *Compare* Distributed Processing

Share Permissions

In Windows NT server security, share permissions can provide a second way to restrict access to shared resources—in addition to file system permissions. Share permissions have the advantage of working with either FAT (file allocation table) or NTFS (New Technology File System) file systems. When both file system and share permissions are being used, NT selects the more restrictive permission setting in any particular instance.

→ *Broader Category* Permissions

Shell, Network

A general term for networking software that runs on a network workstation and gives the workstation the ability to communicate with the server.

→ *See Also* DOS Requester; NOS (Network Operating System)

Shield

In coaxial and twisted-pair cabling, a sheath, generally of foil or braided metal, wrapped around a conductor wire and dielectric (insulator). The shield helps to prevent external signals and noise from interfering with the signal being transmitted through the cable.

→ *See Also* Cable, Coaxial; Cable, Twisted-Pair

Shielded Distributed Data Interface (SDDI)

→ *See* SDDI (Shielded Distributed Data Interface)

Short

In a cable, a condition in which excess current flows between two wires, such as the two wires in a pair, because of an abnormally low resistance between the two wires.

Shortest Path First (SPF)

→ *See* SPF (Shortest Path First)

Sideband

A sideband is a frequency band either just above or just below the frequency for the carrier signal used in the modulation process that converts data into analog signals in a modem. The illustration "Sidebands lie on either side of a carrier frequency" shows this arrangement.

Since the lower and upper sidebands are symmetrical, one of these is sometimes used either as an additional channel or for diagnostic and management signaling.

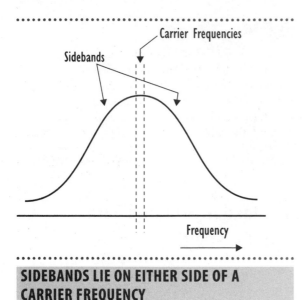

SIDEBANDS LIE ON EITHER SIDE OF A CARRIER FREQUENCY

Signal

An electrical signal takes the form of a change in voltage or current over time. The signal is described by the levels, or amplitudes, that the voltage or current reaches, and by the pattern with which this level changes over time.

The following types of information about amplitudes are distinguished when describing electrical signals:

Peak   The highest level reached by a signal.

Peak-to-peak   The difference between the highest and lowest levels reached by a signal.

Average   A simple arithmetic average of the absolute magnitude of signal levels, without taking positive or negative charge into account.

RMS (root mean square)   A weighted measure of amplitude. This is the value actually used when describing a power supply. For example, in the United States, voltage coming out of the wall outlet is about 117 volts RMS, alternating at 60 times a second (at 60 hertz).

The peak amplitude for our power supply is actually 165 volts.

Peak values represent single values, whereas average values summarize amplitudes over time.

The signal pattern is described as a waveform that represents level over time. Two types of waveforms are used most commonly in networking contexts:

- Sine: The waveform of a "clean" AC signal direct from a reliable power company. Your computer's power supply likes to see such a signal.

- Square: The waveform of a "perfectly encoded" digital bit. Such an ideal waveform is produced with instantaneous voltage or current changes. Ideally, your network interface card or a transceiver sends such a signal along the network.

The illustration "Common waveforms for electrical signals in networks" illustrates these waveforms.

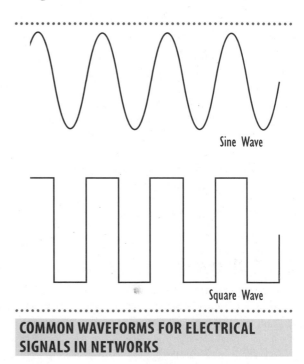

Sine Wave

Square Wave

COMMON WAVEFORMS FOR ELECTRICAL SIGNALS IN NETWORKS

Different electrical properties are associated with the different waveforms. For example, the average and RMS amplitudes for a square wave are equal to the peak; the average amplitude for a sine wave is less than two-thirds that of the peak ($0.637 \times$ peak), and the RMS is $0.707 \times$ peak.

In networking, electrical signals are used in two contexts:

- Power supply: The signal that provides electrical power for a network component. Whatever is providing this signal should be providing a sine wave, *not* a square wave.

- Information transmission: This is the signal that encodes the data or instructions being transmitted. For digital transmissions, the closer this waveform is to a square wave, the better.

For a digital signal, the rise time (time required for the signal to go from 10 to 90 percent of peak strength) determines the shape of the signal. A square wave has a rise time of 0 seconds; in actual signals, the waveform will be more trapezoidal. (The downside counterpart to rise time is fall time.)

In real-world situations, signals come with noise attached. This noise distorts and weakens the signal, and may result in information loss, transmission errors, and electrical malfunction.

Noise also makes the task of signal amplification, or strengthening, more complicated. You cannot just amplify a weakened signal, because this will amplify the noise as well.

Signal, Analog

An analog signal's values are continuous over time. These values represent a level on some variable, such as voltage or intensity, and they range between a minimum and a maximum value. This is in contrast to a digital signal, which takes only a limited number (usually, two) of discrete values.

An analog signal takes the form of a wave, which can be periodic or aperiodic. Periodic signals repeat

in a regular pattern; aperiodic signals do not. The repetition behavior of a periodic signal is measured in cycles per second, or hertz (Hz).

For example, a 50 Hz signal repeats its pattern 50 times a second. Each repetition is a cycle, and consists of a continuous process in which the signal's value changes continuously from a peak to a trough, and back to the peak. The illustration "Features of a periodic signal" on the next page illustrates this type of signal.

The amplitude (volume), frequency (pitch), and phase (starting time) for an analog signal can each be varied.

Signal, Digital

A digital signal's possible levels are represented by discrete values within a limited range. These values are created using sequences of 0 and 1 values. The number of possible values that can be represented depends on the number of bits that are allocated to represent a single value. For example, using eight bits, 256 possible values can be represented.

A digital signal must distinguish between two possible values: 0 and 1. At the electrical level, these values are generally represented as different voltage levels. For example, a 1 might be represented by +5 volts and 0 by zero volts; or a 1 might be represented as *either* +5 or –5 volts, with a 0 represented as 0 volts. Digital signals are sent as square waves, as illustrated in the illustration "Square wave patterns representing digital values."

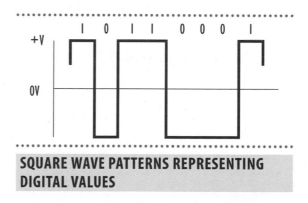

SQUARE WAVE PATTERNS REPRESENTING DIGITAL VALUES

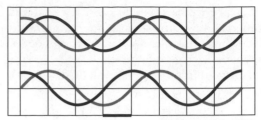

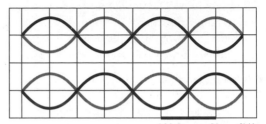

90-Degree Phase Shift

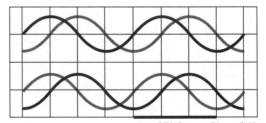

180-Degree Phase Shift

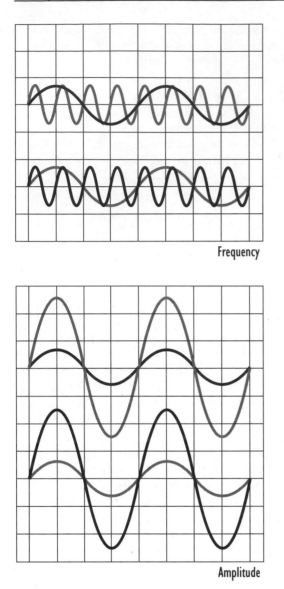

Frequency

Amplitude

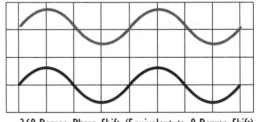

270-Degree Phase Shift

360-Degree Phase Shift (Equivalent to 0-Degree Shift)

FEATURES OF A PERIODIC SIGNAL

Digital signals are somewhat easier to deal with than analog signals. Because of this, digital circuitry is simpler and cheaper. For various reasons, however, digital circuitry will fail much more abruptly.

→ **See Also** Encoding, Signal

Signal, Jam

A jam signal is transmitted by an Ethernet node to indicate that there has been a collision on the network. Collisions are usually caused by two nodes trying to send packets at the same time.

The jam signal consists of a 32- or 48-bit transmission whose contents are unspecified except that the contents cannot be identical to the cyclical redundancy check (CRC) value of the partial packet sent prior to the collision.

Each node involved sends a jam signal, and then waits a random amount of time before trying to access the network again.

Signal Quality Error (SQE)

→ **See** SQE (Signal Quality Error)

Signal-to-Crosstalk Ratio (SCR)

→ **See** SCR (Signal-to-Crosstalk Ratio)

Signal-to-Noise Ratio (SNR)

→ **See** SNR (Signal-to-Noise Ratio)

Simple Workflow Access Protocol (SWAP)

→ **See** Protocol, SWAP (Simple Workflow Access Protocol)

Simplified Access Control (SAC)

→ **See** SAC (Simplified Access Control)

Simplex

A communications mode in which information can travel in only one direction, as, for example, with a tickertape machine. The receiver may be able to send control and error signals, but no data, to the sender. Radio or TV broadcasts are examples of simplex communication.

→ **Compare** Full-Duplex; Half-Duplex

Single-Attachment Concentrator (SAC)

→ **See** SAC (Single-Attachment Concentrator)

Single-Attachment Station (SAS)

→ **See** SAS (Single-Attachment Station)

Single Domain Model

In Windows NT, the single domain model is one of four possible models for organizing and administering networks. In the single domain model, there is only one domain, and all accounts are centralized in that domain. This means that there are no trust relationships to worry about, which simplifies the network administration.

However, if the network gets too large, performance can suffer in the single domain model. This is because the domain controller must manage a huge SAM (security access manager) database.

The other NT domain models are the complete trust domain model, the multiple master domain model, and the single domain model.

→ *Broader Categories* Domain Model; Windows NT

→ *Compare* Complete Trust Domain Model; Master Domain Model; Multiple Master Domain Model

Single Large Expensive Disk (SLED)

→ *See* SLED (Single Large Expensive Disk)

Single-Mode Fiber

Optical fiber designed to allow just a single path of light through the core. The core for a single-mode fiber is extremely thin—less than 10 microns (millionths of a meter)—which makes the signal extremely clean.

→ *See Also* Cable, Fiber-Optic

Single Sign On

→ *See* SSO (Single Sign On)

Single-Step Multimode Fiber

Optical fiber with a core wide enough to allow multiple light paths (modes) through at a time. Unlike graded-index multimode fiber, single-step fiber has only a single layer of cladding, so that there is an abrupt difference in refractive index between fiber core and cladding.

→ *See Also* Cable, Fiber-Optic

Site Server Express

Site Server Express is a component in the Windows NT 4 Option Pack that is used to keep track of the Web pages being hosted by Internet Information Server (IIS).

Skin Effect

When transmitting data at a fast rate over twisted-pair wire, the current tends to flow mostly on the outside surface of the wire. This greatly decreases the cross-section of the wire being used for moving electrons, and thereby *increases* resistance. This, in turn, increases signal attenuation, or loss.

Sky Wave

In radio wave transmissions, a wave that can be transmitted over a great distance before being reflected back to earth. Sky waves, also known as *ionospheric waves*, take advantage of the fact that the ionosphere reflects high-frequency waves in a frequency-dependent manner. The great transmission distances that can be achieved must often use unreliable paths, however.

Slamming

In telephony, slamming is the ethically and legally dubious practice of tricking a subscriber into switching service providers—for example, by making the switch a condition of some special offer. Generally, the information that accepting the offer constitutes the user's consent to be switched is included in a location, form, or size that virtually guarantee that a typical subscriber will not see it—so that the switch will often be made without the subscriber's knowledge.

SLED (Single Large Expensive Disk)

A storage strategy that uses a single, high-capacity disk as the sole storage location. This is the most common strategy, and it is in contrast to the more fault-tolerant RAID (redundant array of inexpensive disks) strategy.

SLIP (Serial Line Internet Protocol)

→ **See** Protocol, SLIP (Serial Line Internet Protocol)

Slots

Slots are part of a media-access method used with some older ring topologies. When using this access method, a ring is divided into a number of fixed-size slots, which circulate around the ring. A slot can be empty or in use. This status is determined by the value of a control bit. When an empty slot passes a node in the ring, the node can access the network by setting the slot's control bit and putting a packet (which contains data and addressing and error checking information) into the slot for transmission.

An advantage of slotted rings is that multiple packets can be transmitted at the same time. A disadvantage is the potential for hogging, in which a particular node uses every empty slot that passes by, thereby preventing nodes downstream from gaining access to the network.

Slotted rings have fallen into disuse as token passing and other access methods have become more popular.

→ **Broader Category** Media-Access Method

→ **Compare** CSMA/CA; CSMA/CD; Demand Priority; Polling; Token Passing

Slotted Ring

A ring topology that uses slots as the media-access method. Slotted-ring networks, such as the Cambridge Ring, were popular in the 1970s, but have largely been replaced by token-ring networks.

Slot Time

In an Ethernet-based architecture, the maximum time that can elapse between the first and last node's receipt of a packet. To ensure that a node can tell whether the packet it transmitted has collided with another packet, a packet must be longer than the number of bits that can be transmitted in the slot time. For Ethernet networks, this is about half a microsecond, which is long enough to transmit at least 512 bits.

SLS (Secondary Link Station)

In environments that use IBM's SDLC (Synchronous Data Link Control) protocol, a secondary link station (or just a *secondary*) is a node that responds to communications initiated by a primary link station (PLS). In SDLC, secondaries cannot initiate communications.

SM (Standby Monitor)

In a Token Ring network, a node that is ready to take over as active monitor (AM), which is the dispenser of the token and de facto network manager in case the AM fails to do its work in a timely and correct manner. A Token Ring network may have several SMs.

→ **See Also** Token Ring

SMAE (Systems Management Application Entity)

In the OSI network management model, the component that implements the network management services and activities at the application level in a node.

→ **See Also** Network Management

Small Computer System Interface (SCSI)

→ **See** SCSI (Small Computer System Interface)

SMAP (Systems Management Application Process)

In the OSI network management model, the software that implements the network-management capabilities in a single node, which may be an ordinary station, a router, a bridge, a front-end processor (FEP), or another type of node.

→ *See* Network Management

Smart Phone

A smart phone is a wireless, multifunction device that, essentially, combines the functions of a PDA (personal digital assistant) and a cellular telephone. The PDA provides such utilities as an address book, calendar or scheduling software, communications capabilities, Internet access, e-mail services, and a Web browser.

Smart phone technology has been available since about 1995, but the market has grown slowly—with annual sales still in the (low) hundreds of thousands. Proponents project sales in the millions within two or three years; critics predict that the technology will never catch on—partly because of the ergonomic difficulties associated with using the devices in some of the ways envisioned.

SMASE (Systems Management Application Service Element)

In the OSI network management model, the component that does the work for a systems management application entity (SMAE).

→ *See* Network Management

SMDS (Switched Multimegabit Data Service)

SMDS is a connectionless high-speed, broadband, packet-switched, wide area network (WAN) service.

This service transmits data over public lines at rates between 1.544 and 44.736Mbps, which is much faster than X.25. SMDS can also run over the physical wiring for a metropolitan-area network (MAN). A special version of SMDS—dubbed "skinny SMDS"—has been developed. This variant operates at 56 or 64Kbps.

Access to the network is over DS1 or DS3 lines. The service conforms to IEEE 802.6 standards. Full SMDS services will be made available gradually, over a several-year period.

SMF (Systems Management Function)

In the OSI network management model, any one of a baker's dozen of services available for managing particular network domains.

→ *See Also* Network Management

SMFA (Systems Management Functional Area)

A term for any one of the five major domains that make up the OSI network management model: accounting management, configuration management, fault management, performance management, and security management.

→ *See Also* Network Management

SMI (Structure of Management Information)

One of the components in the IP (Internet Protocol) network management model. The SMI specifies how information about managed objects is to be represented. The representation uses a restricted version of the ISO's Abstract Syntax Notation One (ASN.1) system.

→ *See Also* Network Management

SMIL (Synchronized Multimedia Integration Language)

SMIL provides a way to include multimedia content on Web sites and to deliver this content even over low-bandwidth connections. SMIL is designed as a cross-platform means of delivering such content to browsers without requiring these to have special plug-ins to handle the content. Effectively, SMIL allows you to include something like a TV show on a Web page.

Objects in SMIL files are defined with temporal parameters so that objects that must operate (play or display) together—for example audio and video objects—will do so in an appropriate manner during display of the Web page. Users watching the contents of an SMIL page can pause the display, rewind it, play it in reverse, and so forth—just as if the users were fiddling with their VCRs or music players.

To enable the precise coordination and synchronization required for satisfactory display, SMIL includes elements that let the author specify whether objects are to be played together (in parallel) or in sequence. The <PAR> and <SEQ> elements are used to specify such details. In addition, SMIL makes extensive use of hyperlinks to coordinate element presentation. Since it is based on XML (eXtensible Markup Language), SMIL makes use of the more powerful hyperlinking methods supported in XML.

SMIL is one of the dozens of applications that have been created using XML, the markup language and development tool that is busy replacing HTML (Hypertext Markup Language) as the main Web development language. The SMIL specification was created by W3C (the World Wide Web Consortium).

→ **Primary Sources** The specifications for SMIL can be found at the W3C Web site, at `http://www.w3.org/TR/PR-smil`.

S/MIME (Secure Multimedia Internet Mail Extensions)

→ *See* Protocol, S/MIME (Secure Multimedia Internet Mail Extensions)

SMS (Storage Management Services)

In Novell's NetWare, SMS is a collection of services for managing data storage and retrieval. These services are provided in a collection of modules and are independent of operating systems and hardware. The following SMS modules are provided:

- SBACKUP, for doing backup and restore operations.
- SMDR (Storage Management Data Requester), for passing commands and information between the backup program and TSAs (target service agents).
- Storage device interface for passing information between SBACKUP and the actual storage devices.
- Device drivers, for controlling the actual behavior of the storage or other devices.
- Server, database, and workstation TSAs (target service agents) for passing requests, commands, and data between SBACKUP and various other components on the network.
- Workstation Manager, for identifying and keeping track of the stations waiting to be backed up.

SMS is also an architecture that third-party backup package vendors can use to enable their backup software to work on a NetWare network.

SMT (Station Management)

In the FDDI network architecture, the component concerned with ensuring that various network elements are operating correctly. The three parts to SMT are frame services, connection management, and ring management.

→ *See Also* FDDI (Fiber Distributed Data Interface)

SMTP (Simple Mail Transfer Protocol)

→ *See* Protocol, SMTP (Simple Mail Transfer Protocol)

SMTP (Simple Mail Transfer Protocol) Service Manager

→ *See* HTML Service Manager

SNA (Systems Network Architecture)

SNA is an all-encompassing architecture designed to enable any IBM machine to communicate with any other. In particular, SNA was developed to enable various machines to communicate with IBM's mainframes. Although SNA was originally introduced in 1974, various capabilities and components have been added over the years.

SNA is both complex and powerful. It can be used to connect machines or networks with very different architectures, provided that both support SNA. It can also be used to pass data between two non-SNA networks.

Various offshoots of SNA (for example, SAA) define standards for application programs, to ensure an interface that can be used within an SNA environment.

SNA was originally released for use in the centralized, master-slave world surrounding IBM mainframes. These machines were used to communicate with terminals (usually dumb terminals), which requested services and resources from the host. All decision making and processing were to be done by the host; all SNA needed to do was enable any type of terminal, controller, printer, or other device to talk to the host. Any interdevice communication would go through the host.

Then came PCs, which are capable of talking to each other directly. In order to enable PCs to communicate with each other without going through the host, IBM added the APPC (Advanced Program-to-Program Communications) capability.

APPC

APPC allows direct communication between certain types of devices (most notably, PCs). To deal with these devices in the SNA hierarchy, a physical unit (type 2.1) and a logical unit (type 6.2) were added. Essentially, a logical unit (LU) is an access point (a logical port) for a device or an application. A physical unit (PU) is a device and software for controlling one or more LUs. PUs and LUs are described in greater detail later in this article.

APPC (or, more precisely, LU 6.2) is a powerful concept because it provides a flexible way to integrate PC networking capabilities with mainframe networking. Allowing direct LU-to-LU connections makes it possible, for example, for two applications *on the same machine* to communicate with each other. This capability also makes it easier to implement client/server computing, in which one part of an application runs on a workstation (the client) and the other part runs on the server.

APPC is actually network-independent, so it can be implemented on non-SNA networks. This independence makes APPC an ideal way to connect dissimilar networks.

SNA as a Layered Architecture

As a layered architecture, SNA divides the world into five main functional layers. It also includes two additional layers as extensions and to make comparisons with the OSI reference model easier.

The illustration "Layers defined for IBM's SNA environment" shows the seven-layer, extended SNA architecture.

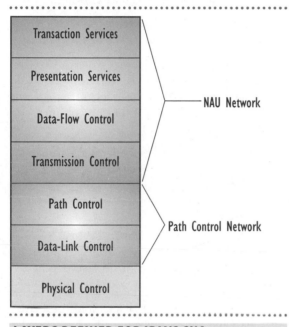

| Transaction Services |
| Presentation Services |
| Data-Flow Control |
| Transmission Control |

NAU Network

| Path Control |
| Data-Link Control |

Path Control Network

| Physical Control |

LAYERS DEFINED FOR IBM'S SNA ENVIRONMENT

Physical Control Layer

The physical interface and medium, as well as the electrical properties of the connection, are specified at the lowest layer, physical control, which is *not defined as part of SNA*.

SNA can support both serial and parallel interfaces, and can use coaxial or fiber-optic cable and, in certain places, twisted-pair cable. For example, hosts (mainframes) and front-end processors (FEPs) generally use a parallel interface; terminals or PCs

generally use a serial interface. Similarly, the connection between a host and a FEP uses either coaxial or fiber-optic cable, but a PC in a network may be connected to a multistation access unit (MAU) using twisted-pair cable.

Data-Link Control Layer

The lowest layer specified in SNA is the data-link control layer. This layer is responsible for reliable transmission of data across the physical connection. Various protocols are supported at this level, including the following:

- SDLC (Synchronous Data Link Control), arguably the most commonly used protocol for this layer

- X.25, for packet-switched networks and for remote connections

- BSC (Bisynchronous Communications), for older IBM hardware

- LLC (Logical-Link Control) sublayer protocol, defined for token ring and other local area networks (LANs) in IEEE 802.2

Path Control Layer

Software at the path control layer creates logical connections between the components associated with specific addresses (NAUs, which are described below). This layer consists of three sublayers:

- Transmission group control, which is responsible for identifying and managing all the links between two nodes.

- Explicit route control, which performs the actual routing (finds a route between the two nodes in a connection).

- Virtual route control, which manages the logical connection (the virtual route) between connected nodes.

Each of the links between nodes can be used as a channel for transmission, and all the links between the same two nodes form a transmission group. Transmission groups make it possible to allocate

S

bandwidth (by assigning more channels to the group) and also to balance the transmission load (by allocating transmissions evenly to unused channels in a group).

Transmission Control Layer

The transmission control layer is for managing (establishing, maintaining, and terminating) sessions between nodes. The transmission control layer is responsible for logical routing. (The path control layer is responsible for physical routing.) Among other things, this layer is responsible for making sure that correct transmissions arrive at their destinations and that they do so in the correct order.

The automatic (and user-transparent) encryption and decryption of data is performed at the transmission control layer.

Data-Flow Control

The data-flow control layer defines the general features of the connection (as opposed to the data-link control layer, which defines the specific details of the data transmission). For example, tasks such as the following are handled at this layer:

- A session is defined as half- or full-duplex.
- Mechanisms for enabling recovery from lost or erroneous data are provided.
- Related data is grouped into units.
- Rules for acknowledging packets are specified (such as whether to acknowledge each packet).
- Data transmission may be halted temporarily and then restarted.

Presentation Services Layer

The presentation services layer is responsible for making sure data reaches its destination in an appropriate form. This may require the following:

- Format conversions, such as between ASCII and EBCDIC

- Formatting, such as to display data on a screen
- Data compression and decompression

Transaction Services Layer

The transaction services layer is the layer at which applications communicate with each other, and at which sessions are requested and initiated. Services provided at this layer include the following:

- Distributed data management (DDM), which enables, for example, a node to use a remote database.
- Exchange of formatted or unformatted documents using IBM's DCA (Document Content Architecture) and DIA (Document Interchange Architecture).
- Store-and-forward capabilities, for e-mail or other message handling systems, using SNA Distribution Services (SNADS).

Layer Groupings

The middle five layers, which are the main SNA layers, can be grouped into two broad categories, each of which is under the control of a different program:

- Path-control network, which consists of layers 2 and 3 (data-link and path control), and is responsible for moving data through the network. These functions are implemented by the ACF/NCP (Advanced Communications Function/Network Control Program), which generally runs on the SNA network's FEP. By relieving the host of these tasks, the NCP helps improve the network's efficiency.
- NAU network, which provides the functions required to control and manage a network. These functions are implemented by the ACF/VTAM (ACF/Virtual Telecommunications Access Method), which generally runs on the host computer.

SNA Components

SNA has an unusual metaphysics in that some components have both physical and logical status. The objects in an SNA world are nodes, which are distinguished as NAUs.

SNA was created to operate in a hierarchical network, in which the mainframe was at the top of the hierarchy, with terminals at the bottom. Three types of nodes are distinguished in SNA networks:

Host This is the mainframe running the network (through the ACF/VTAM software). Each host is in charge of a domain, which consists of one or more subareas.

Communications controller This is an FEP, running the NCP program and the path-control network for the host.

Peripheral These are the establishment and cluster controllers and the terminals.

A NAU is any entity that can be assigned a network address. Three categories of NAU are distinguished. (Remember, SNA network components may be both hardware and software.)

Physical Units (PUs)

PUs are actual physical devices and also the software that runs these devices. A PU is a node in a network, and also the software that manages the node. As a node, a PU is a connection point to a network, and it can support one or more LUs. The five types of PUs are listed in the table "Physical Unit Types." Interestingly, these are numbered 1, 2.0, 2.1, 4, and 5.

Logical Units (LUs)

LUs are the access points for end-user programs (known as SNA users). SNA users get access to network services through an LU. Essentially, an LU is a logical port, rather than a physical one. An LU is associated with a particular application and, in ordinary usage, is generally equated with this application or with the end user.

PHYSICAL UNIT TYPES

PU Type	Description
1	A peripheral node. A now obsolete type that represents certain low-end controllers and terminals.
2.0	A peripheral node. An establishment (IBM 3174) or cluster (3274) controller for 3270 terminals. This node can communicate only with a communications controller, or front-end processor, which is a type 4 PU. The node needs the SSCP to establish a session between two LUs.
2.1	A peripheral node. In addition to all the capabilities of a type 2.0 PU, a type 2.1 PU can communicate with another type 2.1 PU and can support one or more type 6.2 LUs. This software can run in any type of computer, including minicomputers or PCs.
4	A subarea node. A communications controller that serves as a front-end processor for a host computer. A type 4 PU can communicate with all other PU types, including other type 4 PUs. Type 4 PUs include IBM 37xx series machines running ACF/NCP.
5	A host processor, usually a mainframe such as an IBM 370 or 390, running ACF/VTAM as an access method program, and including an SSCP to control the network activity.

In order to make the most effective use of a connection between LUs, several subsystems have been developed, each with its own protocols:

- TSO (time sharing option), which helps make it easier to provide program development services.

- CICS (customer information control system), which supports transaction-processing functions.

- IMS (information management system), which helps make it easier to access and use databases.

- CMS (conversational monitor system), which helps make interactive sessions easier to manage.

Often, you will see these subsystems qualified with virtual storage (VS) in their designation, as in *CMS/VS*.

The LU types are listed in the table "Logical Unit Types." Keep in mind that an LU is both the connection and the software controlling the connection; that is, the LU provides the capabilities required to communicate through the specified connection.

LOGICAL UNIT TYPES

LU Type	Description
0	User-defined LU. Can be used to support terminals or other devices that are not covered in other types.
1	Printers that support SCS (SNA character string) mode. This is true of just about all printers.
2	Terminals that support the 3270 data stream; for example, IBM models 3278 and 3279.
3	Printers that do not support SCS mode, but that do support data stream compatibility mode (support the 3270 data stream).
4	Peer-to-peer communications using SCS mode; for example, between terminals, or between a terminal and a printer that supports SCS.
6.0	Program-to-program communication between applications (such as database programs) that both use CICS. The applications may be running on the same machine.
6.1	Program-to-program communications between applications running CICS/VS and/or IMS/VS.
6.2	General-purpose program-to-program communication. Uses SNA's general data stream for communications. Such communication does not require a host. LU 6.2 allows communication between two type 2.1 PUs, two type 5 PUs, or between a type 2.1 and a type 5 PU.
7	Communications between a host and a terminal that supports SCS or 5250 data stream.

The first four LU types (0 through 3) all involve asymmetrical (master-slave) relationships between a program and the device being controlled. Type 4 LUs may be either program-to-program or program-to-device, and they may use either a master/slave or a peer-to-peer relationship. Type 6.x LUs are generally program-to-program and peer-to-peer.

Within SNA, a single PU can support multiple LUs. One consequence of this is that a terminal (or a PC node) may be able to support multiple applications at the same time, simply by having each application associated with a different LU.

A session between two NAUs generally involves a primary and a secondary NAU, which have somewhat different functions. Even if the relationship is peer-to-peer, there is a primary and a secondary NAU. In that case, the primary NAU is the one that initiates the communication.

System Service Control Points (SSCPs)

SSCPs provide the services needed to manage an entire network or part of one. An SSCP sits on the host computer along with the VTAM control program, and it controls a domain (a collection of PUs and LUs). The SSCP provides access to services, generally through a PU that is running the NCP. As the control program, the SSCP manages sessions between LUs as well as managing the PUs.

Component Relationships

The illustration "Relationship among SNA components" shows how the various types of SNA components can be related.

All SNA networks require an SSCP. This runs on a type 5 PU, along with the VTAM program. The SSCP on the host machine can load and use an NCP program running on a type 4 PU (an FEP).

The FEP may control other PUs, each of which may control one or more LUs. The LUs communicate with each other through sessions (logical and physical paths), which are set up by the SSCP or possibly by the LUs themselves, provided these are type 6.x LUs.

Thus, an end user running a program might attach to an LU at a terminal or through a terminal-emulation program. This LU will be associated with a PU that connects, directly or through intermediate steps, to an FEP and then to the host.

In the case of type 6.*x* LUs—for example, PCs in a Token Ring LAN—the connection need not involve either an FEP or a host.

Links between Devices

SNA supports both local and remote links, depending on how far apart the communicating components are located. Several types of links are commonly used in SNA networks:

Data channels   Very high-speed links (100Mbps or so), which are commonly used between a host and a communication controller or between two hosts. The high bandwidth is achieved by using multiple lower-speed data paths in a single channel. Data channels generally use optical fiber.

SDLC (Synchronous Data Link Control) This protocol can be used for communications between a host and nodes or between two nodes

over telephone lines. SNA also supports the ISO's HDLC (High-level Data Link Control) protocol, which was adapted from SDLC.

BSC (Binary Synchronous Communications) An obsolescent protocol that is supported because some older IBM hardware uses it.

X.25   This protocol is supported for networks that use packet-switching.

Token Ring   PCs can be connected to a host through a Token Ring network. The network's MAU will be connected to the host (or to an FEP).

One way for a PC to communicate with a mainframe or a minicomputer in SNA is by emulating a particular type of terminal. For example, to communicate with an AS/400 midrange computer, a PC would need to emulate either a 5250 or a 3270 terminal; to communicate with a 3090 mainframe, the PC needs to emulate a 3270 terminal.

S

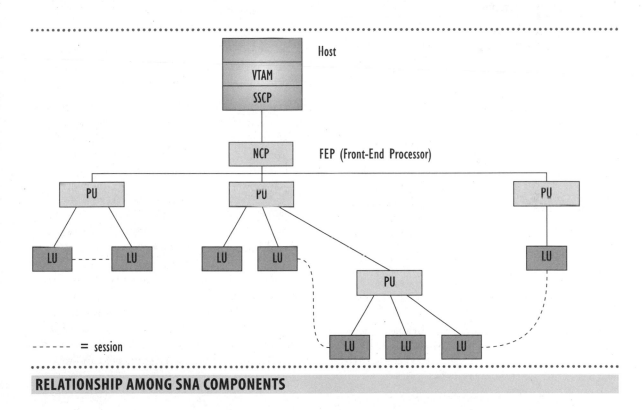

----- = session

RELATIONSHIP AMONG SNA COMPONENTS

SNA Sessions

In SNA, a session is a temporary logical (and physical) link between two NAUs, established for the purpose of communication. The nature of the session and the kinds of information transferred depend on the type of nodes involved. SNA includes sessions for applications and also sessions for network management.

The table "SNA Network Sessions" shows the types of sessions that are allowed in an SNA network. Note that the CP-CP type session is allowed only in networks that use the APPN (Advanced Peer-to-Peer Networking) extension to SNA. This extension allows PUs or LUs to communicate directly, without needing the help of an SSCP on a host machine. Nodes in an APPN-compatible network each serve as their own control points.

SNA NETWORK SESSIONS

Session Type	Description
LU-LU	Communication is between two LUs or between a type 2 LU and a host application. LU-LU sessions are established, maintained, and terminated by the SSCP, unless type 6.x LUs are involved.
PU-PU	Communication is between two PUs. A PU-PU session enables one PU to notify another of an event or problem on the network.
SSCP-LU	Communication is between a host (running the SSCP) and a type 2 LU (a terminal). A SSCP-LU session generally precedes or follows the activation of an LU-LU session by the SSCP.
SSCP-PU	Communication is between a host (running the SSCP) and a type 2.0 PU (an establishment controller). A SSCP-PU session generally precedes or follows the establishment of an SSCP-LU session.
SSCP-SSCP	Communication is between two hosts (both running SSCP), and is generally for the purpose of establishing a session across domains, for example, across networks.
CP-CP	Control point to control point communications. Two such sessions are always established at a time: one for transmission in each direction. A CP-CP session requires APPN.

Type 6.2 LU NAUs were introduced with APPN, and these have proven extremely efficient and flexible. Sessions involving type 6.2 LUs are more efficient because they need to transfer less data in a session, and because both the participants in the session can do error recovery.

LU 6.2 sessions are more flexible because even dissimilar systems can communicate. As a result, numerous vendors have added support for LU 6.2 sessions in their products.

Network Management

IBM's most recent and effective network management tool for SNA networks is NetView. This program monitors an SNA network in four areas:

Performance/Accounting   Parameters such as network response times and delays, and resource availability.

Configuration   NetView keeps a record of the physical components on the network and of the logical relationships among these.

Change   NetView can keep track of any type of change to the network, such as the addition or removal of a hardware or a software item.

Problem   NetView detects and deals with any problems that arise on the network. This management task is carried out in five phases: determination, diagnosis, bypass and recovery, resolution, and tracking and control.

Novell's NetWare Management Agent for NetView provides an interface between a NetWare server and NetView. The connection is through a Token Ring network or through NetWare for SAA. With this connection, an administrator can control the NetWare server from a NetView console and execute certain NetView commands on the server. The NetWare server can also send alarms to the NetView host in case of errors. NetWare Management Agent for NetView makes it possible for two different networks to be connected and managed together.

SNA Character String (SCS)

→*See* SCS (SNA Character String)

SNADS (SNA Distribution Services)

SNADS provides store-and-forward file and document-handling capabilities in an IBM SNA (Systems Network Architecture) environment. SNADS uses APPC (Advanced Program-to-Program Communication) protocols to transport data.

SNA Gateway

An SNA gateway is a gateway that enables PCs and other machines on a PC-based network to communicate with IBM mainframes and minicomputers. The gateway provides translation necessary to enable a PC to talk to a host computer as any of the following:

- A 3270 terminal

- A 3287 printer

- An application that can use the LU 6.2 protocol, which is defined to enable programs to communicate

These capabilities require an adapter card. Among other things, this card provides the required emulation capabilities, for the gateway machine and on behalf of any node that can communicate with the gateway.

Snap-In

A snap-in—also known as a plug-in—is a special-purpose code module that can be connected (snapped in) to an application (for example, a browser) in order to perform a task.

In the Windows NT Options Pack, a snap-in refers to any of the components that snap into Microsoft Management Console and that provide administration for the tools in the Options Pack.

SNA/SDLC (Systems Network Architecture/Synchronous Data Link Control)

A communications protocol used to transfer data between a host and a controller in an SNA environment.

SNDCP (Subnetwork-Dependent Convergence Protocol)

In the OSI specifications for the Internal Organization of the Network Layer (IONL), the type of protocol used at the middle of the three sublayers into which the layer has been subdivided. A SNDCP protocol must handle any details or problems relating to the subnetwork to which the data is being transferred.

SNICP (Subnetwork-Independent Convergence Protocol)

In the OSI specifications for the Internal Organization of the Network Layer (IONL), the type of protocol used at the highest of the three sublayers into which the layer has been subdivided. A SNICP protocol must provide the routing and relaying capabilities needed to get data to its destination. The OSI's CLNP (Connectionless-mode Network Protocol) is an example of an SNICP.

SNR (Signal-to-Noise Ratio)

In a transmission, SNR is the ratio between the signal and noise levels at a given point, usually at the receiving end of the transmission. The SNR value is generally expressed in decibels (dB).

The SNR can be used to determine how long a cable segment can be before the signal loss is unacceptably high. The SNR also helps determine whether a particular type of cable is appropriate for the intended use. Cable testers, such as those manufactured by MicroTest and by Fluke, can help determine whether a particular type of cable is appropriate in a specific environment.

In general, digital signals have a much higher SNR than analog signals.

Socket

In network communications, a socket consists of a port and a network address (for example, an IP, or Internet Protocol, address) for the node on which the port is defined. Together these two elements constitute one end of a network connection. That is, a network connection can be established by a path between two sockets.

More generally, a socket is a general-purpose IPC (interprocess communication) mechanism. It is a logical entity through which a program or process communicates with a network or with another process. Each socket is associated with an address and, usually with some other type of identification.

Sockets were first developed for the UNIX environment, and are part of the BSD UNIX kernel. Sockets are supported, usually in libraries, by other UNIX implementations, for operating systems such as DOS or OS/2, and for network operating systems such as Novell's NetWare and AppleTalk.

Because sockets are generic, different parts of an application can execute on several different machines simultaneously. For example, for a database program, part of the program may run on a file server, which can provide fast access to any of the numerous databases connected to the server. Another part of an application may run on a workstation or on another specialized machine. The program portions communicate with each other using sockets.

Types of socket you may find mentioned in the literature include the following:

- Datagram socket, for sending datagrams (packets used in connectionless delivery systems that do not guarantee delivery).

- Stream socket, a higher-level mechanism that provides a reliable connection (one that guarantees delivery).

- Raw socket, used for access by low-level protocols, and available only to privileged programs.

- DAS (dynamically assigned socket) and SAS (statically assigned socket), used for datagram delivery between nodes in an AppleTalk internetwork.

Socket Client

A process or function associated with a socket in a particular network node. The client is said to "own" the socket; that is, it can make use of the socket to request and receive information and network services.

Socket, NetWare

In Novell's NetWare, a socket is part of an IPX internetwork address. A socket is the destination for an IPX packet. Each socket is associated with a unique value. For most sockets, this value is assigned dynamically; however, certain socket values are reserved for Novell's use.

The table "Reserved NetWare Socket Values" shows the reserved socket numbers and their uses. Note that the socket values are expressed in hexadecimal, or base 16, values.

Third-party developers can reserve socket values for use in the developers' products.

RESERVED NETWARE SOCKET VALUES

Socket Value	Reserved For
451h	NCP (NetWare Control Protocol)
452h	SAP (Service Advertising Protocol)
453h	RIP (Router Information Protocol)
455h	NetBIOS
456h	Diagnostics
8063h	NVT (Novell Virtual Terminal)
4000–6000h	Temporary sockets

Socket Number

In any of various networking environments, such as AppleTalk and Novell's NetWare, a unique value assigned to a socket. The maximum size of such a value depends on the number of bits allocated for the number. For example, AppleTalk socket numbers are 8-bit values. Within this 0–255 range, values between 0 and 127 are reserved by Apple for system devices.

Soft Error

In a token-ring network, an error that is not considered serious or a threat to the performance or continued operation of the network.

→ *Compare* Hard Error

Solaris

Solaris is a UNIX implementation by SunSoft. Solaris is based on SunSoft's own SunOS. SunOS, in turn, is based on UNIX System V Release 4 (SVR4), but adds capabilities such as support for multithreading, symmetric multiprocessing, and real-time processing.

Solaris provides versatile networking support, including support for ONC (Open Network

Computing), TCP/IP, NetWare IPX/SPX, and other protocols. Solaris can mount remote file systems automatically when needed, and it includes utilities for configuring network nodes and for installing software across the entire network from a single machine.

Solaris was implemented originally on Sun's SPARC architecture, but has since been ported to the Intel processor family.

SONET (Synchronous Optical Network)

SONET is a high-speed, fiber-optic system, which provides an interface and transport mechanism for high-speed optical transmission of digital information. At the interface, signals are converted from electrical to optical form (and back to electrical form at the destination).

The electrical portion before and after the SONET is known as a Synchronous Transport Signal (STS). This signal format represents the basic building block for SONET transmissions.

SONET is an ANSI standard. The CCITT counterpart is SDH (Synchronous Digital Hierarchy).

This type of network has the following features:

- Supports transmission rates ranging from 51.84Mbps to 9.953Gbps. In the digital signal (DS) hierarchy, SONET's basic bandwidth is a DS3 (44.736Mbps) channel plus overhead. However, SONET also supports the multiplexing of lower-capacity channels, down to the 64Kbps DS0 channels.

- Uses an 810-byte (6480-bit) frame as its basic transmission unit, and transmits 80,000 of these per second.

- Uses a four-layer hierarchy to implement and manage the transmission of frames between two endpoints.

- Can adjust timing and framing during operation.

S

- Supports drop-and-insert capabilities, which make it easier to identify and remove channels going to different destinations. This makes it feasible to multiplex smaller-capacity (as low as 64Kbps) channels into SONET channels.

- Can be used as a carrier service for ATM (Asynchronous Transfer Mode) or Ethernet networks, DS1 or DS3 lines, or just about any other kind of transmission scheme.

- Is designed to be usable as a carrier service with up-and-coming communications standards and services, such as broadband ISDN (BISDN).

SONET Network Components

The illustration "SONET network components" shows the elements in a SONET network.

The *endpoints* are the source and destination for the DS3 or smaller channels that make up the SONET transmission. The endpoints may represent various types of technologies—ATM, Ethernet, and so forth. These can all be transported over SONET, but they will first be converted to the signal form and packets used for SONET transport. This gathering and conversion process occurs in an *access node*—also known as a *terminal multiplexer*.

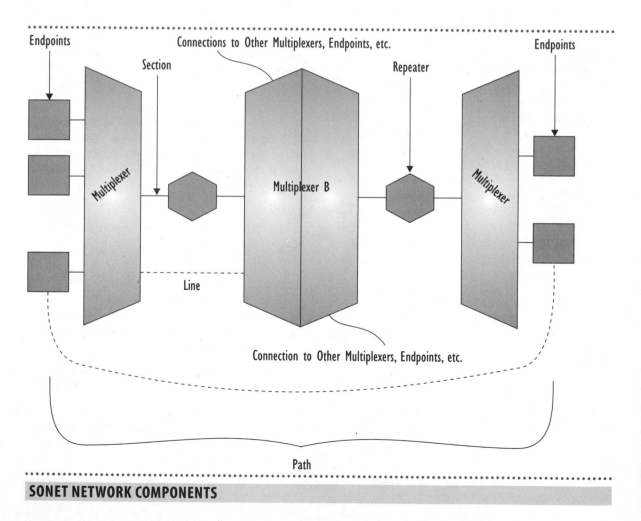

The diverse incoming signals are multiplexed into a single STS-*n* (Synchronous Transport Signal, level *n*) stream. The *n* indicates the level of multiplexing, with a base rate of 51.84Mbps (for *n*=1). Thus STS-3 would be 3 × 51.84Mbps = 155.52Mbps. In the SDH standard, these signals are multiplexed into an STM-*x* (Synchronous Transport Module, level *x*) stream. STM-1 is defined as 155.52Mbps, which corresponds to STS-3.

These electrical signals are multiplexed into optical form by an add/drop multiplexer (ADM). This multiplexer can move payload around for most effective transport. Sometimes the access node also functions as an ADM, in which case the signals coming out will already be in optical form. The optical signal is represented in the optical carrier hierarchy: OC-*x* (for optical carrier, level *x*).

Such ADMs are organized into a ring topology, with redundant elements that allow the topology to survive even if there are breaks at certain places. The topology will also have a digital cross-connect, which can handle streams with different carrier rates. This component is designed to eliminate the need for back-to-back multiplexers, which would be needed to make such shifts between carrier rates.

The paths between the endpoints are constructed of lines, which are, themselves, made from sections. A *section* is a single stretch of fiber-optic cable. The endpoints of a section are transmitters and receivers, which may be in a multiplexer or in a repeater. A repeater simply cleans and strengthens the signal, then sends it on.

A *line* connects two multiplexers. These intermediate multiplexers—generally ADMs—may be connected to other multiplexers or to endpoints. In either case, these multiplexers may route some of the channels to other networks or to endpoints, or they may add channels from endpoints or other lines. Drop-and-insert actions take place at intermediate multiplexers.

SONET Layers

The SONET standard defines four layers to deal with the tasks involved in getting transmissions from one endpoint to another:

Photonic   Cable, signal, and component specifications are defined at this physical layer. Signals are converted between electrical and optical form.

Section   Frames are created at this layer, and these frames are scrambled, if appropriate. The section layer also monitors the transmission for errors.

Line   This layer is responsible for getting frames from one end of a line to the other. Any timing adjustments, adding, or dropping will be made at this level.

Path   This layer is responsible for getting the transmission from the source to the destination; that is, it is responsible for the overall path.

SONET Transmissions

The table "SONET Channel Capacities" shows the channels defined in the SONET transmission hierarchy. The table also shows the equivalent channels as defined in the CCITT SDH standard, which uses STM (synchronous transfer mode) levels.

SONET CHANNEL CAPACITIES

SONET Level	Transmission Rate	STM Level
STS-1/OC-1	51.84Mbps	–
STS-3/OC-3	155.52Mbps	STM-1
STS-9/OC-9	466.56Mbps	STM-3
STS-12/OC-12	622.08Mbps	STM-4
STS-18/OC-18	933.12Mbps	STM-6
STS-24/OC-24	1.244Gbps	STM-8
STS-36/OC-36	1.866Gbps	STM-12
STS-48/OC-48	2.488Gbps	STM-16
STS-96/OC-96	4.877Gbps	STM-32
STS-192/OC-192	9.953Gbps	STM-64

At each endpoint, signals must be converted between electrical and optical forms. STS (synchronous transport signal) and OC (optical carrier) are the designations for the electrical and optical channels, respectively. In the SDH hierarchy, the levels are defined as synchronous transport modes.

SONET Frames

SONET frames have a simple overall structure with complicated details. The illustration "A SONET frame" shows the general structure and provides a glimpse into the details.

The 810 bytes in a frame are grouped into nine 90-byte portions, which are transmitted one after the other. In the illustration, these are represented as nine rows.

Three bytes in each row are overhead; the remaining 87 bytes are data, or payload. The overhead in three of the rows is allocated for monitoring the section; in the remaining six rows it is for the line.

The remaining bytes contain the payloads for the nine rows. This section of the frame is known as the SPE (synchronous payload environment). One column in the SPE is used for path overhead.

In the illustration, enlargements of the overhead sections show the kinds of checking SONET does. Note both the section and line overhead include channels for communicating. These channels are used to send alarms and other administrative information.

The line overhead includes several bytes for pointers. These are used to allow channels to be dropped or added, and even to allow the SPE to be moved.

A Floating Payload

The fast speeds involved in SONET transmissions mean that precise timing and immediate corrections are crucial. Timing adjustments can be made at the end of a line. Generally, such adjustments are minor, on the order of a byte interval or two.

Such adjustments will wreck the structure of a frame. Fortunately, the SPE can be moved around (relative to the frame boundaries), and can even cross frame boundaries.

The floating payload means that timing adjustments can be made at a very fine level. The drop-and-insert capabilities mean that a frame can be reconstructed at a line endpoint, before being sent down another line. This means, in turn, that the SONET channels can be used efficiently.

Source Address (SA)

→ *See* SA (Source Address)

Source Routing

Source routing is a packet-routing strategy used in token ring networks. In a source-routing strategy, the route a packet will take between its source and destination is determined in advance by (or for) the source node.

Packet routes are determined by some type of discovery process, in which the node sends a packet onto the network, then waits for the packet's return. By the time it returns to the source node (as the destination), the packet will have picked up travel stickers from each node visited. The sender will be able to determine a path between sender and destination. This routing information is included when a packet is sent around a token-ring network.

→ *See Also* Routing

Spanning Tree

In a network, a spanning tree is a path or collection of paths that represent connections between nodes. To be called a spanning tree, the tree must cover every possible path in a network.

A minimal spanning tree is one that covers all possible paths, does so with as few segments as possible, and makes sure there are no loops (closed paths) in the network.

The IEEE 802.1 recommendations provide an algorithm for finding a spanning tree in any network.

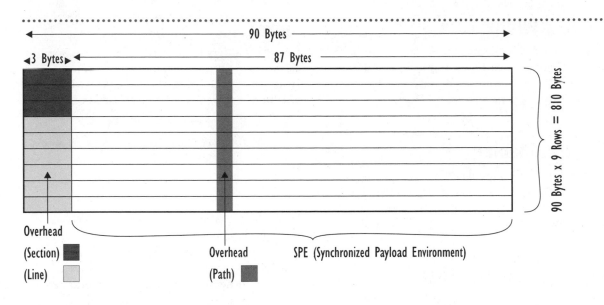

Overhead
(Section)

(Line)

Overhead
(Path)

SPE (Synchronized Payload Environment)

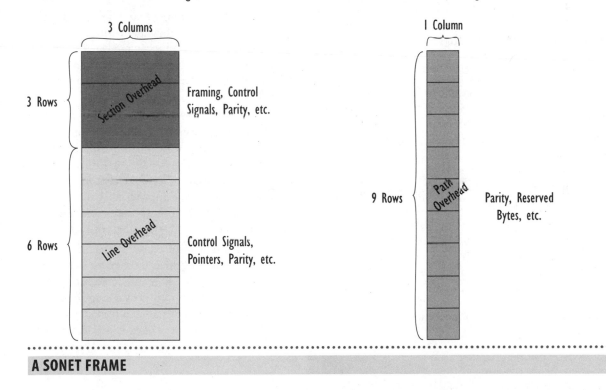

Section and Line Overhead Enlargement

3 Columns

3 Rows

Section Overhead

Framing, Control
Signals, Parity, etc.

6 Rows

Line Overhead

Control Signals,
Pointers, Parity, etc.

Path Overhead Enlargement

1 Column

9 Rows

Path
Overhead

Parity, Reserved
Bytes, etc.

A SONET FRAME

Spectral Width

Spectral width (also known as *laser line width*) is the range of light frequencies (or wavelengths) emitted by a laser. For communications, a narrower width has more desirable properties.

Spectral Shaping

In pulse amplitude modulation (PAM) line coding—that is, in the representation of a data value in electrical form—spectral shaping is a method for optimizing the encoding.

SPF (Shortest Path First)

A routing strategy for passing packets between routers. This strategy is used in Token Ring networks that may include connections to IBM mainframes.

SPID (Service Provider Identification)

ISDN (Integrated Services Digital Network) provides a Basic Rate Interface (BRI) consisting of two 64Kbps B, or bearer, channels and one 16Kbps D, or data, channel. The B channels are used to transmit calls or other information; the D channel is used for control signaling.

The B channels can be accessed separately and used independently. However, sometimes it can be advantageous to aggregate, or bond, them together into a single 128Kbps channel. In order for this to be possible, an ISDN switch (known as the local exchange, or LE) must be able and willing to assign an SPID to the bonded B-channel.

→ **Broader Category** ISDN (Integrated Services Digital Network)

Spike

A very brief, very large increase in voltage. Specifically, a spike occurs when the voltage is more than twice the nominal peak voltage. Spikes (which are also known as *impulses*) are most often caused by lightning strikes.

→ **See Also** Power Disturbances

Splice

In fiber optics, a permanent connection between two cable segments. The splice can be made by fusing the cores from the two cables together or by attaching the cores to each other by mechanical means. In general, a fusion approach works better than a mechanical one.

Split Cable System

A split cable system is a broadband wiring arrangement in which a single cable's bandwidth is divided between transmission and receiving capabilities. Such a wiring system may be used, for example, in a 10Broad36 broadband Ethernet or a broadband (IEEE 802.4) token bus architecture.

In a split cable system, the cable's frequency spectrum is split with, for example, lower frequencies allocated for incoming transmissions and higher frequencies for outgoing signals. At the head end (the transmission source), a frequency converter translates signals into the appropriate bandwidth, and a bidirectional amplifier passes the frequencies to the appropriate channel (input or output).

The bandwidth in a split cable system need not be distributed equally between the two directions. For example, cable television allocates a much larger part of the bandwidth to outgoing signals, since the subscribers need not communicate with the head end. For local area networks (LANs), the distribution should be more even. The following splits are commonly used:

Subsplit Allocates only 25 megahertz (MHz) of bandwidth to transmissions going from node to head end, and over ten times as much bandwidth to output transmissions.

Midsplit Allocates roughly equal bandwidths to incoming and outgoing transmissions. The split uses bandwidths of over 100MHz.

Highsplit Allocates roughly equal bandwidths to incoming and outgoing transmissions. The split uses bandwidths of over 150MHz for both the incoming and outgoing channels.

→ *Compare* Dual Cable System

Split Horizon

When routers communicate with each other to update their routing tables, problems can sometimes arise because the same routing information can get passed around more than once. For example, if router A sends its routing information to router B, there is no reason why router B should include the information from router A when B sends its routing information to A. In fact, there are good reasons for making sure that B does not send A's own routing information back to A—at least not in the form that A originally sent it.

Split horizon is an algorithm that makes it possible to avoid sending back information received from a router. A variant—split horizon with poison(ed) reverse—does send the information back, but in a form that will discourage further processing of the information. In the latter algorithm, router B will send router A's information back to A, but will set the route distances to infinity (which effectively marks the routes as unreachable)—so that router A will not bother looking any further at the information.

Split-Horizon Routing

In an AppleTalk Phase 2 network, a strategy for maintaining routing tables. Basically, the strategy involves passing routing table updates only to nodes or routers that can and will actually use the information.

Split Pair

In twisted-pair wiring, split pair refers to sending a signal over wires from two different pairs instead of over wires in the same pair. Since the pairing is what helps cancel the effects of interference, this advantage is lost with split pairs.

→ *See Also* Wiring Sequence

Splitter

A coupler (an analog device) that breaks a signal into multiple derived signals. An important type of splitter is a wavelength-selective coupler, which splits an incoming signal into outgoing signals based on wavelength.

→ *Compare* Combiner

Spoofing

Spoofing is a network attack strategy in which the attacker uses another node's address as the attacker's own—in order to gain access to the network under assault. This strategy can succeed only if the spoofed address is one that is recognized by the network and is allowed to access it. In networks that use the TCP/IP (Transmission Control Protocol/Internet Protocol) protocol suite, such an attack is known as IP spoofing.

Spooler

A spooler is a program that serves as a buffer for material waiting to be processed by a device, such as a printer. The spooler intercepts material being sent (ostensibly) to a particular port, and can store the material until the spooler is ready for the next transmission. The most common type of spooler used is a print spooler.

On a network, the spooler software may run on a workstation or on the print server. For example, in AppleTalk networks, a *background spooler* runs as a background process on the workstation. Such a spooler sends the print jobs to a file.

In contrast, a *spooler/server* runs on the print server and works by serving as the printer for other applications. The spooler then feeds the print jobs to the real printer.

The term spooler comes from spool, which is an acronym for "simultaneous peripheral operation on line."

SPP (Sequenced Packet Protocol)

A transport level protocol in the XNS protocol suite from Xerox.

SPS (Stand-by Power Supply)

An SPS is an emergency power source that can deliver a limited amount of power to a file server or other device in the event of a blackout (total loss of power).

SPSs are more commonly known as standby UPSs (uninterruptible power supplies). A UPS is a similar, but not identical, device. The main difference is that a UPS always supplies power through a battery, whereas an SPS does so only when there is a power failure.

An SPS includes a battery charger, a battery, and an inverter that can be used to provide the emergency power when necessary. The SPS monitors the power coming in from the power lines. As long as power is coming in, the SPS bypasses the battery component. Instead, the supplied voltage may go through a surge protector and a noise filter before reaching the machine being protected.

Thus, the primary power path in an SPS bypasses the battery, going instead through whatever voltage-cleaning components the SPS has. The secondary path—through a battery charger, a battery, and an inverter—remains idle.

If the SPS detects a blackout, it switches to the battery component. This battery (which must be charged) can provide power for a limited time: anywhere from five minutes to over an hour. The amount of time depends on the capacity of the SPS battery and on the power needs of the system being protected. In any case, there should be enough power to enable a file server to shut down the network in an orderly manner.

The switchover from the primary to the secondary (battery/inverter) path takes a few milliseconds (msec), generally fewer than five or so. This amount of time is short enough to avoid any data loss, since the computer can run for about 50 msec on power stored in its capacitors. This switching time is also lower than the 8.33 msec "half-cycle" time that represents the interval between pulses of power from the power line. One standard (IEEE 446) for switching times specifies that this period should be no longer than a quarter cycle, which is 4.2 msec. (The cycle time comes from the 60 Hz that is the standard rate at which AC power changes polarity in North American power supplies.)

SPSs are generally less expensive than UPSs, but the money saved may prove to be penny wise and pound foolish. This is because an SPS makes extra demands on the system administrator or whoever is in charge of hardware maintenance.

SPS BATTERIES

It is absolutely essential to have a working, fully charged battery available in the event of a power failure. This means the battery must be tested at periodic intervals, and should be fully drained and recharged regularly.

Even if the battery is never used, there will always be some drainage over time. Ironically, drainage increases as the period of non-use does. There's a natural tendency to get complacent the longer one goes without a power outage.

If this leads to looser maintenance, then you could be in for trouble when that blackout finally hits. If the SPS battery hasn't been checked for a long time, the chances become more disconcerting that the battery won't work properly.

Even batteries that are maintained wear out eventually. In general, UPS and SPS batteries should be replaced every three to five years.

→ *Broader Category* Safety Device

→ *Compare* UPS (Uninterruptible Power Supply)

SQCIF (Sub-Quarter Common Intermediate Format)

The Common Intermediate Format (CIF) is the de facto standard for videoconferencing images. This standard specifies a resolution of 352×288 pixels. Two higher- and two lower-resolution variants have also been defined.

The lower-resolution formats are QCIF (for quarter-CIF) and SQCIF (for sub-quarter CIF). QCIF has half the resolution in each dimension (176×144), which yields one-fourth the number of pixels compared to CIF. With an 88×72 resolution, SQCIF is the lowest-resolution variant.

→ *Broader Categories* Videoconferencing

→ *See Also* 4CIF ($4\times$ Common Intermediate Format); 16CIF ($16\times$ Common Intermediate Format);

CIF (Common Intermediate Format); QCIF (Quarter Common Intermediate Format)

SQE (Signal Quality Error)

In an Ethernet 2.0 or 802.3-based network, a signal sent from the transceiver to the attached machine to indicate that the transceiver's collision-detection circuitry is working. SQE (also known as a *heartbeat*) was introduced to identify nodes incapable of detecting collisions.

SQL (Structured Query Language)

SQL (pronounced either as "sequel" or as individual letters) is a language standardized by the ISO for defining and querying relational databases. SQL is widely used as an interface to databases, and almost all database packages now support SQL. Unfortunately not all versions of SQL are the same.

User or application requests are handled as *transactions* by SQL. A transaction may involve one or more SQL actions. SQL must be able to complete a transaction completely or not at all. If a transaction cannot be completed, all the actions already performed must be undone. This provides a measure of data protection.

SQL (Structured Query Language) Server

SQL Server is a database application server from Microsoft for the Windows NT platform. SQL Server will respond to client queries, once there are clients with queries.

The SQL Server package doesn't include client software, which must be created. This can be done using an existing database program—for example, Microsoft Access.

→ *Broader Categories* Database

SRAM (Static Random-Access Memory)

A type of chip memory in which information is stored in flip-flop circuits, which retain their value as long as the power is switched on. This is in contrast to DRAM (dynamic RAM), whose contents must be refreshed periodically. SRAM is faster but much more expensive than DRAM, and is used primarily for cache storage, if at all.

SS (Sampled Servo)

Sampled servo is a compact disc recording technique in which the contents are stored on a single, spiral track.

→ **Compare** CCS (Continuous Composite Servo)

SS7

A standard for out-of-band signaling developed by the CCITT for use in ISDN telephone systems. SS7 (also known as *CCITT 7*) offers fast call setup and sophisticated information and transaction capabilities. For example, SS7 makes call waiting, screening, forwarding, and transfer services available in international networks.

SSCP (System Services Control Point)

A type of node in SNA networks. SSCPs provide the services needed to manage an entire network or part of one.

→ **See Also** SNA (Systems Network Architecture)

SSI (Server-Side Include)

This term is used to refer to any kind of Web services that use embedded HTML tags to create Web documents on the fly—by combining information from multiple other documents. Such SSIs may be delivered upon request or automatically—for example, because the included material may contain announcements or other essential information.

SSL (Secure Socket Layer) Protocol

→ **See** Protocol, SSL (Secure Sockets Layer)

SSO (Single Sign On)

An approach to logins in which a user may need only a single user ID and password in order to access any machine in an enterprise or other network, and even to use any application or service on these machines—provided the user has the appropriate access and usage privileges.

SSS (Server Session Socket)

In an AppleTalk session layer protocol, a field that contains the number of the socket to which the session level packets are to be sent.

Stack Manager

A stack manager is a software process that mediates between a network interface card (NIC) driver and the drivers for higher-level protocols. This type of process is typically loaded in the file server, but may be loaded in a gateway or workstation.

For example, when loaded on a file server, a stack manager could allow the following types of workstations to connect to the server: a DOS workstation running Novell NetWare, a UNIX workstation running TCP/IP, a Macintosh, and an OS/2 workstation running LAN Manager or LAN Server. In this example, the stack manager would need to be able to handle IPX, IP, AppleTalk, and NetBIOS protocols, respectively.

When loaded in a gateway, the stack manager could allow servers from networks running different network operating systems (NOSs) to communicate.

When loaded in a workstation, the stack manager could allow the workstation to access servers running different NOSs. This approach is relatively rare, because the appropriate protocols and shell software must be loaded for each NOS being accessed, in addition to the stack manager.

Stand-Alone Hub

An external hub that requires its own power supply. A stand-alone hub is generally a box with connectors for the nodes that will be attached, and possibly with special connectors for linking to other hubs.

→ **See Also** Hub

Standard Generalized Markup Language (SGML)

→ **See** SGML (Standard Generalized Markup Language)

Standby Monitor (SM)

→ **See** SM (Standby Monitor)

Stand-by Power Supply (SPS)

→ **See** SPS (Stand-by Power Supply)

Star Coupler

A coupler that splits a signal into more than two derived signals, as, for example, in a star topology.

This is in contrast to a tee coupler, which splits an incoming signal into two outgoing signals.

→ **See Also** Coupler

StarGroup

StarGroup is a network operating system (NOS) from AT&T. This NOS is adapted from Microsoft's LAN Manager and runs on UNIX systems, although other versions (such as one for the Macintosh) are available. The NOS provides support for the most common protocol families (TCP/IP and ISO), for SNA (Systems Network Architecture) and asynchronous gateways, routers for X.25 networks, and other capabilities.

StarGroup provides extensive network-management capabilities, and it can report management data to AT&T's UNMA (Unified Network Management Architecture) environment or to NetView running in IBM's NMA (Network Management Architecture).

StarKeeper

A network management system from AT&T. StarKeeper provides centralized management of Datakit VCS and ISN (Information Systems Network) switches.

Start Bit

A bit used to establish timing in asynchronous communications. One or more start bits may be appended to the start of every byte. (Start bits are not required for synchronous communications.)

→ **Compare** Stop Bit

Start Delimiter (SD)

→ **See** SD (Start Delimiter)

STARTUP.NCF

A boot file in a Novell NetWare file server. This file loads the disk driver and name spaces for the server. It can also be used to set other environment variables for the server.

Static Random-Access Memory (SRAM)

→ See SRAM (Static Random-Access Memory)

Static Web Page

A static Web page is an HTML file that remains the same each time it is displayed. Static Web pages are created and then stored on a Web server. The server makes the pages available when a browser requests them.

Static Web pages are in contrast to dynamic Web pages, which are created on the fly whenever they are requested by a browser. Such pages are not stored because they can be created from other elements (such as data or other files, which are read into an HTML framework). The contents from which dynamic Web pages are constructed may change, so on-the-fly construction ensures that the pages are built from the most recent versions of all the elements.

Station Management (SMT)

→ See SMT (Station Management)

Statistical Time Division Multiplexing (STDM)

→ See STDM (Statistical Time Division Multiplexing)

Statistical Multiplexing

A multiplexing strategy in which access is provided only to ports that need or want it. Thus, in any given cycle, one node may have nothing to send, while another node may need to get as much access as possible.

→ See Also Multiplexing

STDA (StreetTalk Directory Assistance)

In StreetTalk, the global network naming system for Banyan's VINES, STDA provides a pop-up window in which a user can see the name of every node or device attached to the network. STDA can also provide addressing facilities for electronic mail and certain types of other information about a particular node or device.

→ See Also StreetTalk

STDM (Statistical Time Division Multiplexing)

A multiplexing technique in which each node is polled and any node with nothing to send is immediately skipped. This helps fill more of the available bandwidth.

→ See Also Multiplexing

STM (Synchronous Transfer Mode)

In broadband ISDN, a transport method that uses time division multiplexing and switching methods to provide each user with up to 50Mbps of bandwidth for synchronous transmissions.

STM (Synchronous Transfer Mode)-*x*

STM-*x* (where *x* is the level) is any of several channel capacities defined in the CCITT's SDH (Synchronous Digital Hierarchy), which is the European equivalent of the ANSI SONET (Synchronous Optical Network) standard.

The STM levels represent multiplexed, 44.736Mbps, DS3 channels + overhead for signaling and framing. For example, the lowest STM capacity, STM-1, has a 155.52Mbps bandwidth, which multiplexes three 51.84Mbps channels. The table "STM-*x* Channel Capacities" shows the rates for the levels in the SDH, as well as the corresponding designations in the SONET hierarchy.

STM-X CHANNEL CAPACITIES

STM Level	Transmission Rate	SONET Level
–	51.84Mbps	STS-1/OC-1
STM-1	155.52Mbps	STS-3/OC-3
STM-3	466.56Mbps	STS-9/OC-9
STM-4	622.08Mbps	STS-12/OC-12
STM-6	933.12Mbps	STS-18/OC-18
STM-8	1.244Gbps	STS-24/OC-24
STM-12	1.866Gbps	STS-36/OC-36
STM-16	2.488Gbps	STS-48/OC-48

Stop Bit

A bit used to indicate the end of a character in asynchronous serial communications. One or more stop bits may be appended to the end of every byte. Older devices needed two stop bits to get themselves set again; newer devices require only one. Stop bits are not required for synchronous communications.

→ *Compare* Start Bit

Storage

Storage—the technology for maintaining a (quasi-) permanent copy of digital materials—has always been essential for computers. Over the years, various technologies have been developed for storing information—including perforated paper tapes and Hollerith (that is, punch) cards. Currently, electromagnetic and optical storage methods are the most popular. Over the next few decades, however, as these technologies reach their limits, the expectation is that chemical, biological, and quantum storage technologies (or, perhaps more accurately, biotechnologies) will become increasingly important, and will probably replace the current ones.

Storage media may provide random or sequential access. Content on a random-access medium can be retrieved in roughly the same amount of time, regardless of where on the medium the content is located. Content on a sequential medium may have significantly different access time, depending on the content's location on the medium. (For example, on a rewound tape, material at the end of the tape requires significantly longer to retrieve than material at the start.)

Content on tape is currently the only sequential medium getting any significant use. (Perforated paper and cards were also sequential media.)

Electromagnetic Storage

Electromagnetic storage technologies use electrical signals to charge or orient elements on a medium. Depending on its orientation, the element will indicate a 0 or 1. The capacity of electromagnetic media depends in part on how densely such elements can be packed without affecting each other.

Electromagnetically stored information is sensitive to corruption and damage from various sources, including heat and cold and—most significantly—strong magnetic fields.

S

Electromagnetic storage technologies currently in use include the following:

- Tape, which requires sequential access, and which can have high capacity (up to 5GB or so). Tape is used almost exclusively as a backup medium.

- Floppy disks, which have a limited capacity (around 1–2MB). Floppies are probably on their way out.

- Hard disks, which have a much higher capacity than floppies (50GB and rising).

- Removable media, which include media for Zip, Jaz, Kangaru, SuperDisk, and other drives of that ilk. The media for these drives have capacities ranging from about 120MB to several GB. For the most part, these media all use proprietary storage formats. Removable hard disks are commonly used for laptop computers.

Optical Storage

Optical storage technology uses lasers to encode and read information. In most cases, bit values are burned onto the medium surface or into a layer just beneath the surface. The disc capacity for optical storage depends in part on the wavelength (and, hence, on the energy) of the laser being used.

Much of the material encoded optically is read-only—for example, on CD-ROM (compact disc read-only memory) and on DVD-ROM (digital versatile disc read-only memory). However, rewritable variants exist for both CD and DVD storage technologies. Not all rewritable variants are compatible with each other; some variants require special hardware.

Optically stored information is impervious to interference from magnetic fields. However, optical storage media can suffer scratches or damage from heat.

Optical storage technologies currently in use include the following:

- CD-ROM, which is a read-only medium with a capacity of about 660MB. CD-ROM

was the first high-capacity software delivery medium, and may be partly responsible for the software bloat that is ubiquitous today. After all, if you have almost a gigabyte of available space to deliver a product, why worry about a few megabytes?

- CD-R (recordable), which is a write-once technology that stores information by changing the optical properties of the disc surface (rather than by burning the bit value into the disc). CD-R discs have a 660MB capacity and can be read in ordinary CD-ROM drives.

- CD-RW (rewritable), which allows discs to be rewritten up to 1000 times. CD-RW discs are written using a somewhat different recording technology, which makes the disc surface less reflective than ordinary CDs. As a result, some CD-ROM drives cannot read CD-RW discs. (Only those with MultiRead capabilities are guaranteed to be able to read CD-RW discs.) CD-RW drives can write to random sections of the disc—so that the disc can be written a bit at a time. However, only newer CD-RW drives can also erase random disc areas.

- DVD-ROM, which is a read-only medium with a capacity of about 4.7GB on each side of a disc. DVD-ROM is generally what is meant when someone speaks simply of DVD in connection with software.

- DVD-R (recordable) is a write-once technology with a capacity of just under 4GB on each side currently, and about 4.7GB per side eventually.

- DVD-RAM is also a write-once technology with a capacity of just under 2.7GB on each side currently, and about 4.7GB per side eventually. The entire disc must be written in a single session.

- DVD+RW (rewritable) is an alternate rewritable DVD technology that allows up to 10,000 rewrites. Unlike DVD-RAM,

DVD+RW discs can be written a little at a time. DVD+RW technology supports up to 3GB on each side of the disc.

- EO (erasable optical) discs, which can store anywhere from about 130MB to over 5GB on a single disc. This surprisingly flexible technology has never caught on.

Network Storage

As multimedia content becomes more pervasive and more widely used, storage requirements—particularly on networks—are increasing rapidly. Storage area networks (SANs) currently offer a promising solution, which is described in the entry for SAN.

→ *See Also* CD (Compact Disc); DVD (Digital Versatile Disc); SAN (Storage Area Network)

Storage Area Network (SAN)

→ *See* SAN (Storage Area Network)

Storage Management Services (SMS)

→ *See* SMS (Storage Management Services)

Store-and-Forward

A messaging technology in which messages can be held for a time—at the source machine, at an intermediate node, or at the destination machine—and then sent on to their destination.

Store-and-Forward Switch

A switch that first checks a packet's integrity before sending it on to its destination port. The switch gets each packet from the input port, looks up the packet's destination (MAC-level) address, and then sends the packet on. To be useful, such a switch

needs enough storage to hold an address table large enough to store every address on the network.

→ *Compare* Cut-Through Switching

STP (Shielded Twisted-Pair)

→ *See* Cable, Twisted-Pair

STREAMS

In Novell's NetWare, STREAMS is a NetWare Loadable Module (NLM) that provides an interface between the NOS (network operating system) and Transport layer protocol stacks, such as Novell's own IPX/SPX, the Internet's TCP/IP, IBM's SNA architecture, and networks that conform to the OSI reference model.

In addition to the STREAMS NLM, one or more other NLMs are needed to provide STREAMS with access to the other protocol stacks. For example, SPXS.NLM and IPXS.NLM provide access to STREAMS for the transport and network layers, respectively; TCPIP.NLM can mediate between STREAMS and the TCP and UDP protocols.

StreetTalk

StreetTalk is the global naming system for Banyan's VINES network operating system (NOS). Street-Talk includes a database that contains all the necessary information about the network and each node or device on it. The database is updated every 90 seconds by every server on the network.

A StreetTalk name may include three levels of identity: item, group, and organization. Item is the most specific. A node or device may get a name at each of these levels, and these names will be separated by an @. For example, Hickory@Dickory @Dock specifies node *Hickory*, which belongs to group *Dickory*, which is part of organization *Dock*.

StreetTalk allows nicknames for nodes and devices.

S

StreetTalk Directory Assistance (STDA)

→See STDA (StreetTalk Directory Assistance)

Structure of Management Information (SMI)

→See SMI (Structure of Management Information)

Structured Query Language (SQL)

→See SQL (Structured Query Language)

Stub Area (SA)

→See SA (Stub Area)

Style Sheets

Style sheets are used to provide layout or structure templates for a document that is being marked up for display, indexing, or other types of processing. The document processing may involve hard copy or—much more commonly these days—an electronic version in one or more files.

Style sheets contain definitions for elements that may appear in the document and include instructions for how these elements may (or must) be handled. Markups in the document can then be limited (more or less) to simply labeling the elements when they appear. When the document is processed, the processor (for example, a browser or an indexing program) reads and parses the style sheet(s) and then deals with the document.

Style sheets make it possible to separate content from structure or form to a much greater extent. This has the following advantages:

- Makes it possible to use the same styles with multiple documents without having to duplicate the style details in each document.

- Makes it possible to use different styles with the same document without having to maintain separate versions of the document for each style.

- Makes it possible to change the details of a style without having to make these changes in each individual document.

- Makes it possible to create special versions of a style for particular purposes—for example, versions of a document that may display or conceal notes or information appropriate only for certain users.

- Makes it possible to combine styles in a document by reading in multiple style sheets.

Style sheets or some analogous means of using templates are provided for many editing and markup tools. For example, HTML (Hypertext Markup Language) supports the use of cascading style sheets (CSS) and XML (eXtensible Markup Language) includes its own eXtensible Style Language (XSL). Word processors such as Microsoft Word or Corel's WordPerfect also include mechanisms for defining and using different styles, as do Web page development tools.

Sub-Distribution Frame (SDF)

→See SDF (Sub-Distribution Frame)

Subnet

Computers in a subnet have IP (Internet Protocol) addresses that are all in the same range. Such address subnets are possible because of the way IP addresses are assigned. These are represented as a sequence of four decimal numbers—for example, 35.185.63.251. These numbers create a hierarchy within which subnets can be defined.

For example, an Internet Service Provider (ISP) might be assigned addresses in the range 44.*x.x.x*. That is, the ISP can assign addresses in the ranges below 44 to customers. For example, the ISP might assign 44.125.*x.x* addresses to a customer (A) who could, in turn, assign addresses below 44.125 to A's clients. Thus, an address such as 44.125.37.128 or 44.125.63.244 would be in a subnet below 44.125. Similarly, addresses such as 44.125.63.25 and 44.125.63.245 would be addresses in a subnet below 44.125.63.

Subnet Layers

In the OSI reference model, the bottom three layers: Physical, Data-Link, and Network. These layers are significant because intermediate systems, which are the devices that relay transmissions between other devices, use only these three layers to pass on transmissions.

→ *See Also* OSI Reference Model

Subnet Mask

In the IP (Internet Protocol) addressing scheme, a group of selected bits whose values serve to identify a subnetwork. All the members of the subnetwork share the mask value. Once identified using the mask, members of this subnet can be referenced more easily. This is also known as an *address mask*.

Subnetwork

Subnetwork is a term for a network that is part of another network, connected through a gateway, bridge, or router. A subnetwork may include both end systems (nodes) and intermediate systems (routers). The nodes in a subnetwork use a single protocol to communicate with each other. The subnetwork is connected to the larger network through an intermediate system, which may use a routing protocol to communicate with nodes outside the subnetwork.

A local area network (LAN), or even a group of LANs, connected by bridges or routers can form a subnetwork. Similarly, a localized X.25 network may be a subnetwork in a larger wide area network (WAN).

Subnetwork, Level *x*

If an internetwork grows too large, routers may be unable to keep track of all the routing information. This can, under some circumstances, cause errors that are very difficult to fix. To avoid such problems, an oversized internetwork can be divided into areas, each consisting of a number of networks. These areas are called *level 1 subnetworks*, and they are managed by level 1 routers.

To a network elsewhere on the internetwork, all the networks included in a particular level *x* network are treated as part of the same network. For example, a giant reference internetwork might include dozens of networks from a single city, with networks in libraries, schools, research labs, and so on. For the outside world, all the networks in a city could be grouped into a level 1 subnetwork.

Transmissions to a machine on one of the networks would be sent to a level 1 router for that city. Routers would have the address of that level 1 router, rather than having addresses for each of the networks in the city.

For really large internetworks, several level 1 subnetworks could be grouped into a level 2 subnetwork, handled by level 2 routers.

Arranging a large internetwork hierarchically in this manner makes it possible to build larger internetworks, because routers need to keep track of less information overall. Also, by partitioning level 1 subnetworks, it is possible to isolate any routing or protocol problems that might arise in a subnetwork.

→ *See Also* Router

Subnetwork-Dependent Convergence Protocol (SNDCP)

→ *See* SNDCP (Subnetwork-Dependent Convergence Protocol)

Subnetwork-Independent Convergence Protocol (SNICP)

→ *See* SNICP (Subnetwork-Independent Convergence Protocol)

Sub-Quarter Common Intermediate Format (SQCIF)

→ *See* SQCIF (Sub-Quarter Common Intermediate Format)

Supergroup

→ *See* Master Group

Surface Test

A surface test is a test of a hard disk's surface for bad blocks (areas in which data may become damaged or lost). This type of test can be done as part of the installation process for most network operating systems.

Some hard disk manufacturers perform these tests prior to shipment. If the test identifies bad blocks, these are labeled as bad and the blocks are included in a bad blocks table, so that a program or operating system will not write anything to these regions of the disk.

A surface test may be destructive or nondestructive. In a destructive test, existing data on the disk will be overwritten and lost. In a nondestructive test, data is moved before the section of the disk is tested.

Surge, Electrical

A short-term increase in voltage. The duration of a surge is longer than for a spike, but the voltage increase is much lower than for a spike. Specifically, a surge occurs if the voltage is more than 10 percent above the nominal RMS voltage for more than $1/120$ second.

→ *See Also* Power Disturbances

Surge, Packet-Switched Network

In packet-switched networks, a surge is a temporary increase in required bandwidth. The increase is measured in relation to a guaranteed bandwidth, known as the *committed information rate* (*CIR*). If you are a subscriber to a packet-switched network, you will be charged for the extra bandwidth.

Surge Suppressor

A surge suppressor is a filter designed to protect computers and other electrical equipment from brief bursts of high voltage, or *surges*. The purpose of a surge suppressor is to deal with the excess voltage and pass on a more normal voltage to the device. Surge suppressors are also known as surge protectors, and less commonly as noise filters.

Surge suppressors differ in the following ways:

- The way in which they deal with the excess voltage

- The speed with which they can deal with the voltage

- The level of voltage they can absorb

- The number of surges they can withstand

- The combinations of power supply wires (hot, neutral, and ground) they protect

Voltage-Diversion Approaches

Less expensive suppressors use a shunt to divert the excess voltage along a separate path. The most popular shunt is a metal-oxide varistor (MOV), and you will see references to "MOV surge suppressors." The shunt approach requires a small amount of time, called the *clamping time*, before the suppressor can go to work.

This grade of surge suppressors is best suited for appliances. Unfortunately, it is also the most widely sold type of surge suppressor. According to some estimates, about 90 percent of surge suppressors are of this type. MOVs have a limited lifetime, and they should be replaced occasionally. How often you will need to replace a MOV depends on the how often it needs to come into service.

A more sophisticated approach uses shunts and noise filtering. This is much more effective (and more expensive) than just a shunt, and it is used in many surge suppressors designed for use with computers.

An isolating design places special components between the power source and the protected device. These devices have particularly high resistance to high voltages, so that the excess signal is effectively blocked by these components. The shunt and noise filtering approach does not require any clamping time or other response delays.

WHAT TO LOOK FOR IN A SURGE SUPPRESSOR

Consider only UL 1449-listed surge suppressors with 6000/330 (or at worst 6000/400) ratings, especially for use on a network.

Surge suppressors are better than no protection for workstations, but they are not adequate for file servers. A file server should have a UPS (uninterruptible power supply) for protection.

A good indicator of a manufacturer's confidence in its equipment is the warranty offered. Some surge suppressors actually have lifetime warranties. For example, American Power Conversion (APC) will, under certain conditions, provide a $25,000 insurance policy for their surge suppressors and other safety devices.

Surge Suppressor Performance

A useful surge suppressor should be fast and effective, reliable and durable.

Underwriters Laboratories has several tests for surge suppressors. The UL 1449 standard sends repeated high-voltage (6000 volts), high-current signals through the surge suppressor, and monitors the voltage that the device lets through.

To be listed, the performance for the first and last tests must be within 10 percent of each other, indicating that the surge protector is durable. Listed devices also get a rating that indicates the voltage that is let through. The best rating is 6000/330 (330 volts are let through with a 6000 volt surge), then 6000/400, 6000/500, and so on.

To be UL-listed, a surge suppressor needs to pass only for the hot-ground wire pair. However, to be really valuable, the suppressor should provide acceptable protection across *each* pair of lines (hot-ground, hot-neutral, and neutral-ground).

Surge suppressors also do line noise filtering. The UL 1283 standard tests a surge protector's ability to suppress noise at various frequencies. However, a UL 1283 listing is less important than a UL 1449 listing, because the type of noise the UL 1283 tests cover should be filtered out by the shields on your computer anyway, in order to meet FCC (Federal Communication Commission) guidelines for emission levels.

Surge suppressors to which you will attach modems, fax machines, or other devices that will communicate over telephone lines must meet additional standards. These surge protectors should also be UL 497A listed.

→ *Broader Category* Safety Device

Sustainable Cell Rate (SCR)

→ *See* SCR (Sustainable Cell Rate)

SVC (Switched Virtual Circuit)

In telecommunications, a circuit, or connection, that is established for a communications session, and that is terminated after the session is over. This is in contrast to a permanent virtual circuit (PVC), which is a connection that is always established.

SWAP (Simple Workflow Access Protocol)

→ *See* Protocol, SWAP (Simple Workflow Access Protocol)

Switch

A switch is a device that connects material coming in with an appropriate outlet. For example, the input may be packets and the outlet might be an Ethernet bus, as in an Ethernet switch. Or the input might be an electronic mail (e-mail) message in cc:Mail format and the output might be to any of a number of other e-mail formats, as with a mail switch.

A switch needs to have a way of establishing the desired connection, and may also need to translate the input before sending it to an output.

There are two main approaches to the task of matching an input with the desired outlet:

- In a matrix approach, each input channel has a predefined connection with each output channel. To pass something from an input to an output is merely a matter of following the connection.

- In a shared memory approach, the input controller writes the material to a reserved area of memory and the specified output channel reads the material from this memory area.

If the connection requires translation, a switch may translate directly or use an intermediate form. For example, a mail switch may use a common format as the storage format. The specified output channel will translate this "generic" format into the format required for the output channel.

In general, switches are beginning to replace earlier, less flexible internetwork links, such as bridges and gateways. For example, a gateway may be able to connect two different architectures, but a switch may be able to connect several.

Because switches do more work than bridges or gateways, switches need more processing power. Switches may have multiple processors, or they may run on a minicomputer for better performance.

Switch Blocking

In telephony and other switching technology, switch blocking refers to a situation in which no path can be established between two parties wishing to communicate. This can happen, for example, if too many people try to make calls (establish connections) at the same time or if certain lines are not released as quickly as expected (so that the fewer available lines cannot meet the demand).

Switch, Data

A location or device in which data can be routed, or switched, to its destination. Data switches are used in switching networks, in which data is grouped and routed on the basis of predetermined criteria.

Switch, Ethernet

An Ethernet switch is a device that can direct network traffic among several Ethernet networks. This type of switch has multiple ports to connect the subnetworks, and it generally has multiple processors to handle the traffic through the switch.

Two types of Ethernet switches are common:

- A store-and-forward switch checks each packet for errors before directing it to the appropriate network. In heavy traffic, this can be time-consuming, and the switch may be overwhelmed; in burst mode, a store-and-forward switch will almost certainly be overwhelmed.

- A cross-point switch directs packets without checking for errors. This type of switch is generally much faster than a store-and-forward switch.

In a sense, an Ethernet switch is just a super-bridge for Ethernet networks.

Switched 56

A 56 kilobit per second, circuit-switched telecommunications service. A switched 56 channel can be leased from long-distance providers, such as AT&T or MCI.

Switched Digital Access

In telecommunications and wide area networking, a mediated connection to long-distance lines. The local carrier mediates the connection, so that the user is connected directly to the local carrier and from there to the long-distance carrier.

→ *Compare* Direct Connect

Switched Backbone

In a switched backbone, a network backbone is implemented in a switch rather than over cable. Each of the key network elements is connected to a port in the switch. Switched backbones are used in flattened networks.

Switched Multimegabit Data Service (SMDS)

→ *See* SMDS (Switched Multimegabit Data Service)

Switched T1

A circuit-switched telecommunications service that provides a 1.544Mbps bandwidth (that is, a T1 line). Transmissions over this line may go through a multiplexer, or channel bank, where they are broken down and transmitted across slower (for example, 64 kilobit per second) channels.

→ *Compare* Switched 56

Switched Virtual Circuit (SVC)

→ *See* SVC (Switched Virtual Circuit)

Switching, Circuit

In circuit switching, a hardware path is set up to establish a connection between two devices. This path stays in effect until the communication is finished, as when one party hangs up the telephone to end a telephone call. Examples of circuit-switching services include the following:

- Switched 56
- Switched T1
- ISDN

→ *Compare* Packet Switching

Switching Element

Switching is the process of getting a packet of data into a node and moving this packet along the appropriate path to the packet's destination. More generally, switching is the process of connecting an input to the appropriate output. The goals are to do this as quickly and as inexpensively as possible.

Switching Tasks

Switching involves three tasks:

Mapping   Identifying the desired output channel

Scheduling   Deciding which packet or packets to send in a time slot

Data forwarding   Delivering the packet to the output once it has been scheduled

The switching process is controlled by a switching element, such as the one shown in the illustration "A switching element."

Switching Element Components

The switching element has three types of components:

- An input controller (IC) for each input channel, or line. This controller's job is to synchronize each input (which may be a message, packet, or cell, depending on the architecture being used) with the internal clock.

- An output controller (OC) for each output channel. This controller's job is to queue and buffer inputs if there are several being routed to the same output channel.

- An interconnection network, which provides a way of getting from any input channel to any output channel.

The interconnection network can take the form of a matrix with a node for each input-output pair. The interconnection can also be provided by a common memory area to which the input controllers write the input and from which the output controllers read and transmit the input. Bus and ring arrangements may also be used to connect input and output channels.

Switching Levels

Switching can take place at any of various levels, and can involve any of the following:

- Hardware circuits, as when making connections for telephone calls

- Messages, such as those in voice and e-mail services, which store a message and forward it to the destination at the appropriate time

- Packets, as in telecommunications services such as X.25 or frame relay

- Cells, as in the ATM network architecture

Cell switching is similar to packet switching, except that it involves fixed-size cells rather than variable-sized packets.

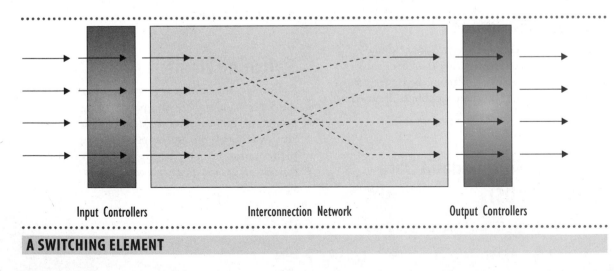

Input Controllers   Interconnection Network   Output Controllers

A SWITCHING ELEMENT

Switching theory, which is concerned with analyzing and optimizing such tasks, is an important and active branch of mathematics, and is likely to grow in prominence as the electronic superhighway is paved.

Switching Hierarchy

In telephony, a hierarchy of switch levels for establishing connections for long-distance calls. Five levels are involved.

→ *See Also* Exchange

Switching, Message

In message switching, a message makes its way from sender to receiver by being passed through intermediate nodes. Each node will store the entire message and forward it to the next node when the opportunity arises. Under certain types of connections, different parts of the message may take different routes to the destination during transmission.

Symmetrical Multiprocessing

In multiprocessing, two or more processors are available to do work. In symmetrical multiprocessing, tasks are assigned to processors in a manner that distributes the workload evenly across processors. By trying not to overwork any processor, symmetrical multiprocessing helps assure that no single processor becomes a performance bottleneck. Because work is distributed evenly among available processors, symmetrical multiprocessing handles the addition of new processors with little problem—that is, symmetrical multiprocessing scales easily.

Symmetrical multiprocessing is in contrast to asymmetrical multiprocessing, in which certain processors are assigned specific tasks, regardless of the relative workloads that result. Asymmetrical multiprocessing is easier to implement than its symmetrical counterpart, but does not scale as well.

Symmetric Digital Subscriber Line (SDSL)

→ *See* SDSL (Symmetric Digital Subscriber Line)

Synchronization

A timing or version comparison and coordination process. The term is used most commonly to refer to actions by which two or more systems are assigned identical times or by which systems agree on the duration of a bit interval (the time required to send one bit). The term has also come to be used to refer to version comparisons, as when replicas of files or database elements are checked to make sure they contain the same information.

Synchronization Rules

Rules used by file servers to control simultaneous access to a file by multiple stations.

Synchronized Multimedia Integration Language (SMIL)

→ *See* SMIL (Synchronized Multimedia Integration Language)

Synchronous

A communications strategy that uses timing to control transmission. A transmission consists of an initial synchronization sequence, followed by a predefined number of bits, each transmitted at a constant rate. Except for the initial synchronization bit, synchronous transmissions do not require any additional bits (as asynchronous methods do). Synchronous transmissions can be fast, but they must be slowed down on noisy lines.

S

Synchronous Digital Hierarchy (SDH)

→*See* SDH (Synchronous Digital Hierarchy)

Synchronous Optical Network (SONET)

→*See* SONET (Synchronous Optical Network)

Synchronous Transfer Mode (STM)

→*See* STM (Synchronous Transfer Mode)

Synchronous Transfer Mode (STM)-*x*

→*See* STM (Synchronous Transfer Mode)-*x*

System Attribute

In a file system, such as the one used by DOS, an attribute (or *flag*) that marks a file or directory as usable only by the operating system.

System Connect

The physical connection to a network or a host computer. For example, the system connect in a thin Ethernet network is through a BNC T-connector attached to the network interface card.

System Fault Tolerance (SFT)

→*See* SFT (System Fault Tolerance)

System Partition

In Windows NT Server environments, files can be stored on a server partition, which merely represents a logical subdivision of the server's hard disk. A hard disk may have one or more server partitions.

A further distinction is made between a boot partition and a system partition. The boot partition refers to the part of the hard disk on which the actual operating system files are stored. The system partition is the active partition (i.e., the partition on which startup activity commences), and it contains hardware specific files that are needed to boot the NT server.

→*Broader Category* Windows NT

System Services Control Point (SSCP)

→*See* SSCP (System Services Control Point)

System Side

The cabling from the computer or network to the distribution frame.

Systems Application Architecture (SAA)

→*See* SAA (Systems Application Architecture)

Systems Management Application Entity (SMAE)

→*See* SMAE (Systems Management Application Entity)

Systems Management Application Process (SMAP)

→ *See* SMAP (Systems Management Application Process)

Systems Management Application Service Element (SMASE)

→ *See* SMASE (Systems Management Application Service Element)

Systems Management Function (SMF)

→ *See* SMF (Systems Management Function)

Systems Management Functional Area (SMFA)

→ *See* SMFA (Systems Management Functional Area)

Systems Network Architecture (SNA)

→ *See* SNA (Systems Network Architecture)

Systems Network Architecture/ Synchronous Data Link Control (SNA/SDLC)

→ *See* SNA/SDLC (Systems Network Architecture/Synchronous Data Link Control)

SystemView

A comprehensive network management package from IBM. The first parts of SystemView were released in 1990, and components are still being developed. Intended as a replacement for NetView, SystemView is more comprehensive, will support more networking models, and will provide greater flexibility in data presentation than NetView.

S

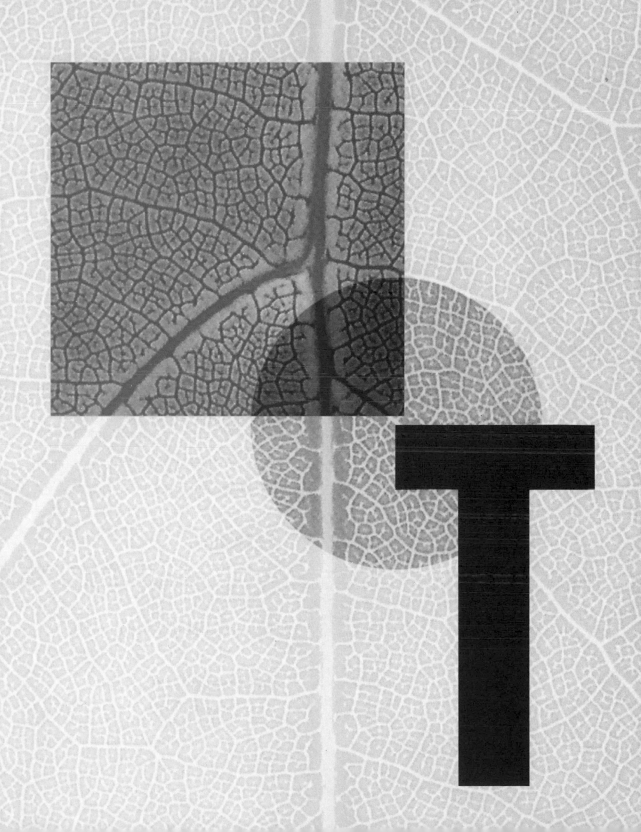

T

Used as an abbreviation for the prefix *tera*, as in THz (terahertz), TB (terabytes), or Tbps (terabits per second). This order of magnitude corresponds to 2^{40}, which is roughly 10^{12}, or trillions (in the United States counting system).

→ **See Also** Order of Magnitude

T1 Carrier

In digital communications, T1 is the carrier used in North America, Australia, and Japan. Although originally developed to transmit voice conversations, T1 is also suitable for data and image transmissions, and it is commonly used for such purposes. T1 has a bandwidth of 1.544Mbps, which comes from two dozen 64Kbps channels, together with one 8Kbps framing channel.

The T1 link was developed by AT&T to increase the number of voice calls that could be handled through the existing cables. A T1 carrier can handle 24 conversations simultaneously, using two wire pairs. One pair is used for sending, and the other for receiving, so that a T1 link can operate in full-duplex mode.

The 24 individual channels are each sampled 8000 times a second, generating an 8 bit value each time. Data from the 24 channels is multiplexed into 192 bit frames, to which a 193rd bit is added for framing purposes. The samples for the 24 channels yield 1.536Mbps, and 8Kbps is added for framing to make the 1.544Mbps capacity for a T1 line. (Actually, in the T1 world, the subscriber only gets 56Kbps of every channel; the service provider steals one bit from each value for control purposes.)

The individual 64Kbps channels are known as DS0 (for Digital Signal, level 0) channels. DS0 channels are the building blocks for a T1 carrier and for even higher-speed links. In DS terms, the 24 DS0 channels make up one DS1 channel. The T1 carrier provides the transmission capabilities for the data in the DS1 channel.

T1 lines can be multiplexed into even faster links. The table "The T1 Digital Carrier Hierarchy" shows the T1 hierarchy. The data rates reflect extra channels for framing, control, or signaling.

THE T1 DIGITAL CARRIER HIERARCHY

Signal Level	Carrier	# T1 Links	Data Rate
DS1	T1	1	1.544Mbps
DS1C	T1C	2	3.152Mbps
DS2	T2	4 (2×T1C)	6.312Mbps
DS3	T3	28 (7×T2)	44.736Mbps
DS4	T4	168 (6×T3)	274.176Mbps

T1 services are still quite expensive. This is partly because they tend to be used for long-distance links and because subscribers must pay a monthly fee based on distance (possibly several dollars per mile). T1 links also have high installation costs.

In Europe, South America, and Mexico, an analogous carrier is defined by the CCITT, designated as E1. This carrier has a bandwidth of 2.048Mbps.

→ **Broader Category** Digital Communications

→ **See Also** E1 Carrier; Fractional T1

T3 Channel

A communications channel with a bandwidth of 44.736Mbps. This channel is the equivalent of 28 T1 channels, or of 672 voice channels, each of 64 kilobits per second. In Europe, this designation has been superseded by the CCITT's DS3 designation.

TA (Terminal Adapter)

A device that mediates between an ISDN (Integrated Services Digital Network) network and devices that are not ISDN-compatible (known as TE2 devices). The TA's output will conform to whichever one of four CCITT standards is appropriate: V.110, V.120, X.30, or X.31.

Table

Information in databases is generally organized in tables whose rows represent records and whose columns represent attributes, or keys. The content of a particular table cell represents the value of a particular record for a specific key.

Tables, as used for database manipulation and management, can be modified in a variety of ways. For example, they may be ordered (sorted on the basis of values for specific keys), extended (by adding new keys to an existing table), combined (by merging two tables with a common key), or refined (by creating a tables using only some of the keys in the original table).

These are just a few of the possible manipulations on database tables. The justifications for such operations derive from various formal disciplines such as mathematics and logic. In addition, database management has profited from theoretical developments in database theory—particularly in connection with relational databases.

→ *Broader Category* Database

Tag Switching

Tag switching is one of several methods that have been developed to speed up the forwarding of layer 3 (network layer) packets over high-speed networking architectures such as ATM (Asynchronous Transfer Mode). Developed by Cisco Systems, tag switching attaches a special label, or tag, to packets that are part of the same flow. (A flow is a sequence of consecutive packets all of which are going to the same destination address.) Once a packet has been identified as part of a flow by its tag, it is not necessary for a router to check its network address and to

generate routing instructions, thereby saving considerable time.

→ *Broader Category* Layer 3 Switching

→ *See Also* IP Switching; Protocol, MPLS (Multiprotocol Layer Switching)

TAG (Technical Advisory Group)

An IEEE committee whose task is to provide general recommendations and technical guidance for other committees. Perhaps the best known TAGS are the 802.7 and 802.8 committees, which are concerned with issues relating to broadband networks and to the use of fiber-optic cabling in networks, respectively.

Talk protocol

→ *See* Protocol, Talk

Tandem

In the PSTN (public switched telephone network) hierarchy, tandems are centers in which trunk-switching is done. In telephone company parlance, a trunk is an aggregate line that carries multiple individual lines—for example, lines from individual subscribers. In the telephone company office hierarchy, the offices at classes 4, 3, 2, and 1 are tandems.

The lines, trunks, and exchanges in the telephone system network are connected via a five-level hierarchy of offices. Class 5 offices are the local exchanges at which calls originate. Individual subscribers are connected to these class 5 central offices.

The class 5 offices are connected to class 4 offices, which are the first level of offices that handle long distance calls. Lines into a class 5 office are combined into trunks, which lead out to a level 4 office.

Trunks from various class 5 offices converge on a class 4 office.

Multiple class 4 offices are combined at—and serviced by—class 3 offices. Each area code is handled by a class 3 office, which is also known as a primary center. Primary centers, in turn, connect to class 2 offices—known as sectional centers. Each sectional center covers a section of the country. Finally, class 2 offices connect to class 1 offices (also known as regional centers).

Tap

An attachment to a transmission or power line. For example, a tap may be used to add a node to a network. Signals can be received or transmitted through a tap. In a thick Ethernet network, a *vampire tap* is one that actually pierces the cable in order to attach a node to the network.

Tape Drive

A tape drive is a sequential access storage device that is often used for backing up hard disk systems. Because of their large capacity (250MB drives are common) and relatively high speed, tape drives are a popular backup medium for networks.

Most network operating systems include servers for using tape drives as a backup medium, either as part of the basic services or through add-on modules.

Types of Tape Drives

Tape drives come in internal and external forms. Some external drives plug into a parallel port, so they are easier to move from machine to machine to do backups.

Although many tape drive manufacturers have their proprietary compression and storage formats, just about all manufacturers support the QIC-80 format, which has become the standard for tape backup.

BUYING TAPES FOR TAPE DRIVES

Formatting tapes for tape drives is a tedious, time-consuming task. For some types of cartridges, it can take a couple of hours to format, mark, and verify a single tape.

If at all possible, buy preformatted tapes. The price difference is small compared with the time and aggravation saved.

Advantages and Disadvantages of Tape Drives as Backup Media

Tape drives and media are an inexpensive way to back up data. They are also suitable for restoring data when you need to restore an entire tape.

Tape as a storage medium suffers when you want to access specific information on a tape. This is because, unlike hard or floppy disk drives or CD-ROM drives, tape is a sequential-access medium (rather than a random-access medium). This means it can take several minutes to get to the material you want to retrieve from the tape.

➞ Broader Category Peripheral

TAPI (Telephony Applications Program Interface)

TAPI is a set of functions developed by Microsoft for integrating PCs and telephone systems. TAPI supports PBX and Centrex systems, as well as conventional lines. It also supports services such as ISDN or cellular technology. TAPI support is built into Windows 95.

TSAPI, Novell's entry, is a main competitor for TAPI.

➞ Broader Category Computer-Telephony Integration

➞ See Also TSAPI (Telephony Services API); Versit

Target

In Novell's NetWare, a server or node that contains data to be backed up or restored. A server or node can be a target only if a Target Service Agent (TSA) is running on the potential target.

→ *See Also* TSA (Target Service Agent)

Target Coding

In a communications context, the coding (representation) used by the application that receives a transmission. In a network, the receiving application must be running on an end system, which is a node capable of using all seven layers in the OSI reference model.

Target Service Agent (TSA)

→ *See* TSA (Target Service Agent)

Target Token Rotation Time (TTRT)

→ *See* TTRT (Target Token Rotation Time)

Tcl (Tool Command Language)

Tcl (pronounced "tickle") is an interpreted scripting language developed by John Ousterhout and intended for controlling and extending the functionality of applications. A common use for Tcl scripts is linking applications—for example, to feed data from one application into another or to process output from a program before feeding the modified material to another program.

Tcl scripts can run in an appropriate shell; or they can be embedded in applications in order to accomplish certain tasks or to enhance the application. The Tcl language is also extensible, allowing programmers to add to the language's constructs

and capabilities by writing such extensions in C, C++, or Java.

Various extensions to Tcl have been created in this way, with the best known being Tk (toolkit). Tk provides resources (buttons, menus, scroll bars, and other widgets, or window objects) for creating graphical user interfaces (GUIs). A related extension—XF—enables a user to create interfaces interactively.

Other Tcl extensions include:

- Tcl-DP (Tcl Distributed Programming), a library of Tcl commands that makes it easier to create distributed programs.

- TclX (Extended Tcl), a library of language extensions that provide such things as online help and debugging facilities, more versatile data structures (for example, key lists, which are similar to structures in C or records in Pascal), and the ability to scan files. Historically, TclX has served as a proving ground for new constructs, with those that are especially popular being incorporated into a newer version of the standard Tcl language.

- Expect, a program that can be used to provide a link to interactive programs—for example, for filling out forms or running ftp (file transfer program) or telnet sessions.

- Ak, a library of audio extensions for Tcl. Ak can be used to record, play back, and otherwise control files using the AudioFile audio system. Ak can also be used to synchronize the presentation of particular information or files in multimedia presentations.

Scriptics Corp. was formed to develop and package commercial versions of the Tcl environment and tools. However, public versions of Tcl continue to be available. You can find more information about Tcl at http://www.tclconsortium.org and at http://www.scriptics.com/resource.

→ *Broader Category* Scripting Language

TCNS (Thomas-Conrad Network System)

TCNS is a 100 megabit per second (Mbps) implementation of the ARCnet architecture, developed by Thomas-Conrad. TCNS can use existing ARCnet drivers, but it also includes drivers to make it usable in any of several operating environments, such as Novell's NetWare, Microsoft's LAN Manager, or Banyan's VINES.

TCNS does require special Network Interface Cards (NICs), however. Special NICs are needed because of the higher transmission speed and also because TCNS uses a different encoding scheme than standard ARCnet.

TCNS can use coaxial, shielded twisted-pair (STP), or fiber-optic cable, but it does not support unshielded twisted-pair (UTP). In order to help increase bandwidth, TCNS uses a 4B/5B translation scheme (which converts four signal bits into a five-bit symbol) and then uses a Nonreturn to Zero, Inverted (NRZI) signal-encoding scheme.

→ *Broader Category* ARCnet

T-Connector

→ *See* Connector, T

TCP (Transmission Control Protocol)

→ *See* Protocol, TCP (Transmission Control Protocol)

TCP/IP (Transmission Control Protocol/Internet Protocol) Suite

TCP/IP is a suite of several networking protocols, developed for use on the Internet. The suite has proven very popular, and it is also used for most UNIX implementations as well as other platforms. The only real competition for the TCP/IP suite is provided by protocols that have been or are being developed for the emerging OSI reference model.

The main protocols in the suite include the following:

- SMTP (Simple Mail Transfer Protocol) provides a simple electronic-mail (e-mail) service. SMTP uses the TCP protocol to send and receive messages.

- FTP (File Transfer Protocol) enables users to transfer files from one machine to another. FTP also uses the services of the TCP protocol at the Transport layer to move the files.

- Telnet provides terminal-emulation capabilities and allows users to log in to a remote network from their computers.

- SNMP (Simple Network Management Protocol) is used to control network-management services and to transfer management-related data.

- TCP (Transmission Control Protocol) provides connection- and stream-oriented, transport-layer services. TCP uses the IP to deliver its packets.

- UDP (User Datagram Protocol) provides connectionless transport-layer service. UDP also uses the IP to deliver its packets.

- IP (Internet Protocol) provides routing and connectionless delivery services at the Network layer. The IP uses packet switching and makes a best effort to deliver its packets.

- ARP (Address Resolution Protocol) provides a mapping between IP (network layer) and hardware (data-link layer) addresses. That is, given an IP address, ARP will determine the hardware address corresponding to it.

- ICMP (Internet Control Message Protocol) handles errors at the network layer. ICMP is actually part of IP.

- HTTP (Hypertext Transfer Protocol) allows Web servers and clients (for example, browsers) to communicate and to exchange requests and files.

TDDI (Twisted-pair Distributed Data Interface)

A network architecture that implements FDDI capabilities and protocols on twisted-pair, copper-based cable.

→ **See Also** CDDI (Copper-based Distributed Data Interface)

TDM (Time Division Multiplexing)

A transmission scheme in which signals from multiple sources are transmitted "simultaneously" by allocating time slices in sequence to each of the signals. This method is generally used for digital communications.

→ **See Also** Multiplexing

TDMA (Time Division Multiple Access)

A strategy for making a communications channel available to multiple parties at a time. The strategy allocates each party a time slot, whose duration depends on the number of parties who want to transmit and on the relative importance of the party to whom the time slot is being allocated. Each party's transmissions must be reassembled at the receiving end.

→ **Compare** CDMA (Cell Division Multiple Access); FDMA (Frequency Division Multiple Access)

TDR (Time Domain Reflectometry)

A diagnostic method in which a signal of known amplitude and duration is sent along a stretch of cable. Depending on the amount of time the signal takes to return and on the cable's nominal velocity of propagation, a measurement instrument can determine the distance the signal traveled and whether there are any shorts or opens in the cable. A *time domain reflectometer* is a device used to test the integrity of a section of cable before the cable is even unwound.

TE (Terminal Equipment)

In digital communications technologies such as ISDN (Integrated Services Digital Network) and the DSL (Digital Subscriber Line) variants (ADSL, HDSL, RADSL, SDSL, and so forth), TE refers to equipment that is at either end of the connection—that is, either at the customer premises or at the telephone company's central office (CO).

Technical Advisory Group (TAG)

→ **See** TAG (Technical Advisory Group)

Technical Office Protocol (TOP)

→ **See** TOP (Technical Office Protocol)

Tee Coupler

A coupler that splits an incoming signal into two outgoing signals. This is in contrast to a star coupler, which splits the signal into more parts. A tee coupler has three ports. These couplers are used in bus topologies.

→ **See Also** Coupler

Telecommunications

Telecommunications refers to the transmission of digital or analog data or voice over electrical or optical lines or using wireless technology. Various standards, methods, and technologies have been developed to accomplish this, and several of these are still in use. The digital/analog distinction can apply independently to both the data format and the transmission method. That is, digital or analog data can each be sent using either digital or analog signaling methods. Special devices may be needed to convert between digital and analog form.

Traditional voice telephone communications use analog signals to send analog content (spoken words) over copper wire—at least for the stretch between the customer premises and the telephone company central office (CO). Once a signal reaches the CO, the signal may be converted to digital form before being passed on to its next destination—particularly if this is an interexchange carrier that provides long distance service.

As stated, analog technologies can also be used to transmit digital data. To do this, a modem is used to translate the digital data into analog form before transmitting the data over the telephone lines. Modems can support various transmission speeds, depending on the standards to which the modems conform. Older, slower modems are based on Bell signaling standards. These support transmission speeds of up to 9600bps (bits per second). Newer, higher speed modems use the V series signaling standards developed by the ITU (International Telecommunications Union), an international standards organization. The V series standards support speeds of up to 56kbps, and even higher for certain modems with special connections.

Digital technologies developed for data communications can also be used for voice transmission. Such digital technologies include ISDN (Integrated Services Digital Network) or DSL (digital subscriber line) services. In general, digital technologies can support higher transmission speeds—in some cases, billions of bits per second.

Various digital communications standards are used, depending on the type of connection and the network architecture involved. For example, ATM (Asynchronous Transfer Mode), FDDI (Fiber Distributed Data Interface), frame relay, and X.25 provide standards for WAN (wide area network) transmission architectures; SONET (Synchronous Optical Network) and STM (Synchronous Transfer Mode) provide transport methods upon which a hierarchy of channel capacities have been developed (as described in the entry for SONET).

Wireless technologies represent both the oldest (messenger, drums, smoke signals) and the newest (cellular, GSM, or global system for mobile communications) telecommunications methods. This area is still in flux, with companies competing to establish their technology as the wireless standard. Transmission speeds for wireless technologies are considerably slower than for copper- or fiber-based transmissions.

→ See Also Digital Communication; GSM (Global System for Mobile Communications); Modem; SONET (Synchronous Optical Network); Telephony; Wireless Communication

Telecommunications Architecture

A telecommunications architecture provides a framework for establishing connections between network elements and for transmitting data between them. Examples of such an architecture include the PSTN (public switched telephone network), ATM (Asynchronous Transfer Mode), and the Internet. Such architectures use some type of switching to create a path for a communications session.

For example, the PSTN uses circuit switching to connect parties in a telephone conversation or to connect an end user to an Internet service provider. In circuit switching, a fixed path is established by reserving the circuits along the path prior to beginning communications. The entire session takes place over these circuits, with each part of the session taking the same path. The circuits along this path are dedicated. That is, these circuits cannot be used for other connections as long as the session lasts. On balance, however, such dedicated circuits can ensure that the connection gets the full bandwidth that is possible across the circuits. In other words, a circuit-switched architecture can provide a desired quality of service (QoS).

In contrast, the Internet is a packet-switched network. In such an architecture, only the endpoints of a connection are fixed. The content for a communication session is broken into packets, which may be different sizes. The packets are transmitted individually, and they may take different paths between source and destination. The packets that make up a transmission are assembled at the destination by an appropriate protocol.

In a packet-switched architecture, intermediate points, or nodes, in a connection can be used for multiple sessions, since packets can be rerouted if a node is not available when needed. Packet-switched architectures generally do not support QoS without special measures. In order to provide QoS in such an architecture, it's necessary to reserve a path prior to transmission. Protocols (such as the Resource Reservation Protocol, or RSVP) have been developed to make this possible.

Cell-switched architectures—for example, Frame Relay and ATM—have features of both circuit- and packet-switched architectures. Such architectures are connection-oriented by default. This means that a path is selected before communications begin—just as in a circuit-switched arrangement. It also means that a cell-switched architecture can support QoS requirements. However, cell-switched networks can also provide a connectionless mode, in which different cells (packets that are all the same size) can take different paths if necessary. QoS is still supported even in connectionless mode, however, because only nodes that can provide the required QoS will be considered when selecting paths.

→ *See Also* ATM (Asynchronous Transfer Mode); Connectionless Service; Connection-Oriented Service; Frame Relay; QoS (Quality of Services)

Telecommuting

Telecommuting refers to a growing trend in which employees use telecommunications technology to access office resources and to do their work from a remote location—usually from home or from a mobile station. Telecommuting is becoming increasingly popular as increases in electronic bandwidth make it more feasible and as congestion in vehicular traffic and in public transportation make it more desirable.

Teleconference

A conference between individuals who are separated by a distance and who are communicating by electronic means. The telecommunications link for a teleconference may be voice only (two-way), one-way video, two-way voice, or two-way video.

Teledisc

Teledisc is a low earth orbit (LEO) satellite project that will use 288 satellites to provide Internet access. Like Iridium, a competitor product from a consortium headed by Motorola, Teledisc requires a huge investment, so it will be a gamble. In light of the recent bankruptcy filing by the Iridium consortium, it remains to be seen how Teledisc will fare.

→ *Broader Category* LEO (Low Earth Orbit) Satellite

→ *See Also* Iridium

Telegraph

The telegraph was the first long-distance electronic communications technology. Developed by Samuel Morse, telegraphy—that is, telegraph communications—used Morse code. This code represents each letter and digit as a unique sequence of dots and dashes—that is, short and long signals.

The sender encodes the individual letters by pressing a key for a short (dot) or long (dash) duration. This produces a change in an electrical current that is transmitted over the telegraph wires. (This serial signal is reproduced by marks on paper at the receiving end.)

Telephone

The telephone is the most widely used communications device in the world, and has led to the creation of the largest net of connections on the planet—more extensive even than the roadway systems of the world. The global network that has been built for voice telephone service has also provided access to the Internet and to other types of telecommunications services (such as fax and telex).

Alexander Graham Bell developed the telephone to make voice communication possible between remote locations. Bell was encouraged to begin his efforts to develop the telephone because he mistranslated statements in a paper by the German physicist Hermann von Helmholtz. These statements led Bell to believe that Helmholtz had already demonstrated the feasibility of capabilities he required for his device—namely the ability to convert acoustic signals to electrical form and vice versa. Although there was no proof of concept, such conversions were possible, and Bell developed the means to accomplish them.

The ability to communicate over long distances by voice has been a major boon for the world's social and economic development in the past 120 or so years. It has made many aspects of commerce and of social interaction easier and faster. However, it is generally agreed that this ability has also been a major bane for at least some of that time—because it has led to such intrusions and time-wasters as telemarketers and telephone tag.

Although they are based on analog technology, the public switched telephone networks (PSTNs) have also been a model for many of the networking principles that underlie the digital global networks that are now replacing PSTNs. For example, the concept of switching is central to many types of data networks. Similarly, disciplines and research areas such as queuing theory and traffic management were originally developed to help plan out wiring for the telephone network, but they have proven indispensible in planning out data networks as well.

The digital networks that are replacing the PSTNs will continue to provide telephony service, but will also provide access to video and other types of data services. As part of this development, the telephone itself is changing. The stand-alone device that began as the bulky, crank-operated box seen in old movies has developed through thematic and design-conscious forms such as the princess and football phones, and can now be shrunk down to a few chips that sit on a card in a PC.

Despite these changes in form and function, the telephone continues to play a central role in communications and in modern civilization.

→ **See Also** CTI (Computer-Telephony Integration); Telephony

Telephone Amplifier

A telephone amplifier is used to increase the sound level in a telephone receiver beyond the level provided by the line power. Such an amplifier must be powered by an adapter or by batteries. However, with such an amplifier, the voice signal level can be increased by 20dB (decibels), as opposed to the 10dB increase provided by line power alone.

Telephone Channel

A telephone channel is simply a path that can carry voice signals. For this purpose, the channel must include the telephone frequency (the range between 300 and 3000Hz).

Telephone Circuit

A telephone circuit makes it possible for parties at either end of a telephone call to communicate. The circuit provides a complete round-trip path for such communications.

Telephone Frequency

In telephony, the frequency range between 0 and 4000 Hz is known as the voice channel, and the band from 300 to 3000Hz is known as the telephone frequency. Voice signals within the telephone frequency are known as in-band signals, and signals between 3000 and 4000 Hz are known as out-of-band signals. The former transmit the voice information, whereas the latter are used for signaling and control purposes. Any frequencies above 4000Hz are filtered out, so that they do not interfere with the voice signals.

Telephone Tag

Telephone tag is a serial communications method in which the participants in the tag leave messages for each other, but don't actually get to communicate directly. Participants generally take turns leaving such messages, but strict alternation is not required. The telephone tag ends when the two participants actually manage to talk directly or when one of them simply stops calling.

Telephone Twisted Pair (TTP)

→ See Cable, Twisted-Pair

Telephony

A term that referred originally to the business of the telephone companies, but that has come to refer to the combination and integration of telephone and networking services. For example, providing a link from a network to the telephone lines and using software to interact with the telephone services can be referred to as telephony.

Telephony Application Programming Interface (TAPI)

→ See TAPI (Telephony Application Program Interface)

Telephony Services Application Programming Interface (TSAPI)

→ See TSAPI (Telephony Services API)

Teleservices

In ISDN (Integrated Services Digital Network), services defined for communications between two endpoints. The following teleservices have been defined:

Telefax Provides facsimile service compliant with the specifications for Group 4 (digital) faxes. The fax is sent on a B (bearer) channel; control signals are sent over the D (data) channel.

Telephony Provides speech communication in 3.1 kilohertz (kHz) bandwidths. The conversion is sent over a B channel; control signals are sent over the D channel.

Teletex Provides text communication capabilities, using standardized character sets, formats, and communication protocols. Users can exchange text at 2400 baud. The user's transmission is over a B channel; control signals are over the D channel. Not to be confused with *teletext*, which is a special type of videotex service.

Telex Provides interactive text communication capabilities. Telex is older and slower than Teletex.

Videotex Provides transmission capabilities for both text and graphics. Videotex services are generally one-directional.

Teletext is a one-directional videotex service in which signals are transmitted from a source during certain "quiet" intervals in a television transmission. Originally intended as a service to provide general information (weather, sports updates, and so on), teletext has not yet caught on with the general public. It is, however, popular in business environments.

→ *Primary Source* CCITT Recommendation I.212

Temperature Sensor

A sensor that monitors the temperature inside the computer. If this rises above a predefined level, the sensor automatically turns on or speeds up the computer's fan.

Terminal

A terminal is a device that can be used to communicate with a host computer, such as a mainframe, but that may lack any independent processing capabilities. Several categories of terminals are defined:

Dumb terminal Lacks any memory or other components needed for doing computations. All processing for the terminal is done by the host or by the host's Front-End Processor (FEP). Dumb terminals have limited flexibility for use, because they are not addressable. This means dumb terminals cannot do line sharing and cannot be polled for requests. These restrictions greatly limit the kind of interactions possible with a dumb terminal.

Smart terminal Has at least limited processing capabilities and can be associated with an address.

Intelligent terminal Has its own processor, can do its own processing, and can even run programs. PCs often serve as intelligent terminals.

In addition, terminals may be used for synchronous or asynchronous communications. Since the requirements for these two different communications strategies are quite different, synchronous and asynchronous terminals may not be compatible.

If the required type of terminal is not available, it is often possible to provide *terminal emulation* through software, hardware, or both. Through an *emulation*, a PC can be turned into a functionally equivalent replica of the required terminal. In general, asynchronous terminals are easier to emulate than synchronous ones.

Terminal Adapter (TA)

→ *See* TA (Terminal Adapter)

Terminal Cluster Controller

A device that connects one or more PCs to a front-end processor for a mainframe computer, most notably in an IBM mainframe network. An alternative uses a gateway to the mainframe.

Terminal Emulation

Terminal emulation is a process by which a computer behaves as if it were a particular model of terminal. For example, terminal emulation may be used in order to enable the PC to communicate with a mainframe machine.

Emulation capabilities can be provided in hardware or software. The use of an emulation adapter card is popular. The speed and performance of these types of boards are sometimes better than for emulation in software, but the price can be prohibitive if many workstations will need to provide access to mainframes.

Terminal Equipment (TE)

→ *See* TE (Terminal Equipment)

Terminal Packet Assembler/ Disassembler (TPAD)

→ *See* PAD (Packet Assembler/Disassembler)

Terminal Server

→ *See* Server, Terminal

Terminate-and-Stay-Resident (TSR) Program

→ *See* TSR (Terminate-and-Stay-Resident) Program

Termination

If a program or other process behaves incorrectly or takes up more than its share of resources, it is sometimes necessary to stop it, in order to allow other processes to do their work. The process of ending such processes is known as termination.

In SCSI (Small Computer System Interface) systems and certain other electrical connections, termination is used to make sure electrical signals do not cause interference when they reach the end of their path. SCSI connections must be terminated at either end in order to ensure that the signals behave properly.

Terminator

A resistor placed at the end of a segment of cable to prevent signals from being echoed or reflected back toward the incoming signal.

TH (Transmission Header)

In SNA networks, an element added to a basic information unit (BIU) at the path control layer. The BIU, together with the TH, form a path information unit (PIU).

→ *See* SNA (Systems Network Architecture)

The Internet Adapter (TIA)

→ *See* TIA (The Internet Adapter)

Thick Ethernet

→ *See* Ethernet

Thin Ethernet

→ *See* Ethernet

Thomas-Conrad Network System (TCNS)

→ *See* TCNS (Thomas-Conrad Network System)

Three-Way Handshake

A three-way handshake is the process used to synchronize activities when two protocols establish a connection. In a three-way handshake, the following occurs:

- The caller sends a packet requesting a connection. This packet may contain communications parameters that specify the terms under which the caller wants to establish a connection.

- To indicate that it is ready to receive, the called node returns a connect confirmation packet. This packet may contain connection parameters that the called node needs or wants. These parameters may be different from those originally sent by the caller.

- To indicate agreement to the called node's terms, the caller sends an acknowledgment packet. This tells the called node that the terms are acceptable and that the caller is ready to proceed. Under certain conditions, the caller may send an ordinary or a special, expedited data packet instead of the acknowledgment.

Note that the *three-way* refers to the number of steps involved rather than to the number of hands. See the Time-Sequence Diagram article for an illustration of the three-way handshake.

Threshold

In network management, an attribute level that is used as a cutoff point between significant or critical and nonsignificant events. For example, an alarm may be given if an error rate goes above a predefined threshold value.

Throughput

A measure of activity or progress in a communications session. The most common measure of throughput is the total number of bits transmitted within a given amount of time, usually a second. This value includes *all* bits transmitted (data, control, and so on), even retransmitted bits. The *effective throughput* is the number of *data* bits transmitted within a given time period.

THT (Token Holding Time)

In FDDI networks, a parameter whose value can be used to adjust access to the network. A high THT value allows a node to keep the token for a long time, which is useful if network activity consists mainly of large file transfers and if rapid access to the network is not critical. In contrast, a small value gives nodes more equal access to the network.

TIA (The Internet Adapter)

The Internet Adapter provides a SLIP (Serial line Internet Protocol) emulator for Unix systems. This emulator makes it possible to run Windows browsers, such as Mosaic, from a Unix shell account. TIA is a shareware program.

TIC (Token Ring Interface Coupler)

A device that enables direct connections from a Token Ring network to various types of mainframe equipment, including front-end processors, AS/400s, and 3174 terminal cluster controllers.

Tight Buffer

In fiber-optic cabling, a layer that is stretched tightly over the cladding to keep the fiber from moving around too much. Tight buffers are commonly used in patch cords and other areas in which the cable is likely to be moved or shaken.

Time Division Multiple Access (TDMA)

→ *See* TDMA (Time Division Multiple Access)

Time Division Multiplexing (TDM)

→ **See** TDM (Time Division Multiplexing)

Time Domain Reflectometry (TDR)

→ **See** TDR (Time Domain Reflectometry)

Time-Out

As a verb, to time-out means to use too much time to respond in a communication situation, usually resulting in the failure of the task that was being performed. For example, a device, such as a modem or a station on a network, can cause a time-out if it does not acknowledge receipt of a transmission from another device.

Time-outs can be caused by transmission errors, delays due to network traffic, and other types of delays. The action taken by the waiting device depends on the configuration. For example, a modem may end the session or retransmit the message.

Time-Sequence Diagram

A time-sequence diagram refers to a technique for graphically representing events over time. In this type of diagram, time is represented on a vertical axis, with the oldest event at the top and the most recent event at the bottom. The information presented horizontally depends on the diagram's content.

"A time-sequence diagram" illustrates an example. The illustration shows a three-way handshake in which sender and receiver go through a request and acknowledgment process before the sender begins transmitting data. To make the sequence clear, the events are numbered.

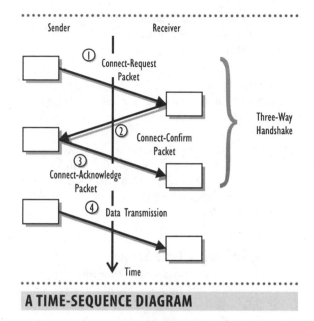

A TIME-SEQUENCE DIAGRAM

Time Synchronization

In Novell's NetWare 4.x and later, time synchronization is a way of ensuring that all servers in a NetWare Directory Services (NDS) Directory are using the same time. Synchronized timing is essential because it provides a way of ordering changes that may have been made to information about objects on the network.

Information about objects changes, as a print queue grows or shrinks, a user changes a password, or an application is executed. Since these changes may be recorded in replicas, it is essential to keep track of the timing and sequence of events when updating the Directory.

NetWare 4.x uses time synchronization for this purpose. In time synchronization, the NDS marks each event that occurs, along with the exact time of its occurrence, with a unique value, known as a *time stamp*.

To make time stamps useful, the network must ensure that all servers are keeping the same time.

T

To do this, special time servers are designated. These time servers provide the "correct" time to other time servers or to workstations.

NetWare 4.x distinguishes three types of time servers that provide time: Single Reference, Reference, and Primary. All other servers that accept time information from these servers are called *secondary* time servers. In any network with more than one time server, the time servers must work together to create a network time. They influence each other until they reach something like an "average" time, and they then deliver this time to all the secondary servers.

Single-Reference Time Server

If one is defined, a Single-Reference time server is the only time server that provides the correct time to all other servers and to workstations. Defining a time server that has such complete authority has two consequences:

- All other servers must be able to contact the Single-Reference time server.

- All other servers on the network must be designated as Secondary time servers, which provide the time information to the workstations.

Single-Reference time servers are generally used for local area networks (LANs), since it is inconvenient (and expensive) when secondary time servers need to make long-distance calls to find out the time.

Reference Time Server

A Reference time server provides a time for all other Primary time servers to work towards as they achieve a network time. A Reference time server may be synchronized with an external time source. It adjusts its internal clock only in relation to such an external source, never to synchronize with other Primary time servers; the Primary servers must adjust to the Reference server.

A network usually has only one Reference time server, and this may or may not be designated as a Single-Reference server. However, if there are two or more Reference servers, each must be synchronized with the same (or with an equivalent) external source. A network probably will not need more than one Reference time server, unless, for example, it has one at each end of a wide area network (WAN) link.

Reference time servers are used when it is important to have a central time source. A Reference (as opposed to a Single-Reference) time server must have at least one other Primary or Reference time server with which to communicate.

Primary Time Server

A Primary time server synchronizes its clock to a Reference or another Primary time server. Primary time servers participate in a vote, along with Reference and other Primary time servers, to determine the common network time. Once this time is set, Primary time servers adjust their clocks to this time. (Reference time servers do not adjust their clocks, since their time is actually used to determine the network time.)

Primary time servers are useful on large networks, particularly on WANs. By putting a Primary time server in each geographic region, you can minimize the amount of telephone access needed to determine the time. Primary time servers provide the time information to secondary time servers and to workstations. (A Reference server is not necessary, but you must have at least two Primary servers.)

Secondary Time Server

A secondary time server gets time information from a Single Reference, Reference, or Primary time server, and provides this information to workstations. Secondary time servers always synchronize their time to that of the time source.

Communications among Time Servers

To enable time servers to find each other, the servers can use the SAP (Service Advertising Protocol) to make themselves known. Because of the small amount of extra network traffic generated by SAP packets, this strategy is recommended for small networks and for networks whose configurations are unlikely to change much. The SAP changes dynamically, as servers and nodes are added or removed.

An alternative is to configure the network explicitly, by specifying the location of all time servers and by specifying which time server each secondary server should contact for information. This strategy is best when the level of SAP traffic begins to impede network performance.

Time-to-Live (TTL)

→ *See* TTL (Time-to-Live)

Tip

One of a pair of twisted wires, with the other wire known as the ring. A four-pair unshielded twisted-pair cable has four tip/ring pairs.

Tk (Toolkit)

→ *See* Tcl (Tool Command Language)

TLS (Transport Layer Security) Encryption

TLS encryption is a security measure used for outgoing mail in Microsoft Internet Information Server (IIS). When TLS encryption is used, TCP packets at the Transport layer are encrypted before transmission.

Token

In some media-access methods, a special packet that is passed from node to node according to a predefined sequence. The node with the token gets to access the network.

Token Bus

Token Bus is a network architecture defined in the IEEE 802.4 specifications. The Token Bus architecture has never been popular for local area networks (LANs) of the type found in most offices. It is, however, widely used in manufacturing contexts.

The Token Bus architecture was inspired, in part, by work relating to the automation of manufacturing tasks. This architecture has, in turn, become the basis for the various types of Manufacturing Automation Protocol (MAP) systems that have been developed to help automate operations in industrial contexts.

The 802.4 specifications include physical layer and Media Access Control (MAC) sublayer details for networks that use a bus topology and use token passing as the media-access method. "Context and properties of Token Bus" summarizes this architecture.

The Token Bus architecture supports the following:

- Both carrier band (single-channel) and broadband networks.

- Operation over either 75-ohm coaxial cable or fiber-optic cable.

- Network speeds of 1, 5, 10, and 20 megabits per second (Mbps), with supported speeds depending on the medium.

- Four priority levels for regulating access to the network medium.

- Four physical layer medium configurations: two carrier bands (full bandwidth), one broadband, and an optical configuration.

Physical Media Configurations

According to the 802.4 standard, Token Bus networks can use any of several configurations at the physical layer, depending on whether the network uses electrical (75-ohm coaxial) or fiber-optic cable and on whether the network uses the entire bandwidth for a single channel. Selection of a configuration also helps determine the allowable transmission speeds and the topology.

The cable for a Token Bus architecture may support a single channel or multiple channels on the same channel. In carrier band configurations, the entire bandwidth is used for a single modulated transmission; multiplexing is not used to get multiple messages onto the same channel. In contrast, broadband configurations support multiple modulated transmissions on the same cable. Each of the channels in a broadband configuration will use a different bandwidth for its transmission.

Single-Channel, Phase-Continuous FSK

A single-channel, phase-continuous configuration uses Frequency Shift Keying (FSK) as the modulation technique. In FSK, different frequencies are used to encode different values. The shift from one frequency to another is accomplished by a gradual, continuous change in the frequency (as opposed to an abrupt switch from one frequency to the other).

This method, which is also known as *phase-continuous carrier band*, is the easiest to implement and the least expensive of the four configurations supported for Token Bus architectures. It can be used even with older cable that may already be installed in a building. The disadvantage is that the top speed is only 1Mbps.

This configuration uses a bus in which all signals are broadcast in all directions. Cable segments are connected using a BNC connector.

Single-Channel, Phase-Coherent FSK

A single-channel, phase-coherent configuration also uses a form of FSK to encode the possible values. In this variant, the frequencies used to encode 1 and 0 values are an integral multiple of the transmission rate. For example, for a 5Mbps transmission rate, a 1 would be encoded as a 5MHz frequency and a 0 would be encoded as 10MHz. For a 10Mbps network, the frequencies would be 10 and 20MHz for 1 and 0, respectively.

Context

Network Architecture
    Ethernet
    ARCnet
    Token Bus ─────────┐
    Token Ring   │
                    ↓

Token Bus Properties

Defined by IEEE 802.4 specifications

Uses token passing as the media-access method

Uses a physical bus topology, but with nodes connected in a logical ring, based on the token-passing sequence

Supports electrical (coaxial) and fiber-optic cable

Supports carrier band and broadband networks

Supports network speeds of up to 20 Mbps

CONTEXT AND PROPERTIES OF TOKEN BUS

This method, which is also known as *phase-coherent carrier band*, is more expensive to implement than the phase-continuous carrier band method. It also supports faster networks: either 5 or 10Mbps. This configuration uses a bus in which all signals are broadcast in all directions. Cable segments are connected using a BNC connector.

Broadband

The primary configuration defined for the Token Bus architecture uses broadband transmissions and a directed bus, or tree, topology. This configuration is based on recommendations from General Motors, whose work on what has since become the MAP helped inspire the 802.4 standard. The broadband configuration also uses many of the principles and methods associated with cable television transmissions.

In a broadband topology, transmissions are assumed to originate in a special node, known as the *head end*. The signals are sent from the head end to the nodes along the network bus or tree.

The broadband configuration uses a modulation technique that varies both the amplitude and the phase (timing offset) of a signal. The phase variation is actually used to reduce the bandwidth required for the channel, thereby making more channels possible within the total bandwidth. The signal may be scrambled before transmission to avoid loss of synchronization during a long stretch in which a signal does not change.

This configuration can support transmission speeds of 1, 5, or 10Mbps. Cable segments are connected using an F connector.

Fiber-Optic ASK

Another Token Bus configuration uses optical fiber as the transmission medium. This configuration uses Amplitude Shift Keying (ASK) as the modulation technique. In ASK, values are encoded as changes in the amplitude, or strength, of the carrier signal. In this configuration, the amplitude change is rather severe: a binary 1 is encoded as a pulse of light, and a 0 is no light (a pulse of darkness, so to speak). To avoid the loss of synchronization during a long period of

light or darkness, data is first encoded using Manchester encoding to ensure value changes.

This configuration uses a star configuration, in which the center of the star may be a node (active star) or a coupler (passive star). In an active star, each node in the star sends its transmissions to the central node, which then broadcasts the transmission to all the other connected nodes. In a passive star, the coupler (signal redirector) at the center is created by fusing the fibers coming from each of the nodes. This fusion creates paths between all nodes, so that any transmission from a node will automatically reach all the other nodes.

Fiber-optic configurations are still the most expensive, but they also support the fastest transmission speeds: 5, 10, and 20Mbps.

Token Bus Operation

Access to the network is determined by the token, a special frame that is passed from node to node in a well-defined sequence. To regulate the sequence in which the token is passed, the nodes involved in the token passing form a logical ring, as shown in "A bus topology with nodes in a logical ring."

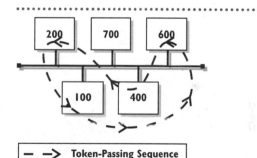

— —> **Token-Passing Sequence**

A BUS TOPOLOGY WITH NODES IN A LOGICAL RING

Each node passes the token to the node with the next lower ring address. In the illustration, the token is passed from node 600 to 400 to 200 to 100. To complete the ring, the node with the lowest address passes to the node with the highest, so that

T

node 100 passes to 600. Notice that node 700 is on the bus but it is not part of the ring. Node 700 can receive messages but cannot send any.

Only the node with the token can transmit. When it has the token, a node can send a packet to whatever node it wishes. For example, with the token, node 400 can send a message to node 600. To do so, 400 just needs to broadcast the packet on the bus. Each node on the bus will check the destination address, but only node 600 will bother to read the packet. Node 400 could just as easily have sent a packet to node 700 in this way.

Once node 400 has finished transmitting, it sends the token to node 300. This node can transmit, if it has anything to say.

When token passing is used as a media-access method, networks need considerable monitoring capabilities to keep track of the token. If a token should be lost or corrupted, the network will use mechanisms for forcing an attempt at token recovery and, failing that, for generating a new token to avoid disrupting the network.

To enable nodes to connect to the ring, "sign-up" opportunities are provided at random intervals. Each node will occasionally ask whether any nodes with lower addresses are interested in joining the ring.

Handling Service Priority Levels

The four priority levels for service supported by the Token Bus architecture are named (from highest priority to lowest) 6, 4, 2, and 0.

To ensure that no node hogs the token, restrictions are placed on the amount of time a node may hold a token. This restriction is called the Token Holding Time (THT).

For each priority level, a maximum Token Rotation Time (TRTx) is specified. For example, a value of TRT2 represents how long the token can take to make its way around the ring while still being able to ensure that packets at priority level 2 will be transmitted.

Token Bus Frames

The 802.4 architecture uses a data frame and several types of control frames. The data frame is used for transmitting information from and to higher levels. Control frames help manage, update, and maintain a network. The token is a control frame that plays a central role. "A Token Bus frame" shows the basic structure of a frame and also how the FC field differs for data and control frames.

1+ Byte	1 Byte	1 Byte	2 or 6 Bytes	2 or 6 Bytes	0+ Bytes	4 Bytes	1 Byte
Preamble	SD	FC	DA	SA	Data	FCS	ED

FC Field for Control Frame

| 0 | 0 | C | C | C | C | C | C |

FC Field for Data Frame

| 0 | 1 | M | M | M | P | P | P |

SD = Starting Delimiter
FC = Field Control
DA = Destination Address
SA = Source Address
FCS = Frame Check Sequence
ED = Ending Delimiter

0 0 = Control Frame
C C C C C C = Type of Control Function (e.g., token, claim token, etc.)

0 1 = Data Frame
M M M = Desired Action (e.g., request and response, request with no response)
P P P = Priority Level

A TOKEN BUS FRAME

Control Frames

For control frames, the following fields are used:

Preamble (1+ bytes) Used to synchronize sender and receiver. More bytes are used for faster transmission speeds. For example, 1 byte of synchronization suffices for 1Mbps networks, but 3 bytes are needed for a 10Mbps transmission.

SD (Start Delimiter, 1 byte) Used to indicate the start of a frame. This byte consists of a signal pattern (xx0x x000) that can never occur as data. In this pattern, the x's represent a signal that is not used for data.

FC (Frame Control, 1 byte) Used to specify information about the frame. The first 2 bits indicate whether it is a data (01) or a control (00) frame. In a control frame, the remaining 6 bits specify the command the frame represents. For the token frame, these bits are 001000, from least to most significant bit. In a data frame, the next 3 bits indicate the status of data and transmission, and the last 3 bits show the frame's priority level (0, 2, 4, or 6). The status bits represent three possibilities: request with no response expected (the default), request with response expected, or response.

DA (Destination Address) Specifies the node to which the token is being passed. Depending on the type of addresses being used, this field will use either 2 or 6 bytes.

SA (Source Address) Specifies the node passing the token. Depending on the type of addresses being used, this field will use either 2 or 6 bytes.

Data For control frames, this may contain special settings or commands. For data frames, this contains the material being transmitted between higher layers. Not all types of frames include this field. For example, the token uses 0 bytes for this field.

FCS (Frame Check Sequence, 4 bytes) Used to check whether the frame was received without error.

ED (End Delimiter) Used to indicate the end of the frame. As with the SD field, this will be a unique signal pattern.

Data Frame

A data frame for the Token Bus architecture has the same basic structure as a control frame:

Preamble Same as for a token frame.

SD (Start Delimiter) Same as for a token frame.

FC (Frame Control) Same as for a token frame, except that this is a data frame.

DA (Destination Address) Same as for token frame.

SA (Source Address) Same as for a token frame.

Data Contains a Protocol Data Unit (PDU) from a higher layer, generally the Logical-Link Control (LLC) sublayer. This field may be over 8000 bytes. The restriction is that the FC, DA, SA, Data, and FCS fields together cannot be larger than 8191 bytes.

FCS (Frame Check Sequence) Same as for a token frame.

ED (End Delimiter) Same as for a token frame.

→ **Broader Category** Network Architecture

→ **See Also** ARCnet; ATM; Ethernet; FDDI; Token Ring

Token-Claiming

In Token Ring LAN topologies, a token-claiming process is used to select an active monitor. Such a claiming process takes place under either of the following conditions:

- If there is a loss of signal.

- If the active monitor does not receive certain test frames it sends out or does not receive other test frames correctly within a specified amount of time.

Token-claiming is also known as *monitor-contention*.

Token Holding Time (THT)

→ *See* THT (Token Holding Time)

Token Passing

Token passing is a deterministic media-access method in which a token is passed from node to node, according to a predefined sequence. A *token* is a special packet, or frame. At any given time, the token can be available or in use. When an available token reaches a node, that node can access the network. "Summary of the token-passing process" shows this method.

A deterministic access method guarantees that every node will get access to the network within a given length of time, usually on the order of a few hundred microseconds or milliseconds. This is in contrast to a probabilistic access method (such as CSMA/CD), in which nodes check for network activity when they want to access the network, and the first node to claim the idle network gets access to it.

Because each node gets its turn within a fixed period, deterministic access methods are more efficient on networks that have heavy traffic. With such networks, nodes using probabilistic access methods spend much of their time trying to gain access and relatively little time actually transmitting data over the network.

Network architectures that support token passing as an access method include ARCnet, FDDI, and IBM's Token Ring.

Token-Passing Process

To transmit, the node first marks the token as in-use, and then transmits a data packet, with the token attached. The packet is passed from node to node, until the packet reaches its destination. The recipient acknowledges the packet by sending the token back to the sender, who then sets the token to idle and passes it on to the next node in the network.

The next recipient is not necessarily the node that is nearest to the token-passing node. Rather, the next node is determined by some predefined rule. For example, in an ARCnet network, the token is passed from a node to the node with the next higher network address.

Networks that use token passing generally have some provision for setting the priority with which a node gets the token. Higher-level protocols can specify that a message is important and should receive higher priority.

Active and Standby Monitors

A network that uses token passing also requires an active monitor (AM) and one or more standby monitors (SMs). The AM keeps track of the token to make sure it has not been corrupted, lost, or sent to a node that has been disconnected from the network. If any of these things happens, the AM generates a new token, and the network is back in business.

The SM makes sure the AM is doing its job and does not break down and get disconnected from the network. If the AM is lost, one of the SMs becomes the new AM, and the network is again in business.

These monitoring capabilities make for complex circuitry on network interface cards that use this media-access method.

→ *Broader Category* Media-Access Method

→ *Compare* CSMA/CA; CSMA/CD; Demand Priority; Polling

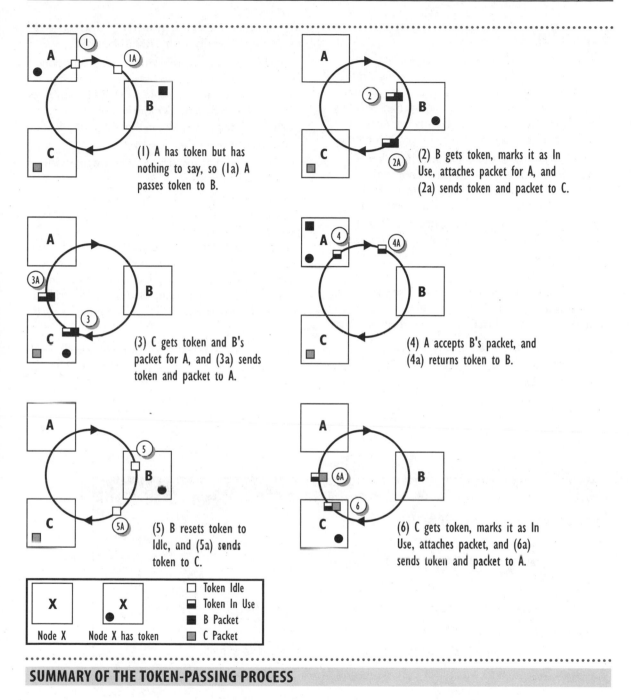

(1) A has token but has nothing to say, so (1a) A passes token to B.

(2) B gets token, marks it as In Use, attaches packet for A, and (2a) sends token and packet to C.

(3) C gets token and B's packet for A, and (3a) sends token and packet to A.

(4) A accepts B's packet, and (4a) returns token to B.

(5) B resets token to Idle, and (5a) sends token to C.

(6) C gets token, marks it as In Use, attaches packet, and (6a) sends token and packet to A.

X Node X	**X** ● Node X has token

☐ Token Idle
▭ Token In Use
■ B Packet
▣ C Packet

SUMMARY OF THE TOKEN-PASSING PROCESS

T

Token Ring

Token Ring is a network architecture that uses a ring network topology and a token-passing strategy to control access to the network. This type of architecture works best with networks that handle heavy data traffic from many users, because of inherent fairness rules in token passing as an access method.

The IEEE 802.5 standard defines the token ring architecture and specifies how this architecture operates at the lowest two layers in the OSI reference model, which are the Physical and Data-Link layers. All Token Ring architectures use the network-access scheme defined by 802.5 and the LLC (Logical-Link Control) sublayer standard defined in an IEEE 802.2 document.

IBM developed its own revised specifications for a token ring architecture. These revisions differ somewhat from the official IEEE 802.5 specifications, but they have become so widely used that discussions of token ring generally mean IBM Token Ring.

IBM is largely responsible for the long-time popularity of the Token Ring architecture because it provides a good way to connect PCs to IBM mainframes. Many of this architecture's more baroque features (such as the frames) are also in the best tradition of the IBM mainframe world.

"Context and properties of token ring" summarizes this architecture.

With token passing as the media-access method, the node that has the token gets to access the network, provided the token is available (not being used to transport a packet) when the node receives it. Unlike the CSMA/CD media-access method that Ethernet networks use, token passing is deterministic. This means each node is guaranteed to get a turn sending packets within a predefined time or number of cycles.

Context

Network Architecture
    Ethernet
    ARCnet
    Token Bus
    Token Ring

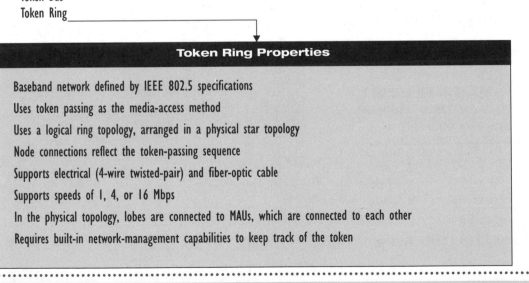

Token Ring Properties

Baseband network defined by IEEE 802.5 specifications

Uses token passing as the media-access method

Uses a logical ring topology, arranged in a physical star topology

Node connections reflect the token-passing sequence

Supports electrical (4-wire twisted-pair) and fiber-optic cable

Supports speeds of 1, 4, or 16 Mbps

In the physical topology, lobes are connected to MAUs, which are connected to each other

Requires built-in network-management capabilities to keep track of the token

CONTEXT AND PROPERTIES OF TOKEN RING

Token ring networks have the following features:

- Use a ring as the logical topology, but a star as the physical topology, or wiring.

- Operate at either 1 or 4Mbps, for IEEE 802.5; operate at either 4 or 16Mbps, for IBM. (Specifications for higher-speed Token Ring networks have been created—including one for a full-duplex Token Ring network that can operate at 32Mbps and one that supports speeds of up to 100Mbps—but these are not catching on as quickly as Token Ring advocates had hoped. As a result, Token Ring technology is losing even more market share to the Ethernet juggernaut, which has introduced 100Mbps and 1Gbps variants during the period when 100Mbps Token Ring was being developed.)

- Use baseband signaling, which means that only one signal travels along the line at a time.

- Use the differential Manchester signal-encoding method. Because this method breaks each bit interval into two signals, the clock speed must be twice the transmission speed in order to attain the maximum bandwidth. Thus, a 4Mbps token ring network needs an 8MHz clock; a 16Mbps network needs a 32MHz clock.

- Use shielded twisted-pair (STP) or unshielded twisted-pair (UTP) cable or fiber-optic cable, but not coaxial cable. The STP has a 150-ohm resistance, and the UTP has a 100-ohm resistance.

- Use four-wire cable, with two of the wires used for the main ring and two for the secondary ring (which can be used if there is a break in the main ring).

- Have each node (called a *lobe* in IBM terminology) connected to a wiring center, called an MAU (Multistation Access Unit). The wiring inside a MAU creates a ring of the attached nodes.

- Allow MAUs to be connected to each other, to create larger rings. Each MAU includes two reserved connectors for making a MAU-MAU connection.

- Allow the use of patch panels, which sit between nodes and MAUs and make it easier to reconfigure the network.

- Require built-in network management facilities, because nodes need to be able to determine whether a token has been corrupted, destroyed, or lost.

- Are controlled by the node that generates the token. This node (which is known as the *active monitor*) is generally the network file server.

Token Ring Components

The components of token ring networks include the network interface card (NIC), cable, MAUs, connectors, media filters, and repeaters.

Token Ring NIC

Token Ring NICs are usually designed for 4Mbps or 16Mbps operation, or for both. NICs that support both speeds generally require you to select a speed by setting DIP switches or through software.

Because Token Ring networks must do constant network monitoring, NICs for this architecture implement an agent in the chip set. This component communicates with stations in various management roles on the network regarding the node's status and network activity.

Several companies make token ring chip sets, and there is some competition to add attractive features to the chip set. This competition also helps drive prices down.

Token Ring Cable

When discussing cabling, the categories defined in the IBM Cable System are generally used. This grouping includes nine types, of which seven are defined. In the literature and in discussions, you will hear references to, for example, Type 1 or Type 3 cable. See the Cable, IBM article for a discussion of this cable system. Note that the IEEE 802.5 specifications do not specify a particular type of cabling.

In a Token Ring network, cable is used for two purposes: for the main ring path (which connects MAUs) and for short runs (lobe to MAU or MAU to patch panel).

STP (IBM Type 1, 2, or possibly 9) cable is generally used for the main ring path. However, the Token Ring specifications also support UTP (for example, Type 3) and fiber-optic (Type 5) cables. For patch or jumper cable, Type 6 cable is commonly used.

MAUs (Multistation Access Units)

MAUs serve as wiring concentrators for several lobes, and they arrange the connections from the lobes into a ring. The IBM 8228 MAU is the "papa" MAU, and most MAUs from other vendors are compatible with this older model. Newer models have more intelligence and monitoring capabilities built into the MAU.

MAUs are simply called *wiring centers* in IEEE 802.5 networks.

Connectors

Token Ring NICs generally have a DB-9 connector for STP cable and may have a modular RJ-45 plug for UTP cable.

MAUs have IBM Data Connectors. This is a special type of connector that self-shorts when disconnected, so that the ring inside the MAU is not broken when a lobe is disconnected. Note that a patch cable for an IBM Token Ring network needs a DB-9 or an RJ-*xx* connector at one end and an IBM Data Connector at the other end.

Media Filter and Repeaters

A media filter is needed if you want to connect UTP cable to a DB-9 connector (which is expecting STP cable) on a NIC. This filter removes the high-frequency signals that arise when using UTP and also adjusts the inputs.

Repeaters serve to extend the maximum cable lengths imposed by various power and noise restrictions in a token ring network. Different types of repeaters are used for the main ring and for lobes.

Token Ring Layout

Although they use a logical ring structure, token ring networks are actually arranged in a star topology, with each node connected to a central hub (the MAU), as illustrated in the "Token Ring layout."

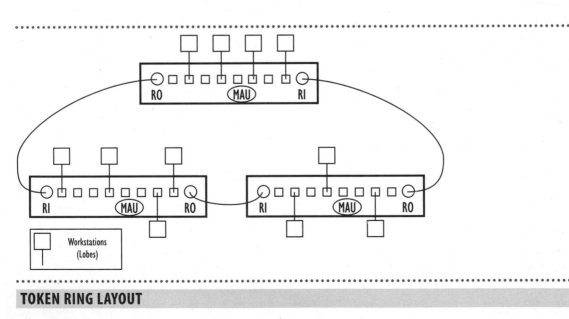

TOKEN RING LAYOUT

Depending on where the MAUs are in relation to the nodes, a node may be connected directly to a MAU or to a wallplate. In the latter case, a cable will go from the wall plate to a patch panel and from there to the MAU. Regardless of whether the connection is direct or roundabout, the link to the MAU is through an IBM Data Connector, so that the node can be removed from the network without disrupting the ring.

MAUs may be connected to each other using special RI (Ring In) and RO (Ring Out) ports on the MAUs. These connections maintain the ring structure across the MAUs. The RO port from one MAU is connected to the RI port of another. Several MAUs may be linked this way. If there are multiple MAUs, the RO port of the last MAU in the series is connected to the RI port of the first MAU to complete the ring.

Assuming everything is connected correctly, the logical layout of the network should have each node (*X*) associated directly with exactly two other nodes:

- The node which passes frames and the token to node X in the ring. This node is X's Nearest Active Upstream Neighbor (NAUN).

- The node to which X passes frames and the token. This destination neighbor is downstream from X. For symmetry, this node can be called the Nearest Active *Down*stream Neighbor (NADN).

The MAU-MAU connection actually creates a primary, or main, ring and a backup ring. If there is a break in the main ring, it may be possible to bypass the break by going through the backup ring.

Token Ring Restrictions and Limitations

As with other network architectures, there are restrictions on the allowable distances between token ring network components and on the number of components allowed on the network.

Token Ring networks have two types of length restrictions: the lobe length and the ring length.

Lobe Length

The lobe length is the distance between a node and a MAU, as follows:

- For Types 1 and 2 cable (both STP), the maximum lobe length is 100 meters (330 feet).

- For types 6 and 9 (also STP), the maximum lobe length is only about 66 meters (220 feet).

- For UTP (such as Type 3 cable), the maximum lobe length is 45 meters (150 feet).

Ring Length

The ring length is the distance between MAUs on the main ring path. Distance calculations and restrictions for this part of a Token Ring network can be complicated. Values depend on the number of repeaters, MAUs, and wiring closets in the network, and these factors are used to compute an Adjusted Ring Length (ARL) for the network.

That caution raised, the following values apply even for simple networks with minimal repeaters, MAUs, and wiring closets:

- For Types 1 and 2 cable, the distance between MAUs can be up to 200 meters (660 feet).

- For Type 3 cable, the distance between MAUs can be up to about 120 meters (400 feet).

- For Type 6 cable, the distance between MAUs can be up to only about 45 meters (140 feet), because this type is intended for use as a patch cable.

- Fiber-optic cable segments can be as long as 1 kilometer (0.6 mile).

There is also a *minimum* distance constraint—lobes must be separated by at least 2.5 meters (8 feet).

Other Token Ring Restrictions

Other restrictions on Token Ring networks include the following:

- At most, three cable segments (separated by repeaters) are allowed in a series.

- Each cable segment must be terminated at both ends and grounded at one end.

- In the IEEE 802.5 specifications, a network can have up to 250 lobes.

- In the IBM Token Ring specifications, a network using STP can have up to 260 lobes; one using UTP can have up to 72 lobes.

- At most, 33 MAUs are allowed on the network.

- A network cannot have nodes operating at different speeds. That is, a network may consist of 4Mbps or 16Mbps lobes, but not both. You can, however, use a bridge to connect a 4Mbps to a 16Mbps token ring network.

- To operate a 16Mbps token ring network, you need cable that is at least at Category 4 in the EIA/TIA-568 classification system.

In many cases, the specific values in the restrictions are imposed because of timing constraints on the network. As such, the quoted values assume a maximal network, so that all signals take the longest possible time to reach their destinations.

In practice, this means that some of the restrictions can be exceeded (but *with caution*), at least slightly, on smaller networks.

Token Ring Operation

In a Token Ring architecture, the token is passed from node to node in a logical ring structure. The token is passed in a fixed direction around the ring. The node with the token is allowed to send a message to another node.

A particular node, usually the network file server, generates the token that starts the network rolling. This node also serves as the Active Monitor (AM) whose job is to keep track of the token and make sure it does not get corrupted or lost. The AM is responsible for several important functions:

- Checking for and detecting lost tokens or frames.

- Monitoring frame transmissions.

- Purging the ring and creating a new token.

- Initiating and monitoring Neighbor Notification (NN).

- Maintaining proper delays in the ring.

- Maintaining the master clock.

Other nodes serve as standby monitors (SMs); their job is to monitor the AM. SMs constantly check for the presence of an AM. If none is detected (or if the AM is not working properly), the SMs go through a token-claiming process to determine a new AM.

Once the ring has been set up, the token-passing process does not require any special intervention from the AM. Each node receives the token from its NAUN and passes it to its NADN.

When a network first starts up, the AM generates a token and initiates a Neighbor Notification (NN) process. This is the process by which each node learns the address of its NAUN and broadcasts its own address to the node's NADN.

Ring nodes can be checked in two different ways for token passing:

- Using *physical ring polling,* each node attached to the network is included, regardless of whether or not that node is currently active (actually logged onto the network).

- Using *active ring polling*, only those nodes that are currently active on the network are included in the token-passing process.

Using the Token

The token is a special type of frame that contains, among other things, a priority value and a monitor setting (which is 0 or 1). A token with a monitor setting of 1 is available for use. Any node with a priority setting greater than or equal to that of the token can grab the token as it goes by on the ring, and then transmit a frame.

When a node has grabbed the token and is going to transmit, the node changes the token's monitor setting to 0 (so no other node will try to grab the token). If the active monitor sees a token with a monitor setting of 1 come around, the AM assumes the token is corrupt, destroys it, and creates a new one.

When a node sends a frame onto the network, the frame includes a destination and a source address. The frame is passed from node to node according to the sequence determined by the ring structure. Each node checks to see whether it is the destination for the frame.

If not, the node passes the frame on. If so, the node saves the source address and the data, computes the Cyclic Redundancy Check (CRC) value, changes some bits in the Frame Status field for the data frame, and passes the frame to the node's NADN.

The frame circulates the ring until it returns to the sender, who checks the Frame Status information to make sure the frame was received correctly. If so, the node releases the token and passes it to the NADN.

During the token-passing process, a lobe may claim an available token, let it pass by unclaimed, or request a higher-priority level for the token. A lobe makes this request by setting the reserved priority bits in the token frame to the desired value. When a lobe requests a higher priority, the lobe records the current token priority value in a buffer.

The token continues to circulate with the priority level and the requested priority settings until any of the following happens:

- A lobe with sufficiently high priority grabs the token.

- The unclaimed token reaches the lobe that generated the token.

- A token with a higher priority raises the requested priority level.

In the second case, the starting lobe destroys the token and generates a new one with priority set to the highest requested level. This new token is then sent around the ring, where it can be claimed by the lobe that requested the higher priority.

A lobe may get the token by requesting a higher priority and then claiming the regenerated token. Once the lobe finishes sending its frame and has the token back, that lobe must restore the token's original priority (the token priority setting when the lobe originally requested the higher priority). In short, it is the sender's responsibility to restore a token to the state it had before the sender used it.

Token Ring Activities

Normal repeat mode is the default operation of a lobe in a Token Ring network. When the network is operating normally, each lobe can deal properly with each frame received, and can pass the frame on correctly.

In addition to normal repeat mode, several special-purpose activities take place only under certain conditions.

Ring Insertion

The five-step ring-insertion process occurs when a lobe wants to join the network. The steps in this process are as follows:

1. Physical connection and lobe media check. The lobe is connected to the network. The connection is checked by having the lobe send a particular type of MAC frame to the MAU and making sure the frame is returned intact.

2. Monitor check. The new lobe checks for the presence of an AM by waiting a specified amount of time to hear one of three types of MAC frames. If the lobe hears one of these frames, it assumes an AM is present and proceeds to the next step. If none of the frames arrives within the specified time, the lobe begins a token-claiming process.

3. Address verification. The lobe checks that its address is unique on the network. This check is also done using a particular type of MAC frame. If successful, the lobe proceeds to the next step; if not, the node disconnects

T

itself from the ring and begins the ring-insertion process again.

4. Neighbor notification. The lobe learns the address of its NAUN and sends its own address to the new lobe's NADN. This process also takes place each time the network is started.

5. Request initialization. The network's Ring Parameter Server (RPS) checks the new lobe's parameters and settings.

NN (Neighbor Notification)

The NN process tells each lobe about the upstream neighbor from which the lobe receives frames and the downstream neighbor to which the lobe transmits them. The process uses the Frame Status and Source Address fields in certain types of MAC frames to assign this information to the appropriate lobes.

The NN process is repeated until each lobe has been involved. The AM begins the process by sending the first MAC frame, and ends the process by copying the last values from the MAC frame sent by the AM's upstream neighbor.

The AM sends an Active Monitor Present (AMP) MAC frame; the remaining lobes (which are all SMs by default) send Standby Monitor Present (SMP) MAC frames. Each frame is received by one lobe, which becomes the sending lobe's downstream neighbor.

Priority Access

Each lobe in a Token Ring network has a priority level (0 is lowest, 7 is highest) whose value determines which tokens the lobe can grab. Priority access is the method by which priority values are assigned to the token frame and to a lobe.

A lobe can grab only a token with a priority level less than or equal to the lobe's. Lobes can request priority levels so that they can get the token.

Ring Purge

In the ring purge process, the AM dissolves the ring and rebuilds it beginning with the token-claiming process. A ring purge happens under any of the following conditions:

- When the token or a frame is lost or corrupted.

- When a particular type of MAC frame is not received within a required amount of time.

- When a particular bit in a frame indicates that a lobe has failed to return the token.

Token Claiming

Through the token-claiming process, an AM is chosen from among the SMs vying for the position. The token-claiming process is initiated under any of the following conditions:

- When the AM does not detect any frames on the ring within a predefined amount of time.

- When an SM cannot detect either an AM or a frame within a predefined amount of time.

- When a new lobe is added to the ring but that lobe does not detect an AM during the ring-insertion process.

The process by which a winner emerges from this contest is reminiscent of certain children's games: lobes release and circulate frames using rules based on relative address values, and the first node to get its own frame back three times becomes the AM.

Beaconing

Beaconing is a signaling process by which lobes announce the occurrence of hard (serious) errors on the network. A lobe can detect such an error in either itself or in its NAUN.

The Beacon MAC frame sent under these circumstances allows the Ring Error Monitor (REM) to determine the fault domain, which is the logical area in which the error most likely occurred. This area consists of the beaconing lobe, that lobe's NAUN, and the cable between these two lobes.

Further diagnostics rely on monitoring statistics from these and other lobes on the ring.

Network Management

Networks with deterministic media-access methods must be able to make sure the selection mechanism is functioning properly at all times. For token ring networks, this means the token must be valid, visible, and circulating.

The mechanism for evaluating the status of the token must also be working correctly. For Token Ring networks, this means that the AM must be doing its work. If one of the token conditions should be violated and the AM should be unable to detect this, the network could become locked.

To make sure this does not happen, the token ring architecture management facilities include some built-in mechanisms: the AM monitors the token, and the other lobes monitor the AM.

Token Ring networks have an extensive set of management capabilities, and each NIC on the network can participate, at least by monitoring network activity. In addition to the AM and SM, token ring networks include several other management functions, and the same node may carry out one or more of these functions:

- The CRS (Configuration Report Server) node collects various performance and other numerical information from the nodes, and passes this information on to the network manager node.

- The RPS (Ring Parameter Server) node monitors the addresses of all nodes on the ring and of the NAUN for each of these nodes, to make sure that all the attachments meet the criteria for a ring. The RPS also sends ring-initialization information to new nodes as they join the ring, and sends the information gathered to the network manager.

- The REM (Ring Error Monitor) node gathers reports of any hard or soft errors on the ring and passes this information on to the network manager. (A hard error is serious, and threatens or impairs the network's continued operation; a soft error is considered minor, and no

threat to the network's normal operation.) The REM also counts soft error frequency to determine whether they happen often enough to be regarded as potentially serious.

- The LBS (LAN Bridge Server) node monitors the functioning of any bridges on the network and keeps track of the activity across these bridges. The LBS also communicates this data to the network manager.

- The LRM (LAN Reporting Mechanism) node provides the network manager with information about any remote servers on the network.

Note that the REM node is dedicated to its error gathering, and it does not generally function as an ordinary workstation on the network. A protocol analyzer program for token ring provides alternatives to or enhancements of the REM's services.

The data collected by each of these management functions is sent to a specially designated node that serves as the network manager. This node's task is to summarize and analyze the collected statistics, and to make adjustments in the network's operations as a result of this information. The network manager's capabilities are generally provided as software.

For network management, IBM Token Ring networks use the NMT (Network Management) protocol, which is defined as part of IEEE 802.5. In contrast, FDDI networks, which also use token passing, use SMT (System Management), a somewhat different management protocol.

Token Ring Frames

Token Ring networks send packets, or frames, around the network. There are only four main types of frames in token ring networks: Token, LLC, MAC, and Abort Sequence frames. (LLC and MAC frames are both considered data frames.) However, there are 25 types of MAC frames. "Token ring frame types" shows the frames.

T

Token Frames
Token frames have three 1-byte fields:

Starting Delimiter Indicates the start of the frame. It contains a pattern of deliberate signal violations, which are signal patterns that do not occur in normal transmissions, to indicate the start of a frame.

Access Control Indicates the type of frame, its priority level, and its status. Three bits specify the frame's priority value; 0 is lowest, 7 is highest. A Token bit is set to 0 if the frame is a token and to 1 otherwise. A Monitor bit is set to 1 by the AM, and to 0 whenever a lobe grabs the token. Three bits can be used by a lobe to request a priority level that is required to get access to the network.

Ending Delimiter Indicates the end of the frame. This field contains a pattern of deliberate signal violations (signal patterns that do not occur in normal transmissions) to indicate the end of a frame.

Abort Sequence Frame
The Abort Sequence frame is used to clear the ring when a faulty frame has been detected. The frame consists of two fields: Starting Delimiter (1 byte)

and Ending Delimiter (1 byte). Both of these are the same as in a Token frame.

Data Frames: Common Fields
Both LLC and MAC frames have the same general structure: a header, an optional information field, and a trailer. The header and trailer for LLC and MAC frames differ only in a few bits; the main differences are in the Information field.

Common Header Fields
In the header, both types of frames have Starting Delimiter (1 byte) and Access Control (1 byte) fields, which are both the same as for a Token frame (except that the Token bit value is 1 in the Access Control field).

The Frame Control field (1 byte) distinguishes LLC and MAC data frames. The first 2 bits indicate whether the frame is a MAC or LLC frame: 00 is MAC, and 01 is LLC. Values of 10 and 11 are reserved. The next 2 bits are reserved. The last 4 bits are control bits. For LLC frames, these bits are reserved for future use. For MAC frames, the control bits indicate whether the frame should be copied to the lobe's regular input buffer (0000) for normal handling or to an "express" buffer (non-zero value) so that the frame is processed immediately by the MAC sublayer.

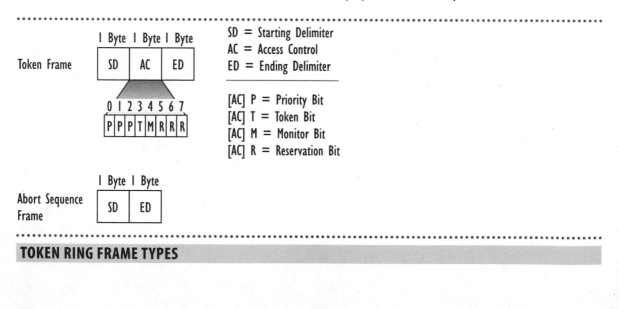

TOKEN RING FRAME TYPES

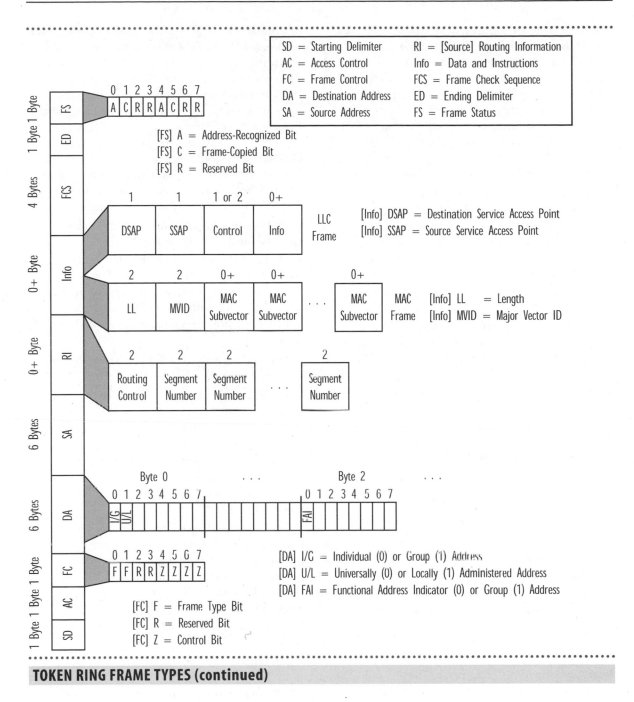

SD = Starting Delimiter   RI = [Source] Routing Information
AC = Access Control   Info = Data and Instructions
FC = Frame Control   FCS = Frame Check Sequence
DA = Destination Address   ED = Ending Delimiter
SA = Source Address   FS = Frame Status

[FS] A = Address-Recognized Bit
[FS] C = Frame-Copied Bit
[FS] R = Reserved Bit

[Info] DSAP = Destination Service Access Point
[Info] SSAP = Source Service Access Point

[Info] LL = Length
[Info] MVID = Major Vector ID

[DA] I/G = Individual (0) or Group (1) Address
[DA] U/L = Universally (0) or Locally (1) Administered Address
[DA] FAI = Functional Address Indicator (0) or Group (1) Address

[FC] F = Frame Type Bit
[FC] R = Reserved Bit
[FC] Z = Control Bit

TOKEN RING FRAME TYPES (continued)

The Destination Address field (6 bytes) indicates the address of the lobe to which the frame is being sent. Certain bits in particular bytes have special significance: Bit 0 in byte 0 indicates whether the address is an individual (0) or a group (1) address. In group addressing, multiple lobes share the same address, for the purpose of communication, so that a frame sent to that location will be received by each lobe that belongs to the group. In individual addressing, each lobe has its own address.

Bit 1 in byte 0 indicates whether the address is administered universally (0) or locally (1). In universal administration, hardware addresses (those assigned to the NIC by the IEEE and the board's manufacturer) are used. In local administration, software or switch-configurable addresses are used.

Bit 0 in byte 2 is special only for locally administered group addresses. This functional address indicator (FAI) bit is 0 if the address is a functional one, and is 1 otherwise. A functional address specifies a lobe with a particular function (Token Ring management or user-defined). The table "Predefined Functional Addresses" indicates predefined addresses for particular lobes.

PREDEFINED FUNCTIONAL ADDRESSES

Address	Server with Address
C00000000001	Active Monitor (AM)
C00000000002	Ring Parameter Server (RPS)
C00000000008	Ring Error Monitor (REM)
C00000000010	Configuration Report Server (CPS)
C00000000100	Bridge
C00000002000	LAN Manager
C00000800000–C00040000000	User-defined servers

The Source Address field (6 bytes) indicates the location of the frame's originator. The I/G and U/L bits are also found in the first byte of the Source Address field.

If the frame is addressed to a lobe on another network—a lobe that must be reached using a bridge or a router—the frame will include a Routing Information field. This field will contain information regarding the bridges or routers through which the frame must pass. If this frame is present, the first 2 bytes are routing control, and the remaining bytes are grouped into pairs, each of which identifies a bridge or router.

Common Trailer Fields

In the trailer, both LLC and MAC frames have a Frame Check Sequence, an Ending Delimiter field, and a Frame Status field.

The Frame Check Sequence field (4 bytes) contains the results of a 32-bit CRC computation by the sender. This value is used to determine whether the frame was received as transmitted. The receiving node also computes a CRC value and compares the computed value with the field's value. If the values match, the frame is assumed to have been received intact.

The Ending Delimiter field (1 byte) is the same as the one used in a Token frame.

The Frame Status field (1 byte) contains information about how the frame fared in its route around the ring. Bits 0 and 4 are Address Recognized bits. These are set to 0 by the sender and are changed to 1 when the destination lobe recognizes the source address. If the frame returns to the sender with these bits still set 0, the sender assumes the destination node is not on the ring.

Bits 1 and 5 are Copied bits. These are 0 by default but are changed to 1 when the destination lobe copies the frame's contents to its input buffer. If the frame is not received correctly, the destination node sets the Address Recognized bits to 1, but leaves the Copied bits set to 0. The sender will know that the destination is on the ring, but that the frame was not received correctly.

The remaining four bits are reserved for future use.

Information Field for LLC Frames

An LLC frame is received from the LLC sublayer defined in the IEEE 802.2 standard. This frame contains the packet from the higher-layer protocol, which is being sent as data to another node.

For such a frame, the Information field is known as the PDU (Protocol Data Unit). The PDU is broken down into the DSAP address, SSAP address, and control components.

The DSAP (Destination Service Access Point) address (1 byte) provides information about the process running at the layer that will be receiving the packet. For example, this value is 0xe0 for Novell's NetWare.

The SSAP (Source Service Access Point) address (1 byte) provides information about the process running at the layer that is sending the packet. Again, this value is 0xe0 for Novell's NetWare.

The control component's (1 or 2 bytes) value indicates the type of data included in the PDU. This may be ordinary user data, supervisory (command) data, or unnumbered data.

If the data format requires sequence numbering—as when the frame is part of a sequence of frames that, together, constitute a message—2 bytes are used for control information. In that case, the second byte indicates the frame's position in the sequence.

If the first bit in the control component is 0, the PDU contains ordinary information, and the control component uses 2 bytes. Such an I-format PDU is used for connection-oriented communications. In an I-format PDU, the next seven bits represent the frame's location in the transmission sequence. The first bit of the second byte is used by the sender to poll the receiver, and by the receiver to respond. The remaining seven bits represent the position in the sequence at which the frame was received.

If the first two bits are 10, the PDU is supervisory, and the control component uses 2 bytes. Such a PDU is used in connection-oriented transmissions (those in which acknowledgments are required). For such an S-format PDU, the next two bits represent any of the following possible values: receive ready (00), reject (01), or receive not ready (10). The next four bits are reserved in this type of PDU. The first bit of the second byte is used for polling and responding (just as for an I-format PDU). The remaining seven bits represent the position in the sequence at which the frame was received.

If the first two bits are 11, the PDU is unnumbered, which may be used for connection-oriented or connectionless services. Such a U-format PDU uses only one byte for the control component. After the 11, such a PDU has two modifier bits (the third and fourth; that is, those in positions 2 and 3), followed by a polling/response bit, followed by three more modifier bits (in positions 5, 6, and 7). The table "Unnumbered PDU Values" shows the possible modifier values used for connection-oriented or connectionless service. Note that certain values appear twice. The interpretation for the value depends on whether the sender or receiver has set the value.

UNNUMBERED PDU VALUES

Value (bit positions: 23567)	Meaning	Communication
00000	UI Command	Connection-oriented
00111	Test Command	Connection-oriented
00111	Test Response	Connection-oriented
11101	XID Command	Connection-oriented
11101	XID Response	Connection-oriented
00010	DISC Command	Connectionless
00110	UA Response	Connectionless
10001	FRMR Response	Connectionless
11000	DM Response	Connectionless
11110	SABME Command	Connectionless

The remainder of the LLC PDU contains data from a higher-level protocol. The length of this component is limited by time constraints on how long a lobe in the ring may hold on to the token. In practice, the PDU generally has fewer than 4500 bytes, and may have just a few hundred.

Information Field for MAC Frames

MAC frames give commands and provide status information. Of the 25 different MAC frame types defined, 15 can be used by ordinary workstations. The remaining types are used by the AM or by special management servers. The table "Token Ring MAC Frame Types" lists the types defined.

The Information field of a MAC frame has three components:

Length (2 bytes) Specifies the length (in bytes) of the MAC control information provided later in the field.

TOKEN RING MAC FRAME TYPES

MAC Frames	Description
Active Monitor Present	The AM generates this frame to initiate the NN process.
Beacon	Any lobe generates this frame when a hard error is detected.
Change Parameters	The CRS generates this to set parameters for a lobe.
Claim Token	Any lobe that wants to participate in the token-claiming process can generate such a frame.
Duplicate Address Test	A new lobe generates this frame to check that the lobe's address will be unique on the ring.
Initialize Ring Station	The RPS generates this in response to the Ring Station Initialization frame generated by a new lobe.
Lobe Test	A new lobe generates this frame to test the connection between the lobe and the MAU.
Remove Ring Station	The CRS generates this to send to a lobe that will be removed from the ring for whatever reason.
Report Active Monitor Error	The AM generates this frame when the AM detects something wrong with itself.
Report NAUN Change	A lobe sends this frame to the CRS when the lobe has been provided with a NAUN address during NN.
Report Neighbor Notification Incomplete	A lobe generates this frame if the lobe does not hear from a NAUN within a predefined amount of time.
Report New Active Monitor	A lobe generates this frame and sends it to the CRS to announce that the lobe is the new AM.
Report Ring Station Address	A lobe sends this frame to the CRS in response to a Request Ring Station Address frame.
Report Ring Station Attachments	A lobe sends this frame to the CRS in response to a Request Ring Station Attachments frame.
Report Ring Station State	A lobe sends this frame to the CRS in response to a Request Ring Station State frame.
Report Soft Error	A lobe generates this frame when the lobe has accumulated more than a predefined number of soft errors, and then sends the frame to the REM.
Report Transmit Forward	A lobe sends this frame to the CRS or to the LAN manager in response to a Transmit Forward frame and to indicate that a path exists from the lobe to the CRS.
Request Ring Station Address	The CRS sends this frame to a lobe when the CRS wants address information from the lobe.
Request Ring Station Attachments	The CRS sends this frame to a lobe to find out what ring functions the lobe can perform.
Request Ring Station State	The CRS sends this frame to a lobe to determine the status of that lobe.
Response	A lobe sends this frame to another lobe to indicate receipt of a frame and to indicate errors in a received frame.
Ring Purge	The AM sends this frame to all lobes to clear the ring and restore Normal Repeat mode.
Ring Station Initialization	A new lobe in the ring generates this frame to announce the lobe's presence and to get any network settings.
Standby Monitor Present	A lobe generates this frame to send to the lobe's NADN as part of the NN process.
Transmit Forward	The CRS or the network manager generates this frame to test the communications path on the network.

Major Vector ID (MVID, 2 bytes) Identifies the function of the frame and of the information in the control information component.

Control Information (0+ bytes) Contains the data and information needed for the frame to do its work.

Extensions and Enhancements

To increase the span of a token ring network, you can use repeaters, additional MAUs, and wiring closets. A repeater enables you to run longer stretches of cable by cleaning and boosting the signal at the repeater. These extensions increase the size of the network while increasing the span.

Bridges and Routers

You can also use bridges and routers to increase the reach of a network by providing access to other networks. A bridge can route frames between two token ring networks; a router can find an "optimal" path for a frame through any number of networks, some of which may have different architectures.

Although Token Ring and Ethernet bridges perform the same functions, they do so differently. Ethernet bridges are also called learning bridges and transparent bridges, because they automatically learn the addresses and network locations of all nodes.

In contrast, Token Ring bridges use source routing. In source routing, the sending lobe first determines the route and then stores this information in the Routing Information field of the frame. The bridge (or router) uses the routing sequence in the field to get the frame to its destination. Because the entire route is stored in the frame, Token Ring bridges can have very high throughput.

Source-routing bridges have a parameter that limits the number of bridges over which a frame can travel. This HCL (Hop Count Limit) prevents a frame from traveling too long on a network.

Early Token Release

Manufacturers also work to improve network performance by adding features to the NIC chip set or

to MAUs. For example, newer token ring NICs support ETR (Early Token Release). This is a token-handling variant that makes it possible to have more than one frame traveling around the ring at a time, while still using only one token.

Essentially, in ETR, the lobe with the token releases it as soon as the lobe has sent its frame (rather than letting the token circulate with the frame). The frame travels around the ring, with the token's blessing, but without the token. The NADN gets the frame and passes it on, if appropriate. However, this lobe also gets the token, which has been marked as available again.

Because it is available, the lobe can grab the token and send its own frame. The lobe will release the frame to its NADN, and will then release the token. This NADN's NADN thus gets the following elements:

- Frame from the original transmitting lobe
- Frame from the original lobe's NADN
- Token

Intelligent MAUs

Manufacturers are making MAUs more intelligent by giving these components more ring monitoring and management capabilities. Some MAUs (such as the LattisNet series from SynOptics) can even manage multiple architectures. Such multiarchitecture MAUs provide routing between the architectures.

Another approach is to make the MAUs more sophisticated at configuring (*and reconfiguring*) themselves, either as lobes are added to the network or on the basis of network activity.

Switched and Dedicated Token Ring

As is the case with other networking architectures, switching technology is becoming increasingly popular. One reason for this is that switches can provide a node with the network's full bandwidth. This helps increase throughput.

Dedicated Token Ring (DTR) provides a direct connection between a node and the token ring switch, so that the node can have the network's full bandwidth.

T

As another aid to speeding up the architecture, the 802.5 committee defined TXI (Transmit Immediate), to speed up the transmission process.

Full-duplex token ring can provide up to 16Mbps in each direction.

Token Ring Tools

Hardware tools that can be useful for setting up and maintaining a token ring network include crimping and line-testing tools. You can use the crimping tool for crimping wire when making connections.

Use a line-testing tool for testing whether a particular section of cable is working properly. This type of tool comes in all forms and prices. At the low end, for about $25, a simple line monitor will tell you if the line is at least intact. At the very high end ($2000+), line-testing tools can do very precise measurements using TDR (Time Domain Reflectometry).

In addition to these, a general set of tools (including screwdrivers, chip extractors, and so on) is also essential.

Advantages of Token Ring

Token Ring networks are easy to connect to IBM mainframe-based networks.

Also, even though there is more overhead when using tokens than when using CSMA/CD as an access method, the performance difference is negligible because the bottleneck in a network with heavy traffic is much more likely to be elsewhere. In heavy traffic, nodes on networks using CSMA/CD (for example) will spend a lot of their time resolving collisions, thus adding to the traffic load.

Disadvantages of Token Ring

Components (for example, NICs) tend to be more expensive than for Ethernet or ARCnet architectures.

Also, the Token Ring architecture is not easy to extend to wide area networks (WANs).

Finally, the Token Ring architecture has not grown as smoothly or as quickly as Ethernet. As a result, Token Ring is waning in popularity, while the Ethernet architecture continues to claim new networking customers.

Resources

The specifications for a token ring architecture are found in IEEE 802.5 documents. Compared with the documentation generated by the 802.3 and 802.4 committees, these documents are quite sparse and relatively superficial.

The entire 802.5 specifications take fewer than 100 pages; by comparison, it takes 107 pages to cover just the physical medium possibilities in the 802.3 specifications.

ASTRAL (Alliance for Strategic Token Ring Advancement and Leadership) was formed to help develop these new technologies and to help get them accepted as standards. They are another source of information.

→ *Broader Category* Network Architecture

→ *Compare* ARCnet; ATM; Ethernet; FDDI

Token Ring Interface Coupler (TIC)

→ *See* TIC (Token Ring Interface Coupler)

TokenTalk

TokenTalk is Apple's implementation of the token ring network architecture for its own AppleTalk environments. TokenTalk has the following features:

- Is defined at the lowest two OSI Reference Model layers: physical and data-link.

- Uses the TokenTalk Link Access Protocol (TLAP) to get access to the network.

- Supports both 4 megabit per second (Mbps) and 16Mbps networks.

→ *Broader Category* AppleTalk; Token Ring

→ *Compare* ARCTalk; EtherTalk; LocalTalk

Toll Office

In the telephone company hierarchy, a toll office is one in which trunks from local exchanges converge and are switched to other offices.

Tool Command Language (Tcl)

→ *See* Tcl (Tool Command Language)

Tool, Network

Tools are devices that make some tasks easier and other tasks possible. Both hardware and software tools are important for creating, running, and maintaining a network.

Several types of hardware tools can be distinguished:

Manufacturing Tools for creating individual components, such as crimpers and dies for attaching wires to connectors, and tools for splicing, polishing, and attaching optical fiber.

Construction Tools for assembling or disassembling systems. For example, screwdrivers can be considered construction tools for attaching connectors.

Testing Tools for testing individual components or for monitoring the performance of a component or system, such as breakout boxes, voltmeters, (milli)ammeters, and line scanners. A versatile piece of equipment, the volt-ohm-milliammeter (VOM) can be used to examine voltage, resistance, and current.

Safety Tools for making sure components are protected against damage from electrical and other dangers. These types of tools are discussed in the Safety Devices article.

Miscellaneous Many special-purpose and jury-rigged tools fit in this category, as do certain "gadgets," or small-scale components that help make things easier. For example, a gadget such as velcro strips can be used to collect and organize cables.

Basic Tool Requirements

The level and range of tools you will need depend on the level of involvement you have with the network. Regardless of the level, a few basic tools will almost certainly make life easier:

- Screwdrivers (flat and Philips head) for opening machines and for attaching connectors.

- Pliers for grasping objects and for tightening and loosening nuts.

- Chip remover for, …yes, removing chips from a circuit board.

- Tweezers (with long arms) for retrieving screws that fall into the back of the computer as you are removing or attaching the guard on an expansion slot.

In addition to these tools, some people might also have use for wire strippers and cutters, and for soldering irons, which may be used to rig up special-purpose circuits or wiring connections.

If you are going to do any troubleshooting at all, you will need a voltmeter or ammeter or both, *with a manual*, to test electrical activity. The manual is essential, because you will need to look up how to connect the meter. Connecting a meter (or any type of testing device) incorrectly can cause serious damage to sensitive circuitry, both yours and the meter's.

T

In general, magnets and hammers are not popular around computers, expansion boards, or peripherals. If you must hammer, do it at the keyboard.

Tools for Installing and Attaching Cable

If you will be involved with installing the cable as well as hooking up the computers, you may need other, more specialized tools.

For example, it is rarely feasible, and even more rarely advisable, to get all your cable pre-cut and pre-attached (to the connectors). You may need to make your own cable, or rather, cable ends. To do this, you need to attach the cable to the connector, make sure the cable and connector fit snugly, and then test the cable.

To attach connectors to cable, you need the following tools:

- A crimping tool, or crimper, for pressing the cable and connector together

- A die for the specified cable/connection pair, to make sure cable and connector fit properly

You can buy preconfigured installation toolkits from vendors such as Jensen Tools or Black Box. These kits can range in price from one or two hundred to several thousand dollars.

If you are actually going to be installing the cable—hanging it in the ceiling or running it through a plenum in a wall or under the floor—you will need industrial-strength tools, since some of the parts you will install may need to support dozens of pounds of cable.

Tools for Testing Cables

Voltmeters and ammeters provide readings (of voltage and current, or amperage, respectively) by tapping into the circuit and recording electrical activity as it occurs. The recorded values may or may not provide details about what is happening along the lines or on the network.

Scanners are much more sophisticated testing tools. Some of the capabilities of top-of-the-line scanners include the following:

- Check for faults (shorts or opens) in a cable

- Test a cable's compliance with any of several network architectures, such as Ethernet, Token Ring, ARCnet, and electronics standards, such as UL (Underwriters Laboratories)

- Monitor performance and electrical activity, given the type of cable and architecture involved

- Test the cable's wiring sequence

- Generate and print a summary of the information obtained

A powerful scanner can test for wire quality (for example, to find the best pair of wires in a cable for a connection), for the quality of the connections between cable segments or between cable and device.

At the lower end, scanners will at least be able to test for noise, crosstalk (in particular, Near End Crosstalk, or NEXT), signal attenuation, resistance, cable length, and so on.

Tools for Installing and Attaching Fiber-Optic Cable

Working with optical fiber creates special requirements not found when dealing with electrical cable. These special requirements, in turn, create a need for special tools.

The procedure for connecting or splicing two sections of fiber is somewhat different than for copper wire.

For connectors, the fiber must be glued into a ferrule (a tube used for guiding the fiber and for keeping it from moving), then the ends must be cut and polished in an appropriate manner. Polishing machines are used to make the fiber ends smooth, and special microscopes can be used to check the polishing job. Even for "high-tech" fiber-optic connections, something as lowly as epoxy is needed to attach the fiber core to the side of a ferrule.

In addition, the same kinds of tools as for copper wire may be needed: cable strippers and pliers for taking the outer sheaths off the cable, crimping tools, and so on. Most fiber-optic installation kits also include a duster (to make sure the pieces of fiber are clean before being joined). Special fluid may also be used to adjust the reflectivity of the fiber or cladding.

For splicing, the fibers are joined directly and permanently. One way of doing this it to fuse the two pieces of fiber together by applying heat to melt the fibers slightly, and then joining them before the fibers cool. Special machines, called fusion splicers, are used to do this.

Tools for Testing Fiber-Optic Cable

Equipment for testing the integrity of fiber-optic cable and the quality of the signal must gather optical (rather than electrical) data. Consequently, special equipment is needed. Ironically, this equipment gets its information from electrical signals. These signals are created by converting the optical signal to electrical form.

An optical power meter is the analog to the VOM mentioned earlier. This device can determine the power of a signal, in decibels (dB), or in decibels referenced to a milliwatt (dBm). The latter provides a standardized way of specifying signal strength.

An Optical Time-Domain Reflectometer (OTDR) serves as the foundation for higher-end cable testers. The optical time-domain reflectometry that underlies this device uses the light scattered back from a signal (or light bounced back for a test signal), and allows sophisticated measurements on the light.

These devices cost several thousand dollars, but can provide valuable information, such as signal loss per unit distance and signal loss at splices or over connectors.

TOP (Technical Office Protocol)

TOP is an architecture that provides standards for the representation and exchange of messages, documents, and other files in office settings. TOP provides APIs (Application Program Interfaces) for a variety of file types, including e-mail, office documents and graphics files. These APIs are built upon the seven-layer OSI reference model.

Like the closely related MAP (Manufacturing Automation Protocol), TOP is an effort to provide standardized protocols and services for use in real-world contexts that involve the reliable and efficient exchange of formatted data or access to such data from remote locations.

TOP APIs

"TOP APIs, OSI layers, and protocols" shows the APIs defined for TOP and also shows how these relate to the OSI reference model layers and to various protocols.

T

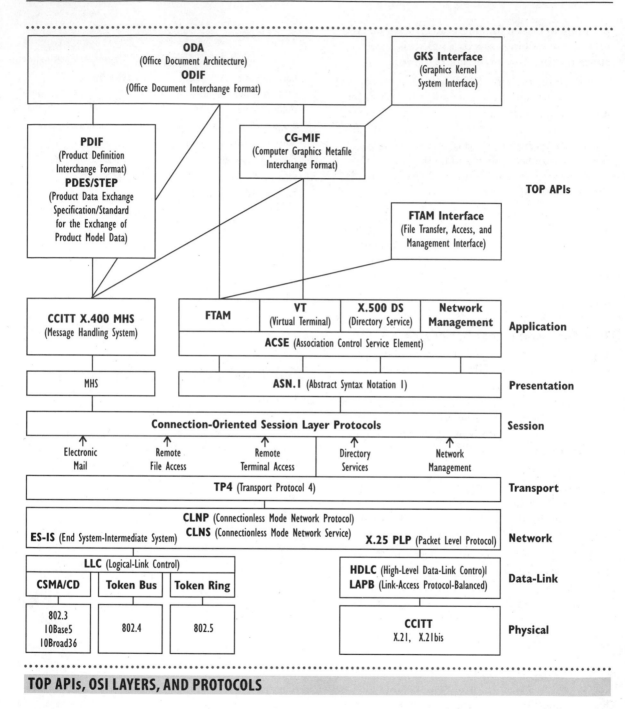

ODA
(Office Document Architecture)
ODIF
(Office Document Interchange Format)

GKS Interface
(Graphics Kernel System Interface)

TOP APIs

PDIF
(Product Definition Interchange Format)
PDES/STEP
(Product Data Exchange Specification/Standard for the Exchange of Product Model Data)

CG-MIF
(Computer Graphics Metafile Interchange Format)

FTAM Interface
(File Transfer, Access, and Management Interface)

CCITT X.400 MHS
(Message Handling System)

FTAM   **VT**
(Virtual Terminal)   **X.500 DS**
(Directory Service)   **Network Management**

Application

ACSE (Association Control Service Element)

MHS   **ASN.1** (Abstract Syntax Notation 1)   **Presentation**

Connection-Oriented Session Layer Protocols   **Session**

Electronic Mail   Remote File Access   Remote Terminal Access   Directory Services   Network Management

TP4 (Transport Protocol 4)   **Transport**

CLNP (Connectionless Mode Network Protocol)
ES-IS (End System-Intermediate System)   **CLNS** (Connectionless Mode Network Service)   **X.25 PLP** (Packet Level Protocol)   **Network**

LLC (Logical-Link Control)
CSMA/CD   **Token Bus**   **Token Ring**

HDLC (High-Level Data-Link Control)
LAPB (Link-Access Protocol-Balanced)   **Data-Link**

802.3
10Base5
10Broad36   802.4   802.5

CCITT
X.21, X.21bis   **Physical**

TOP APIs, OSI LAYERS, AND PROTOCOLS

TOP provides APIs for the following:

- PDIF (Product Definition Interchange Format) provides support for the description standards IGES (Initial Graphics Exchange Standard) and PDES/STEP (Product Description Exchange Standard/Standard for the Exchange of Product Model Data).

- ODA/ODIF (Office Document Architecture/Office Document Interchange Format) provides support for the creation and exchange of formatted and compound documents. (*Compound* documents contain multiple types of content, such as character and vector or raster graphics.) Certain of these formats can be used to create documents for the PDIF APIs.

- CGMIF (Computer Graphics Metafile Interchange Format) provides a vector-based representation for graphics files. This format can be used for describing graphics elements in compound documents.

- GKS (Graphics Kernel System) Interface provides a collection of primitive objects and functions for creating two- and three-dimensional graphics objects. In the TOP architecture, GKS objects are also represented in the CGMIF.

- FTAM (File Transfer, Access, and Management) Interface provides an interface for an FTAM application, which can be used to initiate and carry out the actual file transfer.

OSI Layers in the TOP Architecture

TOP APIs are designed to use protocols and services that conform to existing standards. To help provide flexibility in this use, the bottom four and the top three layers are each treated as a group.

The communications-based layers—from the Physical layer to the Transport layer—support one wide area network (WAN) and three local area network (LAN) architectures: Ethernet (802.3), Token Bus (802.4), and Token Ring (802.5) LAN architectures and the X.25 WAN interface.

TOP supports the Data-Link layer protocols appropriate to the various architectures, including support for the Logical-Link Control (LLC) sublayer specified by IEEE 802.2 for the LAN architectures. The TOP architecture supports connectionless protocols and services at the Network and Transport layers, but also supports the connection-oriented X.25 Packet Level Protocol.

For the application-oriented layers (session, presentation, and application), TOP supports several types of applications:

- Electronic Mail using the CCITT X.400 Message Handling System (MHS)

- Remote File Access using the OSI FTAM protocol

- Remote Terminal Access using the OSI's VT (Virtual Terminal) protocol

- Network directory services using OSI protocols

- Network management services using OSI protocols

Both TOP and MAP are currently undergoing scheduled revisions after a 6-year evaluation period for versions 3 of both TOP and MAP.

Topology, Backbone Bridge

A backbone topology provides a method for using bridges among multiple networks. A backbone topology connects each pair of networks directly using a bridge.

For example, in a three network (A, B, and C) setup, three bridges would be used: to connect A and B, A and C, and B and C. "A backbone bridge topology" illustrates this example.

This connection topology is in contrast to a cascaded bridge topology, in which two bridges are used (A to B and B to C) so that network A needs to go through network B to communicate with network C. A backbone bridge topology saves work for each network; a cascaded bridge topology saves on equipment.

→ *Compare* Topology, Cascaded Bridge

Topology, Bus

Bus refers to a physical and a logical topology. As a logical topology, a bus is distinguished by the fact that packets are broadcast so that every node gets the message at the same time. Ethernet networks are the best examples of a logical bus topology.

As a physical topology, a bus describes a network in which each node is connected to a common line: the backbone, or trunk. A bus usually has the file server at one end, with the main trunk line extending from this point. (Although the metaphor of a backbone is useful, it should not be taken literally; just as in the real world, not all network backbones are straight.) "A bus topology" illustrates this layout.

Nodes are attached to this trunk line, and every node can hear each packet as it goes past. Packets travel in both directions along the backbone, and need not go through the individual nodes. Rather, each node checks the packet's destination address to determine whether the packet is intended for the node.

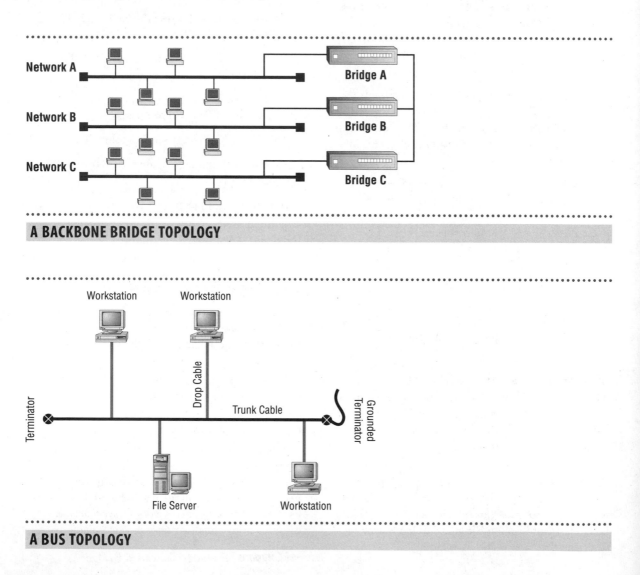

A BACKBONE BRIDGE TOPOLOGY

A BUS TOPOLOGY

When the signal reaches the end of the trunk line, a terminator absorbs the packet to keep it from traveling back again along the bus line, possibly interfering with other messages already on the line. Each end of a trunk line must be terminated, so that signals are removed from the bus when they reach the end.

Thin and thick Ethernet are the best examples of a physical bus topology. Twisted-pair Ethernet (10Base-T Ethernet) uses a logical bus topology, but a star for its physical topology.

In a bus topology, nodes should be far enough apart so that they do not interfere with each other. If the backbone cable is long, it may be necessary to boost the signal strength. The maximum length of the backbone is limited by the size of the time interval that constitutes "simultaneous" packet reception.

Bus Topology Advantages

Bus topologies offer the following advantages:

- A bus uses relatively little cable compared to other topologies, and arguably has the simplest wiring arrangement.

- Since nodes just attach to the main line, it's easy to add or remove nodes from a bus. This makes it easy to extend a bus topology.

- Architectures based on this topology are simple and flexible.

Bus Topology Disadvantages

Bus topology disadvantages include the following:

- Diagnosis/troubleshooting (fault-isolation) can be difficult.

- The bus trunk can be a bottleneck when network traffic gets heavy. This is because nodes can spend much of their time trying to access the network.

Topology, Cascaded Bridge

A cascaded bridge topology is a method for providing bridges among multiple networks. A cascaded topology uses one network (B) as an access point to another network (C) from a third network (A). Thus, instead of providing a direct bridge between A and C, a cascaded bridge topology saves a bridge by making network A go through B to communicate with C. "A cascaded bridge topology" illustrates this layout.

A cascaded topology saves on equipment, but adds to work. This approach is in contrast to a

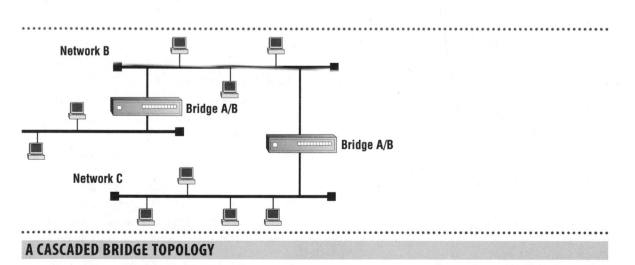

A CASCADED BRIDGE TOPOLOGY

backbone bridge topology, in which there are direct bridges between each pair of networks. In the example, A would be connected directly to B and directly to C with separate bridges, and B would be connected to C with yet another bridge.

→ **Compare** Topology, Backbone Bridge

Topology, Distributed Star

A distributed star topology is a physical topology that consists of two or more hubs, each of which is the center of a star arrangement. "A distributed star topology" illustrates this layout.

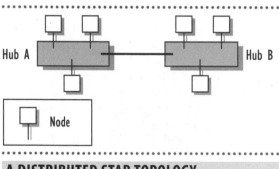

Hub A   Hub B

Node

A DISTRIBUTED STAR TOPOLOGY

This type of topology is common, and it is generally known simply as a *star topology*. A good example of such a topology is an ARCnet network with at least one active hub and one or more active or passive hubs.

Topology, Hybrid

A physical topology that is actually a combination of two or more different physical topologies. The best known example is the star-wired ring topology that is used to implement IBM Token Ring networks.

→ **See Also** Topology, Star-Wired Ring

Topology, Logical

A logical topology defines the logical layout of a network. This specifies how the elements in the network communicate with each other and how information is transmitted, or the path information takes through a network.

The two main logical topologies are bus and ring. These are each associated with different types of media-access methods, which determine how a node gets to transmit information along the network.

In a bus topology, information is broadcast, and every node gets the information at the same time. "Same time" for a bus topology is defined as the amount of time it actually takes a signal to cover the entire length of cable. This time interval limits the maximum speed and size for the network. Supposedly, nodes read only messages intended for them. To broadcast, a node needs to wait until the network is temporarily idle. Ethernet networks are the best examples of a logical bus topology.

In a ring topology, each node hears from exactly one node and talks to exactly one other node. Information is passed sequentially from node to node. In a ring topology, information is passed sequentially, in an order determined by a predefined process. A polling or token mechanism is used to determine who has transmission rights, and a node can transmit only when it has this right. A Token Ring network is the best example of a logical ring topology.

Topology, Mesh

A mesh topology is a physical topology in which there are at least two paths to and from every node. "A mesh topology" illustrates this layout.

This type of topology is advantageous in hostile environments in which connections are easily broken. If a connection is broken in this layout, at least one substitute path is always available.

A more restrictive definition requires each node to be connected directly to every other node. Because of the severe connection requirements, such restrictive mesh topologies are feasible only for small networks.

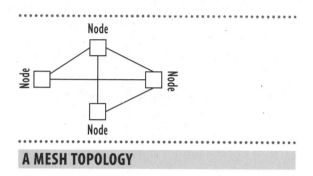

A MESH TOPOLOGY

Topology, Physical

A physical topology defines the wiring layout for a network. This specifies how the elements in the network are connected to each other *electrically*. This arrangement will determine what happens if a node on the network fails.

Categories of Physical Topologies

There are numerous physical topologies, because hybrid topologies are possible. These are created from two or more different physical topologies. Physical topologies fall into three main categories:

- Those which implement a logical bus topology. These include bus, star, and tree topologies. In a star topology, multiple nodes are connected to a central hub. This hub may be connected to another hub or to the network's file server. In a tree topology, two or more buses may be daisy-chained (strung together) or a bus may be split into two or more buses at a hub.

- Those which implement a logical ring topology. Logical ring topologies are implemented by physical rings, which are actually rare in pure form. This is because a physical ring is extremely susceptible to failures. When a node

in a physical ring goes down, the entire network goes down. For this reason, logical rings are generally implemented by a hybrid star-wired ring topology.

- Hybrids, which implement a combination of physical topologies. The best known of these is a star-wired ring, which is used for IBM Token Ring networks. The FDDI architecture also allows a variety of hybrid topologies, such as a dual ring of trees. Hybrid topologies are used to overcome weaknesses or restrictions in one or the other component topology.

The various physical topologies are described in separate articles.

Multipoint versus Point-to-Point Connections

Physical topologies can also be categorized by the manner in which nodes are connected to each other. In particular, they can be categorized by how workstations are connected to a server on the network.

In a point-to-point connection, two nodes are linked directly. A mesh topology is a specific type of point-to-point connection in which there are at least two direct paths to every node. (A more restrictive definition of a mesh topology requires that every node be connected directly to every other node.)

In a multipoint connection (also called a *multidrop connection*), multiple nodes are connected to a single node (for example, to a hub or gateway), which is, in turn, connected to another (for example, to a server or host).

Topology, Ring

A ring topology is a logical and a physical topology. As a logical topology, a ring is distinguished by the fact that packets are transmitted sequentially from node to node, in a predefined order. Nodes are arranged in a closed loop, so that the initiating node is the last one to receive a packet. Token Ring networks are the most widely used example of a logical ring topology.

As a physical topology, a ring describes a network in which each node is connected to two other nodes. Information traverses a one-way path, so that a node receives packets from exactly one node and transmits them to exactly one other node. A packet travels around the ring until it returns to the node that originally sent the packet. In a ring topology, each node can act as a repeater, boosting the signal before sending it on. "A ring topology" illustrates this layout.

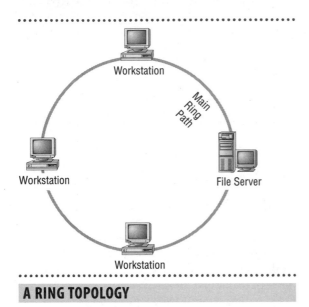

A RING TOPOLOGY

Each node checks whether the packet's destination node matches the node's address. When the packet reaches its destination, the node accepts the message, then sends it back to the sender to acknowledge receipt.

Since ring topologies use token passing to control access to the network, the token is returned to sender with the acknowledgment. The sender then releases the token to the next node on the network. If this node has nothing to say, the node passes the token on to the next node, and so on. When the token reaches a node with a packet to send, that node sends its packet.

Physical ring networks are rare, because this topology has considerable disadvantages compared to a

more practical star-wired ring hybrid, which is described in a separate article.

The advantages of a ring topology are that the cable requirements are fairly minimal, and no wiring center or closet is needed.

The disadvantages of this topology include the following:

- If any node goes down, the entire ring goes down.

- Diagnosis/troubleshooting (fault isolation) is difficult because communication is only one-way.

- Adding or removing nodes disrupts the network.

Topology, Star

A star topology is a physical topology in which multiple nodes are connected to a central component, generally known as a hub. "A star topology" illustrates this layout. Despite appearances, such a wiring scheme actually implements a logical bus topology.

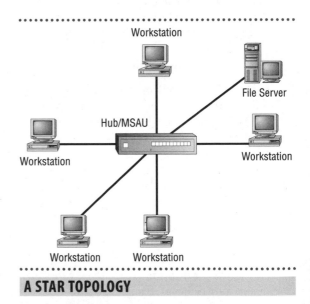

A STAR TOPOLOGY

The hub of a star generally is just a wiring center; that is, a common termination point for the nodes, with a single connection continuing from the hub. In rare cases, the hub may actually be a file server, with all its nodes attached directly to the server.

As a wiring center, a hub may, in turn, be connected to a file server, a wall plate, or to another hub. All signals, instructions, and data going to and from each node must pass through the hub to which the node is connected.

The telephone company wiring system is the best known example of a star topology, with lines to individual subscribers (such as yourself or your employer) coming from a central location. In the LAN world, low impedance ARCnet networks are probably the best example of a star topology.

One advantage of a star topology is that troubleshooting and fault isolation are easy. Also, it is easy to add or remove nodes, and to modify the cable layout.

A disadvantage of this topology is that if the hub fails, the entire network fails. Sometimes a backup central machine is included, to make it possible to deal with such a failure. Also, a star topology requires a lot of cable.

Topology, Star-Wired Ring

A star-wired ring topology, also known as a *hub topology*, is a hybrid physical topology that combines features of the star and ring topologies. Individual nodes are connected to a central hub, as in a star network. Within the hub, however, the connections are arranged into an internal ring. Thus, the hub constitutes the ring, which must remain intact for the network to function. "A star-wired ring topology" illustrates this layout.

The hubs, known as *Multistation Access Units* (*MAUs*) in Token Ring network terminology, may be connected to other hubs. In this arrangement, each internal ring is opened and connected to the attached hubs to create a larger, multi-hub ring.

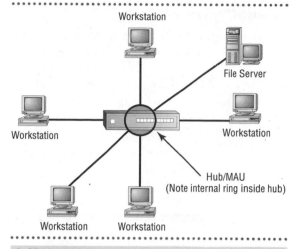

A STAR-WIRED RING TOPOLOGY

The advantage of using star wiring instead of simple ring wiring is that it is easy to disconnect a faulty node from the internal ring. The IBM Data Connector is specially designed to close a circuit if an attached node is disconnected physically or electrically. By closing the circuit, the ring remains intact, but with one less node.

IBM Token Ring networks are the best-known example of a star-wired ring topology at work. In Token Ring networks, a secondary ring path can be established and used if part of the primary path goes down.

The advantages of a star-wired ring topology include the following:

- Troubleshooting, or fault isolation, is relatively easy.

- The modular design makes it easy to expand network, and makes layouts extremely flexible.

- Individual hubs can be connected to form larger rings.

- Wiring to the hub is flexible.

The disadvantage is that, because of the extreme flexibility of the arrangement, configuration and cabling may be complicated.

T

Topology, Tree

A tree topology, also known as a distributed bus or a branching tree topology, is a hybrid physical topology that combines features of star and bus topologies. Several buses may be daisy-chained together, and there may be branching at the connections (which will be hubs). The starting end of the tree is known as the *root* or *head end*. "A tree topology" illustrates this layout.

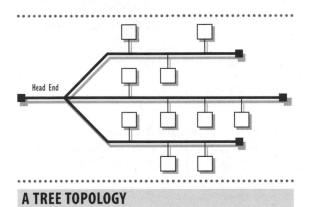

Head End

A TREE TOPOLOGY

This type of topology is used in delivering cable television services.

The advantages of a tree topology are that the network is easy to extend by just adding another branch, and that fault isolation is relatively easy.

The disadvantages are as follows:

- If the root goes down, the entire network goes down.

- If any hub goes down, all branches off of that hub go down.

- Access becomes a problem if the entire conglomerate becomes too big.

ToS (Type of Service)

A field in an IP (Internet Protocol) packet, or datagram, header. The contents of this byte specify the kind of transmission desired, with respect to delay, throughput, and reliability. Part of this byte specifies a priority for the datagram's handling. The details of this field are being reconsidered by the Internet Engineering Task Force (IETF).

TPAD (Terminal Packet Assembler/Disassembler)

→ *See* PAD (Packet Assembler/Disassembler)

TPDDI (Twisted-Pair Distributed Data Interface)

A network architecture, also known as CDDI, that implements the FDDI specifications on electrical (rather than optical) twisted-pair cable. This FDDI variant is being considered by the ANSI FDDI committee (X3T9.5).

TP-PMD (Twisted-Pair, Physical Media Dependent)

The 100 megabit per second, FDDI standard as implemented on unshielded twisted-pair (UTP) cable.

Traceroute

A program that can create a map of the path taken by a packet as it goes from source to destination. Traceroute is used as a tool when troubleshooting a network. See Also RFC 1470 ("FYI on a Network Management Tool Catalog, Tools for Monitoring and Debugging TCP/IP Internets and Interconnected Devices").

Traffic

In networking, the level of network activity. For example, one measure of traffic is the number of messages sent over the network at a given time or within a given interval.

Traffic Descriptor

In the ATM architecture, an element that specifies parameters for a Virtual Channel or Path Connection (VCC or VPC). These parameter values can be negotiated by the entities involved in the connection. A traffic descriptor is also known as a *user-network contract*.

Traffic Management

The ATM (Asynchronous Transfer Mode) networking architecture supports various classes of service and guarantees a negotiated quality of service for a connection. In order to fulfill such guarantees, ATM relies heavily on traffic management methods. In fact, several specifications in the ATM architecture are concerned with traffic management. These include the User-Network-Interface (UNI) specification, The Interim Local Management (ILM) specification, and the ATM Forum Traffic Management specification.

Traffic management strategies and mechanisms work by monitoring the values of several traffic parameters and by taking the required steps to modify these, when necessary. The traffic parameters are as follows:

Minimum cell rate (MCR) The minimum cell transmission rate that the network must guarantee in order for a virtual connection to be established.

Peak cell rate (PCR) The maximum rate at which cells can be transmitted over a virtual connection.

Sustainable cell rate (SCR) The maximum *average* cell transmission rate that can be achieved over a virtual connection.

Maximum burst size (MBS) The longest PCR traffic burst that a virtual connection can support.

Mechanisms for traffic management include traffic policing and shaping—which are both described in their own entries—as well as selective cell discard, forward error correction, explicit forward congestion indication (EFCI), generic flow control, and available bit rate (ABR) flow control.

→ *See Also* Traffic Policing; Traffic Shaping

Traffic Policing

Traffic Policing is one of the traffic management measures used in ATM (Asynchronous Transfer Mode) network technology. Also known as *usage parameter control (UPC)*, traffic policing checks the parameters related to a connection—for example, the validity of virtual path identifiers and virtual channel identifiers (VPIs and VCIs, respectively).

Traffic policing uses one or two leaky buckets to control the flow of traffic. A leaky bucket behaves like a buffer with a hole in it. Cell traffic flows into the bucket, from which it is released, cell by cell, at a rate determined by various connection parameters—for example, minimum cell rate (MCR), peak cell rate (PCR), sustainable cell rate (SCR), and cell-delay variation tolerance (CDVT). For constant bit rate (CBR) traffic, only a single bucket is needed, whereas two buckets are used for variable bit rate (VBR) traffic.

→ *Broader Category* Traffic Management

→ *See Also* Traffic Shaping

Traffic Shaping

In traffic management for ATM (Asynchronous Transfer Mode) networks, traffic shaping is used to

T

modify the properties of cell traffic in order to improve efficiency, while meeting the quality of service (QoS) requirements for the connection. Traffic shaping measures can include such actions as reducing burstiness, removing cell delay variation (CDV), or decreasing the peak cell rate (PCR). Traffic shaping is accomplished using ATM's Generic Cell Rate Algorithm (GCRA), and can be applied at any point in the network.

→ **Broader Category** Traffic Management

→ **See Also** Traffic Policing

Trailer

In packets transmitted on a network, a packet portion that follows the data contained in the packet. Trailer portions generally include error-detection fields (for example, FCS or CRC). Most administrative and control information relevant to the packet is in the packet's *header*, which *precedes* the data portion.

Transaction

A transaction is an interaction between a client and a server. For example, a transaction may be a request, the transfer of data, or the termination of a connection. An ATM (Automated Teller Machine) session is an example of a transaction.

The transaction is the smallest complete action when using SQL (Structured Query Language) to search or modify a database. In SQL, if any step in the transaction cannot be carried out, the entire transaction fails, and all the intermediate steps in the transaction are undone.

Transaction Server

→ **See** Server, Transaction

Transaction Tracking System (TTS)

→ **See** TTS (Transaction Tracking System)

Transceiver

A transceiver, from *trans*mitter/re*ceiver*, is a device that can both receive and transmit a signal. On a network, most computers are connected to the network using a transceiver.

The transceiver may be on a network interface card (NIC), or it may be an external component. For example, the transceiver for a thin Ethernet network is on the NIC. A transceiver for thick Ethernet is external, and it attaches to a drop cable (which goes to the node) and to the network cable.

In fiber-optics, a transceiver is similar to a repeater in that both consist of a transmitter and a receiver. The difference is that these components are in parallel for a transceiver and in series for a repeater (with the receiver first, then the signal-cleaning component, then the transmitter).

In the IEEE specifications, a transceiver is known as a Medium Attachment Unit (MAU), not to be confused with a Multistation Access Unit, which is the MAU in a Token Ring network.

→ **Broader Category** Intranetwork link

→ **See Also** Repeater

Transducer

A transducer is a device that converts energy from one form to another—for example, between acoustic and electrical forms (as in a telephone) or between electrical and optical forms (as in a photodiode).

Transfer Mode

In telecommunications, the manner in which data is transmitted and/or switched in a network. For example, ATM (Asynchronous Transfer Mode) transmits asynchronously, and uses both circuit- and packet-switching techniques to route data.

Transfer Time

In connection with an SPS, the amount of time required to switch to the SPS's auxiliary power in case of a power outage to a network node. Look for times less than 5 milliseconds or so.

→ See Also UPS (Uninterruptible Power Supply); SPS (Standby Power Supply)

Transistor-Transistor Logic (TTL)

→ See TTL (Transistor-Transistor Logic)

Transit Network

A transit network is one that connects to at least two other networks, and that carries traffic for these networks as well as for hosts that might be connected to the transit network. In an internetwork—for example, the Internet—a transit network represents an intermediate-level network that may be connected to the Internetwork backbone at the top, to one or more transit networks in the middle, or to a stub network, or area, at the bottom of the Internetwork hierarchy. A stub area is an element at the lowest level of networks in an Internetwork, since such a network connects only to its own hosts and to exactly one transit network.

Translator

In telephony, a translator is a device that converts digits that are dialed into the routing information needed for setting up a call. In computer programming, a translator is a program that converts material from one form to another. In radio or television programming, a translator is an intermediate station that gets a signal from a primary station, amplifies it, and shifts it to the appropriate frequency range before sending it on to customers.

Transmission Code

A set of rules for representing data, usually characters. Commonly used transmission codes include EBCDIC (an 8-bit code used on all IBM mainframes) and ASCII (a 7-bit code commonly used on PCs).

Transmission Control Protocol (TCP)

→ See Protocol, TCP (Transmission Control Protocol)

Transmission Control Protocol/ Internet Protocol (TCP/IP) Suite

→ See TCP/IP (Transmission Control Protocol/ Internet Protocol) Suite

Transmission Header (TH)

→ See TH (Transmission Header)

Transmission Medium

The physical medium through which a data, voice, or another type of transmission moves to reach its destination. Common transmission media include conductive (usually, copper) wire, optical fiber, and air.

Transmission Mode

A transmission mode describes the manner in which a communication between a sender and a receiver can take place. The following modes are defined:

Simplex Communication goes in one direction only, and the sender can use the entire communication channel. A ticker-tape machine is an example.

Half-duplex Communication can go in both directions, but in only one direction at a time. The sender can use the entire channel. In order to change direction, a special signal must be given and acknowledged. The time required to turn over control to the other side is called the line turnaround (or just turnaround) time. Turnaround time can become significant in certain transmissions. A CB connection is an example.

Full-duplex Communication can go in both directions simultaneously, but each part gets to use only half the channel. Modem connections are an example.

Echo-plex An error-checking mode in which characters typed for transmission are sent back to the screen from the receiver, to permit direct comparison with what was typed.

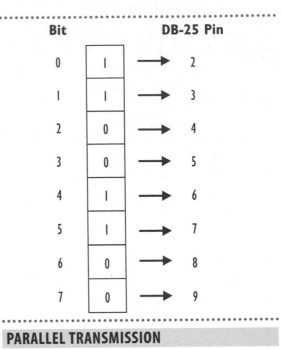

PARALLEL TRANSMISSION

Transmission, Parallel

Parallel is a transmission mode in which the bits that make up a byte are all transmitted at the same time; each bit is transmitted on a different wire. "Parallel transmission" shows this method. This is in contrast to serial transmission, in which bits are transmitted one at a time, in sequence.

Parallel transmissions are commonly used for communicating with printers and external LAN adapters, and for internal communications on the computer's bus.

→ *Compare* Transmission, Serial

Transmission, Serial

Serial is a digital transmission mode in which bytes are broken down into individual bits. These bits are then transmitted one after the other, in a predefined sequence (least to most significant bits, or vice versa). The bits are reassembled into a byte at the receiving end. "Serial transmission, with both least and most significant bits first" shows this method. Serial transmissions are in contrast to parallel transmissions, in which multiple bits are transmitted at the same time, each on different wires.

Serial transmissions are used for communicating with modems (for telecommunications), some printers, and some mouse devices.

→ *Compare* Transmission, Parallel

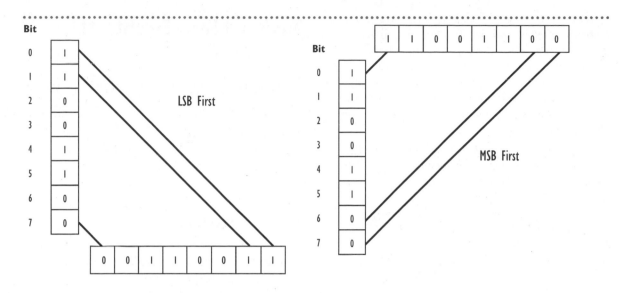

SERIAL TRANSMISSION, WITH BOTH LEAST AND MOST SIGNIFICANT BITS FIRST

Transmission, Single-Frequency

Single-frequency is a transmission method using radio waves. In single-frequency transmissions, the signal is encoded within a narrow frequency range. With such a signal, all the energy is concentrated at a particular frequency range.

A single-frequency signal is susceptible to jamming and eavesdropping. Depending on the frequency range being used, you may need a license to operate a single-frequency network.

Motorola's Altair system is an example of a single-frequency network. These types of radio wave networks operate within a frequency range that requires licensing, but the vendor takes care of that. For the Altair system, Motorola must also assign a frequency within which to operate, to ensure that the network does not interfere with another single-frequency network in the area. The Altair network operates as an Ethernet network.

➔ *Broader Categories* Network, Wireless; Radio Wave Transmission

➔ *Compare* Transmission, Spread-Spectrum

Transmission, Spread-Spectrum

Spread-spectrum is a form of radio transmission in which the signal is distributed over a broad frequency range, or spectrum. The distribution pattern is based on either frequency hopping or on direct sequence coding.

With frequency hopping, a transmitter will send at a particular frequency for a few milliseconds, then switch to another frequency for a few milliseconds, and so on. The frequency sequence is selected at random. The receiver must know the random number sequence and must be able to adjust and fine-tune just as rapidly and accurately as the transmitter. This type of signal is impossible to jam or eavesdrop unless the frequency hopping sequence is known.

With direct-sequence coding, the information to be transmitted is modified by a multibit binary chipping code. The chipping code spreads the signal out over a broader frequency range, with more chips (bits) in the code corresponding to a broader range. As with frequency hopping, this type of transmission is impossible to jam or overhear unless the chipping code is known.

Spread-spectrum signals are extremely unlikely to interfere with other transmissions, since the other transmission would need to be using the same spreading algorithm. Spread-spectrum networks do not require licensing, at least not within the frequency range covered by such products. WaveLAN from NCR, RangeLAN from Proxim, and Netwave from Xircom are examples of networks that use spread-spectrum technology.

→ *Broader Category* Network, Wireless; Radio Wave Transmission

→ *Compare* Transmission, Single-Frequency

Transparent

Used as an adjective in connection with computer use, something that is taken care of without requiring any instructions or attention from the user. For example, the media-access process in a network transmission is transparent to the user.

Transparent Mode

A terminal-display mode in which control characters are displayed literally, rather than being interpreted as commands. For example, in transparent mode, a beep character (Ctrl+G, or ASCII 7) sent to the terminal (or to a PC emulating a terminal) would be displayed as a Ctrl+G character; there would be no beep.

Transport Layer Security (TLS) Encryption

→ *See* TLS (Transport Layer Security) Encryption

Transport Protocol

→ *See* Protocol, Transport

Tree Structure

A tree is a flexible data structure that can be used to represent information that is hierarchically organized, such as a corporate structure or an elimination tournament schedule.

As a data structure, a tree consists of a topmost element called the *root*, and one or more elements that are defined directly below this root.

The root may represent the topmost element in the content area being represented (for example, a corporate head). The root is often left as an abstract entity, which means that it is an element that serves a purpose but that has no particular content associated with it.

The elements below the root are known as *children* of the root. A child element may, itself, be a tree, and the child can have child trees of its own. Or the child element may be an end element, known as a *leaf*. A leaf element has no children.

Directories of various types are often represented using a tree structure. For example, directories for hierarchical file systems, such as the one used by DOS, and for naming services, such as the NetWare Directory Services (NDS) used in NetWare 4.x, are represented using trees.

The NDS contains information about all objects (users, devices, queues, and so on) on the network. This information is stored in the Directory tree, or just Directory (with an uppercase *D*). In the Directory, the topmost element is the root object. Below this are one or more children, known as containers. See the NDS article for more information about the Directory tree.

Tribit

A tribit consists of three bits treated as a single unit. The eight possible tribits are 000, 001, 010, 011, 100, 101, 110, and 111. Similarly, a *dibit* consists of two bit values treated together, and a *quadbit* is a four-bit sequence.

→ **See Also** Dibit; Quadbit

Trit

A trit is a ternary digit. That is, a trit is any of the possible values in a three-valued number system. For example, in the simplest such system, a trit can take on any of the values 0, 1, or 2. In comparison, a bit can have a value of 0 or 1; a quat can have a value of 0, 1, 2, or 3.

Trojan Horse

A program that looks harmless but that contains hidden instructions to destroy files, programs, or File Allocation Tables (FATs). The instructions may be "time bombs," which are triggered by certain dates, times, or user commands.

→ **See Also** Virus; Worm

Trouble Ticket

In network fault management, a trouble ticket is an error log. Trouble tickets are a useful logging method for distributed systems.

When a fault arises somewhere on a distributed network, a nearby administrator may take responsibility for dealing with it. This administrator can fill out a trouble ticket to indicate that the fault has been detected and is being worked on. When the fault has been resolved, the administrator can add the date of the resolution to the trouble ticket.

Trouble tickets can be stored in a problem library, and they can serve as both reference information and performance data.

→ **Broader Category** Network Management

Trunk

In telephony, a trunk refers to a circuit that connects two switching systems—rather than connecting a user to a switching system. For example, trunks connect offices at different levels in the telephone company hierarchy to each other.

The term also refers to the physical lines that connect local exchanges (that is, the offices to which subscribers connect) to toll offices. In this sense, a trunk aggregates multiple user lines into a single channel going to the next office.

Trunk group

In telephony, a trunk group is a collection of trunks serving the same function and connecting the same locations.

Trust-Based Security

In trust-based security, a host decides which networks or hosts to trust, and then accepts certain kinds of materials—for example plug-ins, ActiveX controls, or Java applets—only from those sites. Trust-based security methods were developed by Microsoft and other software vendors in order to enable hosts—for example, Web surfers— to limit the kinds of programs that can execute on the host. This is necessary because processes such as those mentioned can potentially be designed to damage files on the host's machine or to send information stored on the host's machine to another location.

→ **Broader Category** Security

T

TRUSTe

TRUSTe is an organization that monitors the privacy policies and practices of participating Web sites, and that certifies such Web sites if their policies conform to guidelines established by the organization. TRUSTe provides such certification in the form of a trustmark. This mark indicates that the site is willing to publish its policies on how it handles personal data obtained from visitors to the site, and is willing to submit to periodic checks on whether the site is actually adhering to its own policies.

Such a certification helps to give Web users some modicum of control over how information about them is used. Although it is a big step in the right direction, the trustmark system is far from perfect, as attested by recent controversy caused by the discovery that Microsoft (a TRUSTe certified site) was automatically gathering information about users' systems when they registered their software electronically.

TSA (Target Service Agent)

A TSA is a Novell NetWare program that helps move data between a host and a target server. A *host* is any server with storage and a storage controller. A *target* is a server with data to be backed up or restored.

Specifically, a TSA runs on a target and communicates with the SBACKUP utility on the host, as follows:

1. SBACKUP on the host sends a request to the TSA on the target. The TSA translates the request into a form the target's Operating System (OS) will be able to handle.

2. In the second step, the TSA actually passes the request on to the target OS. The target OS performs the appropriate action on the data.

3. The target OS returns any output or results to the TSA, which now converts them into a form suitable for the host. In fact, NetWare uses the SMS (Storage Management Services) to create hardware and operating system-independent representations.

4. The TSA passes the results and data to SBACKUP for the host.

"A TSA at work" shows the elements of a session with SBACKUP and a TSA.

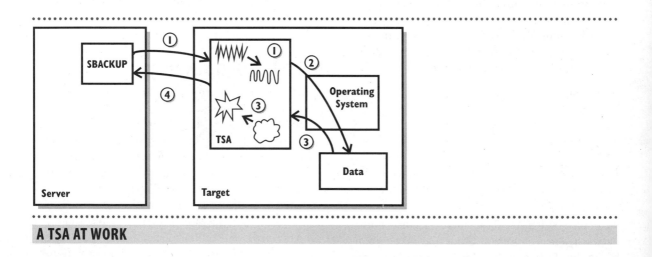

A TSA AT WORK

TSAPI (Telephony Services API)

A collection of functions for communicating with telephones, PBXs, and other telecommunications devices and for enabling networks to make use of these devices. The TSAPI was developed by AT&T and Novell to help bring about true Computer-Telephony Integration (CTI).

→ **Broader Category** CTI (Computer-Telephony Integration)

→ **See Also** TAPI (Telephony API); Versit

TSR (Terminate-and-Stay-Resident) Program

A program that is loaded into memory and stays there, usually dormant, until activated by a condition or a key sequence.

TTL (Time-to-Live)

In packets being routed, the TTL field indicates how long the packet may travel before being discarded as undeliverable. The TTL may be measured in seconds or in hops. The sender sets the TTL value before sending off the packet. This value is decremented under the appropriate circumstances—for example, each time the packet reaches a new node (hops) or every second (time). If the TTL value reaches zero before the packet reaches its destination, the packet may be discarded.

TTL (Transistor-Transistor Logic)

A very fast (versions operating at over 100 megahertz are available) but relatively power-hungry logic family for digital circuitry. Compare TTL with ECL, which is used for very high-speed applications, and CMOS, which is used for applications in which low-power consumption is needed.

TTP (Telephone Twisted-Pair)

→ **See** Cable, Twisted-Pair

TTRT (Target Token Rotation Time)

In FDDI networks, a parameter whose value specifies how long it will take before every node on a network gets access to the token.

TTS (Transaction Tracking System)

TTS is a Novell NetWare software safety mechanism used to protect file integrity in database applications. In TTS, database transactions are carried out completely or not at all.

TTS works using *automatic rollback* to accomplish its tasks. Automatic rollback restores the starting state if a transaction fails before completion. Backing out of a transaction enables the user or application to completely abandon an uncompleted transaction in a database, so that no changes are made to the database. Automatic rollback helps ensure that a record is never changed partially in a transaction.

TTS can help prevent errors under conditions such as the following:

- Loss of power to either the server or the workstation during a transaction

- Other hardware failure in either server or workstation during a transaction

- Hardware failure to a non-node component, such as a cable, hub, or repeater

- Software failure, such as a hung system

TTS works only with files in which information is stored in records and in which record locking can be used. This applies to database files and to some electronic mail and workgroup schedule files. TTS will not work with ordinary text files such as those created with a word processor.

→ **Broader Category** NetWare

Tunnel

A software tunnel provides a way to achieve secure communications over a WAN (wide area network) by using one protocol (known as the transport protocol) to provide encryption and delivery of packets for another protocol (known as the passenger protocol). For example, IPX (Internetwork packet exchange) packets from a NetWare network can be delivered across the Internet or an intranet by encapsulating the IPX packets in an IP (Internet Protocol) packet.

Tunneling

Tunneling is a method for avoiding protocol restrictions by wrapping packets from one protocol in a packet for another, and then transmitting this wrapped, or encapsulated, packet over a network that supports the wrapper protocol.

For example, an SDLC (Synchronized Data Link Control) packet from an SNA (Systems Network Architecture) network expects to be transmitted in a connection-oriented manner (over a predefined path). In contrast, on some local area networks (LANs), packets are transmitted in a connectionless manner (by whatever path is most expedient). To move SDLC packets over LANs, these packets may be wrapped in a TCP/IP protocol.

Similarly, the Apple Internet Router (AIR) can wrap an AppleTalk packet inside X.25 or TCP/IP packets.

Tunneling is also known as *protocol encapsulation* and *synchronous pass-through*.

Turbo FAT Index Table

In the DOS file system as used by NetWare, a turbo FAT (File Allocation Table) index table is created when a file gets too large for an ordinary FAT. The turbo FAT index that Novell's NetWare creates for such a file will speed up access to the file.

TUXEDO

Novell's TUXEDO software provides a high-level interface for client-server and transaction-management services, such as Online Transaction Processing (OLTP). TUXEDO provides a functional layer between applications and database management systems or other transaction-based systems.

The additional layer supplies a common interface that developers can use, and it also provides a buffer between applications and services. This buffer makes it easier to redirect or otherwise filter transmissions, thereby making it easy to protect data. For example, TUXEDO uses the layer to redirect a client's request to an appropriate server, which will handle the transaction. Instead of transmitting data across the network, TUXEDO transmits requests and functions.

Applications communicate using a data-presentation service known as *typed buffers*. Typed buffers provide an intermediate representation for data, which can be translated from and to any format supported by TUXEDO. By separating the applications from the internal representations, TUXEDO helps make network and remote access easier for applications.

Other TUXEDO features and capabilities include the following:

- Use of a naming service, so that clients can refer to services by name, instead of needing to specify the service's location.

- Support for DOS, Microsoft Windows 3.1, OS/2, and Macintosh workstations.

- The ability to transfer data among platforms that differ in the way they represent data (for example, DOS, UNIX, and mainframe environments).

- Support for message queuing by applications.

- Use of an authentication system to verify a user's identity.

- Transaction monitoring and management.

- Replication of servers and services across multiple nodes, to help ensure that the requested services will always be available.

- Support for load balancing, for automatic recovery, and server restarts after a fault.

- Support for service migration, by which a service is moved from one server to another when error or load conditions dictate.

TWAIN

TWAIN technology was developed to increase the versatility of scanners so that they can work with multiple applications, rather than just with the scanner software. TWAIN software connects applications and scanning software, so that images can be scanned directly into an application. The TWAIN drivers—which are part of the scanner software environment—make this possible without requiring the application to interact directly with the scanner.

Although its developers claim it is not, TWAIN has come to be generally regarded as an acronym for "technology without an interesting name."

Twisted-Pair Distributed Data Interface (TPDDI)

→*See* TPDDI (Twisted-Pair Distributed Data Interface)

Twisted-Pair, Physical Media Dependent (TP-PMD)

→*See* TP-PMD (Twisted-Pair, Physical Media Dependent)

Two-Wire circuit

In telephony, a two-wire circuit is one in which transmissions in both directions travel along the same path. Two-wire circuits allow half-duplex communication. This is in contrast to a four-wire circuit, in which transmissions in each direction have their own separate paths, making full duplex operation possible.

Type of Service (ToS)

→*See* ToS (Type of Service)

Typewriter

A *typewriter* is a wireless input device that has fallen into disuse. Typewriters used digital input and a narrowband mechanical transmission scheme. Multicast capabilities were possible with the inclusion of additional media paired with an input template known as carbon paper. Most typewriters supported error correction, which was built into later models. In both the built-in and manual correction schemes, the same BWR (backspace, whiteout, retransmit) algorithm was used.

T

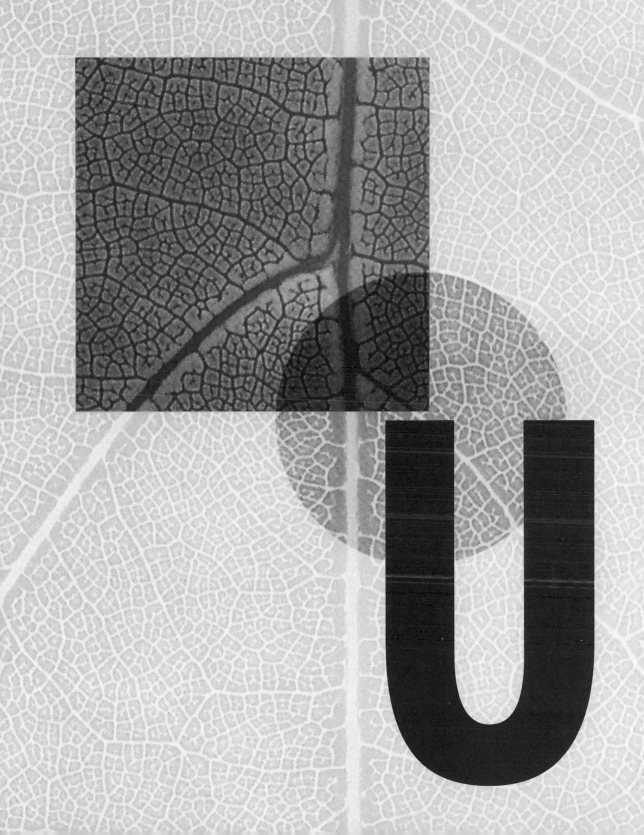

UA (User Agent)

In the CCITT X.400 Message Handling System (MHS), the UA is an application process that provides access for a human user to a Message Transfer System (MTS).

→ *See Also* X.400

UAL (User Access Line)

In an X.25 network, the UAL is the line that provides a connection between a DTE (computer) and a network, with the user's DCE (digital service unit, modem, or multiplexer) serving as the interface to the network.

UAL (User Agent Layer)

In the 1984 version of the X.400 Message Handling System (MHS) recommendations, the UAL is the upper sublayer of the OSI Application layer. Users interact with the UAL, and the UAL, in turn communicates with the MTL (Message Transfer Layer) below it.

→ *See Also* X.400

UAM (User Authentication Method)

In an AppleTalk network, the UAM identifies users for a file server before giving the users access to services. Depending on the authentication method being used, this can be done on the basis of either an unencrypted password sent over the network or of a random number from which the user's password can be derived by decrypting at the server's end.

UART (Universal Asynchronous Receiver/Transmitter)

The UART is the chip that does the nitty-gritty work for serial communications. The UART is located on either the motherboard or on a serial interface card.

UART Functions

The UART performs the following tasks:

- Converts parallel input from a program to serial form for transmission
- Adds any required start, stop, and parity bits to the byte
- Monitors the serial port's status by reading the appropriate control pins
- Controls the timing for the transmission
- Maintains and administrates a buffer to speed up processing
- At the receiving end, strips framing bits from the transmitted character
- At the receiving end, converts serial input to parallel form, before passing the character on to a program

Because of all the tasks a UART needs to do, this component can easily become a bottleneck in a communication. If the data is being transmitted too quickly from the program, the UART may be overrun, so that bits (and even bytes) are lost. To help protect against such loss, UARTs have buffers that can be used to store bits while the UART is tending to other tasks.

UART Versions

The early PCs used the 8-bit 8250 UART, which had 1-byte buffers for receiving and transmitting. Beginning about 1985, when AT clones became available, the 8250 was replaced by the faster, more powerful, 16-bit 16450 UART.

The 16-bit version is capable of transmissions up to 115,200bps. Although this is faster than the best throughput of ordinary modems, the UART must have complete control of the computer's resources to achieve this speed.

To deal with the greater demands imposed on the processor by programs and to make the UART effective even in multiuser and multitasking environments, a new version UART was introduced: the 16550A. Even though this chip represents a major deviation from earlier models, the difference is only internal. In fact, the 16550A plugs into a socket designed for the 16450. (Not all UARTs are in sockets; some are part of the board itself.)

A major difference between the 16450 and 16550 UARTs is the 16-byte buffers (for receiving and transmitting) on a 16550. These buffers are not used until activated by software that can make use of the 16550's features. Until that happens, the 16550 behaves just like a 16450.

The buffers save considerable time because the UART needs to stop transmission much less often. This means the UART must compete less with other devices for the central processing unit's (CPU's) attention. In systems running a multitasking environment or those with high-speed microprocessors (such as the 80486), the faster UART may be the only way to get high-speed communications to work properly.

The 16550 has more intelligent circuitry for checking when it needs to do work and when it needs to signal other devices. In addition, the 16550 can run about 20 percent faster than the 16450. These enhancements give the 16550 UART a 256Kbps throughput under optimal conditions.

UBR (Unspecified Bit Rate)

One of five service classes specified for ATM (Asynchronous Transfer Mode) networks, UBR makes no guarantees concerning speed, quality of service, or anything else. It does, however, make a best effort to deliver cells at the highest available rate. At any given time in a session, UBR will try to use the highest transmission rate that it can—that is, it will try to fill the available bandwidth.

The other service classes are ABR (Available Bit Rate), CBR (Constant Bit Rate), real-time and non-real-time VBR (Variable Bit Rate). Like UBR, ABR is also a best-effort service class. Otherwise, UBR differs from the other four classes, which all use traffic parameters to specify the details of the service class and of the quality of service to be provided; UBR specifies none of these things. The other four classes all use traffic management methods to ensure that they can provide the agreed upon service; UBR does not. Because it does neither traffic management nor error correction, UBR leaves it up to higher-level protocols to control traffic flow and to ensure that all the packets in a transmission make it to their destination without errors.

This is similar to the way packets move on LANs (Local Area Networks): A source node sends packets as quickly as possible when it has the chance. Any error checking and packet sequencing is done by the appropriate protocol at the Transport layer. In fact, one common use for the UBR service class is to provide transport for LAN traffic over ATM networks.

→ *Broader Category* ATM (Asynchronous Transfer Mode)

→ *See Also* ABR (Available Bit Rate); CBR (Constant Bit Rate); VBR (Variable Bit Rate)

UMB (Upper Memory Block)

In the DOS environment, the UMB refers to part or all of the memory in the area between 640KB and 1MB. With the help of memory managers, UMBs are allocated for storing drivers, video or other buffers, and other items, which frees conventional memory and gives programs more room in which to execute.

→ *See Also* Memory

UNA (Upstream Neighbor's Address)

In a Token Ring network, the address of the node from which a given node receives frames. Because of the ring structure, this address is unique at any given time in the network's operation.

→ *See Also* Token Ring

Undervoltage

As in other areas of life, electrical dangers can come from having too much or too little. Collectively, such disturbances are known as overvoltages and undervoltages, respectively. An undervoltage is a condition in which the voltage supply is below its nominal level.

→ *See Also* Power Disturbance

UNI (User-to-Network Interface)

In ATM networks, one of three levels of interface. The other two are Network-to-Network (NNI) and User-to-User (UUI).

In the PSTN (Public Switched Telephone Network) and in other network architectures, a UNI represents the manner in which an end user connects to the network. In the case of the phone network, the connection is over the local loop—the line running between the phone hookup at the customer's premises and a link at the phone company's central office (CO).

Unicast

A unicast refers to a transmission that is sent to a single network address. This is in contrast to a broadcast (sent to all network addresses) and a multicast (sent to selected network addresses).

Unicode

Unicode is a 16-bit character code, which supports up to 64,000 different characters. A 16-bit representation is particularly useful for languages with large alphabets or other basic units (for example, Asian languages). The Unicode specifications were developed by the Unicode Consortium. Most of the commonly used character codes (such as ASCII or EBCDIC) are encoded somewhere in Unicode's databanks and can, therefore, be used.

Character representation using Unicode is in contrast to the code-page strategy currently used in most DOS and Microsoft Windows environments. Each code page is 8 bits and has room for just 256 characters.

The NetWare Directory database in Novell's NetWare 4.*x* uses Unicode format to store information about objects and their attributes.

Unified Messaging

Unified messaging, also known as *integrated messaging*, is a local area network (LAN) based telephony service, in which various kinds of messages or information can be accessed in a transparent manner. The types of information that can be handled include electronic mail (e-mail), fax, image, video, and voice transmissions.

With unified messaging, the telephony services can find and display the messages, regardless of the format. This search-and-display process, known as a *launch*, may require certain applications. For example, the process may need an application that can display a particular type of message. Any required applications will be started up automatically.

Unified Network Management Architecture (UNMA)

→ *See* UNMA (Unified Network Management Architecture)

Uniform Resource Locator (URL)

→ *See* URL (Uniform Resource Locator)

Uniform Service Ordering Code (USOC)

→ *See* USOC (Uniform Service Ordering Code)

Uninterruptible Power Supply (UPS)

→ *See* UPS (Uninterruptible Power Supply)

Union

In database management or processing, a union combines rows from two tables into a single table. The term *union* refers both to the operation of combining tables and to the aggregate table that results.

→ *Compare* Join

Universal Asynchronous Receiver/Transmitter (UART)

→ *See* UART (Universal Asynchronous Receiver/Transmitter)

Universal In-Box

A single location that can be used as a delivery point for all forms of electronic communications for a user, including e-mail, faxes, and other types of messages. A universal in-box makes computer-telephony integration easier to use and more appealing to ordinary users.

Universal Resource Locator (URL)

→ *See* URL (Uniform Resource Locator)

Universal Serial Bus (USB)

→ *See* USB (Universal Serial Bus)

UNIX

UNIX is a 32-bit, multiuser, multitasking operating system. It was originally developed at AT&T's Bell Labs in 1969, to implement a space invaders game on some unused hardware. The operating system has since been implemented on hardware ranging from PCs to Crays; it has acquired hundreds of commands, tools, and utilities over the years.

UNIX development has proceeded along two major strains: the AT&T System releases (with the most recent major release being System V) and the UC Berkeley System Distribution (BSD) releases (with the most recent major release being 4). The various UNIX strains and variants were combined at the UNIX Software Operation (now UNIX Systems Group, a division of Novell). In recognition of the two UNIX strains, the most recent combined version is System V Release 4.2, known as SVR4.2.

The UNIX environment provides several types of networking resources, including the uucp (UNIX-to-UNIX copy) program and the TCP/IP protocol suite. UNIX also makes distributed computing easier, and it forms a major part of the Internet software infrastructure. The X Window System developed at MIT provides the basis of a graphical interface for UNIX.

UNIX variants, work-alikes, and extensions abound. The following is a partial list:

- A/UX (Macintosh)
- AIX (IBM)
- Coherent (Intel)

U

- LINUX (Intel)
- MACH (various)
- MINIX (various)
- NeXTSTEP (NeXT and Intel)
- Solaris (RISC and Intel)
- ULTRIX (DEC)
- UnixWare (Intel)
- Xenix (Intel)
- Yggdrasil (Intel)

Unloading

The process of removing the contents (usually a program, module, or other file) from an allocated area of memory. For example, a program is unloaded from working memory when execution finishes. In Novell's NetWare versions 3.x and 4.x, unloading refers to the unlinking of a NetWare Loadable Module (NLM) from the NetWare operating system.

UNMA (Unified Network Management Architecture)

UNMA is an architecture developed by AT&T to provide a unified framework for AT&T's conception of network management tasks. The UNMA is medium- and vendor-independent, and relies on distributed (rather than centralized, or mainframe-based) processing.

The architecture is based on OSI protocols, serves as an operating environment for AT&T's Accumaster Integrator network management package, and provides a framework for dealing with the nine major management functions in AT&T's model:

- Accounting management
- Configuration management

- Fault management
- Performance management
- Security management
- Integrated control
- Operations support
- Planning capability
- Programmability

The first five of these function areas are identical to those specified in the OSI network management model.

UNMA Components

UNMA consists of five main components:

- A unified user interface, which provides a graphics-based summary of the network's operation. This is the level with which the user interacts directly.

- An integrated network management system, which actually does the network management. In the UNMA, this role is filled by Accumaster Integrator, as described in the next section.

- Element management systems (EMSs), which serve essentially as local network managers. They are managers for a part of the entire network, such as for a local area network (LAN), a mainframe, or a telecommunications link. The integrated management system supervises EMS operation and communicates with these components using the network management protocol.

- A network management protocol (NMP), which is based on OSI protocols and designed to enable the management package to perform all the tasks included in AT&T's definition of network management.

- Network elements, which are the components operating at the user level. In UNMA, a network element can be anything from a node to a LAN, from a modem to a PBX (private branch exchange), an IXC (interexchange carrier), or an entire PTT (Post, Telephone, and Telegraph).

These elements are shown in the figure "Structure of AT&T's UNMA."

Accumaster Integrator

Accumaster Integrator is the actual network management package within UNMA. The package is a "supermanager" in that it can monitor both hardware and logical network activity. Given AT&T's leading role in telecommunications, it should not be surprising that Accumaster Integrator can manage various types of telecommunications setups, including PBXs, X.25 network connections, Dataphone systems, and IXCs, in addition to the usual network elements (nodes, LANs, and so on).

Accumaster Integrator has powerful graphics-based reporting and display capabilities, and it can distinguish between important and noncritical alarms on the network.

Although Accumaster Integrator is based on the OSI network management model, it offers support for other models. In particular, support is available through third-party products for IBM's SNA (Systems Network Architecture) and for the NMA (Network Management Architecture) based on this model. Other products provide support for the SNMP (Simple Network Management Protocol) supported in TCP/IP-based network management.

→ See Also EMA (Enterprise Management Architecture); Network Management; NMA (Network Management Architecture)

U

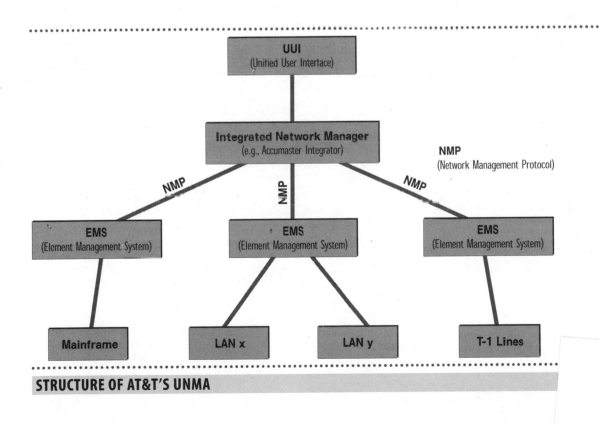

STRUCTURE OF AT&T'S UNMA

Unshielded Twisted-Pair (UTP)

→ *See* Cable, Twisted-Pair

Unspecified Bit Rate (UBR)

→ *See* UBR (Unspecified Bit Rate)

Upgrade

An upgrade provides a mechanism for converting from one version of a program or package to another, more recent, one. For example, Novell supports the following types of upgrades to NetWare 4.*x*:

- Migration, in which servers are converted from NetWare 2.*x* or 3.*x* to NetWare 4.*x* or another netware operating system.

- In-place upgrade, which uses SERVER.EXE to upgrade from NetWare 2.*x* to NetWare 3.*x* and then uses the 4.*x* upgrade programs to continue the upgrade process.

As a verb, upgrade refers to the process of performing the installation of a newer software version or of a more powerful hardware component. Many applications can be upgraded automatically by downloading the appropriate software from the Web and installing it—or even by installing the software directly from the Web. Several software packages—for example Oil Change—check Web sites regularly for newer versions of a user's software, inform the user, and then give the user the opportunity to upgrade to the newer version.

Uplink

In telecommunications, a communications link between one or more earth stations and a satellite; also, the process of transmitting from an earth sta-

tion to the satellite. More generally, the term is also used to refer to a connection that goes from an end user, or subscriber, to a central office or a service provider. This is in contrast to a downlink, which goes from the provider to the subscriber.

These two directions are distinguished from each other because some services are asymmetric. That is, they operate at different speeds in the two directions. Generally, the downlink speed will be higher because most subscribers to service providers expect mainly to download information or materials from the service, and plan to do relatively little uploading of material to the service provider. ADSL (asymmetric digital subscriber line) technology is currently a popular example of an asymmetric service.

→ *Compare* Downlink

Upload

To transfer data (such as a file) from a PC or other machine to a host machine. For example, the target machine may be a mainframe or a bulletin board system (BBS) computer. In general, an upload transfers from a remote machine to a central one. This process requires a communications protocol that both host and recipient can understand and use.

Upper Memory Block (UMB)

→ *See* UMB (Upper Memory Block)

UPS (Uninterruptible Power Supply)

A UPS is an emergency power source that can deliver a limited amount of power to a file server or other device in the event of a blackout (total loss of power).

UPSs are sometimes known as online UPSs to distinguish them from SPSs (standby power supplies), which are also known as *offline UPSs*. An SPS is similar, but not identical, to a UPS. The main difference is that a UPS always supplies power through a battery, whereas an SPS does so only when there is a power failure.

UPS Operation

A UPS provides power to a file server through its battery and an inverter (which converts the battery's direct current to alternating current). That is, a UPS takes power from the lines and uses it to charge a battery. The UPS then feeds the server by sending power from the battery through an inverter, to create the alternating current the computer's power supply expects. The UPS's battery is kept full by a battery charger that is also part of the UPS.

A UPS with a bad battery can actually suck power from the lines as it tries to charge the battery. This can cause voltage sags in other devices. Similarly, a UPS operating in an environment with a low voltage supply will not be able to charge the battery, which may also get drained to provide extra power.

As stated, UPSs typically work as battery chargers during normal operation. Because of this, the UPS may draw more than its share of power if there is something wrong with the battery. This, of course, would be to the detriment of other equipment on the same line.

In a UPS, the primary power path is through the battery. Should the battery stop working, a standard online UPS has a secondary path: the one the power company supplies. In other words, the secondary path is the path that would exist if there were no UPS attached.

UPS Special Features

A UPS should have an inverter shutdown capability, so that the battery will not continue to be drained.

After the UPS has shut down the machine, the battery should also be shut down.

UPSs can be monitored and put to work if necessary. Monitoring capabilities are included in most network operating systems, but they can generally be added if not provided. UPS monitors can record values for various indicators of power requirements and supply. See the "UPS Monitoring" article for more information.

Some UPSs can perform automatic network shutdowns in case of a blackout. This is a great help, because it enables networks to be shut down properly even if no one is around during a power outage. Shutdown capability is often provided in an optional board that is plugged into the server (or whatever machine is being protected).

CONSEQUENCES OF ONLINE POWER

An online power supply has several consequences:

- Since a server will get more than just emergency power from the UPS, the UPS must be able to provide power that is at least as clean as the power company's. In practice, this means the UPS must be able to produce a true sine wave pattern, rather than providing just a square wave as a rough approximation. Ask potential vendors to send you typical wave patterns produced by their devices or check on these for yourself. To do that properly, you'll need an oscilloscope.

- There is a 25 to 30 percent loss of power as it goes through the battery and the inverter. Thus, the UPS must work harder than the power company to supply the file server (or whatever) with its power. (A standby power supply, in contrast, loses only about 2 percent of the power.)

- A busy UPS generates a considerable amount of heat as it loses the power. This heat causes wear and tear on the UPS components, including the battery. This wear shortens the effective lifetime of the components. Some manufacturers house the battery in a separate box to protect it from the heat, and thereby extend the battery's life.

U

Variant Power Supplies

The (online) UPS and the SPS represent two "pure" ends of a spectrum that includes various hybrids and special variants. These hybrids each have their own distinctive features, advantages, and disadvantages:

- An *online without bypass* variant operates like a regular UPS, except that the entire system goes down if the UPS breaks down, because there is no secondary path. This means that the power supply is through the UPS or nothing. Such a device is cheaper to make but riskier to use.

- A *standby online* hybrid always has the inverter online, but puts the battery into action only when necessary. This has the instantaneous switchover of an online UPS and the small power requirements of an SPS. This variant has no secondary path.

- A *line interactive* variant has the inverter and battery always online, but the battery is used only when needed. During normal operation, the inverter charges the battery and feeds the file server. In a blackout, the inverter draws power from the battery to feed the server.

- A *standby ferro* is a standby power supply with a special transformer that protects against noise and overvoltages. This variant has the same power loss and heat generation as an online power supply.

UPS Maintenance

A UPS battery is working all the time, which is going to take its toll. To ensure that the battery is working properly, it is a good idea to test it every few months. It is also important periodically to discharge the battery completely, and then charge it again. Testing and discharging can both be done at the same time.

When you are testing the battery, back up the network before you begin the test. Then follow the recommendations of the UPS manufacturer regarding testing. In most cases, the recommendation will be to pull the plug on the UPS. The effects of just pulling the plug are not exactly the same as in the case of a real power outage. A real power outage is a more severe test. This is because other equipment or machinery connected to the power lines will also be drawing on the last remaining power in case of a real outage—along with the UPS. Nevertheless, such a test is better than none at all. This is a more severe trial than simply pulling the plug. Nevertheless, such a test is better than none.

Even with regular maintenance, UPS batteries need to be replaced every few years.

Centralized versus Distributed UPSs

The device or devices protected by a UPS depend on where the UPS is connected. A centralized UPS is intended to provide power protection for an entire network with a single power supply. This type of UPS is rare, because its power requirements are enormous. Such a UPS must be able to provide more than the total power consumed by the components during normal operation. This is because each node can draw more than 20 times its average power requirements at startup. The UPS battery would be quickly drained each morning as the stations logged in one by one.

The more common solution is to use distributed UPSs, which means a separate UPS for every device that needs special protection. This gets expensive, cluttered, and hot (especially if all the machines are in the same room).

Mainly because of the expense, many locations protect only file servers and possibly certain other key components, such as routers, hubs, or hard disk subsystems.

→ *Broader Category* Safety Device

→ *Compare* SPS (Standby Power Supply)

UPS Monitoring

UPS monitoring is a network operating system (NOS) service that enables the NOS to keep track of an attached UPS, to determine when backup power is being provided. The server can shut down the network before the backup power supply is exhausted.

For ISA (Industry Standard Architecture) and EISA (Extended Industry Standard Architecture) architectures, the UPS monitoring software needs an interface board to do the actual monitoring; with MicroChannel Architecture (formerly MCA) machines, the UPS can be monitored through the mouse port.

Various UPS vendors offer more sophisticated monitoring than the services provided by the NOS. These products may also provide automatic battery tests and power supply diagnostics.

Upstream Neighbor's Address (UNA)

→ *See* UNA (Upstream Neighbor's Address)

Up Time

The time during which a machine or other device is functioning. Even when functioning, a machine is not necessarily available for use, however. This may happen, for example, when the demand for a device makes it impossible to accommodate all the requests. A device that is unavailable because of heavy activity level is still said to be "up."

→ *Compare* Down Time

URL (Uniform Resource Locator)

A URL provides a means of identifying a document on the Internet. The following is an example of a URL:

```
http://cuiwww.unige.ch/meta-index.html
```

This URL has three main parts:

- Information about the document type and about the protocol used to transport it. On the World Wide Web, the most common value is http, as in the example. This indicates that the Hypertext Transfer Protocol (HTTP) is being used—probably to transport a hypertext document written using HTML (Hypertext Markup Language) or XML (eXtensible Markup Language). Other possible values include FTP, Gopher, and file. The protocol information is almost always followed by a colon and two forward slashes (://).

- The next element is the domain name of the machine on which the document is found. In the example, this is cuiwww.unige.ch, which is a Web server at the university of Geneva (unige) in Switzerland (ch).

- The final element is the document's name. This name must be represented as an absolute path to the file. In the example, the document is named meta-index.html, and is found in the root directory of the machine.

URLs are an example of the more general Uniform Resource Identifiers (URIs), which also encompass Uniform Resource Names (URNs). Sometimes, *Universal* is used in place of *Uniform* in these names.

→ *Primary Sources* URLs are discussed in RFC 1738, 1808, and 2368.

URL (Universal Resource Locator)

→ *See* URL (Uniform Resource Locator)

USB (Universal Serial Bus)

The Universal Serial Bus specification is one of several candidates to become *the* serial communications standard for the next millenium (or at least for its first year or two). While it has been around since 1996, USB has become a hot item only in the past year or so. It has several features that make it a good candidate:

Anything goes   USB can connect any type of device you might need—mouse, keyboard, scanner, printer, and so forth.

Lots of room   USB will let you connect up to 127 devices to a single bus.

Ease of use   USB connections are—literally—a snap. To get a device onto the bus, simply plug it into a hub. There's no need to specify any information for the device, reserve any IRQs, or load any drivers. The USB software will take care of all of these details automatically. (A hub is a way for devices to get attached to the bus. Hubs can be connected to other hubs or directly to the bus.)

High speed   USB supports a throughput of 12Mbps, and works with any combination of fast and slow devices.

True bus   Because USB actually is a bus, all devices connected to it can operate any time they need or want to—regardless of whatever other devices are operating at the time.

Hot swap   USB lets you plug devices in when needed, and unplug them when done—even while your system is running.

Power to the devices   USB can provide power to devices along its wires.

USB Elements

A USB configuration includes one host PC, devices and hubs, cables and connectors. Devices must plug into hubs or directly into the host PC; hubs may plug into other hubs or into the host PC. Thus, hubs serve as device concentrators. "An example USB configuration" shows how these elements fit together.

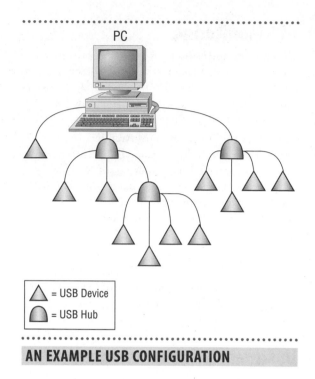

PC

△ = USB Device
⌂ = USB Hub

AN EXAMPLE USB CONFIGURATION

USB Cables and Connectors

USB connections use a special four-wire, color-coded cable. Two of the wires (green and white) are used for data, with one wire carrying a positive signal (green), and the other wire carrying its negative counterpart (white). By using the differential between the two wires as the signal, random noise on either wire will be eliminated. The two data wires are wrapped around each other.

A third wire (red) is used to supply 5 volts of power, which attached devices can draw on. The fourth wire (black) is a ground. The USB specification dictates the wire gauge (thickness) required for cable of different lengths. The maximum length of a cable is 5 meters.

USB connectors can be of type A or type B. For each type of connector, a jack and a plug are defined. One end of a USB cable has an A-plug; the other end has a B-plug. A hub has an A-jack, to which the A-plug on the cable must attach. A device has a B-jack, to which the B-plug on the cable must attach. Simple, isn't it?

USB Transmissions

To communicate with the PC through a USB port, a device simply needs to start transmitting. The bus software processes all the bus signals into packets, which are sent along the bus to the PC. At the receiving end, they will be directed to the appropriate process or device. (On the bus, all communications are broadcast, which means that each packet is sent to each device. Just as in an Ethernet network, each device identifies packets intended for it, and discards any others.)

USB packets contain an 8-bit Sync field, an 8-bit packet identifier (PID), 1032 bytes of data, and a 16-bit CRC (Cyclic Redundancy Check) field. The bits that make up these packets are encoded using NRZI (Non-Return to Zero, Inverted), which is a self-clocking encoding scheme. (A self-clocking scheme is one that includes timing information in the actual signal encoding—for example, by changing the signal level at the midpoint of the signal interval. Self-clocking encoding schemes make it unnecessary to including timing bits.)

The USB signal encoding scheme also uses bit stuffing, which inserts a signal for a zero value after any stream of six consecutive one values. This ensures that there are signal transitions within any 7-bit sequence.

The main competition for USB is probably the IEEE P1394 specification, commonly known as FireWire. Other higher speed serial technologies exist, but these are less standard.

→ **Compare** FireWire

US Classification Levels

The US Classification levels provide a set of classification categories specified by the United States government, and used in datagrams transmitted across the Internet. A datagram's classification level is specified in an 8-bit value. The levels are shown in the table "US Classification Levels."

US CLASSIFICATION LEVELS

Bit Sequence	Level
0000 0001	Reserved
0011 1101	Top secret
0101 1010	Secret
1001 0110	Confidential
0110 0110	Reserved
1100 1100	Reserved
1010 1011	Unclassified
1111 0001	Reserved

Note that 8 bits have been allocated to represent just eight possible classifications (only four of which are currently used). With 8 bits, it is possible to make the values different enough that a receiver could identify a value even if multiple bits in the sequence were incorrect. (In terms of error-correction strategies, the selected bit sequences differ from every other selected sequence in at least four positions.)

Usenet

Usenet is a global news distribution service that relies on the Internet for much of its news traffic. Usenet works by using news servers that agree to share and distribute *newsfeeds* (grouped collections of news articles).

Usenet sites mirror (maintain copies of) or distribute articles from newsgroups, which are named article collections in seven top-level categories, and in thousands of subcategories:

- comp deals with computer science and related topics.

- news contains announcements and information about Usenet and news-related software.

U

- **rec** contains newsgroups for hobbies, arts, crafts, music, and other recreational activities.

- **sci** contains newsgroups concerned with scientific research, advances, and applications for scientific fields other than computer science.

- **soc** deals with topics of social relevance—with "social" defined just about any way you want it to be.

- **talk** contains debate and heated—or long-winded—discussion about controversial topics.

- **misc** contains categories that don't fit into any of the others in the list.

There are thousands of newsgroups that don't fall into any of the Usenet categories. These are grouped under **alt** and several dozen other headings.

User Access Line (UAL)

→ *See* UAL (User Access Line)

User Agent (UA)

→ *See* UA (User Agent)

User Agent Layer (UAL)

→ *See* UAL (User Agent Layer)

User Authentication Method (UAM)

→ *See* UAM (User Authentication Method)

User-Network Contract

In the ATM architecture, a user-network contract (also known as a *traffic descriptor*) is an element that specifies parameters for a virtual channel or path connection (VCC or VPC). These parameter values can be negotiated by the entities involved in the connection.

User Object

In the Novell Directory Services (NDS) for NetWare 4.*x* and later, a User Object is a leaf object that represents a specific user. The following properties are associated with a User Object, and these properties will have specific values for the user:

- User's login name

- User's group membership (if any)

- Home directories, which serve as personal workspaces for the user

- Trustee rights, which control access to directories and files

- Security equivalences, which give a user the same rights as another user has

- Print job configurations

- Account management

- User login scripts

- User account restrictions

→ *See Also* NDS (NetWare Directory Services)

User Profile

A record specifying a user's access and usage rights on a server.

User-to-Network Interface (UNI)

→ *See* UNI (User-to-Network Interface)

USOC (Uniform Service Ordering Code)

A commonly used sequence for wire pairs.

→ *See Also* Wiring Sequence

UTP (Unshielded Twisted-Pair)

→ *See* Cable, Twisted-Pair

uucp

An Application layer protocol for transferring files between UNIX systems. The uucp (for UNIX-to-UNIX copy program) protocol is dial-up and store-and-forward, so that its services are limited. uucp is available for just about every operating environment. It is commonly used as a low-end access protocol for the Internet.

U

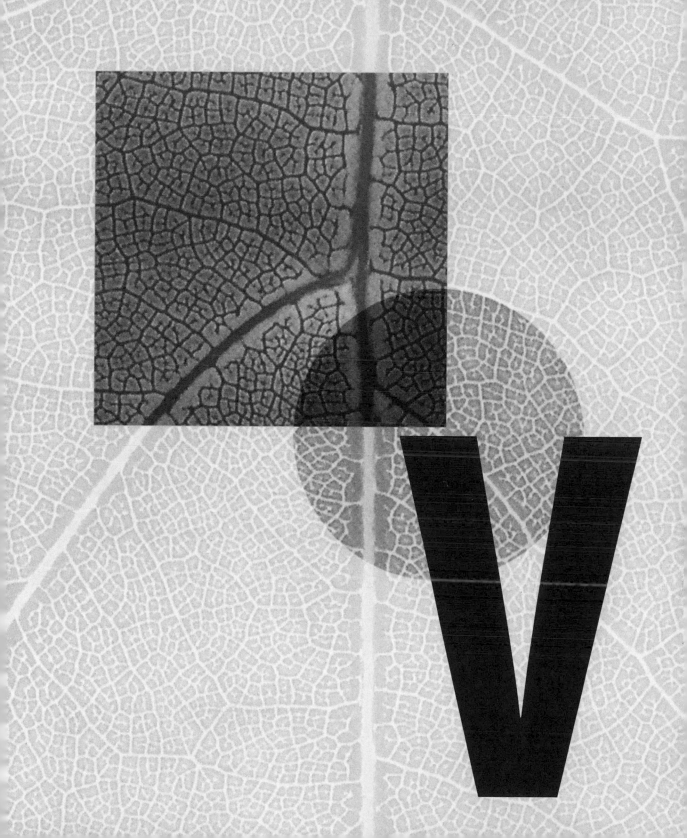

V.xxx

The ITU-T's (International Telecommunications Union—Telecommunication Standardization Sector's) V series recommendations pertain to data communications over the public telephone network. Practically speaking, these recommendations define such things as how computers communicate with modems or multiplexers, and how modems or multiplexers communicate with each other.

More specifically (and more technically), the recommendations address interactions between data terminal equipment (DTE) and data circuit-terminating equipment (DCE). In computer communications, a PC is the DTE, and a modem is the DCE. This means that the recommendations also concern communications between modems.

For the most part, recommendations in this series address features and capabilities at the Physical layer—the lowest layer in the OSI (Open Systems Interconnection) seven-layer model. Some, mostly newer, V series recommendations pertain to the Data-Link layer, which lies between the Physical and Network layers.

The recommendations address such topics as characteristics of the wiring and the electrical signals for communicating across the Physical layer (for example, at different speeds), the functions of the interchange circuits in the physical interface between DCE and DTE, synchronous versus asynchronous communications, error correction, and data compression.

Table "Selected V Series Recommendations" summarizes some of these recommendations.

V.90

The ITU-T (International Telecommunications Union—Telecommunication Standardization Sector) V.90 recommendations define modem technology capable of downstream (that is, provider to subscriber) speeds of 56Kbps and upstream speeds of 33.6Kbps. In practice, the downstream speed cannot be higher than 53Kbps, because of signal power restrictions imposed by the FCC (Federal Communications Commission). And, in harsh reality, even the 53Kbps speed is all but impossible to reach.

The V.90 recommendations were developed and eventually ratified in order to put an end to the standards wars being waged by two incompatible 56Kbps chip designs—x2 technology from US Robotics (now part of 3Com) and the K56flex technology from Rockwell International and Lucent Technology. Because these technologies were (and still are) incompatible with each other, potential customers were hesitant to buy 56K modems for fear they would back the wrong "standard" and end up with the modem equivalent of a Betamax VCR or an eight-track tape player.

The adoption of the V.90 recommendations ensure that all new modems will be able to communicate with each other. However, these new modems are still all built using chip sets based on either x2 or K56flex technology. This means that older modems will only be able to communicate with some V.90 modems—those whose underlying chip set matches that of the older modem.

→ **See Also** 56K Modem

Value Added Network (VAN)

→ **See** VAN (Value Added Network)

Value-Added Process (VAP)

→ **See** VAP (Value-Added Process)

VAN (Value Added Network)

A commercial network that includes services or features added to existing networks. Users can buy access to these VANs.

SELECTED V SERIES RECOMMENDATIONS

Recommendation	Description
V.1	Defines encoding for 0s and 1s under different conditions.
V.2	Specifies the maximum power output for equipment and the maximum power over telephone lines.
V.4	Specifies the structure of signals for asynchronous communication using the 7-bit IA5 (international alphabet 5).
V.5	Specifies signal rates (600, 1200, 2400, 4800, and 9600bps) for synchronous communication over the public (switched) telephone system.
V.6	Specifies signal rates (600, 1200, 2400, 4800, 9600, and 14,400bps) for synchronous communication over leased telephone lines.
V.7	Provides definitions for essential terms.
V.10	Specifies electrical characteristics for unbalanced circuits.
V.11	Specifies electrical characteristics for balanced circuits.
V.21	Defines a 300bps full-duplex modem for use on a general switched (that is, public) telephone network.
V.22 (V.22bis)	Defines a 1200bps (2400bps) full-duplex modem for use on a general switched (that is, public) telephone network.
V.23	Defines a 600bps or 1200bps modem for use on a general switched (that is, public) telephone network.
V.24	Defines functions of the interchange circuits between DTE and DCE.
V.25, V.25bis	Specifies conventions for automatic calling and answering, with V.25bis addressing serial transmission.
V.26	Defines a 2400bps modem for use on four-wire leased telephone lines.
V.26bis	Defines a 2400bps modem for use on a general switched (that is, public) telephone network.
V.26ter	Defines a 2400bps full-duplex modem for use on a general switched (that is, public) telephone network or over dedicated, two-wire leased telephone lines.
V.27	Defines a 4800bps modem (with manual equalizer) for use on leased telephone lines.
V.27bis	Defines a 2400bps or 4800bps modem (with automatic equalizer) for use on leased telephone lines.
V.27ter	Defines a 2400bps or 4800bps modem for use on general switched telephone lines.
V.28	Specifies electrical characteristics of interface between DTE and DDE.
V.29	Defines a 9600bps modem for use in four-wire leased telephone lines.
V.31	Defines a current loop interface for 75bps transmissions.
V.32	Defines a 9600bps full-duplex modem for use on general switched and leased telephone lines.
V.33	Defines a 14,400bps modem for use on four-wire leased telephone lines.
V.42	Converts from asynchronous to synchronous transmission, detects errors, and retransmits erroneous data. Implements LAPM (link access procedure for modems).
V.42bis	Provides data compression capabilities.
V.54	Provides a loop test device for modems.
V.57	Provides a data set for testing high signal rates.
V.90	Defines a modem capable of 56Kbps downstream speeds for use over general switched telephone lines.
V.100	Specifies an interconnection between public data networks (PDNs) and the Public Switched Telephone Network (PSTN).
V.110	Specifies interface between V series DTEs and ISDN (Integrated Services Digital Network) networks.
V.230	Defines signaling, synchronization, timing, and wiring to enable internetworking between ISDN and a series modem.

V

VAP (Value-Added Process)

In Novell's NetWare 2.*x*, a process that runs on top of the network operating system to provide additional services, without interfering with normal network operations. A VAP can run only on a network server or on a router.

→ *Compare* NLM (NetWare Loadable Module)

Variable Bit Rate (VBR)

→ *See* VBR (Variable Bit Rate)

Variable-Length Subnet Mask (VLSM)

→ *See* VLSM (Variable-Length Subnet Mask)

VBI (Vertical Blank Interval)

A nonvisible component of the signal sent to televisions, the VBI is currently used only for closed captioning. But, the VBI can also be used for signaling other purposes. A new product—Malachi, from En Technology—will use the VBI for downloading software to users.

VBR (Variable Bit Rate)

In ATM networks, a VBR connection transmits at varying rates, such as in bursts. VBR connections use class B, C, or D services, and are used for data (as opposed to voice) transmissions, whose contents are not constrained by timing restrictions.

VBR service can be provided for real-time or nonreal-time delivery, depending on the type of service requested. VBR is only one of several quality of service (QoS) classes, with the others being ABR (available bit rate), CBR (constant bit rate), and UBR (unspecified bit rate).

→ *Broader Category* ATM (Asynchronous Transfer Mode)

→ *See Also* ABR (Available Bit Rate); CBR (Constant Bit Rate); UBR (Unspecified Bit Rate)

VBScript

VBScript is Microsoft's scripting language, and is an alternative to Netscape's JavaScript language. Like JavaScript, VBScript is used mainly for creating scripts to produce special effects in Web documents—for example, HTML (Hypertext Markup Language) files.

VBScript is based on—in fact, is a proper subset of—Visual Basic. In addition, VBScript is an ActiveX scripting engine, which means it can be used to create and use ActiveX controls and that it can communicate with any other ActiveX scripting engine.

→ *Broader Category* Scripting Language

→ *See Also* JavaScript

VC (Virtual Channel)

In Asynchronous Transfer Mode (ATM) and other cell- or packet-switching network architectures, a virtual channel is a one-way logical connection between two adjacent (ATM) nodes. VCs are associated with virtual paths (VPs), which are routes over the physical connection between two adjacent (ATM) nodes. Up to 4096 VCs can be assigned to each virtual path, and up to 256 virtual paths can be created on each physical link.

To distinguish individual channels and paths, each virtual channel is assigned a virtual channel identifier (VCI) and each virtual path is assigned a unique virtual path identifier (VPI). For a particular VP, each VCI must be unique; the same VCI values can, however, be used in two different VPs. The identifiers at the two adjacent nodes being connected must be the same. That is, VCI3 for VPI6 going from node A to the adjacent node, B, must have the same identifiers at both ends. However, if the physical connection continues—for example, from node B to node C—the same channels and paths can have different identifiers for the link between B and C.

A virtual channel connection (VCC) is the term used for the concatenated chain of VCs between adjacent nodes that, together, serve to create an end-to-end connection. Similarly, the concatenation of VPs to establish an end-to-end connection is known as a virtual path connection (VPC).

→ **Broader Category** ATM (Asynchronous Transfer Mode)

→ **See Also** VP (Virtual Path)

VC (Virtual Circuit)

In long-distance communications, a virtual circuit is a temporary connection between two points. This type of circuit will appear as a dedicated line to the user, but will actually be using packet switching to accomplish transmissions. The virtual circuit is maintained as long as the connection exists. A different virtual circuit may be established each time a call is made.

Virtual circuits are used in contrast to leased lines, in which a dedicated connection between two particular points is always available. X.25 and frame relay both use virtual circuits.

In the X.25 environment, a virtual circuit is a logical connection between a DTE (computer) and a DCE (digital service unit, modem, or multiplexer). This type of connection can be a switched virtual circuit (SVC) or a permanent virtual circuit (PVC). The SVC can connect to a different DTE at the other end each time. The PVC always connects to the same DTE at the other end.

VC (Voice Channel)

In the PSTN (Public Switched Telephone Network), a voice channel refers to a line in a trunk cable or in the local loop that can be used to carry a voice signal. Strictly speaking, a voice channel represents a one-directional line. Two voice channels together—one in each direction—make up a voice circuit (which is also abbreviated VC). That is, a voice channel is a one-way connection, whereas a voice circuit is a two-way connection.

→ **See Also** VC (Voice Circuit)

VC (Voice Circuit)

In the PSTN (Public Switched Telephone Network), a voice circuit is a two-way connection between two end users. Such a circuit is made up of two unidirectional voice channels (also abbreviated VC).

→ **See Also** VC (Voice Channel)

VCC (Virtual Channel Connection)

In ATM (Asynchronous Transfer Mode) network architectures, a VCC is a logical connection between two entities (which may be users or networks). A VCC is created by chaining together virtual channels (VCs), which are logical connections between adjacent nodes. The VCC is the basic switching level for ATM, and is analogous to a virtual circuit (VC) in an X.25 network.

VCCs have the following features:

- May be switched (established as needed) or dedicated (semipermanent).

- Preserve the order in which cells are transmitted; that is, if cells A, B, and C are transmitted in that sequence, they are received in the same order at the other end.

- Provide a quality of service (QoS) that is specified by parameters concerning such features as variations in cell delays and cell losses (in relation to total cells transmitted).

- Have performance parameters that can be negotiated by the entities involved in a connection.

The parameters that apply for a VCC are specified in a *traffic descriptor*, also called a *user-network contract*. Although the details have not yet been standardized, a user-network contract is expected to specify values such as peak transmission rate and maximum burst length.

A group of VCCs can be allocated for the same connection, to provide the desired bandwidth for the connection. This type of VCC cluster is known as a *virtual path connection* (*VPC*). All channels in a given VPC are routed together, which helps reduce management overhead. Certain VCCs in a VPC may be reserved for network use.

→ **Broader Category** ATM (Asynchronous Transfer Mode)

VCI (Virtual Channel Identifier)

In an ATM (Asynchronous Transfer Mode) network, a VCI is a value associated with a virtual channel (VC)—that is, with a logical connection between adjacent nodes. Such virtual channels are grouped together within virtual paths (VPs). Within a virtual path, a given VCI value must be unique. The same VCI value may, however, be used in a different VP. VCI values are used to route cells between source and destination.

→ **Broader Category** ATM (Asynchronous Transfer Mode)

→ **Compare** VPI (Virtual Path Identifier)

VCPI (Virtual Control Program Interface)

An interface developed by Quarterdeck Systems, Phar Lap Software, and other vendors. VCPI provides specifications to enable DOS programs to run in protected mode on 80386 and higher machines and to execute cooperatively with other operating environments (most notably, DESQview). As the first *DOS extender*, VCPI became a *de facto* standard. VCPI is incompatible with DPMI (DOS Protected Mode Interface), an alternative DOS extender standard developed by Microsoft.

VDSL (Very High Speed Digital Subscriber Line)

VDSL represents the most likely future of DSL technology. It offers the highest speed of all the DSL variants, and it uses a fiber-optic connection—unlike the other variants, which use the telephone company's local analog loop for their transmissions.

VDSL supports downstream speeds ranging from 13Mbps to over 50Mbps, depending on how far the customer is from the phone company's local exchange. The 13Mbps speed is supported over distances as long as 4500 feet, whereas the highest speed is supported only for stretches of 1000 feet or less. Upstream speeds for VDSL are 1.5Mbps and higher.

VDSL technology will require the next generation of digital loop carriers—that is, fiber running (almost) to the home.

→ **Broader Category** DSL (Digital Subscriber Line)

→ **Compare** ADSL (Asymmetric Digital Subscriber Line)

Velocity of Propagation (VOP)

→ *See* VOP (Velocity of Propagation)

Vendor Independent Messaging (VIM)

→ *See* VIM (Vendor Independent Messaging)

Veronica (Very Easy Rodent-Oriented Netwide Index to Computerized Archives)

An Internet service for gopher environments. Veronica searches all gopher servers for any menus that contain items that match specified search criteria. The string specifying the search criteria can include substrings and also Boolean operators (AND, NOT, OR).

→ *See Also* Gopher

Versit

A consortium formed by Apple, AT&T, IBM, and Siemens Rolm Communications to create a specification for CTI (Computer-Telephony Integration). This would enable computers, networks, and PDAs (personal digital assistants) to communicate with telephones, PBXs, and other devices. To help bring this about, the Versit participants are developing specifications for an application program interface (API) for telephony. This is a set of functions that make possible communications between computers and telephony devices.

→ *See Also* TAPI (Telephony API); TSAPI (Telephony Services API)

Vertical Blank Interval (VBI)

→ *See* VBI (Vertical Blank Interval)

Very High Speed Digital Subscriber Line (VDSL)

→ *See* VDSL (Very High Speed Digital Subscriber Line)

Very Small Aperture Terminal (VSAT)

→ *See* VSAT (Very Small Aperture Terminal)

VESA (Video Electronics Standards Association)

An association of video adapter and display manufacturers, which has developed standards for display formats (such as the Super VGA graphics standard) and also for a system bus, called the VL, or VESA local, bus. Like its main competitor, the PCI bus, the VL bus standard is capable of 64-bit operation and can also support much faster clock speeds than earlier bus designs.

VGM (Voice-Grade Media)

→ *See* Cable, Voice-Grade

Videoconferencing

Videoconferencing refers to multiparty communications involving both video and audio. Videoconferencing may use special-purpose hardware, ordinary telephone services, or computer-based

V

hardware and software. Until recently, acceptable quality video and sound required huge (for the period) bandwidths. This situation has improved as image and voice compression methods have become more efficient.

A video codec (coder/decoder) is needed for translating between the video images and their digital representation. Standards and specifications for videoconferencing and also for codecs and the information they must process are formulated in the CCITT H.200 and H.300 series of documents.

Video Electronics Standards Association (VESA)

→ *See* VESA (Video Electronics Standards Association)

Video on Demand (VoD)

→ *See* VoD (Video on Demand)

VIM (Vendor Independent Messaging)

VIM is an API (Application Program Interface) for use between application programs and the various types of messaging-related services available. Applications include programs such as electronic mail (e-mail), scheduling, and workflow. Services include message store-and-forward and directory services.

Details of the API depend on the service being provided. For example, when used for directory or messaging services, VIM allows use of multiple databases (known as *address books*) and either direct or indirect addressing when specifying a message recipient.

The VIM API was developed by a consortium of vendors, including Apple, Borland, Lotus, and Novell. VIM is comparable in function to Microsoft's MAPI (Messaging API) and also to the XDS (X.500 Directory Services) API from X/Open and the X.400 API Association.

VINES (Virtual Networking System)

VINES is a distributed network operating system (NOS) from Banyan Systems. It is built on a UNIX operating environment and shares many of that operating system's features, including its distributed nature and its extensibility. However, VINES is flexible and can deal with most of the popular operating and networking environments. Moreover, the UNIX system is covered by VINES and is unavailable, so that any networking or system services must be provided by VINES.

VINES can support up to four network interface cards (NICs) per server. If the cards support different topologies, VINES can automatically perform any necessary protocol binding or translation when moving packets between the LANs supported by different cards. Protocol binding is accomplished using Microsoft's NDIS (Network Driver Interface Specification). This provides a standard interface for NIC, or adapter, drivers, so that multiple adapters can be connected, each with access to the available protocol stacks.

VINES provides access to files and directories across the network. The VINES file system (VFS) can support views compatible with any of several popular file systems, including those for DOS, OS/2, and Macintosh environments. This means that workstations running these environments can keep their files in native format. VINES also provides locking and synchronization capabilities to ensure that multiple users do not try to access the same material at the same time.

Other VINES features and services include the following:

- Support for multiple servers and enterprise networks.

- Backup and archiving capabilities, including support for various types of backup media.

- Support for named pipes, sockets, and NetBIOS emulation to provide connectivity in a range of environments.

- Drivers for, and shared access to, various physical devices (hard disks and other storage media, printers, communications equipment, and so on).

- Network-wide security services that provide user authentication services and that use access rights lists associated with files and resources to determine who is allowed to use which resources. A VINES administrator can also specify when and how each user may use a file or resource.

- Both local and network-wide management and monitoring capabilities, including the optional ability to monitor (in real time) the network from the server console or from any network PC. Basic or optional management components can provide statistics about both local area network (LAN) and wide area network (WAN) interfaces.

- Server-to-server connections for LANs or WANs. WAN connections can be over X.25, ISDN, T1, SNA, dial-up, or leased lines.

- Support for the VINES protocol stack and optional support for other popular protocol stacks, including OSI, TCP/IP, and AppleTalk stacks. In addition, VINES offers NetBIOS emulation, which provides generic support for other layered networking environments.

- Intelligent messaging (IM), which provides a generalized information transfer capability

that encompasses electronic mail and message handling, bulletin board systems, calendar, scheduling, and reporting activity, fax services, and workflow automation. The IM service supports a proprietary Banyan Mail Service (BMS) as well as many popular third-party mail packages for DOS, Macintosh, Microsoft Windows, and other environments.

- Symmetric multiprocessing capabilities, which support multiple processors working independently of each other, but all communicating with the NOS. This allows the NOS to allocate different tasks to different processors.

- Asynchronous communication capabilities for remote networking and optional gateway services for communicating with SNA and other networking environments. The ICA (Intelligent Communications Adapter) provides serial connections from a VINES server to other environments, including mainframe hosts, public or private data networks, or other VINES servers. The VINES ATE (Asynchronous Terminal Emulation) services allow workstations to connect to mainframe hosts.

"VINES architecture" on the following page shows the main protocols supported in the VINES architecture.

Much of the flexibility and power of VINES can be attributed to the fact that VINES services are all coordinated with the StreetTalk Directory service. StreetTalk is a distributed and replicated global directory service that provides users with transparent access to resources anywhere on the network, regardless of the server providing the resource. The NetWare Directory Services (NDS) in Novell's NetWare 4.x provide comparable network services. These global directory services are in contrast to server-based naming services, such as the NetWare bindery, which is used in NetWare versions 3.x and earlier.

VINES comes in several versions, ranging from a five-user version to one that will handle an unlimited number of nodes. In addition, a symmetric multiprocessing version is available for use on servers with multiple central processing units (CPUs).

Virtual

Ad hoc, as in a virtual circuit, which is created as needed, or in virtual memory, which can be taken from an available buffer for temporary use when needed.

Virtual Channel (VC)

→ *See* VC (Virtual Channel)

Virtual Channel Connection (VCC)

→ *See* VCC (Virtual Channel Connection)

Virtual Channel Identifier (VCI)

→ *See* VCI (Virtual Channel Identifier)

Layer 7: Application Layer	VINES File Service	VINES Applications Services	
Layer 6: Presentation Layer	VINES Remote Procedure Calls (RPCs)	Server Message Block (SMB)	
Layer 5: Session Layer	Socket Interface		
Layer 4: Transport Layer	VINES Interprocess Communications (VIPC)	VINES Sequenced Packet Protocol (VSPP)	Transmission Control Protocol (TCP)	User Datagram Protocol (UDP)
Layer 3: Network Layer	VINES Internet Protocol (VIP)	VINES Internet Control Protocol (VICP)	Internet Protocol (IP)	X.25
Layer 2: Data-Link Layer	Network Driver Interface Specification (NDIS)	X.25 HDLC	
Layer 1: Physical Layer	Network Interface Card and Cabling		

VINES ARCHITECTURE

Virtual Circuit (VC)

→ *See* VC (Virtual Circuit)

Virtual Control Program Interface (VCPI)

→ *See* VCPI (Virtual Control Program Interface)

Virtual Directory

→ *See* Directory, Virtual

Virtual LAN (VLAN)

→ *See* VLAN (Virtual LAN)

Virtual Loadable Module (VLM)

→ *See* VLM (Virtual Loadable Module)

Virtual Local Area Network (VLAN)

→ *See* VLAN (Virtual LAN)

Virtual Networking System (VINES)

→ *See* VINES (Virtual Networking System)

Virtual Path (VP)

→ *See* VP (Virtual Path)

Virtual Path Connection (VPC)

→ *See* VPC (Virtual Path Connection)

Virtual Path Identifier (VPI)

→ *See* VPI (Virtual Path Identifier)

Virtual Private Network (VPN)

→ *See* VPN (Virtual Private Network)

Virtual Reality Modeling Language (VRML)

→ *See* VRML (Virtual Reality Modeling Language)

Virtual Telecommunications Access Method (VTAM)

→ *See* VTAM (Virtual Telecommunications Access Method)

Virtual Terminal (VT)

→ *See* VT (Virtual Terminal)

Virus

A virus is a small bit of computer code that is self-replicating and that is designed to hide inside other programs. The virus travels with these programs, and it is invoked whenever the program is invoked. Because the virus is self-replicating, it will make a

V

copy of itself whenever the program is invoked, and it can then infest other programs or files.

In addition to self-replication, the virus may also include instructions to cause unexpected effects or damage to a computer or its files. There are thousands of different viruses loose, and new ones appear almost daily. Virus scanning and destruction programs must be updated periodically to handle new viruses as they appear.

Viruses can be categorized by where they reside and by how they work. Viruses generally infect either or both of two locations:

- File viruses infect files—generally executable ones. When these files are executed or opened, the virus begins to spread. Macro viruses are a particular type of file virus that infect macros in applications such as Microsoft Word or Excel. Such viruses are now the most common viruses, and a recent macro virus—Melissa—infected hundreds of thousands of computers.

- Boot sector viruses infect the disk's boot sector. This means that they will replicate every time the machine boots.

- Multipartite viruses infect both locations.

A few of the strategies used by viruses include:

- Stealth viruses, which modify system functions or seize interrupts in order to help hide the virus. Whenever a program, such as a virus scanning program, requests the co-opted function, the virus intercepts the call and handles the response.

- Polymorphic viruses, which change themselves whenever they replicate to confound anti-virus programs that look for distinctive signatures (bit patterns) of known viruses. Encrypted viruses may be considered a special case of polymorphic virus: everything in the virus is encrypted except for the code needed to decrypt the virus prior to activating it. This decryption code may be altered each time.

- Armored viruses, which try to take defensive measures when a program tries to disassemble or otherwise analyze the virus.

→ **See Also** Trojan Horse; Worm

VLAN (Virtual LAN)

A virtual LAN refers to a local area network that is configured on the basis of network addresses or some other grouping criterion. Such virtual networks can be configured on the fly, and will be made up of nodes in a larger, physical network.

VLANs are generally configured and administered through switches or routers, and they can help cut down on network traffic because only packets intended for the VLAN are passed to the LAN's nodes. However, this traffic reduction comes at a price. Since addresses for the VLAN nodes will not necessarily be contiguous, a switch or router could end up having to check many long lists of arbitrary addresses in order to decide whether a node belongs to a VLAN.

Various solutions to this VLAN member identification problem have been proposed and are being tried. One of the more widely used measures is known as packet tagging—in which packets belonging to a VLAN are identified by added bits, known as *tags*.

VLM (Virtual Loadable Module)

In Novell NetWare environments, a VLM is a module that runs on a DOS workstation and that enables the workstation to communicate with the server. Two classes of VLMs are defined: a *child VLM* handles a group of functions for a particular implementation, and a *multiplexer VLM* finds the appropriate child VLM for a given task.

The VLMs listed in the table "NetWare 4.x VLMs" are used in the NetWare 4.x DOS Requester. These VLMs are loaded and managed by a DOS Requester module named VLM.EXE.

NETWARE 4.x VLMS

VLM	Function
AUTO.VLM	Used to reconnect automatically to the server if a connection has been lost. AUTO.VLM rebuilds the connection and its configuration information when the malfunctioning device is back on line. Currently, AUTO.VLM works only with NetWare 4.x Directory Services, but will eventually support Bindery Services (for earlier NetWare versions).
BIND.VLM	Used for Bindery Services from NetWare 3.x and earlier. Either NDS.VLM or BIND.VLM or both will be loaded, depending on the kinds of NetWare servers on the network.
CONN.VLM (Connection Table Manager)	Maintains the connections and connection information for the DOS Requester and allocates these connections. Anywhere between 2 and 50 connections can supported, and the number can be set during configuration. The default is 8, because this is the maximum number of connections supported by the network shell program used with NetWare 3.x. CONN makes the table information available to other modules and can also provide statistics for network management.
FIO.VLM (File Input/Output)	Used for accessing files on the network. FIO.VLM provides file cache capabilities for more efficient access, Large Internet Packets (LIP) for more flexible packaging of transmissions, and Packet Burst mode for more efficient transmission.
GENERAL.VLM	Contains various functions used in other modules. Functions are available to provide server, queue, and connection information, to handle search drive mappings, and to deal with machine names.
IPXNCP.VLM	Builds the appropriate packets and passes these packets to the IPX protocol for transmission over the network. IPXNCP.VLM is a child process that is managed by TRAN.VLM.
NDS.VLM	Used for NetWare 4.x Directory Services. Either NDS.VLM or BIND.VLM or both will be loaded, depending on the kinds of NetWare servers on the network.
NETX.VLM	Used to provide compatibility with utilities from pre-4.x NetWare versions. This module need not be loaded if the network involves only NetWare 4.x servers or if only applications (but no NetWare utilities) from earlier versions are called.
NMR.VLM (NetWare Management Responder)	Uses VLM.EXE's memory management capabilities to load and provide diagnostic capabilities for management software. NMR can gather information about the workstation configuration and also about the ODI services.
NWP.VLM (NetWare Protocol)	Uses child modules to connect to available services and to handle logins and logouts.
PNW.VLM	Used with Personal NetWare servers.
PRINT.VLM	Provides printer redirection for both Bindery and NetWare Directory Services.
REDIR.VLM	Serves as the DOS Redirector for the VLM architecture.
RSA.VLM	Provides packet encryption capabilities based on the RSA algorithm.
SECURITY.VLM	Used to provide security features. This module provides a message digest algorithm to help provide protection at the Transport layer.
TRAN.VLM	Provides the ability to handle different Transport layer protocols. By default, TRAN has only the IPXNCP.VLM module to manage, but others can be added by third parties. TRAN is a multiplexer VLM.

V

Since VLM.EXE is just a TSR (terminate-and-stay-resident) program manager, any TSR program written to conform to the VLM specifications can be treated as a module, which means that the VLM capabilities can be extended.

→ *See Also* DOS Requester

VLSM (Variable-Length Subnet Mask)

Because of the rate at which IP (Internet Protocol) addresses were being used up, various measures were developed to slow the address depletion rate, by making more efficient use of IP address classes or by finding ways to add an extra level to the address hierarchy. One way of adding an extra layer is by subnet masking—in which a specific collection of bits serves as a mask to identify all members of a given subnetwork under a base class address.

VLSM goes one step further by making it possible to create more than one subnet mask for a given class address and also subnet masks of different sizes. By getting more use out of a given class address, subnet masking and VLSM help cut down on the number of entries in routing tables, which can sometimes lead to very large time savings.

VoD (Video on Demand)

VoD is a content delivery service that will be able to provide any requested materials (more or less) immediately. VoD is expected to become the content delivery mechanism of the future.

Prior to the VoD era, however, VoD's somewhat slower cousin, near video on demand (NVoD) is expected to replace the currently used pay-per-view (PPV). With NVoD, a subscriber can get access to materials within at most a half hour or so, depending on how often the content provider checks requests. NVoD will, itself, most likely be replaced by true VoD.

→ *Compare* NVod (Near Video on Demand)

Voice Channel (VC)

→ *See* VC (Voice Channel)

Voice Circuit (VC)

→ *See* VC (Voice Circuit)

Voice Mail

Voice mail provides a system for recording, storing, retrieving, and delivering electronic voice messages.

Volume

In networking, a volume refers to the highest level in a file server's directory and file structure. For example, a large hard disk can be divided into several volumes during installation of the network operating system. Conversely, a volume may be distributed over multiple disks.

In Novell's NetWare, a volume is a fixed amount of physical hard disk space. The SYS volume is created automatically during NetWare installation. Other NetWare volumes can be created using INSTALL.

A NetWare volume can be divided logically into directories, and physically into volume segments. Volume segments can be on different hard disks, and each volume can have up to 32 volume segments. A hard disk can have at most eight volume segments. In NetWare versions 3.*x* and later, it is possible to add segments to a volume, provided that there is sufficient storage and there are not too many entries to add.

When the NetWare server boots, each available volume is mounted. *Mounting* makes the volume visible to the operating system and also loads certain information for the subsequent use of the volume.

VOP (Velocity of Propagation)

In a network, a value that indicates the signal speed, as a proportion of the maximum speed theoretically possible. This value varies with cable and with architecture. Values for electrically based local area networks range from about 60 to 85 percent of maximum.

→ *See Also* NVP (Nominal Velocity of Propagation)

VP (Virtual Path)

In the ATM (Asynchronous Transfer Mode) network architecture, a virtual path is a route over a physical connection between two adjacent ATM nodes. VPs are important elements of an ATM connection: a connection is created by combining virtual paths in the appropriate way.

Virtual paths are instantiated over the physical lines connecting the adjacent nodes. Up to 256 VPs can be defined over a single physical line.

VPs are, themselves, made up of logical connections, known as virtual channels (VCs). Such VCs are one directional connections, and up to 4096 VCs can be established for a single VP.

Because VPs are defined only between adjacent nodes, a single VP rarely manages to connect the two parties involved in a communication. That is, a single VP rarely provides an end-to-end connection. However, VPs can be chained, or concatenated, to produce an end-to-end route between the nodes involved in the communication. Such a chain of VPs is known as a virtual path connection (VPC).

Each VP is assigned a unique identifier, known as a virtual path identifier (VPI). Analogously, each VC in a VP is assigned a unique virtual channel identifier (VCI). The same VCI can be used in a different VP.

The VPI value must be the same at both ends of the connection. For example, if nodes A and B are adjacent, VPI 6 at the A end of a connection must also be VPI 6 at the B end. The route created for VPI 6 may be continued in a different VPI—for example, VPI 3—in the next VP on the virtual path connection.

→ *Broader Category* ATM (Asynchronous Transfer Mode)

→ *See Also* VC (Virtual channel)

VPC (Virtual Path Connection)

In ATM (Asynchronous Transfer Mode) network architectures, a VPC provides an end-to-end route for a cluster of logical connections between a source and a destination node (which may be end nodes or network nodes). The VPC is built up of shorter routes between adjacent nodes. These "neighbor" routes are known as virtual paths (VPs). Thus, an end-to-end route is created by stringing together the appropriate VPs.

Each VP can be made up of as many as 4096 logical connections between adjacent nodes. Such a connection is known as a virtual channel (VC). A string of VPs can make a VPC between source and destination; in the same way, the appropriate string of VCs can establish a logical connection between source and destination. Such a VC chain is known as a virtual channel connection (VCC).

→ *Broader Category* ATM (Asynchronous Transfer Mode)

→ *See Also* VCC (Virtual Channel Connection)

VPI (Virtual Path Identifier)

In an ATM (Asynchronous Transfer Mode) network, a VPI is a value associated with a particular virtual path—that is, with a physical route between adjacent nodes. VPI values must be unique for a given physical link.

→ *Broader Category* ATM (Asynchronous Transfer Mode)

→ *See Also* VCI (Virtual Channel Identifier); VP (Virtual Path)

V

VPN (Virtual Private Network)

A VPN is a way of creating a private and secure connection over a public network. VPNs are used, for example, if a connection must be made over a public network—most notably, over the Internet—and if the connection will need to carry sensitive materials that must be protected from anyone who might try to peek. The virtual network is made private by encrypting all materials while they pass over the Internet, and also by attaching digital signatures to them in order to prevent tampering. The materials are sent using the standard Internet protocol suite (TCP/IP and so forth), with the encrypted materials encapsulated in IP packets.

At either end of the VPN there will be a VPN gateway, whose job it is to convert between the cleartext, or open, version of the corporate materials and their encrypted form. The original transmission is encrypted and signed by the *originating VPN gateway*, and then encapsulated in IP packets, which are sent to the receiving VPN gateway. This network node removes the IP envelope (strips the header, and so forth), decrypts the material, and sends it on—once again on the physical private network—to its destination. This process of sending encrypted material encapsulated in a native protocol is known as *tunneling*. "VPN components" shows how these elements fit together.

The encryption for VPNs takes place at the Network layer, unlike the Secure Socket Layer (SSL), which provides encryption capabilities at the higher, Transport layer. VPN encryption is preferable to using SSL because the encapsulation will work even in environments that do not support SSL.

Export limitations on encryption methods allowed for U.S. companies can be a potential problem if the ends of the VPN are in different countries. This is not likely to be a problem for long, however, in light of a recent U.S. Supreme Court ruling that effectively treated encryption algorithms as equivalent to speech and, therefore, not subject to the restrictions imposed by the government.

→ *Broader Category* Security

→ *See Also* Encapsulation; Protocol, SSL (Secure Socket Layer)

VRML (Virtual Reality Modeling Language)

VRML is a language for creating three-dimensional scenes for use on the World Wide Web. The language provides several primitive shapes (box, cone, cylinder, and sphere), along with language

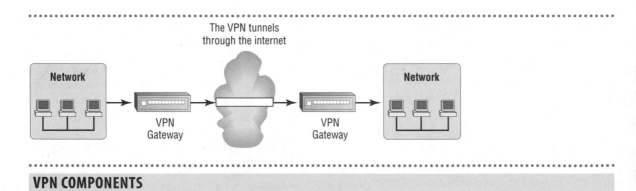

The VPN tunnels
through the internet

Network

VPN
Gateway

VPN
Gateway

Network

VPN COMPONENTS

constructs for specifying an object's location (in an absolute coordinate system or in relation to another object), color, orientation, and shape.

VRML is extensible in that a developer can define new constructs and actions, simply by combining existing ones or by writing out complete explicit instructions. VRML is also scalable in that scenes of arbitrary sizes can be created—at least as far as the language is concerned. Finally, and perhaps most importantly, VRML is composable. This means that an object or a scene can be used in another object or scene. If this is done, the embedded element will contain all the information from the original version of the object or scene. This "full detail property" holds true regardless of how many levels deep something is nested.

VRML 1 was developed in 1995, from an idea by Tim Berners-Lee for a language originally known as Virtual Reality Markup Language—a name that was changed to Virtual Reality Modeling Language very early on. Many of VRML's constructs and file properties are based on the Inventor language originally developed at Silicon Graphics (now SGI). VRML 1 lacked animation, which has been added in VRML 2.

A VRML-compliant browser—for example, CosmoPlayer—is necessary to display VRML files. VRML scenes are displayed as they would appear to a camera or other viewing device whose location and orientation can be specified.

VSAT (Very Small Aperture Terminal)

A relatively small (up to about 2 meters) satellite dish, used for digital communications.

VT (Virtual Terminal)

In the OSI Reference Model, virtual terminal is an Application layer service that makes it possible to emulate the behavior of a particular terminal. This type of emulation enables an application to communicate with a remote system, such as a mainframe or minicomputer host, without needing to worry about the type of hardware sending or receiving the communications. The virtual terminal provides an intermediate base with which both the host and the PC can communicate.

The host will use the host's native language to communicate with the PC through the virtual terminal. The virtual terminal will convert any communications from the host into an intermediate form and then into a form compatible with the protocols the PC is using.

OSI Classes of Service for Virtual Terminals

The OSI virtual terminal services specify what properties and capabilities a virtual terminal should have. The OSI specifies three classes of virtual terminal service:

Basic: A text-oriented service that provides basic capabilities such as line editing, scrolling, and so on. Basic mode can also handle certain block- or page-oriented commands.

Forms: A text-oriented service with access to certain predefined form templates and with the ability to communicate with forms-based terminals (such as the IBM 3270 terminals).

Graphics: A service that provides graphics capabilities and that can handle image-oriented terminals.

Other Virtual Terminal Choices

In addition to these classes of service, virtual terminal also offers choices for the following:

Modes of operation: Half-duplex or full-duplex. In half-duplex, transmissions go in only one direction at a time, so that only one party can send at a time. In full-duplex, both sides can be talking simultaneously.

V

Delivery control method: None, simple, or quarantine. In simple delivery control, the user can request delivery of any undelivered packets. In quarantine delivery control, the data is held until explicitly released.

Echo control: Remote or local.

→ *Primary Sources* ISO documents 9040 and 9041

→ *Broader Category* ASE (Application Service Element)

VTAM (Virtual Telecommunications Access Method)

In IBM's SNA (Systems Network Architecture) environment, software that controls the communications services. VTAM runs on a mainframe under IBM's MVS or VM operating systems and supports several popular communications protocols, including Token Ring and SDLC (Synchronous Data Link Control).

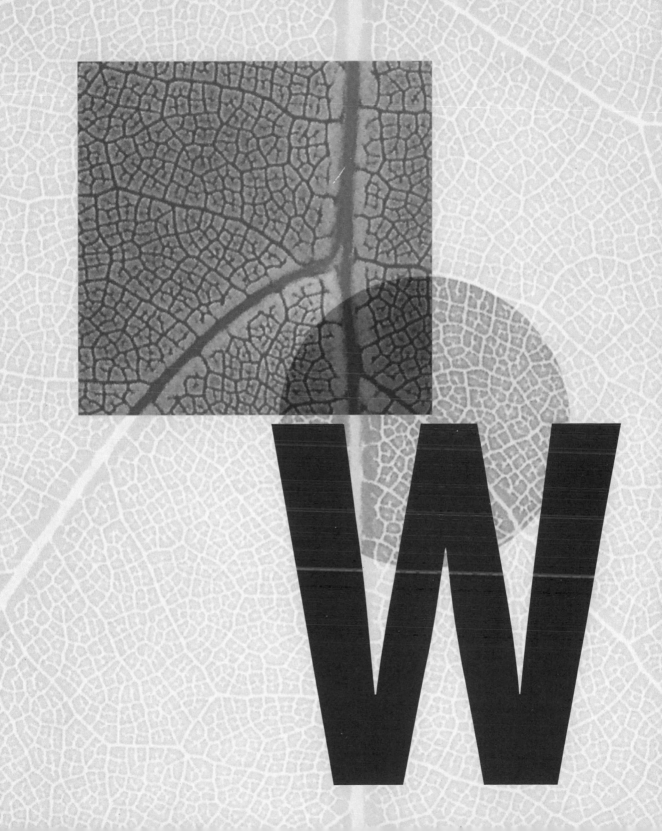

W3C (World Wide Web Consortium)

The W3C is the body that oversees the development of Web-based documents and standards. It is the de facto standards body for Web-based publishing languages—for example, HTML (Hypertext Markup Language) and the up-and-coming XML (eXtensible Markup Language). For information on W3C activities and publications, you can start at the organization's home page:

`http://www.w3.org`

WAIS (Wide Area Information Service)

On the Internet, a service that can search specified locations (*sources*) for files that contain specified terms (*keywords*). WAIS (pronounced "weighs") returns a list of files that satisfy the search criteria. WAIS allows the use of one or more keywords, which can be combined using simple relationships (AND, OR, or NOT).

WAN (Wide Area Network)

A WAN is a network whose elements may be separated by distances great enough to require telephone communications. The WAN supports communications between such elements. For most WANs, the long-distance bandwidth is relatively slow: on the order of kilobits per second (kbps) as opposed to megabits per second (Mbps) for local area networks (LANs). For example, an Ethernet LAN has a 10Mbps bandwidth; a WAN using part or all of a T1 carrier has a bandwidth determined by the number of 64Kbps channels the WAN is using—up to 24 such channels, for a maximum T1 bandwidth of 1.544Mbps (including control bits).

There is no specified upper limit to the radius of a WAN, but in practice, machines distributed over areas larger than a state almost certainly belong to different networks that are connected to each other.

Such a setup is known as an *internetwork*. Thus, although they are simply called WANs, these are more accurately wide area *inter*networks (WAIs). One of the oldest, best-known, and most widely used examples of a WAI is the Department of Defense's ARPAnet, from which we have inherited many of the important concepts and protocols used in networking.

Centralized versus Distributed WANs

WANs can be centralized or distributed. A centralized WAN generally consists of a mainframe (or minicomputer) host, connected over telephone or dedicated lines to terminals at remote sites. The terminals are usually dumb. Centralized WANs generally use polling to control access to the network.

A distributed WAN may include intelligent nodes, which are nodes that have processing capabilities independent of their connection to a host mainframe. The ARPAnet was one of the first distributed WANs.

WANs do not always involve mainframes. In fact, WANs consisting solely of PC-based networks (such as Novell NetWare LANs) are fairly common.

WAN Connection Approaches

Three types of approaches are used to connect WANs:

- Circuit switching, which provides a fixed connection (at least for the duration of a call or session), so that each packet takes the same path. Examples of this approach include ISDN, Switched 56, and Switched T1.

- Packet switching, which establishes connections during the transmission process, so that different packets from the same transmission may take different routes and may arrive out of sequence at the destination. Examples of this approach are X.25, Frame Relay, and ATM.

- Leased lines, which can provide a dedicated connection for private use.

Watchdog

In Novell's NetWare, a special packet used to make sure a workstation is still connected to the NetWare server. A watchdog packet is sent if the server has not heard from a node in a predefined amount of time. If the workstation does not respond to any of the repeated requests within a preset amount of time, the server assumes the workstation is no longer connected and clears the entry for the station in the network configuration file.

WATS (Wide Area Telecommunication Service)

A long-distance service that provides discounted rates. WATS lines may be inbound, outbound, or both. Inbound and outbound services require separate subscriptions, but may share the same line. The 1-800 service is the best-known example of WATS service.

Wavelength

The distance an electrical or light signal travels in a single cycle. Specific wavelengths or wavelength ranges may be used to encode particular transmissions. For light signals, there is an inverse relationship between wavelength and frequency: the greater the wavelength, the smaller the frequency, and vice versa.

Wavelength Division Multiplexing (WDM)

→ **See** WDM (Wavelength Division Multiplexing)

Wavelength-Selective Coupler

A splitter coupler breaks a light signal into multiple derived signals. An important type of splitter is a wavelength-selective coupler, which splits an incoming signal into outgoing signals based on wavelength.

→ **See Also** Coupler

WBC (Wideband Channel)

In an FDDI network, a WBC is a channel with a bandwidth of 6.144Mbps. The FDDI bandwidth can support 16 WBCs. In FDDI-II, a WBC can be allocated either for packet- or circuit-switched service.

If it is used for packet-switched service, the channel is merged with the other WBCs allocated this way. This aggregate is known as the *packet data channel*. This is the channel that transmits data in an FDDI network, The channel has a minimum bandwidth of 768Kbps and a maximum of about 99Mbps.

If a WBC is used for circuit-switched service, it may be allocated entirely to a single connection, or the WBC may be broken into slower channels, each of which can then be used to connect a different pair of nodes.

WBEM (Web-Based Enterprise Management)

WBEM (pronounced "web um") is an initiative whose goal is to provide a vendor-independent set of definitions for network management data. Any WBEM-compliant vendor will be able to use these definitions to describe their products and to collect

W

information for monitoring and managing their network.

The original WBEM guidelines were developed in 1996 by a group of five major vendors: BMC Software, Cisco Systems, Compaq Computer, Intel, and Microsoft. They turned the project over to the Desktop (now Distributed) Management Task Force (DMTF) in 1998, and that group has been in charge of developing the specifications and ancillary elements since then.

The two main components underlying the WBEM initiative are the Common Information Model (CIM) and eXtensible Markup Language (XML). The CIM makes it possible to provide a common language for any network management elements that need to be monitored or described. XML will make it possible to automate much of the monitoring, and will also make it possible to process the information in more (and, hopefully, more useful) ways.

It remains to be seen whether WBEM will catch on, or whether it will simply go the way of other efforts at automating data management. The need for such a platform-independent description works in WBEM's favor, as does the tremendous influence wielded by the initiative's original sponsors.

WDM (Wavelength Division Multiplexing)

A multiplexing method in which different signals are transmitted at different wavelengths along the same wire or fiber.

→ *See Also* Multiplexing

Web-Based Enterprise Management (WBEM)

→ *See* WBEM (Web-Based Enterprise Management)

WebCrawler

WebCrawler is a search engine for the World Wide Web. A search engine is a program that can search an index to find pages that contain the strings or expressions specified by the user.

WebCrawler was developed by Brian Pinkerton at the University of Washington and uses *Web robots*, which are somewhat intelligent programs designed to retrieve information from the Web. (Web robots are examples of *knowbots*, which are information retrieval programs.)

When building an index of Web pages, WebCrawler uses several knowbots at a time. Each knowbot begins with one or more documents and determines all the links from those documents. The knowbot's goal is to identify and index all the links in the original documents, then all the links in the documents to which the original documents connect, and so on. The information retrieved by the knowbots is indexed, and this is the database WebCrawler searches when a user accesses it with a query.

The WebCrawler home page contains an interesting example of netiquette (considerate behavior on the Internet). When searching through Web pages, the knowbots can use either of two strategies: depth first or breadth first. The first way involves searching down and following links to their conclusion. In practice, this means that the knowbot will be retrieving lots of pages from the same site—effectively hogging the site, and perhaps preventing other Web searchers from accessing the pages at that location.

In contrast, the breadth first strategy used by Pinkerton's knowbots means that they move from site to site. This is not a big deal on the Internet—that is, it doesn't necessarily make the search process any slower. It does, however, avoid tying up what may be a popular resource.

Web Home Page

A Web home page is the starting point for a hypertext document accessible through the World Wide

Web. Home pages may belong to individuals, corporations, or other organizations. They can be used to:

- Provide access to information about a concept or product.

- Provide information about a company and its products.

- Provide information about an individual.

- Provide quick access to pages that are of interest to the page's owner.

- Provide ways to enter and request information.

Web Interface Definition Language (WIDL)

→ *See* WIDL (Web Interface Definition Language)

Web Map

A Web map is a diagram—actually a tree or other graph structure—that shows the layout of a Web site.

Web Publishing

Web publishing refers to the creation of documents for viewing and distribution over the World Wide Web or over a corporate intranet or extranet. The basic component of a Web publishing project is a Web page. This is generally a text file annotated using either of the two main languages for creating Web documents: HTML (Hypertext Markup Language) or XML (eXtensible Markup Language).

There are several ways to create Web pages, including the following:

- Embedding raw HTML or XML instructions into a text file created with an ordinary text editor.

- Using an HTML or XML editor, which can generate the appropriate markup instructions in response to menu selections or other actions by the file's creator. Many word processing packages—for example Word and Word-Perfect—have editing modes in which you can generate HTML files.

- Using a more powerful Web page creation program, such as DrumBeat, FrontPage, or DreamWeaver, which can generate not only markup instructions but can also do fancy Web publishing things such as generating scripts, creating image maps (screen images that will produce different responses to mouse clicks on different sections of the image), or otherwise making the resulting Web page flashier (and presumably more interesting) and better able to make use of the available resources. These programs can create an entire Web site, which may contain dozens or even hundreds of pages.

To make Web pages fancier, all the basic tools generally must be supplemented with special-purpose programs—for example, to create animation files or to make files smaller (and, therefore, able to load or download in less time), to check the Web page, and so forth. Clearly some basic tools will need more supplementing than others.

In most cases, the Web page file is created with the expectation that it will be viewed by interested surfers using their browsers. This expectation is reasonable with HTML documents; however, the much more powerful XML opens up all sorts of other possibilities for interacting with a Web page.

HTML markups are designed to specify the document *layout* for a display program such as a browser; in fact, HTML markups are pretty much limited to doing only this. In contrast, XML markups are designed to specify the document *structure* for any program that might want access to specific elements within this structure; in fact, document layout is often a secondary issue for an XML file—something that can even be left to HTML tools. Still, a browser will often be set loose on an XML file. XML documents

W

can be fed, with appropriate layout instructions (for example, in a style sheet), to a browser for display.

Beefing Up the Basic Document

The basic text file can be extended by including various elements in the file—for example, links to other files that can be retrieved and displayed if the user clicks on a hotspot linked to such a file. These files can be image, animation, or other types of multimedia files; they can also be other Web documents or specific sections of such documents. In XML documents, the links can be to a greater variety of elements, including particular structural components in a file (the third item in a particular list, for example).

A Web page can also be enhanced through the use of various programming approaches—including script files, Java applets (and servlets, which are similar to applets except that they execute on the server's side), and ActiveX controls. Such scripts, programs, or modules can produce the most powerful effects—particularly if they can use the Document Object Model (DOM) that underlies Dynamic HTML (currently the most powerful variant of HTML).

With such programming access, Web documents can be made to do just about anything that can be written into a program or script. However, there are practical limitations on several levels—as described later.

HTML files can also be enhanced through the use of cascading style sheets (CSS). These are files that can be used to define style elements—that is document layout elements—for use by the browser. The use of style sheets makes an HTML file more flexible because the style sheet makes possible a certain degree of separation between form and content. Multiple style sheets can be used with a single document, and they can be cascaded—that is, used in succession or for different parts of the document.

By taking the style instructions out of a document, it makes the document easier to read and, more important, easier to change—for example, if a different look is desired for the document. To achieve the new look, simply associate a different style sheet with the HTML file.

The use of style sheets also helps by making the style sheets reusable. The same style sheets can be used to make different documents look the same.

XML documents offer more possibilities from the start, because XML marks up a document's structure. By identifying structural elements, programs that interact with the XML file can get access to any marked information in the document. This means that databases can be searched and content can be retrieved. Information also can be delivered using push technology through channels. Or the document may simply be displayed—just like an HTML file. Of course, with XML, the document could just as easily be displayed on a screen, a printer, or even on a pager or cell phone display.

XML documents are more likely to be mined or massaged for their content—with that content being packaged and delivered to whatever source or application has requested it. And, as developers and consumers think of new ways to mine information, XML applications can be built to accomplish them. Thus, XML will bring about a radical redefinition of Web publishing in the next few years.

Issues in Web Publishing

While scripts, applets and ActiveX controls can do all sorts of things on a Web page, there are limits to what these (relatively simple) programming tools can do. To do fancy things requires either a sophisticated program or lots of supporting data files. These elements somehow need to make their way down to the client's machine.

The main obstacle to using the programs or supplying data is bandwidth. No matter how fancy a Web site is, few surfers are going to wait several minutes for all the required elements to download. So Web page developers must either tone down their ambitions or find faster ways to deliver the material.

There are dozens of products on the market designed to streamline or improve some aspect of Web page creation or delivery—including Macromedia Shockwave and Fireworks. There are also several excellent packages for creating Web pages—for example, HomeSite, ColdFusion, Drumbeat 2000, Dreamweaver 2, and Macromedia Director.

In the next few years, bandwidth problems are likely to be resolved, as high-speed networking and telecommunications become more widespread. Also, the development of XML applications and the expected spread of XML will introduce all sorts of new twists into Web content delivery. Finally, the intensification of competition for Web users' attention will lead to even more outrageous efforts to make one's Web pages stand out from the crowd.

Web publishing is going to get interesting.

Web Robot

A Web robot is an electronic assistant programmed to retrieve information on the World Wide Web. Web robots are examples of *knowbots* (from knowledge robot), which are intelligent retrieval programs.

Several search engines on the Web use Web robots—for example, Oliver McBryan's Word Wide Web Worm (WWWW) and Brian Pinkerton's WebCrawler. Such programs use Web robots to index documents specified on a list. The robot then follows up all links in these documents, all links in the follow-up documents, and so forth.

Web robots are also known as *Web crawlers* and *digital agents*.

Web Server

→ *See* Server, Web

Web Toaster

A Web toaster is a Web server that operates over public telephone lines by making a call to establish a connection, and then never hanging up. That is, rather than operating over a dedicated line, a Web toaster tries to maintain a permanent connection over a public line.

Needless to say, such servers are not very popular at the ISP (Internet Service Provider) that is giving the server access to the Internet. After all, it is the ISP's phone line that is being tied up. Many ISPs explicitly prohibit such practices.

Whiteboard

A term used to describe products that use only software to provide conferencing capabilities that enable conference members to work cooperatively on a document.

White Pages Directory

On the Internet, a database containing name and address information for users on a server or network. White pages directories may be found through the Gopher and the Whois servers. The user-based white pages are in contrast to the service-oriented yellow pages.

Wide Area Information Service (WAIS)

→ *See* WAIS (Wide Area Information Service)

Wide Area Network (WAN)

→ *See* WAN (Wide Area Network)

Wide Area Telecommunication Service (WATS)

→ *See* WATS (Wide Area Telecommunication Service)

W

Wideband Channel (WBC)

→ *See* WBC (Wideband Channel)

WIDL (Web Interface Definition Language)

WIDL provides a way to automate the interactions between Web elements—that is, HTML or XML files—and applications. WIDL can be used, for example, to identify and select elements from a Web document (or session). This information can be used to generate a robot program—in Java, JavaScript, VBScript, or whatever language is used by a particular WIDL implementation.

Originally developed as a way to give applications access to Web sites, WIDL has been split into two components in the most recent release (WIDL 3). One specification describes the IDL (Interface Definition Language) and the second one specifies the document-mapping component.

The document-mapping component sits between the IDL and Web documents. The document mapping establishes a binding between the raw data in a document or document element and a message that can be passed back through the IDL to whatever application requires it.

Both the document mapping and the IDL components were created using XML. That makes WIDL an XML application. In fact, WIDL is one of dozens of XML applications that have been created and are already being widely used. Others include Microsoft's Channel Definition Format (CDF), which can be used to deliver material using push technology, and the Open Software Description (OSD), which can be used to automate the distribution of software—upgrades, for example.

→ *Broader Category* XML (eXtensible Markup Language)

→ *See Also* CDF (Channel Definition Format)

WIN (Wireless In-Building Network)

A wireless network that is confined to a single building.

Window

In the context of optical communications, a wavelength region that has a relatively high transmittance (transmission capability) and that is surrounded by regions with low transmittancy. Such window regions are used for transmissions.

In the context of general communications, a window represents a time slot—usually known as a floating window—during which a receiving node must send back an acknowledgment in order to avoid retransmission of packets that have arrived since the last acknowledgment. The size of the floating window determines how often the receiving node must acknowledge packet receipt. In the extreme—that is, in a window of size 1—each packet must be acknowledged.

A window can also refer to a functional area of the screen within which an application, process, or thread executes. The window may simply display, and then disappear when its work is done, or the window may require input from a user—as in a dialog box. In that case, the window will stay until the user gives the required response. In the Microsoft Windows environment, only one window can be active at a time. The active window is said to be in focus or modal.

Windows

This refers to a family of operating system products from Microsoft, which are described in separate entries. The main products in the line include the now fading Windows 3.x, Windows for Workgroups, Windows 95/98 (Windows 9x), Windows NT, and Windows 2000.

Windows 3.x and Windows for Workgroups, its network-enabled counterpart, are 16-bit systems and are no longer being supported. Windows 95 and, more recently, Windows 98 are the 32-bit stand-alone successors to Windows 3.x; together, the 32-bit systems have come to be known as Windows 9x.

Windows NT (for New Technology) is Microsoft's network operating system for running server-based networks (as opposed to the peer networks that Windows for Workgroups supports). The current version, NT4, is the end of the line under this name. NT5, the next release, has been renamed Windows 2000, and it represents a convergence of the NT and 9x lines.

This convergence is expected to do away with existing file incompatibilities between NT and 9x, which use different file systems. Unfortunately, Windows 2000 will do this by introducing a file system that is incompatible with current ones. Several versions of Windows 2000 will cover a range of operating environments (client, server, enterprise server).

→ **See Also** Windows 9x, Windows 2000, Windows for Workgroups; Windows NT

Windows 95

→ **See** Windows 9x

Windows 98

→ **See** Windows 9x

Windows 9x

Windows 9x refers to either the Windows 95 or the Windows 98 operating systems that were released in 1995 and 1998, respectively. In this article, I'll refer to the Windows 9x operating system because Windows 95 and Windows 98 have the same fundamental design and architecture. Where there are substantive differences, the individual operating

systems will be distinguished. In general, Windows 98 offers better integration of components, some optimization, improved tools, an integrated browser—the infamous Internet Explorer of Justice Department lawsuit fame—and a more versatile file system as an option.

Windows 95 was the long awaited successor to the DOS and Windows 3.1 environments. Unlike Windows 3.1, which is just a graphical user interface that runs on top of DOS, Windows 95 and 98 are operating systems that run with a special version of DOS. Specifically, Windows 9x is a 32-bit operating system with a graphical interface, built-in network support (including support for the most popular protocol stacks), and a flat memory space.

Windows 9x supports preemptive multitasking and multithreading. Multitasking refers to the ability to work on more than one task almost simultaneously; preemptive indicates that the multitasking is under the operating system's control. That is, Windows 9x decides when to switch processor time to a new task. This is in contrast to *cooperative multitasking,* in which applications are responsible for handing off task control properly to the next allocation. (Windows 3.1 uses cooperative multitasking.) Multithreading means that Windows can be running multiple parts of a program, provided the program is written properly.

Windows 9x is back compatible with its 16-bit predecessors, DOS and Windows 3.x. This means it can run properly behaved (and even some badly behaved) DOS and Windows programs. In fact, Windows 9x offers several ways to run DOS programs, with different degrees of DOS autonomy (see below).

The Windows 9x Environment

Like Windows 3.1, Windows 9x has a graphical interface. Beyond that, the two don't have much in common. For example, the Program Manager from Windows 3.1 has been replaced by a desktop metaphor and a Start button. Applications or folders—formerly directories—on the desktop are accessible by clicking on the corresponding icons.

W

Programs and files are also accessible through the Start button, which is found in the corner of the Windows screen.

Various interface niceties and additions make it easier to move around and accomplish things. For example, *shortcuts* are simple ways to start a task. Another component—Explorer—provides all the capabilities of File Manager and then some. Explorer provides easy access to the contents of all the devices accessible from your computer. Internet Explorer, which is integrated into Windows 98, extends these capabilities to the Web, and provides browsing, download, and other capabilities for Internet connections.

Context menus are accessible by right-clicking on the mouse. They show what options are available in the context in which the right button was clicked. For example, if you right-click on a file or folder, the context menu might give you the opportunity to do such things as rename, delete, move, copy, print, scan for viruses, and so forth. If you right-clicked on a compressed file, you might also have the opportunity to decompress the file.

Windows 9x includes support for Plug and Play, in which the operating system detects new hardware automatically, and lets you specify where it should get the drivers for the new device. While still far from perfect, the Plug-and-Play support built into Windows 98 is a great improvement over earlier versions, since you rarely need to fiddle with interrupts and buffer addresses in Windows 9x.

Windows 9x also includes a system tray, which is an area of the Taskbar from which programs can be launched quickly, and where frequently used programs can be kept while not needed.

My Computer provides easy access to various details and levels of your computer. Most of the resources and information are accessible by other means. The true benefit of My Computer is gathering everything in one location.

In a networking context, My Briefcase enables you to make sure that you always have the most current versions of files on the computer you're using. This makes it easier to move from machine to machine without having to worry about version control all the time.

Windows 9x supports installable file systems and long file names. Installable file systems means that the operating system can, or will be able to, understand and use different types of file organizations. Windows 95 supports only the DOS FAT (File Allocation Table) system and VFAT (virtual FAT), which is the Windows 95 extension of FAT. The Windows 95 FAT is 16 bits—that is, it is FAT16. Windows 98 also supports a 32-bit FAT32 system.

Long file name support means that Windows 9x names are not limited to the 8.3 (name.extension) format used by DOS and Windows 3x files. Be aware, however, that files with long names may not be accessible to DOS programs and may, in fact, be destroyed, corrupted, or lost by certain kinds of DOS programs.

Windows 9x contains new utilities, including the following:

- CD Player, which lets you play audio CDs on your computer's CD-ROM drive. With CD Player you can control track sequence, speed, etc.

- Fax, which lets you send and receive faxes.

- HyperTerminal, which is a full-featured communications package which replaces Terminal from earlier Windows versions.

- Phone Dialer, which lets you dial a number using your modem and then speak to the party on a regular telephone. With Phone Dialer you can log calls automatically.

- Sound Recorder, which lets you record through a microphone connected to the PC.

- WordPad, which is a word processor for editing unformatted files (.INF, .INI, or.TXT, for example), and also Word for Windows files. WordPad replaces Write.

Other Windows 9x Components

Windows 9x includes two major components, one of which has created considerable controversy. These components are Microsoft Exchange and the controversial Microsoft Network (MSN).

Microsoft Exchange

Microsoft Exchange provides a central location for handling all messaging functions—electronic mail, Internet or information service traffic, faxes, etc. Microsoft Exchange can serve both as a repository and as a launch center for messages. That is, Exchange can store messages in an Inbox until the user is ready to deal with them; it can also send outgoing messages using whatever services the user specifies. Exchange can even forward messages between message functions. For example, you can send an e-mail message or a downloaded file as a fax.

In order to use Microsoft Exchange, however, it must first be configured and connected. For example, your computer should be connected to a network and you must be registered with the mail and fax services on the network. If you use online services you must also enter information about these. E-mail addresses and other access information should be entered in the Exchange address book which, incidentally, can serve as a common address book for all your messaging activities.

Microsoft Network

Microsoft's online service package is included with Windows 9x, and this has led to loud protests from other developers and vendors. These groups claim that Microsoft is getting an undue advantage by being able to include MSN with the operating system, and making it easy for users to register with the service.

MSN provides the usual gamut of services currently expected of online service providers:

- Electronic mail service

- Chat forums for online conversations and bulletin boards for message exchanges

- Access to the Internet, and even to America Online

- Libraries of articles, programs, graphics, and other types of files

- Information services about various topics, including news, finances, and weather

- Information about new Microsoft products

While MSN is an online service, Microsoft is also positioning MSN as a Web portal—that is, as a Web access point for subscribers. Users can customize their portals—to get updates on information channels that users select.

Running Windows 9x

When you start up Windows 9x, you can control—to some extent—the environment to which you'll boot by doing the following:

- Pressing F4 during the boot process will load the operating system you used prior to installing Windows 9x, provided you left the system on your computer. For example, if this was DOS, you can run Windows 3.1 on top of it.

- Pressing F5 will boot a *fail-safe* version of Windows 9x. This is a version with a minimal system and with only essential drivers. Use this boot when you're having configuration difficulties.

- Pressing F8 will get you a menu from which you can select how you want to boot. With Windows 95, you get two seconds to do this after the POST (power-on self test) is completed; in Windows 98, you have to be quicker. The options you get on this menu depend on what other operating systems are still installed on your machine and on whether your machine is connected to a network.

W

- Holding down the left Ctrl key during bootup will bring up a Boot menu from which you can start a different operating system—DOS, Windows NT, or Windows 3x.

Once you're in Windows 9x, you can still run DOS programs. There are three ways to do this:

- From an MS-DOS prompt, which runs your program in a Windows 9x DOS window. In this mode Windows 9x plays DOS.

- In MS-DOS Mode, which shuts down Windows 9x but runs the version of DOS that works with Windows 9x.

- From earlier versions of DOS, provided these are still installed on your system.

Windows 9x also provides another nice feature: Remote Access Service (RAS). This allows you to call into a network or a stand-alone machine (that also supports RAS) from a remote location. The machine from which you logged in can then operate as a network client, just as if it were onsite, except that transmissions will be considerably slower. A machine using the RAS functions as a remote node communicating with a network. Such connections generally involve a modem, which can be a bottleneck because of the relatively low-transmission speeds. Given this, the quality of a RAS connection will depend on the nature of the connection. If the remote machine is just giving instructions, so that most of the work is being done at the remote location, then the slow modem connection will play a minor role. On the other hand, if the session involves transferring large files, then the modem can be a painful bottleneck.

Windows 9x and Networking

Windows 9x provides other networking capabilities in addition to MSN. It provides built-in support for peer-to-peer networking, and also supports several of the most common protocol stacks: TCP/IP, IPX/SPX, NetBEUI, and both NDIS and ODI driver interfaces (for network adapter cards).

In supporting the Internet Protocol Stack (TCP/IP), Windows 9x also supports several of the Internet services, including FTP (File Transfer Protocol), Telnet (a remote terminal emulation protocol), SLIP and PPP (serial access protocols).

In short, Windows 9x makes your computer ready for work on just about any kind of network.

Windows 2000

Windows 2000 is the official name for the much-discussed next version of Microsoft's Windows operating system. Windows 2000—or WIN2000, as it is sometimes known—is intended as a successor to both the Windows 9x line of software (consisting of the Windows 95 and Windows 98 releases) and Microsoft's Windows NT line of networking software (which is currently in version NT4). At the time this entry was being written, Windows 2000 is due to be released in the third quarter of 1999. So, by the time you read this, Windows 2000 either will be available or there will be a new official release date. "Windows family tree" shows the relationship among the various Windows versions.

Although intended to replace both operating system lines, Windows 2000 has much more in common with the NT family than with Windows 9x, and it is arguable whether the Windows 9x line will truly be integrated in WIN2000. For example, Windows 2000 and NT4 share the same Registry database, and they use the same file system. Because of the differences, the upgrade from a Windows 9x machine may prove to be difficult. In fact, Microsoft recommends that Windows 9x users who plan to upgrade should do so by first upgrading to Windows NT4 Workstation, which is the NT client software. From that platform, upgrading to Windows 2000 is much more straightforward—but still not necessarily automatic.

Windows 2000 Versions

Windows 2000 will come in four basic versions, each aimed at a different segment of the networking market.

- Windows 2000 Professional will be the lowest-common denominator system. It will replace

Windows NT Client software and also the Windows 9*x* platforms.

- Windows 2000 Server will be the basic server software, which will replace Windows NT Server.

- Windows 2000 Advanced Server will cover more complex networks with multiple domains. This package will replace Windows NT Server for the Enterprise. Windows 2000 subsumes Microsoft's Domain model under its Active Directory component, and it uses the Internet's Domain Name System (DNS) for naming network elements. In fact, the domain model may even be more flexible under Active Directory than in its current form.

- Windows 2000 Datacenter Server is specially designed for networks that have very large databases or data warehouses attached.

Windows 2000 Features

Windows 2000 is a huge operating system—with estimates claiming it includes as many as 60 million lines of code. The files for a late beta version require about twice as much space as the Windows NT4 system. This will shrink before the final version, but the end product will almost certainly still be quite a bit larger than NT4.

Some of this size is actually due to new features, which are designed to make Windows 2000 more robust, more powerful, and more flexible. Only the final product will show whether these goals have been accomplished. A later section contains a brief discussion of some of the more significant new features or advancements included in Windows 2000. First, however, is a summary of some of the features Windows 2000 shares with Windows 9*x* and NT.

Common Features

The operating systems share many features. In just about all cases, Windows 2000 improves on the feature.

- Windows 2000 uses the same Registry and can use the same file system (NTFS 4) as Windows NT. This is one reason upgrades from NT to Windows 2000 are easier than those from Windows 9*x*. The Windows 9*x* Registry structure is different.

W

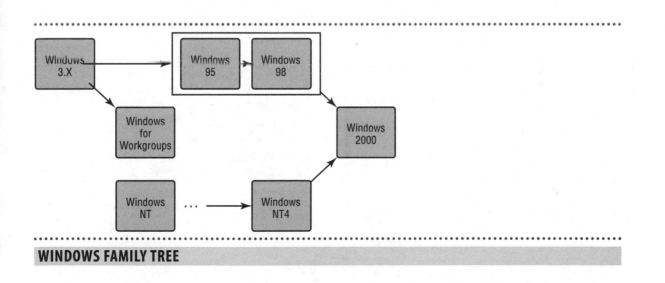

WINDOWS FAMILY TREE

- Like both predecessor lines, Windows 2000 supports Plug and Play for attaching devices to the system. However, this is implemented differently in Windows 2000 than it is in earlier versions, so devices that work on your current system will not necessarily work immediately in the new environment. Microsoft maintains a Hardware Compatibility List that shows all the hardware that has been tested and found to work with Windows 2000.

- Windows 2000 uses the same desktop metaphor as the two predecessor lines, and retains the main features and components that have been introduced over successive versions of both lines. These include the Start menu, Explorer, context menus, and so forth. However, in general these components are improved in Windows 2000.

Improvements and Differences

Many of Windows 2000's most noteworthy features are actually improvements on existing ones. They are, nevertheless, important because they affect much of a user's interactions with the operating system.

Thus, Windows 2000 has a greatly improved Start menu. It is easier to use and to modify—for example to sort or rename entries. A particularly nice feature is the Start menu's ability to monitor what programs you use and how frequently you use them. Based on this information, the Start menu items will be rearranged to put the commonly used programs at the top and to hide infrequently used programs.

Other niceties include the addition of a My Pictures folder as a default place to keep image files and a My Network Places folder to store references to frequently visited Web sites or other network locations. The latter folder replaces the Network Neighborhood folder in Windows 9x.

Explorer is greatly improved and even supports customizable toolbars. The Find command has been replaced by a Search command, which is much more powerful and easy to use. It supports Boolean search specifications (AND, OR, NOT)—with the help of Microsoft Index Server—and behaves like a search command on the Web.

The application installer may prove to be the most satisfying feature of Windows 2000. The installer will help eliminate two of the biggest inconveniences plaguing Windows:

- The tendency of applications to install files in the Windows directory during installation

- The tendency of applications to replace DLL files with their versions during installation

The installer will prevent both of these behaviors. Applications will be able to store their DLL files in the application's directory.

Windows 2000 will include a Network wizard that will make it much easier for users to connect to a network or to the Internet. The wizard will help establish a connection by having the user answer questions.

Windows 2000 Server's Active Directory is a globally distributed directory service. It is based on the X.500 directory standards, but includes some proprietary extensions. With Active Directory, Windows 2000 will be able to provide hierarchical, distributed directory services for NT networks and internetworks, and will be able to work with other directory services based on open standards (for example, Novell Directory Services, or NDS). Windows 2000 Server will also use the Domain Name System (DNS) for identifying network resources—making the integration between network and Internet stronger. In many ways, this is the most important change in Windows 2000.

Windows 2000 Server includes the widely used Kerberos authentication server to provide security during login. This is a more powerful security measure than NT currently provides. In NT 4, Microsoft's extensions to the Challenge Handshake Authentication Protocol (CHAP)—known as MS-CHAP—is the most restrictive measure. However, WIN2000 will use a version of Kerberos that is not compatible with earlier Windows implementations. This means that clients running Win9x or even Windows NT will need to use a less stringent authentication service.

As stated, Windows 2000 can use the same file system as Windows NT—namely, NTFS 4. However, Windows 2000 also provides NTFS 5, which is incompatible with NTFS 4 but which provides support for both Encrypted and Distributed File Systems (EFS and DFS, respectively). This file system is more powerful than NTFS 4, but a move to NTFS 5 is irreversible. That is, it is not possible to return to an NTFS 4 system without reformatting the hard disk. Once again, Microsoft lures its customers down a path of no return.

Windows 2000 Issues

Windows 2000 promises a lot, but it remains to be seen what will actually be delivered. Currently, two big issues relating to the final release of Windows 2000 are how big Windows 2000 will be and how much memory it will realistically require. The most recent specifications from Microsoft call for a minimum of 64MB of RAM, with 128MB recommended. Past experience suggests that this means that—realistically—128MB are needed to function adequately, and 192MB or 256MB are recommended.

There are also likely to be a number of irate and/or confused customers at first—because Windows 2000 seems to be picky about hardware support in some cases. This is expected to be much less of a problem once the final release is ready. Nevertheless, it is likely that some older hardware will have to be put out to cyberpasture.

Finally, the upgrade to Windows 2000 is currently much more complex than earlier upgrades. Installing Active Directory has proven particularly challenging. Again, many of the installation problems should disappear before the final release, but things will still be tricky.

Microsoft's Windows 2000 Server home page is at `http://www.microsoft.com/windows/server/default.asp`. You'll also find information about

various topics related to Windows 2000 at `http://www.windows2000.org`.

→ *Compare* Windows 9x; Windows NT

→ *See Also* Active Directory

Windows CE

Windows CE is an implementation of a Windows operating system for handheld and palmtop computers. To date, Windows CE products have not caught on as Microsoft and its partners had hoped. The two main reasons for this are the astounding success of 3Com's Palm-series of handheld computers, and the lack of enthusiasm for Windows CE in reviews and in the market.

The PalmPilot and its successors have done so well that other handheld designs have not managed to make any significant inroads into the handheld computer market.

Windows for Workgroups

Microsoft's Windows for Workgroups is an extension of Microsoft Windows 3.1 that provides peer-to-peer networking capabilities. These capabilities make it easier to share files, directories, and resources among multiple machines.

Windows for Workgroups differs from traditional peer-to-peer networking packages (such as LANtastic or NetWare Lite) in that a Windows for Workgroups machine can be either a server or a workstation, depending on the context. In fact, a computer can be a server for one machine and a workstation when dealing with a different machine. This is similar to newer peer-based networking software (such as Novell's Personal NetWare and Hayes Microcomputer's LANstep). Windows for Workgroups also has more sophisticated security capabilities.

Windows for Workgroups requires a network interface card (NIC), or a network adapter for each

W

node, and the appropriate cabling. These components are needed to create the physical network over which the software will work. Windows for Workgroups supports Ethernet (thick, thin, and twisted-pair versions) and Token Ring network adapters.

In addition to enhancements on many of the features provided by Windows 3.1, Windows for Workgroups provides the following features:

- File, directory, application, and printer sharing. Shared directories are marked with a special icon in the File Manager. The owner of a file or directory can see who is using the file at a given time.

- Support for passwords and other access restrictions to directories. Only shared directories are visible to network components. The owner of a directory can set the following access restrictions on the directory: no access allowed, read access only, password required for access, or full access.

- Connectivity with servers for Novell NetWare and for Microsoft LAN Manager.

- Toolbars to simplify commands.

The Windows for Workgroups package also includes the following programs:

- Microsoft Mail, a program that provides electronic mail (e-mail) services. In addition to being able to send and receive mail, users can do file transfer by attaching files to messages.

- Schedule+, a program that serves both as a personal calendar and notebook, and also as a group scheduling tool. Schedule+ uses Microsoft Mail for deliveries and also relies on certain Mail files for address and membership information.

- Chat, an accessory for communicating in real time with another user. Unlike Mail, which provides a store-and-forward capability, Chat sessions are live. They take place on a split screen in which one window is for the user's writing, and the other is for receiving information.

- Net Watcher, an accessory to determine how local network resources are being used by other members of a workgroup.

- WinMeter, an accessory to report on central processing unit (CPU) usage. WinMeter reports the proportion of processing that is network-based.

Windows Internet Name Service (WINS)

→ *See* WINS (Windows Internet Name Service)

Windows NT

Microsoft's Windows NT is a 32-bit, preemptive, multitasking operating system with built-in networking capabilities and security services. Windows NT is designed to be portable, and runs on CISC (Complex Instruction Set Computing), RISC (Reduced Instruction Set Computing), and symmetric multiprocessor computer architectures. Windows NT's modular design makes it easier to extend by adding new modules, and also easier to port to other machines by isolating hardware-dependent elements in separate modules.

The Windows NT architecture consists of the following components:

- The Hardware Abstraction Layer (HAL) is software that serves as the interface to particular hardware at one end, but provides a hardware-independent interface to other Windows NT components. The HAL is generally provided by the hardware manufacturer.

- The kernel manages the most fundamental tasks: thread dispatching, hardware-exception handling, and processor synchronization. The kernel also implements low-level, hardware-dependent functions. Processes running in the kernel cannot be preempted.

- The Windows NT Executive provides an interface between the environment subsystems in the outside world (of users and other machines) and the kernel. The Executive provides several types of services, as shown in "Windows NT architecture."

- Environment subsystems, which represent environments that might want to run on top of Windows NT. Supported subsystems include those for OS/2, POSIX, and Win32 (which is the Windows NT subsystem).

- VDMs (Virtual DOS Machines), which provide support for DOS or for 16-bit Windows

applications by creating virtual machines and then implementing the desired environment within such a machine.

I/O Manager is first among equals in the Executive component breakdown. This element provides a cache manager, file system support, and a common interface for device and higher-level network drivers.

Windows NT Networking

The Windows NT networking architecture has a layered design that makes it easier to provide support for multiple networking environments. Through use of generic interfaces, Windows NT also provides support for environment combinations across the layers. "Windows NT and OSI layers" shows how Windows NT's networking components relate to the layers in the OSI reference model.

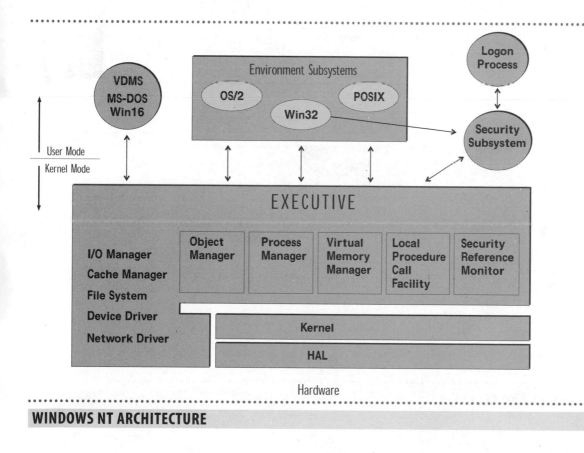

WINDOWS NT ARCHITECTURE

The device drivers at the bottom of the architecture provide the interface to particular hardware. These drivers can work with multiple Transport layer protocols, because of the NDIS (Network Device Interface Specification) interface. NDIS enables any of the protocol stacks supported to communicate with any NDIS-conformant network interface card (NIC), and allows any NIC to communicate with supported protocol stacks.

Windows NT supports several Transport layer protocol stacks:

- NBF (NetBEUI Format), which is used in OS/2-based network operating systems (such as LAN Manager and LAN Server).

- TCP/IP (Transport Control Protocol/Internet Protocol), which is used in UNIX and other environments. Support for TCP/IP enables a Windows NT computer to function as a TCP/IP client.

- NWLink, which is a version of Novell's IPX/SPX protocols. With NWLink, a Windows NT machine can function as a NetWare client.

- DLC (Data Link Control), which provides access to mainframe environments.

The Transport Driver Interface (TDI) provides the second boundary at which it is possible to mix

OSI Layer	Component
Application	Environment Subsystems
Presentation	Providers
	Executive Services
Session	Redirector / Server
Transport	TDI
Network	Transport Protocols: NBF (NetBEUI), TCP/IP, DLC, NWLink (IPX/SPX)
Data-Link	NDIS
Physical	NIC Drivers

WINDOWS NT AND OSI LAYERS

and match networking environments. The protocol stacks below this interface can be used in sessions with any valid server or redirector.

At the Session layer, the Windows NT redirector and server components provide the functionality for the workstation and server, respectively. These components are implemented as file system drivers. Redirectors for both NT and other networking environments can be loaded simultaneously, so that a Windows NT machine can be connected to other networks. For example, redirectors for Novell's NetWare and Banyan's VINES are available.

A provider is also needed for each network supported through a redirector. The provider operates at the Session and Application layers, in contrast to the redirector, which operates at the Session layer.

Windows NT includes support for distributed applications, such as mail, scheduling, and database services. Applications can use NetBIOS, Windows Sockets, named pipes, mail slots, and remote procedure calls (RPCs) to provide or communicate with distributed applications.

Servers and Advanced Servers

Depending on the size and purpose of a Windows NT network, it may consist of workgroups or of domains. A *workgroup* is a group of users who shares information and resources. A workgroup network consists of a server and several workstations. Windows NT Workstation will support network clients, and could be used in a workgroup.

A *domain* consists of one or more servers with a common security policy and a shared user database. The server in charge of such a network is known as a *domain controller*. A domain controller must run the Windows NT Server software, which was called Windows NT Advanced Server in early versions. To handle larger networks—particularly those with multiple domains—Microsoft provides NT Server for the Enterprise.

Windows NT Servers provide support for additional client types. In particular, Windows NT Servers support Macintosh and RAS (Remote Access Service) clients. The latter makes it possible

for remote PCs to get full access to the Windows NT network. The RAS capabilities include security, with authentication of all remote access clients.

Windows NT computers can be NetWare clients, and Windows NT Servers can function as application servers for the NetWare network. Because of its support for TCP/IP and for distributed computing, a Windows NT network can work with UNIX systems. Similarly, support for the DLC (Data Link Control) protocol makes it possible to connect Windows NT networks and IBM mainframes.

As stated, Windows NT Server for the Enterprise can be used for networks with multiple domains, each of which may have its own server. In such a network, one server will be designated the *primary domain controller (PDC)*. This server will be responsible for logon security—authenticating users and passwords. A synchronized replica of the account and security information will be stored on a second machine—known as the *backup domain controller (BDC)*.

Windows NT Security

Security and authentication checks are made during the login process (which uses a secure communications channel) and also during network operations (for example, when a user or process needs to access a service). Windows NT supports several levels of security requirements, which can be used to provide access for different kinds of users who need access to different types of materials.

At the lowest end, NT servers can allow anonymous logins, which require no passwords and no authentication. Such access may be provided for outsiders who may wish to, for example, visit a company's Web site. Such users should, of course, not be able to get anywhere near materials that the company wants to keep private.

At the high end, NT uses Microsoft's variant of the Challenge Handshake Authentication Protocol (CHAP)—known as MS-CHAP. This is Microsoft's most stringent logon process for NT Server. This

W

type of authentication works only with NT clients. Windows 2000, the successor to NT4, will include the widely used Kerberos authentication server to implement security.

In addition to the security process during login, Windows NT includes a local security subsystem and a Security Reference Monitor. The monitor is part of the Windows NT Executive, and it is responsible for making sure the local security subsystem's requirements are enforced.

The Future of Windows NT

NT4, the current version, is the last one that will appear under the NT name. Microsoft had originally planned to release NT5 this year (actually, last year, but who's counting). Instead, the product has been renamed Windows 2000, and it will be released as an evolutionary next step for both the NT and the Windows 9x architectures. Windows 2000 will be released in several versions to handle the different kinds of hosts that might run the machine: stand-alone computers, clients, servers, and enterprise servers.

➜ *Compare* NetWare; NOS (Network Operating System)

➜ *See Also* Windows 2000; Windows 9x

Windows NT Challenge/Response Authentication and Encryption

➜ *See* Protocol, CHAP (Challenge Handshake Authentication Protocol)

Windows NT Security Domain

A Windows NT security domain is a grouping of connected servers, all of whom use the same security accounts database.

Windows Scripting Host

In the Windows NT, 95, and 98 environments, the Windows Scripting Host is a component that makes it possible to run the VBScript and JScript (Microsoft's implementation of JavaScript) programs directly under the operating systems—that is, even if neither Microsoft Internet Information Server (IIS) nor Active Server Pages are being used.

With the Windows Scripting Host you can also write scripts to automate various types of tasks, including logins, administrative tasks, file translations, and HTML file generation.

WINS (Windows Internet Name Service)

In the Windows NT operating system, WINS is a name server—that is, a program that performs name lookups and address resolution for names referenced on a network or internetwork. In particular, WINS is a name server for NetBIOS names. These use a naming system and format that is popular on various Microsoft and IBM networks. NetBIOS names (for example, \\myname) are in contrast to Internet domain names (for example, www.myname.com). WINS translates between NetBIOS names and IP (Internet Protocol) addresses; the Internet Domain Name Service (DNS) translates between Internet domain names and IP addresses.

Note that WINS is an *Inter*net name service. This is important for NT networks that are connected to other networks. A WINS name server gathers and stores name and address information from any network to which the server has access. Once the information is on a WINS, access to resources on other networks can become available—assuming the appropriate file and access permissions are present.

Name services on NT networks are provided through programs known as *network browsers*, which generally do not get information about names and resources on other networks—unless there is a WINS that can provide it.

→ *Broader Category* Windows NT

Winsock

Winsock (for Windows sockets) is the name given to an API (Application Program Interface) that implements the TCP/IP protocol stack in a Windows environment. Windows programs—for example, the Chameleon Sampler or commercial programs from NetManage and other companies—that provide access to the Internet must all have access to a TCP/IP stack. Most of these programs use some version of Winsock.

Wireless Components

Wireless networks use the same functional components as networks that use a physical medium. Specifically, wireless nodes need transmitters and receivers, just like wired nodes.

However, wireless components may take somewhat different forms and may turn up in unusual locations in wireless networks. For example, a network may use antennas located at strategic points to broadcast and capture signals across the network. In wireless communications, each node may have its own antenna, or a single antenna may serve a limited area. Antennas will generally be placed in open, unobstructed areas in order to avoid objects that can block incoming or outgoing signals.

→ *Broader Category* Hardware

→ *See Also* Network, Wireless

Wireless Communication

Wireless communication refers to any of several communications technologies that rely on open-air transmission. Wireless communication methods can be grouped into two main categories—those that use radio waves and those that use infrared signals—with variants within these. These categories cover two different frequency ranges in the electromagnetic spectrum:

- Radio waves cover a seemingly wide frequency range—from a few hundred KHz (kilohertz) to about 20GHz (gigahertz). Most radio wave communications use frequencies somewhere between 900MHz (megahertz) to about 6GHz—a frequency band that has been divided into three regions described in a later section.

- Infrared signals really cover a huge frequency band—from 300GHz to about 430THz (terahertz)—that is, to the threshold of the visible spectrum.

Wireless Communications: General Features

Wireless communications methods need to use some sort of waveform to transmit signals. On these waveforms, either analog or digital signals can be transmitted. In other words, wireless communications can be either analog or digital in form. The signal to be transmitted will be modulated by adding a base carrier signal.

Wireless transmissions may travel through thin air—that is without using a wire medium—but they require physical equipment to do so. Wireless communications require the following components to work, in addition to components that will transform bits into signals at one end and signals into bits at the other.

Transmitter Any element that wants to have something to say in wireless communication must be able to send signals.

W

Receiver Any element that wants to hear what's going on in a wireless communication must be able to receive signals.

These minimal elements are often combined into a single transceiver—for transmitter/receiver. However, such minimal equipment will work only for relatively short-distance communications—the electronic equivalent of conversing by yelling across the street. To work over longer distances, a wireless communications architecture needs some additional components. These components are mainly responsible for relaying, cleaning, or amplifying signals.

A wireless communications setup may also include antennas, cell towers, relay stations, satellites, walls and ceilings. These components pass signals one from one portion of the communication path to the next. Many of these components also clean and strengthen the signal as it passes through the component. For example, a cell tower passes a signal from one coverage region to another. In infrared networks, signals are often bounced off walls or ceilings to reach their destination. Clearly, in such networks, the signal will not get massaged or amplified.

Some wireless communications are actually only portions of a longer communication chain that includes wired media. For example, if a cellular phone user wants to call someone's home phone, the call will go from the user's cell phone to the cellular service's base station by wireless communication. The base station will be connected by wire to a telephone company office, and the call will continue over an ordinary telephone connection between the cellular base station and the callee's home phone.

Communications Using Radio Waves

Any long-distance wireless communications—for example, cellular telephony—will use radio waves. In fact, just about any type of wireless communication other than short-distance communications will use radio waves. Such radio-based communications can take any of several forms. These are distinguished by the manner in which the signal is transmitted.

Narrowband

Radio wave signals can be transmitted over a broad or narrow frequency range. The latter is known as narrowband transmission. This is how radio stations broadcast—at their frequency. Unless someone else is broadcasting in the same frequency range in that area, such signals will suffer little interference. However, the likelihood of frequency overlap (and, therefore, of interference) goes up as the number of parties transmitting in the frequency range increases. Because of this, the FCC (Federal Communications Commission) regulates what ranges may be used and what kind of signal power is allowed in various locations – for both radio broadcasts and for individuals communicating using radio waves.

Narrowband transmissions are, of course, public. Anyone tuned to the frequency on which a communication is taking place will be able to listen in. The fact that it is a crime to do so deters only non-criminals.

Spread Spectrum

More commonly, radio communications use spread-spectrum modulation. In this method, a transmission is spread out over a frequency range. The transmission uses one frequency for a short period, then moves to another frequency for a short period, and so on. There are two main strategies for doing this:

Direct sequence In direct-sequence spread spectrum, the data signal is combined with a higher rate sequence—known as the chipping code—to increase the signal's resistance to interference. In addition, the transmission will use different slices of the allowed frequency range in succession.

Frequency hopping In frequency hopping, the data signal is moved from frequency to frequency in a pattern determined by a special hopping code. The listener must know the hopping code in order to be able to tune in on the appropriate signals at each moment. Such a transmission is very difficult to intercept or to jam—unless one knows the hopping code.

ISM

Radio-based communications generally use any of three frequency bands that are available for unlicensed use. These bands had previously been reserved for use in industrial, scientific, and medical contexts. These ISM bands, as they have been called, cover the following frequency ranges:

- Industrial (I-band): 902MHz—928MHz

- Scientific (S-band) : 2.40GHz—2.4835GHz

- Medical (M-band) : 5.725GHz—5.850GHz

All three bands are used in North and South America; only the S-band is used in the rest of the world. Most cellular telephone services with international aspirations operate in the S-band. In the United States, on the other hand, the I-band is also quite popular for cellular phones.

Infrared Communication

Infrared communications use infrared components to transmit and receive signals over a relatively limited range. Such transmissions use a frequency range just below the visible light spectrum. These waves require a line of sight connection between sender and receiver or between each of these and a common cell or target (which may be a wall or ceiling).

An infrared signal can be focused or diffuse, and the transmission may be reflected or point to point. A focused signal is transmitted in only a single direction. This may be directly toward its target receiver; or the signal may be beamed at a surface and reflected off this to a receiver. A focused signal can travel over a greater range but only to a specific target. In contrast, a diffuse signal travels in multiple directions, but is much weaker in each direction. As a result, the range of a diffuse signal is much smaller than for a focused signal.

Transmissions that use reflection fall into two categories:

- *Directed transmissions* use a common central target, and all transceivers bounce and read signals off this target. A directed transmission

is useful if the network configuration stays constant (if nodes do not move around). There are generally restrictions on the number of transceivers that can see the target and the range over which these transceivers are distributed.

- *Diffuse transmissions* bounce the signal off everyday objects so that the target can change if necessary. This newer technology is useful if nodes are moved around a great deal.

In contrast to reflected transmissions, a point-to-point transmission aims the signal directly at the target.

Advantages

Advantages of infrared transmissions include the following:

- Components are relatively inexpensive.

- Very high bandwidths are possible.

- Signals can be reflected off surfaces (such as walls) so that direct line of sight is not necessary.

- Transmissions can be multidirectional.

- No license is required for infrared networks.

Disadvantages of Infrared Communications

Disadvantages of infrared transmissions include the following:

- Transmission distance is limited.

- Transmission cannot penetrate walls.

- Possible health risks from infrared radiation.

- Atmospheric conditions (such as rain or fog) can attenuate the signal.

Wireless Markup Language (WML)

→ *See* WML (Wireless Markup Language)

W

Wireless Modem

A modem that transmits over a wireless network, rather than over telephone lines.

→ *See Also* Modem

Wire, Solid

Solid wire is electrical wire whose central, conducting element is a single strand of (usually) copper or some other conductive material. This is in contrast to stranded wire, whose conductor wire consists of dozens, perhaps hundreds, of thin copper strands wrapped tightly around each other.

Wire, Stranded

Electrical wire whose central, conducting element consists of many thin strands of (usually) copper or some other conductive material. These strands are rolled tightly around each other. This is in contrast to solid wire, whose conductor wire consists of a single, (relatively) large diameter copper (or other conductive) wire.

Wiring Center

Wiring center is a general term for any of several components that serve as common termination points for one or more nodes and/or other wiring centers. The wiring center will connect to a higher-level wiring collector, to either an intermediate distribution frame (IDF) or a main distribution frame (MDF).

Functions of Wiring Centers

The main functions of a wiring center are electrical. The wiring center collects lines in a common location, in order to continue the connection more easily from there. Any network-specific features or benefits (such as signal routing flexibility) are likely to be the result of special intelligence or capabilities built into the wiring center.

Collecting multiple cables at a common location makes the following tasks easier:

- Installing cabling
- Tracking down faults
- Cleaning and boosting signals (if appropriate)
- Controlling (limiting) the transmission of packets and the dissemination of information
- Dealing with any necessary electrical conversions involving particular nodes

Over time, various capabilities and services have migrated from the server to wiring centers. This helps decrease the server's workload. It also makes certain security measures easier to implement. For example, an intelligent hub can send a packet to its destination and can broadcast a nonsense packet to nondestination nodes. In networks such as Ethernet and ARCnet, all packets are broadcast to all nodes. Nodes are supposed to ignore packets not intended for the nodes, but there is no way to prevent an eavesdropping node from reading everything that comes through.

Types of Wiring Centers

Hubs, concentrators, and MAUs (multistation access units) have all been referred to as wiring centers. In part, terminology is tied to network architecture.

MAU is the term for a common termination point in a Token Ring network. Individual nodes (or lobes, in Token Ring terminology) can connect to the MAU in whatever sequence is most convenient. Internally, the MAU orders the connected lobes to produce a ring structure, as required by the network architecture.

MAUs have two additional ports, called RI (ring in) and RO (ring out), through which they can be connected to other MAUs. These ports make it possible to maintain the ring structure over the larger, multi-MAU network.

Hub is the term for a component that serves as a termination point for multiple nodes that all use the same network architecture (for example, Ethernet or ARCnet). Hubs differ in the amount of intelligence they have and in whether they can boost a signal.

A *concentrator* is a "superhub," which can connect lines from different architectures and with different cabling. For example, a concentrator may be used as the termination point for the nodes on multiple networks, and these networks may use different architectures.

The boundaries between the two are fuzzy, but the main differences between hubs and concentrators are in the number of nodes the component can handle, the number of network architectures it can handle, and the component's price.

Hubs, concentrators, and MAUs represent the basic wiring centers. There are all sorts of exotic variants of these types, with specialized capabilities and properties added by vendors.

→ **Broader Categories** Hardware; Intranetwork Link

→ **See Also** Concentrator; Hub

Wiring Closet

In a premises wiring layout, a wiring closet is one in which cables are gathered, usually in one or more punch-down blocks or in a distribution frame. These cables connect the various areas in an office or building to the central wiring, and from there to the telephone or power company wiring.

Wiring, Legacy

Wiring that is already installed in a business or residence. This wiring may or may not be suitable for networking purposes.

Wiring, Premises

A wiring system that provides the "behind the scenes" wiring for an entire house or office building. This wiring generally runs between outlets and any wiring centers or distribution frames. Users connecting devices to the outlets need to provide the cables to do so.

Wiring Sequence

In twisted-pair cabling, the wiring sequence is the order in which the wire pairs are attached to pins in the connector. (In a pair of wires, one wire is known as the *tip* and the other as the *ring*.)

Several standard wiring sequences exist, as shown in the illustration "Commonly used wiring sequences."

Each of the standard schemes was developed by a different organization or standards committee, and each is intended for different purposes:

- USOC (Uniform Service Ordering Code) is a sequence originally developed by the telephone company. The tip/ring pairs are nested, with tip 1 and ring 1 (denoted as T1 and R1, respectively) occupying the middle two connections. In an 8-wire (4-pair) arrangement, these correspond to wires 4 and 5. This pair is nested inside T2 and R2, which is nested inside T3 and R3, and so on. The advantage of such nesting is that a 6-wire plug (such as an RJ-12) can be plugged into an 8-wire jack (such as an RJ-45).

- The 10BaseT sequence is used in Ethernet networks running over unshielded twisted-pair (UTP) cable. Note that, by design, the middle pair (wires 4 and 5) is not used, because voice connections are generally made in this tip/ring pair in telephone cable. By not using these wires, the 10BaseT sequence is compatible with 3- or 4-pair telephone cable (at least with respect to wiring).

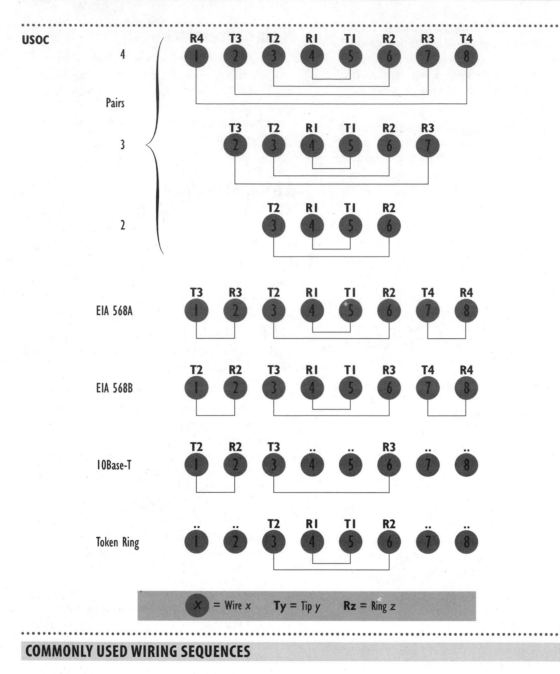

COMMONLY USED WIRING SEQUENCES

- The Token Ring sequence is used in Token Ring networks. The sequence uses pairs 1 and 2 in the four center locations. Note that this wiring scheme makes it impossible to use telephone cable for both voice and a Token Ring network at the same time.

- The EIA-568A sequence was developed as part of the EIA/TIA-568 specifications for UTP. This particular variant was designed to be backward-compatible with the USOC sequence, at least for 4-wire cable (T1/R1 and T2/R2). The remaining two pairs are grouped at opposite sides of the cable.

- The EIA-568B sequence is also used as the sequence for AT&T's Premises Distribution System (PDS). This is a widely used configuration, in part because it is compatible with the wiring sequence specified for 10BaseT network cabling.

The interference-protection properties of twisted-pair cable come from *pairing* the wires. The advantages of pairing are lost if a signal is carried over wires from two different pairs. This is known as the *split-pair* problem, and can happen if one wiring sequence (such as USOC) is used in a situation that calls for a different sequence (such as Ethernet). For example, the T2 and R2 pair for 10BaseT Ethernet would be split over two pairs in a USOC wiring sequence.

CABLE QUALITY

It is important to find out which wiring scheme is being used in any cable you plan to use or buy, and to make sure all the cable uses the same scheme.

Try to make sure the connector and wire types have been matched correctly. A "piercing" connector may not penetrate the solid wire, which means the attachment is more likely to become loose and flaky with time, particularly if the wire is frequently bent or subjected to other stresses near the connector end.

The chances of connector and cable being mismatched are greater with cheaper cable. *Let the buyer beware.*

WML (Wireless Markup Language)

WML is an XML (eXtensible Markup Language) application that is part of the Wireless Application Protocol (WAP) suite. The WAP suite was created to provide wireless devices with tools to access networks and the Internet.

WML was created to help in specifying user interfaces and content for various narrowband wireless devices such as cellular phones, PDAs, and pagers. The language was designed with the shortcomings of such devices in mind. In particular, the language tries to get around such limitations as a (relatively) slow narrowband connection, limited display capabilities, and limited memory and computing power.

→ *Broader Category* XML (eXtensible Markup Language)

→ *See Also* Protocol WAP (Wireless Application Protocol)

Workflow Software

Software for describing or managing the steps needed to complete a transaction or other type of task. Examples of workflow software include flow-charting and other "electronic pencil" programs, CASE (computer-assisted software engineering) or CAM (computer-assisted manufacturing) software, and programs based on an underlying model of management or process, such as software for automating the steps in a manufacturing or an assembly context.

Workgroup

A workgroup is a group of individuals who share files, data, and possibly applications. Workgroups are generally defined around an office, a project, or a group of tasks. The individuals who make up a workgroup may change as a project (for example) progresses or as tasks change.

W

Workgroup members can use local area networks (LANs), electronic mail (e-mail), or other message-handling services to share information. Some applications (such as database, spreadsheet, and word processing programs) come in special workgroup versions that are specifically designed to allow such collaborative interactions. In other cases, an ordinary application may use an engine program that provides workgroup capabilities for the application.

In addition to allowing users to share information, many workgroup programs can also exchange information easily with other applications. Workgroup programs are often combined into suites that encompass a range of computing tasks. (Note that the different applications in such a suite may be associated with different members of a workgroup if the workgroup is formed by task.)

The Borland Office for Windows package is an example of a suite of workgroup programs. The package includes workgroup versions of Paradox for Windows, Quattro Pro, and WordPerfect in a single environment. (The latter two products are now owned by Novell.) Borland Office programs uses an Object Exchange (OBEX) engine to drive the Workgroup Desktop. Users and applications can exchange information by going through the Workgroup Desktop.

Workstation

In a PC network, a workstation is a client machine. In general, a workstation is a consumer of network services, although it is not uncommon for a workstation to serve as a special-purpose server, such as a server for a printer or backup tape drive.

In general, workstations can be viewed as interchangeable units, which need not be particularly powerful unless they are being used for a resource-intensive purpose. In contrast, a file server should be a high-speed, powerful machine that can deal with dozens of requests at once.

Each workstation needs a network interface card (NIC) that is compatible with the workstation's hardware and with the NIC used by the network's server. External and PCMCIA NICs are available, so that even a machine with minimal capabilities (such as a palmtop) can be used as a workstation. Laptops have some important advantages as workstations—most notably, portability—and are becoming more common in networks.

Unlike a server (which runs a network operating system, or NOS), a workstation runs a special type of program that coordinates operations with the workstation's native operating system. The details of this program's operation depend on the type of workstation software involved. For example, a network shell program performs the following tasks:

- Intercepts all user and application commands

- Determines whether the command is for the local operating system (such as DOS, OS/2, or UNIX) or for the network

- Routes the command to the local operating system or to the NIC for processing and transmission onto the network

- Passes transmissions from the network (via the NIC) to the application running on the workstation

In contrast, a program such as the NetWare DOS Requester used in NetWare 4.*x* functions much differently. The DOS Requester consists of about a dozen Virtual Loadable Modules (VLMs), each of which is responsible for certain tasks related to networking and also to the coordination of operations between the operating system and the Requester. For example, the DOS Requester includes VLMs for handling network security, file access, protocol management, redirecting tasks based on communications with the operating system, and so on. See the VLM article for a summary of the individual modules.

The better communication between DOS and a Requester (as opposed to a shell) means less redundancy in functions, which saves memory and also helps improve performance.

For the most part, workstation programs communicate at the Network layer of the OSI reference model, and they use protocols such as Novell's IPX or the Internet's IP to communicate with the driver for the NIC. Certain Requester modules operate at the Transport layer.

In general, a workstation does not need to know much about the resources on a network, other than that they are available. This information is available from the server, which will generally mediate between the workstation and a particular resource.

→ *Broader Category* Computer

→ *Compare* Server

Workstation, Diskless

A diskless workstation is designed specifically for use on networks. It has no disk drive (either floppy or hard), but it does have a keyboard, screen, some memory, booting instructions in ROM, and a network interface card (NIC).

The workstation software needed to connect to the network must be loaded somehow, either from ROM (read-only memory) or from the server. In the latter case, the software is loaded through the NIC. Most NICs have a socket into which a bootable ROM chip can be inserted, to enable the diskless workstation to boot without help from the server.

A diskless workstation is closed, which means there is no way to upload anything from the workstation or download anything to it. A diskless workstation cannot pass a virus onto the network,

LAPTOPS AS WORKSTATIONS

Laptops can serve as workstations on a LAN, but special adapters or measures are usually necessary. There are several ways to connect a laptop to a LAN: through a docking station, external LAN adapter, or a PCMCIA card.

A docking station is essentially an expansion box that turns a laptop into a desktop. You can also use a docking station to connect a laptop to a larger display or to a better keyboard. The docking station has expansion slots, into which you can put whatever types of cards you want. To use the attached laptop on a LAN, you need to plug a NIC into one of the expansion slots. Docking stations are hardware-dependent, and they generally work with only a single model laptop from a single manufacturer.

An external LAN adapter (NIC) attaches to the laptop's parallel port. This can be pocket size (portable) or desk size. The desk size version may support multiple types of cable in the same unit; the pocket size adapter will have room for only a single type of connector.

External NICs generally include a pass-through parallel port, which provides an additional parallel port to replace the one bound to the external adapter. (Note, however, that this additional port will be accessible only if it can be assigned a valid and accessible address.) The pocket size adapter does not include a parallel port; the adapter can be used with a parallel port multiplexer, however. Because they communicate through the parallel port, external adapters don't need an address and IRQ line, which make setup much easier. External adapters use the IEEE addressing algorithm (just like other types of NICs), so they get node addresses just like any other machine.

Unlike a docking station, external NICs are hardware-independent (as is the case for ordinary NICs). This makes it possible to use such adapters with just about any laptop.

External adapters are slower because the parallel port is slower. Fortunately, these adapters won't slow down other network activity, because such tasks as token passing are handled right onboard (without going to the port).

Prices for an external NIC depend on the protocol being supported. ARCnet is cheapest, Token Ring is most expensive.

PCMCIA cards make it possible to link a smaller computer (such as a notebook) to a network.

Newer laptops have the EPP (enhanced parallel port), which supports burst speeds of up to 16Mbps. Support for this port is built into Intel's 386.25 SL chip set, which is currently popular for laptops.

W

nor can a user bootleg software off the network. Because of this, diskless workstations afford greater security than ordinary workstations. For this reason, such workstations are popular in networks where security is a problem or where it is crucial.

Beyond increased security, diskless workstations have little to offer. They are not significantly cheaper than ordinary PCs, but have much more limited utility. Because the instructions in ROM are generally tied to a particular release of the networking software, the ROM chip must be upgraded every time there is a change in software versions. At $50 or more per node, such an upkeep cost is considerable. However, they may provide greater reliability of the nodes, because there are no drives to get dirty or break down.

World Wide Web Consortium (W3C)

→ *See* W3C (World Wide Web Consortium)

Worm

A program that is designed to infiltrate an operating system and to keep replicating itself. Eventually, there are so many copies of the worm floating around that the computer cannot do any work, and a system crash results.

→ *See Also* Trojan Horse; Virus

WOS (Workstation Operating System)

The native operating system on a workstation in a network. Whereas the file server will run a network operating system, workstations can generally continue to run their usual operating systems. The networking software can run as Terminate-and-Stay Resident (TSR) programs or as applications on top of the WOS.

WOSA (Windows Open Services Architecture)

A system-level interface for connecting applications to services (regardless of whether these services are provided on a network).

WWW (World Wide Web)

The World Wide Web has grown from a distributed document lending service for a group of high-energy physicists to the world's largest library—at least in geographical extent. WWW—known simply as the Web—is the name for a network of links to hypertext documents. Documents are known as *Web pages*, and the starting point in a document or for a corporation is known as the *home page*.

Information about the documents and access to them are controlled and provided by Web servers. At the user's end, a Web client takes the user's requests and passes them on to the server. Such a client is generally a *browser* program—that is, a hypertext reader program. Browsers and server communicate using a transfer protocol—generally HTTP (Hypertext Transfer Protocol). Netscape Navigator, various flavors of Mosaic, and Cello are all examples of Web browsers.

Web pages are identified by their URLs (Uniform Resource Locators), which are a form of Web address and document description. For example, the following is the URL for the Sybex home page:

`http://www.sybex.com`

This URL has two components. The first part (`http`) indicates the protocol being used for the documents to be retrieved. In this case, the `http` refers to the hypertext transfer protocol, which is used to transport hypertext files across the Internet. Other protocols that are generally handled by browsers include FTP and Gopher.

The second part specifies the domain name for the machine on which the home page is found. In this case it's a machine named `sybex.com`, which is accessed through a Web server (`www`).

Searching and Accessing the Web

There are currently over 800 million documents on the Web, and about two dozen publishers are competing with each other to sell products that make it easy for users with Internet accounts to add to this by setting up their own Web pages.

There are various online resources for searching the Web. Some are organized by content, and others use search engines to carry out open-ended queries.

Search Engine Index

Undoubtedly one of the most useful Web tools available is a document containing links to search engines on the WWW. If you're just getting started, or if you've forgotten what's available, then this is the Web page you should visit first:

```
http://cuiwww.unige.ch/meta-index.html
```

Yahoo!

Yahoo! is one of the first information sources for the Web, and is still one of the most popular. It is organized by topics but also allows users to search by keywords. By having you narrow down your search to a content area, Yahoo! can speed up its work. Yahoo!'s home page is

```
http://www.yahoo.com
```

WWWW

The World Wide Web Worm, or the Worm, is one of the most popular Web search engines. It works by sending out a *Web robot* to search through Web pages. The robot searches and indexes all documents on its list, all documents to which there are links from the original documents, all links from the links, etc. It is located at

```
http://www.cs.colorado.edu/home/
mcbryan/WWWW.html
```

NIKOS

NIKOS (New Internet KnOwledge System) is a text-based search engine developed by California Polytechnic Institute and Rockwell Network

Systems. When it returns its results, NIKOS orders them on the basis of how relevant they are likely to be. The NIKOS home page is

```
http://www.rns.com/cgi-bin/nikos
```

Harvest

Harvest is an example of what may be the next generation of Web searchers: a program that indexes Web page content as well as titles, authors, and key words. It is billed as an information discovery and access system, and is an experiment in finding and delivering complex information efficiently.

Harvest uses a two-level search process to make things more efficient. At the information end, *gatherers* have relatively specific search tasks based on user queries. The gatherers return their results to *brokers*, who organize and package the information for the consumers, or users.

Brokers are monitored, and if a broker gives out the same information frequently, that information is copied to a cache by a special server program known as a *replicator*. By caching the information, Harvest uses fewer resources the next time someone wants that information. The Harvest home page is

```
http://rd.cs.colorado.edu/harvest/
```

The Growth of the Web

The WWW is growing at an astounding pace. From a few thousand Web pages in 1989, the Web has grown to over 800 million (and counting). Averaged, this amounts to over 200,000 documents per day—over 2.5 per second—during the entire period. In fact, the Web is growing at a considerably faster pace now. For example, in the previous edition of this book, the growth rate was only about 3000 documents per day, or a mere 2 documents per minute, on average. (Isn't it marvelous what interesting facts number can provide.)

This growth is likely to continue for a while, especially as new users master their Web Publishing kits and load their own Web pages.

W

→ *See Also* Browsers; HTML (Hypertext Markup Language)

→ *Primary Sources* One useful place to start finding out about WWW is with the FAQ (Frequently Asked Questions) file. This is available from

```
http://sunsite.unc.edu/boutell/faq/
www_faq.html
```

Any of the Web Kits described in Appendix B also provide helpful information about the WWW and about interesting pages.

WWWW (World Wide Web Worm)

A search program for the World Wide Web . WWWW was developed by Oliver McBryan at the University of Colorado, and it works by sending out a Web robot to search documents. The robot begins by searching documents on a list, then searching all documents accessible through the original documents, etc.

The home page for WWWW is

```
http://www.cs.colorado.edu/home/
mcbryan/WWWW.html
```

Other search engine products include Lycos, Magellan, NIKOS, WebCrawler, and Yahoo!.

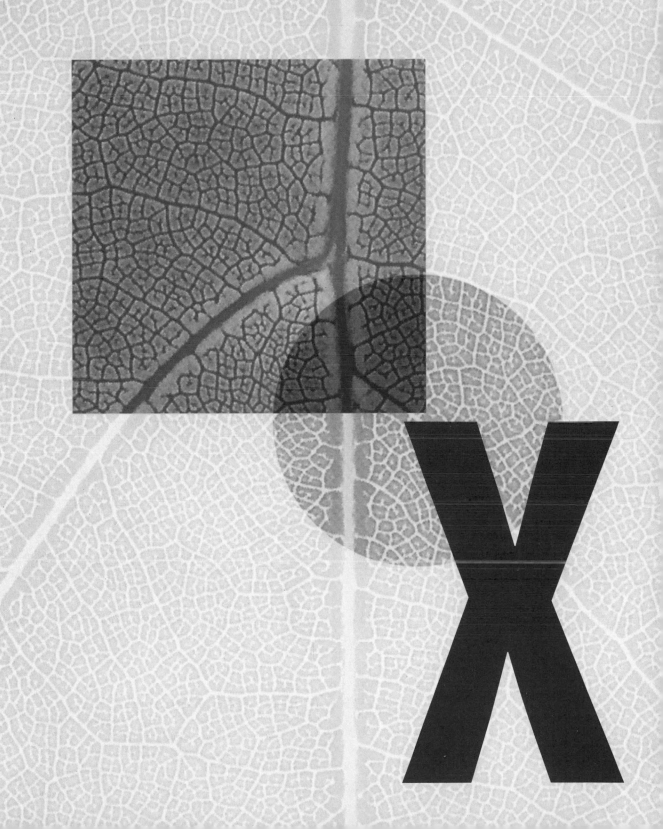

X.xxx

The ITU's (International Telecommunications Union) X series of recommendations provides specifications and protocols for data transmission over public networks.

In particular, various documents in the series specify data transmission services and interfaces, signaling and switching methods, the OSI (Open Systems Interconnection) layers, and messaging handling and directory services—to name just a few of the topics addressed. Many of the specifications concern the operation of DTEs (data terminal equipment) and DCEs (data circuit-terminating equipment) or the interface between them. A PC is an example of a DTE, and a modem is an example of a DCE.

Table "Selected X Series Recommendations" summarizes some of these recommendations.

X0 Band

This is a frequency band in the 7–8GHz range that is used primarily for military and microwave communications.

X2

X2 is the name for a 56Kbps modem technology originally developed by US Robotics (now part of 3COM). It was one of the two incompatible technologies that fought it out for control of the 56K modem market. Both X2 and the competing 56Kflex technology (from Rockwell) have been officially superseded by the international V.90 modem standard, which was adopted in 1998.

However, the 56K modem market is still confusing because the pre-V.90 technologies have not disappeared. V.90 modems are built on chips sets based on either X2 or K56flex technology, which means that a given V.90 modem will support V.90 connections and either X2 or K56flex connections, but not both. This is useful because some ISP providers are still not finished switching over to V.90 technology so that connections sometimes must still rely on

such prestandard connections. Of course, it's not so handy if your X2 modem tries to talk to the ISP's K56flex modems.

Note that the X2 technology has no connection with the X.xxx series of recommendations.

→ See Also 56K Modem

X.25

X.25 is a set of recommendations defined by the CCITT for transmitting data over a packet-switched network. It provides a CCITT-standard *interface* to packet-switched networks and has become the most widely used interface for wide area networks (WANs).

This interface encompasses the three lower layers in the OSI reference model. At the Physical layer, the X.25 standard assumes an X.21 interface, but can also support V.35 and the EIA RS232-D interfaces. At the Data-Link layer, X.25 assumes LAPB (Link Access Protocol, Balanced) is being used, but also supports other protocols, such as the older LAP and IBM's Bisync (BSC) protocol. At the Network layer, X.25 uses PLP (Packet-Level Protocol).

X.25 is suitable for data (but not voice) transmissions. It defines procedures for exchanging data between a DTE (such as a computer) and the network. The connection to this network is represented by a DTE, which may be a modem, multiplexer, or PAD (packet assembler/disassembler). Asynchronous devices (such as a PC) can be connected to the X.25 network through the use of a PAD. Specifications for the operation of a PAD—which assembles characters into packets at one end, disassembles them back into characters at the other end, and handles various call setup and breakdown tasks—are defined in the X.3 specification.

X.25 uses LCNs (logical channel numbers) to distinguish the connections between DTEs at either end of a communication. These LCNs make it possible to send a packet into a packet-switched network at one end (with no control over the packet's journey) and then to pick the packet out at the receiving end.

SELECTED X SERIES RECOMMENDATIONS

Recommendation	Description
X.1	Defines international service classes for users of public data networks (PDNs).
X.2	Defines international data transmission services and user facilities for PDNs. Used by other X series recommendations.
X.3	Defines a packet assembly/disassembly (PAD) facility in PDNs.
X.10	Specifies how DTEs interface with various types of networks (packet-switched, circuit-switched, and leased-circuit).
X.15	Provides definitions related to PDNs.
X.20	Defines the interface between DTEs and DCEs for start/stop transmissions on the PDN.
X.20bis	Specifies use—over PDNs—of DTEs connected to asynchronous, full-duplex V series modems.
X.21	Defines the interface between DTEs and DCEs for synchronous communications on the PDN.
X.21bis	Specifies use—over PDNs—of DTEs connected to synchronous, full-duplex V series modems.
X.24	Specifies definitions for interchange circuits between DTEs and DCEs on PDNs.
X.25	Specifies interface between DTEs and DCEs operating in packet mode when connected to PDNs by a dedicated circuit.
X.30	Defines ISDN support for X.21- and X.21bis-based DTEs.
X.31	Defines ISDN support for DTEs operating in packet mode.
X.32	Defines interface between DTEs and DCEs operating in packet mode and accessing a packet-switched PDN (PSPDN) or a circuit-switched PDN (CSPDN).
X.61	Specifies the data user part of signaling system 7 (SS7).
X.75	Specifies call control procedures and data transfer systems between PSPDNs.
X.81	Defines internetworking between ISDN (Integrated Services Digital Network) and a CSPDN.
X.82	Defines internetworking between CSPDN and PSPDN.
X.121	Specifies an international numbering plan for PDNs.
X.122	Specifies a numbering plan for internetworking between a PSPDN and either a PSTN (Public Switched Telephone Network) or ISDN.
X.140	Specifies general quality of service (QoS) parameters for communications over PDNs.

Recommendation	Description
X.141	Specifies general principles for detecting and correcting errors in PDNs.
X.150	Specifies rules for testing PDNs using test loops between DTEs and DCEs.
X.200	Specifies the OSI reference model).
X.208	Specifies ASN.1 (Abstract Syntax Notation 1).
X.209	Specifies basic encoding rules for ASN.1.
X.210	Specifies conventions for layer service definitions in the OSI reference model.
X.211	Specifies service definitions for the Physical layer.
X.212	Specifies service definitions for the Data-Link layer.
X.213	Specifies service definitions for the Network layer.
X.214	Specifies service definitions for the Transport layer.
X.215	Specifies service definitions for the Session layer.
X.216	Specifies service definitions for the Presentation layer.
X.217, X.218, X.219	Specify service definitions for the Application layer.
X.224	Specifies Transport layer protocol.
X.225	Specifies Session layer protocol.
X.226	Specifies Presentation layer protocol.
X.227, X.228, X.229	Specify Application layer protocols
X.300	Specifies general principles for internetworking between PDNs or between a PDN and another network.
X.400	Provides overview of message handling systems (MHS) and services.
X.402	Specifies an overall architecture for MHS.
X.411	Provides abstract service definition for MTS (message transfer system).
X.413	Provides abstract service definition for MS (message store).
X.419	Specifies protocol definitions for MHS.
X.500	Provides overview of concepts, models, and services provided by the Directory.
X.501	Defines Directory Models.
X.509	Specifies an authentication framework—in this case, for the use of certificates.
X.519	Provides protocol specifications for the Directory Models.

X

The interface supports transmission speeds of up to 64Kbps. The 1992 revision of the X.25 recommendations has increased the throughput to 2Mbps, but this faster X.25 is not yet widely used. X.25 also has a relatively high overhead for error checking and packet sequencing.

X.25 does *not* specify how a packet should be shipped across the network. In fact, X.25 has nothing at all to say about the details of the network transmissions. The WAN itself is represented as a network "cloud" (an assumed connection). X.25 is responsible for getting packets into that cloud at one end and for retrieving them at the other end.

X.75

X.25 provides an interface that allows an end user to connect to a packet-switched public data network (PDN). With this connection, communication is possible with another user on the same network. This communication may take place over a network cloud.

In contrast, X.75 provides an interface for connecting two packet-switched PDNs (PSPDNs)—that is, between two networks—or for establishing a connection between a PSPDN and ISDN (Integrated Services Digital Network). X.75 effectively makes internetwork connections possible. At the Physical layer, this interface operates at 64Kbps by default, but it can also use a 2.048Mbps rate. X.75 uses the HDLC (High-level Data Link Control) protocol at the Data-Link layer.

X.400

X.400 is a message handling standard defined by the CCITT. X.400 has been through two major versions and a revision.

- The original 1984 draft, referred to as X.400/84, provides the basic definitions and model. This version has been implemented for years. Unfortunately, the model has major shortcomings.

- A 1988 version, referred to as X.400/88, addresses most of the major flaws in the 1984 draft, but is not yet widely implemented.

A round of revisions in 1992 addressed additional flaws and ambiguities, and also defined two new types of message contents: EDI (Electronic Data Interchange) messages for use in business transactions and record keeping, and voice messages.

The notion of a Message Handling System (MHS) figures prominently in both versions, but the details of an MHS are somewhat different. Similarly, both versions include a Message Transfer Service (MTS) as an MHS component, but the contents of this MTS differ.

The X.400/84 version dealt only with MHS interfaces for end-users. In X.400/88, an MHS is an object that has interfaces for communicating with end-users, with other CCITT and special services, and possibly with other networks.

The X.400 recommendations series addresses the contents and workings of the MHS, and the manner in which the MHS communicates with outside entities. The documents say nothing about how to implement these recommendations.

The MHS contains several other objects as components, including the MTS. The illustration "1984/1988-version composite of the structure of an MHS" shows the structure of an MHS. Shaded portions are included only in X.400/88; the remaining elements are included in both versions.

X.400 Components

The MHS consists of the following elements:

UA (User Agent) An application process (AP) that provides an end-user with access to the MTS. UAs are used in both versions.

AU (Access Unit) A process that provides a gateway between the MTS and other CCITT services. AUs are used in only the 88 version.

PDAU (Physical Delivery Access Unit) A type of AU that provides a gateway between the

MTS and services that involve physical delivery. PDAUs are used in only the 88 version.

MS (Message Store)   An archive used as temporary storage for messages until they can be forwarded to their destination. The Message Store Access Protocol (MSAP) is used to communicate with this store. MSs are used in only the 88 version.

MTS (Message Transfer System)   A process that transfers messages between users. The MTS relies on its own components (MTAs) to accomplish this transfer. MTSs are used in both versions.

MTA (Message Transfer Agent)   A component of the MTS, the MTA forwards messages to another MTA or the destination entity (which may be a UA, MS, AU, or PDAU). MTAs are used in both versions, but the details differ.

MHS Element Distribution

The MHS elements can be distributed in several ways. These variants differ in the location of MTAs and of the elements that provide interfaces for the MHS (for example, UAs and AUs). The 1984 version provides only UAs for such interfaces.

The elements can be distributed as follows:

- Only interfaces on the machine, as when workstations access the MHS through a server. In this case, the server has the MTA, and the workstations need to run only user agents.

- Only MTA on the machine, such as on the server that is providing MHS access to the workstations described in the previous item.

- MTA and interfaces on the same machine, as when the access is through a terminal.

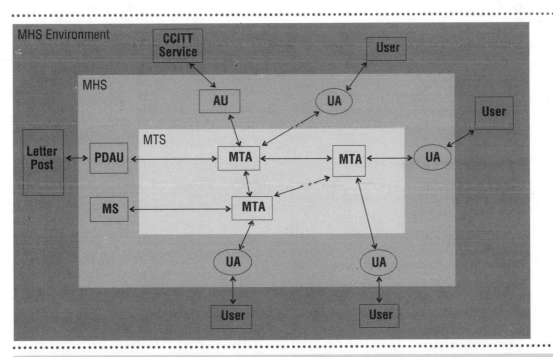

1984/1988-VERSION COMPOSITE OF THE STRUCTURE OF AN MHS

Management Domains

To make electronic mail (e-mail) truly useful, it must be global, which means the MHS must be able to span the entire world. In order to deal with a worldwide MHS, X.400 defines management domains (MDs).

A management domain is a limited—but not necessarily contiguous—area whose message handling capabilities operate under the control of a management authority. Two types of management domains are defined:

ADMD (Administration Management Domain) A network area operated by the CCITT. For example, an ADMD may be a national Post, Telegraph, and Telephone (PTT) service.

PRMD (Private Management Domain) A network area operated by a private organization, such as a university campus or a state university system.

ADMDs can connect PRMDs, but a PRMD cannot connect two ADMDs.

X.400 and the OSI Reference Model

The relationship between X.400 and the OSI reference model depends on the X.400 version. The 1984 version covered the Presentation and Application layers. In addition, X.400/84 subdivided the Application layer into an upper user agent layer (UAL) and a lower message transfer layer (MTL). Users interact with the UAL, and the UAL, in turn communicates with the MTL below it. User agent entities (UAEs) carry out the layer-related functions at the UAL. The 1984 version defines the interpersonal messaging protocol (known as P2) for communications between UAEs.

The 1988 version discards the sublayers and confines the definition of the model to the Application layer. This makes it much easier to implement the 1988 version.

X.400 and Electronic Commerce

One of the major accomplishments of the 1988–1992 sessions was the creation of the X.435

standard. This document defines a messaging system for electronic data interchange (EDI), which is a standard that businesses have adopted for their use. X.435 specifies EDI services, as well as defining EDI messages, agents, and message stores.

It is expected that more and more businesses will begin using EDI for their business transactions and internal record keeping. If that happens, business will move to EDI at an even faster rate, because companies get the most benefits from EDI when their clients also use it.

→ **Primary Sources** The ITU X.400 series of documents define the MHS. For example, X.400 provides an overview of MHS; X.402 describes the architecture, X.411 and X.413 describe the abstract services, and X.419 describes the protocols. Several of the F.400 documents are also relevant.

X.500

The CCITT X.500 Directory Services specifications provide standards and guidelines for representing, accessing, and using information stored in a Directory. In this context, a Directory contains information about objects. These objects may be files (as in a file system directory listing), network entities (as in a network naming service such as Banyan's StreetTalk, Novell's NetWare Directory Services, or Windows 2000's Active Directory), or other types of entities. To distinguish an X.500 Directory from the more commonly encountered file system directory, in Novell's literature, the X.500 variant is written with uppercase *D*.

Functions of a Directory Service

X.500 Directory Services are Application-layer processes. Directory services can be used for various tasks, including the following:

- Providing a global, unified naming service for all elements in a network.

- Translating between network names and addresses.

- Providing descriptions of objects in a directory. The descriptions are listings of attributes and values associated with the objects.

- Providing unique names for all objects in the Directory. All aliases for an object evaluate to the object's unique name.

Depending on the context in which the Directory service is being used, the information may be organized as a name space or as an address book. The latter format is used in electronic mail (e-mail) or messaging services, and is more likely to be tied to a particular product.

Directory Information Bases (DIBs)

The information for a Directory service is stored in a Directory Information Base (DIB). This information is organized in terms of entries and attributes. The entries correspond to the objects in a network; the attributes correspond to properties associated with the objects. The information is represented using ASN.1 (Abstract Syntax Notation 1).

Information in the DIB is organized in a tree structure, known as the Directory Information Tree (DIT). The DIT represents the logical organization of the Directory's contents. Each node in the tree represents an object type. Intermediate nodes (elements with subtrees derived from them) generally serve an organizational function. The subtrees of such an intermediate node represent objects derived from the node's object type. Leaf nodes, which are elements with no subtrees, correspond to specific objects. The illustration "An example of a DIT" shows a tree.

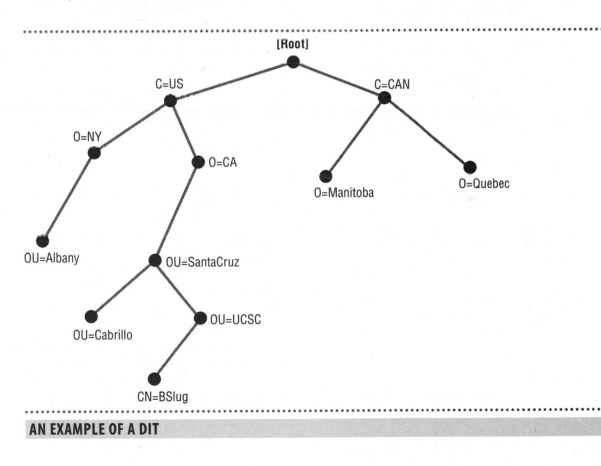

AN EXAMPLE OF A DIT

The Relative Distinguished Name (RDN) is among the attributes associated with each object in a Directory. The RDN specifies an object's local name, which may or may not be unique. In the example in the figure, C=US is an RDN, as are OU=UCSC and CN=B Slug. Because there are restrictions on the ways objects in a Directory can be related to each other, the labels associated with each object provide information about the object's relative location in the DIT:

- C, which represents Country, and is the highest (most general) grouping field in the DIT. Such a field can be located only directly below the root.

- O, which represents Organization, and is the next most general grouping field (after Country). If present, an O field must be located either directly below the root or directly below a Country node.

- OU, which represents Organizational Unit, and is an intermediate-level grouping field. An OU field can appear only below an O field.

- CN, which represents Common Name, and is the bottom-level field. A CN field can be used only with a leaf node.

The rules specifying allowable locations for different fields are part of the schema for a Directory. A schema represents the rules that define the types of relationships allowed between objects in the Directory. Although they are mentioned in the 1988 version, only the 1992 X.500 includes formal elaboration of the schema rules.

Each object has a unique location in the DIT. To identify an object uniquely, you just need to specify all the names on the path to the object. To do this, list every RDN on the path from the root to the object. This chain of RDNs is the object's unique Distinguished Name, or DN. In the figure, C=US, O=CA, OU=Santa Cruz, OU=UCSC, CN=B Slug is the DN for the leaf element named CN=B Slug.

A DIB may be distributed across a network or an internetwork. To simplify access and use, parts or all of a Directory may be replicated at multiple locations in a network or internetwork. When replicas exist, decisions need to be made about how to handle updates. Three possibilities exist for making changes to the Directory:

- No changes are allowed to either the original or any replicas.

- Changes must be made in the original, which must then periodically inform all replicas of the update. This is known as a master/shadow arrangement, because shadow is a term for a replica. This concept was introduced in the 1992 X.500 specifications.

- Changes may be made in either the original or in a replica. Other locations will be updated on whatever schedule is in effect. For some networks, updates must be immediate; for others, updates are made at periodic intervals. This is known as a peer-to-peer update mechanisms. Despite the same name, such a mechanism is not necessarily related to a peer-to-peer network.

A DIB may modified or updated frequently. If replicas are also being modified, then synchronization of the changes is essential. Synchronization ensures that all versions of the Directory information are up to date, and that everyone is using the same version. The actual updating depends on the availability of a common time frame as a reference. The reference time need not be correct; it just has to be shared by the DIB and all replicas. See the Time Synchronization article for an example of the use of reference times.

Using DIBs

To access the information in a DIB, X.500 provides Directory User and Directory System Agents (DUAs and DSAs, respectively). An end user can get information from a Directory service by working through a DUA. The DUA communicates with a DSA, whose task is to access and deal with the actual DIB. The DUA communicates with a DSA using a DAP (Directory Access Protocol).

Communication between DUA and DSA uses any of three ports that are defined in X.500: Read, Search, or Modify. (A *port* is an access to a service from the perspective of the user of a protocol.) Each of these ports can handle a limited number and range of actions:

- The Read port can handle Read, Compare, and Abandon.

- The Search port can handle List and Search.

- The Modify port can handle Add Entry, Remove Entry, Modify Entry, and Modify RDN.

In some cases, particularly with a distributed Directory, DSAs may use each other for help. Such interactions use the DSP (Directory System Protocol). The illustration "Accessing a DIB" shows these elements. In addition to the two protocols shown in the figure, the 1992 X.500 specifications introduce two new protocols, both of which are used for interactions between DSAs: DISP (Directory Information Shadowing Protocol) and DOP (Directory Operational Binding Management Protocol).

The 1988 version of the X.500 recommendations relied on the authentication services to prevent unauthorized access to Directory information or elements. The 1992 revision adds access controls as a mechanism. With this, a Directory can have access control lists associated with it. These lists determine who is allowed access to Directory elements and also the kinds of access that will be allowed.

X.500 Security Measures

To help ensure that unauthorized users do not get access to the DIB, steps are taken to authenticate each user. The X.500 authentication framework specifies two levels of authentication:

- Simple authentication, which requires just a valid password from the user.

- Strong authentication, which uses encryption to help safeguard information.

In addition, the authentication framework supports the use of digital signatures to help prevent message or information forgery, and the use of

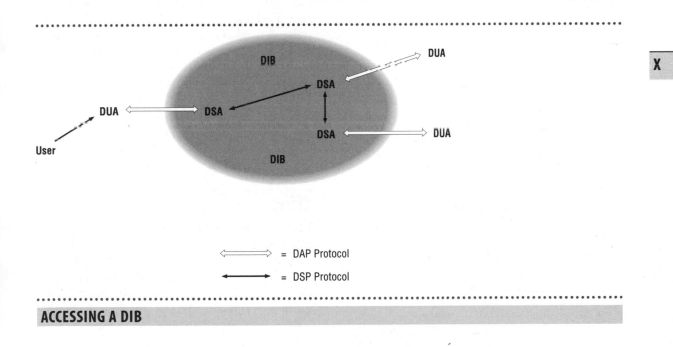

```
⇐====⇒  = DAP Protocol
◄────►  = DSP Protocol
```

ACCESSING A DIB

certificates (public keys with enciphered information) to ensure that the encryption keys are unique and known only to authorized parties.

The State of X.500

Directories of the sort defined in X.500 have been around a long time. For example, the Domain Naming Service in the Internet community and Novell's NetWare Directory Services (NDS) in version 4.*x* of NetWare provide such services; Active Directory in Microsoft's soon-to-be-released Windows 2000 will provide them.

Such Directory or naming services generally adopt the X.500 architecture (entries and attributes organized in a tree structure) and some amount of the X.500 functionality. The ASN.1 notation is less likely to be adapted in such implementations.

Implementation of X.500 specifications has been slow partly because developers were waiting for the 1992 revisions for both X.500 and for the X.400 Message Handling Services (MHS), which rely heavily on X.500 services. Now that updates to both the MHS and the Directory Services standards have appeared, the expectation is that such services will be implemented more rapidly.

→ *See Also* NDS (NetWare Directory Services); StreetTalk; X.400

xB/tB Encoding

*x*B/tB encoding is a general label for any of several data-translation schemes that can serve as a preliminary to signal encoding in telecommunications or networking contexts.

In *x*B/tB, every group of *x* bits is represented as a *y*-bit symbol. This symbol is associated with a bit pattern that is then encoded using a standard signal encoding method (usually NRZI).

The following are commonly used translation schemes of this sort:

- 4B/5B, used in FDDI networks

- 5B/6B, used in the 100BaseVG fast Ethernet standard proposed by Hewlett-Packard

- 8B/10B, used in SNA (Systems Network Administration) networks

XDR (External Data Representation)

An abstract (machine-independent) syntax for describing data structures. XDR was developed by Sun Microsystems as part of their Network File System (NFS), and it is comparable in function to the Abstract Syntax Notation One (ASN.1) used in the OSI reference model.

Xerox Network System (XNS)

→ *See* XNS (Xerox Network System)

XJACK

XJACK is a special connector on a PCMCIA (Personal Computer Memory Card International Association) card that makes it possible to plug a telephone wall jack connector directly into the modem on the card. Such modems are used in laptop and notebook computers, and are often difficult to keep connected in a secure manner. XJACK makes a secure connection possible.

XJACK is a registered trademark of MegaHertz Corporation, a subsidiary of US Robotics (which is now owned by 3Com).

XLink

XLink is one of the two components that are used to handle links in an XML (eXtensible Markup Language) document—that is, to resolve references and to retrieve the appropriate materials. The other component is XPointer, which knows how to manage the versatile pointers (links) that are allowed in XML documents.

Both of these components are actually special-purpose languages: XLink for linking (surprise, surprise), and XPointer for managing link references. You can find the specifications for XLink and XPointer at the following URLs:

http://www.w3.org/TR/WD-xlink

http://www.w3.org/TR/WD-xptr

These URLs generally have the most recent draft of the specifications.

→ **Broader Category** XML (eXtensible Markup Language)

→ **See Also** XPointer

XML (eXtensible Markup Language)

XML is poised to revolutionize the presentation and distribution of content on the World Wide Web and elsewhere—and by the time you read this, it may already have done so. XML is a markup language that can be used to create XML applications. These are other markup languages that can be used to identify and represent the structure of specific types of documents. Although the same kinds of elements are involved as with HTML (Hypertext Markup Language)—Web documents and a markup language—things are very different in XML documents because the markups have a different purpose and significance.

A document marked up with HTML tags is basically marked up with layout guidelines. The document elements that are marked by HTML tags relate to the way the content is to be presented—for example, a heading, list, or table are all displayed differently when they are encountered in an HTML file. HTML tags are essentially suggestions to the browser as to how to interpret a section of document for display.

In contrast, the markups in an XML document correspond to structural elements that have been defined for a document of that type. With this kind of markup, the document can not only be displayed—just like an HTML file—but it can also be taken apart for specific purposes, rearranged, or otherwise

manipulated by an appropriate program. This is possible because the tags in the document indicate how elements relate to each other, which implicitly determines how they can or need to be related to each other after modification.

In many instances, the same elements will be marked up in both HTML and XML documents—for example, headings and subheadings, lists, and so forth. However, in an HTML document, subheadings under a particular heading have no relationship to each other or to the heading under which they are found. Beyond displaying the subheadings in the same way (and probably displaying the heading differently), there is nothing a browser can do with the elements.

In contrast, in an XML document the subheadings under a particular heading are children of the heading—in the tree structure that underlies the document—and are siblings of each other. (This genealogical terminology is standard when discussing hierarchically arranged data structures such as trees.) By retaining the relationship among the elements, XML markups give applications hooks by which they can access more meaningful document elements.

With the advent of Dynamic HTML (DHTML), HTML browsers can be made to behave on the basis of document interrelationships—but only if instructed to do so by a script, applet, or ActiveX control. This is because each element on a DHTML page is an accessible object, and so an outside program can traverse the elements until it reaches the required one. Once the element is in focus, the program can give the browser instructions on what to do with the element.

XML's Roots and Features

An important feature of XML is that it is extensible. That is, you can create new markup elements and rules. This means that XML can be used to create a markup language that is appropriate for any kind of content. Such fabricated markup languages are known as XML applications—a somewhat different use of the term than you may be used to seeing, but one that is not as different as it seems at first glance.

X

HTML is, in fact, such an application—but it is not an XML application. HTML is actually an SGML application. SGML stands for Standard Generalized Markup Language, and it is the language that provides the roots for both HTML and XML. However, whereas HTML is an SGML application (a set of markup tags created using SGML's construction rules), XML is an SGML subset (an abridged version of the SGML construction rules).

In fact, XML is almost as powerful as SGML, but much less complex. For example, the XML specification is about 50 pages long, compared to the SGML specification, which is over 500 pages long. XML is a streamlined version of SGML that is designed for publishing and manipulating documents over the Internet. Illustration "The evolution of markup languages" shows how the various products are related.

SGML is essentially a version of GML—developed for IBM by Charles Goldfarb and others—adopted as an international standard. HTML was created as an SGML application, but it could just as easily have been created by XML—as indicated by the dashed line connecting XML and HTML in the figure. Note that XML is just a smaller SGML.

An XML document consists of a content (text) file marked up with permissible language constructs, and supplemented with certain other files. The language constructs include document elements, element attributes, and entities. One of the files contains rules that specify what the permissible elements are for the text file; another file may provide display guidelines for a browser.

Document Elements

XML document markups include tags that mark the start and end of elements contained in the document. What constitutes an element in a particular document will depend on the content of the document. For example, if the document is a course catalog, one document element might be department. Within a department, there might be one or more faculty members listed; there will also be courses listed. These—department, faculty member, and course—are all elements. A faculty member element will include a name element, one or more research interest elements, and possibly other (sub)elements. A course element will include subelements for course

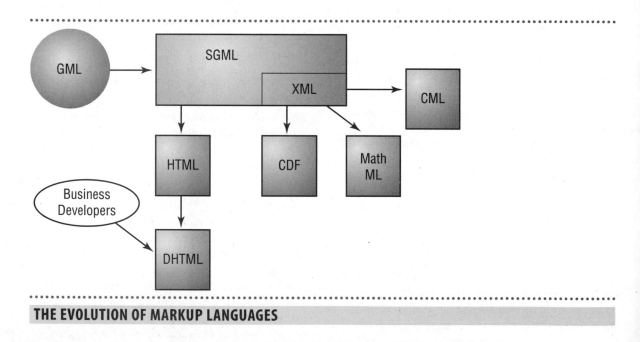

THE EVOLUTION OF MARKUP LANGUAGES

number, instructor, meeting times, prerequisites, number of credits, and so forth.

Note that elements can be nested inside of other elements. Note also that some elements might occur a variable number of times in a particular context. For example, some faculty members might have more research interests than others, some courses might have more sections than others, and some departments might have more faculty members than others.

The elements that are allowed in a course catalog are specified in a Document Type Definition (DTD) file. DTDs are discussed at greater length below. For now, it's enough to know that a DTD specifies in complete detail what types of elements can occur in a document, where each element type can (or must) occur, what type of information can be associated with each element type, what attributes (properties or qualifiers) are associated with each element type, and what possible values can be associated with each attribute. The structure of a document is defined completely in a DTD.

Element attributes

Elements may be qualified by attributes associated with the element. An attribute is a property or feature associated with a particular element type. Each attribute can take on a limited range of values, which must be specified when defining the attribute in the DTD. For example, a course might include an attribute where one can specify whether the course is required for a particular major. An attribute can have a default value associated with it—so that if the attribute is not specified for a particular element, the default value can be assumed. For example, no required attribute might by default evaluate to a NO—that is, a course is not required unless otherwise specified.

Entities

An XML document can also include entities, which are essentially elements that represent special characters, common phrases or special values, or references to materials outside the file. For example, the entity lt can be used to represent the less-than character (<), which is a special character in XML and which, therefore, cannot simply be included as ordinary text. To get around this restriction—that is, to be able to use a less-than symbol in a document—you must use the following:

```
&lt;
```

When it encounters this in a XML document, an XML parser or processor will replace it with the less-than character in its output file—where the character will not cause confusion. Entities can be defined to represent values that will be repeated in the document—for example, a book title, company name, address, and so forth.

DTDs

A DTD file contains a formal definition of each element that is allowed in a document, and shows exactly where in the document an element can be used. The DTD specifies the components out of which each element is made—which could be other elements or data of a type specified in the DTD. The DTD also contains information about the possible values for any attributes associated with any of the document elements.

When an XML parser or processor checks an XML file, it compares the markups in the document against the document structure defined by the DTD. If the elements and attributes are used appropriately in the document, the document is syntactically correct and a valid document in relation to the DTD. Because of DTDs, XML files must adhere much more closely to syntax rules. Sloppiness may be tolerated in HTML files, but never in an XML file.

Other XML Components

Like HTML files, XML documents can include links. However, HTML links are limited to simple types of connections—to another document or to a specific location in the same or another document. The target of any link to a specific section in an HTML document must have an appropriate label. All HTML links go in one direction only.

X

In contrast, XML links are much more powerful, and can be much more complex. In XML, links can be bidirectional, can point to multiple objects at the same time, and can point to arbitrary structural elements in a document—for example, the fourth item in a bulleted list in a section with a specified name.

To handle such links, the XML environment includes two supplementary components: XLink and XPointer. XLink is, in fact, a linking language, and was originally known as eXtensible Link Language (XLL). Similarly, XPointer is actually a pointer language that can be used to specify target elements in relation to parent or child document elements.

For actually rendering, or displaying, an XML document, some type of style sheet can be used with the XML document. XML documents can work with any of the following:

- The cascading style sheets (CSS1 and CSS2) defined for and used with HTML documents.

- Style sheets created using the international standard Documentation Style and Semantics Specification language (DSSSL), which is actually designed for SGML documents.

- Style sheets created using the eXtensible Style Language (XSL) intended for use with XML documents.

XML Applications

Just as SGML gave us HTML, XML has given us dozens of specialized markup languages. Some of these have produced documents that have affected millions of Web users and even ordinary people going about their daily routines.

For example, the entertainment, business, sports, and other channels that have become such hot attractions on the Internet are actually delivered using push technology to provide updated materials and a channel definition to provide a route for delivery. Channel services are provided using the Microsoft Channel Definition Format (CDF), which is an XML application.

Financial packages such as Microsoft Money and Intuit Quicken are able to communicate with financial institutions and even to exchange information with such institutions. These programs are also able to exchange information with each other. All of this communication and interoperation is made possible because the parties involved all use Open Financial Exchange (OFX or OFE) as a common vocabulary. Like CDF, OXF is an XML application.

CDF and OFX are both specialized vocabularies that have been created to make it possible to organize and deliver specific kinds of material. A CDF document—that is, a channel—must be able to determine what relevant material is new, and must be able to package and deliver this material to subscribers. Since subscribers don't all log on with the same frequency, what's new for one subscriber is not necessarily new for another. Nevertheless, each subscriber gets material that is tailored to that subscriber's logon history.

The channel delivery server manages this with no difficulty—because the program responsible for retrieving and packaging the channel content knows how to identify content items in the database or other data store from which the content will be obtained. The program also knows how to determine which items are more recent than the subscriber's last channel delivery, which are of interest to the subscriber and, therefore, which items need to be packaged and delivered to the subscriber. The packaging of the content may rely on the information provided by the item's structure and also on the structure of the delivery format.

CDF and OFX are just two of the dozens of special purpose markup languages that have been created in the past few years. All of these derive their utility from the fact that XML makes it possible to specify structural information about the content of interest, which is necessary for knowing how things must fit together.

For example, this is why applications such as MathML (Mathematical Markup Language) and CML (Chemical Markup Language) are feasible. Since it's possible to specify precisely and completely how equations or chemical molecules are put together, it's possible to provide rules for constructing such elements in documents. These rules can be written in a form that is human readable but that also provides enough information to an application to understand the rules. Such an application might be a printer or a browser, whose job is to "display" the content on paper or on a screen, respectively.

Other XML applications include the following:

OSD (Open Software Description)   A vocabulary for describing and distributing software over the Internet. OSD makes it possible to specify enough information about the software (version, configuration, and so forth) that installation and upgrades can be automated. OSD is actually an SGML application that is being revised as an XML application.

SMIL (Synchronized Multimedia Integration Language)   A vocabulary for specifying how to include various types of multimedia in Web documents. The included materials can be "displayed" (that is, played or executed) together, in succession, at certain intervals, for particular durations, etc. The elements and attributes available in SMIL make it possible to specify such things in an unambiguous (to both computer and human) manner.

RDF (Resource Description Framework)   A vocabulary for describing various kinds of Web metadata—that is, information *about* the content (security settings, copyright notices, cross-referencing or keyword information, and so forth).

TML (Tutorial Markup Language)   A vocabulary for creating and working with instructional materials, presenting, administering, and scoring tests, and tracking student performance.

CKML (Conceptual Knowledge Markup Language)   A vocabulary for representing knowledge, and for creating models of decision making and reasoning.

The table "XML Topics and Applications" contains URLs (Uniform Resource Locators) for information about some example XML applications and about XML and its various components.

→*Compare* HTML (Hypertext Markup Language)

XML TOPICS AND APPLICATIONS

XML Topic/Application	URL	Comments
XML	http://www.w3.org/XML	W3C's home page for XML information and activity
XML resources	http://www.sil.org/sgml/xml.html	A starting point for access to tons of XML resources; check in often
XML resources	http://www.xmlinfo.com	Another excellent starting point; check in often
XML resources	http://www.xml.com	Yet another excellent source
XML applications (various examples)	http://www.schema.net	Lots of examples
XML software	http://xmlsoftware.com	Find out about available XML-related software
BsML (Bioinformatic Sequence ML)	http://www.topogen.com/sbir/rfc.html	For sequencing DNA, RNA, and proteins

X

Continued on next page

XML TOPICS AND APPLICATIONS (continued)

XML Topic/Application	URL	Comments
CDF (Channel Definition Format)	http://www.microsoft.com/standards/cdf.htm	Delivers channel content using push technology
CKML (Conceptual Knowledge ML)	http://asimov.eecs.wsu.edu/WAVE/Ontologies/CKML/CKML-DTD.html	For learning, reasoning, and decision making
CML (Chemical Markup Language)	http://www.venus.co.uk/omf/cml	For chemical content
EAD (Encoded Archival Description)	http://www.loc.gov.ead	Library of Congress application
GedML (Genealogical Data in XML)	htp://home.iclweb.com/icl2/mhkay/gedml.html	For genealogy databases
HTTP DRP (Distribution and Replication Protocol)	http://www.w3.org/TR/NOTE-drp-19970825.html	Makes HTTP more efficient and reliable for distributing materials over the Internet
ICE (Information and Content Exchange)	http://www.vignette.com/Products/ice/Item/0,1669,5226,00.html	Automates exchange and management of assets by business partners
IMS Metadata Specification	http://www.imsproject.org/md_overview.html	Enables delivery and management of high-quality training materials over the Internet
JSML (Java Speech ML)	http://java.sun.com/products/java-media/speech/forDevelopers/JSML	Marks up text for delivery using speech synthesizers and the Java Speech API (JSAPI)
MathML (Mathematical ML)	http://www.w3.org/Math	For handling equations and other math content
MCF (Meta Content Framework)	http://www.w3.org/TR/NOTE-MCF-XML.html	For dealing with metacontent (that is, content about content)
NFF (Notes Flat File)	http://www.digitome.com	Provides intermediate data representation for importing material into Lotus Notes
OFX (Open Financial Exchange)	http://www.ofx.net	Provides standards for exchanging financial information
OML (Ontology ML)	http://asimov.eecs.wsu.edu/WAVE/Ontologies/OML/OML-DTD.html	Marks documents for machine reading
OpenTag	http://www.opentag.org/otspecs.htm	Provides common method for marking different file types
OSD (Open Software Description)	http://www.microsoft.com/standards/osd	For electronic software distribution and upgrading
OTP (Open Trading Protocol)	http://www.otp.org:8080	Enables secure trading of securities and stocks over the Internet

Continued on next page

XML TOPICS AND APPLICATIONS (continued)

XML Topic/Application	URL	Comments
PGML (Precision Graphics ML)	http://www.w3.org/TR/1998/NOTE-PGML	Provides a 2-D, precision graphics language that produces vector graphics (as opposed to bitmaps)
RDF (Resource Description Framework)	http://www.w3.org/RDF	Provides a framework for working with metadata (ratings, site maps, security settings, and so forth)
RELML (Real Estate Listings ML)	http://www.openmls.com http://www.4thworldtele.com	Provides tools for managing multiple listing services
SMIL (Synchronized Multimedia Integration Language)	http://www.w3.org/AudioVideo/Activity.html	For incorporating multimedia content into documents
TIM (Telecommunications Interchange Markup)	http://www.atis.org/atis/tcif/ipi/5tc60hom.htm	Provides a mechanism for dealing with standards and information relating to the selling, buying, and use of telecommunications equipment
TML (Tutorial ML)	http://www.ilrt.bris.ac.uk/mru/netquest/tml/about/aboutlang.html	For creating and handling instructional materials, tests, tracking, etc.
TMX (Translation Memory Exchange)	http://www.lisa.org/tmx/tmx.htm	Allows easier exchange of translation memory data
UXF (UML Exchange Format)	http://www.yy.cs.keio.ac.jp/~suzuki/project/uxf	For handling material using the Unified Modeling Language (UML)
VXML (Voice XML)	http://www.voxml.mot.com/voxml.html	Speech synthesis
WAP (Wireless Application Protocol)	http://www.wapforum.org	Standards for wireless network transmissions
WebDAV (Distributed Authoring and Versioning on the WWW)	http://www.ics.uci.edu/~ejw/authoring	Uses HTTP for working with Web pages from remote locations
WIDL (Web Interface Description Language)	http://www.webmethods.com/technology/widl description.html	Specifies interfaces for automating Web transactions
XBEL (XML Bookmark Exchange Language)	http://www.python.org/topics/xml/xbel/docs/html/xbel.html	Provides a language for exchanging bookmarks among browsers
XML-Data	http://www.microsoft.com/standards/xml/xmldata.htm	An alternative to the use of DTDs with XML documents
XML/EDI (XML/Electronic Data Interchange)	http://www.xmledi.net	Combines XML with EDI

X

Xmodem

Xmodem is a popular file transfer protocol available in many off-the-shelf and shareware communications packages, as well as on many bulletin board systems (BBSs).

Xmodem divides the data for the transmission into blocks. Each block consists of the start-of-header character, a block number, 128 bytes of data, and a checksum.

An extension to Xmodem, called *Xmodem-CRC*, adds a more stringent error-checking method by using a cyclical redundancy check (CRC) to detect transmission errors.

→ *See Also* Kermit; Ymodem; Zmodem

XMS (Extended Memory Specification)

Microsoft's specifications for extended memory. In order to access extended memory, programs should use an XMS driver (for example, HIMEM.SYS).

→ *See Also* Memory

XNS (Xerox Network System)

XNS is a proprietary protocol suite from Xerox Corporation. It was developed as part of the original Ethernet development project, and several currently popular protocols—for example Novell's IPX (Internetwork Packet Exchange)—are based on protocols from the XNS suite.

XON/XOFF

In asynchronous communications, characters used to control the flow of data. The XOFF (ASCII 19, or Ctrl-S) tells the sender to stop transmitting until further notice; the XON (ASCII 17, or Ctrl-Q) tells the sender to resume transmission after an XOFF.

XPointer

Along with XLink, XPointer is one of the two components used to handle links and their attendant pointers in XML (eXtensible Markup Language) documents. Unlike HTML (Hypertext Markup Language) links, which can point in only one direction, and which can do little more than connect two locations, XML links can be two-directional, can point to multiple locations with a single link, and can even point to arbitrary document elements, regardless of whether these elements are labeled with names (as they must be for an HTML link to be able to reach them).

Both XLink and XPointer actually are special-purpose languages—the former for linking, and the latter for resolving referents in document files. Each of these components has its own specification.

You can find the XLink specification at

`http://www.w3.org/TR/WD-xlink`

and the XPointer specification at

`http://www.w3.org/TR/WD-xptr`

→ *Broader Category* XML (eXtensible Markup Language)

XSL (eXtensible Style Language)

XSL is a style sheet mechanism intended for use with XML (eXtensible Markup Language) documents. It can be used to specify the layout of an XML file for a browser. XSL can also be used to convert an XML file to HTML (Hypertext Markup Language) or to other markup language formats.

XSL is one of three style sheet mechanisms that can be used with XML. The others are cascading style sheets (CSS) and Document Style Semantics and Specification language (DSSSL). The CSS mechanism—currently consisting of CSS1 and CSS2, for levels 1 and 2, respectively—was originally created for use with HTML; DSSSL is an international layout standard that was designed for use with SGML (Standard Generalized Markup

Language). Of the three, only XSL was designed specifically for use with XML documents.

The advantage of using a style sheet mechanism with XML documents is that it allows content and form to be kept separate. This makes both the content and the layout instructions easier to read, maintain, and change. It also makes it possible to reuse layouts with different documents without having to type them into each document. To do this, it's just necessary to include the appropriate style sheet file with the document file.

XSL is described only in a W3C (World Wide Web Consortium) note—as opposed to the 300-page specification for DSSSL. XSL is not yet considered a specification. You can find the XSL note at

```
http://www.w3.org/TR/NOTE-XSL.html
```

→ *Broader Category* XML (eXtensible Markup Language)

X Window

X Window is a windowing system developed for UNIX environments. Generally known simply as X, it consists of a client, a server, and a communications link that connects the two. The server software controls the I/O (input/output) devices (display, keyboard, and mouse); the client is a program that can communicate with the server to make X Window–based requests. Since the client is generally an application, it will probably perform other functions as well—for example, acting as a database manager or an e-mail program.

The communications link uses the X protocol, which is similar to protocols in the TCP/IP (Transmission Control Protocol/Internet Protocol) stack, and which can support X Window client-server communications on a single machine (using interprocess communication, or IPC) or communications between a client and server over a network (using a link such as Ethernet, X.25, or Token Ring).

Once an X Window system has been set up, users can access any X-compliant application anywhere on the network, and can display the output on the user's machine. X is platform independent, so that the user need not worry about where the application is running, so long as the machine supports the X Window protocol.

An X Window manager is a special client program that is responsible for such tasks as creating, resizing, and removing windows, managing overlapping windows, and converting windows into icons (when minimizing) and vice versa. Essentially, the X Window manager provides the operations needed for a GUI (graphical user interface). Open Look and Motif are two commonly used X Window managers.

Various versions of X Window have been implemented. Of these, X11, a version used in MIT's Project Athena is arguably the best known.

X

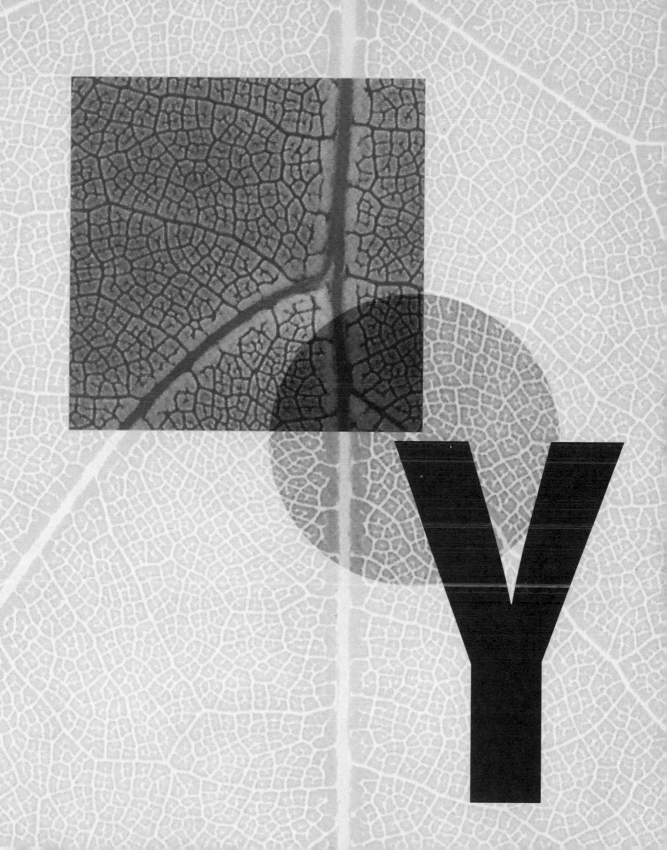

Y2K Bug

If you are reading this, the Y2K (year 2000) bug—also known as the millenium bug—probably was not the death-knell of the civilized world as some had predicted. The Y2K bug refers to a problem that will arise on January 1, 2000 (01-01-00) because an unknown number of computers and other processor-controlled devices will think it's January 1, 1900. An unknown percentage of those devices will begin to behave in incorrect ways. Depending on how big the unknown values are, on where the misbehaving devices are, and on how they misbehave, the Y2K bug could be either a minor (albeit exorbitantly expensive) inconvenience or a major catastrophe (costly as well as expensive).

The main source of the problem stems from the use of two digit codes to represent the year. In the earliest computers, this was done to save precious memory or storage. Over time, it became common practice to do this. Now, however, with the chronometer about to turn over two extra digits, the year value will become ambiguous in millions—perhaps billions—of electronic places (date stamps in files, lines of code, soda dispensers, switches for train lines over which needed parts are being shipped, pacemakers, nuclear defense computers, nuclear offense computers, and so forth).

Corporations and governments worldwide have spent hundreds of billions of dollars trying to address this issue, and the total costs of dealing with the Y2K problem may approach one trillion dollars worldwide. And these expenses have been almost entirely for preventative measures (along with some money for liability insurance—although some insurance providers will not write policies for Y2K liability insurance). Expenses after the beginning of 2000 may be even greater if the failures are in key locations.

Outcomes in the first trials by fire have been encouraging for companies, municipalities, and states whose fiscal years have begun already—that is, whose computers are already in their year 2000. Most of these cases have caused little more than inconvenience. However, there are still major industries (and major countries) for which the little available Y2K information is either unreliable or discouraging.

The uncertainties surrounding the Y2K bug have spawned some very successful industries—including the Y2K book writing industry, the survival foods and supplies industries, and the Y2K video and software industries. They have also given pundits and consultants much to drum up business about, and litigation lawyers much to smile about. COBOL programmers have earned a new cachet, and many people are perhaps a bit more paranoid and edgy than they might normally be.

… And if you are not reading this?

Yahoo!

Yahoo! is one of the oldest search engines on the World Wide Web, and is now also one of the more successful Web portals—initial access points to the Web. To see for yourself, go to `http://www.yahoo.com`.

Yellow Cable

Yellow cable is a coaxial cable that is often used when a line needs to be tapped for some reason. The tap used with such cable is known as a vampire tap, and the cable gets its name from its yellow cover.

Yellow Pages (YP)

→ **See** YP (Yellow Pages)

Ymodem

Ymodem is a popular file transfer protocol available in many off-the-shelf and shareware communications packages, as well as on many bulletin board systems (BBSs). Ymodem is a variation of the Xmodem protocol.

This protocol divides the data to be transmitted into blocks. Each block consists of the start-of-header character, a block number, one kilobyte of data, and a checksum. Ymodem also incorporates the capabilities to send multiple files in the same session and to abort file transfer during the transmission.

Ymodem's larger data block results in less overhead for error control than required by Xmodem;

however, if the block must be retransmitted because the protocol detects an error, there is more data to resend.

→ *See Also* Kermit; Xmodem; Zmodem

YP (Yellow Pages)

The Yellow Pages are a network directory service from Sun. The service allows system administrators on UNIX platforms to manage databases that are distributed over a network. RPCs (remote procedure calls) allow administrators to work with the databases. For various reasons, the name Yellow Pages has been changed to NIS (network information services).

Y

ZAW (Zero Administration for Windows)

ZAW is a feature in Windows 2000 (formerly known as Windows NT 5) that is expected to centralize the administration of PCs on a Windows 2000 network. It will simplify configuration and maintenance, and will also make it possible to upgrade software packages and to install new packages.

Once completed, ZAW is expected to work with Windows 98 as well, but only Windows 2000 machines will be able to take full advantage of all ZAW features.

→ **Compare** Z.E.N.works (Zero Effort Networks)

Z.E.N.works (Zero Effort Networks)

Z.E.N.works (Zero Effort Networks) is a server-based, directory-enabled software package from Novell. It is designed to help NetWare administrators manage network applications and workstations. Z.E.N.works provides centralized administration and control over user profiles on Windows NT or Windows 9x workstations, and also over Windows policies (including any special Y2K policies).

By providing users with access to resources through Z.E.N.works, the resources can be linked with the user's login ID and profile—so that the user can access the resource from any workstation. Such centralized control also makes it possible to configure printers easily and to create inventories of hardware. Software distribution and updates can be automated and carried out with Z.E.N.works.

Z.E.N.works is derived from two earlier Novell products: Novell Application Launcher (NAL) and Novell Workstation Manager. To the capabilities of these two programs, Novell has added remote help desk services and troubleshooting capabilities.

→ **Broader Category** NetWare

→ **Compare** ZAW (Zero Administration for Windows)

Zero Administration for Windows (ZAW)

→ **See** ZAW (Zero Administration for Windows)

Zero Byte Time Slot Interchange

In telecommunications systems using T1 lines, zero byte time slot interchange is a compression technique in which a byte containing all zeros will be dropped and replaced with information indicating that the action was taken.

Zero-Slot LAN

A zero-slot LAN is a local area network (LAN) that uses one of the existing serial or parallel ports on the computer rather than a special network interface card (NIC) plugged into the computer's expansion bus.

Because zero-slot LANs can transmit only as fast as the computer's output port, they are considerably slower than networks that use network-specific hardware and software. The maximum length of each cable segment is also severely limited, so zero-slot LANs can connect only two or three computers.

The advantage of a zero-slot LAN is its low cost compared with dedicated network systems; however, the prices of newer peer-to-peer networks are beginning to negate this advantage.

ZIS (Zone Information Socket)

In an AppleTalk network, a socket (access point) associated with the zone information protocol (ZIP) services.

ZIT (Zone Information Table)

In an AppleTalk network, a ZIT maps the zone name(s) associated with each subnetwork in a network or internetwork.

Zmodem

A popular file transfer protocol available in many off-the-shelf and shareware communications packages, as well as on many bulletin board systems. Zmodem is similar to Xmodem and Ymodem but is designed to handle larger data transfers with fewer errors. Zmodem also includes a feature called checkpoint restart, which allows an interrupted transmission to resume at the point of interruption, rather than starting again at the beginning of the transmission.

→ *See Also* Kermit; Xmodem; Ymodem

Zone

In an AppleTalk network or internetwork, a logical subset of nodes which, together, form a subdivision. This is similar to the concept of a domain in Windows NT networking environments. A zone can have a name associated with it, and a node can be part of one or more zones. The zone name is used to simplify routing and service advertising. A zone can encompass multiple networks and can cross network boundaries (that is, apply to parts of several networks).

An area served by a DNS (Domain Name Service) server is also known as a zone. Such zones are defined, for example, for the Internet. The Internet's hierarchical structure supports various levels of domain names. The top level zones include the well-known `.com`, `.org`, `.net`, `.edu`, `.int`, and `.mil`; the country codes; codes for the U.S. states; and also the new top-level domains that were added in the past year (for example, `.arts`, `.firm`, `.info`, `.nom`, `.rec`, `.store`, and `.web`).

Zone Information Protocol (ZIP)

→ *See* Protocol, ZIP (Zone Information Protocol)

Zone Information Socket (ZIS)

→ *See* ZIS (Zone Information Socket)

Zone Information Table (ZIT)

→ *See* ZIT (Zone Information Table)

Zulu Time

Zulu time is a term used in the military and also in navigation contexts to refer to Coordinated Universal Time (CUT, formerly known as Greenwich Mean Time, or GMT). (CUT is often abbreviated as UTC, on the basis of the French term.)

Zulu time is expressed using a 24 hour clock (0–12 is AM, 13–24 is PM) and a predefined format. When used in the military, a Z is added to the end of the time value. For example, 1545Z refers to 3:45PM.

Z

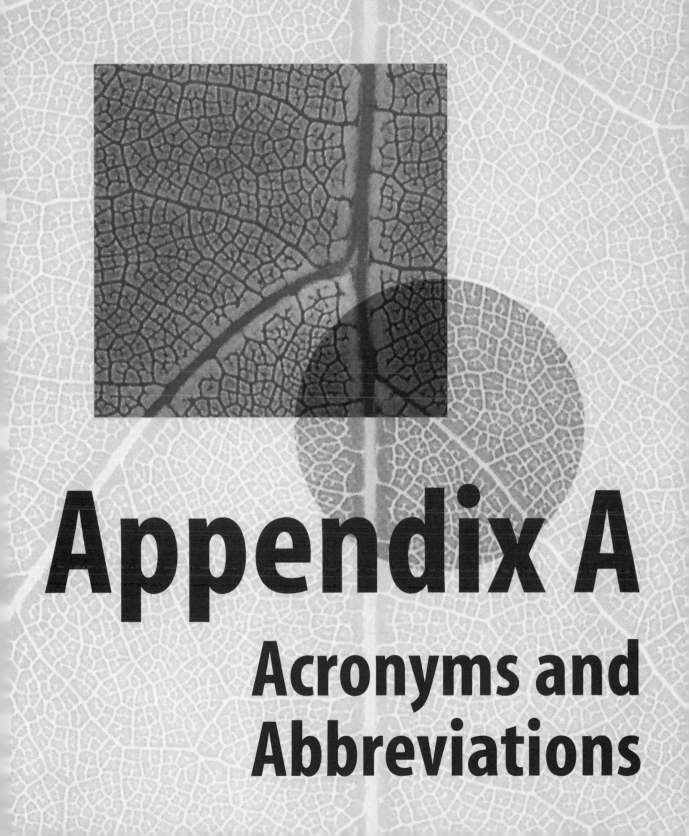

Appendix A

Acronyms and Abbreviations

Acronyms and Abbreviations

It has been said that with only a thousand different words you can express any idea in English. If this is true, then the following acronym list has enough entries to make several languages. Acronyms have become a language of their own, and they are bandied about and used just like ordinary words. Because they have become such an integral part of any discussion related to computer topics, particularly to networking, we have tried to provide a list that is as comprehensive as possible. The list has grown by several thousand entries since the first edition, and the acronym/abbreviation population grows daily. If you can't find an acronym here, try finding it at either of the following locations on the Internet:

http://www.ucc.ie/info/net/acronyms/acro.html or http://www.acronymfinder.com

16CIF	16x Common Intermediate Format	AAP	Applications Access Point
32BFA	32-bit File Access	AAP	Association of American Publishers
3DES	Triple Data Encryption Standard	AAR	Automatic Alternate Routing
3DMF	3-D Metafile	AARNet	Australian Academic Research Network
3DTF	3-D Trading Floor	AARP	AppleTalk Address Resolution Protocol
3GL	3rd Generation Language	AAT	Average Access Time
3LS	Third Layer Switching	AAU	Audio Access Unit
3M	Minnesota Mining and Manufacturing	AAUI	Apple Attachment Unit Interface
4CIF	4x Common Intermediate Format	AB	Abort Session
4GL	4th Generation Language	AB	Area Border
4WCD	4-Wire Conditioned Diphase	ABAP	Advanced Business Application Programming
A	Ampere	ABATS	Automatic Bit Access Test System
A/D	Analog/Digital	ABBET	A Broad Based Environment for Test
A3D	Aureal 3D	ABC	Atanasoff-Berry Computer
AA	Application Association	ABCD	ABC-Disney
AA	Auto Answer	ABEL	Advanced Boolean Expression Language
AAA	Autonomous Administrative Area	ABI	Application Binary Interface
AAAI	American Association for Artificial Intelligence	ABIOS	Advanced Basic Input / Output System
AAC	Autonomous Activation Condition	ABIST	Automatic Built-in Self Test
AACE	Association for the Advancement of Computing in Education	ABM	Anything but Microsoft
		ABM	Asynchronous Balanced Mode
AAI	Administration Authority Identifier	ABM	Authentication Billing Manager
AAL	ATM Adaptation Layer	ABME	Asynchronous Balanced Mode Extended
AALM	ATM Adaptation Layer Management	ABP	Alternate Bipolar
AAL-PCI	ATM Adaptation Layer Protocol Control Information	ABR	Answer Bid Ratio
AAL-SDU	ATM Adaptation Layer Service Data Unit	ABR	Area Border Router
AALx	AAL Protocol X (x=1, 2, 3, 4, or 5)	ABR	Available Bit Rate
AAM	Application Activity Model	ABS	Average Busy Season
AAP	Alternate Access Providers	ABT	Abort Timer

ABT	Answer Back Tone
AC	Accept Session
AC	Access Control
AC	Acoustic Coupler
AC	Alternating Current
AC	Application Context
AC	Association Control
AC	Audio Circuitry
AC'97	Audio Codec '97
ACA	American Cryptogram Association
ACA	Automatic Circuit Assurance
ACAP	Application Configuration Access Protocol
ACB	Access (or Application) Control Block
ACBH	Average Consistent Busy Hour
ACBS	Advanced Commercial Banking System
ACC	Audio Communication Controller
ACC	Automatic Callback Calling
ACCM	Asynchronous Character Control Map
ACCS	Automated Calling-Card Service
ACD	Adaptive Call Distributor
ACD	Automatic Call Distributor (or Distribution)
ACDF	Access Control Decision Function
ACDI	Asynchronous Communication Device Interface
ACE	Access Connection Element
ACE	Access Control Encryption (or Entry)
ACE	Adaptive Communication Environment
ACE	Advanced Computing Environment
ACE	Adverse Channel Enhancement
ACE	American Council for Education
ACE	Asynchronous Communication Element
ACEF	Access Control Enforcement Function
ACELP2	Adaptive Code Excited Linear Predictive Coding 2
ACET	Advisory Committee on Electronics and Telecommunications
ACF	Access Control Field (or File)
ACF	Advanced Communications Function
ACF/NCP	Advanced Communications Function/Network Control Program
ACF/TCAM	Advanced Communications Function/Telecommunications Access Method
ACF/VTAM	Advanced Communications Function/Virtual Telecommunications Access Method
ACF/VTAME	Advanced Communications Function/Virtual Telecommunications Access Method Entry
ACH	Automated Clearing House
ACH CCD	Automated Clearing House Cash Concentration or Disbursement
ACI	Access Control Information
ACIA	Access Control Inner Areas
ACIA	Asynchronous Communication Interface Adapter
ACID	ActiveX Control Insertion Device
ACID	Atomicity, Consistency, Isolation, and Durability
ACK	Acknowledgment
ACK0	Positive Acknowledgment
ACK1	Positive Acknowledgment
ACL	Access Control List
ACL	Advanced CMOS Logic
ACM	Address Complete Message
ACM	Advanced Computer Modeling
ACM	Association for Computing Machinery
ACM	Audio Compression Manager
ACME	Application Creation Made Easy
ACOG	Atlanta Committee for the Olympic Games
ACOL	Atlantic Canada Online
ACP	Access Control Points
ACP	Allied Communications Publication
ACP	Americans for Computer Privacy
ACP	Ancillary Control Process
ACPI	Advanced Configuration and Power (Management) Interface
ACPM	Association Control Protocol Machine
ACR	Abandon Call and Retry
ACR	Allowed Cell Rate
ACR	Attenuation to Crosstalk Ratio
ACR	Available (or Allowed) Bit Rate
ACRC	Advanced Cisco Router Configuration
ACS	Academic Computer Specialist
ACS	Access Control Store
ACS	Advanced Communications System
ACS	Asynchronous Communications Server

APP
A

ACSA	Access Control Specific Area
ACSE	Application (or Association) Control Service Element
ACSNET	Australian Computer Science Network
ACSP	Access Control Specific Point
ACT	Activity (bit)
ACT	Association for Commuter Transportation
ACT	Association for Competitive Technology
ACTAS	Alliance of Computer-Based Telephony Application Suppliers
ACTGA	Attendant Control of Trunk Group Access
ACTIUS	Association of Computer Telephone Integration Users and Suppliers
ACTLU	Activate Logical Unit
ACTPU	Activate Physical Unit
ACTS	Advanced Communication Technologies and Services
ACTS	Automated Computer Time Service
ACTS	Automatic Coin Telephone System (or Service)
ACTT	Advanced Communications Timekeeping Technology
ACU	Autocall Unit
ACU	Automatic Calling Unit
AD	Activity Discard
AD	Addendum
AD	Administrative Domain
ADA	Activity Discard Acknowledgment
ADA	Ancillary Device Adapter
ADAPSO	Association of Data Processing Service Organizations
ADAPT+	Adaptive Digital Access Protocol
ADB	Apple Desktop Bus
ADC	Advanced Data Control
ADC	Analog-to-Digital Converter
ADC	Analysis Date Concentrator
ADCCP	Advanced Data Communications Control Procedures
ADCU	Association of Data Communications Users
ADDMD	Administrative Directory Management Domain
ADF	Access Control Decision Function
ADF	Application Description File
ADI	Access Control Decision Information
ADI	Application Directory
ADIC	Advanced Digital Information Corporation

ADM	Adaptive Delta Modulation
ADM	Add/Drop Multiplexer
ADMD	Administration Management Domain
ADN	Advanced Digital Network
ADO	ActiveX Data Object
ADP	Adapter Control Block
ADP	Application Distribution Protocol
ADP	Automatic Data Processing
ADPCM	Adaptive Differential Pulse Code Modulation
ADS	Active Directory Services
ADS	Application Delivery Services
ADSI	Active Directory Services Interface
ADSI	Analog Display Services Interface
ADSL	Asymmetric (or Asymmetrical) Digital Subscriber Line
ADSP	AppleTalk Data Stream Protocol
ADT	Abstract Data Type
AE	Activity End
AE	Application Entity
AEA	Activity End Acknowledgment
AEA	American Electronics Association
AEB	Analog Expansion Bus
AEC	Adaptive Echo Cancellation
AEC	Architecture, Engineering, and Construction
AEF	Access Control Enforcement Function
AEF	Address Extension Facility
AEIMP	Apple Event Interprocess Messaging Protocol
AEP	Advanced E-mail Protector
AEP	AppleTalk Echo Protocol
AEP	Application Environment Profile
AET	Application Entity Title
AF	Address Field
AF	Alignment Field
AF	Audio Frequency
AF	Auxiliary Facility
AFC	Advanced Fibre Communications
AFC	Application Foundation Class
AFC	Automatic Frequency Control
AFI	AppleTalk Filing Interface

AFI	Authority and Format Identifier	AIP	Association of Internet Professionals
AFII	Association for Font Information Interchange	AIR	Adaptive Increase Rate
AFIPS	American Federation of Information Processing Societies	AIR	Apple Internet Router
		AIS	Action Information Services
AFM	Active Fax Messaging	AIS	Advanced Integrated Synthesis
AFNOR	Association Francaise De Normalisation	AIS	Alarm Indication Signal
AFP	Advanced Function Printing	AIS	Automatic Intercept System
AFP	AppleTalk Filing Protocol	AIS-E	Alarm Indication Signal, External
AFRP	ARCNET Fragmentation Protocol	AIT	Advanced Intelligent Tape
AFS	Andrew File System	AITT	Acadia Institute for Teaching and Technology
AFSK	Audio Frequency Shift Keying	AIU	Access Interface Unit
AFT	Application File Transfer	AIU	American Insurance Underwriters
AGBH	Average Group Busy Hour	AIX	Advanced Interactive Executive
AGC	Automatic Gain Control	AK	Acknowledge
AGP	Accelerated Graphics Port	AKA	Also Known As
AGS	Asynchronous Gateway Server	AL	Access Link
AH	Authentication Header	AL	Alignment field
AHT	Average Holding Times	AL	Application Layer
AI	Artificial Intelligence	AL	Availability Level
AI	Authentication Information	AL x	Availability Level x
AIA	Aerospace Industries Association	ALAP	ARCTalk Link Access Protocol
AIAG	Automotive Industry Action Group	ALAP	As Late As Possible
AIC	Application Interpreted Constructs	ALEC	Alternate Local Exchange Carrier
AIChE	American Institute of Chemical Engineers	ALFT	Action-Level Fault Tolerance
AID	Attention Identifier	ALI	Automatic Location Information
AIFF	Advanced Integrated File Format	ALM	AppWare Loadable Module
AIFF	Amiga Image File Format	ALO	At Least Once
AIFF	Audio Interchange (or Interface) File Format	ALP	Abstract Local Primitive
AIIM	Association for Information and Image Management	ALPS	Advanced Logistics and Procurement System
		ALR	Advanced Logic Research
AIM	Analog Intensity Modulation	ALS	Application Layer Structure
AIM	Apple, IBM, Motorola (Alliance)	ALT	Automatic Link Transfer
AIM	Application Integration Module	ALTS	Association for Local Telecommunications Services
AIM	Asset Information Manager	ALU	Application Layer User
AIM	Asynchronous Interface Module	ALU	Arithmetic Logical Unit
AIM	ATM Inverse Multiplexer	AM	Accounting Management
AIN	Advanced Intelligent Network	AM	Active Monitor
AIO	Asynchronous Input/Output	AM	Amplitude Modulation
AIOD	Automatic Identification of Outward Dialing	AM/PSK	Amplitude Modulation with Phase Shift Keying

AMA	Automatic Message Accounting		ANX	Automotive Network Exchange
AMD	Advanced Micro Devices		AO/DI	Always On / Dynamic ISDN
AME	Asynchronous Modem Eliminator		AOC	Audio Operator Console
AMF	Account Metering Function		AOCE	Apple Open Collaborative Environment
AM-FDM	Aamplitude Modulated-Frequency Division Multiplexed		AOL	America Online
AMH	Application Message Handling		AOM	Application OSI Management
AMI	Alternate Mark Inversion		AOP	Association of Online Professionals
AMII	Agile Manufacturing Information Infrastructure		AOS	Alternate (or Automated) Operator Service
AMIS	Audio Messaging Interchange Standard		AOS	Alternate Option Selection
AMM	Agent Management Module		AOS	Automated Office Systems
AMO	Aggregation Managed Object		AOSIP	Airline Open Systems Interconnection Profile
AMP	Active Monitor Present		AOW	Asia and Oceania Workshop
AMPS	Advanced Mobile Phone Service		AOWS	Asia-Oceanic Workshop
AMS	American Management Systems		AP	Administrative Point
AMS	Applications Management Specification		AP	Application Process
AMS	Audiovisual Multimedia Service		AP	Application Profile
AMT	Address Mapping Table		AP	Application Protocol
AMT	Advanced Manufacturing Technology		AP	Associative Processor
AMVFT	Amplitude Modulated Voice Frequency Telegraph		APA	Advertising Photographers of America
AM-VSB	Amplitude Modulation Vestigial Sideband		APAR	Authorized Program Analysis Report
AN	Access Network (or Node)		APB	Alpha Primary Bootstrap
ANBH	Average Network Busy Hour		APC	Adaptive Predictive Coding
ANC	Active Noise Cancellation		APC	Asynchronous Procedure Call
ANC	African National Congress		APCC	American Public Communications Council
AND	Automatic Network Dialing		APCI	Application-layer Protocol Control Information
ANDOS	All-or-Nothing Disclosure of Secrets		APCT	Advanced PC Technologies
ANF	AppleTalk Networking Forum		APCUG	Association of Personal Computer User Groups
ANI	Automatic Number Identification		APD	Avalanche Photodiode
ANM	Advanced Network Management		APDU	Application Protocol Data Unit
ANM	Answer Message		API	Application Program Interface
ANN	Auditing Network Needs		APIA	Application Program Interface Association
ANR	Active Noise Reduction		APK	Amplitude Phase Keying
ANS	Advanced Network & Services		APL	A Programming Language
ANS	American National Standard		APLI	ACSE Presentation Library Interface
ANSA	Advanced Network Systems Architecture		APLT	Advanced Private Line Termination
ANSC	American National Standards Committee		APM	Advanced Power Management
ANSI	American National Standards Institute		APNY	Advertising Photographers of New York
ANTC	Advanced Networking Test Center		APP	Application
			APP	Application Portability Profile

APPC	Advanced Program-to-Program Communications
APPC/PC	Advanced Program-to-Program Communications/Personal Computers
APPI	Advanced Program-to-Program Internetworking
APPL	Application Program
APPN	Advanced Peer-to-Peer Networking
APPN EN	Advanced Peer-to-Peer Network End Node
APPN IN	Advanced Peer-to-Peer Network Interchange Node
APPN NN	Advanced Peer-to-Peer Network Network Node
APR	Analogy Port Adapter, with Ringing
APR	Annual Percentage Rate
APS	Application Processing Services
APS	Asynchronous Protocol Specification (Alliance)
APS	Automatic Protection Switching
APSO	Audio Precision System One
APT	Application Process Title
APT	Application Programmer's Toolkit
APTS	Advanced Public Transportation
APU	Audio Presentation Unit
AQS	Advanced Queuing Systems
AR	Action Request
AR	Activity Resume
ARA	Attribute Registration Authority
ARAP	AppleTalk Remote Access Protocol
ARCV	Association for Really Cruel Viruses
ARD	Application Remote Database
ARDIS	Advanced National Radio Data Service
ARE	All Routes Explorer
ARF	Absolute Radio Frequency
ARF	Alarm Reporting Function
ARF	Automatic Reconfiguration Facility
ARFCN	Absolute Radio Frequency Channel Number
ARGO	A Really Good Open System Interconnection
ARI	Address Recognized Indicator bit
ARL	Access Rights List
ARL	Adjusted Ring Length
ARL	Attendant Release Loop
ARLL	Advanced Run-Length Limited
ARM	Application Reference Model

ARM	Asynchronous Response Mode
ARO	After Receipt of Order
ARP	Address Resolution Protocol
ARPA	Advanced Research Projects Agency
ARPANET	Advanced Research Projects Agency Network
ARQ	Automatic Repeat Request
ARR	Attributes for Representing Relationships
ARR	Automatic Repeat Request
ARS	Alternate (also, Automatic) Route Selection
ART	Asynchronous Remote Takeover
ART	Automatic Revision Tracking
ARTT	Asynchronous Remote Takeover Terminal
ARU	Audio Response Unit
AS	Activity Start
AS	Application System
AS/400	Application System/400
ASA	Adaptive Server Anywhere
ASA6	Adaptive Server Anywhere 6
ASAI	Adjunct Switch Application Interface
ASAP	As Soon As Possible
ASB	Asynchronous Balanced Mode
ASB	Autonomous System Boundary
ASBR	Autonomous System Boundary Router
ASC	Accredited Standards Committee
ASCD	Association for Supervision and Curriculum Development
ASCII	American Standard Code for Information Interchange
ASDC	Abstract Service Definition Convention
ASDU	Application-layer Service Data Unit
ASE	Adaptive Server Enterprise
ASE	Application Service Element
ASI	Adapter Support Interface
ASI	Alternate Space Inversion
ASI	Application Software Interface
ASI	Automatic Switch Interface
ASIC	Application-Specific Integrated Circuit
ASIS	American Society for Industrial Security
ASK	Amplitude Shift Keying

APP
A

ASM	Address Space Management (or Manager)
ASMO	Advanced Storage Magneto-Optical
ASMP	American Society of Media Photographers
ASN	Abstract Syntax Notation
ASN	Advance Ship Notice
ASN.1	Abstract Syntax Notation One
ASO	Application Service Object
ASP	Abstract Service Primitive
ASP	Active Server Pages
ASP	AppleTalk Session Protocol
ASP	Application Service Provider
ASP	Association of Shareware Publishers
ASPI	Advanced SCSI Programming Interface
ASQ	American Society for Quality
ASQ/SD	American Society for Quality, Software Division
ASR	Answer Seizure Ratio
ASR	Automated Service Representative
ASR	Automatic Send/Receive
ASR	Automatic Speech Recognition
AST	Asynchronous System Trap
ASTC	Advanced Simulation Technologies Conference
ASTLVL	Asynchronous System Trap Level
ASTM	American Society for Testing Materials
ASTRAL	Alliance for Strategic Token Ring Advancement and Leadership
ASUG	American SAP Users Group
ASVD	Analog Simultaneous Voice/Data
ASYNC	Asynchronous Transmission
AT	Abatement Threshold
AT	Acceptance Test
AT	Advanced Technology
AT&T	American Telephone and Telegraph
ATA	ARCnet Trade Association
ATA	AT Attachment
ATAPI	AT Attachment Packet Interface
ATAS	Analog Test Access System
ATASPI	AT Attachment Software Programming Interface
ATB	All Trunks Busy
ATC	Authorized Training Center

ATD	Association of Telecommunications Dealers
ATD	Asynchronous Time Division
ATDM	Asynchronous Time Division Multiplexing
ATDP	Attention Dial Pulse
ATDT	Attention Dial Tone
ATE	Asynchronous Terminal Emulation
ATEC	Authorized Training Education Center
ATIS	Advanced Traveler Information Systems
ATIS	Alliance for Telecommunications Industry Solutions
ATL	Active Template Library
ATM	Abstract Test Method
ATM	Asynchronous Transfer Mode
ATM	Automatic Teller Machine
ATM CSU/DSU	ATM Channel Service Unit / Data Service Unit
ATMARP	Asynchronous Transfer Mode Address Resolution Protocol
ATME	Automatic Transmission Measuring Equipment
ATMMIB	ATM Management Information Base
ATM-SAP	ATM Service Access Point
ATM-SDU	Asynchronous Transfer Mode Service Data Unit
ATMVCC	Asynchronous Transfer Mode Virtual Channel Connection
ATP	Advanced Technology Program
ATP	AppleTalk Transaction Protocol
ATP	Application Transaction Processing
ATP	Application Transfer Program
ATPS	AppleTalk Print Services
ATQ	AppleTalk Transition Queue
ATR	Advanced Telecommunications Research
ATRP	Agricultural Technology Research Program
ATS	Abstract Test Suite
ATT	Applied Transmission Technologies
ATTIS	AT&T Information Systems
ATU	ADSL Termination Unit
ATU-C	ADSL-3 Terminal Unit At CO
ATU-R	ADSL-3 Terminal Unit At Remote Site
ATV	Automatic Transfer Vehicle
ATX	ATM Turbo Exchange
AU	Access (or Adaptive) Unit

AU	Administrative Unit	BBC	Broadband Bearer Capability
AUC	Authentication Center (or Certificate)	BBH	Bouncing Busy Hour
AUG	Administrative Unit Group	BBS	Bulletin Board System
AUI	Attachment (also, Auxiliary) Unit Interface	BC	Begin Chain
AU-i	Administrative Unit-i	BC	Blind Copy
AUP	Acceptable Use Policy	BC	Block Check
AURP	AppleTalk Update Routing Protocol	BCC	Basic Concurrency Constraint
AUTODIN	Automatic Digital Network	BCC	Bellcore Client Company
AUU	ATM User-to-User (flag)	Bcc	Blind Carbon (also, Courtesy) Copy
AV	Audio-Visual	BCC	Block Check Character
AVA	Attribute Value Assertion	BCD	Binary Coded Decimal
AVCS	Advanced Vehicle Control Systems	BCD	Blocked Calls Delayed
AVD	Alternative Voice/Data	BCDBS	Broadband Connectionless Data Bearer Service
AVI	Audio Visual Interleaved	BCECA	British Chemical Engineering Contractors Association
AVN	Automated Voice Network		
AVS	Advanced Vector Synthesis	BCER	Business Coalition for Education Reform
AVS	APPC/VM VTAM Support	BCH	Blocked Calls Held
AVT	Application Virtual Terminal	BCH	Bose-Chadhuri-Hocquenghem
AVT	Applied Voice Technology	BCM	Basic Call Model
AW	Administrative Weight	BCN	Backbone Concentrator Node
AWACS	Airborne Warning and Control System	BCN	Backward Congestion Notification
AWC	Association for Women in Computing	BCN	Beacon
AWG	American Wire Gauge	BCNU	Be Seeing You
AWT	Abstract Window(ing) Toolkit	BCOB	Broadband Class of Bearer
B	Busy	BCP	Broadband Communications Products
B2B	Business to Business	BCP	Bulk Copy Program
B8ZS	Bipolar with 8 Zero Substitution	BCP	Business Communications Project
BAC	Basic Access Control	BCP	Byte-Control Protocols
BACC	Billing and Customer Care	BCR	Blocked Calls Released
BACM	Basic Access Control Model	BCS	Basic Combined Subset
BAIS	Bell Atlantic Internet Solutions	BCS	Business Communications Systems
BAPI	Bridge Application Program Interface	BCVT	Basic Class Virtual Terminal
BAS	Basic Activity Subset	BCW	Burst Code-Word
BAS	Bit-rate Allocation Signal	BDE	Borland Database Engine
BASIC	Beginners All-Purpose Symbolic Instruction Code	BDK	Bean Development Kit
BASize	Buffer Allocation Size	BDLC	Burroughs Data Link Control
BAUD	Bits At Unit Density	BDN	Bell Data Network
BB	Begin Bracket	BDR	Backup Designated Router
BB&N	Bolt, Beranek & Newman	BDS	Building Distribution System

APP
A

BDT	Bureau of Telecommunications Development
BEC	Backward Error Correction
BECN	Backward Explicit Congestion Notification
BEITA	Business Equipment and Information Technology Association
Bellcore	Bell Communications Research
BEM	Bug-Eyed Monster
BER	Basic Encoding Rules
BER	Bit Error Rate (or Ratio)
BER	Box Event Records
BERT	Bit Error Rate Tester
BETag	Beginning-End Tag
BF	Boundary (or Bridge) Function
BF	Framing Bit
BFOC	Bayonet Fiber Optic Connector
BFR	Big Fast Router
BFT	Binary File Transfer
BFt	Terminal Framing Bit
BGP	Border Gateway Protocol
BGT	Broadcast and Group Translators
BHCA	Busy Hour Call Attempts
BIA	Burned-In Address
BIAS	Burroughs Integrated Adaptive System
BIB	Bus Interface Board
B-ICI	B-ISDN Intercarrier Interface
B-ICI	Broadband Inter-Carrier Interface
BICI SAAL	Broadband Inter-Carrier Interface Signaling ATM Adaptation Layer
BICMOS	Bipolar Complementary Metal-Oxide Semiconductor
BICSI	Building Industry Construction Standards Institute
BIH	Bureau International De L'Heure (International Time Bureau)
BIM	Business and Information Modeling (Task Group)
BIMOS	Bipolar Metal-Oxide Semiconductor
BIND	Berkeley Internet Name Domain
BIOS	Basic Input/Output System
BIP	Bit Interleave Parity
BIPS	Billion Instructions Per Second
BIP-x	Bit Interleaved Parity-X

BIS	Bracket Initiation Stopped
BIS	Business Intelligence Systems
BISDN	Broadband Integrated Services Digital Network
B-ISDN	Broadband Integrated Services Digital Network
B-ISDN PRM	B-ISDN Protocol Reference Model
B-ISPBX	B-ISDN Private Branch Exchange
BISSI	Broadband Inter-Switching System Interface
B-ISUP	Broadband ISDN User's Part
Bisync	Binary Synchronous Control
BISYNC	Bisynchronous (or Binary Synchronous) Communications
BIT	Basic Interconnection Test
BIT	Binary Digit
BITNET	Because It's Time Network
BIU	Basic Information Unit
BIU	Bus Interface Unit
BKERT	Block Error Rate Tester
BLAST	Bell Labs Layered Space-Time
BLAST	Blocked Asynchronous/Synchronous Transmission
BLER	Block Error Rate (or Ratio)
BLERT	Block Error Rate Tester
BLF	Busy Lamp Field
B-LLI	Broadband Lower Layer Information
BLNT	Broadband Local Network Technology
BLOB	Binary Large Object
BLSR	Bidirectional Line Switched Ring
BLU	Basic Link Unit
BMA	Broadcast Multiple Access
BMAF	Bellcore automatic Message Accounting Format
BMOS	Bytex Matrix Operating System
BMP	Bitmap
BMS	Banyan Mail Services
BMS	Basic Mapping Support
BMU	Basic Measurement Unit
BN	Backward Notification
BN	Boundary Node
BN	Bridge Number
BNA	Burroughs Network Architecture
BNC	Bayonet Nut (also, Navy) Connector

BNC	Bayonet-Neill-Concelnan		BRMTP	Batch Simple Message Transfer Protocol
BNF	Backus-Naur Form		BRP	Business Recovery Plan
BNN	Boundary Network Node		BRS	Big Red Switch
BNT	Broadband Network Termination		BS	Back Space
B-NT1	B-ISDN Network Termination 1		BS	Base Station
B-NT2	B-ISDN Network Termination 2		BSA	Basic Service Arrangement
BOA	Basic Object Adapter		BSC	Base Station Controller
BOC	Bell Operating Company		BSC	Binary Synchronous (or Bisync) Communication
BOC	Bureau of the Census		BSC	Binary Synchronous Control
BOF	Birds Of a Feather		BSD	Berkeley Software Distribution
BOI	Basic Operators Interface		BSDL	Boundary Scan Description Language
BOM	Beginning of Message		BSE	Basic Service Element
BOM	Bill of Materials		BSHR	Bidirectional Self-Healing Ring
BONDING	Bandwidth on Demand Interoperability Group		BSI	British Standards Institute
BONM	Business-Oriented Network Management		BSN	Broadband Service Node
BONT	Broadband Optical Network Termination		BSR	Board of Standards Review
BOOTP	Bootstrap Protocol		BSRF	Basic System Reference Frequency
BOP	Bit-Oriented Protocol		BSS	Basic Synchronized Subset
BOPS	Billion Operations Per Second		BSS	Broadband Switching System
BOT	Beginning of Tape (or Text or Transmission)		BSVC	Broadcast Switched Virtual Connection
BOTI	Business On The Internet		BT	British Telecom
BPB	BIOS Parameter Block		BT	Bulk Transfer (Service Class)
BPB FAT	BIOS Parameter Block File Allocation Table		BT	Burst Tolerance
BPDU	Bridge Protocol Data Unit		BTA	Basic Trading Area
BPF	Band-Pass Filter		BTA	Business Technology Association
BPI	Bits per Inch		B-TA	B-ISDN Terminal Adapter
BPL	Break Point Location		BTAG	Begin Tag
BPNRZ	Bipolar Non-Return-to-Zero		Btag	Beginning tag
BPP	Bridge Port Pair		BIAM	Basic Telecommunications Access Method
BPR	Business Process Reengineering (or Redesign)		BTE	Broadband Terminal Equipment
BPRZ	Bipolar Return-to-Zero		B-TE1	B-ISDN Terminal Equipment 1
bps	Bits Per Second		B-TE2	B-ISDN Terminal Equipment 2
Bps	Bytes Per Second		BTL	Backplane Transceiver Logic
BPSK	Binary Phase Shift Keying		BTL	Bipolar-Transistor Logic
BPSS	Bell Packet Switching System		BTM	Bulk Transfer and Manipulation (service Class)
BPV	Bipolar Violation		BTR	Bit Transfer Rate
BRA	Basic Rate Access		BTS	Base Transceiver Station
BRB	Be Right Back		BTU	Basic Transmission Unit
BRI	Basic Rate Interface		BTV	Business Television

APP
A

BTW	by the Way		CalREN	California Research and Education Network
BUAF	Big Ugly ASCII Font		CALS	Computer-Aided Acquisition and Logistic Support
BUAG	Big Ugly ASCII Graphic		CAM	Channel (or Common) Access Method
BUGS	Bad, Ugly, Good, or Splendid		CAM	Computer Association of Manufacturers
BUS	Broadcast and Unknown Server		CAM	Computer-Assisted (or Aided) Manufacturing
BVT	Build Verify Test		CAM	Content-Addressable Memory
BW	Bacteriological Warfare		CAMA	Centralized Automatic Message Accounting
BW	Bandwidth		CAMC	Customer Access Maintenance Center
BW	Business (Information) Warehouse		CAMIS	Countywide Acquisition Management Information System
C	Container			
C/AIM	Center for Advanced Instructional Media		CAMP	Corporate Association for Microcomputer Professionals
C/SCC	Computer/Standards Coordinating Committee (IEEE Computer Society)		CAN	Campus-Area Network
CA	Cell Arrival		CAN	Central Administration and Naming
CA	Cellular Automata		CAP	Carrierless Amplitude/Phase
CA	Certificate (or Certification) Authority		CAP	Competitive Access Provider
CA	Channel Adapters (or Attachment)		CAP	Computer-Aided Publishing
CA	Computer Appliance		CAP	Customer Administration Panel
CAB	Cabinet		CAPI	Cryptography Applications Programming Interface
CAC	Call Administration Control		CARL	Colorado Alliance of Research Libraries
CAC	Canadian Advisory Committee		CARO	Computer Antivirus Research Organization
CAC	Carrier Access Code		CARP	Cache Array Routing Protocol
CAC	Connection Admission Control		CAS	Centralized Attendant System (or Service)
CACS	Customer Administration Communication System		CAS	Communicating Application Specification
CAD	Computer Access Device		CASE	Common Application Service Element
CAD	Computer-Aided Design		CASE	Computer-Assisted Software Engineering
CAD/CAM	Computer-Aided Design/Computer-Aided Manufacturing		CAST	China Association for Science and Technology
CADD	Computer-Assisted (or Aided) Design and Drafting		CAT	Common Authentication Technology
CAD-FEM	Computer-Assisted (or Aided) Design Finite Element Modeling		CAT	Core Architecture Team
			CATV	Cable Television
CAE	Common Application Environment		CATV	Community Antenna Television
CAE	Computer-Assisted (or Aided) Engineering		CAU	Controlled Access Unit
CAF	Channel Auxiliary Facility		CAU/LAM	Controlled Access Unit/Lobe Attachment Module
CAFM	Computer-Aided Facility Management		CAV	Constant Angular Velocity
CAH	Certificate Authority Hierarchy		CAV-ID	Computer-Aided Victim Identification
CAI	Common Air Interface		CAVT	Computer-Assisted Virtual Testing
CAI	Computer-Aided Instruction		CB	Citizens Band
CALC	Customer Access Line Charge		CB	Conference Bridge
CALEA	Communications Assistance for Law Enforcement Act		CBC	Certified Business Credential

CBC	Cipher Block Chaining
CBCPD	Cipher Block Chaining of Plaintext Difference
CBDS	Connectionless Broadband Data Service
CBE	Certified Banyan Engineer
CBEMA	Computer and Business Equipment Manufacturers' Association
CBF	Computer-Based Fax
CBI	Certified Banyan Instructor
CBIA	Cost-Benefit Impact Analysis
CBMS	Computer-Based Messaging System
CBO	Continuous Bitstream-Oriented
CBQ	Class-Based Queuing
CBR	Constant (or Continuous) Bit Rate
CBS	Certified Banyan Specialist
CBS	Complete Business Solutions
CBT	Computer-Based Training
CBT	Core-Based Tree
CBW	Crypt Breaker's Workbench
CBX	Central Branch Exchange
CBX	Computerized Branch Exchange
CC	Carbon (or Courtesy) Copy
CC	Chain Command
CC	Clearing Center
CC	Cluster Controller
CC	Connection Confirm
CC	Continuity Cell
CC	Country Code
CCA	Conceptual (or Common) Communication Area
CCAF	Call Control Access (or Agent) Function
CCB	Channel (or Connection) Control Block
CCC	Clear Channel Capability
CCD	Cash Concentration and Disbursement
CCDN	Corporate Consolidated Data Network
CCDP	Cisco Certified Data Professional
CCE	Collaborative Computing Environment
CCEP	Commercial COMSEC Endorsement Program
CCF	China Computer Federation
CCF	Connection (or Call) Control Function
CCH	Control Channel

CCH	Harmonization Coordination Committee
CCH/SP	CCH Permanent Secretariat
CCI	Carrier-to-Carrier Interface
CCI	Client Communication Interface
CCIA	Computer and Communication Industry Association
CCIE	Cisco Certified Internetwork Expert
CCIR	Comité Consultatif Internationale De Radiocommunications (International Consultative Committee for Radio Communications)
CCIRN	Coordinating Council on International Research Networks
CCIS	Common Channel Interoffice Signaling
CCITT	Consultative Committee for International Telegraphy and Telephony
CCL	Connection Control Language
CCM	Check Cashing Machine
CCN	Community Care Network
CCNA	Cisco Certified Network Associate
CCNP	Cisco Certified Network Professional
CCO	Context Control Object
CCPS	Consultative Council for Postal Studies
CCR	Commitment, Concurrency, and Recovery
CCR	Current Cell Rate
CCR	Customer Controlled Reconfiguration
CCRSE	Commitment, Concurrency, and Recovery Service Element
CCS	Centum (hundreds) Call Seconds
CCS	Common Channel Signal (or Signaling)
CCS	Common Communications Support
CCS	Console Communication Service
CCS	Continuous Composite Servo
CCS7	Common Channel Signaling 7
CCSA	Common Control Switching Arrangement
CCSS7	Common Channel Signaling System 7
CCSSO	Council of Chief State School Officers
CCT	CNMA Conformance Testing
CCTA	Central Computer and Telecommunications Agency
CCTV	Closed-Circuit TV
CCU	Central (or Communications) Control Unit
CCW	Channel Command Word

APP
A

CD	Capability Data	CDS	Central Directory Server
CD	Carrier Detect	CDS	Conceptual Data Store
CD	Chain Data	CDS	Current Directory Structure
CD	Change Directory	CDSA	Common Data Security Architecture
CD	Collision Detection	CDT	Cambridge Display Technology
CD	Committee Draft	CDT	Cell Delay Tolerance
CD	Compact Disc	CDT	Center for Democracy and Technology
CD	Current Data	CDV	Cell Delay Variation
CD+G	Compact Disc Plus Graphics	CDVT	Cell Delay Variation Tolerance
CDA	Capability Data Acknowledgment	CD-WO	Compact Disc, Write Once
CDC	Control Data Corporation	CE	Classic Edition
CDCCP	Control Data Communications Control Procedure	CE	Communications Entity
CDCD	Cambridge Distributed Computing System	CE	Connection Element
CD-DA	Compact Disc, Digital Audio	CEBI	Conditional End Bracket Indicator
CDDI	Copper Distributed Data Interface	CEC	Commission of European Communities
CDE	Common Desktop Environment	CEI	Cable & Electrical Interface
CD-E	Compact Disc Erasable	CEI	Comparably Efficient Interconnection
CDF	Channel Definition Format	CEI	Connection Endpoint Identifier
CDF	Configuration Data Flow	CELI	Computer-Enhanced Learning Initiative
CDFS	Compact Disc (or CD-ROM) File System	CELP	Code Excited Linear Predictive Coding
CDI	Change Direction Indicator	CEN	Comité Européen De Normalisation (European Committee for Standardization)
CDI	Custom Device Interface		
CD-I	Compact Disc Interactive	CENELEC	Comité Européen De Normalisation Électrique (European Committee for Electrical Standardization)
CDM	Custom Device Module		
CDMA	Code Division Multiple Access		
CDO	Community Dial Office	CENTREX	Central Exchange
CDPD	Cellular Digital Packet Data	CENTS	Customer Events System
CDR	Call Detail Recording	CEO	Chief Executive Officer
CD-R	Compact Disc Recordable	CEP	Certificate Enrollment Protocol
CDRAM	Cached Dynamic Random Access Memory	CEP	Connection Endpoint
CDRFS	Compact Disc Recordable File System	CEPI	Connection Endpoint Identifier
CDRH	Center for Devices and Radiological Health	CEPT	Comite Europeen Des Administrations Des Postes Et Des Telecommunications (European Committee for the Administration of Post and Telecommunications)
CDRM	Cross-Domain Resource Manager		
CD-ROM	Compact Disk-Read Only Memory		
CD-ROM XA	Compact Disc-Read Only Memory, Extended Architecture		
		CEQ	Customer Equipment
CDRSC	Cross-Domain Resource	CER	Canonical Encoding Rule
CD-RTOS	Compact Disc Real-Time Operating System	CER	Cell Error Rate (or Ratio)
CD-RW	Compact Disc Rewritable	CERT	Computer Emergency Response Team
		CES	Circuit Emulation Service
		CET	Computer-Enhanced Telephony
		CF	Control Function

CF	Conversion Facility
CF-2	Compact Flash 2
CFAC	Call Forwarding All Calls
CFB	Cipher Feedback
CFGR	Configuration
CFO	Chief Financial Officer
CFP	Computer Freedom and Privacy
CFV	Call for Votes
CGA	Color Graphics Adapter
CGI	Common Gateway Interface
CGI	Computer Graphics Interface
CGM	Computer Graphics Metafile
CGMIF	Computer Graphics Metafile Interchange Format
CGPM	General Conference on Weights and Measures
CGSA	Cellular Geographic Serving Area
CH	Correspondent Host
CHAP	Challenge Handshake Authentication Protocol
CHI	Computer-Human Interaction
CHILL	CCITT High-Level Language
CHPID	Channel Path Identifier
CHRP	Common Hardware Reference Platform
CHT	Call Holding Time
CI	Certified Instructor
CI	Component Integration
CI	Computer Interconnect
CI	Congestion Indicator (or Indication)
CI	Connect Indication
CI	Control In
CI	Copy Inhibit
C-i	Container-I
CIAC	Computer Incident Advisory Capability
CIB	CRC-32 Indicator Bit
CIBC	Canadian Imperial Bank of Commerce
CICS	Customer Information Control System (also, Communication Subsystem)
CICSPARS	CICS Performance Analysis Reporting System
CID	Command (or Connection) Identifier
CIDR	Classless Interdomain Routing
CIE	Commercial Internet Exchange

CIE	Commission Internationale De L'Eclairage
CIE	Customer-Initiated Entry
CIF	Cell Information Field
CIF	Common Intermediate Format
CIGOS	Canadian Interest Group on Open Systems
CIJE	Current Index to Journals in Education
CILab	Components Integration Laboratories
CIM	Common Information Model
CIM	CompuServe Information Manager
CIM	Computer-Integrated Manufacturing
CIMAP	Circuit Installation Maintenance Access Package
CIME	Customer Installation Maintenance Entities
CIMITI	Center for Information Management and Information Technology Innovation
CIO	Chief Information Officer
CIP	Carrier Identification Parameter
CIPX	Compressed IPX (Protocol)
CIR	Committed Information Rate
CIR	Communications Industry Researchers
CIRC	Cross-Interleaved Reed-Solomon Code
CIS	CompuServe Information Services
CIS	Customer Information System
CIS	Customer Interaction Software
CISC	Complex Instruction Set Computer
CITEC	Center for Information Technology & Communications
CIU	Communications Interface Unit
CIUG	California ISDN Users' Group
CIWA	Certified Internet Webmaster Administrator
CIX	Commercial Internet Exchange
CL	Connectionless
CLA	Central Legitimization Agency
CLASS	Cooperative Library Agency for Systems and Services
CLASS	Custom Local-Area Signaling (or Switching) Services
CLAW	Common Link Access to Workstation
CLB	Common Logic Board
CLEC	Competitive Local Exchange Carrier
CLI	Call-Level Interface
CLI	Command Line Interface

CLI	Connectionless Internetworking	CMIP	Common Management Information (also, Interface) Protocol
CLIB	C Library	CMIPDU	Common Management Information Protocol Data Unit
CLID	Calling Line Identification	CMIPM	Common Management Information Protocol Machine
CLIP	Calling Line Identification Presentation		
CLIR	Calling Line Identification Restriction	CMIS	Common Management Information (also, Interface) Service
CLIST	Command List		
CLLM	Consolidated Link-Layer Management	CMISE	Common Management Information Service Element
CLM	Career Limiting Move	CML	Chemical Markup Language
CLNAP	Connectionless Network Access Protocol	CML	Current-Mode Logic
CLNP	Connectionless Network Protocol	CMM	Capability (also Compatibility) Maturity Model
CLNS	Connectionless-Mode Network Service	CMOL	CMIP Over Logical Link Control
CLP	Cell Loss Priority	CMOS	Complementary Metal-Oxide Semiconductor
CLR	Cell Loss Ratio	CMOT	Common Management Information Services and Protocol Over TCP/IP
CLS	Clear Screen		
CLS	Connectionless Service	CMR	Cell Misinsertion Rate
CLSDST	Close Destination	CMS	Color Management System
CLSF	Connectionless Service Functions	CMS	Conversational Monitor System
CL-TK	Claim Token	CMT	Connection Management
CLTP	Connectionless Transport Protocol	CMYK	Cyan, Magenta, Yellow, Black
CLTS	Connectionless Transport Service	CN	Common Name
CLU	Command Line Utility	CN	Common Node
CLU	Control Logical Unit	CN	Community Network
CLV	Constant Linear Velocity	CN	Connect
Cm	Centimeter	CN	Copy Network
CM	Configuration Management	CN	Country Name
CM	Connection Machine	CN	Customer Network
CM/2	Communications Manager for OS/2	CNA	Certified NetWare Administrator
CMA	Communication Managers Association	CNC	Concentrator
CMC	Common Mail (or Messaging) Calls	CNCP	Canadian National-Canadian Pacific
CMC	Common Mezzanine Card	CNE	Certified NetWare Engineer
CMC	Communication Management Cupcake	CNEPA	CNE Professional Association
CMC	Computer-Mediated Communication	CNET	Centre National dÉtudes Des Telecommunications (National Center for the Study of Telecommunications)
CMC	Connection Management Computer		
CMD	Charge-Modulation Device	CNI	Certified NetWare Instructor
CME	Center for Media Education	CNI	Coalition for Networked Information
CME	Circuit Multiplication Equipment	CNIDR	Clearinghouse for Networked Information Discovery and Retrieval
CME	Component Management Entity		
CMI	Coded Mark Inversion	CNM	Communication (or Customer)Network Management

CNMA	Communications Network for Manufacturing Applications
CNMI	Communication Network Management Interface
CNMS	Compaq Network Management Software
CNN	Composite Network Node
CNOS	Computer Network Operating System
CNRI	Corporation for National Research Initiatives
CNRS	Centre Nationale De Recherche Scientifique (National Center for Scientific Research)
CNS	Cisco Networking Services
CNS	Complementary Network Services
CNS/AD	Cisco Networking Services / Active Directory
CNT	Communications Name Table
CO	Central Office
CO	Connection Oriented
CO	Customer Owned
CoA	(RARE) Council of Administration
COA	Care-of-agent
COAX	Coaxial Cable
COB	Central Office Building
COBOL	Common Business-Oriented Language
COC	Central Office Connections
COCF	Connection-Oriented Convergence Function
COCOM	Coordinating Committee for Multilateral Export Control
COCOT	Customer-Owned Coin-Operated Telephone
COD	Connection-Oriented Data
CODASYL	Computer Data Systems Language
CODASYL-DBTG	Computer Data Systems Language-Data Base Task Group
CODEC	Coder/Decoder
CODLS	Connection-Mode Data Link Service
COH	Connection Overhead
COI	Connection-Oriented Internetworking
COIN	Columbia Online Information Network
COLD	Computer Output to Laser Disc
COLP	Connected Line Identification Presentation
COLR	Connected Line Identification Restriction
COLT	Connection Optimized Link Technology
COM	Common (or Component) Object Model
COM	Computer Output Microfilm
COM	Continuation of Message
COMBS	Customer-Oriented Message Buffer System
COMPU-SEC	Computer Security
COMSEC	Communications Security
COMSPEC	Command Specifier
COMTI	Component Object Model Transaction Integrator
CON	Concentrator
CONCERT	Communications for North Carolina Education, Research, and Technology
CONF	Confirm
CONS	Connection Oriented Network Service
COO	Chief Operations Officer
COOTS	Conference on Object Oriented Technologies and Systems
COPP	Connection-Oriented Presentation Protocol
COPS	Computer Oracle and Password System
COPS	Connection-Oriented Presentation Service
COR	Confirmation of Receipt
CORA	Canadian OSI Registration Authority
CORBA	Common Object Request Broker Architecture
CORE	Council of Registrars
COS	Call Originate Status
COS	Class of Service
COS	Corporation for Open Systems
COSAC	Canadian Open Systems Applications Criteria
COSE	Common Open Software Environment
COSE	Common Operating System Environment
COSINE	Cooperation for Open Systems Interconnection Networking-Europe
COSM	Class of Service Manager
COSMOS	Computer System for Mainframe Operations
COSN	Consortium for School Networking
CoSQ	Cost of Software Quality
COSS	Connection-Oriented Session Service
COSSS	Committee on Open Systems Support Services
COT	Central Office Trunks
COTF	Classroom of the Future
COTP	Connection-Oriented Transport Protocol
COTS	Commercial Off-the-Shelf (Software)

APP
A

COTS	Connection-Oriented Transport Service
COV	Carrier Over Voice
COW	Character-Oriented Windows
CP	Circularly Polarized
CP	Common Part
CP	Connect Presentation
CP	Connection Processor
CP	Control Point (or Program)
CP	Customer Premises
CPA	Connect Presentation Accept
CPAAL5	Common Part of ATM Adaptation Layer- 5
CPAN	Comprehensive Perl Archive Network
CPC	Certified Professional Credential
CPC	Cheap Personal Computer
CPC	Cost-per-Click
CPCB	Control Program (or Point) Control Block
CPCI	Compact Peripheral Component Interface
CPCS	Common Part Convergence Sublayer
CPCS-SDU	Common Part Convergence Sublayer Service Data Unit
CPCS-UU	Common Part Convergence Sublayer User-to-User Indication
CPD	Computer Privacy Digest
CPE	Convergence Protocol Entity
CPE	Customer Premises Equipment
CPF	Call Processing Facility
CPF	Control Program Facility
CPFM	Continuous Phase Frequency Modulation
CPH	Characters Per Hour
CPI	Common Part Indicator
CPI	Common Programming Interface
CPI	Computer to PABX (Private Automatic Branch Exchange) Interface
CPI	Computer-to-PBX (Private Branch Exchange) Interface
CPIC	Common Programming Interface for Communications
CPI-C	Common Programming Interface for Communications
CPI-C	Common Programming Interface with C Language

CPIW	Customer-Provided Inside Wiring
CPL	Call-Processing Logic
C-plane	Control plane
CPM	Cost-Per-Minute
CPM	Cost-per-Thousand
CPMS	Control Point Management Services
CPMU	COSINE Project Management Unit
CPN	Calling Party Number
CPN	Customer Premises Network (or Node)
CPODA	Contention Priority-Oriented Demand Assignment
CPP	Certified Perfect Partners
CPR	Connect Presentation Reject
CPS	Cash Paymaster Services
CPS	Characters (or Cycles) Per Second
CPSR	Computer Professionals for Social Responsibility
CPU	Central Processing Unit
CPUC	California Public Utilities Commission
CQE	Certified Quality Engineer
CR	Carriage Return
CR	Command Response
CR	Connect Request
CRC	Cyclic Redundancy Check
CRCG	Common Routing Connection Group
CREN	Corporation for Research and Educational Networking
CRF	Cable Retransmission Facility
CRF	Communication-Related (also, Connection-Related) Function
CRF(VC)	Virtual Channel Connection-Related Function
CRF(VP)	Virtual Path Connection-Related Function
CRL	Certificate Revocation List
CRLF	Carriage Return, Line Feed
CRM	Cell Rate Margin
CRM	Customer Relationship Management
CRQ	Call Request
CRS	Cell Relay Service
CRS	Configuration Report Server
CRSO	Cellular Radio Switching Office
CRT	Cathode Ray Tube

CRV	Call Reference Value	CS-MUX	Circuit-Switching Multiplexer
CS	Carrier Selection	CSN	Carrier Service Node
CS	Check Sequence	CSN	Colorado Supernet
CS	Circuit Switching	CSNET	Computer Science Network
CS	Configuration Services	CSNW	Client Services for NetWare
CS	Console	CSO	Central Services Organization
CS	Convergence Sublayer	CSO	Central Switching Office
CS	Coordinated Single-Layer	CSO	Composite Second Order
CS1	Capability Set 1	CSO	Computing Services Office
CS2	Capability Set 2	CSP	Commerce Solution Provider
CSA	Canadian Standards Association	CSP	Communications Scanner Processor
CSA	Carrier (also, Common) Service Area	CSPDN	Circuit-Switched Public Data Network
CSA	Common Storage Area	CS-PDU	Convergence Sublayer Protocol Data Unit
CSB	Computer Simulation in Business	CSPP	Computer Systems Policy Project
CSC	Computer Sciences Corporation	CSPRSG	Cryptographically Secure Pseudo-Random Sequence Generator
CSC	Customer Service Consortium		
CSCW	Computer-Supported Cooperative Work	CSPS	Constrained System Parameter Stream
CSDC	Circuit-Switched Digital Capability	CSQA	Certified Software Quality Analyst
CSDN	Circuit Switched Data Network	CSR	Cell Missequenced Ratio
CSE	(Wordperfect) Certified System Engineer	CSR	Centrex Station Rearrangement
CSE	Coordinated Single-Layer Embedded	CSR	Customer Service Record
CSELT	Centro Studi E Laborateri Telecommunicazioni (Telecommunications Study Center and Laboratory)	CSR	Customer Service Representative
		CSRSS	Client Server Runtime Subsystem
CSF	Cell Switch Fabric	CSS	Conceptual Signaling and Status
CSF	Critical Success Factor	CSS	Control Signaling and Status (Store)
CSFS	Cable Signal Fault Signature	CSS	Controlled Slip Second
CSI	Convergence Sublayer Indication	CSSFE	Controlled Slip Second, Far End
CSIS	Center for Strategic and International Studies	CSTA	Computer-Supported Telephony (also, Telecommunications) Application
CSL	Call Support Layer		
CSL	Computer Systems Laboratory	CSTB	Computer Science and Telecommunications Board
CSLIP	Compressed Serial Line Interface Protocol	CSTC	Computer Security Technology Center
CSMA	Carrier Sense Multiple Access	CSTE	Certified Software Test Engineer
CSMA/CA	Carrier Sense Multiple Access/Collision Avoidance	CSTO	Computer Systems Technology Office
CSMA/CD	Carrier Sense Multiple Access/Collision Detection	CSU	Central Switching Unit
CSMA/CP	Carrier Sense Multiple Access/Collision Prevention	CSU	Channel Service Unit
CSMA/CR	Carrier Sense Multiple Access with Collision Resolution	CSU/DSU	Channel Service Unit/Data Service Unit
		CSV	Comma-Separated Variable
CSMC	Communications Services Management Council	CSW	Client Services Workstation
CS-MUX	Carrier-Switched Multiplexer	CT	Collection Time

APP
A

CT	Computer Telephony
CT	Cordless Telephone
CTAK	Cipher Text Auto Key
CTB	Communications Toolbox
CTB	Composite Triple Beat
CTC	Channel-to-Channel
CTCA	Channel-to-Channel Adapter
CTCP	Communication and Transport Control Program
CTD	Cell Transfer Delay
CTD	Cumulative Transit Delay
CTD	Cumulative Trauma Disorder
CTE	Computer Telephony Engineer
CTERM	Command Terminal Protocol
CTERM	Communications Terminal (protocol)
CTF	Central Tabulating Facility
CTG	Clock Tone Generator
CTI	Computer-Telephony Integration
CTIP	Commission on Computing, Telecommunications, and Information Policies
CTL	Control
CTNE	Compañia Telefónica Nacional De España (National Telephone Company of Spain)
CTO	Chief Technical (or Technology) Officer
CTP	Cambridge Technology Partners
CTRG	Collaboration Technology Research Group
CTS	Carpal Tunnel Syndrome
CTS	Clear to Send
CTS	Common Transport Semantics
CTS	Communications Technology Satellite
CTS	Conformance Testing Service
CTS-LAN	Conformance Testing Service Local Area Network
CTSM	Conformance Test System Manual
CTS-WAN	Conformance Testing System for Wide Area Networks
CTTC	Coax to the Curb
CTTH	Coax to the Home
CTV	Cell Tolerance Variation
CTX	Corporate Trade Exchange
CU	See You
CUA	Channel Unit Address

CUA	Common User Access
CUCRIT	Capital Utilization Criterion
CUG	Cluster (also, Closed) User Group
CUI	Common User Interface
CUL	See You Later
CUT	Control Unit Terminal
CV	Code Violation
CVCP	Code Violation, CP-Bit Parity
CVCRC	Code Violation, Cyclical Redundancy Check
CVFE	Code Violation, Far End
CVO	Commercial Vehicle Operation
CVP	Code Violation, "P" Bit
CVRAM	Cached Video Random Access Memory
CVS	Caller Verification System
CVSD	Continuous Variable Slope Delta Modulation
CVT	Communications Vector Table
CVTC	Conversational Voice Technologies Corporation
CW	Call Waiting
CWARC	Canadian Workplace Automation Research Center
CWI	Centrum Voor Wiskunde En Informatica (Center for Mathematics and Informatics)
CWIS	Campus Wide Information System
CWS	Corporate Workflow Solutions
D	Destination
D3D	Direct 3D
DA	Data Available
DA	Demand Assignment
DA	Desk Accessory
DA	Destination Address
DA/FDMA	Demand Assignment, Frequency Division Multiple Access
DA/TDMA	Demand Assignment, Time Division Multiple Access
DAA	Data Access Arrangement
DAC	Data Authentication Code
DAC	Digital-to-Analog Converter
DAC	Dual Attachment Concentrator
DACD	Directory Access Control Domain
DACL	Discretionary Access Control List
DACS	Digital Access and Cross-Connect System

DACTPU	Deactivate Physical Unit		DBK	Definition Block
DAD	Desktop Application Director		DBMS	Database Management System
DAD	Draft Addendum		DBR	DOS Boot Record
DAE	Digital Audio Extraction		DBS	Data Base Service
DAF	Destination Address Field		DBS	Direct (or Digital) Broadcast Satellite
DAF	Directory Authentication Framework		DBTG	Data Base Task Group
DAF	Distributed Application Framework		DBX	Digital Branch Exchange
DAK	Data Acknowledge		DC	Data Chaining
DAL	Data Access Language		DC	Direct Current
DAL	Data Access Line		DC	Disconnect Confirm
DAM	Data Access Manager		DC	Distribution Center
DAM	Draft Amendment		DCA	Defense Communications Agency
DAMA	Demand (or Data) Assigned Multiple Access		DCA	Digital Communication Associates
DAN	Departmental Area Network		DCA	Document Content Architecture
DAO	Data Access Object		DCA	Dynamic Channel Assignment
DAO	Disk-at-Once		DCAA	Dual Call Auto Answer
DAP	Directory (or Data) Access Protocol		DCB	Data Control Block
DAP	Document Application Profile		DCB	Directory Cache Buffer
DARPA	Defense Advanced Research Projects Agency		DCB	Disk Coprocessor Board
DARTnet	Defense Advanced Research Testbed Network		DCC	Data Communications Channel
DAS	Disk Array Subsystem		DCC	Data Country Code
DAS	Dual Address Space		DCC	Digital Compact Cassette
DAS	Dual-Attachment Station		DCC	Distributed Computing and Communications
DAS	Dynamically Assigned Sockets		DCD	Data Carrier Detect
DASD	Direct Access Storage Device (hard Disk in IBMese)		DCE	Data Circuit-Terminating Equipment
DASS	Design Automation Standards Subcommittee		DCE	Data Communications Equipment
DASS	Distributed Authentication Security Service		DCE	Distributed Computing Environment
DAT	Digital Audio Tape		DCEC	Defense Communications Engineering Center
DAT	Duplicate Address Test		DCE-RPC	Distributed Computing Environment Remote Procedure Call
DAT	Dynamic Address Translation		DCF	Data Communications Function
DATC	Drake Authorized Training Centers		DCF	Distributive Computing Facility
dB	Decibel		DCI	Display Control Interface
DB2/2	Data Base 2 for OS/2		DCIU	Data Communications Interface Unit
DBA	Database Accelerator (or Administrator)		DCL	Digital Command Language
dba	Doing Business As		DCME	Digital Circuit Multiplication Equipment
DBCS	Double-Byte Character Set		DCMS	Digital Circuit Multiplication System
DBF	Database File		DCN	Data Communication Network
DBF	Dynamic Beam Forming		DCO	Digitally Controlled Oscillator
DBI	Database Interface			

APP
A

DCOM	Distributed Component Object Model
DCP	Digital Communications Protocol
DCPSK	Differentially Coherent Phase Shift Keying
DCR	Direct Current Resistance
DCS	Data Circuit Switches
DCS	Defined Context Set
DCS	Desktop Color Separation
DCS	Digital Cellular System
DCS	Digital Cross-Connect System
DCS	Distributed Computing System
DCSS	Discontinuous Shared Segment
DCT	Discrete Cosine Transform
DD	Depacketization Delay
DDA	Domain Defined Attribute
DDB	Directory (also, Distributed) Database
DDBMS	Distributed Database Management System
DDCMP	Digital Data Communications Messaging Protocol
DDD	Direct Distance Dialing
DDDB	Distributed Directory Database
DDE	Dynamic Data Exchange
DDF	Data Description File
DDFII	Data Description File for Information Interchange
DDGL	Device-Dependent Graphics Layer
DDI	Direct Dialing in
DDK	Device Development Kit
DDL	Data Definition (or Description) Language
DDL	Data Direct Link
DDM	Direction Division Multiplexing
DDM	Distributed Data Management
DDMA	Distributed Direct Memory Access
DDN	Defense Data (or Department) Network
DDName	Data Definition Name
DDN-NIC	Defense Data Network-Network Information Center
DDNS	Dynamic Domain Name Service
DDP	Data Description Packet
DDP	Datagram Delivery Protocol
DDP	Distributed Data Processing
DDR	Data Descriptive Record
DDS	Dataphone Digital Service

DDS	Digital Data Service
DDS	Digital Directory System
DDS	Direct Digital Service
DDS	Document Distribution Services
DE	Directory Entry
DE	Discard Eligibility
DEA	Data Encryption Algorithm
DEA	Directory Entry Attribute
DEB	Directory Entry Block
DEC	Digital Equipment Corporation
DECdns	DEC Distributed Name Service
DECdts	Digital Equipment Corporation Distributed Time Service
DECmcc	DEC Management Control Center
DECnet	Digital Equipment Corporation Network Architecture
DECT	Digital European Cordless Telecommunications
DECUS	Digital Equipment Computer Users Society
DEF	Direct Equipment Failure
DEK	Data Encryption (also, Exchange) Key
DELNI	Digital Equipment Corporation Local Network Interconnect
DELTA	Distributed Electronic Telecommunications Archive
DEM	Dynamic Enterprise Modeler
DEMPR	DEC Multiport Repeater
DEMUX	Demultiplexer
DEN	Directory Enabled Network
DER	Distinguished Encoding Rules
DES	Data Encryption Standard
DES	Destination End System
DES	Discrete Event Simulation
DES	Distributed End System
DESIRE	Directory of European Information Security Standard Requirements
DET	Directory Entry Table
DEUNA	Digital Ethernet Unibus Network Adapter
DF	Don't Fragment
DFB	Distributed Feedback (laser)
DFC	Data Field Channel
DFC	Data Flow Control

DFD	Data Flow Diagram	DIGS	Device-Independent Graphics Services
DFEP	Diagnostic Front End Processor	DII COE	Defense Information Infrastructure Common Operating Environment
DFI	Digital Signal Processing Format Identifier		
DFL	Distributed Feedback Laser	DIN	Deutsches Institut Fur Normung (German Institute for Standardization)
DFN	Deutsches Forschungsnetz (German Research Network)		
		DIP	Dual In-Line Package
DFR	Document Filing and Retrieval	DIPE	Distributed Interactive Processing Environment
DFRC	Dryden Flight Research Center	DIR	Direct Inbound Routing
DFS	Distributed File System	DIS	Distributed Interactive Simulation
DFSK	Differential Frequency Shift Keying	DIS	Draft International Standard
DFSM	Dispersion Flattened Signal Mode	DISA	Data Interchange Standards Association
DFT	Discrete Fourier Transform	DISA	Defense Information Systems Agency
DFT	Distributed Function Terminal	DISA	Direct Inward Switch Access
DFT	Drive Fitness Test	DISC	Disconnect
DFWMAC	Distributed Foundation Wireless Medium Access Control	DISERF	Data Interchange Standards Education and Research Foundation
DGM	Data-Grade Media	DISN	Defense Information Systems Network
DGR	Dynamic Growth and Reconfiguration	DISOSS	Distributed Office Supported System
DGSE	Direction Générale De La Securité	DISP	Directory Information Shadow Protocol
DH	DMPDU Header	DISP	Draft International Standardized Profile
DHA	Destination Hardware Address	DIT	Directory Information Tree
DHCP	Dynamic Host Configuration Protocol	DIU	Distribution Interchange Unit
DI	Data In	DIVE	Direct Interface Video Extension
DI	Delete Inhibit	DIVE API	Direct Interface Video Extension API
DI	Desktop Integrator	DIW	D-Inside Wire
DI	Document Imaging	DIX	Diqital, Intel, Xerox
DIA	Document Interchange Architecture	DKA	Digital Knowledge Assets
DIB	Device-Independent Bitmap	DL	Data Link
DIB	Directory Information Base	DL	Distribution List
DIBI	Device Independent Backup Interface	DLA	Defense Logistic Agency
DIC	Data Integrity Check	DLC	Data Link Control
DID	Destination ID	DLC	Digital Loop Carrier
DID	Direct Inward Dialing	DLC	Dynamic Load Control
DIF	Data (or Documentation) Interchange Format	DLCEP	Data Link Connection Endpoint
DIF	Digital Interchange Format	DLCF	Data Link Control Field
DiffServ	Differentiated Services	DLCI	Data Link Connection Identifier
DIG	Domain Information Groper	DLE	Data Link Escape
DIGI	Deutsche Interessengemeinschaft Internet (German Special Interest Group for Internet)	DLL	Data Link Layer
		DLL	Dynamic Link Library
DIGL	Device-Independent Graphics Layer	DLM	Data Line Monitor

APP
A

DLO	Data Line Occupied
DLP	Digital Light Processing
DLPDU	Data Link Protocol Data Unit
DLPI	Data-Link Provider Interface
DLS	Data Link Services
DLS	Document Library Services
DLS	Downloadable Sample
DLSAP	Data Link-Layer Service Access Point
DLSDU	Data Link-Layer Service Data Unit
DLSw	Data Link Switching
DLT	Digital Linear Tape
DLTG	Delegate Liaison Task Group
DLU	Dependent (or Destination) Logical Unit
DLUR	Dependent Logical Unit Requestor
DLUS	Dependent Logical Unit Server
DM	Delta Modulation
DM	Desktop Management
DM	Disconnected Mode
DM	Document Manipulation (service Class)
DMA	Direct Memory Access
DMA	Document Management Alliance
DMAC	Direct Memory Access Controller
DMD	Differential Mode Delay
DMD	Directory Management Domain
DMDD	Distributed Multiplexing Distributed Demultiplexing
DME	Direct Memory Execution
DME	Distributed Management Environment
DMI	Definition of Management Information
DMI	Desktop Management Interface
DMI	Digital Media (or Multiplexed) Interface
DMI	Distributed Management Interface
DML	Data Manipulation Language
DMO	Domain Management Organization
DMPDU	Derived Medium Access Control Protocol Data Unit
DMS	Defense Messaging System
DMS	Distributed Mail (or Memory) System
DMS	Document Management Service
DMSP	Distributed Mail System Protocol
DMT	Discrete Multitone

DMTF	Desktop Management Task Force
DMUX	Double Multiplexer
DN	Digital (or Distribution) Network
DN	Distinguished Name
DNA	Digital (also, Distributed) Network Architecture
DNA	Distributed Internet Applications Architecture
DNA	Dynamic Network Administration
DNBNS	Dynamic NetBIOS Name Service
DNC	Democratic National Committee
DNC	Digital Node Controller
DNC	Dynamic Network Controller
DNDS	Distributed Network Design System
DNHR	Dynamic Nonhierarchical Routing
DNIC	Data Network Identification Code
DNIS	Dialed Number Identification Service
DNP	Distributed Network Processing
DNR	Data Network Routing
DNS	Domain Name System
DO	Data Out
DOAM	Distributed Office Applications Model
DOAPI	DOS Open API
DOC	Declaration of Conformity
DOC	Distributed Object Computing
DOC	Dynamic Overload Control
DOCS	Data Over Cable Service
DOCSIS	Data Over Cable Service Interface Specification
DOD	Department of Defense
DOD	Direct Outward Dialing
DOE	Department of Energy
DOIT	Disabilities, Opportunities, Internetworking, Technology
DOM	Document Object Model
DOMF	Distributed Object Management Facility
DOMS	Distributed Object Management System
DOMSAT	Domestic Satellite Service
DONACS	Department of the Navy Automation and Communication System
DOP	Directory Operational Protocol
DOS	Disk Operating System

DOV	Data Over Voice		DRP	Distributed Resource Processing
DOW	Distributed Object Web		DRPF	Decimal Reference Publication Format
DP	Data Processing		DRS	Data Rate Selector
DP	Demarcation Point		DRSLST	Directed Search List
DP	Detection Point		DS	Dansk Standardiseringsrad (Danish Board for Standardization)
DP	Draft Proposal			
DP	Dual Processor		DS	Deferrable Server
DPA	Demand Protocol Architecture		DS	Desired State
DPA	Document Printing Application		DS	Digital Section
dpANS	Draft Proposed American National Standard		DS	Directory (also, Digital) Service
DPC	Data Processing Center		DS	Distributed Single-layer
DPC	Deferred Procedure Call		DS	Document Storage
DPCM	Differential Pulse Code Modulation		DS	Draft Standard
DPDU	Data Link Layer Protocol Data Unit		DS0	Digital Signal, Level 0
DPE	Digital Phone Set Emulation		DS1	Digital Signal, Level 1
DPG	Dedicated Packet Group		DS1C	Digital Signal, Level 1C
DPI	Dots Per Inch		DS2	Digital Signal, Level 2
DPL	Dedicated Private Line		DS3	Digital Signal, Level 3
DPL	Distribution Services Primary Link		DS3 PLCP	Digital Signal, Level 3 Physical Layer Convergence Protocol
DPLL	Digital Phase-Locked Loop			
DPMI	DOS Protected Mode Interface		DS4	Digital Signal, Level 4
DPMS	Display Power Management Signaling		DSA	Dedicated Switched Access
DPMS	DOS Protected Mode Services		DSA	Destination Software Address
DPO	Dial Pulse Originating		DSA	Digital (Equipment Corporation) Storage Architecture
DPSK	Differential Phase Shift Keying			
DPT	Dial Pulse Terminating		DSA	Digital Signature Algorithm
DQDB	Distributed Queue Dual Bus		DSA	Directory Service (or System) Agent
DR	Data Repository		DSA	Directory System Alert
DR	Definite Response		DSA	Distributed Systems Architecture
DR	Delivery Report		DSAP	Data Link Service Access Point
DR	Disconnect Request		DSAP	Destination Service Access Point
DR	Dynamic Reconfiguration		DSB	Double Sideband
DRAM	Dynamic Random-Access Memory		DSBFC	Double Sideband Full Carrier
DRDA	Distributed Relational Data Architecture		DSBSC	Double Sideband Suppressed Carrier
DRDS	Dynamic Reconfiguration Data Set		DSC	Data Stream Compatibility
DRM	Disaster Recovery Manager		DSC	Digital Still Camera
DRN	Data Routing Network		DSC	Direct Satellite Communications
DRP	DECnet Routing Protocol		DSC	Document Structure Conventions
DRP	Directory Replication Protocol		DSD	Data Structure Definition
			DSD	Direct Store Delivery

APP
A

DSDS	Dataphone Switched Digital Service
DSE	Data Switching Equipment
DSE	Data-Specific Entry
DSE	Data-Switching Exchange
DSE	Distributed Single-layer Embedded
DSE	Distributed System Environment
DSE	DSA Specific Entry
DSI	Digital Speech Interpolation
DSID	Destination Signaling Identifier
DSL	Digital Subscriber Line
DSLO	Distributed System License Option
DSM	Dedicated Server Module
DSM	Digital Storage Media
DSM	Distributed State Machine
DSM	Distributed Switching Matrix
DSM	Distributed Systems Management
DSMA	Digital Sense Multiple Access
DSN	Data Source (also, Store) Name
DSN	Delivery Status Notification
DSO	Data Source Object
DSOM	Distributed System Object Model
DSOM	Distributed Systems Operation and Management
DSP	Defense Standardized Profit
DSP	Digital Signal Processor
DSP	Directory System Protocol
DSP	Domain Specific Part
DSPU	Downstream Physical Unit
DSR	Data Set Ready
DSS	Decision Support Systems
DSS	Department of Social Services
DSS	Digital Signal (or Signature) Standard
DSS	Digital Subscriber Service
DSS	Direct Station Selection
DSS	Directory and Security Server
DSS	Domain SAP Service
DSS/BLF	Direct Station Selection/Busy Lamp Field
DSS-1	Digital Subscriber Signaling System 1
DSSI	Digital (DEC) Small Systems Interconnect
DSSS	Direct Sequence Spread Spectrum

DSSSL	Document Style, Semantics, and Specification Language
DSTINIT	Data Services Task Initialization
DSTU	Draft Standard for Trial Use
DSU	Data Service Unit
DSU	Digital Services Unit
DSU/CSU	Data Service Unit/Channel Service Unit
DSUN	Distribution Services Unit Name
DSVD	Digital Simultaneous Voice Data
DSX	Digital Signal Cross-connect
DSx	Digital Signal, Level X ($x = 0, 1, 1C, 2, 3,$ or 4)
DSX1/3	Digital Signal Cross-connect Between Levels 1 and 3
DT	Data
DT	Data Transfer
DT	Detection Threshold
DT	DMPDU Trailer
DTAM	Document Transfer and Manipulation
DTAM-PM	Document Transfer and Manipulation Protocol Machine
DTAMSE	Document Transfer and Manipulation Service Element
DTAS	Digital Test Access System
DTD	Document Type Definition
DTE	Data Terminal Equipment
DTE	Domain Type Enforcement
DTI	Department of Trade and Industry (UK)
DTI	Digital Telephony Interface
DTM	Direct Transaction Mapping
DTMF	Dual Tone Multifrequency
DTP	Desktop Publishing
DTP	Distributed Transaction Processing
DTR	Data Terminal Ready
DTR	Dedicated Token Ring
DTR	Draft Technical Report
DTS	Data Transfer System
DTS	Decoding Time Stamp
DTS	Digital Termination Service
DTS	Digital Theater Surround
DTS	Digital Transmission System
DTSS	Digital Time Synchronization Service

DTSX	Data Transport Station for X.25		EASINet	European Academic Supercomputer Initiative Network
DTV	Digital Television		EAW	Eastern Acoustic Works
DU	Data Unit		FAX	Electronic Automatic Exchange
DUA	DIrectory User Agent		EAX	Environmental Audio Extensions
DUAL	Diffusing Update Algorithm		EB	End Bracket
DUN	Dial-Up Networking		EB	Erlang B
DUNCE	Dial-Up Network Connection Enhancer		EBCDIC	Extended Binary Coded Decimal Interchange Code
DUT	Delft University of Technology		EBIOS	Extended BIOS
DUV	Data Under Voice		EBN	Extended Border Node
DV	Digital Video		EBONE	European Backbone
DVD+RW	Digital Versatile (or Video) Disc Rewritable		EBPR	eBusiness Process Re-Engineering
DVD-R/W	Digital Versatile (or Video) Disc-Read/Write		EC	Electronic Commerce
DVD-ROM	Digital Versatile (or Video) Disc-Read only Memory		EC	European Community (or Commission)
DVE	Digital Video Effect		ECAT	Electronic Commerce Action Team
DVI	Digital Video Interactive		ECB	Electronic Cookbook
DVMRP	Distance Vector Multicast Routing Protocol		ECC	Enhanced Error Checking and Correction
DVT	Destination Vector Table		ECC	Error-Correcting Code
DWDM	Dense Wave(length) Division Multiplexing		ECC SDRAM	Error Checking and Correction Synchronous Dynamic Random Access Memory
DWI	Direct Wall Interface		ECE	Economic Commission for Europe
DWO	Digital Waveform Oscillator		ECELP	Enhanced Code Excited Linear Predictive Coding
DX	Directory Exchange		ECF	Enhanced Connectivity Facilities
DXC	Digital Cross-Connect		ECH	Echo Canceller with Hybrid
DXF	Drawing Exchange Format		ECITC	European Committee for Information-Technology Testing and Certification
DXI	Data Exchange Interface		ECL	Emitter-Coupled Logic
E	Voltage (or Electromotive Force, in Volts)		ECL	End Communication Layer
E/O	Electro-optical		ECM	Error-Correcting Mode
EA	Enterprise Architecture		ECMA	European Computer Manufacturers Association
EA	Expedited Acknowledgment		ECN	Explicit Congestion Notification
EA	Extended Attribute		ECNE	Enterprise Certified NetWare Engineer
EA	External Access (equipment)		ECO	Echo-Controlled Object
EAB	Extended Addressing Bit		ECOS	Extended Communications Operating System
EAN	Electronic Article Number		ECP	Extended Capabilities Port
EAN	European Academic Network		ECPA	Electronic Communications Privacy Act
EAOG	European ADMD Operators Group		ECR	Efficient Consumer Response
EAP	Enterprise Architecture Planning		ECS	Egyptian Computer Society
EAP	Extensible Authentication Protocol		ECS	Enterprise Communications Server
EARN	European Academic and Research Network		ECS	Event Control Server
EAROM	Electrically Alterable Read-Only Memory			
EAS	Extended Area Service			

APP
A

ECSA	Exchange Carriers Standards Association
ECTEI	European Conference of Telecommunications and Electronics Industries
ECTF	Enterprise Computer Technology (or Telephony) Forum
ECTP	Ethernet Configuration Test Protocol
ECTS	European Computer Trade Show
ECU	European Currency Unit
ED	End(ing) Delimiter
ED	EWOS Document
ED	Exception (or Expedited) Data
EDA	Electronic Document Authorization
EDA	Embedded Document Architecture
EDAC	Error Detection and Correction
E-DDP	Extended Datagram Delivery Protocol
EDE	Encrypt-Decrypt-Encrypt
EDF	Execution Diagnostic Facility
EDFA	Erbium-Doped Fiber Amplifiers
EDGAR	Electronic Data Gathering, Analysis, and Retrieval
EDGAR	Electronic Data Gathering, Archiving, and Retrieval
EDI	Electronic Data Interchange
EDIA	Electronic Data Interchange Association
EDICUSA	Electronic Data Interchange Council of the United States
EDIF	Electronic Data Interchange Format
EDIFACT	Electronic Data Interchange for Finance, Administration, Commerce, and Transport
EDIM	Electronic Data Interchange User Agent Message
EDIME	Electronic Data Interchange Messaging Environment
EDIMG	Electronic Data Interchange Messaging
EDIMS	Electronic Data Interchange Messaging System
EDI-MS	Electronic Data Interchange Message Store
EDIN	Electronic Data Interchange Notification
EDIUA	Electronic Data Interchange User Agent
EDL	Edit Decision List
EDLIS	Exchange of Dylan Lyrics Internet Service
EDM	Electronic Document Management
EDMD	Electronic Document Message Directory
EDN	Expedited Data Negotiation
EDO	Extended Data Out

EDODRAM	Extended Data Out Dynamic Random Access Memory
EDORAM	Extended Data Out Random Access Memory
EDOSRAM	Extended Data Out Static Random Access Memory
EDOVRAM	Extended Data Out Video Random Access Memory
EDP	Electronic Data Processing
EDRAM	Enhanced Dynamic Random Access Memory
EDSD	Electronic Document Segment Directory
EEB	Extended Erlang B
EEC	European Economic Community (or Commission)
EEI	External Environment Interface
EEMA	Electrical and Electronic Manufacturing Association
EEMA	European Electronic Mail Association
EEMAC	Electrical and Electronic Manufacturing Association of Canada
EEMS	Enhanced Expanded Memory Specification
EEO	Equal Employment Opportunity
EEPG	European Engineering Planning Group
EEPROM	Electrically Erasable Programmable Read-Only Memory
EER	Enhanced E-R (Data Model)
EETDN	End-to-End Transit Delay Negotiation
EETLA	Extraordinarily Extended Three Letter Acronym
EFCI	Explicit Forward Congestion Indicator (or Indication)
EFD	Event Forwarding Discriminator
EFD	Exchange Forms Designer
EFF	Electronic Frontier Foundation
EFLA	Extended Four Letter Acronym
EFM	Eight-to-Fourteen Modulation
EFS	Encrypted (or External) File System
EFS	End Frame Sequence
EFS	Error Free Second
EFS	Extended Facility Set
EFT	Electronic Funds Transfer
EFTA	European Free Trade Association
EG	Envelope Generator
EG	Experts Group
EGA	Enhanced Graphics Adapter
EG-CAE	Experts Group for Command Application Environment

EG-CT	Experts Group for Conformance Testing
EG-DIR	Experts Group on Directory
EG-FT	Experts Group on File Transfer
EG-LIB	Experts Group for Library
EG-LL	Experts Group for Lower Layers
EG-MHS	Experts Group for MHS
EG-MMS	Experts Group for Manufacturing Message Specification
EG-NM	Experts Group for Network Management
EG-ODA	Experts Group for Office Document Architecture
EGP	Exterior Gateway Protocol
EG-TP	Experts Group on Transaction Processing
EG-VT	Experts Group on Virtual Terminal
EHA	European Harmonization Activity
EHF	Extremely High Frequency
EHLLAPI	Extended High-level Language Applications Program Interface
EIA	Electronic Industries Alliance (Association)
EIA/TIA	Electronics Industry Association / Telecommunications Industry Association
EIB	Enterprise Information Base
EIBA	European Internet Business Association
EIC	Enterprise Interaction Center
EID	Electronic Imaging Division
EIES	Electronic Information Exchange System
EIGRP	Enhanced IGRP
EINET	Enterprise Integration Network
EINOS	Enhanced Interactive Network Optimization System
EIP	Enterprise Information Portal
EIR	Equipment Identity Register
EIR	Excess Information Rate
EIRP	Effective Isotropic Radiated Power
EIS	Electronic Information Security
EIS	Executive Information Systems
EISA	Extended Industry Standard Architecture
EIT	Encoded Information Type
EIUF	European ISDN Users' Forum
EJB	Enterprise JavaBeans
EKE	Encrypted Key Exchange
EKS	Enterprise Knowledge Solutions

EKTS	Electronic Key Telephone System
ELAN	Emulated (also, ESPRIT) Local Area Network
ELAP	EtherTalk Link Access Protocol
ELEPL	Equal Level Echo Path Loss
ELF	Extremely Low Frequency
ELS	Entry Level System
EMA	Electronic Mail Association
EMA	Electronic Messaging Association
EMA	Element Management Agent
EMA	Enterprise Management Architecture
EMA	Enterprise Marketing Automation
EMB	Embedded Memory Block
EMC	Electromagnetic Capacity
EMC	Electronic Medical Claims
EMF	Electromotive Force
EMI	Electromagnetic Interference
EMIT	Embedded Micro Interface Technology
EMM	Expanded Memory Manager
EMO	Enterprise Management and Operations
EMOS1	East Mediterranean Optical System 1
EMP	Electromagnetic Pulse
EMP	Emergency Management Port
EMPC	Electromagnetic Pulse Cannon
EMPM	Electronic Manuscript Preparation and Markup
EMPT	Electromagnetic Pulse Transformer
EMS	Event Management Service
EMS	Expanded Memory Specification
EMU	European Monetary Union
EMUG	European MAP/TOP Users' Group
EMWAC	European Microsoft Windows NT Academic Center
EMX	Enterprise Mail Exchange
EN	End Node
EN	European Norm
ENA	Extended Network Addressing
ENC	Eisenhower National Clearinghouse
ENDEC	Encoder/Decoder
ENDIF	Enterprise Network - Data Interconnectivity Family (Working Group)
ENE	Enterprise Networking Event

APP
A

ENIAC	Electronic Numeric Integrator and Calculator
ENQ	Inquiry
ENS	Enterprise Naming (also, Network) Service
ENS	European Nervous System
ENSDU	Expedited Network Service Data Unit
ENTELEC	Energy Telecommunications and Electrical Association
EO	Electro-optics
EO	End Office
EO	Erasable Optic
EOA	End of Address
EOB	End of Burst
EOC	Embedded Operations Channel
EOC	End of Content
EOF	Extremely Old Fart
EOI	End of Interrupts
EOM	End of Message
EON	End of Number
EOS	Element of Service
EOS	Enterprise Object Software
EOT	End of Text (or Transmission or Tape)
EOTC	European Organization for Testing and Certification
EP	Echo Protocol
EP	Emulation Program
EP	Extended Play
EPA	Environmental Protection Agency
EPABX	Electronic Private Automatic Branch Exchange
EPHOS	European Procurement Handbook for Open Systems
EPIC	Electronic Privacy Information Center
EPNOA	European Public Network Operators Association
EPOS	Electronic Point of Sale
EPP	Enhanced Parallel Port
EPRI	Electrical Power Research Institute
EPROM	Erasable Programmable Read-Only Memory
EPS	Encapsulated PostScript
EPSCS	Enhanced-Private Switched Communications Service
EPSF	Encapsulated PostScript Format
EPSS	Electronic Performance Support System

EQEEB	Equivalent Queue Extended Erlang B
ER	Energy Research
ER	Error
ER	Exception Response
ER	Explicit Route
E-R	Entity-Relationship (Data Model)
ERA	Entity-Relationship-Attribute
ERAS	Enhanced Remote Access Service (or Server)
ERD	Event Report Discriminator
ERE	Echo Return Loss
EREP	Environmental Recording, Editing, and Printing
ERF	Event Report Function
ERIC	Educational Resources Information Service
ERL	Echo Return Loss
ERL	Environmental Research Laboratories
ERLL	Enhanced Run Length Limited
ERM	Enterprise Reference Model
ERM	Enterprise Relationship Management
ERM	Explicit Rate Marking
ERMF	Event Report Management Function
ERP	Enterprise Resource Planning
ERP	Error-Recovery Procedure
ERS	Evaluated Receipt Settlement
ERT	Equivalent Random Theory
ES	End System
ES	Errored Second
ESA	Enhanced Subarea Addressing
ESA	Enterprise System Architecture
ESA	Errored Second, Type A
ESA	European Space Agency
ESAFE	Errored Second, Type A, Far End
ESB	Errored Second, Type B
ESBFE	Errored Second, Type B, Far End
ESCON	Enterprise System Connection Architecture
ESCP	Errored Second, CP-bit Parity
ESCR	Elementary Stream Clock Reference
ESCRC	Errored Second, Cyclic Redundancy Check
ESD	Electronic Software Distribution
ESD	Electrostatic Discharge

ESDI	Enhanced Small Device Interface
ES-ES	End System to End System
ESF	Extended Superframe Format
ESFE	Errored Second, Far End
ESH	End-System Hello
ESI	End System Identifier
ES-IS	End System to Intermediate System
ESL	Electronic Software Licensing
ESL	Enhanced Signaling Link
ESM	Enterprise Storage Manager
ESMR	Enhanced Specialized Mobile Radio
ESMTP	Extended Simple Mail Transfer Protocol
ESN	Electronic Serial Number
ESN	Electronic Switched Network
ESnet	Energy Sciences Network
ESP	Encapsulating Security Payload (or Protocol)
ESP	Enhanced Service Provider
ESP	Enhanced Services Platform
ESP	Enterprise Service Provider
ESP	Enterprise Storage Platform
ESP	Errored Second, P-bit
ESPRIT	European Strategic Project for Research on Information Technology
ESS	Electronic Switching System
ESTELLE	Extended State Transition Language
ET	Exchange Termination
ETAG	End Tag
ETB	End of Text (or Transmission) Block
ETCO	European Telecommunications Consultancy Organization
ETCOM	European Testing for Certification of Office and Manufacturing Equipment
ETE	End-to-End
ETG	EWOS Technical Guide
ETHICS	Effective Technical and Human Implementation of Computer-based Systems
ETIS	Electronic Telephone Inquiry System
ETL	Electronic Testing Laboratory
ETLA	Extended Three Letter Acronym
ETN	Electronic Tandem Network

ETR	Early Token Release
ETRI-PEC	Electronics and Telecommunications Research Institute-Protocol Engineering Center
ETS	European Telecommunications Standards
ETS	Executable Test Suite
ETSDU	Expedited Transport Service Data Unit
ETSI	European Telecommunications Standards Institute
ETTM	Electronic Toll and Traffic Management
ETX	End of Text
EUNET	European UNIX Network
EUROSINET	European Open System Interconnect Network
EUTELSAT	European Telecommunications Satellite
EUUG	European UNIX Users Group
EUV	Extreme Ultraviolet
EV	Extreme Value
EVE	European Videoconferencing Equipment
EVE	Extensible VAX Editor
EVE	Extreme Value Engineering
E-VPN	Enterprise Virtual Private Network
EVS	European Videoconferencing Service
EWAS	Ergonomic Work Assessment System
EWICS	European Workshop on Industrial Computer Systems
EWOS	European Workshop for Open Systems
EWP	Enterprise Workshop Planning
EWTA	Enterprise-Wide Technical Architecture
EX	Expedited
EXLIST	Exit List
EXM	Exit Message
EXOS	Extension Outside
EXT	External Trace
F	Flag
f2f	Face to Face
FACT	Federation of Automated Coding Technologies
FAD	Frame Assembler/disassembler
FADU	File Access Data Unit
FAIS	Factory Automation Interconnection System
FAL	File Access Listener
FAM	File system Activity Monitor
FAN	Facility Area Network

FAP	Format and Protocol		FDM	Frequency Division Multiplexing
FAPL	Format and Protocols Language		FDMA	Frequency Division Multiple Access
FAQ	Frequently Asked Questions		FDR	Field Definition Record
FAQL	Frequently Asked Question List		FDT	Formal Description Technique
FAR	False Acceptance Rate		FDX	Full Duplex
FARNET	Federation of American Research Networks		FE	Framework (or Function) Element
FAS	Frame Alignment Sequence		FEA	Finite Element Analysis
FAT	File Allocation (also, Access) Table		FEBE	Far End Block Error
FAX	Facsimile		FEC	Field Entry Condition
FBE	Free Buffer Enquiry		FEC	Forward Error Correction
FC	Feedback Control		FECN	Forward Explicit Congestion Notification
FC	Frame Check (or Control)		FED-STD	Federal Standard
FCA	Fiber Channel Association		FEE	Fast Elliptic Encryption
FC-AL	Fibre Channel Arbitrated Loop		FEE	Field Entry Event
FCB	File Cache Buffer		FEI	Field Entry Instruction
FCC	Federal Communications Commission		FEICO	Field Entry Instruction Control Object
FCCSET	Federal Coordinating Council on Science, Engineering and Technology		FEIR	Field Entry Instruction Record
			FEM	Finite Element Modeling
FC-EL	Fibre Channel Enhanced Loop		FEP	Front End Processor
FCG	Format Computer Graphics		FEPCO	Field Entry Pilot Control Object
FCI	Frame Copied Indicator Bit		FEPG	Federal Engineering Planning Group
FCIC	Florida Crime Information Center		FEPR	Field Entry Pilot Record
FCRC	Federated Computing Research Conference		FER	Field Entry Reaction
FCS	Fast Circuit Switching		FERF	Far End Receive Failure
FCS	Fiber Channel Standard		FERPM	FTAM Error Recovery Protocol Machine
FCS	Frame Check Sequence		FES	Fixed End System
FCSI	Fiber Channel Systems Initiative		FEXT	Far End Crosstalk
FC-x	Fibre Channel, level x ($x = 0, 1, 2, 3,$ or 4)		FF	Fone Friend
FD	Flat Display		FF	Form Feed
FDCO	Field Definition Control Object		FFOL	FDDI Follow-On LAN
FDD	Frequency Division Duplex(ing)		FFS	Flash File System
FDDI	Fiber Distributed Data Interface		FFT	Fast Fourier Transform
FDDI-FO	Fiber Distributed Data Interface Follow-On		FFT	Final Form Text
FDFA	Federal Department of Foreign Affairs		FG	Frame Ground
FDHM	Full Duration Half Maximum		FG	Functional Group
FDI	Format Directory		FGND	Frame Ground
FDL	Facility Data Link		FH	Frame Handler
FDL	File Definition Language		FHD	Fixed-Head Disk
FDLE	Florida Department of Law Enforcement		FI	File Interchange

FI/CO	Financial Operations and Control	FNPRM	Further Notice of Proposed Rule Making
FICC	Federation of Insurance and Corporate Counsel	FNS	FDDI Network Service
FID	Format Identifier	FO	Fiber Optics
FIF	Fractal Image Format	FOAF	Friend of a Friend
FIFO	First In, First Out	FOC	Fiber Optic Communications
FIGS	Figures Shift	FOCC	Forward Control Channel
FIM	Fiber Interface Module	FOCS	Foundations of Computer Science
FIN	Finish Flag	FOD	Fax-on-Demand
FIPS	Federal Information Processing Standard	FOD	Format Office Document
FIR	Fast Infrared	FoIP	Fax over Internet Protocol
FIR	Finite Impulse Response	FOIRL	Fiber Optic Inter-Repeater Link
FIRL	Fiber-optic Inter-Repeater Link	FOOBAR	FTP Operation Over Big Address Records
FIRST	Forum on Incident Response and Security Teams	FOPG	Federal Networking Council Open Systems Interconnection Planning Group
FISUS	Fill In Signal Unit		
FITL	Fiber In the Loop	FOT	Frequency of Optimum Traffic
FIU	Fingerprint Identification Unit	FOTS	Fiber Optic Transmission System
FIX	Federal Information (also, Internet) Exchange	FOX	Field Operational X.500
FL	First Level	FP	Floating Point
FLAG	Fiber-Optic Link Around the Globe	FP	Framing Protocol
FLAP	FDDITalk Link Access Protocol	FP	Functional Profile
FLIH	First-Level Interrupt Handler	FPASD	Facsimile Packet Assembler/Disassembler
FLIP	Fast Local Internet Protocol	FPF	Facility Parameter Field
FLP	Fast Link Pulse	FPGA	Field Programmable Gate Array
FM	Fault (or Function) Management	FPLMTS	Future Public Land Mobile Telecommunication System
FM	Frequency Modulation		
FM	Functional Model	FPM	Fast Page Mode
FMBS	Frame-Mode Bearer Service	FPODA	Fixed Priority-Oriented Demand Assignment
FMD	Function Management Data	FPS	Fast Packet Switching
FM-FDM	Frequency Modulated-Frequency Division Multiplexed	FPS	Frames Per Second
		FPSNW	File and Print Service for NetWare
FMH	Function Management Header	FPU	Floating Point Unit
FMS	File Management System	FQA	Frequently Questioned Acronym
FMV	Full Motion Video	FQDN	Fully Qualified Domain Name
FMVFT	Frequency Modulation Voice Frequency Telegraph	FQPCID	Fully Qualified Procedure Correlation Identifier
FN	Finish	FR	Frame Relay
FN	Forward Notification	FR\&O	First Report and Order
FNC	Federal Networking Council	FRAD	Frame Relay Access Device
FNOI	Further Notice of Inquiry	FRAD	Frame Relay Assembler / Disassembler
FNP	Front-End Network Processor	FRAM	Ferroelectric Random Access Memory

APP
A

FREDMAIL	Free Educational Electronic Mail		FTS	Frontline Test System
FRF	Frame Relay Forum		FTSC	Federal Telecommunications Standards Committee
FRFH	Frame Relay Frame Handler		FTTC	Fiber to the Curb
FRI	Frame Relay Interface		FTTH	Fiber to the Home
FRICC	Federal Research Internet Coordination Committee		FTTN	Fiber to the Node
FRMR	Frame Reject		FU	Functional Unit
FRR	False Rejection Rate		FUBAR	Fouled Up Beyond All Recognition
FRS	Flexible Route Selection		FUI	Fake User Interface
FRS	Frame Relay Service		FUNI	Frame User Network Interface
FRSE	Frame Relay Switching Equipment		FWHM	Full Width At Half Maximum
FR-SSCS	Frame Relaying Service-Specific Convergence Sublayer		FWIW	For What It's Worth
FRTE	Frame Relay Terminal Equipment		FX	Foreign Exchange
FS	File Server		FYI	For Your Information
FS	Frame (or Full) Status		G	Giga-
FS	Functional Standard		G.O.O.D	Get out of Debt
FSB	Front Side Bus		GA	Genetic Algorithm
FSD	Fixed Shroud Duplex		GA	Go Ahead
FSF	Free Software Foundation		GAA	Gallium Arsenide
FSG	Format Standard Generalized Markup Language		GAN	Global Area Network
FSIOP	File Server I/O Processor		GAO	Government (or General) Accounting Office
FSK	Frequency Shift Keying		GAP	Gateway Access Protocol
FSL	Free Space Loss		GAP	Generic Address Parameter
FSM	Finite State Machine		GATED	GATE Daemon
FSN	Full Service Network		Gb	Gigabit
FSP	File Service Process		GB	Gigabyte
FSS	Fully Separated Subsidiary		Gbps	Gigabits Per Second
FSTG	Functional Standardization Taxonomy Group		GBps	Gigabytes Per Second
FSTV	Free Speech Television		GBS	Goal-Based Scenario
FSU	File Support Utility		GCID	Global Call Identifier
FT	Fault Tolerant (or Tolerance)		GCID-IE	Global Call Identifier—Information Element
Ft	Foot		GCM	Generalized Control Model
FT1	Fractional T1		GCR	Gray Component Replacement
FTAM	File Transfer, Access, and Management		GCR	Group Coded Recording
FTF	Face to Face		GCRA	Generic Cell Rate Algorithm
FTL	Flash Translation Layer		GCS	Group Control System
FTP	File Transfer Protocol		gd\&r	Grinning, Ducking, and Running
FTS	Federal Telecommunications System		GDAP	Government Document Application Profile
FTS	File Transfer Service		GDC	Georgia Department of Corrections
			GDDM	Graphical Data Display Manager

GDES	Generalized Data Encryption Standard		GNP	Gross National Product
GDI	Graphics Device Interface		GNU	GNU's Not UNIX
GDMI	Generic Definition of Management Information		GO	Geometrical Optics
GDMO	Guidelines for the Definition of Managed Objects		GOAS	Ground Operator Assistant System
GDP	Gross Domestic Product		GOES	Geostationary Orbit Environment Satellite
GDS	Generalized Data Stream		GoS	Grade of Service
GDS	Graphics Data Syntax		GOSIP	Government Open Systems Interconnection Profile
GE	Group of Experts		GPC	Graphics Performance Characterization Committee
GEA	Gigabit Ethernet Alliance		GPD	General Purpose Discipline
GEIS	General Electric Information Services		GPIB	General Purpose Interface Bus
GEM	Generalized Event Monitoring		GPL	General Public License
GEM	Global Enterprise Manager		GPN	Government Packet Network
GEM	Graphics Environment Manager		GPS	Global Positioning Satellite (or Service)
GEMDES	Government Electronic Messaging and Document Exchange Service		GPV	General Public Virus
			GQ	Generation Qualifier
GEN	Generation		GR/PS	Graphical Representation/ Phrase Representation
GFC	Generic Flow Control		GRC	Generic Reference Configuration
GFH	Global Failure Handler		GRD	GOSIP Register Database
GFI	General Format Identifier		GRE	Generic Routing Encapsulation
GFID	General Format Identifier		GRIN	Graded Indices
GFLOP	Billions of Floating Point Operations		GS	General Synthesizer
GGP	Gateway-to-Gateway Protocol		GSA	General Services Administration
GHz	Gigahertz		GSM	Global Satellite Mobile
GID	Group ID		GSM	Global State Manager
GIF	Gauntlet Internet Firewall		GSM	Global System for Mobiles
GIF	Graphic Interchange Format		GSM	Groupe Spécial Mobile
GIGO	Garbage In, Garbage Out		GSMP	General Switch Management Procotol
GILC	Global Internet Liberty Campaign		GSN	Government Satellite Network
GIMPS	Great Internet Mersenne Prime Search		GSNW	Gateway Services for NetWare
GIO	Generic Interface of Operation		GSR	Gigabit Switch Router
GIS	Geographic Information System		GSS	Generic Security Services
GKS	Graphical Kernel System		GSS/RSS	Generation Support Statement/Reception Support Statement
GL	Generation Language (eg, 4GL)			
GMHS	Global Message Handling Service		GSTN	General Switch Telephone Network
GMSC	Gateway Mobile Services Switching Center		GT	Give Token
GMT	Greenwich Mean Time		GTA	Give Token Acknowledgment
GN	Given Name		GTA	Government Telecommunications Agency
GNM	Generic Network Model		GTC	Give Token Confirm
GNMP	Government Network-Management Profile		GTE	General Telephone and Electronics

APP

A

GTF	Generalized Trace Facility
GTIS	Government Telecommunications and Informatics Services
GTN	Government Telecommunications Network
GUI	Graphical User Interface
GUID	Globally Unique Identifier
GUS	Guide to the Use of Standards
GWNCP	Gateway Network Control Program
GWSSCP	Gateway System Services Control Point
H	Hexadecimal
HA	Header Authentication
HA	Highly Available (or High Availability)
HAA	Home Address Agent
HAI	Host Adapter Interface
HAL	Hardware Abstraction Layer
HALO	High Altitude Long Operation
HAM	Host Adapter Module
HAM	Hybrid Access Method
HAN	House Area Network
HAND	Have A Nice Day
HASE	High-Assurance Systems Engineering
HASP	Hardware / Software Avionic System Performance
HASP	Houston Automatic Spooling Priority
HAVi	Home Audio-Video Interoperability
HBA	Host Bus Adapter
HC	Hyperchannel
HCD	Hardware Configuration Definition
HCFA	Health Care Finance Administration
HCL	Hardware Compatibility List
HCL	Hop Count Limit
HCS	Hard Clad Silica
HCS	Header Check Sequence
HCS	Health Care System
HCSS	High-Capacity Storage System
HD	Hard Disk
HD DVD	High Density Digital Video Disc
HDB3	High-Density—Three Zeros
HDCD	High Density Compact Disc
HDI	Help Desk Institute

HDL	Hardware Description Language
HDLC	High-Level Data Link Control
HDPA	Help Desk Professionals Association
HDR EXT	Header Extension
HDSL	High-bit-rate Digital Subscriber Line
HDT	Host Digital Terminal
HDTV	High Definition Television
HD-WDM	Wave Division Multiplexing
HDX	Half Duplex
HE	Head End
HEC	Header Error Control (or Correction or Check)
HEC	Higher Education Consortium
HEL	Header Extension Length
HEMP	High-altitude Electromagnetic Pulse
HEMS	High-Level Entity Monitoring System
HERF	High Energy Radio Frequency
HES	Home Entertainment System
Hex	Hexadecimal
HF	High Frequency
HFC	Hybrid Fiber-optic Coaxial (networks)
HFCop	Hybrid Fiber / Copper
HFO	High-Frequency Oscillator
HFS	Hierarchical File System
HFSM	Hierarchical Finite State Machine
HGC	Hercules Graphics Card
HICOM	High Technology Communication
HID/LOD	High-Density/ Low-Density Tariff
HiFD	High-Capacity Floppy Disk
HILI	Higher-Level Interface
HIMSS	Healthcare Information Management Systems Society
HIPERLAN	High-Performance Local Area Network
HIPPI	High-Performance Parallel Interface
HiPPI FP	High-Performance Parallel Interface Framing Protocol
HiPPI LE	High-Performance Parallel Interface Link Encapsulation
HiPPI MI	High-Performance Parallel Interface Memory Interface
HiPPI PH	High-Performance Parallel Interface Physical

HiPPI SC	High-Performance Parallel Interface Switch Control
HiPPI ST	High-Performance Parallel Interface Scheduled Transfer
HI-SAP	Hybrid Isochronous-MAC Service Access Point
HL7	Health Industry Level 7
HLC	Higher Layer Compatibility
HLF	Higher-layer Function
HLL	High-Level Language
HLLAPI	High-Level Language Application Program Interface
HLPI	Higher Level Protocol Identifier
HLR	Home Location Register
HLS	Hue, Lightness, Separation
HMA	High Memory Area
HMI	Hub Management Interface
HMI	Human-Machine Interface
HML	Human-Machine Language
HMM	Hidden Markov Model
HMMO	Hypermedia Managed Object
HMMP	Hypermedia Management Protocol
HMMS	Hypermedia Management Schema
HMOM	Hypermedia Object Manager
HMP	Host Monitoring Protocol
HMUX	Hybrid Multiplexer
HMVIP	Hybrid Multi-Vendor Integration Protocol
HN	Host-to-Network
HNDS	Hybrid Network Design System
HOB	Hierarchical Operational Binding
HOL	Head of Line
HomePNA	Home Phone Networking Alliance
HP	Hewlett-Packard
HPAD	Host Packet Assembler/Disassembler
IIPC	Hand-Held Personal Computer
HPC	High-Performance Computing
HPC FMS	High-Performance Computing File Management System
HPCA	High-Performance Computing Act
HPCC	High-Performance Computing and Communications
HPCMP	High-Performance Computing Modernization Program
HPF	High-Pass Filter

HPFS	High-Performance File System
HPGL	Hewlett-Packard Graphics Language
HPIB	Hewlett-Packard Interface Bus
HPM	High-Power Microwave
HPN	High-Performance Network
HPPI	High-Performance Parallel Interface
HPR	High-Performance Routing
HPSS	High-Performance Switching System
HPT	Human Performance Technology
Hr	Hour
HRC	Hybrid Ring Control
HREF	Hypertext Reference
HRPF	Hexadecimal Reference Publication Format
HRTF	Head-Related Transfer Function
HRX	Hypothetical Reference Connection
HS	Half Session
HSB	Hue, Saturation, and Brightness
HSC	Hierarchical Storage Controller
HSDC	High-Speed Data Card
HSDN	High-Speed Data Network
HSI AN	High-Speed Local Area Network
HSM	Hardware-Specific Module
HSM	Hierarchical Storage Management (or Manager)
HSSI	High-Speed Serial Interface
HSTR	High-Speed Token Ring
HSV	Hue/saturation/value
HT	Horizontal Tab
HTML	Hypertext Mark-up Language
HTTP	Hypertext Transfer Protocol
HTTP-NG	Hypertext Transfer Protocol, Next Generation
HVAC	Heating, Ventilation, and Air Conditioning
HWD	Height Width Depth
Hz	Hertz
I	Current (in Amperes)
I	Increment
I	Information
I/G	Individual/Group
I/O	Input/Output
IA	Implementer's (or Implementation) Agreement

APP
A

IA	Intelligent Agent
IA	International Alphabet
IA	Intra-Area
IA5	International Alphabet 5
IAA	Initial Address Acknowledgement
IAB	Internet Activities Board
iABI	Intel Application Binary Interface
IAC	Inter-Application Communication
IAC	International Advisory Committee
IAC	Interpret As Command
IACA	Intra-Application Communication Area
IADCS	Interactivity Defined Context Set
IAHC	International Ad Hoc Committee
IAL	Intel Architecture Lab
IAM	Initial Address Message
IAN	Integrated Analog Network
IANA	Internet Assigned Numbers Authority
IANAL	I Am Not A Lawyer
IAOG	International ADMD Operators Group
IAP	Inner Administrative Point
IAP	Internet Access Provider
IAPP	Industrial Automation Planning Panel
IAR	Initial Address Reject
IAS	Interactive Application System
IAU	International Astronomical Union
IB	Indicator Bit
IBCN	Integrated Broadband Communication Network
IBIS	I/O Buffer Information Specification
IBM	International Business Machines
IBMCS	IBM Cabling System
IBMNM	IBM Network Management
IBT	Internet-Based Training
IC	Input Controller
IC	Integrated Circuit
IC	Interchange (or Interexchange) Carrier
IC	Internet Commerce
ICA	Independent Computing Architecture
ICA	Intelligent (also, Integrated) Communications Adapter

ICA	Intelligent Console Architecture
ICA	International Communications Association
ICAC	Industrial Commercial Advisory Council
ICADD	International Committee for Acceptable Document Designs
ICANN	Internet Corporation for Assigned Names and Numbers
ICC	Initiation Condition Check
ICC	International Chamber of Commerce
ICC	International Color Consortium
ICC	International Communication Conference
ICC	International Connectors and Cable
ICC	International Control Center
ICCA	Independent Computer Consultants Association
ICCB	Internet Configuration Control Board
ICCE	International Conference on Computers in Education
ICCF	Interactive Computing and Control Facility
ICD	Installable Client Driver
ICD	International Code Designator
ICE	Information and Content Exchange
ICF	International Cryptography Framework
ICF	Isochronous Convergence Function
ICI	Incoming Call Identification
ICI	Interexchange Carrier Interface
ICI	Interface Control Information
ICIP	Interchange Carrier Interface Protocol
ICLID	Incoming Called Identification
ICLS	International Conference on the Learning Sciences
ICM	Image Color Matching (or Management)
ICMP	Internet Control Message Protocol
ICN	International Cooperating Network
ICOS	International Club for Open Systems
ICOT	ISDN Conformance Testing
ICP	Initial Connection Protocol
ICP	Intelligent Call Processor
ICP	Interconnect Control Program
ICP	International Center of Photography
ICP	Internet Control Protocol
ICP	Interprocess Communications Protocol

ICPT	Intercept Tone
ICR	Intelligent Call Router
ICR	Intelligent Character Recognition
ICRC	Introduction to Cisco Router Configuration
ICS	Integrated Client Services
ICSA	International Computer Security Association
ICST	Institute for Computer Science and Technology
ICSU	Internal Channel Service Unit
ICSW	ISDN CPE and Software Workgroup
ICTYBTIWHTKY	I Could Tell You But Then I Would Have to Kill You
ICV	Integrity Check Value
ICW	Interrupt Continuous Wave
ID	Identifier
ID	Internet Draft
I-D	Internet Draft
IDA	Indirect Data Addressing
IDA	Integrated Digital Access
IDAPI	Integrated Database Application Programming Interface
IDC	Insulation Displacement Contact
IDC	International Data Corporation
IDC	International Direct Connection
IDCMA	Independent Data Communication Manufacturers' Association
IDCT	Inverse Discrete Cosine Transform
IDD	International Direct Dialing
IDDS	Innosoft Distributed Directory Server
IDE	Integrated (or Intelligent) Drive Electronics
IDE	Integrated Development Environment
IDF	Intermediate Distribution Frame
IDG	Inter-Dialog Gap
IDI	Initial Domain Identifier
IDL	Interface Definition Language
IDM	Integrated Diagnostic Modem
IDMS	Image and Document Management Services
IDN	Integrated Digital Network
IDN	Interface Definition Notation
IDP	Initial Domain Part
IDP	Integrated Detector Pre-amplifier

IDP	Internet Datagram Protocol
IDP	Internetwork Datagram Packet (or Protocol)
IDPR	Interdomain Policy Routing
IDRA	International Digital Radio Association
IDRP	Inter-Domain Routing Protocol
IDS	Integrated Digital Systems
IDSA	Interactive Digital Software Association
IDSL	ISDN Digital Subscriber Line
IDT	Interrupt Descriptor (also, Dispatch) Table
IDU	Interface Data Unit
IDV	Intel Device View
IE	Information Element
IE	Internet Explorer
IEC	Interexchange Carrier
IEC	International Electrotechnical Commission
IEE	Institute of Electrical Engineers
IEEE	Institute of Electrical and Electronics Engineers
IEEE-USA/CCIP	IEEE Committee on Communications and Information Policy
IEICE	Institute of Electronics, Information, and Communication Engineers
IEN	Internet Engineering (also, Experiment) Note
IEPG	Intercontinental Engineering Planning Group
IES	Information Exchange System
IESG	Internet Engineering Steering Group
IETF	Internet Engineering Task Force
IEV	International Electrotechnical Vocabulary
IF	Intermediate Frequency
IFC	Internet Foundation Class
IFG	Interframe Gap
IFIP	International Federation for Information Processing
IFMP	Ipsilon Flow Management Protocol
IFOBS	International Forum on Open Bibliographic Systems
IFPI	International Federation of the Phonographic Industry
IFRB	International Frequency Registration Board
IFS	Installable File System
IFS	Internal File System
IFU	Interworking Functional Unit

APP
A

IFYCSEM	Integrated First-Year Curriculum in Science, Engineering, and Mathematics
IGC	Institute for Global Communications
IGC	Interactive Gaming Council
IGES	Initial Graphics Exchange Specification
IGMP	Internet Group Management Protocol
IGN	IBM Global Network
IGOSS	Industry and Government Open Systems Specification
IGP	Interior Gateway Protocol
IGRP	Internet Gateway Routing Protocol
IHL	Internet Header Length
IHMC	Institute for Human and Machine Cognition
I-H-U	I Heard You
IIA	Information Interchange Architecture
IIJ	Internet Initiative Japan
IIM	Inventory Information Management
IINREN	Interagency Interim National Research and Education Network
IIOP	Internet InterORB Protocol
IISG	Investment Intelligence Systems Group
IIW	ISDN Implementors' Workshop
IK	Interchange Key
IK	Inverse Kinematics
IKE	IBM Kiosk for Education
IKE	Internet Key Exchange
IKMP	Internet Key Management Protocol
IKP	Internet Keyed Payment
ILAC	International Laboratory Accreditation Conference
ILD	Injection Laser Diode
ILEC	Incumbent Local Exchange Carrier
ILMI	Interim Link Management Interface
ILS	Internet Locator Service
ILU	Independent Logical Unit
IM	Instant Message
IM	Intelligent Messaging
IM	Intensity Modulation
IMAC	Isochronous Media Access Control
IMAP	Internet Message Access Protocol
IMC	Internet Mail Consortium

IMC	Internet Multicast Channel
IMCO	In My Considered Opinion
IMHO	In My Humble Opinion
IMIL	International Management Information Library
IML	Initial Microcode Load
IMNERHO	In My Not Even Remotely Humble Opinion
IMNSHO	In My Not So Humble Opinion
IMO	In My Opinion
IMP	Information Management Plan
IMP	Interface Message Processor
IMPACT	Information Market Policy Actions
IMPATT	Impact Avalanche and Transit Time
IMPDU	Initial MAC Protocol Data Unit
IMPS	Interface Message Processors
IMR	Intensive Mode Recording
IMR	Internet Monthly Report
IMS	Image Management Service (or Solutions)
IMS	Information Management Systems
IMS	Internet Map Server
IMS/VS	Information Management System/Virtual Storage
IMSI	International Mobile Subscriber Identity
IMSP	Independent Manufacturer Support Program
IMSP	Interactive Mail Support Protocol
IMTS	Improved Mobile Telephone Service
IM-UAPDU	Interpersonal Messaging User Agent Protocol Data Unit
IMVOD	Impulse VOD
In	Inch
IN	Integrated (or Intelligent) Network
IN	Interchange Node
InARP	Inverse Address-Resolution Protocol
InATMARP	Inverse Asynchronous Transfer Mode Address Resolution Protocol
INC	Integrated Network Connect
INCA	Integrated Network Communication Architecture
IND	Indication
INFOSEC	Information Systems Security
INIT	Initials
INMARSAT	International Maritime Satellite Service Organization

INN	Intermediate Network Node	IPI	Initial Protocol Identifier
INS	International Network Services	IPI	Intelligent Peripheral Interface
INSI	Intra-Network Switching Interface	IPICS	ISP Implementation Conformance System
INT	Interrupt	IPL	Initial Program Load
INTAP	Interoperability Technology Association for Information Processing	IPL	Interactive Services Primary Layer
INTELSAT	International Telecommunications Satellite Organization	IPM	Impulses per Minute
		IPM	Interpersonal Messaging
INTIAA	Internet Industry Association of Australia	IPMI	Intelligent Platform Management Interface
INTUG	International Telecommunications Users' Group	IPMI	IP Multicast Initiative
INWATS	Inward Wide Area Telephone Service	IPMS	Interpersonal Messaging Service (or System)
IO	Input/Output	IPM-UA	Interpersonal Messaging User Agent
IOC	Input/Output Control	IPN	Integrated Packet Network
IOC	Interoffice Channel	IPN	Interpersonal Notification
IOCDS	Input/Output Configuration Data Set	IPng	Internet Protocol, Next Generation
IOCP	Input/Output Control (or Configuration) Program	IPR	Isolated Pacing Response
IOD	Identified Outward Dialing	IPRA	Internet Policy Registration Authority
IOM	Input/Output Module	IPRL	ISPICS Requirements List
ION	Integrated On-Demand Network	IPS	Image Processing Server
IONL	Internal Organization of the Network Layer	IPS	Information Processing System
IOP	Input/Output Processor	IPS	Instructions per Second
IOP	Interoperability	IPSEC	Internet Protocol Security
IOPD	Input/Output Problem Determination	IPSIT	International Public Sector Information Technology
IOPM	Input / Output Permission Bitmap	IPSJ	Information Processing Society of Japan
IOS	Intermediate Open System	IPSS	Integrated Performance Support System
IOS	Internetwork Operating System	IPS-SMG	i-Planet Solution Surf and Mail Gateway
IOUGA	International Oracle Users Group – Americas	IPT	Internet Protocol Telephony
IP	Intelligent Peripheral	IPv4	Internet Protocol version 4
IP	Internet Protocol	IPv6	Internet Protocol version 6
IPA	International Prepress Association	IPX	Internetwork Packet Exchange
IPAE	Internet Protocol Address Encapsulation	IPX/SPX	Internetwork Packet Exchange/Sequenced Packet Exchange
IPC	Interprocess Communication	IQ	Information Quality
IPCP	Internet Protocol Internet Protocol	I-Q	Inter-quartile
IPCS	Interactive Problem Control System	IR	Infrared
IPD	Internet Protocol Datagram	IR	Internet (or Internetwork) Router
IPDS	Intelligent Printer Data Stream	IR	Internet Registry
IPDU	Internetwork Protocol Data Unit	IRB	Integrated Routing and Bridging
IPE	In-band Parameter Exchange	IRC	International Record Carrier
IPE	Intelligent Peripheral Equipment	IRC	Internet Relay Chat

IRD	Information Resource Dictionary
IrDA	Infrared Data Association
IRDG	InterResearch and Development Group
IRDS	Information Resource Dictionary System
IRF	Inherited Rights Filter
IRF	Intermediate Routing Function
IRL	Inter-Repeater Link
IRM	Inherited Rights Mask
IRN	Intermediate Routing Node
IRP	Internal Reference Point
IRQ	Interrupt Request Line
IRQL	Interrupt Request Level
IRSG	Internet Research Steering Group
IRTF	Internet Research Task Force
IRV	International Reference Version
IS	Industrial Simulation
IS	Information Store (or Systems)
IS	Integrated Services
IS	Intermediate System
IS	International (also, Internet) Standard
ISA	Industry Standard Architecture
ISAAC	Industry Standard Architecture Adapter Card
ISACA	Information Systems Audit and Control Association
ISAKMP	Internet Security Association Key Management Protocol
ISAM	Indexed Sequential Access Method
ISAPI	Internet Server (or Services) Application Programming Interface
ISBX	Integrated Services Business Exchange
ISC	International Switching Center
ISC	Intersystem Communications in CICS
ISCA	Intelligent Synchronous Communications Adapter
ISCC	Intelligent System Control Console
ISCF	Inter-System Control Facility
ISD	International Subscriber Dialing
ISDN	Integrated Services Digital Network
ISDN-UP	Integrated Services Digital Network User Part
ISE	Integrated Storage Element
ISH	Intermediate-System Hello

ISI	Information Sciences Institute
ISI	Inter-Symbol Interference
IS-IS	Intermediate System to Intermediate System
ISLUA	International SL-1 Users' Association
ISM	Industrial, Scientific, and Medical
ISN	Information Systems Network
ISN	Initial Sequence Number
ISN	Internet Society News
ISO	International Standardization Organization
ISO/CS	International Standardization Organization Central Secretariat
ISOC	Internet Society
ISODE	International Standardization Organization Development Environment
ISORM	International Standardization Organization Reference Model
ISP	Integrated Signal Processor
ISP	International Standard (or Standardized) Profile
ISP	Internet (or Information) Service Provider
ISPATS	International Standardized Profile Abstract Test Suite
ISPBX	Integrated Service Private Branch Exchange
ISPC	International Sound-Program Center
ISPCON	Internet Service Provider Convention
ISPETS	International Standardized Profile Executable Test Suite
ISPF	Interactive System Productivity Facility
ISPICS	International Standardized Profile Implementation-Conformance Statement
ISPIXIT	ISP Protocol Implementation Extra Information for Testing
ISPSN	Initial Synchronization Point Serial Number
ISPT	Instituto Superiore Poste E Telecommunicazioni (Superior Institute for Post and Telecommunications)
ISPX	ISDN Private Branch Exchange
ISQL	Interactive Structured Query Language
ISR	Intermediate Session Routing (or Router)
ISR	Interrupt Service Routine
ISRC	International Standard Recording Code
ISS	International Space Station

ISS	Internet Security Scanner (or Systems)
ISSB	Information Systems Standards Board
ISSI	Interswitching System Interface
ISSO	Information Systems Security Organization
ISTE	International Society for Technology in Education
ISU	Integrated Service Unit
ISUP	ISDN User Part
ISV	Independent Software Vendor
IT	Information Technology
IT	Information Type
IT	Intelligent Terminal
ITA	Industry Technical Agreement
ITA	International Telegraph Alphabet
ITAA	Information Technology Association of America
ITAEGC	Information Technology Advisory Experts' Group on Certification
ITAEGS	Information Technology Advisory Experts' Group on Standardization
ITAEGT	Information Technology Advisory Experts' Group on Telecommunications
ITB	Intermediate Text Block
ITC	Independent Telephone Company
ITCA	International Teleconferencing Association
ITCAP	Information Technology College Accreditation Program
ITCC	Information Technology Consultative Committee
ITDM	Intelligent Time-Division Multiplexer
ITE	Information Technology Equipment
ITFS	Instructional Television Fixed Service
ITI	Industrial Technology Institute
ITI	Information Technology Industry
ITI	Interactive Terminal Interface
ITIMS	In-service Transmission Impairment Measurement Set
ITR	Internet Talk Radio
ITRC	Information Technology Requirements Council
ITS	Institute for Telecommunication Sciences
ITS	Internet Telephony Server
ITS	Invitation to Send
ITSB	Image Technology Standards Board

ITSC	Inter-regional Telecommunications Standards Conference
ITSEC	Information Technology Security Evaluation Criteria
ITSP	Information Technology and System Planning
ITSP	Internet Telephony Service (or Solution) Provider
ITS-SP	Internet Telephony Server for Service Providers
ITSTC	Information Technology Steering Committee
ITT	Invitation to Transmit
ITTA	Information Technology Talent Association
ITU	International Telecommunications Union
ITUA	Independent T1 Users' Association
ITU-T	International Telecommunications Union, Telecommunications Sector
ITV	Interactive Television
ITXC	Internet Telephony Exchange Carrier
IUCV	Interuser Communication Vehicle
IUMA	Internet Underground Music Archive
IUPAC	International Union of Pure and Applied Chemistry
IUT	Implementation Under Test
IUW	ISDN User's Workshop
IVC	Integrated Visual Computing
IVD	Integrated Voice and Data
IVDMS	Integrated Voice and Data Multiplexers
IVDS	Interactive Video and Data Service
IVDT	Integrated Voice/Data Terminal
IVDTE	Integrated Voice/Data Terminal Equipment
IVHS	Intelligent Vehicle Highway Systems
IVMO	Initial Value Managed Object
IVOD	Interactive Voice on Demand
IVP	Instant Virus Product Kit
IVR	Interactive Voice Response
IVS	Interactive Video Service
IVSN	Interactive Video Services Network
IVT	Interrupt Vector Table
IW	Information Warehouse
IWBNI	It Would Be Nice If
IWF	Interworking Function
IWR	Interactive Web Response
IWU	Intermediate Working Unit

APP
A

IWU	Internetworking Unit
IXC	Interexchange Carrier or Channel
IXI	International X.25 Interconnect
IYFEG	Insert Your Favorite Ethnic Group
Jail	Just Another Image Library
JAIN	Java Advanced Intelligent Network
JAM	Just A Minute
JANET	Joint Academic Network
JBCL	JavaBeans Component Library
JBIG	Joint Bi-level Imaging Group
JBOD	Just a Bunch of Discs
JBPC	Java-Based Pipeline Connection
JCE	Java Cryptography Extensions
JCG	Joint Coordination Group
JCL	Job Control Language
JDA	Joint Development Agreement
JDBC	Java Database Connectivity
JDK	Java Development Kit
JDMK	Java Dynamic Management Kit
JEDEC	Joint Electronic Device Engineering Council
JEDI	Joint Electronic Data Interchange
JEDI	Joint Environment for Digital Imaging
JEMA	Japanese Electric Machinery Association
JES	Job Entry Subsystem
JES 2	Job Entry Subsystem 2
JES 3	Job Entry Subsystem 3
JFC	Java Foundation Class
JIPS	JANET Internet Protocol Service
JISC	Japanese Industrial Standards Committee
JIT	Just in Time
JITC	Joint Interoperability Test Center
JITEC	Joint Information Technology Experts Committee
JMAPI	Java Management Application Programming Interface
JMS	Java Message Service
JMUG	Japanese MAP/TOP User Group
JNDI	Java Naming and Directory Interface
JNDS	Java Naming and Directory Specification
JNI	Java Native Interface

JNT	Joint Network Team
JPEG	Joint Photographic Experts Group
JRAG	Joint Registration Advisory Group
JSA	Japan Standards Association
JSAPI	Java Speech Application Programming Interface
JSDK	Java Servlet Development Kit
JSIMS	Joint Simulation System
JSML	Java Speech Markup Language
JSS	JavaScript Style Sheet
JTAG	Java Technical Advisory Group
JTAPI	Java Telephony Application Programming Interface
JTAV	Joint Total Asset Visibility
JTC	Joint Technical Committee
JTC1	Joint Technical Committee 1
JTM	Job Transfer and Manipulation
JUG	Java Users Group
Jughead	Jonzy's Universal Gopher Hierarchy Excavation and Display
JUNET	Japanese UNIX Network
JVM	Java Virtual Machine
JVTOS	Joint Viewing and Tele-Operation Service
k	Kilo
KAK	Key-Auto-Key
KAU	Key Station Adapter Unit
Kb	Kilobit
KB	Kilobyte
Kbps	Kilobits Per Second
KBps	Kilobytes Per Second
KDC	Key Distribution Center
KDD	Kokusai Denshin Denwa
KDS	Keyboard Display Station
KHz	Kilohertz
KIS	Knowbot Information Service
KISS	Keep It Safely Secure
KISS	Keep It Simple, Stupid
km	Kilometer
KM	Knowledge Management
KMP	Key Management Protocol
KNI	Katmai New Instruction

KR	Knowledge Repository
KSC	Kennedy Space Center
KSH	KornShell
KSO	Keyboard Send Only
KSR	Keyboard Send and Receive
KST	Kelly Space & Technology
KSU	Key Service Unit
KTS	Key Telephone System
KTU	Key Telephone Unit
KVA	Kilovolt-amps
KWH	Kilowatt Hour
L	Length
L2F	Layer 2 Forwarding
L2TP	Layer 2 Tunneling Protocol
LAA	Locally-Administered Address
LAB	Latency Adjustment Buffer
LAB	Line Attachment Base
LAD	Local Area Disk
LAL	Leased Access Line
LAM	Lobe Attachment Module
LAMA	Local Automatic Message Accounting
LAN	Local Area Network
LAN/RM	Local Area Networks Reference Model
LANAO	LAN Automation Option
LANDA	Local Area Network Dealer Association
LANE	Local Area Network Emulation
LANRES	Local Area Network Resource Extension Services
LANSUP	LAN Adapter NDIS Support
LAP	Link Access Procedure (or Protocol)
LAPB	Link Access Procedure, Balanced
LAPD	Link Access Procedure, D Channel
LAPM	Link Access Procedure, Modem
LAPS	LAN Adapter and Protocol Support
LAPX	Link Access Procedure, Half Duplex
LASER	Light Amplification by Stimulated Emission of Radiation
LAT	Local Area Transport
LATA	Local Access and Transport Area
LAVC	Local Area VAX Cluster

LAWN	Local Area Wireless Network
LB	Leaky Bucket
LBRV	Low Bit Rate Voice
LBS	LAN Bridge Server
LBT	Listen Before Talk
LC	Link Control
LC	Local Channel
LCC	Lost Calls Cleared
LCCM	LANClient Control Manager
LCD	Learner-Centered Design
LCD	Line Current Disconnect
LCD	Liquid Crystal Display
LCD	Lost Calls Delayed
LCF	Lightweight Client Framework
LCF	Log Control Function
LCGN	Logical Channel Group Number
LCI	Logical Channel Identifier (or Identification)
LCID	Language Code Identifier
LCM	Line Concentrating Module
LCM	Logical Control Module
LCN	Logical Channel Number
LCP	Link Control Protocol
LCR	Least Cost Routing
LCR	Line Control Register
LCS	Laboratory for Computer Science
LCT	Last Compliance Time
LCW	Link Code Word
LD	LAN Destination
LD	Laser Diode
LDAP	Lightweight Directory Access Protocol
LDCM	LANDesk Client Manager
LDDI	Local Distributed Data Interface
LDDP	Local Directory Database
LDDS	Limited Distance Data Service
LDM	Limited Distance Modem
LDN	Listed Directory Number
LE	LAN Emulation
LE	Link Encapsulation
LE	Local Exchange

APP
A

LEA	Light Extender Amplifier		LIMS	Lotus, Intel, Microsoft Specifications
LEAF	Law-Enforcement Access Field		LINC	Laboratory Instrumentation Computer
LEARP	LAN Emulation Address Resolution Protocol		LINX	London Internet Exchange
LEC	LAN Emulation Client		LIP	Large Internet Packet
LEC	Local Exchange Carrier		LIP	Loop Initialization Protocol
LECC	Layered Error-Correction Code		LIPS	Lightweight Internet Person Schema
LECID	LAN Emulation Client Identifier		LIPX	Large Internetwork Packet Exchange
LECS	LAN Emulation Configuration Server		LIT	Line Insulation Test
LED	Light-Emitting Diode		LIU	Line Interface Unit
LEN	Large Extension Node		LIV	Link Integrity Violation
LEN	Low-End Network		LIVT	Link Integrity Verification Test
LEN	Low-Entry Networking		LIW	Long Instruction Word
LEN EN	Low-End Network End Node		LL	Length Identifier
LEOS	Low Earth Orbit Satellite		LL2	Link Level 2
LEP	Light Emitting Polymer		LLAP	LocalTalk Link Access Protocol
LES	LAN Emulation Server		LLATMI	Lower-layer Asynchronous Transfer Mode Interface
LF	Largest Frame		LLC	Logical Link Control
LF	Line Feed		LLC	Lower Layer Compatibility
LF	Low Frequency		LLC/SNAP	Logical Link Control, Subnetwork Access Protocol
LFC	Local Function Capabilities		LLC1	Logical Link Control Type 1
LFH	Local Failure Handler		LLC2	Logical Link Control Type 2
LFM	Link Framing Module		LLCS	Logical Link Control Security
LFN	Long Fat Network		LLI	Lower-Layer Identification
LFO	Low-Frequency Oscillator		LLP	Lower Layer Protocol
LFSID	Local Form Session Identifier		LLPDU	Logical Link Protocol Data Unit
LFSR	Linear Feedback Shift Register		LLS	LAN-Like Switching
LGC	Line Group Controller		LLSIG	Lower Layer Special Interest Group
LGN	Logical Group Number		LLWANP	LAN-to-LAN Wide Area Network Program
LH	Link Header		LM	Layer Management
LHT	Long Holding Time		LMDS	Local Multipoint Distribution Service
LI	Length Indicator		LME	Layer-Management Entity
LIB	Line Interface Base		LMI	Local Management Interface
LIC	Line Interface Coupler		LMMP	LAN/MAN Management Protocol
LID	Local Injection/Detection		LMMS	LAN/MAN Management Service
LIDB	Line Information Database		LMS	Least Mean Square
LIFO	Last In, First Out		LMU	LAN Manager for UNIX
LIJP	Leaf-Initiated Join Parameter		LMX	L Multiplex
LIM	Line Interface Module		LNA	Low Noise Amplifier
LIM	Lotus, Intel, Microsoft		LND	Local Number Dialing

LNM	LAN Network Manager		LSA	Limited Space-charge Accumulation
LNP	Local Number Portability		LSA	Link State Advertisement
LNRU	Like New Repair and Update		LSAP	Link Service Access Point
LO	Line Occupancy		LS-API	Licensing Server Application Program Interface
LOB	Line of Business		LSB	Least Significant Bit (or Byte)
LoC	Lines of Code		LSB	Lower Sideband
LOC	Loss of Cell Delineation		LSCU	Link Service Data Unit
LOCIS	Library of Congress Information Service		LSD	Line Sharing Device
LOCKD	LOCK Daemon		LSE	Local Single-layer Embedded
LOD	Level of Detail		LSE	Local System Environment
LOF	Loss of Frame		LSEL	Link Selector
LOHP	Labor Occupational Health		LSI	Large Scale Integration
LOL	Laughing Out Loud		LSL	Link Support Layer
LOS	Line of Sight		LSM	Local State Manager
LoS	Loss of Signal		LSN	Logical Session Number
LOTOS	Language for Temporal Ordering Specification		LSP	Link State Packet
LP	Linearly Polarized		LSPID	Link State Packet Identifier
LPAR	Logical Partition		LSR	Leaf Setup Request
LPC	Linear Predictive Coding		LSRR	Loose Source and Record Route
lpd	Line Printer Daemon		LSS	Low-Speed Scanner
LPDA	Link Problem Determination Application		LSSU	Link Status Signal Unit
LPDU	Logical Link Control Protocol Data Unit		LSU	Link-State Update
LPF	Low-Pass Filter		LT	Line (or Local or Loop) Termination
LPM	Lines per Minute		LT	Lower Tester
LPN	Local Packet Network		LTA	Line Turnaround
LPP	Lightweight Presentation Protocol		LTB	Last Trunk Busy
LPR	Line Printer		LTD	Local Test Desk
LPVS	Link Packetized Voice Server		LTE	Line Terminating Entity (or Equipment)
LQA	Line Quality Analysis		LTE	Local Telephone Exchange
LR	Loudness Rating		LTH	Length Field
LRC	Longitudinal Redundancy Check		LTM	LAN Traffic Monitor
LRD	Long-Range Dependence		LTO	Linear Tape Open
LRM	LAN Reporting Mechanism		LTRS	Letter Shift
LRP	Linux Router Project		LTSS	Long Term Station Statistics
LRU	Least Recently Used		LU	Logical Unit
LS	Licensing Service		LUA	Logical Unit Application
LS	Link Station		LUT	Look-Up Table
LS	Local Single-layer		LUW	Logical Units of Work
LS/LC	Line Stabilizer/Line Conditioner		LVD	Low-Voltage Differential

LWER	Lightweight Encoding Rules
LWG	LAN WorkGroup
LWS	Linear Whitespace
LWSP	Logical White Space
LWT	Listen While Talk
M	Mandatory
M	Mega-
m	Meter
M/SET	Mathematics/Science Education and Technology
MA	Maintenance and Adaptation
MA	Medium Adaptor
MAA	Major Acknowledgment
MAA	Mathematical Association of America
MAAP	Management and Administration Panels
MAC	Medium Access Control
MAC	Message Authentication Code
MAC	Move/Add/Change
MAC	Multiplexed Analog Components
MAC	Multiply/Accumulate
MACE	Macintosh Audio Compression and Expansion
MACF	Multiple Association Control Function
MACSTAR	Multiple Access Customer Station Rearrangement
MACU	Multidrop Auto Call Unit
MADE	Manufacturing Automation and Design Engineering
MAE	MERIT Access Exchange
MAFP	Multicast Attribute Framing Protocol
MAN	Metropolitan Area Network
MAP	Major Point
MAP	Manufacturing Automation Protocol
MAP	Mobile Application Part
MAP/TOP	Manufacturing Automation Protocol/Technical and Office Protocol
MAPDU	Management Application Protocol Data Unit
MAPI	Mail (also, Messaging) Application Program Interface
MARC	Machine-Readable Cataloging
Marvel	Management Aggregation and Visualizaton Environment
MAS	Meridian Authentication Services
MASC	Mobitex Asynchronous Communications (protocol)

MASE	Message Administration Service Element
MAT	Meridian Administration Tools
MATD	Maximum Acceptable Transit Delay
MathML	Mathematics Markup Language
MATR	Minimum Average Time Requirement
MAU	Medium Attachment Unit
MAU	Multistation Access Unit
MAW	Microsoft At Work
Mb	Megabit
MB	Megabyte
MB	Memoryless Behavior
mb/s	Megabits Per Second
MBA	MASSBUS Adapter
MBA	Master of Business Administration
MBE	Molecular-Beam Epitaxy
Mbps	Megabits Per Second
MBps	Megabytes Per Second
MBR	Master Boot Record
MBS	Maximum Burst Size
MBZ	Must Be Zero
MBZS	Maximum Bandwidth Zero Suppression
MC	Machine Congestion
MC	Multi-Chain
MCA	MicroChannel Architecture
MCAE	Mechanical Computer Assisted (or Aided) Engineering
MCC	Microelectronics and Computer Technology Corporation
MCC	Mission Control Center
MCD	Maintenance Cell Description
MCF	Medium Access Control Convergence Function
MCF	Meta Content Format
MCG	Motorola Computer Group
MCGA	Multi-Color Graphics Array
MCI	Media Control Interface
MCI	Microwave Communications Inc.
MCI	Multimedia Command Interface
MCIS	Microsoft Commercial Internet System
MCO	Multiplexer Control Option

MCP	MAC Convergence Protocol		MEGO	My Eyes Glaze Over
MCP	Microsoft Certified Professional		MERL	Managed Extended Private Line
MCPS	Microsoft Certified Product Specialist		MERS	Most Economic Route Selection
MCR	Minimum Cell Rate		MES	Manufacturing Execution System
MCR	Monitor Console Routine		M-ES	Mobile End System
MCS	Maintenance Control Subsystem		MESA	Manufacturing Execution System Association
MCS	Microsoft Cluster Server		MF	Mediation Function
MCTD	Mean Cell Transfer Delay		MF	Medium (or Multiple) Frequency
MCU	Mobile Control Unit		MF	More Fragments
MCU	Multipoint Control Unit		MFA	Management Functional Areas
MCVD	Modified Chemical Vapor Deposit		MFD	Master File Directory
MD	Make Directory		MFJ	Modified Final Judgment
MD	Management Domain		MFM	Modified Frequency Modulation
MD	Mediation Device		MFOTS	Military Fiber-Optic Transmission System
MD	Mini-Disc		MFS	Macintosh File System
MD	Multiple Dissemination		MFS	Message Formatting Service
MD5	Message Digest 5		MFS	Microsoft File System
MDA	Monochrome Display Adapter		MFT	Mixed Form Text
MDAC	Microsoft Data Access Component		MFTP	Multicast File Transfer Protocol
MDBS	Mobile Data Base Station		MG	Motor Generators
MDBS	Mobile Database System		MH	Message Handling
MDC	Manipulation Detecting Code		MH	Mobile Host
MDD	Multidimensional Database		MHD	Moving Head Disk
MDF	Main Distribution Frame		MHF	Mobile Home Function
MDI	Multiple Document Interface		MHP	Message Handling Protocol
MDIS	Mobile Data Intermediate System		MHS	Message Handling System (or Service)
MD-IS	Mobile Data, Intermediate System		MHS-SE	Message Handling System Service Element
MDN	Mobile Data Network		MHTS	Message Handling Test System
MDR	Message Detail Recording		MHz	Megahertz
MDS	Mail Delivery System		MI	Memory Interface
MDS	Multiple Dataset System		Mi	Mile
MDS	Multipoint Distribution Service		MIA	Minor Acknowledgment
MDSE	Message Delivery Service Element		MIB	Management (also, Message) Information Base
MDSL	Multirate Digital Subscriber Line		MIB	Medical Information Bus
MDTS	Modem Diagnostic and Test System		MIC	Medium Interface Cable (also, Connector)
ME	Mapping Entity		MIC	Message Identification Code
ME	Mobile Equipment		MIC	Message Integrity Check
MEA	Mail-Enabled Application		MICB	Meridian Integrated Conference Bridge
MED	Maximum Excess Delay		MICR	Magnetic Ink Character Recognition

MICS	Management Information Conformance Statement	MLS	Multi-Level Security
MID	Message ID	MLS	Multiple Listing Service
MID	Multiplexing Identifier	MLT	Multiple Logical Terminals
MIDA	Message Interchange for Distributed Application	Mm	Millimeter
MIDI	Musical Instrument Digital Interface	MMAC	Multimedia Access Center
MIF	Management Information File (or Form or Format)	MMBLS	Market Maker Business Language
MIFF	Management Information Format File	MMC	Microsoft Management Console
MII	Media Independent Interface	MMC	Multimedia Marketing Council
MIL	Management Information Library	MMD	Multimedia Document
MILNET	Military Network	MMDF	Multichannel Memorandum Distribution Facility
MIL-STD	Military Standard	MMDS	Multichannel Multipoint Distribution Service
MIM	Management Information Model	MMF	Multimode Fiber
MIMC	Massachusetts Interactive Media Council	MMFS	Manufacturing Message Format Standard
MIME	Multi-purpose Internet Mail Extension	MMHS	Military Message Handling System
MIMS	Meridian Intranet Meeting Software	MMI	Man-Machine Interface
Min	Minute	MMJ	Modified Modular Jack
MIN	Mobile Identification Number	MML	Man-Machine Language
MIN	Multi-path Interconnection Network	MML	Mathematical Markup Language
MIN	Multiple Interaction Negotiation	MMO	Mobile Module
MIN	Multistage Interconnection Networks	MMPM/2	Multimedia Presentation Manager/2
MIND	Modular Interactive Network Designer	MMS	Manufacturing Message Service
MIO	Multiple Port Information Outlet	MMS	Manufacturing Message Specification (or Standard)
MIP	Minor Point	MMS	Market Management System
MIPS	Millions of Instructions Per Second	MMS	Microsoft Merchant Server
MIR	Maximum Information Rate	MMT	Multimedia Multiparty Teleconferencing
MIRAN	Meridian Integrated Recorded Announcer	MMTA	Multimedia Telecommunications Association
MIS	Management Information Systems	MMU	Memory Management Unit
MIT	Management Information Tree	MMVF	Multimedia Video File Format
MIT	Massachusetts Institute of Technology	MMX	Multimedia Extensions
MITI	Ministry of International Trade and Industry	MNCS	Multipoint Network Control System
MJPEG	Motion Joint Photographic Experts Group	MNDS	Multi-Network Design System
MLA	Master License Agreement	MNP	Microcom Networking Protocol
MLFA	Machine-learned Fragment Analysis	MO	Magneto-Optical
MLI	Multiple Link Interface	MO	Managed Object
MLID	Multiple Link Interface Driver	MOAC	Message Origin Authentication Check
MLN	Main Listed Number	MOAS	Master Optical Access Switch
MLP	Multilink Procedures	MOC	Manufacturing Outreach Center
MLPP	Multilevel Precedence and Preemption	MOC	Mission Operations Computer
MLPPP	Multilink Point-to-Point Protocol	MOCS	Managed-Object Conformance Statement

MODEM	Modulator Demodulator		MPDU	Message Protocol Data Unit
MOFTEC	Ministry of Foreign Trade and Economic Cooperation		MPEG	Moving Pictures Experts Group
MOLI	Microsoft Online Institute		MPEG-3	Moving Pictures Experts Group, Audio Layer 3
MOLIS	Minority Online Information Service		MPG	Multiplayer Game
MOM	Message-Oriented Middleware		MPG	Multiple Preferred Guests
MONET	Multiwavelength Optical Network		MPI	Multiple Protocol Interface
MOO	Multi-User Simulated Environment, Object-Oriented		MPIX	Metropolitan Phoenix Internet Exchange
MOOSE	Multi-User Object-Oriented Shared Environment		MPL	Multi-Schedule Private Line
MOP	Maintenance (also, Management) Operations Protocol		M-Plane	Management Plane
			MPLS	Multi-Protocol Label Switching
MOP	Maintenance Operation Protocol		MPOA	Multi-Protocol Over Asynchronous Transfer Mode
MorF	Male or Female		MPP	Massively Parallel Processor (or Processing)
MOS	Mean Opinion Score		MPP	Multiple-Protocol Package
MOS	Metal Oxide Semiconductor		MPPC	Microsoft Point-to-Point Compression
MOSFET	Metal Oxide Semiconductor Field Effect Transistor		MPR	Multi-Port Repeater
MOSPF	Multicast Open Shortest Path First Protocol		MPR	Multi-Protocol Router
MOSS	Maintenance and Operator Subsystem		MPSA	Multiprocessor Server Architecture
MOSS	MIME Object Security Services		MPST	Memory Process Scheduling Table
MOT	Managed Object to Test		MPT	Ministry of Posts and Telecommunications
MOT	Means of Testing		MPT	Multi-Port Transceiver
MOTAS	Member of the Appropriate Sex		MPTM	Multi-Party Test Method
motd	Message of the Day		MPTN	Multi-Protocol Transport Network
MOTIS	Message-Oriented Text Interchange System		MPU	Multiprocessor Unix
MOTOS	Member of the Opposite Sex		MPW	Macintosh Programmer's Workbench
MOTSS	Member of the Same Sex		MPX	Multiplexer
MOV	Metal Oxide Varistor		MQ	Message Queue (or Queuing)
MP	Machine Processable		MQE	Managed Query Environment
MP	Managing Process		MQI	Message Queuing Interface
MP	Mobile Professional		MR	Magnetoresistive
MP	Modem Port		MR	Message Retrieval
MP	Multilink PPP (Point-to-Point Protocol)		MRCI	Microsoft Real-time Compression Interface
MP	Multiprocessing		MRCP	Microsoft Real-time Compression Format
MP Spec	Multiprocessing Specification		MRCS	Multi-rate Circuit Switching
MP3	MPEG, Audio Layer 3		MRI	Magnetic Resonance Imaging
MPAF	Midpage Allocation Field		MRM	Maximum Rights Mask
MPC	Mass-Produced Code (Generator)		MRO	Multi-Region Operation
MPC	Multipath Channel		MRP	Manufacturing Requirements Planning
MPCC	Multiprotocol Communications Controller		MRP	Multicast Routing Protocol
MPDT	Multi-Peer Data Transmission		MRPII	Manufacturing Resource Planning

MRSE	Message Retrieval Service Element	MSOH	Multiplex Section Overhead
MS	Management Services	MSP	Maintenance Service Provider
MS	Message Store	MSP	Message Security Protocol
MS	Meta-signaling	MSP	Microsoft Paintbrush
Ms	Millisecond	MSP	Mid-level Service Provider
MS	Mobile Station	MSP	Modular Switching Peripheral
MS	More Segments	MSS	MAN Switching System
MS&T	Modeling, Simulation, and Training	MSS	Maritime Satellite Service
MSA	Metropolitan Service Area	MSS	Mass Storage Service
MS-AIS	Multiplex Section Alarm Indication Signal	MSS	Metropolitan Switching System
MSAP	MAC Service Access Point	MSS	Mobile Satellite Service
MSAP	Management Service Access Point	MSS	Modem Substitution Switch
MSAP	Message Store Access Protocol	MSS	Multi-protocol Switched Services
MSAT	Mobile Satellite	MSSE	Message Submission Service Element
MSAU	Multi-Station Access Unit	MSSSE	Message Submission and Storage Service Element
MSB	Most Significant Bit (or Byte)	MST	Minimum Spanning Tree
MSC	Mobile (Services) Switching Center	MST	Multiplex Slotted and Token Ring
MSCP	Mass Storage Control Protocol	MSU	Management Service Unit
MSD	Microwave Semiconductor Device	MSU	Message Signal Unit
MSDN	Microsoft Developer's Network	MSU	Microsoft University
MSDOS	Microsoft Disk Operating System	MSU	Modem-Sharing Unit
MSDSL	Microsoft Digital Subscriber Line	MSVC	Meta-Signaling Virtual Channel
MSDTC	Microsoft Distributed Transaction Coordinator	MT	Machine Translation
MSF	Measurement Summarization Function	MT	Measured Time
MSF	Mobile Serving Function	MT	Message Transfer (or Type)
MS-FERF	Multiplex Section Far End Receive Failure	MTA	Mail Transfer Alias
MSG	Message	MTA	Major Trading Area
MSHP	Maintain System History Program	MTA	Message Transfer Agent
MSI	Medium Scale Integration	MTACP	Magnetic Tape Ancillary Control Process
MSI	Multiple Station Interface	MTAE	Message Transfer Agent Entity
MSK	Modulation Shift Keying	MTAU	Metallic Test Access Unit
MSL	Mirrored-Server Link	MTBF	Mean Time Between Failures
MSM	Matrix Switch Module	MTBSO	Mean Time Between Service Outages
MSM	Multi-Site Manager	MTC	Man Tended Capability
MSMQ	Microsoft Message Queue (or Queuing)	MTC	Manufacturing Technology Center
MSN	Microsoft Network	MTC	MIDI Time Code
MSN	Monitoring (cell) Sequence Number	MTCN	Minimum Throughput Class Negotiation
MSN	Multiple Systems Networking	MTL	Message Transfer Layer
MSNF	Multiple Systems Networking Facility	MTO	Many-To-One

MTP	Message Transfer Part (also, Protocol)	NACHA	National Automated Clearinghouse Association
MTR	Minimum Time Requirement	NACK	Negative Acknowledgement
MTS	Message Telecommunications Service	NACS	NetWare Asynchronous Communications Server (or Services)
MTS	Message Transfer Service		
MTS	Microsoft Transaction Server	NACT	National Applied Computer Technologies
MTS	Mobile Telephone Service	NAD	Network Activity Display
MTSE	Message Transfer Service Element	NADF	North American Directory Forum
MTSL	Message Transfer Sublayer	NAEB	North American EDIFACT Board
MTSO	Mobile Telephone Switching Office	NAEC	Novell Authorized Education Center
MTTA	Multi-Tenant Telecommunications Association	NAEP	National Assessment of Educational Progress
MTTR	Mean Time to Repair	NAK	Negative Acknowledgment
MTTSR	Mean Time to Service Restoration	NAL	Novell Application Launcher
MTU	Maximum Transmission Unit	NAM	Network Access Method
MTU	Message Transfer Unit	NAM	Numerical Assignment Modules
MTX	Mobile Telephone Exchange	NAMAS	National Measurement Accreditation Services
MUD	Multi-User Dimension (or Dungeon)	NAMPS	National Advanced Mobile Phone Service
MUF	Maximum Urgency First	NAMS	Network Analysis and Management System
MUF	Maximum Usable Frequency	NAMTUG	North American MAP/TOP Users' Group
MULTICS	Multiplexed Information and Computing Service	NAN	Neighborhood (also, National) Area Network
MUP	Multiple Uniform Naming Convention Provider	NANP	North American Numbering Plan
MUS	Multiuser System	NANPA	North American Nature Photography Association
MUSE	Multi-User Simulated Environment	NAP	Network Access Point
MUSH	Multi-User Simulated Hallucination	NAPLPS	North American Presentation Level Protocol Syntax
MUX	Multiplexer	NARA	National Archives and Records Association
MVC	Model-View Controller	NARM	National Association of Recording Merchandisers
MVC	Multicast Virtual Circuit	NARUC	National Association of Regulatory Utilities Commission
MVI	Major Vector Identifier		
MVID	Major Vector ID	NAS	Network Access Server (also, Signaling)
MVIP	Multi-Vendor Integration Protocol	NAS	Network Application Support
MVL	Major Vector Length	NAS	Network-Attached Storage
MVS	Multiple Virtual Storage	NASA	National Aeronautics and Space Administration
MVS/TSO	Multiple Virtual Storage/Time Sharing Option	NASC	Novell Authorized Service Center
MVS/XA	Multiple Virtual Storage/Extended Architecture	NASI	NetWare Asynchronous Services Interface
MVT	Multiprogramming with Variable Number of Tasks	NASTD	National Association of State Telecommunications Directors
MX	Mail Exchanger		
N	Normal	NAT	Network Address Translation
NA	Numerical Aperture	NATA	National Association of Testing Authorities
NAC	Network Access Controller	NATA	North American Telecommunications Association
NAC	Network Applications Consortium	NATD	National Association of Telecommunication Dealers
		NATD	North American Association of Telecom Dealers

APP
A

NAU	Network Access Unit
NAU	Network Addressable Unit
NAUN	Nearest Active (or Addressable) Upstream Neighbor
NAV	Norton Anti-Virus
NAW	National Association of Webmasters
NBEC	Non-Bell Exchange Carrier
NBMA	Non-Broadcast Multiple Access
NBP	Name Binding Protocol
NBS	National Bureau of Standards
NC	Network Connection
NC	Numerical Control (or Controller)
NCB	Network (also, Node) Control Block
NCC	National Computing Center
NCC	Network Control (or Coordination) Center
NCCF	Network Communications Control Facility
NCCUSL	National Conference of Commissioners on Uniform State Laws
NCD	Network Computing Device
NCEP	Network Connection Endpoint
NCF	NetWare Command File
NCIC	National Crime Information Center
NCIC	Network Control Interface Channel
NCL	Network Control Language
NCL	Null Convention Logic
NCM	Network Connection Management
NCMS	National Center for Manufacturing Science
NCMS	Network Control and Management System
NCO	National Coordination Office
NCO/HPCC	National Coordination Office High Performance Computing and Communications
NCP	NetWare Core Protocol
NCP	Network Control Program (also, Point)
NCR	National Cash Register
NCR-DNA	NCR-Distributed Network Architecture
NCS	National Communications Systems
NCS	NetWare Connect Services
NCS	Network Computing (also, Control) System
NCSA	National Center for Supercomputing Applications
NCSA	National Computer Security Association

NCSC	National Computer Security Center
NCSI	Network Communications Services Interface
NCSL	National Computer Systems Laboratory
NCT	Network Control Terminal
NCT	Noise Cancellation Technologies
NCTE	Network Channel Termination Equipment
NCTM	National Council of Teachers of Mathematics
NCU	National Currency Unit
NCUG	National Centrex Users' Group
ND	Network Digit
NDD	NetWare Directory Database
NDF	NCP/EP Definition Facility
NDIS	Network Driver Interface Specification
NDL	Network Database Language
NDM	Network Data Manager
NDM	Network Database Management
NDMS	NetWare Distributed Management Services
NDN	Non-Delivery Notification
NDPS	NetWare Distributed Print Services
NDPS	Novell Distributed Print Services
NDS	NetWare Directory Services
NDT	Net Data Throughput
NDTS	Network Diagnostic and Test System
NE	Network Element
NEAP	Novell Education Academic Partner
NEAT	Novell Easy Administration Tool
NEBS	Network Equipment Building System
NEC	National Electric Code
NEF	Network Element Function
NEI	Network Entity Identifier
NEMA	National Electrical Manufacturers Association
NEP	Noise-Equivalent Power
NESC	National Electric Safety Code
NEST	Novell Embedded Systems Technology
NET	Network Engineering Technologies
NET	Network-Entity Title
NET	Norme Européenne De Telecommunications (European Standard for Telecommunications)
NetBEUI	NetBIOS Extended User Interface

NetBIOS	Network Basic Input/Output System
NetDDE	Network Dynamic Data Exchange
NETID	Network ID
NETUCON	NetWare Users' Conference
NEWS	Network Error Warning System
NEXT	Near End Crosstalk or Near End Differential Crosstalk
NF	Not Finished
NFF	No Form Feed
NFPA	National Fire Protection Association
NFS	Network File System
NG	NuKE (Randomic Life) Generator
NGDLC	Next Generation Digital Line Carrier
NGI	Next Generation Internet
NGIO	Next Generation Input / Output
NGN	Next Generation Network
NGV	NuKE (Randomic Life) Generator Virus
NH	Non-busy Hour
NHOB	Non-specific Hierarchical Operational Binding
NHRP	Next Hop Routing (or Resolution) Protocol
NI	Network Interface
NIA	Network Interoperability Alliance
NIB	Node Identification (or Initialization) Block
NIC	Network Information Center
NIC	Network Interface Card
NICE	Network Information and Control Exchange
NID	Network Interface Device
NID	Next ID
NIE	Neurons in Excess
NIF	Network Information File
NII	National Information Infrastructure
NIIT	National Information Infrastructure Testbed
NIM	Network Interface Module
NiMH	Nickel Metal Hydride
NIMQ	Not in My Queue
NIOD	Network Inward/Outward Dialing
NIOSH	National Institute of Occupational Safety and Health
NIS	Names Information Socket
NIS	Network Information Server (or Services)
N-ISDN	Narrowband ISDN

NISO	National Information Standards Association
NIST	National Institute of Standards and Technology
NIST-APP	National Institute of Standards and Technology-Application Portability Profile
NIU	Network Interface Unit
NIUF	National ISDN Users Forum
NIUF	North American ISDN Users' Forum
NJE	Network Job Entry
NL	Network Layer
NLDM	Network Logical Data Manager
NLETS	National Law Enforcement Telecommunications System
NLM	NetWare Loadable Module
NLP	NetWare Lite Protocol
NLP	Normal Link Pulse
NLPID	Network Level Protocol Identifier
NLS	National Language Support
NLSP	NetWare Link Service Protocol
NLU	Natural Language Understanding
Nm	Nanometer
NM	Network Management
NMA	NetWare Management Agent (also, Architecture)
NMC	Network Management Center
NMC	NuView Management Console
NMCC	Network Management Control Center
NME	Network Management Entity
NMF	Network Management Forum
NMI	Non-Maskable Interrupt
NMP	Network Management Protocol
NMPA	National Music Publisher Association
NMR	NetWare Management Responder
NMRC	Nomad Mobile Research Center
NMS	National Market Systems
NMS	NetWare Management System
NMS	Network Management System (or Station)
NMSIG	Network Management Special Interest Group
NMSL/C	NetWare Management Server Link/Cable Option
NMSL/F	NetWare Management Server Link/Fiber Option
NMT	Nordic Mobile Telephone

NMTS	National Message Transfer System
NMU	Network Management Unit
NMVT	Network Management Vector Transport
NMX	Narrowline Media Exchange
NN	Negative Notification
NN	Network Node
nn	No News
NND	National Number Dialing
NNI	Netherlands Normatization Institute
NNI	Network-Node Interface
NNI	Network-to-Network Interface
NNM	Network Node Manager
NNS	NetWare Name Service
NNT	NetView-NetView Task
NNTP	Network News Transfer Protocol
NNTPD	Network News Transfer Protocol Daemon
NOAA	National Oceanic and Atmospheric Administration
NOC	Network Operations Center
NOF	Node Operator Facility
NOI	Notice of Inquiry
NOMS	Network Operations Management Symposium
NOOP	Network OSI Operations
NOS	Network Operating System
Np	Neper
NP	Network Provider (also, Performance)
NP	New Project
NP	Next Page
NPA	NetWare Peripheral Architecture
NPA	Network Professional Association
NPA	Numbering Plan Area
NPAI	Network Protocol Address Information
NPAP	Network Printing Alliance Protocol
NPB	Name Binding Protocol
NPC	Network Parameter Control
NPC	North Pacific Cable
NPCI	Network Protocol Control Information
NPDA	Network Problem Determination Application
NPDU	Network Protocol Data Unit
NPF	Network Partitioning Facility

NPI	Network Peripherals Incorporated
NPL	National Physical Laboratory
NPM	NetView Performance Monitor
NPRM	Notice of Proposed Rule Making
NPSI	Network Packet Switch Interface
NPTN	National Public Telecommunications (or Telecomputing) Network
NR	Negative Response
NR	Number of Receives
NRE	Non-Recurring Engineering Expense
NREN	National Research and Education Network
NRF	National Retail Federation
NRL	Naval Research Laboratory
NRLG	NuKE Random Life Generator
NRM	Network Resource Management
NRM	Normal Response Mode
NRS	Name Registration Scheme
NRZ	Non-Return to Zero
NRZI	Non-Return to Zero, Inverted
NRZ-L	Non-Return to Zero-Level
Ns	Nanosecond
NS	Network Service (or Signaling)
NS	Number of Sends
NSA	National Security Agency
NSA	Next Station Addressing
NSAI	National Standards Authority of Ireland
NSAP	Network Service Access Point
NSAPI	Netscape Services (or Server) Application Programming Interface
NSC	National Service Center
NSCC	National Securities Clearing Corporation
NSDU	Network Protocol Service Unit
NSE	Network Support Encyclopedia
NSEL	Network Selector
NSEP	National Security and Emergency Preparedness
NSF	National Science Foundation
NSF	Network Search Function
NSFnet	National Science Foundation Network
NSHEC	North Suburban Higher Education Consortium

NSI	NASA Science Internet
NSI	Network Solutions Incorporated
NSM	NetWare Services Manager
NSP	NATO Standardized Profile
NSP	NetWare Lite Sideband Protocol
NSP	Network Service Part (SS7)
NSP	Network Service Provider
NSP	Network Services Protocol
NSPC	National Sound Program Center
NSR	Network Surveillance and Reconfiguration
NSR	Non-Source Routed
NSRC	Network Startup Resource Center
NSS	Nodal Switching System
NSS	Novell Storage Services
NSSA	Not So Stubby Area
NSSDU	Normal Session Service Data Unit
NSSII	Network Supervisory System I
NSSN	National Standards Systems Network
NSSR	Non-Specific Subordinate Reference
NSW	Norton Safe on the Web
NT	Network Termination
NT	New Technology
NT1	Network Termination 1
NT12	Network Termination 1+2
NT2	Network Termination 2
NTD	Network Tools for Design
NTFS	New Technology (NT) File System
NTI	Novell Technology Institute
NTIA	National Telecommunication and Information Administration
NTIA/USA	National Telecommunication and Information Administration/USA
NTIS	National Technical Information Service
NTM	Network Traffic Management
NTN	Network Terminal Number
NTO	Network Terminal Option
NTP	Network Time Protocol
NTPF	Number of Terminals Per Failure
NTS	NetWare Technical Support

NTS	Network Telesystems
NTS	Network Tracking System
NTSA	Networking Technical Support Alliance.
NTSC	National Television Systems Committee
NTT	Nippon Telegraph and Telephone
NTU	Network Terminating Unit
NUA	Network Users' Association
NUC	NetWare Unix Client
NUCFS	NetWare UNIX Client File System
NUI	NetWare Users International
NUI	Network User Identification
NURB(S)	Non-Uniform Rational B-Spline
NVE	Network-Visible Entity
NVLAP	National Voluntary Laboratory Accreditation Program
NVOD	Near-Realtime Voice (or Video) on Demand
NVP	Network Voice Protocol
NVP	Nominal Velocity of Propagation
NVRAM	Non-Volatile Random Access Memory
NVT	Novell (also, Network) Virtual Terminal
NVTS	Network Virtual Terminal Service
NWI	New Work Item
NWRESD	Northwest Regional Education Service District
NWS	National Weather Service
NYIP	New York Institute of Photography
NYNMA	New York New Media Association
NYSE	New York Stock Exchange
NYSERNet	New York State Education and Research Network
O	Optional
O	Organization
O&M	Operation and Maintenance
O/R	Originator/Recipient
OA	Office Automation
OA	Operator Assistance
OAAC	Objects and Attributes for Access Control
OAC	Operational Amplifier Characteristics
OAI	Open Application Interface
OAM	Operation and Maintenance

APP

A

OAM	Operations, Administration, and Maintenance (Functions)
OAM&P	Operations, Administration, Maintenance, and Provisioning
OAMC	Operation and Maintenance Center
OAMC	Operation, Administration, and Maintenance Center
OAPDE	Open Architecture Predictive Dialing Engine
OAS	Open Application Server
OASIS	Online Access to the Standards Information Service
OASP	Open Access Signaling Protocol
OAUG	Oracle Application Users Group
OBEX	Object Exchange
OBI	Online Book Initiative
OBI	Open Buying on the Internet
OC	Optical Carrier
OC	Output Controller
OC1	Optical Carrier, Level 1
OCA	Open Communication Architecture
OCB	Out-going Calls Barred
OCC	Other Charges or Credits
OCC	Other Common Carriers
OCE	Open Collaborative Environment
OCF	Open Card Framework
OC-i	Optical Carrier, Level I
OCL	Object Constraint Language
OCLC	Online Computer Learning (also Library) Center
OCM	Originating Call Model
OCR	Optical Character Recognition
OCR/ICR	Optical Character Recognition / Intelligent Character Recognition
OCS	Operator Console Services
OCX	OLE Control Extension
OCX	OLE Custom Control
ODA	Open (also Office) Document Architecture
ODBC	Open Database Connectivity
ODBMS	Object DBMS
ODD	Operator Distance Dialing
ODETTE	Organization for Data Exchange by Teletransmission in Europe
ODI	Open Data-link Interface

ODIF	Office Document Interchange Format
ODINSUP	Open Data-link Interface/Network Driver Interface Specification Support
ODK	Office Developers Kit
ODL	Object Definition Language
ODMA	Open Document Management API
ODMG	Object Data Management Group
ODN	Optical Distribution Network
ODP	Open Distributed Processing
ODR	Optical Drivers and Receivers
ODS	Object Data Store
ODS	Open Data Services
ODSS	Object Data Store Segment
OE	Original Edition
OECD	Organization for Economic Cooperation and Development
OEDIPE	OSI EDI for Energy Providers
OEIC	Optoelectronic Integrated Circuit
OEM	Original Equipment Manufacturer
OFB	Output Feedback
OFBNLF	Output Feedback with A Nonlinear Function
OFE	Open Financial Exchange
OFNP	Optical Fiber, Non-conductive Plenum
OFNR	Optical Fiber, Non-conductive Riser
OFTEL	Office of Telecommunications
OFTP	ODETTE File Transfer Protocol
OFX	Open Financial Exchange
OGT	Outgoing Trunk
OH	Off Hook
OHP	On-Hold Plus
OHQ	Off-Hook Queue
Oic	Oh, I See
OID	Object Identifier
OIF	Optical Internetworking Forum
OIM	Optical Index Modulation
OIM	OSI Internet Management
OIT	Object Identifier Tree
OIW	OSI Implementers Workshop
OLAP	Online Analytical Processing

OLCP	Online Complex Processing
OLE	Object Linking and Embedding
OLE-DB	Object Linking and Embedding for Databases
OLI	Originating Line Information
OLRT	Online Real Time
OLT	Optical Line Termination
OLTP	Online Transaction Processing
OLU	Originating Logical Unit
OM	Object Management
OM	Optical Modulator
OMA	Object Management Association (or Architecture)
OMAP	Operations, Management, and Administration Part (SS7)
OMC	Operations and Maintenance Center
OMF	Object Management Function
OMG	Object Management Group
OMI	Open Messaging Interface
OMP	Optimized Multipath
OMS	Open Management System
OMT	Object Modeling Technique
ONA	Open Network Architecture
ONC	Open Network Computing
ONE	Open Network Environment (or Expandable)
ONI	Operator Number Identification
ONITA	Of No Interest to Anybody
ONMS	Open Network Management System
ONN	Open Network Node
ONP	Open Network Provision
ONPT	Office National des Postes et Telecommunications (National Office for Post and Telecommunications)
ONU	Optical Network Unit
OO	Over and Out
OOBE	Out-of-Box Experience
OOD	Object-Oriented Design
OODB	Object-Oriented Database
OOF	Out of Frame
OOK	On-Off Keying
OOP	Object-Oriented Programming
OOPSLA	Object-oriented Programming, Systems, Languages, and Applications

OOS	Out of Service
OOSE	Object-Oriented Software Engineering
OOUI	Object-Oriented User Interface
OPCR	Original Program Clock Reference
OPDU	Operation Protocol Data Unit
OPEN	Open Protocol Enhanced Network
OPI	Open Press Interface
OPM	Organization and Procedures Manual
OPNDST	Open Destination
OPRA	Options Pricing Reporting Authority
OPS	Off Premises Station
OPS	Open Profiling Standard
OPSEC	Open Platform for Secure Enterprise Connectivity
OPX	Off Premises Extension
OQL	Object Query Language
O-QPSK	Offset Quadrature Phase Shift Keying
ORAP	O/R Address Prefix
ORB	Object Request Broker
ORM	Operation Resource Management
OROM	Optical Read-only Memory
O-ROM	Optical Read-only Memory
ORT	Overload Recovery Time
ORWG	Open Routing Working Group
OS	Operating System
OS/2	Operating System/2
OS/400	Operating System/400 (for AS/400)
OS/NE	Operating System / Network Element
OSA	Open Scripting (also, Solutions) Architecture
OSA	Optivity Service Accounting
OSAK	OSI Application Kernel
OSC	Operating System Control
OSD	On-Screen Display
OSD	Open Software Distribution
OSE	Open Systems Environment
OSF	Open Software Foundation
OSF	Operations Systems Function
OSI	Open Systems Interconnection
OSI/CS	OSI Communications Subsystem
OSID	Origination Signaling Identifier

APP
A

OSIE	OSI Environment
OSILL	Open System Interconnection, Lower Layers
OSINet	OSI Network
OSIRM	Open Systems Interconnection Reference Model
OSIUL	Open System Interconnection, Upper Layers
OSME	Open Systems Message Exchange
OSNS	Open Systems Network Services
OSPF	Open Shortest Path First
OSPF-OMP	Open Shortest Path First – Optimized Multipath
OSR	OEM Service Release
OSS	Operational Support System
OSS	Operator Services System
OSSWG	Office System Standards Work Group
OSTA	Optical Storage Technology Association
OSTC	Open Systems Testing Consortium
OSTP	Office of Science and Technology Policy
OSWS	Operating System Workstation
OT	Onset Threshold
OTA	Office of Technology Assessment
OTDR	Optical Time Domain Reflectometer
OTL	OSI Testing Liaison
Otoh	On the Other Hand
OTQ	Out-going Trunk Queuing
Otth	On the Third Hand
OU	Organizational Unit
OUI	Organizational Unit Identifier
OURS	Open User Recommended Solution
OVD	Optical Video Disk
OW/AF	Object Windows for AppWare Foundation
OWAS	Oracle Web Application Server
OWF	One-Way Function
OWF	Optimum Working Frequency
OWRTS	Open-Wire Radio Transmission System
OWTL	Open-Wire Transmission Line
OXF	Open Exchange Format
P	Preamble
P&S	Publish and Subscribe
P/F	Poll/Final Bit
P1	Protocol 1 (Message Transfer Function in X.400)

P2	Protocol 2 (Interpersonal Messaging in X.400)
P3	Protocol 3 (Submission and Delivery Protocol in X.400)
P3P	Platform for Privacy Preferences
P5	Protocol 5 (Teletext Access Protocol in X.400)
P7	Protocol 7 (Message Store Access Protocol in X.400)
PA	Pre-Arbitrated
PA	Public Address
PAA	Peer Access Approval
PABX	Private Automatic Branch Exchange
PAC	Privilege Attribute Certificate
PACA	Picture Agency Council of America
PACCEPT	Presentation Accept
PACS	Picture Archiving and Communication System
PAD	Packet Assembler/ Disassembler
PAE	Peer Access Enforcement
PAEB	Pan American EDIFACT Board
PAF	Prearbitrated Function
PAGODA	Profile Alignment Group for Office Document Architecture
PAI	Protocol Address Information
PAIX	Palo Alto Internet Exchange
PAL	Phase Alternate Line
PAL	Printer Application Language
PAM	Pulse Amplitude Modulation
PAN	Peripheral Area Network
PAN	Personal Area Network
PANS	Pretty Amazing New Stuff
PAP	Password Authentication Protocol
PAP	Printer Access Protocol
PAR	Peak-to-Average Ratio
PAR	Positive Acknowledgment with Retransmission
PAR	Project Authorization Request
PARADISE	Piloting A Researcher's Directory Service in Europe
PARC	Palo Alto Research Center
PAS	Publicly Available Specification
PASP	Public Service Answering Point
PATG	Procedures and Awareness Task Group
PATS	Parameterized Abstract Test Suite

PAX	Private Automatic Exchange	PCS	Personal Communications Services
PB	Petabyte	PCS	Plastic Clad Silica
P-BEST	Production-Based Expert System Toolset	PCSA	Personal Computer System Architecture
PBN	Peripheral Border Node	PCSN	Private Circuit-Switching Network
PBX	Private Branch Exchange	PCT	Private Communications Technology
PC	Path Control	PCTE	Portable Common Tools Environment
PC	Payload CRC	PCTR	Protocol Conformance Test Report
PC	Personal Computer	PCU	Packet Control Unit
PC	Priority Control	PCVS	Point to Point Switched Virtual Connection
PC	Protocol Count	PD	Packetization (also, Propagation) Delay
PCA	Policy Certification Authority	PD	Physical Delivery
PCA	Program Calibration Area	PD	Public Domain
PCAMI	Personal Computing Asset Management Institute	PDA	Personal Digital (also, Data) Assistant
PCB	Printed Circuit Board	PDAD	Proposed Draft Addendum
PCCU	Physical Communications Control Unit	PDAM	Proposed Draft Amendment
PCE	Presentation Connection Endpoint	PDAU	Physical Delivery Access Unit
PCEI	Presentation Connection Endpoint Identifier	PDB	Process Data Block
PCEO	Personal Computer Enhancement Operation	PDC	Packet Data Channel
PCEP	Presentation Connection Endpoint	PDD	Physical Device Driver
PCF	Point Coordination Function	PDES	Parallel Discrete Event Simulation
PCI	Peripheral Component Interface	PDES	Product Data Exchange Standard
PCI	Presentation Context Identifier	PDF	Package (also, Printer) Definition File
PCI	Program (or Protocol) Control Information	PDF	Portable Document Format
PCI	Program-Controlled Interruption	PDF	Program Development Facility
PCI	Programmable Communication Interface	PDG	Phillips Design Group
PCI	Protocol Control Information	PDH	Plesiochronous Digital Hierarchy
PCI-X	Peripheral Component Interface – Extended	PDIAL	Public Dial-up Internet Access List
PCL	Printer Control Language	PDIF	Product Definition Interchange Format
PCM	Pulse Code Modulation	PDISP	Proposed Draft International Standardized Profile
PCM / TDM	Pulse Code Modulated / Time Division Multiplex	PDL	Page Description Language
PCMCIA	Personal Computer Memory Card International Association	PDM	Packet Division Multiplexing
		PDM	Parlance Document Manager
PCN	Personal Communications Network	PDM	Pulse Duration Modulation
PCO	Point of Control and Observation	PDN	Packet (also, Public) Data Network
PCONNECT	Presentation Connect	PDN	Passive Distribution Network
PCPM	Programmable Call Progress Monitoring	PDP	Parallel Data Processor
PCR	Peak Cell Rate	PDP	Professional Developer's Program
PCR	Program Clock Reference	PDP	Programmable Data Processor
PCS	Performance Centered System	PDS	Parallel Data Structure

PDS	Phase Distortion Synthesis
PDS	Physical Delivery Service
PDS	Premises Distribution System
PDS	Processor Direct Slot
PDTR	Proposed Draft Technical Report
PDU	Packet (or Payload or Protocol) Data Unit
PDV	Presentation Data Value
PEB	PCM Expansion Bus
PEB	Phone Set Emulation Board
PEBCAK	Problem Exists Between Computer and Keyboard
PEDI	Protocol for Electronic Data Interchange
PELS	Picture Elements
PEM	Privacy Enhanced Mail
PEN	Public Electronic Network
PEP	Packet Exchange Protocol
PEP	Platform Environment Profile
PEPY	Presentation Element Parser, YACC
PER	Packed Encoding Rules
PER	Program Event Recording
PERL	Practical Extraction and Report Language
PERT	Program Evaluation and Review Technique
PES	Packetized Elementary Stream
PES	Proposed Encryption Standard
PET	Page Entry
PETS	Parameterized Executable Test Suite
PFD	Privacy Forum Digest
PFEP	Programmable Front-End Processor
PFM	Pulse Frequency Modulation
PGA	Professional Graphics Adapter
PGA	Programmable Gate Array
PGF	Presentation Graphics Feature
PGI	Parameter Group Identifier
PGL	Professional Gaming League
PGML	Precision Graphics Markup Language
PGP	Pretty Good Privacy
PH	Packet Handler (or Handling)
PH	Packet Header
PhC	Physical-Layer Connection
PhCEP	Physical Connection Endpoint

PHIGS	Programmer Hierarchical Interactive Graphics System
PhL	Physical Layer
PhPDU	Physical Layer Protocol Data Unit
PhS	Physical-Layer Service
Ph-SAP	Physical-Layer Service Access Point
PhSDU	Physical-Layer Service Data Unit
PHY	Physical Layer
PI	Parameter Identifier
PI	Peripherals Interface
PI	Protocol Identification
PIA	Peripheral Interface Adapter
PIC	Personal Identification Code
PIC	Personal Intelligent Communicators
PIC	Point-in-Call
PIC	Primary Interexchange Carrier
PIC	Programmable Interrupt Controller
PICS	Protocol Implementation Conformance Statement
PICT	Picture
PID	Packet (also, Protocol) Identifier
PID	Personal ID
PIDX	Petroleum Industry Data Exchange
PIE	Pocket Internet Explorer
PIF	Phase Interface Fading
PIF	Program Information File
PIFT	Protocol Interbank File Transfer
PIM	Personal Information Manager
PIM	Port Interface Module
PIM	Protocol-Independent Multicast
PIM-DM	Protocol-Independent Multicast – Dense Mode
PIM-SM	Protocol-Independent Multicast – Standard Mode
PIN	Personal Identification Number
PIN	Positive Intrinsic Negative Photodiode
PIN	Procedure Interrupt Negative
Pine	Pine Is Not Elm
Ping	Packet Internet Groper
PIO	Programmed Input / Output
PIP	P Internet Protocol
PIP	Program Initialization Parameters

PIR	Protocol Independent Routing		PM	Physical Medium
PIT	Programmable Interrupt Timer		PM	Presentation Manager
pita	Pain in the Arse		PM	Protocol Machine
PITR	Product Inter-operation Test Report		PMA	Performance Measurement Analysis
PIU	Path Information Unit		PMA	Physical Medium Attachment
PIXEL	Picture Element		PMA	Program Memory Area
PIXIT	Protocol Implementation Extra Information for Testing		PMAC	Packet Media Access Controller
PJL	Printer Job Language		PMBX	Private Manual Branch Exchange
PKCS	Public Key Cryptographic Services		PMD	Physical Medium (or Media) Dependent
PKCS	Public Key Cryptography System (or Standard)		PML	Permitted Maximum Level
PKE	Public Key Encryption		PMMU	Paged Memory Management Unit
PKI	Public Key Infrastructure		PMN	Performance Monitoring
PKP	Public Key Partners		PMS	Pantone Matching System
PL	PAD Length		PMS	Public Message Service
PL	Payload Length		PMSP	Preliminary Message Security Protocol
PL	Physical (also, Presentation) Layer		PMT	Packet-Mode Terminal
PL	Private Line		PMT	Photo Multiplier Tube
PL	Programming Language		PMTU	Path Maximum Transmission Unit
PLAF	Pluggable Look-and-Feel		PMX	Packet Multiplexer
PLC	Programmable Logic Controller		PMX	Private Message Exchange
PLCP	Physical Layer Convergence Procedure (or Protocol)		PN	Personal Name
PLD	Phase Lock Demodulator		PN	Positive Notification
PLIP	Parallel Line Internet Protocol		PNA	Private Network Adapter
PLK	Primary Link		PNAP	Private Network Access Point
PLL	Phase-Locked Loop		PNC	Personal Number Calling
PLM	Photo Lab Management		PND	Present Next Digit
PLMN	Public Land Mobile Network		PNG	Portable Network Graphic
PL-OAM	Physical Layer Operation and Maintenance (cell)		PNIC	Private Network Identification Code
plokta	Press Lots of Keys to Abort		PNM	Physical Network Management
PLP	Packet-Layer Protocol (or Procedure)		P-NNI	Private Network-to-Network Interface
PLP	Packet-Level Protocol		PnP	Plug and Play
PLS	Physical Layer Signaling		PNSQC	Pacific Northwest Software Quality Conference
PLS	Primary Link Station		POA	Post Office Agent
PLSAP	Physical Layer Service Access Point		POAC	Probe Origin Authentication Check
PLU	Primary Logical Unit		PoF	Proof of Failure
PLV	Production Level Video		POH	Path Overhead
PM	Performance Management		POI	Path Overhead Indicator
PM	Phase Modulation		POI	Program Operator Interface
			POL	Participant Online

APP
A

PON	Passive Optical Network
POP	Point of Presence
POP	Post Office Protocol
POP3	Post Office Protocol, Version 3
POPL	Proceedings on Programming Languages
POS	Packet over SONET
POS	Passive Optical Splitter
POS	Point of Sale
POSI	Promoting OSI
POSIX	Portable Operating System Interface Extension
POST	Power On Self-Test
POT	Point of Termination
POTS	Plain Old Telephone Service
POV	Point of View
POWER	Performance Optimization with Enhanced RISC
PPA	Professional Photographers of America
PPC	Program-to-Program Communication
PPCI	Presentation Protocol Control Information
PPDU	Presentation Protocol Data Unit
PPL	Plain Position Indicator
PPL	Programmable Protocol Language
PPM	Pages Per Minute (or Month)
PPM	Presentation Protocol Machine
PPM	Principal Period Maintenance
PPM	Pulse Position Modulation
PPN	Private Packet Network
PPO	Primary Program Operator
PPP	Point to Point Protocol
PPPI	Production Planning Process Industries
PPP-MP	Point-to-Point Protocol – Multiprotocol
PPS	Packets (or Pulses) Per Second
PPS	Path Protection Switching
PPSDN	Public Packet-Switched Data Network
PPSN	Public Packet Switched Network
PPTM	Protocol Profile Testing Methodology
PPTP	Point-to-Point Tunneling Protocol
PR	Prepare
PR/SM	Processor Resource/Systems Manager
PRA	Parabolic Reflector Antenna

PRA	Primary Rate Access
PRAM	Parameter RAM
PRB	Packet Receive Buffer
PRB	Procedures Review Board
PRDMD	Private Directory-Management Domain
PREFUSE	Presentation Refuse
PRG	Purge
PRI	Primary Rate Interface
PRID	Protocol Identifier
PRM	Protocol Reference Model
PRMD	Private Mail (or Management) Domain
PRML	Partial-Response Maximum-Likelihood (technology)
PROFS	Professional Office System
PROM	Programmable Read-only Memory
P-ROM	Partial Read-only Memory
PRTM	Printing Response Time Monitor
PS	PostScript
PS	Presentation Service
PS	Print Server
PS	Proposed Standard
PS/2	Personal System 2
PS/VP	Personal System/Value Point
PSAP	Presentation Service Access Point
PSAP	Public Safety Answering Point
PSC	Print Server Control
PSC	Protection Switching Circuit
PSC	Public Service Commission
PSD	Power Spectral Density
PSD	Protection Switching Duration
PSDN	Packet-Switched Data Network
PSDN	Public Switched Data Network
PSDU	Presentation Service Data Unit
PSE	Packet Switching Exchange
PSE	Power Series Expansion
PSEB	Phone Set Emulation Board
PSEL	Presentation Selector
PSH	Push Flag
PSI	Packet Switching Interface

PSI	Performance Summary Interval		PTTXAU	Public Teletex Access Unit
PSI	Process to Support Interoperability		PTXAU	Public Telex Access Unit
PSI	Program-Specific Information		PU	Physical (also, Presentation) Unit
PSID	Product-Set Identification		PUC	Public Utility Commission
PSK	Phase Shift Keying		PUC/PSC	Public Utility Commission / Public Service Commission
PSM	Phase Shift Modulation		PUCP	Physical Unit Control Point
PSN	Packet Switched Network (or Node)		PUMS	Physical Unit Management Service
PSN	Packet Switching Node		PUT	Program Update Tape
PSN	Private Switching Network		PV	Parameter Value
PSNB	Packet Switched Network		PVC	Polyvinyl Chloride
PSP	Payphone Service Provider		PVC	Private (or Permanent) Virtual Circuit
PSP	Presentation Services Process		PVCC	Permanent Virtual Channel Connection
PSPDN	Packet Switched Public Data Network		PVD	Point of Video Delivery
PSR	Previous Slot Read		PVN	Private Virtual Network
PSRG	Privacy and Security Research Group		PVPC	Permanent Virtual Path Connection
PSS	Performance Support Solution		PVT	Permanent Virtual Terminal
PSTN	Public Switched Telephone Network		PWA	Premises Wiring Administrator
PSU	Peak Simultaneous Range		PWGSC	Public Works and Government Services Canada
PSW	Program Status Word		PWL	Power Indicator
PT	Pass Through		PWM	Pulse Width Modulation
PT	Payload Type		PWSS	Programmable Workstation
PT	Please Token		PXE	Preboot Execution
PTAN	Performance Testing Alliance for Networks		Q	Queue
PTC	Positive Temperature Coefficient		QA	Queue Arbitrated
PTC	Public Telephone Companies		QAF	Queued Arbitrated Function
PTE	Path Terminating Entity		QAI	Quality Assurance Institute
PTF	Program Temporary Fix		QAM	Quadrature Amplitude Modulation
PTI	Payload Type Identifier		QBE	Query by Example
PTLXAU	Public Telex Access Unit		QC	Quiesce Complete
PTM	Packet Transfer Mode		QCD	Quarterly Charm Deficiency
PTM	Pulse Time Modulation		QCIF	Quarter Common Intermediate Format
PTN	Personal Telecommunications Number		QD	Queuing Delay
PTN	Public Telephone Network		qdu	Quantization Distortion Unit
PTNX	Private Telecommunications Network Exchange		QEC	Quiesce At End of Chain
PTP	Point-To-Point		QFA	Quick File Access
PTR	Pointer		QFC	Quantum Flow Control
PTS	Presentation Time Stamp		QIC	Quarter-Inch Cartridge
PTS	Profile Test Specification		QLLC	Qualified Link Level Control
PTT	Post, Telephone, and Telegraph			

APP
A

QLLC	Qualified Logical Link Control
QMF	Query Management Facility
QoS	Quality of Service
qotd	Quote of the Day
QPA	Quad-Port Acceleration
QPSK	Quadrature Phase Shift Keying
QPSX	Queued Packet and Synchronous Circuit Exchange
QPW	Quattro Pro for Windows
QR	Quick Response
QTAM	Queued Telecommunications Access Method
QWEST	Quantum-Well Envelope State Transition
QWL	Quantum-Well Laser
R	Reminder
R	Reserved
R	Resistance (in Ohms)
RA	Rate Adapter
RA	Read Audit
RA	Recognition Arrangement
RA	Registration Authority
RA0	Rate Adapter 0
RA1	Rate Adapter 1
RA2	Rate Adapter 2
RAB	Record Access Block
RAC	Remote Access
RACE	Research and Development of Advanced Communication in Europe
RACF	Resource Access Control Facility
RAD	Rapid Application Development
RADAR	Radio Detection and Ranging
RADCOM	Radio Communications
RADIUS	Remote Authentication Dial-In User Service
RADSL	Rate Adaptive Digital Subscriber Line
RAG	Registration and Advisory Group
RAI	Remote Alarm Indicator
RAID	Redundant Array of Inexpensive Disks
RAM	Random-Access Memory
RAM	Remote Access Manager
RAMDAC	Random Access Memory Digital-to-Analog Converter

RARC	Regional Administrative Conference
RARE	Reseaux Associes Pour La Recherche Europeenne (Associated Network for European Research)
RARP	Reverse Address Resolution Protocol
RAS	Remote Access Services
RBHC	Regional Bell Holding Company
RBOC	Regional Bell Operating Company
RBone	Reservation Backbone
RBS	Robbed Bit Signaling
RC	Routing Control
RCA	Radio Corporation of America
RCA	Remote Computer Access
RCAC	Remote Computer Access Communications Service
RCC	Routing Control Channel
RCD	Receiver-Carrier Detector
RCF	Remote Call Forwarding
RCMD	Remote Command
RCS	Resource Constructor Set
RCV	Receiver
RD	Receive Data
RD	Remove Directory
RD	Request A Disconnect
RD	Route Descriptor
RD	Routing Domain
RDA	Remote Database (also, Document) Access
RDAU	Remote Data Access Unit
RDBMS	Relational (also, Remote) Database Management System
RDC	Remote Data Concentrator
RDF	Rate Decrease Factor
RDF	Resource Description Framework
RDI	Remote Defect Identification (or Indication)
RDI	Restricted Digital Information
RDL-SQL	Relational Database Language-Structured Query Language
RDM	Remote Document Management
RDN	Relative Distinguished Name
RDO	Remote Data Object
RDP	Reliable Data Protocol
RDP	Remote Desktop (or Display) Protocol

RDRAM	Rambus Dynamic Random Access Memory		RG	Rapporteur Group
RDS	Remote Data Scope (also, Service)		RG	Regenerator
RDT	Rapid Deployment Team		RGB	Red, Green, Blue
RDT	Recall Dial Tone		RGO	Royal Greenwich Observatory
RDT	Referenced Data Transfer		RH	Request (or Response) Header
RDT	Resource Definition Table		RHOB	Relevant Hierarchical Operational Binding
RE	Reference Equivalent		RI	Reference Implementation
RE	Routing Element		RI	Rename Inhibit
REA	Rural Electrification Administration		RI	Ring In
REC	RARE Executive Committee		RI	Ring Indication
RECC	Reverse Control Channel		RI	Routing Indicator (or Information)
RECFMS	Record Formatted Maintenance Statistics		RIAA	Recording Industry Association of America
REJ	Reject		RIB	Routing Information Base
REL	Release Message		RID	Relative Identifier
RELML	Real Estate Listings Markup Language		RIF	Routing Information Field
REM	Ring Error Monitor		RII	Route Information Indicator
REMF	Reverse Electromagnetic Force		RIM	Request Initialization Mode
REN	Ringer Equivalence Number		RIP	Router (or Routing) Information Protocol
REQ	Request		RIPE	Reseaux IP Europeens (European IP Networks)
RER	Residual Error Rate		RIPEM	Riordan's Privacy Enhanced Mail
RES	Reserved		RIPng	Routing Information Protocol, Next Generation
RESP	Response		RISC	Reduced Instruction Set Computing
RESYNC	Resynchronization		RISE	Retrieval and Interchange of Standards in Europe
RET	Resolution Enhancement Technology		RJ	Registered Jack
RETLA	Really Extended Three Letter Acronym		RJ	Reject
REXX	Restructured Extended Executor		RJE	Remote Job Entry
RF	Radio Frequency		RL	Real Life
RF	Remote Fault		RLC	Release Complete
RFC	Radio Frequency Choke		RLCM	Remote Line Concentrating Module
RFC	Request for Comments		RLIN	Research Libraries Information Network
RFD	Regional Frequency Divider		RLL	Run-Length Limited
RFD	Request for Discussion		RLM	Remote Line Module
RFI	Radio Frequency Interference		RLN	Remote LAN Node
RFI	Request for Information		RLS	Recursive Least Square
RFP	Request for Proposal		RLS	Remote Line Switch
RFQ	Request for Quote		RLSD	Received Line Signal Detector
RFS	Remote File Server (or System)		RLT	Release Link Trunking
RFT	Revisable Format Text		RM	Rate Monotonic
RG	Radio Government		RM	Reference Model

RM	Resource Manager (or Management)
RMATS	Remote Maintenance and Testing System
RMDM	Reference Model of Data Management
RMF	Remote Management Facility
RMHS	Remote Message Handling Service
RMI	Remote Method Invocation
RM-ODP	Reference Model for Open Distributed Processing
RMON	Remote Network Monitoring
RMON-MIB	Remote Network Monitoring Management Information Base
RMP	Reliable Multicast Protocol
RMS	Record Management Services
RMS	Repetitive Motion Syndrome
RMS	Root Mean Square
RMT	Ring Management
rn	Read News
RN	Receipt Notification
RN	Reference Noise
RNAA	Request Network Address Segment
RNE	Reseau National D'Essai (National Network for Testing)
RNR	Receiver Not Ready
RO	Receive (or Repair) Only
RO	Remote Operations
RO	Ring Out
ROAC	Report Origin Authentication Check
ROAD	Routing and Addressing (Group)
RODM	Resource Object Data Manager
RODNI	Record-On-Demand via Network Interface
ROER	Remote Operations Error
rofl	Rolling on the Floor, Laughing
ROH	Receiver Off-Hook
ROI	Return on Investment
ROIV	Remote Operations Invoke
ROLAP	Relational Online Analytic Processing
ROLC	Routing Over Large Clouds
ROM	Read-Only Memory
ROPM	Remote Operations Protocol Machine
RORE	Remote Operations Return Error

RORJ	Remote Operations Reject
RORS	Remote Operations Response
ROS	Read-Only Store
ROS	Remote Operations Service
ROSE	Remote Operations Service Element
ROTFL	Rolling on the Floor Laughing
ROTL	Remote Office Test Line
ROW	Rest of the World
RP	Radio Frequency
RP	Rotate-Plane
RPC	Registered Protective Circuitry
RPC	Remote Procedure Call
RPE	Remote Peripheral Equipment
RPG	Remote Password Generator
RPG	Report Program Generator
RPL	Remote Procedure (or Program) Load
RPL	Request Parameter List
RPM	Revolutions Per Minute
RPOA	Recognized Private (or Public) Operating Agency
RPQ	Request for Price Quotation
RPS	Ring Parameter Server (or Service)
RPU	Redundant Power Unit
RQC	Repair and Quick Clean
RR	Ready to Receive
RR	Receive Ready
RRD	Revised Resistance Design
RRIP	Rock Ridge Interchange Protocol (Specifications)
RRISI	Realtors Regional Information System, Inc.
RRQ	Read Request
RRT	Reverse Recovery Time
RS	Recommended Standard
RS	Relay System
RS	Remote Single-Layer
RS	Resume Session
RS	Ring Station
RS-#	Recommended Standard #
RSA	Resume Acknowledgment
RSA	Rivest, Shamir, Adleman

RSA-PPDU	Resynchronize Acknowledge Presentation Protocol Data Unit		RTFM	Read the FLWO (Four-letter Word Omitted) Manual
RSC	Remote Switching Center		RTM	Read the Manual (also, Monitor)
RSCS	Remote Spooling and Control Subsystem		RTMP	Routing Table Maintenance Protocol
RSCV	Route Selection Control Vector		RTNR	Ringing Tone No Reply
RSE	Remote Single-Layer Embedded		RTO	Real-Time Object
RSF	Remote Support Facility		RTOAC	Reliable Transfer Open Accept
RSI	Repetitive Stress Injury		RTORJ	Reliable Transfer Open Reject
RSL	Received Signal Level		RTORQ	Reliable Transfer Open Request
RSN	Real Soon Now		RTOS	Real-Time Operating System
RSO	Regional Standards Organization		RTP	Real-time Transport Protocol
RSOH	Regenerator Section Overhead		RTP	Routing Update Protocol
RSP	Response		RTP/RTCP	Real-time Transport Protocol / Real-time Control Protocol
RS-PCM	Resynthesized Pulse Code Modulation		RTPM	Reliable Transfer Protocol Machine
RS-PPDU	Resynchronize Presentation Protocol Data Unit		RTR	Ready to Receive
RSPX	Remote Sequenced Packet Exchange		RTS	Reliable Transfer Service
RSRB	Remote Source-Route Bridging		RTS	Request to Send
RSS	Route Selection Services		RTS	Residual Time Stamp
RST	Reset Flag		RTSE	Reliable Transfer Service Element
RSU	Remote Switching Unit		RTSP	Real-Time Streaming Protocol
Rsvd	Reserved		RTT	Round-Trip Time
RSVP	Resource Reservation Protocol		RTTI	Runtime Type ID
RSX	Real-time Resource Sharing Executive		RTTP	Reliable Transfer Token Response
RT	Reliable Transfer		RTU	Remote Test Unit
RT	Report		RTU	Right to Use
RT	Routing Table (or Type)		RU	Remote Unit
RT	Total Resistance		RU	Request (or Response) Unit
RTA	Resident Technology Advisor		RUA	Remote User Agent
RTAB	Reliable Transfer Abort		RUIP	Remote User Information Program
RTBM	Read the Bloody Manual		RUR	Repair, Update, Refurbish
RTBX	Real-Time Bandwidth Exchange		RVI	Reverse Interrupt
RTC	RARE Technical Committee		RW	Read-Write
RTC	Real-Time Clock		RWCC	Regional Workshop Coordinating Committee
RTCP	Real-Time Control Protocol		RWSCC	Regional Workshop Coordinating Committee
RTCS	Real-Time Computing System		RZ	Return to Zero
RTDS	Real-Time Data System		RZI	Return to Zero, Inverted
RTEL	Reverse Telnet		S	Second
RTF	Rich Text Format		S	Shareable
RTFAQ	Read the Frequently Asked Questions		S	Source

APP
A

S/MIME	Secure Multipurpose Internet Mail Extensions	SAO	Software Association of Oregon
S/PDIF	Sony/Philips Digital Interchange Format	SAP	Service Access Point
SA	Sequenced Application	SAP	Service Advertising Protocol
SA	Source Address	SAPI	Service Access Point Identifier
SA	Study Administration	SAPI	Speech Application Programming Interface
SA	Subarea	SAR	Segmentation and Reassembly
SA	System Attendant	SARC	Symantec Anti-Virus Research Center
SAA	Specific Administrative Area	SARF	Security Alarm Reporting Function
SAA	Standards Association of Australia	SARM	Set Asynchronous Response Mode
SAA	Systems Application Architecture	SAS	Secure Authentication Services
SAAL	Signaling ATM Adaptation Layer	SAS	Single-Attachment Station
SAB	Subnetwork-Access Boundary	SAS	Statistically Assigned Sockets
SABM	Set Asynchronous Balanced Mode	SAS	SWITCH Access System
SABME	Set Asynchronous Balanced Mode Extended	SASE	Special Application Service Element
SABRE	Semi-Automatic Business Research Environment	SASFE	SEF/AIS Alarm Signal, Far End
SAC	Simplified Access Control	SASI	Shugart Associates System Interface
SAC	Single-Attachment Concentrator	SASL	Secure Authentication Socket Layer
SACF	Single Association Control Function	SASL	Simple Authentication and Security Layer
SACK	Selective Acknowledgment	SASO	Saudi Arabian Standards Organization
SACL	System Access Control List	SATAN	Security Analysis Tool for Auditing Networks
SACSS	State Automated Child Support System	SATC	Software Assurance Technology Center
SAF	Secure Authentication Facility	SATF	Security Audit Trail Function
SAF	Single Association Control Function Auxiliary Facility	SATF	Shared-Access Transfer Facility
SAF	Spectral Analysis Facilities	SATS	Selected Abstract Test Suite
SAF	Subnetwork Access Facility	SAW	Surface Acoustic Wave
SAFE	Security and Freedom through Encryption	SBA	Set Buffer Address
SAFENET	Survivable Adaptable Fiber-optic Embedded Network	SBC	Single Board Computer
		SBC	System Broadcast Channel
SAF-TE	SCSI-Accessed Fault-Tolerant Enclosure	SBCS	Single-Byte Character Set
SAG	SQL (Structured Query Language) Access Group	SBE	Small Business Edition
SAGE	Semi-Automatic Ground Environment	SBI	Stop Bracket Initiation
SAIL	Speedy Asymmetric Internet Link	SBK	System Builder's Kit
SAK	Selective Acknowledgment	SBS	Satellite Business Systems
SALI	Source Address Length Indicator	SBS	Small Business Services (or Server)
SALMON	SNA Application Monitor	SBT	System Backup Tape Drive
SAMBE	Set Asynchronous Mode Balanced Extended	SC	Session Connection (or Control)
SAMMS	Standard Automated Material Management System	SC	Single-Chain
SAN	Storage Area Network	SC	Subcommittee
SAO	Single Association Object	SC	Subscriber (or Session) Connector

SC	Switch Control
SCA	Short Code Address
SCA	Subsidiary Communication Authorization
SCA	Systems Communication Architecture
SCADA	Supervisory Control and Data Acquisition
SCAI	Switch to Computer Application Interface
SCAM	SCSI Configured Automatically (sometimes, "Automagically")
SCARLET	Synchronous Communications Accessing Live Event Television
SCB	Session Control Block
SCC	Satellite Communications Control
SCC	Specialized Common Carrier
SCC	Standards Council of Canada
SCCP	Signaling Connection Control Part
SCE	Service Creation Environment
SCE	System Control Element
SCEF	Service Creation Environment Function
SCEP	Session Connection Endpoint
SCF	Service Control Function
SCFM	Sub-Carrier Frequency Modulation
SCIF	Single-Console Image Facility
SCL	Switch to Computer Link
SCM	Session Connector Manager
SCM	Session Control (or Connection) Manager
SCM	Software Configuration Management
SCN	Seattle Community Network
SCO	Santa Cruz Operation
SCP	Service (or System) Control Point
SCP	Session Control Properties
SCPC	Single Channel Per Channel
SCR	Secure Conversion
SCR	Silicon Control Rectifiers
SCR	Sustainable Cell Rate
SCS	Satellite Communications Systems
SCS	Shanghai Computer Society
SCS	Silicon Controlled Switches
SCS	SNA Character String
SCS	Society for Computer Simulation

SCS	SWITCH Central System
SCS	System Communication Services
SCS	System Conformance Statement
SCSA	Signal Computing System Architecture
SCSI	Small Computer System Interface
SCTO	Soft Carrier Turn-Off
SCTR	System Conformance Test Report
SCUSA	Standards Council of the USA
SCW	Setup Computer Wizard
SD	Start Delimiter
SD	Start Frame Delimiter
SD	Switching Delay
SDA	Security Domain Authority
SDA	Swappable Data Area
SDAP	Standard Document Application Profile
SDD	Software Description Database
SDDI	Shielded Data Distributed Interface
S-DDP	Short Datagram Delivery Protocol
SDE	Submission and Delivery Entity
SDF	Screen Definition Facility
SDF	Service Data Function
SDG	Software Development Group
SDH	Synchronous Digital Hierarchy
SDI	Supplier Declaration of Inter-operation
SDIF	SGML Document Interchange Format
SDIF	Standard Document Interchange Format
SDK	Software Developer's Kit
SDL	Specification and Description Language
SDL	System Description Language
SDL/GR	Specification and Description Language/Graphical Representation
SDL/PR	Specification and Description Language/Phrase Representation
SDLC	Synchronous Data Link Control
SDM	Space-Division Multiplexing
SDMI	Secure Digital Music Initiative
SDN	Software Defined Network
SDNS	Secure Data Network System
SDO	Standards Development Organization

SDP	Security Development Platform
SDRAM	Synchronous Dynamic Random Access Memory
SDRP	Source Demand Routing Protocol
SDS	Sun Directory Services
SDS	Synchronous Data Services
SDSAF	Switched Digital Services Applications Forum
SDSE	Shadowed Directory Service Area Specific Entry
SDSL	Symmetric Digital Subscriber Line
SDT	Start Data Traffic
SDT	Structured Data Transfer
SDU	Service Data Unit
SDV	Switched Digital Video
SE	Session Entity
SE	Status Enquiry
SE	Sweden
SE	Switching Element
SEA	SoftSolutions Enterprise Administrator
SEA	System Enhancement Associates
SEAL	Simple and Efficient Adaptation Layer
SEAS	Solaris Easy Access Server
SEB	Site Event Buffer
Sec	Second
SEC	Single Edge Contact
SECAM	Systeme En Couleur Avec Memoire (Color System With Memory)
SECG	Standards for Efficient Cryptography Group
SEE	Search Equipment Exchange
SEF	Source Explicit Forwarding
SEF	Standard Exchange Format
SEF/AIS	Severely Errored Framing/Alarm Indication Signal
SEFS	Severely Erred Framing Seconds
SEHK	Stock Exchange of Hong Kong
SEI	Software Engineering Institute
SEK	Swedish Electrical Commission
SEL	Selector
SEMT	Symposium on Elementary Mathematics Teaching
SEN	Software Engineering Notes
SeOS	Security for Open Systems
SESFE	Severely Errored Second, Far End

SESP	Severely Errored Second, Path
SET	Secure Electronic Transaction
SET	Shock-Excited Tones
SETS	Selected Executable Test Suite
SF	Single Frequency
SF	Summarization Function
SF	Switching Fabric
SFA	Sales Force Automation
SFD	Simple Formattable Document
SFD	Start of Frame Delimiter
SFET	Synchronous Frequency Encoding Technique
SFI	Single Frequency Interface
SFNOI	Second Further Notice of Inquiry
SFQL	Structured Full-text Query Language
SFS	Shared File System
SFS	Suomen Standardisoimisliitto (Standards Association of Finland)
SFT	System Fault Tolerance
SFU	Store and Forward Unit
SG	Study Group
SGFS	Special Group on Functional Standardization
SGISP	Special Group on International Standardized Profiles
SGM	Segmentation Message
SGML	Standard Generalized Markup Language
SGML-B	Standard Generalized Markup Language-Binary
SGMP	Simple Gateway Management (or Monitoring) Protocol
SGND	Signal Ground
SGRAM	Synchronous Graphics Random Access Memory
SH	Segment Header
SH	Shared
SH	Switch Hook
SHA	Secure Hash Algorithm
SHAMU	Secure Highly Available Mobile demo Unit
SHF	Super-High Frequency
SHR	Self-Healing Ring
SHT	Short Holding Time
SHTTP	Secure Hypertext Transfer (or Transport) Protocol
SI	SPDU Identifier

SI	Step Index
SIA	Securities Industry Association
SIA	Stable Implementation Agreements
SIC	Standard Industrial Codes
SICS	Service Implementation Conformance Statement
SID	Signaling Identifier
SID	Source Identifier
SID	Sudden Ionospheric Disturbance
SID	Switch Interface Device
SIDF	Standard Interface Data Format
SIDF	System Independent Data Format
SIF	Standard (or Source) Input Format
SIG	Special Interest Group
SIGCHI	Special Interest Group on Human-Computer Interaction
SIGCOMM	Special Interest Group on Data Communications
SIIA	Software and Information Industry Association
SIL	Semiconductor Injection Laser
SILS	Standard for Interoperable LAN Security
SIM	Set Initialization Mode
SIM	Society for Information Management
SIMD	Single Instruction / Multiple Data
SIMM	Single In-line Memory Module
SIMP	Satellite Information Message Protocol
SIMS	Sun Internet Mail Server
SINA	Static Integrated Network Access
SIO	Security Information Object
SIO	Start Input/Output
SIP	Switched multi-megabit data service Interface Protocol
SIPP	Simple Internet Protocol Plus
SIPP	Single In-Line Pin Package
SIR	Signal (to Co-channel) Interference Ratio
SIR	Speaker Independent Recognition
SIR	Sustained Information Rate
SIS	Service Incident Standard
SIS	Standardiserings-kommissionen in Sverige (Swedish Standards Committee)
SIS	Strategic Information Systems
SIS	Structured Information Store

SITA	Society for International Telecommunications for Aeronautics
SITE	Society for Information Technology and Teacher Education
SIVR	Speaker-Independent Voice Recognition
SKID	Secret Key Identification
SKIP	Simple Key Management for Internet Protocols
SL	Session Layer
SL	Sink Loss
SLA	Service-Level Agreement
SLA/SLM	Service-Level Agreement / Service-Level Management
SLC	Semiconductor Laser Configurations
SLC	Subscriber Line Concentrator
SLED	Single Large Expensive Disk
SLI	Scanline Interleave
SLI	Suppress Length Indication
SLIC	Standard Language for Implementation Conventions
SLIP	Serial Line Internet Protocol
SLM	Service-Level Management
SLM	Spatial Light Modulator
SLR	Service Level Reporter
SLS	Sequential Logic Systems
SLU	Secondary Logical Unit
SM	Session Manager
SM	Standby Monitor
SM	Synchronous Multiplexer
SM	System Management
SMA	Sub-Miniature Assembly
SMAE	Systems Management Application Entity
SMAF	Service Management Access (or Agent) Function
SMAP	Systems Management Application Process
SMART	Self-Monitoring Analysis and Reporting Technology
SMAS	Switched Maintenance Access System
SMASE	Systems Management Application Service Element
SMATV	Satellite Master Antenna Television
SMB	Server Message Block
SMB	Small to Medium-sized Business
SMC	Secretariat Management Committee

APP
A

SMC	Sleep Mode Connection		SMS	Service-Management System
SMC	Solaris Management Console		SMS	Short Message Services
SMC	Standard Microsystems Corporation		SMS	Storage Management Services (also, Subsystem)
SMD	Storage Module Device		SMS	Systems Management Server
SMDI	Simple Message Desk Interface		SMS/800	Service Management System / 800
SMDL	Standard Music Description Language		SMSA	Standard Metropolitan Statistical Area
SMDR	Station Message Detail Recording		SMSDI	Storage Management Services Device Interface
SMDR	Storage Management Data Requester		SMSP	Storage Management Services Protocol
SMDS	Switched Multimegabit Data Service		SMT	Station Management
SME	Society of Manufacturing Engineers		SMTP	Simple Mail Transfer Protocol
SME	Storage Management Engine		SN	Sequence Number
SME	Subject Matter Expert		SN	Subarea Node
SMF	Service (also, Systems) Management Function		SN	Subnetwork
SMF	Simple Message Format		SNA	Systems Network Architecture
SMF	Single-Mode Fiber		SNA/SDLC	Systems Network Architecture/Synchronous Data Link Control
SMF	Standard Message (or Messaging) Format			
SMF	Standard MIDI File		SNAcF	Subnetwork Access Function
SMFA	Systems Management Functional Area		SNAcP	Subnetwork Access Protocol
SMG	Surf and Mail Gateway		SNADS	Systems Network Architecture Distribution Services
SMI	Structure of Management Information		SNAP	Subnetwork Access Protocol
SMI	System Management Interrupt		SNARE	Subnetwork Address-Resolution Entity
SMIB	Stored Message Information Base		SNCP	Single Node Control Point
SMIB	System Management Information Base		SNDCF	Subnetwork-Dependent Convergence Facility
SMIL	Synchronized Multimedia Integration Language		SNDCP	Subnetwork-Dependent Convergence Protocol
SMIS	Specific Management Information Service		SNERT	Sexually Nerdish Expressively Recidivistic Troll
SMISE	Specific Management Information Service Element		SNI	SNA Network Interconnection (or Interface)
SMK	Shared Management Knowledge		SNI	Subscriber-to-Network Interface
SMM	Segment Management Module		SNICF	Subnetwork-Independent Convergence Facility
SMO	System Management Overview		SNICP	Subnetwork-Independent Convergence Protocol
SMOR	Storage Manager on ROM		SNMP	Simple Network Management Protocol
SMP	Session Management Protocol		SNMPv2	Simple Network Management Protocol version 2
SMP	Standby Monitor Present		SNP	Sequence Number Protection
SMP	Symmetric Multiprocessing		SNP	Subnetwork Access Protocol
SMP	System Modification Program		SNPA	Subnetwork Point of Attachment
SMPDU	Service Message Protocol Data Unit		SNR	Signal-to-Noise Ratio
SMPDU	System Management Protocol Data Unit		SNRM	Set Normal Response Mode
SMPTE	Society of Motion Picture and Television Engineers		SNS	Satellite Navigation System
SMR	Specialized Mobile Radio		SNS	Secondary Network Server
SMRT	Signal Message Rate Timing		SO	Significant Other

SOA	Safe Operating Area
SOA	Semiconductor Optical Amplifier
SOAP	Simple Object Access Protocol
SOES	Small Order Execution System
SOGITS	Senior Officials' Group for Information Technology Standardization
SOGT	Senior Officials' Group for Telecommunications
SOH	Section Overhead
SOH	Start of Header
SOHO	Small Office/Home Office
SOM	Scripting Object Model
SOM	Start of Message
SOM	System Object Model
SOMA	Semantic Object Modeling Approach
SON	Sent (or Send) Outside the Node
SONET	Synchronous Optical Network
SOP	Standard Operating Procedure
SOX	Small Office Exchange
SP	Security Protocol
SP	Service Provider
SP	Signaling Point
SP	Space Character
SP	System Performance
SPA	Software Publishers Association
SPAG	Standards Promotion and Application Group
SPAN	System Performance Analysis
SPARC	Scalable Performance Architecture
SPARC	Standards Planning and Review Committee
SPC	Signaling Point Code
SPC	Stored Program Control
SPCS	Service Point Command Service
SPD	Serial Presence Detect
SPDL	Standard Page Description Language
SPDU	Session Protocol Data Unit
SPE	Synchronous Payload Envelope
SPEC	Standard Performance Evaluation Cooperative (or Corporation)
SPEDE	SAMMS Procurement by Electronic Data Exchange
SPF	Shortest Path First
SPI	Security Profile Inspector
SPI	Subsequent Protocol (or Profile) Identifier
SPICE	Software Process Improvement and Capability Determination
SPID	Service Profile (or Protocol) Identifier
SPIRIT	Service Provider Integrated Requirements for Information Technology
SPL	Scenario Programming Language
SPL	Service Provider Link
SPM	Session Protocol Machine
SPMF	Servo Play-Mode Function
SpMs	Spontaneous Methods
SPN	Signal Processor Network
SPN	Subscriber Premises Network
SPOOL	Simultaneous Peripheral Operation On-Line
SPP	Sequenced Packet Protocol
SPS	Stand-by Power Supply
SPSN	Synchronization-Point Serial Number
SPTS	Single Program Transport Stream
SPTV	Still Picture Television
SPVC	Semi-Permanent Virtual Circuit
SPX	Sequenced Packet Exchange
SQCIF	Sub-Quarter Common Intermediate Format
SQD	Signal Quality Detector
SQE	Signal Quality Error
SQE	Software Quality Engineer
SQL	Structured Query Language
SQLJ	Structured Query Language for Java
SQUID	Super-conducting Quantum Interference Device
SR	Source Routing
SR/TLB	Source-Route Translational Bridging
SRAM	Static Random Access Memory
SRB	Source Route Bridging
SRDF	Symmetric Remote Data Facility
SREJ	Selective Reject
SRES	Signed Response
SRF	Specialized Resource Function
SRF	Specifically Routed Frame
SRGB	Sustained Red Green Blue

APP
A

SRH	SNARE Request Hello
SRI	Stanford Research Institute
SRL	Singing Return Loss
SRM	Security Reference Monitor
SRM	Self-Routing Module
SRM	Storage Resource Management
SRM	System Resource Manager
SRQ	Service Request Queue
SRS	Shared Registry System
SRT	Source Routing Transparent
SRT	Source-Route Transparent Bridging
SRTS	Synchronous Residual Time Stamp
SR-UAPDU	Status Report-User Agent Protocol Data Unit
SS	Sampled Servo
SS	Server-to-Server
SS	Session Service
SS	Signaling System
SS	Sporadic Server
SS	Start/Stop
SS	Switching System
SS6	Signaling System 6
SS7	Signaling System 7
SSA	Serial Storage Architecture
SSA	Subschema Specific Area
SSAP	Session (also, Source) Service Access Point
SSB	Single Sideband
SSBSC	Single Sideband Suppressed Carrier
SSCF	Service Specific Coordination Function
SSCOP	Service Specific Connection Oriented Protocol
SSCP	System Services Control Point
SSCS	Service Specific Convergence Sublayer
SSDU	Session Service Data Unit
S-SEED	Symmetric Self-Electro-Optic Effect Device
SSEL	Session Selector
SSF	Service Switching Function
SSI	Server-Side Insert (or Include)
SSI	Small-Scale Integration
SSI	Subsystem Support Interface
SSL	Secure Socket Layer

SSM	Single-Segment Message
SSM	Stochastic Sequential Machine
SSN	Switched Service Network
SSO	Single Sign On
SSO	Structure, Sequence, and Organization (of A Program)
SSP	Service Specific Part
SSP	Service Switching Point
SSP	System Support Program
SSPA	Software Support Professionals Association
SSPI	Security Support Provider Interface
SSS	Server Session Socket
SST	Single Sideband Transmitter
SSTDMA	Spacecraft Switched Time Division Multiple Access
ST	Scheduled Transfer
ST	Segment Type
ST	Sequence Terminal
ST	Slot Type
ST	Straight Tip
STA	Serial Test Async
STA	Spanning Tree Algorithm
STAC	Software Testing Assurance Corporation
STACK	Start Acknowledgement
STANAG	Standard Agreement
STB	Start of Text Block
STC	Serial Test ComProbe
STC	Switching and Testing Center
STC	System Time Clock
STD	Standard
STD	Subscriber Trunk Dialing
STD	Synchronous Time Division
STD	System Time Decoder
STDA	StreetTalk Directory Assistance
STDM	Statistical Time Division Multiplexing
STE	Signal Terminal Equipment
STE	Spanning Tree Explorer
STEP	Secure Tunnel Establishment Protocol
STEP	Software Test and Evaluation Panel
STEP	Standard for the Exchange of Product Model Data

STF	Standard Transaction Format
STI	Single Tuned Interstage
STL	Standard Template Library
STM	Station Management
STM	Synchronous Transfer (or Transport) Mode
STMF	State Management Function
STM-i	Synchronous Transport Module I
STO	Security Through Obscurity
STP	Service Transaction Program
STP	Shielded Twisted Pair
STP	Signal Transfer Point
STR	Synchronous Transmit Receive
STS	Shared Tenant Service
STS	Synchronous Time Stamp
STS	Synchronous Transport Signal
STS-1	Synchronous Transport Signal 1
STS-3c	Synchronous Transport System, with Level 3 Concatenated
STS-i	Synchronous Transport Signal, Level I
STT	Secure Transaction Technology
STT	Set-Top Terminal
STV	Subscription Television
STX	Specialty Telecommunications Exchange
STX	Start of Text
SU	Service User
SU	Signaling Unit
SUA	Stored Upstream Address
SUABORT	Session User Abort
SUDS	Software Updates Distribution Service
SUSP	System Use Sharing Protocol
SUT	System Under Test
SVA	Shared Virtual Area
SVC	Signaling Virtual Channel
SVC	Switched Virtual Call
SVC	Switched Virtual Circuit (or Connection)
SVC	Switched Voice Circuit
SVCI	Switched Virtual Circuit Identifier
SVD	Simultaneous Voice/Data
SVEC	Silicon Valley Engineering Council

SVGA	Super VGA
SVI	Subvector Identifier
SVID	System V Interface Definition
SVIP	Silicon Valley Internet Partners
SVL	Subvector Length
SvMs	Service Methods
SVP	Switched Virtual Path
SVPI	Subvector Parameter
SVR	(UNIX) System V Release
SVRAM	Synchronous Video Random Access Memory
SVS	Switched Virtual Circuit
SVVS	System V Verification Suite
Sw	Switch
SWAIS	Simple Wide Area Server
SWAN	Satellite (or Secure) Wide-Area Network
SWAP	Simple Workflow Access Protocol
SWC	Serving Wire Center
SWG	Special Working Group
SWIFT	Society for Worldwide International Financial Telecommunications
SWO	Standards Writing Organization
SWRL	Southwest Regional Labs
SXS	Step-by-Step Switch
SYN	Synchronize Flag
SYNC	Synchronization
SYSCON	System Configuration
T	Tera
T	Time
TA	Terminal Adapter
TA	Time Arrival
TA	Transferred Account
TAAS	Trunk Answer From Any Station
TA-BA	Trunk Bridger Amplifier
TAC	Technical Advisory Committee
TAC	Technical Assistance Center
TAC	Terminal Access Controller
TACACS	Terminal Access Controller Access Control System
TACIT	Transition and Coexistence Including Testing (Working Group)

APP
A

TACS	Total Access Communication System
TADP	Tests and Analyses of Data Protocols
TAF	Terminal Access Facility
TAG	Technical Ad Hoc Group
TAG	Technical Advisory Group
TAG	Technical Assessment (Task) Group
TANSTAAFL	There Ain't No Such Thing as a Free Lunch
TAO	Telephony Application Object
TAO	Track-at-Once
TAP	Telelocator Alphanumeric Protocol
TAP	Trace Analysis Program
TAPI	Telephony Application Program (or Programming) Interface
TARR	Test Action Request Receiver
TARS	Transaction Archives and Reporting System
TAS	Telephone Access Server
TAS	Telephone Answering Service
TAS	TotalNet Advanced Server
TASI	Time Assignment Speech Interpolation
TAT	Theoretical Arrival Time
TAT	Trans-Atlantic Telecom
TAU	Telematic Access Unit
Tb	Terabit
TB	Terabyte
TB	Transparent Bridging
TB	Treasury Board
TBC	Time-Base Corrector
TBC	Token Bus Controller
TBI	Technology and Business Integrators
TBITS	Treasury Board Information Technology Standard
Tbps	Terabits Per Second
TBps	Terabytes Per Second
TBS	Treasury Board Secretariat
TC	Technical Committee
TC	Terminal Controller
TC	Test Conductor
TC	Transaction Capabilities
TC	Transmission Control (also, Convergence)
TC	Transmission Convergence Sublayer

TC	Transport Connection
TCA	Telecommunications Association
TCAM	Telecommunications Access Method
TCAP	Transaction Capabilities Application Product
TCAP	Transaction Capability Application Part
TCB	Task (or Transmission) Control Block
TCC	Transmission Control Code
TCCC	Technical Committee for Computer Communications
TCE	Transit Connection Element
TCEP	Transport Connection Endpoint
TCG	Teleport Communications Group
TCH	Traffic Channel
TCI	Test Cell Input
TCIF	Telecommunications Industry Forum
Tcl	Tool Command Language [pronounced "tickle"]
TCM	Terminating Call Model
TCM	Time Compression Multiplexing
TCM	Trellis Coded Modulation
TCN	Telecommunications Networks
TCN	Throughput Class Negotiation
TCNS	Thomas-Conrad Network System
TCO	Test Cell Output
TCO	Total Cost of Ownership
TCP	Test Coordination Procedure
TCP	Transmission Control Protocol
TCP/IP	Transmission Control Protocol/Internet Protocol
TCRF	Transit Connection-Related Function
TCS	Transmission Convergence Sublayer
TCS-1	Trans-Caribbean System-1
TCSEC	Trusted Computer System Evaluation Criteria
TCT	Terminal Control Table (in CICS)
TCU	Transmission Control Unit
TCU	Trunk Coupling Unit
TD	Technology Division
TD	Transmit Data
TD	Typed Data
TDB	Task Database
TDC	Tabular Data Control
TDCC	Transportation Data Coordinating Committee

TDD	Time Division Duplex (also, Duplexing)	TFA	Transparent File Access
TDDI	Twisted-pair Distributed Data Interface	TFH	Timing Failure Handler
TDED	Trade Data Elements Directory	TFP	TOPS Filing Protocol
TDF	Trunk Distribution Frame	TFT	Thin-Film Transistor
TDI	Transit Delay Indication	TFTP	Trivial File Transfer Protocol
TDI	Transport Device (or Driver) Interface	TFUI	Touch-and-Feel User Interface
TDID	Trade Data Interchange Directory	TG	Task Group
TDJ	Transfer Delay Jitter	TG	Transmission Group
TDM	Time Division Multiplexing	TGB	Trunk Group Busy
TDM	Topology Database Manager	TGS	Ticket-Granting Server (or Service)
TDMA	Time Division Multiple Access	TGT	Ticket-Granting Ticket
TDO	Technology Development Organization	TGW	Trunk Group Warning
TDR	Time Domain Reflectometer	TH	Transmission Header
TDS	Tabular Data Stream	THD	Ten High Day
TDS	Transit Delay Selection	THD	Total Harmonix Distortion
TDSAI	Transit Delay Selection and Indication	THEnet	Texas Higher Education Network
TE	Terminal Equipment	THT	Token Hold Timer
TE1	Terminal Equipment Type 1	THT	Token Holding Time
TE2	Terminal Equipment Type 2	THz	Terahertz
TEC	Technical Evaluation Committee	TI	Time In
TEC	Tivoli Enterprise Console	TIA	Telecommunications Industry Association
TEDIS	Trade Electronic Data Interchange System	TIA	Telematic Internetworking Application
TEHO	Tail End Hop Off	TIA	The Internet Adapter
TEI	Terminal End-point Identifier	TIAS	Telematic Internetworking Abstract Service
TELCO	Telephone Company	TIB	Task Information Base
TELNET	Telecommunications Network	TIC	Token-ring Interface Coupler
TELSET	Telephone Set	TID	Transaction ID
TEM	Transverse Electromagnetic	TID	Traveling Ionospheric Disturbance
TEM	Trusted Enterprise Manager	TIE	Translated Image Environment
TEMPEST	Transient Electromagnetic Pulse Emanation Standardizing	TIFF	Tagged Image File Format
		TIMS	Transmission Impairment Measuring Sets
TEN	Telephone Equipment Network	TIMSS	Third International Mathematics and Science Study
TEN	Terribly Expensive Network	TIP	Terminal Interface Package (also, Processor)
TEP	Transport Endpoint	TIRIS	Texas Instruments Registration and Information System
TERC	Technology Education Research Center		
TERC	Telecom Equipment Remarketing Council	TIRPC	Transport Independent Remote Procedure Call
TERC	Telecommunications Equipment Re-marketing Council	TIS	Transaction Information System
		TIS	Tribune Information Services
TEXEL	Texture Element	TIS	Trusted Information System

TISSEC	Transactions on Information and System Security	TNC	Threaded Neill-Concelnan (also Nut) Connector
TIU	Telematic Internetworking Unit	TNG	The Next Generation
TIU	Trusted Interface Unit	TNIC	Transit Network Identification Code
Tk	Toolkit	TNS	Transaction Network Service
TL	Transport Layer	TNS	Transit Network Selection
TLA	Three Letter Acronym	TO	Test Object
TLAP	TokenTalk Link Access Protocol	TO	Time Out
TLD	Top-Level Domain	TOD/DOW	Time of Day / Day of Week
TLF	Trunk Line Frame	TOI	Transfer of Information
TLFF	Technical Level Feeders Forum	TOP	Technical and Office Protocol
TLI	Transport Layer (or Library) Interface	TOS	Technical and Office Systems
TLMA	Telematic Agent	ToS	Type of Service
TLMAU	Telematic Access Unit	TP	Terminal Portability
TLP	Transmission Level Point	TP	Transaction Processing
TLR	Tie-Line Reconciliation	TP	Transport Protocol
TLSPP	Transport Layer Sequenced Packet Protocol	TP	Twisted Pair
TLV	Type-Length-Value	TP0	Transport Protocol Class 0
TLX	Telex	TP1	Transport Protocol Class 1
TLXAU	Telex Access Unit	TP2	Transport Protocol Class 2
TM	Terminal Management	TP3	Transport Protocol Class 3
TM	Traffic Management	TP4	Transport Protocol Class 4
TMA	Technology Management Associates	TPA	Telematic Protocol Architecture
TME	Tivoli Management Environment	TPA	Trading Partner Agreement
TMF	Test Management Function	TPAD	Terminal Packet Assembler/Disassembler
TMM	Transmission Monitoring Machine	TPC	Transaction Processing Performance Council
TMN	Telecommunications Management Network	TPC	Trans-Pacific Cable
TMP	Test-Management Protocol	TPCC	Third-Party Call Control
TMPDU	Test-Management Protocol Data Unit	TPC-D	Transaction Processing Performance Council Benchmark D
TMS	Telecommunications Message Switcher		
TMS	Telephone Management System	TPDDI	Twisted Pair Distributed Data Interface
TMS	Time-Multiplexed Switching	TPDU	Transport Protocol Data Unit
TMSCP	Tape Mass Storage Control Program	TPE	Transmission Path Endpoint
TMSI	Temporary Mobile Subscriber Identity	TPE	Twisted-Pair Ethernet
TM-SWG	Traffic Management (Sub-Working Group)	TPEG	Transport Protocol Expert Group
TMU	Transmission Message Unit	TPF	Transaction Processing Facility
TN	Transport Network	TPI	Transport Protocol Interface
TNC	Terminal Node Connector (also, Controller)	TPPMD	Twisted Pair, Physical Media Dependent
TNC	The Networking Center	TPS	Transactions Per Second
TNC	Threaded Navy Connector	TPS	Two-processor Switch

TPSP	Transaction Processing Service Provider		TSDS	Transaction Set Development System
TPSU	Transaction Processing Service User		TSDU	Transport-layer Service Data Unit
TPSUI	Transaction Processing Service User Invocation		TSE	Terminal Switching Exchange
TPT	Third-Party Transfer		TSEL	Transport Selector
TPTAE	Third-Party Transfer Application Entity		TSGR	Transport Systems Generic Requirements
TP*x*	Transport Protocol, Class X (*x*=0, 1, 2, 3, or 4)		TSI	Time-Slot Interchange
TQM	Total Quality Management		TSMC	Taiwan Semiconductor Manufacturing Company
TR	Technical Report		TSO	Terminating Service Office
TR	Test Responder		TSO	Time-Sharing Option
TR	Token Ring		TSO/E	Time Sharing Option/Extension
TR	Tributaries		TSP	Telephony Services Platform
TRA	Telecommunications Resellers Association		TSPS	Traffic Service Position System
TRA	Token-Ring Adapter		TSR	Telemarketing Service Representative
TRAC	Technical Recommendation Application Committee		TSR	Terminate and Stay Resident
TRADACOMS	Trading Data Communications Standards		TSS	Time-Sharing System
TRAPS	Telemetry/Radar Acquisition and Processing System		TSS	Transmission Subsystem
TRIB	Transmission Rate in Bits		TSS&TP	Test Suite Structure and Test Purposes
TRIL	Token Ring Interoperability Lab		TSSDU	Typed Data Session Service Data Unit
TRIP	Transcontinental ISDN Project		TT	Time-Triggered
TRMS	Treasury Risk Management System		TTA	Telecommunication Technology Association
TROPIC	Token Ring Protocol Interface Controller		TTC	Telecommunications Technical Committee
TRS	Topology and Routing Services		TTC	Telecommunications Technology Council
TRSS	Token Ring Subsystem		TTCN	Tree and Tabular Combined Notation
TRT	Telephone Response Technologies		TTCN.GR	Tree and Tabular Combined Notation, Graphical Representation
TRT	Token Rotation Timer		
TS	Time Slot (also, Stamp)		TTCN.MP	Tree and Tabular Combined Notation, Machine Processable
TS	Traffic Shaping		
TS	Transaction Services		TTD	Target Transit Delay
TS	Transport Service (also, Stream)		TTD	Temporary Text Delay
TS	Transport Stream		TTL	Time to Live
TSA	Target Service Agent		TTL	Transistor-Transistor Logic
TSA	Technical Support Alliance		TTN	Tandem Tie-line Network
TSAF	Transport Services Access Facility		TTP	Telephone Twisted Pair
TSAP	Transport Service Access Point		TTP	Timed-Token Protocol
TSAPI	Telephony Server Application Programming Interface		TTP	Transport Test Platform
TSAPI	Telephony Services Application Program Interface		TTRT	Target Token Rotation Time
			TTRTO	Time-Triggered Real-Time Object
TSC	Transmission Subsystem Controller		TTS	Text to Speech
TSCF	Target System Control Facility		TTS	Transaction Tracking System

APP

A

TTTN	Tandem Tie-Trunk Network
TTX	Teletex
TTXAU	Teletex Access Unit
TTY	Teletypewriter
TTYL	Talk to You Later
TU	Tributary Unit
TUBA	TCP and UDP Over Bigger Addresses
TUCC	Triangle University Computing Center
TUG	TeX User's Group
TUG	Tributary Unit Group
TUG-i	Tributary Unit Group-i
TUI	Telephone (or Telephony) User Interface
TU-i	Tributary Unit-i
TUP	Telephone User Part
TUR	Traffic Usage Recorder
TUXEDO	Transactions for Unix Extended for Distributed Operations
TV	Television
TVA	Time Variant Amplifier
TVC	Trunk Verification by Customer
TVF	Time Variant Filter
TVRO	Television Receive Only
TVS	Trunk Verification by Station
TVX	Valid Transmission Timer
TWA	Two-Way Alternate
TWAIN	Toolkit Without An Important Name
TWIG	Technical Wizard Interest Group
TWS	Two-Way Simultaneous
TWX	Teletypewriter Exchange
TXI	Transmit Immediate
TXK	Telephone Exchange Crossbar
TXS	Telephone Exchange Strowger
TYMNET	Timeshare Inc. Network
TZD	Time Zone Difference
U/L	Universal/Local
UA	Universal Access
UA	Unnumbered Acknowledgment
UA	Unsequenced Application
UA	User Account (or Agent)

UAE	User Agent Entity
UAL	User Agent Layer
UAM	User Authentication Method
UAOS	User Alliance for Open Systems
UAPDU	User Agent Protocol Data Unit
UART	Universal Asynchronous Receiver Transmitter
UAS	Unavailable Second
UASFE	Unavailable Second, Far End
UASL	User Agent Sublayer
UAWG	Universal ADSL Working Group
UBCIM	Universal Bibliographic Control/International MARC
UBR	Unspecified Bit Rate
UCA	Utilities Communication Architecture
UCAID	University Corporation for Advanced Internet Development
UCB	Unit Control Block
UCB	University of California, Berkeley
UCC	Uniform Code Council
UCC	Uniform Commercial Code
UCD	Uniform Call Distribution
UCL	University College, London
UCO	Universal Communications Object
UCR	Undercolor Removal
UCS	Uniform Communications Standard (also, System)
UCS	Universal Component System
UCS/WINS	Uniform Communication System/Warehouse Information Network Standard
UCW	Ubit Control Word
UD	Unit Data
UDA	Universal Data Access
UDF	Universal Disk Format
UDF	User-Defined Function
UDI	Unrestricted Digital Information
UDLC	Universal Data Link Control
UDP	User Datagram Protocol
UDSL	Universal Digital Subscriber Line
UDT	Unstructured Data Transfer
UDT	User-Defined Type
UE	User Element

UFS	UNIX File System
UHF	Ultra-High Frequency
UI	Unit Interval
UI	UNIX International
UI	Unnumbered Information (also, Interrupt)
UI	User Interface
UI/PSS	User Interface and Performance Support Solution
UID	User ID
UIS	Ubiquitous Information Systems
UIS	Universal Information Services
UKRA	United Kingdom Registration Authority
UL	Underwriters' Laboratories
UL	Urban Legend
UL	User Location
ULA	Upper-Layer Architecture
ULCC	University of London Computing Centre
ULCT	Upper-Layer Conformance Testing
ULP	Upper Layer Protocol (or Process)
UMA	Universal Management Agent
UMB	Upper Memory Block
UME	UNI Management Entity
UML	Unified Modeling Language
UMPDU	User Message Protocol Data Unit
UMTS	Universal Mobile Telecommunications System
UMTS	Universal Mobile Telephone Service
UN	United Nations
UN/ECE	United Nations Economic Commission for Europe
UNA	Upstream Neighbors Address
UNC	Uniform (or Universal) Naming Convention
UNH	University of New Hampshire
UNI	User-Network Interface
UNII	Unlicensed National Information Infrastructure
UNISON-1	Unidirectional Synchronous Optical Network 1
UNJEDI	United Nations Joint EDI
UNMA	Unified Network Management Architecture
UNO	Network Object
UNSM	UN/EDIFACT Standard Message
UNTDI	United Nations Trade Data Interchange
UoD	Universe of Discourse

UoW	Unit of Work
UP	Unnumbered Poll
UP	User Part
UPC	Uniform (also, Universal) Product Code
UPC	Usage Parameter Control
U-Plane	User Plane
UPS	Uninterruptible Power Supply
UPT	Universal Personal Telecommunications
UPTN	Universal Personal Telecommunication Number
UPU	Universal Postal Union
URG	Urgent
URG	Urgent Flag
URI	Uniform Resource Identifier
URL	Uniform Resource Locators
URN	Uniform Resource Name
URSI	Union Radio-Scientifique Internationale (International Union of Radio Sciences)
USA	Undedicated Switch Access
USACM	United States Association for Computing Machinery
USART	Universal Synchronous/Asynchronous Receiver/Transmitter
USB	Universal Serial Bus
USB	Upper Sideband
USE	UnixWare Support Encyclopedia
USF	Universal Service Fund
USHR	Unidirectional Self-Healing Ring
USITA	United States Independent Telephone Association
USL	UNIX System Laboratories
USNC	United States National Committee
USO	UNIX Software Operation
USOC	Uniform Service Order Code
USP	United States Pharmacopia
USRA	Universities Space Research Association
USRT	Universal Synchronous Receiver Transmitter
USS	Unformatted System Services
USV	User Services
UT	Universal Time
UT	Unsequenced Terminal
UT	Upper Tester

APP

A

UTAM	Unlicensed Transition and Management
UTC	Universal Coordinated Time
UTC	Universal Time Coordinated
UTOPIA	Universal Test and Operations PHY Interface for ATM
UTP	Unshielded Twisted Pair
UTTP	Unshielded Telephone Twisted Pair
UUCP	UNIX to UNIX Copy Program
UUS	User-to-User Signaling
UVM	Universal Virtual Machine
V	Voltage (in volts)
V+TU	Voice Plus Teleprinter Unit
VAB	Visual Application Builder
VAC	Value-Added Carrier
VAC	Voltage AC
VAD	Value-Added Distributor
VADS	Value-Added Data Services
VADSL	Very high-rate Asymmetric Digital Subscriber Line
VAG	VRML Architecture Group
VAIO	Video Audio Integrated Operation
VAMPIRE	Voice-Actuated Medical Practice Image
VAN	Value-Added Network
VAP	Value-Added Process
VAR	Value-Added Reseller
VARP	VINES Address Resolution Protocol
VAS	Value-Added Service
VAS	Video Application Signaling
VAST	Variable Architecture Synthesis Technology
VAU	Video Access Unit
VAX	Virtual Address Extension
VAXBI	VAX Bus Interface
VB	Visual Basic
VB	VoiceBridge
VBA	Visual Basic for Applications
VBNS	Very high-performance Backbone Network Service
VBR	Variable Bit Rate
VBS	Visual Basic Script
VBX	Visual Basic (custom) Control
VBX	Visual Basic Extension
VC	Virtual Call (or Channel)

VC	Virtual Circuit
VC	Virtual Container
VC	Voice Channel (also, Circuit)
VCAPI	Voice Communications Application Programming Interface
VCC	Virtual Channel Connection
VCCE	Virtual Channel Connection Endpoint
VCI	Virtual Channel Identifier
VCI	Virtual Circuit (or Connection) Identifier
VC-i	Virtual Container I
VCL	Virtual Channel Link
VCL	Virus Creation Lab
VCM	Visual Call Management
VCNS	VTAM Common Network Services
VCPI	Virtual Control Program Interface
VCS	Virtual Circuit Switch
VCS	Virus Control System
VDA	Variable Digital Amplifier
VDC	Voltage DC
VDD	Virtual Device Driver
VDD	Virtual Display Device
VDF	Variable Digital Filter
VDI	Virtual Device Interface
VDM	Virtual DOS Machine
VDMAD	Virtual Direct Memory Access Device
VDMM	Virtual DOS Machine Manager
VDS	Virtual DMA (Direct Memory Access) Services
VDSL	Very High Speed Digital Subscriber Line
VDT	Video Dialtone
VDT	Video Display Terminal
VDU	Video Display Unit
Veronica	Very Easy Rodent-Oriented Net-wide Index to Computerized Archives
VERS	Virtual Environment for Reconstructive Surgery
VESA	Video Equipment Standards Association
VEST	VAX Environment Software Translator
VEX	Video Extensions for X-Windows
VF	Voice Frequency
VFAT	Video File Allocation Table

VFRP	VINES Fragmentation Protocol
VFS	VINES File System
VFS	Virtual File Store (or System)
VFT	Voice Frequency Telegraph
VfW	Video for Windows
VG	Voice Grade
VGA	Video Graphics Array
VHF	Very High Frequency
VIC	Voting Information Center
VICP	VINES Internet Control Protocol
VIM	Vendor Independent Messaging
VIMS	Visual Interactive Molecular Simulation
VINES	Virtual Networking System
VIP	Versatile Interface Processor
VIP	Video Information Provider
VIP	VINES Internet Protocol
VIP	Visual Information Processing
VIPC	VINES Interprocess Communications
VIPER	Virus Interface for Protective Early Response
VIP-NI	Video Information Provider Network Interface
VIT	VTAM Internal Trace
VITAL	Virtually Integrated Technical Architecture Lifecycle
VIU	Video Information User
VIU-NI	Video Information User Network Interface
VIW	VIP-video Information Warehouse
VKD	Virtual Keyboard Device
VL	VESA Local
VL	Virtual Link
VLAN	Virtual Local Area Network
VLDB	Very Large Database
VLF	Very Low Frequency
VLF	Virtual Look Aside Facility
VLM	Virtual Loadable Module
VLR	Visitor Location Register
VLSI	Very Large-Scale Integration
VLSM	Variable Length Subnet Mask
VM	Virtual Machine (also, Memory)
VM	Voice Messaging
VM/CMS	Virtual Machine/Conversation Monitor System

VM/ESA	Virtual Machine/Enterprise Systems Technology
VM/SP	Virtual Machine/System Product
VM/SP HPO	Virtual Machine/System Product, High-Performance Option
VM/XA	Virtual Machine/Extended Architecture
VMBP	Virtual Machine Break Point
VMD	Virtual Manufacturing Device
VMD	Virtual Mouse Device
VMDBK	Virtual Machine Definition Block
VMI	Vendor-Managed Inventory
VML	Vector Markup Language
VMM	Virtual Machine Manager
VMS	Virtual Memory System
VMS	Voice Message System
VMT	Virtual Memory Table
VMTP	VDT Message Transfer Part
VMTP	Versatile Message Transaction Protocol
VMTP-T	VDT Message Transfer Part Translator
VNA	Virtual Network Architecture
VNET	Virtual Network
VNL	Via Net Loss
VNLF	Via Net Loss Factor
VO	Virtual Operator
VoATM	Voice over Asynchronous Transfer Mode
VOD	Video on Demand
VoFR	Voice over Frame Relay
VoIP	Voice over Internet Protocol
VOM	Volt-Ohm-Meter
VOOPE	Visual Object-Oriented Programming Environment
VOP	Velocity of Propagation
VOS	Voice Operating System
VOTS	VAX OSI Transport Service
VP	Virtual Path
VP/VC	We Play, We Chat
VPC	Virtual Path Connection
VPCE	Virtual Path Connection Endpoint
VPCI/VCI	Virtual Path Connection Identifier/Virtual Channel Identifier
VPI	Virtual Path Identifier

APP
A

VPICD	Virtual Programmable Interrupt Control Device
VPIM	Voice Profile for Internet Mail
VPL	Virtual Private (or Path) Link
VPN	Virtual Private Network
VPU	Video Presentation Unit
VP-VCI	Virtual Path-Virtual Channel Identifier
VQ	Vector Quantizer
VR	Virtual Router
VRAM	Video Random Access Memory
VRBL	Virtual Reality Behavior Language
VRC	Vertical Redundancy Check
VRD	Virtual Retinal Display
VRM	Voltage Regulator Module
VRML	Virtual Reality Modeling Language
VRMP	Vitria Reliable Multicast Protocol
VRPWS	Virtual Router Pacing Window Size
VRTP	VINES Routing Update Protocol
VRU	Voice Response Unit
VRUP	VINES Routing Update Protocol
VS	Virtual Storage (also, Scheduling)
VS/VD	Virtual Source / Virtual Destination
VSAM	Virtual Index Sequential Access Method
VSAM	Virtual Storage Access Method
VSAT	Very Small Aperture Terminal
VSB	Vestigial Sideband
VSCCP	VDT Signaling Connection Control Part
VSCP	VDT Session Control Part
VSCS	VM/SNA Console Support
VSE	Virtual Storage Extended
VSE/ESA	Virtual Storage Extended/Enterprise System Architecture
VSF	Voice Store-and-Forward
VSL	Voyetra Synth Layering
VSM	Virtual Storage Manager
VSPC	Visual Storage Personal Computing
VSPP	VINES Sequenced Packet Protocol
VSTM	Very Slow Time Machine
VSWR	Voltage Standing Wave Radio
VT	Vertical Tab
VT	Virtual Terminal (also, Tributary)
VTAM	Virtual Telecommunication Access Method
VTC	Virus Test Center
VTD	Virtual Timer Device
VTE	Virtual Terminal Environment
VTOA	Voice Telephony over ATM
VTP	Virtual Terminal Protocol
VTPM	Virtual Terminal Protocol Machine
VTPP	Variable Team Pricing Plan
VTS	Virtual Tape Servers
VTS	Virtual Telemanagement System
VTS	Virtual Terminal Service
VTST	Virtual Terminal Service Element
VU	Volume Unit
VVIEF	VAX Vector Instruction Emulation Facility
VxD	Virtual Device Driver
VXD	Virtual Device Driver
VxFS	Veritas File System
VXML	Voice Extensible Markup Language
W3C	World Wide Web Consortium
WA	Write Audit
WACA	Write Access Connection Acceptor
WACIA	Write Access Connection Initiator
WACK	Wait for Acknowledgment
WAIS	Wide-Area Information Service
WAITS	Wide-Area Information Transfer System
WAIUG	Washington-area ISDN Users' Group
WAN	Wide Area Network
WANDD	Wide Area Network Device Driver
WAP	Wireless Application Protocol
WARC	World Administrative Radio Conference
WAS	Web Application Server
WATR	Western Aeronautical Test Range
WATS	Wide Area Telephone Service
WAVAR	Write Access Variable
WBC	Wideband Channel
WBEM	Web-Based Enterprise Management
WBS	Work Breakdown Structure
WCC	World Congress on Computing

WCCP	Web Cache Control Protocol		WORM	Write Once, Read Many
W-CDMA	Wideband Code Division Multiple Access		WOS	Workstation Operation System
WCET	Worst-Case Execution Times		WOSA	Windows Open System Architecture
WCP	UNIX-to-UNIX Copy Program		WP	White Pages
WD	Working Document (or Draft)		WP	Working Party
WDM	Wavelength Division Multiplexing		WPG	WordPerfect Graphics
WDM	Windows Driver Model		WPM	Words per Minute
WDMA	Wavelength Division Multiple Access		WPS	Workplace Shell
WELAC	Western Europe Laboratory Accreditation Cooperation		WRAM	Windows Random Access Memory
			WRED	Weighted Random Early Detection
WELL	Whole Earth 'Lectronic Link		WRQ	Write Request
WEP	Well-known Entry Point		WRT	With Respect to
WfM	Wired for Management		WRU	Who Are You
WFMTUG	World Federation of MAP/TOP Users' Group		WSF	Workstation Function
WFQ	Weighted Fair Queuing		WTAPI	Writing Tools Application Program Interface
WfW	Windows for Workgroups		WTDM	Wavelength Time Division Multiplexing
WG	Working Group		WTO	World Trade Organization
WIBNI	Wouldn't It Be Nice If		WTS	Windows NT Terminal Server
WIDL	Web Interface Definition Language		WTSC	World Telecommunication Standardization Conference
WIMP	Windows Icons, Mice (or Menu), and Pointers			
WIN	Wireless Intelligent Network		WUI	Western Union International
WIN	Wissenschaftsnetz (Science Network)		WWMCCS	Worldwide Military Command and Control System
WinCAPI	Windows Cryptography Application Programming Interface		WWW	World Wide Wait
			WWW	World Wide Web
WINCS	WWMCCS Intercomputer Network Communication Subsystem		WWW-SQL	World Wide Web Structured Query Language
			WWWW	World Wide Web Worm
WINDO	Wide Information Network for Data Online		WYSIAYG	What You See Is All You Get (whizzy-egg)
WinHEC	Windows Hardware Engineering Conference		WYSIWYG	What You See Is What You Get (whizzy-wig)
WINS	Warehouse Information Network Standard		X	the X Window System
WINS	Windows Internet Name Service		XA	Exchange Access
WINS	Windows Naming Service		XA	Extended Architecture
WIPO	World Intellectual Property Organization		XALS	Extended Application-Layer Structure
WKSH	Windowing Korn Shell		XAPIA	X.400 API Association
WLL	Wireless Local Loop		XCF	Cross-system Coupling Facility
WMC	Workflow Management Coalition		XDF	Extended Distance Facility
WMF	Workload Monitoring Function		Xdm	X Display Manager
WMRM	Write Many, Read Many		XDR	External Data Representation
WND	Workgroup Networks Division		Xds	X Display Server
WNIM	Wide Area Network Interface Module		XDS	X/Open Directory Services API
WOAPI	Windows Open Application Program Interface			

APP
A

*X*DSL	*x* Digital Subscriber Line		XSSDU	Expedited Session Service Data Unit
XEMS	X/Open Event Management Service		XT	Extended Technology
XFCN	External Function		XTC	External Transmit Clock
XFDL	Extensible Forms Description Language		XTI	X/Open Transport-layer Interface
XID	Exchange ID		XTP	Express Transfer Protocol
XIP	Execute in Place		YAA	Yet Another Acronym
XIWT	Cross-Industry Working Team		YAA	Yet Another Agreement
XLL	Extensible Link Language		YABA	Yet Another Bloody Acronym
XMH	X Mail Handler		YABS	Yet Another Benchmark Suite
XMIT	Transmit		YAFIYGI	You Asked for It, You Got It
XML	Extensible Markup Language		YAHOO	Yet Another Hierarchically Officious Oracle
XML-RPC	Extensible Markup Language Remote Procedure Call		YAUN	Yet Another UNIX Nerd
XML-SOAP	Extensible Markup Language Simple Object Access Protocol		YHBT	You Have Been Trolled
			YHBT. YHL. HAND.	You Have Been Trolled. You Have Lost. Have A Nice Day.
XMS	Extended Memory Specification		YHL	You Have Lost
XNA	Xerox Network Architecture		YMMV	Your Mileage May Vary
XNS	Xerox Network Services		YMU	Y-Net Management Unit
XO	Exactly Once		YP	Yellow Pages
XOFF	Transmitter Off		YR	Yeah, Right
XON	Transmitter On		ZAC	Zero Administration Client
XP	Extended Pointer		ZAK	Zero Administration Kit
XPD	Cross Polarization Discrimination		ZAW	Zero Administration initiative for Windows
XPG	X.400 Promotion Group		ZEN	Zero Effort Network
XPG	X/Open Portability Guide		ZIF	Zero Insertion Force
XPSDU	Expedited Presentation Service Data Unit		ZIP	Zone Information Protocol
XQL	Xtructured Query Language		ZIS	Zone Information Socket
XRF	Extended Recovery Facility		ZIT	Zone Information Table
XSL	Extensible Style Language		ZMA	Zone Multicast Access

Appendix B
Bibliography and Other Resources

There are thousands of books about networking, telecommunications, and related topics. The standards organizations alone have produced hundreds of documents. In addition, there are many other types of information sources. These sources include consultants, periodicals, technical reports and newsletters, training centers, films, and, of course, the Internet itself—especially the World Wide Web.

Primary Sources

Three classes of primary sources can be helpful to network developers, administrators, and users:

- Documents and recommendations from standards committees and other organizations.

- Internal manufacturers' documentation about architectures and about software or hardware products.

- Manufacturers' and vendors' technical reports and research papers about products, protocols, and standards.

All of these types of information are available over the Internet. Be aware, that some of the information—particularly standards documentation—will cost money.

Standards Documentation

Copies of standards documents are available either from the committees or organizations themselves or from their distributors. The following list provides information on how to contact some of these sources. This list covers only the major standards organizations; later in this appendix you'll find a list that also includes special purpose standards committees and forums. We have tried to make certain the information in the list is correct and up-to-date, but things change. So don't be surprised if you try to contact one of these sources and find that the phone number, or even the address, has changed.

ANSI (American National Standards Institute)

11 West 42ns Street, 13th Floow
New York, NY 10036
USA
Phone: 1-212-642-4900
Fax: 1-212-302-1286
http://www.ansi.org

CSA (Canadian Standards Association) International

178 Rexdale Boulevard
Etobicoke, Ontario M9W 1R3
CANADA
Phone: 1-416-747-2620
Fax: 1-416-747-4292

http://www.csa.ca

ECMA (European Computer Manufacturers Association)

114 Rue de Rhone
CH1204 Geneva
SWITZERLAND
Phone: 011 41 22 35 3634
Fax: 011 41 22 86 5231

http://www.ecma.org

EIA (Electrical Industries Alliance)

2500 Wilson Boulevard
Arlington, VA 22201
USA
Phone: 1-703-907-7500
Fax: 1-703-907-7501

http://www.eia.org

FIPS (Federal Information Processing Standard)

U.S. Department of Commerce
National Technical Information Service
5285 Port Royal Road
Springfield, VA 22161
USA

IEEE (Institute of Electrical and Electronics Engineers)

345 East 47th Street
New York, NY 10017
USA
Phone: 1-212-705-7900

http://www.ieee.org

ISO (International Standardization Organization)

Central Secretariat
1 Rue de Varembe
Case Postale 56
CH-1211 Geneva
SWITZERLAND
Phone: 011 41 22 749 0111
Fax: 011 41 22 733 3430

http://www.iso.ch

ITU (International Telecommunications Union)

Place de Nations
CH1211 Geneva 20
SWITZERLAND
Phone: 011 41 22 99 511
Fax: 011 41 22 33 7256

http://www.itu.int

NIST (National Institute for Standards and Technology) Library

Gaithersburg, MD 20899
USA
Phone: 1-301-975-2000

TIA (Telecommunications Industry of America)

2500 Wilson Boulevard
Arlington, VA 22201
USA
Phone: 1-703-907-7700
Fax: 1-703-907-7727

http://www.eia.org

UL (Underwriters Laboratories)

333 Pfingsten Road
Northbrook, IL 60061
USA
Phone: 1-847-272-8800
Fax: 1-847-272-8129

http://www.ul.com

Other Sources for Standards and Recommendations

The following resellers and distributors also provide documentation from standards committees:

Global Engineering Documents

1990 M Street NW, Suite 400
Washington, DC 20036
(800) 854-7179

Information Handling Services

PO Box 1154
15 Inverness Way East
Englewood, CO 80150
(800) 525-7052; (303) 790-0600

Phillips Business Information

1201 Seven Locks Road, Suite 300
Potomac, MD 20854
(800) 777-5006

United Nations Bookshop

General Assembly Building
Room GA 32B
New York, NY 10017
(800) 553-3210; (212) 963-7680

InfoMagic, Inc.

11950 N. Highway 89
Flagstaff, AZ 86004
(800) 800-6613; (520) 526-9565
Fax: (520) 526-9573
E-mail: info@infomagic.com
Web: http://www.infomagic.com

APP
B

InfoMagic sells CDs containing various documentation, including the RFCs that serve as standards in the Internet community and much of the ITU (formerly, the CCITT) documentation. While there are gaps in the standards, the 2-CD collection is well organized, and indispensable if you need to consult any of the included documents often, or if you'll need any number of the documents.

They also have discs containing various Internet tools, and *World Wide Catalog*, an interesting disc about the World Wide Web that can be used even if you don't have an Internet account.

The discs, which are updated every six months or so, cost about $30–$40. While you can get the materials yourself, it would take you weeks to do so.

Secondary Sources

The following books are informative secondary sources about topics related, broadly or narrowly, to networking or to the Internet. These are by no means the only good sources for such information, but they do provide a start for readers who want to go beyond this book. The references range from introductory to advanced treatments. Some of the books include CDs:

Albritton, John. *Cisco IOS Essentials* (1999, McGraw-Hill)

Anonymous. *Maximum Security,* 2nd edition (1998, Sams)

Aviram, Mariva H. *XML for Dummies Quick Reference* (1998, IDG Books)

Bach, Maurice J. *The Design of the UNIX Operating System* (1986, Prentice-Hall).

Ben-Natan, Ron. *CORBA on the Web* (1998, McGraw-Hill)

Blacharski, Dan. *Maximum Bandwidth* (1997, Que)

Black, Uyless. *Emerging Communications Technologies,* 2nd edition (1997, Prentice-Hall)

Black, Uyless. *OSI: A Model for Computer Communications* (1991, Prentice-Hall).

Black, Uyless. *The V Series Recommendations* (1991, McGraw-Hill).

Black, Uyless. *The X Series Recommendations* (1991, McGraw-Hill).

Blum, Daniel J & Litwack, David M. *The E-Mail Frontier* (1995, Addison-Wesley).

Boumphrey, Frank. *Professional Style Sheets for HTML and XML* (1998, Wrox Press)

Bradner, Scott O. & Mankin, Allison (eds). *IPng: Internet Protocol Next Generation* (1996, Addison-Wesley)

Brown, Kevin, Brown, Kenyon & Brown, Kyle. *Mastering Lotus Notes* (1995, Sybex).

Brown, Wendy E. & Simpson, Colin MacLeod (eds.). *The OSI Dictionary of Acronyms and Related Abbreviations* (1993, McGraw-Hill).

Cady, Glee Harrah & McGregor, Pat. *Mastering the Internet* (1995, Sybex).

Cedeno, Nancy. *The Internet Tool Kit* (1995, Sybex).

Chappell, Laura (ed). *Advanced Cisco Router Configuration* (1999, Cisco Press)

Chappell, Laura. *Novell's Guide to NetWare LAN Analysis* (1993, Novell Press).

Chappell, Laura A. & Spicer, Roger L. *Novell's Guide to Multiprotocol Networking* (1994, Novell Press).

Cheong, Fah-Chun. *Internet Agents* (1995, New Riders)

Cheswick, William R & Bellovin, Steven M. *Firewalls and Internet Security* (1994, Addison-Wesley).

Clarke, David James IV. *Novell's CNA Study Guide* (1993, Novell Press).

Cole, Marion. *Telecommunications* (1999, Prentice-Hall)

Coleman, Pat & Dyson, Peter. *Mastering Intranets, the Windows 95/NT Edition* (1997, Sybex)

Colonna-Romano, John & Srite, Patricia. *The Middleware Source Book* (1995, Digital Press).

Comer, Douglas E. *Internetworking with TCP/IP,* Volume 1, 2nd edition (1991, Prentice-Hall).

Coulouris, George, Dollimore, Jean & Kindberg, Tim. *Distributed Systems: Concepts and Design,* 2nd edition (1994, Addison-Wesley).

Cowart, Robert. *Mastering Windows 95* (1995, Sybex).

Currid, Cheryl C. & Saxon, Stephen. *Novell's Guide to NetWare 4.0 Networks* (1993, Novell Press).

Derfler, Frank, Jr. *PC Magazine Guide to Connectivity,* 2nd edition (1992, Ziff-Davis Press).

Donald, Lisa & Chellis, James. *MCSE: NT Server 4 in the Enterprise,* 2nd edition (1998, Sybex)

Duntemann, Jeff, Pronk, Ron & Vincent, Patrick. *Web Explorer Pocket Companion* (1995, Coriolis Group).

Dyson, Peter. *Mastering OS/2 Warp* (1995, Sybex).

Dyson, Peter. *Novell's Dictionary of Networking* (1994, Novell Press).

Eckel, Bruce. *Thinking in Java* (1998, Prentice-Hall) There is also a very useful course on learning Java programming on CD available in conjunction with this book. See the book for details.

Eddy, Sandra E. *XML in Plain English* (1998, M&T Books)

Ernst, Warren. *Presenting ActiveX* (1996, Sams

Esposito, Dino. *Instant DHTML Scriptlets* (1998, Wrox Press)

Evans, Tim. *Building an Intranet* (1996, Sams)

Flanagan, William A. *The Guide to T-1 Networking,* 4th edition (1990, Telecom Library).

Francis, Brian et al. *Beginning Active Server Pages 2.0* (1998, Wrox Press)

Freedman, Alan. *The Computer Glossary,* 6th edition (1993, Amacom).

Garfinkel, Simson. *PGP: Pretty Good Privacy* (1995, O'Reilly & Associates).

Gaskin, James E. *The Complete Guide to NetWare 4.1* (1995, Sybex).

Gerber, Barry. *Mastering Microsoft Exchange Server 5.5,* 3rd edition (1998, Sybex)

Goldfarb, Charles F. & Prescod, Paul. *The XML Handbook* (1998, Prentice-Hall)

Goralski, Walter. *ADSL and DSL Technologies* (1998, McgRaw-Hill)

Graham, Ian. *HTML Sourcebook* (1995, John Wiley & Sons).

Green, James Harry. *The Business One Irwin Handbook of Telecommunications,* 2nd edition (1992, Irwin).

Hagen, Bill von. *SGML for Dummies* (1997, IDG Books)

Halsall, Fred. *Data Communications, Computer Networks, and OSI,* 3rd edition (1994, Addison-Wesley).

Hart-Davis, Guy. *Word 97 Macro & VBA Handbook* (1997, Sybex)

Hebrawi, Baha. *OSI Upper Layer Standards and Practice* (1993, McGraw-Hill).

Hecht, Jeff. *Understanding Fiber Optics* (1987, Sams).

Holzner, Steven. *XML Complete* (1998, McGraw-Hill)

Homer, Alex & Ullman, Chris. *Instant IE4 Dynamic HTML Programmer's Reference* (1997, Wrox Press)

Horn, Delton T. *Basic Electronics Theory,* 4th edition (1994, Tab Books)

APP
B

Howe, Denis. *Free On-Line Dictionary of Computing* (1993, Denis Howe). Available on the Internet by FTP or Gopher from wombat.doc.ic.ac.uk (146.169.22.42).

Hoffman, Paul E. *The Internet Instant Reference*, 2nd edition (1995, Sybex).

Homer, Alex, Ullman, Chris & Wright, Steve. *Instant HTML Programmer's Reference* (1997, Wrox Press)

Hopkins, Gerald L. *The ISDN Literacy Book* (1995, Addison-Wesley).

Hughes, Jeffrey F & Thomas, Blair W. *Novell's QuickPath to NetWare 4.1 Networks* (1995, Sybex).

Huitema, Christian. *Routing in the Internet* (1995, Prentice-Hall).

Jerram, Peter. *The Web at Work* (1996, Novell Press)

Jordan, Larry & Churchill, Bruce. *Communications and Networking for the IBM PC and Compatibles,* 4th edition (1992, Brady).

Kadambi, Jayant, Crayford, Ian & Kalkunte, Mohan. *Gigabit Ethernet* (1998, Prentice-Hall)

Kearns, David & Iverson, Brian. The Complete Guide to Novell Directory Services (1998, Sybex)

Kernighan, Brian W. & Ritchie, Dennis M. *The C Programming Language* (1978, Prentice-Hall)

Khan, Ahmed S. *The Telecommunications Fact Book and Illustrated Dictionary* (1992, Delmar Publishers).

Kientzle, Tim. *Internet File Formats* (1995, Coriolis Group)

Kuruppillai, Rajan, Dontamsetti, Mahi & Cosentino, Fil J. *Wireless PCS* (1997, McGraw-Hill)

Lammle, Todd, Lammle, Monica & Chellis, James. *MCSE: TCP/IP for NT Server 4 Study Guide,* 3rd edition (1996, Sybex)

Leinwand, Allan & Fang, Karen. *Network Management, a Practical Perspective* (1993, Addison-Wesley).

Lemay, Laura. Teach Yourself Web Publishing with HTML 4 in a Week, 4th edition (1997, Sams)

Lemay, Laura & Perkins, Charles L. *Teach Yourself Java 1.1 in 21 Days* (1997, Sams)

Linnell, Dennis. *The SAA Handbook* (1990, Addison-Wesley).

Loshin, Peter. Extranet Design and Implementation (1997, Sybex)

Lynch, Daniel C. & Rose, Marshall T. *Internet System Handbook* (1993, Addison-Wesley).

Mara, Mary Jane. *VBScript Sourcebook* (1997, John Wiley & Sons)

Margulies, Edwin. *Client Server Computer Telephony* (1994, Flatiron Publishing).

Marrin, Chris. *Teach Yourself VRML 2 in 21 Days* (1997, Sams)

Matthews, Carole Boggs & Matthews, Martin. *Windows 95 Instant Reference* (1995, Sybex).

Mattison, Rob. *Data Warehousing* (1996, McGraw-Hill)

McFedries, Paul. *Windows 98 Unleashed* (1998, Sams)

McGrath, Sean. *XML by Example* (1998, Prentice-Hall)

McGraw, Gary & Felten, Edward W. *Java Security: Hostile Applets, Holes, and Antidotes* (1997, John Wiley & Sons)

Messmer, Hans-Peter. *The Indispensable PC Hardware Book,* 2nd edition (1995, Addison-Wesley)

Microsoft Press. *Computer Dictionary* (1991, Microsoft Press).

Miller, Mark A. *Internetworking* (1991, M&T Books).

Miller, Mark A. *LAN Protocol Handbook* (1992, M&T Books).

Miller, Mark A. *Troubleshooting Internetworks* (1991, M&T Books).

Miller, Mark A. *Troubleshooting TCP/IP* (1992, M&T Books).

Minasi, Mark. *The Complete PC Upgrade & Maintenance Guide,* 8th edition (1997, Sybex)

Minasi, Mark, Anderson, Christa, & Creegan, Elizabeth. *Mastering Windows NT Server 3.5* (1995, Sybex).

Minasi, Mark, Christiansen, Eric & Shapar, Kristina. *Expert Guide to Windows 98* (1998, Sybex)

Minoli, Daniel. Video *Dialtone Technology* (1995, McGraw-Hill)

Motorola. *The Basics Book of Frame Relay* (1993, Addison-Wesley).

Motorola. *The Basics Book of Information Networking* (1992, Addison-Wesley).

Motorola. *The Basics Book of ISDN,* 2nd edition (1992, Addison-Wesley).

Motorola. *The Basics Book of OSI and Network Management* (1993, Addison-Wesley).

Motorola. *The Basics Book of X.25 Packet Switching,* 2nd edition (1992, Addison-Wesley).

Nellist, John G. *Understanding Telecommunications and Lightwave Systems: An Entry-Level Guide,* 2nd edition (1996, IEEE Press)

Newton, Harry, *Newton's Telecom Dictionary*, 7th edition (1994, Flatiron Publishing).

Odom, Wendell. *CCNA Exam Certification Guide* (1999, Cisco Press)

Ousterhout, John K. *Tcl and the Tk Toolkit* (1994, Addison-Wesley).

Partridge, Greg. *Gigabit Networking* (1994, Addison-Wesley).

Pecar, Joseph A., O'Connor, Roger J. & Garbin David A. *The McGraw-Hill Telecommunications Factbook* (1993, McGraw-Hill).

Perkins, Charles, Strebe, Matthew & Chellis, James. *MCSE: NT Workstation 4 Study Guide,* 2nd edition (1996, Sybex)

Perlman, Radia. *Interconnections: Bridges and Routers* (1992, Addison-Wesley).

Piscitello, David M. & Chapin, A. Lyman. *Open Systems Networking: TCP/IP and OSI* (1993, Addison-Wesley).

Pitts-Moultis, Natanya & Kirk, Cheryl. *XML Black Book* (1999, Coriolis Group)

Plattner, B. et al. *X400 Message Handling* (1991, Addison-Wesley).

Potts, William F. *McGraw-Hill Data Communications Dictionary* (1993, McGraw-Hill).

Purcell, Lee & Mara, Mary Jane. *The ABCs of JavaScript* (1997, Sybex)

Quigley, Ellie. *Perl by Example* (1995, Prentice-Hall)

Radicati, Sara. *X.500 Directory Services* (1994, Van Nostrand Reinhold).

Ridge, Peter M. *The Book of SCSI* (1995, No Starch Press)

Rosch, Winn. *Hardware Bible,* Premier Edition (1997, Sams)

Russell, Deborah & Gangemi, G.T. Sr. *Computer Security Basics* (1991, O'Reilly & Associates).

Sackett, George C. & Metz, Christopher Y. *ATM and Multiprotocol Networking* (1997, McGraw-Hill)

Sapien, Mike & Piedmo, Greg. *Mastering ISDN* (1997, Sybex)

Saunders, Stephen. The McGraw-Hill High-Speed LANs Handbook (1996, McGraw-Hill)

Savetz, Kevin, Randall, Neil & Lepage, Yves. *MBone: Multicasting Tomorrow's Internet* (1996, IDG Books)

Schatt, Sam. *Understanding Local Area Networks*, 3rd edition (1993, Sams).

Schatt, Stan. *Understanding Network Management* (1993, Windcrest).

Schmidt, Friedhelm. *The SCSI Bus and IDE Interface* (1995, Addison-Wesley)

Schneier, Bruce. *Applied Cryptography*, 2nd edition (1996, John Wiley & Sons).

Schulman, Andrew. *Unauthorized Windows 95, Developer's Resource Kit* (1994, IDG Books).

Sidhu, Gursharan S., Andrews, Richard F. & Oppenheimer, Alan B. *Inside AppleTalk*, 2nd edition (1990, Addison-Wesley).

Simpson, Alan, Olson, Elizabeth & Weisskopf, Gene. *The Compact Guide to PerfectOffice* (1995, Sybex).

Sochats, Ken & Williams, Jim. *The Networking and Communications Desk Reference* (1992, Sams).

Stallings, William. *Handbook of Computer-Communications Standards* (1987, Macmillan).

Stallings, William. *Local and Metropolitan Area Networks*, 4th edition (1993, Macmillan).

Stallings, William. *Networking Standards: A Guide to OSI, ISDN, LAN, and MAN Standards* (1993, Addison-Wesley).

Stallings, William. *SNMP, SNMPv2, and CMIP* (1993, Addison-Wesley).

Sterling, Donald J. Jr. *Technician's Guide to Fiber Optics*, 2nd edition (1993, Delmar).

Stern, Morgan & Rasmussen, Tom. Building Intranets on NT, NetWare and Solaris: An Administrator's Guide (1997, Sybex)

Stevens, W. Richard. *TCP/IP Illustrated, Volume 1: The Protocols* (1994, Addison-Wesley).

St. Laurent, Simon. *Cookies* (1998, McGraw-Hill)

Strayer, W. Timothy, Dempsey, Bert J & Weaver, Alfred C. *XTP: The Xpress Transfer Protocol* (1992, Addison-Wesley).

Strebe, Matthew & Perkins, Charles. *MCSE: Internet Information Server 4 Study Guide*, 2nd edition (1998, Sybex)

Strebe, Matthew, Perkins, Charles & Moncur, Michael G. *NT Network Security* (1998, Sybex)

Stroustrup, Bjarne. *The Design and Evolution of C++* (1994, Addison-Wesley)

Tanenbaum, Andrew S. *Computer Networks* (1988, Prentice-Hall).

Tauber, Daniel A., Kienan, Brenda & Towers, J. Tarin. *Surfing the Internet with Netscape Communicator 4* (1997, Sybex)

Taylor, D. Edgar. *The McGraw-Hill Internetworking Handbook* (1995, McGraw-Hill).

Thomas, Robert M. *Introduction to Local Area Networks*, 2nd edition (1997, Sybex)

Tittel, Ed, Mikula, Norbert & Chandak, Ramesh. *XML for Dummies* (1998, IDG Books)

Trowt-Bayard, Toby. *Videoconferencing: the Whole Picture* (1994, Flatiron Publishing)

Vacca, John. *The Cabling Handbook* (1998, Prentice-Hall)

Wall, Larry & Schwartz, Randal L. *Programming Perl* (1991, O'Reilly & Associates)

Wright, Gary R. & Stevens, W Richard. *TCP/IP Illustrated, Volume 2: The Implementation* (1995, Addison-Wesley).

Yggdrasil Computing. *The Linux Bible: The GNU Testament*, 4th, expanded ed (1998, Yggdrasil).

Internet Resources

The Internet, the world's largest network, grows at a faster pace than its local counterparts. Given its popularity, it's not surprising that new products and resources are appearing daily. Probably the best place to learn about the Internet is on the Internet itself. There are thousands of documents, programs, and other resources accessible through the World Wide Web or by other means. In this section, you will find a list of Web sites you can check for information about various topics related to networking and to the Internet. The list can provide only a start—since there is no way to cover the more than 800 million Web pages currently out there.

In many cases—particularly in the case of corporations and service providers—the URL represents a home page. You can use this as a starting point for various more refined searches. For example, the Microsoft home page gets you access to product information, to information about various Microsoft technologies (such as ActiveX, COM and DCOM, and so forth), and to software patches and other downloads.

A Search Tool

When searching for specific information in Web pages, it is helpful to have some type of tool that can help locate the content in a Web page. One program that works quite well for this purpose is dtSearch from DT Software. You can use it as a standalone program – to search through files on your own machine. The program can also be used to build a search form on a web site. That is, dtSearch can be installed to enable users to search through a web site when the users visit that web site. For information about dtSearch, check at http://www.dtsearch.com.

URLs for Forums and Standards-Related Organizations

The following list includes URLs for various forums, organizations, and interest groups concerned with developing specifications or warehousing information about topics related to networks and networking. If no group is listed for a topic in which you're interested, try a URL of the form: http://www.YOUR_TOPIC_HERE.org or http://www.YOUR_TOPIC_HERE.com. Who knows, you may get lucky.

ACM (Association for Computing Machinery): `http://www.acm.org`

ADSL (Asymmetric Digital Subscriber Line) Forum: `http://www.adsl.com`

ANSI (American National Standards Institute): `http://www.ansi.org`

ATIS (Association for Telecommunications Industry Solutions): `http://www.atis.org`

Austin Common Standards Revision Group: `http://www.opengroup.org/austin/`

Biometrics Consortium: `http://www.biometrics.org`

Broadband Wireless Association: `http://www.broadband-wireless.org`

DISA (Data Interchange Standards Association): `http://www.disa.org`

DMTF (Distributed Management Task Force): `http://www.dmtf.org`

ECML (Electronic Commerce Modeling Langugage): `http://www.ecml.org`

ECTF (Enterprise Computer Telephony Forum): `http://www.ectf.org`

EFF (Electronic Frontier Foundation): `http://www.eff.org`

EIA (Electronic Industries Alliance): `http://www.eia.org`

EPIC (Electronic Privacy Information Center): `http://www.epic.org`

GEA (Gigabit Ethernet Alliance): `http://www.gigabit-ethernet.org`

HiPPI (High Performance Parallel Interface): `http://www.hippi.org`

HNF (High-Performance Networking Forum): `http://www.hnf.org`

APP
B

IAB (Internet Architecture Board):
http://www.iab.org

IANA (Internet Assigned Numbers Authority):
http://www.iana.org

ICANN (The Internet Corporation for Assigned
Names and Numbers):
http://www.icann.org

IETF (Internet Engineering Task Force):
http://www.ietf.org

IMC(Internet Mail Consortium:
http://www.imc.org

International Biometrics Group:
http://www.biometricgroup.com

ISO (International Standardization Organization):
http://www.iso.ch

ISOC (Internet Society): http://www.isoc.org

ITU (International Telecommunications Union):
http://www.itu.int

Java: http://www.java.org

JPEG (Joint Photographic Experts Group):
http://www.jpeg.org

Linux: http://www.linux.org

Linux Standard Base:
http://www.linuxbase.org

MMTA (Multimedia Telecommunications
Association):
http://www.mmta.org

MPEG (Motion Picture Experts Group):
http://www.mpeg.org

NACHA (National Automated Clearing House
Association): http://www.nacha.com

NEMA (National Electronic Manufacturers
Association): http://www.nema.org

NGIO (Next Generation I/O) Forum:
http://www.ngioforum.org

NISO (National Information Standards
Organization): http://www.niso.org

NIST (National Institute for Standards and
Technology): http://www.nist.gov

OMG (Object Management Group):
http://www.omg.org

PCI (Peripheral Component Interconnect):
http://www.pcisig.com

PCMCIA (Personal Computer Memory
Card International Association):
http://www.pcmcia.org

Perl: http://www.perl.org

Python: http://www.python.org

SCSI (Small Computer System Interface):
http://www.scsi.org

SIA (Securities Industry Association):
http://www.sia.com

SONET (Synchronous Optical Network):
http://www.sonet.com

Standards Organizations (miscellaneous
information): http://www.standards.ieee
.org/(faqs/othstdsorgs.html)

Telecommunications Standards Groups (various):
http://www.naturalmicrosystems.com/
nmss/nmsweb.nsf/tech/stndorgs

TIA (Telecommunications Industry Association):
http://www.eia.org

UMC (Unified Messaging Consortium):
http://www.unified-msg.com

USENIX Standards: http://www.usenix
.org/about/standards.html

W3C: http://www.w3.org

WAP (Wireless Application Protocol) Forum:
http://www.wapforum.org

XML (eXtensible Markup Language):
http://www.xml.org

Corporate and ISP-Related URLs

@Home: http://www.home.net/home

Adobe Systems: http://www.adobe.com

Adaptec: http://www.adaptec.com

Apple Computer: http://www.apple.com

AT&T: http://www.att.com

3Com: http://www.3com.com

Bell Atlantic: http://www.bellatlantic.com

BellSouth: http://www.bellsouth.com

Berk-Tek: http://www.berktek.com

Borland: http://www.borland.com

Cabletron: http://www.cabletron.com

Caldera Systems:
http://www.calderasystems.com

Cisco Systems: http://www.cisco.com

Compaq: http://www.compaq.com

Computer Associates: http://www.cai.com

Corel Systems http://www.corel.com

Dell Computer: http://www.dell.com

EarthLink: http://www.earthlink.com

eBay: http://www.ebay.com

Ericsson: http://www.ericsson.com

Etrade: http://www.etrade.com

Fluke Technologies: http://www.fluke.com

Gateway Computer: http://www.gateway.com

Hewlett-Packard: http://www.hp.com

IBM: http://www.ibm.com

Intel: http://www.intel.com

ISS (Internet Security Systems):
http://www.iss.net

Lotus: http://www.lotus.com

Lucent Technologies: http://www.lucent.com

Macromedia: http://www.macromedia.com

MCI: http://www.mci.com

MediaOne:
http://www.mediaoneexpress.com

MicroGrafx: http://www.micrografx.com

Micron Electronics: http://www.micron.com

Microsoft: http://www.microsoft.com

MindSpring: http://www.mindspring.com

Netscape: http://home.netscape.com

Network Associates: http://www.nai.com

Novell: http://www.novell.com

Oracle Systems: http://www.oracle.com

Pacific Bell: http://www.pacbell.com

RealNetworks: http://www.real.com

Red Hat Software: http://www.redhat.com

RSA Data Security: http://www.rsa.com

Silicon Graphics: http://www.sgi.com

Southwestern Bell: http://www.swbell.com

Sprint: http://www.sprint.com

Sun Microsystems: http://www.sun.com

SuSE Linux: http://www.suse.com

Sybex Publishing: http://www.sybex.com

Tivoli Systems: http://www.tivoli.com

U S West: http://www.uswest.com

UUNET: http://www.uunet.com

VocalTec: http://www.vocaltec.com

Xerox: http://www.xerox.com

APP
B

Search-Engine and Portal-Related URLs

AltaVista: http://www.altavista.com

About.com: http://www.about.com

America Online: http://www.aol.com

CompuServe 2000:
http://www.compuserve.com

Excite: http://www.excite.com

Google:
http://www.google.stanford.edu.com

HotBot: http://www.hotbot.com

InfoSeek: http://www.infoseek.go.com

Lycos: http://www.lycos.com

MSN: http://home.microsoft.com

Northern Light:
http://www.northernlight.com

Web Crawler: http://www.webcrawler.com

Yahoo!: http://www.yahoo.com

Publication and Periodical-Related URLs

Byte Magazine (electronic version):
http://www.byte.com

Computer Telephony Magazine:
http://www.computertelephony.com

Computerworld: www.computerworld.com

Data Communications: http://www.data.com

DV (Digital Video) Magazine:
http://www.dv.com

e-business Advisor:
http://www.advisor.com/E-Business

Enterprise Development:
http://www.enterprisedev.com

Information Week:
http://www.informationweek.com

Infosecurity Magazine:
http://www.infosecurity.com

Internet Week: http://www.internetwk.com

Java Pro: http://www.java-pro.com

Linux Journal:
http://www.linuxjournal.com

NetObjects: http://www.netobjects.com

Network Computing Magazine:
http://www.networkcomputing.com

Network Magazine:
http://www.networkmagazine.com

PC Computing: http://www.pccomputing.com

PC Magazine: http://www.pcmag.com

PC World: http://www.pcworld.com

Teleconnect Magazine:
http://www.teleconnect.com

Web Techniques:
http://www.webtechniques.com

Windows Magazine: http://www.winmag.com

Ziff-Davis publications: http://www.zdnet.com

Topic-Related URLs

ADSL standards:
http://www.adsl.com/adsl_forum.html

Anonymous browsing/privacy:
http://www.anonymizer.com

Cable modems:
http://www.cablemodeminfo.com

Computer dictionary: http://www.whatis.com

Computer dictionary:
http://pcwebopedia.com

Computer magazines: http://www.cmpnet.com

Computer-related information:
http://www.cnet.com

CORBA FAQ:
`http://www.cerfnet.com/~mpcline/`
`Corba-FAQ`

CORBA/IIOP specifications:
`http://www.omg.org`

DOM: `http://www.w3.org/DOM`

Expert advice: `http://www.allexperts.com`

Expert advice:
`http://www.experts-exchange.com`

FAQ list (maintained by Thomas Boutell):
`http://www.boutell.com/faq/`

File system hierarchy standard:
`http://www.pathname.com/fns/`

Help manuals: `http://help-site.com`

How-to information: `http://www.learn2.com`

HTML specifications:
`http://www.w3.org/TR/WD-html40`

Information Technology (IT):
`http://www.planetit.com`

Internet Public Library: `http://www.ipl.org`

Internet resources for developers:
`http://www.dc.net/ilazar`

Introduction to the Internet:
`http://www.learnthenet.com`

Introduction to the WWW:
`http://www.newbie-u.com`

Internet commerce statistics:
`http://www.thestandard.com`

Java: `http://java.sun.com/index.html`

Miscellaneous dictionaries, and so forth:
`http://www.onelook.com`

Online learning: `http://www.digitalthink.com`

Online learning: `http://www.webproforum.com`

Open Trading Protocol: `http://www.iotp.org`

PC Information: `http://www.pcguide.com`

PCI (Peripheral Component Interconnect)
specification: `http://www.pcisig.com`

Resources for developers: `http://www.devx.com`

RFC list: `http://www.landfield.com/`
`rfcs/rfc-titles.html`

Technology information: `http://techweb.com`

Tips: `http://www.tipworld.com`

Tutorials: `http://cires.colorado.edu/`
`people/peckham.scott/tutors.html`

Virtual Library: `http://www.vlib.org`

Virus Myths: `http://www.kumite.com`

Web Design tps & resources:
`http://www.projectcool.com`

Windows 2000: `http://www.windows2000.org`

WWW information: `http://www.yahoo.com/`
`Computers/`

XHTML: `http://www.xhtml.org`

XML RPC (Remote Procedure Call):
`http://www.xmlrpc.com`

XML specification:
`http://www.w3.org/TR/REC-xml`

Miscellaneous Sources

Other sources of information are available to meet
several needs:

- Getting basic background and general
  information, either about an area or a specific
  product.

- Getting more advanced information and
  training.

- Staying up-to-date on what is going on in an
  area or with a product.

APP
B

Background Information

For general background information or a basic introduction, and for relatively stable information, the most useful resources are books, films, online tutorials, and introductory workshops or seminars. Introductory courses are often available through local user groups, universities, and schools.

Advanced Training

Courses or workshops at conferences or through professional training centers are excellent resources for more advanced or specialized training. Vendors may either provide such training through their own divisions or may certify third-party trainers.

For example, Novell, Cisco, Microsoft, and other vendors authorize training centers to give courses leading to recognition as a certified administrator or other type of technical expert about the vendor's product line.

In some regions, advanced training may also be available through local user groups or local universities. This is more likely in areas with large user groups (such as Boston or New York) or where many people are employed in the computer industry.

Index

Note to the Reader: Page numbers in **bold** indicate the principal discussion of a topic. Page numbers in *italic* indicate illustrations.

Here's What You'll Get on the CD:

Two Complete Books!

The Network Press Encyclopedia of Networking's accompanying CD contains the entire text of two essential networking reference books:

- *The Network Press Encyclopedia of Networking,* Third Edition, by Werner Feibel

- The *Dictionary of Networking*, Third Edition, by Peter Dyson

The Encyclopedia of Networking in PDF

On the enclosed CD, you'll find the entire text of *The Network Press Encyclopedia of Networking*, complete with figures and tables, in the convenient Adobe Portable Document Format (PDF). The full text provides you with a portable, quick electronic reference.

To view the PDF files, you'll also find on the CD the Adobe Acrobat Reader 4 software for the following platforms:

- Windows (including 95, 98, and NT)

- Linux